Postcolonial Studies

Also available:

Postcolonial Studies

An Anthology

EDITED BY PRAMOD K. NAYAR

WILEY Blackwell

This edition first published 2016
Editorial material and organization © 2016 John Wiley & Sons Ltd

Registered Office
John Wiley & Sons, Ltd, The Atrium, Southern Gate, Chichester, West Sussex, PO19 8SQ, UK

Editorial Offices
350 Main Street, Malden, MA 02148-5020, USA
9600 Garsington Road, Oxford, OX4 2DQ, UK
The Atrium, Southern Gate, Chichester, West Sussex, PO19 8SQ, UK

For details of our global editorial offices, for customer services, and for information about
how to apply for permission to reuse the copyright material in this book please see our website
at www.wiley.com/wiley-blackwell.

Library of Congress Cataloging-in-Publication Data

Postcolonial studies : an anthology / edited by Pramod K. Nayar.
     pages   cm
   Includes bibliographical references and index.
     ISBN 978-1-118-78099-2 (cloth) – ISBN 978-1-118-78100-5 (pbk.)   1. Postcolonialism in
literature.   2. Postcolonialism.   3. Globalization in literature.   4. Globalization.
5. Transnationalism in literature.   6. Transnationalism.
I. Nayar, Pramod K., editor.
   PN56.P555P674 2016
   809'.93358–dc23

                                               2015019934

A catalogue record for this book is available from the British Library.

Cover image: Hawara checkpoint, West Bank. Photo © Loay Abu Haykel / Reuters / Corbis

Set in 10.5/13pt Dante by SPi Global, Pondicherry, India
Printed and bound in Malaysia by Vivar Printing Sdn Bhd

1   2016

Contents

Preface

This anthology is determinedly interdisciplinary in nature. Scholars from anthropology, international relations, history, publishing, sociology, gender studies, philosophy of science, film and media studies, political science, and the "postcolonial ubiquitous" – literary studies – add the heft of methodological diversity to the field we have come to call "postcolonial studies." The aim here is to not only open up these many routes into the postcolonial but also to foreground how different disciplines bring their own politics, whether about cultural hybridity or political economy, into the analyses.

While traditional fields of analysis such as literature, identity politics, agency, the nation-state, and representationality, continue to find their space in the volume, a considerable amount of emphasis has been laid on emergent domains and analytic practices. Essays on environmentalism and the "slow violence" (Rob Nixon's term) of neocolonial corporate activities in the formerly colonized regions, electronic empires and the exploitative nature of the digital economy that enmeshes the "Third World" in new forms of debt, labor, and resource-sharing, digital archivization, torture, identity politics online, postcolonial-feminist epistemologies in science and technology constitute, therefore, the expanded field of postcolonial studies in this volume.

While postcolonialism remains contested in theory and in practice, the breadth of thinkers united in the task of foregrounding common histories of racialized oppression and political readings of texts, and committed to pluralist, emancipatory-liberatory ethics of identity and politics that the volume brings together indicates that the field thrives in precisely its diversity and contested nature.

PKN
Hyderabad, India
April 2014

Acknowledgments

My gratitude in different measures (all of you *know* the quantum owed to each of you) to: Emma Bennett at Wiley Blackwell for her interest, the months of discussion over the project before finalization, and her helpful suggestions; Deirdre Ilkson, Wiley Blackwell, who fielded several queries with speed and efficiency; Ben Thatcher, Wiley Blackwell, for being significantly helpful at the production stage; parents and parents-in-law, Nandini and Pranav for being grounded at all times so as to ensure the everyday is smoothened out, and for their constant support; V. Premlata for regularly sending me stuff to read; Saradindu Bhattacharya for sourcing materials at short notice; friends, for their affection and (the usual) bewildered interest at my self-imposed workload: Ajeet, Neelu, Ibrahim, Walter; and Anna, who yet again demonstrated with characteristic loyalty and warmth that the projects existing as fantasies in my head *are* realistic, necessary, and doable.

Introduction

Postcolonialism has never been as relevant as it is today, and the present volume, in its disciplinary range and methodological depth, seeks to demonstrate the validity of this claim. Postcolonialism, as the theoretical-philosophical wing of the condition of postcoloniality (and a postcoloniality caught up in the circuits of amplified globalization) that offered, not in the too distant past, modes of reading the colonial archives, continues to offer the politically relevant methodological-analytical tools needed to deal with new social, economic, cultural, and political contexts and situations. This has also meant a massive expansion *within* postcolonial studies, in terms of its temporal limits, geographical territories covered, genres, and sites of analysis. We see now postcolonialism's influence on anthropology, history, political science, science and technology studies, and media and new media studies.

To return first briefly to the traditional concerns of postcolonial studies. We have seen since the 1990s examinations of the diverse apparatuses of Empire. The imperial apparatuses of knowledge-making and subsequent dominance that have come in for attention now include mapping and cartography (Edney 1997), publishing (Davis, in this volume), health and medicine (Arnold 1993, Levine 2003) mathematical sciences (Bishop 1990), English language and literature (Vishwanathan 1989, Trivedi 1993), nature and horticulture (Drayton 2000), art and museums (Barringer and Flynn 1998, Eaton 2006). Racial-cultural stereotypes (including cannibalism or the vulnerable native woman) and their links with imperial ideologies continue to be one of the pillars of postcolonial literary criticism (Hulme 1992, Guest 2001). Much of this work of postcolonialism has consisted, right from Edward Said, of reading discourses as political acts with material effects, while a slow recognition, owing much to the work of Homi Bhabha (1994), of the instability and ambivalence of colonial discourses has made its appearance in postcolonial studies since the 1990s. The effects, postcolonial studies has shown, organized the colonizers' perception of the racial-cultural Other, the colonial structure, and interracial relations, and constructed the very subjectivities of the colonizer and the colonized.

Postcolonial Studies: An Anthology, First Edition. Edited by Pramod K. Nayar.
Editorial material and organization © 2016 John Wiley & Sons, Ltd.
Published 2016 by John Wiley & Sons, Ltd.

Alongside these scrupulous deconstructions of colonial structures of dominance, postcolonial studies also locates moments and movements of resistance, subversion, and buried knowledges in Africa, Asia, and South America. Famously associated with the Subaltern Studies group this approach in excavating knowledges subjugated by colonialism has revealed unexpected and radical forms of the political in the colonial period. Indigenous science, cultural practices, and forms of knowledge are being recuperated in the work of scholars like Seema Alavi (2008), who trace counter- and local traditions of thought in, say, medicine that had been rendered invisible during the colonial period. Postcolonial studies has shown how colonial dominance was very often countered, in unobtrusive ways perhaps, but significant nevertheless, by theories of domestic purity (Partha Chatterjee's work on the colonial domestic sphere [1993] comes to mind here) or spirituality. It has also enabled us to better understand the extraordinary hybrid identities produced within the crucible of colonialism where social reform, the domestic sphere, education, and political thought in the colony often emerged as a result of the conjunction of local traditions and Western education.

Beyond this attention to colonial and counter- or anti-colonial discourses, postcolonialism since the 1990s has seen two significant shifts. The first is the shift toward a transnationalization of European histories, the second, extending the first shift to the contemporary age, an increased attention to locating the politics, problems, and processes of the postcolony within the contexts of globalization, neocolonialism, and decolonization.

Both these shifts might be subsumed under a new, or emergent, methodological rubric of postcolonial studies: an emphasis on exchanges, links, hybridities of racial, national, and cultural relations of "West" and "East" that is increasingly replacing the *hierarchic binary* of "West versus East" of early postcolonial studies, just as the belief in a strident colonial discourse has, since the 1990s, been replaced by the sense of an "uncertain colonial." Under the impact of influential, if often controversial, works such as Janet Abu-Lughod's *Before European Hegemony* (1989), David Cannadine's *Ornamentalism* (2002), John Hobson's *The Eastern Origins of Western Civilization* (2004), Catherine Hall's *Civilizing Subjects* (2002), Antoinette Burton's *At the Heart of the Empire* (1998), Linda Colley's *Britons* (1992) and *Captives* (2004), and Ian Buruma and Avishai Margalit's *Occidentalism* (2006), scholars have begun to locate *connections* and mutually influential exchanges between East and West, even though these exchanges might be asymmetrical and uneven.

I. Europe's Transnational Pasts

Postcolonialism has engineered a major turn in evaluating the many pasts of England/ Europe and the nations in Africa, Asia, and South America. We can think of this turn as a transnationalization of the study of European and English history, literary as well as political, a shift also signaled in the introduction to another anthology on postcolonialism (Loomba et al. 2008: 4).

"Transnationalization" in postcolonial studies today is at once a material condition as well as an interpretive method: it focuses on material exchanges and linkages and offers a way of reading literary-cultural texts (Nayar forthcoming). It makes a strong case for seeing imperialism as not a unidirectional or center–periphery phenomenon but as a messy, mutually constitutive state of affairs where the periphery was very often located within the heart of imperial metropolises. European history and literature and even Europe's political identity, these works informed by postcolonialism demonstrate, were always multicultural and the result of cultural exchanges even as these exchanges were unequal and asymmetric like the economic transactions. But we are getting ahead of the story of postcolonialism's transnationalization of Europe.

Postcolonialism's focus on race, race relations, and race-informed social, cultural, and political formations in history has, first and foremost, pushed back the temporal bookends of the Empire to a stage – the medieval, the Renaissance and the early modern – where commentators have discerned a (racialized) proto-imperial imaginary in English texts. The work of Walter Cohen (2004), Jonathan Gil Harris (1998, 2004), Richmond Barbour (2003), Kim Hall (1995), Dirk Hoerder (2002), Lisa Jardine (1996), Jardine and Brotton (2000), and other scholars, and collections such as *The Postcolonial Middle Ages* (Jeffrey Jerome Cohen 2001) and *Companion to the Global Renaissance* (Singh 2009), have altered our perceptions of a purely *European* Renaissance or *English* Early Modern. The early modern, to snatch up one period of English history, was, in such interpretations, a *transnational* Early Modern, even as the preliminary concerns of an imperial variety – revolving around race and racial purity, mostly – make their presence felt, according to these new readings, in the period's texts. Anxieties over race manifest in literary-cultural texts as concerns with trade, national-cultural boundaries, pathology, material artifacts, plants and plant products (tobacco), complexion/skin color, edible products (coffee, tea), object-spectacles (the curiosity cabinet) and Other bodies (Native American, African). The study of transnationalization has thus tracked an imperial and racial *imagination* to a period when the Empire was not even in the offing although, as some have argued, England always suffered from an "imperial envy" (MacLean 2001). In the process it shows how these early moments of imperialism had already begun its messy negotiations in materiality and in discourse with multiculturalism and cultural diversity-difference, and in many cases co-opted this heterogeneity into its structures, in trade and in governance (Daniel Vitkus' work [2006, 2007] on Turkey in the Early Modern period would be an example of such studies).

The greater emphasis on cultural exchanges, dissolving boundaries and linkages within every historical age, that demonstrate how national and cultural identities were organized around the presence of the "foreign" ensure that the West/East relation is no longer seen as a hierarchic binary. England's journeys and the flow of "foreign" products and people from all over the world into its geopolitical as well as cultural borders were *constitutive* of its identity. Transnationalist readings claim not only a multicultural Renaissance or Enlightenment but also a constant racialized engagement of Europe with its Other in the formation of intellectual ideas of humanism, aesthetics such as the sublime, or literary forms such as the novel. Similar interpretations for later periods and intellectual currents, such as the Enlightenment (*The Postcolonial Enlightenment*, Carey and Festa 2009) or modernism (Saikat Majumdar, *Prose of the World*, 2013), in European history have appeared since the late 1990s and early 2000s.

Narrowing the focus, feminist histories, such as Clare Midgley's (2007) or Philippa Levine's (2003, 2004), have shown how Europe's own radical and emancipatory movements – such as the women's suffragette movement of the late nineteenth century – emerged partly due to the reformers' engagement with their colonized "sisters" and the latter's social conditions. The discourses of amelioration (in slavery but also in emancipatory and reform movements) owe their existence, the above commentators demonstrate, to the imperial contexts of Europe in the late nineteenth century.

Whether it is the study of the Native American in British literature (Fulford 2006) or the "Noble Savage" (Bickham 2005), excavating transnational cultures has meant an alertness to the intertwined economies of race, profit, and cultural difference. Critics informed by postcolonial studies also detect counter-colonialisms and "reverse colonialisms" within British literature and culture, seeing in invasion themes and multicultural metaphors an anxiety about shifting cultural borders and the imminent threat of cultural mixing (Arata 1990, Keep and Randall 1999, Favour 2000, McLaughlin 2000). Others point to odd conjunctions and connections that have aligned anti-imperial whites with the freedom struggles of Asia and Africa (Gandhi 2006). Reading "counterflows to colonialism," to borrow the title of Michael Fisher's exemplary work (2004), these critics make a persuasive case for *not* regarding the Empire as one constituted by a simple East/West binary or a unidirectional flow of white men and women toward colonies, but rather constituted as a transaction.

Central to such transnational transactions that "make" an England or a Europe are fields opening up in postcolonialism, such as material cultures or travel cultures. Commentators (Franey 2003, Daly 2011) demonstrate how the rhetoric of consumption or object biographies in English literature owed their origins to racialized *discourses* of cultural practices, acquisition, and social prestige. European arrangements of domestic décor, food and drink, and sartorial fashion were all made possible, as these studies have shown, by the thriving mercantile and cultural links with Asia, Africa, China and East Asia, and South America. Right from Aphra Behn, literary scholars note, Oriental Caribbean and Arab products – whether jewelry or edibles – have enabled the English (and Europeans) to construct their identities in particular ways right from the eighteenth century. Thus chinoiserie (Porter 2002), tea (Kowaleski-Wallace 1994), and Kashmiri shawls (Daly 2002, Zutshi 2009) were integral to the making of an *English* identity.

The geographical scope of postcolonial studies has expanded in intricate and interesting ways. For a long time postcolonial studies was concerned mainly with Asia and Africa and Europe's cultural engagements with the people of these regions. China in European culture, from the early modern period downwards, has come in for attention (Chang 2010). More recently, the Palestine/Israel question, South America, and Ireland have figured in postcolonial studies. The Other in such studies is not always the Black or the Brown or the Yellow. Attention is now being paid to Europe's internal colonialisms – of, say, Gypsies and east Europeans (Bardi 2006, Matthews 2010), even as postcolonial methods of interpretation enable powerful new readings of Irish national identity. This shift to Europe's internal colonialisms has demonstrated how racial discourse has been appropriated in order to subjugate races within Europe itself.

II. The Postcolony's Transnational Present

Postcolonialism's new emphasis on connections and exchanges rather than hierarchic binaries between the West and the East has also contributed to a better understanding of contemporary contexts of the "postcolony."

Postcolonialism informs studies of new developments in technology and techno-cultures. Racialized science and new domains within technoscience, such as genetic racism, have been examined from a postcolonial perspective for the subtle, and some-times not so subtle, reiterations of colonial ideology (Nayar 2006, Merson in this volume). But by far the most important shift within academia that postcolonial studies has advanced is in studies of globalization and neocolonialism. In one sense replicating the shift toward transnational histories of imperial Europe, globalization studies, via postcolonial studies, examine the new economic, political, and cultural configurations of the "postcolony" as embedded simultaneously within the local and the global, situated within the space of "flows" (a term popularized by social scientists such as Arjun Appadurai [1996]) of capital, resources, and people, while geographers like Denis Cosgrove (2001) map the cultural history of the globe itself in European cultures.

Postcolonial studies has demonstrated how colonial dominance has morphed into a more insidious neocolonialism in the context of globalization. Millions of people in the "Third World" continue to be deprived of basic necessities and lose their cultural-economic-political sovereignties due to the alignment of local (i.e., postcolonial) governments/business interests with those from the Euro-American segment of the world. Globalization, which calls for new forms of labor, produces new classes and structures of regulation, training, and workplace cultures. Call-center and Business Process Outsourcing (BPO) services produce racialized forms of (hybrid) identity (Shome 2006) and entail newer forms of exploitation of labor from the Global South (Poster, in this volume). Techno-cultures informed by science are racialized and gendered (Harding, in this volume). Work in the hard sciences and biomedicine, such as Fatimah Jackson's (1999) on the Human Genome Project revealing its assumptions about race, opens up a useful line of exploration for postcolonial studies. Ecology, environment, and development have also been studied, as a result of postcolonialism, for their role in new forms of the Empire (Comaroff and Comaroff 2001). "Slow violence" (Nixon, in this volume) in South American or African nations is perpetrated by the First World's transnational corporations and through the material contexts of mining, trade, and dumping. Global "connections" in such matters, and in such forms, have come in for attention as well (Tsing 2007, Gorasevski 2012).

The decolonization project, therefore, in Africa, South America, or Asia, and its complications, is examined for its dual legacies of colonization and anti-colonial struggle. That these legacies – what Robert Young in "Postcolonial Remains" (in this volume) calls "the hidden rhizomes of colonialism's historical reach" – are also quite often embodied in political issues of fundamentalism, cultural xenophobia, or separatism in postcolonial nations draws postcolonial critics in political science, literary-cultural studies, and philosophy. Balancing these necessities and legacies with cultural globalization (Ghosh 2010), cosmopolitanism (Appiah 2006), and its resultant cultural hybridization (Werbner, in this volume) has engaged postcolonial critics since the 1990s at least. The tensions, in the globalized postcolony, between new cultural hybridities and the campaigns for cultural-religious purity, the multiple religious and sectarian conflicts but also the campaigns for greater freedoms, have engaged the sustained interest of postcolonial studies (Varshney 2002, Dabashi 2012). Witnessing the acrimonious debates, for example around the *hijab* in France or the Sikh turban in Canada (Puar 2008), the postcolonial has debated the difficult balance between cultural rights, national identity, and globalized cultures (Menon 2005).

Decolonization has also meant dealing with contentious gender issues, especially as these connect to questions of religious identity, theology, and reproductive rights. These have been at the forefront of debates in Islamic cultures and in societies dealing with massive shifts (especially) in gender roles, legal reforms that empower women, and educational reforms (McFadden 2005). In other cases, focusing on women and gender issues after 9/11, critics have begun to speak of transnational solidarities and communities of women (Marchand 2009, Jabri in this volume).

Whether such a decolonization actually happens has itself been debated from the time of Frantz Fanon. Critics like Walter Mignolo (in this volume) and Robert Young (in this volume) have called into question the route decolonization takes, even as they propose a new (cosmopolitan) role for the formerly colonized nations. A few see the emergence of a "postcolonial capitalism" in the age of global capital (Mezzadra 2011). Others see imperialism cast in the form of humanitarian aid or intervention continuing to produce racialized violence in parts of the world, and cultures seeking decolonization in the form of sovereignty or even cultural rights. In the wake of 9/11 such racialized violence, enabled and empowered by colonial fantasies this time in the USA, produces horrific results such as Abu Ghraib (Richter-Montpetit, in this volume), once again reiterating the enormous power – economic, military, and cultural – of the Western world over the peoples of other races, which often manifests not only as torture but also as cultural humiliation and violence (Rejali 2004).

Postcolonialism has contributed to a better understanding of European-colonial and postcolonial literary forms and themes as well, whether in the *Bildungsroman* (Esty 2007), the novel (Azim 1993), or travel writing (Leask 2002, Youngs 2010) and canonical English literary traditions like Romantic poetry (Leask 1993, Makdisi 1998). Critics now trace the impact of the colony, or the world, on the rise and development of these genres and forms. Thus Srinivas Aravamudan (2005) shows how the English novel in the eighteenth century arose from an engagement with the French and European "romances." This kind of work demonstrates how European forms arose at least partially in response to other traditions and in the context of transnational linkages.

Postcolonialism in academia has also contributed in no small measure to the enthusiasm for writings from the formerly colonized nations, indigenous people, and marginalized communities, making the genre both commercially profitable but also a source of not inconsiderable cultural capital. However, alongside this incorporation of the writings from formerly colonized nations into "South Asian" or "postcolonial" syllabi and publishing, there also emerges a line of critique of this trend. The "postcolonial exotic," as Graham Huggan and "re-orientalism" as Lisa Lau (in this volume) study it, offers up ethnographic fictions, authentic "marginal" cultures, and literatures produced by the formerly colonized people themselves. Migrant and diasporic writing from Hanif Kureishi, Salman Rushdie, Mohsin Hamid, Khaled Hossaini, and Marjane Satrapi has thus been a major constituent of literary publishing, literary awards, and film adaptations, as Huggan and Lau demonstrate. Postcolonialism also draws attention to the ways in which contemporary minority, marginalized, and migrant authors "fit" into First World demands of such "Third World writers" (the subject of the famous Fredric Jameson–Aijaz Ahmad debate, in this volume). Such a commercialization and commodification of "Third World" cultures in the form of diasporic-migrant writing or ethnic chic has been seen as part of the new globalization that extends an older Orientalism and mercantile imperialism.

Combining a traditional postcolonial studies concern with the transnationalist frame results in studies of what can be thought of as historical globalizing projects. Global humanitarian projects initiated in Europe from the eighteenth century are now viewed through a postcolonial lens, and it has been demonstrated how (implicit) ideologies of racial-moral superiority informed these projects then (Lester 2000) and complicate processes of globalization today. Versions of this global humanitarian imaginary also enabled the British to fashion themselves in particular ways (Ferguson 1992).

Others, like Joseph Slaughter (2007), have commented on the links between theories of universal human rights and the rise of particular forms of fiction, both founded on particular *Western* notions of the individual, which were then deemed to be universal. Concerns about alternative ideas of sovereignty, selfhood, and identity have continued in contemporary studies of Aboriginal or Native American policies in Australia, Canada, and the USA, even as the "Third World" refugee emerges as a problematic and paradigmatic ethical figure in rethinking questions of neocolonialism, migration, and globalization (Ong 2003). The indigenous peoples' demands for compensation (for their displacement, dispossession, and extermination by the white races in the colonial period) or for land rights to ancestral sites of their communities have found (academic and political) support in postcolonial studies.

But studies of globalization through the postcolonial lens also means addressing the pernicious nature of informational capitalism and eEmpires (Cooppan, 2008, Raley in this volume) as well as forms of resistance and subaltern appropriations of these new technologies (Nayar 2011). Postcolonial studies has turned to the world of digital cultures to examine how everyday lives, diasporic identities, and communities are built online (Franklin 2001). In many cases (Povinelli, in this volume) digital technologies have helped establish, or reinforce, traditional storytelling and local knowledge productions.

That globalization has also meant a globalization of both terrorism and interventionary / restorative / preemptive war is now established as a truism within postcolonial studies, as indicated by essays in a special issue (48.3) in 2012 of the *Journal of Postcolonial Writing* devoted to the "Orientalism after 9/11" and an earlier special issue (2010) on "Literary Responses to the War on Terror" (46.3–4). Questions of racial difference, migration, Islam and world cultures, and of course the notorious Samuel Huntington thesis about the "clash of civilizations," have been foregrounded in postcolonial studies in the decade following 9/11 (see Koshy 2008, Ray 2008). How 9/11 manifests as subtext to postcolonial writers – including celebrity authors like Khaled Hossaini or Kamila Shamsie – has become the subject of literary studies (Bernard 2010, Hartnell 2010).

Debates around the globalization studies–postcolonialism dynamic have inevitably centered on the US role in world affairs (Pease 2008) even as Jenny Sharpe (2008) and Aihwa Ong (2003), among others, have interrogated the nature of American multiculturalism, the role of refugees, and the continuing racial divide. Bringing the American dimension into the analytics, since at least 9/11 and Hardt and Negri's *Empire* (2000), has added an extra layer to postcolonial studies not only because of the American role in neocolonialism but also because of the part the nation plays in global humanitarian regimes, media networks, and popular culture much of which have their rhizomatic connections deep in Asia, Africa, and South America.

***

This volume captures these two major shifts, and the concomitant expansion, within postcolonial studies. The essays demonstrate the depth of imperial intervention, the continued influences of imperial domination in new forms and modalities in the globalized age, and the transnational roots of European identity and cultural practices even as they examine the apparatuses of Empire. The collection combines the traditional loci of postcolonial studies – colonial discourses – with an intensive engagement with continuing colonialisms, new domains for reworked, better-disguised colonialisms, and a wider geographical scope in the study of these relations of various parts and races of the world.

References

Abu-Lughod, Janet. *Before European Hegemony: The World System, AD 1250–1350.* New York: Oxford University Press, 1989.

Alavi, Seema. *Islam and Healing: Loss and Recovery of an Indo-Muslim Medical Tradition, 1600–1900.* London: Palgrave Macmillan, 2008.

Appadurai, Arjun. *Modernity at Large.* Minneapolis: University of Minnesota Press, 1996.

Appiah, Kwame Anthony. *Cosmopolitanism: Ethics in a World of Strangers.* New York: W. W. Norton, 2006.

Arata, Stephen D. "The Occidental Tourist: *Dracula* and the Anxiety of Reverse Colonization," *Victorian Studies* 33.4 (1990), 621–625.

Arnold, David. *Colonizing the Body: State Medicine and Epidemic Disease in Nineteenth-Century India.* New Delhi: Oxford University Press, 1993.

Aravamudan, Srinivas. "Fiction/Translation/Transnation: The Secret History of the Eighteenth-Century Novel," in P. R. Backscheider and C. Ingrassia (eds.), *A Companion to the Eighteenth-Century English Novel and Culture.* Oxford: Blackwell, 2005, 48–74.

Azim, Firdous. *The Colonial Rise of the Novel.* New York: Routledge, 1993.

Barbour, Richmond. *Before Orientalism: London's Theatre of the East 1576–1626.* Cambridge: Cambridge University Press, 2003.

Bardi, Abigail R. "The Gypsy as Trope in Victorian and Modern British Literature," *Romani Studies* 5, 16.1 (2006), 31–42.

Barringer, Tim and T. Flynn, eds. *Colonialism and the Object: Empire, Material Culture and the Museum.* London: Routledge, 1998.

Bernard, Anna. "Another Black September? Palestinian Writing after 9/11," *Journal of Postcolonial Writing* 46.3–4 (2010), 349–358.

Bhabha, Homi K. *The Location of Culture.* London: Routledge, 1994.

Bickam, T. O. *Savages Within the Empire: Representations of American Indians in Eighteenth-Century Britain.* Oxford: Clarendon Press, 2005.

Bishop, Alan. "Western Mathematics: The Secret Weapon of Cultural Imperialism," *Race and Class* 32.2 (1990), 51–65.

Burton, Antoinette. *At the Heart of the Empire: Indians and the Colonial Encounter in Late Victorian Britain.* Berkeley: University of California Press, 1998.

Buruma, Ian, and Avishai Margalit. *Occidentalism: The West in the Eyes of Its Enemies.* New York: Penguin, 2006.

Cannadine, David. *Ornamentalism: How the British Saw Their Empire.* London: Penguin, 2002.

Carey, Daniel, and Lynn Festa, eds. *The Postcolonial Enlightenment: Eighteenth-Century Colonialism and Postcolonial Theory.* Oxford: Oxford University Press, 2009.

Chang, E. H. *Britain's Chinese Eye: Literature, Empire, and Aesthetics in Nineteenth-Century Britain.* Stanford: Stanford University Press, 2010.

Chatterjee, Partha. *The Nation and Its Fragments.* Princeton, NJ: Princeton University Press, 1993.

Cohen, Jeffrey Jerome, ed. *The Postcolonial Middle Ages.* London: Palgrave Macmillan, 2001.

Cohen, Walter. "The Literature of Empire in the Renaissance," *Modern Philology* 102.1 (2004), 1–34.

Colley, Linda. *Britons: Forging the Nation, 1707–1837.* New Haven: Yale University Press, 1992.

Colley, Linda. *Captives: Britain, Empire, and the World, 1600–1850.* New York: Random House, 2004.

Comaroff, Jean, and John L. Comaroff. "Naturing the Nation: Aliens, Apocalypse and the Postcolonial State," *Journal of Southern African Studies* 27.3 (2001), 621–651.

Cooppan, Vilashini. "The Ruins of Empire: The National and Global Politics of America's Return to Rome," in Ania Loomba et al. (eds.), *Postcolonial Studies and Beyond.* Ranikhet: Permanent Black, 2008, 80–100.

Cosgrove, Dennis. *Apollo's Eye: A Cartographic Genealogy of the Earth in the Western Imagination.* Baltimore: Johns Hopkins University Press, 2001.

Dabashi, Hamid. *The Arab Spring: The End of Postcolonialism.* New York: Zed, 2012.

Daly, Suzanne. "Kashmir Shawls in Mid-Victorian Novels," *Victorian Literature and Culture* 30.1 (2002), 237–256.

Daly, Suzanne. *The Empire Inside: Indian Commodities in Victorian Domestic Novels*. Ann Arbor: University of Michigan Press, 2011.

Drayton, Richard. *Nature's Government: Science, Imperial Britain, and the "Improvement" of the World* [2000]. Hyderabad: Orient Longman, 2005.

Eaton, Natasha. "Nostalgia for the Exotic: Creating an Imperial Art in London, 1750–1793," *Eighteenth-Century Studies* 39.2 (2006), 227–250.

Edney, Mathew. *Mapping an Empire: The Geographical Construction of British India, 1753–1843*. Chicago: University of Chicago Press, 1997.

Esty, Jed. "The Colonial *Bildungsroman*: 'The Story of an African Farm' and the Ghost of Goethe," *Victorian Studies* 49.3 (2007), 407–430.

Favour, L. J. "The Foreign and the Female in Arthur Conan Doyle: Beneath the Candy Coating," *English Literature in Transition* 43.4 (2000), 398–409.

Ferguson, Moira. *Subject to Others: British Women Writers and Colonial Slavery 1670–1834*. London: Routledge, 1992.

Fisher, Michael. *Counterflows to Colonialism: Indian Travellers and Settlers in Britain, 1600–1857*. New Delhi: Permanent Black, 2004.

Franey, Laura. *Victorian Travel Writing and Imperial Violence: British Writing of Africa 1855–1902*. Basingstoke: Palgrave, 2003.

Franklin, M. I. "Postcolonial Subjectivities and Everyday Life Online," *International Feminist Journal of Politics* 3.3 (2001), 387–422.

Fulford, Tim. *Romantic Indians: Native Americans, British Literature, and Transatlantic Culture 1756–1830*. Oxford: Oxford University Press, 2006.

Gandhi, Leela. *Affective Communities: Anticolonial Thought and the Politics of Friendship*. Delhi: Permanent Black, 2006.

Ghosh, Bishnupriya. "Looking through Coca-Cola: Global Icons and the Popular," *Public Culture* 18.1 (2010), 332–368.

Gil Harris, Jonathan. *Foreign Bodies and the Body Politic: Discourses of Social Pathology in Early Modern England*. Cambridge: Cambridge University Press, 1998.

Gil Harris, Jonathan. *Sick Economies: Drama, Mercantilism, and Disease in Shakespeare's England*. Philadelphia: University of Pennsylvania Press, 2004.

Gillies, John. *Shakespeare and the Geography of Difference*. Cambridge: Cambridge University Press, 1994.

Gorasevski, Ellen. "Wangari Maathai's Emplaced Rhetoric: Green Global Peacebuilding," *Environmental Communication* 6.3 (2012), 290–307.

Guest, K., ed. *Eating their Words: Cannibalism and the Boundaries of Cultural Identity*. Albany: State University of New York Press, 2001.

Hall, Catherine. *Civilizing Subjects: Metropole and Colony in the English Imagination 1830–1867*. Chicago: University of Chicago Press, 2002.

Hall, Kim. *Things of Darkness: Economies of Race and Gender in Early Modern England*. Ithaca, NY: Cornell University Press, 1995.

Hardt, Michael and Antonio Negri. *Empire*. Cambridge, MA: Harvard University Press, 2000.

Hartnell, Anna. "Moving through America: Race, Place and Resistance in Mohsin Hamid's *The Reluctant Fundamentalist*," *Journal of Postcolonial Writing* 46.3–4 (2010), 336–348.

Hobson, John M. *The Eastern Origins of Western Civilization*. Cambridge: Cambridge University Press, 2004.

Hoerder, Dirk. *Cultures in Contact: World Migrations in the Second Millennium*. Durham, NC: Duke University Press, 2002.

Huggan, Graham. *The Postcolonial Exotic: Marketing the Margins*. London: Routledge, 2002.

Hulme, Peter. *Colonial Encounters: Europe and the Native Caribbean, 1492–1797* [1986]. London: Routledge, 1992.

Jackson, Fatimah L. "African-American Responses to the Human Genome Project," *Public Understanding of Science* 8.3 (1999), 181–191.

Jardine, Lisa. *Worldly Goods: A New History of the Renaissance*. New York: W. W. Norton, 1996.

Jardine, Lisa, and Jerry Brotton. *Global Interests: Renaissance Art between East and West*. London: Reaktion, 2000.

Keep, Christopher, and Don Randall. "Addiction, Empire, and Narrative in Arthur Conan Doyle's *The Sign of the Four*," *Novel* 32.3 (1999), 207–222.

Koshy, Susan. "Postcolonial Studies after 9/11: A Response to Ali Behdad," *American Literary History* 20.1–2 (2008), 300–303.

Kowaleski-Wallace, Beth. "Tea, Gender, and Domesticity in Eighteenth-Century England," *Studies in Eighteenth-Century Culture* 23 (1994), 131–145.

Leask, Nigel. *English Romantic Writers and the East: Anxieties of Empire*. Cambridge: Cambridge University Press, 1993.

Leask, Nigel. *Curiosity and the Aesthetics of Travel Writing: "From an Antique Land"*. New York: Oxford University Press, 2002.

Lester, Alan. "Obtaining the 'Due Observance of Justice': The Geographies of Global Humanitarianism," *Environment and Planning D* 20.3 (2000), 277–293.

Levine, Philippa. *Prostitution, Race and Politics: Policing Venereal Disease in the British Empire*. New York: Routledge, 2003.

Levine, Philippa. *Gender and Empire*. Oxford: Oxford University Press, 2004.

Levine, Philippa. "Naked Truths: Bodies, Knowledge, and the Erotics of Colonial Power," *Journal of British Studies* 52.1 (2013), 5–25.

Loomba, Ania, Suvir Kaul, Matti Bunzl, Antoinette Burton, and Jed Esty. "Beyond What? An Introduction," in Ania Loomba et al. (eds.), *Postcolonial Studies and Beyond* [2005]. Ranikhet: Permanent Black, 2008, 1–38.

Makdisi, Saree. *Romantic Imperialism: Universal Empire and the Culture of Modernity*. Cambridge: Cambridge University Press, 1998.

McFadden, Patricia. "Becoming Postcolonial: African Women Changing the Meaning of Citizenship," *Meridians* 6.1 (2005), 1–22.

McLaughlin, Joseph. *Writing the Urban Jungle: Reading Empire in London from Doyle to Eliot*. Charlottesville : University Press of Virginia, 2000.

MacLean, Gerald. "Ottomanism before Orientalism? Bishop King Praises Henry Blount, Passenger in the Levant," in Ivo Kamps and Jyotsna G. Singh (eds.), *Travel Knowledge: European "Discoveries" in Early Modern England*. Basingstoke: Palgrave Macmillan, 2001, 85–96.

Majumdar, Saikat. *Prose of the World: Modernism and the Banality of Empire*. New York: Columbia University Press, 2013.

Marchand, Marianne H. "The Future of Gender and Development after 9/11: Insights from Postcolonial Feminism and Transnationalism," *Third World Quarterly* 30.5 (2009), 921–935.

Matthews, Jodie. "Back Where They Belong: Gypsies, Kidnapping and Assimilation in Victorian Children's Literature," *Romani Studies* 5, 20.2 (2010), 137–159.

Mbembe, Achille. "Provisional Notes on the Postcolony," *Africa: Journal of the International African Institute* 62.1 (1992), 3–37.

Menon, Nivedita. "Between the Burqa and the Beauty Parlour: Globalization, Cultural Nationalism, and Feminist Politics," in Ania Loomba et al. (eds.), *Postcolonial Studies and Beyond* [2005]. Ranikhet: Permanent Black, 2008, 206–225.

Mezzadra, Sandro. "How Many Histories of Labour? Towards a Theory of Postcolonial Capitalism," *Postcolonial Studies* 14.2 (2011), 151–170.

Midgley, Clare. *Feminism and Empire*. London: Routledge, 2007.

Nayar, Pramod K. "The Rhetoric of Biocolonialism: Genomic Projects, Culture and the New Racisms," *Journal of Contemporary Thought* 24 (2006), 131–148.

Nayar, Pramod K. "The Digital Dalit: Subalternity and Cyberspace," *Sri Lanka Journal of the Humanities* 37.1–2 (2011).

Nayar, Pramod K. *Transnationalism in English Literature: Shakespeare to the Modern* Routledge, forthcoming.

Ong, Aihwa. *Buddha in Hiding: Refugees, Citizenship, and the New America*. Berkeley: University of California Press, 2003.

Pease, Donald E. "US Imperialism: Global Dominance without Colonies," in Henry Schwarz and Sangeeta Ray (eds.), *A Companion to Postcolonial Studies*. Oxford: Wiley-Blackwell, 2008, 203–220.

Porter, David. "Monstrous Beauty: Eighteenth-Century Fashion and the Aesthetics of the Chinese Taste," *Eighteenth-Century Studies* 35.3 (2002), 395–411.

Puar, Jasbir K. " 'The Turban Is Not a Hat': Queer Diaspora and Practices of Profiling," *Sikh Formations* 4.1 (2008), 47–91.

Ray, Sangeeta. "Postscript: Popular Perceptions of Postcolonial Studies after 9/11," in Henry Schwarz and Sangeeta Ray (eds.), *A Companion to Postcolonial Studies*. Malden, MA: Wiley-Blackwell, 2008, 574–583.

Rejali, D. "The Real Shame of Abu Ghraib", *Time*, May 20, 2004. http://content.time.com/time/nation/article/0,8599,640375,00.html (accessed March 9, 2015).

Sharpe, Jenny. "Postcolonial Studies in the House of US Multiculturalism," in Henry Schwarz and Sangeeta Ray (ed.), *A Companion to Postcolonial Studies*. Oxford: Wiley-Blackwell, 2008, 112–122.

Shome, Raka. 2006. "Thinking Through the Diaspora: Call Centers, India, and a New Politics of Hybridity' [2006]. In Pramod K. Nayar (ed.), *The New Media and Cybercultures Anthology*. Oxford: Wiley-Blackwell, 2012, 151–165.

Singh, Jyotsna G., ed. *A Companion to the Global Renaissance: English Literature and Culture in the Era of Expansion*. Oxford: Wiley-Blackwell, 2009.

Slaughter, Joseph. *Human Rights, Inc.: The World Novel, Narrative Form and International Law*. New York: Fordham University Press, 2007.

Trivedi, Harish. *Colonial Transactions: English Literature and India*. Manchester: Manchester University Press, 1993.

Tsing Anna L. *Friction: An Ethnography of Global Connection*. Princeton, NJ: Princeton University Press, 2007.

Varshney, Ashutosh. *Ethnic Conflict and Civic Life: Hindus and Muslims in India*. New Haven: Yale University Press, 2002.

Vishwanathan, Gauri. *Masks of Conquest: Literary Study and British Rule in India*. New York: Columbia University Press, 1989.

Vitkus, Daniel. "Turks and Jews in *The Jew of Malta*," in G. A. Sullivan, Jr., P. Cheney and A. Hadfield (eds.), *Early Modern Drama: A Critical Companion*. Oxford: Oxford University Press, 2006, 61–71.

Vitkus, Daniel. "Adventuring Heroes in the Mediterranean: Mapping the Boundaries of Anglo-Islamic Exchange on the Early Modern Stage," *Journal of Medieval and Early Modern Studies* 37.1 (2007), 75–95.

Walsh, Judith. *Domesticity in Colonial India: What Women Learned When Men Gave Them Advice.* New York: Rowman & Littlefield, 2004.

Youngs, Tim. "Pushing against the Black/White Limits of Maps: African American Writings of Travel," *English Studies in Africa* 53.2 (2010), 71–85.

Zutshi, C. " 'Designed for Eternity': Kashmiri Shawls, Empire, and Cultures of Production and Consumption in Mid-Victorian Britain," *The Journal of British Studies* 48.02 (2009), 420–440.

Part One
Framing the Postcolonial

The essays in this, the opening section of the volume, carry some of the classic texts that "made" the discipline of postcolonial studies and the methodologies of postcolonial theory. Many of the older essays here deal with questions of identity, nationhood, and the nature of colonial discourses. These essays instituted lines of inquiry, and have been reproduced here for a sense of continuity. Frantz Fanon examines the nature of "blackness," pointing to the objectification of the black body by the European which the black man then internalizes so that he is "sealed" (as Fanon calls it) into the object-condition of being black. Homi Bhabha argues for the fractured nature of colonial discourses. Bhabha's work calls into question any coherent and unified sense of colonial discourse and passive colonized response, thus marking a major shift in the evaluation of the former. Edward Said's epochal *Orientalism*, from which we reproduce here the introduction, defined the sweeps and swathes of colonial discourse. Said's work offered a methodology for reading the political aesthetic of European writing, and so has played a key role in literary and cultural examinations of the colo-

nial era. Fredric Jameson's identikit declarations on postcolonial literatures that nearly set an agenda for reading and writing "postcolonially" find their riposte in Aijaz Ahmad's nuanced reading of the condition of postcoloniality and the imperatives of allegory that Jameson prescribes. Separated by some years, and even decades, the later essays in this section throw up new questions, domains, and concerns for the postcolonial project and thereby set the agenda for new debates to emerge. Gayatri Spivak extends her thinking on the "subaltern" to consider the singularities of the very term and the "subject." Yet, even as Spivak calls for a more scrupulous attention to the subaltern minus the universalisms, Dipesh Chakrabarty positions postcolonial criticism, with all its foregrounding of the local and the particular, within global-universal and contemporary concerns, such as global warming. Enlightenment universalisms come up against local contexts and differences, but retain considerable purchase here. Robert Young's essay, like Chakrabarty's, seeks to establish new mandates for postcolonial studies, arguing that the postcolonial *remains*. Young's

Postcolonial Studies: An Anthology, First Edition. Edited by Pramod K. Nayar.
Editorial material and organization © 2016 John Wiley & Sons, Ltd.
Published 2016 by John Wiley & Sons, Ltd.

essay foregrounds the necessity of retaining the postcolonial political stance in the age of continuing empires for its focus on emancipation. Lisa Lau's essay makes a case for the Oriental who/that capitalizes upon the identity "Third World" – to bring back that rhetorical-polemical label – in order to obtain cultural purchase in the global literary marketplace.

In the age of globalized postcolonial authors, issues of representation such as the ones Lau raises, are crucial in understanding the politics behind authorship, publishing, and academic study. Some of the issues and debates inaugurated by Young, Lau, and Chakrabarty will find supporting and contestatory arguments in the essays in subsequent sections.

1 The Fact of Blackness

Frantz Fanon

"Dirty nigger!" Or simply, "Look, a Negro!"

I came into the world imbued with the will to find a meaning in things, my spirit filled with the desire to attain to the source of the world, and then I found that I was an object in the midst of other objects.

Sealed into that crushing objecthood, I turned beseechingly to others. Their attention was a liberation, running over my body suddenly abraded into nonbeing, endowing me once more with an agility that I had thought lost, and by taking me out of the world, restoring me to it. But just as I reached the other side, I stumbled, and the movements, the attitudes, the glances of the other fixed me there, in the sense in which a chemical solution is fixed by a dye. I was indignant; I demanded an explanation. Nothing happened. I burst apart. Now the fragments have been put together again by another self.

As long as the black man is among his own, he will have no occasion, except in minor internal conflicts, to experience his being through others. There is of course the moment of "being for others," of which Hegel speaks, but every ontology is made unattainable in a colonized and civilized society. It would seem that this fact has not been given sufficient attention by those who have discussed the question. In the *Weltanschauung* of a colonized people there is an impurity, a flaw that outlaws any ontological explanation. Someone may object that this is the case with every individual, but such an objection merely conceals a basic problem. Ontology—once it is finally admitted as leaving existence by the wayside—does not permit us to understand the being of the black man. For not only must the black man be black; he must be black in relation to the white man. Some critics will take it on themselves to remind us that this proposition has a converse. I say that this is false. The black man has no ontological

Frantz Fanon, "The Fact of Blackness," in *Black Skin, White Masks*, translated by Charles Lam Markmann. New York: Grove Press, 1967, pp. 82–108. Reproduced in the UK by permission of Éditions du Seuil and in the rest of the world by permission of Grove/Atlantic, Inc.

Postcolonial Studies: An Anthology, First Edition. Edited by Pramod K. Nayar.
Editorial material and organization © 2016 John Wiley & Sons, Ltd.
Published 2016 by John Wiley & Sons, Ltd.

resistance in the eyes of the white man. Overnight the Negro has been given two frames of reference within which he has had to place himself. His metaphysics, or, less pretentiously, his customs and the sources on which they were based, were wiped out because they were in conflict with a civilization that he did not know and that imposed itself on him.

The black man among his own in the twentieth century does not know at what moment his inferiority comes into being through the other. Of course I have talked about the black problem with friends, or, more rarely, with American Negroes. Together we protested, we asserted the equality of all men in the world. In the Antilles there was also that little gulf that exists among the almost-white, the mulatto, and the nigger. But I was satisfied with an intellectual understanding of these differences. It was not really dramatic. And then. …

And then the occasion arose when I had to meet the white man's eyes. An unfamiliar weight burdened me. The real world challenged my claims. In the white world the man of color encounters difficulties in the development of his bodily schema. Consciousness of the body is solely a negating activity. It is a third-person consciousness. The body is surrounded by an atmosphere of certain uncertainty. I know that if I want to smoke, I shall have to reach out my right arm and take the pack of cigarettes lying at the other end of the table. The matches, however, are in the drawer on the left, and I shall have to lean back slightly. And all these movements are made not out of habit but out of implicit knowledge. A slow composition of my *self* as a body in the middle of a spatial and temporal world—such seems to be the schema. It does not impose itself on me; it is, rather, a definitive structuring of the self and of the world—definitive because it creates a real dialectic between my body and the world.

For several years certain laboratories have been trying to produce a serum for "denegrification"; with all the earnestness in the world, laboratories have sterilized their test tubes, checked their scales, and embarked on researches that might make it possible for the miserable Negro to whiten himself and thus to throw off the burden of that corporeal malediction. Below the corporeal schema I had sketched a historico-racial schema. The elements that I used had been provided for me not by "residual sensations and perceptions primarily of a tactile, vestibular, kinesthetic, and visual character,"[1] but by the other, the white man, who had woven me out of a thousand details, anecdotes, stories. I thought that what I had in hand was to construct a physiological self, to balance space, to localize sensations, and here I was called on for more.

"Look, a Negro!" It was an external stimulus that flicked over me as I passed by. I made a tight smile.

"Look, a Negro!" It was true. It amused me.

"Look, a Negro!" The circle was drawing a bit tighter. I made no secret of my amusement.

"Mama, see the Negro! I'm frightened!" Frightened! Frightened! Now they were beginning to be afraid of me. I made up my mind to laugh myself to tears, but laughter had become impossible.

I could no longer laugh, because I already knew that there were legends, stories, history, and above all *historicity*, which I had learned about from Jaspers. Then, assailed at various points, the corporeal schema crumbled, its place taken by a racial epidermal schema. In the train it was no longer a question of being aware of my body in the third person but in a triple person. In the train I was given not one but two, three places. I had already stopped being amused. It was not that I was finding febrile coordinates in the world. I existed triply: I occupied space. I moved toward the other … and the eva-nescent other, hostile but not opaque, transparent, not there, disappeared. Nausea. …

I was responsible at the same time for my body, for my race, for my ancestors. I subjected myself to an objective examination, I discovered my blackness, my ethnic characteristics; and I was battered down by tom-toms, cannibalism, intellectual deficiency, fetishism, racial defects, slave-ships, and above all else, above all: "Sho' good eatin'."

On that day, completely dislocated, unable to be abroad with the other, the white man, who unmercifully imprisoned me, I took myself far off from my own presence, far indeed, and made myself an object. What else could it be for me but an amputa-tion, an excision, a hemorrhage that spattered my whole body with black blood? But I did not want this revision, this thematization. All I wanted was to be a man among other men. I wanted to come lithe and young into a world that was ours and to help to build it together.

But I rejected all immunization of the emotions. I wanted to be a man, nothing but a man. Some identified me with ancestors of mine who had been enslaved or lynched: I decided to accept this. It was on the universal level of the intellect that I understood this inner kinship—I was the grandson of slaves in exactly the same way in which President Lebrun was the grandson of tax-paying, hard-working peasants. In the main, the panic soon vanished.

In America, Negroes are segregated. In South America, Negroes are whipped in the streets, and Negro strikers are cut down by machine-guns. In West Africa, the Negro is an animal. And there beside me, my neighbor in the university, who was born in Algeria, told me: "As long as the Arab is treated like a man, no solution is possible."

"Understand, my dear boy, color prejudice is something I find utterly foreign. … But of course, come in, sir, there is no color prejudice among us. … Quite, the Negro is a man like ourselves. … It is not because he is black that he is less intelligent than we are. … I had a Senegalese buddy in the army who was really clever. …"

Where am I to be classified? Or, if you prefer, tucked away?

"A Martinican, a native of 'our' old colonies."

Where shall I hide?

"Look at the nigger! … Mama, a Negro! … Hell, he's getting mad. … Take no notice, sir, he does not know that you are as civilized as we. …"

My body was given back to me sprawled out, distorted, recolored, clad in mourning in that white winter day. The Negro is an animal, the Negro is bad, the Negro is mean, the Negro is ugly; look, a nigger, it's cold, the nigger is shivering, the nigger is shivering because he is cold, the little boy is trembling because he is afraid of the nigger, the nigger is shivering with cold, that cold that goes through your bones, the handsome little boy is trembling because he thinks that the nigger is quivering with rage, the little white boy throws himself into his mother's arms: Mama, the nigger's going to eat me up.

All round me the white man, above the sky tears at its navel, the earth rasps under my feet, and there is a white song, a white song. All this whiteness that burns me. …

I sit down at the fire and I become aware of my uniform. I had not seen it. It is indeed ugly. I stop there, for who can tell me what beauty is?

Where shall I find shelter from now on? I felt an easily identifiable flood mounting out of the countless facets of my being. I was about to be angry. The fire was long since out, and once more the nigger was trembling.

"Look how handsome that Negro is! …"

"Kiss the handsome Negro's ass, madame!"

Shame flooded her face. At last I was set free from my rumination. At the same time I accomplished two things: I identified my enemies and I made a scene. A grand slam. Now one would be able to laugh.

The field of battle having been marked out, I entered the lists.

What? While I was forgetting, forgiving, and wanting only to love, my message was flung back in my face like a slap. The white world, the only honorable one, barred me from all participation. A man was expected to behave like a man. I was expected to behave like a black man—or at least like a nigger. I shouted a greeting to the world and the world slashed away my joy. I was told to stay within bounds, to go back where I belonged.

They would see, then! I had warned them, anyway. Slavery? It was no longer even mentioned, that unpleasant memory. My supposed inferiority? A hoax that it was better to laugh at. I forgot it all, but only on condition that the world not protect itself against me any longer. I had incisors to test. I was sure they were strong. And besides. …

What! When it was I who had every reason to hate, to despise, I was rejected? When I should have been begged, implored, I was denied the slightest recognition? I resolved, since it was impossible for me to get away from an *inborn complex*, to assert myself as a BLACK MAN. Since the other hesitated to recognize me, there remained only one solution: to make myself known.

In *Anti-Semite and Jew* (p. 95), Sartre says: "They [the Jews] have allowed themselves to be poisoned by the stereotype that others have of them, and they live in fear that their acts will correspond to this stereotype. … We may say that their conduct is perpetually overdetermined from the inside."

All the same, the Jew can be unknown in his Jewishness. He is not wholly what he is. One hopes, one waits. His actions, his behavior are the final determinant. He is a white man, and, apart from some rather debatable characteristics, he can sometimes go unnoticed. He belongs to the race of those who since the beginning of time have never known cannibalism. What an idea, to eat one's father! Simple enough, one has only not to be a nigger. Granted, the Jews are harassed—what am I thinking of? They are hunted down, exterminated, cremated. But these are little family quarrels. The Jew is disliked from the moment he is tracked down. But in my case everything takes on a *new* guise. I am given no chance. I am overdetermined from without. I am the slave not of the "idea" that others have of me but of my own appearance.

I move slowly in the world, accustomed now to seek no longer for upheaval. I progress by crawling. And already I am being dissected under white eyes, the only real eyes. I am *fixed*. Having adjusted their microtomes, they objectively cut away slices of my reality. I am laid bare. I feel, I see in those white faces that it is not a new man who has come in, but a new kind of man, a new genus. Why, it's a Negro!

I slip into corners, and my long antennae pick up the catch-phrases strewn over the surface of things—nigger underwear smells of nigger—nigger teeth are white—nigger feet are big—the nigger's barrel chest—I slip into corners, I remain silent, I strive for anonymity, for invisibility. Look, I will accept the lot, as long as no one notices me!

"Oh, I want you to meet my black friend.… Aimé Césaire, a black man and a university graduate. … Marian Anderson, the finest of Negro singers. … Dr. Cobb, who invented white blood, is a Negro. … Here, say hello to my friend from Martinique (be careful, he's extremely sensitive). …"

Shame. Shame and self-contempt. Nausea. When people like me, they tell me it is in spite of my color. When they dislike me, they point out that it is not because of my color. Either way, I am locked into the infernal circle. I turn away from these inspectors of the Ark before the Flood and I attach myself to my brothers, Negroes like myself. To my horror, they too reject me. They are almost white. And besides they are about to marry white women. They will have children faintly tinged with brown. Who knows, perhaps little by little. …

I had been dreaming.

"I want you to understand, sir, I am one of the best friends the Negro has in Lyon."

The evidence was there, unalterable. My blackness was there, dark and unarguable. And it tormented me, pursued me, disturbed me, angered me.

Negroes are savages, brutes, illiterates. But in my own case I knew that these statements were false. There was a myth of the Negro that had to be destroyed at all costs. The time had long since passed when a Negro priest was an occasion for wonder. We had physicians, professors, statesmen. Yes, but something out of the ordinary still clung to such cases. "We have a Senegalese history teacher. He is quite bright. … Our doctor is colored. He is very gentle."

It was always the Negro teacher, the Negro doctor; brittle as I was becoming, I shivered at the slightest pretext. I knew, for instance, that if the physician made a mistake it would be the end of him and of all those who came after him. What could one expect, after all, from a Negro physician? As long as everything went well, he was praised to the skies, but look out, no nonsense, under any conditions! The black physician can never be sure how close he is to disgrace. I tell you, I was walled in: No exception was made for my refined manners, or my knowledge of literature, or my understanding of the quantum theory.

I requested, I demanded explanations. Gently, in the tone that one uses with a child, they introduced me to the existence of a certain view that was held by certain people, but, I was always told, "We must hope that it will very soon disappear." What was it? Color prejudice.

> It [colour prejudice] is nothing more than the unreasoning hatred of one race for another, the contempt of the stronger and richer peoples for those whom they consider inferior to themselves, and the bitter resentment of those who are kept in subjection and are so frequently insulted. As colour is the most obvious outward manifestation of race it has been made the criterion by which men are judged, irrespective of their social or educational attainments. The light-skinned races have come to despise all those of a darker colour, and the dark-skinned peoples will no longer accept without protest the inferior position to which they have been relegated.[2]

I had read it rightly. It was hate; I was hated, despised, detested, not by the neighbor across the street or my cousin on my mother's side, but by an entire race. I was up against something unreasoned. The psychoanalysts say that nothing is more traumatizing for the young child than his encounters with what is rational. I would personally say that for a man whose only weapon is reason there is nothing more neurotic than contact with unreason.

I felt knife blades open within me. I resolved to defend myself. As a good tactician, I intended to rationalize the world and to show the white man that he was mistaken.

In the Jew, Jean-Paul Sartre says, there is

> a sort of impassioned imperialism of reason: for he wishes not only to convince others that he is right; his goal is to persuade them that there is an absolute and unconditioned value to rationalism. He feels himself to be a missionary of the universal; against the universality of the Catholic religion, from which he is excluded, he asserts the "catholicity" of the rational, an instrument by which to attain to the truth and establish a spiritual bond among men.[3]

And, the author adds, though there may be Jews who have made intuition the basic category of their philosophy, their intuition

> has no resemblance to the Pascalian subtlety of spirit, and it is this latter—based on a thousand imperceptible perceptions—which to the Jew seems his worst enemy. As for Bergson, his philosophy offers the curious appearance of an anti-intellectualist doctrine constructed entirely by the most rational and most critical of intelligences. It is through argument that he establishes the existence of pure duration, of philosophic intuition; and that very intuition which discovers duration or life, is itself universal, since anyone may practice it, and it leads toward the universal, since its objects can be named and conceived.[4]

With enthusiasm I set to cataloguing and probing my surroundings. As times changed, one had seen the Catholic religion at first justify and then condemn slavery and prejudices. But by referring everything to the idea of the dignity of man, one had ripped prejudice to shreds. After much reluctance, the scientists had conceded that the Negro was a human being; *in vivo* and *in vitro* the Negro had been proved analogous to the white man: the same morphology, the same histology. Reason was confident of victory on every level. I put all the parts back together. But I had to change my tune.

That victory played cat and mouse; it made a fool of me. As the other put it, when I was present, it was not; when it was there, I was no longer. In the abstract there was agreement: The Negro is a human being. That is to say, amended the less firmly convinced, that like us he has his heart on the left side. But on certain points the white man remained intractable. Under no conditions did he wish any intimacy between the races, for it is a truism that "crossings between widely different races can lower the physical and mental level. … Until we have a more definite knowledge of the effect of race-crossings we shall certainly do best to avoid crossings between widely different races."[5]

For my own part, I would certainly know how to react. And in one sense, if I were asked for a definition of myself, I would say that I am one who waits; I investigate my surroundings, I interpret everything in terms of what I discover, I become sensitive.

In the first chapter of the history that the others have compiled for me, the foundation of cannibalism has been made eminently plain in order that I may not lose sight of it. My chromosomes were supposed to have a few thicker or thinner genes representing cannibalism. In addition to the *sex-linked*, the scholars had now discovered the *racial-linked*.[6] What a shameful science!

But I understand this "psychological mechanism." For it is a matter of common knowledge that the mechanism is only psychological. Two centuries ago I was lost to humanity, I was a slave forever. And then came men who said that it all had gone on far too long. My tenaciousness did the rest; I was saved from the civilizing deluge. I have gone forward.

Too late. Everything is anticipated, thought out, demonstrated, made the most of. My trembling hands take hold of nothing; the vein has been mined out. Too late! But once again I want to understand.

Since the time when someone first mourned the fact that he had arrived too late and everything had been said, a nostalgia for the past has seemed to persist. Is this that lost original paradise of which Otto Rank speaks? How many such men, apparently rooted to the womb of the world, have devoted their lives to studying the Delphic oracles or exhausted themselves in attempts to plot the wanderings of Ulysses! The pan-spiritualists seek to prove the existence of a soul in animals by using this argument: A dog lies down on the grave of his master and starves to death there. We had to wait for Janet to demonstrate that the aforesaid dog, in contrast to man, simply lacked the capacity to liquidate the past. We speak of the glory of Greece, Artaud says; but, he adds, if modern man can no longer understand the *Choephoroi* of Aeschylus, it is Aeschylus who is to blame. It is tradition to which the anti-Semites turn in order to ground the validity of their "point of view." It is tradition, it is that long historical past, it is that blood relation between Pascal and Descartes, that is invoked when the Jew is told, "There is no possibility of your finding a place in society." Not long ago, one of those good Frenchmen said in a train where I was sitting: "Just let the real French virtues keep going and the race is safe. Now more than ever, national union must be made a reality. Let's have an end of internal strife! Let's face up to the foreigners (here he turned toward my corner) no matter who they are."

It must be said in his defense that he stank of cheap wine; if he had been capable of it, he would have told me that my emancipated-slave blood could not possibly be stirred by the name of Villon or Taine.

An outrage!

The Jew and I: Since I was not satisfied to be racialized, by a lucky turn of fate I was humanized. I joined the Jew, my brother in misery.

An outrage!

At first thought it may seem strange that the anti-Semite's outlook should be related to that of the Negrophobe. It was my philosophy professor, a native of the Antilles, who recalled the fact to me one day: "Whenever you hear anyone abuse the Jews, pay attention, because he is talking about you." And I found that he was universally right— by which I meant that I was answerable in my body and in my heart for what was done to my brother. Later I realized that he meant, quite simply, an anti-Semite is inevitably anti-Negro.

You come too late, much too late. There will always be a world—a white world— between you and us. … The other's total inability to liquidate the past once and for all. In the face of this affective ankylosis of the white man, it is understandable that I could have made up my mind to utter my Negro cry. Little by little, putting out pseudopodia here and there, I secreted a race. And that race staggered under the burden of a basic element. What was it? *Rhythm!* Listen to our singer, Léopold Senghor:

> It is the thing that is most perceptible and least material. It is the archetype of the vital element. It is the first condition and the hallmark of Art, as breath is of life: breath, which accelerates or slows, which becomes even or agitated according to the tension in the individual, the degree and the nature of his emotion. This is rhythm in its primordial purity, this is rhythm in the masterpieces of Negro art, especially sculpture. It is composed of a theme—sculptural form—which is set in opposition to a sister theme, as inhalation is to exhalation, and that is repeated. It is not the kind of symmetry that gives rise to monotony; rhythm is alive, it is free. … This is how rhythm affects what is least intellectual in us, tyrannically, to make us penetrate to the spirituality of the object; and that character of abandon which is ours is itself rhythmic.[7]

Had I read that right? I read it again with redoubled attention. From the opposite end of the white world a magical Negro culture was hailing me. Negro sculpture! I began to flush with pride. Was this our salvation?

I had rationalized the world and the world had rejected me on the basis of color prejudice. Since no agreement was possible on the level of reason, I threw myself back toward unreason. It was up to the white man to be more irrational than I. Out of the necessities of my struggle I had chosen the method of regression, but the fact remained that it was an unfamiliar weapon; here I am at home; I am made of the irrational; I wade in the irrational. Up to the neck in the irrational. And now how my voice vibrates!

> Those who invented neither gunpowder nor the compass
> Those who never learned to conquer steam or electricity
> Those who never explored the seas or the skies
> But they know the farthest corners of the land of anguish
> Those who never knew any journey save that of abduction
> Those who learned to kneel in docility
> Those who were domesticated and Christianized
> Those who were injected with bastardy. …

Yes, all those are my brothers—a "bitter brotherhood" imprisons all of us alike. Having stated the minor thesis, I went overboard after something else.

> … But those without whom the earth would not be the earth
> Tumescence all the more fruitful
> than
> the empty land
> still more the land
> Storehouse to guard and ripen all
> on earth that is most earth
> My blackness is no stone, its deafness
> hurled against the clamor of the day
> My blackness is no drop of lifeless water

on the dead eye of the world
My blackness is neither a tower nor a cathedral
It thrusts into the red flesh of the sun
It thrusts into the burning flesh of the sky
It hollows through the dense dismay of its own pillar of patience.[8]

Eyah! the tom-tom chatters out the cosmic message. Only the Negro has the capacity to convey it, to decipher its meaning, its import. Astride the world, my strong heels spurring into the flanks of the world, I stare into the shoulders of the world as the celebrant stares at the midpoint between the eyes of the sacrificial victim.

But they abandon themselves, possessed, to the essence of all things, knowing nothing of externals but possessed by the movement of all things

uncaring to subdue but playing the play of the world
truly the eldest sons of the world
open to all the breaths of the world
meeting-place of all the winds of the world
undrained bed of all the waters of the world
spark of the sacred fire of the World
flesh of the flesh of the world, throbbing with the very movement of the world![9]

Blood! Blood! … Birth! Ecstasy of becoming! Three-quarters engulfed in the confusions of the day, I feel myself redden with blood. The arteries of all the world, convulsed, torn away, uprooted, have turned toward me and fed me.

"Blood! Blood! All our blood stirred by the male heart of the sun."[10]

Sacrifice was a middle point between the creation and myself—now I went back no longer to sources but to The Source. Nevertheless, one had to distrust rhythm, earth-mother love, this mystic, carnal marriage of the group and the cosmos.

In *La vie sexuelle en Afrique noire*, a work rich in perceptions, De Pédrals implies that always in Africa, no matter what field is studied, it will have a certain magico-social structure. He adds:

All these are the elements that one finds again on a still greater scale in the domain of secret societies. To the extent, moreover, to which persons of either sex, subjected to circumcision during adolescence, are bound under penalty of death not to reveal to the uninitiated what they have experienced, and to the extent to which initiation into a secret society always excites to acts of *sacred love*, there is good ground to conclude by viewing both male and female circumcision and the rites that they embellish as constitutive of minor secret societies.[11]

I walk on white nails. Sheets of water threaten my soul on fire. Face to face with these rites, I am doubly alert. Black magic! Orgies, witches' sabbaths, heathen ceremonies, amulets. Coitus is an occasion to call on the gods of the clan. It is a sacred act, pure, absolute, bringing invisible forces into action. What is one to think of all these manifestations, all these initiations, all these acts? From ever direction I am assaulted by the obscenity of dances and of words. Almost at my ear there is a song:

> First our hearts burned hot
> Now they are cold
> All we think of now is Love
> When we return to the village
> When we see the great phallus
> Ah how then we will make Love
> For our parts will be dry and clean.[12]

The soil, which only a moment ago was still a tamed steed, begins to revel. Are these virgins, these nymphomaniacs? Black Magic, primitive mentality, animism, animal eroticism, it all floods over me. All of it is typical of peoples that have not kept pace with the evolution of the human race. Or, if one prefers, this is humanity at its lowest. Having reached this point, I was long reluctant to commit myself. Aggression was in the stars. I had to choose. What do I mean? I had no choice. …

Yes, we are—we Negroes—backward, simple, free in our behavior. That is because for us the body is not something opposed to what you call the mind. We are in the world. And long live the couple, Man and Earth! Besides, our men of letters helped me to convince you; your white civilization overlooks subtle riches and sensitivity. Listen:

Emotive sensitivity. *Emotion is completely Negro as reason is Greek*.[13] Water rippled by every breeze? Unsheltered soul blown by every wind, whose fruit often drops before it is ripe? Yes, in one way, the Negro today is richer *in gifts than in works*.[14] But the tree thrusts its roots into the earth. The river runs deep, carrying precious seeds. And, the Afro-American poet, Langston Hughes, says:

> I have known rivers
> ancient dark rivers
> my soul has grown deep
> like the deep rivers.

The very nature of the Negro's emotion, of his sensitivity, furthermore, explains his attitude toward the object perceived with such basic intensity. It is an abandon that becomes need, an active state of communion, indeed of identification, however negligible the action—I almost said the personality—of the object. A rhythmic attitude: The adjective should be kept in mind.[15]

So here we have the Negro rehabilitated, "standing before the bar," ruling the world with his intuition, the Negro recognized, set on his feet again, sought after, taken up, and he is a Negro—no, he is not a Negro but the Negro, exciting the fecund antennae of the world, placed in the foreground of the world, raining his poetic power on the world, "open to all the breaths of the world." I embrace the world! I am the world! The white man has never understood this magic substitution. The white man wants the world; he wants it for himself alone. He finds himself predestined master of this world. He enslaves it. An acquisitive relation is established between the world and him. But there exist other values that fit only my forms. Like a magician, I robbed the white man of "a certain world," forever after lost to him and his. When that happened, the white man must have been rocked backward by a force that he could not identify, so little used as he is to such reactions. Somewhere beyond the objective world of farms and banana trees and rubber trees, I had subtly brought the real world into being. The essence of the world was my fortune. Between the world and me a relation of coexistence was established. I had discovered the primeval One. My "speaking hands" tore at the hysterical throat of the world. The white man had the anguished feeling that I was escaping from him and that I was taking something with me. He went through my pockets. He thrust probes into the least circumvolution of my brain. Everywhere he found only the obvious. So it was obvious that I had a secret. I was interrogated; turning away with an air of mystery, I murmured:

Tokowaly, uncle, do you remember the nights gone by
When my head weighed heavy on the back of your patience or
Holding my hand your hand led me by shadows and signs
The fields are flowers of glowworms, stars hang on the bushes, on the trees
Silence is everywhere
Only the scents of the jungle hum, swarms of reddish bees that overwhelm the
    crickets' shrill sounds,
And covered tom-tom, breathing in the distance of the night.
You, Tokowaly, you listen to what cannot be heard, and you explain to me what the
    ancestors are saying in the liquid calm of the constellations,
The bull, the scorpion, the leopard, the elephant, and the fish we know,
And the white pomp of the Spirits in the heavenly shell that has no end,
But now comes the radiance of the goddess Moon and the veils of the shadows fall.
Night of Africa, my black night, mystical and bright, black and shining.[16]

I made myself the poet of the world. The white man had found a poetry in which there was nothing poetic. The soul of the white man was corrupted, and, as I was told by a friend who was a teacher in the United States, "The presence of the Negroes beside the whites is in a way an insurance policy on humanness. When the whites feel that they have become too mechanized, they turn to the men of color and ask them for a little human sustenance." At last I had been recognized, I was no longer a zero.

I had soon to change my tune. Only momentarily at a loss, the white man explained to me that, genetically, I represented a stage of development: "Your properties have been exhausted by us. We have had earth mystics such as you will never approach. Study our history and you will see how far this fusion has gone." Then I had the feeling that I was repeating a cycle. My originality had been torn out of me. I wept a long time, and then I began to live again. But I was haunted by a galaxy of erosive stereotypes: the Negro's *sui generis* odor … the Negro's *sui generis* good nature … the Negro's *sui generis* gullibility. …

I had tried to flee myself through my kind, but the whites had thrown themselves on me and hamstrung me. I tested the limits of my essence; beyond all doubt there was not much of it left. It was here that I made my most remarkable discovery. Properly speaking, this discovery was a rediscovery.

I rummaged frenetically through all the antiquity of the black man. What I found there took away my breath. In his book *L'abolition de l'esclavage* Schoelcher presented us with compelling arguments. Since then, Frobenius, Westermann, Delafosse—all of them white—had joined the chorus: Ségou, Djenné, cities of more than a hundred thousand people; accounts of learned blacks (doctors of theology who went to Mecca to interpret the Koran). All of that, exhumed from the past, spread with its insides out, made it possible for me to find a valid historic place. The white man was wrong, I was not a primitive, not even a half-man, I belonged to a race that had already been working in gold and silver two thousand years ago. And too there was something else, something else that the white man could not understand. Listen:

What sort of men were these, then, who had been torn away from their families, their countries, their religions, with a savagery unparalleled in history?

Gentle men, polite, considerate, unquestionably superior to those who tortured them—that collection of adventurers who slashed and violated and spat on Africa to make the stripping of her the easier.

The men they took away knew how to build houses, govern empires, erect cities, cultivate fields, mine for metals, weave cotton, forge steel.

Their religion had its own beauty, based on mystical connections with the founder of the city. Their customs were pleasing, built on unity, kindness, respect for age.

No coercion, only mutual assistance, the joy of living, a free acceptance of discipline.

Order—Earnestness—Poetry and Freedom.

From the untroubled private citizen to the almost fabulous leader there was an unbroken chain of understanding and trust. No science? Indeed yes; but also, to protect them from fear, they possessed great myths in which the most subtle observation and the most daring imagination were balanced and blended. No art? They had their magnificent sculpture, in which human feeling erupted so unrestrained yet always followed the obsessive laws of rhythm in its organization of the major elements of a material called upon to capture, in order to redistribute, the most secret forces of the universe. ...[17]

Monuments in the very heart of Africa? Schools? Hospitals? Not a single good burgher of the twentieth century, no Durand, no Smith, no Brown even suspects that such things existed in Africa before the Europeans came. ...

But Schoelcher reminds us of their presence, discovered by Caillé, Mollien, the Cander brothers. And, though he nowhere reminds us that when the Portuguese landed on the banks of the Congo in 1498, they found a rich and flourishing state there and that the courtiers of Ambas were dressed in robes of silk and brocade, at least he knows that Africa had brought itself up to a juridical concept of the state, and he is aware, living in the very flood of imperialism, that European civilization, after all, is only one more civilization among many—and not the most merciful.[18]

I put the white man back into his place; growing bolder, I jostled him and told him point-blank, "Get used to me, I am not getting used to anyone." I shouted my laughter to the stars. The white man, I could see, was resentful. His reaction time lagged interminably. ... I had won. I was jubilant.

"Lay aside your history, your investigations of the past, and try to feel yourself into our rhythm. In a society such as ours, industrialized to the highest degree, dominated by scientism, there is no longer room for your sensitivity. One must be tough if one is to be allowed to live. What matters now is no longer playing the game of the world but subjugating it with integers and atoms. Oh, certainly, I will be told, now and then when we are worn out by our lives in big buildings, we will turn to you as we do to our children—to the innocent, the ingenuous, the spontaneous. We will turn to you as to the childhood of the world. You are so real in your life—so funny, that is. Let us run away for a little while from our ritualized, polite civilization and let us relax, bend to those heads, those adorably expressive faces. In a way, you reconcile us with ourselves."

Thus my unreason was countered with reason, my reason with "real reason." Every hand was a losing hand for me. I analyzed my heredity. I made a complete audit of my ailment. I wanted to be typically Negro—it was no longer possible. I wanted to be white—that was a joke. And, when I tried, on the level of ideas and intellectual activity, to reclaim my negritude, it was snatched away from me. Proof was presented that my effort was only a term in the dialectic:

> But there is something more important: The Negro, as we have said, creates an anti-racist racism for himself. In no sense does he wish to rule the world: He seeks the abolition of all ethnic privileges, wherever they come from; he asserts his solidarity with the oppressed of all colors. At once the subjective, existential, ethnic idea of *negritude* "passes," as Hegel puts it, into the objective, positive, exact idea of *proletariat*. "For Césaire," Senghor says, "the white man is the symbol of capital as the Negro is that of labor. ... Beyond the black-skinned men of his race it is the battle of the world proletariat that is his song."
>
> That is easy to say, but less easy to think out. And undoubtedly it is no coincidence that the most ardent poets of negritude are at the same time militant Marxists.
>
> But that does not prevent the idea of race from mingling with that of class: The first is concrete and particular, the second is universal and abstract; the one stems from what Jaspers calls understanding and the other from intellection; the first is the result of a psychobiological syncretism and the second is a methodical construction based on experience. In fact, negritude appears as the minor term of a dialectical progression: The theoretical and practical assertion of the supremacy of the white man is its thesis; the position of negritude as an antithetical value is the moment of negativity. But this negative moment is insufficient by itself, and the Negroes who employ it know this very well; they know that it is intended to prepare the synthesis or realization of the human in a society without races. Thus negritude is the root of its own destruction, it is a transition and not a conclusion, a means and not an ultimate end.[19]

When I read that page, I felt that I had been robbed of my last chance. I said to my friends, "The generation of the younger black poets has just suffered a blow that can never be forgiven." Help had been sought from a friend of the colored peoples, and that friend had found no better response than to point out the relativity of what they were doing. For once, that born Hegelian had forgotten that consciousness has to lose itself in the night of the absolute, the only condition to attain to consciousness of self. In opposition to rationalism, he summoned up the negative side, but he forgot that this negativity draws its worth from an almost substantive absoluteness. A consciousness committed to experience is ignorant, has to be ignorant, of the essences and the determinations of its being.

Orphée Noir is a date in the intellectualization of the *experience* of being black. And Sartre's mistake was not only to seek the source of the source but in a certain sense to block that source:

> Will the source of Poetry be dried up? Or will the great black flood, in spite of everything, color the sea into which it pours itself? It does not matter: Every age has its own poetry; in every age the circumstances of history choose a nation, a race, a class to take up the torch by creating situations that can be expressed or transcended only through Poetry; sometimes the poetic impulse coincides with the revolutionary impulse, and sometimes they take different courses. Today let us hail the turn of history that will make it possible for the black men to utter "the great Negro cry with a force that will shake the pillars of the world" (Césaire).[20]

And so it is not I who make a meaning for myself, but it is the meaning that was already there, pre-existing, waiting for me. It is not out of my bad nigger's misery, my bad nigger's teeth, my bad nigger's hunger that I will shape a torch with which to burn down the world, but it is the torch that was already there, waiting for that turn of history.

In terms of consciousness, the black consciousness is held out as an absolute density, as filled with itself, a stage preceding any invasion, any abolition of the ego by desire. Jean-Paul Sartre, in this work, has destroyed black zeal. In opposition to historical becoming, there had always been the unforeseeable. I needed to lose myself completely in negritude. One day, perhaps, in the depths of that unhappy romanticism. ...

In any case I *needed* not to know. This struggle, this new decline had to take on an aspect of completeness. Nothing is more unwelcome than the commonplace: "You'll change, my boy; I was like that too when I was young ... you'll see, it will all pass."

The dialectic that brings necessity into the foundation of my freedom drives me out of myself. It shatters my unreflected position. Still in terms of consciousness, black consciousness is immanent in its own eyes. I am not a potentiality of something, I am wholly what I am. I do not have to look for the universal. No probability has any place inside me. My Negro consciousness does not hold itself out as a lack. It *is*. It is its own follower.

But, I will be told, your statements show a misreading of the processes of history. Listen then:

> Africa I have kept your memory Africa
> you are inside me
> Like the splinter in the wound
> like a guardian fetish in the center of the village
> make me the stone in your sling
> make my mouth the lips of your wound
> make my knees the broken pillars of your abasement
> AND YET
> I want to be of your race alone

workers peasants of all lands ...
... white worker in Detroit black peon in Alabama
uncountable nation in capitalist slavery
destiny ranges us shoulder to shoulder
repudiating the ancient maledictions of blood taboos
we roll away the ruins of our solitudes
If the flood is a frontier
we will strip the gully of its endless
covering flow
If the Sierra is a frontier
we will smash the jaws of the volcanoes
upholding the Cordilleras
and the plain will be the parade ground of the dawn
where we regroup our forces sundered
by the deceits of our masters
As the contradiction among the features
creates the harmony of the face
we proclaim the oneness of the suffering
and the revolt
of all the peoples on all the face of the earth
and we mix the mortar of the age of brotherhood
out of the dust of idols.[21]

Exactly, we will reply, Negro experience is not a whole, for there is not merely *one* Negro, there are *Negroes*. What a difference, for instance, in this other poem:

The white man killed my father
Because my father was proud
The white man raped my mother
Because my mother was beautiful
The white man wore out my brother in the hot sun of the roads
Because my brother was strong
Then the white man came to me
His hands red with blood
Spat his contempt into my black face
Out of his tyrant's voice:
"Hey boy, a basin, a towel, water."[22]

Or this other one:

My brother with teeth that glisten at the compliments of hypocrites
My brother with gold-rimmed spectacles
Over eyes that turn blue at the sound of the Master's voice
My poor brother in dinner jacket with its silk lapels
Clucking and whispering and strutting through the drawing rooms of Condescension
How pathetic you are
The sun of your native country is nothing more now than a shadow

On your composed civilized face
And your grandmother's hut
Brings blushes into cheeks made white by years of abasement and *Mea culpa*
But when regurgitating the flood of lofty empty words
Like the load that presses on your shoulders
You walk again on the rough red earth of Africa
These words of anguish will state the rhythm of your uneasy gait
I feel so alone, so alone here![23]

From time to time one would like to stop. To state reality is a wearing task. But, when one has taken it into one's head to try to express existence, one runs the risk of finding only the nonexistent. What is certain is that, at the very moment when I was trying to grasp my own being, Sartre, who remained The Other, gave me a name and thus shattered my last illusion. While I was saying to him:

"My negritude is neither a tower nor a cathedral,
it thrusts into the red flesh of the sun,
it thrusts into the burning flesh of the sky,
it hollows through the dense dismay of its own pillar of patience …"

while I was shouting that, in the paroxysm of my being and my fury, he was reminding me that my blackness was only a minor term. In all truth, in all truth I tell you, my shoulders slipped out of the framework of the world, my feet could no longer feel the touch of the ground. Without a Negro past, without a Negro future, it was impossible for me to live my Negrohood. Not yet white, no longer wholly black, I was damned. Jean-Paul Sartre had forgotten that the Negro suffers in his body quite differently from the white man.[24] Between the white man and me the connection was irrevocably one of transcendence.[25]

But the constancy of my love had been forgotten. I defined myself as an absolute intensity of beginning. So I took up my negritude, and with tears in my eyes I put its machinery together again. What had been broken to pieces was rebuilt, reconstructed by the intuitive lianas of my hands.

My cry grew more violent: I am a Negro, I am a Negro, I am a Negro. …

And there was my poor brother—living out his neurosis to the extreme and finding himself paralyzed:

THE NEGRO: I can't, ma'am.
LIZZIE: Why not?
THE NEGRO: I can't shoot white folks.
LIZZIE: Really! That would bother them, wouldn't it?
THE NEGRO: They're white folks, ma'am.
LIZZIE: So what? Maybe they got a right to bleed you like a pig just because they're white?
THE NEGRO: But they're white folks.

A feeling of inferiority? No, a feeling of nonexistence. Sin is Negro as virtue is white. All those white men in a group, guns in their hands, cannot be wrong. I am guilty. I do not know of what, but I know that I am no good.

THE NEGRO: That's how it goes ma'am. That's how it always goes with white folks.

LIZZIE: You too? You feel guilty?

THE NEGRO: Yes ma'am.[26]

It is Bigger Thomas—he is afraid, he is terribly afraid. He is afraid, but of what is he afraid? Of himself. No one knows yet who he is, but he knows that fear will fill the world when the world finds out. And when the world knows, the world always expects something of the Negro. He is afraid lest the world know, he is afraid of the fear that the world would feel if the world knew. Like that old woman on her knees who begged me to tie her to her bed:

"I just know, Doctor: Any minute that thing will take hold of me."

"What thing?"

"The wanting to kill myself. Tie me down, I'm afraid."

In the end, Bigger Thomas acts. To put an end to his tension, he acts, he responds to the world's anticipation.[27]

So it is with the character in *If He Hollers Let Him Go*[28]—who does precisely what he did not want to do. That big blonde who was always in his way, weak, sensual, offered, open, fearing (desiring) rape, became his mistress in the end.

The Negro is a toy in the white man's hands; so, in order to shatter the hellish cycle, he explodes. I cannot go to a film without seeing myself. I wait for me. In the interval, just before the film starts, I wait for me. The people in the theater are watching me, examining me, waiting for me. A Negro groom is going to appear. My heart makes my head swim.

The crippled veteran of the Pacific war says to my brother, "Resign yourself to your color the way I got used to my stump; we're both victims."[29]

Nevertheless with all my strength I refuse to accept that amputation. I feel in myself a soul as immense as the world, truly a soul as deep as the deepest of rivers, my chest has the power to expand without limit. I am a master and I am advised to adopt the humility of the cripple. Yesterday, awakening to the world, I saw the sky turn upon itself utterly and wholly. I wanted to rise, but the disemboweled silence fell back upon me, its wings paralyzed. Without responsibility, straddling Nothingness and Infinity, I began to weep.

Notes

[1] Jean Lhermitte, *L'Image de notre corps* (Paris, Nouvelle Revue critique, 1939), p. 17.

[2] Sir Alan Burns, *Colour Prejudice* (London, Allen and Unwin, 1948), p. 16.

[3] *Anti-Semite and Jew* (New York, Grove Press, 1960), pp. 112–113.

[4] *Ibid.*, p. 115.

[5] Jon Alfred Mjoen, "Harmonic and Disharmonic Race-crossings," The Second International Congress of Eugenics (1921), *Eugenics in Race and State*, vol. II, p. 60, quoted in Sir Alan Burns, *op. cit.*, p. 120.

[6] In English in the original. (Translator's note.)

[7] "Ce que l'homme noir apporte," in Claude Nordey, *L'Homme de couleur* (Paris, Plon, 1939), pp. 309–310.

[8] Aimé Césaire, *Cahier d'un retour au pays natal* (Paris, Présence Africaine, 1956), pp. 77–78.

[9] *Ibid.*, p. 78.

[10] *Ibid.*, p. 79.

[11] De Pédrals, *La vie sexuelle en Afrique noire* (Paris, Payot), p. 83.

[12] A. M. Vergiat, *Les rites secrets des primitifs de l'Oubangui* (Paris, Payot, 1951), p. 113.

[13] My italics—F.F.

[14] My italics—F.F.

15. Léopold Senghor, "Ce que l'homme noir apporte," in Nordey, *op. cit.*, p. 205.

16. Léopold Senghor, *Chants d'ombre* (Paris, Editions du Seuil, 1945).

17. Aimé Césaire, Introduction to Victor Schoelcher, *Esclavage et colonisation* (Paris, Presses Universitaires de France, 1948), p. 7.

18. *Ibid.*, p. 8.

19. Jean-Paul Sartre, *Orphée Noir*, preface to *Anthologie de la nouvelle poésie nègre et malgache* (Paris, Presses Universitaires de France, 1948), pp. xl ff.

20. *Ibid.*, p. xliv.

21. Jacques Roumain, "Bois-d'Ebène," Prelude, in *Anthologie de la nouvelle poésie nègre et malgache*, p. 113.

22. David Diop, "Le temps du martyre," in *ibid.*, p. 174.

23. David Diop, "Le Renégat."

24. Though Sartre's speculations on the existence of The Other may be correct (to the extent, we must remember, to which *Being and Nothingness* describes an alienated consciousness), their application to a black consciousness proves fallacious. That is because the white man is not only The Other but also the master, whether real or imaginary.

25. In the sense in which the word is used by Jean Wahl in *Existence humaine et transcendence* (Neuchâtel, La Baconnière, 1944).

26. Jean-Paul Sartre, *The Respectful Prostitute*, in *Three Plays* (New York, Knopf, 1949), pp. 189, 191. Originally, *La Putain respectueuse* (Paris, Gallimard, 1947). See also *Home of the Brave*, a film by Mark Robson.

27. Richard Wright, *Native Son* (New York, Harper, 1940).

28. By Chester Himes (Garden City, Doubleday, 1945).

29. *Home of the Brave*.

2 Introduction to *Orientalism*

Edward Said

I

On a visit to Beirut during the terrible civil war of 1975–1976 a French journalist wrote regretfully of the gutted downtown area that "it had once seemed to belong to … the Orient of Chateau-briand and Nerval."[1] He was right about the place, of course, especially so far as a European was concerned. The Orient was almost a European invention, and had been since antiquity a place of romance, exotic beings, haunting memories and landscapes, remarkable experiences. Now it was disappearing; in a sense it had happened, its time was over. Perhaps it seemed irrelevant that Orientals themselves had something at stake in the process, that even in the time of Chateaubriand and Nerval Orientals had lived there, and that now it was they who were suffering; the main thing for the European visitor was a European representation of the Orient and its contemporary fate, both of which had a privileged communal significance for the journalist and his French readers.

Americans will not feel quite the same about the Orient, which for them is much more likely to be associated very differently with the Far East (China and Japan, mainly). Unlike the Americans, the French and the British—less so the Germans, Russians, Spanish, Portuguese, Italians, and Swiss—have had a long tradition of what I shall be calling *Orientalism*, a way of coming to terms with the Orient that is based on the Orient's special place in European Western experience. The Orient is not only adjacent to Europe; it is also the place of Europe's greatest and richest and oldest colonies, the source of its civilizations and languages, its cultural contestant, and one of its deepest and most recurring images of the Other. In addition, the Orient has helped to define Europe (or the West) as its contrasting image, idea, personality, experience. Yet none of this Orient is merely imaginative. The Orient is an integral part of European *material*

Edward W. Said, *Orientalism*. New York: Pantheon Books, 1978, pp. 1–28. © 1978 Edward W. Said. Used by permission of Pantheon Books, an imprint of the Knopf Doubleday Publishing Group, a division of Random House LLC.

Postcolonial Studies: An Anthology, First Edition. Edited by Pramod K. Nayar.
Editorial material and organization © 2016 John Wiley & Sons, Ltd.
Published 2016 by John Wiley & Sons, Ltd.

civilization and culture. Orientalism expresses and represents that part culturally and even ideologically as a mode of discourse with supporting institutions, vocabulary, scholarship, imagery, doctrines, even colonial bureaucracies and colonial styles. In contrast, the American understanding of the Orient will seem considerably less dense, although our recent Japanese, Korean, and Indochinese adventures ought now to be creating a more sober, more realistic "Oriental" awareness. Moreover, the vastly expanded American political and economic role in the Near East (the Middle East) makes great claims on our understanding of that Orient.

It will be clear to the reader (and will become clearer still throughout the many pages that follow) that by Orientalism I mean several things, all of them, in my opinion, interdependent. The most readily accepted designation for Orientalism is an academic one, and indeed the label still serves in a number of academic institutions. Anyone who teaches, writes about, or researches the Orient—and this applies whether the person is an anthropologist, sociologist, historian, or philologist—either in its specific or its general aspects, is an Orientalist, and what he or she does is Orientalism. Compared with *Oriental studies* or *area studies*, it is true that the term *Orientalism* is less preferred by specialists today, both because it is too vague and general and because it connotes the high-handed executive attitude of nineteenth-century and early-twentieth-century European colonialism. Nevertheless books are written and congresses held with "the Orient" as their main focus, with the Orientalist in his new or old guise as their main authority. The point is that even if it does not survive as it once did, Orientalism lives on academically through its doctrines and theses about the Orient and the Oriental.

Related to this academic tradition, whose fortunes, transmigrations, specializations, and transmissions are in part the subject of this study, is a more general meaning for Orientalism. Orientalism is a style of thought based upon an ontological and epistemological distinction made between "the Orient" and (most of the time) "the Occident." Thus a very large mass of writers, among whom are poets, novelists, philosophers, political theorists, economists, and imperial administrators, have accepted the basic distinction between East and West as the starting point for elaborate theories, epics, novels, social descriptions, and political accounts concerning the Orient, its people, customs, "mind," destiny, and so on. *This* Orientalism can accommodate Aeschylus, say, and Victor Hugo, Dante and Karl Marx. A little later in this introduction I shall deal with the methodological problems one encounters in so broadly construed a "field" as this.

The interchange between the academic and the more or less imaginative meanings of Orientalism is a constant one, and since the late eighteenth century there has been a considerable, quite disciplined—perhaps even regulated—traffic between the two. Here I come to the third meaning of Orientalism, which is something more historically and materially defined than either of the other two. Taking the late eighteenth century as a very roughly defined starting point Orientalism can be discussed and analyzed as the corporate institution for dealing with the Orient—dealing with it by making statements about it, authorizing views of it, describing it, by teaching it, settling it, ruling over it: in short, Orientalism as a Western style for dominating, restructuring, and having authority over the Orient. I have found it useful here to employ Michel Foucault's notion of a discourse, as described by him in *The Archaeology of Knowledge* and in *Discipline and Punish*, to identify Orientalism. My contention is that without examining Orientalism as a discourse one cannot possibly understand the enormously systematic discipline by which European culture was able to manage—and even produce—the

Orient politically, sociologically, militarily, ideologically, scientifically, and imaginatively during the post-Enlightenment period. Moreover, so authoritative a position did Orientalism have that I believe no one writing, thinking, or acting on the Orient could do so without taking account of the limitations on thought and action imposed by Orientalism. In brief, because of Orientalism the Orient was not (and is not) a free subject of thought or action. This is not to say that Orientalism unilaterally determines what can be said about the Orient, but that it is the whole network of interests inevitably brought to bear on (and therefore always involved in) any occasion when that peculiar entity "the Orient" is in question. How this happens is what this book tries to demonstrate. It also tries to show that European culture gained in strength and identity by setting itself off against the Orient as a sort of surrogate and even underground self.

Historically and culturally there is a quantitative as well as a qualitative difference between the Franco-British involvement in the Orient and—until the period of American ascendancy after World War II—the involvement of every other European and Atlantic power. To speak of Orientalism therefore is to speak mainly, although not exclusively, of a British and French cultural enterprise, a project whose dimensions take in such disparate realms as the imagination itself, the whole of India and the Levant, the Biblical texts and the Biblical lands, the spice trade, colonial armies and a long tradition of colonial administrators, a formidable scholarly corpus, innumerable Oriental "experts" and "hands," an Oriental professorate, a complex array of "Oriental" ideas (Oriental despotism, Oriental splendor, cruelty, sensuality), many Eastern sects, philosophies, and wisdoms domesticated for local European use—the list can be extended more or less indefinitely. My point is that Orientalism derives from a particular closeness experienced between Britain and France and the Orient, which until the early nineteenth century had really meant only India and the Bible lands. From the beginning of the nineteenth century until the end of World War II France and Britain dominated the Orient and Orientalism; since World War II America has dominated the Orient, and approaches it as France and Britain once did. Out of that closeness, whose dynamic is enormously productive even if it always demonstrates the comparatively greater strength of the Occident (British, French, or American), comes the large body of texts I call Orientalist.

It should be said at once that even with the generous number of books and authors that I examine, there is a much larger number that I simply have had to leave out. My argument, however, depends neither upon an exhaustive catalogue of texts dealing with the Orient nor upon a clearly delimited set of texts, authors, and ideas that together make up the Orientalist canon. I have depended instead upon a different methodological alternative—whose backbone in a sense is the set of historical generalizations I have so far been making in this Introduction—and it is these I want now to discuss in more analytical detail.

II

I have begun with the assumption that the Orient is not an inert fact of nature. It is not merely *there*, just as the Occident itself is not just *there* either. We must take seriously Vico's great observation that men make their own history, that what they can know is what they have made, and extend it to geography: as both geographical and cultural entities—to say nothing of historical entities—such locales, regions, geographical sectors as "Orient" and "Occident" are man-made. Therefore as much as the West itself, the Orient is an idea that has a history and a tradition of thought, imagery, and vocabulary that have given it reality and presence in and for the West. The two geographical entities thus support and to an extent reflect each other.

Having said that, one must go on to state a number of reasonable qualifications. In the first place, it would be wrong to conclude that the Orient was *essentially* an idea, or a creation with no corresponding reality. When Disraeli said in his novel *Tancred* that the East was a career, he meant that to be interested in the East was something bright young Westerners would find to be an all-consuming passion; he should not be interpreted as saying that the East was *only* a career for Westerners. There were—and are—cultures and nations whose location is in the East, and their lives, histories, and customs have a brute reality obviously greater than anything that could be said about them in the West. About that fact this study of Orientalism has very little to contribute, except to acknowledge it tacitly. But the phenomenon of Orientalism as I study it here deals principally, not with a correspondence between Orientalism and Orient, but with the internal consistency of Orientalism and its ideas about the Orient (the East as career) despite or beyond any correspondence, or lack thereof, with a "real" Orient. My point is that Disraeli's statement about the East refers mainly to that created consistency, that regular constellation of ideas as the pre-eminent thing about the Orient, and not to its mere being, as Wallace Stevens's phrase has it.

A second qualification is that ideas, cultures, and histories cannot seriously be understood or studied without their force, or more precisely their configurations of power, also being studied. To believe that the Orient was created—or, as I call it, "Orientalized"—and to believe that such things happen simply as a necessity of the imagination, is to be disingenuous. The relationship between Occident and Orient is a relationship of power, of domination, of varying degrees of a complex hegemony, and is quite accurately indicated in the title of K. M. Panikkar's classic *Asia and Western Dominance*.[2] The Orient was Orientalized not only because it was discovered to be "Oriental" in all those ways considered common-place by an average nineteenth-century European, but also because it *could be*—that is, submitted to being—*made* Oriental. There is very little consent to be found, for example, in the fact that Flaubert's encounter with an Egyptian courtesan produced a widely influential model of the Oriental woman; she never spoke of herself, she never represented her emotions, presence, or history. *He* spoke for and represented her. He was foreign, comparatively wealthy, male, and these were historical facts of domination that allowed him not only to possess Kuchuk Hanem physically but to speak for her and tell his readers in what way she was "typically Oriental." My argument is that Flaubert's situation of strength in relation to Kuchuk Hanem was not an isolated instance. It fairly stands for the pattern of relative strength between East and West, and the discourse about the Orient that it enabled.

This brings us to a third qualification. One ought never to assume that the structure of Orientalism is nothing more than a structure of lies or of myths which, were the truth about them to be told, would simply blow away. I myself believe that Orientalism is more particularly valuable as a sign of European-Atlantic power over the Orient than it is as a veridic discourse about the Orient (which is what, in its academic or scholarly form, it claims to be). Nevertheless, what we must respect and try to grasp is the sheer knitted-together strength of Orientalist discourse, its very close ties to the enabling socio-economic and political institutions, and its redoubtable durability. After all, any system of ideas that can remain unchanged as teachable wisdom (in academies, books, congresses, universities, foreign-service institutes) from the period of Ernest Renan in the late 1840s until the present in the United States must be something more formidable than a mere collection of lies. Orientalism, therefore, is not an airy European fantasy about the Orient, but a created body of theory and practice in which, for many generations, there has been a considerable material investment. Continued investment made Orientalism, as a system of knowledge about the Orient, an accepted grid for filtering through the Orient into Western consciousness, just as that same investment multiplied—indeed, made truly productive—the statements proliferating out from Orientalism into the general culture.

Gramsci has made the useful analytic distinction between civil and political society in which the former is made up of voluntary (or at least rational and noncoercive) affiliations like schools, families, and unions, the latter of state institutions (the army, the police, the central bureaucracy) whose role in the polity is direct domination. Culture, of course, is to be found operating within civil society, where the influence of ideas, of institutions, and of other persons works not through domination but by what Gramsci calls consent. In any society not totalitarian, then, certain cultural forms predominate over others, just as certain ideas are more influential than others; the form of this cultural leadership is what Gramsci has identified as *hegemony*, an indispensable concept for any understanding of cultural life in the industrial West. It is hegemony, or rather the result of cultural hegemony at work, that gives Orientalism the durability and the strength I have been speaking about so far. Orientalism is never far from what Denys Hay has called the idea of Europe,[3] a collective notion identifying "us" Europeans as against all "those" non-Europeans, and indeed it can be argued that the major component in European culture is precisely what made that culture hegemonic both in and outside Europe: the idea of European identity as a superior one in comparison with all the non-European peoples and cultures. There is in addition the hegemony of European ideas about the Orient, themselves reiterating European superiority over Oriental backwardness, usually overriding the possibility that a more independent, or more skeptical, thinker might have had different views on the matter.

In a quite constant way, Orientalism depends for its strategy on this flexible *positional* superiority, which puts the Westerner in a whole series of possible relationships with the Orient without ever losing him the relative upper hand. And why should it have been otherwise, especially during the period of extraordinary European ascendancy from the late Renaissance to the present? The scientist, the scholar, the missionary, the trader, or the soldier was in, or thought about, the Orient because he *could be there*, or could think about it, with very little resistance on the Orient's part. Under the general heading of knowledge of the Orient, and within the umbrella of Western hegemony over the Orient during the period from the end of the eighteenth century, there emerged a complex Orient suitable for study in the academy, for display in the museum, for reconstruction in the colonial office, for theoretical illustration in anthropological, biological, linguistic, racial, and historical theses about mankind and the universe, for instances of economic and sociological theories of development, revolution, cultural personality, national or religious character. Additionally, the imaginative examination of things Oriental was based more or less exclusively upon a sovereign Western consciousness out of whose unchallenged centrality an Oriental world emerged, first according to general ideas about who or what was an Oriental, then according to a detailed logic governed not simply by empirical reality but by a battery of desires, repressions, investments, and projections. If we can point to great Orientalist works of genuine scholarship like Silvestre de Sacy's *Chrestomathie arabe* or Edward William Lane's *Account of the Manners and Customs of the Modern Egyptians*, we need also to note that Renan's and Gobineau's racial ideas came out of the same impulse, as did a great many Victorian pornographic novels (see the analysis by Steven Marcus of "The Lustful Turk"[4]).

And yet, one must repeatedly ask oneself whether what matters in Orientalism is the general group of ideas overriding the mass of material—about which who could deny that they were shot through with doctrines of European superiority, various kinds of racism, imperialism, and the like, dogmatic views of "the Oriental" as a kind of ideal and unchanging abstraction?—or the much more varied work produced by almost uncountable individual writers, whom one would take up as individual instances of authors dealing with the Orient. In a sense the two alternatives, general and particular, are really two perspectives on the same material: in both instances one would have to deal with pioneers in the field like William Jones, with great artists like Nerval or Flaubert. And why would it not be possible to employ both perspectives together, or one after the other? Isn't there an obvious danger of distortion (of precisely the kind that academic Orientalism has always been prone to) if either too general or too specific a level of description is maintained systematically?

My two fears are distortion and inaccuracy, or rather the kind of inaccuracy produced by too dogmatic a generality and too positivistic a localized focus. In trying to deal with these problems I have tried to deal with three main aspects of my own contemporary reality that seem to me to point the way out of the methodological or perspectival difficulties I have been discussing, difficulties that might force one, in the first instance, into writing a coarse polemic on so unacceptably general a level of description as not to be worth the effort, or in the second instance, into writing so detailed and atomistic a series of analyses as to lose all track of the general lines of force informing the field, giving it its special cogency. How then to recognize individuality and to reconcile it with its intelligent, and by no means passive or merely dictatorial, general and hegemonic context?

III

I mentioned three aspects of my contemporary reality: I must explain and briefly discuss them now, so that it can be seen how I was led to a particular course of research and writing.

1. *The distinction between pure and political knowledge.* It is very easy to argue that knowledge about Shakespeare or Wordsworth is not political whereas knowledge about contemporary China or the Soviet Union is. My own formal and professional designation is that of "humanist," a title which indicates the humanities as my field and therefore the unlikely eventuality that there might be anything political about what I do in that field. Of course, all these labels and terms are quite unnuanced as I use them here, but the general truth of what I am pointing to is, I think, widely held.

One reason for saying that a humanist who writes about Wordsworth, or an editor whose specialty is Keats, is not involved in anything political is that what he does seems to have no direct political effect upon reality in the everyday sense. A scholar whose field is Soviet economics works in a highly charged area where there is much government interest, and what he might produce in the way of studies or proposals will be taken up by policymakers, government officials, institutional economists, intelligence experts. The distinction between "humanists" and persons whose work has policy implications, or political significance, can be broadened further by saying that the former's ideological color is a matter of incidental importance to politics (although possibly of great moment to his colleagues in the field, who may object to his Stalinism or fascism or too easy liberalism), whereas the ideology of the latter is woven directly into his material—indeed, economics, politics, and sociology in the modern academy are ideological sciences—and therefore taken for granted as being "political."

Nevertheless the determining impingement on most knowledge produced in the contemporary West (and here I speak mainly about the United States) is that it be nonpolitical, that is, scholarly, academic, impartial, above partisan or small-minded doctrinal belief. One can have no quarrel with such an ambition in theory, perhaps, but in practice the reality is much more problematic. No one has ever devised a method for detaching the scholar from the circumstances of life, from the fact of his involvement (conscious or unconscious) with a class, a set of beliefs, a social position, or from the mere activity of being a member of a society. These continue to bear on what he does professionally, even though naturally enough his research and its fruits do attempt to reach a level of relative freedom from the inhibitions and the restrictions of brute, everyday reality. For there is such a thing as knowledge that is less, rather than more, partial than the individual (with his entangling and distracting life circumstances) who produces it. Yet this knowledge is not therefore automatically nonpolitical.

Whether discussions of literature or of classical philology are fraught with—or have unmediated—political significance is a very large question that I have tried to treat in some detail elsewhere.[5] What I am interested in doing now is suggesting how the general liberal consensus that "true" knowledge is fundamentally nonpolitical (and conversely, that overtly political knowledge is not "true" knowledge) obscures the highly if obscurely organized political circumstances obtaining when knowledge is produced. No one is helped in understanding this today when the adjective "political" is used as a label to discredit any work for daring to violate the protocol of pretended suprapolitical objectivity. We may say, first, that civil society recognizes a gradation of political importance in the various fields of knowledge. To some extent the political importance given a field comes from the possibility of its direct translation into economic terms; but to a greater extent political importance comes from the closeness of a field to ascertainable sources of power in political society. Thus an economic study of long-term Soviet energy potential and its effect on military capability is likely to be commissioned by the Defense Department, and thereafter to acquire a kind of political status impossible for a study of Tolstoi's early fiction financed in part by a foundation. Yet both works belong in what civil society acknowledges to be a similar field, Russian studies, even though one work may be done by a very conservative economist, the other by a radical literary historian. My point here is that "Russia" as a general subject matter has political priority over nicer distinctions such as "economics" and "literary history," because political society in Gramsci's sense reaches into such realms of civil society as the academy and saturates them with significance of direct concern to it.

I do not want to press all this any further on general theoretical grounds: it seems to me that the value and credibility of my case can be demonstrated by being much more specific, in the way, for example, Noam Chomsky has studied the instrumental connection between the Vietnam War and the notion of objective scholarship as it was applied to cover state-sponsored military research.[6] Now because Britain, France, and recently the United States are imperial powers, their political societies impart to their civil societies a sense of urgency, a direct political infusion as it were, where and whenever matters pertaining to their imperial interests abroad are concerned. I doubt that it is controversial, for example, to say that an Englishman in India or Egypt in the later nineteenth century took an interest in those countries that was never far from their status in his mind as British colonies. To say this may seem quite different from saying that all academic knowledge about India and Egypt is somehow tinged and impressed with, violated by, the gross political fact—and yet *that is what I am saying* in this study of Orientalism. For if it is true that no production of knowledge in the human sciences can ever ignore or disclaim its author's involvement as a human subject in his own circumstances, then it must also be true that for a European or American studying the Orient there can be no disclaiming the main circumstances of *his* actuality: that he comes up against the Orient as a European or American first, as an individual second. And to be a European or an American in such a situation is by no means an inert fact. It meant and means being aware, however dimly, that one belongs to a power with definite interests in the Orient, and more important, that one belongs to a part of the earth with a definite history of involvement in the Orient almost since the time of Homer.

Put in this way, these political actualities are still too undefined and general to be really interesting. Anyone would agree to them without necessarily agreeing also that they mattered very much, for instance, to Flaubert as he wrote *Salammbô*, or to H. A. R. Gibb as he wrote *Modern Trends in Islam*. The trouble is that there is too great a distance between the big dominating fact, as I have described it, and the details of everyday life that govern the minute discipline of a novel or a scholarly text as each is being written. Yet if we eliminate from the start any notion that "big" facts like imperial domination can be applied mechanically and deterministically to such complex matters as culture and ideas, then we will begin to approach an interesting kind of study. My idea is that European and then American interest in the Orient was political according to some of the obvious historical accounts of it that I have given here, but that it was the culture that created that interest, that acted dynamically along with brute political, economic, and military rationales to make the Orient the varied and complicated place that it obviously was in the field I call Orientalism.

Therefore, Orientalism is not a mere political subject matter or field that is reflected passively by culture, scholarship, or institutions; nor is it a large and diffuse collection of texts about the Orient; nor is it representative and expressive of some nefarious "Western" imperialist plot to hold down the "Oriental" world. It is rather a *distribution* of geopolitical awareness into aesthetic, scholarly, economic, sociological, historical, and philological texts; it is an *elaboration* not only of a basic geographical distinction (the world is made up of two unequal halves, Orient and Occident) but also of a whole series of "interests" which, by such means as scholarly discovery, philological reconstruction, psychological analysis, landscape and sociological description, it not only creates but also maintains; it *is*, rather than expresses, a certain *will* or *intention* to understand, in some cases to control, manipulate, even to incorporate, what is a manifestly different (or alternative and novel) world; it is, above all, a discourse that is by no means in direct, corresponding relationship with political power in the raw, but rather is produced and exists in an uneven exchange with various kinds of power, shaped to a degree by the exchange with power political (as with a colonial or imperial establishment), power intellectual (as with reigning sciences like comparative linguistics or anatomy, or any of the modern policy sciences), power cultural (as with orthodoxies and canons of taste, texts, values), power moral (as with ideas about what "we" do and what "they" cannot do or understand as "we" do). Indeed, my real argument is that Orientalism is—and does not simply represent—a considerable dimension of modern political-intellectual culture, and as such has less to do with the Orient than it does with "our" world.

Because Orientalism is a cultural and a political fact, then, it does not exist in some archival vacuum; quite the contrary, I think it can be shown that what is thought, said, or even done about the Orient follows (perhaps occurs within) certain distinct and intellectually knowable lines. Here too a considerable degree of nuance and elaboration can be seen working as between the broad superstructural pressures and the details of composition, the facts of textuality. Most humanistic scholars are, I think, perfectly happy with the notion that texts exist in contexts, that there is such a thing as intertextuality, that the pressures of conventions, predecessors, and rhetorical styles limit what Walter Benjamin once called the "overtaxing of the productive person in the name of ... the principle of 'creativity,'" in which the poet is believed on his own, and out of his pure mind, to have brought forth his work.[7] Yet there is a reluctance to allow that political, institutional, and ideological constraints act in the same manner on the individual author. A humanist will believe it to be an interesting fact to any interpreter of Balzac that he was influenced in the *Comédie humaine* by the conflict between Geoffroy Saint-Hilaire and Cuvier, but the same sort of pressure on Balzac of deeply reactionary monarchism is felt in some vague way to demean his literary "genius" and therefore to be less worth serious study. Similarly—as Harry Bracken has been tirelessly showing—philosophers will conduct their discussions of Locke, Hume, and empiricism without ever taking into account that there is an explicit connection in these classic writers between their "philosophic" doctrines and racial theory, justifications of slavery, or arguments for colonial exploitation.[8] These are common enough ways by which contemporary scholarship keeps itself pure.

Perhaps it is true that most attempts to rub culture's nose in the mud of politics have been crudely iconoclastic; perhaps also the social interpretation of literature in my own field has simply not kept up with the enormous technical advances in detailed textual analysis. But there is no getting away from the fact that literary studies in general, and American Marxist theorists in particular, have avoided the effort of seriously bridging the gap between the superstructural and the base levels in textual, historical scholarship; on another occasion I have gone so far as to say that the literary-cultural establishment as a whole has declared the serious study of imperialism and culture off limits.[9] For Orientalism brings one up directly against that question—that is, to realizing that political imperialism governs an entire field of study, imagination, and scholarly institutions—in such a way as to make its avoidance an intellectual and historical impossibility. Yet there will always remain the perennial escape mechanism of saying that a literary scholar and a philosopher, for example, are trained in literature and philosophy respectively, not in politics or ideological analysis. In other words, the specialist argument can work quite effectively to block the larger and, in my opinion, the more intellectually serious perspective.

Here it seems to me there is a simple two-part answer to be given, at least so far as the study of imperialism and culture (or Orientalism) is concerned. In the first place, nearly every nineteenth-century writer (and the same is true enough of writers in earlier periods) was extraordinarily well aware of the fact of empire: this is a subject not very well studied, but it will not take a modern Victorian specialist long to admit that liberal cultural heroes like John Stuart Mill, Arnold, Carlyle, Newman, Macaulay, Ruskin, George Eliot, and even Dickens had definite views on race and imperialism, which are quite easily to be found at work in their writing. So even a specialist must deal with the knowledge that Mill, for example, made it clear in *On Liberty* and *Representative Government* that his views there could not be applied to India (he was an India Office functionary for a good deal of his life, after all) because the Indians were civilizationally, if not racially, inferior. The same kind of paradox is to be found in Marx, as I try to show in this book. In the second place, to believe that politics in the form of imperialism bears upon the production of literature, scholarship, social theory, and history writing is by no means equivalent to saying that culture is therefore a demeaned or denigrated thing. Quite the contrary: my whole point is to say that we can better understand the persistence and the durability of saturating hegemonic systems like culture when we realize that their internal constraints upon writers and thinkers were *productive*, not unilaterally inhibiting. It is this idea that Gramsci, certainly, and Foucault and Raymond Williams in their very different ways have been trying to illustrate. Even one or two pages by Williams on "the uses of the Empire" in *The Long Revolution* tell us more about nineteenth-century cultural richness than many volumes of hermetic textual analyses.[10]

Therefore I study Orientalism as a dynamic exchange between individual authors and the large political concerns shaped by the three great empires—British, French, American—in whose intellectual and imaginative territory the writing was produced. What interests me most as a scholar is not the gross political verity but the detail, as indeed what interests us in someone like Lane or Flaubert or Renan is not the (to him) indisputable truth that Occidentals are superior to Orientals, but the profoundly worked over and modulated evidence of his detailed work within the very wide space opened up by that truth. One need only remember that Lane's *Manners and Customs of the Modern Egyptians* is a classic of historical and anthropological observation because of its style, its enormously intelligent and brilliant details, not because of its simple reflection of racial superiority, to understand what I am saying here.

The kind of political questions raised by Orientalism, then, are as follows: What other sorts of intellectual, aesthetic, scholarly, and cultural energies went into the making of an imperialist tradition like the Orientalist one? How did philology, lexicography, history, biology, political and economic theory, novel-writing, and lyric poetry come to the service of Orientalism's broadly imperialist view of the world? What changes, modulations, refinements, even revolutions take place within Orientalism? What is the meaning of originality, of continuity, of individuality, in this context? How does Orientalism transmit or reproduce itself from one epoch to another? In fine, how can we treat the cultural, historical phenomenon of Orientalism as a kind of *willed human work*—not of mere unconditioned ratiocination—in all its historical complexity, detail, and worth without at the same time losing sight of the alliance between cultural work, political tendencies, the state, and the specific realities of domination? Governed by such concerns a humanistic study can responsibly address itself to politics *and* culture. But this is not to say that such a study establishes a hard-and-fast rule about the relationship between knowledge and politics. My argument is that each humanistic investigation must formulate the nature of that connection in the specific context of the study, the subject matter, and its historical circumstances.

2. *The methodological question.* In a previous book I gave a good deal of thought and analysis to the methodological importance for work in the human sciences of finding and formulating a first step, a point of departure, a beginning principle.[11] A major lesson I learned and tried to present was that there is no such thing as a merely given, or simply available, starting point: beginnings have to be made for each project in such a way as to *enable* what follows from them. Nowhere in my experience has the difficulty of this lesson been more consciously lived (with what success—or failure—I cannot really say) than in this study of Orientalism. The idea of beginning, indeed the act of beginning, necessarily involves an act of delimitation by which something is cut out of a great mass of material, separated from the mass, and made to stand for, as well as be, a starting point, a beginning; for the student of texts one such notion of inaugural delimitation is Louis Althusser's idea of the *problematic*, a specific determinate unity of a text, or group of texts, which is something given rise to by analysis.[12] Yet in the case of Orientalism (as opposed to the case of Marx's texts, which is what Althusser studies) there is not simply the problem of finding a point of departure, or problematic, but also the question of designating which texts, authors, and periods are the ones best suited for study.

It has seemed to me foolish to attempt an encyclopedic narrative history of Orientalism, first of all because if my guiding principle was to be "the European idea of the Orient" there would be virtually no limit to the material I would have had to deal with; second, because the narrative model itself did not suit my descriptive and political interests; third, because in such books as Raymond Schwab's *La Renaissance orientale*, Johann Fück's *Die Arabischen Studien in Europa bis in den Anfang des 20. Jahrhunderts*, and more recently, Dorothee Metlitzki's *The Matter of Araby in Medieval England*[13] there already exist encyclopedic works on certain aspects of the European-Oriental encounter such as make the critic's job, in the general political and intellectual context I sketched above, a different one.

There still remained the problem of cutting down a very fat archive to manageable dimensions, and more important, outlining something in the nature of an intellectual order within that group of texts without at the same time following a mindlessly chronological order. My starting point therefore has been the British, French, and American experience of the Orient taken as a unit, what made that experience possible by way of historical and intellectual background, what the quality and character of the experience has been. For reasons I shall discuss presently I limited that already limited (but still inordinately large) set of questions to the Anglo-French-American experience of the Arabs and Islam, which for almost a thousand years together stood for the Orient. Immediately upon doing that, a large part of the Orient seemed to have been eliminated—India, Japan, China, and other sections of the Far East—not because these regions were not important (they obviously have been) but because one could discuss Europe's experience of the Near Orient, or of Islam, apart from its experience of the Far Orient. Yet at certain moments of that general European history of interest in the East, particular parts of the Orient like Egypt, Syria, and Arabia cannot be discussed without also studying Europe's involvement in the more distant parts, of which Persia and India are the most important; a notable case in point is the connection between Egypt and India so far as eighteenth- and nineteenth-century Britain was concerned. Similarly the French role in deciphering the Zend-Avesta, the pre-eminence of Paris as a center of Sanskrit studies during the first decade of the nineteenth century, the fact that Napoleon's interest in the Orient was contingent upon his sense of the British role in India: all these Far Eastern interests directly influenced French interest in the Near East, Islam, and the Arabs.

Britain and France dominated the Eastern Mediterranean from about the end of the seventeenth century on. Yet my discussion of that domination and systematic interest does not do justice to (a) the important contributions to Orientalism of Germany, Italy, Russia, Spain, and Portugal and (b) the fact that one of the important impulses toward the study of the Orient in the eighteenth century was the revolution in Biblical studies stimulated by such variously interesting pioneers as Bishop Lowth, Eichhorn, Herder, and Michaelis. In the first place, I had to focus rigorously upon the British-French and later the American material because it seemed inescapably true not only that Britain and France were the pioneer nations in the Orient and in Oriental studies, but that these vanguard positions were held by virtue of the two greatest colonial networks in pre-twentieth-century history; the American Oriental position since World War II has fit—I think, quite self-consciously—in the places excavated by the two earlier European powers. Then too, I believe that the sheer quality, consistency, and mass of British, French, and American writing on the Orient lifts it above the doubtless crucial work done in Germany, Italy, Russia, and elsewhere. But I think it is also true that the major steps in Oriental scholarship were first taken in either Britain and France, then elaborated upon by Germans. Silvestre de Sacy, for example, was not only the first modern and institutional European Orientalist, who worked on Islam, Arabic literature, the Druze religion, and Sassanid Persia; he was also the teacher of Champollion and of Franz Bopp, the founder of German comparative linguistics. A similar claim of priority and subsequent pre-eminence can be made for William Jones and Edward William Lane.

In the second place—and here the failings of my study of Orientalism are amply made up for—there has been some important recent work on the background in Biblical scholarship to the rise of what I have called modern Orientalism. The best and the most illuminatingly relevant is E. S. Shaffer's impressive *"Kubla Khan" and The Fall of Jerusalem*,[14] an indispensable study of the origins of Romanticism, and of the intellectual activity underpinning a great deal of what goes on in Coleridge, Browning, and George Eliot. To some degree Shaffer's work refines upon the outlines provided in Schwab, by articulating the material of relevance to be found in the German Biblical scholars and using that material to read, in an intelligent and always interesting way, the work of three major British writers. Yet what is missing in the book is some sense of the political as well as ideological edge given the Oriental material by the British and French writers I am principally concerned with; in addition, unlike Shaffer I attempt to elucidate subsequent developments in academic as well as literary Orientalism that bear on the connection between British and French Orientalism on the one hand and the rise of an explicitly colonial-minded imperialism on the other. Then too, I wish to show how all these earlier matters are reproduced more or less in American Orientalism after the Second World War.

Nevertheless there is a possibly misleading aspect to my study, where, aside from an occasional reference, I do not exhaustively discuss the German developments after the inaugural period dominated by Sacy. Any work that seeks to provide an understanding of academic Orientalism and pays little attention to scholars like Steinthal, Müller, Becker, Goldziher, Brockelmann, Nöldeke—to mention only a handful—needs to be reproached, and I freely reproach myself. I particularly regret not taking more account of the great scientific prestige that accrued to German scholarship by the middle of the nineteenth century, whose neglect was made into a denunciation of insular British scholars by George Eliot. I have in mind Eliot's unforgettable portrait of Mr. Casaubon in *Middle-march*. One reason Casaubon cannot finish his Key to All Mythologies is, according to his young cousin Will Ladislaw, that he is unacquainted with German scholarship. For not only has Casaubon chosen a subject "as changing as chemistry: new discoveries are constantly making new points of view": he is undertaking a job similar to a refutation of Paracelsus because "he is not an Orientalist, you know."[15]

Eliot was not wrong in implying that by about 1830, which is when *Middlemarch* is set, German scholarship had fully attained its European pre-eminence. Yet at no time in German scholarship during the first two-thirds of the nineteenth century could a close partnership have developed between Orientalists and a protracted, sustained *national* interest in the Orient. There was nothing in Germany to correspond to the Anglo-French presence in India, the Levant, North Africa. Moreover, the German Orient was almost exclusively a scholarly, or at least a classical, Orient: it was made the subject of lyrics, fantasies, and even novels, but it was never actual, the way Egypt and Syria were actual for Chateaubriand, Lane, Lamartine, Burton, Disraeli, or Nerval. There is some significance in the fact that the two most renowned German works on the Orient, Goethe's *Westöstlicher Diwan* and Friedrich Schlegel's *Über die Sprache und Weisheit der Indier*, were based respectively on a Rhine journey and on hours spent in Paris libraries. What German Oriental scholarship did was to refine and elaborate techniques whose application was to texts, myths, ideas, and languages almost literally gathered from the Orient by imperial Britain and France.

Yet what German Orientalism had in common with Anglo-French and later American Orientalism was a kind of intellectual *authority* over the Orient within

Western culture. This authority must in large part be the subject of any description of Orientalism, and it is so in this study. Even the name *Orientalism* suggests a serious, perhaps ponderous style of expertise; when I apply it to modern American social scientists (since they do not call themselves Orientalists, my use of the word is anomalous), it is to draw attention to the way Middle East experts can still draw on the vestiges of Orientalism's intellectual position in nineteenth-century Europe.

There is nothing mysterious or natural about authority. It is formed, irradiated, disseminated; it is instrumental, it is persuasive; it has status, it establishes canons of taste and value; it is virtually indistinguishable from certain ideas it dignifies as true, and from traditions, perceptions, and judgments it forms, transmits, reproduces. Above all, authority can, indeed must, be analyzed. All these attributes of authority apply to Orientalism, and much of what I do in this study is to describe both the historical authority in and the personal authorities of Orientalism.

My principal methodological devices for studying authority here are what can be called *strategic location*, which is a way of describing the author's position in a text with regard to the Oriental material he writes about, and *strategic formation*, which is a way of analyzing the relationship between texts and the way in which groups of texts, types of texts, even textual genres, acquire mass, density, and referential power among themselves and thereafter in the culture at large. I use the notion of strategy simply to identify the problem every writer on the Orient has faced: how to get hold of it, how to approach it, how not to be defeated or overwhelmed by its sublimity, its scope, its awful dimensions. Everyone who writes about the Orient must locate himself vis-à-vis the Orient; translated into his text, this location includes the kind of narrative voice he adopts, the type of structure he builds, the kinds of images, themes, motifs that circulate in his text—all of which add up to deliberate ways of addressing the reader, containing the Orient, and finally, representing it or speaking in its behalf. None of this takes place in the abstract, however. Every writer on the Orient (and this is true even of Homer) assumes some Oriental precedent, some previous knowledge of the Orient, to which he refers and on which he relies. Additionally, each work on the Orient *affiliates* itself with other works, with audiences, with institutions, with the Orient itself. The ensemble of relationships between works, audiences, and some particular aspects of the Orient therefore constitutes an analyzable formation—for example, that of philological studies, of anthologies of extracts from Oriental literature, of travel books, of Oriental fantasies—whose presence in time, in discourse, in institutions (schools, libraries, foreign services) gives it strength and authority.

It is clear, I hope, that my concern with authority does not entail analysis of what lies hidden in the Orientalist text, but analysis rather of the text's surface, its exteriority to what it describes. I do not think that this idea can be overemphasized. Orientalism is premised upon exteriority, that is, on the fact that the Orientalist, poet or scholar, makes the Orient speak, describes the Orient, renders its mysteries plain for and to the West. He is never concerned with the Orient except as the first cause of what he says. What he says and writes, by virtue of the fact that it is said or written, is meant to indicate that the Orientalist is outside the Orient, both as an existential and as a moral fact. The principal product of this exteriority is of course representation: as early as Aeschylus's play *The Persians* the Orient is transformed from a very far distant and often threatening Otherness into figures that are relatively familiar (in Aeschylus's case, grieving Asiatic women). The dramatic immediacy of representation in *The Persians* obscures the fact that the audience is watching a highly artificial enactment of what a non-Oriental has made into a symbol for the whole Orient. My analysis of the Orientalist text therefore places emphasis on the evidence, which is by no means invisible, for such representations *as representations*, not as "natural" depictions of the Orient. This evidence is found just as prominently in the so-called truthful text (histories, philological analyses, political treatises) as in the avowedly artistic (i.e., openly imaginative) text. The things to look at are style, figures of speech, setting, narrative devices, historical and social circumstances, *not* the correctness of the representation nor its fidelity to some great original. The exteriority of the representation is always governed by some version of the truism that if the Orient could represent itself, it would; since it cannot, the representation does the job, for the West, and *faute de mieux*, for the poor Orient. "Sie können sich nicht vertreten, sie müssen vertreten werden," as Marx wrote in *The Eighteenth Brumaire of Louis Bonaparte*.

Another reason for insisting upon exteriority is that I believe it needs to be made clear about cultural discourse and exchange within a culture that what is commonly circulated by it is not "truth" but representations. It hardly needs to be demonstrated again that language itself is a highly organized and encoded system, which employs many devices to express, indicate, exchange messages and information, represent, and so forth. In any instance of at least written language, there is no such thing as a delivered presence, but a *re-presence*, or a representation. The value, efficacy, strength, apparent veracity of a written statement about the Orient therefore relies very little, and cannot instrumentally depend, on the Orient as such. On the contrary, the written statement is a presence to the reader by virtue of its having excluded, displaced, made supererogatory any such *real thing* as "the Orient." Thus all of Orientalism stands forth and away from the Orient: that Orientalism makes sense at all depends more on the West than on the Orient, and this sense is directly indebted to various Western techniques of representation that make the Orient visible, clear, "there" in discourse about it. And these representations rely upon institutions, traditions, conventions, agreed-upon codes of understanding for their effects, not upon a distant and amorphous Orient.

The difference between representations of the Orient before the last third of the eighteenth century and those after it (that is, those belonging to what I call modern Orientalism) is that the range of representation expanded enormously in the later period. It is true that after William Jones and Anquetil-Duperron, and after Napoleon's Egyptian expedition, Europe came to know the Orient more scientifically, to live in it with greater authority and discipline than ever before. But what mattered to Europe was the expanded scope and the much greater refinement given its techniques for receiving the Orient. When around the turn of the eighteenth century the Orient definitively revealed the age of its languages—thus outdating Hebrew's divine pedigree—it was a group of Europeans who made the discovery, passed it on to other scholars, and preserved the discovery in the new science of Indo-European philology. A new powerful science for viewing the linguistic Orient was born, and with it, as Foucault has shown in *The Order of Things*, a whole web of related scientific interests. Similarly William Beckford, Byron, Goethe, and Hugo restructured the Orient by their art and made its colors, lights, and people visible through their images, rhythms, and motifs. At most, the "real" Orient provoked a writer to his vision; it very rarely guided it.

Orientalism responded more to the culture that produced it than to its putative object, which was also produced by the West. Thus the history of Orientalism has both an internal consistency and a highly articulated set of relationships to the dominant culture surrounding it. My analyses consequently try to show the field's shape and internal organization, its pioneers, patriarchal authorities, canonical texts, doxological ideas, exemplary figures, its followers, elaborators, and new authorities; I try also to explain how Orientalism borrowed and was frequently informed by "strong" ideas, doctrines, and trends ruling the culture. Thus there was (and is) a linguistic Orient, a Freudian Orient, a Spenglerian Orient, a Darwinian Orient, a racist Orient—and so on. Yet never has there been such a thing as a pure, or unconditional, Orient; similarly, never has there been a nonmaterial form of Orientalism, much less something so innocent as an "idea" of the Orient. In this underlying conviction and in its ensuing methodological consequences do I differ from scholars who study the history of ideas. For the emphases and the executive form, above all the material effectiveness, of statements made by Orientalist discourse are possible in ways that any hermetic history of ideas tends completely to scant. Without those emphases and that material effectiveness Orientalism would be just another idea, whereas it is and was much more than that. Therefore I set out to examine not only scholarly works but also works of literature, political tracts, journalistic texts, travel books, religious and philological studies. In other words, my hybrid perspective is broadly historical and "anthropological," given that I believe all texts to be worldly and circumstantial in (of course) ways that vary from genre to genre, and from historical period to historical period.

Yet unlike Michel Foucault, to whose work I am greatly indebted, I do believe in the determining imprint of individual writers upon the otherwise anonymous collective body of texts constituting a discursive formation like Orientalism. The unity of the large ensemble of texts I analyze is due in part to the fact that they frequently refer to each other: Orientalism is after all a system for citing works and authors. Edward William Lane's *Manners and Customs of the Modern Egyptians* was read and cited by such diverse figures as Nerval, Flaubert, and Richard Burton. He was an authority whose use was an imperative for anyone writing or thinking about the Orient, not just about Egypt: when Nerval borrows passages verbatim from *Modern Egyptians* it is to use Lane's authority to assist him in describing village scenes in Syria, not Egypt. Lane's authority and the opportunities provided for citing him discriminately as well as indiscriminately were there because Orientalism could give his text the kind of distributive currency that he acquired. There is no way, however, of understanding Lane's currency without also understanding the peculiar features of *his* text; this is equally true of Renan, Sacy, Lamartine, Schlegel, and a group of other influential writers. Foucault believes that in general the individual text or author counts for very little; empirically, in the case of Orientalism (and perhaps nowhere else) I find this not to be so. Accordingly my analyses employ close textual readings whose goal is to reveal the dialectic between individual text or writer and the complex collective formation to which his work is a contribution.

Yet even though it includes an ample selection of writers, this book is still far from a complete history or general account of Orientalism. Of this failing I am very conscious. The fabric of as thick a discourse as Orientalism has survived and functioned in Western society because of its richness: all I have done is to describe parts of that fabric at certain moments, and merely to suggest the existence of a larger whole, detailed, interesting, dotted with fascinating figures, texts, and events. I have consoled myself with believing that this book is one installment of several, and hope there are scholars and critics who might want to write others. There is still a general essay to be written on imperialism and culture; other studies would go more deeply into the connection between Orientalism and pedagogy, or into Italian, Dutch, German, and Swiss Orientalism, or into the dynamic between scholarship and imaginative writing, or into the relationship between administrative ideas and intellectual discipline. Perhaps the most important task of all would be to undertake studies in contemporary alternatives to Orientalism, to ask how one can study other cultures and peoples from a libertarian, or a nonrepressive and nonmanipulative, perspective. But then one would have to rethink the whole complex problem of knowledge and power. These are all tasks left embarrassingly incomplete in this study.

The last, perhaps self-flattering, observation on method that I want to make here is that I have written this study with several audiences in mind. For students of literature and criticism, Orientalism offers a marvelous instance of the interrelations between society, history, and textuality; moreover, the cultural role played by the Orient in the West connects Orientalism with ideology, politics, and the logic of power, matters of relevance, I think, to the literary community. For contemporary students of the Orient, from university scholars to policymakers, I have written with two ends in mind: one, to present their intellectual genealogy to them in a way that has not been done; two, to criticize—with the hope of stirring discussion—the often unquestioned assumptions on which their work for the most part depends. For the general reader, this study deals with matters that always compel attention, all of them connected not only with Western conceptions and treatments of the Other but also with the singularly important role played by Western culture in what Vico called the world of nations. Lastly, for readers in the so-called Third World, this study proposes itself as a step towards an understanding not so much of Western politics and of the non-Western world in those politics as of the *strength* of Western cultural discourse, a strength too often mistaken as merely decorative or "superstructural." My hope is to illustrate the formidable structure of cultural domination and, specifically for formerly colonized peoples, the dangers and temptations of employing this structure upon themselves or upon others.

The three long chapters and twelve shorter units into which this book is divided are intended to facilitate exposition as much as possible. Chapter One, "The Scope of Orientalism," draws a large circle around all the dimensions of the subject, both in terms of historical time and experiences and in terms of philosophical and political themes. Chapter Two, "Orientalist Structures and Restructures," attempts to trace the development of modern Orientalism by a broadly chronological description, and also by the description of a set of devices common to the work of important poets, artists, and scholars. Chapter Three, "Orientalism Now," begins where its predecessor left off, at around 1870. This is the period of great colonial expansion into the Orient, and it culminates in World War II. The very last section of Chapter Three characterizes the shift from British and French to American hegemony; I attempt there finally to sketch the present intellectual and social realities of Orientalism in the United States.

3. *The personal dimension.* In the *Prison Notebooks* Gramsci says: "The starting-point of critical elaboration is the consciousness of what one really is, and is 'knowing thyself' as a product of the historical process to date, which has deposited in you an infinity of traces, without leaving an inventory." The only available English translation inexplicably leaves Gramsci's comment at that, whereas in fact Gramsci's Italian text concludes by adding, "therefore it is imperative at the outset to compile such an inventory."[16]

Much of the personal investment in this study derives from my awareness of being an "Oriental" as a child growing up in two British colonies. All of my education, in those colonies (Palestine and Egypt) and in the United States, has been Western, and yet that deep early awareness has persisted. In many ways my study of Orientalism has been an attempt to inventory the traces upon me, the Oriental subject, of the culture whose domination has been so powerful a factor in the life of all Orientals. This is why for me the Islamic Orient has had to be the center of attention. Whether what I have achieved is the inventory prescribed by Gramsci is not for me to judge, although I have felt it important to be conscious of trying to produce one. Along the way, as severely and as rationally as I have been able, I have tried to maintain a critical consciousness, as well as employing those instruments of historical, humanistic, and cultural research of which my education has made me the fortunate beneficiary. In none of that, however, have I ever lost hold of the cultural reality of, the personal involvement in having been constituted as, "an Oriental."

The historical circumstances making such a study possible are fairly complex, and I can only list them schematically here. Anyone resident in the West since the 1950s, particularly in the United States, will have lived through an era of extraordinary turbulence in the relations of East and West. No one will have failed to note how "East" has always signified danger and threat during this period, even as it has meant the traditional Orient as well as Russia. In the universities a growing establishment of area-studies programs and institutes has made the scholarly study of the Orient a branch of national policy. Public affairs in this country include a healthy interest in the Orient, as much for its strategic and economic importance as for its traditional exoticism. If the world has become immediately accessible to a Western citizen living in the electronic age, the Orient too has drawn nearer to him, and is now less a myth perhaps than a place crisscrossed by Western, especially American, interests.

One aspect of the electronic, postmodern world is that there has been a reinforcement of the stereotypes by which the Orient is viewed. Television, the films, and all the media's resources have forced information into more and more standardized molds. So far as the Orient is concerned, standardization and cultural stereotyping have intensified the hold of the nineteenth-century academic and imaginative demonology of "the mysterious Orient." This is nowhere more true than in the ways by which the Near East is grasped. Three things have contributed to making even the simplest perception of the Arabs and Islam into a highly politicized, almost raucous matter: one, the history of popular anti-Arab and anti-Islamic prejudice in the West, which is immediately reflected in the history of Orientalism; two, the struggle between the Arabs and Israeli Zionism, and its effects upon American Jews as well as upon both the liberal culture and the population at large; three, the almost total absence of any cultural position making it possible either to identify with or dispassionately to discuss the Arabs or Islam. Furthermore, it hardly needs saying that because the Middle East is now so identified with Great Power politics, oil economics, and the simple-minded dichotomy of freedom-loving, democratic Israel and evil, totalitarian, and terroristic Arabs, the chances of anything like a clear view of what one talks about in talking about the Near East are depressingly small.

My own experiences of these matters are in part what made me write this book. The life of an Arab Palestinian in the West, particularly in America, is disheartening. There exists here an almost unanimous consensus that politically he does not exist, and when it is allowed that he does, it is either as a nuisance or as an Oriental. The web of racism, cultural stereotypes, political imperialism, dehumanizing ideology holding in the Arab or the Muslim is very strong indeed, and it is this web which every Palestinian has come to feel as his uniquely punishing destiny. It has made matters worse for him to remark that no person academically involved with the Near East— no Orientalist, that is—has ever in the United States culturally and politically identified himself wholeheartedly with the Arabs; certainly there have been identifications on some level, but they have never taken an "acceptable" form as has liberal American identification with Zionism, and all too frequently they have been radically flawed by their association either with discredited political and economic interests (oil-company and State Department Arabists, for example) or with religion.

The nexus of knowledge and power creating "the Oriental" and in a sense obliterating him as a human being is therefore not for me an exclusively academic matter. Yet it is an *intellectual* matter of some very obvious importance. I have been able to put to use my humanistic and political concerns for the analysis and description of a very worldly matter, the rise, development, and consolidation of Orientalism. Too often literature and culture are presumed to be politically, even historically innocent; it has regularly seemed otherwise to me, and certainly my study of Orientalism has convinced me (and I hope will convince my literary colleagues) that society and literary culture can only be understood and studied together. In addition, and by an almost inescapable logic, I have found myself writing the history of a strange, secret sharer of Western anti-Semitism. That anti-Semitism and, as I have discussed it in its Islamic branch, Orientalism resemble each other very closely is a historical, cultural, and political truth that needs only to be mentioned to an Arab Palestinian for its irony to be perfectly understood. But what I should like also to have contributed here is a better understanding of the way cultural domination has operated. If this stimulates a new kind of dealing with the Orient, indeed if it eliminates the "Orient" and "Occident" altogether, then we shall have advanced a little in the process of what Raymond Williams has called the "unlearning" of "the inherent dominative mode."[17]

Edward Said

Notes

1 Thierry Desjardins, *Le Martyre du Liban* (Paris: Plon, 1976), p. 14.

2 K. M. Panikkar, *Asia and Western Dominance* (London: George Allen & Unwin, 1959).

3 Denys Hay, *Europe: The Emergence of an Idea*, 2nd ed. (Edinburgh: Edinburgh University Press, 1968).

4 Steven Marcus, *The Other Victorians: A Study of Sexuality and Pornography in Mid-Nineteenth Century England* (1966; reprint ed., New York: Bantam Books, 1967), pp. 200–19.

5 See my *Criticism Between Culture and System* (Cambridge, Mass.: Harvard University Press, forthcoming).

6 Principally in his *American Power and the New Mandarins: Historical and Political Essays* (New York: Pantheon Books, 1969) and *For Reasons of State* (New York: Pantheon Books, 1973).

7 Walter Benjamin, *Charles Baudelaire: A Lyric Poet in the Era of High Capitalism*, trans. Harry Zohn (London: New Left Books, 1973), p. 71.

8 Harry Bracken, "Essence, Accident and Race," *Hermathena* 116 (Winter 1973): 81–96.

9 In an interview published in *Diacritics* 6, no. 3 (Fall 1976): 38.

10 Raymond Williams, *The Long Revolution* (London: Chatto & Windus, 1961), pp. 66–7.

11 In my *Beginnings: Intention and Method* (New York: Basic Books, 1975).

12 Louis Althusser, *For Marx*, trans. Ben Brewster (New York: Pantheon Books, 1969), pp. 65–7.

13 Raymond Schwab, *La Renaissance orientale* (Paris: Payot, 1950); Johann W. Fück, *Die Arabischen Studien in Europa bis in den Anfang des 20. Jahrhunderts* (Leipzig: Otto Harrassowitz, 1955); Dorothee Metlitzki, *The Matter of Araby in Medieval England* (New Haven, Conn.: Yale University Press, 1977).

14 E. S. Shaffer, *"Kubla Khan" and The Fall of Jerusalem: The Mythological School in Biblical Criticism and Secular Literature, 1770–1880* (Cambridge: Cambridge University Press, 1975).

15 George Eliot, *Middlemarch: A Study of Provincial Life* (1872; reprint ed., Boston: Houghton Mifflin Co., 1956), p. 164.

16 Antonio Gramsci, *The Prison Notebooks: Selections*, trans. and ed. Quintin Hoare and Geoffrey Nowell Smith (New York: International Publishers, 1971), p. 324. The full passage, unavailable in the Hoare and Smith translation, is to be found in Gramsci, *Quaderni del Carcere*, ed. Valentino Gerratana (Turin: Einaudi Editore, 1975), 2: 1363.

17 Raymond Williams, *Culture and Society, 1780–1950* (London: Chatto & Windus, 1958), p. 376.

3   Of Mimicry and Man
The Ambivalence of Colonial Discourse

Homi K. Bhabha

Mimicry reveals something in so far as it is distinct from what might be called an itself that is behind. The effect of mimicry is camouflage.… It is not a question of harmonizing with the background, but against a mottled background, of becoming mottled – exactly like the technique of camouflage practised in human warfare.

Jacques Lacan, 'The line and light', *Of the Gaze*.[1]

It is out of season to question at this time of day, the original policy of a conferring on every colony of the British Empire a mimic representation of the British Constitution. But if the creature so endowed has sometimes forgotten its real significance and under the fancied importance of speakers and maces, and all the paraphernalia and ceremonies of the imperial legislature, has dared to defy the mother country, she has to thank herself for the folly of conferring such privileges on a condition of society that has no earthly claim to so exalted a position. A fundamental principle appears to have been forgotten or overlooked in our system of colonial policy – that of colonial dependence. To give to a colony the forms of independence is a mockery; she would not be a colony for a single hour if she could maintain an independent station.

Sir Edward Cust, 'Reflections on West African affairs …
addressed to the Colonial Office', Hatchard, London 1839

The discourse of post-Enlightenment English colonialism often speaks in a tongue that is forked, not false. If colonialism takes power in the name of history, it repeatedly exercises its authority through the figures of farce. For the epic intention of the civilizing mission, 'human and not wholly human' in the famous words of Lord

Homi K. Bhabha, "Of Mimicry and Man: The Ambivalence of Colonial Discourse," in *The Location of Culture*. Abingdon: Routledge, 1994, pp. 121–131. Reproduced by permission of Taylor & Francis Books UK.

Postcolonial Studies: An Anthology, First Edition. Edited by Pramod K. Nayar.
Editorial material and organization © 2016 John Wiley & Sons, Ltd.
Published 2016 by John Wiley & Sons, Ltd.

Rosebery, 'writ by the finger of the Divine'[2] often produces a text rich in the traditions of *trompe-l'œil*, irony, mimicry and repetition. In this comic turn from the high ideals of the colonial imagination to its low mimetic literary effects mimicry emerges as one of the most elusive and effective strategies of colonial power and knowledge.

Within that conflictual economy of colonial discourse which Edward Said[3] describes as the tension between the synchronic panoptical vision of domination – the demand for identity, stasis – and the counter-pressure of the diachrony of history – change, difference – mimicry represents an *ironic* compromise. If I may adapt Samuel Weber's formulation of the marginalizing vision of castration,[4] then colonial mimicry is the desire for a reformed, recognizable Other, *as a subject of a difference that is almost the same, but not quite*. Which is to say, that the discourse of mimicry is constructed around an *ambivalence*; in order to be effective, mimicry must continually produce its slippage, its excess, its difference. The authority of that mode of colonial discourse that I have called mimicry is therefore stricken by an indeterminacy: mimicry emerges as the representation of a difference that is itself a process of disavowal. Mimicry is, thus the sign of a double articulation; a complex strategy of reform, regulation and discipline, which 'appropriates' the Other as it visualizes power. Mimicry is also the sign of the inappropriate, however, a difference or recalcitrance which coheres the dominant strategic function of colonial power, intensifies surveillance, and poses an immanent threat to both 'normalized' knowledges and disciplinary powers.

The effect of mimicry on the authority of colonial discourse is profound and disturbing. For in 'normalizing' the colonial state or subject, the dream of post-Enlightenment civility alienates its own language of liberty and produces another knowledge of its norms. The ambivalence which thus informs this strategy is discernible, for example, in Locke's Second Treatise which *splits* to reveal the limitations of liberty in his double use of the word 'slave': first simply, descriptively as the locus of a legitimate form of ownership, then as the trope for an intolerable, illegitimate exercise of power. What is articulated in that distance between the two uses is the absolute, imagined difference between the 'Colonial' State of Carolina and the Original State of Nature.

It is from this area between mimicry and mockery, where the reforming, civilizing mission is threatened by the displacing gaze of its disciplinary double, that my instances of colonial imitation come. What they all share is a discursive process by which the excess or slippage produced by the *ambivalence* of mimicry (almost the same, *but not quite*) does not merely 'rupture' the discourse, but becomes transformed into an uncertainty which fixes the colonial subject as a 'partial' presence. By 'partial' I mean both 'incomplete' and 'virtual'. It is as if the very emergence of the 'colonial' is dependent for its representation upon some strategic limitation or prohibition *within* the authoritative discourse itself. The success of colonial appropriation depends on a proliferation of inappropriate objects that ensure its strategic failure, so that mimicry is at once resemblance and menace.

A classic text of such partiality is Charles Grant's 'Observations on the state of society among the Asiatic subjects of Great Britain' (1792)[5] which was only superseded by James Mills's *History of India* as the most influential early nineteenth-century account of Indian manners and morals. Grant's dream of an evangelical system of mission education conducted uncompromisingly in the English language, was partly a belief in political reform along Christian lines and partly an awareness that the expansion of company rule in India required a system of subject formation – a reform of manners, as Grant put it – that would provide the colonial with 'a sense of personal identity as we know it'. Caught between the desire for religious reform and the fear that the Indians might become turbulent for liberty, Grant paradoxically implies that it is the 'partial' diffusion of Christianity, and the 'partial' influence of moral improvements which will construct a particularly appropriate form of colonial subjectivity. What is suggested is a process of reform through which Christian doctrines might collude with divisive caste practices to prevent dangerous political alliances. Inadvertently, Grant produces a knowledge of Christianity as a form of social control which conflicts with the enunciatory assumptions that authorize his discourse. In suggesting, finally, that 'partial reform' will produce an empty form of 'the *imitation* [my emphasis] of English manners which will induce them [the colonial subjects] to remain under our protection'.[6] Grant mocks his moral project and violates the Evidence of Christianity – a central missionary tenet – which forbade any tolerance of heathen faiths.

The absurd extravagance of Macaulay's 'Minute' (1835) – deeply influenced by Charles Grant's 'Observations' – makes a mockery of Oriental learning until faced with the challenge of conceiving of a 'reformed' colonial subject. Then, the great tradition of European humanism seems capable only of ironizing itself. At the intersection of European learning and colonial power, Macaulay can conceive of nothing other than 'a class of interpreters between us and the millions whom we govern – a class of persons Indian in blood and colour, but English in tastes, in opinions, in morals and in intellect'[7] – in other words a mimic man raised 'through our English School', as a missionary educationist wrote in 1819, 'to form a corps of translators and be employed in different departments of Labour'.[8] The line of descent of the mimic man can be traced through the works of Kipling, Forster, Orwell, Naipaul, and to his emergence, most recently, in Benedict Anderson's excellent work on nationalism, as the anomalous Bipin Chandra Pal.[9] He is the effect of a flawed colonial mimesis, in which to be Anglicized is *emphatically* not to be English.

The figure of mimicry is locatable within what Anderson describes as 'the inner compatibility of empire and nation'.[10] It problematizes the signs of racial and cultural priority, so that the 'national' is no longer naturalizable. What emerges between mimesis and mimicry is a *writing*, a mode of representation, that marginalizes the monumentality of history, quite simply mocks its power to be a model, that power which supposedly makes it imitable. Mimicry *repeats* rather than *re-presents* and in that diminishing perspective emerges Decoud's displaced European vision of Sulaco in Conrad's *Nostromo* as:

> the endlessness of civil strife where folly seemed even harder to bear than its ignominy … the lawlessness of a populace of all colours and races, barbarism, irremediable tyranny…. America is ungovernable.[11]

Or Ralph Singh's apostasy in Naipaul's *The Mimic Men*:

> We pretended to be real, to be learning, to be preparing ourselves for life, we mimic men of the New World, one unknown corner of it, with all its reminders of the corruption that came so quickly to the new.[12]

Both Decoud and Singh, and in their different ways Grant and Macaulay, are the parodists of history. Despite their intentions and invocations they inscribe the colonial text erratically, eccentrically across a body politic that refuses to be representative, in a narrative that refuses to be representational. The desire to emerge as 'authentic' through mimicry – through a process of writing and repetition – is the final irony of partial representation.

What I have called mimicry is not the familiar exercise of *dependent* colonial relations through narcissistic identification so that, as Fanon has observed,[13] the black man stops being an actional person for only the white man can represent his self-esteem. Mimicry conceals no presence or identity behind its mask: it is not what Césaire describes as 'colonization-thingification'[14] behind which there stands the essence of the *présence Africaine*. The *menace* of mimicry is its *double* vision which in disclosing the ambivalence of colonial discourse also disrupts its authority. And it is a double vision that is a result of what I've described as the partial representation/ recognition of the colonial object. Grant's colonial as partial imitator, Macaulay's translator, Naipaul's colonial politician as play-actor, Decoud as the scene setter of the *opéra bouffe* of the New World, these are the appropriate objects of a colonialist chain of command, authorized versions of otherness. But they are also, as I have shown, the figures of a doubling, the part-objects of a metonymy of colonial desire which alienates the modality and normality of those dominant discourses in which they emerge as 'inappropriate' colonial subjects. A desire that, through the repetition of *partial presence*, which is the basis of mimicry, articulates those disturbances of cultural, racial and historical difference that menace the narcissistic demand of colonial authority. It is a desire that reverses 'in part' the colonial appropriation by now producing a partial vision of the colonizer's presence; a gaze of otherness, that shares the acuity of the genealogical gaze which, as Foucault describes it, liberates marginal elements and shatters the unity of man's being through which he extends his sovereignty.[15]

I want to turn to this process by which the look of surveillance returns as the displacing gaze of the disciplined, where the observer becomes the observed and 'partial' representation rearticulates the whole notion of *identity* and alienates it from essence. But not before observing that even an exemplary history like Eric Stokes's *The English Utilitarians and India* acknowledges the anomalous gaze of otherness but finally disavows it in a contradictory utterance:

> Certainly India played *no* central part in fashioning the distinctive qualities of English civilisation. In many ways it acted as a disturbing force, a magnetic power placed at the periphery tending to distort the natural development of Britain's character.[16] (My emphasis)

What is the nature of the hidden threat of the partial gaze? How does mimicry emerge as the subject of the scopic drive and the object of colonial surveillance? How is desire disciplined, authority displaced?

If we turn to a Freudian figure to address these issues of colonial textuality, that form of difference that is mimicry – *almost the same but not quite* – will become clear. Writing of the partial nature of fantasy, caught *inappropriately*, between the unconscious and the preconscious, making problematic, like mimicry, the very notion of 'origins', Freud has this to say:

Their mixed and split origin is what decides their fate. We may compare them with individuals of mixed race who taken all round resemble white men but who betray their coloured descent by some striking feature or other and on that account are excluded from society and enjoy none of the privileges.[17]

Almost the same but not white: the visibility of mimicry is always produced at the site of interdiction. It is a form of colonial discourse that is uttered *inter dicta*: a discourse at the crossroads of what is known and permissible and that which though known must be kept concealed; a discourse uttered between the lines and as such both against the rules and within them. The question of the representation of difference is therefore always also a problem of authority. The 'desire' of mimicry, which is Freud's 'striking feature' that reveals so little but makes such a big difference, is not merely that impossibility of the Other which repeatedly resists signification. The desire of colonial mimicry – an interdictory desire – may not have an object, but it has strategic objectives which I shall call the *metonymy of presence*.

Those inappropriate signifiers of colonial discourse – the difference between being English and being Anglicized; the identity between stereotypes which, through repetition, also become different; the discriminatory identities constructed across traditional cultural norms and classifications, the Simian Black, the Lying Asiatic – all these are *metonymies* of presence. They are strategies of desire in discourse that make the anomalous representation of the colonized something other than a process of 'the return of the repressed', what Fanon unsatisfactorily characterized as collective catharsis.[18] These instances of metonymy are the non-repressive productions of contradictory and multiple belief. They cross the boundaries of the culture of enunciation through a strategic confusion of the metaphoric and metonymic axes of the cultural production of meaning.

In mimicry, the representation of identity and meaning is rearticulated along the axis of metonymy. As Lacan reminds us, mimicry is like camouflage, not a harmonization of repression of difference, but a form of resemblance, that differs from or defends presence by displaying it in part, metonymically. Its threat, I would add, comes from the prodigious and strategic production of conflictual, fantastic, discriminatory 'identity effects' in the play of a power that is elusive because it hides no essence, no 'itself'. And that form of *resemblance* is the most terrifying thing to behold, as Edward Long testifies in his *History of Jamaica* (1774). At the end of a tortured, negrophobic passage, that shifts anxiously between piety, prevarication and perversion, the text finally confronts its fear; nothing other than the repetition of its resemblance 'in part': [Negroes] are represented by all authors as the vilest of human kind, to which they have little more pretension of resemblance *than what arises from their exterior forms*' (my emphasis).[19]

From such a colonial encounter between the white presence and its black semblance, there emerges the question of the ambivalence of mimicry as a problematic of colonial subjection. For if Sade's scandalous theatricalization of language repeatedly reminds us that discourse can claim 'no priority', then the work of Edward Said will not let us forget that the 'ethnocentric and erratic will to power from which texts can spring'[20] is itself a theatre of war. Mimicry, as the metonymy of presence is, indeed, such an erratic, eccentric strategy of authority in colonial discourse. Mimicry does not merely destroy narcissistic authority through the repetitive slippage of difference and desire. It is the process of the *fixation* of the colonial as a form of cross-classificatory, discriminatory knowledge within an interdictory discourse, and therefore necessarily raises the question of the *authorization* of colonial representations; a question of authority that goes beyond the subject's lack of priority (castration) to a historical crisis in the conceptuality of colonial man as an *object* of regulatory power, as the subject of racial, cultural, national representation.

'This culture ... fixed in its colonial status', Fanon suggests, '[is] both present and mummified, it testified against its members. It defines them in fact without appeal.'[21] The ambivalence of mimicry – almost but not quite – suggests that the fetishized colonial culture is potentially and strategically an insurgent counter-appeal. What I have called its 'identity-effects' are always crucially *split*. Under cover of camouflage, mimicry, like the fetish, is a part-object that radically revalues the normative knowledges of the priority of race, writing, history. For the fetish mimes the forms of authority at the point at which it deauthorizes them. Similarly, mimicry rearticulates presence in terms of its 'otherness', that which it disavows. There is a crucial difference between this *colonial* articulation of man and his doubles and that which Foucault describes as 'thinking the unthought'[22] which, for nineteenth-century Europe, is the ending of man's alienation by reconciling him with his essence. The colonial discourse that articulates an *interdictory* otherness is precisely the 'other scene' of this nineteenth-century European desire for an authentic historical consciousness.

The 'unthought' across which colonial man is articulated is that process of classificatory confusion that I have described as the metonymy of the substitutive chain of ethical and cultural discourse. This results in the *splitting* of colonial discourse so that two attitudes towards external reality persist; one takes reality into consideration while the other disavows it and replaces it by a product of desire that repeats, rearticulates 'reality' as mimicry.

So Edward Long can say with authority, quoting variously Hume, Eastwick and Bishop Warburton in his support, that: 'Ludicrous as the opinion may seem I do not think that an orangutang husband would be any dishonour to a Hottentot female.'[23]

Such contradictory articulations of reality and desire – seen in racist stereotypes, statements, jokes, myths – are not caught in the doubtful circle of the return of the repressed. They are the effects of a disavowal that denies the differences of the other but produces in its stead forms of authority and multiple belief that alienate the assumptions of 'civil' discourse. If, for a while, the ruse of desire is calculable for the uses of discipline soon the repetition of guilt, justification, pseudo-scientific theories, superstition, spurious authorities, and classifications can be seen as the desperate effort to 'normalize' *formally* the disturbance of a discourse of splitting that violates the rational, enlightened claims of its enunciatory modality. The ambivalence of colonial authority repeatedly turns from *mimicry* – a difference that is almost nothing but not quite – to *menace* – a difference that is almost total but not quite. And in that other scene of colonial power, where history turns to farce and presence to 'a part' can be seen the twin figures of narcissism and paranoia that repeat furiously, uncontrollably.

In the ambivalent world of the 'not quite/not white', on the margins of metropolitan desire, the *founding objects* of the Western world become the erratic, eccentric, accidental *objets trouvés* of the colonial discourse – the part-objects of presence. It is then that the body and the book lose their part-objects of presence. It is then that the body and the book lose their representational authority. Black skin splits under the racist gaze, displaced into signs of bestiality, genitalia, grotesquerie, which reveal the phobic myth of the undifferentiated whole white body. And the holiest of books – the Bible – bearing both the standard of the cross and the standard of empire finds itself strangely dismembered. In May 1817 a missionary wrote from Bengal:

> Still everyone would gladly receive a Bible. And why? – that he may lay it up as a curiosity for a few pice; or use it for waste paper. Such it is well known has been the common fate of these copies of the Bible. ... Some have been bartered in the markets, others have been thrown in snuff shops and used as wrapping paper.[24]

Notes

[1] J. Lacan, 'The line and the light', in his *The Four Fundamental Concepts of Psychoanalysis*, Alan Sheridan (trans.) (London: The Hogarth Press and the Institute of Psycho-Analysis, 1977), p. 99.

[2] Cited in E. Stokes, *The Political Ideas of English Imperialism* (Oxford: Oxford University Press, 1960), pp. 17–18.

[3] E. Said, *Orientalism* (New York: Pantheon Books, 1978), p. 240.

[4] S. Weber, 'The sideshow, or: remarks on a canny moment', *Modern Language Notes*, vol. 88, no. 6 (1973), p. 112.

[5] C. Grant, 'Observations on the state of society among the Asiatic subjects of Great Britain', *Sessional Papers of the East India Company*, vol. X, no. 282 (1812–13).

[6] ibid., ch. 4, p. 104.

[7] T. B. Macaulay, 'Minute on education', in W. Theodore de Bary (ed.) *Sources of Indian Tradition*, vol. II (New York: Columbia University Press, 1958), p. 49.

[8] Mr Thomason's communication to the Church Missionary Society, 5 September 1819, in *The Missionary Register*, 1821, pp. 54–5.

[9] B. Anderson, *Imagined Communities* (London: Verso, 1983), p. 88.

[10] ibid., pp. 88–9.

[11] J. Conrad, *Nostromo* (London: Penguin, 1979), p. 161.

[12] V. S. Naipual, *The Mimic Men* (London: Penguin, 1967), p. 416.

[13] F. Fanon, *Black Skin, White Masks* (London: Paladin, 1970), p. 109.

[14] A. Césaire, *Discourse on Colonialism* (New York: Monthly Review Press, 1972), p. 21.

[15] M. Foucault, 'Nietzche, genealogy, history', in his *Language, Counter-Memory, Practice*, D. F. Bouchard and S. Simon (trans.) (Ithaca: Cornell University Press, 1977), p. 153.

[16] E. Stokes, *The English Utilitarians and India* (Oxford: Oxford University Press, 1959), p. xi.

[17] S. Freud, 'The unconscious' (1915), *SE*, XIV, pp. 190–1.

[18] Fanon, *Black Skin, White Masks*, p. 103.

[19] E. Long, *A History of Jamaica*, 1774, vol. II, p. 353.

[20] E. Said, 'The Text, the world, the critic', in J. V. Harari (ed.) *Textual Strategies* (Ithaca: Cornell University Press, 1979), p. 184.

[21] F. Fanon, 'Racism and culture', in his *Toward the African Revolution*, H. Chevalier (trans.) (London: Pelican, 1967), p. 44.

[22] M. Foucault, *The Order of Things* (New York: Pantheon Books, 1971), part II, ch. 9.

[23] Long, *History of Jamaica*, p. 364.

[24] *The Missionary Register*, May 1817, p. 186.

4 Scattered Speculations on the Subaltern and the Popular

Gayatri Chakravorty Spivak

Subaltern is to popular as gender is to sex, class to poverty, state to nation. One word inclines to reasonableness, the other to cathexis – occupation through desire. 'Popular' divides between descriptive (as in presidential or TV ratings), evaluative (not 'high', both a positive and a negative value, dependent on your 'politics'), and contains 'people', a word with immense range, from 'just anyone', to the 'masses' (both a positive and a negative political value, depending on your politics). The reasonable and rarefied definition of the word subaltern that interests me is: to be removed from all lines of social mobility.

The disciplinary interest of literary criticism is in the singular and the unverifiable. In 'Can the Subaltern Speak?' it was the peculiar and singular subalternity of the young Bhubaneswari Bhaduri that seemed of interest.[1] Her story was my mother Sivani Chakravorty's testimony. The question of veridicality – of the evidentiary status of testimony, sometimes taken for granted in unexamined oral history – has to be thought of here.

Gilles Deleuze's notion of singularity is both complex and simple. In its simplest form, the singular is not the particular because it is an unrepeatable difference that is, on the other hand, repeated – not as an example of a universal but as an instance of a collection of repetitions. Singularity is life as pure immanence, what will be, of this life, as life. As the name Bhubaneswari Bhaduri became a teaching text, it took on this imperative – repeat as singular –, as does literature.[2]

If the thinking of subalternity is taken in the general sense, its lack of access to mobility may be a version of singularity. Subalternity cannot be generalised according to hegemonic logic. That is what makes it subaltern. Yet it is a category and therefore repeatable. Since the general sense is always mired in narrow senses,

Gayatri Chakravorty Spivak, "Scattered Speculations on the Subaltern and the Popular." *Postcolonial Studies*, 8(4), 2005: 475–486. Reproduced by permission of Taylor & Francis Ltd.

Postcolonial Studies: An Anthology, First Edition. Edited by Pramod K. Nayar.
Editorial material and organization © 2016 John Wiley & Sons, Ltd.
Published 2016 by John Wiley & Sons, Ltd.

any differentiations between subalternity and the popular must thus concern itself with singular cases and thus contravene the philosophical purity of Deleuze's thought.[3]

The starting point of a singular itinerary of the word 'subaltern' can be Antonio Gramsci's 'Southern Question' rather than his more general discussions of the subaltern. I believe that was the basic starting point of the South Asian Subaltern Studies collective – Gramsci, a Communist, thinking beyond capital logic in terms of unequal development. Subsequently, Partha Chatterjee developed a nuanced reading of both Gramsci and Foucault.[4]

It is from 'Some Aspects of the Southern Question', then, that we can move into Ranajit Guha's 'On Some Aspects of the Historiography of Colonial India'.[5] 'Subaltern' in the early Guha was the name of a space of difference. And the word was indistinguishable from 'people'. Although Guha seems to be saying that the words 'people' and 'subaltern' are interchangeable, I think this is not a substantive point for him. At least in their early work, the members of the Subaltern Studies collective would not quarrel with the notion that the word 'subaltern' and the idea of the 'popular' do not inhabit a continuous space. Yet their failure to make this distinction has led to a certain relaxing of the word 'subaltern' that has undermined its usefulness. The slide into the 'popular' may be part of this.

Subalternity is a position without identity. It is somewhat like the strict understanding of class. Class is not a cultural origin, it is a sense of economic collectivity, of social relations of formation as the basis of action. Gender is not lived sexual difference. It is a sense of the collective social negotiation of sexual differences as the basis of action. 'Race' is not originary; it assumes racism. Subalternity is where social lines of mobility, being elsewhere, do not permit the formation of a recognisable basis of action. The early subalternists looked at examples where subalternity was brought to crisis, as a basis for militancy was formed. Even then colonial and nationalist historiography did not recognise it as such. Could the subaltern speak, then? Could it have its insurgency recognised by the official historians? Even when, strictly speaking, they had burst the outlines of subalternity? This last is important. Neither the groups celebrated by the early subalternists nor Bhubaneswari Bhaduri, in so far as they had burst their bonds into resistance, were in the position of subalternity. No one can say 'I am a subaltern' in whatever language. And subaltern studies will not reduce itself to the historical recounting of the details of the practice of disenfranchised groups and remain a study of the subaltern.

Subalternity is where social lines of mobility, being elsewhere, do not permit the formation of a recognisable basis of action. Both Gramsci and Guha imply this, of course. But I came to it through Marx.

I came to it through the very well-known and often misunderstood passage in the *Eighteenth Brumaire*, where Marx is talking about class formation in two ways, about how the same group of people are, and are not, a class, depending upon whether they have a consciousness of class. Marx comes to the conclusion that small peasant proprietors in France are a class, to use contemporary language, as a constative, but not as a performative. It is in that connection that he writes: 'They cannot represent themselves; they must be represented'. That passage, about the difference between the two ways of being a class, was what gave me a sense of what I later learned to call the difference between subalternity and agency. Agency was the name I gave to institutionally validated action, assuming collectivity, distinguished from the formation of the subject, which exceeds the outlines of individual intention. (Marx is not, of course, speaking of subject-formation.) The idea of subalternity became imbricated with the idea of non-recognition of agency. Did Marx intend this? I believe so. When I came across Bhubaneswari's story, this Marxian resource, already in hand, produced the account that a woman's resistance in extremis was not recognised.

The line from the Marx passage to Bhubaneswari Bhaduri can be discerned if we look at Marx's German. The best English translation goes: 'They are therefore incapable of asserting their class interest in their own name'. In the German it is, 'Sie sind daher unfähig, ihr Klasseninteresse im eigenen Namen […] geltend zu machen'.[6] Because of the absence of infrastructural institutions, which are the condition and effect of class-consciousness, 'they could not make their class-interest count', to have what they are saying and doing be recognised as such.

The early subalternists accepted this type of situation as the challenge of their new historiography. Their sources were the texts of an elite that was constituted by this non-recognition. They could not therefore deduce subalternity from the textual or archival evidence. They solved the problem by putting forward a 'negative consciousness'.[7] And I, instead of noticing that they were finessing the problem, said they were using essentialism strategically. But essentialism is always used strategically, to bypass or acknowledge difference. Today, realising that subalternity is a position without identity – that like the value-form it is contentless –, I cannot think that the project is to fill it with a 'negative' essence. Subaltern content takes on identity, names itself 'people'. 'People' becomes a slogan too quickly. To appreciate Gramsci's vision, we must know that, outside of such politics, subalternisation does not stop. I have not been able to get my hands on Peter Hallward's book. But I understand he thinks this is just too non-specific and therefore not political.[8] Some people think an interest in the subaltern takes us away from secularism. I have tried to answer that charge in 'Terror: A Speech after 9/11'.[9]

To want to hegemonise the subaltern, of which the subalternist revision of historiography is an important but relatively autonomous part, transforms the academic intellectual into a 'permanent persuader'.[10] The subalternists, having chosen to persuade a change in nineteenth-century historiography, exhausted that vein when the project became a part of curricula. They seem now engaged in excellent postcolonial exercises away from the subaltern classes. Alternatively, there is some recounting of the details of the practice of disenfranchised groups. This is useful work, but only constative, there is no effort here to touch the subaltern or, with the energy with which historio-graphic practice is questioned, to question the political strategy that appropriates the disenfranchised. Contemporary political conduct does not even rise to the status of the texts of the elite in earlier work. It is not decoded and contrasted to that which it subverts: the conformity of the subaltern to its own social norms.

The oral version of what became 'Can the Subaltern Speak?', entitled 'Power and Desire', was presented before I had read the first volume of Subaltern Studies. Perusal of that book and the subsequent meeting with the collective represented such a change in intellectual direction that it led to the placement of a collective (rather than singular) initial theoretical coding upon the phenomenon of sati-reform: white men are saving brown women from brown men. That incendiary sentence, come back to haunt our time, does not apply to the status of the reform itself, of course. In the essay the reform is called 'in itself admirable!'[11] In order for the presuppositions of the reform to reach the affective field of the popular, however, a kind of involvement with subaltern female subjectivity had to be undertaken that was inconsonant with colonialism and indeed the postcolonial state, and today with the practices of the international civil society. The focus of subalternity in the essay remained the singular woman who attempted to send the reader a message, as if her body were a 'literary' text. The message of the woman who hanged herself was one of unrecognisable resistance, an unrecognisable refusal of victimage by reproductive heteronormativity. As already mentioned, I had learnt the importance of making unrecognisable resistance recognisable from 'The Eighteenth Brumaire', a rather different recognition from the one touted by today's liberal multiculturalism.[12]

The only criticism of the subaltern studies group in 'Deconstructing Historiography' was that they were gender-blind. In the next volume, Ranajit Guha produced 'Chandra's Death', where the dead woman also remained singular.[13] There too the theme is reproduction. But the woman is a victim, without even the minimal activity of suicide.

What I am suggesting today, then, is that constative subaltern studies, radical in its place and time, was questioning colonial, nationalist, as well as Marxist historiography. Its connection to the performative was to attempt to expand the horizons of historiography. I am suggesting that their focus on the bringing into crisis of subalternity *by* the subaltern, and its non-recognition because they could not make it *count* for such historians as Eric Hobsbawm, who called such activity 'pre-political', inevitably called for another kind of 'setting-to-work', to which most of them did not rise. I am suggesting that Gramsci also called for such a setting-to-work in his conception of the organic intellectual. The call is for another performativity, a contamination of the outlines of historiography by its own place in history, so that the subaltern is not merely protected by 'negative consciousness', as the new historiography continues endlessly to read the archives against the grain. Such reading of the archives is, of course, useful, but only, at best, for correcting the constative.

In *Primitive Rebels*, Eric Hobsbawm enters into the intimacy of the ethnographer with the communities he describes as 'pre-political'. He believes in accessing the mindset of the other, getting 'a "feel" for' them, yet he finds comfort in knowing that some of his subjects will never read his books.[14] This is disciplinary protection of another kind. In my interdisciplinary intervention, I began to see (this is, of course, an abreactive stereotyping of myself) that, however ethnographic his practice, Hobsbawm did at least call them pre-political, not pre- or para-historical, nor merely anthropological, so perhaps he was not quite as culpable as the nationalist historiography that could not make these people count as history. Yet Hobsbawm too was stopping the problem of the unrepresentability of the subaltern (position) with no more than ethnographic regret.

Gramsci, the thinker of subalternity as an amendment of mere capital logic, had, in his figuration of the organic intellectual, given us an idea of expanding the horizon of historiography as an activity. In an extended consideration, I would question the figure of the 'organic', but that would not lead to a disagreement with Gramsci's general point.

This is not the place to launch an analysis of Gramsci's notion of subalternity. Suffice it to say that Gramsci's subaltern is not as impervious as the one I have been discussing. There are at least two reasons for this. First, Gramsci's thought-world was mono-gendered. And, subalternity as position without identity computed differently in a world where the role of the Communist party as envisaged by Gramsci in his jail cell was significantly different from anything that either ourselves or the early subalternists could imagine. One insight, however, is still useful: 'The intellectuals are the dominant group's "deputies" exercising the subaltern functions of social hegemony and political government'.[15] I add here Raymond William's dynamic sense of the 'dominant' as defined by its ceaseless appropriation of the emergent, as it divides itself into mere alternative and actively oppositional.[16] Hobsbawm's and the early subalternists' limiting of the subaltern within the historiographical may be seen as such an appropriation. By contrast, it was the intention of saving the singular oppositional that the example of Bhubaneswari Bhaduri taught me so long ago. That message in her body led outside disciplinary limits.

Gramsci's description of the organic intellectual fits the vast network of US tertiary education well: 'the "organic" intellectuals which every new class creates alongside itself and elaborates' – Gramsci uses this word in the strong sense of 'working through' – 'in the course of its development, are for the most part 'specialisations' of partial aspects of the [...] activity of the new social type which the new class has brought into prominence'.[17]

I think it can be argued that there is such a connection between the gradual emergence of a global secessionist managerial class, a self-styled international civil society of self-selected moral entrepreneurs with no social contract – with the transference of power from Britain to the United States in the middle of the last century – and the transmogrification of the subaltern into the humanist figure of the 'people', a noun that cannot enter into singularity. As the political passes into management, our conjuncture needs 'people', a pluralised general category that has no necessary class-description.[18] In a broad understanding, the subaltern historian as the historian of the popular is the organic intellectual of the class-shuffle between the old and new imperial worlds. Gramsci had loosened class-logic to think of bringing the subaltern into hegemony. This new development annuls both class-logic and the Gramscian task.

In so far as one can examine one's own production, I situate my concern with subalternity within this narrative. One must think that this can help produce an effort not to be helplessly confined within one's class-culture of origin, an effort not to be fully determined by history. One recalls with embarrassment Gramsci's furofher description: 'The mode of being of the new intellectual can no longer consist in eloquence, which is an exterior and momentary mover of feelings and passions, but in active participation in practical life, as constructor, organizer, "permanent persuader" [...]'.[19] This may seem too radical if your goal is the constative, but there is no gainsaying that Gramsci is looking to 'generat[e] by a joint and simultaneous grafting [...] of the performative and the constative'.[20] I defend this effort by quoting Gramsci further, and questioning both 'the position assumed by the social complex of intellectuals [whose philosophy] can be defined as the expression of that social utopia by which the intellectuals think of themselves as 'independent, autonomous, endowed with a character of their own, etc', and, on the other hand, those old-style new historiographers who have forgotten that 'school is the instrument through which intellectuals of various levels are elaborated'.[21]

What we are speaking of, then, is the bringing of the subaltern from the deduced subject of crisis to the logic of agency. Can this be equated with the activation of singularity into multiplicity (see Note 18)? I think not.

Singularity was a questioning of the universal-particular dyad. The singular is repeated, with a difference. That is how the 'human' is repeated-in-difference in single humans, prior to the construction of personhood or individuality. It is a powerful concept, anchored in good sense, questioning both universalism and identitarianism. Such differently repeated singularities collectively are a multiplicity. This is not an empirical collective, not, in other words, a multitude. As long as we remember these are ways of thinking, always inclined to the empirical, we can continue to work. If we reduce them to the empirical alone, turn subaltern into popular, we are merely disputatious chroniclers.

If the repetition of singularity that gives multiplicity is the repetition of difference, agency calls for the putting aside of difference. Agency presumes collectivity, which is where a group acts by synecdoche: the part that seems to agree is taken to stand for the whole. I put aside the surplus of my subjectivity and metonymise myself, count myself as the part by which I am connected to the particular predicament so that I can claim collectivity, and engage in action validated by that very collective. A performative contradiction connects the metonymy and the synecdoche into agential identity.[22] All calls to collectivity are metonymic because attached to a situation. And they work by synecdoche. Now in order to be able to restrict singularity by agential intuition, an immense labor of infrastructural change, to make resistance count (*geltend*), to make it recognisable, must be undertaken. This is where humanities education kicks in, sees the way reasonable agency is nestled in the permission to be figurative – the right to the metonym/synecdoche political performance of collectivity. I will give an example in a moment. But let me say here that this is where the humanities can reclaim a part of history for the 'human' as it plays with qualitative social science. To mistake this for classical humanism is to ignore history and politics. The outlines of historiography must be contaminated if it wishes to continue as subalternist. Making something count is not counting things, on the way to quantification.

I have said that the 'singular', as it combats the universal-particular binary opposition, is not an individual, a person, an agent; multiplicity is not multitude. If, however, we are thinking of potential agents, when s/he is not publicly empowered to put aside difference and self-synecdochise to form collectivity, the group will take difference itself as its synecdochic element. Difference slides into 'culture', often indistinguishable from 'religion'. And then the institution that provides agency is reproductive heteronormativity (RHN). It is the broadest and oldest global institution. You see now why just writing about women does not solve the problem of the gendered subaltern, just as chronicling the popular is not subaltern studies. In search of the subaltern I first turned to my own class: the Bengali middle class: Bhubaneshwari Bhaduri and Mahasweta Devi. From French theory that is all I could do. But I did not remain there. In the middle class, according to Partha Chatterjee, Bhubaneshwari Bhaduri was metaleptically substituting effect for cause and producing an idea of national liberation by her suicide. Chatterjee's argument is that an idea of national liberation was produced by, so-called, terrorist movements.[23] It was a frightening, solitary, and 'Clytemnestra-like' project for a woman.

In the subsequent years the gendered subaltern, for me, kept moving down the social strata. Class is not the exact word here because we are speaking of an area beside capital logic. Relative autonomy does not apply here, first, because autonomy is a marked concept. Secondly, because, in the common-place agential sense, there is minimal agential autonomy in engendered subalternity. My discussion of Mahasweta Devi's 'Doulati the Bountiful' in *Outside in the Teaching Machine*, describes a literary representation of the female subaltern as holding up the rural economy.[24] This downward trajectory came to relate to home working, permanent casuals, more orthodox doubts of the Marxist analysis of the female laboring body as the agent of production.

As you can see, however, in what I am writing today, the problems that emerged out of 'Can the Subaltern Speak?', – the problem of subject-ship and agency, and the call to build 'infrastructure' in the colloquial, not the Marxist sense, so that agency would emerge –, have not left me. At that stage already, I saw agency as institutional validation, whereas subject formation exceeded the borders of the intending subject, to put it brutally briefly. And I saw reproductive heteronormativity as the broadest global institution. Now, in addition, I see agency as the play of self-synecdochising in a metonym. To 'restore rights to the people' without laying the groundwork for this (political) will can be well-intentioned but only that, and only at best.

In general, the leaders of collectivities – 'good' or 'bad' – have the right to the metonym/synecdoche complex. That the rank and file do not, sometimes gets overlooked. That I believe is the difference between 'good' and 'bad' movements. My foray into teacher-training for the subaltern is because they also are citizens, *the* name for hegemony. In order to work for them, I set aside my differences – Columbia Professor, dollar income, classed caste-birth, and all that comes with it. I synecdochise myself as nothing but a citizen of India, which is where my students, their parents and relatives, and I, can form a collectivity, in search of agency. On the other hand, they are not, mentally or materially (the two bleed into each other), free to put aside their differences. The effort is to build infrastructure so that they can, when necessary, when the public sphere calls for it, synecdochise themselves without identitarian exploitation (sometimes well-meaning but equally destructive), from above. The solution, as I see it, is not to celebrate or deny difference, but find out what specific case of inequality brings about the use of difference and who can deny it on occasion. The solution is also not to create 'a politics of recognition' where this problematic is altogether ignored.[25] The solution cannot come to us from the international civil society, self-selected moral entrepreneurs who distribute philanthropy without democracy.[26] I believe the existing debates about contingency and universality have not taken into account.[27]

Here is another example, from the other end of the spectrum. Donald Pease the Americanist has suggested that, in the wake of 9/11, with civil liberties constrained by the Patriot Act and the general atmosphere of suspicion and fear, the will of the citizen of the United States has become separated from the state.[28] This too is a kind of subalternity because the part is no longer part of the whole, and therefore the power to self-synecdochise has been taken away. Bruce Ackerman had suggested some years ago that, 'We the people' in the United States polity are not engaged on an ordinary day. It is only when there are transformative Supreme Court decisions and popular mandates that they act.[29] And now Donald Pease was suggesting that even that has been changed. He, however, was not able to see that RHN kicks in here as well. Although the citizen is subalternised inside the nation-state – the United States –, outside in the world, agency is reclaimed, again and again, and across the political spectrum, generally in the name of gender. Gender is the alibi for much US interference abroad. That has as little persuasiveness for the thinking of subalternity as a position without identity as does gender-oppression in the name of cultural difference. 'People' will play into both these extremes. If we grasp subalternity as a position without identity we will think of building infrastructure for agency. Ethical sameness cannot be compromised. The point is to have access to the situation, the metonym, through a self-synecdoche that can be withdrawn when necessary rather than confused with identity.

I hesitate to talk about my teacher-training efforts, because they seem so minute. But, if I am going to suggest that the task is to take Hobsbawm a step further, to make the anthropologist construct her object as a teacher for a different end, learn to learn from below, *from* the subaltern, rather than only study him(her), I have to make an attempt. In this audience, I can call it 'fieldwork'. Then you can take a small example and people will not dismiss you. In this audience I can call it 'case studies'. It is a small undertaking going on for fifteen years and it has its place in the movement of the subaltern as I am describing it. My project has become more and more not only to study the subaltern (always in the sense of 'cut-off from lines of social mobility') but to learn (as from figuration – because I am a literary person) from them in order to be able to devise a philosophy of education that will develop, for want of a better expression (since I do not write about this fieldwork, generalisable phrases do not come immediately), the 'habits of democratic behavior', or 'rituals of democratic behavior', or 'intuition of the public sphere'.

By now it should be clear that 'insertion into the public sphere' means for me the effort to create the possibility of metonymising oneself for making oneself a synecdoche, a part of a whole, so that one can claim the idea of the state belonging to one. The particular collectivity claimed here is citizenship: the state can be seen as being in the citizen's service through access to this collectivity. This abstract agential self-perception is a non-dependent intuition of the public sphere, not as *'ma-baap'* but as a claimable right. This is hopelessly idealistic, especially in the context of a repressive state, in the current era of globalisation where the state is more and more reconfigured as not the agent of redistribution, but the agent of repression; and the model is not accountability, but management. The idea of relating to the state in a country as multi-lingual and multi-cultural, as many-leveled as India –and to a degree such differences exist everywhere –, unless you want to go through nationalism/fascism, you must be able to metonymise/synecdochise yourself, understand the part by which you are connected to that abstract whole so that you can claim it. It is not even the right to metonymise oneself, it is the possibility. This kind of work can only be a supplement to much more quick-fix, problem-solving work. But if it isn't there then subalternisation remains in place and accounts of popular practice as political society remain constative.

This is where the responsibilities of borrowing Gramsci's word has brought me. It is the next stage of the work with a trajectory of the subaltern. Not to study the subaltern, but to learn. I am a humanities teacher, not a historian or anthropologist. Therefore, those disciplinary habits are not easily mine. I have fallen into a reading task: to learn from these collectivities enough to suture rights thinking into the torn cultural fabric of responsibility; or, to vary the concept-metaphor, activate a dormant ethical imperative. The text is text-ile. To suture here is to weave, as in invisible mending.[30] The work takes me to the break up of rural welfare in China, and the transformation of indigenous knowledge in South Africa. And this brings me to the new subaltern, about whom I have written elsewhere.

So far I have spoken of the old subaltern, withdrawn from lines of social mobility, in terms of an educational enterprise that in a supplementary way tries to release the possibility of self-abstraction, self-synecdoche. Merely trying to release the possibility – it will not happen in the classroom tomorrow. By infrastructure, I had earlier meant the effort to establish, implement and monitor structures that allow subaltern resistance to be located and heard. In the interim years, through the electronic circuits of globalisation, the subaltern has become greatly permeable. Much of a pastiche of 'global' culture is lexicalised in a fragmentary fashion in the underclass public world. (To lexicalise is to separate a linguistic item from its appropriate grammatical system into the conventions of another grammar.) But the permeability I speak of is the exploitation of the global subaltern as source of intellectual property without the benefit of benefit-sharing,[31] pharmaceutical patenting and social dumping. There is no permeability in the opposite direction. That is where the permanent effort of infrastructural involvement is called for. I am not speaking of organising international conferences with exceptionalist 'examples' of subalternity to represent collective subaltern will. The subaltern has no 'examples'. The exemplary subaltern is hegemonised, even if (and not necessarily) in bad faith. This must be distinguished from the desperate and hardly perceptible effort at faking subaltern collective initiative by the leaders of counter-globalist resistances. I have called it 'feudality' without 'feudalism'. I do not think it is a good idea at this point to take a real position against it, because I know where the desperation comes from.

Here too I will speak of tapping subjectship for the sake of agency, as in teacher training among the subaltern. For what we need is not only legitimate benefit-sharing. We need also to prepare the field for sharing, however incomplete. Professor Hayden, whom I cite in Note 31, speaks of Mexico. I have some experience of South Africa in terms of the transformation of indigenous knowledge into intellectual property. My limited experience would tell me that even as organisations such as the *Indigenous Knowledge Systems of South Africa Trust* are trying to make benefit-sharing equitable, they remain complicit with the idea that the transformation of indigenous knowledge systems into data is an unquestioned good, and that there need be no attention paid, beyond the descriptive attention of anthropology and archeology, to how these knowledge systems can supplement the imagination of the global. The only alternative seems to be to say, 'This is as good as what the heritage of the European world calls science'. I do talk about the problem with the Hindu nationalist claim, in India, that the ancient texts of the Vedas offer us 'Vedic science'.[32] The problem of the Hindu right is not that it cares for Vedic science, but that it uses it to prove that it is best, it can oppress others in its name, that India belongs to it. The Hindu right is not subaltern![33] The traditional healers in South Africa cannot be immediately compared to the Bharatiya Janata Party, although the fear of religious violence should be always around the corner. From within the humanities, I want to claim the traditional healer's sense of all history as a big now, I want to claim the sense of myth as being able to contain history, and keep detranscendentalising belief into the imagination. Turn the traditional healers' performative into performance, through training, curriculum, and curatorial practice, not just transform it into data. (This is easier and more common than transforming subaltern elementary education, where the 'traditional' is in play as deep background.) The unintended consequence of this can become an appropriation for religious fundamentalism, just as the intended consequence of the data-transformation is exploitation. This is the cleft stick for the new subalternist.

To historicise the subaltern, then, is not to write the history of the singular. It is the active, scrupulous, and vigilant contamination of historiography from the constative through the disciplinary performative into the field of the historical possibility of what we can only call the present. Here the difference between the old and the new subaltern is only conjunctural. The category of the 'popular' seems altogether tame when compared to this dynamic. I hope you will move with me.

Notes

1. Gayatri Chakravorty Spivak, *A Critique of Postcolonial Reason: Toward a History of the Vanishing Present*, Cambridge: Harvard University Press, 1999, pp 306–311.

2. Gilles Deleuze, *The Logic of Sense*, Mark Lester with Charles Stivale (trans), Constantin V. Boundas, ed., New York: Columbia University Press, 1990. See also Antonio Negri, 'Spinoza's Anti-Modernity', Charles T. Wolfe (trans) *Graduate Faculty Philosophy Journal* 18(2), 1995, pp 1–15, where singularity is related to Spinoza's notion of ethical singularity. All reading carries this imperative, but literature admits to this most readily.

3. Here Derrida is once again useful. 'Shibboleth: For Paul Celan', *Midrash and Literature*, Geoffrey H. Hartman and Sanford Bunick, eds, New Haven: Yale University Press, 1986, p 325.

4. Partha Chatterjee, *Nationalist Thought and the Colonial World: A Derivative Discourse?*, Minneapolis: University of Minnesota Press, 1993, pp. 24, 29–30, 43–50.

5. Ranajit Guha, 'On Some Aspects of the Historiography of Colonial India' in *Subaltern Studies I: Writings on South Asian History and Society*, Ranajit Guha, ed., New Delhi: Oxford Univ. Press, 1982.

6. Karl Marx, *Surveys from Exile*, David Fernbach (trans), Vintage: New York, 1974, p 239; Marx-Engels *Werke*, Berlin: Dietz, 1982, vol. 8, p 198.

7. Gayatri Chakravorty Spivak, 'Subaltern Studies: Deconstructing Historiography', in *Subaltern Studies IV* (1985), p 330.

8. Peter Hallward, *Absolutely Postcolonial: Writing Between the Singular and the Specific*, New York: Manchester University Press, 2001.

9. Gayatri Chakravorty Spivak, 'Terror: A Speech after 9/11', *boundary 2* 31(2), 2004, p 81–111.

10. Antonio Gramsci, 'The Intellectuals', in *Selections from the Prison Notebooks*, Quintin Hoare and Geoffrey Nowell-Smith (trans), New York: International Publishers, 1971, p 10.

11. In a much revised form (that phrase was never revised), it is now to be found in Spivak, *A Critique*, p 290.

12. Charles C. Taylor, *Multiculturalism and the 'Politics of Recognition'*, Amy Gutmann, ed., Princeton: Princeton University Press, 1992.

13. Ranajit Guha, 'Chandra's Death', in *Subaltern Studies V*, New Delhi, Oxford University Press, 1987, pp 135–165.

14. Eric Hobsbawm, *Primitive Rebels: Studies in Archaic Forms of Social Movement in the 19th and 20th Centuries* Manchester: Manchester University Press, 1959, pp v, vi.

15. Antonio Gramsci, 'The Intellectuals', p 12.

16. Raymond Williams, 'Base and Superstructure in Marxist Cultural Theory' in *Marxism and Literature*, Oxford: Oxford University Press, 1985, pp 121–128.

17. Gramsci, 'The Intellectuals', p 6.

18. Here the current subalternists and their critics, the authors of *Empire*, meet. 'Multitude' is as dangerous a hypostatization of singularity, as 'people' is of subalternity.

19. Gramsci, 'The Intellectuals', p 10.

20. Derrida, *Politics of Friendship*, George Collins (trans), New York: Verso, 1997, p 32; translation modified. I have suppressed 'without a proper body' because that may not have been part of Gramsci's plan. That such efforts have no identity is a problem for historian and political activist alike. This is where the imagination of the humanities, the aesthetic that judges without an objective concept (I paraphrase Kant) is useful for work.

21. Gramsci, 'The Intellectuals', pp. 8, 10.

22. The classic analysis is in Derrida, 'Declarations of Independence', Thomas W. Keenan and T. Pepper (trans), *New Political Science* 15 (Summer 1986), pp 3–19.

23. Unpublished conversation.

24. Gayatri Chakravorty Spivak, *Outside in the Teaching Machine*, New York: Routledge, 1993, pp 78–95.

25. Charles Taylor, *Multiculturalism and the 'Politics of Recognition'*, Amy Gutman, ed., Princeton: Princeton University Press, 1992.

26. Alas the United Nations noble Millennium Project suffers from this. I do not mean to denigrate its awesome scope and the good intentions of its framers.

27. There is a good discussion of the debate in James Penney, '(Queer) Theory and the Universal Alternative', *Diacritics* 32.2 (Summer 2002), pp 3–41. I cannot lay claim to Penney's theoretical sophistication. But I offer my approach as an open-ended response to Penney's important question: 'if we acknowledge that Left-leaning cultural criticism has in the last decade or so reached a virtual consensus that the Foucault-style postmodern emphasis on difference, specificity, and particularity necessarily features either (a) a socioeconomic short circuit misrecognizing the fact that,

by virtue of the lack of closure of the general social field (the barred Other for Lacanians, the structural necessity of suture / articulation for the "radical democrats"), any expression of a "particular" political interest always manifests either an implicit "call" to the universal or a formally necessary "gesture" of universalization, how is the very concept of the universal to be elaborated?' (p 9).

28 Donald E. Pease, 'The Global Homeland State: Bush's Biopolitical Settlement', *boundary 2* 30(3) (Fall, 2003), pp 1–18.

29 Bruce A. Ackerman, *We the People, Vol 1: Foundations*, Cambridge: Harvard University Press, 1991, and *We the People, Vol 2: Transformations*, Cambridge: Harvard University Press, 1998.

30 I am told that a Pakistani poet has also used the metaphor of invisible mending or *rafu*. There is no copyright on metaphors. The task is to set it to work.

31 For one example of this among many, see Corinne Heyden, *When Nature Goes Public: the Making and Unmaking of Bioprospecting in Mexico*, Princeton: Princeton University Press, 2003, and 'Benefit-sharing: The Public at Stake', paper presented at 'Contested Commons / Trespassing Publics'. A Conference on Inequalities, Conflicts and Intellectual Property, 6–8 January 2005 in New Delhi, India.

32 This seems to be the main argument against the subalternists offered by Sumit Sarkar, *Beyond Nationalist Frames: Relocating Postmodernism, Hindutva, History*, New Delhi: Permanent Black, 2002, Meera Nanda, *Prophets Facing Backwards: Postmodern Critiques of Science and Hindu Nationalism in India*, New Brunswick: Rutgers University Press, 2003, and against Spivak by Hallward, *Absolutely Postcolonial: Writing Between the Singular and the Specific*, New York: Palgrave, 2001. Who can deny that the phrase 'position without identity' has a 'postmodernist' smell? I

hope by distinguishing it from the abstract-posing-as-concrete menace of the 'people', I have been able to make a case for our position.

33 Professor Romila Thapar drew my attention to Shrinivas Tilak, 'Taking Back Hindu Studies', http://sulekha.com/expressions/articledesc.asp?cid = 307085. This piece is an excellent example of how the so-called diasporic re-lexicalises material into the grammar of 'the West and the rest', as understood by the upwardly class mobile hyphenated immigrant in the metropole. I wrote an entire book analysing this phenomenon: *A Critique of Postcolonial Reason*. Tilak has not read this book. He seems not to have read 'Can the Subaltern Speak?' either, since he does not cite it. If he had read it, he could hardly have missed the fact that it was a harsh critique of the *Dharma-Shastra* staging of *sati*. It is amusing that, although he takes me as his authority, he also participates in the general anti-intellectual putdown of Spivak: 'One cautionary note! Spivak can be unnecessarily dense and obtuse when approached for the first time. A good stepping stone and guide to her thought is Gayatri Chakravorty Spivak by Stephen Morton (2003). He also provides a comprehensive bibliography of her works updated to 2003 (including her famous 1985 essay "Can the Subaltern Speak? Speculations on Widow-Sacrifice")'. In other words, Mr Tilak can credit a 'Western' interpretation of an 'authentic Indian' scholar when it suits him! The only thing I can say about this dangerous nonsense is that, when I was offered Stephen Morton's book by a colleague, I was chagrined by his representation of me, especially where he attempts to explain my attitude to war in the last pages of his book! Needless to say, I was not offered the chance to read the book in manuscript. One is not altogether responsible for one's readers!

5 Third-World Literature in the Era of Multinational Capitalism

Fredric Jameson

Judging from recent conversations among third-world intellectuals, there is now an obsessive return of the national situation itself, the name of the country that returns again and again like a gong, the collective attention to "us" and what we have to do and how we do it, to what we can't do and what we do better than this or that nationality, our unique characteristics, in short, to the level of the "people." This is not the way American intellectuals have been discussing "America," and indeed one might feel that the whole matter is nothing but that old thing called "nationalism," long since liquidated here and rightly so. Yet a certain nationalism is fundamental in the third world (and also in the most vital areas of the second world), thus making it legitimate to ask whether it is all that bad in the end.[1] Does in fact the message of some disabused and more experienced first-world wisdom (that of Europe even more than of the United States) consist in urging these nation states to outgrow it as fast as possible? The predictble reminders of Kampuchea and of Iraq and Iran do not really seem to me to settle anything or suggest by what these nationalisms might be replaced except perhaps some global American postmodernist culture.

Many arguments can be made for the importance and interest of non-canonical forms of literature such as that of the third world,[2] but one is peculiarly self-defeating because it borrows the weapons of the adversary: the strategy of trying to prove that these texts are as "great" as those of the canon itself. The object is then to show that, to take an example from another non-canonical form, Dashiell Hammett is really as great as Dostoyevsky, and therefore can be admitted. This is to attempt dutifully to wish away all traces of that "pulp" format which is constitutive of sub-genres, and it invites immediate failure insofar as any passionate reader of Dostoyevsky will know at once, after a few pages, that those kinds of satisfactions are not present. Nothing is

Fredric Jameson, "Third-World Literature in the Era of Multinational Capitalism." *Social Text*, 15, 1986: 65–88. Reproduced by permission of Duke University Press.

Postcolonial Studies: An Anthology, First Edition. Edited by Pramod K. Nayar.

to be gained by passing over in silence the radical difference of non-canonical texts. The third-world novel will not offer the satisfactions of Proust or Joyce; what is more damaging than that, perhaps, is its tendency to remind us of outmoded stages of our own first-world cultural development and to cause us to conclude that "they are still writing novels like Dreiser or Sherwood Anderson."

A case could be built on this kind of discouragement, with its deep existential commitment to a rhythm of modernist innovation if not fashion-changes; but it would not be a moralizing one—a historicist one, rather, which challenges our imprisonment in the present of postmodernism and calls for a reinvention of the radical difference of *our own* cultural past and its now seemingly old-fashioned situations and novelties.

But I would rather argue all this a different way, at least for now[3]: these reactions to third-world texts are at one and the same time perfectly natural, perfectly comprehensible, *and* terribly parochial. If the purpose of the canon is to restrict our aesthetic sympathies, to develop a range of rich and subtle perceptions which can be exercised only on the occasion of a small but choice body of texts, to discourage us from reading anything else or from reading those things in different ways, then it is humanly impoverishing. Indeed our want of sympathy for these often unmodern third-world texts is itself frequently but a disguise for some deeper fear of the affluent about the way people actually live in other parts of the world—a way of life that still has little in common with daily life in the American suburb. There is nothing particularly disgraceful in having lived a sheltered life, in never having had to confront the difficulties, the complications and the frustrations of urban living, but it is nothing to be particularly proud of either. Moreover, a limited experience of life normally does not make for a wide range of sympathies with very different kinds of people (I'm thinking of differences that range from gender and race all the way to those of social class and culture).

The way in which all this affects the reading process seems to be as follows: as western readers tastes (and much else) have been formed by our own modernisms, a popular or socially realistic third-world novel tends to come before us, not immediately, but as though already-read. We sense, between ourselves and this alien text, the presence of another reader, of the Other reader, for whom a narrative, which strikes us as conventional or naive, has a freshness of information and a social interest that we cannot share. The fear and the resistance I'm evoking has to do, then, with the sense of our own non-coincidence with that Other reader, so different from ourselves; our sense that to coincide in any adequate way with that Other "ideal reader"—that is to say, to read this text adequately—we would have to give up a great deal that is individually precious to us and acknowledge an existence and a situation unfamiliar and therefore frightening—one that we do not know and prefer *not* to know.

Why, returning to the question of the canon, *should* we only read certain kinds of books? No one is suggesting we should *not* read those, but why should we not also read other ones? We are not, after all, being shipped to that "desert island" beloved of the devisers of great books lists. And as a matter of fact—and this is to me the conclusive nail in the argument—we all do "read" many different kinds of texts in this life of ours, since, whether we are willing to admit it or not, we spend much of our existence in the force field of a mass culture that is radically different from our "great books" and live at least a double life in the various compartments of our unavoidably fragmented society. We need to be aware that we are even more fundamentally fragmented than that; rather than clinging to this particular mirage of the "centered subject" and the unified personal identity, we would do better to confront honestly the fact of fragmentation on a global scale; it is a confrontation with which we can here at least make a cultural beginning.

A final observation on my use of the term "third world." I take the point of criticisms of this expression, particularly those which stress the way in which it obliterates profound differences between a whole range of non-western countries and situations (indeed, one such fundamental opposition—between the traditions of the great eastern empires and those of the post-colonial African nation states—is central in what follows). I don't, however, see any comparable expression that articulates, as this one does, the fundamental breaks between the capitalist first world, the socialist bloc of the second world, and a range of other countries which have suffered the experience of colonialism and imperialism. One can only deplore the ideological implications of oppositions such as that between "developed" and "underdeveloped" or "developing" countries; while the more recent conception of northern and southern tiers, which has a very different ideological content and import than the rhetoric of development, and is used by very different people, nonetheless implies an unquestioning acceptance of "convergence theory"—namely the idea that the Soviet Union and the United States are from this perspective largely the same thing. I am using the term "third world" in an essentially descriptive sense, and objections to it do not strike me as especially relevant to the argument I am making.

* * *

In these last years of the century, the old question of a properly world literature reasserts itself. This is due as much or more to the disintegration of our own conceptions of cultural study as to any very lucid awareness of the great outside world around us. We may therefore—as "humanists"—acknowledge the pertinence of the critique of present-day humanities by our titular leader, William Bennett, without finding any great satisfaction in his embarrassing solution: yet another impoverished and ethnocentric Graeco-Judaic "great books list of the civilization of the West," "great texts, great minds, great ideas."[4] One is tempted to turn back on Bennett himself the question he approvingly quotes from Maynard Mack: "How long can a democratic nation afford to support a narcissistic minority so transfixed by its own image?" Nevertheless, the present moment does offer a remarkable opportunity to rethink our humanities curriculum in a new way—to re-examine the shambles and ruins of all our older "great books," "humanities," "freshman-introductory" and "core course" type traditions.

Today the reinvention of cultural studies in the United States demands the reinvention, in a new situation, of what Goethe long ago theorized as "world literature." In our more immediate context, then, any conception of world literature necessarily demands some specific engagement with the question of third-world literature, and it is this not necessarily narrower subject about which I have something to say today.

It would be presumptuous to offer some general theory of what is often called third-world literature, given the enormous variety both of national cultures in the third world and of specific historical trajectories in each of those areas. All of this, then, is provisional and intended both to suggest specific perspectives for research and to convey a sense of the interest and value of these clearly neglected literatures for people formed by the values and stereotypes of a first-world culture. One important distinction would seem to impose itself at the outset, namely that none of these cultures can be conceived as anthropologically independent or autonomous, rather, they are all in various distinct ways locked in a life-and-death struggle with first-world cultural imperialism—a cultural struggle that is itself a reflexion of the economic situation of such areas in their penetration by various stages of capital, or as it is sometimes euphemistically termed, of modernization. This, then, is some first sense in which a study of third-world culture necessarily entails a new view of ourselves, from the outside, insofar as we ourselves are (perhaps without fully knowing it) constitutive forces powerfully at work on the remains of older cultures in our general world capitalist system.

But if this is the case, the initial distinction that imposes itself has to do with the nature and development of older cultures at the moment of capitalist penetration, something it seems to me most enlightening to examine in terms of the marxian concept of modes of production.[5] Contemporary historians seem to be in the process of reaching a consensus on the specificity of feudalism as a form which, issuing from the break-up of the Roman Empire or the Japanese Shogunate, is able to develop directly into capitalism.[6] This is not the case with the other modes of production, which in some sense must be disaggregated or destroyed by violence, before capitalism is able to implant its specific forms and displace the older ones. In the gradual expansion of capitalism across the globe, then, our economic system confronts two very distinct modes of production that pose two very different types of social and cultural resistance to its influence. These are so-called primitive, or tribal society on the one hand, and the Asiatic mode of production, or the great bureaucratic imperial systems, on the other. African societies and cultures, as they became the object of systematic colonization in the 1880s, provide the most striking examples of the symbiosis of capital and tribal societies; while China and India offer the principal examples of another and quite different sort of engagement of capitalism with the great empires of the so-called Asiatic mode. My examples below, then, will be primarily African and Chinese; however, the special case of Latin America must be noted in passing. Latin America offers yet a third kind of development—one involving an even earlier destruction of imperial systems now projected by collective memory back into the archaic or tribal. Thus the earlier nominal conquests of independence open them at once to a kind of indirect economic penetration and control—something Africa and Asia will come to experience only more recently with decolonization in the 1950s and 60s.

Having made these initial distinctions, let me now, by way of a sweeping hypothesis, try to say what all third-world cultural productions seem to have in common and what distinguishes them radically from analogous cultural forms in the first world. All third-world texts are necessarily, I want to argue, allegorical, and in a very specific way: they are to be read as what I will call *national allegories*, even when, or perhaps I should say, particularly when their forms develop out of predominantly western machineries of representation, such as the novel. Let me try to state this distinction in a grossly over-simplified way: one of the determinants of capitalist culture, that is, the culture of the western realist and modernist novel, is a radical split between the private and the public, between the poetic and the political, between what we have come to think of as the domain of sexuality and the unconscious and that of the public world of classes, of the economic, and of secular political power: in other words, Freud versus Marx. Our numerous theoretical attempts to overcome this great split only reconfirm its existence and its shaping power over our individual and collective lives. We have been trained in a deep cultural conviction that the lived experience of our private existences is somehow incommensurable with the abstractions of economic science and political dynamics. Politics in our novels therefore is, according to Stendhal's canonical formulation, a "pistol shot in the middle of a concert."

I will argue that, although we may retain for convenience and for analysis such categories as the subjective and the public or political, the relations between them are wholly different in third-world texts, even those which are seemingly private and invested with a properly libidinal dynamic—necessarily project a political dimension in the form of national allegory: *the story of the private individual destiny is always an allegory of the embattled situation of the public third-world culture and society*. Need I add that it is precisely this very different ratio of the political to the personal which makes such texts alien to us at first approach, and consequently, resistant to our conventional western habits of reading?

I will offer, as something like the supreme example of this process of allegorization, the first masterwork of China's greatest writer, Lu Xun, whose neglect in western cultural studies is a matter of shame which no excuses based on ignorance can rectify. "Diary of a Madman" (1918) must at first be read by any western reader as the protocol of what our essentially psychological language terms a "nervous breakdown." It offers the notes and perceptions of a subject in intensifying prey to a terrifying psychic delusion, the conviction that the people around him are concealing a dreadful secret, and that that secret can be none other than the increasingly obvious fact that they are cannibals. At the climax of the development of the delusion, which threatens his own physical safety and his very life itself as a potential victim, the narrator understands that his own brother is himself a cannibal and that the death of their little sister, a number of years earlier, far from being the result of childhood illness, as he had thought, was in reality a murder. As befits the protocol of a psychosis, these perceptions are objective ones, which can be rendered without any introspective machinery: the paranoid subject observes sinister glances around him in the real world, he overhears tell-tale conversations between his brother and an alleged physician (obviously in reality another cannibal) which carry all the conviction of the real, and can be objectively (or "realistically") represented. This is not the place to demonstrate in any detail the absolute pertinence, to Lu Xun's case history, of the pre-eminent western or first-world reading of such phenomena, namely Freud's interpretation of the paranoid delusions of Senatspräsident Schreber: an emptying of the world, a radical withdrawal of libido (what Schreber describes as "world-catastrophe"), followed by the attempt to recathect by the obviously imperfect mechanisms of paranoia. "The delusion-formation," Freud explains, "which we take to be a pathological product, is in reality an attempt at recovery, a process of reconstruction."[7]

What is reconstructed, however, is a grisly and terrifying objective real world beneath the appearances of our own world: an unveiling or deconcealment of the nightmarish reality of things, a stripping away of our conventional illusions or rationalizations about daily life and existence. It is a process comparable, as a literary effect, only to some of the processes of western modernism, and in particular of existentialism, in which narrative is employed as a powerful instrument for the experimental exploration of reality and illusion, an exploration which, however, unlike some of the older realisms, presupposes a certain prior "personal knowledge."

The reader must, in other words, have had some analogous experience, whether in physical illness or psychic crisis, of a lived and balefully transformed real world from which we cannot even mentally escape, for the full horror of Lu Xun's nightmare to be appreciated. Terms like "depression" deform such experience by psychologizing it and projecting it back into the pathological Other; while the analogous western literary approaches to this same experience—I'm thinking of the archetypal deathbed murmur of Kurtz, in Conrad's "Heart of Darkness," "The horror! the horror!"—recontains precisely that horror by transforming it into a rigorously private and subjective "mood," which can only be designated by recourse to an aesthetic of *expression*—the unspeakable, unnameable inner feeling, whose external formulation can only designated it from without, like a symptom.

But this representational power of Lu Xun's text cannot be appreciated properly without some sense of what I have called its allegorical resonance. For it should be clear that the cannibalism literally apprehended by the sufferer in the attitudes and bearing of his family and neighbors is at one and the same time being attributed by Lu Xun himself to Chinese society as a whole: and if this attribution is to be called "figural," it is indeed a figure more powerful and "literal" than the "literal" level of the text. Lu Xun's proposition is that the people of this great maimed and retarded, disintegrating China of the late and post-imperial period, his fellow citizens, are "literally" cannibals: in their desperation, disguised and indeed intensified by the most traditional forms and procedures of Chinese culture, they must devour one another ruthlessly to stay alive. This occurs at all levels of that exceedingly hierarchical society, from lumpens and peasants all the way to the most privileged elite positions in the mandarin bureaucracy. It is, I want to stress, a social and historical nightmare, a vision of the horror of life specifically grasped through History itself, whose consequences go far beyond the more local western realistic or naturalistic representation of cut-throat capitalist or market competition, and it exhibits a specifically political resonance absent from its natural or mythological western equivalent in the nightmare of Darwinian natural selection.

Now I want to offer four additional remarks about this text, which will touch, respectively, on the libidinal dimension of the story, on the structure of its allegory, on the role of the third-world cultural producer himself, and on the perspective of futurity projected by the tale's double resolution. I will be concerned, in dealing with all four of these topics, to stress the radical structural difference between the dynamics of third-world culture and those of the first-world cultural tradition in which we have ourselves been formed.

I have suggested that in third-world texts such as this story by Lu Xun the relationship between the libidinal and the political components of individual and social experience is radically different from what obtains in the west and what shapes our own cultural forms. Let me try to characterize this difference, or if you like this radical reversal, by way of the following generalization: in the west, conventionally, political commitment is recontained and psychologized or subjectivized by way of the public-private split I have already evoked. Interpretations, for example, of political movements of the 60s in terms of Oedipal revolts are familiar to everyone and need no further comment. That such interpretations are episodes in a much longer tradition, whereby political commitment is re-psychologized and accounted for in terms of the subjective dynamics of *ressentiment* or the authoritarian personality, is perhaps less well understood, but can be demonstrated by a careful reading of anti-political texts from Nietzsche and Conrad all the way to the latest cold-war propaganda.

What is relevant to our present context is not, however, the demonstration of that proposition, but rather of its inversion in third-world culture, where I want to suggest that psychology, or more specifically, libidinal investment, is to be read in primarily political and social terms. (It is, I hope, unnecessary to add that what follows is speculative and very much subject to correction by specialists: it is offered as a methodological example rather than a "theory" of Chinese culture.) We're told, for one thing, that the great ancient imperial cosmologies identify by analogy what we in the west analytically separate: thus, the classical sex manuals are at one with the texts that reveal the dynamics of political forces, the charts of the heavens at one with the logic of medical lore, and so forth.[8] Here already then, in an ancient past, western antinomies—and most particularly that between the subjective and the public or political—are refused in advance. The libidinal center of Lu Xun's text is, however, not sexuality, but rather the oral stage, the whole bodily question of eating, of ingestion, devoration, incorporation, from which such fundamental categories as the pure and the impure spring. We must now recall, not merely the extraordinary symbolic complexity of Chinese cuisine, but also the central role this art and practice occupies in Chinese culture as a whole. When we find that centrality confirmed by the observation that the very rich Chinese vocabulary for sexual matters is extraordinarily intertwined with the language of eating; and when we observe the multiple uses to which the verb "to eat" is put in ordinary Chinese language (one "eats" a fear or a fright, for example), we may feel in a somewhat better position to sense the enormous sensitivity of this libidinal region, and of Lu Xun's mobilization of it for the dramatization of an essentially social nightmare—something which in a western writer would be consigned to the realm of the merely private obsession, the vertical dimension of the personal trauma.

A different alimentary transgression can be observed throughout Lu Xun's works, but nowhere quite so strikingly as in his terrible little story, "Medicine." The story potrays a dying child—the death of children is a constant in these works—whose parents have the good fortune to procure an "infallible" remedy. At this point we must recall both that traditional Chinese medicine is not "taken," as in the west, but "eaten," and that for Lu Xun traditional Chinese medicine was the supreme locus of the unspeakable and exploitative charlatanry of traditional Chinese culture in general. In his crucially important *Preface* to the first collection of his stories,[9] he recounts the suffering and death of his own father from tuberculosis, while declining family reserves rapidly disappeared into the purchase of expensive and rare, exotic and ludicrous medicaments. We will not sense the symbolic significance of this indignation unless we remember that for all these reasons Lu Xun decided to study western medicine in Japan—the epitome of some new western science that promised collective regeneration—only later to decide that the production of culture—I am tempted to say, the elaboration of a political culture—was a more effective form of political medicine.[10] As a writer, then, Lu Xun remains a diagnostician and a physician. Hence this terrible story, in which the cure for the male child, the father's only hope for survival in future generations, turns out to be one of those large doughy-white Chinese steamed rolls, soaked in the blood of a criminal who has just been executed. The child dies anyway, of course, but it is important to note that the hapless victim of a more properly state violence (the supposed criminal) was a *political* militant, whose grave is mysteriously covered in flowers by absent sympathizers of whom one knows nothing. In the analysis of a story like this, we must rethink our conventional conception of the symbolic levels of a narrative (where sexuality and politics might be in homology to each other, for instance) as a set of loops or circuits which intersect and overdetermine each other—the enormity of therapeutic cannibalism finally intersecting in a pauper's cemetery, with the more overt violence of family betrayal and political repression.

This new mapping process brings me to the cautionary remark I wanted to make about allegory itself—a form long discredited in the west and the specific target of the Romantic revolution of Wordsworth and Coleridge, yet a linguistic structure which also seems to be experiencing a remarkable reawakening of interest in contemporary literary theory. If allegory has once again become somehow congenial for us today, as over against the massive and monumental unifications of an older modernist symbolism or even realism itself, it is because the allegorical spirit is profoundly discontinuous, a matter of breaks and heterogeneities, of the multiple polysemia of the dream rather than the homogeneous representation of the symbol. Our traditional conception of allegory—based, for instance, on stereotypes of Bunyan—is that of an elaborate set of figures and personifications to be read against some one-to-one table of equivalences: this is, so to speak, a one-dimensional view of this signifying process, which might only be set in motion and complexified were we willing to entertain the more alarming notion that such equivalences are themselves in constant change and transformation at each perpetual present of the text.

Here too Lu Xun has some lessons for us. This writer of short stories and sketches, which never evolved into the novel form as such, produced at least one approach to the longer form, in a much lengthier series of anecdotes about a hapless coolie named Ah Q, who comes to serve, as we might have suspected, as the allegory of a certain set of Chinese attitudes and modes of behavior. It is interesting to note that the enlargement of the form determines a shift in tone or generic discourse: now everything that had been stricken with the stillness and emptiness of death and suffering without hope—"the room was not only too silent, it was far too big as well, and the things in it were far too empty"[11]—becomes material for a more properly Chaplinesque comedy. Ah Q's resiliency springs from an unusual—but we are to understand culturally very normal and familiar—technique for overcoming humiliation. When set upon by his persecutors, Ah Q, serene in his superiority over them, reflects: "'It is as if I were beaten by my own son. What is the world coming to nowadays …' Thereupon he too would walk away, satisfied at having won."[12] Admit that you are not even human, they insist, that you are nothing but an animal! On the contrary, he tells them, I'm worse than an animal, I'm an insect! There, does that satisfy you? "In less than ten seconds, however, Ah Q would walk away also satisfied that he had won, thinking that he was after all 'number one in self-belittlement,' and that after removing the 'self-belittlement' what remained was still the glory of remaining 'number one.'"[13] When one recalls the remarkable self-esteem of the Manchu dynasty in its final throes, and the serene contempt for foreign devils who had nothing but modern science, gunboats, armies, technology and power to their credit, one achieves a more precise sense of the historical and social topicality of Lu Xun's satire.

Ah Q is thus, allegorically, China itself. What I want to observe, however, what complicates the whole issue, is that his persecutors—the idlers and bullies who find their daily pleasures in getting a rise out of just such miserable victims as Ah Q—they too are China, in the allegorical sense. This very simple example, then, shows the capacity of allegory to generate a range of distinct meanings or messages, simultaneously, as the allegorical tenor and vehicle change places: Ah Q is China humiliated by the foreigners, a China so well versed in the spiritual techniques of self-justification that such humiliations are not even registered, let alone recalled. But the persecutors are also China, in a different sense, the terrible self-cannibalistic China of the "Diary of a Madman," whose response to power-lessness is the senseless persecution of the weaker and more inferior members of the hierarchy.

All of which slowly brings us to the question of the writer himself in the third world, and to what must be called the function of the intellectual, it being understood that in the third-world situation the intellectual is always in one way or another a political intellectual. No third-world lesson is more timely or more urgent for us today, among whom the very term "intellectual" has withered away, as though it were the name for an extinct species. Nowhere has the strangeness of this vacant position been brought home to me more strongly than on a recent trip to Cuba, when I had occasion to visit a remarkable college-preparatory school on the outskirts of Havana. It is a matter of some shame for an American to witness the cultural curriculum in a socialist setting which also very much identifies itself with the third world. Over some three or four years, Cuban teenagers study poems of Homer, Dante's Inferno, the Spanish theatrical classics, the great realistic novels of the 19th-century European tradition, and finally contemporary Cuban revolutionary novels, of which, incidentally, we desperately need English translations. But the semester's work I found most challenging was one explicitly devoted to the study of the role of the intellectual as such: the cultural intellectual who is also a political militant, the intellectual who produces both poetry and praxis. The Cuban illustrations of this process—Ho Chi Minh and Augustino Nieto—are obviously enough culturally determined: our own equivalents would probably be the more familiar figures of DuBois and C.L.R. James, of Sartre and Neruda or Brecht, of Kollontai or Louise Michel. But as this whole talk aims implicitly at suggesting a new conception of the humanities in American education today, it is appropriate to add that the study of the role of the intellectual as such ought to be a key component in any such proposals.

I've already said something about Lu Xun's own conception of his vocation, and its extrapolation from the practice of medicine. But there is a great deal more to be said specifically about the *Preface*. Not only is it one of the fundamental documents for understanding the situation of the third world artist, it is also a dense text in its own right, fully as much a work of art as any of the greatest stories. And in Lu Xun's own work it is the supreme example of the very unusual ratio of subjective investment and a deliberately depersonalized objective narration. We have no time to do justice to those relationships, which would demand a line-by-line commentary. Yet I will quote the little fable by which Lu Xun, responding to requests for publication by his friends and future collaborators, dramatizes his dilemma:

> Imagine an iron house without windows, absolutely indestructible, with many people fast sleep inside who will shortly die of suffocation. But you know that since they will die in their sleep, they will not feel the pain of death. Now if you cry aloud to wake a few of the lighter sleepers, making those unfortunate few suffer the agony of irrevocable death, do you think you are doing them a good turn?[14]

The seemingly hopeless situation of the third-world intellectual in this historical period (shortly after the founding of the Chinese Communist Party, but also after the bankruptcy of the middle-class revolution had become apparent)—in which no solutions, no forms of praxis or change, seem conceivable—this situation will find its parallel, as we shall see shortly, in the situation of African intellectuals after the achievement of independence, when once again no political solutions seem present or visible on the historical horizon. The formal or literary manifestation of this political problem is the possibility of narrative closure, something we will return to more specifically.

In a more general theoretical context—and it is this theoretical form of the problem I should now like at least to thematize and set in place on the agenda—we must recover a sense of what "cultural revolution" means, in its strongest form, in the marxist tradition. The reference is not to the immediate events of that violent and tumultuous interruption of the "eleven years" in recent Chinese history, although some reference to Maoism as a doctrine is necessarily implicit. The term, we are told, was Lenin's own, and in that form explicitly designated the literacy campaign and the new problems of universal scholarity and education: something of which Cuba, again, remains the most stunning and successful example in recent history. We must, however, enlarge the conception still further, to include a range of seemingly very different preoccupations, of which the names of Gramsci and Wilhelm Reich, Frantz Fanon, Herbert Marcuse, Rudolph Bahro, and Paolo Freire, may give an indication of their scope and focus. Overhastily, I will suggest that "cultural revolution" as it is projected in such works turns on the phenomenon of what Gramsci called "subalternity," namely the feelings of mental inferiority and habits of subservience and obedience which necessarily and structurally develop in situations of domination—most dramatically in the experience of colonized peoples. But here, as so often, the subjectivizing and psychologizing habits of first-world peoples such as ourselves can play us false and lead us into misunderstandings. Subalternity is not in that sense a psychological matter, although it governs psychologies; and I suppose that the strategic choice of the term "cultural" aims precisely at restructuring that view of the problem and projecting it outwards into the realm of objective or collective spirit in some non-psychological, but also non-reductionist or non-economistic, materialistic fashion. When a psychic structure is objectively determined by economic and political relationships, it cannot be dealt with by means of purely psychological therapies; yet it equally cannot be dealt with by means of purely objective transformations of the economic and political situation itself, since the habits remain and exercise a baleful and crippling residual effect.[15] This is a more dramatic form of that old mystery, the unity of theory and practice; and it is specifically in the context of this problem of cultural revolution (now so strange and alien to us) that the achievements and failures of third-world intellectuals, writers and artists must be replaced if their concrete historical meaning is to be grasped. We have allowed ourselves, as first-world cultural intellectuals, to restrict our consciousness of our life's work to the narrowest professional or bureaucratic terms, thereby encouraging in ourselves a special sense of subalternity and guilt, which only reinforces the vicious circle. That a literary article could be a political act, with real consequences, is for most of us little more than a curiosity of the literary history of Czarist Russia or of modern China itself. But we perhaps should also consider the possibility that as intellectuals we ourselves are at present soundly sleeping in that indestructable iron room, of which Lu Xun spoke, on the point of suffocation.

The matter of narrative closure, then, and of the relationship of a narrative text to futurity and to some collective project yet to come, is not, merely a formal or literary-critical issue. "Diary of a Madman" has in fact two distinct and incompatible endings, which prove instructive to examine in light of the writer's own hesitations and anxieties about his social role. One ending, that of the deluded subject himself, is very much a call to the future, in the impossible situation of a well-nigh universal cannibalism: the last desperate lines launched into the void are the words, "Save the children …" But the tale has a second ending as well, which is disclosed on the opening page, when the older (supposedly cannibalistic) brother greets the narrator with the following cheerful remark: "I appreciate your coming such a long way to see us, but my brother recovered some time ago and has gone elsewhere to take up an official post." So, in advance, the nightmare is annulled; the paranoid visionary, his brief and terrible glimpse of the grisly reality beneath the appearance now vouchsafed, gratefully returns to the realm of illusion and oblivion therein again to take up his place in the space of bureaucratic power and privilege. I want to suggest that it is only at this price, by way of a complex play of simultaneous and antithetical messages, that the narrative text is able to open up a concrete perspective on the real future.

* * *

I must interrupt myself here to interpolate several observations before proceeding. For one thing, it is clear to me that *any* articulation of radical difference—that of gender, incidentally, fully as much as that of culture—is susceptible to appropriation by that strategy of otherness which Edward Said, in the context of the Middle East, called "orientalism." It does not matter much that the radical otherness of the culture in question is praised or valorized positively, as in the preceding pages: the essential operation is that of differentiation, and once that has been accomplished, the mechanism Said denounces has been set in place. On the other hand, I don't see how a first-world intellectual can avoid this operation without falling back into some general liberal and humanistic universalism: it seems to me that one of our basic political tasks lies precisely in the ceaseless effort to remind the American public of the radical difference of other national situations.

But at this point one should insert a cautionary reminder about the dangers of the concept of "culture" itself: the very speculative remarks I have allowed myself to make about Chinese "culture" will not be complete unless I add that "culture" in this sense is by no means the final term at which one stops. One must imagine such cultural structures and attitudes as having been themselves, in the beginning, vital responses to infrastructural realities (economic and geographic, for example), as attempts to resolve more fundamental contradictions—attempts which then outlive the situations for which they were devised, and survive, in reified forms, as "cultural patterns." Those patterns themselves then become part of the objective situation confronted by later generations, and, as in the case of Confucianism, having once been part of the solution to a dilemma, then become part of the new problem.

Nor can I feel that the concept of cultural "identity" or even national "identity" is adequate. One cannot acknowledge the justice of the general poststructuralist assault on the so-called "centered subject," the old unified ego of bourgeois individualism, and then resuscitate this same ideological mirage of psychic unification on the collective level in the form of a doctrine of collective identity. Appeals to collective identity need to be evaluated from a historical perspective, rather than from the standpoint of some dogmatic and placeless "ideological analysis." When a third-world writer invokes this (to us) ideological value, we need to examine the concrete historical situation closely in order to determine the political consequences of the strategic use of this concept. Lu Xun's moment, for example, is very clearly one in which a critique of Chinese "culture" and "cultural identity" has powerful and revolutionary consequences—consequences which may not obtain in a later social configuration. This is then, perhaps, another and more complicated way of raising the issue of "nationalism" to which I referred earlier.

As far as national allegory is concerned, I think it may be appropriate to stress its presence in what is generally considered western literature in order to underscore certain structural differences. The example I have in mind is the work of Benito Perez Galdos—the last and among the richest achievements of 19th century realism. Galdos' novels are more visibly allegorical (in the national sense) than most of their better-known European predecessors:[16] something that might well be explained in terms of Immanuel Wallerstein's world-system terminology.[17] Although 19th century Spain is not strictly *peripheral* after the fashion of the countries we are here designating under the term third world, it is certainly *semi-peripheral* in his sense, when contrasted with England or France. It is therefore not terribly surprising to find the situation of the male protagonist of *Fortunata y Jacinta* (1887)—alternating between the two women of the title, between the wife and the mistress, between the woman of the upper-middle classes and the woman of the "people"—characterized in terms of the nation-state itself, hesitating between the republican revolution of 1868 and the Bourbon restoration of 1873.[18] Here too, the same "floating" or transferable structure of allegorical reference detected in Ah Q comes into play: for Fortunata is also married, and the alternation of "revolution" and "restoration" is likewise adapted to her situation, as she leaves her legal home to seek her lover and then returns to it in abandonment.

What it is important to stress is not merely the wit of the analogy as Galdos uses it, but also its optional nature: we can use it to convert the entire situation of the novel into an allegorical commentary on the destiny of Spain, but we are also free to reverse its priorities and to read the political analogy as metaphorical decoration for the individual drama, and as a mere figural intensification of this last. Here, far from dramatizing the identity of the political and the individual or psychic, the allegorical structure tends essentially to separate these levels in some absolute way. We cannot feel its force unless we are convinced of the radical difference between politics and the libidinal: so that its operation reconfirms (rather than annuls) that split between public and private which was attributed to western civilization earlier in our discussion. In one of the more powerful contemporary denunciations of this split and this habit, Deleuze and Guattari argue for a conception of desire that is at once social and individual.

How does a delirium begin? Perhaps the cinema is able to capture the movement of madness, precisely because it is not analytical or regressive, but explores a global field of coexistence. Witness a film by Nicholas Ray, supposedly representing the formation of a cortisone delirium: an overworked father, a high-school teacher who works overtime for a radio-taxi service and is being treated for heart trouble. He begins to rave about the educational system in general, the need to restore a pure race, the salvation of the social and moral order, then he passes to religion, the timeliness of a return to the Bible, Abraham. But what in fact did Abraham do? Well now, he killed or wanted to kill his son, and perhaps God's only error lies in having stayed his hand. But doesn't this man, the film's protagonist, have a son of his own? Hmmm. … What the film shows so well, to the shame of psychiatrists, is that every delirium is first of all the investment of a field that is social, economic, political cultural, racial and racist, pedagogical, and religious: the delirious person applies a delirium to his family and his son that overreaches them on all sides.[19]

I am not myself sure that the objective consequences of this essentially social and concrete gap, in first-world experience, between the public and the private can be abolished by intellectual diagnosis or by some more adequate theory of their deeper interrelationship. Rather, it seems to me that what Deleuze and Guattari are proposing here is a new and more adequate *allegorical* reading of this film. Such allegorical structures, then, are not so much absent from first-world cultural texts as they are *unconscious*, and therefore they must be deciphered by interpretive mechanisms that necessarily entail a whole social and historical critique of our current first-world situation. The point here is that, in distinction to the unconscious allegories of our own cultural texts, third-world national allegories are conscious and overt: they imply a radically different and objective relationship of politics to libidinal dynamics.

* * *

Now, before turning to the African texts, I remind you of the very special occasion of the present talk, which is concerned to honor the memory of Robert C. Elliott and to commemorate his life's work. I take it that the very center of his two most important books, *The Power of Satire* and *The Shape of Utopia*,[20] is to be found in his pathbreaking association of satire and the utopian impulse as two seemingly antithetical drives (and literary discourses), which in reality replicate each other such that each is always secretly active within the other's sphere of influence. All satire, he taught us, necessarily carries a utopian frame of reference within itself; all utopias, no matter how serene or disembodied, are driven secretly by the satirist's rage at a fallen reality. When I spoke of futurity a moment ago, I took pains to withhold the world "utopia," which in my language is another word for the socialist project.

But now I will be more explicit and take as my motto an astonishing passage from the novel *Xala*, by the great contemporary Senegalese novelist and film-maker Ousmane Sembène. The title designates a ritual curse or affliction, of a very special kind, which has been visited on a prosperous and corrupt Senegalese businessman at the moment in which, at the height of his fortune, he takes to himself a beautiful young (third) wife. Shades of *The Power of Satire*!, the curse is of course, as you may have guessed, sexual impotence. The Hadj, the unfortunate hero of this novel, desperately explores a number of remedies, both western and tribal, to no avail, and is finally persuaded to undertake a laborious trip into the hinterland of Dakar to seek out a shaman of reputedly extraordinary powers. Here is the conclusion of his hot and dusty journey in a horse-drawn cart:

> As they emerged from a ravine, they saw conical thatched roofs, grey-black with weathering, standing out against the horizon in the middle of the empty plain. Free-ranging, skinny cattle with dangerous-looking horns fenced with one another to get at what little grass there was. No more than silhouettes in the distance, a few people were busy around the only well. The driver of the cart was in familiar territory and greeted people as they passed. Sereen Mada's house, apart from its imposing size, was identical in construction with all the others. It was situated in the center of the village whose huts were arranged in a semi-circle, which you entered by a single main entrance. The village had neither shop nor school nor dispensary; there was nothing at all attractive about it in fact [Ousmane concludes, then he adds, as if in afterthought, this searing line:] There was nothing at all attractive about it in fact. Its life was based on the principles of community interdependence.[21]

Here, then, more emblematically than virtually any other text I know, the space of a past and future utopia—a social world of collective cooperation—is dramatically inserted into the corrupt and westernized money economy of the new post-independence national or comprador bourgeoisie. Indeed, Ousmane takes pains to show us that the Hadj is not an industrialist, that his business is in no sense productive, but functions as a middle-man between European multinationals and local extraction industries. To this biographical sketch must be added a very significant fact: that in his youth, the Hadj was political, and spent some time in jail for his nationalist and pro-independence activities. The extraordinary satire of these corrupt classes (which Ousmane will extend to the person of Senghor himself in *The Last of the Empire*) is explicitly marked as the failure of the independence movement to develop into a general social revolution.

The fact of nominal national independence, in Latin America in the 19th century, in Africa in the mid-20th, puts an end to a movement for which genuine national autonomy was the only conceivable goal. Nor is this symbolic myopia the only problem: the African states also had to face the crippling effects of what Fanon prophetically warned them against—to receive independence is not the same as to take it, since it is in the revolutionary struggle itself that new social relationships and a new consciousness is developed. Here again the history of Cuba is instructive: Cuba was the last of the Latin American nations to win its freedom in the 19th century—a freedom which would immediately be taken in charge by another greater colonial power. We now know the incalculable role played in the Cuban Revolution of 1959 by the protracted guerrilla struggles of the late 19th century (of which the figure of José Martí is the emblem); contemporary Cuba would not be the same without that laborious and subterranean, one wants to say Thompsonian, experience of the mole of History burrowing through a lengthy past and creating its specific traditions in the process.

So it is that after the poisoned gift of independence, radical African writers like Ousmane, or like Ngugi in Kenya, find themselves back in the dilemma of Lu Xun, bearing a passion for change and social regeneration which has not yet found its agents. I hope it is clear that this is also very much an aesthetic dilemma, a crisis of representation: it was not difficult to identify an adversary who spoke another language and wore the visible trappings of colonial occupation. When those are replaced by your own people, the connections to external controlling forces are much more difficult to represent. The newer leaders may of course throw off their masks and reveal the person of the Dictator, whether in its older individual or newer military form: but this moment also determines problems of representation. The dictator novel has become a virtual genre of Latin American literature, and such works are marked above all by a profound and uneasy ambivalence, a deeper ultimate sympathy for the Dictator, which can perhaps only be properly accounted for by some enlarged social variant of the Freudian mechanism of transference.[22]

The form normally taken by a radical diagnosis of the failures of contemporary third-world societies is, however, what is conventionally designated as "cultural imperialism," a faceless influence without representable agents, whose literary expression seems to demand the invention of new forms: Manuel Puig's *Betrayed by Rita Hayworth* may be cited as one of the most striking and innovative of those. One is led to conclude that under these circumstances traditional realism is less effective than the satiric fable: whence to my mind the greater power of certain of Ousmane's narratives (besides *Xala*, we should mention *The Money-Order*) as over against Ngugi's impressive but problematical *Petals of Blood*.

With the fable, however, we are clearly back into the whole question of allegory. *The Money-Order* mobilizes the traditional Catch-22 dilemma—its hapless protagonist cannot cash his Parisian check without identity papers, but since he was born long before independence there are no documents, and meanwhile the money-order, uncashed, begins to melt away before an accumulation of new credits and new debts. I am tempted to suggest, anachronistically, that this work, published in 1965, prophetically dramatizes the greatest misfortune that can happen to a third-world country in our time, namely the discovery of vast amounts of oil resources—something which as economists have shown us, far from representing salvation, at once sinks them incalculably into foreign debts they can never dream of liquidating.

On another level, however, this tale raises the issue of what must finally be one of the key problems in any analysis of Ousmane's work, namely the ambiguous role played in it by archaic or tribal elements. Viewers may perhaps remember the curious ending of his first film, *The Black Girl*, in which the European employer is inconclusively pursued by the little boy wearing an archaic mask; meanwhile such historical films as *Ceddo* or *Emitai* seem intent on evoking older moments of tribal resistance either to Islam or to the west, yet in a historical perspective which with few exceptions is that of failure and ultimate defeat. Ousmane cannot, however, be suspected of any archaizing or nostalgic cultural nationalism. Thus it becomes important to determine the significance of this appeal to older tribal values, particularly as they are more subtly active in modern works like *Xala* or *The Money-Order*.

I suspect that the deeper subject of this second novel is not so much the evident one of the denunciation of a modern national bureaucracy, but rather the historical transformation of the traditional Islamic value of alms-giving in a contemporary money economy. A Muslim has the duty to give alms—indeed, the work concludes with just such another unfulfilled request. Yet in a modern economy, this sacred duty to the poor is transformed into a frenzied assault by free-loaders from all the levels of society (at length, the cash is appropriated by a westernized and affluent, influential cousin). The hero is literally picked clean by the vultures; better still, the unsought for, unexpected treasure fallen from heaven at once transforms the entire society around him into ferocious and insatiable petitioners, in something like a monetary version of Lu Xun's cannibalism.

The same double historical perspective—archaic customs radically transformed and denatured by the superposition of capitalist relations—seems to me demonstrable in *Xala* as well, in the often hilarious results of the more ancient Islamic and tribal institution of polygamy. This is what Ousmane has to say about that institution (it being understood that authorial intervention, no longer tolerable in realistic narrative, is still perfectly suitable to the allegorical fable as a form):

> It is worth knowing something about the life led by urban polygamists. It could be called geographical polygamy, as opposed to rural polygamy, where all the wives and children live together in the same compound. In the town, since the families are scattered, the children have little contact with their father. Because of his way of life the father must go from house to house, villa to villa, and is only there in the evenings, at bedtime. He is therefore primarily a source of finance, when he has work.[23]

Indeed, we are treated to the vivid spectacle of the Hadj's misery when, at the moment of his third marriage, which should secure his social status, he realizes he has no real home of his own and is condemned to shuttle from one wife's villa to the other, in a situation in which he suspects each of them in turn as being responsible for his ritual affliction. But the passage I have just read shows that—whatever one would wish to think about polygamy in and of itself as an institution—it functions here as a twin-valenced element designed to open up historical perspective. The more and more frenzied trips of the Hadj through the great city secure a juxtaposition between capitalism and the older collective tribal form of social life.

These are not as yet, however, the most remarkable feature of *Xala*, which can be described as a stunning and controlled, virtually text-book exercise in what I have elsewhere called "generic discontinuities."[24] The novel begins, in effect, in one generic convention, in terms of which the Hadj is read as a comic victim. Everything goes wrong all at once, and the news of his disability suddenly triggers a greater misfortune: his numerous debtors begin to descend on someone whose bad luck clearly marks him out as a loser. A comic pity and terror accompanies this process, though it does not imply any great sympathy for the personage. Indeed it conveys a greater revulsion against the privileged new westernized society in which this rapid overturning of the wheel of fortune can take place. Yet we have all been in error, as it turns out: the wives have not been the source of the ritual curse. In an abrupt generic reversal and enlargement (comparable to some of the mechanisms Freud describes in "The Uncanny"), we suddenly learn something new and chilling about the Hadj's past:

> "Out story goes back a long way. It was shortly before your marriage to that woman there. Don't you remember? I was sure you would not. What I am now" (a beggar in rags is addressing him) "what I am now is your fault.

Do you remember selling a large piece of land at Jeko belonging to our clan? After falsifying the clan names with the complicity of people in high places, you took our land from us. In spite of our protests, our proof of ownership, we lost our case in the courts. Not satisfied with taking our land you had me thrown into prison."[25]

Thus the primordial crime of capitalism is exposed: not so much wage labor as such, or the ravages of the money form, or the remorseless and impersonal rhythms of the market, but rather this primal displacement of the older forms of collective life from a land now seized and privatized. It is the oldest of modern tragedies, visited on the Native Americans yesterday, on the Palestinians today, and significantly reintroduced by Ousmane into his film version of *The Money-Order* (called *Mandabi*), in which the protagonist is now threatened with the imminent loss of his dwelling itself.

The point I want to make about this terrible "return of the repressed," is that it determines a remarkable generic transformation of the narrative: suddenly we are no longer in satire, but in ritual. The beggars and the lumpens, led by Sereen Mada himself, descend on the Hadj and require him to submit, for the removal of his *xala*, to an abominable ceremony of ritual humiliation and abasement. The representational space of the narrative is lifted to a new generic realm, which reaches back to touch the powers of the archaic even as it foretells the utopian destruction of the fallen present in the mode of prophecy. The word "Brechtian," which inevitably springs to mind, probably does inadequate justice to these new forms which have emerged from a properly third-world reality. Yet in light of this unexpected generic ending, the preceding satiric text is itself retroactively transformed. From a satire whose subject-matter or content was the ritual curse visited on a character within the narrative, it suddenly becomes revealed as a ritual curse in its own right—the entire imagined chain of events becomes Ousmane's own curse upon his hero and people like him. No more stunning confirmation could be adduced for Robert C. Elliott's great insight into the anthropological origins of satiric discourse in real acts of shamanistic malediction.

I want to conclude with a few thoughts on why all this should be so and on the origins and status of what I have identified as the primacy of national allegory in third-world culture. We are, after all, familiar with the mechanisms of auto-referentiality in contemporary western literature: is this not simply to be taken as another form of that, in a structurally distinct social and cultural context? Perhaps. But in that case our priorities must be reversed for proper understanding of this mechanism. Consider the disrepute of social allegory in our culture and the well-nigh inescapable operation of social allegory in the west's Other. These two contrasting realities are to be grasped, I think, in terms of *situational consciousness*, an expression I prefer to the more common term materialism. Hegel's old analysis of the Master-Slave relationship[26] may still be the most effective way of dramatizing this distinction between two cultural logics. Two equals struggle each for recognition by the other: the one is willing to sacrifice life for this supreme value. The other, a heroic coward in the Brechtian, Schweykian sense of loving the body and the material world too well, gives in, in order to continue life. The Master—now the fulfillment of a baleful and inhuman feudal-aristocratic disdain for life without honor—proceeds to enjoy the benefits of his recognition by the other, now become his humble serf or slave. But at this point two distinct and dialectically ironic reversals take place: only the Master is now genuinely human, so that "recognition" by this henceforth sub-human form of life which is the slave evaporates at the moment of its attainment and offers no genuine satisfaction. "The truth of the Master," Hegel observes grimly, "is the Slave; while the truth of the Slave, on the other hand, is the Master." But a second reversal is in process as well: for the slave is called upon to labor for the master and to furnish him with all the material benefits befitting his supremacy. But this means that, in the end, only the slave knows what reality and the resistance of matter really are; only the slave can attain some true materialistic consciousness of his situation, since it is precisely to that that he is condemned. The Master, however, is condemned to idealism—to the luxury of a placeless freedom in which any consciousness of his own concrete situation flees like a dream, like a word unremembered on the tip of the tongue, a nagging doubt which the puzzled mind is unable to formulate.

It strikes me that we Americans, we masters of the world, are in something of that very same position. The view from the top is epistemologically crippling, and reduces its subjects to the illusions of a host of fragmented subjectivities, to the poverty of the individual experience of isolated monads, to dying individual bodies without collective pasts or futures bereft of any possibility of grasping the social totality. This placeless individuality, this structural idealism which affords us the luxury of the Sartrean blink, offers a welcome escape from the "nightmare of history," but at the same time it condemns our culture to psychologism and the "projections" of private subjectivity. All of this is denied to third-world culture, which must be situational and materialist despite itself. And it is this, finally, which must account for the allegorical nature of third-world culture, where the telling of the individual story and the individual experience cannot but ultimately involve the whole laborious telling of the experience of the collectivity itself.

I hope I have suggested the epistemological priority of this unfamiliar kind of allegorical vision; but I must admit that old habits die hard, and that for us such unaccustomed exposure to reality, or to the collective totality, is often intolerable, leaving us in Quentin's position at the end of *Absalom, Absalom!*, murmuring the great denial, "I don't hate the Third World! I don't! I don't! I don't!"

Even that resistance is instructive, however; and we may well feel, confronted with the daily reality of the other two-thirds of the globe, that "there was nothing at all attractive about it in fact." But we must not allow ourselves that feeling without also acknowledging its ultimate mocking completion: "Its life was based on the principles of community interdependence."

Notes

[1] The whole matter of nationalism should perhaps be rethought, as Benedict Anderson's interesting essay *Imagined Communities* (London: Verso, 1983), and Tom Nairn's *The Breakup of Britain* (London: New Left Books, 1977) invite us to do.

[2] I have argued elsewhere for the importance of mass culture and science fiction. See "Reification and Utopia in Mass Culture," *Social Text* no. 1 (1979), 130–148.

[3] The essay was written for an immediate occasion—the third memorial lecture in honor of my late colleague and

friend Robert C. Elliot at the University of California, San Diego. It is essentially reprinted as given.

4 William Bennett, "To Reclaim a Legacy," Text of a report on the Humanities, *Chronicle of Higher Education*, XXIX, 14 (Nov. 28, 1984), pp. 16–21.

5 The classic texts are F. Engels, *The Origin of the Family, Private Property and the State* (1884) and the earlier, but only more recently published section of Marx's *Grundrisse*, often called "Pre-capitalist economic formations," trans. Martin Nicolaus (London: NLB/Penguin, 1973), pp. 471–514. See also Emmanuel Terray, *Marxism and "Primitive" Societies*, trans. M. Klopper, (New York: Monthly Review, 1972); Barry Hindess and Paul Hirst, *Pre-Capitalist Modes of Production* (London: Routledge and Kegan Paul, 1975); and Gilles Deleuze and Felix Guattari, "Savages, Barbarians, Civilized Men," in *Anti-Oedipus*, trans. R. Hurley, M. Seem, H.R. Lane, (Minneapolis: University of Minnesota press, 1983), pp. 139–271.

Besides mode-of-production theory, whose validity is in any case widely debated, there have also appeared in recent years a number of important synthesizing works on third-world history as a unified field. Three works in particular deserve mention: *Global Rift*, by L.S. Stavrianos (Morrow, 1981); *Europe and the People without History*, by Eric R. Wolf (California, 1982), and *The Three Worlds*, by Peter Worsley (Chicago, 1984). Such works suggest a more general methodological consequence implicit in the present essay but which should be stated explicitly here: first, that the kind of comparative work demanded by this concept of third-world literature involves comparison, not of the individual texts, which are formally and culturally very different from each other, but of the concrete situations from which such texts spring and to which they constitute distinct responses; and second, that such an approach suggests the possibility of a literary and cultural comparatism of a new type, distantly modelled on the new comparative history of Barrington Moore and exemplified in books like Theda Skocpol's *States and Social Revolutions* or Eric Wolf's *Peasant Revolutions of the 20th Century*. Such a new cultural comparatism would juxtapose the study of the differences and similarities of specific literary and cultural texts with a more typological analysis of the various socio-cultural situations from which they spring, an analysis whose variables would necessarily include such features as the interrelationship of social classes, the role of intellectuals, the dynamics of language and writing, the configuration of traditional forms, the relationship to western influences, the development of urban experience and money, and so forth. Such comparatism, however, need not be restricted to third-world literature.

6 See for example, Perry Anderson, *Lineages of the Absolutist State* (London: New Left Books, 1974), pp. 435–549.

7 Sigmund Freud, "Psychoanalytic Notes on an Autobiographical Account of a Case of Paranoia," trans. James Strachey, *The Standard Edition of the Complete Psychological Works of Sigmund Freud* (London: Hogarth, 1958), Volume XII, p. 457.

8 See for example Wolfram Eberhard, *A History of China*, trans. E.W. Dickes, (Berkeley: University of California Press, 1977), p. 105: "When we hear of alchemy, or read books about it we should always keep in mind that many of these books can also be read as books of sex; in a similar way, books on the art of war, too, can be read as books on sexual relations."

9 Lu Xun, *Selected Stories of Lu Hsun*, trans. Gladys Yang and Yang Hsien-yi (Beijing: Foreign Languages Press, 1972), pp. 1–6.

10 Ibid., pp. 2–3.

11 Ibid., p. 40.

12 Ibid., p. 72.

13 Ibid. I am indebted to Peter Rushton for some of these observations.

14 Ibid., p. 5.

15 Socialism will become a reality, Lenin observes, "when the *necessity* of observing the simple, fundamental rules of human intercourse" has "become a habit." (*State and Revolution* [Beijing: Foreign Languages Press, 1973], p. 122.)

16 See the interesting discussions in Stephen Gilman, *Galdós and the Art of the European Novel: 1867–1887* (Princeton: Princeton University Press, 1981).

17 Immanuel Wallerstein, *The Modern World System* (New York: Academic Press, 1974).

18 For example: "El Delfin habia entrado, desde los últimos dias del 74, en aquel periodo sedante que seguia infaliblemente a sus desvarios. En realidad, no era aquello virtud, sino casancio del pecado; no era el sentimiento puro y regular del orden, sino el hastio de la revolución. Verificábase en él lo que don Baldomero habia dicho del pais: que padecia fiebres alternativas de libertad y de paz." *Fortunata y Jacinta* (Madrid: Editorial Hernando, 1968), p. 585 (Part III, chapter 2, section 2).

19 Deluze and Guattari, op. cit., p. 274.

20 Princeton University Press, 1960; and University of Chicago Press, 1970, respectively.

21 Sembène Ousmane, *Xala*, trans. Clive Wake, (Westport, Conn.: Lawrence Hill, 1976), p. 69.

22 I am indebted to Carlos Blanco Aguinaga for the suggestion that in the Latin American novel this ambivalence may be accounted for by the fact that the archetypal Dictator, while oppressing his own people, is also perceived as *resisting* North American influence.

23 *Xala*, op. cit., p. 66.

Fredric Jameson

24 "Generic Discontinuities in Science Fiction: Brian Aldiss'
Starship," *Science Fiction Studies* #2 (1973), pp. 57–68.

25 *Xala*, op. cit., pp. 110–111.

26 G.W.F. Hegel, *The Phenomenology of Mind*, trans. A.V. Miller,
(Oxford: Oxford University Press, 1977): Section B, Chapter
IV, Part A-3, "Lordship and Bondage," pp. 111–119. The
other basic philosophical underpinning of this argument is
Lukács' epistemology in *History and Class Consciousness*
according to which "mapping" or the grasping of the
social totality is structurally available to the dominated
rather than the dominating classes. "Mapping" is a term I
have used in "Postmodernism, or, the Cultural Logic of
Late Capitalism," (*New Left Review* #146 [July-August,
1984], pp. 53–92). What is here called "national allegory" is
clearly a form of just such mapping of the totality, so that
the present essay—which sketches a theory of the
cognitive aesthetics of third-world literature—forms a
pendant to the essay on postmodernism which describes
the logic of the cultural imperialism of the first world and
above all of the United States.

6 Jameson's Rhetoric of Otherness and the "National Allegory"

Aijaz Ahmad

In assembling the following notes on Fredric Jameson's "Third-World Literature in the Era of Multinational Capital," I find myself in an awkward position. If I were to name the *one* literary critic/theorist writing in the US today whose work I generally hold in the highest regard, it would surely be Fredric Jameson. The plea that generates most of the passion in his text—that the teaching of literature in the US academy be informed by a sense not only of "western" literature but of "world literature"; that the so-called literary canon be based not upon the exclusionary pleasures of dominant taste but upon an inclusive and opulent sense of heterogeneity—is of course entirely salutary. And, I wholly admire the knowledge, the range of sympathies, he brings to the reading of texts produced in distant lands.

Yet this plea for syllabus reform—even his marvelously erudite reading of Lu Xun and Ousmane—is conflated with, indeed superseded by, a much more ambitious undertaking which pervades the entire text but which is explicitly announced only in the last sentence of the last footnote: the construction of "a theory of the cognitive aesthetics of third-world literature." This "cognitive aesthetics" rests, in turn, upon a suppression of the multiplicity of significant difference among and within both the advanced capitalist countries and the imperialised formations. We have, instead, a binary opposition of what Jameson calls the "first" and the "third" worlds. It is in this passage from a plea for syllabus reform to the enunciation of a "cognitive aesthetics" that most of the text's troubles lie. These troubles are, I might add, quite numerous.

There is doubtless a personal, somewhat existential side to my encounter with this text, which is best clarified at the outset. I have been reading Jameson's work now for roughly fifteen years, and at least some of what I know about the literatures and cultures of Western Europe and the US comes from him; and because I am a marxist, I had always thought of

Aijaz Ahmad, "Jameson's Rhetoric of Otherness and 'National Allegory'." *Social Text*, 17, 1987: 3–25.
Reproduced by permission of Duke University Press.

Postcolonial Studies: An Anthology, First Edition. Edited by Pramod K. Nayar.
Editorial material and organization © 2016 John Wiley & Sons, Ltd.
Published 2016 by John Wiley & Sons, Ltd.

Aijaz Ahmad

us, Jameson and myself, as birds of the same feather even though we never quite flocked together. But, then, when I was on the fifth page of this text (specifically, on the sentence starting with "All third-world texts are necessarily…" etc.), I realized that what was being theorised was, among many other things, myself. Now, I was born in India and I am a Pakistani citizen; I write poetry in Urdu, a language not commonly understood among US intellectuals. So, I said to myself: *"All? … necessarily?"* It felt odd. Matters got much more curious, however. For, the farther I read the more I realized, with no little chagrin, that the man whom I had for so long, so affectionately, even though from a physical distance, taken as a comrade was, in his own opinion, my civilizational Other. It was not a good feeling.

I

I too think that there *are* plenty of very good books written by African, Asian and Latin American writers which are available in English and which must be taught as an anti-dote against the general ethnocentricity and cultural myopia of the humanities as they are presently constituted in these United States. If some label is needed for this activity, one may call it "third-world literature." Conversely, however, I also hold that this phrase, "the third world," is, even in its most telling deployments, a polemical one, with no theoretical status whatsoever. Polemic surely has a prominent place in all human discourses, especially in the discourse of politics, so the use of this phrase in loose, polemical contexts is altogether permissible. But to lift the phrase from the register of polemics and claim it as a basis for producing theoretical knowledge, which presumes a certain rigor in constructing the objects of one's knowledge, is to misconstrue not only the phrase itself but even the world to which it refers. I shall argue, therefore, that there is no such thing as a "third-world literature" which can be constructed as an internally coherent object of theoretical knowledge. There are fundamental issues—of periodisation, social and linguistic formations, political and ideological struggles within the field of literary production, and so on—which simply cannot be resolved at this level of generality without an altogether positivist reductionism.

The mere fact, for example, that languages of the metropolitan countries have not been adopted by the vast majority of the producers of literature in Asia and Africa means that the vast majority of literary texts from those continents are unavailable in the metropoles, so that a literary theorist who sets out to formulate "a theory of the cognitive aesthetics of third-world literature" shall be constructing ideal-types, in the Weberian manner, duplicating all the basic procedures which orientalist scholars have historically deployed in presenting their own readings of a certain tradition of "high" textuality as *the* knowledge of a supposedly unitary object which they call "the Islamic civilization." I might add that literary relations between the metropolitan countries and the imperialised formations are constructed very differently than they are among the metropolitan countries themselves. Rare would be a literary theorist in Europe or the US who does not command a couple of European languages other than his/her own; and the frequency of translation, back and forth, among European languages creates very fulsome circuits for the circulation of texts, so that even a US scholar who does not command much beyond English can be quite well grounded in the various metropolitan traditions.

Linguistic and literary relations between the metropolitan countries and the countries of Asia and Africa, on the other hand, offer three sharp contrasts to this system.

Rare would be a modern intellectual in Asia or Africa who does not know at least one European language; equally rare would be, on the other side, a major literary theorist in Europe or the United States who has ever bothered with an Asian or African language; and the enormous industry of translation which circulates texts among the advanced capitalist countries comes to the most erratic and slowest possible grind when it comes to translation from Asian or African languages. The upshot is that major literary traditions—such as those of Bengali, Hindi, Tamil, Telegu and half a dozen others from India alone—remain, beyond a few texts here and there, virtually unknown to the American literary theorist. Consequently, the few writers who happen to write in English are valorized beyond measure. Witness, for example, the characterization of Salman Rushdie's *Midnight's Children* in the *New York Times* as "a Continent finding its voice"—as if one has no voice if one does not speak in English. Or, Richard Poirier's praise for Edward Said in *Raritan Quarterly* which now adorns the back cover of his latest book: "It is Said's great accomplishment that thanks to his book, Palestinians will never be lost to history." This is the upside-down world of the *camera obscura*: not that Said's vision is itself framed by the Palestinian experience but that Palestine would have no place in history without Said's book! The retribution visited upon the head of an Asian, an African, an Arab intellectual who is of any consequence and who writes in English is that he/she is immediately elevated to the lonely splendour of a "representative"—of a race, a continent, a civilization, even the "third world." It is in this general context that a "cognitive theory of third-world literature" based upon what is currently available in languages of the metropolitan countries becomes, to my mind, an alarming undertaking.

I shall return to some of these points presently, especially to the point about the epistemological impossibility of a "third-world literature." Since, however, Jameson's own text is so centrally grounded in a binary opposition between a first and a third world, it is impossible to proceed with an examination of his particular propositions regarding the respective literary traditions without first asking whether or not this characterization of the world is itself theoretically tenable, and whether, therefore, an accurate conception of *literature* can be mapped out on the basis of this binary opposition. I shall argue later that since Jameson defines the so-called third world in terms of its "experience of colonialism and imperialism," the political category that necessarily follows from this exclusive emphasis is that of "the nation," with nationalism as the peculiarly valorized ideology; and, because of this privileging of the nationalist ideology, it is then theoretically posited that "all third-world texts are necessarily … to be read as … national allegories." The theory of the "national allegory" as the metatext is thus inseparable from the larger Three Worlds Theory which permeates the whole of Jameson's own text. We too have to begin, then, with some comments on "the third world" as a theoretical category and on "nationalism" as the necessary, exclusively desirable ideology.

II

Jameson seems aware of the difficulties in conceptualising the global dispersion of powers and populations in terms of his particular variant of the Three Worlds Theory ("I take the point of criticism," he says). And, after reiterating the basic premise of that theory ("the capitalist first world"; "the socialist bloc of the second world"; and "countries that have suffered colonialism and imperialism"), he does clarify that he does not uphold the specifically Maoist theory of "convergence" between the United States and the Soviet Union. The rest of the difficulty in holding this view of the world is elided, however, with three assertions: that he cannot find a "comparable expression"; that he is deploying these terms in "an essentially descriptive way"; and that the criticisms are at any rate not "relevant." The problem of "comparable expression" is a minor matter, which we shall ignore; "relevance," on the other hand, is the central issue and I shall deal with it presently. First, however, I want to comment briefly on the matter of "description."

More than most critics writing in the US today, Jameson should know that when it comes to a knowledge of the world, there is no such thing as a category of the "essentially descriptive"; that "description" is never ideologically or cognitively neutral; that to "describe" is to specify a locus of meaning, to construct an object of knowledge, and to produce a knowledge that shall be bound by that act of descriptive construction. "Description" has been central, for example, in the colonial discourse. It was by assembling a monstrous machinery of descriptions—of our bodies, our speech-acts, our habitats, our conflicts and desires, our politics, our socialities and sexualities—in fields as various as ethnology, fiction, photography, linguistics, political science—that the colonial discourse was able to classify and ideologically master the colonial subject, enabling itself to transform the descriptively verifiable multiplicity and difference into the ideologically felt hierarchy of value. To say, in short, that what one is presenting is "essentially descriptive" is to assert a level of facticity which conceals its own ideology and to prepare a ground from which judgments of classification, generalisation and value can be made.

As we get to the substance of what Jameson "describes," I find it significant that first and second worlds are defined in terms of their production systems (capitalism and socialism, respectively), whereas the third category—the third world—is defined purely in terms of an "experience" of externally inserted phenomena. That which is constitutive of human history itself is present in the first two cases, absent in the third one. Ideologically, this classification divides the world between those who make history and those who are mere objects of it; elsewhere in the text, Jameson would significantly re-invoke Hegel's famous description of the master/slave relation to encapsulate the first/third world opposition. But analytically, this classification leaves the so-called third world in a limbo; if only the first world is capitalist and the second world socialist, how does one understand the third world? Is it pre-capitalist? Transitional? Transitional between what and what?

But then there is also the issue of the location of particular countries within the various "worlds." Take, for example, India. Its colonial past is nostalgically rehashed on US television screens in copious series every few months, but the India of today has all the characteristics of a capitalist country: generalised commodity production, vigorous and escalating exchanges not only between agriculture and industry but also between Departments I and II of industry itself, technical personnel more numerous than that of France and Germany combined, and a gross industrial product twice as large as that of Britain. It is a very miserable kind of capitalism, and the conditions of life for over half of the Indian population (roughly 400 million people) are considerably worse than what Engels described in *Conditions of the Working Class in England*. But India's steel industry did celebrate its hundredth anniversary a few years ago, and the top eight of her multinational corporations are among the fastest growing in the world, active as they are in numerous countries, from Vietnam to Nigeria. This economic base is combined, then, with unbroken parliamentary rule of the bourgeoisie since independence in 1947, a record quite comparable to the length of Italy's modern record of unbroken bourgeois-democratic governance, and superior to the fate of bourgeois democracy in Spain and Portugal, two of the oldest colonising countries. This parliamentary republic of the bourgeoisie in India has not been without its own lawlessnesses and violences, of a kind and degree now not normal in Japan or Western Europe, but a bourgeois political subjectivity *has* been created for the populace at large. The corollary on the left is that the two communist parties (CPI and CPM) have longer and more extensive experience of regional government, within the republic of the bourgeoisie, than all the eurocommunist parties combined, and the electorate that votes ritually for these two parties is probably larger than the communist electorates in all the rest of the capitalist world.

So, does India belong in the first world or the third? Brazil, Argentina, Mexico, South Africa? And ...? But we *know* that countries of the Pacific rim, from South Korea to Singapore, constitute the fastest growing region within global capitalism. The list could be much longer, but the point is that the binary opposition which Jameson constructs between a capitalist first world and a presumably pre- or non-capitalist third world is empirically ungrounded.

III

I have said already that if one believes in the Three Worlds Theory, hence in a "third world" defined exclusively in terms of "the experience of colonialism and imperialism," then the primary ideological formation available to a leftwing intellectual shall be that of nationalism; it will then be possible to assert, surely with very considerable exaggeration but nonetheless, that "all third-world texts are necessarily ... *national allegories*" (emphases in the original). This exclusive emphasis on the nationalist ideology is there even in the opening paragraph of Jameson's text where the only choice for the "third world" is said to be between its "nationalisms" and a "global American postmodernist culture." Is there no other choice? Could not one join the "second world," for example? There used to be, in the marxist discourse, a thing called socialist and/or communist culture which was neither nationalist nor postmodernist. Has that vanished from our discourse altogether, even as the name of a desire?

Jameson's haste in totalising historical phenomena in terms of binary oppositions (nationalism/postmodernism, in this case) leaves little room for the fact, for instance, that the only nationalisms in the so-called third world which have been able to resist US cultural pressure and have actually produced any alternatives are the ones which are already articulated to and assimilated within the much larger field of socialist political practice. Virtually all others have had no difficulty in reconciling themselves with what Jameson calls "global American postmodernist culture"; in the singular and sizeable case of Iran (which Jameson forbids us to mention on the grounds that it is "predictable" that we shall do so), the anti-communism of the Islamic nationalists has produced not social regeneration but clerical fascism. Nor does the absolutism of that opposition (postmodernism/nationalism) permit any space for the simple idea that nationalism itself is not some unitary thing with some pre-determined essence and value. There are hundreds of nationalisms in Asia and Africa today; some are progressive, others are not. Whether or not a nationalism will produce a progressive cultural practice depends, to put it in Gramscian terms, upon the political character of the power bloc which takes hold of it and utilises it, as a material force, in the process of constituting its own hegemony. There is neither theoretical ground nor empirical evidence to support the notion that bourgeois nationalisms of the so-called third world will have any difficulty with postmodernism; they *want* it.

Yet, there *is* a very tight fit between the Three Worlds Theory, the over-valorization of the nationalist ideology, and the assertion that "national allegory" is the primary, even exclusive, form of narrativity in the so-called third world. If this "third world" is *constituted* by the singular "experience of colonialism and imperialism," and if the only possible response is a nationalist one, then what else is there that is more urgent to narrate than this "experience"; in fact, there is *nothing else* to narrate. For, if societies here are defined not by relations of production but by relations of intra-national domination; if they are forever suspended outside the sphere of conflict between capitalism (first world) and socialism (second world); if the motivating force for history here is neither class formation and class struggle nor the multiplicities of intersecting conflicts based upon class, gender, nation, race, region and so on, but the unitary "experience" of national oppression (if one is merely the *object* of history, the Hegelian slave) then what else *can* one narrate but that national oppression? Politically, we are Calibans, all. Formally, we are fated to be in the poststructuralist world of repetition with difference; the same allegory, the nationalist one, re-written, over and over again, until the end of time: "all third-world texts are necessarily…"

IV

But one could start with a radically different premise, namely the proposition that we live not in three worlds but in one; that this world includes the experience of colonialism and imperialism on both sides of Jameson's global divide (the "experience" of imperialism is a central fact of all aspects of life inside the US from ideological formation to the utilisation of the social surplus in military-industrial complexes); that societies in formations of backward capitalism are as much constituted by the division of classes as are societies in the advanced capitalist countries; that socialism is not restricted to something called the second world but is simply the name of a resistance that saturates the globe today, as capitalism itself does; that the different parts of the capitalist system are to be known not in terms of a binary opposition but as a contradictory unity, with differences, yes, but also with profound overlaps. One immediate consequence for literary theory would be that the unitary search for "a theory of cognitive aesthetics for third-world literature" would be rendered impossible, and one would have to forego the idea of a meta-narrative that encompasses all the fecundity of real narratives in the so-called third world. Conversely, many of the questions that one would ask about, let us say, Urdu or Bengali traditions of literature may turn out to be rather similar to the questions one has asked previously about English/American literatures. By the same token, a *real* knowledge of those other traditions may force US literary theorists to ask questions about their own tradition which they have heretofore not asked.

Jameson claims that one cannot proceed from the premise of a real unity of the world "without falling back into some general liberal and humanistic universalism." That is a curious idea, coming from a marxist. One should have thought that the world was united not by liberalist ideology—that the world was not at all constituted in the realm of an Idea, be it Hegelian or humanist—but by the global operation of a single mode of production, namely the capitalist one, and the global resistance to this mode, a resistance which is itself unevenly developed in different parts of the globe. Socialism, one should have thought, was not by any means limited to the so-called second world (the socialist countries) but a global phenomenon, reaching into the farthest rural communities in Asia, Africa and Latin America, not to speak of individuals and groups within the United States. What gives the world its unity, then, is not a humanist ideology but the ferocious struggle of capital and labor which is now strictly and fundamentally global in character. The prospect of a socialist revolution has receded so much from the practical horizon of so much of the metropolitan left that the temptation for the US left intelligentsia is to forget the ferocity of that basic struggle which in our time transcends all others. The advantage of coming from Pakistan, in my own case, is that the country is saturated with capitalist commodities, bristles with US weaponry, borders on China, the Soviet Union and Afghanistan, suffers from a proliferation of competing nationalisms, and is currently witnessing the first stage in the consolidation of the communist movement. It is difficult, coming from there, to forget that primary motion of history which gives to our globe its contradictory unity: a notion that has nothing to do with liberal humanism.

As for the specificity of cultural difference, Jameson's theoretical conception tends, I believe, in the opposite direction, namely, that of homogenisation. Difference between the first world and the third is absolutised as an Otherness, but the enormous cultural heterogeneity of social formations within the so-called third world is submerged within a singular identity of "experience." Now, countries of Western Europe and North America have been deeply tied together over roughly the last two hundred years; capitalism itself is so much older in these countries; the cultural logic of late capitalism is so strongly operative in these metropolitan formations; the circulation of cultural products among them is so immediate, so extensive, so brisk that one could sensibly speak of a certain cultural homogeneity among them. But Asia, Africa, and Latin America? Historically, these countries were never so closely tied together; Peru and India simply do not have a common history of the sort that Germany and France, or Britain and the United States, have; not even the singular "experience of colonialism and imperialism" has been in specific ways same or similar in, say, India and Namibia. These various countries, from the three continents, have been assimilated into the global structure of capitalism not as a single cultural ensemble but highly differentially, each establishing its own circuits of (unequal) exchange with the metropolis, each acquiring its own very distinct class formations. Circuits of exchange among them are rudimentary at best; an average Nigerian who is literate about his own country would know infinitely more about England and the United States than about any country of Asia or Latin America or indeed about most countries of Africa. The kind of circuits that bind the cultural complexes of the advanced capitalist countries simply do not exist among countries of backward capitalism, and capitalism itself, which is dominant but not altogether universalised, does not yet have the same power of homogenisation in its cultural logic in most of these countries, except among the urban bourgeoisie.

Of course, great cultural similarities also exist among countries that occupy analogous positions in the global capitalist system, and there are similarities in many cases that have been bequeathed by the similarities of socio-economic structures in the pre-capitalist past. The point is not to construct a typology that is simply the obverse of Jameson's, but rather to define the material basis for a fair degree of cultural homogenisation among the advanced capitalist countries and the lack of that kind of homogenisation in the rest of the capitalist world. In context, therefore, one is doubly surprised at Jameson's absolute insistence upon difference and the relation of otherness between the first world and the third, and his equally insistent idea that the "experience" of the "third world" could be contained and communicated within a single narrative form.

By locating capitalism in the first world and socialism in the second, Jameson's theory freezes and de-historicises the global space within which struggles between these great motivating forces actually take place. And, by assimilating the enormous heterogeneities and productivities of our life into a single Hegelian metaphor of the master/slave relation, this theory reduces us to an ideal-type and demands from us that we narrate ourselves through a form commensurate with that ideal-type. To say that all third-world texts are necessarily this or that is to say, in effect, that any text originating within that social space which is *not* this or that is not a "true" narrative. It is in this sense above all, that the category of "third-world literature" which is the site of this operation, with the "national allegory" as its metatext as well as the mark of its constitution and difference, is, to my mind, epistemologically an impossible category.

V

Part of the difficulty in engaging Jameson's text is that there is a constant slippage, a recurrent inflation, in the way he handles the categories of his analysis. The specificity of the first world, for example, seems at times to be predicated upon the postmodernist moment, which is doubtless of recent origin, but at other times it appears to be a matter of the capitalist mode of production, which is a much larger, much older thing; and, in yet another range of formulations, this first world is said to be coterminal with "western civilization" itself, obviously a rather primordial way of being, dating back to antiquity ("Graeco-Judaic," in Jameson's phrase) and anterior to any structuration of productions and classes as we know them today. *When* did this first world become first, in the pre-Christian centuries, or after World War II?

And, at what point in history does a text produced in countries with "experience of colonialism and imperialism" become a *third-world text*? In one kind of reading, only texts produced *after* the advent of colonialism could be so designated, since it is colonialism/imperialism which constitutes the third world as such. But, in speaking constantly of "the west's other"; in referring to the tribal/tributary and the Asiatic modes as the theoretical basis for his selection of Lu Xun (Asian) and Sembene (African) respectively; in characterising Freud's theory as a "western or first-world reading" as contrasted with ten centuries of specifically Chinese distributions of the libidinal energy which are said to frame Lu Xun's texts—in deploying these broad epochal and civilizational categories, Jameson suggests also that the difference between the first world and the third is itself primordial, rooted in things far older than capitalism as such. If, then, the first world is the same as "the west" and the "Graeco-Judaic," one has an alarming feeling that the *Bhagvad Geeta*, the edicts of Manu, and the Quran itself are perhaps third-world texts (though the Judaic elements of the Quran are quite beyond doubt, and much of the ancient art in what is today Pakistan is itself Graeco-Indic).

But there is also the question of *space*. Do all texts produced in countries with "experience of colonialism and imperialism" become, by virtue of geographical origin, third-world texts? Jameson speaks so often of *"all"* third-world texts, insists so much on a singular form of narrativity for third-world literature, that not to take him literally is to violate the very terms of his discourse. Yet, one knows of so many texts from one's own part of the world which do not fit the description of "national allegory" that one wonders why Jameson insists so much on the category *"all."* Without this category, of course, he cannot produce *a* theory of third-world litera-ture. But is it also the case that he means the opposite of what he actually says: not that "all third-world texts are to be read ... as national allegories" but that *only* those texts which give us national allegories can be admitted as authentic texts of third-world literature, while the rest are excluded by definition? Hence, one is not quite sure whether one is dealing with a fallacy ("all third-world texts are" this or that) or with the Law of the Father (you must write *this* if you are to be admitted into my theory).

These shifts and hesitations in defining the objects of one's knowledge are based, I believe, on several confusions, one of which I shall specify here. For, if one argues that the third world is constituted by the "experience of colonialism and imperialism," one must also recognise the two-pronged action of the colonial/imperialist dynamic: the forced transfers of value *from* the colonialised/imperialised forma-tions, and the intensification of capitalist relations *within* those formations. And if capitalism is not merely an externality but also a shaping force within those formations, then one must conclude also that the separation between the public and the private, so characteristic of capitalism, has occurred there as well, at least in some degree and especially among the urban intelligentsia which produces most of the written texts and which is itself caught in the world of capitalist commodities. With this bifurcation must have come, at least for some of the producers of texts, the individuation and personalisation of libidinal energies, the loss of access to "concrete" experience, and the consequent experience of self as isolated, alienated entity incapable of real, organic connection with any collectivity. There must be texts, perhaps numerous texts, that are grounded in this desolation, bereft of any capacity for the kind of allegorisation and organicity that Jameson demands of them. The logic of Jameson's own argument (i.e., that the third world is constituted by "experience of colonialism and imperialism") leads necessarily to the conclusion that at least some of the writers of the third world itself must be producing texts characteristic not of the so-called tribal and Asiatic modes but of the capitalist era as such, much in the manner of the so-called first world. But Jameson does not draw that conclusion.

He does not draw that conclusion at least partially because this so-called third world is to him suspended outside the modern systems of production (capitalism and socialism). He does not quite say that the third world is pre- or non-capitalist, but that is clearly the implication of the contrast he establishes, as for example in the following formulation:

> ... one of the determinants of capitalist culture, that is, the culture of the western realist and modernist novel, is a radical split between the private and the public, between the poetic and the political, between what we have come to think of as the domain of sexuality and the unconscious and that of the public world of classes, of the economic, and of secular political power: in other words, Freud versus Marx. ...
>
> I will argue that, although we may retain for convenience and for analysis such categories as the subjective and the public or political, the relations between them are wholly different in third-world culture.

It is noteworthy that "the radical split between the private and the public" is distinctly located in the capitalist mode here, but the *absence* of this split in so-called third-world culture is not located in any mode of production—in keeping with Jameson's very definition of the Three Worlds. But Jameson knows what he is talking about, and his statements have been less ambiguous in the past. Thus, we find the following in his relatively early essay on Lukács:

> In the art works of a preindustrialized, agricultural or tribal society, the artist's raw material is on a human scale, it has an immediate meaning. ... The story needs no background in time because the culture knows no history; each generation repeats the same experiences, reinvents the same basic human situations as though for the first time. ... The works of art characteristic of such societies may be called concrete in that their elements are all meaningful from the outset ... in the language of Hegel, this raw material needs no *mediation*.
>
> When we turn from such a work to the literature of the industrial era, everything changes ... a kind of dissolution of the human sets in. ... For the unquestioned ritualistic time of village life no longer exists; there is henceforth a separation between public and private ... (*Marxism And Form*, pp. 165–67.)

Clearly, then, what was once theorised as a difference between the pre-industrial and the industrialized societies (the unity of the public and the private in one, the separation of the two in the other) is now transposed as a difference between the first and third worlds. The idea of the "concrete" is now rendered in only slightly different vocabulary: "third-world culture ... must be situational and materialist despite itself." And it is perhaps that other idea—namely that "preindustrialized ... culture knows no history; each generation repeats the same experience"—which is at the root of now suspending the so-called third world outside the modern modes of production (capitalism and socialism), encapsulating the experience of this third world in the Hegelian metaphor of the master/slave relation, and postulating a unitary form of narrativity (the national allegory) in which the "experience" of this third world is to be told. In both texts, the theoretical authority that is invoked is, predictably, that of Hegel.

Likewise, Jameson insists over and over again that the *national* experience is central to the cognitive formation of the third-world intellectual and that the narrativity of that experience takes the form exclusively of a "national allegory," but this emphatic insistence on the category "nation" itself keeps slipping into a much wider, far less demarcated vocabulary of "culture," "society," "collectivity" and so on. Are "nation" and "collectivity" the same thing? Take, for example, the two statements which seem to enclose the elaboration of the theory itself. In the beginning we are told:

> All third-world texts are necessarily, I want to argue, allegorical, and in a very specific way: they are to be read as what I will call *national allegories*, even when, or perhaps I should say, particularly when their forms develop out of predominantly western machineries of representation, such as the novel.

But at the end we find the following:

> ... the telling of the individual story and the individual experience cannot but ultimately involve the whole laborious telling of the experience of the collectivity itself.

Are these two statements saying the same thing? The difficulty of this shift in vocabulary is that one may indeed connect one's personal experience to a "collectivity"—in terms of class, gender, caste, religious community, trade union, political party, village, prison—combining the private and the public, and in some sense "allegorizing" the individual experience, without involving the category of "the nation" or necessarily referring back to the "experience of colonialism and imperialism." The latter statement would then seem to apply to a much larger body of texts, with far greater accuracy. By the same token, however, this wider application of "collectivity" establishes much less radical difference between the so-called first and third worlds, since the whole history of realism in the European novel, in its many variants, has been associated with ideas of "typicality" and "the social," while the majority of the written narratives produced in the first world even today locate the individual story in a fundamental relation to some larger experience.

If we replace the idea of the nation with that larger, less restricting idea of collectivity, and if we start thinking of the process of allegorisation not in nationalistic terms but simply as a relation between private and public, personal and communal, then it also becomes possible to see that allegorisation is by no means specific to the so-called third world. While Jameson overstates the presence of "us," the "national allegory," in the narratives of the third world, he also, in the same sweep, understates the presence of analogous impulses in US cultural ensembles. For, what else are, let us say, Pynchon's *Gravity's Rainbow* or Ellison's *The Invisible Man* but allegorisations of individual—and not so individual—experience? What else could Richard Wright and Adrienne Rich and Richard Howard mean when they give to their books titles like *Native Son* or *Your Native Land, Your Life* or *Alone With America*? It is not only the Asian or the African but also the American writer whose private imaginations must *necessarily* connect with experiences of the collectivity. One has only to look at black and feminist writing to find countless allegories even within these postmodernist United States.

Aijaz Ahmad

VI

I also have some difficulty with Jameson's description of "third-world literature" as "non-canonical," for I am not quite sure what that *means*. Since the vast majority of literary texts produced in Asia, Africa and Latin America are simply not available in English, their exclusion from the US/British "canon" is self-evident. If, however, one considers the kind of texts Jameson seems to have in mind, one begins to wonder just what mechanisms of canonisation there *are* from which this body of work is so entirely excluded.

Neruda, Vallejo, Octavio Paz, Borges, Fuentes, Marquez *et al.* (i.e., quite a few writers of Latin American origin) *are* considered by the American academy as major figures in modern literature. They, and even their translators, have received the most prestigious awards (the Nobel for Marquez, for instance, or the National Book Award for Eshleman's translation of Vallejo) and they get *taught* quite as routinely in literature courses as their German or Italian contemporaries might be, perhaps more regularly in fact. Soyinka was recently canonised through the Nobel Prize and Achebe's novels are consistently more easily available in the US book market than are, for example, Richard Wright's. Edward Said, a man of Palestinian origin, has had virtually every honor the US academy has to offer, with distinct constituencies of his own; *Orientalism*, at least, gets taught widely, across several disciplines—more widely, it seems, than the work of any other leftwing literary/cultural critic in this country. V.S. Naipaul is now fully established as a major English novelist, and he does come from the Caribbean; he *is*, like Borges, a "third-world writer." Salman Rushdie's *Midnight's Children* was awarded the most prestigious literary award in England and *Shame* was immediately reviewed as a major novel, almost always favorably, in virtually all the major newspapers and literary journals in Britain and the US. He is a major presence on the British cultural scene and a prized visitor to conferences and graduate departments on both sides of the Atlantic. The blurbs on the Vintage paperback edition of *Shame*—based partly on a quotation from the *New York Times*—compare him with Swift, Voltaire, Stern, Kafka, Grass, Kundera and Marquez. I am told that a PhD dissertation has been written about him at Columbia already. What else *is* canonisation, when it comes to modern, contemporary, and in some cases (Rushdie, for example) relatively young writers?

My argument is not that these reputations are not well-deserved (Naipaul is of course a different matter), nor that there should not be *more* such canonisations. But the representation of this body of work in Jameson's discourse as simply "non-canonical" (i.e., as something that has been altogether excluded from the contemporary practices of high textuality in the US academy) does appear to over-state the case considerably.

Jameson later speaks of "non-canonical forms of literature such as that of the third world," compares this singularized *form* to "another non-canonical form" in which Dashiell Hammett is placed, and then goes on to say:

> Nothing is to be gained by passing over in silence the radical difference of non-canonical texts. The third-world novel will not offer the satisfactions of Proust or Joyce; what is more damaging than that, perhaps, is its tendency to remind us of outmoded stages of our own first-world cultural development

and to cause us to conclude that "they are still writing novels like Dreiser and Sherwood Anderson."

Now, I am not sure that realism, which appears to be at the heart of Jameson's characterization of "third-world literature" in this passage, is quite as universal in *that* literature or quite as definitively superseded in what Jameson calls "first-world cultural development." Some of the most highly regarded US fictionists of the present cultural moment, from Bellow and Malamud to Grace Paley and Robert Stone, seem to write not quite "like Dreiser and Sherwood Anderson" but surely within the realist mode. On the other hand, Cesaire became so popular among the French surrealists because the terms of his discourse were contemporaneous with their own, and Neruda has been translated by some of the leading poets of the US because he is even formally not "outmoded." Novelists like Marquez or Rushdie have been so well received in the US/British literary circles precisely because they do not write like Dreiser or Sherwood Anderson; the satisfactions of their outrageous texts are not those of Proust or Joyce but are surely of an analogous kind, delightful to readers brought up on modernism and postmodernism. Cesaire's *Return to the Native Land* is what it is because it combines what Jameson calls a "national allegory" with the formal methods of the Parisian avant-garde of his student days. Borges is of course not seen in the US any longer in terms of his Latin American origin; he now belongs to the august company of the significant moderns, much like Kafka.

To say that the canon simply does not admit any third-world writers is to misrepresent the way bourgeois culture works, i.e., through selective admission and selective canonisation. Just as modernism has now been fully canonised in the museum and the university, and as certain kinds of marxism have been incorporated and given respectability within the academy, certain writers from the "third world" are also now part and parcel of the literary discourse in the US. Instead of claiming straightforward exclusion, it is perhaps more useful to inquire as to how the principle of selective incorporation works in relation to texts produced outside the metropolitan countries.

VII

I want to offer some comments on the history of Urdu literature, not in the form of a cogent narrative, less still to formulate a short course in that history, but simply to illustrate the kind of impoverishment that is involved in the *a priori* declaration that "all third-world texts are necessarily … to be read as national allegories."

It is, for example, a matter of some considerable curiosity to me that the Urdu language, although one of the youngest linguistic formations in India, had nevertheless produced its first great poet, Khusrow, in the 13th century, so that a great tradition of poetry got going, but then it waited roughly six centuries before beginning to assemble the first sizeable body of prose narratives. Not that prose itself had not been there; the earliest prose texts in Urdu date back to the 8th century, but those were written for religious purposes and were often mere translations from Arabic or Farsi. Non-seminarian and non-theological narratives—the ones that had to do with the pleasures of reading and the etiquettes of civility—began appearing much, much later, in the last decade of the 18th century. Then, over two dozen of them got published during the next ten years. What inhibited that development for so long, and why did it happen precisely at that time? Much of that has to do with complex social developments that had gradually led to the displacement of Farsi by Urdu as the language of educated, urban speech and of prose writing in certain regions of Northern India.

That history we shall ignore, but a certain material condition of that production can be specified: many, though by no means all, of those prose narratives of the 1810s got written and published for the simple reason that a certain Scotsman, John Gilchrist, had argued within his own circles that employees of the East India Company could not hope to administer their Indian possessions on the basis of Persian alone, and certainly not English, so that Fort William College was established in 1800 for the education of the British in Indian languages, mainly in Urdu of which Gilchrist was a scholar and exponent. He hired some of the most erudite men of his time and got them to write whatever they wanted, so long as they wrote in accessible prose. It was a stroke of genius, for what came out of that enterprise was the mobilisation of the whole range of vocabularies existing at that time—the *range* of vocabularies were in keeping with the pedagogical purpose—and the construction of narratives which either transcribed the great classics of oral literature or condensed the fictions that already existed in Arabic or Farsi and were therefore part of the cultural life of the North Indian upper classes. Thus, the most famous of these narratives, Meer Amman's *Bagh-o-Bahar*, was a condensation, in superbly colloquial Urdu, of the monumental *Qissa-e-Chahar Dervish*, which Faizi, the great scholar, had composed some centuries earlier in Farsi, for the amusement of Akbar, the Mughal king who was almost an exact contemporary of the British Queen, Elizabeth.

But that was not the only impulse and the publishing house of Fort William College was in any case closed within a decade. A similar development was occurring in Lucknow, outside the British domains, at exactly the same time; some of the Fort William writers had themselves come from Lucknow, looking for alternative employment. Rajab Ali Beg Saroor's *Fasana-e-A'jaib* is the great classic of this other tradition of Urdu narrativity (these were actually not two different traditions but parts of the same, some of which got formed in the British domains, some not). In 1848, eight years before it fell to British guns, the city of Lucknow had twelve printing presses, and the consolidation of the narrative tradition in Urdu was inseparable from the history of those presses. The remarkable thing about all the major Urdu prose narratives which were written during the half century in which the British completed their conquest of India is that there is nothing in their contents, in their way of seeing the world, which can be reasonably connected with the colonial onslaught or with any sense of resistance to it. By contrast, there is a large body of *letters* and even of poetry which documents that colossal carnage. It is as if the establishment of printing presses and the growth of a reading public for prose narratives gave rise to a kind of writing whose only task was to preserve in books at least some of that Persianized culture and those traditions of orality which were fast disappearing. It is only in this negative sense that one could, by stretching the terms a great deal, declare this to be a literature of the "national allegory."

The man, Pandit Naval Kishore, who gave to the language its first great publishing house, came somewhat later, however. His grandfather had been employed, like many upper caste Hindus of the time, in the Mughal ministry of finance; his own father was a businessman, genteel and affluent but not rich. Naval Kishore himself had a passion for the written word; but like his father and grandfather, he also understood money. He started his career as a journalist, then went on to purchasing old hand-written manuscripts and publishing them for wider circulation. Over time, he expanded into all sorts of fields, all connected with publishing, and gave to Urdu its first great modern archive of published books. Urdu, in turn, showered him with money; at the time of his death in 1895, his fortune was estimated at one crore rupees (roughly a hundred million British pounds). He *had* to publish, I might add, more than national allegories, more than what came out of the experience of colonialism and imperialism, to make that kind of money.

But let me return to the issue of narration. It is a matter of some interest that the emergence of what one could plausibly call a novel came more than half a century *after* the appearance of those early registrations of the classics of the oral tradition and the re-writing of Arabic and Farsi stories. Sarshar's *Fasana-e-Azad*, the most opulent of those early novels, was serialised during the 1870s in something else that had begun emerging in the 1830s: regular Urdu newspapers for the emergent middle classes. Between the traditional tale and the modern novel, then, there were other things, such as newspapers and sizeable reading publics, much in the same way as one encounters them in a whole range of books on English literary history, from Ian Watt's *The Rise of the Novel* to Lennard J. Davis' more recent *Factual Fictions*. And I have often wondered, as others have sometimes wondered about Dickens, if the structure of Sarshar's novel might not have been very different had it been written not for serialisation but for direct publication as a book.

Those other books, independent of newspapers, came too. One very prolific writer, whose name as it appears on the covers of his books is itself a curiosity, was Shams-ul-Ulema Deputy Nazir Ahmed (1831–1912). The name was actually Nazir Ahmed; "Shams-ul-Ulema" literally means a Sun among the scholars of Islam and indicates his distinguished scholarship in that area; "Deputy" simply refers to the fact that he had no independent income and had joined the Colonial Revenue Service. His training in Arabic was rigorous and immaculate; his knowledge of English was spotty, since he had had no formal training in it. He was a prolific translator, of everything: the Indian Penal Code, the Indian Law of Evidence, the Quran, books of astronomy. He is known above all as a novelist, however, and he had one anxiety above all others: that girls should get modern education (in which he represented the emergent urban bourgeoisie) and that they nevertheless remain good, traditional housewives (a sentiment that was quite widespread, across all social boundaries). It was this anxiety that governed most of his fictions.

It is possible to argue, I think, that the formative phase of the Urdu novel and the narratives that arose alongside that novel, in the latter part of the 19th century and the first decades of the 20th, had to do much less with the experience of colonialism and imperialism as such and much more with two other kinds of pressures and themes: (a) the emergence of a new kind of petty bourgeois who was violating all established social norms for his own pecuniary ends (Nazir Ahmed's own *Ibn-ul-Vaqt*—"Time-Server," in rough English approximation—is a classic of that genre); and (b) the status of women. Nazir Ahmed of course took conservative positions on both these themes and was prolific on the latter. But there were others as well. Rashid-ul-Khairi, for example, established a very successful publishing house, the Asmat Book Depot, which published hundreds of books for women and children, as well as the five journals that came into my family over two generations: *Asmat, Khatoon-e-Mashriq, Jauhar-e-Nisvan, Banat*, and *Nau-Nehal*. English approximations for the latter four titles are easier to provide: "Woman of the East," "Essence of Womanhood," "Girls" (or "Daughters"), and "Children." But the first of these titles, *Asmat*, is harder to render in English, for the Urdu usage of this word has many connotations, from virginity to honor to propriety, in a verbal condensation which expresses inter-related preoccupations. That these journals came regularly into my family for roughly forty years is itself significant, for mine was not, in metropolitan terms, an educated family; we lived in a small village, far from the big urban centers, and I was the first member of this family to finish high school or drive an automobile. That two generations of women and children in such a family would be part of the regular readership of such journals shows the social reach of this kind of publishing. Much literature, in short, revolved around the issues of femininity and propriety, in a very conservative sort of way.

But then there were other writers as well, such as Meer Hadi Hassan Rusva who challenged the dominant discourse and wrote his famous *Umrao Jan Ada* about those women for whom Urdu has many words, the most colorful of which can be rendered as "women of the upper chamber": women to whom men of property in certain social milieux used to go for instruction in erotic play, genteel manner, literary taste, and knowledge of music. The scandal of Rusva's early 20th-century text is its proposition that since such a woman depends upon no one man, and because many men depend on her, she is the only relatively free woman in our society. He obviously did not like Nazir Ahmed's work, but I must also emphasize that the ironic and incipient "feminism" of this text is not a reflection of any westernisation. Rusva was a very traditional man and was simply tired of certain kinds of moral posturing. Meanwhile, the idea that familial repressions in our traditional society were so great that the only women who had any sort of freedom to make fundamental choices for themselves were the ones who had no "proper" place in that society—that subversive idea was to re-appear in all kinds of ways when the next major break came in the forms of Urdu narrativity, in the 1930s, under the banner not of nationalism but of the Progressive Writers Union which was a cultural front of the Communist Party of India and had come into being directly as a result of the united front policy of the comintern after 1935.

Critical realism became the fundamental form of narrativity thereafter, for roughly two decades. "Nation" was certainly a category used in this narrative, especially in the non-fictional narrative, and there was an explicit sense of sociality and collectivity, but the categories that one deployed for that sense of collectivity were complex and several, for what critical realism demanded was that a critique of others (anti-colonialism) be conducted in the perspective of an even more comprehensive, multi-faceted critique of ourselves: our class structures, our familial ideologies, our management of bodies and sexualities, our idealisms, our silences. I cannot think of a single novel in Urdu between 1935 and 1947, the crucial year leading up to decolonisation, which is in any direct or exclusive way about "the experience of colonialism and imperialism." All the novels that I know from that period are predominantly about other things: the barbarity of feudal landowners, the rapes and murders in the houses of religious "mystics," the stranglehold of moneylenders upon the lives of peasants and the lower petty bourgeoisie, the social and sexual frustrations of school-going girls, and so on. The theme of anti-colonialism is woven into many of those novels but never in an exclusive or even dominant emphasis. In fact, I do not know of *any* fictional narrative in Urdu, in the last roughly two hundred years, which is of any significance and any length (I am making an exception for a few short stories here) and in which the issue of colonialism or the difficulty of a civilizational encounter between the English and the Indian has the same primacy as, for example, in Forster's *A Passage To India* or Paul Scott's *The Raj Quartet*. The typical Urdu writer has had a peculiar vision, in which he/she has never been able to construct fixed boundaries between the criminalities of the colonialist and the brutalities of all those indigenous people who have had power in our own society. We have had our own hysterias here and there, far too many in fact, but there has never been a sustained, powerful myth of a primal innocence, when it comes to the colonial encounter.

The "nation" indeed became the primary ideological problematic in Urdu literature at the moment of independence, for our independence too was peculiar: it came together with the partition of our country, the biggest and possibly the most miserable migration in human history, the biggest bloodbath in the memory of the sub-continent: the gigantic fratricide conducted by Hindu, Muslim and Sikh communalists. Our "nationalism" at this juncture was a nationalism of mourning, a form of valediction, for what we witnessed was not just the British policy of divide and rule, which surely was there, but our own willingness to break up our civilizational unity, to kill our neighbors, to forego that civic ethos, that moral bond with each other, without which human community is impossible. A critique of others (anti-colonial nationalism) receded even further into the background, entirely overtaken now by an even harsher critique of ourselves. The major fictions of the 50s and 60s—the shorter fictions of Manto, Bedi, Intezar Hussein; the novels of Qurrat ul Ain, Khadija Mastoor, Abdullah Hussein—came out of that refusal to forgive what we ourselves had done and were still doing, in one way or another, to our own polity. There was no quarter given to the colonialist; but there was none for ourselves either. One *could* speak, in a general sort of way, of "the nation" in this context, but not of "nationalism." In Pakistan, of course, there was another, overriding doubt: were we a nation at all? Most of the leftwing, I am sure, said No.

VIII

Finally, I also have some difficulty with the way Jameson seems to understand the epistemological status of the dialectic. For, what seems to lie at the heart of all the analytic procedures in his text is a search for, the notion that there *is*, a unitary determination which can be identified, in its splendid isolation, as the source of all narrativity: the proposition that the "third world" is a *singular* formation, possessing its own unique, unitary force of determination in the sphere of ideology (nationalism) and cultural production (the national allegory).

Within a postmodernist intellectual milieu where texts are to be read as the utterly free, altogether hedonistic plays of the signifier, I can well empathise with a theoretical operation that seeks to locate the production of texts within a determinate, knowable field of power and signification. But the idea of a *unitary* determination is in its *origins* a pre-marxist idea. I hasten to add that this idea is surely present in a number of Marx's own formulations as well as in a number of very honorable, highly productive theoretical formations that have followed, in one way or another, in Marx's footsteps. It is to be seen in action, for example, even in so recent a debate as the one that followed the famous Dobb-Sweezy exchange and which came to be focused on the search for a "prime mover" (the issue of a unitary determination in the rise of the capitalist mode of production in Western Europe). So, when Jameson implicitly invokes this particular understanding of the dialectic, he is in distinguished company indeed.

But there is, I believe, a considerable space where one could take one's stand between (a) the postmodernist cult of utter non-determinacy and (b) the idea of a unitary determination which has lasted from Hegel up to some of the most modern of the marxist debates. For, the main thrust of the marxist dialectic, as I understand it, is comprised of a *tension* (a mutually transformative relation) between the problematic of a final determination (of the ideational content by the life-process of material labor, for example) and the utter historicity of multiple, interpenetrating determinations, so that, in Engels' words, the "outcome" of any particular history hardly ever corresponds to the "will" of *any* of those historical agents who struggle over that outcome. Thus, for example, I have said that what constitutes the unity of the world is the global operation of the capitalist mode of production and the resistance to that mode which is ultimately socialist in character. But this constitutive fact does not operate in the same way in all the countries of Asia and Africa. In Namibia, the imposition of the capitalist mode takes a directly colonial form, whereas the central fact in India is the existence of stable and widespread classes of capitalist society within a post-colonial bourgeois polity; in Vietnam, which has already entered a post-capitalist phase, albeit in a context of extreme devastation of the productive forces, the character of this constitutive dialectic is again entirely different. So, while the problematic of a "final determination" is surely active in each case it is constituted differently in different cases, and literary production must, on the whole, reflect that difference.

What further complicates this dialectic of the social and the literary is that most literary productions, whether of the "first world" or of the "third," are not always available for that kind of direct and unitary determination by any one factor, no matter how central that factor is in constituting the social formation as a whole. Literary texts are produced in highly differentiated, usually very over-determined contexts of competing ideological and cultural clusters, so that any particular text of any complexity shall always have to be placed within the cluster that gives it its energy and form, before it is totalised into a universal category. This fact of over-determination does not mean that individual texts merely float in the air, or that "totality" as such is an impossible cognitive category. But in any comprehension of totality, one would always have to specify and historicize the determinations which constitute any given field; with sufficient knowledge of the field, it *is* normally possible to specify the principal ideological formations and narrative forms. What is not possible is to operate with the few texts that become available in the metropolitan languages and then to posit a complete singularization and transparency in the process of determinacy, so that all ideological complexity is reduced to a single ideological formation and all narratives are read as local expressions of a metatext. If one does that, one shall produce not the knowledge of a totality, which I too take to be a fundamental cognitive category, but an idealization, either of the Hegelian or of the positivist kind.

What I mean by multiple determinations at work in any text of considerable complexity can be specified, I believe, by looking briefly at the problem of the cultural location of Jameson's own text. This is, ostensibly, a first-world text; Jameson is a US intellectual and identifies himself as such. But he is a US intellectual of a certain kind; not everyone is able to juxtapose Ousmane and Deleuze so comfortably, so well; and he debunks the "global American culture of postmodernism" which he says is *the* culture of his country. His theoretical framework, moreover, is marxist, his political identification socialist—which would seem to place this text in the second world. But the particular energy of his text—its thematics, its relation with those other texts which give it its meaning, the very narrative upon which his "theory of cognitive aesthetics" rests—takes him deep into the third world, valorizing it, asserting it, filiating himself with it, as against the politically dominant and determinant of his own country. Where do *I*, who do not believe in the Three Worlds Theory, in which *world* should I place his text: the first world of his origin, the second world of his ideology and politics, or the third world of his filiation and sympathy? And, if "all third-world texts are necessarily" this or that, how is it that his own text escapes an exclusive location in the first world? I—being who I am—shall place it *primarily* in the global culture of socialism (Jameson's second world—my name for a global resistance) and I shall do so not by suppressing the rest (his US origins, his third world sympathies) but by identifying that which has been central to all his theoretical undertakings for many years.

These obviously are not the only determinations at work in Jameson's text. I shall mention only two others, both of which are indicated by his silences. His is, among other things, a *gendered* text. For, it is inconceivable to me that *this* text could have been written by a US *woman* without some considerable statement, probably a full-length discussion, of the fact that the bifurcation of the public and the private, and the necessity to re-constitute that relation where it has been broken, which is so central to Jameson's discussion of the opposition between first-world and third-world cultural practices, is indeed a major preoccupation of first-world women writers today, on both sides of the Atlantic. And, Jameson's text is determined also by a certain *racial* milieu. For, it is equally inconceivable to me that *this* text could have been written by a *black* writer in the US who would not also insist that black literature of this country possesses this unique third-world characteristic that it is replete with national allegories (more replete, I personally believe, than is Urdu literature).

I point out the above for three reasons. One is to strengthen my proposition that the ideological conditions of a text's production are never singular but always several. Second, even if I were to accept Jameson's division of the globe into three worlds, I would still have to insist, as my references not only to feminism and black literature but to Jameson's own location would indicate, that there is right here, within the belly of the first world's global postmodernism, a veritable third world, perhaps two or three of them. Third, I want to insist that within the unity that has been bestowed upon our globe by the irreconcilable struggle of capital and labour, there are increasingly those texts which cannot be easily placed within this or that world. Jameson's is not a first-world text, mine is not a third-world text. We are not each other's civilizational Others.

7 Re-Orientalism
The Perpetration and Development of Orientalism by Orientals

Lisa Lau

Introducing Re-Orientalism

Almost three decades ago, Edward Said identified and articulated the processes of Orientalism, the relationship of power and dominance where the Oriental was submitted to being made the Oriental. As illustration of the concept, Said used the example of Flaubert's encounter with an Egyptian courtesan, "which produced a widely influential model of the Oriental woman; she never spoke of herself, she never represented her emotions, presence, or history. He spoke for and represented her. He was foreign, comparatively wealthy, male, and these were historical facts of domination that allowed him not only to possess Kuchuk Hanem physically but to speak for her and tell his readers in what way she was 'typically Oriental'" (Said 1978: 6). Said's argument was that Flaubert's situation in relation to Kuchuk Hanem illustrated a parallel situation to that between the Occident and the Orient.

Orientalism has long been evident in the literature written about South Asia from the days of colonialism, which began with non-South Asians writing and representing the Indian Sub-Continent and its people. However, even in contemporary South Asian literature in English by South Asians, the process of Orientalism can be seen to be still occurring. The curious development over these few recent decades is that Orientalism is no longer only the relationship of the dominance and representation of the Oriental by the non-Oriental or Occidental, but that this role appears to have been taken over (in part at least) by other Orientals, namely, the diasporic authors. This process of Orientalism by Orientals is what I will be terming as 'Re-Orientalism' for the purposes of this article, which is the same relationship of the powerful speaking for and representing the other, who is all but consigned to subalternism. In Re-Orientalism, we have the curious case in

Lisa Lau, "Re-Orientalism: The Perpetration and Development of Orientalism by Orientals." *Modern Asian Studies*, 43(2), 2009: 571–590. Reproduced by permission of Cambridge University Press.

Postcolonial Studies: An Anthology, First Edition. Edited by Pramod K. Nayar.
Editorial material and organization © 2016 John Wiley & Sons, Ltd.
Published 2016 by John Wiley & Sons, Ltd.

which the positionality of the powerful is simultaneously that of the insider and out-sider, where the representing power can be simultaneously self and other.

Because diasporic writers are based mainly in the Occident, some may regard this simply as Orientalism, as it has ever been, but I would argue that there has been a difference, because these diasporic authors can be identified as Orientals to some extent, culturally, ethnically, etc. They are not completely alien to the Orient, but derive both ancestry and identity from the Orient (and indeed many have very immediate and strong links to the Orient). However, they are located outside of the Orient, and relative to the writers based within South Asia, diasporic South Asian writers are in a position of power and dominance, particularly where the issue of literary representation and image construction is concerned.

Even the most cursory of observations will note the dominance of this literary sub-genre by the diasporic authors, which, for working purposes, we can designate as those based outside South Asia. In a previous article, I have already argued that apparently "… it is predominantly the diasporic women writers who are the creators and keepers of the global literary image of South Asian culture, and this trend looks set to continue" (Lau 2005: 238). In terms of sheer numbers, not to mention visibility and accessibility, the output of the diasporic authors simply overwhelms that of the home authors[1] (those writing from within South Asia), and in the literary arena, the very positionality of these diasporic authors has enabled them, voluntarily or otherwise, to re-orientalise.

This issue is an increasingly sensitive one, as can be seen from Perera's volatile response to Salgado's article about Sri Lankan writers; Salgado is quoted as having said, "Their [migrant writers'] residence in metropolitan centres and access to Western publishers gives them an international readership and the potential for publicity that is the envy of their counterparts in Sri Lanka …" (Salgado 2004: 6). Perera's tart response is that "Sri Lankan writers are not necessarily 'envious' of their expatriate counter-parts' success … but they are justifiably aggrieved when those whose artistic integrity is occasionally compromised because they have become pawns of the publishing industry are given undue prominence. The manner in which Salgado has constructed the above sentence and its tone suggests (perhaps unintentionally) that she is in some way amused by the Sri Lankan writers' apparent discomfiture" (Perera 2005: 241). The testiness of Perera's response indicates fairly strong undercurrents of dissatisfaction and even indignation over the disadvantageous or adverse positionality of home writers relative to their diasporic or expatriate counterparts.

Re-Orientalism is perhaps, in part, an extension of the totalisation[2] that had always been present in the literature, imposing the culture, values, attitudes, etc., of a select minority as representative of the diverse majority. This article focuses on the sub-genre of contemporary South Asian women's literature in English to illustrate my points. The reins of domi-nant representation may have shifted hands from the foreign, male subject to the diasporic, semi-Oriental female, but the Orient continues to be orientalised. It is exactly as Said explained that "Orientalism depends for its strategy on this flexible positional superiority … in a whole series of possible relationships with the Orient without ever losing him the relative upper hand" (Said 1978: 7). Re-Orientalism observes that while this 'him' can be taken on by different parties, the relationship of unequal power relations has not changed.

At this juncture I must add that it is not my contention that the diasporic authors necessarily have any insidious intention, or consciously conceived aim, to re-orientalise, but that it is precisely their positionality, both individual and collective positionality, that has rendered this process of Re-Orientalism so widespread as to be almost inevitable in the genre.

Nevertheless, intentional or otherwise, representations of South Asia, of South Asian culture, and particularly of South Asian women by the women writers – representations which emphasise and explore the sensitivities, mindsets, expectations, characteristics of South Asian women – are being largely created from without South Asia by the diasporic writers, and imposed upon South Asia as representative of their identity, or at least, a significant part of their identity construction.

Culturally and socially speaking, the problem of representation has always been one which has plagued this region, from the regional scale to the local. India's neighbours have feared the cultural dominance of India, and Indians themselves have felt threatened by the linguistic, cultural, religious dominance from various subgroups and communities. Meenakshi Mukherjee articulated her fear of the erasure of the diversity of India, identifying the threat as coming from "the category of writers called 'The Third World Cosmopolitans,' who are globally visible, who are taught in postcolonial classrooms the world over, and who are hailed in the review pages of Western journals as interpreters and authentic voices of the non-Western world [who] hardly ever include a writer from India who does not write in English" (Mukherjee 2000). Apart from the issue of India's multi-lingual literary heritage, even if we are considering only the literature written in English, Mukherjee would still have cause to be concerned that it may still be the case that those taught in postcolonial classrooms the world over, hailed and feted by the Western world as interpreters and authentic voices, may still not include a writer from within South Asia.[3]

This is not to suggest that diasporic authors are all inaccurate and write distorted depictions; indeed, world literature owes some of its excellent pieces to very great South Asian authors who happen to be diasporic authors: Anita Desai, Amitav Ghosh, Rohinton Mistry, V. S. Naipaul, Michael Ondaatje, Salman Rushdie, Vikram Seth, to name but a few. However, this article focuses on the most recent developments, over the last 5 years, in the English literature produced by South Asian women writers, and an interesting, if slightly disturbing, trend seems to be emerging.

This article begins by identifying some of the patterns in the recent publications of South Asian women's writing, and proceeds to discuss some problematic trends emerging in this sub-genre which further muddy the already-troubled waters of representation and authenticity.

Analysis of Recent Trends in South Asian Women's Literature

This section analyses the publication of literature written in English from 2002 to 2006 (Table 1).

This table does not attempt to be a comprehensive list of all the writings in English by South Asian women in the last half decade, but it does compile a fair representation of the publications that are fairly well known, discussed on Internet forums and sites, and at least reasonably accessible, available either online and/or in major booksellers in the United Kingdom. The intention of a quick perusal of such a table is to observe trends, not attempt to produce statistical evidence.

Table 1 South Asian Women's Fiction 2002–2006

Re-Orientalism

Author	Year	Title	Publisher	Currently based in
Deepa Agarwal	2002	*If the Earth Should Move*	Srishti	India
Thalassa Ali	2002	*A Singular Hostage*	Bantam	USA
Brinda Charry	2002	*The Hottest Day of the Year*	Penguin	India
Daya de Silva	2002	*The Days We Wished Would Never Come*	Vishva Lekha	Sri Lanka
Chitra Divakaruni	2002	*The Vine of My Desire*	Doubleday-Random House, New York	USA
Shama Futehally	2002	*Reaching Bombay Central*	Viking, Delhi	India
Yasmin Gooneratne	2002	*Masterpiece and Other Stories*	Indialog, New Delhi, India	Australia
Manju Kapur	2002	*A Married Woman*	India Ink	India
Bharti Kirchner	2002	*Darjeeling*	St. Martin's Press	USA
Vikay Lakshmi	2002	*Pomegranate Dreams*	Indialog, New Delhi, India	USA
Sharon Maas	2002	*Peacocks Dancing*	Harper Collins	UK
Amulya Malladi	2002	*A Breath of Fresh Air*	Ballantine	Denmark
Anita Nair	2002	*Ladies Coupe*	Chatto & Windus, London	India
Meera Nair	2002	*Video: Stories*	Pantheon	USA
Kavery Nambisan	2002	*On Wings of Butterflies*	Penguin	India
Amulya Malladi	2002	*A Breath of Fresh Air*	Ballantine, USA	Denmark
Preeti Singh	2002	*Circles of Silence*	Hodder & Stoughton, GB	India
Indu Sundaresan	2002	*The Twentieth Wife*	Pocket Books, USA	USA
Susan Viswanathan	2002	*The Visiting Moon*	India Ink	India
Nalini Warrior	2002	*Blues From the Malabar Coast*	TSAR Books	Canada
Monica Ali	2003	*Brick Lane*	Granta	UK
Shinie Antony	2003	*Barefoot and Pregnant*	Rupa, New Delhi	India
Rupa Bajwa	2003	*The Sari Shop*	Viking-Penguin, UK	India
Kavita Daswani	2003	*For Matrimonial Purposes*	Penguin Putnam	USA
Githa Hariharan	2003	*In Times of Siege*	Viking, Delhi	India
S. Mitra Kalita	2003	*Suburban Sahibs*	Rutgers University Press	USA
Manju Kapur	2003	*A Married Woman*	Faber & Faber	India
Sorayya Khan	2003	*Noor*	Penguin	USA
Bharti Kirchner	2003	*Pastries*	St. Martin's Press	USA
Jhumpa Lahiri	2003	*The Namesake*	Houghton Mifflin, New York	USA
Shoba Narayan	2003	*Monsoon Diary*	Random House	USA
Cauvery Madhavan	2003	*The Uncoupling*	Penguin	Ireland
Amulya Malladi	2003	*The Mango Season*	Piatkus, London	Denmark
Rani Manicka	2003	*The Rice Mother*	Viking, London	UK
Bharati Mukherjee	2003	*Desirable Daughters*	Theia, USA	USA

(Continued)

Lisa Lau

Table 1 (Continued)

Author	Year	Title	Publisher	Currently based in
Preethi Nair	2003	*One Hundred Shades of White*	Harper Collins, London	UK
Manjula Padmanabhan	2003	*Kleptomania*	Penguin, India	India
Qaisra Sharaz	2003	*Typhoon*	Black Amber, London	UK
Sara Suleri	2003	*Boys Will Be Boys*	University of Chicago Press	USA
Kalpana Swaminathan	2003	*Ambrosia for Afters*	Penguin, India	India
Indu Sundaresan	2003	*The Feast of Roses*	Atria, USA	USA
K. R. Usha	2003	*The Chosen*	Penguin, India	India
Vasanthi Victor	2003	*When Peacocks Dance*	Trade Paperback	USA
Samina Ali	2004	*Madras on Rainy Days*	Farrar, Straus and Giroux, NY	USA
Thalassa Ali	2004	*A Beggar at the Gate*	Bantam	USA
Shauna Singh Baldwin	2004	*The Tiger's Claw*	Knopf	Canada
Kankana Basu	2004	*Vinegar Sunday*	Indialog	India
Nonda Chatterjee	2004	*The Strawberry Patch*	Penguin, India	India
Kavita Daswani	2004	*The Village Bride of Beverly Hills*	Penguin Putnam	USA
Anita Desai	2004	*The Zig Zag Way*	Houghton Mifflin	India-USA
Shashi Deshpande	2004	*Moving On*	Penguin, ND	India
Chitra Divakaruni	2004	*Queen of Dreams*	Doubleday-Random House	USA
Hina Haq	2004	*Sadika's Way*	Academy Chicago Publishers	USA
Miriam Karim	2004	*My Little Boat*	Penguin India	India
Sikeena Karmali	2004	*A House by the Sea*	Vehicle Press, Montreal	Uzbekistan
Uzma Aslam Khan	2004	*Trespassing*	Harper Collins	Pakistan
Sharon Maas	2004	*The Speech of Angels*	Harper Collins	UK
Amulya Malladi	2004	*Serving Crazy with Curry*	Ballantine	Denmark
Manorama Mathai	2004	*Whispering Generations*	Srishti Publishers, Delhi	India
Jaishree Misra	2004	*Afterwards*	Penguin	UK
Preethi Nair	2004	*Beyond Indigo*	Harper Collins, London	UK
Maniza Naqvi	2004	*Stay With Me*	Sama Publishers, Pakistan	USA
Lakshmi Persaud	2004	*Raise the Lanterns High*	AmberBlack Books	UK
Sebha Sarwar	2004	*Black Wings*	Alhamra Publishings, Islamabad	USA

Table 1   (*Continued*)

Author	Year	Title	Publisher	Currently based in
Sonia Singh	2004	*Goddess for Hire*	Harper Collins	USA
Thrity Umrigar	2004	*First Darling of the Morning*	Harper Collins, New Delhi	USA
Neela Vaswani	2004	*Where the Long Grass Bends*	Sarabande Books	USA
Usha Alexander	2005	*Only the Eyes Are Mine*	Frog Books, Mumbai, India	USA
Shinie Antony	2005	*Kardamom Kisses*	Rupa, New Delhi	India
Shinie Antony	2005	*Planet Polygamous: 36 Tales of Infidelity*	Indialog, New Delhi	India
Abha Dawesar	2005	*Babyji*	Anchor	USA
Nilani de Silva	2006	*Monsoon Dreams*	Books Surge LLC	Denmark
Amulya Malladi	2005	*Song of the Cuckoo Bird*	Ballantine	Denmark
Rani Manicka	2005	*Touching Earth*	Hodder & Stoughton	UK
Shani Mootoo	2005	*He Drown She in the Sea*	Grove Press	Canada
Bharati Mukherjee	2005	*The Tree Bride*	Hyperion	USA
Anita Nair	2005	*Mistress*	Penguin, India	India
Asita Prabushankar	2005	*Beyond the Call of Voice*	Frog Books, Mumbai, India	USA
Kamila Shamsie	2005	*Broken Verses*	Harcourt	Pakistan-UK-USA
Lavanya Sankaran	2005	*The Red Carpet*	Dial Press, Random House	India
Thalassa Ali	2006	*The Companions of Paradise*	Bantam	USA
Kiran Desai	2006	*The Inheritance of Loss*	Atlanta Monthly Press	USA
Sonia Faleiro	2006	*The Girl*	Penguin Viking	India
Thrity Umrigar	2006	*The Space Between Us*	William Morrow	USA

It is not possible to classify in a black and white manner as to which authors are diasporic, which are sojourner authors,[4] and which are home authors, but the right-most column on the table informs us as to where the author is (currently) based. In many cases, these diasporic authors are first-generation diaspora, who have been born, bred, even educated in South Asia before migrating abroad for studies and/or career purposes. Only in a very few instances are these authors of the second generation of diasporic South Asians.

The most obvious trend to be observed over these last 5 years is the consistent one that the diasporic authors are continuing to easily outnumber the home authors, in some cases, by quite a large margin. Their dominance on the literary scene of this sub-genre is unmistakable and undeniable, not only in terms of the weight of numbers, but also in terms of distribution, promotion, marketing and availability of their writings. In some cases, such as in 2004, the ratio of diasporic authors to home authors seems overwhelming; of the twenty-four authors listed in 2004, only six are based in

South Asia (five in India and one in Pakistan), with the majority of the diasporic authors seeming to be based in the United States.

Not only are the South Asian-based authors in clear minority, the higher profile books are more likely to be the diasporic ones, which are simply better marketed, more widely distributed and generally available in major booksellers, and consequently, better known. Penguin India[5] has been responsible for bringing many of the home authors' works to global attention (or at least to global accessibility) and introducing new authors to the reading public, intentionally giving opportunities as they do to debut writers. Were it not for Penguin India, this table would contain significantly fewer home writers than it already does.

Amongst the home authors, Indian authors were prevalent, with Pakistani authors (or authors of Pakistani descent) beginning to come to the fore more than ever before, and just within this list, there are over half a dozen: Thalassa Ali, Hina Haq, Sorayya Khan, Uzma Aslam Khan, Kamila Shamsie, Qaisa Sharaz, and Sara Suleri. The significant presence of Pakistani writers in the recent years would reward further research, but the case nevertheless remains that even though there may be some new strengths emerging amongst the home authors of non-Indian descent, only one of these Pakistani authors (Uzma Aslam Khan) is actually based in Pakistan. (Shamsie is based in Pakistan, the United Kingdom and the United States, making her perhaps more a sojourner author than a diasporic author.) The others are diasporic authors, with five of the seven listed here currently based in the United States.

Another trend we could observe from this table is that a fair number of these authors are producing books quite prolifically, even within this short period of less than 5 years, many have written two or more books: Shinie Antony publishing in 2003, and two books in 2005, Amulya Malladi also publishing three novels in 2002, 2003, 2005, and a good number of authors managing two publications in this 5-year period: Anita Nair (2002, 2005), Thrity Umrigar (2004, 2006), Chitra Divakaruni (2002, 2004), Indu Sundaresan (2002, 2003), Thalassa Ali (2002, 2004), Kavita Daswani (2003, 2004), Rani Manicka (2003, 2005), Bharati Kirchner (2002, 2003). These, of course, do not include those with other publications also appearing close on the heels of others prior to 2002. This may indicate a remarkable demand for more in this sub-genre which the publishers are trying to supply, and apparently from a relatively limited pool of authors.

The list contains a reasonable combination of 'old-timers' like Anita Desai, Shashi Deshpande, Bharati Mukherjee, who have been publishing steadily for several decades, and of debutants, Samina Ali, Brinda Charry, Lavanya Shankar, and others. This indicates that there is space and opportunity for development in this sub-genre, but the significant fact is that most of the space and opportunity is currently being occupied by diasporic writers.

The clear trend of the diasporic authors having dominance in numbers is in itself a matter of interest rather than concern, but the consequences of this trend may well be that not only have diasporic authors taken on the construction and representation of South Asian women's identity on the global literary arena and skewed the portrait, but that the sheer weight of their presence and volume of their voices may be gradually relegating the home authors ever closer to subalternism. It can hardly be thought that there are simply more and better South Asian women writers in the diaspora than there are to be found within South Asia, but clearly some writers are geographically better located to have access to publication of literature written in English, and thus, by virtue of their positionality, are able to re-orientalise South Asia.

As said before, many diasporic South Asian authors have in the past made valuable contributions to the body of South Asian literature in English, but the remainder of this article focuses on analysing the problematic techniques of some South Asian women writers, who have in recent years employed writing techniques which are particularly insidious in the process of Re-Orientalism, and which provoke the rise of its negative effects. And, what are these negative effects? They are not far different from the problems Said identified with Orientalism: "My fears are distortion and inaccuracy, or rather the kind of inaccuracy produced by too dogmatic a generality and too positivistic a localized focus" (Said 1978: 8).

The Problems of Re-Orientalism

Ironically, although as can be easily seen, in terms of sheer numbers and availability, diasporic writers overwhelm this writing scene, in many cases, diasporic literature displays internal insecurities, particularly over self-identity. Diasporic authors are, of course, having to negotiate the hybridity of their cultures, the multiplicity of their attachments and allegiances, "obliged to deal in broken mirrors, some of whose fragments have been irretrievably lost", as Rushdie (1983: 76) notes. "Shaken about the globe, we live out our fractured lives. Enticed or fleeing, we re-form ourselves, taking on partially the coloration of our new backgrounds. Even our tongues are alienated and rejoined – a multiplicity that creates richness and confusion" (Seth 2005: 403). The fragmented nature of the definition of self, the nostalgia, the learnt chameleon abilities, the sense of looking back or referencing a distant place, of being strangers in a strange land whether they are in the East or West, has naturally led a number of diasporic South Asian women writers to be notably prickly concerning the thorny issue of authenticity.

Some deal with this issue constructively, seeking to learn, requesting that their manuscripts and ideas be double checked, asking local residents of South Asia whether they have described and represented rituals, traditions, cultural and regional practices accurately and as they currently stand, in sum, looking to expertise from within South Asia to provide confirmation, and in a sense, further authentication. There are others which simply sidestep this issue and regard it as no issue at all.

However, there are still others who employ techniques in claiming authenticity, which result in adverse effects, because these techniques seek less to negotiate and tease out the complications and nuances of identities, than to stridently depict South Asian women and culture oversimplistically, stereotypically, and often sensationally. They are perhaps those who play to the gallery and target a readership that, they comfortably suppose, has little or no knowledge of South Asian customs and cultures. It is these techniques which re-orientalise the genre of South Asian literature in a particularly heavy-handed manner, which I identify as being problematic, contributing as they do to distortion and inaccuracy, and indeed, the kind produced by "too dogmatic a generality" and "too positivitistic a localised focus" (Said 1978: 8).

Not all methods of Re-Orientalism are necessarily damaging ones in terms of representation even if they do reinforce the dominance of a certain group, but in terms of contemporary diasporic writings (English) by South Asian women writers, there are a few troubling trends emerging that could, if they became too prevalent, seriously distort the representations in a way which could be harmful to both genre and the wider identity and image construction of South Asian women.

The remainder of this article therefore focuses on three characteristic problems within contemporary diasporic South Asian women's literature, each of which exacerbates the damaging processes of re-orientalising.

The First Problem: The Necessity of Being Recognisably South Asian

One common distortion of the images constructed by diasporic South Asian women writers occurs because of the overemphasis on being South Asian, and the almost rigid depiction of adherence of fictional South Asian characters to traditional ideals associated with South Asia. It is almost as if in an attempt to over-compensate and pre-emptively defend accusations of not being a 'real' South Asian, plotlines, narratives and characters in writings by quite a number of diasporic South Asian women writers are under pressure[6] to demonstrate so-called recognisably 'South Asian characteristics'. This is in stark contrast to the literature by home South Asian writers, where the South Asian context just happens to be the background, the setting in which the narrative just happens to occur, rather than being the reason for the narrative in a deterministic fashion.

To take an example by way of illustration, I will discuss and compare two contemporary novels: the first by Anita Nair, an Indian author based in Bangalore, and whose *Ladies Coupe* was published in 2001, and the other by a diasporic Indian author, Amulya Malladi, who published *The Mango Season* in 2003.

Ladies Coupe is almost a montage of short stories. It begins with a protagonist who wishes to change her life completely, and begins by making what is, for her, an unusual journey alone, from her home in Bangalore to Kanyakumari. In the course of the long train journey, the protagonist meets five other women who ride in her carriage. These passengers tell their life stories to one another, and this sets the protagonist contemplating her own life. The six women come from various different situations and walks of life – some are married (with varying degrees of happiness), some are mothers, one is still a schoolgirl, most of them are middle- or upper-class women, but one of them is poor and uneducated. Nair provides her reader with a range of women and a spectrum of different stories and experiences. The fact that they are all Indian women does not prevent them from having very diverse lives and fortunes from one another, and also from having private and even secret lives. In fact, they merely seem to happen to be Indian women, and while this identity colours their experiences, it in no way determines them, let alone reducing the range of their experiences.

This is diametrically different from Malladi's *The Mango Season*, which on the very first page, in its prologue, we read, "Even though I was raised in a society where arranged marriage was the norm, I always thought it was barbaric to expect a girl of maybe twenty-one years to marry a man she knew even less than the milkman ..." (Malladi 2003: 1). It is revealing that the author feels the need to explain that "arranged marriage is the norm", an explanation one would seldom, if ever, come across in the writings by home Indian writers, where if something is the norm, it is hardly necessary to highlight it any further. This explicit and deliberate explanation of cultural norms is one of the defining characteristics of diasporic writing, and one of its most distinctive features. It is also one of the reasons why diasporic writing so often comes across as rather heavy handed.

The Mango Season is about an Indian girl who had been studying in the United States for 7 years, and at the late but still marriageable age of 27, is engaged to an African American man. The plot focuses on her returning to her home and family in India to break this news to them, news which she dreads will come as a blow to a family of Telegu Brahmins living in Andhra Pradesh, who want to marry their family members to others of the same caste, from the same state, and also Telegu speaking. The entire story and the life of the protagonist is apparently centred around the fact that she is Indian, with all the non-negotiable cultural baggage that being an Indian girl is made out to bring. The Re-Orientalism of this novel seems motivated by the need to make the protagonist and her family recognisably Indian and displaying ostentatiously Indian behavioural traits, such as being completely intolerant of their daughters marrying outside race and caste. Like all stereotypes, this depiction contains partial truths but omits significant conditions, subtleties and differences. The constant rehashing of a handful of stereotypes which supposedly accord with the expected representation of Indians is part of the damaging workings of Re-Orientalism as practiced by a fair number of diasporic South Asian women writers.

In both these novels, the protagonists are depicted as wishing to break the mould, wanting to do things which are conventionally frowned upon but which they are convinced would bring them individual happiness. In both stories, the protagonists take this step, and encounter various forms of protests and dismay and anger from family members, but the difference is in how this is portrayed. *Ladies Coupe* told a realistic and engaging tale of humans interacting and conflicting, whereas *The Mango Season* sensationalised the 'defiance', depicted the cultural conventions as insurmountable barriers, and placed the notion of 'Indian culture' at the centre of the conflict, as the reason for the conflict. This implicit insistence on there being such an entity as 'Indian culture', and moreover such a rigid, fixed, definitive one, is exactly the over-dogmatic generality Said wrote of, but nevertheless a fairly common representation of India and Indians as imposed on them by diasporic Indian women writers.

The Second Problem: Generalisations and Totalisations

A second and oft-occurring problem with the writings of diasporic South Asian women writers is the inclination to generalise with totalisations, sweeping statements appearing more the norm than the exception. For example, in her short story "Stop the Insanity", Bella Mayani writes, "Coming from a generation in which you are in purdah till the wedding night and then become a servant for his family and less than human for your husband ..." Another such example by Qirone Adhikary reads, "Being excitable, passionate, tempestuous – in a word, Bangali [sic] – she starts telling her story, interspersed by sobs, hyperventilation, hysteria, hair-pulling and chest-pounding."

These generalisations serve to reinforce fables and stereotypes of Indian women being bound in perpetual servitude, and Indians as a race being hysterical and histrionic people. In making such statements, some diasporic South Asian women writers are seen to be propagating certain cultural images, implying and sometimes quite explicitly, that may apply only in a certain section of society, is in fact the norm in the wider

South Asian community. In circulating stereotypes, pandering to clichés, carelessly totalising, writers like Mayani and Adhikary play a role in providing skewed and/or misleading information on South Asian, re-orientalising in damaging ways.

It is probable that this negative re-orientalisation by diasporic South Asian women writers via sweeping generalisations and thus glaring inaccuracies not to mention painful distortions may not entirely be with the cold commercial intent of exoticising in order to increase sales, nor even to brandish their colour and ethnicity as trophies. Being themselves in the less-than-comfortable position of constantly re-negotiating their own identities, these writers may have an unwritten agenda to simultaneously claim insider knowledge (and status), while somehow distancing themselves enough to claim the position of knowledgeable representative or emissary.

These diasporic writers wish to claim that they have the best of both worlds, implicitly offering themselves to a western readership as a guide and translator of South Asian customs, wishing to gain credibility as having authentic accounts to impart, but not wanting for a moment to be confused with being a local South Asian. To secure the latter end, rather simplistic strategies tend to be employed, such as firmly demonstrating a criticism of backward traditions and patriarchal oppressions, and equally firmly demonstrating a love of what is regarded as western ideals of equality, individual autonomy, freedom of speech, etc.

The Third Problem: Truth Claims

It is increasingly common in the last decade for South Asian women writers, both home and diasporic ones, to write novels blurring the boundaries between fiction and autobiography. In itself, this technique is not one which necessarily adversely impacts the process of Re-Orientalism. Authors such as Manju Kapur (*Difficult Daughters*, 1998), Manjula Padmanabhan (*Getting There*, 2000), Thrity Umrigar (*First Darling of the Morning*, 2004) have written thoughtful and sensitively handled stories drawing richly from their own lives, and, in thus doing, have stretched the genre to include some exciting new spaces.

However, there are a number of diasporic authors who have employed the blurring of boundaries between fiction and autobiography in exploitative ways, enabling a very skewed representation to be mainstreamed by virtue of possessing a 'truth claim'. A 'truth claim' is the case of an author writing a tale that very closely resembles his or her own life-story, a tale which usually glorifies and justifies the actions of the protagonist, but a tale which is written under the guise of being fiction. Some writers even go so far as to issue vociferous disclaimers to the effect that this is not biographical writing although the plot corresponds extremely closely to their lives. So while the writing remains ostentatiously fiction, it can implicitly claim a larger degree of authenticity and validity through the closeness of personal experience. (This closeness of personal experience is made known to the reader, who is given enough information to easily notice the resemblance between the author's biography and the fiction.) The staking or establishing of this truth claim, even though implicit, renders the representation more powerful and influential than is proportionate, further contributing to the distorted representation of South Asian women, further re-orientalising.

In this section, I will use two examples to illustrate cases of diasporic authors making 'truth claims'. These two instances are also cases in which the writing deliberately increases the chasm between 'the West' and India, further relegating India into the position of 'the other', further compelling Indian culture into 'otherness'.

The first is example is Jaishree Misra's writings, author of *Ancient Promises*, *Accidents Like Love and Marriage*, and *Afterwards*. Misra is a Keralite who grew up in an army family in Delhi, and who in her own words, "did fall in love at seventeen … lost my teenage sweetheart to an English University and arranged marriage." After a 10-year period of silence, Misra met her sweetheart "in circumstances not dissimilar to those described in the book [*Ancient Promises*], effectively ending my marriage". Misra has a daughter with a learning disability. She moved to England when she was 32.

Ancient Promises, Misra's debut novel published in 2000, tells Janaki's story; a Keralite who grew up in Delhi with what was seen as modern western social influences and a relatively 'free' lifestyle. At 17, Janaki who fell in love but elected to give up her love relationship in order to please her parents and also because her boyfriend intended to go abroad to study at an English university. Janaki's loving parents arranged a prestigious marriage for her with a 'traditional' Keralite, an arrangement that would require her to reside in a joint-family system and to interact in a culture and language relatively alien to her. The story unfolds predictably enough that Janaki becomes an unhappy daughter-in-law and wife, and although not abused or deprived by her husband or in-laws, she is emotionally unfulfilled, socially alienated, and feels unappreciated and unwanted. When a mentally handicapped daughter is born to her, Janaki grows more defiant of her in-laws and resolves to take her daughter away to a country where facilities for her care and education are better. Coincidentally discovering her ex-lover now works in England, Janaki leaves her husband to join her lover and eventually, after a struggle, manages to take her daughter with her to start a new life in England with her ex-lover.

The reader can hardly help but be aware that the plot closely echoes Misra's own life story, especially since the novel includes a few paragraphs in 'Author's Note' describing Misra's life.

Misra states, "I am not Janu [Janaki's nickname], just as no character is ever the one it is based on." This seems an inadvertent admission that Janaki was at least based on Misra's own character. She also claims, "While I had, obviously, a husband and in-laws in my first marriage, I wish to state quite clearly that they bear no resemblance to the corresponding characters in the book." The interesting thing to note in this disclaimer is the phrase "corresponding characters", rather than just 'characters'.

Questions will invariably be raised as to how Misra's 'corresponding character', Janaki, was handled in the novel, and with what intentions. Were Misra's vindication and defense of Janaki's actions and choices a deliberate vindication and defence of her own?[7] On being asked how much of her story was true, Misra apparently "took refuge in the non-committal reply" that her novel was "*semi*-autobiographical" (Misra 2000: 307). Misra writes that as a new novelist, the truth was something she did not "especially wish to be bothered with". She thought it "mundane, restrictive" and discovered fiction was "quite simply much more fun" (Misra 2000: 307). Misra appears to reject responsibility for the biographical elements in her writing by simply disclaiming and denying it. Simple rejection of her originally held ethics and responsibilities also appears to be Janaki's method of dealing with life; 'corresponding' perhaps, to her author's method?

Remarkably, Misra uses the plot of her life story not only in one of her novels but in yet another. *Afterwards*, published in 2004, begins with broadly the same plot and characters as *Ancient Promises*. In *Afterwards*, the story begins with a young Indian man from England who goes to stay in India for a short period of time, becomes greatly attracted to his neighbour, Maya, a lovely young woman with a mentally handicapped daughter, and whose husband largely neglects her. The young woman runs off to England with Rahul, the protagonist, bringing her daughter with her in hope of giving her daughter a better future in a country where her disability could be better addressed. The desertion of her husband, marriage, and life in India by Maya is portrayed in the same rose-tinted manner as Janaki's desertion and adultery. The rest of *Afterwards* deals with the events following the sudden death of Maya, the young woman, in a car accident, and how Rahul deals with her passing, and with the daughter who survives her.

Misra is not the only diasporic South Asian author to employ this technique of blurring fact and fiction in an insidious manner. Nilani de Silva is a diasporic Sri Lankan author who has just published her debut novel, *Monsoon Dreams*, in which the life of the glorified heroine closely resembles de Silva's own life experiences. Nilani de Silva grew up in Sri Lanka, did her master's degree in England, and now lives in Stockholm with her husband and three children: one daughter and two sons. This information is provided on the back cover of her book along with her photograph.

The protagonist of *Monsoon Dreams*, Anushka, also grew up in Sri Lanka. Anushka goes to the United Kingdom without visa or destination for her trip, is put in a detention camp for 3 weeks, and deported back to Sri Lanka. She then goes back to the United Kingdom a few years on (having thrown away her passport with "Deported" stamped in it and acquired a new one) to do a master's course in Leicester University. The novel's concluding chapters tell us that Anushka meets a Swede, gets married, moves to Sweden to live, and has an apparently perfect family life with her husband and three children: one daughter and two sons. de Silva concludes the novel with Anushka flying back to Sri Lanka with her husband and children, and, after being cast out, ostracised and despised by her Sri Lankan friends and family for two decades, she is welcomed back with open arms and apparent delight, and she is feted and admired universally – no explanations are provided.

Presenting semi-autobiographical stories as fiction, with their implicit truth claims, confers validity and authenticity on stories which may not be representative, adding to the distortion of the portrait being collectively painted of Indian culture and Indian women's lives by the diasporic writers. The Re-Orientalism in these cases is particularly insidious because South Asia is always placed in juxtaposition as not only The Other, but practically 'The Opposite' of the West, emphasising the exotica elements of South Asian culture. These diasporic authors, using their semi-autobiographical fiction, speak for and present a South Asia which they lay claim to have insider knowledge of, re-orientalising South Asian society and consigning it to an increasingly subaltern position.

Concluding Thoughts

It is a slightly curious situation which has arisen that inheriting a legacy of Orientalism, Orientals should then themselves be guilty of perpetrating Orientalism. Said already noted that even Orientalism in the past had not been without the consent of Orientals, nor were Orientalists all Westeners, but active and widespread Re-Orientalism is a relatively recent development, at least on the literary scene in the South Asian genre. Said noted that "Each age and society recreates its 'Others'" (Said 1978: 332), and it seems in this age that the body of diasporic South Asian writing is at least partly responsible for Re-Orientalism, for continuing to keep the Orient as 'The Other'. This is one of the salient differences between the writings of diasporic and home South Asian women writers that this sense of 'othering' South Asia is usually notably absent from the productions of the home authors.

This article does not seek to point the finger of accusation at all diasporic South Asian women writers, and indeed there are some who far from re-orientalising, have actually knit the different elements of two seemingly opposing cultures onto a single and wider framework. Moreover, it is also understood that diasporic authors necessarily have different concerns from home authors, consequently different themes in their writings, for after all, "A theory or idea that travels to different contexts get partly or fully accommodated or incorporated, and is 'to some extent transformed by its new uses, its new position in a new time and place'… transformed by the reception context, their meanings, reproduced and reshaped to fit local agendas" (Amireh and Majaj 2000: 3).

Diasporic South Asian women's writings which frequently discuss the negotiation of a hyphenated identity, feeling as Lahiri puts it, "intense pressure to be … loyal to the old world and fluent in the new, approved of on either side of the hyphen" (Lahiri 2006), may be more conducive to understanding the diasporic search for and construction of identities, and the balancing of hybridities and multiple realities, than as a representation of South Asia or South Asian women.

However, the influences on and preoccupations of diasporic writing have resulted in much of this literature insistently setting up South Asia and 'the West' as binaries. The presence and voices of diasporic South Asian women writers have been so dominant within the genre that in terms of how South Asia is constructed in narrative, it continues to be set in opposition to 'the West', thereby locking both into stereotypes, continuing to define the Orient relative to the Occident, in a word, to Re-Orientalise. At its worst, this has resulted in skewed, distorted and dogmatically generalised representations of South Asia, its culture and its women's positionalities in particular.

It is somehow mildly ironic that when the opportunity arose to move away from Orientalism, the direction some diasporic authors have chosen to move in is Re-Orientalism.

Notes

[1] As defined in a previous article, the term home author implies that "the writer resides within South Asia, or is a national of a South Asian country. It is not possible to ascertain the nationality of every diasporic writer, but the purpose of this differentiation between home and diasporic writers is less to determine the political status of the authors, and more to register the geographical residences and locations of the writers, which goes a long way in influencing the writing" (Lau 2005).

[2] Defined by Uma Narayan as casting values or practices which pertain only to specific privileged groups within the community as values of the "culture" as a whole.

[3] The one exception may be Arundhati Roy's novel, *The God of Small Things*, which has been globally acknowledged.

[4] Writers who travel frequently from within South Asia to other countries, living and working and dividing their life and time between two or more countries.

Lisa Lau

⁵ On their website, they state that "Penguin Books India is the largest English language trade publisher in the subcontinent." (http://www.penguinbooksindia.com/home.asp 19/01/06)
⁶ It is not clear where the source(s) of this pressure lies.
⁷ For example, When Janaki, still married and mother of a toddler, meets her ex-lover after 9 years apart and goes with him the very same afternoon to his house for sexual intercourse, Misra elects to describe it thus: "I succumbed wholly and entirely to Arjun and to my own being, without the slightest feeling of fear or shame ....."

References

Amulya Malladi, *The Mango Season* (London: Piatkus, 2003).

Anita Nair, *Ladies Coupe* (London: Chatto & Windus, 2002).

Edward Said, *Orientalism* (Harmondsworth: Penguin, 1978).

Edward Said, 'Travelling theory' in Amireh and Majaj (eds.), *Going Global: The Transnational Reception of Third World Women Writers* (New York and London: Garland Publishing, 2002). Wellesley Studies in Critical Theory, Literary History, and Culture. Vol. 27.

Jaishree Misra, *Ancient Promises* (London: Penguin, 2000).

Jaishree Misra, *Afterwards* (India: Penguin, 2004).

Jumpa Lahiri, 'My two lives' in *Newsweek*, March 6, 2006, http://www.msnbc.msn.com/id/11569225/site/newsweek/.

Lisa Lau, 'Making the difference: The differing presentations and representations of South Asia in the contemporary fiction of home and diasporic South Asian women writers' in *Modern Asian Studies*, Vol. 39, No. 1 (2005), pp. 249–269.

Manju Kapur, *Difficult Daughters* (Kent: Faber & Faber, 1998).

Manjula Padmanabhan, *Getting There* (London: Picador, 2000).

Meenakshi Mukherjee, *The Perishable Empire. Essays on Indian Writing in English* (New Delhi, India: Oxford University Press, 2000).

Minoli Salgado, 'Writing Sri Lanka, reading resistance: Shyam Selvadurai's Funny Boy and A. Sivanandan's When Memory Dies' in *Journal of Commonwealth Literature*, Vol. 39, No. 1 (2004), pp. 5–18.

Nilani de Silva, *Monsoon Dreams* (Colombo: Vijitha Yapa, 2006).

Salman Rushdie, *The Eye of the Beholder. Indian Writing in English* (London: Commonwealth Institute, 1983).

S. W. Perera, 'Sri Lanka' in *Journal of Commonwealth Literature*, Vol. 40, No. 4 (2005) pp. 235–251.

The Women of South Asian Descent Collective, *Our Feet Walk the Sky. Women of the South Asian Diaspora* (San Francisco: Aunt Lute, 1993).

Thrity Umrigar, First Darling of the Morning. Selected Memories of an Indian Childhood (New Delhi, India: HarperCollins, 2004).

Uma Narayan, *Dislocating Cultures. Identities, Traditions and Third-World Feminism* (New York: Routledge, 1998).

Vikram Seth, *Two Lives* (London: Little Brown, 2005).

8   Postcolonial Remains

Robert JC Young

WHAT REMAINS OF THE POSTCOLONIAL? Has it already perished, leaving only its earthly relics, forgotten books, abandoned articles floating in cyberspace, remnants of yellowing conference programs? So one might think on reading the obituary announced by *PMLA* in 2007: "The End of Postcolonial Theory?"[1] There, a group of apparently former postcolonial critics pronounced "it" over. The members of the forum, for the most part, discussed postcolonial theory as if it were an entirely American phenomenon, and even there, as something of interest only to English departments. In that Anglophone characterization, the forum concurred with the more recent view of the French political scientist and director of research at the prestigious Centre national de la recherche scientifique (CNRS) in Paris, Jean-François Bayart—except that for Bayart the postcolonial is far too alive, prompting him to write a whole book objecting to postcolonial theory as an unpleasant Anglo-Saxon intrusion into the purity of French thought.[2] Despite its noisy appearance in contemporary French intellectual culture, Bayart dismisses the postcolonial by claiming that its sources are entirely French, even if its identity is Anglo-Saxon, which therefore makes "postcolonial theory" altogether superfluous.

The desire to pronounce postcolonial theory dead on both sides of the Atlantic suggests that its presence continues to disturb and provoke anxiety: the real problem lies in the fact that the postcolonial remains. Why does it continue to unsettle people so much? The aspiring morticians of the postcolonial concur in scarcely relating it to the world from which it comes and for which it claims to speak: that outside Europe and North America. The desired dissolution of postcolonial theory does not mean that poverty, inequality,

Robert JC Young, "Postcolonial Remains." *New Literary History*, 43(1), 2012: 19–42. © 2012 *New Literary History*, The University of Virginia. Reproduced by permission of Johns Hopkins University Press.

exploitation, and oppression in the world have come to an end, only that some people in the U.S. and French academies have decided they do not want to have to think about such things any longer and do not want to be reminded of those distant invisible contexts which continue to prompt the transformative energies of the postcolonial.

"Postcolonialism" is not just a disciplinary field, nor is it a theory which has or has not come to an end. Rather, its objectives have always involved a wide-ranging political project—to reconstruct Western knowledge formations, reorient ethical norms, turn the power structures of the world upside down, refashion the world from below. The postcolonial has always been concerned with interrogating the interrelated histories of violence, domination, inequality, and injustice, with addressing the fact that, and the reasons why, millions of people in this world still live without things that most of those in the West take for granted. Clean water, for example. This is not to say that "the West" is an undifferentiated economic and social space, and nor, of course, are those countries outside the West, as economic booms transform nations such as Brazil, China, and India into new dynamics that contribute to a shifting of paradigms of economic and political power that have certainly modified the sensibility of colonial dependency.[3] Far from being over, the twenty-first century is already the century of postcolonial empowerment. The widespread anxiety that this produces provides a further reason why Western academics want to deny the realities of the postcolonial.

The postcolonial will remain and persist, whether or not it continues to find a place in the U.S. academy, just as it did not need academia to come into existence. Postcolonial theory came from outside the United States,[4] and has never involved a singular theoretical formation, but rather an interrelated set of critical and counterintuitive perspectives, a complex network of paronymous concepts and heterogeneous practices that have been developed out of traditions of resistance to a global historical trajectory of imperialism and colonialism. If anti- and postcolonial knowledge formations were generated by such circumstances, peripheral as they may seem to some metropolitan intellectuals, now, as in the past, the only criterion that could determine whether "postcolonial theory" has ended is whether, economic booms of the so-called "emerging markets" notwithstanding, imperialism and colonialism in all their different forms have ceased to exist in the world, whether there is no longer domination by nondemocratic forces (often exercised on others by Western democracies, as in the past), or economic and resource exploitation enforced by military power, or a refusal to acknowledge the sovereignty of non-Western countries, and whether peoples or cultures still suffer from the long-lingering aftereffects of imperial, colonial, and neocolonial rule, albeit in contemporary forms such as economic globalization.[5] Analysis of such phenomena requires shifting conceptualizations, but it does not necessarily require the regular production of new theoretical paradigms: the issue is rather to locate the hidden rhizomes of colonialism's historical reach, of what remains invisible, unseen, silent, or unspoken. In a sense, postcolonialism has always been about the ongoing life of residues, living remains, lingering legacies.[6]

The British Prime Minister David Cameron, for example, forgot to consult his Special Advisor in Postcolonial Studies before he led his November 2010 trade and business delegation to China, a delegation billed as the biggest ever in British history. Cameron clearly had not been reading Amitav Ghosh's 2009 novel, *Sea of Poppies*, either.[7] When the British ministers arrived at the Great Hall of the People in Beijing for the reception, they wore their Remembrance Day poppies in their jacket lapels, as people in Britain do every year in the week running up to Remembrance Sunday. The poppies symbolize the sacrifice of more than a million servicemen who have died on active service since the First World War. The flowers reminded the Chinese, however, of a rather different poppy—the opium poppy, and therefore the Opium Wars fought by Britain against China in 1839–42 and 1856–60, which among other things, led to the concession of the British colony of Hong Kong. When Prime Minister Cameron and the British delegation arrived wearing their poppies in November 2010, the Chinese officials asked that they remove them, since they considered these poppies "inappropriate." In an echo of the famous incident when the British ambassador Earl McCartney refused to kowtow before the Emperor in 1793, Cameron refused to back down and insisted on wearing his poppy. When he followed this refusal with a lecture on human rights, the historical irony was apparent to all but himself.

Whereas the British often forget the Opium Wars, just as Austria, France, Germany, Italy, Japan, Russia, the United Kingdom, and the United States forget the international "eight-nation alliance" sent to Peking to put down the Boxer "Rebellion" in 1898–1901, in China the historical injustices of its semicolonial past lingers on in official memory, repeated tirelessly to every tourist who visits the Summer Palace in Beijing, where visitors are reminded that the original was destroyed by British and French troops in 1860. The perpetrators of violence forget far sooner than those subjected to their power. Derrida used to argue that there will always be something "left over" and in that sense the postcolonial will always be left over. Something remains, and the postcolonial is in many ways about such unfinished business, the continuing projection of past conflicts into the experience of the present, the insistent persistence of the afterimages of historical memory that drive the desire to transform the present.

The postcolonial remains: it lives on, ceaselessly transformed in the present into new social and political configurations. One marker of its continuing relevance is the degree to which the power of the postcolonial perspective has spread across almost all the disciplines in the humanities and social sciences, from classics to development theory to law to medieval studies to theology—even sociology, under the encouragement of postcolonial-minded scholars such as Arjun Appadurai and Paul Gilroy, has abandoned its former narrow national focus to turn to an interest in globalization in the present.[8] So many disciplines have been, so to speak, postcolonialized, along with the creation of related subdisciplines such as diaspora and transnational studies, that this remarkable dispersal of intellectual and political influence now makes it difficult to locate any kind of center of postcolonial theory: reaching into almost every domain of contemporary thought, it has become part of the consciousness of our era. Inevitably, in each discipline in which it has been taken up, the postcolonial has been subtly adapted and transformed in different ways—in sociology's turn to globalization, for example, the historical perspective so fundamental to postcolonial studies gets largely removed. But how has the postcolonial itself changed in response to the historical transformations that have been occurring in the last decades, and, even more to the point, how should it change in the future? What conditions and situations have risen to a new visibility? What have been the greatest challenges to postcolonial analysis? And, continuing in the necessary mode of perpetual autocritique, what aspects of its own theoretical framework have limited the reach of its own radical politics?

In a reconsideration of the role of the postcolonial in the era of the twenty-first century that attempts to begin to answer these questions, I will focus on contemporary issues that have involved what can be characterized as the politics of invisibility and of unreadability: indigenous struggles and their relation to settler colonialism, illegal migrants, and political Islam. None of these fall within the template of the classic paradigm of anticolonial struggles, but they all involve postcolonial remains as well as prompting political insights that show the extent to which the postcolonial remains. What can be learned from them? They all invoke historical trajectories that have hitherto been scarcely visible, but which offer potential resources for critiques and transformations of the present. Since political Islam has highlighted questions of religion and secularism, I consider the example of the history of practices of toleration in Islamic societies, in which otherness is included rather than excluded. This in turn prompts the need for significant theoretical revision of a problematic concept appropriated by postcolonial theory from philosophy and anthropology: the idea of the Other.

I. The Politics of Invisibility

What has changed in the twenty-first century, from a postcolonial perspective? To answer the question in the first instance conceptually rather than historically, what the postcolonial eye can see more clearly now are the ways in which, like the conflictual meanings of Cameron's poppy, postcolonial remains operate in a dialectic of invisibility and visibility.

One of the most influential theoretical innovations of postcolonial theory has been the appropriation and reconceptualization of Antonio Gramsci's concept of subaltern classes.[9] Modified and typically singularized into the idea of the subaltern, this concept has enabled subaltern historians and cultural critics to recover a whole arena of historical agency that had remained invisible while history was written according to exclusive protocols of nationalist movements or class conflict. The preoccupation with the subaltern can be interpreted more generally to suggest the extent to which the postcolonial has always been concerned with a politics of invisibility: it makes the invisible visible. This is entirely paradoxical to the extent that its object was never, in fact, invisible, but rather the "invisible visible": it was not seen by those in power who determine the fault lines between the visible and the invisible. Postcolonialism, in its original impulse, was concerned to make visible areas, nations, cultures of the world which were notionally acknowledged, technically there, but which in significant other senses were not there, rather like the large letters on the map that Jacques Lacan characterizes as the structure of the unconscious. To take a simple example, until very recently, histories of "the world" were really histories of European expansion. Even today, so-called "world literature" is only belatedly being transformed from its long historical containment within the same Eurocentric paradigm. So the politics of invisibility involves not actual invisibility, but a refusal of those in power to see who or what is there. The task of the postcolonial is to make the invisible, in this sense, visible.

Within academia, this task begins with the politics of knowledge, with articulating the unauthorized knowledges, and histories, of those whose knowledge is not allowed to count. In the world beyond, politics itself often involves a practice of acting in order to make the invisible visible so that its injustices can be redressed. A postcolonial perspective will be more alert in detecting the signs of such transformations, but it, too, can be belated in its recognition of the campaigns of subaltern historical agents. This would be the case with indigenous struggles, which have only recently come to be regarded as a central issue for postcolonial politics. The obvious reason for this is that, drawing from the history of anticolonialism that formed part of so many national narratives of emancipation, postcolonial studies did not give equal weight to the history of indigenous activism in what are, for the most part, long-standing postcolonial countries, such as those of North and South America. At the same time, there was a political-theoretical issue: indigenous activism uses a whole set of paradigms that do not fit easily with postcolonial presuppositions and theories—for example, ideas of the sacred and attachment to ancestral land. This disjunction, however, only illustrates the degree to which there has never been a unitary postcolonial theory—the right of return to sacred or ancestral land, for example, espoused by indigenous groups in Australia or the Palestinian people, never fitted easily with the postmodern Caribbean celebration of delocalized hybrid identities.[10] Postcolonial theory has always included the foundational and the antifoundational at the same time, indeed, it could be characterized by the fact that it has simultaneously deployed these apparently antithetical positions, a feature entirely missed by those who criticize it either as being too Marxist or alternatively too postmodern, though the fact that it is criticized on both counts is indicative. Suspicions about the foundations of established truths are not necessarily incompatible with, and indeed are more likely to be prompted by, the memories of an empirical, experienced history of colonial rule.[11]

While it is debatable whether the "third world" as such exists today, there is little doubt that the fourth world emphatically remains. With the demise of the third, the fourth world has risen to a new prominence, its issues thrown into starker visibility. At the beginning of the twenty-first century, a transformation was underway in the long history of continued contesting resistance by tribal peoples, a history whose written articulation began with Bartolomé de Las Casas's *A Short Account of the Destruction of the Indies* (1542), whose institutional initiatives included the setting up of the Aborigines' Protection Society by Thomas Hodgkin in 1837, and which culminated many years later in the global political campaign that produced the UN Declaration on the Rights of Indigenous Peoples in 2007.[12] The scope of indigenous struggles, and the ways in which they have been articulated through the power of the UN Declaration and by the use of the internet and other media as a means of facilitating transnational affiliations and forms of political organization, has meant that in a new and powerful way, indigenous peoples have been able to assert themselves effectively and very visibly within an international arena against the power of the sovereign states that have oppressed them for centuries. The narrative of emancipation whose goal was national liberation through the Leninist model of the capture of the central state apparatus has been supplemented by a political dynamic that in earlier decades was only visible to radical intellectuals such as the Peruvian socialist José Carlos Mariátegui.[13] Despite these successes, however, oppressive forms of "fourth-world" internal colonialism continue to operate on every continent of the earth, particularly with respect to exploitation of natural resources that shows scant regard to the lives and lands of indigenous peoples. Who, though, is authorizing such exploitation? Thinking indigenous struggles through a postcolonial frame points to a topic that has remained comparatively neglected: settler colonialism.

In the arena of postcolonial studies, settler colonialism has managed, through its invocation of the tradition of colonial nationalism, to affiliate itself to the emancipatory narratives of anticolonial struggles—witness the widely circulated *The Empire Writes Back* of 1989, which assimilates all forms of colonial liberation into a single narrative of freedom from the imperial metropolis.[14] What this passes over is the degree to which settler colonies themselves practiced a form of "deep colonialism," a term recently revived by Lorenzo Veracini, which underscores the extent to which the achievement of settler self-governance enforced the subjection of indigenous peoples and indeed increased the operation of oppressive colonial practices against them.[15] In almost any settler colony one can think of, settler liberation from colonial rule was premised on indigenous dispossession. The emancipatory narrative of postcolonialism was not accessible to those who remained invisible within it. Indeed for them, national emancipation produced a more overpowering form of colonial rule, often enforced by a special contract for indigenous peoples distinct from that between settlers and metropolis.

The postcolonial question that remains is how indigenous emancipation, that is the acquisition of land and rights not mediated or already conditioned by the terms of settler emancipation from which indigenous people were excluded, can be achieved. It also becomes clear that the same paradigm of sovereignty through dispossession applies to many nonsettler colonies, where indigenous minorities or historically excluded groups have found the freedom of a postcolonial sovereignty to mean comparable or even worse forms of oppression than under colonial rule, even if the political structure is that of a democracy. One leading marker of the nationalist drive for domination over heterogeneous peoples can often be located in the history of the language policies of the independent national state. What we need to recognize now is that the postcolonial narrative of emancipation and the achievement of sovereignty was in many cases deeply contradictory. The civil wars and the often continuing civil unrest that, in many cases, followed independence have often been the product of the nationalist creation of a deep colonialism that has sought to make indigenous people or other minorities invisible.

Today this practice has in certain respects become more widespread with respect to other kinds of minorities across the world. As some minorities make themselves conspicuous, others must live their lives unseen. Paradoxically, it can often be the visible minorities who are in certain respects invisible. In Beirut, when you go to a restaurant, the waiters who serve you will generally be local people, of one sort or another. But hidden below, and only visible when you go downstairs and glance into the kitchens, you see that those cooking and washing up are Bangladeshi. While indigenous peoples have been making themselves visible, a new tricontinental has developed. Not this time the militancy of the Organization of Solidarity of the People of Africa, Asia, and Latin America (OSPAAL) that was developed in the 1960s, but a new subaltern tricontinental of migrants from the poorer countries of Africa, Asia, and Latin America, often fleeing state or other forms of violence, moving around the world in search of jobs and livelihood. These people form an invisible tricontinental diaspora, made up of refugees, internally displaced persons, stateless persons, asylum seekers, economic migrants, illegal migrants, irregular migrants, undocumented migrants, illegal aliens. They remain almost invisible, working in unregulated conditions in building sites, hotel kitchens, brothels, cleaning lavatories, on farms, until for a moment they are thrown into sharp relief: when the media reports that the boat onto which too many are crowded has capsized off Lampedusa during the journey from Libya to Italy or off the coast of Morocco on the way to Spain or off the coast of Sudan on the way to Saudi Arabia or shipwrecked on the Australian coast at the end of the journey from Sri Lanka. These invisible migrants only move into visibility when they die in this way, or when they are arrested by border police or when they suddenly appear in their thousands fleeing war, as in the case of those who fled to the borders of Egypt and Tunisia from Libya in the spring of 2011—or when they are demonized by politicians in election campaigns. Otherwise, they remain as the invisible support system of the economies of Western countries, the Middle East, and elsewhere, hidden in their fugitive illegality or kept separate in workers' compounds, visible only in the fruit and vegetables they have picked that are bought at the supermarket, or the sleek skyscraper that rises on the distant horizon. Invisible until the moment, as imagined in the 2004 film *A Day Without a Mexican*, when the "illegals" suddenly disappear and the whole of California grinds to a halt. How do you make the invisible visible? the film asks. The answer: you take it away.

The problem with *A Day Without a Mexican*, on the other hand, is that it encourages the idea that migration is just a Western issue, whereas the reality is that, of the 43 million displaced people in the world, the great majority find themselves in poorer countries outside the West. From a Western perspective, these are the really invisible invisible people. Many of them are children. Often without papers or documentation, they are denied the basic rights of the nation-state and are left only with the interminable inaccessibility of the dream of self-emancipation. Whereas migration theorists tend to examine migration issues generated through specific case studies, postcolonial theory can provide a theoretical and historical framework for understanding new phenomena such as the globalization of migration, and for thinking through the question of how to reformulate the emancipatory aims of anticolonial struggle outside the parameters of the nation-state. Today, it is no longer a question of a formal colonizer-colonized relation. That is for the most part over, though versions of it persist in the settler colonies, and its legacy continues to inflect attitudes, assumptions, and cultural norms in the world beyond. What we have instead is something almost more brutal, because there is no longer even a relation, just those countless individuals in so many societies, who are surplus to economic requirements, redundant, remaindered, condemned to the surplusage of lives full of holes, waiting for a future that may never come, forced into the desperate decision to migrate illegally across whole continents in order to survive.[16] The postcolonial question now is how to make the dream of emancipation accessible for all those people who fall outside the needs of contemporary modernity.

II.   Unreadable Islam

The second shift in the visible landscape of postcolonial studies involves a comparable transformation, in which the struggles of people who were visible but not seen or taken seriously by global populations in positions of power and their political and cultural leaders have moved into political prominence—with the re-emergence of radical Islam. As with indigenous struggles, this political story goes far back into the colonial era, and it is also one that the fight for national sovereignty, which formally ended the period of colonial rule, left in different ways unresolved. The resurgence of

Islam and of indigenous struggles both developed out of remainders, the living-on remnants of the conflicts of the past. The two "new" political issues that postcolonial studies has begun to engage with more actively in recent years are in fact two of the oldest, once regarded as outmoded and finished, but which refused to die. What was repressed and left without resolution has re-emerged, articulated in new forms. And what disconcerts Westerners the most is when it becomes starkly visible: hence the Western obsession with women who choose to assert their beliefs visibly by wearing the veil.

While the question of representing or covering (up) Islam was always central to the work of Edward W. Said, it was not a major preoccupation of postcolonial studies as a whole in its first twenty or so years of existence. If, since its inception in academic form with Said's *Orientalism* in 1978, postcolonial thinking broadly defined has become integrated within dominant cultural and institutional practices, then one reason why it found relatively easy acceptance was because it tended to sideline not only the Israel-Palestine conflict, but also the question of Islam and the role of religion in anticolonial struggle more generally—this despite the fact that *Orientalism* was published just a year before the Iranian revolution of 1979.[17] Postcolonial activism transforming the Eurocentrism and ingrained cultural assumptions of the West and advocating greater tolerance and understanding of people who displayed ethnic and cultural differences received a dramatic setback, however, with the political reactions that followed the 9/11 attacks on the United States in 2001.

At this point, a different history of the twentieth century was thrown into a violent visibility, highlighting not the "world" and "cold" wars, or the anticolonial struggles of Africa, Asia, and Latin America, but focusing instead on the Iranian Revolution in 1979 and the Israel-Palestine conflict, together with related events such as the Russian invasion of Afghanistan. The Caribbean model of creolization and hybridity, championed so effectively by postcolonial theorists and adapted without too much difficulty to Britain's own earlier models of integration with respect to the Irish, other Catholics, Jews, and other minorities, or with respect to American hyphenated minority identities, no longer seemed so obviously appropriate as a way forward.[18] The fact that Salman Rushdie, the best-known advocate for the new hybridized cultural model, had come into conflict with Muslims across the world with the controversy around *The Satanic Verses* that erupted in 1989 was transformed from what had at the time seemed like a particular incident epitomizing the clash of artistic and religious values into a symptomatic and indicative marker in this newly visible history.

In retrospect, the arguments around *The Satanic Verses* demonstrate the degree to which the new forms of Islam were effectively unreadable to those in the West. What had been little noticed was that Islam had also been changing—a difference highlighted in the contrast between the Iranian Revolution, which developed into an attempt to transform Iran into a properly Muslim state, and the Rushdie controversy ten years later, which revolutionized traditional configurations of Islamic activism. In so far as both events were precipitated from Iran, many assumed that the Revolution and the fatwa were part of the same Islamic "fundamentalism" that had been identified in the militant Islamic political parties in Algeria, Egypt, and Pakistan, entirely missing the point that the former were Shiite and the latter Sunni. Despite the amply funded Wahhabi Islamism promoted from Saudi Arabia, the Rushdie controversy was the first moment in the production of a new syncretic configuration of Islam, whose only connection with Wahhabism was its transnationalism, albeit of a rather different kind.[19]

Westerners tend to read all forms of radical Islam as the same, that is, as fundamentalism, itself ironically a Western concept, as is wittily suggested in Mohsin Hamid's *The Reluctant Fundamentalist* of 2007.[20] The *Satanic Verses* controversy was taken to initiate a conflict between the new Western cultural language of hybridity and the language of the pure, of a fundamentalist Islam. Instead the controversy signaled the appearance of a new hybrid Islam, marked by the fact that the Shia fatwa was supported internationally all over the Muslim world by people and groups whose own ideologies were radically different from each other, including Sunni Wahhabi and fundamentalist groups such as Jamaah al-Islamiyyah of Egypt or the Jamaat-e Islami of Pakistan. As Faisal Devji has persuasively argued, the international reach of the agitation against Rushdie was the first sign of a new globalized form of Islam, whose next major manifestation would be spectacularly launched with 9/11.[21] What Devji calls the "democratic" tendency of Al Qaeda, eschewing all traditional forms of Muslim authority, drawing on an international range of supporters, and employing a heady eclectic mixture of Muslim motifs, often more Shiite than Sunni despite its Sunni identity, marks the emergence of a new heterogeneous Islam whose objective, far from being focused on the traditional takeover of control of the individual nation-state on the Leninist, anticolonialist, or Islamist model, involves the liberation of the "Holy Land" of Islam from a century of Western domination and pins its hope on a transnational utopia created through the return of the Caliphate.

Far from being "fundamentalist," Al Qaeda is a dialectical product of the long-standing interaction of Islam with the West, as eclectic in its ideology as in the provenance of its often Westernized operatives, and for that reason it sees the West as its own intimate enemy and draws on a form of anticolonial rhetoric to establish its objectives, even if these are transnational rather than national. It was hardly surprising, in this context, to discover that Osama Bin Laden spent his time in hiding videotaping himself watching videos of himself on TV. Al Qaeda's political objectives are equally bound to its antagonist, preoccupied as it is with the historical grievance of the history of Western imperialism in the Middle East. In his public statements, Bin Laden explicitly traced the origins of Al Qaeda's grievance back to the dismemberment of the Ottoman Empire in 1919 and the abolition of the Ottoman Caliphate by the new National Assembly of Atatürk's Turkey on 3 March 1924. Already by 1919, the French and British occupation of Istanbul had produced the "terrorist" or military response of the Khilafat Movement across Asia Minor and, particularly, British India, and in some respects Al Qaeda represents a modern recreation of that extraordinary transnational campaign.[22] Its irreverence for tradition, and its secularization of Islam, suggests that in certain ways Al Qaeda could be seen as one of the many factors that encouraged the Arab Spring of 2011 by breaking the deadlock between Islamic fundamentalism and repressive auto-cracies operating as Western fiefdoms. While the Arab Spring has remained predominantly national in terms of political objectives, it has also involved an insistent transnationalism in its outlook, with demands for democratic participa-tion arising across almost every nation in the region. We should not be surprised that, as in any history of anticolonial or antiauthoritarian struggle, the results have varied, depending on the particular situation in each country. What is clear, however, is that Islamic cultures are not, and have never been, characterizable according to a singular form of Islam, even if this idea persists in Western perceptions.

While an intense interest in postcolonial theory has developed in Islamic countries, in 2001 Islam was just as unreadable for most postcolonial theorists in the West as for everyone else.[23] The development of Islamism in its diverse configurations as a contemporary oppositional discourse and practice to Western interests in the Middle East caught postcolonial studies off-guard. Developed out of the secular tradition of Marxism, in which religion was deemed to merit little serious attention, postcolonial studies has had comparatively little to say about the diverse modalities of Islamic resistance effected through unorthodox global formations in the present or the past, focusing for the most part on what is presented as the new Western imperialism in Afghanistan and Iraq. On the assumption that Al Qaeda and fundamentalisms of various kinds can all be identified with each other and identified with the return of religion to the sphere of the political, one major response has involved an interest in secularism. Contemporary work on secularism originally developed in the context of the rise of Hindutva ideology in India, and in many ways, India's Shiv Sena can be regarded as the Hindu equivalent of Afghanistan and Pakistan's Taliban. The problem, however, with much work on secularism has been that it begins from a stance that is already committed to secularism itself. This means that it takes a position within the political as well as philosophical spectrum of the very situation that it seeks to resolve, for the separation of the religious from the worldly is exactly what is being contested.[24] What are the alternatives to a secularism whose claim to stand outside the conditions of belief is seen by some to be partial rather than impartial? What can secularism learn from nonsecular societies, where secular practices may nevertheless still figure in significant ways in an alternative configuration with the religious? One approach has been to interrogate the concept and philosophy of religion, as in the work of Talal Asad.[25] Another would be to re-examine different concepts and practices of social and political toleration within nonsecular societies, for toleration is a concept which, as we shall see, is by no means exclusively identifiable with secularism or the West—indeed Western secularism can itself produce intolerant behavior, such as the banning of the niqab in France. In the face of forms of communalism that in many different countries of the world such as India, Pakistan, Sri Lanka, Iran, Israel-Palestine, Northern Ireland, may have a fundamentally religious basis, there are limits to what Western secularism, and the liberal forms of toleration that are often assumed to follow from it, can offer. How can populations learn again how to live with each other without the imposition of state secularism? What can be learned from the historical example of nonsecular societies? It is here that a postcolonial interest in alternative cultural forms and in histories that are given limited attention in the West can be constructive. This may need to begin with thinking the unthinkable.

Even though I have spent most of my life writing against imperialism in various ways, it is time for some forms of empire to be re-examined in at least one respect: empire's structure of government was necessarily organized around the accommodation of diversity, albeit according to an imperial hierarchy.[26] Empire was destroyed by the principle of nationalism, the drawback of which was often an intolerant principle of autonomous ethnic or cultural homogeneity that tended to disallow heterogeneity and difference, seeing them as a problem to be resolved or eliminated.

The huge (and unbearably costly, in terms of human life) movements of peoples at the times of the institution of the nation-states of Greece and Turkey, India and Pakistan, Israel and Palestine, are all material indicators of the antinomy between the modern concept of the nation and the ability of empires to sustain the diversity that preceded nation formation. An earlier example would be the expulsion of the Jews and Muslims at the time of the *Reconquista* in Spain in 1492.

III. *Convivencia*

What can nations, which represent the modern political form of the state, learn from the empires which they replaced? The initial drive to homogeneity within many post-colonial nation-states is in many cases only now (if at all) beginning to shift towards the cultivation of heterogeneity and toleration of difference, something that was fundamental to the practice of empire. I am not necessarily thinking of the British empire, though it was certainly a bizarrely heterogeneous institution, negotiating its diversity in the first instance by discounting other differences in favor of rank.[27] Today, in a world in which Islam is automatically connected by those in the West with fundamentalism and terrorism, there is an often-forgotten history that remains particularly relevant as a long-standing achievement of equitable relations between different communities, different people living in the same place, tolerating each other's differences. While Islamic Spain constitutes one of the reference points for Al-Qaeda's unorthodox *longue durée* account of Islamic history—a preoccupation that it shares, uncharacteristically, with Salman Rushdie—in the West it is rarely acknowledged that, prior to the Canadian invention of multiculturalism in the 1970s, the major and historically by far the longest example of successful multiculturalism in Europe was the Islamic state of al-Andalus in the tenth century, during the eight hundred odd years of Muslim rule in Spain. This has never been adequately acknowledged in Western assumptions of the superiority of its recent political systems. It was under the Caliphate of Cordoba (929–1031) that Cordoba became one of the greatest cities of medieval Europe and the Near East, a beacon of learning rivaled in that era only by Baghdad, with the largest library in Europe serving as the effective conduit of Arabic, Greek, and Latin philosophy and science into Renaissance Europe.[28]

What was unusual about Cordoba, certainly compared to other parts of Europe at that time, was that it was a multicultural society comprising Muslims, Jews, and Christians living peaceably together—*Convivencia*—and even engaging with each other convivially, for it was scholars of all religions who facilitated the reception and translation of the great philosophical texts into Arabic and the composition of classic writings such as Maimonides' *Guide for the Perplexed*, the major text of Kabbalah, the *Zohar*, and the Arabic rhymed prose narrative of Ibn al-Astarkuwi.[29] This intellectual work was the product of the environment created during the rule of Abd-ar-Rahman III (912–961) when, despite wars with the Christian kingdoms to the north, tolerance and freedom of religion was instituted as the marker of Islamic rule. Al-Andalus involved a thriving commercial as well as intellectual culture, one in which Muslims, Jews, and Christians lived together in a relative equanimity that would be unparalleled in Christian Europe until the last decades of the twentieth century. This is the world portrayed in the concluding pages of Rushdie's *The Moor's Last Sigh* (1995). J. M. Coetzee has commented on what he calls Rushdie's "provocative thesis": "that the Arab penetration of Iberia, like the later Iberian penetration of India, led to a creative mingling of peoples and cultures; that the victory of Christian intolerance in Spain was a tragic turn in history; and that Hindu intolerance in India bodes as ill for the world as did the sixteenth-century Inquisition in Spain."[30] The tolerant society of al-Andalus remains Europe's most sustained and successful experiment in communal living in a pluralistic society; yet, because it occurred under Muslim rule, it merits little discussion among analysts of multiculturalism or toleration today.[31] Similarly, there has been little discussion of contemporary Arab multiculturalism, such as can be found in some of the Gulf States, one of the closest modern equivalents to al-Andalus in political terms in a number of respects (including autocracy as well as tolerance of diversity). States such as Qatar, in which migrant noncitizens make up as much as three-quarters of the population, are producing complex, heterogeneous new cultural formations very different from Western multiculturalisms, even as they struggle to adjust to (or repress) demands for democracy, human and workers' rights. For similar reasons, there has been comparatively little analysis of the Islamic millet system, in which different communities were allowed to rule themselves under their own legal codes, despite the fact that remnants of its legacy lives on today in certain respects in many formerly Ottoman or Muslim countries, including Bangladesh, Egypt, Greece, India, Iran, Iraq, Israel, Jordan, Lebanon, Pakistan, Palestine, and Syria. Once again, we encounter postcolonial remains, hidden beneath the surface of modern national states, but living on, the past persisting in the present, but in what ways (legal, political, and social), with what effects—and with what possibilities for the future?

Although it is hardly the preferred narrative of the BJP, even today one still sometimes hears the claim being made in India that before British rule the different communities lived in harmony together, and that it was the British who destroyed this amicable concord with their divide-and-rule policy. If this were at all true, that time must refer to the Mughal era, when much of India was ruled on the basis of the Islamic *dhimma* system. There is not space here to analyze that institution in any substantial way, and I am certainly not proposing it as a model (but then which models are not imperfect?). The *dhimma* system was hardly a system of equal human rights and citizenship as we would think of them today, and there are many examples of abuses of various sorts in different places, or of limits to the forms and degrees of tolerance that it offered. However, the fact remains that, as even Bernard Lewis remarks, up until the end of Ottoman rule there were no large-scale massacres of Jews or Christians in Muslim lands comparable to those that took place in Europe.[32] Christians and Jews were not forced to submit to the harsh options of conversion, expulsion, or death offered to Muslims and Jews at the time of the *Reconquista* in Spain 1492. A system of fundamentally tolerant living together in difference obtained. When British Indian troops entered Baghdad in March 1917, there were more Jews living in the city than Arabs. The extraordinary cultural and ethnic heterogeneity of cities such as Alexandria or Smyrna at that time has now been completely lost, but the destruction of those heterogeneous societies has not formed part of postcolonial critique. While Europeans were engaging in a thousand years of internecine strife, with incessant war between states conducted in Europe and beyond, and perennial persecution of religious and racial minorities, the Islamic societies that stretched around the other side of the Mediterranean managed to create a long-lasting system of comparative tolerance of diversity and cultural syncretism that was only destroyed by European imperial greed and the rise of nationalism in the nineteenth century.

Wendy Brown has argued that tolerance is less an ethic or a virtue than a structure and discourse of power and a structure of governmentality, as if to expose its hidden flaw.[33] The *dhimma* system never pretended otherwise—it was a form of government—but this did not mean that its tolerance was not based on, or practiced without, a fundamentally ethical structure. Given the politico-religious framework, we might call this system one of dissent—the "absence of collective unanimous opinion"—the very opposite of the typical model of nationalism. It involved a system of coexisting dissenting communities: each community at variance with each other in its opinions, customs, and beliefs, while nevertheless respecting the autonomy of the other. It was not, in the manner of Jacques Rancière, dissensus in the sense of a fissure within the polity.[34] The structure of dissent was the fundamental basis of how the system was organized, not the oppositional form of the political to the juridical. If tolerance of others is a central aspect of communal organization, it would make no sense if there were no conflict, for tolerance means to endure, suffer, put up with, involving an ethics not only of acts, but of restraint, of forbearance in the face of forms of unsettling of the self, the disruptive ethos of being placed in translation.[35] Tolerance implies an active concept of duty as a primary part of any ethical life; its precepts become unreadable within an exclusively individualistic rights-based discourse. If, in practice, tolerance must always be qualified, nevertheless, like forgiveness, tolerance only has meaning if it is imprescriptible, unconditional, and unqualified at the same time.[36] These heterogeneous and aporetic divisions were fundamental to the *dhimma* system—the Muslims put up with the Christians and Jews, the Christian and Jews suffered the rule of the Muslims. Yet within this unsettling and imperfect cosmopolitan dissensus, tolerance, respect, and a mode of mutual living found its place.

Though we now tend to promote tolerance as a way of solving or avoiding social and political strife, the idea of an underlying conflict was fundamental to the idea of tolerance which forms the basis for the liberal Western tradition that was gradually instituted from the sevententh century onwards. We find it laid out most notably in John Locke's "Letter Concerning Toleration" of 1689.[37] Locke's letter proposed a radical solution to the question of religious differences and the role of the state. Whereas Thomas Hobbes had taken what we might call, anachronistically, the nationalist perspective and advocated the need for homogeneity of religion for the successful nondisruptive functioning of the state, Locke took the opposite view, and argued that it was more probable that dissent, and a plurality of religious groups, would create stability and prevent civil unrest. Locke argued that any attempt by the state to repress other religions is in fact more likely to produce civil unrest than if it allows them to proliferate. The state becomes stronger through the tolerance of heterogeneity, weaker by repressing it. Giving one church the authority of the state is insufficient. One of the logical paradoxes of Protestantism, Locke argued, is that one church does not possess enough authority to condemn another. His example, significantly, comes from two rival churches residing in Constantinople: "To make things clear by an example, let us imagine two churches at Constantinople, one of Remonstrants, the other of Antiremonstrants. Would anyone say that either church has the right to take away the liberty or property of those who disagree with them (as happens elsewhere), or to punish them with exile or death because they have different doctrines or rituals?

Robert JC Young

The Turks meanwhile say nothing and laugh up their sleeves at the cruelty of Christians beating and killing each other."[38]

In the founding philosophical text on tolerance in English, Locke thus contrasts the forbearing and tolerant behaviour of the Turks with the inhuman cruelty of the intolerant, warring Christian sects. Tolerance is typically considered to be both a Western virtue and a Western invention. But it is significant that two of its greatest theorists, Locke in the seventeenth century, and Voltaire in his entry on toleration in the *Philosophical Dictionary* in the eighteenth,[39] both invoke the Islamic world of their time as an example of the kind of tolerance that they are proposing. Although modern commentators, such as Will Kymlicka, argue that the Islamic and the European traditions comprise two entirely different models, the second was nevertheless developed from knowledge of the practices of the first.[40] Islam always provided the great example for the Reformation and Enlightenment proponents of tolerance. Can that example be retrieved for today?

IV. The Other

Tolerance requires that there be no "other," that others should not be othered. We could say that there can be others, but there should be no othering of "the other." Critical analysis of subjection to the demeaning experience of being othered by a dominant group has been a long-standing focus for postcolonial studies, initiated by Frantz Fanon in his *Black Skin, White Masks* (1952).[41] Central to postcolonial critique has been the observation that implicit in the idea of "the other" is a distinction between the modern (the same) and the residue that is nonmodern (the other). Yet people regarded as being outside modernity, or outside the West, are still frequently described and categorized in terms of the concept and the term of "the other."

You can find examples everywhere. Linda Colley, for example, in *Britons: Forging the Nation*, invokes a whole consensual body of late twentieth-century thought when she writes that, "Britishness was super-imposed over an array of differences in response to contact with the Other, and above all in response to conflict with the Other."[42] No one, of course, in the nineteenth century talked about people as "Other," with a Sartrean or Lacanian capital O. It is one thing to claim that so-called "Britishness was superimposed over an array of differences." However, when Colley adds "in response to contact with the Other," she conflates the historical event of contact with diverse peoples around the world with a contemporary, late twentieth-century characterization of these diverse peoples as "the Other." Why describe the contact of the British with a vast array of different peoples around the world, made British by virtue of being made subjects of the British Empire, as an encounter with "the Other," a concept that serves to repeat the very perspective that Colley is criticizing?

The casual use of this concept has led to the odd perpetuation of the very category that postcolonial theorists have been challenging for many years—a colonial remainder that resurfaces sometimes even within the rhetoric of the postcolonial. For everywhere we look today we still read or hear about "the other." "This is all very well," commented a member of the audience after a panel discussion on postcolonialism in which I participated in New York, "but where is the other? Hasn't this panel continued to exclude the very others that it is supposed to be championing?" There were two possible responses to this question. The first would have been to point to the "race" or ethnicity, that is the visible otherness, of various panel members that the questioner had clearly not registered. The other response, which was the one I made, was to point out that there is, or should be, no "other" as such, only individuals or groups who have been, or feel that they have been, othered by society. The idea that there is a category of people, implicitly third-world, visibly different to the casual eye, essentially different, and "other," is itself a product of racial theory, its presuppositions drawn from the discriminatory foundations of modernity.[43] The legacy of this, of course, is the existence of minorities, who struggle for full participation within a society that continues to other them as "the other."

Othering is what the postcolonial should be trying to deconstruct, but the tendency to use the concept remains: the often-posed question of how "we" (implicitly the majority or dominant group) can know "the other," who remains implicitly unknowable and unapproachable, or how "the other" can be encouraged to represent itself in its otherness rather than merely be represented as other, is simply the product of having made the discriminatory conceptual distinction in the first place. It accepts the discriminatory gesture of social and political othering that it appears to contest. The question is not how to come to know "the other," but for majority groups to stop othering minorities altogether, at which point minorities will be able to represent themselves as they are, in their specific forms of difference, rather than as they are othered.

Another way of putting this would be to say that in some theoretical and even historical discourse since the 1980s, there has been an unexamined conflation of two ideas: first, the invention of the "other" as a philosophical category of the philosophy of consciousness from Hegel onwards, in which the other is, in fact, not essentially different but the very means through which the individual becomes aware of him or herself, and vice versa (a formulation developed most actively in recent times by Sartre, Levinas, and Lacan); and second, the category of whole cultural or ethnic groups as "other" which has been the product, as well as the object of, anthropological inquiry, in a formulation that goes back at least to John Beattie's *Other Cultures* (1964).[44] For postcolonial studies an early example was Tzvetan Todorov's *The Conquest of America: The Question of the Other* of 1982, followed by his *Nous et les autres* [*On Human Diversity*] of 1989.[45] The founding conference of the field of postcolonial studies, held at the University of Essex in 1984, was programmatically called "Europe and its Others." As the conference title suggests, the philosophical, anthropological, and geographical had by then become conflated. The critical question raised by delegates at the conference was to what extent that title described a historical situation—the ways in which Europe "othered" non-Europeans—and to what extent it was being used as a description of the present, without implying any critical perspective. Since that time, the term "the other" has come to designate both the individual and the group whose unknown, exotic being remains the object of postcolonial desire—a desire that seeks to reach the very unknowable that it has itself conjured up. To that degree, the concept of "the other" simply continues the founding conceptual framework of modernity, in which a portion of humanity entered modernity towards the end of the eighteenth century, at least in Kant's account, while the rest of humanity was relegated to the status of an immature, primitive, and scarcely human "other."[46]

The concept of the other, in short, simply comprises the modern form of the category of the primitive, notwithstanding the fact that the latter has been critically interrogated for many years by Bruno Latour and others.[47] There have been specific anthropological and philosophical critiques of the idea of the Other, such as Johannes Fabian's *Time and the Other* (1983),[48] or Levinas's life-long critique of Hegel, or Derrida's essays on Levinas, but these critiques have not prevented the continuing, often unnuanced, use of this idea even in postcolonial studies—the very field in which the concept has also been thoroughly interrogated and unpicked. Levinas, for example, begins by arguing that in Hegel, even the achievement of knowledge of the other is tainted, because the other then loses its otherness and becomes the same. The result of this line of argument is an extended pursuit of the absolute other, the other that will remain untainted, which Levinas, in a catachrestic gesture, calls "face."[49] Levinas thus offers us the other *plus ultra*, truly othered, respectfully. His idea of the authentic other has been attractive to those who, in a well-meaning way, have been pursuing the attempt to break down modernity's same-other distinction by coming to know or represent the culturally other or by encouraging this other to represent itself. In fact, however, any such attempt ironically only perpetuates the divisive category in which "the other" must always remain incomprehensible. As soon as you have employed the very category of "the other" with respect to other peoples or societies, you are imprisoned in the framework of your own predetermining conceptualization, perpetuating its form of exclusion.

This is the substance of Derrida's 1964 critique of Levinas in "Violence and Metaphysics," where Derrida argues, as Gabriela Basterra puts it, that "if the other is absolutely exterior, if it is separated from the self by an untraversable distance, how does one know that the other exists?"[50] To which the answer is, only by having created the concept in the first place. In *Otherwise than Being* (1972), therefore, Levinas revised his position to develop a new way of understanding the relation to the other, for him a question of both ethics and politics, by tracing it through the remains of its derangement of the self, "the restlessness of the same disturbed by the other."[51] "The psyche is the other in the same," Levinas argues, in a move which brings him closer to Hegel as well as Freud.[52] Levinas's move to "auto-heteronomy," a philosophy of the same, but a same that has been heterogenized with the recognition that sameness must be determined and unsettled by the other against which it defines itself, has, however, made little impact on the discourse of postcolonial studies. In philosophical terms, there should be no difference between any of the various "others" who resides outside the domain of individual subjectivity—the politics of recognition is once again a self-fulfilling paradigm that only seeks to cure the illness that it has itself created. There are really two categories here: others whom "we" know or do not know, and others whom "we" do not know at all, those who are not even recognized as strangers but generically classified as *the* other.[53]

The time has come for postcolonial scholars to rethink the category of the other according to Levinas's later positions, or according to the arguments of Jean-Luc Nancy, Giorgio Agamben, and others that alterity is not something produced as a form of exclusion but fundamental to being itself, which must always involve "being singular plural" from the very first. Until people rethink the idea of the other in this way, the most useful thing that Postcolonial Studies could do to achieve its aim of mutual understanding and universal equality would be to abandon the category of "the other" altogether.[54] Not all—if indeed any—forms of difference require the absoluteness of the category of "the other," unless that otherness is chosen by the subject him or herself to describe a situation of historical discrimination which requires challenge, change, and transformation. No one is so different that their very difference makes them unknowable. Othering was a colonial strategy of exclusion: for the postcolonial, there are only other human beings.

NEW YORK UNIVERSITY

Notes

I am grateful to Dipesh Chakrabarty, Tanya Fernando, Achille Mbembe, Parvati Nair, and Rita Felski and the editors of *New Literary History*, for comments on the ideas or earlier drafts of this essay.

1   Editor's Column, "'The End of Postcolonial Theory?' A Roundtable with Sunil Agnani, Fernando Coronil, Gaurav Desai, Mamadou Diouf, Simon Gikandi, Susie Tharu, and Jennifer Wenzel," *PMLA* 122, no. 3 (2007): 633–51.

2   Jean-François Bayart, *Les études postcoloniales, un carnaval académique* (Paris: Karthala, 2010). For a response, see Robert J. C. Young, "Bayart's Broken Kettle," *Public Culture* 23, no. 1 (2011): 167–75.

3   The claim that the economic rise of India and China outdates the postcolonial forgets that rapid economic development in Asia is hardly new as a phenomenon: China and India are in fact latecomers, the latest in a long line of countries that have experienced such economic booms—they were preceded in Asia by Japan, Malaysia, Singapore, South Korea, and Taiwan. And yet the postcolonial has hardly become irrelevant to these post-boom "tiger" cultures: indeed, a preoccupation with postcoloniality has only intensified there.

4   See Robert J. C. Young, *Postcolonialism: An Historical Introduction* (Oxford: Blackwell, 2001).

5   Arif Dirlik, *Global Modernity: Modernity in the Age of Global Capitalism* (London: Paradigm Publishers, 2007).

6   Cf. Paul Gilroy, *After Empire: Melancholia or Convivial Culture?* (Abingdon: Routledge, 2004); Achille Mbembe, *Sortir de la grande nuit. Essai sur l'Afrique décolonisée* (Paris: La Découverte, 2010).

7   Amitav Ghosh, *Sea of Poppies* (London: John Murray, 2008).

8   Arjun Appadurai, ed., *The Social Life of Things: Commodities in Cultural Perspective* (Cambridge: Cambridge Univ. Press, 1986); Catherine Keller, Michael Nausner, and Mayra Rivera, eds., *Postcolonial Theologies: Divinity and Empire* (St. Louis, MO: Chalice Press, 2004); Lorna Hardwick and Carol Gillespie, eds., *Classics in Postcolonial Worlds* (Oxford: Oxford Univ. Press, 2007); Piyel Haldar, *Law, Orientalism, and Postcolonialism: The Jurisdiction of the Lotus Eaters* (London: Routledge-Cavendish, 2007); Lisa Lampert-Weissig, *Medieval Literature and Postcolonial Studies* (Edinburgh: Edinburgh Univ. Press, 2010); Cheryl McEwan, *Postcolonialism and Development* (London: Routledge, 2008).

9   For a differentiation between the Gramscian and postcolonial concepts of the subaltern, see Robert J. C. Young, "Il Gramsci meridionale," in *The Postcolonial Gramsci*, ed. Neelam Srivastava and Baidik Bhattacharya (New York: Routledge, 2012), 17–33.

10 Stuart Hall, "Cultural Identity and Diaspora," in *Identity: Community, Culture, Difference*, ed. Jonathan Rutherford (London: Lawrence and Wishart, 1990), 222–37.

11 Cf. Linda Tuhiwai Smith, *Decolonizing Methodologies: Research and Indigenous Peoples* (London: Zed Books, 1999).

12 Bartolomé de Las Casas, *A Short Account of the Destruction of the Indies* [1542], trans. Nigel Griffin (London: Penguin, 1992); UN Declaration: *http://www.un.org/esa/socdev/unpfii/en/drip.html*.

13 José Carlos Mariátegui, *Seven Interpretive Essays on Peruvian Reality*, trans. Marjory Urquidi (Austin: Univ. of Texas Press, 1971).

14 Bill Ashcroft, Gareth Griffiths, and Helen Tiffin, *The Empire Writes Back: Theory and Practice in Post-Colonial Literatures* (London: Routledge, 1989).

15 Lorenzo Veracini, *Settler Colonialism: A Theoretical Overview* (Basingstoke: Palgrave Macmillan, 2010); Mike Davis, *Planet of Slums* (London: Verso, 2006).

16 Cf. Yto Barrada, *A Life Full of Holes: The Strait Project* (London: Autograph, 2005); Craig Jeffrey, *Timepass: Youth, Class, and the Politics of Waiting in India* (Stanford, CA: Stanford Univ. Press, 2010).

17 Edward W. Said, *Orientalism* (London: Routledge & Kegan Paul, 1978).

18 See Robert J. C. Young, *The Idea of English Ethnicity* (Oxford: Blackwell, 2008).

19 Olivier Roy, *Globalized Islam: The Search for a New Ummah*, 2nd ed. (New York: Columbia Univ. Press, 2004).

20 Mohsin Hamid, *The Reluctant Fundamentalist* (New York: Harcourt, 2007).

21 Faisal Devji, *Landscapes of the Jihad: Militancy, Morality, Modernity* (London: Hurst, 2005).

22 Al Qaeda is not the first globalized or transnational anti-colonial campaign: that distinction belongs to the Irish. See Robert J. C. Young, "International Anti-Colonialism: The Fenian Invasions of Canada," in *Studies in Settler Colonialism: Politics, Identity and Culture*, ed. Fiona Bateman and Lionel Pilkington (Basingstoke: Palgrave Macmillan, 2011), 75–89.

23 The controversies surrounding Saba Mahmood's *Politics of Piety: The Islamic Revival and the Feminist Subject* (Princeton, NJ: Princeton Univ. Press, 2005) are indicative of the West's difficulties in reading the forms of Islamic belief.

24 Derrida characteristically puts the question more subtly, asking "if this word [secularism] has a meaning other than in the religious tradition that it maintains in claiming to escape it." Jacques Derrida, *On Cosmopolitanism and Forgiveness*, trans. Mark Dooley and Michael Hughes (London: Routledge, 2001), 46. Cf. Judith Butler, *Precarious Life: The Powers of Mourning and Violence* (London: Verso, 2004), 144.

25 Talal Asad, *Formations of the Secular: Christianity, Islam, Modernity* (Stanford, CA: Stanford Univ. Press, 2003).

26 For an extended discussion of how empires managed difference, see Jane Burbank and Frederick Cooper, *Empires in World History: Power and the Politics of Difference* (Princeton, NJ: Princeton Univ. Press, 2011).

27 David Cannadine, *Ornamentalism: How the British Saw Their Empire* (New York: Oxford Univ. Press, 2002).

28 Souleymane Bachir Diagne, *Comment philosopher en Islam?* (Paris: Panama, 2008); George Makdisi, *The Rise of Humanism in Classical Islam and the Christian West: With Special Reference to Scholasticism* (Edinburgh: Edinburgh Univ. Press, 1990).

29 Gil Anidjar, *"Our Place in al-Andalus": Kabbalah, Philosophy, Literature in Arab Jewish Letters* (Stanford, CA: Stanford Univ. Press, 2002). The argument for the *Convivencia* was first proposed in modern times by Américo Castro in *España en su historia. Cristianos, moros y judíos* (Buenos Aires: Editorial Losada, 1948); for recent more critical views, see David Nirenberg, *Communities of Violence: Persecution of Minorities in the Middle Ages* (Princeton, NJ: Princeton Univ. Press, 1996), and Maya Soifer, "Beyond *Convivencia*: Critical Reflections on the Historiography of Interfaith Relations in Christian Spain," *Journal of Medieval Iberian Studies* 1, no. 1 (2009): 19–35. On the role of al-Andalus in the culture of memory of Arab, Jewish, and Hispanic peoples, see Stacy N. Beckwith, ed., *Charting Memory: Recalling Medieval Spain* (New York: Garland, 1999); the prominence of the imagined memory of al-Andalus in the poetry of Mahmoud Darwish is of obvious relevance to the wider implications of my argument. In that context, see also Michelle U. Campos, *Ottoman Brothers: Muslims, Christians and Jews in Early Twentieth-Century Palestine* (Stanford, CA: Stanford Univ. Press, 2011).

30 J. M. Coetzee, "Palimpsest Regained," review of *The Moor's Last Sigh*, by Salmon Rushdie, *The New York Review of Books*, March 21, 1996, http://www.nybooks.com/articles/archives/1996/mar/21/palimpsest-regained/?page=1.

31 Hasan Hanafi, "Alternative Conceptions of Civil Society: A Reflective Islamic Approach" in *Alternative Conceptions of Civil Society*, ed. Simone Chambers and Will Kymlicka (Princeton, NJ: Princeton Univ. Press, 2002), 171–89.

32 Bernard Lewis, *The Multiple Identities of the Middle East* (London: Weidenfeld & Nicholson, 1998), 127.

33 Wendy Brown, *Regulating Aversion: Tolerance in the Age of Identity and Empire* (Princeton, NJ: Princeton Univ. Press, 2006).

34 Jacques Rancière, *Dissensus: On Politics and Aesthetics*, trans. Steven Corcoran (London: Continuum, 2010).

35 Anidjar, *Our Place in al-Andalus*, 14.

36 Cf. Derrida, *On Cosmopolitanism and Forgiveness*, 44–45. Space prevents me here from discussing Gandhi's ideas and practice of tolerance.

37 "A Letter Concerning Toleration" (1689) in *John Locke on Toleration*, ed. Richard Vernon (Cambridge: Cambridge Univ. Press, 2010).

38 "A Letter," 13–14.

39 Voltaire, *Philosophical Dictionary*, trans. Theodore Besterman (Harmondsworth, UK: Penguin, 1972).

40 Will Kymlicka, *Multicultural Citizenship: A Liberal Theory of Minority Rights* (Oxford: Oxford Univ. Press, 1995), 82.

41 Frantz Fanon, *Black Skin, White Mask*, trans. Charles Lam Markmann (London: Pluto Press, 1986).

42 Linda Colley, *Britons: Forging the Nation, 1707–1837* (New Haven: Yale Univ. Press, 1992), 6.

43 Paul Gilroy, *Against Race: Imagining Political Culture beyond the Color Line* (Cambridge, MA: Harvard Univ. Press, 2000).

44 John Beattie, *Other Cultures: Aims, Methods and Achievements in Social Anthropology* (London: Cohen & West, 1964).

45 Tzvetan Todorov, *The Conquest of America: The Question of the Other*, trans. Richard Howard (New York: Harper & Row, 1984); *Nous et les autres: La réflexion française sur la diversité humaine* (Paris: Seuil, 1989), translated as *On Human Diversity: Nationalism, Racism, and Exoticism in French Thought*, trans. Catherine Porter (Cambridge, MA: Harvard Univ. Press, 1993).

46 Immanuel Kant, "What is Enlightenment?" in *Foundations of the Metaphysics of Morals and What is Enlightenment?* trans. Lewis White Beck, 2nd ed. rev. (New York: Macmillan, 1990).

47 Bruno Latour, *We Have Never Been Modern*, trans. Catherine Porter (Cambridge, MA: Harvard Univ. Press, 1993); Adam Kuper, *The Invention of Primitive Society: Transformations of an Illusion* (London: Routledge, 1988); Marianna Torgovnick, *Gone Primitive: Savage Intellects, Modern Lives* (Chicago: Univ. of Chicago, 1990).

48 Johannes Fabian, *Time and the Other: How Anthropology Makes Its Object* (New York, Columbia Univ. Press, 1983).

49 Emmanuel Levinas, *Totality and Infinity: An Essay on Exteriority*, trans. Alphonso Lingis (Pittsburgh, PA: Duquesne Univ. Press, 1969).

50 Gabriela Basterra, "Auto-Heteronomy, or Levinas' Philosophy of the Same," *Graduate Faculty Philosophy Journal* 31, no. 1 (2010): 114; Jacques Derrida, "Violence and Metaphysics," in *Writing and Difference*, trans. Alan Bass (Chicago: Univ. of Chicago Press, 1978), 97–192. Derrida makes a similar argument in his critique of Foucault's *Madness and Civilization*, "Cogito and the History of Madness," also collected in *Writing and Difference*: if

Foucault is speaking on behalf of a madness that he claims has been reduced to silence, Derrida asks, how can he avoid participating in the very structure of exclusion that he is criticizing?

51 Emmanuel Levinas, *Otherwise than Being, or, Beyond Essence*, trans. Alphonso Lingis (The Hague: Nijhoff, 1981), 25.

52 Levinas, *Otherwise*, 112.

53 Cf. Sara Ahmed, *Strange Encounters: Embodied Others in Post-coloniality* (London: Routledge, 2000), 21. Though not questioning the category as such, Ahmed provides a critique of the abstract use of the concept of "the other" by emphasizing the fact that the stranger is always embodied in any encounter.

54 Giorgio Agamben, The Coming Community, trans. Michael Hardt (Minneapolis: Univ. of Minnesota Press, 1993); Jean-Luc Nancy, The Inoperative Community, trans. Peter Connor, Lisa Garbus, Michael Holland, and Simona Sawhey (Minneapolis: Univ. of Minnesota Press, 1991); Being Singular Plural, trans. Robert D. Richardson and Anne E. O' Byrne (Stanford, CA: Stanford Univ. Press, 2000).

9 Postcolonial Studies and the Challenge of Climate Change

Dipesh Chakrabarty
For Homi K. Bhabha

HOWEVER WE COME TO THE QUESTION of postcolonial studies at this historical juncture, there are two phenomena, both topics of public debate since the early 1990s, that none of us can quite escape in our personal and collective lives at present: globalization and global warming. All thinking about the present has to engage both. What I do in this essay is to use some of the recent writings of Homi K. Bhabha to illustrate how a leading contemporary postcolonial thinker imagines the figure of the human in the era of what is often called "neoliberal" capitalism, and then enter a brief discussion of the debate on climate change to see how postcolonial thinking may need to be stretched to adjust itself to the reality of global warming. My ultimate proposition in this essay is simple: that the current conjuncture of globalization and global warming leaves us with the challenge of having to think of human agency over multiple and incommensurable scales at once.

The nineteenth century left us with some internationalist and universal ideologies, prominent among them Marxism and liberalism, both progenies in different ways of the Enlightenment. Anticolonial thought was born of that lineage. The waves of decolonization movements of the 1950s and 60s were followed by postcolonial criticism that was placed, in the universities of the Anglo-American countries at least, as brother-in-arms to cultural studies. Together, cultural studies and postcolonial criticism fed into the literature on globalization, though globalization studies, as such, also drew on developments in the cognate disciplines of sociology, economics, and anthropology. Now we have a literature on global warming and a general sense of an environmental crisis that is no doubt mediated by the inequities of capitalist development, but it is a crisis that faces humanity as a whole. In all these moves, we are left with three images of the human: the universalist-Enlightenment view of the human as potentially the same

Dipesh Chakrabarty, "Postcolonial Studies and the Challenge of Climate Change." *New Literary History*, 43(1), 2012: 1–18. © 2012 *New Literary History*, The University of Virginia. Reproduced by permission of Johns Hopkins University Press.

Postcolonial Studies: An Anthology, First Edition. Edited by Pramod K. Nayar.
Editorial material and organization © 2016 John Wiley & Sons, Ltd.
Published 2016 by John Wiley & Sons, Ltd.

everywhere, the subject with capacity to bear and exercise rights; the postcolonial-postmodern view of the human as the same but endowed everywhere with what some scholars call "anthropological difference"—differences of class, sexuality, gender, history, and so on. This second view is what the literature on globalization underlines. And then comes the figure of the human in the age of the Anthropocene, the era when humans act as a geological force on the planet, changing its climate for millennia to come. If critical commentary on globalization focuses on issues of anthropological difference, the scientific literature on global warming thinks of humans as constitutively one—a species, a collectivity whose commitment to fossil-fuel based, energy-consuming civilization is now a threat to that civilization itself. These views of the human do not supersede one another. One cannot put them along a continuum of progress. No one view is rendered invalid by the presence of others. They are simply disjunctive. Any effort to contemplate the human condition today—after colonialism, globalization, and global warming—on political and ethical registers encounters the necessity of thinking disjunctively about the human, through moves that in their simultaneity appear contradictory.

But since I come to all these questions as someone trained in the discipline of history, allow me to approach them via this discipline and by way of a brief historical detour. And I apologize in advance for the slight intrusion of the autobiographical at this point, for I was also a witness to the history I recount here. My entry into the field of post-colonial studies, quite fittingly for someone interested in the theme of belatedness, was late.[1] Postcolonial ideas, as we know, took by storm departments of English literature in the Anglo-American academe in the 1980s. Now when I look at back on it, postcolonial studies seem to have been a part, initially at least, of a cultural and critical process by which a postimperial West adjusted itself to a long process of decolonization that perhaps is not over yet. After all, it cannot be without significance that what brought Stuart Hall, Homi Bhabha, and Isaac Julien together to read Fanon in the London of the late 1980s and the 1990s was the struggle against racism in a postimperial Britain, a struggle sometimes given official backing by the radical Greater London Council and hosted by the Institute of Contemporary Art.[2]

The American scene with regard to postcolonial studies was admittedly somewhat different. Edward Said wrote *Orientalism* (1978) out of his sense of involvement in the Palestinian struggle and Gayatri Spivak, I assume, was responding in part to the culture wars on American campuses about opening up core curriculum (as at Stanford in the late 1980s) and redefining the literary canon when she introduced the Indian feminist writer Mahasweta Devi to academic readers in the United States. Australian developments that I personally witnessed in these years drew on both English and North-American instances. I got drawn into debates about "culture as distinction" and about the literary canon that took place in the meetings of the Arts Faculty at the University of Melbourne in the late 1980s. A leading scholar in those debates was Simon During, a pioneer in what was then emerging as the field of cultural studies.[3] The University of Essex conferences on postcolonial studies had just taken place. I was aware of During's involvement in those conferences. Lata Mani, then a graduate student with the History of Consciousness Program at the University of California–Santa Cruz, had published a path-breaking paper on "sati" in one of their proceedings volumes.[4] But the volumes still had not impacted the world of historians. We began to publish *Subaltern Studies* in India in 1983 without much awareness of postcolonial literary criticism. I remember

Simon During returning to Melbourne in the mid-80s from a postcolonialism conference overseas and asking me if I knew of the work of Homi Bhabha. I answered, with some surprise but as any educated newspaper-reading Indian would have answered in those days, "Sure, a major Indian Atomic Research Centre is named after him. He was one of our best physicists; but why would you be interested in him?" That was the day the other Homi Bhabha entered my life, as a problem of mistaken identity, through a stand-in, as a question of difference *within* the identity "Homi Bhabha" (to mimic my dear friend who bears that name).

Subaltern Studies, the historiographical movement with which I was associated, emerged out of anti-, and not postcolonial, thought. We were a bunch of young men (initially men) interested in Indian history and were in some ways disillusioned with the nationalisms of our parents. The two Englishmen in the group, David Arnold and David Hardiman, were anti-imperial in their political outlook and rejected the dominantly proimperial historiography that came out of England. The Indian members of the group were disappointed and angry about the Indian nation's failure to deliver the social justice that anticolonial nationalism had promised. Our historiographical rebellion raised many interesting methodological issues for Indian history and for history in general. Ranajit Guha, our mentor, could easily be seen as one of the pioneers of the so-called linguistic turn in the discipline of history though, it has to be acknowledged, Hayden White had already raised many of the most pertinent issues in the 1970s.[5] Our analyses of subaltern histories were deeply influenced by Guha's infectious enthusiasm for structuralism of the kind that was associated with Barthes, Jakobson, and Levi-Strauss, a structuralism of the kind that was associated with Barthes, Jakobson, and Levi-Strauss, a structuralism one could also associate with Hayden White and with an early moment of cultural studies—especially in Britain where the New Accent series of publications emphasized the importance of structuralism, and where Guha was originally based. Gramsci—with a selection of his prison notebooks translated into English in 1971—had softened the Stalinist edges of our Indo-British Marxism and attuned us to the importance of the popular, and Mao—many of the historians in the group had earlier been involved in the Maoist movement that took place in India between 1967 and 1971—had helped us to think of the peasant as a modern revolutionary subject. But we did not encounter postcolonial thought until Spivak brought our group into contact with her deconstructionist variety of Marxism and feminism, and made us confront our theoretical innocence in proposing to make the subaltern the "subject" of his or her own history. As we pondered the challenge she posed to the group and embraced its consequences, we crossed over from being merely anticolonial historians (with incipient critiques of the nation-state form) to being a part of the intellectual landscape of postcolonial criticism.

What was the difference? one might ask. The difference was signaled by Spivak's epochal essay "Can the Subaltern Speak?" that she had begun to draft in response to the *Subaltern Studies* project and before our first meeting with her took place.[6] The human in our anticolonial mode of thinking was a figure of sovereignty. We wanted to make the peasant or the subaltern the subject of his or her history, period. And we thought of this subject in the image of the autonomous rights-bearing person with the same access to representation in national and other histories as others from more privileged backgrounds enjoyed. A straightforward plea for social justice underlay our position, just as it did in a variety of Marxist, feminist, or even liberal histories. And like

Fanon, we saw the subaltern classes as claiming their humanity through revolutionary upheavals. Becoming human was for us a matter of becoming a subject.[7]

This was why Spivak's exercise in "Can the Subaltern Speak?" was so salutary. It challenged the very idea of the "subject" that *Subaltern Studies* and much anticolonial thought celebrated and invited us to write deconstructive histories of subjecthood.

This critique of the subject was not the same as that performed by Althusserian antihumanism of the 1960s and 70s that so riled E. P. Thompson, the great humanist historian of the last century.[8] Postcolonial critique of the subject was actually a deeper turning towards the human, a move best exemplified for me in the work of Homi Bhabha. It was a turn that both appreciated difference as a philosophical question and at the same time repudiated its essentialization by identity politics.[9] That single move—channeled not through identity politics but through difference philosophies— connected postcolonial thinking to thinking about the human condition in the age of globalization.

To appreciate the close political relations that existed between "rights" thinking and the body of postcolonial thought that drew on the post-structuralist critique of the subject, we have to get beyond some of the fruitless debates of the 1990s. I think it was a mistake of the Left on both sides of the postmodern divide in the 1990s to think of these two different figurations of the human—the human as a rights-bearing subject and the figure of the human glimpsed through the critique of the subject—as somehow competing with each other in a do-or-die race in which only the fittest survived. The critique of the subject did not make the idea of the autonomous subject useless any more than the critique of the nation-state made the institution of the nation-state obsolete. What I have learnt from postcolonial thinkers is the necessity to move through contradictory figures of the human, now through a collapsing of the person and the subject as in liberal or Marxist thought, and now through a separation of the two. Before I discuss what forces us to engage in such border-crossing in our thinking, let me illustrate the fleet-footed movement I am speaking of by turning to some recent writings of Homi K. Bhabha.

The Human in Postcolonial Criticism Today

Listen to Bhabha writing of the new subaltern classes of today, "the stateless," "migrant workers, minorities, asylum seekers, [and] refugees" who "represent emergent, undocumented lifeworlds that break through the formal language of 'protection' and 'status' because"—he says, quoting Balibar—"they are *neither insiders [n]or outsiders, or (for many of us) … insiders officially considered outsiders.*"[10] Classic Bhabha, one would have thought, this turning over of the outside into the inside and vice versa. Yet it is not the "cosmopolitan claims of global ethical equivalence" that Bhabha reads into these new subalterns of the global capitalist order. His eyes are fixed as much on the deprivation that the human condition suffers in these circumstances as they are on the question of rights: "As insiders/outsiders they damage the cosmopolitan dream of a 'world without borders' … by opening up, *in the midst of* international polity, a complex and contradictory mode of being or surviving somewhere in between legality and incivility. It is a kind of no-man's land that, in the world of migration, shadows global success … it substitutes cultural survival in migrant *milieux* for full civic participation."[11]

"Full civic participation"—one can see at once the normative horizons on which Bhabha has set his sights. They are indeed those that acknowledge that our recognition of the human condition in the everyday does not *eo ipso* negate questions of social justice. On the contrary. Bhabha, of course, acknowledges the fact that the politics of (cultural) survival often takes the place of "full civic participation" in the lives of these new subalterns of the global economy. But he has to move between these poles (survival versus civic participation) to see the subaltern politics of cultural survival not only as a zone of creativity and improvisation—which it is—but also as an area of privation and disenfranchisement. It will be interesting, then, to see how it is precisely this freedom that Bhabha claims for himself to think contradictorily—to think mobility (survival) and stasis (civic participation) at the same time—that allows him to turn the tables on his erstwhile critics, Michael Hardt and Antonio Negri, who found in "nomadism and miscegenation" "figures of virtue, the first ethical practices on the terrain of Empire," since, they argued, "circulation" or "deterritorialisation" were steps towards the goal of global citizenship that entailed "the struggle against the slavery of belonging to a nation, an identity and a people, and thus the desertion from sovereignty and the limits it places on subjectivity" were for them and this reason "entirely positive" developments.[12] "Such an emancipatory ideal," writes Bhaba, "—so fixated on the *flowing*, borderless, global world—neglects to confront the fact that migrants, refugees, or nomads do not merely circulate." Rather, he goes on to point out:

> They need to settle, claim asylum or nationality, demand housing and education, assert their economic and cultural rights, and seek the status of citizenship. It is salutary, then, to turn to less "circulatory" forms of the economy like trade and tariffs, or taxes and monetary policy—much less open to postmodern metaphoric appropriation—to see how they impact on the global imaginary of diasporic cultural studies. Positive global relations depend on the protection and enhancement of these national "territorial" resources, which should then become part of the "global" political economy of resource redistribution and a transnational moral economy of redistributive justice.[13]

The point of these long quotations is simply to show how juxtaposed and crossed-over remain the two figures of the human in these discussions by Bhabha: the human of the everyday who illustrates the human condition as the embodiment of what Bhabha once called "difference within"—the insider as the outsider and vice versa—the human who improvises and survives, and the human who asserts his or her cultural and economic rights in the expectation of being the sovereign figure of the citizen some day.

This constant movement between normative and onto-existential images of the human in Bhabha's prose is an index of the human predicament produced by dominant forms of globalization. Bhabha turns to Hannah Arendt to explain this predicament. Arendt had once argued that the very creation of a "One World" through the positing of so many "peoples" organized into nation-states produced the problem of statelessness, not from "a lack of civilization" but as "the perverse consequence of the political and cultural conditions of modernity."[14] Modernity created this new "savage" condition of many human beings, the condition of being declared stateless if they could not be identified with a nation-state, forcing them to fall back on the politics of survival. Today, it is not simply the arrangement of nation-states that creates this condition of stateless, illegal migrants, guest workers, and asylum seekers. It is a deeper predicament produced by both the globalization of capital and the pressures of demography in poorer countries brought about by the unevenness of postcolonial development. Whether you read Mike Davis on *The Planet of Slums* or documents produced by Abahlali baseMjondolo, the shack-dwellers' movement in Durban, South Africa, it is clear that today's capitalism feeds off a large pool of migrant, often illegal, labor that is cast aside by many as "surplus population"—a process that deprives these groups of the enjoyment of any social goods and services, while their labor remains critical to the functioning of the service sector in both advanced and growing economies.[15] At the same time, it has to be acknowledged, refugees and asylum seekers are produced also by state-failures connected to a whole series of factors: economic, political, demographic, and environmental. Together, these groups, today's subaltern classes, embody the human condition negatively, as an image of privation. No ethnography of their everyday lives can access its object positively through the figure of the citizen. Yet our normative horizons, belonging as we analysts do to one or another kind of civil society, cannot but depend on the measure of "cultural and economic rights" and "full civic participation," even as any real possibility of effective citizenship for all humans seems increasingly remote. Do not one billion human beings already live without access to proper drinking water? When will the illegal Bangladeshi and North-African workers one encounters on the streets of Athens, Florence, Rome, Vienna, Paris, London—not to speak of illegal Bangladeshi labor in the informal sectors of India and Pakistan—become full-fledged European citizens? There is one predicament of our thinking, however, that speaks to the contradictions of our lifeworlds today. Our normative horizons, unlike those of Marx's classical writings, say, give us no vantage point from which we could not only judge but also describe and know these classes, while ethnographies of what the marginal, the poor, and the excluded actually do in order to survive yield no alternative norms for human societies that are still in the grip of large and centralizing institutions, corporations, and bureaucracies.[16]

This disjuncture is at its most acute now in what progressive European theorists such as Etienne Balibar or Sandro Mezzadra write by way of placing refugees, asylum seekers, and illegal immigrants in European history, politics, and policy.[17] It may or may not surprise the reader to know that Europe today is dotted with detention centers for these unwelcome people. The number of such centers exceeds one hundred and they extend outside Europe into North Africa.[18] Europe has adopted border protection policies that are reminiscent of those pursued by the United States or Australia, except that in Europe the borders, if a detention camp is indeed a border, are as much inside Europe as outside. It is this indeterminacy of borders that has led Balibar to make the observation that if the nineteenth century was the time when European imperialism made frontiers into borders by exporting the border-form outside Europe, we stand today on the threshold of an age when borders are becoming frontiers again.[19]

However, reading Balibar and Mezzadra on these questions makes it clear that their writing is caught in tension between two tendencies: on the one hand they have to acknowledge the historical and current barbarisms that have in the past acted as a foundation of European "civilization" and continue to do so to some extent even in the present; on the other hand they have to appeal to the highest utopians ideals of their civilizational heritage in order to imagine into being a vibrant European polity that not only practices the ethics of hospitality and responsibility that Derrida, Levinas, and others have written about, but that also grounds itself in a deep acceptance of the plurality of human inheritances inside its own borders.[20] It is no wonder, then, that European intellectuals, whether discussing refugees from outside Europe or internal migrants from the ex-colonies and the question of "Eastern Europe," are increasingly debating postcolonial theory and are even producing their own readers and translations of postcolonial writings.[21] Europe today is clearly a new frontier of postcolonial studies—and not because the classical peasant-subaltern subject can be found in Europe. No, it is because the new subalterns of the global economy—refugees, asylum seekers, illegal workers—can be found all over Europe and it is by making these groups the object of his thinking that Homi Bhabha arrives at a figure of the human that is constitutionally and necessarily doubled and contradictory.

Let me now turn to the issue of global warming to consider how it challenges us to imagine the human.

The Human in the Anthropocene

If the problem of global warming or climate change had not burst in on us through the 2007 Report of the Intergovernmental Panel on Climate Change (IPCC), globalization would have been perhaps the most important theme stoking our thoughts about being human. But global warming adds another challenge. It calls us to visions of the human that neither rights talk nor the critique of the subject ever contemplated. This does not, as I said before, make those earlier critiques irrelevant or redundant, for climate change will produce—and has begun to produce—its own cases of refugees and regime failures.[22] The effects of climate change are mediated by the global inequities we already have. So the two visions of the human that I have already outlined—the universalist view of global justice between human individuals imagined as having the same rights everywhere and the critique of the subject that poststructuralism once promoted—will both remain operative. In discussing issues of climate justice, we will thus necessarily go through familiar moves: criticize the self-aggrandizing tendencies of powerful and rich nations and speak of a progressive politics of differentiated responsibilities in handling debates about migration, legal or illegal. Indeed, one of the early significant tracts to be written on the problem and politics of global warming was authored by two respected Indian environmental activists who gave it the title, *Global Warming in an Unequal World: A Case of Environmental Colonialism*.[23] The science and politics of climate change have not rendered these moves irrelevant or unnecessary; but they have become insufficient as analytical strategies.[24]

Consider the challenge that climate science poses to humanists. Climate scientists raise a problem of scale for the human imagination, though they do not usually think through the humanistic implications of their own claim that, unlike the changes in climate this planet has seen in the past, the current warming is anthropogenic in nature. Humans, collectively, now have an agency in determining the climate of the planet as a whole, a privilege reserved in the past only for very large-scale geophysical forces. This is where this crisis represents something different from what environmentalists have written about so far: the impact of humans on their immediate or regional environments. The idea of humans representing a force on a very large geological scale that impacts the whole planet is new. Some scientists, the Nobel-winning Paul J. Crutzen at the forefront, have proposed the beginning of a new geological era, an era in which human beings act as a force determining the climate of the entire planet all at once. They have suggested that we call this period "the Anthropocene" to mark the end of the Holocene that named the geological "now" within which recorded human history so far has unfolded.[25] But who is the "we" of this process? How do we think of this collective human agency in the era of the Anthropocene?

Scientists who work on the physical history of the universe or on the history of the earth's climate in the past no doubt tell certain kinds of histories. But in Gadamerian or Diltheyan terms, they *explain* and are not required to *understand* the past in any humanist sense. Every individual explanation makes sense because it relates to other existing explanations. But a cognitive exercise is not "understanding" in the Gadamerian sense, and until there is an element of the latter, we do not have history, not human history at least. Which is why, usually, a purely "natural" history of climate over the last several million years would not be of much interest to a postcolonial historian who works on human history.

What is remarkable about the current crisis is that climate scientists are not simply doing versions of natural history. They are also giving us an account of climate change that is neither purely "natural" nor purely "human" history. And this is because they assign an agency to humans at the very heart of this story. According to them, current *global* (and not regional) climate changes are largely human induced. This implies that humans are now part of the natural history of the planet. The wall of separation between natural and human histories that was erected in early modernity and reinforced in the nineteenth century as the human sciences and their disciplines consolidated themselves has some serious and long-running cracks in it.[26]

The ascription of a geological agency to humans is a comparatively recent development in climate science. One of the earliest references I could find of scientists assigning to humans a role in the geophysical process of the planet was in a paper that the University of California, San Diego, oceanographer Roger Revelle and the University of Chicago geophysicist H. E. Suess coauthored in the geophysics journal *Tellus* in 1957. "Human beings are now carrying out a large-scale geophysical experiment of a kind that could not have happened in the past nor be reproduced in the future," they wrote. "Within a few centuries we are returning to the atmosphere and oceans the concentrated organic carbon stored in the sedimentary rocks over hundreds of millions of years. This experiment, if adequately documented, may yield a far-reaching insight into the processes determining weather and climate."[27] The Environmental Pollution Panel of the U.S. President's Science Advisory Committee expressed the opinion in 1965 that "through his worldwide industrial civilization, Man is unwittingly conducting a vast geophysical experiment. Within a few generations, he is burning fossil fuel that slowly accumulated in the earth over the past 500 million years." They went on to warn: "The climatic changes that may be produced by the increased CO_2 content could be deleterious from the point of view of human beings."[28] Even as late as 1973, the Committee on Atmospheric Sciences of the National Academy of Science said: "Man clearly has no positive knowledge of the magnitude or the manner in which he is presently changing the climate of the earth. There is no real question that inadvertent modification of the atmosphere is taking place."[29]

We can thus see a progress or inflation, if you like, in the rhetoric of climate scientists. Man was an experimenter on a geophysical scale in the 1950s; by the 1990s, he was a geophysical force himself. Silently and implicitly, climate scientists have doubled the figure of the human as the agent of anthropogenic global warming (AGW). Humans put out greenhouse gases in the atmosphere and the biosphere. Here the picture of the human is how social scientists have always imagined humans to be: a purposeful biological entity with the capacity to degrade natural environment. But what happens when we say humans are acting like a geophysical force? We then liken humans to some nonhuman, nonliving agency. That is why I say the science of anthropogenic global warming has doubled the figure of the human—you have to think of the two figures of the human simultaneously: the human-human and the nonhuman-human. And that is where some challenges lie for the postcolonial scholar in the humanities.

The first challenge is the scale on which scientists invite us to imagine human agency. Consider the point that, collectively, we are now capable of affecting the climate of this planet and changing it, as the geophysicist David Archer says, for the next one hundred thousand years.[30] Such numbers usually function as operators with which we manipulate information. We do not understand them without training. Scientists are aware of this problem and do what historians do to bring vast scales within the realm of understanding: appeal to human experience. The Australian social and environmental historian Tom Griffiths recently published a splendid history of the Antarctic. But how does a social historian go about writing a *human* history of an uninhabited and uninhabitable vast expanse of snow and ice? Griffiths does what all good historians do: go to the experience that past humans have already had of such a region in order to write a human history of this place. He consults the private papers of historical explorers, looks at their letters to see how they experienced the place, and intercalates his reading of these documents with leaves from his own diary of traveling to the South Pole. This is how the Antarctic gets humanized. We use the metaphoric capacity of human language and visual records to bring its ice within the grasp of human experience. The Australian explorer Douglas Mawson went to the Antarctic for the years 1911–14, having just become engaged to a Paquita Delprat of Broken Hill in Western Australia. In one of her love-lorn letters to Mawson, Delprat wrote: "Are you frozen? In heart I mean …. Am I pouring out a little of what is in my heart to an iceberg? … Can a person remain in such cold and lonely regions however beautiful and still love warmly?" Mawson reassured her that her love had warmed her "proxy iceberg" and that "he felt less cold this time."[31] It is through such interleaving of experiences and through the employment of figures of speech—some telling metaphors and similes—that we make a human history of the empty vastness and ice of the South Pole.

Scientists interested in creating an informed public around the crisis of climate change make a very similar appeal to experience. For reasons of space, I will illustrate the point with an example from David Archer's book *The Long Thaw*. Archer distills out of his analysis a problem that turns around the explanation/understanding distinction I mentioned earlier. Human beings cannot really imagine beyond a couple of generations before and after their own time, he says. "The rules of economics, which govern much of our behavior," he writes, "tend to limit our focus to even shorter time frames," for the value of everything gets discounted in decades.[32] Archer faces the problem that humans may not care for the science he is telling us about. One hundred thousand years is too far—why should we care for people so far into the future? "How would it feel," Archer asks, trying to translate geological units into human scales, "if the ancient Greeks, for example, had taken advantage of some lucrative business opportunity for a few centuries, aware of potential costs, such as, say, a [much] stormier world, or the loss of … agricultural productivity to rising sea levels—that could persist to this day?"[33] I find it remarkable as a historian that Archer, a socially concerned paleoclimatologist, should be asking us to extend to the future the faculty of understanding that historians routinely extend to humans of the recorded past.

But this is also where we encounter a real problem of interpretation. We write of pasts through the mediation of the experience of humans of the past. We can send humans, or even artificial eyes, to outer space, the poles, the top of Mount Everest, to Mars and the Moon and vicariously experience that which is not directly available to us. We can also—through art and fiction—extend our understanding to those who in future may suffer the impact of the geophysical force that is the human. But we cannot ever experience ourselves as a geophysical force—though we now *know* that this is one of the modes of our collective existence. We cannot send somebody out to experience in an unmediated manner this "force" on our behalf (as distinct from experiencing the impact of it mediated by other direct experiences—of floods, storms, or earthquakes, for example). This nonhuman, forcelike mode of existence of the human tells us that we are no longer simply a form of life that is endowed with a sense of ontology. Humans have a sense of ontic belonging. That is undeniable. We used that knowledge in developing both anticolonial (Fanon) and postcolonial criticism (Bhabha). But in becoming a geophysical force on the planet, we have also developed a form of collective existence that has no ontological dimension. Our thinking about ourselves now stretches our capacity for interpretive understanding. We need nonontological ways of thinking the human.

Bruno Latour has complained for a long time that the problem with modern political thought is the culture / nature distinction that has allowed humans to look on their relationship to "nature" through the prism of the subject / object relationship.[34] He has called for a new idea of politics that brings together—as active partners into our arguments—both humans and nonhumans. I think what I have said adds a wrinkle to Latour's problematic. A geophysical force—for that is what in part we are in our collective existence—is neither subject nor an object. A force is the capacity to move things. It is pure, nonontological agency. After all, Newton's idea of "force" went back to medieval theories of impetus.[35]

Climate change is not a one-event problem. Nor is it amenable to a single rational solution. It may indeed be something like what Horst Rittel and Melvin Webber, planning theorists, once called a "wicked problem," an expression they coined in 1973 in an article entitled "Dilemmas in a General Theory of Planning" published in *Policy Sciences* "to describe a category of public policy concern that [while susceptible to a rational diagnosis] defied rational and optimal solutions," because it impinged on too many other problems to be solved or addressed at the same time.[36] Besides, as Mike Hulme, a climate researcher, points out: "This global solution-structure also begs a fundamental question which is rarely addressed in the respective fora where these debates and disagreements surface: What is the ultimate performance metric for the human species, what is it that we are seeking to optimise? Is it to restabilise population or to minimise our ecological footprint? Is it to increase life expectancy, to maximise gross domestic product, to make poverty history or to increase the sum of global happiness? Or is the ultimate performance metric for humanity simply survival?"[37]

Given that it is difficult to foresee humanity arriving at a consensus on any of these questions in the short-term future, even while scientific knowledge about global warming circulates more widely, it is possible that the turn towards what Ulrich Beck calls a "risk society" will only be intensified in the current phase of globalization and global warming. As we cope with the effects of climate change and pursue capitalist growth, we will negotiate our attachments, mediated no doubt through the inequities of capitalism, knowing fully that they are increasingly risky.[38] But this also means that there is no "humanity" that can act as a self-aware agent. The fact that the crisis of climate change will be routed through all our "anthropological differences" can only mean that, however anthropogenic the current global warming may be in its origins, there is no corresponding "humanity" that in its oneness can act as a political agent. A place thus remains for struggles around questions on intrahuman justice regarding the uneven impacts of climate change.

This is to underline how open the space is for what may be called the politics of climate change. Precisely because there is no single rational solution, there is the need to struggle to make our way in hitherto uncharted ways—and hence through arguments and disagreements—toward something like what Latour calls "the progressive composition of a common world."[39] Unlike the problem of the hole in the ozone layer, climate change is ultimately all about politics. Hence its openness as much to science and technology as to rhetoric, art, media, and arguments and conflicts conducted through a variety of means. The need then is to think the human on multiple scales and registers and as having both ontological and nonontological modes of existence.

With regard to the climate crisis, humans now exist in two different modes. There is one in which they are still concerned with justice even when they know that perfect justice is never to be had. The "climate justice" historiography issues from this deeply human concern. Climate scientists' history reminds us, on the other hand, that we now also have a mode of existence in which we—collectively and as a geophysical force and in ways we cannot experience ourselves—are "indifferent" or "neutral" (I do not mean these as mental or experienced states) to questions of intrahuman justice. We have run up against our own limits as it were. It is true that as beings for whom the question of Being is an eternal question, we will always be concerned about justice. But if we, collectively, have also become a geophysical force, then we also have a collective mode of existence that is justice-blind. Call that mode of being a "species" or something else, but it has no ontology, it is beyond biology, and it acts as a limit to what we also are in the ontological mode.

This is why the need arises to view the human simultaneously on contradictory registers: as a geophysical force and as a political agent, as a bearer of rights and as author of actions; subject to both the stochastic forces of nature (being itself one such force collectively) and open to the contingency of individual human experience; belonging at once to differently-scaled histories of the planet, of life and species, and of human societies. One could say, mimicking Fanon, that in an age when the forces of globalization intersect with those of global warming, the idea of the human needs to be stretched beyond where postcolonial thought advanced it.

In Conclusion

A little more than half a century ago, "an earth-born object made by man"—the Sputnik—orbited the planet in outer space, "in the proximity of the heavenly bodies as though it had been admitted tentatively to their sublime company." The author of these words, Hannah Arendt, thought that this event foretold a fundamental change in the human condition. The earth had been "unique in the universe in providing human beings with a habitat in which they can move and breathe without effort and without artifice," but now clearly science was catching up with a thought that "up to then had been buried in the highly non-respectable literature of science fiction." The Sputnik could be the first "step toward escape from man's imprisonment to the earth." "Should the emancipation and the secularization of the modern age," asked Arendt, "... end with [a] ... fateful repudiation of an Earth who was the Mother of all living creatures under the sky?"[40] Still, Arendt's reading of this change in the human condition was optimistic. A critic of "mass society," she saw the danger of such a society mainly in spiritual terms. A "mass society" could "threaten humanity with extinction" in spirit by rendering humans into a "society of laborers."[41] But it was in the same "mass society"—"where man as a social animal rules supreme"—that "the survival of the species could [now] be guaranteed on a world-wide scale," thought Arendt.[42] The Sputnik was the first symbol, for her, of such optimism regarding the survival of the human species.

Today, with the crisis of anthropogenic climate change coinciding with multiple other crises of planetary proportions—of resources, finance, and food, not to speak of frequent weather-related human disasters—we know that the repudiation of the earth has come in a shape Arendt could not have even imagined in the optimistic and modernizing 1950s. Humans today are not only the dominant species on the planet, they also collectively constitute—thanks to their numbers and their consumption of cheap fossil-fuel-based energy to sustain their civilizations—a geological force that determines the climate of the planet much to the detriment of civilization itself. Today, it is precisely the "survival of the species" on a "world-wide scale" that is largely in question. All progressive political thought, including postcolonial criticism, will have to register this profound change in the human condition.

Notes

A draft of this essay was presented as a lecture at the University of Virginia in December 2010. Thanks to my audience and to the anonymous readers of the journal for constructive criticisms. Special thanks are due to Rita Felski for the original invitation to write this essay and for her helpful suggestions. I am grateful to Homi K. Bhabha for making some of his recent writings available to me and for many discussions of the issues raised here.

1 See my "Belatedness as Possibility: Subaltern Histories, Once Again" in *The Indian Postcolonial: A Critical Reader*, ed. Elleke Boehmer and Rosinka Chaudhuri (New York: Routledge, 2011), 163–76.

2 I discuss these developments in "An Anti-Colonial History of the Postcolonial Turn: An Essay in Memory of Greg Dening," Second Greg Dening Memorial Lecture (Melbourne,

Australia: Department of History, The University of Melbourne, 2009),11–13.

3 During gives his own account of these times in his introduction to *The Cultural Studies Reader*, ed. Simon During (New York: Routledge, 1993).

4 Lata Mani, "The Production of an Official Discourse on Sati In Early Nineteenth Century Bengal," in *Europe and Its Others*, ed. Frances Barker and others (Colchester: Univ. of Essex Press, 1985), 1:107–27. The book was published in two volumes out a conference held at Essex in July 1984 on the subject of "the Sociology of Literature."

5 See Ranajit Guha, *Elementary Aspects of Peasant Insurgency in Colonial India* (Delhi: Oxford Univ. Press, 1983) and Hayden White, *Metahistory: The Historical*

Imagination in Nineteenth-Century Europe (Baltimore: Johns Hopkins Univ. Press, 1973). I have tried to bring Guha and White together in my essay "Subaltern History as Political Thought" in *Colonialism and Its Legacies*, ed. Jacob T. Levy with Marion Iris Young (Lanham, MD: Lexington Books, 2011), 205–18.

6 Gayatri Chakravorty Spivak, "Can the Subaltern Speak?" in *Marxism and the Interpretation of Culture*, ed. Cary Nelson and Lawrence Grossberg (Chicago: Univ. of Illinois Press, 1988), 271–313.

7 Guha's *Elementary Aspects* was the best illustration of this proposition.

8 On all this, see E. P. Thompson, *The Poverty of Theory and Other Essays* (New York: Monthly Review Press, 1978).

9 The *locus classicus* for this position is still Homi K. Bhabha, *The Location of Culture* (London: Routledge, 1994). See Homi K. Bhabha, "Global Pathways" (unpublished).

10 Homi K Bhabha, "Notes on Globalization and Ambivalence" in *Cultural Politics in a Global Age: Uncertainty, Solidarity and Innovation*, ed. David Held, Henrietta L. Moore, Kevin Young (Oxford: Oneworld, 2008), 39.

11 Bhabha, "Notes," 39–40.

12 Michael Hardt and Antonio Negri, *Empire* (Cambridge, MA: Harvard Univ. Press, 2000), 361–62, cited in Homi K. Bhabha, "Our Neighbours, Ourselves: Contemporary Reflections on Survival" (unpublished), 3. For Hardt and Negri's critique of Bhabha and of postcolonialism generally, see *Empire*, 137–59.

13 Bhabha, "Our Neighbours," 3–4.

14 Bhabha paraphrasing Arendt in "Notes," 38.

15 Bhabha, "Notes." Mike Davis, *Planet of Slums* (London: Verso, 2006). For details on the Abahlali base Mjondolo movement, see their website *http://www.abahlali.org/*.

16 I read Partha Chatterjee's *Politics of the Governed: Reflections on Popular Politics in Most of the World* (New York: Columbia Univ. Press, 2004) as symptomatic of this predicament.

17 See Manuela Bojadžijev and Isabelle Saint-Saëns, "Borders, Citizenship, War, Class: A Discussion with Étienne Balibar and Sandro Mezzadra," *New Formations* 58 (2006): 10–30.

18 See the map reproduced in Rochona Majumdar, *Writing Postcolonial History* (New York: Bloomsbury Academic, 2010), 15. Thanks to Sandro Mezzadra for bringing these maps to my and Majumdar's attention.

19 Etienne Balibar, "Europe: An 'Unimagined' Frontier of Democracy," *Diacritics* 33, no. 3–4 (2003): 36–44. Also Etienne Balibar, *We the People of Europe? Reflections on Transnational Citizenship*, trans. James Swenson (Princeton, NJ: Princeton Univ. Press, 2004), 7.

20 See Balibar, *We the People of Europe?* and note 21 below.

21 Gerhard Stilz and Ellen Dengel-Janic, eds., *South Asian Literatures* (Trier: WVT Wissenschaftslicher Verlag, 2010);

Sandro Mezzadra, *La Condizione Postcoloniale: storia e politica nel presente globale* (Verona: Ombre Corte, 2008).

22 See the recent documentary film *Climate Refugees* (2009) made by Michael P. Nash. *http://www.climaterefugees.com/*.

23 Sunita Narain and Anil Agarwal, *Global Warming in an Unequal World: A Case of Environmental Colonialism* (Delhi: Centre for Science and Environment, 1991)

24 For an elaboration of this point, see my essay "Verändert der Klimawandel die Geschichtsschreibung?" *Transit* 41 (2011): 143–63.

25 I discuss historiographical and some philosophical implications of the Anthropocene hypothesis in my essay, "The Climate of History: Four Theses," *Critical Inquiry* 35, no. 2 (2009): 197–222. See also Will Steffen, Paul J. Crutzen, and John R. McNeill, "The Anthropocene: Are Humans Now Overwhelming the Great Forces of Nature?" *Ambio* 36, no. 8 (2007): 614–21 and the special issue of *Philosophical Transactions of the Royal Society* edited by Jan Zalasiewicz, Mark Williams, Alan Haywood, and Michael Ellis, "The Anthropocene: A New Epoch of Geological Time?" (2011): 835–41.

26 For elaboration, see my "Climate of History."

27 R. Revelle and H. E. Suess, "Carbon Dioxide exchange between atmosphere and ocean and the question of an increase in atmospheric CO_2 during the past decades," *Tellus* 9 (1957): 18–27, cited in *Weather and Climate Modification: Problems and Prospects*, vol. 1, summary and recommendations. Final Report of the Panel on Weather and Climate Modification to the Committee on Atmospheric Sciences, National Academy of Sciences, National Research Council (Washington: National Academy of Sciences, 1966), 88–89.

28 *Restoring the Quality of Our Environment (Report of the Environmental Pollution Panel, President's Science Advisory Committee)* (Washington: The White House, 1965), Appendix Y4, 127.

29 *[Report of the] Committee on Atmospheric Sciences*, National Research Council (Washington, DC: National Academy of Sciences, 1973), 160.

30 David Archer, *The Long Thaw: How Humans are Changing the Climate of the Planet for the Next 100,000 years* (Princeton, NJ: Princeton Univ. Press, 2010).

31 Tom Griffiths, *Slicing the Silence: Voyaging to Antarctica* (Cambridge, MA: Harvard Univ. Press, 2007), 200.

32 Archer, *The Long Thaw*, 9.

33 Archer, *The Long Thaw*, 9–10.

34 Bruno Latour, *Politics of Nature: How to Bring the Sciences into Democracy*, trans. Catherine Porter (Cambridge, MA: Harvard Univ. Press, 2004). Also see the debate between David Bloor and Bruno Latour: Bloor, "Anti-Latour," and Latour, "For David Bloor … And Beyond," in *Studies in History and Philosophy of Science* 30, no. 1 (1999): 81–112 and 113–29.

35 J.Bruce Brackenridge, *The Key to Newton's Dynamics: The Kepler Problem and the Principia* (Berkeley and Los Angeles: Univ. of California Press, 1995)

36 Quoted in Michael Hulme, *Why We Disagree About Climate Change: Understanding Controversy, Inaction, and Opportunity* (Cambridge: Cambridge Univ. Press, 2009), 334. Here is a contemporary definition of a "wicked problem": "A wicked problem is a complex issue that defies complete definition, for which there can be no final solution, since any resolution generates further issues, and where solutions are not true or false or good or bad, but the best that can be done at the time. Such problems are not morally wicked, but diabolical in that they resist all the usual attempts to resolve them." Valerie A. Brown, Peter M. Deane, John A Harris, and Jaqueline Y. Russell, "Towards a Just and Sustainable Future," in *Tackling Wicked Problems: Through the Transdisciplinary Imagingation*, ed. Valerie A. Brown, John A. Harris, and Jaqueline Y. Russell (London, Washington: Earthscan, 2010), 4.

37 Hulme, *Why We Disagree*, 336.

38 Ulrich Beck, "The Naturalistic Misunderstanding of the Green Movement: Environmental Critique as Social Critique," in *Ecological Politics in an Age of Risk*, trans. Amos Weisz (Cambridge: Polity, 1995), 36–57. See also the discussion in Ursula K. Heise, *Sense of Place and Sense of Planet: The Environmental Imagination of the Global* (New York: Oxford Univ. Press, 2008), chap. 4.

39 Latour, *Politics of Nature*, 47

40 Hannah Arendt, *The Human Condition*, 2nd ed., introduction by Margaret Canovan (1958; Chicago: Univ. of Chicago Press, 1998), 1–2.

41 Arendt, *The Human Condition*, 46.

42 Arendt, *The Human Condition*, 46.

Part Two
The Question of History and Historical Subjects

Since the first moments of the discipline of postcolonial studies, critics have been concerned with the history of the colonized, the project of colonial historiography, and the emerging history of the present, globalized world. This section brings together essays that address the H-question even as they examine the subject – colonizer, colonized – that is forged in the crucible of colonialism and its narrative accounts. While some essays concern themselves with the historical past, others study the forms of history-writing and representations within today's postcolonial societies as the latter seek to not only come to terms with their colonial/slavery/racialized pasts but also to chart their concerns in the globalized era. Lorenzo Veracini's essay turns to the historical consciousness of settler colonies in Australia, where the dynamics of amnesia (of the historical past) and reclamation (of the historical past) are played out with an overriding emphasis on "heritage." The tensions of retrieving and preserving memory from the colonized past to which Veracini draws attention have resonances for other postcolonial nations as well. Fernando Coronil uses Latin America and its decolonization process to propose a dialogue between the study of postcolonialism (understood as historical transformations after political independence), and the analysis of contemporary imperialism/neocolonialism within what he considers a major shift from Eurocentrism to "globalcentrism," and thus brings to the forefront matters of politics and culture in the messy histories of the present. Barbara Weinstein's essay argues that the rise of new kinds of history – world history, for example – working alongside postcolonial studies returns us to the "grand narrative" tradition, even as, ironically, postcolonialism concerns itself with microhistories. Like Chakrabarty or Young in the preceding section and Coronil here, Weinstein points to the universal versus particular tensions attending postcolonial history-writing. Ruth Mayer makes a case for the revisionist representations of the Middle Passage in the visual arts, literature, and pop music that, she claims, might be termed "Afrofuturism." Paying attention to strategies of representation, Mayer argues that the recuperation of the past is achieved by aligning it with contemporary forms of displacement and migration even as the representation itself takes on fantastic and even surreal forms.

Postcolonial Studies: An Anthology, First Edition. Edited by Pramod K. Nayar.
Editorial material and organization © 2016 John Wiley & Sons, Ltd.
Published 2016 by John Wiley & Sons, Ltd.

10   Historylessness
Australia as a Settler Colonial Collective

Lorenzo Veracini

Most cabbies would confirm that 'Australia has little history'. This is remarkable; how can one explain this often repeated trope? While having 'little' history should be understood in the sense that Australia has a short chronology (as dialogically opposed to 'Old Europe', for example), this refrain could also be understood as a way of expressing a perception that Australia is, relatively speaking, an especially 'historyless' society. This article understands a recurring reference to a lack of a 'dense' past as one discursive feature related to a number of specific constraints typical of settler colonial ideological formations.

Perceiving a lack of history, a lack of conflict, and a classless circumstance are related. As well as historyless (and despite contradicting evidence) Australia has a long tradition of being represented as an exceptionally egalitarian and classless society (again, as dialogically opposed to 'Old England'). A classless political order would be characterised by a lack of conflict that would in turn produce no history. This article interprets this claim as another discursive feature typical of settler colonial rhetorical traditions. Mythologies about egalitarian societies inhabiting 'quiet' continents, and the reality of underdeveloped historiographies, are related to the long lasting resilience of a settler colonial consciousness. The first section of this article outlines an approach to the historical consciousness of settler colonial political traditions; the second section focuses on Australian historiographies.

History and 'Settler Society'

Settler colonial political traditions have recurrently imagined a settler collective as the establishment of a worldly 'city on the hill': a locale where history could and had to be abandoned as a way of organising a regenerated body politic (religious zealots

Lorenzo Veracini, "Historylessness: Australia as a Settler Colonial Collective." *Postcolonial Studies,* 10(3), 2007: 271–285. Reprinted by permission of Taylor & Francis Ltd.

establishing themselves in New England recurrently construed their migration as 'rebirth'). An ideal society built elsewhere had to validate a specific representation of a traditional world by anti-politically leaving Old World history behind. In the context of an Anglophone tradition of settler colonialism, it was an idealised and 'pristine countryside cast timelessly in the early 18th century', as epitomised by Wordsworth's 'perfect Republic of Shepherds and Agriculturalists', and by rhetorical representations of 'the fall of the yeomanry'.[1] Images of neotraditional futures informed other national approaches to settler colonial practice. It was the 'intense desire to construct a preindustrial, agrarian vision of Germany', for example, that informed policies aiming at creating a new/old Germany in South West Africa.[2] And yet, a settler society is especially a society 'to come', where tradition and new beginnings would necessarily be closely intertwined. Nietzsche's warning against antiquarianism and against an insistence on new departures is especially appropriate in the case of settler colonial regimes.[3]

A settler anthropological revolution had to produce social collectives entirely projected towards the future and express a determination to reject historical and political precedents (while at the same time re-establishing new/truer traditional forms). As a result, forgetting can be understood as one trait of settler colonial collectives. Indeed, historical oblivion is one structural feature of the settler colonial mind. On this point, historiographer Eviatar Zerubavel, author of *Time Maps*, quotes Berl Katznelson, one 'of Zionism's leading visionaries':

> we cultivate oblivion and are proud of our short memory. ... And the depth of our insurrection [in Zionist parlance: settlement] we measure by our talent to forget. ... The more rootless we see ourselves, the more we believe that we are more free, more sublime. ... It is roots that delay our upward growth [in Israeli parlance: settlement].[4]

Patrick Wolfe, on the other hand, has perceptively detected settler colonialism's propensity for 'selective amnesia' and 'solipsistic narratives':

> This kind of selective amnesia would seem to be particularly congenial to settler-colonial nationalism. After all, settler colonialism strives for the elimination of the native in favour of an unmediated connection between the settlers and the land—hence the notion of building clone-like fragments of the mother country in the wilderness. In this fantasy, nobody else is involved, just settlers and the natural landscape. Such a situation is clearly conducive to solipsistic narratives.[5]

In settler colonial contexts, however, a rhetorical reference to lack of history coexists with a competing—and equally recurring—reclamation of history, and an enhanced attention to the marking of a new experience (US historian Edmund S Morgan defined Puritan New England as a 'most self-conscious society') is often associated with a corresponding need to reject existing political and historical orders.[6] While the tension between the prospect of establishing *another* society (a new Europe endowed with its unbroken history) and the possibility of a society that is *other* (a social experiment capable of leaving history behind) is indeed a recurring feature of settler colonial political traditions, the establishment of a settler polity is recurrently framed in terms of a civilising effort.

As well as being negated, 'history' becomes at the same time a crucial legitimising marker in the struggle against Indigenous people (who are perceived as having none) and against the possibility of degeneration in frontier conditions (ongoing anxieties about the possibility of Europeans 'going native' and thus rejecting their 'history' are always part of a settler cultural horizon).[7] Frantz Fanon wrote authoritatively about the ways in which a reference to history is one fundamental refrain of colonial and settler colonial discourse:

> The settler makes his history; his life is an epoch, an Odyssey. He is the absolute beginning: 'This land was created by us'; he is the unceasing cause: 'If we leave, all is lost, and the country will go back to the Middle Ages'. Over against him torpid creatures, wasted by fevers, obsessed by ancestral customs, form an almost inorganic background for the innovating dynamism of colonial mercantilism.

> The settler makes history and is conscious of making it. And because he constantly refers to the history of his mother country, he clearly indicates that he himself is the extension of that mother country. Thus the history which he writes is not the history of the country which he plunders but the history of his own nation in regard to all that she skims off, all that she violates and starves.[8]

This displacement—being somewhere and making the history of another locale—underscores a somewhat distorted relationship with history that is typical of a settler colonial state of mind.

The founding texts of settler political traditions outline the establishment of a body politics that operates in a historyless reality. Tocqueville's *Democracy in America*, for example, focuses on the encounter between a settler group and the exceptional geography it settles (a scenario that facilitates the establishment of an agrarian society of equals). It narrates the unique combination of a land that is unframed by social relations (a wilderness waiting to be cultivated) and a settler collective (which is also assumed to be divested of any prior social determination): a people without history in a place without history.[9] Moreover, as Ayse Deniz Temiz's outline of his account of a settler foundation remarks, the 'transition from the state of nature to the social state is incomparably smoother in Tocqueville's exceptional case' (as opposed to the Hobbesian transfer of power to the sovereign, or Rousseau's social contract).

> [The] state of law does not rule out the natural state, but emerges alongside it. For the law does not arise as a collective response to a conflict which it takes upon itself to dissipate, rather it emerges spontaneously, so to say, as supplement to a conflict-free natural state.[10]

Tocqueville's assertion of a non-detectable shift from a state of nature responds to Locke's notion that 'in the beginning all the world was America' (it is 'settlement' that supersedes a natural state, and it is an original settler appropriation—enclosure—that defines and precedes the inception of historical processes).[11] Despite their differences, both Locke and Tocqueville assumed that settlers are natural men engaged in building a settled life in a historical locales.

On the other hand, a need to break away from historical orders is a recurring feature of debates pertaining to the establishment of settler polities. In his analysis of settler colonialism Anthony Moran notes how what he defines as a discourse of "newness" was the 'staple of nineteenth-century and early twentieth-century settler nationalists', proclaiming that 'settler colonies or nations were new societies free of the problems, the traditions and the class distinctions that bedevilled the "old world"', that the '"absence" of history and tradition meant that settlers could build their own utopias without hindrances'.[12] This is a long lasting and widely held notion shared, among others, by Malthus, Tocqueville and Marx—who had all emphasised, for example, how the United States, uncluttered by feudal vestiges, and ecclesiastical burdens, was a locale where a bourgeois order was at the same time the 'natural' and the foundational organisation of society. Australasian league secretary Gilbert Wright even suggested in 1853 that Australia should reject 'Old World' history as a means to emphasise a discontinuity between historical and settler colonial orders: 'We should aim at nationa lity—at individuality—at a character. We should not blend our associations with the histories of the Old World. Why not have an era—a chronology of our own?'[13]

Parallel to a utopian drive to build an ideal society, there is another structural reason why reference to history would not constitute an effective legitimating discursive trope in settler colonial contexts. In these formations and in typically Lockean fashion, possession flows from improvement and it is labour expended on the land rather than an historical or an ancestral relation to it that can sustain an exclusive claim.[14] Victimologies allow suffering (rather than, for example, prior ownership, an ancestral connection, or an aristocratic background) to become an essential vehicle for legitimacy in a settler colonial context.[15] As a result, settler colonial discourses emphasise victimology and displace history; and settler groups emphasise suffering as a strategy for legitimising their claims to country (i.e. the myth and the reality of the 'struggle with the land'; 'this place was empty, we built it'; 'we are its beginning, therefore it has no previous history'—all classic settler accounts). These discursive constructions require at the same time a parallel denigration of later migrant victimologies (i.e. 'they did not have it as tough as we did') and a constant reinforcement of the notion of an Indigenous non-relationship with the land (i.e. 'they are nomads', 'they did not use this place', etc.). In a settler colonial historiographical order, it is not only settler histories that are denied; Indigenous and migrant histories are also repressed in order to sustain a settler claim to an *original* and *exclusive* relationship with the land. In turn, these constraints do inform migrant historiographies, and the historiography of Indigenous experiences, centred around a discursive reaffirmation of the 'we had it quite tough too' and 'we also built this country' refrains on the one hand, and forced to continuously reite rate Indigenous survival and the very existence of Indigenous pasts on the other.[16]

As founders of political orders that see themselves carrying an inherent and unprecedented sovereignty (unlike migrants, who are appellants *vis-à-vis* political systems that are already established), settlers are often engaged in avoiding a reproduction of the political structures characterising the Old World: settler societies recurrently display a determination to become exemplary societies.[17] As a result, settler narrative forms generally determine a type of emplotment in which the establishment of a settler community ends up being at the same time the beginning and the end of history: no real history can be admitted to have happened before a foundational moment that, because of the constituent character of a regenerated body politics, would not be followed by history either. If the development/validation of an ideal society merely follows an originally ideal foundation, history as conflict (a notion shared by Whig interpretations of history as the unfolding of the opposing 'interests' and by Marxist understandings of class struggle) cannot have a place in settler historiographical perceptions.

Indeed, while settler societies are political determinations that declaratively reject the possibility of a class system, yet alone the presence of class conflict, a historyless circumstance must be a situation where contradictions have been ultimately resolved. Donald Denoon's seminal and comparative article on settler societies and their historiographies argued against neglecting 'class' as a category of historical enquiry:

> [t]he historiography of many of these [settler] societies is replete with exceptionalist arguments: social classes may have existed in nineteenth century Europe, but not in regions of recent settlement where social mobility was very rapid; in this society people alternated between two kinds of employment, so classes did not form; or the society was so small and so homogeneous culturally, that class divisions were marginal. Social class could be defined as a phenomenon which occurs everywhere except 'here' [...].[18]

Of course he had a point: classes did exist—even in settler societies—and shaped the way people lived; and he set out to demonstrate it.[19] The consistent pattern of rhetorical reference he detected in the settler colonial polities included in his research, however, also pointed to a typically settler colonial reluctance to perceive a settler society as a classed body politic.

The Historiography of an Impossible History

The need to represent Australia as a settler colonial collective has shaped Australian historiographies and contributed to a historiography systematically intent on displacing conflict. While these considerations are suggestive rather than exhaustive, I am not suggesting that Australia was ever exclusively a settler society, or that no historical works were ever produced. The purpose, however, is to highlight a number of recurring interpretative impasses in a context in which, generally speaking, the expectation was that Australia should have a special history and that this uniqueness was that there would be little of it, and where conflicting necessities produce a situation in which history is claimed and denied at the same time. The aim is to explore the delayed consolidation of a historiography that recurrently faces contradictory needs: doing away with history and making good claims to land and new social orders and, *at the same time*, developing meaningful histories and/or histories that could be appropriate for national purposes.[20] A preoccupation with history (hence, an enhanced concern for memorials, and an emphasis on textbook history, historical novels and films, etc.) continuously coexisted with a parallel and contradictory need to downplay it.[21]

There is a long lasting Australian tradition of surprised shock in the face of 'Old World' history and conflict cropping up from within. John Hirst, for example, perceptively noted what he defines as a uniquely Australian determination to repress visible sectarian strife from public life after riots followed Orangist marches in Melbourne in 1846 (he also noted a related and equally 'distinctly Australian response to class conflict': the Arbitration Court).[22] T H Irving's classic 1970s account of 1850s and 1860s Australian political life detected a flow of 'editorial surprise that European feuds could still break out in Australia's benign society' (this was after an Irish immigrant shot and slightly wounded a member of the Royal family in 1868).[23] While this could be understood as a truly Australian reflex, other episodes could be mentioned in this tradition of perception: the Kisch affair, for example, and all the way down to the Cronulla riots of 2005.[24] According to this narrative frame of reference, history does not generate within Australia and its unwanted manifestations also emanate from elsewhere and have to be stopped on their way in—on inbound ships, in international waters, at the beach.[25]

Some positively reclaimed a lack of history and insisted on the possibility that a new beginning would produce an especially egalitarian society (or, conversely, regretted that Australia had failed to fulfil the promise of a truly egalitarian polity and had become classed); others sorely lamented a lack of a civilised (steeped in history) lifestyle. While these are obviously contradicting perspectives, these patterns of opinion share an original perception of an Australian distinctive historyless quality. The long lasting influence of dismissive notions like the 'Cultural Cringe' and of a widespread percep-tion that cultural and other standards are defined elsewhere should also be mentioned in this context.[26] Historiographical orders emphasising a remarkable lack of conflict were only slowly eroded, with the gradual emergence throughout the twentieth century of a fully articulated historiography. Labour history, in particular the work of historian Brian Fitzpatrick, the detection and exploration of sectarian division within the social body (Manning Clark, for example, would challenge obvious omissions, and explore the contradiction between what he defined as 'the Catholic and Protestant view of the world' in the process of abandoning what he called the 'comforters of the past'), women's history, and Aboriginal history were all eventually integrated in the context of a steadily expanding scholarship.[27] A delayed pattern of historiographical consolidation, and traditional structures of reference that remain entrenched in public perception, however, should be the subject of historiographical investigation.

Indeed, reclaiming a lack of history as a defining feature of a new (settler) polity (the 'young and free', that is, the 'young and *therefore* free' refrain, a counterpoint to earlier but not unrelated constructions of the ancient rights of 'freeborn Englishmen', free beyond doubt because enjoying a truly ancient right) is one recurring theme of reflections pertaining to Australia. Percy Reginald Stephensen's 1936 radical nationalist manifesto entitled *The Foundations of Culture in Australia*, for example, emphasised how Australia was 'a country *without* any castles or ruins [a country endowed with] thou-sands of square miles of ground *not* staled by history and tradition'. He also expressed another widely accepted notion: in the case of an Australian nation it was 'race' and 'place' (both typically unchanging elements) and, symptomatically, *not* history that would interact in giving birth to a new national type. He called for the absorption by settlers of the spirit of a place as a way to establish a new national type, which he called: 'the true indigenous Australians'.[28] While settlers recurrently represent them-selves as truly native in an attempt to indigenise their claims against Indigenous, migrant and metropolitan others, Stephensen's argument constitutes an exemplary indication that a settler project is *especially* about replacement.[29]

A stress on a lack of political conflict—the myth of the 'Quiet Continent'—is a recurring and long lasting theme of an Australian historiography and would characterise its settler narrative orders.[30] Could a generalised neglect of Indigenous pasts and a parallel disregard for the sectarian and ethnic tension between Irish Catholic and English Protestant, for example, be one result of a settler-determined inclination to erase conflict and history and a function of a typically settler colonial narrative structure? In this tradition, Australia is often represented as a comparatively successful site for a settler colonial experiment, as a locale uniquely apt for the exercise of a settler colonial project (indeed, the need to represent country as 'quiet' is a theme that can be detected in most settler colonial traditions: after all, settling is about pacification). Representations of Australian landscapes as a 'sleeping garden' implied a country awaiting settlers, awaiting an act of settlement so natural that it could be understood as not needing an act of conquest.[31] While in settler colonial narrative structures there is an ongoing need to elide violent encounters and conflict, Australian historiographies often express a radicalised version of this tendency: Keith Windschuttle's anxious reaffirmation that the British colonisation of Australia 'was the least violent of all Europe's encounters with the New World', for example, should be framed in the context of a narrative need to project images of a peaceful process in a pacified country.[32]

Elision of conflict *within* the polity in an Australian context is matched by a related emphasis on the capacity to pick up a fight overseas, as epitomised by the historiographical myth of ANZAC promoted by Ernest Scott and C E W Bean, for example.[33] Ann Curthoys has convincingly remarked how '[i]n Australian popular political culture, commemoration of war displaces the political formation of the nation through Federation as the emotional locus of a sense of nationhood'.[34] This reversal of normal patterns of national observance could be understood as one consequence of a settler-determined need to represent Australians as history-making people provided they make it somewhere else. While a settler-determined vision of history necessitates that Australia as a settler society be somewhat outside of history, a celebration of ANZAC becomes a way to fulfil the apparently contradictory necessity of constructing a national history and at the same time maintaining that history happens overseas.[35] Referring to New Zealand, James Belich noted that how 'independence is demonstrated by a disastrous attack on a place one has never heard of, occupied by people who have never heard of New Zealand, on the instructions of another country, has yet to be satisfactorily explained'.[36] This may hold true of Australia as well; at the same time, however, as psycho-analytic practice suggests, displacement is often one outcome of the necessity of dealing with competing impulses.[37]

There are other features characterising the long lasting development of an Australian historiography that would sustain this approach. Uneasiness towards the convict 'stain' and a successive recuperation of convict pasts, for example, share a reluctance in accounting for historical transformation. University of Sydney based historian George Arnold Wood's initial and seminal 'recuperation' of convicts was a way of projecting a struggle between a settler colonial democracy in the making, and the political constraints of a foreign 'imperial' power. While erasure and repression of a convict past had previously been functional to the establishment of a settler colonial project, a later recuperation of convict pasts was also functional to the display of settler images. The more successful the earlier process of erasure had been, the more seamless the obverse process of inclusion could now be. Since Australia had been successful in establishing a unique settler colonial order, convicts could now be retroactively included in the settler colonial project that had been established by way of their exclusion. While Wood rejected an inclination to avoid discussing the convict 'stain', he was able to project a settler order that included convicts in his powerfully defusing definition, 'generally criminals of a low rank', and emphasised their role in nation building and their opposition to the interests of a corrupt English aristocracy. It was a class-ridden 'Old World' society that had produced a classless settler society: 'Is it not clearly a fact that the atrocious criminals remained in England, while their victims, innocent and manly, founded the Australian democracy?', he rhetorically asked.[38] It was discontinuity, the history of a transition between two diametrically opposed exemplary societies—concentrationarian 'Botany Bay' and utopian 'Australia'—that was erased in the process. No major change—no history—had occurred: convicts could be seen as equipped with the determinants required for the building of a settler society because a liberal settler society had eventually been built.[39]

An historiographical emphasis on 'white Australia' can also be construed as a rejection of the possibility of history. Keith Hancock, for example, had supported the necessity of defending a settler colonial order and symptomatically collapsed national and settler identity. Restrictions against non-Europeans were justified because what Australians fear, he had written, 'is not physical conquest by another race, but rather the internal decomposition and degradation of their own civilisation'.[40] While a seamless shift between an appraisal of racial discourse and an assessment of a settler democratic tradition can only be understood in the context of a settler colonial order where the racial identification of an exclusive social body is also one essential prerequisite for the effective enjoyment of an inherent right to sovereign self-governance, an accent on race constitutes an important way of rejecting history in a context where there can be no significant national or class articulations in 'white' fragments, and where racial orders could be construed as immutable.[41]

'Australian legend' and settler colonial narrative structures are also related. R M Crawford's original notion of an Australian 'legend' could be construed as a settler colonial trope articulating Australia *through difference* as a 'new' (settler) world intrinsically different from the old one.[42] In *Australia* Crawford became concerned with a set of images purportedly emanating from life on the land, and with an attempt to distinguish a historyless Australian experience and 'type' (facing the outback, disrespectful of human pretentiousness, at times cynical). While 'legend' is located by definition outside of historical processes, this characteristic also emerged from Russel Ward's influential rendition of the 'Australian legend'.[43] As it suggests that Australia is a special place where 'prophecy' better than history can best describe the particular character of a unique polity, Geoffrey Serle's *From Deserts the Prophets Come* also fits in with this historiographical pattern.[44]

Finally, the 'great Australian silence' and the conditions of its supersession should be mentioned in the context of a brief outline of a repressed historiography. Its nature may also stem from a contradictory need to represent a historyless history, as settler colonial historiographical regimes would not easily allow for the acknowledgement of a history of Indigenous people before or after invasion (again, this is because the settler colonial project is premised on the denial of Indigenous presences *and* because a settler project is not supposed to produce historical dynamics, especially a history of violent confrontation and land wars).[45] It is not a coincidence that Indigenous history was literally repatriated from overseas by C D Rowley and

W E H Stanner working in Papua New Guinea and developing the structures that would allow a successive incorporation of an Aboriginal history within public discourse.[46] History and colonialism were happening overseas: they had to be 'smuggled in' by scholars (it is significant that both Stanner and Rowley were not historians) who were in a position to finally bypass the conceptual blockages embedded in a settler colonial conception of history.

Conclusion: *Historia Nullius*

'Heritage' emerges as the only non-unsettling form of history in a settler determined political body.[47] A disinclination to deal with history as process (as opposed to history as residue) is confirmed, for example, by a propensity to emphasise heritage rather than transformation. Prime Minister John Howard's recent insistence that history emphasise what he defines as an 'objective record of achievement' confirms this pattern of perception.[48] These approaches are, after all, a negation of history that identifies the present with the past.[49] On the contrary, history could be a situation where the past is seen as insisting dialectically on the present; as Eric Hobsbawm has noted, 'The past is another country, but it has left its mark on those who once lived there.'[50] Whereas in the case of 'heritage' (understood as legacy, or inheritance) the focus is on the present and the object is the past, in a settler colonial narrative system the only possible history remains a continuous and unbroken succession of developmental passages—literally, a 'record of achievement'.[51] Criticising Windschuttle ended up becoming a true Australian historiographical genre; and whereas a number of scholars have endeavoured with success to show how he is not an excellent historian, or a fair assessor of historical work, the fact that his reasoning is not historical has not yet been emphasised.[52] Windschuttle deploys a logic that collapses the present with what he perceives/supposes/wishes to be the past:

> Ever since they were founded in 1788, the British colonies in Australia were civilised societies governed by both morality and laws that forbade the killing of the innocent. The notion that the frontier was a place where white men could kill blacks with impunity ignores the powerful cultural and legal prohibitions on such action.[53]

That is: no Aboriginal person is presently being hunted down, we claim an absolute identification with our settler colonial heritage (we are civilised now and we always were), we cannot therefore accept that Indigenous people *could* have been killed at any time (good people *like us*/good people *that are us* could not have allowed that to happen). Unlike history, this is especially an exercise in identification. Yet again, if one feels that Australia should not have much history, *all* history looks like a fabrication.[54]

John Farrell's 1889 officially sanctioned and celebratory composition entitled *Australia* associates an emphasis on pacified surroundings with the suggestion that a land that escaped horrors endemic elsewhere would express God's will that earthly redemption might be found. *Australia* evocatively displays a number of widely held notions: Australia was inherently different from anywhere else, it had no history, and as a settler society (by now forgetful of a painful colonial past) would have none.

Farrell was explicit about a historylessness that precedes and follows settlement; it seems appropriate to quote at length:

'And once again will they, with eyes unheeding
His sacrifice, uplift their guilty hands
Each to his brother, and with rage exceeding,
And lust and vengeance, desolate the lands;
But this one land', so mused He, the Creator,
'This will I bless, and shield from all the woe,
That worthier among men, in ages later,
May find it pure, and, haply, hold it so!'

So, sweet Australia, fell a benediction
Of sleep upon thee, where no wandering breath
Might come to tell thee of the loud affliction
Of cursing tongues, and clamouring hosts of death;
So with the peace of His great love around thee,
And rest that clashing ages could not break,
Strong prying eyes of English seekers found thee,
Strong English voices cried to thee 'Awake!'

For them a continent, undreamed of, peerless—
A realm for happier sons of theirs to be,
One spot preserved, unspotted, bloodless, tearless,
Beyond the rim of an enchanted sea
Lay folded in the soft compelling languor
Of warm south airs, as an awaiting bride,
While strife and hate, and culminating anger
Raged through the far-off nations battle-dyed.

Here no dread vestiges stood up imprinted
With evil messages and brands of Cain,
No mounds of death or walls of refuge dinted
With signs that Christ had lived and died in vain;
No chill memorials here proclaimed the story
Of kinship stricken for and murders done;
Here was a marvel and a separate glory
One land whose history had not begun!

One unsown garden fenced by sea-crags sterile,
Whose mailed breasts pushed back strong-breasted waves,
From all the years of fierce unrest and peril,
And slaves, and lords, and broken blades, and graves;
One gracious freehold for the free, where only
Soft dusky feet fell, reaching not thy sleep
One field inviolate, untroubled, lonely
Across the dread of the uncharted deep![55]

A land that is awoken by the appearance of a settler collective, a land that remains historyless ('worthier' men would 'hold it so') and 'One gracious freehold for the free'—possibly as good a definition as any of a settler colonial determination—are key to Farrell's emphasis on the typically messianic settler colonial trait of endeavouring the establishment of an earthly redeemed polity.

A settler beginning is the beginning of history, but it is also its end. And if a 'gracious freehold' is seen as crucially epitomising a settler colonial end of history, no wonder that native title can be upsetting: it denies any graciousness and it demonstrates that it was not free—that many had to pay dearly. It is similarly unsurprising that the notion of the stolen generations can be so upsetting: stolen children also deny graciousness and demonstrate that it was not free—that many lost their freedom. Most importantly, native title and stolen generations deny the end of history, and crucially reintroduce historical process in the picture (for example, as the history of partial enforcement and locally selective of *terra nullius* in various parts of Australia; yes, *terra nullius* does exist, and it does have a history).[56]

Farrell's summation of an historical *tabula rasa* amounted to a type of *historia nullius* as much indispensable for the discursive practices of a settler colonial collective as its counterpoint dealing with real estate. Absence, excision, silences, amnesia and other defensive formations can all be interpreted as discursive necessities of a (settler colonial) need to emphasise the anti-political impossibility of conflict, class struggle, sectarian divisions, Indigenous survival, ethnic strife, etc. Previous to the intellectual shifts that began in the 1960s an Australian historiography would often attempt the writing of an impossible history.

Notes

[1] John L Comaroff, 'Images of Empire, Contests of Conscience: Models of Colonial Domination in South Africa', *American Ethnologist* 16, 1989, p 667.

[2] Daniel Joseph Walther, *Creating Germans Abroad: Cultural Policies and National Identity in Namibia*, Athens: Ohio University Press, 2002, p 183. Although it does not distance itself from the colonial dimension and language of German South West Africa, Walther's book remains a source of information pertaining to a specific example of a settler colonial project.

[3] See Friedrich Nietzsche, 'On the Uses and Disadvantages of History for Life', in Friedrich Nietzsche, *Untimely Meditations*, Cambridge: Cambridge University Press, 1983, pp 59–64.

[4] Quoted in Eviatar Zerubavel, *Time Maps: Collective Memory and the Social Shape of the Past*, Chicago: University of Chicago Press, 2003, p 93. Of course, parallel to this rejection of history, Zionism consistently expressed a determination to repossess history. It is important to note how dialectically opposed impulses coexisted and coalesced in the formation of different political traditions.

[5] Patrick Wolfe, 'Islam, Europe and Indian Nationalism: Towards a Postcolonial Transnationalism', in Ann Curthoys and Marilyn Lake (eds), *Connected Worlds: History in Transnational Perspective*, Canberra: ANU E-Press, 2005, p 235.

[6] Edmund S Morgan, *The Genuine Article: A Historian Looks at Early America*, New York: Norton, 2005, p 23.

[7] See, for example, Eric R Wolf, *Europe and the People Without History*, Berkeley: University of California Press, 1982.

[8] Frantz Fanon, *The Wretched of the Earth*, London: Penguin, 1967, pp 39–40.

[9] See Alexis de Tocqueville, *Democracy in America*, New York: Perennial Classics, 2000, and Cheryl B Welch, *de Tocqueville*, Oxford: Oxford University Press, 2001. The impact this narrative had on settler political traditions should not be underestimated, as it directly shaped Turnerian notions of 'frontier' democracy, for example, and, by way of analogy and identification, other settler entities as well.

[10] Ayse Deniz Temiz, 'Dialogues with *A Forgetful Nation*: Genealogy of Immigration Discourses in the US', *borderlands e-journal* 5(3), 2006. The URL for this article is: http://www.borderlandsejournal.adelaide.edu.au/vol5no3_2006/temiz_behdad.htm

11 See John Locke, *Two Treatises of Government: A Critical Edition with an Introduction and Apparatus*, New York: Cambridge University Press, 1965 [1690],# 48, 49.

12 Anthony Moran, 'As Australia Decolonizes: Indigenizing Settler Nationalism and the Challenges of Settler/ Indigenous Relations', *Ethnic and Racial Studies* 25, 2002,p 1016.

13 Quoted in T H Irving, '1850–70', in Francis K Crowley (ed.), *A New History of Australia*, Melbourne: W Heinemann, 1974, p 133. For various reasons not entirely unrelated to a perceived need to enact an anthropological revolution, other regimes would also symbolically mark their breaking away from historical orders. Both Fascist Italy and Gaddafi's Libya, for example, would enact a separate chronology.

14 Isn't it interesting that a most reasonable implication of this logic, that settlers degrading and/or defacing the land with poor environmental management should be dispossessed, has not yet been argued?

15 Ann Curthoys's work on Australian victimologies quotes anthropologist Andrew Lattas, who 'examined how Australian nationalist discourses emphasize a struggle in which the pioneer, the explorer and the artist all *suffer* as they seek to possess the land', and where 'White settler suffering [...] becomes a means for conferring right of ownership to the land.' Ann Curthoys, 'Expulsion, Exodus and Exile in White Australian Historical Mythology', *Journal of Australian Studies* 61, 1999, p 3.

16 For examples of how these interpretative necessities informed scholarly research, see, respectively: Gianfranco Cresciani, *The Italians in Australia*, New York: Cambridge University Press, 2003, which concludes a long trajectory of inscription of ethnic migrant histories within national historiographical orders; Lorna Lippmann, *Generations of Resistance: The Aboriginal Struggle for Justice*, Melbourne: Longman Cheshire, 1981; and Lyndall Ryan, *The Aboriginal Tasmanians*, Brisbane: University of Queensland Press, 1981.

17 This definition of settler endeavours (a characterisation focusing on a particular set of political traditions) differs from other approaches to the study of settler colonial forms, where emphasis is placed on the political ascendancy of 'fragment'-establishing newcomers. See, for example, Louis Hartz (ed.), *The Founding of New Societies: Studies in the History of the United States, Latin America, South Africa, Canada, and Australia*, New York: Harcourt, Brace & World, 1964.

18 Donald Denoon, 'Understanding Settler Societies', *Historical Studies* 18(73), 1979, pp 526–527.

19 In *The Fatal Shore*—which outsells all other history books on Australia—Robert Hughes subverted this trope by concluding that, on the contrary, 'the question of class was all pervasive and pathological'. Robert Hughes, *The Fatal Shore*, New York: Knopf, 1987, p 323.

20 On a number of specific constraints characterising history writing in Australia, see Ann Curthoys, 'Does Australian

History Have a Future?' *Australian Historical Studies* 118, 2002, pp 140–152. For an early detection of an Australian inclination to forget, see Bernard Smith's groundbreaking *The Spectre of Truganini*, Sydney: Australian Broadcasting Commission, 1980, especially pp 17–25.

21 In his analysis of the anti-transportation movement, a key moment in the transition to an Australian settler colonial order, John Hirst detected a particular sensitivity to history: while he noted how its promoters were 'very conscious they were making history' he also recorded how, immediately after the movement's victory, 'John West, one of its Tasmanian leaders, wrote its history'. John Hirst, *Convict Society and its Enemies: A History of Early New South Wales*, Sydney: George Allen & Unwin, 1983, pp 212, 216.

22 John Hirst, 'Australia's Absurd History', in John Hirst, *Sense and Nonsense in Australian History*, Melbourne: Black Inc., 2005, pp 14, 16.

23 Irving, '1850–70', pp 163–164.

24 On the 'Kisch affair' see, for example, Heidi Zogbaum, *Kisch in Australia: The Untold Story*, Melbourne: Scribe Publications, 2004. A perceptive reconstruction of the Cronulla riots is presented in Suvendrini Pereira, 'Race Terror, Sydney, December 2005', *borderlands e-journal*, 5(1), 2006. The URL for this essay is: http://www.borderland sejournal.adelaide.edu.au/vol5no1_2006/perera_raceter ror.htm

25 I am not suggesting that sectional, class, or ethnic strife should be promoted; a peculiar and long lasting pattern of perception assuming that these conflicts are intrinsically un-Australian, however, should be the subject of further exploration.

26 See A A Phillips, *The Cultural Cringe*, Melbourne: Melbourne University Press, 2006. Here one could also mention historian Keith Hancock's recurring ridicule of Australian mediocrity and of an Australian incapacity of producing 'history'—a possible case in point in the phenomenology of narrative envy.

27 See Brian Fitzpatrick, *A Short History of the Australian Labor Movement*, Melbourne: Rawson's Bookshop, 1944; Manning Clark, 'Rewriting Australian History', in Manning Clark, *Occasional Writings and Speeches*, Melbourne: Fontana Books, 1980, pp 4, 10; Miriam Dixson, *The Real Matilda: Woman and Identity in Australia, 1788–1975*, Melbourne: Penguin, 1976; and Anne Summers, *Damned Whores and God's Police: The Colonization of Women in Australia*, Melbourne: Penguin, 1975. For an outline of the evolution of Aboriginal history as a field of historical enquiry, see Lorenzo Veracini, 'A Prehistory of Australia's History Wars: The Evolution of Aboriginal History during the 1970s and 1980s', *Australian Journal of History and Politics* 52, 2006, pp 439–454.

28 Quoted in Anthony Moran, 'As Australia Decolonizes: Indigenizing Settler Nationalism and the Challenges of Settler/Indigenous Relations', *Ethnic and Racial Studies*

25, 2002, pp 1019, 1020. For a definition of settler colonialism as essentially a project of replacement, see Patrick Wolfe, *Settler Colonialism and the Transformation of Anthropology: The Politics and Poetics of an Ethnographic Event*, London: Cassell, 1999.

29 One example of how settler narratives often replicate a settler colonial need to enforce replacement is provided by an interpretation of *Waltzing Matilda* as a settler story, where the process of indigenization of the settler is completed and a settler logic of replacement is carried to its full logical extent (i.e. there is no Aboriginal presence whatsoever—except for an Aboriginal terminology that has been comprehensively, and significantly, appropriated and made truly own). In *Waltzing Matilda* the settler *is* the 'native': 'nomadically' inhabiting what is constructed as a pristine idyll before experiencing in succession the passages that would constitute a history of the Aboriginal experience: invasion, the clash of competing claims, a decision to fight against overwhelming odds rather than surrender to a claim that is perceived as ultimately illegitimate, extermination, and eventual haunting of country, are all elements of its narrative structure. And since a settler consciousness has entirely replaced an Indigenous presence, *Waltzing Matilda* is especially the story of an Indigenous dispossession. Crucially, its political imaginary is also a typically settler one, with a marked emphasis on an anti-aristocratic political message. Rejecting the possibility of establishing an aristocratic regime and its claims, however, is a rejection of history in this context, as any aristocratic regime by definition legitimises rule by reference to precedent and to historical realities. For a recent analysis of *Waltzing Matilda*'s story and its relation to interpreting Australian history, see Inga Clendinnen, 'The History Question: Who Owns the Past', *Quarterly Essay* 23, 2006, especially pp 3–8. See also Matthew Richardson, *Once a Jolly Swagman: The Ballad of Waltzing Matilda*, Melbourne: Melbourne University Press, 2006.

30 See, for example, Douglas Pike, *Australia: The Quiet Continent*, Cambridge: Cambridge University Press, 1962. Indeed, for a long time 'Australia' was the standard title for a history book, as if a description of place could exhaust the history of an inherently historyless locale.

31 For examples of this pattern of perception, see Paul Carter, *Road to Botany Bay: An Essay in Spatial History*, London: Faber and Faber, 1987, and Simon Ryan, *The Cartographic Eye: How Explorers Saw Australia*, Cambridge: Cambridge University Press, 1996. Elsewhere, settler political traditions could not possibly lay claim to a 'quiet land' and a celebration of frontier violence became a feature of national mythologies (in the US, for example). In these instances, however, the 'quietness' trope re-emerges *after* the 'closing' of troubled frontiers, when the establishment of a settled/settler order can be finally pursued.

32 Keith Windschuttle, *The Fabrication of Aboriginal History*, Sydney: Macleay Press, 2002, p 3.

33 Ernest Scott, *A Short History of Australia*, London: Oxford University Press, 1916; C E W Bean, *Official History of Australia in the War of 1914–1918*, Sydney: Angus and Robertson, 1921–1942. See also Donald Denoon, 'The Isolation of Australian History', *Historical Studies* 87, 1986, pp 252–260.

34 Ann Curthoys, 'Expulsion, Exodus and Exile in White Australian Historical Mythology', *Journal of Australian Studies* 61, 1999, p 12.

35 On Anzac memorials, see Ken Inglis, *Sacred Places: War Memorials in the Australian Landscape*, Melbourne: Miegunyah Press/Melbourne University Press, 1998. On war and memory in Australia, see Liz Reed, *Bigger than Gallipoli: War, History, and Memory in Australia*, Nedlands: University of Western Australia Press, 2004.

36 James Belich, 'Colonization and History in New Zealand', in Robin W Winks (ed.), *The Oxford History of the British Empire: Historiography*, vol. V, Oxford: Oxford University Press, 1999, p 185.

37 See also Marilyn Lake, 'Monuments, Manhood and Colonial Dependence: The Cult of Anzac as Compensation', in Marilyn Lake (ed.), *Memory, Monuments and Museums: The Past in the Present*, Melbourne: Melbourne University Press, 2006.

38 G A Wood, 'Convicts', *Journal of the Royal Australian Historical Society* VIII(IV), 1922, p 187.

39 John Hirst's 1983 book on New South Wales convict society, a contribution to the 'normalising school' on convict society, argues a similar conclusion by way of a different process: it was not a democratic tradition that should be upheld but had to struggle against British repression; on the contrary, it was a democratic tradition that should be upheld *and* one that could flourish under British rule (i.e. concentrationarian Australia was never a brutalised society). See John Hirst, *Convict Society and its Enemies: A History of Early New South Wales*, Sydney: Allen & Unwin, 1983.

40 W K Hancock, *Australia*, London: Ernest Benn Ltd, 1930, p 80.

41 South African historian George McCall Theal's reconciliation of British and Boer experiences had performed a similar narrative shift in a South African context. His massive production epitomises a settler historiography, with a shift towards race and towards appraising a conflict between civilisation and barbarism. Leonard Thompson, for example, concludes that 'Theal was a settler historian par excellence'. Leonard Thompson, *The Political Mythology of Apartheid*, New Haven: Yale University Press, 1985, p 56.

42 R M Crawford, *Australia*, London: Hutchinson's University Library, 1952.

43 Russel Ward, *The Australian Legend*, Melbourne: Oxford University Press, 1958.

44 Geoffrey Serle, *From Deserts the Prophets Come: The Creative Spirit in Australia 1788–1972*, Melbourne: Heinemann, 1973. Indeed, even Manning Clark's recurring reference to a

tragic register could be seen as one type of displacement, where an Australian history can only exist on the provision that it be recognised as the unfolding of a tragedy.

[45] However, in *Looking for Blackfellas' Point*, Mark McKenna provides a related and complementary argument. As well as forgetting and erasure, settler narratives can construe an active denial of responsibility, one result of a settler community's need to 'create history in their own image'. One consequence of this narrative requirement is that even acknowledgment of Indigenous destruction becomes a discursive device by which the Indigenous presence is placed in an irretrievable and unrecoverable past—a way to confirm that Indigenous people do not have a place in settler histories. See Mark McKenna, *Looking for Blackfellas' Point: An Australian History of Place*, Sydney: UNSW Press, 2002, p 94.

[46] See Veracini, 'A Prehistory of Australia's History Wars', p 454.

[47] See, for example, John Moloney, *Australia: Our Heritage*, Melbourne: Australian Scholarly, 2006.

[48] See John Howard's remarks in his 2006 Australia Day speech on the need to present a structured narrative and abandon a 'fragmented stew of themes and issues'. Howard quoted in Inga Clendinnen, 'The History Question: Who Owns the Past', *Quarterly Issue* 23, 2006, p 2. Clendinnen was about to participate in a 'History Summit' on the reformation of the teaching of Australian history organized by federal Education Minister Julie Bishop.

[49] The outstanding success of TV series like 'The Colony', where contemporary Australians are asked to fully immerse themselves in nineteenth-century circumstances, is a case in point. See Belinda Gibbon, *The Colony: The Book from the Popular SBS Living History Series*, Sydney: Random House Australia, 2006.

[50] Eric Hobsbawm, *Interesting Times: A Twentieth-century Life*, London: Abacus, 2003.

[51] Clendinnen insightfully summarises this approach as the 'triumph of British explorers and settlers in overcoming the recalcitrant land […] smoke rising from slab huts, the sound of axes ringing through the blue air, and so on'. See Clendinnen, 'The History Question', p 3.

[52] See, for example, Robert Manne, 'In Denial: The Stolen Generation and the Right', *Quarterly Essay* 1, 2001; Robert Manne (ed.), *Whitewash: On Keith Windschuttle's Fabrication of Aboriginal History*, Melbourne: Black Inc., 2003; and Stuart Macintyre and Anna Clark, *The History Wars*, Melbourne: Melbourne University Press, 2003.

[53] Keith Windschuttle, 'The Break-up of Australia', *Quadrant*, November 2000. This article is also available at: http://www.sydneyline.com/Massacres%20Part%20Two.htm

[54] See Keith Windschuttle, *The Fabrication of Aboriginal History*, Sydney: Macleay Press, 2002, p 3.

[55] John Farrell, 'Australia', quoted in Ian Turner (ed.), *The Australian Dream: A Collection of Anticipations about Australia from Captain Cook to the Present Day*, Melbourne: Sun Books, 1968, pp 236–237.

[56] For an anxious—and ultimately unconvincing—attempt to deny its very existence, see Michael Connor, *The Invention of Terra Nullius: Historical and Legal Fictions on the Foundation of Australia*, Sydney: Macleay Press, 2005.

11   Latin American Postcolonial Studies and Global Decolonization

Fernando Coronil

Given the curiously rapid rise to prominence of "postcolonial studies" as an academic field in Western metropolitan centers since the late 1980s, it is to be expected that its further development would involve efforts, like this one, to take stock of its regional expressions. Yet, while the rubric "Latin American postcolonial studies" suggests the existence of a regional body of knowledge under that name, in reality it points to a problem: there is no corpus of work on Latin America commonly recognized as "postcolonial." This problem is magnified by the multiple and often diverging meanings attributed to the signifier "postcolonial," by the heterogeneity of nations and peoples encompassed by the problematical term "Latin America," by the thoughtful critiques that have questioned the relevance of postcolonial studies for Latin America, and by the diversity and richness of reflections on Latin America's colonial and postcolonial history, many of which, like most nations in this region, long predate the field of postcolonial studies as it was developed in the 1980s. How then to identify and examine a body of work that in reality does not appear to exist? How to define it without arbitrarily inventing or confining it? How to treat it as "postcolonial" without framing it in terms of the existing postcolonial canon and thus inevitably colonizing it?

These challenging questions do not yield easy answers. Yet they call attention to the character of "postcolonial studies" as one among a diverse set of regional reflections on the forms and legacies of colonialism, or rather, colonia / isms. In light of the worldwide diversity of critical thought on colonialism and its ongoing aftermath, the absence of a corpus of Latin American postcolonial studies is a problem not of studies on Latin America, but between postcolonial and Latin American studies. I thus approach this discussion of Latin American postcolonial studies – or, as I prefer to see it, of postcolonial

Fernando Coronil, "Latin American Postcolonial Studies and Global Decolonization," in *Worlds and Knowledges Otherwise*. WKO and the Center for Global Studies and the Humanities, Duke University, 2013.

Fernando Coronil

studies in the Americas – by reflecting on the relationship between these two bodies of knowledge.

While its indisputable achievements have turned postcolonial studies into an indispensable point of reference in discussions about old and new colonialisms, this field can be seen as a general standard or canon only if one forgets that it is a regional corpus of knowledge whose global influence cannot be separated from its grounding in powerful · metropolitan universities; difference, not deference, orients this discussion. Rather than subordinating Latin American studies to postcolonial studies and selecting texts and authors that may meet its standards and qualify as "postcolonial," I seek to establish a dialogue between them on the basis of their shared concerns and distinctive contributions. This dialogue, as with any genuine exchange even among unequal partners, should serve not just to add participants to the "postcolonial discussion," but also to clarify its assumptions and transform its terms.

My discussion is divided into four sections: (a) the formation of the field of postcolonial studies; (b) the place of Latin America in postcolonial studies; (c) responses to postcolonial studies from Latin Americanists; and (d) open-ended suggestions for deepening the dialogue between postcolonial and Latin American studies. By focusing on exchanges between these fields, I have traded the option of offering close readings of selected texts and problems for the option of engaging texts that have addressed the postcolonial debate in terms of how they shape or define the fields of postcolonial and Latin American studies.

Postcolonial Studies

Despite a long history of critical reflections on modern colonialism originating in reactions to the conquest and colonization of the Americas, "post-colonialism" as a term and as a conceptual category originates in discussions about the decolonization of African and Asian colonies after the Second World War. At that time, "postcolonial" was used mostly as an adjective by sociologists and political scientists to characterize changes in the states and economies of excolonies of the "Third World," a category that was also created at that time. This regional focus was already present in French sociologist George Balandier's analysis of "the colonial situation" (1951) as well as in later debates about the "colonial" and "postcolonial state" (Alavi 1972; Chandra 1981), the "colonial mode of production" (Alavi et al. 1982), or the "articulation of modes of production" (Wolpe 1980; Berman and Londsale 1992). Although Latin America was considered part of the Third World, because most of its nations had achieved political independence during the first quarter of the nineteenth century, it was only tangentially addressed in these discussions about decolonization that centered on the newly independent nations of Africa and Asia.

As "old" postcolonial nations that had faced the problem of national development for a long time, the key word in Latin American social thought during this period was not colonialism or postcolonialism, but "dependency." This term identified a formidable body of work developed by leftist scholars in the 1960s, designed to understand Latin America's distinct historical trajectory and to counter modernization theory. Riding atop the wave of economic growth that followed the Second World War, modernization theory presented capitalism as an alternative to socialism and argued than achieving modernity would overcome obstacles inhering in the economies, cultures, and subjective motivations of the peoples of the "traditional" societies of the Third World. W. W. Rostow's The Stages of Economic Growth (1960), revealingly subtitled A Non-Communist Manifesto, was a particularly clear example of modernization theory's unilinear historicism, ideological investment in capitalism, and teleological view of progress.

In sharp contrast, dependency theorists argued that development and underdevelopment are the mutually dependent outcomes of capitalist accumulation on a world scale. In their view, since underdevelopment is the product of development, the periphery cannot be modernized by unregulated_ capitalism but through an alteration of its polarizing dynamics. This basic insight into the mutual constitution of centers and peripheries was rooted in Argentinian economist Raul Prebisch's demonstration that unequal trade among nations leads to their unequal development. Formulated in the 1940s, Prebisch's critique of unequal exchange has been considered "the most influential idea about economy and society ever to come out of Latin America" (Love 1980: 46). His insights were integrated into "structural" reinterpretations of social and historical transformation in Latin America by Fernando Enrique Cardoso, Enzo Faletto, Anibal Quijano, Theotonio Dos Santos, Rui Mauro Marini, and many other "dependency" theorists; as Cardoso (1977) noted, their work was "consumed" in the United States as "dependency theory" associated with the work of Andre Gunder Frank.

The world-wide influence of dependency declined after the 1970s. Dependency theory was criticized for its one-dimensional structuralism and displaced by the postmodern emphasis on the textual, fragmentary and indeterminate; its Eurocentric focus on state-centered development and disregard of racial and ethnic divisions in Latin American nations has been a focus of a recent critique (Grosfoguel 2000). Despite its shortcomings, in my view the dependency school represents one of Latin America's most significant contributions to postcolonial thought within this period, auguring the post-colonial critique of historicism, and providing conceptual tools for a much needed postcolonial critique of contemporary imperialism. As a fundamental critique of Eurocentric conceptions of history and of capitalist development, dependency theory undermined historicist narratives of the "traditional," "transitional," and "modern," making it necessary to examine postcolonial and metropolitan nations in relation to each other through categories appropriate to specific situations of dependency.

Starting around three decades after the Second World War, the second usage of the term "postcolonial" developed in the Anglophone world in connection with critical studies of colonialism and colonial literature under the influence of postmodern perspectives. This change took place during a historical juncture formed by four intertwined world-wide processes: the increasingly evident shortcomings of Third-World national development projects; the breakdown of really existing socialism; the ascendance of conservative politics in Britain (Thatcherism) and the United States (Reaganism); and the overwhelming appearance of neoliberal capitalism as the only visible, or at least seemingly viable, historical horizon. During this period, postcolonial studies acquired a distinctive identity as an academic field, marked by the unusual marriage between the metropolitan location of its production and the anti-imperial stance of its authors, many of whom were linked to the Third World by personal ties and political choice.

Fernando Coronil

In this second phase, while historical work has centered on British colonialism, literary criticism has focused on Anglophone texts, including those from Australia and the English-speaking Caribbean. The use of postmodern and poststructuralist perspectives in these works became so intimately associated with postcolonialism that the "post" of postcolonialism has become identified with the "post" of postmodernism and poststructuralism. For instance, a major postcolonial Reader argues that "postcolonial studies is a decidedly new field of scholarship arising in Western universities as the application of post-modern thought to the long history of colonising practices" (Schwarz 2000: 6).

In my view, equally central to postcolonialism has been the critical application of Marxism to a broad spectrum of practices of social and cultural domination not reducible to the category of "class." While marked by idiosyncratic traces, its identifying signature has been the convergence of these theoretical currents – Marxist and postmodern/poststructuralist – in studies that address the complicity between knowledge and power. Edward W. Said's integration of Gramscian and Foucauldian perspectives in his path-breaking critique of Orientalism (1978) has been widely recognized as foundational for the field. A similar tension between Marxism and poststructuralism animates the evolving work of the South Asian group of historians associated with Subaltern Studies, the strongest historiographical current of postcolonial studies.

Postcolonial critique now encompasses problems as different as the formation of minorities in the United States and African philosophy. But while it has expanded to new areas, it has retreated from analyzing their relations within a unified field; the fragmentary study of parts has taken precedence over the systemic analysis of wholes. Its critique of the grand narratives of modernity has led to skepticism towards any grand narrative, not always discriminating between Eurocentric claims to universality and the necessary universalism arising from struggles against world-wide capitalist domination (Amin 1989; Lazarus 1999a).

As the offspring of a tense marriage between anti-imperial critique and metropolitan privilege, postcolonial studies is permeated by tensions that also affect its reception, provoking sharply different evaluations of its significance and political implications. While some analysts see it as an academic commodity that serves the interests of global capital and benefits its privileged practitioners (Dirlik 1994), others regard it as a paradigmatic intellectual shift that redefines the relationship between knowledge and emancipatory politics (Young 2001). This debate helps identify what in my view is the central intellectual challenge postcolonial studies has raised: to develop a bifocal perspective that allows one, on the one hand, to view colonialism as a fundamental process in the formation of the modern world without reducing history to colonialism as an all-encompassing process and, on the other hand, to contest modernity and its Eurocentric forms of knowledge without presuming to view history from a privileged epistemological standpoint.

In this light, the apparently simple grammatical juxtaposition of "post" and "colonial" in "postcolonial studies" serves as a sign to address the murky entanglement of knowledge and power. The "post" functions both as a temporal marker to refer to the problem of classifying societies in historical time and as an epistemological sign to evoke the problem of producing knowledge of history and society in the context of imperial relations.

Given this genealogy, it is remarkable but understandable that debates and texts on or from Latin America do not figure significantly in the field of post-colonial studies as it has been defined since the 1980s. As Peter Hulme (1996) has noted, Said's canonical Culture and Imperialism (1993) is emblematic of this tendency: it centers on British and French imperialism from the late nineteenth century to the present; its geographical focus is limited to an area stretching from Algeria to India; and the role of the United States is restricted to the post Second World War period, disregarding this nation's origin as a colonial settlement of Britain, Spain, and France, the processes of internal colonialism through which Native Americans were subjected within its territory, and its imperial designs in the Americas and elsewhere from the nineteenth century to the present.

The major Readers and discussions on postcolonial studies barely take Latin America into account. One of the earliest attempts to discuss post-colonial literatures as a comprehensive field, The Empire Writes Back: Theory and Practice in Post-Colonial Literatures (Aschroft, Griffiths, and Tiffin 1989), acknowledges a focus on Anglophone literatures. Even so, its extensive sixteen-page bibliography, including "all the works cited in the text, and some additional useful publications" (22.4), fails to mention even a single text written on Latin America or by a Latin American author. The book treats Anglophone literatures, including those produced in the Caribbean, as if these literatures were not cross-fertilized by the travel of ideas and authors across regions and cultures-or at least as if the literatures resulting from the Iberian colonization of the Americas had not participated in this exchange.

This exclusion of Latin America was clearly reflected in the first general anthology of postcolonial texts, Colonial Discourse and Postcolonial Theory (P. Williams and Chrisman 1993), whose thirty-one articles include no author from Iberoamerica. Published two years later, The Post-colonial Studies Reader (Aschroft, Griffiths and Tiffin 1995), reproduces the Anglo-centric perspective that characterizes their earlier The Empires Writes Back, but this time without the justification of a topical focus .on English literatures. The Reader features eighty-six texts divided into fourteen thematic sections, including topics such as nationalism and hybridity, which have long concerned Latin American thinkers. While some authors are repeated under different topics (Bhabha appears three times, Spivak twice), the only author associated with Latin America is Jose Rabasa, whose contribution is a critical reading of Mercator's Atlas, a topic relevant but not specific to Latin America.

The marginalization of Latin America is reproduced in most works on postcolonial-ism published since then. For example, Leela Gandhi's Post-colonial Theory: A Critical Introduction (1998) does not discuss Latin American critical reflections or include even a single reference to Latin American thinkers in its extensive bibliography. While Relocating Postcolonialism (Goldberg and Quayson 2002) "relocates" the postcolonial through the inclusion of such topics as the cultural politics of the French radical right and the construction of Korean-American identities, it maintains the exclusion of Latin America by having no articles or authors associated with this area. This taken-for-granted exclusion appears as well in a dialogue between John Comaroff and Homi Bhabha that introduces the book. Following Comaroff's suggestion, they provide a historical frame for "postcoloniality" in terms of two periods: the decolonization of the Third World marked by India's independence in 1947 and the hegemony of neoliberal capitalism signaled by the end of the Cold War in r989 (Goldberg and Quayson 2002: 15).

In contrast, two recent works on postcolonialism include Latin America within the postcolonial field, yet their sharply different criteria highlight the problem of discerning the boundaries of this field. In an article for a book on the postcolonial debate in Latin America, Bill Aschroft (whose co-edited book, as has been mentioned above, basically excludes Latin America) presents Latin America as "modernity's first born" and thus as a region that has participated since its inception in the production of postcolonial discourses (r999). He defines postcolonial discourse comprehensively as "the discourse of the colonized" produced in colonial contexts; as such, it does not have be "anticolonial" (r4–r5). He presents Menchu's I, Rigoberta Menchu and Juan Rulfo's Pedro Paramo as examples that reveal that the transformative strategies of postcolonial discourse, strategies which engage the deepest disruptions of modernity, are not limited to the recent colonized" (28). While his comprehensive definition of the field includes Latin American discourses from the conquest onwards, his examples suggest a narrower field defined by more discriminating but unexamined criteria.

The second text is Robert Young's Postcolonialism: An Historical Introduction (200r). While Young (like Aschroft) had not discussed Latin America in a previous work (White Mythologies, 1990) that had served to sacralize Said, Bhabha, and Spivak as the foundational trinity of postcolonial studies, in his new book he gives such foundational importance to Latin America and to the Third World that he prefers to name the field "tricontinentalism," after the Tricontinental conference held in Havana in 1966 (200r: 57). Young recognizes that postcolonialism has long and varied genealogies, but he finds it necessary to restrict it to anticolonial thought developed after formal political independence has been achieved: "Many of the problems raised can be resolved if the postcolonial is defined as coming after colonialism and imperialism, in their original meaning of direct-rule domination" (57). Yet Young distinguishes further between the anticolonial thought of the periphery and the more theoretical thought formed at the heart of empires "when the political and cultural experience of the marginalised periphery developed into a more general theoretical position that could be set against western political, intellectual and academic hegemony and its protocols of objective knowledge" (65). Thus, even successful anticolonial movements "did not fully establish the equal value of the cultures of the decolonised nations." "To do that," Young argues, "it was necessary to take the struggle into the heart-lands of the former colonial powers" (65).

Young's suggestive discussion of Latin American postcolonial thought leaves unclear the extent to which its anticolonialism is also "critical" in the sense he ascribes to metropolitan reflections. Young discusses Latin American postcolonial thought in two brief chapters. The first, "Latin America I: Mariategui, Transculturation and Cultural Dependency," is divided into four sections: "Marxism in Latin America," an account of the development of communist parties and Marxist thinkers in the twentieth century, leading to the Cuban revolution; "Mexico 1910," a presentation of the Mexican revolution as precursor of tricontinental insurrections against colonial or neo-colonial exploitation; "Mariategui," a discussion of Mariategui's role as one of Latin America's most original thinkers, highlighting his innovative interpretation of Peruvian reality; and "Cultural Dependency," an overview of the ideas of some cultural critics which, for brevity's sake, I will reduce to a few names and to the key concepts associated with their work: Brazilian Oswald de Andrade's "anthropophagy;' (the formation of Latin American identity through the "digestion" of world-wide cultural formations); Cuban Fernando Ortiz's "transculturation" (the transformative creation of cultures out of colonial confrontations); Brazilian Roberto Schwarz's "misplaced ideas" (the juxtaposition in the Americas of ideas from different times and societies); and Argentinian Nestor Garcia Canclini's "hybrid cultures" (the negotiation of the traditional and the modern in Latin American cultural formations).

Young's second chapter, "Latin America II: Cuba-Guevara, Castro, and the Tricontinental," organized around the centrality of Cuba in the development of post-colonial thought, is divided into three sections: "Compañero: Che Guevara," focuses on Guevara's antiracism and radical humanism; "New Man" relates Guevara's concept of "the new man" to Jose Marti's proposal of cultural and political independence for "Our America" and to

Roberto Fernandez Retamar's Calibanesque vision of mestizaje; and the "Tricontinental," which presents the "Tricontinental Conference of Solidarity of the Peoples of Africa, Asia and Latin America" held in Havana in 1966 as the founding moment of postcolonial thought; in Young's words, "Postcolonialism was born with the Tricontinental" (2001: 213).

While Young's selection is comprehensive and reasonable, its organizing criteria are not sufficiently clear; one can easily imagine a different selection involving other thinkers and anticolonial struggles in Latin America. Despite the significance he attaches to theoretical reflections from metropolitan centers, Young makes no mention of the many Latin Americanists who, working from those centers or from shifting locations between them and Latin America, have produced monumental critiques of colonialism during the same period as Said, Bhabha, and Spivak – for example, Enrique Dussel, Anibal Quijano, and Walter Mignolo, among others.

The contrasting positions of Ashcroft and Young reveal the difficulty of defining postcolonial studies in Latin America. At one extreme, we encounter a comprehensive discursive field whose virtue is also its failing, for it must be subdivided to be useful. At the other extreme, we encounter a restricted domain that includes an appreciative and impressive selection of authors, but that needs to be organized through less discretionary criteria. Whether one adopts an open or a restricted definition of Latin American postcolonial studies, however, what is fundamental is to treat alike, with the same intellectual earnestness, all the thinkers and discourses included in the general field of postcolonial studies, whether they are produced in the metropolitan centers or in the various peripheries, writing or speaking in English or in other imperial and sub-altern languages. Otherwise, the evaluation of post-colonial thought risks reproducing within its midst the subalternization of peoples and cultures it claims to oppose.

Latin American Studies and Postcolonial Studies

It is understandable that the reception of postcolonial studies among Latin Americanists should have been mixed. Many thinkers have doubted the appropriateness of postco-lonial studies to Latin America, claiming that post-colonial studies responds to the academic concerns of metropolitan universities, to the specific realities of Asia and

Africa, or to the position of academics who write about, not from, Latin America, and disregard its own cultural traditions (Achugar 1998; Colas 1995; IZlor de Alva 1992, 1995; Moraiia 1997; Perez 1999; and Yudice I996). Klor de Alva has presented the most extreme critique, arguing that colonialism and postcolonialism are "(Latin) American mirages," for these terms, "as they are used in the relevant literature," or "as commonly understood today," properly apply only to marginal populations of indigenes, not to the major non-Indian core that has formed the largely European and Christian societies of the American territories since the sixteenth century. For him, its wars of independence were not anticolonial wars, but elite struggles inspired in European models that maintained colonial inequalities.

This argument, in my view, has several problems: it takes as given the standard set by discussions of the Asian and African colonial and postcolonial experiences; it assumes too sharp a separation between indigenous and non-indigenous peoples in America; it adopts a restricted conception of colonialism derived from a homogenized reading of Northern European colonialism and an idealized image of the effectiveness of its rule; it disregards the importance of the colonial control of territories in Iberian colonialism; it pays insufficient attention to the colonial control of populations in the high-density indigenous societies of Mexico, Peru, and Central America and in plantations run by imported slave labor in the Caribbean and Brazil; and it fails to see the similarity between the wars of independence and the decolonizing processes of Asia and Africa, which also involved the preservation of elite privilege and the reproduction of internal inequalities (what Pablo Gonzalez Casanova [r965] and Rodolfo Stavenhagen [1965) have theorized for Latin America as "internal colonialism"). Rather than presenting one set of colonial experiences as its exclusive standard, a more productive option would be to pluralize colonialism – to recognize its multiple forms as the product of a common historical process of Western expansion.

An influential debate on colonial and postcolonial studies in a major journal of Latin American studies was initiated by Patricia Seed, a historian of colonial Latin America, who presented the methods and concepts of colonial and postcolonial discourse as a significant breakthrough in social analysis. According to Seed (1991), postcolonial studies' critique of conceptions of the subject as unitary and sovereign, and of meaning as transparently expressed through language, recasts discussions of colonial domination that are simplistically polarized as resistance versus accommodation by autonomous subjects. Two years later in the same journal, three literary critics questioned her argument from different angles. Hernan Vidal expressed misgivings about "the presumption that when a new analytic and interpretative approach is being introduced, the accumulation of similar efforts in the past is left superseded and nullified," which he called "technocratic literary criticism" (r 993: II?). Rolena Adorno (1993), echoingi Klor de Alva's argument, argued for the need to recognize the distinctiveness of Latin America's historical experience, suggesting that colonial and postcolonial discourse may more properly apply to the historical experience of Asia and Africa. Walter Mignolo (1993) for his part, argued for the need to distinguish among three critiques of modernity: postmodernism (its internal expression), postcolonialism (its Asian and African modality), and postoccidentalism (its Latin American manifestation). Yet far from regarding postcolonialism as irrelevant for Latin America, he suggested that we treat the former as liminal space for developing knowledge from our various loci of enunciation. Mignolo has developed his ideas of "postoccidentalism" (building on its original conception by Fernandez Retamar [1974), and on my own critique of "occidentalism" [Coronil 1996)) in his pathbreaking Local Histories I Global Designs (:woo), a discussion of the production of non-imperial knowledge that draws on wide-ranging Latin American reflections, in particular Quijano's notion of the "coloniality of power" (2000) and Enrique Dussel's critique of Eurocentrism (1995).

Subaltern Studies has been widely recognized as a major current in the postcolonial field. While historians developed Subaltern Studies in South Asia, literary theorists have played a major role in the formation of Subaltern Studies in the Latin American context. Around the time of the Seed debate, the Latin American Subaltern Studies Group was founded at a meeting of the Latin American Studies Association in 1992. Unlike its South Asian counterpart, after which it was named, it was initially composed of literary critics, with the exception of Seed and two anthropologists who soon thereafter left the group. Its "Founding Statement" offered a sweeping overview of major stages of Latin American studies, rejecting their common modernist foundations and celebrating the South Asian critique of elitist representations of the subaltern. However, unlike the South Asian Group, formed by a small group of historians organized around a coherent historiographical and editorial project centered on rewriting the history of India, this group, mostly composed of literary critics, was characterized by its diverse and shifting membership and the heterogeneity of their disciplinary concerns and research agendas. While the publications of its members have not fitted within traditional disciplinary boundaries, they have privileged the interpretation of texts over the analysis of historical transformations. The group's attempt to represent the subaltern has typically taken the form of readings of texts produced by authors considered subaltern or dealing with the issue of subalternity. In its decade-long life (I myself participated in the second half of it), the group stimulated efforts to rethink the intellectual and political engagements that had defined the field of Latin American studies.

While centered on literary studies, Subaltern Studies has been considered a major source of postcolonial historiography in Latin America. In a thoughtful discussion entitled "The Promise and Dilemma of Subaltern Studies: Perspectives from Latin American History" published in a forum on Subaltern Studies in a major history journal, historian Florencia Mallon (1994) examines the consumption and production of Subaltern Studies in Latin America and evaluates the tensions and prospects of this field. Her account focuses on historical works, making explicit reference to the contributions of scholars based in the United States who have made significant use of the categories or methods associated with Subaltern Studies. She highlights Gil Joseph's pioneering use of Guha's work on India's peasantry in his examination of banditry in Latin America (Joseph 1990), noting that it moved discussion beyond simplistic oppositions that reduced bandits to either resisters or reproducers of given social orders.

In her review Mallon does not address Subaltern Studies in literary and cultural criticism (perhaps because she does not find this work properly historical), but she does offer a critique of the Latin American Subaltern Studies Group's "Founding Statement," noting its ungrounded dismissal of historiographical work on subaltern sectot's in Latin America. She makes a similar critique of the more substantial article by Seed, the one historian of the group (already discussed here). Objecting to Seed's presentation of members of the "subaltern studies movement" as leaders of the "postcolonial discourse movement," Mallon offers ample references to recent historical work on politics, ethnicity, and the state from the early colonial period to the twentieth century that "had begun to show that all subaltern communities were internally differentiated and conflictual and that subalterns forged political unity or consensus in painfully contingent ways" (1994: 1500).

Mallon's erudite discussion expands the scope of Subaltern Studies, but it does not sufficiently clarify why certain historical works should be considered part of the "subaltern" or "postcolonial" movement. Since studies on the social and cultural history of subaltern sectors ("history from below") and subaltern/postcolonial studies share subalternity as a subject matter and employ similar theories and methods, the lines separating them are some-times difficult to define. Yet South Asian subaltern historiography has sought to distinguish itself from social and cultural history by attaching singular significance to the critique of historicist and Eurocentric assumptions, problematizing the role of power in fieldwork and in the construction of archives, and interrogating such central historiographic categories as the "nation," the "state," "consciousness," and "social actors." The historiographical subaltern project has been marked by the tension between its constructivist aim, which necessarily involves the use of representational strategies not unlike those of social and cultural history, and its deconstructivist strategy, which entails questioning the central categories of historical research and interrupting the narratives of the powerful with those expressed by subaltern actors.

Mallon casts the "dilemma" of Latin American Subaltern Studies in terms of the tension between (Gramscian) Marxist and postmodern perspectives (a tension frequently noted in discussions about South Asian Subaltern Studies). She proposes to solve this dilemma by placing the Foucauldian and Derridean currents of postmodern criticism "at the service of a Gramscian project" (1994: 1515). Perhaps her subordination of deconstruction-so central to subaltern history-to the Gramscian project-so fundamental to social and cultural history-helps account for her insufficient attention to the difference between these fields.

This difference is central for John Beverley, one of the founders of the Latin American Subaltern Studies Group, who in his writings argues for the superiority of subaltern perspectives over non-subalternist ones of the subaltern (1993, 1999', 2000). Deploying criteria that for him define a subalternist perspective, he criticizes Mallon's Peasant and Nation. The Making of Post-colonial Mexico and Peru (1995), arguing that, despite her intentions, she appears as an omniscient narrator engaged in a positivist representational project that uses subaltern accounts to consolidate rather than interrupt the biographies of the nation, re-inscribing rather than deconstructing the official biographies of these nations.

In a sophisticated discussion of Subaltern Studies and Latin American history, Ecuadorian historian Guillermo Bustos (2002) uses Mallon and Beverley as a focal point to assess the relation between these two bodies of knowledge. While sympathetic to Mallon's discussion of this topic in "The Promise and Dilemma of Subaltern Studies" (1994), Bustos notes the Anglo-centric and metropolitan focus of her discussion, and suggests the inclusion of a more representative sample of work produced in Latin America; her only reference is to Andeanist historian Flores Galindo, which Bustos complements by mentioning three related Andeanists: Assadourian, Colmenares, and Rivera Cusicanqui. Like Beverley, Bustos recognizes the need to distinguish between social history and subalternist perspectives. While Beverley, however, uses this distinction to evaluate Mallon's work in terms of the standards of Subaltern Studies, Bustos uses it to caution against assuming the superiority of a subaltern perspective, recalling Vidal's critique of "techno-cratic literary criticism" (1993).

Bustos's proposal is to turn claims about the theoretical and political superiority of any perspective into questions answerable through concrete analysis. He exemplifies this option through a subtle reading of Mallon's Peasant and Nation (1995) that demonstrates the complexity of her narrative, including her attempt to engage in dialogical relation with her informants and fellow historians. While distancing himself from Beverley's critique, Bustos endorses Tulio Halperin Donghi's observation that Mallon's presentation of other perspectives does not prevent her from assuming (as in common practice) the superiority of her own professional account. His point is thus neither to criticize nor to defend Mallon's work, but to refine the dialogue between Subaltern Studies and Latin American historiography. He develops his argument by discussing other texts, including related attempts to break away from accounts organized as "the biography of the nation-state," based on the critical use of multiple voices and sources (Chiaramonti 1997; Coronil 1997; Thurner 1997). In agreement with Italian historian Carlo Ginzburg, Bustos proposes that we meet the postmodern challenge not by making "evidence" impossibly suspect, but by following, as Paul Ricoeur suggests, the "traces that left from the past, take its place and represent it" (Bustos 2002:15). Needless to say, the challenge remains how to retrieve and interpret these traces.

Postcolonial historical studies also received attention in Latin America in a book published in Bolivia, Debates Post Coloniales. Una Introducción a los Estudios de la Subalternidad (1999) ("Postcolonial Debates. An Introduction to Studies of Subalternity"), edited by historians Silvia Rivera Cusicanqui and Rossana Barragan and composed of translations of a selection of nine essays by South Asian authors. In their introduction Rivera Cusicanqui and Barragan make only tangential reference to the Latin American Subaltern Studies Group, and none to the work of its members. They are critical of its "Founding Statement" for reducing the contributions of the South Asian group to an assortment of ethnographic cases that "exemplify from the South the theory and the broad conceptual guidelines produced in the North" (1997: 13). They also criticize Mallon's article on Subaltern Studies both for its inattention to a long Latin American tradition of critical work on colonialism and postcolonialism, and for reducing South Asian Subaltern Studies "to a questionable Gramscian project on behalf of which one should place the whole postmodern and poststructuralist debate" (13).

Their own interpretative effort is centered on underlining the significance of South Asian Subaltern Studies for Latin American historiography, emphasizing the innovative importance of the poststructuralist perspectives informing the South Asian scholarship. Their brief discussion of Latin American work highlights three critical currents: the Argentinian school of economic history represented by Enrique Tandeter, Carlos Sempat Assadourian, and Juan Carlos Garavaglia, distinguished by its transformation of Marxist and Gramscian categories through a confrontation with the specificities of Indian labor in the Potosi area; the studies of peasant insurgency and oligarchic rule carried out by the Taller de Historia Oral Andina (Workshop of Andean Oral History) and by such influential scholars as Alberto Flores Galindo and Rene Zavaleta; and the studies of "internal colonialism" initiated by Mexican sociologist Pablo Gonzalez Casanova in the 1960s (and, I should add, Rodolfo Stavenhagen). Their call for a "South/South" dialogue at the same time avoids a dismissal of the "North," warning against the danger present in "certain academic Latin American circles" of adopting new theories and discarding "our own intellectual traditions-and Marxism is one of them – for this impoverishes and fragments the Latin American debate" (Rivera Cusicanqui and Barragan 1999: 19). Their horizontal dialogue establishes a common ground between postcolonial studies and Latin American historiography on colonialism and postcolonialism, yet presents Subaltern Studies as the product of an "epistemological and methodological rupture" (17). If Subaltern Studies is postcolonial, its "post" is the post of postmodernism and poststructuralism.

A variant of this view is presented by philosophers Santiago Castro-G6mez and Eduardo Mendieta in their thoughtful introduction to an important book of essays written by Latin Americanists published in Mexico under the Latin American postcolonial, studies and global decolonization title Teorias sin disciplina. Latino americanismo, postcolonialidad y globalización en debate (1998) ("Theories without Discipline. Latino Americanism, Postcoloniality and Globalization in Debate"). Focusing on the relationship between critical thought and the historical context of its production, Castro-G6mez and Mendieta seek to determine the specific character of postcolonial studies. They draw a distinction between "anticolonial discourse," as produced in Latin America by Las Casas, Guaman Poma de Ayala, Francisco Bilbao, and Jose Enrique Rod6, and "postcolonial discourse," as articulated by Said, Spivak, and Bhabha. For them, anticolonial discourse is produced in "traditional spaces of action," that is, "in situations where subjects formed their identities in predominantly local contexts not yet subjected to intensive processes of rationalization" (as described by Weber and Habermas). They argue that postcolonial theories, in contrast, are produced in "post-traditional contexts of action," that is, "in localities where social subjects configure their identities interacting with processes of global rationality and where, for this reason, cultural borders become porous" (16–17) For them, this distinction has political implications: while anticolonialist discourse claims to speak for others and seeks to dismantle colonialism deploying colonial categories, postcolonial discourse historicizes its own position, not to discover a truth outside interpretation, but to produce truth effects that unsettle the field of political action. It follows that radical politics lies not in anticolonial work that defines struggles with the categories at hand, thus confirming the established order, but in intellectual work that deconstructs them in order to broaden the scope of politics. From this perspective, the "post" of postcolonialism turns out to be an anti-anticolonial "post" at the service of decolonizing decolonization.

This position has the merit of offering a clear definition of postcolonialism. In my view, it raises several questions. Its distinction between anticolonial and postcolonial discourse risks reproducing the tradition/modernity dichotomy of modernization theory, turning the convulsed and rapidly changing social worlds of Las Casas, Guaman Poma, or Bilbao into stable "traditional" societies of limited rationality, in contrast to the globally rational worlds that engender postcolonial theorists and their superior discourses. By treating deconstruction as a theoretical breakthrough that supersedes previous critical efforts-now relegated to less rational traditional contexts-this position also risks becoming an expression of

Vidal's "technocratic literary criticism."Spivak's dictum that "Latin America has not participated in decolonization" (1993: 57) is perhaps an extreme expression of this risk. While Castro-G6mez and Mendieta acknowledge the "irritation" of those who recognize that Latin American thinkers have "long shown interest in the examination of colonialism," they seem to accept this risk as an inevitable consequence of the radical theoretical and methodological novelty of post-colonial studies (1998: 20).

By contrast, Cuban public intellectual Roberto Fernandez Retamar's discussion of Latin American decolonizing struggles, originally offered as a lecture for a course on Latin American thought in Havana, can be seen in part as a response to Spivak's dictum, which, according to him, wins the prize for epitomizing the problem of Latin America's exclusion from postcolonial studies (1996). It is impossible to summarize his already tight synthesis, organized around thirteen interrelated themes identified by key phrases or ideas that embody political and intellectual movements, such as "Independence or death." Suffice it here to indicate that his presentation links together political struggles and intellectual reflections as part of a single process of decolonization. Thus he joins the Haitian revolution, wars of independence, the Mexican revolution, the Cuban revolution, and the movements of the Zapatistas and the "Madres de Ia Plaza de Mayo" with such diverse intellectual struggles as literary modernism, theology and philosophy of liberation, dependency theory, pedagogy of the oppressed, Latin American historiography, and testimonio. His wide selection of authors and texts celebrates the originality and heterogeneous sources informing self-critical reflections from the Americas. His examples are too numerous to mention here, but they include Venezuelans Simon Rodriguez and Andres Bello, Mexicans Leopolda Zea and Octavio Paz, Brazilians Oswald de Andrade and Darcy Ribeiro, and Cubans Jose Marti and Fernando Ortiz. He highlights the contemporary importance of Rigoberta Menchu and Subcomandante Marcos as articulating in new ways the decolonizing projects of indigenous and national sectors in Guatemala and Mexico. Fernandez Retamar is not concerned with defining or erasing the boundaries bet-ween Latin American and postcolonial critical thought, but with appreciating their shared engagement with decolonization.

The difference between Mendieta/Castro-G6mez and Fernandez Retamar, like that between Ashcroft and Young, reveals the difficulty of defining the relation between postcolonial and Latin American reflections on colonialism and its aftermath. As in Bustos's discussion of the Mallon/Beverley exchange, a dialogue between these intel-lectual traditions requires not only clearer classificatory efforts, but also closer reading of texts, in order to refine the criteria that define these fields. A treatment of authors who are not considered part of the postcolonial canon as postcolonial thinkers may help us appreciate different modalities of critical reflexivity, as Castro-Klaren has done through her subtle reading of Guaman Poma and of the Inca Garcilaso de Ia Vega (1999, 2001). Or perhaps, as Hulme suggests, "the real advantage of considering distant figures like Ralph Waldo Emerson or Andres Bello as postcolonial writers is that this leads us to read them as if they were new" (1996: 6). A particularly productive option is to engage the postcolonial debate through studies of specific postcolonial encoun-ters, as in the pioneering integration of theoretical reflection and detailed historical case studies of US-Latin American relations in the collection edited by Joseph, LeGrand, and Salvatore (!999).

Fernando Coronil

Latin American Elephants in the Americas?

This discussion has made evident how difficult it is to define "Latin American postcolonial studies." As in the well-known parable of the elephant and the wise blind scholars (each of whom visualizes the elephant as a different creature by the part he or she feels), this field, like the wider field of postcolonial studies itself, can be represented in as varied a manner as there are different perspectives from which it can be "seen." If this parable shows that knowledge of reality is always partial and inconclusive, its use to reflect on Latin American postcolonial studies raises two more fundamental points.

First, the peculiar object of postcolonial studies is not a natural entity, like an elephant, or even a social subject regarded as sharing the cultural world of the observer, but one formed as a colonized object, an inferior and alien "Other" to be studied by a superior and central "Self." Since the "elephant" can speak, the problem is not just to represent it but to create conditions that would enable it to represent itself. From the perspective of postcolonial studies, analysis should involve not just self-reflection (an inherent dimension of any serious intellectual enterprise), or granting subjectivity to the social subject studied (as anthropologists and cultural historians have typically sought to do), but the integration of these two analytical endeavors into one unified intellectual project directed at countering this unequal, colonizing relationship. Its epistemology is not just representational but transformative; it uses representational strategies to counter the hierarchies and assumptions that turn some subjects into objects of knowledge for allegedly superior subjects.

Second, insofar as postcolonial studies appears as the most evolved critique of colonialism, it tends to invalidate or diminish the significance of reflections on colonialism developed from other locations and perspectives. If the wise scholars were to act wisely, they would not privilege their respective views of the elephant or isolate it from other creatures. As a reflection on the relationship between postcolonial and Latin American studies, the parable appears as a literal story, the absence of indigenous elephants in the Americas justifying the identification of postcolonial studies with scholarship on Africa and Asia.

If we take the parable literally, since the only elephants that exist in the Americas are imported ones, artificially confined in zoos or circuses so as to protect them from an inhospitable terrain, we may have the desire to see only those rare creatures who have managed to mimic their Asian or African counterparts-our Latin American "elephants." Refusal is another option. Following thinkers who justifiably object to the ease with which metropolitan ideas become dominant in Latin America, or who unjustifiably see Latin America as a self-fashioned and bounded region and argue in defense of its autochthonous intellectual productions (but doing so typically in metropolitan languages and with arguments supported by theories which were once considered "foreign"), one could reject the attempt to define Latin American postcolonial studies, restricting postcolonial studies to other continents and regarding it as an imperial "import" that devalues "local" Latin American knowledge.

In my opinion, the view that restricts postcolonial reflexivity to certain currents of Western intellectual theory, as well as the position that treats postcolonial studies as another foreign fad that undermines local knowledge, reinforces both the field's theoretical and ethnographic provincialism and its de facto exclusion of Latin America.

These two sides of a protected parochial coin prevent us from taking advantage of the global circulation of postcolonial studies as a potent intellectual currency for the exchange and development of perspectives on colonialism and its legacies from different regions and intellectual traditions.

The problem is not simply, as some Latin American critics of postcolonialism have suggested, that Latin Americanists should be drawing on Kusch or Jorge Luis Borges as much as on Said or Derrida, but that knowledge should be global and acknowledge the world-wide conditions of its production. Just as Kusch drew on Heidegger, and Derrida was inspired by Jorge Luis Borges, Said and Ortiz developed independently of each other, fifty years apart, a contrapuntal view of the historical formation of cultures and identities that disrupts the West/rest dichotomy (Coronil 1995). Critical responses to colonialism from different locations take different but complementary forms. While from an Asian perspective it has become necessary to "provincialize" European thought (Chakrabarty 2000a), from a Latin American perspective it has become indispensable to globalize the periphery: to recognize the world-wide formation of what appear to be self-generated modern metropolitan centers and backward peripheries.

As it has been defined so far, the field of postcolonial studies tends to neglect the study of contemporary forms of political domination and economic exploitation. Recognized by many as one of the field's founders, Edward Said has distanced himself from it, saying that he does not "belong to that," and arguing that "postcolonialism is really a misnomer" that does not sufficiently recognize the persistence of neocolonialism, imperialism, and "structures of dependency" (2002: 2). Said's concerns, so central to Latin American thought, highlight the importance of expanding postcolonial studies by building on Latin American critical traditions.

If the relationship between colonialism and modernity is the core problem for both postcolonial and Latin American studies, the fundamental contribution of Latin American studies is to recast this problem by setting it in a wider historical context. The inclusion of Latin America in the field of postcolonial studies expands its geographical scope and also its temporal depth. A wider focus, spanning from Asia and Africa to the Americas, yields a deeper view, revealing the links between the development of modern colonialism by Northern European powers and its foundation in the colonization of the Americas by Spain and Portugal. This larger frame modifies prevailing understandings of modern history. Capitalism and modernity, so often assumed both in mainstream and in postcolonial studies to be a European process marked by the Enlightenment, the dawning of industrialization, and the forging of nations in the eighteenth century, can be seen instead as a global process involving the expansion of Christendom, the formation of a global market and the creation of transcontinental empires since the sixteenth century. A dialogue between Latin American and postcolonial studies ought not to be polarizing, and might range over local histories and global designs, texts and their material contexts, and subjective formations and structures of domination.

This dialogue should bring to the forefront two interrelated areas of significant political relevance today: the study of postcolonialism itself, strictly understood as historical transformations after political independence, and the analysis of contemporary imperialism. Ironically, these two areas, so central to Latin American thought, have been neglected by postcolonial studies. At the juncture of colonialism's historical dusk and the dawn of new forms of imperial domination, the field tends to recollect colonialism rather than its eventualities. Building on a long tradition of work on post-independence Latin America, I have argued for the need to distinguish "global" from "national" and "colonial" imperialism as a phase characterized by the growing abstraction and generalization of imperial modes of political and economic control (Coronil 2003). Drawing on postcolonial studies, I have proposed to understand what I call "occidentalist" representations of cultural difference under global imperialism as involving a shift from "eurocentrism" to "globalcentrism." I see globalcentrism as entailing representational operations that: (a) dissolve the "West" into the market and crystallize it in less visible transnational nodules of concentrated financial and political power; (b) lessen cultural antagonisms through the integration of distant cultures into a common global space; and (c) emphasize subalternity rather than alterity in the construction of cultural difference. In an increasingly globalized world, US and European dominance is achieved through the occlusion rather than the affirmation of radical differences between the West and its others (Coronil 2000: 354).

This dialogue should also redefine the terms of postcolonial studies. Postcolonialism is a fluid and polysemic category, whose power derives in part from its ability to condense multiple meanings and refer to different locations. Rather than fix its meaning through formal definitions, I have argued that it is more productive to develop its significance through research into and analysis of the historical trajectory of societies and populations subjected to diverse modalities of imperial power (Coronil 1992: 101). In the spirit of a long tradition of Latin American transcultural responses to colonialism and "digestive" appropriation of imperial cultures, I thus opt for what I call "tactical postcolonialism." While Spivak's notion of "strategic essentialism" serves to fix socially constructed identities in order to advance political ends, tactical postcolonialism serves to open up established academic knowledge towards open-ended liberatory possibilities. It conceives "postcolonialism" not as a fenced territory but as an expanding field for struggles against colonial and other forms of subjection. We may then work not so much within this field, as with it, treating it with Ortiz as a "transcultural" zone of creative engagements, "digesting it" as Andrade may playfully do, approaching it as a liminal locus of enunciation as Mignolo suggests, in order to decolonize knowledge and build a genuinely democratic world, "a world which would include many worlds," as Subcomandante Marcos and the Zapatistas propose.

Note

This chapter reflects the lively discussions of a postgraduate seminar on postcolonialism and Latin American thought that I taught during the summer of 2002. at the Universidad Andina Simon Bolivar, Ecuador. My gratitude to all. Thanks also to Genese Sodikoff and Julie Skurski for help with the editing of this chapter.

Works Cited

Achugar, Hugo 1998. "Leones, cazadores historiadores. A propósito de las politicas de la memoria y del conocimiento". Teorfas sin disciplina. Postcolonialidad y globalización en debate. Eds. Santiago Castro-Gómez and Eduardo Mendieta.

Adorno, Rolena 1993. "Reconsidering Colonial Discourse for Sixteenth and Seventeenth-Century Spanish America". Latin American Research Review. 28.3: 135–52.

Alavi, Hamza 1972. "The State in Post-Colonial Societies". New Left Review 74:59–81.

Amin, Samir 1989. Eurocentrism. Trans. Russell Moore. New York: Monthly Review Press.

Ashcroft, Bill 1999. "Modernity's First Born: Latin America and Post-Colonial Transformation". El debate de la postcolonialidad en Latinoamerica. Eds. Alfonso de Toro and Fernando de Toro. Madrid: Iberoamericana: 13–30.

Balandier, George 1951. "La situation coloniale: Approache theorique". Cahiers internationaux de sociologie. 11.51: 44–79.

Barker, Francis, Peter Hulme and Margaret Iversen, eds. 1994. Colonial Discourse/Postcolonial Theory. Manchester and New York: Manchester University Press.

Beverley, John 1993. Against Literature. Minneapolis: University of Minnesota Press.

—— 1999. Subalternity and Representation. Arguments in Cultural Theory.

Bustos, Guillermo 2002. "Enfoque subalterno e historia latinoamericana: nación y escritura de la historia en el debate Iviallon-Beverley". Unpublished manuscript.

Cardoso, Fernando Henrique 1977. "The Consumption of Dependency Theory in the United States". Latin American Research Review. 12.3: 7–24.

Castro-Gómez, Santiago and Eduardo Mendieta, eds. 1998. Teorias sin disciplina. Latinoamericanismo, postcolonialidad y globalización en debate. Mexico: Miguel Angel Porrua.

Castro-Klaren, Sara 1999. "Mimicry Revisited: Latin America, Post-colonial Theory and the Location of Knowledge". El debate de la postcolonialidad en Latinoamerica. Eds. Alfonso de Toro and Fernando de Toro. Madrid: Iberoamericana: 137–64.

—— 2001. "Historiography on. the Ground: The Toledo Circle and Guaman Poma". The Latin American Subaltern Studies Reader. Ed. Ileana Rodriguez. Durham and London: Duke University Press.

Chakrabarty, Dipesh 2000a. Provincializing Europe: Postcolonial Thought and Historical Difference. Princeton: Princeton University Press.

Chandra, Bipan 1980. "Karl Marx, His Theories of Asian Societies and Colonial Rule. Sociological Theories: Race and Colonialism. Paris: UNESCO.

Colas, Santiago. "Of Creole Symptons, Cuban Fantasies, and Other Latin American Postcolonial Ideologies". Publications of the Modern Language Association of America 110.3: 382–96.

Coronil, Fernando 1992. "Can Postcoloniality be Decolonized? Imperial Banality and Postcolonial Power". Public Culture 5.1: 89–108.

—— 1995. "Introduction: Transculturation and the Politics of Theory: Countering the Center, Cuban Counterpoint". Cuban Counterpoint: Tobacco and Sugar. Fernando Ortiz. Durham and London: Duke University Press: ix–lvi.

—— 1996. "Beyond Occidentalism: Towards Nonimperial Geohistorical Categories". Cultural Anthropology 11.1: 52–87.

—— 1997. The Magical State: Nature, Money, and Modernity in Venezuela. Chicago: University of Chicago Press.

—— 2000. "Towards a Critique of Globalcentrism: Speculations on Capitalism's Nature". Public Culture 12.2 351–74.

—— 2003. "Globalización liberal o Imperialismo Global: cinco piezas para armar el rompecabezas del presente". Temas: 2004.

Dirlik, Arif 1994. "The Postcolonial Aura: Third World Criticism in the Age of Global Capitalism". Critical Inquiry 20.2: 328–56.

Durham and London: Duke University Press.

—— 2000. "The Dilemma of Subaltern Studies at Duke". Nepantla: Views from the South 1.1:

Dussel, Enrique 1995. The Invention of the Americas. Trans. Michael D. Barber. New York: Continuum.

—— 1998. "Beyond Eurocentrism: The World-System and the Limits of Modernity". The Cultures of Globalization. Eds. Fredric Jameson and Masao Miyoshi. Durham and London: Duke University Press: 3–31.

Fanon, Frantz 1965 The Wretched of the Earth [1961]. Trans. Constance Farrington. New York: Grove Press.

Fernandez Retamar, Roberto 1974. "Nuestra America y el Occidente". Casa de las Americas XVI.98: 36–57.

—— 1996. "Pensamiento de Nuestra America: autoreflexines y propuestas". Casa de las Americas XXXVII.204: 41–56.

Gandhi, Leela 1998. Postcolonial Theory: A Critical Introduction. New York: Columbia University Press.

Gareth Griffiths and Helen Tiffin 1989. The Empire Writes Back: Theory and Practice in Post-Colonial Literatures. London and New York: Routledge.

—— eds. 1995. The Postcolonial Studies Reader. London and New York: Routledge.

Goldberg, Theo and Ato Quayson, eds. 2002. Relocating Postcolonialism. Oxford: Blackwell.

Gonzalez Casanova, Pablo 1965. "Internal Colonialism and National Development". Studies in Comparative International Development 1.4: 27–37.

Grosfoguel, Ramon 2000. "Developmentalism, Modernity and Dependency in Latin America". Nepantla. 1.2: 347–74.

Hulme, Peter. 1989. "La teoria postcolonial y la representación de la cultura en las Americas". Casa de las Americas 36.202: 3–8.

Klor de Alva, Jorge 1992. "Colonialism and Postcolonialism as (Latin) American Mirages". Colonial Latin American Review. 1–.1–2: 3–23.

—— 1995. "The Postcolonization of the (Latin) American Experience: A Reconsideration of 'Colonialism,' 'Postcolonialism,' and 'Mestizaje'". After Colonialism: Imperial Histories and Postcolonial Predicaments. Ed. Cyan Prakash. Princeton: Princeton University Press: 240–75.

Lazarus, Neil 1999. Nationalism and Cultural Practice in the Postcolonial World. Cambridge: Cambridge University Press.

Mallon, Florencia 1994. "The Promise and Dilemma of Subaltern Studies: Perspectives from Latin American History". American Historical Review 99.5: 1491–515.

—— 1995. Peasant and Nation. The Making of Postcolonial Mexico and Peru. Berkeley: University of California Press.

Mexico: Miguel Angel Porrua: 271–85.

Mignolo, Walter D. 1993. "Colonial and Postcolonial Discourse: Cultural Critique or Academic Colonialism?" Latin American Research Review 28.3: 120–34.

—— 2000. Local Histories/Global Designs: Coloniality, Subaltern Knowledges, and Border Thinking. Princeton: Princeton University Press.

Morafia, Mabel 1997. "El boom del subalterno". Revista de critica cultural" 15: 48–53. Nkrumah, Kwame 1965. Neo-Colonialism: The Last Stage of Imperialism. London: Thomas Nelson.

Perez, Alberto Julian 1999. "El poscolonialismo y la inmadurez de los pensadores hispanoamericanos". El debate de la postcolonialidad en Latinoamerica. Eds. Alfonso de Toro and Fernando de Toro. Madrid: Iberoamericana: 199–213.

Quayson, Ato 2000. Postcolonialism: Theory, Practice or Process? Cambridge and Oxford: Polity Press.

Quijano, Anibal 2000. "Colonialidad del poder, eurocentrismo y America Latina". La colonialidad del saber: eurocentrismo y ciencias sociales. Perspectivas Latinoamericanas. Ed. Edgardo Lander. Buenos Aires: CLASCO: 201–46.

Rivera Cusicanqui, Silvia and Rossana Barragan, eds. 1999. Debates post coloniales. Una introducci6n a los estudios subalternos. La Paz: Sephis/Aruwiyri.

Rodriguez, Ileana, ed. 2001. The Latin American Subaltern Studies Reader. Durham and London: Duke University Press.

Said, Edward W. 1978 Orientalism. New York: Random House.

—— 1993. Culture and Imperialism. New York: Alfred A. Knopf.

—— 2002. "A Conversation with Neeldari Bhattacharya, Suvir Kaul and Ania Loomba". Relocating Postcolonialism. Eds. Theo Goldberg and Ato Quayson. Oxford: Blackwell: 1–14.

Salih, Tayeb 1969. Season of Migration from the North. Trans. Denys Johnson- Davies. London: Heinemann.

Sangari, Kumkum 1990. "The Politics of the Possible" The Nature and Context of Minority Discourse. Eds. Abdul JanMohamed and David Lloyd. New York: Oxford University Press: 216–245.

San Juan, Epifanio 1998. Beyond Postcolonial Theory. New York: St. Martins.

Schwarz, Henry 2000. "Mission Impossible: Introducing Postcolonial Studies in the U.S. Academy". A Companion to Postcolonial Studies. Eds. Henry Schwarz and Sangeeta Ray. Oxford: Blackwell: 1–20.

—— and Sangeeta Ray, eds. 2000. A Companion to Postcolonial Studies. Oxford: Blackwell.

Seed, Patricia 1991. "Colonial and Postcolonial Discourse". Latin American Research Review 26.3: 181–200.

Stavenhagen, Rodolfo 1965. "Classes, Colonialism and Acculturation. Essay on a System of Inter-Ethnic Relations in Mesoamerica". Studies in Comparative International Development 1.6: 53–77.

Vidal, Hernan 1993. "The Concept of Colonial and Postcolonial Discourse: A Perspective from Literary Criticism". Latin American Research Review 28.3: 113–19.

Wolpe, Harold, ed. 1980. The Articulation of Modes of Production. London: Routledge and Kegan Paul.

Young, Robert 1990. White Mythologies: Writing History and the West. London and New York: Routledge.

—— 2001. Postcolonialism: An Historical Introduction. Cambridge: Blackwell. Yudice, George 1996. "Puede hablarse de la postmodernidad en America Latina". Revista Critica Literaria Latinoamericana 15.29: 105–28.

12   History Without a Cause?
Grand Narratives, World History, and the Postcolonial Dilemma

Barbara Weinstein

Among the many historical conventions that went out of fashion in the wake of the linguistic and/or cultural turn was the grand explanatory narrative rooted in an interpretive tradition that typically traced an arc from causes to consequences. [1] A chorus of criticism consigned the grand or meta-narrative to the dustbin of historiography, if not history. Linguistic theorists like Hayden White seemed to challenge historians' cherished notions of interpretive truth by stressing the resemblance between historical and fictional narratives; postmodernists of various stripes questioned whether historical narratives could escape the teleological tendencies of the master narrative of the Western/liberal tradition; and recently a leading postcolonial theorist has denounced all historicism, broadly defined, as incurably eurocentric. [2]

As will be discussed in the following essay, this has led to the virtual abandonment of the grand narrative tradition among historians of a strong theoretical bent, and a clear preference for microhistories that avoid or refuse any systematic notion of causation. But I will also argue that there are other, simultaneous developments in the field of history – specifically the growing appeal of world history and, perhaps ironically, the rise of postcolonial studies – which have revived or sustained an interest in the grand historical narrative. My purpose in addressing this issue is not to endorse an uncritical return to the grand narrative tradition, but to consider what we lose if we abandon it altogether, to indicate how it still implicitly influences historical writing even by those who apparently renounce it, and to suggest that, perhaps, we might imagine new ways to narrate the past and to address the question, "Why?" without reverting to excessively positivist master-narratives.

Barbara Weinstein, "History Without a Cause? Grand Narratives, World History, and the Postcolonial Dilemma." *International Review of Social History*, 50(1), 2005: 71–93. Reproduced by permission of Cambridge University Press.

The Cultural Turn and The Decline of Causation

The turn to the new cultural history, in the United States and elsewhere, witnessed a decline in the production of research concerned with the causes of an event or a particular historical process, which has also implied a decline in a certain form of explanatory narrative. These days it is difficult to find a serious and theoretically engaged historian addressing a theme such as "the causes of the French Revolution", or "or the causes of the American Civil War", or "the origins of capitalist relations of production in New England". A book such as David W. Blight's celebrated *Race and Reunion: the Civil War in American Memory* might discuss the putative causes of the Civil War in terms of different discursive positions and how they related to the struggle over how to "remember" the Civil War, but he never explicitly indicates a historiographical preference for one causal narrative over another.[3]

The near erasure of such questions (except as raw material for discourse analysis) so hotly debated just a few decades ago, even during the heyday of the new social history, can be explained, in part, by the skepticism of today's historians with regard to grand narratives in general and, the ample criticism of the historian who positions him/herself as the omniscient narrator, imposing (his/her) narrative order upon the disorder and multiplicity of histories, and by that token ignoring or erasing other narratives and silencing other voices.[4] Beyond this, once we have accepted the notion that all narratives have embedded in them a series of interpretive decisions, how can we construct a coherent narrative without falling into the teleological temptation? By the same token, if we accept the notion of the "instability of the subject", how can we narrate a history of the workers? Or of women? Or of gays?[5] If the very meanings attributed to these words/categories are historically unstable, whose story are we telling? All of these doubts and criticisms, many of them quite reasonable, have ended up devaluing, even de-legitimizing, a certain type of explanatory narrative, concerned with causes and consequences.

Furthermore, for those historians who were immersing themselves in the new cultural history, especially in its early phase, there was the unpleasant memory of another type of "cultural history", with its tendency to essentialize culture, and to treat it as a factor that determined the destiny of a particular collectivity. It was precisely the whiff of eurocentrism, and even racism, of this older cultural history – that presupposed that certain cultures had an aptitude for modernity, economic progress, rational citizenship, while others did not – that moved previous generations to prefer social and economic history, to the detriment of cultural history, and to treat the cultural sphere as always reducible to the social and the material.[6] Therefore, a return to an explanatory/historicist narrative in which culture would serve as the foundation for explanation, in the positivist sense, was something to be avoided at all cost.[7]

It was the rejection of this essentialized view of culture that made the new cultural history "new". And at the moment when the cultural turn first manifested itself clearly in the US historical profession, perhaps the most important source of theoretical inspiration was the field of anthropology, and more specifically, the work of Clifford Geertz.[8] Certainly, he was not the only influence – even North American historians, with their reputation for provincialism, were reading Foucault, Derrida, and Bourdieu.[9] But Geertz's method, his "thick description", was particularly influential. Derived from symbolic anthropology, this interpretive method insisted that all social activity took place within a web of meanings, and that symbols/texts should be read and interpreted in their own context, using the internal logic of the local system. Obviously, "explanation" formed part of the Geertzian project; in his own words, "it is explication I am after, construing social expressions on their surface enigmatical".[10] At the same time, Geertz made a distinction between explanation as interpretation and as the enumeration of general causes; according to Geertz, "culture is not a power, something to which social events, behaviors, institutions or processes can be causally attributed; it is a context, something within which they can be intelligibly – that is, thickly – described".[11]

One implication of this widespread adaptation of anthropological methods to historical research was the eclipse of the longstanding concern with "change over time", and the emergence of a preference for sychronic, rather than diachronic, themes. The tendency now was to examine "a small piece of time", an instant, a snapshot. A certain variant of microhistory, focused on a specific historical anecdote, became the analytical raw material, *par excellence*, for the new cultural history.[12] Books and articles based on some minor episode – minor but bursting with significance – proliferated. A pioneering and quintessential example was *The Great Cat Massacre and Other Episodes in French Cultural History*, by Robert Darnton; in the title essay of this collection, Darnton took an initially puzzling vignette – the hilarity provoked among Parisian artisans at the killing of the pet cats of their master's wife – to explore a shift in social and cultural mores in pre-Revolutionary Paris. There has since been a steady stream of such studies; one recently announced on the back cover of the *American Historical Review*, by Jeffrey Freedman, is described in the following terms:

> *A Poisoned Chalice* tells the story of a long-forgotten criminal case: the poisoning of the communion wine in Zurich's main cathedral in 1776. The story is riveting and mysterious, but it is also far more than just a good story. The affair became a cause célèbre, the object of a lively public debate that focused on the problem of evil.
>
> By following the thoughts and actions of Europeans as they struggled to comprehend an act of inscrutable evil, this book brings to life a key episode in the history of the German Enlightenment – an episode in which the Enlightenment was forced to interrogate the very limits of reason itself.

And the ad ends with an endorsement from the distinguished historian Anthony Grafton who declares the book "a small masterpiece: the distilled essence of cultural history".[13]

In these studies, the old explanatory narrative, concerned with causes, origins, and consequences, has given way to a new "micronarrative", of very brief duration, concentrated on a particular (and often previously "obscure") event that, if well chosen, offers us a bonanza of cultural meanings. The latter no longer refers to causes or origins, and with regard to consequences, the most they might indicate is a range of new cultural/historical possibilities. This, among other factors, makes the appeal of the anecdote entirely understandable. Aside from easing the whole process of archival research, it has a double attraction: at first glance, it offers a (relatively) pure piece of the past – though it would be more accurate to think of the anecdote as a fragment of a narrative.[14] Perhaps more important, the anecdote is reasonably compatible with the methods of symbolic anthropology.

This is not to say that all of the acolytes of Clifford Geertz in the historical profession have cultivated the same terrain. To be sure, there are many examples of studies inspired by his *oeuvre* that diverge from this pattern. Here I will just cite two studies – of very different themes and lengths – that illustrate this diversity. One focuses on an era whose parameters entirely escape the confines of "anecdotal history", and the other is explicitly concerned with the question of change over time.

The first is the recent monograph by Eric Van Young on popular revolts in the era of the independence wars in Mexico. In contrast to the majority of works on this theme, *The Other Rebellion* does not seek to provide a unified explanation for the wars of independence, or their causes; on the contrary, Van Young rejects explanatory "models" for tending to homogenize the various categories of the colonial population that reacted in highly heterogeneous ways to the struggle against Spanish colonialism. Instead of speaking of causes, Van Young privileges what we might call Geertzian preoccupations, concentrating on the cultural meanings of the revolts for their participants. For example, when the peasants or villagers of a certain region speak of the king, what does the figure of the king signify for them? Van Young thus argues that the subaltern groups that participated in these revolts acted within a web of symbols, rites, and discourses that were very distinct from those that fueled the revolt against the Crown among more privileged (creole) sectors of the population. Again, the broad canvas on which Van Young interprets popular revolts (or popular quiescence) makes this a study of wider-ranging implications than a strictly "anecdotal" approach. But at the same time, it could be described as anecdotal history writ large – which may explain why the book is 700-plus pages long.[15]

The second work that is clearly influenced by Geertz, but that escapes the confines of the historical anecdote, is a fascinating article recently published in the *American Historical Review* titled "From Majesty to Mystery: Change in the Meanings of Black Madonnas from the Sixteenth to Nineteenth Centuries".[16] As the very title indicates, the author, Monique Scheer, is explicitly concerned with change over time. But the particular nature of that concern reflects her immersion in anthropological methods. Refusing to dwell on the question of why these madonnas – a group of images widely known in Europe since the medieval era – were black in color (an issue she persuasively dismisses as a positivist distraction), Scheer focuses, instead, on the shifting meanings attributed to the color of these madonnas in different historical eras, culminating in the nineteenth century. In other words, the article explores how various commentators, in different historical-cultural contexts, noted/explained (or not) the color of these madonnas.

Scheer demonstrates that, prior to the eighteenth century, the tendency was to interpret the madonnas' dark color as a sign of the antiquity and authenticity of these images, and, especially among popular groups, an indication of their miraculous qualities. Beginning in the late eighteenth century, one can perceive a significant shift in the perceptions of the madonnas, which cease to be statues that are black in color and become, instead, images of a black, or even African, woman. This change in perception is attributed by the author to two broad transformations occurring during this period. One, predictably, is the construction of racial categories that leads those commenting upon the black madonnas to associate blackness with dark skin and racial difference. The other is the secularization of European society, which allows those commenting upon the madonnas to see them not as sacred (and even less, as miraculous), but as works of human artistry whose color demands a scientific/rational explanation. The images become a "mystery", but in a new materialist sense, rather than the previous religious sense. Many nineteenth-century commentators, befuddled by the idea of an "African" Mary, ultimately conclude that the color was an accident, the result of accumulated candle fumes in churches and cathedrals.[17]

Scheer openly acknowledges her debt to Geertz in the very body of the article; she notes the importance of works on this subject by various art historians, but insists that her "approach to this question is not as a member of their discipline. Rather, it is informed by principles of symbolic anthropology." Scheer's article, at first glance, seems to demonstrate that Geertz's methods are not incompatible with a consideration of change over time. Yet, contrary to the author's claims, what gives the article interpretive coherence is not the Geertzian method employed, but its reference to a grand historical narrative that furnishes the explanatory elements for the changes over time highlighted in the essay. It is the emergence of "race" as a category for organizing human populations and the secularization of European society that provides the explanatory framework for change over time. To be sure, the attention to race as a central concept in post-Enlightenment European culture indicates that this is a revised version of the standard macro-narrative of "Western civilization", but it is nonetheless a grand narrative, and one that is so thoroughly taken for granted in the elaboration of the article's conclusions that it does not merit even a reference in the footnotes. In other words, far from discarding the master narrative, or disengaging from concepts of causation, this article (and not just this article) treats it as so thoroughly embedded in our cultural frameworks that it does not even require acknowledgement. What we have is not the rejection of the master narrative, but its complete and utter triumph as the historian's "common sense".

To be sure, we cannot expect an author focused on the history of a specific set of religious artifacts to rethink the entire narrative of modern (Western-centered) history. What we can expect from historians working in this vein is an explicit acknowledgement that they are invoking a well-established narrative of causation, for only then can we come to grips with its "common-sense" status, and begin to question and rethink the assumptions that inform this grand narrative. Again, the attention to race as a crucial category of "modern" knowledge indicates the subtle transformations in that narrative. These days it would be difficult to equate or celebrate certain western trends with the "march of progress". Even with these significant modifications, however, it still seems dubious to speak unproblematically of "modernity" or "secularization" from the eighteenth century on as generators of symbols and meanings, or as constructing a historical context that is fixed and stable. Geertz's approach may provide a fruitful means of exploring the meanings of rituals and relations in colonial and postcolonial societies, but it tells us little about the history of colonialism as a process, as a system, or as an ongoing power relationship that can be unstable and continually contested.[18]

This translation of cultural-anthropological methods to events of the past will certainly continue to inform historical research, but one can also perceive a sense that this approach, in its current conceptualization, is reaching exhaustion, and for various reasons. Lynn Hunt, who organized the now classic anthology on the cultural turn in the historical profession (*The New Cultural History*, 1989), recently co-edited another collection titled (unsurprisingly) *Beyond the Cultural Turn* (1999). Perusing the articles in the latter anthology, or in recent issues of the journal *History and Theory*, one can

Barbara Weinstein

perceive a range of motives and impulses for going "beyond" cultural-anthropological methods.[19] First, there are considerations of a practical order. For Geertz and his followers everything is a text, and thus his method can be similarly applied to a contemporary ritual witnessed by an anthropologist, or one that took place in the eighteenth century and was recorded in a document of that era. But the inevitably fragmentary nature of the historical evidence, the additional levels of mediation between the event and the interpreter/spectator, and the lack of easy access to a multiplicity of "informants" means that only rarely can the interpretation of a text produced in the past have the richness and multiple layers of meaning that characterize the best cultural-anthropological studies.[20]

Is All The World an Anecdote?

More relevant to the point of this essay, I think we can also perceive an inchoate yearning to return to a more encompassing narrative that would open possibilities for thinking anew about origins and consequences. This is not necessarily a desire to return to a positivist approach to history, with its laws of causation, but rather to revisit long-term processes and great historical events (a category undergoing continual revision), and discuss the question of origins in new ways.[21] There is a perceptible nostalgia for macrohistorical thinking that would permit us to address the broader implications of the operations of signification that have occupied so much space in recent historical research. The incessant debate over the possibility or impossibility of locating a sphere of sociability or social action that is not reducible to the cultural sphere (a debate that I think has been an intellectual dead end) is probably best explained as a symptom of this desire to pierce the limits set on historical narrative by the new cultural history and to escape the cramped confines of postmodernism generally.[22]

There are many areas of history where the question of reviving grand narratives has been raised, but perhaps the one where it is of most obvious relevance is in the burgeoning field of world history. In the remainder of this essay, I will explore both the opportunities and challenges presented by the field of world history for those historians interested in reviving and rethinking grand narratives, and the intersection between these tendencies and the concerns raised by historians working in the relatively new area of postcolonial studies.[23] Obviously, "world history" is not itself a new field, but what I am referring to in this essay is what might be called the "new" world history, an area of research and teaching that is profoundly marked by the historical and historiographical moment of its resurgence.

In the first place, it is important to note that world history, in its current form, is above all a pedagogical field; there are still relatively few historians who would classify themselves as doing research in world history. Indeed, one of the ongoing criticisms of this area of concentration is precisely that it does not share the degree of specialization and professionalization that characterizes other fields or subfields (something that is not necessarily seen as a problem by those who are proponents of world history).[24] While no field of history is entirely detached from a pedagogical mission, in the case of world history, this is, at least for now, the primary focus of the field.[25] At first glance it may seem entirely predictable that this sort of course would proliferate at a moment of intense globalization; however, this alone would not explain the particular form that world history courses are generally taking. It is only possible to fully appreciate its pedagogical purposes by acknowledging what kind of academic course/discourse world history is meant to supplement, or even supplant.[26] Increasingly, this would be the venerable course known by various names – Western civilization, the rise of the West – and increasingly criticized for its association with a narrative of the "triumph of the West". World history, in its current paradigmatic form, is not conceived of as a mere amplification of the "Western Civ" course. Rather, one of its principal purposes is precisely to rethink the place of the West in the macrohistorical narrative.

Practitioners of world history are developing various strategies to "decenter" the West, or to cite the phrase of subaltern studies historian, Dipesh Chakrabarty, to "provincialize Europe". And in most cases, for obvious (pedagogical) reasons, they involve a narrative that is explanatory and/or macro-historical.[27] One strategy with rather clear political implications is to insist that the only "advantage" that Europe enjoyed in the competition for global hegemony was its capacity to colonize and enslave – to exploit other cultures that, though sometimes more sophisticated, were poorly prepared for the depredations and barbarities of the Europeans.[28] In a sense, this argument simply inverts the traditional discourse of European superiority based on Europe's supposed enlightenment – free thinking, free trade, self-discipline, and scientific temperament – a discourse that can still claim active and eminent defenders.

In recent years, two prominent figures of the "old" world history – Alfred Crosby and David Landes – have published books, widely acclaimed in some circles, that reproduce the lineaments of the narrative of a West triumphant due to its more democratic or scientific sensibilities. As one critic put it, they work within the narrative tradition of the "Great Explanandum" – the key to explaining the alleged "uniqueness" of the West.[29] Landes's book, *Wealth and Poverty of Nations: Why Some Are So Rich and Some So Poor* (1998), is especially audacious in its unrestricted endorsement of the euro-centric narrative. For one small example, listen to Landes's argument in favor of a "cultural" interpretation of European dominance: "If we have learned anything from the history of economic development, it is that culture makes all the difference [...] what counts is work, thrift, honesty, patience, tenacity."[30]

This appeal to a "cultural" explanation (which in other parts of Landes's book is not quite as blatantly eurocentric as the lines quoted above) is obviously referring to an older cultural history, with its monolithic and essentialized notion of culture. The problem with those historical works that argue just the opposite – that the cultural qualities that made possible European hegemony were greed, brutality, barbarity – is that they are operating with the same deterministic and simplistic notion of culture, and the same assumption about Western "uniqueness", but now with a negative valence.[31] It is an approach that serves to demonize the West, but not to decenter or provincialize it, contrary to their claims.

Another strategy for "provincializing Europe" that is gaining influence in the field of world history denies "culture" any significant role in the process of the West's ascension, and focuses instead on questions of political economy presumably not reducible to cultural attributes. This approach is exemplified by two recent historical works comparing European and Chinese economic development: Kenneth Pomeranz, *The Great Divergence: China, Europe and the Making of the Modern World Economy*, and Roy Bin Wong, *China Transformed: Historical Change and the Limits of European Experience*. The argument in both books is principally comparative and conjunctural, reminiscent of the explanatory methods of the Annales School. The two authors, both specialists in Chinese history, insist that the level of China's development at the end of the eighteenth century was roughly comparable to that of western Europe, including Great Britain. Whether with regard to the standard of living, technology, maritime commerce, or state and bureaucratic organization, the similarities were greater than the differences.[32] Therefore, someone observing these two societies at the end of that century would hardly conclude that western Europe – and its cousin in the New World, the United States – would rapidly establish unquestioned global hegemony in the following century.

According to these two historians, the explanation for the unexpected "triumph" of the West cannot be attributed principally to a difference in culture or mentality, long-term factors that are useless for explaining a sudden and dramatic divergence. Instead of the intrinsic qualities cited by Landes and Crosby, Pomeranz and Bin Wong insist on the importance of contingent factors; for example, Britain's access to the natural resources of the New World and its capacity to export its excess population, as well as conjunctures that permitted Europe to consolidate its economic position and take full advantage of new technologies of production and power.

One apparent problem with this approach for those teaching and researching world history is that it transforms a unipolar world (the West) into a bipolar world – China and western Europe.[33] But more important for our purposes here is the methodological aspect of these studies. Again, in both cases there is a lack of engagement with cultural history, old or new. It is ironic that these two studies – so bold in their criticism of the traditional historiography and its notion of Western cultural superiority – are based on approaches that are not at all methodologically innovative. Yet, this is not so puzzling when we consider that those historians involved in methodological innovation and current theoretical debates, as noted earlier, have been accustomed to avoiding these types of macrohistorical questions.[34] Margaret Jacob, in commenting on Alfred Crosby's study of the supposedly unique Western disposition for quantification, opens her remarks by acknowledging this avoidance:

> For my generation of historians […] the big questions in Western or world history became strangely unfashionable. None is bigger than the question of what were the factors that made Western hegemony possible. Indeed, the very notion of Western hegemony, of the domination of much of the world by Western political or economic power from roughly 1800 to 1970, may be said to be so fraught with anger or guilt as to be almost untouchable.[35]

In effect, recent years have witnessed an odd disjuncture between the political and methodological inclinations of historians. On the one hand, there is the renewed emphasis on world history and the revision of macronarratives of Western exception-alism; on the other hand, cultural history and the micronarratives continue to occupy (if not monopolize) the terrain of methodological innovation. There have been some tentative efforts toward linking one concern with the other. In a recent commentary on the studies by Pomeranz and Bin Wong, the historian of India, David Ludden, noted that chronicles of British imperialism written in the first half of the nineteenth century rarely remarked on the differences or inequalities in economic conditions between England and India; the theme of inequality typically appeared in descriptions of different social sectors *internal* to each society, and not divergences between metropolis and colony. Even the great famine in nineteenth-century India had its "European" counterpart in the similarly horrific Irish potato famine of 1846–1847, with the key difference being that the Irish enjoyed the option of transatlantic emigration.[36]

India, however, also suffered its "great divergence". In 1818, when James Mill published his magnum opus on the history of British India, there was not a single reference to British economic superiority. Three decades later, Karl Marx could refer to this superiority as an established and unquestionable fact. Although Ludden's narrative of India's descent into what would eventually be called underdevelopment initially appears to be following the same path as Pomeranz's and Bin Wong's studies, Ludden briskly takes a linguistic turn, concerning himself with the discourses of difference and inequality that constructed a global order in which England and India played very distinctive roles, and that increasingly associated the "poverty" of a particular people with its supposed incapacity or ill-preparedness for modernity. There also emerged the new disposition to equate the parameters of an economy with the borders of the nation; instead of colonialism producing a system conceptualized as a single entity, it became routine to think of England as a rich land and India as a poor land, and one whose people did not (and could not) harbor the hope of sharing the standard of living enjoyed by the average British citizen.

The Postcolonial Dilemma

These insights – Ludden's attempt to understand the economic condition of modern India as a result not just of "objective" and quantifiable factors, but of new language and categories – serve as a bridge to the preoccupations of historians working in the area of postcolonial studies. With their roots in subaltern studies, many of these scholars define their project as an effort to rethink history from the point of view of the postcolonial world, including the ex-metropolis. Different from the earlier notion of neocolonialism, a fundamentally materialist concept, these historians recognize the anticolonial struggle and formal political independence as marking significant ruptures with the past, but at the same time recognize that decolonization will be incomplete, even illusory, in a world where imperialism, racism, and ethnocentrism persist in other forms, and where hybridity makes the formation of an autonomous cultural sphere unimaginable.[37]

Beginning with that loose set of assumptions, this diverse group of historians has in common a strong critical concern with the meta-narrative of progress that places Europe at the center of all historical processes – a meta-narrative that, despite the reproofs of postmodernists and disdain of new cultural historians, still hovers over historiographical debates and thoroughly informs public discourse. In the widely acclaimed *Provincializing Europe: Postcolonial Thought and Historical Difference*, Dipesh Chakrabarty presents the question in a refreshingly frank manner: he laments that he and other historians of Asia (and one could substitute Africa or Latin America) need to pay attention to the scholarly production of their European colleagues, but that the latter need not take into account the scholarly production of South Asian, or African, or Latin American historians. Shifting to a more elevated plane of debate, he makes a similar point in different form: while there may be other, documentable ways of representing the self or community outside "Europe", these "will never enjoy the privilege of providing the meta-narratives or teleologies (assuming that there cannot be a narrative without at least an implicit teleology) of our histories".[38] For Chakrabarty, historicism – and especially the "narrative of transition" – will always end up referring to a Europe that is the originating source for modernity, the nation and, above all, reason.

It is important to note that Chakrabarty, despite his thoroughgoing criticism of the eurocentric narrative, does not intend to denounce, *grosso modo*, the historical implications of the Enlightenment and the Age of Reason. In the very final paragraph of his book, he makes a point of insisting, yet again, that "provincializing Europe cannot ever be a project of shunning European thought" – indeed, he characterizes that thought, without irony, as "a gift to us all".[39] Furthermore, he insists that the eurocentric historical narrative, that identifies Europe as the axis of all progress, cannot be viewed as a mere imposition of European imperialism; on the contrary, he cites Third World nationalisms – modernizing discourses par excellence – as active partners with "the West" in the dissemination of this narrative. Hence, the real challenge for Chakrabarty – and for other scholars of postcolonial studies – is to imagine a means of rejecting historicism, whose theoretical subject is always "Europe", without discarding the categories of political modernity associated with European history.

To demonstrate just how difficult it is to escape the historicist trap, Chakrabarty concentrates his criticism not on works, such as those by David Landes and Alfred Crosby, that exalt exceptional European virtues, and whose arguments are relatively easy to refute, but on studies by historians for whom he has great admiration. For example, he discusses the famous essay by E.P. Thompson on "Time, Work-Discipline and Industrial Capitalism". In this essay Thompson not only describes the process by which the English worker is obliged to internalize the discipline associated with industrial work rhythms, but also contends that the same is happening, or will happen to, the Third World worker, with the only difference between the English and, say, Indian worker being the passage of secular/historical time. In this respect, the Thompson article is an excellent example of the problematic tendency cited by Chakrabarty: "The modern" continues to be understood "as a *known history*, something which has *already happened elsewhere*, and which is to be reproduced, mechanically or otherwise, with a local content".[40]

To be sure, Chakrabarty is even more critical of the early writings of his own colleagues from the subaltern studies school. He disapprovingly cites the foreword of the very first issue of *Subaltern Studies*, which announced the group's project as:

> [...] the study of this *historic failure of the nation to come to its own*, a failure due to the *inadequacy* of the bourgeoisie as well as the working class to lead it into a decisive victory over colonialism [...] *it is the study of this failure which constitutes the central problematic of the historiography of colonial India.*

Although the majority of his colleagues today would not overtly reiterate this discourse of "failure", Chakrabarty insists that the tendency to read Indian history in terms of something that is lacking, of something incomplete, of something inadequate continues to influence the historical narrative, and guarantees that the Indian narrative of transition will always remain "grievously incomplete".[41]

What, then, is the alternative that Chakrabarty offers? In *Provincializing Europe* there are four chapters that explore aspects of Indian cultural and political life, and of Indian customs and traditions (some of them very recently invented) that, from his point of view, cannot be easily assimilated into a historicist narrative. He begins his analysis by citing Paul Veyne's distinction between "singularity" and "specificity".[42] The specific is an example of a general tendency, and thus easily lends itself to an explanatory narrative. The black madonnas discussed above would be an excellent instance of "specificity", because the meanings they produced changed over time in a predictable manner, once they were situated within a narrative of secularization and racial classification linked to the birth of modernity. In contrast, Chakrabarty seeks out forms of sociability or social practices that are, in his view, singularities – that is, they resist assimilation into a historicist narrative.

These chapters are certainly intriguing, but they are far from addressing the problem that Chakrabarty himself identified as the central issue. Indeed, even if we accept these practices as singularities (and I suspect many readers will not be entirely convinced of this), the result is a series of cultural fragments that serve only to demonstrate that the history of India is not merely a variation of European narrative history. But this does not necessarily advance the mission of "provincializing Europe". After all, the eurocentric perspective boasts a long tradition of situating elements of "oriental" culture outside of its historicist narrative; in this respect, Chakrabarty's argument sometimes seems to run the risk of replicating an "orientalist" discourse that would certainly represent no challenge whatsoever to the eurocentric vision of the world.[43]

Despite the cogency of his criticism, it is difficult, within the logic of Chakrabarty's argument, to discern a strategy that opens the possibility of Europe becoming a province, rather than the center, of history. In a sense, the author is doubly caught in a trap of his own creation. He fully accepts, at the outset, that Indian culture is hybridized and that there is no prospect of writing an autonomous (non-Westernized) narrative of Indian history. According to Chakrabarty, "the very colonial crucible in which Bengali modernity originated ensured that it would not be possible to fashion a historical account of the birth of this modernity without reproducing some aspect of European narratives of the modern subject".[44] Moreover, he insists that all historical narrative – indeed, the very preoccupation with history, which he regards as a "rational-secular discipline", defined by the capacity to see past time as separate from present time – inevitably has as its referent a Europe associated with reason and progress. Apparently, for Chakrabarty, there does not exist the possibility of writing a macro-historical narrative of India that could replace the narrative of colonialism.

He illustrates this argument by citing an episode involving the noted Indian intellectual B.R. Ambedkar, active during the era of formal colonialism. In a 1916 presentation at Columbia University on the practices of *sati* and child marriage, Ambedkar lamented the complete absence of historical studies of these practices that could explain "the *causes of their origin* and existence".[45] Chakrabarty alludes to the words of this venerable scholar (and champion of the untouchables) as if they virtually speak for themselves as an indictment of Ambedkar; clearly, the latter had fallen into the grave error of historicist thinking, and had given in to the (allegedly) Western temptation to ask, and to seek to know, "why"? Yet, while few scholars today would argue, in a positivist vein, that historical research could provide a definitive answer to the questions posed, do we really want to contend that such questions defy any and all historicization? If so, we run the risk of reproducing one of the key discursive underpinnings of European colonialism, conceptualizing "non-Western" societies as "the people without history", to cite Eric Wolf's memorably mordant phrase.[46]

The New Macro-History?

In this regard, it is important to note that not all historians working in the vein of post-colonial studies share the position advocated by Chakrabarty. At least one of the essays in the volume *Beyond the Cultural Turn* offers an alternative perspective on the dilemma of the postcolonial historian. The author, Steven Feierman – an eminent scholar of African history – is also concerned with the project of provincializing Europe, but he suggests a very different strategy for its implementation. Like Chakrabarty, Feierman opens with a criticism of historians who have attempted to recuperate the "authentic voices" of the African past, and approvingly cites the consensus among historians and anthropologists of the region about the hybridity of African culture, and the consequent futility of any search for "authenticity". Instead, the new cultural history of Africa has explored the extensive and complex interaction between dominant practices (of colonialism, capitalism, and Christianity), and the local practices defined as "African".[47] After enumerating, with a tone of apparent approval, the various studies in this vein, Feierman then shifts to a more critical tone, and it seems worthwhile to cite this passage in its entirety:

> These innovative contributions are fascinating when taken individually, but they present a profound problem of historical representation when aggregated into a regional historical narrative. The studies of commodities (or of Christian sin) in one place, and then another, and then another can be aggregated only on the basis of their shared relationship to the relevant European category: they cannot be placed within a larger or more general African narrative. What is African inevitably appears in a form which is local and fragmented, and which has no greater depth than the time of colonial conquest, or the moment just before it.[48]

Or to cite the words of the editors of the anthology, Feierman's essay indicates the pitfalls of "focusing exclusively on the micro level" which "may just leave untouched all the usual macro accounts of the sweeping success of colonial conquest and capitalist expansion".[49]

While both Feierman and Chakrabarty are troubled by the resistance of historical Europe to "provincialization", when it comes to potential strategies for breaking down that resistance, the former arrives at the opposite conclusion from his colleague in South Asian history. Referring to his own research on the African tradition of public and collective healing – a tradition repeatedly repressed and revived – Feierman calls for the construction of an African macrohistorical narrative that would privilege the history of bodily practices, which he believes would not easily fit within the European linear-narrative framework. Unlike Chakrabarty, Feierman believes that such practices, though presenting significant difficulties for narrative historical representation, would not completely confound the historian's capacity to construct genuinely new narratives. He readily admits that any "regional macrohistory" that resulted from this effort would be very problematic – perhaps as much as the eurocentric narrative – but insists that the only means to begin provincializing Europe would be to create alternative points of reference that are not defined, in the last instance, by the colonial/hegemonic narrative.[50] In short, Feierman is looking for a way out of the postcolonial dilemma through the creation of multiple macrohistorical narratives, instead of through the postmodern rejection of the very notion of macrohistory.

My intention here is not to endorse unreservedly Steven Feierman's intriguing proposal. I think it is indeed likely that any effort to construct a regional macrohistory will either end up essentializing African culture, or will unduly minimize the impact of European culture. But between the nearly total rejection of historical narrative – and especially any attempt to explain "why?" – which I would define as Chakrabarty's position, and Feierman's optimism with regard to the capacity for innovation of the historical imagination, I have to go with Feierman.

For historians of Latin America – my own area of specialization – the project of "provincializing Europe" has been an especially vexing one, given Latin America's uneasy place within the postcolonial paradigm.[51] The region's long history of colonialism and contact, and ambivalence about Western vs non-Western identity, has meant that few historians would venture to emulate Chakrabarty's search for "singularities" not easily assimilated into historicist narratives, or to adopt Feierman's notion of a macrohistory based on practices that transcend the colonial experience.[52] At the same, Latin Americanists themselves have a long history of challenging historical models that locate all agency in the European metropolis; a leading example is Steve J. Stern's now classic critique of Immanuel Wallerstein's world-systems theory.[53] Latin Americanists have also expressed unease about an excessive reliance on "European" or "North American" theories and thinkers, as Michiel Baud incisively discussed in an earlier issue of this journal.[54] Yet such preoccupations have been significant mainly for scholarly work within Latin America and have had limited ramifications for a rethinking of grand narratives. In a recent forum on Latin America's place in world history, it was generally agreed that the region tends to get short shrift once the narrative/analytical frame broadens beyond the western hemisphere.[55]

Even so, there are some innovative lines of historical interpretation among Latin Americanists that have the potential to contribute to the "provincialization of Europe". One is a critique of the diffusion model of intellectual history. In this model of knowledge dissemination, ideas have an identifiable point of origin and radiate out from the center to the periphery. Sites such as Latin America, therefore, only come into possession of this knowledge belatedly – after it is well-established in Europe and North America – and are often portrayed as misinterpreting or misapplying these new (delayed) ideas. This presumed pattern of "first Europe (successfully), then everyone else (incompletely)" is precisely the narrative/explanatory model that inclines Chakrabarty to forsake historicism altogether. But another, less drastic, way to respond is to reject the very notion that "ideas" have fixed and identifiable points of origin, or that they spread in unilinear fashion.

Julyan Peard, in her study of the nineteenth-century *tropicalista* school of medicine in Bahia, contends that these medical researchers' location within the tropics moved them to question, before their Europe-based colleagues, the fatalistic notion that tropical climate, in and of itself, caused disease and degeneration. Again, given their location, it made sense that the *tropicalistas* were more eager to discover ways in which medical knowledge could intervene to ameliorate health conditions in the tropics than their counterparts in Britain or France – though as medical personnel in those countries became more directly engaged in colonial ventures, they began to pursue similar lines of inquiry. The *tropicalistas*, situated in a society where people of color constituted a majority, also adopted a less rigid and deterministic view of race as a factor in the health of nations when compared with Europe-based medical researchers.[56]

In a closely related vein, Nancy Stepan's study of the eugenics movement in Latin America rejects the idea that Latin American intellectuals and scientists simply misinterpreted or distorted concepts transferred from Europe to Brazil, Mexico, or Argentina. Rather, she describes a process of appropriation whereby these concepts are both adopted and adapted to local circumstances. Though such adaptations, which rejected more biologically determinist versions of eugenics, may have been based, technically speaking, on "bad science", they were neither arbitrary nor counterproductive in the Latin American context.[57] Furthermore, Peard and Stepan are not just narrating instances of local variation, which would be intriguing for specialists but irrelevant to a larger historical narrative. Rather, I would argue that, once we dispense with "point of origin" as a principal concern, we can start to think in terms of the circulation of ideas and practices, and of multiple "contact zones" where modifications adopted in one location, previously identified as on the periphery, can serve to break down orthodoxies (about the scientific foundations of "race" or the causes of disease) in another, more "central", location.[58]

Another line of historical research on Latin America, involving a re-examination of the origins of modernity and the idea of race, challenges the eurocentric narrative from a different angle. Historical anthropologist Irene Silverblatt, in her newly-published *Modern Inquisitions*, contests the claim that the modern notion of race emerges in the post-Enlightenment nineteenth century, arguing instead that it is a product of first-wave Iberian colonialism, and more specifically, of the Inquisition's campaigns to persecute "Judaizers" and to catalogue indigenous peoples. In Silverblatt's study, the concept of race is not just the "barbaric underside" of modernity, but rather is a key constitutive element of modernity, inseparable from the new ways of perceiving the world. In other words, it is not a blemish on the face of modernity – it is the very face of the modernity that emerges in the context of Europe's "civilizing mission".[59]

Back to The Future: Concluding Remarks

The scholarly debate over whether or how to go about provincializing Europe has emerged at a moment when the dilemmas of the postcolonial condition are ever more difficult to ignore, both in the former colonies and in the "Western" nations. The presence of immigrants from the erstwhile empires is ever more apparent and unsettling. And the discord over whether the societies of western Europe (and, with some modifications, North America) can absorb people whose cultures and practices are characterized as "non-Western" is increasingly fierce. Thus, the project of provincializing Europe is, simultaneously, a historical discourse about the postcolonial past and present, and an instrument for constructing a still-undefined future. If we leave unchallenged and intact the eurocentric narrative, the future is clear: gradually, these new collectivities – South Asian, Arab, African, Caribbean – will (or will have to) assimilate to the lifeways and values of the "modern and democratic" societies of the West, leaving behind those customs and values that are not congruent with a certain construction of modernity and citizenship.[60]

Should this assimilationist scenario remain the dominant one, the grand narrative of the rise of the West, and the colonial discourse it spawned, will endure virtually unaltered despite the nearly universal repudiation of the imperial past.[61] Chakrabarty, in referring to British colonial discourse in India, cites two key foundational elements – the concept of progress and the "woman question" – in the construction of Western superiority, and these elements continue to be fundamental to the assimilationist discourse of the postcolonial era. To offer just one small example, an article in a July 2003 edition of the *New York Times* reported on the "honor killing" of a young woman in a rural region of Turkey.[62] The case of the murdered woman is profoundly tragic, and she deserves our unreserved sympathy; I thoroughly agree with Chakrabarty in his criticism of cultural relativism, and his insistence that "we need universals to produce critical readings of social injustices".[63] At the same time, it is impossible to ignore the eurocentric (and racist) implications of the way the *Times* reporter presented the issue: according to the article, the debate over legislation to combat killings "in defense of honor" forms part of an attempt "to resolve a question that has been discussed for centuries about Turkey's place in the world: in Europe or in the Middle East". Who could doubt that, in this formulation, Europe represents "progress and civilization" and the Middle East represents "backwardness and barbarity"? As long as this binary – and the grand historical narrative that sustains it – continues informing our visions of the world, Europe will indeed continue to resist all attempts at its provincialization.

Notes

1 In some discussions of this issue, narrative is equated with "event history", but here I am following Paul Ricoeur's argument that all history takes some kind of narrative form. The distinction I would draw is between grand narratives structured by an explanatory arc from causes to consequences, and the smaller-scale interpretive narratives associated with a certain type of microhistory. For a discussion of these issues, see Peter Burke, "History of Events and Revival of Narrative", in *idem* (ed.), *New Perspectives on Historical Writing* (University Park, PA, 2001), 2nd edn, pp. 283–300. On the lack of precision in drawing the boundaries between micro and macro-analysis, see Fritz Ringer, "Max Weber on Causal Analysis", *History and Theory*, 41 (2002), p. 175; on narrative and causation, see Jürgen Peters, "New Historicism: Postmodern Historiography between Narrativism and Heterology", *History and Theory*, 39 (2000),pp. 21–38.

2 On Hayden White, see Karen Halttunen, "Cultural History and the Challenge of Narrativity", in V. Bonnell and L. Hunt (eds), *Beyond the Cultural Turn* (Berkeley, CA, 1999), pp. 165–166; Roger Chartier, "The Chimera of the Origin: Archeology, Cultural History and The French Revolution", in J. Goldstein (ed.), *Foucault and the*

Writing of History (Oxford, 1994), pp. 167–186; Chris Lorenz, "Can Histories be True? Narrativism, Positivism, and the 'Metaphorical Turn'", *History and Theory*, 37 (1998), pp. 309–329; Dipesh Chakrabarty, *Provincializing Europe: Postcolonial Thought and Historical Difference* (Princeton, NJ, 2000).

3 David W. Blight, *Race and Reunion: The Civil War in American Memory* (Cambridge, MA, 2001). Any attentive reader, however, quickly discerns a disapproving tone reserved for narratives that served as apologia for the Confederate position.

4 For an excellent discussion of these issues, see Halttunen, "Cultural History and the Challenge of Narrativity", pp. 165–181; see also Barbara Weinstein, "A Pesquisa sobre Identidade e Cidadania nos EUA: da Nova História Social à Nova História Cultural", *Revista Brasileira de História*, 18:35 (1998), pp. 227–246.

5 For a classic discussion of the instability of identity categories, see Joan W. Scott, "Gender: A Useful Category of Analysis", in *idem*, *Gender and the Politics of History* (New York, 1988).

6 David Landes, whose work treats culture as a set of stable, measurable, enduring attributes that causes some societies

to prosper and others to languish, presents himself as more courageous than other scholars who, presumably for fear of being thought politically incorrect, shrink from this (older) cultural explanation because "it has a sulfuric odor of race and inheritance, an air of immutability". Landes apparently feels that reference to other factors attenuates the potentially racist implications of his arguments; David S. Landes, *Wealth and Poverty of Nations: Why Some Are So Rich and Some Are So Poor* (New York, 1998), p. 516.

7   Geraldo Mártires Coelho, "Qué história cultural?" (unpublished ms.) has an excellent discussion of the nationalist/romanticist roots of the "old" cultural history.

8   My discussion of Geertz and the new cultural history owes much to the following works: Richard Biernacki, "Method and Metaphor after the New Cultural History", in Bonnell and Hunt, *Beyond the Cultural Turn*, pp. 62–92, William Roseberry, "Balinese Cockfights and the Seduction of Anthropology", in *idem*, *Anthropologies and Histories* (New Brunswick, NJ, 1989), pp. 17–29, and Joyce Appleby, Margaret Jacob, and Lynn Hunt, *Telling the Truth About History* (New York, 1994), ch. 6.

9   Bonnell and Hunt, "Introduction", *Beyond the Cultural Turn*, pp. 1–5. Geertzian "thick description" was by no means the only option among cultural-anthropological approaches. See the essays in Sherry B. Ortner (ed.), *The Fate of "Culture": Geertz and Beyond* (Berkeley, CA, 1999).

10   Clifford Geertz, *The Interpretation of Cultures* (New York, 1973), p. 5.

11   *Ibid.*, p. 14.

12   Robert Darnton, a trendsetter for this historical fashion, very recently published an article in the *New York Review of Books* that summarizes some of the major contributions in what I am calling "anecdote history", and which he calls (perhaps more flatteringly) "incident analysis". "It Happened One Night", *NYRB*, 51:11 (24 June 2004), pp. 60–64. Darnton usefully distinguishes between the "microhistory" associated with the Annales School and social history methods, "event history", with its narrow interpretive goals, and what he calls "incident analysis". Even among the studies he cites, and others that might belong in this category, there is considerable variation, with some being more focused on the cultural analysis of a particular episode, while others use an episode mainly to punctuate a broader historical narrative. For an example of the latter, see Emilia Viotti da Costa, *Crowns of Glory, Tears of Blood: The Demerara Slave Rebellion of 1823* (New York, 1994).

13   Jeffrey Freedman, *A Poisoned Chalice* (Princeton, NJ, 2002). This advertisement appeared on the back cover of the *American Historical Review*, 107:2 (2002).

14   This insight comes from Stephen Greenblatt, cited in Peters, "New Historicism", p. 38.

15   Eric Van Young, *The Other Rebellion* (Stanford, CA, 2001).

16   Monique Scheer, "From Majesty to Mystery: Changes in the Meanings of Black Madonnas from the Sixteenth to

the Nineteenth Century", *American Historical Review*, 107 (2002), pp. 1412–1440.

17   *Ibid.*, p. 1435.

18   The most trenchant critique of Geertz in this vein can be found in Roseberry, "Balinese Cockfights and the Seduction of Anthropology", pp. 26–29. According to Roseberry, in Geertz's work "culture as text is removed from the historical process that shapes it and that it in turn shapes"; p. 28. For an appreciation and critique of Clifford Geertz's impact on the discipline of history, see Biernacki, "Method and Metaphor".

19   See Ann Kane, "Reconstructing Culture in Historical Explanation: Narratives as Cultural Structure and Practice", *History and Theory*, 39 (2000), pp. 311–330.

20   Simon Schama, in his 1991 tour de force, *Dead Certainties (Unwarranted Speculations)*, encountered the problem of constructing a historical narrative with insufficient evidence, and ended up supplementing his evidence with an explicitly fictional narrative, not to demonstrate the common structures of the two narratives, but because he did not have at his disposal any other "text" that would permit access to the discourses or practices of those involved in the crime being investigated.

21   Here, Roger Chartier serves both as a critic of an older approach to causation, and as a source of new ideas about "origins". In his words: "It is now less important to know whether the event was already present in the ideas that announced it, prefigured it, or demanded it than it is to recognize changes in belief and sensibility that would render such a rapid and profound destruction of the old political and social order decipherable and acceptable. In this sense, attributing 'cultural origins' to the French Revolution does not by any means establish the Revolution's causes; rather, it pinpoints certain of the conditions that made it possible because it was conceivable." Roger Chartier, *The Cultural Origins of the French Revolution* (Durham, NC, 1991), p. 2.

22   Bonnell and Hunt, "Introduction", *Beyond the Cultural Turn*, pp. 6–8; Geoff Eley, "Is All the World a Text?", in Terrence J. McDonald (ed.), *The Historic Turn in the Human Sciences* (Ann Arbor, MI, 1996).

23   Among the recent anthologies on postcolonialism, see Gyan Prakash (ed.), *After Colonialism* (Princeton, NJ, 1995); Frederick Cooper and Ann L. Stoler (eds), *Tensions of Empire: Colonial Cultures in a Bourgeois World* (Berkeley, CA, 1997); Mark Thurner and Andrés Guerrero (eds), *After Spanish Rule* (Durham, NC, 2004).

24   According to Eric Wolf, "a major obstacle to the development of a new perspective lies in the very fact of specialization itself"; Eric Wolf, *Europe and the People without History* (Berkeley, CA, 1982), p. 19.

25   There has been an enormous output of textbooks in world history, but the production of monographic studies is still relatively small. An important exception is Lauren Benton, *Law and Colonial Cultures: Legal Regimes in World History,*

1400–1900 (Cambridge, 2002). There is also a journal, *World History*, entirely devoted to the field, a World History Association, and an annual prize for the best book in the area of world history. In addition, there are increasing numbers of scholars who would describe themselves as Atlantic historians and address some of the same issues.

26 For an introduction to this "new" world history, see Ross E. Dunn (ed.), *The New World History* (Boston, MA, 2000).

27 However, most would not go as far in the direction of "big history" as Jared Diamond, *Guns, Germs and Steel: The Fates of Human Societies* (New York, 1997), or other scholars who seek a single variable that can explain massive, long-term historical developments. See the cogent criticism of this trend in Susan K. Besse, "Placing Latin America in Modern World History Textbooks", *Hispanic American Historical Review*, 83 (2004), pp. 411–422.

28 James M. Blaut. *The Colonizer's Model: Geographical Diffusionism and Eurocentric History* (New York, 1993); André Gunder Frank, *ReOrient: Global Economy in the Asian Age* (Berkeley, CA, 1998), both cited in Joel Mokyr, "Eurocentricity Triumphant", *American Historical Review*, 104 (1999), pp. 1241–1246.

29 Roger Hart, "The Great Explanandum", *American Historical Review*, 105 (2000), pp. 486–493.

30 Landes, *Wealth and Poverty of Nations*, pp. 516, 523, as cited in Mokyr, "Eurocentricity Triumphant", p. 1243. For a (critical) discussion of Landes's book see "Review Essays: Explaining European Dominance", *American Historical Review*, 104 (1999), pp. 1240–1257. Crosby's volume is a less ostensibly congratulatory, but still emphasizes "unique" Western characteristics; Alfred Crosby, *The Measure of Reality: Quantification and Western Society, 1250–1600* (Cambridge, MA, 1997). For a particularly unapologetic study that revives conventional forms of cultural determinism, see Thomas Sowell, *Conquests and Cultures: An International History* (New York, 1998).

31 This is not to say that I disagree with historians who claim that slavery and colonialism played a significant role in the "rise" of the West, though I regard this, in the first instance, as an empirical question that defies precise calculation. See, for example, Eric Williams, *Capitalism and Slavery* (Chapel Hill, NC, 1944).

32 Kenneth Pomeranz, *The Great Divergence: China, Europe and the Making of the Modern World Economy* (Princeton, NJ, 2000); Roy Bin Wong, *China Transformed: Historical Change and the Limits of the European Experience* (Ithaca, NY, 1997).

33 Patrick Manning, "Introduction to *AHR* Forum: Asia and Europe in the World Economy", *American Historical Review*, 107 (2002), pp. 419–424.

34 One exception would be Patricia Seed, whose work – though increasingly speculative and unpersuasive – does represent an attempt to use cultural studies methods for the consideration of world-historical problems. See her *Ceremonies of Possession in Europe's Conquest of the New World, 1492–1640* (Cambridge, 1995), and *American Pentimento: The Invention of Indians and the Pursuit of Riches* (Minneapolis, MI, 2001).

35 Margaret Jacob, "Thinking Unfashionable Thoughts, Asking Unfashionable Questions", *American Historical Review*, 105 (2000), pp. 494–500; idem, "Science Studies after Social Construction: The Turn toward the Comparative and the Global", in Bonnell and Hunt, *Beyond the Cultural Turn*, pp. 95–120.

36 David Ludden, "Modern Inequality and Early Modernity", *American Historical Review*, 107 (2002), pp. 470–480. To be more specific, the Irish had the slim but significant advantage of being able to emigrate as free, rather than bonded, laborers.

37 Robert Young, *Postcolonialism: An Historical Introduction* (Cambridge, 2001).

38 Chakrabarty, *Provincializing Europe*, p. 37. Throughout the book, Chakrabarty makes it clear that he is referring to a "hyper-real" Europe rather than a specific set of nations or populations.

39 *Ibid.*, p. 255.

40 The discussion of Thompson's essay is in *ibid.*, p. 48; the second part of the quote (in *ibid.*, p. 39) is from the Australian historian, Meaghan Morris.

41 *Ibid.*, pp. 31–32. For a similar discussion in the Latin American postcolonial context of this notion of a historical "not yet", see Mark Thurner, "After Spanish Rule: Writing Another After", in Thurner and Guerrero, *After Spanish Rule*, pp. 12–57.

42 *Ibid.*, p. 82. On this distinction, see Paul Veyne, *Writing History: Essays on Epistemology* (Middletown, CT, 1984), p. 56.

43 A similar criticism can be found in Jacques Pouchepadass's review of Chakrabarty, *Provincializing Europe*, in *History and Theory*, 41 (2002), pp. 381–391.

44 Chakrabarty, *Provincializing Europe*, p. 148.

45 *Ibid.*, p. 248. Italics are Chakrabarty's.

46 Wolf, *Europe and the People without History*.

47 Feierman, "Colonizers, Scholars, and the Creation of Invisible Histories", in Hunt and Bonnell, *Beyond the Cultural Turn*, pp. 184–185. Feierman indicates the anthropological roots of this historiographical turn in the work of Jean and John Comaroff.

48 *Ibid.*, p. 185.

49 Hunt and Bonnell, "Introduction", in *Beyond the Cultural Turn*, p. 20.

50 Feierman, "Colonizers, Scholars, and the Creation of Invisible Histories", p. 207.

51 For a discussion of Latin America's place within postcolonial studies, see Thurner, "After Spanish Rule: Writing Another After".

52 There are some partial exceptions; a work that has a similar proposal (to Feierman's) for Mexican history is Thomas Benjamin, "A Time of Reconquest: History, the Maya Revival, and the Zapatista Rebellion in Chiapas", *American Historical Review*, 105 (2000), pp. 417–450.

53 Steve J. Stern, "Feudalism, Capitalism, and the World-System in the Perspective of Latin America and the Caribbean", *American Historical Review*, 93 (1988), pp. 829–872.

54 Michiel Baud, "History, Morality, and Politics: Latin American Intellectuals in a Global Context", *International Review of Social History*, 48 (2003), pp. 55–78.

55 "Forum: Placing Latin America in World History", *Hispanic American Historical Review*, 84 (2004), pp. 391–446.

56 Julyan G. Peard, "Tropical Disorders and the Forging of a Brazilian Medical Identity", *Hispanic American Historical Review*, 77 (1997), pp. 1–44. For a more extensive discussion of these issues, see her *Race, Place, and Medicine: The Idea of the Tropics in Nineteenth-Century Brazilian Medicine* (Durham, NC, 2000). I am using the somewhat awkward "Europe-based", rather than European, deliberately. Several of the *tropicalistas* were Europeans residing in Bahia, but once again, their point of origin was less significant than the fact of their identification with the local medical community. I make a similar point about discourses of rationalization and productivity in my *For Social Peace in Brazil: Industrialists and the Remaking of the Working Class in São Paulo, 1920–1964* (Chapel Hill, NC, 1996), p. 7.

57 Nancy Leys Stepan, *"The Hour of Eugenics": Race, Gender, and Nation in Latin America* (Ithaca, NY, 1991).

58 The concept of "contact zones", derived from the work of Mary Louise Pratt, is discussed in Gilbert M. Joseph, "Close Encounters: Toward a New Cultural History of US–Latin American Relations", p. 5, in Joseph, Catherine LeGrand, and Ricardo Salvatore (eds), *Close Encounters of Empire* (Durham, NC, 1998). These contact zones are not divorced from unequal relations of power, but that power inequality does not mean that knowledge exchange is entirely unidirectional.

59 Irene Silverblatt, *Modern Inquisitions: Peru and the Colonial Origins of the Civilized World* (Durham, NC, 2004).

60 Most contemporary (Western) public discussions of these "customs and values" treat them primarily as impediments to assimilation, and their practitioners as irrationally, if not dangerously, clinging to tradition. Few academic studies have seriously questioned these assumptions, or explored the meanings of religious practice in these new contexts. One outstanding exception is Aisha Khan's study of race and religious identity in Trinidad, in which she argues that religious rituals "are sites of dynamism rather than simply static repetitions", and that the search for knowledge through religion is crucial to allowing South Asian communities in Trinidad to be "agents of their own futures" in a context of cultural mixing; Aisha Khan, *Callaloo Nation: Metaphors of Race and Religious Identity among South Asians in Trinidad* (Durham, NC, 2004), p. 229.

61 I think this continues to be the case despite the recent embrace of the imperialist ethos by some eminent historians. See Niall Ferguson, *Empire: The Rise and Demise of the British World Order and the Lessons for Global Power* (New York, 2004).

62 "'Honor Killings' Defy Turkish Efforts to End Them", *New York Times*, 13 July 2003, p. 3, emphasis added.

63 Chakrabarty, *Provincializing Europe*, p. 254.

13   "Africa as an Alien Future"
The Middle Passage, Afrofuturism, and Postcolonial Waterworlds

Ruth Mayer

1

At one point in *Amistad*, Stephen Spielberg's 1997 filmic epos about the historical revolt on the Spanish slaver by that name, we witness the desperate efforts of Cinque (Djimon Hounsou), the leader of the African rebels, to escape from the American soldiers who have come across them. Cinque first tries to get away swimming, but is overtaken by a boat. This is when he chooses to take another course, letting himself sink deeper and deeper into the water, the camera tracing his drift to the bottom of the sea – a movement which is suddenly and violently interrupted, when his body refuses to be drowned, forcing its way back up to the surface, where Cinque is promptly pulled into the boat of his American captors.

The scene is fascinating because it is both utterly hopeless and absurdly enticing: for once, Cinque's way out is obviously no way out, his effort at getting away a suicidal undertaking. But on the other hand, and simultaneously, the scene is replete with an aura of a total escape, absolute freedom. Briefly, Cinque seems to have drifted into a realm where the laws of the land do not hold. Of course, once the African comes back to the surface, Spielberg's film sets out to steer an altogether different course, leaving the underwater world and its strange logic behind and turning to the world of American law and order. This world, by contrast, is presented as neat and linear, and it is here where the initial conflict is finally resolved.

With this, *Amistad* manages to downplay precisely the aspects at the heart of the horrors of slavery, the fact that thousands of people were dragged into a world which could not possibly make sense to them, and from which they could not escape other than at the risk of self-annihilation. This is what the underwater scene briefly captures

Ruth Mayer, "'Africa as an Alien Future': The Middle Passage, Afrofuturism, and Postcolonial Waterworlds." *Amerikastudien/American Studies*, 45(4), 2000: 555–566. Used by permission of Ruth Mayer.

Postcolonial Studies: An Anthology, First Edition. Edited by Pramod K. Nayar.
Editorial material and organization © 2016 John Wiley & Sons, Ltd.
Published 2016 by John Wiley & Sons, Ltd.

early in the film, and it is no accident that it presents one of the film's most unreal scenes. But then, to capture events that were never documented in writing by the ones who experienced them might very well require another structure than the realist ones of representation. All narratives around the Middle Passage are invariably and necessarily speculative, and the more so today, over one hundred years after the fact. And thus fantastic, mythic, or grotesque narratives seem so much more adequate to tackle the estrangement and *angst* erupting in its wake.

This is, at any rate, the course a series of recent reenactments of the Middle Passage take, brought forth by artists working in most diverse fields. All of these revisions, as different as they are, concentrate on the fantasy spaces in-between and nowhere at all, spaces that present themselves as mixed-up, ambivalent, floating. The most obvious of these in-between spaces is, of course, the sea, this paradigmatic space of openness and indeterminacy which gains so radically contradictory connotations once it becomes the setting for abduction, violation, enslavement, and revolt. Placed into the context of the Middle Passage, the ocean becomes the 'oceanic,' as Hortense Spillers argued: "… removed from the indigenous land and culture and not-yet 'American' either, these captive persons, without names that their captors would recognize, were in movement across the Atlantic, but they were also *nowhere* at all."[1]

When reenacted from the perspective of today, the last decades of the twentieth century, the Middle Passage acquires a whole set of new connotations, the theme of enforced displacement and violent abduction merging with other, more contemporary, scenarios of migration, dislocation, and contact. Paul Gilroy's study *The Black Atlantic* set out most impressively to trace the imageries of travel in the African diaspora, imageries which often enough managed to translate the starkly negative into accounts of liberation and self-fashioning, rewriting the past from the vantage point of the present.[2]

It is in the contemporary arts – literature, installation art, pop music – that such transformations become most obvious, and it is here that the passages between Africa and the Caribbean are most glaringly reenacted and transformed. In such reenactments, "the metaphor of travel is emptied of a purely retrospective thrust, in which the ship is envisioned as the vehicle of an original abduction or of the return to an original territory. Now the metaphor, especially in contemporary youth cultures of the African diasporas, is opened up to harbor all kinds of notions of development, mutation and crossover."[3] By consequence, speculations and fantasies arise which move ceaselessly back and forth through time and space, between cultural traditions and geographical time zones, and thus "between Africa as a lost continent in the past and between Africa as an alien future."[4]

2

"There are no stories of the middle passage. One hundred million people were stolen and sold from their homes, shipped across the world, and not a single story of that journey survives."[5] The photographer and installation artist Carrie Mae Weems is very well aware of the perils of representing the Middle Passage. To avoid the pitfalls of 'porno-troping'[6] and retrospective exculpation, she focuses on the very logic of recollection and reconstruction in her turn to black history. In an installation concluded in 1995, *Untitled* (Sea Island Series), Weems approaches the entangled histories of Africa and America from a markedly contemporary perspective, juxtaposing photographs and folk narratives from the Gullah Islands off the coast of Georgia and South Carolina, to present a picture of the past inflected with the knowledge of the present.

The bulk of the series consists of large-format landscape photographs combined with text panels. But Weems also takes resort to a device familiar from another series, entitled, tellingly, *Commemorating* (1992), in which she imprinted cheap ceramic dinner plates with the names of famous Americans. In her Sea Island series, she uses dinner ware to display general reflections about the project under the joint heading "Went looking for Africa." One such dinner plate inscription reads:

WENT LOOKING FOR AFRICA and found Africa here in the proverbs of McIntosh in the voices of Sapelo in the songs of St. Simons Along the highways of Jekyll in the gardens of Johns in the grave-yards of Hilton Head

By dint of this approach, Africa and America are no longer conceived of as geographical entities, to be neatly separated, but as convoluted concepts, flightlines of beliefs, memories, and projections that are far too intersected to be told apart. Africa is engrained in the very core of American culture, its language, its folklore, its soil. Characteristically, Weems expresses this insight both verbally and formally, the dinner ware figuring as an emblem of commemoration, invested with a significance that is visible only at second glance and to the initiate, as Houston Baker remarked: "The dishes are memory, and they are luxury. They pass through generations as family inheritance. Carrie Mae Weems reclaims such ceramics for the everyday uses of cultural conversation."[7]

The Gullah Islands, once the last illegal resort for slavery in the United States, epitomize a central predicament of contemporary African-American culture: the fact that black history is both there and not there, evident in countless traces, scars, and memories, yet largely submerged when it comes to written accounts and first-person documentations of the past from the viewpoint of the victims. To come to pass in its own right, the African presence in the United States has to be pried away from the mainstream culture of which it has become an integral part–not by choice, but by necessity, as Samuel Delany pointed out:

… until fairly recently, as a people we were systematically forbidden any images of our past. . . . every effort conceivable was made to destroy all vestiges of what might endure as African social consciousness. When, indeed, we say that this country was founded on slavery, we must remember that we mean, specifically, that it was founded on the systematic, conscientious, and massive destruction of African cultural remnants. That some musical rhythms endured, that certain religious attitudes and structures seem to have persisted, is quite astonishing, when you study the efforts of the white, slave-importing machinery to wipe them out.[8]

Weems's series can be seen as an effort to remobilize these remnants and draw them to our attention, "reassembling traces of the past into new, if only temporary, unities."[9] The same idea motivated a later project, in which she documented the traces of New World slavery in West Africa. Both projects evince that in the field of the visual and narrative arts the project of excavating an African past will invariably deviate from its anthropological and historiographical premises and venture into the realm of fantasy and myth to compensate for the lack of concrete and indubitable material. Time and again in the Sea Islands series, the rhetoric of historical fact is replaced with the vernacular of personal fantasies and sense impressions.

In *Untitled* (Ebo Landing), a triptych of two silver prints and a text panel, Weems displays two scenic views of the island St. Simons, framed in black and mounted one over the other. In between the photographs she inserted a panel set in circular print:

> EBO LANDING One midnight at high tide a ship bringing in a cargo of Ebo (Ibo) men landed at Dunbar Creek on the Island of St. Simons. But the men refused to be sold into slavery; joining hands together they turned back toward the water, chanting, "the water brought us, the water will take us away." They all drowned, but to this day when the breeze sighs over the marshes and through the trees, you can hear the clank of chains and echo of their chant at Ebo Landing.

Here the African past becomes a ghostly present, and a collution of different time spheres sets in which is all the more disconcerting for the detached and depersonalized representation of the event. The Ibo men appear in strange isolation, because their enslavers do not come into view and because the Africans' desperate act is related not so much as a tragic group suicide than as a weird and moving ritual. The photographs emphasize this aura of timeless detachment or suspension of time and place: the marshland at view a curious mixture of water and earth, and the entire setup of irregular palm trees and lush vegetation looking as 'African' as it is 'American.' The Ibos' act seems to have fundamentally affected the land, giving vent to a haunting that is intricately connected with the region's history – its function as a port for slave ships and its plantation culture–even if, or precisely because, this history turns into fantasy and myth.

The same collution of history and myth, the repressed cruel past and a seemingly enlightened present, runs through a much earlier text which traces the horrors of the Middle Passage while well aware of the impossibility of representing the viewpoint of its victims: Herman Melville's "Benito Cereno" (1855).[10] After all, Melville's novella figures forth a "spectral marionette show,"[11] presenting the slave ship along the lines of gothic horror as a haunted place in the middle of nowhere:

> Always upon first boarding a large and populous ship at sea, especially a foreign one, with a nondescript crew such as Lascars or Manilla men, the impression varies in a peculiar way from that produced by first entering a strange house with strange inmates in a strange land. Both house and ship – the one by its walls and blinds, the other by its bulwarks like ramparts – board from view their interiors till the last moment: but in the case of the ship there is this addition; that the living spectacle it contains, upon its sudden and complete disclosure, has, in contrast with the blank ocean which zones it, something of the effect of enchantment. The ship seems unreal; these strange costumes, gestures, and faces, but a shadowy tableau just emerged from the deep, which directly must receive back what it gave.[12]

These observations foreshadow the story's later revelation of a pervasive masquerade enacted on the ship, a revelation which leaves no doubt that the phenomena which "[emerge] from the deep," are not necessarily more truthful or significant than the "blank" surface they disrupt. To the contrary, their uncanny effect might reside exclusively in their meaninglessness, the "spectacle" or "shadowy tableau" only the more frightening because it has lost any melodramatic significance: it does not permit itself to be read.[13]

In fact, it is only against the backdrop of the high seas, the 'blank ocean,' that the spectacle of social and cultural interaction (the "nondescript" foreign crew, presumably under American leadership) fully reveals its cruel, uncanny, and absurd character. In "Benito Cereno," the sea figures not as the land's opposite, but as its epitome: here the incongruities of the land – most notably the system of slavery – are too conspicuous to be entirely ignored. And this is where Melville's novella calls to mind Weems's installation which likewise associates the sea with a repressed and gruesome past – the Ibos' death by drowning. But while for Melville the 'blank sea,' just like the 'tableau' of the land, ultimately does not make sense, because it is an empty melodrama or tautological masquerade, Weems turns it into a meaningful entity. In her enactment, the sea turns from blankness to myth – the history of slavery mixed up with the myths of Africa bringing about the dead men's return and their haunting takeover. Where Melville discloses a dead end, Weems's horror scenario figures as a point of departure for a new symbolic repertoire.

With this, Weems posits herself firmly in a postcolonial scene which insists upon reading established dichotomies of meaning and insignificance, essence and blankness against the grain, siding with the 'nondescript crew,' or the drowned ones whose viewpoint is irretrievably lost, by implementing another concept of history and historiography. In Derek Walcott's poem "The Sea is History," this new notion of history is associated with a new beginning out of the pain and horror of the Middle Passage, a new beginning stemming from the victims, the drowned slaves:

> Where are your monuments, your battles, martyrs?
> Where is your tribal memory? Sirs,
> in that grey vault. The sea. The sea
> has locked them up. The sea is history
> ………
> Sir it is locked in them sea-sands
> out there past the reef's moiling shelf,
> where the men-o'-war floated down;
> strop on these goggles, I'll guide you there myself.[14]

Insisting that the ocean's "blank pages" are not as empty as they seem, Walcott's poem fashions the very history it then sets out to pronounce in the last line: "in the salt chuckle of the rocks / with their sea pools, there was the sound / like a rumor without any echo / of History, really beginning."[15] Black diasporic history, it seems, is a thing of the future, not of the past, a subject of fantasies, dreams and speculations – the currents and changes of the sea – which is created in the process of its recuperation.

Thus, Walcott refutes Melville's notion of the ocean as irretrievably 'blank.' But even more importantly, his turn to the sea as both a burial ground *and* the space of a new beginning, just like Weems's enactment of memory as survival, indicates that the subject matter of black history requires a methodology of its own, new goggles, if you will, that make readable what seemed blank and reveal the ghosts of the past at loose in the present world. It is precisely the openness and indeterminacy of the sea, its 'oceanic' quality of the *'nowhere at all'* as Hortense Spillers had it, which privileges this space for a pervasive revision from the vantage point of present needs and desires. This is why the underwater world, the submarine, gains so much attention in turn: by contrast to the chartered and mapped high seas, this world below emerges as a realm beneath existing lines of power and signification, an ambivalent space, "neither European nor Caribbean, neither metropolitan nor colonial, neither within the 'West' nor without it," as Ian Baucom wrote[16] – a fantasy space which is always as much of the future as it is of the past.

3

We must not forget that the futuristic fantasy spaces in black culture are always also spaces of retreat from very real pressures, testifying – if often only indirectly – to these pressures and their traumatic effects. "Black people live the estrangement that science fiction writers imagine,"[17] Greg Tate noted, and for that matter it is no accident that so much black art that currently deals with this 'life feeling' is not only clearly futuristic, but also, and just as clearly, highly morbid – telling ghost stories and tales of haunting. The British director John Akomfrah thus cast this peculiar obsession with the past as an obsession with the dead: "I think necrophilia is at the heart of black filmmaking." To come up with a history of one's own against the pull of oblivion and decay – to enforce the return of the repressed – is to face some ugly truths:

> The most powerful moment, for me, in my earlier film *Testament*, is the very end and the very beginning, which are both images of death, stultification, atrophy. When she goes to the graveyard and buries her father, or when the man walks into the river, which is a wish-fulfilment of death, a drowning wish going on there. There is a level of morbidity which I think people have to realise in the quest for identity. Identities are a morbid business.[18]

Of course, Akomfrah's emphasis on a morbid black imagination is, to a certain extent, polemic – pitted against all-too-familiar stylizations of blackness as mindlessly joyful, happy-go-lucky and a-historical. But there is more to the obsession with the alien and the uncanny in black culture than sheer provocation, as Weems's and Walcott's ghost stories exemplify, and as comes even more trenchantly to the fore in contemporary pop-cultural turns to the Middle Passage and its imagery of travel and displacement. It is in this context, the workings of pop culture, that the spirits and ghosts of yore turn into quite contemporary figures of horror and haunting: aliens, extraterrestrians, creatures from the deep.

> Could it be possible for humans to breathe underwater? A fetus in its mother's womb is certainly alive in an aquatic environment.
> During the greatest holocaust the world has ever known, pregnant America-bound African slaves were thrown overboard by the thousands during labor for being sick and disruptive cargo. Is it possible that they could have given birth at sea to babies that never needed air?

Recent experiments have shown mice able to breath liquid oxygen. Even more shocking and conclusive was a recent instance of a premature human infant saved from certain death by breathing liquid oxygen through its underdeveloped lungs.

These facts combined with reported sightings of gill men and swamp monsters in the coastal swamps of the Southeastern United States make the slave trade theory startlingly feasible.[19]

These are excerpts from the liner notes to the album *The Quest* by the Detroit electronic duo Drexciya, a project which has for many years fashioned itself around similar ruminations about 'Drexciyans' – sea creatures of a superior submarine civilization invading the United States systematically.[20] Obviously, this narrative epitomizes the logic sketched above, from the move to the sea as an alternative history deeply infused with fantasy and myth, to the evocation of aliens arising out of alienation, up to the morbid imagery of creatures between death and life and beyond identification, which the entire album then sets out to consolidate.

The narrative of the liner notes is, after all, the only 'information' we are given about the album. The music tells no story, apart from disjointed bits and pieces of lyrics that not so much add up to a narrative, but disorient and confuse. Instead of learning more about the Drexciyans, we are literally forced into an underwater world, a sound pattern meshing together the synthetic and the natural, bubble tones and electronic scales which could be called breathtaking in more than one sense. An aesthetics of alienation takes hold, as Kodwo Eshun has argued:

> ...there is no singer, no redemption, no human touch. Far from rehumanizing electronics, Drexciyan fiction exacerbates this dehumanization, populating the world with impalpable hallucinations that get on your nerves. ... At Love Parade and Tribal Gathering you can still hear DJs saying electronic music is universal music. The frequencies can unite us all in a tonal consensus. After listening to Drexciya, it's audible that if electronics ever unites, then it does so through obfuscation. It communicates through mystification.[21]

By dint of this reading, electronic music could become *the* vehicle for dissent in a Deleuzian control society, which operates not "by confining people, but through continuous control and instant communication."[22] Drexciya seem to comply exemplarily with Deleuze's demand for "vacuoles of noncommunication, circuit breakers," which the French critic deemed indispensable to "elude control."[23] For Eshun, Drexciya's aesthetics of alienation forms the blueprint for a new form of cultural interaction and contact: "Each track title... functions as a component in an electronic mythology which the listener assembles.... A new geography of morals."[24]

Of course, such enthusiasm about the potential of music to bring forth a fundamental disruption, a new mythology, must always face up to the 'fluidity' of musical expression – the fact that music, even when not purely instrumental, is so much more ambivalent than any other artistic medium, especially when it comes to ideological positions and projections. It is, after all, by way of lyrics, liner notes, performance, and artistic comments both on and off stage that this ideological dimension enters the field of music. By consequence, the political and social effects of music turn out to be a matter of style – highly unstable, open to all kinds of adaptations, revisions, and appropriations.[25]

While I hesitate thus to join into the enthusiastic chorus of critics like Eshun and celebrate electronic music as the manifestation of an altogether new 'post-human' form of expression, I do believe that Drexciya's style politics are indicative of an interesting turn, as they produce self-destroying narratives, fictions that strain against the conventional pull of identification and closure.

Seen that way, the effect of mystification evoked by Eshun is very well given in Drexciya, but located on an altogether different level, as it is inscribed in the very interaction of instrumental music and the narratives around it. While the narratives, presenting the Drexciyans as social outcasts and fighters from below, offer patterns of identification – if markedly fantastic ones – the music takes these patterns apart, moving between recognizable structures (the underwater sounds) and pure noise and thus discouraging any attempt at making sense eventually, erecting a code that cannot be deciphered.

Of course, Drexciya are not the first musical act to come up with this strategy. Indeed, their aesthetics can be traced back to the free jazz experiments of Sun Ra and his Arkestra, not only with regard to musical, but also to conceptual developments. Time and again, the space narratives evoked in this context ran analogous in their effect to the musical strategy of free jazz to move from established harmonies to sudden transgressions and to confront closure with chaos. Just like the music veers between signification and rupture, so the space narratives establish recognizable structures only to disavow them in turn: "… they have thrown their own identities into question, taking on a multitude of costumes and alter egos, each of them is a myth-making, alias-taking, self-styled postindustrial shaman," writes John Corbett on Sun Ra's and other musicians' 'space madness.'[26] By consequence, the aliens and extraterrestrians invoked by so many black musical projects of the 1950s and 1960s are not to be understood as neat inversions of the dominant value system, but as more extensive tactics of confusion–instead of "only turning around the relation of 'us' against 'them,' and other binaries," Diedrich Diederichsen wrote, "most of these artists tend to mess up the entire matrix of binary distinctions."[27]

In the works of contemporary artists, this technique of 'messing up' has become a much more strategic – and theoretical – affair than in, say, Sun Ra's fantastical mythology. This comes not only to the fore in musical projects from Drexciya to DJ Spooky and 4hero, but also in the films of John Akomfrah, the fiction of Darius James or the art of Keith Piper. All of these artists, together with many more, have been subsumed under the heading "Afrofuturism,"[28] as all of them focus one way or another on the intersecting imageries of pastness and future in black culture, setting out not so much to rewrite the history of the African diaspora, but to systematically deconstruct it, rendering Africa an 'alien future,' as Kodwo Eshun put it in John Akomfrah's film to the movement, *Last Angel of History* (1995). The aliens and monsters haunting Afrofuturist narratives explode the confines of historiography and realism, collapsing established patterns of signification and identification, and put forth undecipherable codes and fractured images.

One prominent means of generating the atmosphere of alienation so characteristic for many of these works is technology. In Drexciya's *Quest*, synthetic sounds imitate natural ones, sounding almost, but not altogether, the same, so that the underwater world disclosed seems strange in several respects – a sphere underneath the human world which is at the same time a realm outside of nature: artificial, alien, and uncanny.

In the work of the British installation artist Keith Piper, similar strategies of technological alienation are employed, and again the result is the collapse of long-standing symbolic systems – not in order to replace them, but to expose them in their constructedness and arbitrariness. And once more aquatic imagery, or what Kobena Mercer called the aesthetics of "oceanic feeling,"[29] is at the heart of these techniques of alienation, and deconstruction: certainties are set afloat, and stable identities go down the drain.

Piper's installation falls into three parts, all of them opening up different time frames to trace the interrelations between black British history and the African diaspora. One such part, "The Ghosts of Christendom," reflects the Middle Passage between Africa and the Caribbean, and leaves no doubt that Piper, too, conceives of black history as also being always a horror story. The ship called Jesus is the *Jesus of Lubeck*, the first official British vessel to take part in the slave trade, sent off by Queen Elizabeth in 1564, and figuring forth the intricate convolution of religion and politics, spirituality and ideology at heart of colonial history and the history of slavery likewise, as we learn from an inscription on a tombstone displayed in the exhibition. And yet, religious history is not to be written along the lines of domination and subjugation alone, as Piper's project evinces: "[T]he slave ship called Jesus has experienced a mutiny of radical proportions. The same Africans for which the ship had been a mechanism of imprisonment had seized control of the helm and were steering the ship in a totally different direction."[30]

The exhibition, which comprises a variety of different representational techniques, unfolds around a series of huge computer-montaged transparencies mounted on light-boxes to simulate stained-glass church windows. Here, the obviously high-tech emulates the ancient, the up-to-date and the traditional enmeshed with each other, while African and Western symbols and emblems appear in intimate interlinkage. This effect is driven home most impressively in a montage showing the feet of a black crucified body on a cross-shaped frame, hanging over a water-filled basin with a broken mirror inside. Ian Baucom has read this installation as a strategy of enforcing an impossible point of view, another means of pulling us under water:

> Looking down into these waters, we see not simply a reflection of the agonized black body which hangs above, we see that bleeding figure as if from beneath, from below the surface of the water. Manipulating a trick of light to reverse our optic of inspection and to reposition our space of observation, Piper's installation displaces the viewing subject, draws us beneath the water to gaze at the scene of violence played out above. The work forces us, if only for a moment, to occupy the submarine.[31]

If this relocation of the perspective is definitely one effect of the installation, there is more to it. The tormented black body on the cross, just like the entire exhibition, points to a deep skepticism *vis-à-vis* the very symbolic systems at work here: the selfsame system – Christianity – which triggered the history of suffering figures now as a means of representing it. With this, Piper for once does invert a set of dominant signs and symbols, as his catalog essay indicates. But he also goes beyond mere inversion, pinpointing the difficulty of representing positively what happened and what happens in the history of cultural contact and race relations. After all, the installation is not content with relating a clear-cut 'other' story of salvation and redemption; it does not merely 'blacken' the imagery of Christianity. The doubly fractured reflection of the black body we see in the water instead brings about the shortcomings of such neat reversals, which merely turn around prefabricated value systems, ideologies, and props, and thus add speculations to speculations: fragments of meaning and knowledge that are as broken up and distorted as the body reflected in the water. Thus Piper's installation seems to comment on the other projects I presented here; all of them collapsing past, present, and future, and all of them interlinking historiographical and mythical rhetoric and imagery, not so much in order to reconstruct a lost history (as did Spielberg's *Amistad*), but to dismantle the established one and give scope to altogether different, highly fantastic scenarios instead, which are as much of the future as they are of the past. In any case we end up with strange sights – alien, aquatic, artificial – which force us not only to reconsider the past, but most of all the present we like to take for granted.

Notes

[1] Hortense Spillers, "Mama's Baby, Papa's May-be: An American Grammar Book," *Within the Circle: An Anthology of African American Literary Criticism from the Harlem Renaissance to the Present*, ed. Angelyn Mitchell (Durham, NC: Duke UP, 1994) 454–81, 466. On the Middle Passage in African-American literature, see also Wolfgang Binder, "Uses of Memory: The Middle Passage in African-American Literature," *Slavery in the Americas*, ed. Wolfgang Binder (Würzburg: Königshausen & Neumann, 1993) 539–64 Carl Pedersen, "Middle Passages: Representation of the Slave Trade in Caribbean and African-American Literature," *Massachusetts Review* 34:2 (1993): 225–39.

[2] Cf. Paul Gilroy, *The Black Atlantic: Modernity and Double Consciousness* (London: Verso, 1993).

[3] Diedrich Diederichsen, "Verloren unter Sternen: UFOs, Aliens und das Mothership," *Globalkolorit: Multikulturalismus und Populärkultur*, ed. Ruth Mayer and Mark Terkessidis (St. Andrä-Wördern: Hannibal, 1998) 237–52; 239–40 (my translation).

[4] Kodwo Eshun in an interview in *Last Angel of History*, dir. John Akomfrah, with Edward George, researchers: Kodwo Eshun and Floyd Webb (Death Audio Film Production 1995).

[5] Carrie Mae Weems – quoted in Maren Stange, "Memory and Form in Recent African American Photography: From *12 Million Black Voices* to Carrie Mae Weems," unpublished manuscript 10-11.

[6] The term 'porno-troping' is Hortense Spillers's and refers to the spectacular enactment of black suffering and pain for an audience both shocked and thrilled by it. Cf. Spillers 67.

[7] Houston A. Baker, Jr., "Islands of Identity: Inside the Pictures of Carrie Mae Weems," *Carrie Mae Weems: In These Islands. South-Carolina – Georgia* (exhibition catalog) (University of Alabama Sarah Moody Gallery of Art, 1995) 12–19; 16.

[8] Mark Dery, "Black to the Future: Interviews with Samuel R. Delany, Greg Tate, and Tricia Rose," *The South Atlantic Quarterly* 92.4 (Fall 1992): 735–78; 747.

[9] Stange, "Memory and Form in Recent African American Photography" 12.

[10] Herman Melville, "Benito Cereno" (1855), *Billy Budd, Sailor and Other Stories* (Harmondsworth: Penguin, 1970) 217–307.

[11] Michael P. Rogin, *Subversive Genealogy: The Politics and Art of Herman Melville* (Berkeley:U of California P, 1983) 209.

[12] Melville 221–22.

[13] On the logic of melodrama, which "demonstrates over and over that the signs of ethical forces can be discovered and can be made legible," see Peter Brooks, *The Melodramatic Imagination: Balzac, Henry James, Melodrama, and the Mode of Excess* (1976; New Haven, CT: Yale UP, 1995) 20.

[14] Derek Walcott, "The Sea is History," *Poems 1965–1980* (London: Jonathan Cape, 1980) 237–40; 237, 238.

[15] Walcott 238, 240.

[16] Ian Baucom, "Charting the 'Black Atlantic,'" *Postmodern Culture* 8.1 (1997): http://muse.jhu.edu/journals/post modern_culture/v008/8.1baucom.html.

[17] Mark Dery, "Black to the Future" 767–768.

[18] Kass Banning, "Feeding Off the Dead: Necrophilia and the Black Imaginary. An Interview with John Akomfrah," *Borderlines* 29–30 (Winter 1993): 33.

[19] Drexciya, *The Quest* (Detroit: Submerge, 1997), liner notes.

[20] For an analysis of the act and its aesthetics see Kodwo Eshun, "Fear of a Wet Planet," *The Wire* (January 1998): 19–20. I came across Eshun's piece through *Loving the Alien: Science Fiction, Diaspora, Multikultur*, ed. Diedrich

Diederichsen (Berlin: ID Verlag, 1998), in which a German version of this text appeared.

[21] Eshun, "Fear of a Wet Planet" 20.

[22] Gilles Deleuze, "Control and Becoming" (Conversation with Toni Negri, 1990), *Negotiations, 1972–1990*, trans. Martin Joughin (New York: Columbia UP, 1995) 169–76; 174.

[23] Deleuze 175.

[24] Eshun, "Fear of a Wet Planet" 20. For a more detailed discussion of electronic music and its cultural potential, see Eshun's *More Brilliant Than the Sun: Adventures in Sonic Fiction* (London: Quartet Books, 1997).

[25] On this issue, especially with regard to so-called 'protest music,' see Simon Frith, *Performing Rites: On the Value of Popular Music* (Oxford: Oxford UP, 1996); and my "Pop As a Difference Engine: Music, Markets, and Marginality," *Simulacrum America*, ed. Elisabeth Kraus and Carolin Auer (Rochester, NY: Camden House, 2000).

[26] John Corbett, "Brothers from Another Planet: The Space Madness of Lee 'Scratch' Perry, Sun Ra, and George Clinton," *Extended Play: Sounding Off from John Cage to Dr. Funkenstein* (Durham, NC: Duke UP, 1994) 7–24; 7.

[27] Diederichsen, "Verloren unter Sternen," 242 (my translation). On this aesthetics and its implications see, apart from Corbett and Diederichsen, the contributions to *Loving the Alien*, ed. Diederichsen, especially Tobias Nagl's "'I wonder if heaven's got a ghetto': Aliens, Ethnizität und der SF-Film," and Renée Green's "Leidige Liebe: My Alien / My Self – Readings at Work," 68-87, 134–51.

[28] For a definition of the – awkward – term 'Afrofuturism' and an introduction to the development at its outset, see Mark Dery, "Black to the Future," 735–43.

[29] Kobena Mercer, "Witness at the Crossroads: An Artist's Journey in Post-colonial Space," *Keith Piper: Relocating the Remains* (exhibition catalog) (London: Institute of International Visual Arts, 1997) 13–85: 79.

[30] Cf. Keith Piper, *A Ship Called Jesus* (exhibition catalog) (Birmingham: Ikon Gallery, 1991) unpaginated.

[31] Baucom, unpaginated.

Part Three
Language, Literacy, Education

That colonialism relied heavily upon the hegemonic power of European languages and literature is now a truism. The essays in this section study the apparatuses of this hegemonic power, even as they trace the continuing legacies of the educational, linguistic, and literary structures of the colonial era into the postcolony. From publishing to pedagogy, the essays here show how language and literacy have played crucial roles in colonization and now need to be deployed differently for the purposes of decolonization, and in order to address the crises of postcolonial sovereignty, self-determination, democratic processes, and globalization. Narayana Chandran ponders over the social, cultural, political, and economic purchase English as a language possesses in contemporary India – even as debates about the "former colonial masters' language" and the "European values inherited" by virtue of "using" the language rage among English teachers, and in colleges and syllabi. Touring the landscape of pedagogy, research, and institutions where English language and literature are taught and learnt, Chandran stresses the need for a

language that facilitates critical thinking. Continuing this concern with postcolonial language and pedagogy Ajay Heble calls for connecting classroom work with social concerns and issues, to provide a more ethical frame for teaching in the face of the increasing corporatization of the institutions of knowledge-production. With postcolonialism's emphasis on emancipation and situated knowledges, the classroom becomes the site of ideological battles over language and history, as Heble notes. One such institution of knowledge production in the colonial age was publishing, and Caroline Davis' essay on the Oxford University Press in South Africa traces the internal and external battles the company faced. The profits that accrued from preparing educational texts meant, she argues, that anti-apartheid texts were scarce in their publishing lists, although, she notes, there was considerable cultural capital to be obtained from publishing books for the white academic audience. Scott Richard Lyons is also interested in knowledge production when he argues that Native Americans have come to distrust the

Postcolonial Studies: An Anthology, First Edition. Edited by Pramod K. Nayar.
Editorial material and organization © 2016 John Wiley & Sons, Ltd.
Published 2016 by John Wiley & Sons, Ltd.

written word (in the colonizer's language) because of the "duplicitous interrelationships between writing, violence, and colonization." What Native Americans (and by extension other formerly colonized peoples) seek from language is the freedom to determine their own communicative needs and the languages of public discourse – what Lyons calls "rhetorical sovereignty."

14   On English from India
Prepositions to Post-Positions

K. Narayana Chandran

I

IF FELICITY ROSSLYN'S ESSAY on the English literature degree of the new century has evoked so wide a spectrum of views around the English-teaching world, it poses, rather unwittingly, a query to the wrong entity. For, among the numerous subjects of professional study at a university, English prepares students not just for a career, but for life. Look around, and you will see someone who has studied English successfully managing a career or business for which no specific orientation is yet available in the standard curricula of our universities, least of all requiring a degree in English. I have heard it said in India, not without some truth to the claim, that with good English you don't just make a living, you can make a killing.

The strength of English, I believe, is not entirely owing to our own initiatives in rethinking the subject from time to time, but also in part to English itself, posing challenges to those who profess it, making it necessary for them to rethink what it is and how best to teach it in the radically evolving curricula of the new universities. *English Now* of the *Quarterly* will, therefore, appear another forty years from now, yet again, as a theme. None of us will perhaps see that number or contribute to its discussion, a prospect none the less cheerful for that reason. For I have often marvelled at the enormous possibilities available to us as teachers of the subject to constitute and reconstitute it as we go along. The 'Crisis' debates on the English curriculum of the last two decades notwithstanding, about 9 million students are currently learning English at Indian colleges and universities. The Indian public does not seem to know or care whether we are teachers of language or literature, whether we teach English or 'certain abhorrent English values' in the process, whether or not what we do in the classes will

K. Narayana Chandran, "On English from India: Prepositions to Post-Positions." *Cambridge Quarterly*, 35(2), 2006: 151–168. Used by permission of Oxford University Press.

help our young people become responsible individuals or citizens. This widespread ignorance about what constitutes university English, or what it does (apart from the widely laughable notion that it 'develops personality'), mercifully shields us, I believe, from public outrage. English is certainly synonymous with university education in India. A command of English is indispensable for advanced learning in any major subject other than Indian languages. And still, in some quarters, there is a widely held belief in the proverbial 'humanising' power of literature, thanks perhaps to English teachers.

The teacher of English in Indian colleges and universities is a special person, more looked up to than most other teachers. (We decry and promote, don't we, colonial paradigms at once?) We are again grateful that English teachers have often been spared the 'utility' questions educational administrators routinely ask our colleagues. For everyone in India somehow seems agreed that English is a privileged language, and that it is really worth the effort to learn it. [1] Teachers, therefore, are required to teach it. The only reservation I have sometimes heard aired is about the *quality* of English teachers and teaching. English is certainly the most coveted among the humanities subjects in any university. While the pressure on us to perform, therefore, is quite considerable, there is another sort of pressure we feel within ourselves, the need to balance the realistic and the unrealistic demands of the profession of English in India. In what follows I shall discuss teaching in advanced centres of English, mostly departments where students pursue postgraduate studies and research.

It is not unusual at all for many of us to begin our professional journey at certain crossroads of indeterminacy, strife, and division. We begin, in other words, where all ladders begin – at the foot of an ivory tower, as teachers of language. How often do young teachers of English wonder when they will graduate into teachers of literature, into preceptors of nobler and loftier things than simple predicates and prepositions? Few teachers love language, let alone love teaching it; the 'dirty' work of the English department is usually reserved for the junior hands who mostly feel unfairly treated until they are able to grab commanding positions of rank and superiority. Which is to admit that literature gives us *pleasure* – whether we talk about it in a class, or read it as students, or just think about it. I shall return to this idea a little later.

To complete this familiar picture, let me add another detail, even though it does not seem to me applicable to or endemic in all parts of India. In metropolitan universities and colleges today the number of members of the English faculty who would swear by their own literatures is very small. But the fact that such teachers are also on our rolls can't be ignored. In most English departments in India, some teachers are quite committed to literature in their own language. A few also write in, and translate from and into, Indian languages. My sketch of an English teacher in India will be complete if you take further into account such appropriate and legitimate differentia as minority religion, caste, gender, sexual orientation, language, region, physical disability, and class. What is more, there is perhaps no language in India other than English that is taught by people who represent the richly diverse socio-cultural-linguistic traditions of our country.

Long before Western criticism or theory began worrying about the nuances of English as an academic discipline, India's national leaders had indeed been concerned about this new language, what it might do in the long run to divide us culturally. Some of them even recommended strengthening our resolve not to give up our languages for English or vice versa. I don't think anyone will regret that resolve. Our languages and literatures have indeed grown with English in the fifty-odd years after our independence. The emergence of a distinct stream of creative and critical writing in English by Indians is another important development in post-independent India. So what we have now, available for teaching, is a body of English texts nearly three to four times bigger than that with which we began in the mid-nineteenth century. That is what we call *English*.

Let us look at what constitutes *English* – the name of our subject; the designation of our profession; the language of our formal pedagogy, speech, writing, enunciation, and interpretation; the official address of our department; the discipline to which we owe institutional and personal allegiance; the sign and substance of our semiotic excursions; and, more narrowly, a linguistic subculture whose steady growth some nationalists here watch with fascinated alarm. There are many things we seem to have been doing with English, some of them quite splendidly. Of course we teach English language and literature. (Under the aegis of the British Council in the 1960s and early 1970s, some of our colleagues even used to teach language *through* literature!) We continue to teach 'communication', 'skills', and 'empowerment' courses in English, quite apart from the 'remedial' lessons. At advanced levels, we believe we could teach courses in elementary rhetoric, discourse analysis, basic theories in linguistics, stylistics, and pragmatics. 'English literature' has now begun to recede as a terrain far away and long ago, but *English* is, happily, going strong. Most English postgraduate programmes in our universities offer a wide range of texts and authors from the sixteenth century to our own time, among them even non-English authors and texts in English translation, both canonical and non-canonical. Like the texts we teach, the arguments for teaching and the methods recommended for reading them still emanate from the Anglo-American book markets. Most of them are do-it-yourself texts with or without commentaries. *English* is also literature, para-literature, sub-literature, anti-literature, or non-literature, according to your understanding of the subject. Of course custom, you may recall, had much earlier made it quite legitimate for the English teacher to appropriate drama as literature. The circumambience of the stage has further legitimised the study in English of all sorts and manners of performance, from the Punch and Judy show to the *Paavakkoothu* of South India. I do not know whether it ought to warm the cockles of Indian English hearts to read other Anglocentric signs of the age such as a recent spate of feature, documentary, and children's films and television serials in English (and occasionally in 'Hinglish') from Mumbai and abroad. I know for a fact that some of our young people watch them with some interest. Nor has this phenomenon gone entirely unnoticed by students of English. In my university a young researcher earned his M.Phil. last year for a dissertation on the 'Social Life of English in India' during the last two decades, the enabling myths of which he has gathered by examining Indian English fiction and Indian English film as 'correspondent genres'.

English today is not only the language we teach but also the subject that enables us to make subtle and tough-minded readers of our wards. I do not know of any subject taught in India that practises theory and presentational skills at one go as an integral and introspective exercise quite as frankly and courageously as English. We encourage our students to think and analyse the historical and ontological status of the texts they read, and how best to read them. When they begin to do that, other questions relating to their professional pursuit of English and literature follow. The whole gamut of 'reading relations' involving authors, the print media, and the reading public; writers in Indian and other languages; texts in synchronic and diachronic contexts; literature among other arts and other forms of writing; criteria for the literary as opposed to the popular and mass productions; literature as constituting culture and vice versa; the construction of hegemonic paradigms through writing that advance and perpetuate crude versions of nationalism; and, above all, the complicity of literary texts in stereotyping, and in reinforcing those stereotypes about certain races and castes, about women and children, and about geographical regions and their cultures – these, and other similar questions, we hope, relate students to the texts they read. Those texts, again, relate them further on to the larger realities of culture and society in India, a large part of it in their own languages, in their own making. They begin to perceive all this, I believe, for the first time in their English classroom.

II

Thus far my 'story' has been somewhat celebratory. I do not, however, think that the new and reoriented theoretical approaches of the last two decades have set a new agenda wholly suitable for our aspirations, or put us on an exemplary course worth pursuing. Here I must admit to a general confusion that seems to have plagued most Indian students about what Western theory is – what it has been for the West, and what it might, if anything, mean for those who live there. Literary theory arose in the West as a result of a serious rethinking on the part of Anglo-American establishments about their higher education. Increasingly their students seemed alienated from the subjects they studied, and from those who taught them. Larger numbers of the Anglo-American population who went to school began to find English to be not as unquestionably theirs as their parents and grand-parents had found it. Of course I am being very selective here about the students and English. I shall quote a paragraph from an American book that pinpoints student enrolment in major US universities as being quite as decisive as some other factors in causing them to 'fall into theory':

> Nowadays ... the most talented minority students are actively recruited by the most prestigious Ivy League colleges, and no teacher can assume that his or her class will consist entirely or even primarily of white male students of Western European origin, or that the female students are less ambitious than the males. At the same time that higher education has been opened up to far more Americans, the massive loss of high-paying manufacturing jobs has made it more and more difficult for people to achieve the 'American dream' of financial well-being without a white-collar job, to which a college degree – at the bare minimum – has become the ticket. As competition for professional jobs has intensified, so have the attractions of 'identity politics': the feeling of solidarity with other women, other gays, other African Americans, other 'ethnics' in a world still dominated by white males. Within the university, these feelings manifest themselves in demands for a more culturally diverse curriculum, a greater inclusion of women, African Americans, gays, and other minorities in reading lists, and an identity politics of interpretation.[2]

My purpose is not to list, point by point, the different circumstances that gave rise to theory in the West and in India to show why Indian students ought to have no interest in them. Far from it. We certainly ought to compare notes whenever that becomes possible because, given the centrality of English, its fortunes in English-speaking countries will provide useful information for all of us. But that, alas, does not seem to be the case with the curricular reformers in India, who have time and again over recent years tried to refashion English reading habits. Apart from in-house seminars and symposia where the more knowledgeable talk to the less fortunate of our colleagues, I cannot recall a single public debate of a meaningful and reforming kind at any national forum on Indian higher education, not least on the centrality of English in the university curriculum. That the reforms in English, such as they are, have gone on apace largely ignoring the non-metropolitan teachers and students throughout the country, quite unmindful of the costs and maintenance of decent libraries and digital connectivity, of poor faculty resources and scholarly communications available to them, only adds to the general confusion among a large community of teachers and students who are still perplexed about 'theory' and what benefits it might bring them.

First, Indian students need decent training in English at the undergraduate and postgraduate levels. We seem to imagine that students somehow pick up the language as they go along; that they can read, think, and write in English on their own; and that texts in European theory (some of them in convoluted English translations) are as good as any other in developing these skills. At the postgraduate level, especially, we assume that students have enough English to cope with the texts and commentaries on them, the language required to meet all the exigencies of their curriculum. This, so far as I can see, is not true at all. If we are honest and serious about the theory we read and recommend for our MA students we shall immediately see that the ideas therein are to an extent translatable into plain English, but that the best of them are presented in highly nuanced arguments, and that the finely chopped logical and linguistic assumptions that make their theory work, work *in* and *through* language. In other words, speculations in theory demand answering speculations from us. We can't even begin to speculate in a weak language. Take, for example, Stanley Fish on the *text*, or Derrida on 'Structure, Sign, and Play'. Both essays are in fact serious takes on language, how language works in situations where assumptions governing it are not necessarily alike or shared by all its users. Now this is very advanced and circumspect thinking about language which cautions us against our routine notions that words have single/singular meanings, and our presumption that desires point always and only in one direction. If such texts do not tell our students anything about language, or about the 'politics' of language which we assume they understand, it is because their *English*, the medium through which they imagine what language is, is itself very poor. I do not think that our students are deficient in intelligence or imagination. When I have my doubts about such things, I encourage them to read English essays and poems, and fine short reflections in prose by contemporary writers on current subjects. The results are not disappointing when our expectations are modest. They have their heads and hearts in the right place, and respond quite earnestly and enthusiastically to words and ideas. They can see very well, as we do, when a text is challenging some patently absurd orthodoxy or the other, or inveighing loudly against evils (capitalism, public corruption, patriarchy, consumerism, or the repressive state). That alone is not enough. They should be able to perceive and give expression to such perceptions on their own – those subtle operations of the word as well, as when a vastly superior creative rhetoric or discursive manoeuvre belies crucial facts, or when texts conceal real motives with artful verbal upholstery. Certainly they need help with English. In other words, I have no difficulty as a teacher in beginning from where they are in terms of their response – we might begin to build a story together, or develop a decent argument, or at least feel contented that both parties, the teacher and the class, are going somewhere together. Of course, complete agreement on what I tell them, or what they hazard as commentary or explanation, is another matter. How English, or any language for that matter, *works* – at once as discourse, and as a critique of it – is rather slow to be formulated in a student's intellectual and emotional experience. I take it that this needs no belabouring.

Second, I am rather uncomfortable about another 'fallout' of theory. Modular theory purveyed by textbooks and digests appears to have divided English departments in India, both within themselves and across the country, into different worlds and classes. There is a widespread belief in the liberating and empowering potential of theory. By 'post'ing and 'positioning' themselves outside our curricular home, metropolitan centres of English hope that they will be better able to watch their enemies who, among many, include nationalists and neocolonists. After many years of such purported vigil I haven't yet heard of any arrests. What intrigues me most about this paranoia is the undiminished craze for more and more Anglo-American textbooks and manuals that tell us how to decolonise ourselves. Now the divisions. On one side of this divide are teachers who refuse to do what all teachers of English, in my view, ought to do all the time – be basically conscious of the fact that English is, and will remain for many years to come, a language of power and special privilege to those who can afford university education in India. It is only fair that those who profess English in India acknowledge this right away and train their students in *the language* first – and not merely in the 'skills' – before they encourage them to embark on theoretically ambitious journeys. (Language, alas, does not follow. Other things follow language.) While teaching the English language, we shall do so with an enabling perspective of it. English, in other words, will not now be seen by our students or by us as having any of the innate superiority or facility it was once presumed to have during colonial times. On the other side are our English *language* teachers, routinely badly treated by the establishment, who do not somehow seem to be quite happy with what they are doing, and how they are doing it. (Is it merely or conceptually accidental that the teachers of 'English as a *second* language' are often seen as only 'second' to the first and foremost teachers – of English literature?) The other, if more regrettable, divide I have noticed is among students who leave the academy with a poor knowledge of both the language and the literature they have 'Mastered,' and the select few, formally qualified to pursue research/teaching careers and accredited by the Indian UGC, who are least inclined to teach the language, or to improve their own English through undertaking tasks they ought to set for themselves. The very poor writing produced by our budding researchers merits urgent attention by experts who recommend advances in the English curriculum. Like English in our vast country of differences, theory in our universities has united us to fall, and divided us to stand.

Third, it is troubling to see certain assumptions to which a wrong-headed view of theory has given currency in our departments of languages and literatures. The foremost of these is a set of assumptions about literature itself. Briefly, these assumptions amount to discounting or denying literature its rightful place, its value as a discipline. Those who have recently discovered other disciplines, or those few who prefer to teach English as one of the 'social sciences', tell us in so many words that literature, as we have known and loved it, simply isn't there. It does not exist any more. Or, to be fair to the nuances of their argument, there is no *itself* about literature, because it is subsumed in other discourses, and it may not really matter ultimately to establish the *literary* as it exists. To talk about literature is, therefore, to court near-heresy in some quarters. I do not know whether mine is a problem peculiar to those of us in India who did not learn English first, but rather one of the Indian languages. I can't recall when it was in my private history of reading that I first recognised what I was reading merely for pleasure was in fact *sāhityam*, a word that basically means, for most Indians who know it, 'that which is *sahita*, that which goes naturally with you; that to which you are drawn by instinct and inclination; inhabitation', etc. Another meaning of *sāhitya* of which I am particularly fond is 'the state of *sahita*, of being with someone, and together'. That which militates against my individual and social nature is always outside my *sāhitya*. Which is to say, the 'pleasure' *sāhitya* gives me includes the reassurance that I am not alone, neither above nor below, in this world. I am happy, and feel privileged, to be counted as one among the many like me. My 'pleasure', therefore, certainly cannot originate from writing that manipulates my responses, for example by either extolling imperialist ideologies or decrying them; by trivializing human differences; or by mocking suffering, no matter whose. What I can't agree with being 'disagreeable', it is only fair that I do not inflict it on my wards. I can neither entertain ideas that force conformity or belittle intellectual challenges, nor be entertained by them. If my own reading does not help me remove ideological cataracts from my pedagogical vision, I cannot see how it would help uninitiated readers make any sense of their exercises, let alone of the texts 'prescribed' for them. The study of a subject can generate scepticism towards many things, but the subject can least afford to be sceptical of its own uses. I should imagine that that is true of most students who pursue English studies in India.

I hope not to be misunderstood. In the first flush of theory, especially of a crudely positivist kind, most young readers here were encouraged to learn a new set of terms for the old, 'problematise' their arguments,[3] keep up with the jargon, give their support to the crusades and jihads of professional groups, textualise and postcolonialise nearly everything to the point of tedium or ridicule. In short, teachers in metropolitan colleges and universities began to purvey a sort of 'grim reading' all over the place, so much so that reading anything became a self-flagellating exercise. All English texts became stories of oppression and exploitation. Any kind of criticism or theory, or any model thereof, is apt to be used unimaginatively in the class-room, by paying no attention whatever to our immediate situations and goals. These goals, to my mind, will be to cast our relationships with English anew, re-evaluate the role of English *among* our languages today, and so situate discourses in English and our languages to the extent that we are able to see ourselves as participants rather than regular benefactors and recipients of 'study materials' from abroad. Why, we never ask, do our students need to read English novels or poems 'differently'? Why, again, are we keen on demonstrating that these texts have all along been deceiving us, that they are now saying the opposite of what they seem to have been saying until we came upon the scene? And what crucial differences have *we* seen in the texts we have set for them to read? Or did we set them indeed *for* those precious 'differences' stashed away in the subtexts we want our students to appreciate, reject, or condemn? Have we made our students aware of 'differences' among themselves? (A related question on English *as* privilege: why do other students feel that students of English are 'different'? Many students of English in Indian universities finish their two years on campus without ever so much as talking to their batch-mates in other language departments.) The diehard postcolonial theorists among us are not bad people, but they hardly command the means and measures that Indian knowledge of such theory should give them. I cannot help suspecting that the 'meanings' they give to relations of power and difference are not ours, so much so that those meanings have much the same faults as those presumed to have been generated by an 'ideal' system they seem now to judge and disparage. When Indian writers in English, for example, tell beautiful stories or celebrate the world in poetry quite regardless of those contestatory paradigms that fill conference papers and polemical criticism, those writers are given short shrift in courses and discussions that privilege the restrictive paradigms of the nation and narration.[4] These paradigms, again, do not fit their apparatus when someone like Harold Pinter, wholly British and wholly anti-imperial, shows us, in plays like *Mountain Language* and *One for the Road*, how the very language of our discipline can harbour imperialistic assumptions and can violate one's right to speak another language, or can sometimes oppress its own speakers. ('Silence' in Pinter, I tell my students, is perhaps a welcome respite for us from an English we seem to understand only too well!) The votaries of 'postcoloniality' mean well, I think, when they build or demolish thin disciplinary walls both within and without the departments they inhabit and begin to withdraw themselves into their respective compartments. Of course they mean well, but, like the man in the following remark, they don't quite know how to: 'My husband is all for sex education. He just doesn't have the right way to *talk* about it with the children. He gets too vulgar right away.'

III

No language can be imported and adapted like a toy or a computer programme that can be easily manipulated or reset for native purposes. Even so, many English teachers here sometimes see English as a Cartesian machine that our users seem to botch up while assembling it. The only merit in this line of thinking, as I see it, is the light it throws on our comparative gain and loss in the modern literatures of India. English accounts for about 90 per cent of the comparative literature (Comp. Lit.) programmes in our universities. These programmes, however, have not quite made it, despite the rich languages and the richer human resources we have in our centres of learning. Many projects have been flourishing under the aegis of Comp. Lit. in English: translation and translation studies; studies of parallelism and influence; philological exercises bringing older texts to light; cross-cultural reading of texts, authors, and traditions; and some attempts at grouping and realigning our periods and movements *à la* Western periods and movements, and, very preciously, the comparative and progressive history of Indian ideas. Historical and literary methods are notoriously difficult to harness in a single study, and so are the various necessary methods germane to disciplines such as linguistics, philosophy, art, sociology, anthropology, ecology and ekistics, politics, and myth-and-folklore studies to which a comparatist adverts. And each of these disciplines, in turn, over the last century, has grown all the richer in scholarly scope and application by cultivating the 'local', 'regional', and 'national' in its methods and materials. Studies of the social life of English India will, therefore, be at a serious disadvantage unless *comparative* perspectives involving these disciplines enable them at every stage. We have nevertheless been trying, and that is the good news from the vicinity. But we must still wait for real achievements. The achievers, to my mind, will be those who can command at least one Indian language with scholarly ease and proficiency (the language into which one is born) and can use English at least with no fear of it getting the better of them (the language one has grown up with alongside the first). Of course the able comparatists know that both languages need constant nurturing, and not because professional advancements are due or the Anglo-American markets have found outsourcing potential in their departments. All this, especially the deficiency/imbalance of English and Indian languages as perceived in metropolitan English classes, has received some attention before,[5] but I believe it would help matters if we recognised the basic and essential requirements of our comparative research involving English as often as we can.

Is Comp. Lit. a level-playing field in India? I doubt it. Few among the teachers of English who realise this will, however, have the temerity to assert that they are comparatists first, and teachers of English second. No one knows why, in that case, we need a separate building and budget for Comp. Lit. courses. Cannot teachers of English indulge Comp. Lit. as a hobby and save precious money? Well, many of them have indeed been doing this, and asking no additional wages for the love of reading their literatures besides the mandatory English canon they must teach. That last phrase might sound more onerous, even unpleasant, than I want our necessary task to seem, but I do not want, again, to be understood as saying that all teachers of English in our colleges and universities are quite happy teaching English with absolutely no reference to the languages and cultures of India's everyday life. As a matter of fact, a good many of our best scholars have cared less for 'comparative' gains than have had a genuine love and respect for the sheer wealth of traditions in India that seem to have challenged their professional commitment to English. Comparative games in literature are often played on that necessitous ground of rejection and reform, exile and utopia, where certainties of region, religion, caste and creed, or even putative identities of gender, origin, and existence simply do not apply, or apply only to divert players from their set goals. I have no doubt that the best Indian comparatists, like those in other countries, leave 'home' in multiple senses and fully appreciate the logic that writers understand only too well, as Gertrude Stein did when she said: 'I am an American and I have lived half my life in Paris, not the half that made me but the half that made what I made.'

English is that language of voluntary exile for most comparatists in India, and for those living abroad now but who once had the English-of-India as part of their intellectual baggage. That, to my mind, explains at least two things about our English. Those students who take English seriously, no matter where or what subjects they study, are those who are seriously contemplating exile. Those who teach them English are already exiles from the home ground of their cultures and languages by choice or forced circumstances, a fate most teachers of languages recognise to be theirs the world over. Most of them, again, love their languages but teach another, a language not theirs. In Hugo Hofmannsthal's 'Gollicismes' we hear him say: 'I truly believe that no one, not even poets, loves his language so much as the exiled.'[6]

For our bid for a comparative poetics in India is perhaps much older than we imagine. Sanskrit, and sometimes Persian, played that mediatory role instead of

234

K. Narayana Chandran

today's English. (Was Sanskrit anybody's mother tongue?) It shouldn't surprise anyone either that English presents itself as the best medium and message of our comparative exercises. English is a language towards which our academic appeal continues to remain steadily strange and 'other' and yet rather necessary for our pursuits if we want to take our findings far and wide, within and without our country. Furthermore, English provides a number of models, its own and those drawn upon from other languages, for our comparative research, each of them modernised and kept up to date, for free, by professional bodies abroad. Of course we cannot patent any of these for obvious reasons, and none of these will become 'ours' some day. For we have not yet given up some of those highly restrictive and hide-bound Western approaches and methods in reading our cultural traditions as simply ours. Amartya Sen has adverted to the persistence of our 'exoticist, magisterial, and curatorial 'habits which an imperialist regime of scholarship had developed and sustained for the colonies'.[7] Now to perform our comparative tasks in English will necessarily involve some such risk. The Indian comparatists are apt either to sound patronising, like high priests of a culture far superior to ours, or to become a shade defensive in espousing Western theoretical models. They might pass for people from another country speaking to the 'Indians' whose languages suffer the ignominy of poor translations beside the strong and pure English in and as itself. A part of this situation, I believe, will improve once we earnestly take up and finish the project Sujit Mukherjee had proposed time and again in his two important books, *Towards a Literary History of India* (1975) and *Some Positions on a Literary History of India* (1981). 'A literary history of India', argues Mukherjee in the latter monograph, 'is not meant for the writers of Indian literature nor its readers, but for the literary critic. This includes the teacher a well as the student of literature in India, not only of Indian literature. Both need to be reminded as well as assured of their literary past in order to make their present preoccupations more meaningful.'[8] The other part of the situation will improve, I believe, when we begin to use English against itself as a weapon for a relentless critique of the power and authority that this language has unfortunately come to command globally.

How shall we try to do this? I shall suggest one way. The immediate demands on our comparative studies have never been more pressing than now, what with the voices from near and far urging us to take good care of our cultural archives. (We have persuaded ourselves, rather irrationally, to believe that the Ford Foundation will help us in all this!) Indian literary classics, and documents in the history of many of our humanist disciplines, are seeking new digital homes. All texts preserved in paper-print are awaiting re-edited digital format, access, and dissemination across this country and outside it. Such a project will by itself be 'comparative' in the senses that combine professional strengths in the history of our languages and regions; in the theory and practice of editing, textual scholarship, and bibliography. Digital textualities have, I assume, brought Indian languages much closer than ever before. We shall hope that the speakers of these languages will work towards an Indian national archive of various traditions, large and small, and network them digitally. I would even suggest that our real comparative harvest will begin only when the dynamic relations and functions that comprise literary and other discourses become clearer to some future student of ours browsing a sumptuous digital archive. If the real sociality of texts is hard to imagine in print, screen technologies will demonstrate it audiovisually to begin with. How do we ever begin to contemplate all this now, without English? History is now and *English*.

A couple of related questions, and an aside. Why on earth do Indians feel compelled to translate *all* of India for the English-knowing world? When English is the 'target language', the target somehow remains rather devotedly and steadfastly Anglo-American. Are not Indians within their cultural and linguistic rights to keep some core cultural texts only for *their* use and sustenance? Let them, therefore, learn to keep as theirs some material traditions of texts and local knowledge as cultural capital that will not change hands unless those who want them badly are prepared to painstakingly learn Indian languages, as some Western students of Indian culture have assiduously done. If, as a nation, we perceive some potential loss to, or misrepresentation of, our capital gains owing to unsuccessful translation, paraphrase, commentary, or comparison, we shall command the good and honest sense to keep them untouched but still yielding reasonable returns for ourselves, the 'insider traders'. Put differently, Indians ought to guard themselves against letting English play its notoriously superior role as a 'master language' showing every translation, and sometimes every well-meaning effort to translate, in a poorer light. Translation *into* English of any text from the erstwhile colonies cannot but betray some signs of repression of their languages, a phenomenon very shrewdly noticed by Walter Benjamin when he discusses the reciprocity of all languages in translation, a kinship among languages that is constituted by an inevitable tension between conflict and complementarity. But the terms of reception in English have changed all over again in postcolonial Europe and North America, a fact to which Elleke Boehmer alerts us when he remarks that the scholarly institutions in the West 'have accepted without question the permeability of other cultures to Western understanding'.[9] Translators and their readers can only see that which is 'lost in translation', mostly what they call the *spirit* or *soul* of the original, but they seem to forget that *they* can be so awfully lost in translation as well. It might, therefore, be advisable to stop exercising English for 'other' purposes when there is a lot more *for* English to learn from other languages and cultures.

IV

Treat any book, Proust once remarked, as a pair of glasses directed to the outside; if they don't suit you, find another pair. No theory will change you, unless you change it. As Gilles Deleuze says, theory is 'necessarily an instrument of combat'. How true. But what if professionally weak hands wield this 'instrument of combat'? In most pedagogic exercises that purportedly offer radical alternatives to, or promise exit paradigms from, Anglocentric (en)closures, and the 'position papers' they graduate into, I can only sense a helpless reading of signs taken literally for wonders. I seem headed for the precincts of some truly insightful felicity or delectable breakthrough, but ultimately I seem stuck somewhere, unable to articulate how I lost my speech and capacity for action while navigating a large ocean of thoughts and ideas. Have we been reading too many *signs* lately? It is not accidental, I think, that a sort of dumb semiotics tourism has grown apace, an insight we owe to Don DeLillo's *White Noise*:

Soon signs started appearing. THE MOST PHOTOGRAPHED BARN IN AMERICA. We counted five signs before we reached the site. There were forty cars and a tour bus in the makeshift lot … Murray maintained a prolonged silence, occasionally scrawling some notes in a little book. 'No one sees the barn,' he said finally. A long silence followed. 'Once you've seen the signs about the barn, it becomes impossible to see the barn … We've agreed to be part of a collective perception. This literally colors our vision. A religious experience in a way, like all tourism'.[10]

Where the fun of reading has disappeared to, and how we might regain it, are questions to which I shall now return. There is a lot of fun – or if 'pleasure' sounds more appropriate here, then pleasure – yet to be had in theory. Postcolonial studies have only begun to see how the fortunes of English in India have been so different from what the colonisers had supposed. When Indian writers, on their own, have freed themselves from the shackles of English, they have given us the best writing we like. There is, of course, some writing of this kind in English as well, especially by writers who have struck the springs of the historical imagination of our provinces. The amazing tenacity of our local people to generate and sustain an assemblage of images, thoughts, myths, etc. owes nothing at all to English modernity. There is fun to be had, again, in reading English writers who are aware of the world, rather than of only Britain, America, or the so-called Commonwealth. The fun here must be the great relief we experience in reading writers from various worlds and historical periods in relationships that form within ourselves – Aristophanes and Guy Davenport, Bhartruhari and Barthes, Indian folk tales and Miroslav Holub – with no constricting agenda or mandate that obliges us to *compare*, or the primary-secondary-tertiary worlds presented to us as eternally locked in a ferocious combat of dominance and resistance. In other words, programmed writing of the kind that is meant to please, or to measure up to standards set for national or international awards, will not please anyone except the writers themselves, or the jury that selects them for literary prizes. I refuse to admit any texts to my survey courses that do not please their readers. Granted that the 'survey' is a serious limitation, even at the postgraduate level, I usually select such texts from tried and tested anthologies, and end up making another anthology for our reading. While teaching 'English Literature and Thought: 1700 to 1798' – to take a survey course I have occasionally had to teach much against my preference – I include a handsome variety of William Blake, whose 'postcolonial' ideas before their time engage us for some classes. Blake, let us recall, cast Urizen as an imperialist by projecting the alarming rise of a universal empire. Blake's London is no mere geographical location, famous as the capital of a powerful empire, but an emblematic storehouse of power relations supplying perhaps a model for the East India Company, a template, so to speak, of transworld capitalism and exploitative labour. Since Blake was not obliged to answer whether the *post* in 'post-modern' is the same as the *post* in 'postcolonial', he knew that on the empires of the mind the sun never sets. The counterparts of Urizenic reason, however, appear time and again in writers like Achebe, Walcott, Coetzee, García Márquez, Gordimer, and Silko, but my students and I have found it advantageous to meet Blake's Urizen in *The Marriage of Heaven & Hell* itself.

Let me propose at least two important and allied considerations of curricular theory since I have mentioned one course, and an author whom I consider 'essential reading' in that course. While I do not see any theory to be above suspicion or scrutiny as I have suggested, I want to add that no theory of the slightest consequence for our studies is uncritical of itself. My first consideration, therefore, relates to our *thinking about the course contents*, which seems to me just as important as the texts we consider important to be included in (and excluded from) each course. Students will benefit, I think, from knowing *why* they are reading certain texts in such and such courses, *what* considerations in the first place guided the inclusion of a set of ideas and texts in their curriculum. A corollary to this would be the students being able to ask us what 'readings' are, how we arrive at them the way we do, and perhaps being able to agree as well that cleverness and tact in 'positioning' ourselves as this and that against this female author, and that African American writer, will take them only thus far and no further. No 'reading' that is meant to please others will please us. We are not reading machines but sentient creatures whose pleasure is as respectable and legitimate as that of writers and the theorists who canvass strategies and positions for themselves. *Thinking about the course contents*, therefore, will constitute a course by itself, like 'Literary Criticism and Theory', but a course that will in effect be metacritical to the degree to which it asks questions from within, as it were. Those questions will be central to our critical and pedagogical practices. The answers to these questions will not be given to students by way of lectures, but we shall seek to formulate them with our students. If we handle this course with reasonable imagination and enterprise, our 'answers' will clearly tell us where we live and what we live for. Our motives and methods of reading literature (and crucially, *in* English, *among* Indian languages) will become much clearer than ever, and therefore more amenable to correction and reform.[11]

My second consideration follows from the first which I have adumbrated above. We shall have practically *no* use, again, for a theory that does not enable us to think critically about it. In an Indian classroom, for instance, Bharata's *nātya*, Kshemendra's *aucitya*, the new-critical shibboleths, Walter Benjamin's *aura*, Roland Barthes's *jouissance*, or Kristeva's *chora* will make no sense if they are merely terms to be learned by rote and reproduced in exam or research papers. They must, rather, be presented as inherently contentious ideas and assumptions, which were by no means filled with the intent of being 'settled' by those who introduced them. Such terms are best considered the crossroads, rather than the termini, of sense. By *unsettling* meanings – meanings not only of words that name certain phenomena or strategies but also of the vast resources of interpretation they occasion in readers the world over – do we advance our knowledge of theory. And English, the language of global spread and power, is the language in which Indians receive and address those terms. This, in fact, more than doubles our burden. We have our languages which have shaped our consciousness as well, to a greater degree in the case of some individuals and groups than English has. We owe those languages as much attention and critical nurturing as we have chosen to invest in English. How poorly we have reconciled Western theory to our sensibilities can be seen if we examine the writing in Indian languages during the last thirty years or so by those of us who dabble in theory for professional purposes. Teaching Western theoretical concepts and keeping pace with world critical thinking has seemed an additional burden teachers of English in India have been carrying for at least the last fifty years. If the best writers in Indian languages, however, do not seem beholden to English in any noticeable way for telling them and their readers what appropriate the-oretical concepts to sound, and what engaging themes to mount in what they write,

K. Narayana Chandran

those who profess English in India ought to be glad that they do not. Of course Indian writers know their job, and have been doing quite well for themselves, despite the departments of English and the curricular models they canvass. English, therefore, must shed its greatness as an *other* language and share the common ground of Indian realities (which include its professional teaching and research) with the languages of India. And this new commerce should extend beyond mere translations into and critical reception in English.

Many exciting, and some challenging, possibilities exist for English now. No one has yet finished writing. We still have a use, I think, for the humble prepositions that used to put us on our guard in the English classrooms of our small towns even as we debate what *post*-positions Indian colonialist history should take. Our students are only beginning to read. And all this is happening at a time when, all over the world, our earlier exceptionalist literary subjectivity is fast becoming an expansive digital subjectivity under the aegis of English. But there is reading. That is the beauty of teaching language and literature. That applies in equal measure to all classes of students, in England, India, and other parts of the world. We must develop, alongside reading habits, the capacity of our students to *imagine* literature, to *imagine* language. I believe that this capacity for boundless potentiality alone will save them many steps. Unless we reach out, however tentatively, to such possibilities, we might be in danger of turning our profession of English into a reckless industry.

Notes

1 The reasons for the continued dominance of English in our free country are many, and are far too complicated to list here. A fairly good discussion of this subject is available in Aijaz Ahmed's 'Languages of Class, Ideologies of Immigration', ch. 2 of *In Theory: Classes, Nations, Literatures* (Bombay 1991), esp. pp. 74–7.

2 David H. Richter, introduction to id. (ed.), *Falling into Theory: Conflicting Views on Reading Literature* (Boston 1994) pp. 1–11: 7–8.

3 More endemic perhaps is *problematic*, a word understood naively as a topic to be debated or a theme to be pursued rather than a conceptual field that gives coherence to a text, a framework to which the text responds and in which it generates its effects. We discern the nature and workings of a problematic through a 'symptomatic reading' of the constitutive exclusions and denegations of texts. See, in particular, Louis Althusser, *Reading Capital*, trans. Ben Brewster (London 1970), and *For Marx*, trans. Ben Brewster (London 1977).

4 For a detailed and enlightening discussion of this phenomenon, see Neil Lazarus, 'The Politics of Postcolonial Modernism', in Ania Loomba et al. (eds.), *Postcolonial Studies and Beyond* (Delhi 2005) pp. 423–38.

5 Of the many discussions, I have particularly in mind Meenakshi Mukherjee's 'Teaching Literature to a Sub-Culture', *The Times of India*, 12 Dec. 1976, and the various responses it evoked in the paper's 'Open Forum' for 26 Dec., 15 and 23 Jan., and 6 Feb. 1977. For her later and revised views on E- and non-E students of the English classes in metropolitan universities, see 'The Unhoused Sensibility: Responding to English Literature in India', in B. Narsing Rao and Kadir Zaman (eds.,), *Modern Thought and Contemporary Literary Trends* (Hyderabad 1982) pp. 183–92.

6 Quoted in Denis Holler, 'Letter from Paris (Foreign Mail)', *Poetics Today*, 17/3 (Fall 1996) p. 376.

7 Amartya Sen, 'Indian Traditions and the Western Imagination', *Daedalus* (Spring 1997) pp. 1–26.

8 Sujit Mukherjee, *Some Positions on a Literary History of India* (Mysore 1981) p. 81.

9 Elleke Boehmer, *Colonial and Postcolonial Literature* (Oxford 1995) p. 24.

10 Don DeLillo, *White Noise* (New York 1985) p. 12.

11 A similar view regarding course contents seems to have inspired Vincent B. Leitch's list of heuristic devices for the benefit of students in 'Theory Heuristics: Short Guide for Students', available at the Vincent B. Leitch homepage.

15   Rhetorical Sovereignty
What do American Indians Want from Writing?

Scott Richard Lyons

After years of colonization, oppression, and resistance, American Indians are making clear what they want from the heretofore compromised technology of writing. Rhetorical sovereignty, a people's control of its meaning, is found in sites legal, aesthetic, and pedagogical, and composition studies can both contribute to and learn from this work.

> *Now, brothers and sisters… the white man has his ways. Oh gracious me, he has his ways. He talks about the Word. He talks through it and around it. He builds upon it with syllables, with prefixes and suffixes and hyphens and accents. He adds and subtracts and divides and multiplies the Word. And in all of this he subtracts the Truth. And, brothers and sisters, you have come to live in the white man's world. Now the white man deals in words, and he deals easily, with grace and sleight of hand. And in his presence, here on his own ground, you are as children, mere babes in the woods.*
>
> —N. Scott Momaday (*House*, 93–94)

> *A student asked, "Can Essential Nature be destroyed?"*
> *Coyote said, "Yes, it can."*
> *The student asked, "How can Essential Nature be destroyed?"*
> *Coyote said, "With an eraser."*
> —Robert Aitken

In *My People the Sioux*, Luther Standing Bear recounts the moment when he and other children arrived at the Carlisle Indian School and received for the first time the

Scott Richard Lyons, "Rhetorical Sovereignty: What Do American Indians Want from Writing?" *College Composition and Communication*, 51(3), 2000: 447–468. Reproduced by permission of the National Council of Teachers of English.

Scott Richard Lyons

European implements of writing. "Although we were yet wearing our Indian clothes," Standing Bear writes, "we were marched into a school room, where we were each given a pencil and slate. We were seated at single desks. We soon discovered that the pencils made marks on the slate" (*Sioux* 136). Pulling their blankets over their heads to conceal both slate and the marks they would make upon them, a child's act of modesty, the children's first impulse was to draw scenes from their recently departed home life—"a man on a pony chasing a buffalo, or a boy shooting birds in a tree, or it might be one of our Indian games"—and when finished, "we dropped our blankets down on the seat and marched up to the teacher with our slates to show what we had drawn" (*Sioux* 136). Picture these children withdrawing into their blankets with a curious new technology, concealing their texts from each other and the teacher until just the right moment, then emerging from their blankets proud and eager to share the fruits of their labor. They were, at least until this point, the same children, and the marks they made were earnest representations of their lives. Shortly thereafter, however, this same technology would be used to change them:

> One day when we came to school there was a lot of writing on one of the black-boards. We did not know what it meant, but our interpreter came into the room and said, 'Do you see all these marks on the blackboard? Well, each word is a white man's name. They are going to give each one of you one of these names by which you will hereafter be known.' None of the names were read or explained to us, so of course we did not know the sound or meaning of any of them. (*Sioux* 136–37)

These arbitrary, meaningless names were selected by students who were given a pointer by the teacher; the chosen name was then written on cloth and sewed on the back of each student's shirt. Standing Bear recalls how the first boy to choose a name looked back at the others "as much as to say…'Is it right for me to take a white man's name?'" (*Sioux* 137). But Standing Bear himself "took the pointer and acted as if I were about to touch an enemy" (*Sioux* 137), counting coup on the text, so to speak, and probably eliciting laughter in support of his mock bravery from the other kids. "Soon we all had names of white men sewed on our backs" (*Sioux* 137).

That laughter, which is not in Standing Bear's book but remains my guess, my desire, would nonetheless be short-lived, as is known by anyone familiar with the boarding school story. As David Wallace Adams tells it in *Education for Extinction*, this tale "constitutes yet another deplorable episode in the long and tragic history of Indian-white relations"—specifically, the development of education designed to promote "the eradication of all traces of tribal identity and culture, replacing them with the commonplace knowledge and values of white civilization" (336, 335). This forced replacement of one identity for another, a cultural violence enabled in part through acts of physical violence, was in so many ways located at the scene of writing. More horrific than most scenes of writing, however, the boarding school stands out as the ultimate symbol of white domination, even genocide, through assimilation in the American Indian experience. And although Standing Bear and others would recall multiple forms of Indian resistance, from torching schools to running away to counting coup on the Western text, the duplicitous interrelationships between writing, violence, and colonization developed during the nineteenth-century—not only in the boarding schools but at the signings of hundreds of treaties, most of which were dishonored by whites—would set into motion a persistent distrust of the written word in English, one that resonates in homes and schools and courts of law still today. If our respect for the Word remains resolute, our faith in the written word is compromised at best.

> The duplicitous interrelationships between writing, violence, and colonization developed during the nineteenth-century…would set into motion a persistent distrust of the written word in English.

What do Indians want from writing? Certainly something other than the names of white men sewn to our backs. And for its part, resistance to assimilation through the acts of writing should entail something more than counting coup on the text (or for that matter, torching the school). I suggest that our highest hopes for literacy at this point rest upon a vision we might name *rhetorical sovereignty*. Sovereignty, of course, has long been a contested term in Native discourse, and its shifting meanings over time attest to an ongoing struggle between Americans and the hundreds of Indian nations that occupy this land. Our claims to sovereignty entail much more than arguments for tax-exempt status or the right to build and operate casinos; they are nothing less than our attempt to survive and flourish as a people. Sovereignty is the guiding story in our pursuit of self-determination, the general strategy by which we aim to best recover our losses from the ravages of colonization: our lands, our languages, our cultures, our self-respect. For indigenous people everywhere, sovereignty is an ideal principle, the beacon by which we seek the paths to agency and power and community renewal. Attacks on sovereignty are attacks on what it enables us to pursue; the pursuit of sovereignty is an attempt to revive not our past, but our possibilities. Rhetorical sovereignty is the inherent right and ability of *peoples* to determine their own communicative needs and desires in this pursuit, to decide for themselves the goals, modes, styles, and languages of public discourse. Placing the scene of writing squarely back into the particular contingency of the Indian rhetorical situation, rhetorical sovereignty requires of writing teachers more than a renewed commitment to listening and learning; it also requires a radical rethinking of how and what we teach as the written word at all levels of schooling, from preschool to graduate curricula and beyond. In what follows, I hope to sketch out some preliminary notes toward the praxis that is rhetorical sovereignty. I begin with a discussion of the concept of sovereignty, followed by a dialogue between the fields of composition and rhetoric and Native American studies, concluding with some very general recommendations for expanding our canons and curricula. My argument is motivated in part by my sense of being haunted by that little boy's backward glance to those other Indian children: *Is it right for me to take a white man's name?*

Sovereignty is (also) rhetorical

Sovereignty, as I generally use and understand the term, denotes the right of a people to conduct its own affairs, in its own place, in its own way. The concept of sovereignty originated in feudal Europe, and as a term it arrived to the English language by way of

France; *souverain* signified a ruler accountable to no one save himself or God (Duchacek 47). Early modern European monarchs employed the language of sovereignty to secure their grip on state power in the face of a threatening nobility and papacy. A declaration of one's right to rule, a monarch's claim to sovereignty "stood as a ringing assertion of absolute political authority at home, one that could imply designs on territory abroad" (Fowler and Bunck 5). As modern nations and states underwent their various forms of development, the concept was consistently deployed to address not only domestic authority at home but a state's relative independence from *and among* other states; thus, sovereignty came to mean something systemic and relational. A sovereign's power was generally a force understood in relation to other sovereigns in the emerging international scene; hence, "a sovereign was to respect the sovereignty of its peers" (Fowler and Bunck 6). As political institutions continued to develop under modernity, the meanings of sovereignty changed with them, signifying such matters as the right to make and enforce laws, notions of political legitimacy and international recognition, and national self-determination. While the meanings of sovereignty have shifted and continue to shift over time, the concept has nonetheless carried with it a sense of locatable and recognizable power. In fact, the location of power has depended upon the crucial act of recognition—and vice versa.

> Rhetorical sovereignty is the inherent right and ability of peoples to determine their own communicative needs and desires.

From the early moments of first contact on this continent, the construction of Indian and non-Indian senses of sovereignty was a contested and contradictory process. It was also a rhetorical one. Although there is no possible way to describe its many and complicated logics in necessary detail here, we can see that for at least two centuries following Columbus, "European states were compelled to recognize and engage Indian nations as political actors in their diplomatic activities" (Berman 128). They did this in large part through making treaties with Indian nations, a process that created a relationship between groups of "an international rather than internal character," even in sites of severe colonizing activity (Berman 129). This acknowledged sense of Indian national sovereignty was so strong among European states that it actually became a means of legitimizing European claims to new world resources; a territorial dispute between the English and the Dutch, say, might be settled by one side producing a treaty with the sovereign nation who actually owned the land (Berman 132). After the American revolution, the United States maintained the practice of treaty-making with Indian nations begun by European powers, and "from the beginning of its political existence, recognized a measure of autonomy in the Indian bands and tribes" (Prucha, *Treaties* 2). During the years 1778–1868, the U.S. signed and ratified some 367 treaties with Indian nations, all of which presumed a sense of sovereignty on the part of Indian groups. About two-thirds of those treaties were land deals, and as Prucha points out, "cession of Indian lands … was an indication of Indian sovereignty over those lands, and the recognition by the United States of Indian ownership to the lands remaining strengthened the concept" (*Treaties* 4). You can't give up what you don't own, after all; nor can you buy what's already yours.

However, the Americans would gradually assume a dominant stance in Indian-white relations, leading to an erosion of Native sovereignty that Prucha credits to over-whelming American military strength, growing Indian economic dependence on white goods, and treaty provisions that left stipulations to be carried out by Congress (Prucha, *Treaties* 6–7). After the American revolution, it wasn't long before the nation-to-nation stance Indians and their interlocutors had operated from was simultaneously attacked and affirmed in a couple of landmark U.S. Supreme Court cases concerning the Cherokee of Georgia facing removal in the early nineteenth century. In *Cherokee Nation v. Georgia* (1831), Chief Justice John Marshall's famous pronouncement of the Cherokees as a "domestic dependent nation" constituted the United States' first major, unilateral reinterpretation of Indian sovereignty, one further tinkered with a year later by the same court in *Worcester v. Georgia* (1832). In the former opinion, Marshall deemed the Cherokees limited in their claim to sovereignty, seeing them as a nation not-quite-foreign, but suggested nonetheless that the Cherokees still formed "a distinct political society, separated by others, capable of managing its own affairs and governing itself" (Prucha, *Documents* 58). This somewhat glaring contradiction was explained in the latter decision, where Marshall opined that "Indian nations had always been considered as distinct, independent political communities, retaining their original natural rights, as the undisputed possessors of the soil, from time immemorial, *with the single exception* imposed by irresistible power" (Prucha, *Documents* 60; emphasis mine). In other words, while recognizing Indian sovereignty in terms we can fairly describe as eternal and absolute, the Supreme Court's decisions on the Cherokee cases ultimately caved in to what would become a persistent, uniquely American, and wholly imperialist notion of recognition-from-above. The United States could limit Cherokee sovereignty simply because it could, and it could because it is the United States. American exceptionalism won the day, thanks to its "irresistible power," and while U.S. plenary power wouldn't become fully articulated in a legal sense until *United States v. Kagama* in 1886, it found its rhetorical groundwork laid solidly in the Cherokee cases of the 1830s.

In a sense, these cases exemplify what we might call rhetorical imperialism: the ability of dominant powers to assert control of others by setting the terms of debate. These terms are often definitional—that is, they *identify* the parties discussed by describing them in certain ways. Take, for example, Marshall's rather self-reflective analysis of the language of sovereignty in his *Worcester v. Georgia* opinion:

> … 'treaty' and 'nation' are words of our own language, selected in our diplomatic and legislative proceedings … having each a definite and well-understood meaning. We have applied them to Indians, as we have applied them to the other nations of the earth. They are applied to all in the same sense. (Prucha, *Documents* 60)

In short, Indians are defined here as fellow nations requiring treaties. Yet in *Cherokee Nation v. Georgia*, Marshall wrote that "the term foreign nation" *wasn't* quite applicable to Indian nations, suggesting instead that the Cherokee Nation's "relation to the United States resembles that of a ward to his guardian." This was because Indians—"savages" newly arrived on "civilization's" fresh path—were "in a state of pupilage" (Prucha, *Documents* 59). More than an agonistic legal contest over sovereign rights, the language of this decision shows Indian people being completely redefined by their interlocutors: a ward or pupil—that is, a child—is quite a different animal than a fellow nation in the community of sovereigns. As the exercise of rhetorical imperialism, Marshall's meta-phors effectively paved the way for the United States to assume a position of political *paternalism* over Indian nations that has thrived up to this very day—chalk one up for the "Great White Father." The lesson here seems obvious: namely, he who sets the terms sets the limits. And likewise the rewriting of Indian sovereignty would continue over time. As Prucha points out, the word "tribe" increasingly came to replace "nation" in treaties, substituting one highly ideological European word for another, and with the Abolition of Treaty-Making Act of 1871, a powerful little rider tacked on to an Indian appropriations bill that formally ended the practice of treaty-making, "treaties" henceforth came to be called "agreements" by the authoring Americans (Prucha, *Treaties* 4, 211–13). From "sovereign" to "ward," from "nation" to "tribe," and from "treaty" to "agreement," the erosion of Indian national sovereignty can be credited in part to a rhetorically imperialist use of writing by white powers, and from that point on, much of the discourse on tribal sovereignty has nit-picked, albeit powerfully, around terms and definitions.

> The United States could limit Cherokee sovereignty simply because it could, and it could because it is the United States.

None of this stopped Indian exercises of sovereignty—it just threw things into different modes and sites of contest, for instance, that of language and representation. Not to downplay the tremendous cost to Indian people these struggles for sovereignty have entailed, but I want to point out that the dominant stance achieved by the Americans must continue to be seen as merely that—dominant, not omnipotent—which is far from saying all things are said and done. Indian nations still possess, and are still recognized to possess, varying and constantly shifting degrees of sovereignty. While hegemonic versions of the American Indian story implying the obverse continue to be told in schools, scholarship, and popular culture—generally in the past tense—discourses of resistance and renewal have never ceased in Indian country, and these marginalized narratives of the continuing struggle for Indian sovereignty are making themselves more and more visible in public representations and talk. It's worthwhile to note how so much of this struggle, from treaties to court cases to the growing popularity of Native American literature—has taken place at what we might call the colonized scene of writing: a site of contact-zone rhetoric in its fullest sense. One way of approaching this site is to find in American legal, political, and cultural written discourses recurrent, yet ambivalent, assaults on Native sovereignty answered by recurrent, yet subordinate, defenses and redefinitions of the same by Indians. These textual exchanges are eminently rhetorical: arguments motivated by highly ideological conflations and intertwinings of motives, beliefs, and assumptions that do not lend themselves to a sense of consensually-derived conclusions. One reason for this is certainly due to power imbalances between whites and Indians, but another seems owing to truly salient differences in cultural understandings of what it means to be political human beings. That is, I want to suggest that the rhetorics of sovereignty advanced by both Indian and non-Indian people often claim to be talking about the same thing, when actually they differ considerably.

For example, for Western powers after the Enlightenment, the meaning of sovereignty became contingent upon freshly-formed conceptions of the modern nation-state and new bourgeois ideologies of the individual. The former was a legal-political understanding of the right to popular self-governance freed from the shackles of older forms of monarchical sovereignty, the latter a new subjectivity enjoyed and defended by the bourgeoisie. Both were generated from a desire to develop and protect the idea of private property. In this context, for a thinker like Kant, sovereignty became essentially procedural, the exercise of reason and public critique generated by the bourgeoisie who as "the people" construct the nation-state through the act of making coercive laws, and subsequently as "sovereign" coerce through them as a *nation* and are coerced by them as *individuals* ("Metaphysics" 142). Sovereignty for Kant was a largely technical process of communicative rationality ultimately designed to benefit and control solitary monads; hence, the nation-state became something of an instrument. Sovereignty rested primarily with the "public," itself constituted by the communicating mass of wholly "private" individuals acting out of self-interest (Kant, "Enlightenment" 55–7; see also Habermas). The dialectic of private and public constituted the business of the nation-state, even while resting upon a series of exclusions (for example, of gender, race, and class) that belied its utopian claims to equality, as public sphere theorists have demonstrated (see Fraser; Ryan). But ultimately, for the young United States of the Enlightenment, sovereignty was exercised through the communicative procedures developed and maintained by individuals who, through reason, would form the public and run the nation-state (Eley).

By contrast, Indians who entered into treaties as nations are better understood as representing themselves as a *people:*

> The idea of the people is primarily a religious conception, and with most American Indian tribes it begins somewhere in the primordial mists. In that time the people were gathered together but did not yet see themselves as a distinct people. A holy man had a dream or a vision; quasi-mythological figures of cosmic importance revealed themselves, or in some other manner the people were instructed. They were given ceremonies and rituals that enabled them to find their place on the continent. (Deloria and Lytle 8)

A people is a group of human beings united together by history, language, culture, or some combination therein—a community joined in union for a common purpose: the survival and flourishing of the people itself. It has always been from an understanding of themselves as a people that Indian groups have constructed themselves as a nation. In *The Power of Identity*, Manuel Castells defines nations as "cultural communes constructed in people's minds and collective memory by the sharing of history and political projects," adding a political dimension to a sense of peoplehood (51). In his analysis, nations, with or without states, tend to be organized around the sensual cultural material of peoples—for example, language—and the First Nations were and are no exception (Castells 31). "Indians had a good idea of nationhood," Deloria and Lytle write, defining the exercise of nationhood as "decision-making that is free and uninhibited within the community" and suggesting it was always conducted out of regard for the survival and flourishing of the people (8, 13). In that sense, the making of political decisions by Indian people hasn't been the work of a nation-state so much as that of a *nation-people*. The sovereignty of individuals and the privileging of procedure are less important in the logic of a nation-people, which takes as its supreme charge the sovereignty of the group through a privileging of its traditions and culture and continuity.

One example of a nation-people might be found in the system of Cherokee towns prior to their formal and essentially forced incorporation as a nation-state in the early nineteenth century, itself a desperate political maneuver in the face of impending removal. Some sixty in all, traditional Cherokee towns in Georgia were generally decentralized but loosely linked through language and kinship, each village ultimately retaining its own sense of independence (Champagne 25). As both people and nation, "the Cherokees found unity in an overarching principle that governed their behavior in both domestic and foreign affairs." Namely, "Cherokees believed that human beings had the responsibility for maintaining cosmic order by respecting categories and maintaining boundaries" (Perdue 56). These categories and boundaries were often derived from mythological understandings of their culture but were also open to democratic contest in council houses (Champagne 29). This was no nation of individuals, nor one reducible to procedure; rather, the Cherokees found their national identity and interests in the concept of the people. Reason, deployed regularly and at will in council-house decision making, did not militate against their understandings of themselves as a group; nor was reason contingent upon a sense of privacy. Rather, reason and rationality were deployed always with an idealistic eye toward the betterment of the people, including but not limited to the individuals which constituted it, through the practices of tradition and culture.

Another, more cosmopolitan example of a nation-people is the Haudenosaunee, or Iroquois League, which was actually a consciously constructed confederation of *different* peoples based upon the principle of peaceful coexistence. As Onandaga leader and professor Oren Lyons tells it, "Haudenosaunee political organization demonstrated that a form of participatory democracy was possible on a fairly large geographic scale," and what's striking in his account is how democratic procedures were constructed into a "primordial" myth that spoke to and of multiple cultures (32). Linked by the story of the Peacemaker and the practice of respectful communication, the Haudenosaunee were—and remain—a *multicultural* nation-people (34–42). "Since the beginning of our memory," Lyons writes, "this distinctiveness has been seen as a foundation for mutual respect; and we have therefore always honored the fundamental right of peoples and their societies to be different" (42). Here, too, the traditions of the people coexisted with the exercise of a communal, communicative rationality:

> The logic of a nation-people … takes as its supreme charge the sovereignty of the group through a privileging of its traditions and culture and continuity.

> Indian decision-making processes at the local level required the free input of information and advice for these processes to work at all. Any proposal brought to the Haudenosaunee was carried to each of the nations, where it was discussed either in clan or general meetings; the sentiments of the nation were then carried by the principal chiefs to the confederate council … and the chiefs had the authority to negotiate details of a proposed agreement according to their own judgment and in line with political reality. (Lyons 32)

Thus conceived, Haudenosaunee sovereignty is probably best understood as the right of a people to exist and enter into agreements with other peoples for the sole purpose of promoting, not suppressing, local cultures and traditions, even while united by a common political project—in this case, the noble goal of peace between peoples.

In the context of the colonized scene of writing, the distinction between a nation-state and a nation-people might get at the root of why Indians and non-Indians tend to view things like treaties so differently even today. "In almost every treaty," Deloria and Lytle write, "the concern of the Indians was the preservation of the people": that is, the successful perpetuation of life, land rights, community, and cultural practice (8). Sovereignty in this regard is concerned not only with political procedures or individual rights but with a whole way of life. Non-Indian reductions of Indian claims to sovereignty as arguments for "self-governance"—that is, for a degree of local financial and political control modeled after western governmental systems—obscures this holistic people-oriented emphasis. "Self-government is not an Indian idea," write Deloria and Lytle. "It originates in the minds of non-Indians who have reduced the traditional ways to dust" (15). Self-governance is certainly the work of a state but not necessarily that of a people; a people requires something more. However, while self-governance alone may not constitute the whole part and parcel of sovereignty, it nonetheless remains a crucial component. "I believe that the future of our nations is singularly dependent upon our ability to self-govern," writes Robert B. Porter. "If we can do this, then all of our other problems—the loss of language and culture, the need for economic stability, and the preservation of tribal sovereignty—can then be addressed and, hopefully, resolved" (73). What we might need, then, is an understanding of the twin pillars of sovereignty: the power to self-govern and the affirmation of peoplehood. For without self-governance, especially in America, the people fragment into a destructive and chaotic individualism, and without the people, there is no one left to govern and simply nothing left to protect.

And so it has been with both self-governance and the people in mind that Indians have been advancing new rhetorics of sovereignty—both to themselves and to outside powers—and some of these have found their way into the academy. In *We Talk, You Listen*, Deloria explicitly addresses the concept in a chapter entitled "Power, Sovereignty, and Freedom." Suggesting that "few members of racial minority groups have realized that inherent in their peculiar experience on this continent is hidden the basic recognition of their power and sovereignty," Deloria argues for action at the group level to replace legal claims for self-determination "since power cannot be given and accepted" (115); rather, it must be first asserted and then recognized. As Robert Warrior points out, Deloria's is a "process-centered definition of sovereignty," one contingent upon the renewal of groups at the community level (91). From this reading of Deloria, Warrior has advanced his own concept of "intellectual sovereignty," a process devoted to community renewal through the paying of attention to the American Indian intellectual tradition, one he lays out in the form of a materialist history (1–3). While I question the end game of a project promoting Indian intellectuals studying Indian intellectuals, Warrior's work still has much to offer in a mainstream academic culture still obsessed with canonicity. Warrior has been praised for this work by Elizabeth Cook-Lynn, who finds most other critics, including some Natives, afraid to take on the nationalist implications of sovereignty in their critical theory and work (90–91). Cook-Lynn also criticizes mainstream multiculturalism, which she argues "has not and will not cast much light on the centuries-long struggle for sovereignty faced by the people" because it remains "in conflict with the concept of American Indian sovereignty, since it emphasizes matters of spirituality and culture" divorced from national recognition (91). Mainstream multiculturalism is not sovereignty *per se* because it abstracts its sense of culture from the people and from the land, and while it may indeed affirm the rightful and creative existence of Indian cultures and peoples among others, it tends not to discuss that other pillar of sovereignty: self-government. Mainstream multiculturalism may focus on the *people* but typically not the *nation* and thus isn't necessarily the practice or honoring of Indian sovereignty.

> Mainstream multiculturalism is not sovereignty per se because it abstracts its sense of culture from the people and from the land.

In all three of these thinkers, the rhetoric of sovereignty takes on a decidedly nationalistic cast, but while they all advocate focusing on action at the community level, none of them can adequately be described as purely separatist. Rather, in explicit opposition to this, Warrior calls for Indians to "withdraw without becoming separatists, being willing to reach out for the contradictions within our experience and open ourselves to the pain and the joy of others" (124). Rather than representing an enclave, sovereignty here is the ability to assert oneself renewed—in the presence of others. It is a people's right to rebuild, its demand to exist and present its gifts to the world. Also key to these thinkers' rhetorics of sovereignty is an adamant refusal to disassociate culture, identity, and power from the *land*, and it is precisely this commitment to place that makes the concept of rhetorical sovereignty an empowering device for all forms of community. While most Indians have a special relationship with the land in the form of an actual land base (reservations), this relationship is made truly meaningful by a consistent cultural refusal to interact with that land as private property or purely exploitable resource. Land, culture, and community are inseparable in Indian country, which might explain Native resistance to such policies as the Dawes Allotment Act of a century ago, which tried to transform Indians into bourgeois whites by making them property-holding farmers. This cultural resistance has consistently been made in objection to the way such policies divide Indian communities and disrupt traditional culture with radically individualist ideologies, and whenever I see community activists of whatever stripe—Black, Hmong, working-class, etc.—making arguments on behalf of "our community" in the face of apparently naked economic self-interest, I think those, too, are claims to sovereignty made by different groups. But most important, as voices of the people, scholars like Deloria, Warrior, and Cook-Lynn are asserting themselves as members of sovereign Indian nations, deploying power and seeking recognition at the colonized scene of writing.

I have gone on (and perhaps on and on) about the concept of sovereignty because I think it is not well understood by most non-Indian scholars and teachers. I also think the idea has something to offer the discourses of multiculturalism and critical race theory, or to anyone who sides with the oppressed or who works for community renewal, because of its applicability to the many contested sites (and actual places) of power in multiple senses: legal, cultural, intellectual, material, and so on. Sovereignty is a concept that has a history of contest, shifting meanings, and culturally-specific rhetorics. A reclamation of sovereignty by any group remains, as Deloria argues above, a recognition of that group's power—a recognition made by both self and other. It is not something "new" or, worse, something "given" by dominant groups, and for the sake of the people, we might all do well to contemplate what that might mean.

Rhetorical sovereignty at the C & R ranch

All of which brings me back to where I started: what do American Indians want from writing? At stake in this discussion are the peoples defined by the writing itself; thus one important tenet of rhetorical sovereignty would be to allow Indians to have some say about the nature of their textual representations. The best way to honor this creed would be to have Indian people themselves do the writing, but it might also be recognized that some representations are better than others, whoever the author. On that note, a quick perusal through the composition and rhetoric literature of the past few years shows a growing interest in American Indians and a general concern for including Native knowledges and voices in classrooms and curricula that should be commended. But some of this work hinders rhetorical sovereignty by presenting readers with Indian stereotypes, cultural appropriation, and a virtual absence of discourse on sovereignty and the status of Indian nations—that is, with a kind of rhetorical imperialism. Sometimes this writing has been done with all the best of intentions, but on that note it might be good to recall that Chief Justice Marshall, the original architect of limited sovereignty for Indians, was generally considered a very pro-Indian thinker in his day—to Indian-hating President Andrew Jackson's continual dismay—even as Marshall was busy composing the foundational documents for American imperialist control over tribes. So without getting into where good intentions sometimes lead, let me say for now that some of our most prominent work on Indians is not yet part of the solution.

Take, for example, the recent publication of George Kennedy's *Comparative Rhetoric: An Historical and Cross-Cultural Introduction*. Kennedy, who has taught me so much in his books about classical Greek and Roman rhetoric and who I continue to honor as a great scholar of those subjects, has now seen fit to locate rhetoric in nature and to place its history on a developmental, essentially evolutionary, model, the entire scheme of which seems to be based upon Western stereotypes of the Other. Divided into two sections, the oral and the literate, the study begins with an investigation of the rhetoric of animals, including bird calls, and works its way "up" through the language of "oral" indigenous people, then through the literacy of Egyptians, Chinese, Indians (from India) to its grand finale in the civilizations of Greece and Rome. In that order, African Americans are not even mentioned, which Kermit Campbell might have criticized more strongly in his mainly positive review of the "pioneering" work (174). It's worth noting that this evolutionary study actually works backwards in time; most of Kennedy's examples of "North American Indian Rhetoric" (Chapter 5), for example, are taken from the nineteenth century, a particularly devastating yet rhetorically profuse time for most Native people. Why Kennedy didn't acknowledge the overwhelming proliferation of *writing* by Native people during that century—not the least of which can be found in the many tribal newspapers of those years, for instance, in the bilingual *Cherokee Phoenix* of the 1820s—probably owes itself to the deeply ingrained stereotypes of Indians as 1) essentially oral creatures, and 2) existing only in an imagined savage past. Both of those persistent stereotypes are examined together in *Forked Tongues: Speech, Writing, and Representation in North American Indian Texts* by David Murray, who points out that in communicative exchanges between Indians and whites, "the cultural translation is all one-way, and the penalty to the subordinate group for not adapting to the demands of the dominant group is to cease to exist" (6). Thus, the logic Kennedy employs in his study might lead some to the conclusion that a writing Indian is no Indian at all.

In addition to the effect of making questions of sovereignty a moot point, Kennedy's erasure of real Indians serves other agendas as well. Finding in "early human language" a "connecting link" between the rhetoric of animals and that of oral (but not literate) humans, Kennedy has basically provided a theory of the Missing Link located within the speech of the people (2). The result is a quiet assumption that Indians are something less than human, if something more than animals. I don't know how else to take his comparison of red deer stags and "Eskimos" (by which I think he means Inuit):

> In a previous chapter I described the rhetoric of red deer stags in seeking rights to mate with females—vocal encounters, stalking, and fights with their horns if one animal does not give way. A similar sequence has characterized Eskimo quarrels over women: insults, threatening gestures, and fights in the form of butting or wrestling contests. (77)

And here I thought all that butting and wrestling was something we did for fun. What Inuit *women* might have to say about this characterization of their dating life notwithstanding, I have to ask if this is really where we want to go in the study of comparative rhetorics. Cultural evolutionism, a nineteenth-century phenomenon associated with early anthropologists like Lewis Henry Morgan (who studied "the vanishing Indian"), has long been used to justify an ideology of savagery-barbarism-civilization, which in turn has always operated to the detriment of Indian peoples (see Berkhofer, 49–61). To locate Indian rhetoric at an early point on the Great Chain of Speaking not only ignores *this* kind of speech for a claim about *that* kind, the results of which may be de-humanizing, but by implication also suggests that today's Indian peoples are probably not real anymore. I suppose Kennedy wanted to find oral eloquence and the like among Indian cultures, but through his desire, and his acceptance and perpetuation of stereotypes, he seems to have lost sight of actually existing indigenous people and has uncharacteristically misplaced rhetoric.

The oral-literate binary—which I apparently (and mistakenly) had thought dismantled by now—also lurks ominously in Bruce Ballenger's "Methods of Memory: On Native American Storytelling." Ballenger appropriates what he calls an "'Indian way' of remembering" to make sense of his own life and writing, "methods" he locates in Native oral traditions (790; 792–3). Of course, his access to this oral tradition is enabled completely through the reading of Native *writers*, but never mind: the point of the article, it seems to me, is to grab and make use of what even Ballenger admits does not belong to him with the express purpose of "creat[ing] the 'whole story' of myself" (795). In other words, the "Indian way" serves as a kind of supplemental technology to aid and abet the construction of Ballenger's self as a sovereign, unique individual: a highly literate white man with all the benefits and privileges therein. "It is always the 'I'—not the 'we'—that concerns me most," Ballenger writes, adding that what distinguishes him from real Indians is his motivation for "self-expression" (795). Not unlike Tonto, then, the Indian is there for the taking as a kind of helper and teacher in the white man's quest to Know Thyself. Since Ballenger's essay on Native American storytelling isn't about Native Americans at all, but rather about what Ballenger apparently

feels free to *take* from Natives, we must find in this writing the logic of cultural imperialism. Wendy Rose has argued that by "appropriating indigenous cultures and distorting them for its own purposes … the dominant society can neatly eclipse every
aspect of contemporary native reality, from land rights to issues of religious freedom"
(404). Indeed, Ballenger's own expansive familiarity with Indian writers did not lead
him to discuss any of the issues facing the people today (and which are often represented in the novels he reads); on the contrary, he seems to accept things as they are.
One particularly troubling moment for me was his discussion of place in Native literature; after making the solid claim that Indians "tend to see the land as something with
a presence"—fair enough—Ballenger goes on to recall his times on the shores of Lake
Michigan, formerly and in some cases still Anishinabe country, remembered by him
"with a kind of reverence" as, in his word, "unpeopled" (798). The actual history of
peopling and unpeopling on those shores would be a worthwhile thing to investigate.

> To locate Indian rhetoric at an early point on the Great Chain of Speaking …
> suggests that today's Indian peoples are probably not real anymore.

> Not unlike Tonto, then, the Indian is there for the taking as a kind of helper and
> teacher in the white man's quest to Know Thyself.

Ballenger's essay is perhaps a sensitive one to criticize because it is interspersed with
some painful recollections of his childhood. But I have some painful recollections of
my own, as many Native people do. Right now I'm thinking of my two young Ojibwe
cousins who committed suicide in the same year—one in his early twenties, the other
barely approaching his teens—two deaths that might be attributed to a kind of self-
hatred experienced by many Indian youths today who find themselves trapped in
colonial wreckage: poverty, violence, a racist dominant culture that hates and excludes
them. Consider the findings of a recent study on American Indian crime produced by
the Justice Department which found that "American Indians are victims of violent
crime at a rate of more than double that of the rest of the population" ("American").
In seven out of ten of those episodes, the offender is non-Indian. The report also stated
that the number of American Indians per capita in state and federal prisons is some
thirty-eight percent above the national average; the rate in local jails is four times the
national average. The arrest rate for alcohol-related offenses is more than twice the
rate for the total population ("American"). Or consider the fact that "Native people
endure the poorest quality of life in this country," because of which "1,000 more Native
men, women, and children die each year than would be expected if they were living in
the same conditions as white America." (This, remember, out of a total population of
only 1.5 million.) "If these same conditions existed throughout the total population of
our country, 150,000 more American people would die *each year*" (Charleston 17;
emphasis in original). Nobody ever wants to appropriate stuff like that.

Rhetorical sovereignty, however, compels us to face it. It is always the "we"—not
the "I"—that concerns me most, and my particular motivation is the pursuit of social
justice. Or let's simply call it sanity in an age of unchecked American imperialism,
rampant consumer capitalism on an unprecedented global scale, haphazard and unsustainable depletions and abuses of natural resources, naked European and American
aggression around the globe, racism, sexism, homophobia, and the ever-widening gap
between rich and poor in America and everywhere. In contexts such as these, there are

very good reasons to fight for indigenous rights. Indigenous people, who in some senses are now forming a global movement (seen, for example, in growing international indigenous support for the Zapatista movement in Chiapas), may constitute the world's most adamant refusal of current expansions of global capitalism and imperialism that plague so many and benefit so few. As groups like Greenpeace have argued:

> Native people's homelands encompass many of the planet's last tracts of wilderness—ecosystems that shelter millions of endangered species, buffer the global climate, and regulate hydrological cycles.… Even without considering questions of human rights and the intrinsic value of cultures, indigenous survival is a matter of crucial importance. We in the world's dominant cultures simply can not sustain the Earth's ecological health without the help of the world's endangered cultures. (qtd. in Owens 233)

However, the people themselves are among those endangered species. Brazil alone has lost something like 90 tribes this century, and over half of all remaining 6,000 indigenous languages worldwide will become extinct in the next (Owens 233). Unless the people can prevent that from happening.

Composition and rhetoric certainly isn't going to stop it, although we can do some things that might have us play a more meaningful role—which brings me back yet again to the question: what do Indians want from writing? So far, I hope to have identified a few things Indians generally do *not* want from writing: stereotypes, cultural appropriation, exclusion, ignorance, irrelevance, rhetorical imperialism. The people want sovereignty, and in the context of the colonized scene of writing, rhetorical sovereignty. As the inherent right and ability of peoples to determine their own communicative needs and desires in the pursuit of self-determination, rhetorical sovereignty requires above all the presence of an Indian voice, speaking or writing in an ongoing context of colonization and setting at least some of the terms of debate. Ideally, that voice would often employ a Native language. "Language, in particular, helps to decolonize the mind," writes the Hawaiian nationalist Haunani-Kay Trask. "Thinking in one's own cultural referents leads to conceptualizing in one's own world view which, in turn, leads to disagreement with and eventual opposition to the dominant ideology" (54). The crucial subject of Native language in literacy research cannot be taken up here, except perhaps to say *nindozhibii'igemin*. But while it's hard to predict what that Indian voice would say in our many and varied classrooms—most of them Indian-free, some located at tribal colleges, others constituting dynamic contact-zones of their own—I can point to scholarly work in a couple of sites that might help us orient our commitment to rhetorical sovereignty and imagine new practices.

One location of rhetorical sovereignty that should be of interest to rhetoricians is the Tribal Law and Government Center, based at the University of Kansas Law School and directed by Seneca legal scholar (and former Attorney General of the Seneca Nation) Robert B. Porter. Focusing its energies on the study and development of tribal law (which is not the same thing as federal Indian law but rather the law of sovereign Indian nations), the Center sponsors the Indian Law Institute each summer for tribal officials, a yearly conference, and a specialization in tribal law within the law program. Of particular interest for our purposes, the Center has been sponsoring annual rearguments of some of the most powerful federal legal decisions in the history of Indian sovereignty, for example, *Cherokee Nation v. Georgia* and *Lone Wolf v. Hitchcock*. Under the auspices of the "Supreme Court of the American Indian Nations," these retrials are conducted by a distinguished array of Indian and non-Indian lawyers and judges, and the briefs they produce are published along-side the original opinions and briefs and are available for study and teaching (Ayana, Guhin, Yazzie). Critical pedagogues, contact-zone theorists, and post/anti-colonial rhetoricians might take note of these powerful Indian countersentences to colonialism; after all, these reargued indigenous responses to legal and political history constitute an ongoing and dynamic practice of rhetorical sovereignty, and we could teach them.

Another key site of rhetorical sovereignty is the report produced by the Indian Nations At Risk Task Force (INARTF), "Toward True Native Education: A Treaty of 1992," which was commissioned by the Department of Education in 1990. INARTF was a 14-member committee established by U.S. Secretary of Education Lauro Cavazos and directed by Choctaw education professor, G. Mike Charleston. With two exceptions it was an Indian committee, and the document they produced is a classic example of the exercise of rhetorical sovereignty. First, as its title suggests, the report announces itself as a *treaty*, one designed to put an end to the "secret war" (also referred to as a "cold war") waged against indigenous peoples (Charleston 15–16). Distinguishing the metaphor of war from other more dominant ones in liberal and educational discourse—for example, the idea of an Indian "plight" and the notion of a "tug-of-war" between cultures—the report justifies the war metaphor on two accounts. First, this "war is over the continued existence of tribal societies of American Indians and Alaska Natives"; that is, at issue isn't so much the curing of Indian ills or celebration of diversity but rather a recognition of Indian sovereignty. Second, war is *stopped* by treaties between mutually recognized sovereign entities (16). The "Treaty of 1992," then, offers an educational theory inseparable from a recognition of sovereignty and a plea to stop the violence as well. Arguing that "school has become the weapon of choice for non-Native societies" to attack tribal sovereignty in all of its manifestations, the report distinguishes three types of Indian education. *Pseudo Native education* is "a process that diligently attempts to teach Native students the standard American curriculum needed to assimilate into American society" (19–20). *Quasi Native education* is "an education that sincerely attempts to make American education more culturally relevant and supportive of Native students and Native communities" through the teaching of Native cultural trinkets like "legends, history, and Native words" (27). *True Native education* rejects any "division between school climate and culture and … community climate and culture," replacing hierarchical models of curricula and pedagogy with a concerted community effort, envisioned by the committee as a circle (40, 31). What true Native education calls for in the final analysis is nothing less than the formal institutionalization of rhetorical sovereignty.

> We should be teaching the treaties and federal Indian laws as rhetorical texts themselves.

This rethought education remains insistent upon dialogue, land, and the continuation of the people, so we should all consider the implications of another metaphor in the INARTF report: the "new Ghost Dance." Invoking the first Ghost Dance movement of a century ago, a prophetic religious movement praying for the return of Indian power (answered by whites with the brutal slaughter of Chief Big Foot's band of Lakota at the Wounded Knee massacre of 1890), the Treaty of 1992 insists that the "new Ghost Dance calls Native *and* non-Native people to join together and take action." For non-Native participants, the new Ghost Dance "requires a major change in their behaviors, attitudes, and values"; for Natives, much of the work will be decolonization of the mind and self (28). Educators "need to teach the reasons for the hundreds of treaties and agreements between the various tribes and the United States" and promote "a basic understanding, respect, and appreciation for American Indian and Alaskan Native cultures" to all students (29). Altogether, this approach would work for "a revival of tribal life and the return of harmony among all relations of creation" (28). I can think of no better document than this to help us begin the work of rhetorical sovereignty in our field and start answering the question of what Indians want from writing. The metaphors of the INARTF report—treaty, war, Ghost Dance—are carefully chosen signifiers that aim to cast into full relief the fault lines of Indian-white interaction in America, and the report should be read as an extended hand, not a fist, in the very serious pursuit of a people's sovereignty. How will we respond?

I suggest we begin by prioritizing the study of American Indian rhetoric—and the rhetoric of the Indian—in our graduate curricula and writing programs, focusing on the history of both secret and not-so-secret wars in the contact-zone. We should be teaching the treaties and federal Indian laws as rhetorical texts themselves, situating our work within both historical and contemporary contexts. We should also study the ideologies of Indianness and Manifest Destiny that have governed it all. No student should encounter a Native American text without having learned something about Indian peoples' historical and ongoing struggles for sovereignty, and teachers of Native students in particular should create a space for those kinds of discussions. This work would continually examine one's relationship to Indian sovereignty, as well as expand our canons and current knowledge in ways that would hopefully make them more relevant to and reflective of actual populations on this land. On that note, I also think this site should be read and taught not in separation from other groups, but alongside the histories, rhetorics, and struggles of African-Americans and other "racial" or ethnic groups, women, sexual minorities, the disabled, and still others, locating history and writing instruction in the powerful context of American rhetorical struggle.

Ideally, this work should focus on local and community levels in hopes of lending support to the work already being done there. "There" is sometimes difficult to locate, I realize, but every university and school exists in a place, on a land, with a history and a community of struggle: every place has its peoples. For example, the Cincinnati-Tristate region where I went to graduate school, and which sometimes struck me as the most Indian-free zone I had ever seen, actually boasts a Native population of 2,365 people ("American"). Who are they, what is their history, and what are they facing now? Some of them are certainly homeless, and so their history might be read in the context of a current struggle. In that place, on that land, members of the local arts community have proposed moving the Drop-Inn Center, the area's largest homeless shelter, away from a gentrifying neighborhood so arts patrons won't have to look at the poor and despondent on their way to the concert (Knight 1). Considering geographer Neil Smith's contention that gentrifying inner-city neighborhoods like this one (Over-the-Rhine) constitute "the new frontier"—the site of increasing white "settlement" to the displacement of the "savages" who live there—it's perfectly reasonable to conclude that the Cincinnati controversy is nothing less than another debate over *removal*. What could be more teachable than this in the pursuit of sovereignty?

Ethnographers and service-learning theorists have already begun the valuable work of theorizing community-based pedagogy, but my hopes are also pinned on classroom theories oriented toward the formation of *publics*. Susan Wells has provided our best thinking so far toward these ends, arguing for and theorizing writing instruction geared toward "public literate action" (334). Wells would rethink publicly-oriented writing classrooms in four different ways: 1) as a version of the public sphere, 2) as a site for the study of public discourse, 3) as a place to produce student writing that might actually enter public space, and 4) as a location for the examination of how academic discourses and disciplinary knowledges intervene in the public (338–39). Read alongside the INARTF recommendations in the context of rhetorical sovereignty, her proposals sound vital to me, for sovereignty has always been on some level a public pursuit of recognition. A focus on American Indian publics is especially appropriate now in the fresh wake of two rather substantial Indian victories in the public, both of which have everything to do with literacy and rhetoric, reading and writing and arguing. The first is the April 1999 Supreme Court upholding of the 1837 Chippewa Treaty in Minnesota that guarantees my own people the right to hunt and fish on ceded lands (*Minnesota v. Mille Lacs Band*). The second is the federal Trademark Trial and Appeal Board's disrecognition of the Washington Redskins trademark, a move that could cost that organization millions of dollars in lost (because unprotected) revenues and, hence, provides a financial incentive to change the name (Rich 3). These victories were won by Native people who learned how to fight battles in both court and the culture-at-large, who knew how to read and write the legal system, interrogate and challenge cultural semiotics, generate public opinion, form publics, and create solidarity with others. That behind each of these victories were contests over the acts of reading and writing is obvious; what needs to be underscored is that both are also victories of rhetorical sovereignty. Both initiatives arose from the grassroots, each in their own way fought over questions of land and identity, and the ultimate outcome of both was an honoring of "a whole way of life," another productive step in the perpetuation of the people. Shouldn't the teaching of (American Indian) rhetoric be geared toward these kinds of outcomes?

Sovereignty has always been on some level a public pursuit of recognition.

Ningiigid, nindinawe: I speak, I speak like the people with whom I live.

That's what I want from writing. My particular desire asks a lot, I know, from teachers and students and readers and writers and texts. It wants to read history through a contemporary lens and continually beckon forth the public. It asks everyone, especially teachers, to think carefully about their positions, locations, and alignments: the differences and connections between sovereignty and solidarity. It wishes to reinscribe the land and reread the people; it cries for revision. However, without some turn in the current assault on affirmative action, I suspect all talk on rhetorical sovereignty will likely happen away from the university. Luther Standing Bear, writing in the 1930s, knew as much in his push for rhetorical sovereignty in American schools. "The Indian," he wrote, "should become his own historian, giving his account of the race—fewer and fewer accounts of the wars and more of statecraft, legends, languages, oratory, and philosophical conceptions" (*Eagle* 254). What did Standing Bear, formerly that little boy who once counted coup on the classroom text, want from writing? "No longer should the Indian be dehumanized in order to make material for lurid and cheap fiction to embellish street-stands," he *wrote*. "Rather, a fair and correct history of the native American should be incorporated in the curriculum of the public school" (*Eagle* 254).

Is it right for me to take a white man's name? The answer, it would seem, has always been no. But that refusal has never meant giving up or going away; rather, a No over there can sometimes enable Yes over here. The ability to speak both—indeed, to speak at all—is the right and the theory and the practice and the poetry of rhetorical sovereignty. *Ningiigid, nindinawe:* I speak, I speak like the people with whom I live.

Works Cited

Adams, David Wallace. *Education for Extinction: American Indians and the Boarding School Experience, 1875–1928*. Lawrence: U of Kansas P, 1995.

Aitken, Robert. "Essential Nature." *Coyote's Journal*. Eds. James Koller, "Gogisgi" Carroll Arnett, Steve Nemirow, and Peter Blue Cloud. Berkeley: Wingbow, 1982. 47.

"American Indians' Victim Rate Double Norm." *Cincinnati Enquirer* 15 Feb. 1999: A3.

Ayana, James. "Brief of Lone Wolf, Principal Chief of the Kiowas, to the Supreme Court of the American Indian Nations." *The Kansas Journal of Law and Public Policy* 7.1 (Winter 1997): 117–45.

Ballenger, Bruce. "Methods of Memory: On Native American Storytelling." *College English* 59 (1997): 789–800.

Berkhofer, Robert F., Jr. *The White Man's Indian: Images of the American Indian from Columbus to the Present*. New York: Vintage, 1978.

Berman, Howard R. "Perspectives on American Indian Sovereignty and International Law, 1600–1776." *Exiled in the Land of the Free: Democracy, Indian Nations, and the U.S. Constitution*. Eds. Chief Oren Lyons and John Mohawk. Santa Fe: Clear Light Publishers, 1992. 125–88.

Calhoun, Craig, ed. *Habermas and the Public Sphere*. Cambridge: MIT P, 1994.

Campbell, Kermit. "Rev. of *Comparative Rhetoric: An Historical and Cross-Cultural Introduction,* by George A. Kennedy." *Rhetoric Review* 17 (1998): 170–74.

Castells, Manuel. *The Power of Identity*. Oxford: Blackwell, 1997.

Champagne, Duane. *Social Order and Political Change: Constitutional Governments among the Cherokee, the Choctaw, the Chickasaw, and the Creek*. Stanford: Stanford UP, 1992.

Charleston, G. Mike. "Toward True Native Education: A Treaty of 1992. Final Report of the Indian Nations At Risk Task Force." *Journal of American Indian Education* 33.2 (1994): 7–56.

Cherokee Nation v. Georgia, 30 U.S. 1. U.S. Supreme Court. 1831.

Cook-Lynn, Elizabeth. "The American Indian Fiction Writers: Cosmopolitanism, Nationalism, the Third World, and First Nation Sovereignty." *Why I Can't Read Wallace Stegner and Other Essays: A Tribal Voice*. Madison: U of Wisconsin P, 1996. 78–98.

Deloria, Vine, Jr. *We Talk, You Listen: New Tribes, New Turf*. New York: Macmillan, 1970.

Deloria, Vine, Jr., and Clifford M. Lytle. *The Nations Within: The Past and Future of American Indian Sovereignty*. Austin: U of Texas P, 1984.

Duchacek, Ivo D. *Nations and Men: International Politics Today*. New York: Holt, Rinehart and Winston, 1966.

Eley, Geoff. "*Nations, Publics, and Political Cultures: Placing Habermas in the Nineteenth Century*." Calhoun 289–339.

Fowler, Michael Ross, and Julie Marie Bunck. *Law, Power, and the Sovereign State: The Evolution and Application of the Concept of Sovereignty*. University Park: Pennsylvania State UP, 1995.

Fraser, Nancy. "*Rethinking the Public Sphere: A Contribution to the Critique of Actually Existing Democracy*." Calhoun 109–42.

Guhin, John P. "Brief of Ethan A. Hitchcock, Secretary of the Interior, to the Supreme Court of the American Indian Nations." *The Kansas Journal of Law and Public Policy* 7.1 (Winter 1997): 146–69.

Habermas, Jurgen. *The Structural Transformation of the Public Sphere: An Inquiry into a Category of Bourgeois Society*. Trans. Thomas Burger. Cambridge: MIT P, 1989.

Kant, Immanuel. "An Answer to the Question: 'What is Enlightenment?'" *Political Writings*. 2nd Eng. ed. Ed. Hans Reiss. Trans. H. B. Nisbet. Cambridge: Cambridge UP, 1991. 54–60.

——. "The Metaphysics of Morals: Introduction to the Theory of Right." *Political Writings*. 2nd Eng. ed. Ed. Hans Reiss. Trans. H. B. Nisbet. Cambridge: Cambridge UP, 1991. 131–75.

Kennedy, George A. *Comparative Rhetoric: An Historical and Cross-Cultural Introduction*. New York: Oxford UP, 1998.

Knight, Susan. "New Arts Center Proposal Pits the Rich against the Poor." *Streetvibes, The Tri-State's Homeless Grapevine*. March 1999:1–3.

Lone Wolf v. Hitchcock. 187 U.S. 553. U.S. Supreme Court. 1903.

Lyons, Oren. "The American Indian in the Past." *Exiled in the Land of the Free: Democracy, Indian Nations, and the U.S. Constitution*. Eds. Chief Oren Lyons and John Mohawk. Santa Fe: Clear Light Publishers, 1992. 13–42.

Minnesota v. Mille Lacs Band of Chippewa Indians, 97 U.S. 1337. U.S. Supreme Court. 1999.

Momaday, N. Scott. *House Made of Dawn*. New York: Harper, 1989.

Murray, David. *Forked Tongues: Speech, Writing, and Representation in North American Indian Texts*. Bloomington: Indian UP, 1991.

Owens, Louis. *Mixedblood Messages: Literature, Film, Family, Place*. Norman: U of Oklahoma P, 1998.

Perdue, Theda. *The Cherokee Removal: A Brief History with Documents*. New York: Bedford, 1995.

Porter, Robert B. "Strengthening Tribal Sovereignty through Government Reform: What Are the Issues?" *The Kansas Journal of Law and Public Policy* 7.1 (1997): 72–105.

Prucha, Francis Paul. *American Indian Treaties: The History of a Political Anomaly*. Berkeley: U of California P, 1994.

——, ed. *Documents of United States Indian Policy*. 2nd ed. Lincoln: U of Nebraska P, 1990.

Rich, Sue. "'Redskins' and 'Indian Red' No More." *The Circle: Native American News and Arts*. Apr. 1999: 3.

Rose, Wendy. "The Great Pretenders: Further Reflections on Whiteshamanism." *The State of Native America: Genocide, Colonization, Resistance*. Ed. M. Annette Jaimes. Boston: South End, 1992. 403–22.

Ryan, Mary. *"Gender and Public Access: Women's Politics in Nineteenth-Century America."* Calhoun 259–88.

Smith, Neil. *The New Urban Frontier: Gentrification and the Revanchist City*. New York: Routledge, 1996.

Standing Bear, Luther. *Land of the Spotted Eagle*. Boston: Houghton Mifflin, 1933.

——. *My People the Sioux*. Lincoln: U of Nebraska P, 1975.

Trask, Haunani-Kay. *From a Native Daughter: Colonialism and Sovereignty in Hawai'i*. Monroe, GA: Common Courage, 1993.

Warrior, Robert Allen. *Tribal Secrets: Recovering American Indian Intellectual Traditions*. Minneapolis: U of Minnesota P, 1995.

Wells, Susan. "Rogue Cops and Health Care: What Do We Want from Public Writing?" *College Composition and Communication* 47 (1996): 325–41.

Worcester v. Georgia, 31 U.S. 515, 562. U.S. Supreme Court. 1832.

Yazzie, Robert. "Opinion: Cherokee Nation v. Georgia." *The Kansas Journal of Law and Public Policy* 7.1 (1997): 159–73.

16 Histories of Publishing under Apartheid

Oxford University Press in South Africa

Caroline Davis

Historically discredited players who, only a few years ago, could talk the language of fundamental pedagogics (based on the National Party's ideology of Christian National Education) now present themselves as torch-bearers of liberation, democracy and progressive education. (Glenn Moss)[1]

My intention in this article is to contribute towards writing the histories of publishers in apartheid South Africa. There are several histories in circulation of independent publishers in this period, of Ravan Press, Skotaville, Taurus, Ad Donker, Renoster Books, Batalaur and David Philip.[2] These publications emphasise the publishers' conflict with the state, their challenge of censorship legislation and their success in discovering new, marginalised authors. Educational publishers, by contrast, have been more circumspect about their histories in South Africa. For example, the officially commissioned *Oxford University Press: An Informal History* by Peter Sutcliffe, with its self-described 'episodic approach and its concentration on a few outstanding indivi duals', privileges the work of the Press in Oxford and London, but is virtually silent about the work of Oxford University Press (OUP) in South Africa.[3]

I explore here the relation between culture and commerce in the work of OUP's Cape Town branch in the apartheid period. Pierre Bourdieu's distinction between economic and cultural capital provides a useful vocabulary for understanding the work of the press in South Africa. OUP's global strategy in the second half of the twentieth century corresponded closely with his model, whereby the restricted field of cultural production, 'oriented to the accumulation of symbolic capital', contrasts with the large-scale field of economic production, which confers 'priority on distribu-tion, on immediate and temporary success, measured for example by the print run'.[4]

Caroline Davis, "Histories of Publishing under Apartheid: Oxford University Press in South Africa." *Journal of Southern African Studies*, 37(1), 2011: 79–98. Reprinted by permission of Taylor & Francis Ltd.

Bourdieu describes these fields as distinct: while he acknowledges that it is possible for a publishing firm to attempt to have 'two different economies coexisting within it, one turned to production and research … the other oriented to the exploitation of assets', in his opinion this is an irreconcilable position: '[o]ne can easily conceive of the contradictions that result from the incompatibilities between the two economies'.[5] However, OUP, in common with other large commercial publishers, integrated both strategies within its publishing programme, and supported its prestigious, uneconomic lists through mass-market, commercial lists. Indeed, this interdependent system of generating economic and cultural capital was established on a global scale by OUP in the second half of the twentieth century. It involved the subsidisation of the academic, Oxford-based Clarendon Press by profits from the London-managed educational publishing wing, which sold large numbers of school textbooks to African and Asian markets. The principle was that the centre would be economically supported by the periphery. By the 1960s, the overseas branches were required to adhere to the standing instruction from the Delegates (Oxford University's governing board of OUP): 'the branches' obligation to be profitable overall remains and … branch managers are controlled by a need for balance and restraint in branch publishing programmes'.[6] The impact of this directive at the national level in South Africa is my point of departure, as I examine the question of how OUP represented its cultural and commercial activities in the country.

This history of OUP in South Africa under apartheid is based on official and unofficial archival records, oral testimonies and written branch histories. The background to the Cape Town branch's post-war publication strategy is first considered, followed by a discussion of the development of its general list alongside its educational list in the 1950s and 1960s, and the dilemmas and contradictions entailed in this twofold policy. The article then reviews the change of management approach towards South Africa in 1970 and the ensuing crisis in the branch and conflicts in London and Oxford. It concludes with an overview of the impact of this strategy in the period 1971 to 1994.

OUP's Vision for South Africa, 1928–1947

The London Publisher of OUP, Humphrey Milford, sent Eric Parnwell, OUP's 'expert in education overseas', to South Africa in 1928 to report on the situation in the Cape Town branch and to conduct a tour of the African colonies.[7] The Cape Town branch had opened in March 1915, under the management of Charles Mellor, and operated as a sales office for OUP and other agency publications.[8] Parnwell was expected to identify a new direction for the branch in the continent and seek out new markets. Parnwell's report on his 'African tour' of 1928 is an illuminating document that sets out his vision for OUP's expansion in Africa:

> I have a vision … of Oxford African Primers in the hands of these squatting boys, in mission schools, in town and village, in bush schools far out in the blue where native teachers, only a little less heathen than their pupils, are struggling to make a greater Africa. This is not only 'uplift', it is also a sound business proposition, because each book will be paid for![9]

In this document, Parnwell articulated his plan for a racially-stratified publishing policy in South Africa. He came to the conclusion that in South Africa the publications of the Clarendon Press would be suitable only for the white English-speaking minority, and he regarded the 'European' educational market as saturated by local publishers. The main area for expansion in Southern Africa he identified as the provision of books for the South African and British colonial governments' 'Native Education' programmes, potentially embracing 5.5 million Africans in the Union and one million in Southern Rhodesia. However, despite Parnwell's enthusiasm to enter this market, there is no archival evidence that the plan was successful. On a return trip to Africa in 1943, he wrote that the 'Native and European' trade in South Africa was far surpassed by the trade in West Africa.[10] In the same year, the Press managers agreed with Parnwell that development of the branch was limited by its failure to move rapidly into 'Native Education'.[11]

The Press had difficulty entering this market in South Africa due to the lack of funding and central organisation of these schools. Elsewhere in British Colonial Africa, OUP worked closely with the Colonial Education department to supply schoolbooks, but as a self-governing dominion, South Africa's education system was independent of the Colonial Office. African education in the Union was handled by the four provincial education departments, each of which worked independently, and was seriously under-funded by government from 1910 to 1948, with the result that only 30 per cent of African children received any schooling. Expenditure for white pupils was about ten times as much as for African pupils. African education was therefore left in the hands of church groups and missions, many of which had their own printing presses for publishing their own textbooks, which restricted the opportunities for commercial publishers.[12] In 1926, in South Africa there were 2,702 schools run by church groups and missions, and only 68 state schools for black students.[13] This situation continued into the early 1950s, when, for example, only about one per cent of schools in the Cape were state provided (24 out of 2,296).[14] Hyslop argues that the mission schools were incapable of meeting demand, and as a result 'failed both the potential pupils they excluded and the minority of actual pupils they took in'.[15]

Parnwell thus anticipated the market for schoolbooks for 'Native Education' as early as the 1920s, and the foundations were laid in the 1930s and 1940s. However, his strategy was slow to be realised, and it was not until the advent of Bantu Education that the Press was able to achieve mass publishing of schoolbooks for black South Africans.

Academic and Educational Publishing, 1946–1962

In 1946, OUP in Cape Town was converted from a sales office to a publishing branch. Fred Cannon continued as Trade Manager, and Leo Marquard was appointed as the new Educational Manager with a brief to bring out 'special books for Africa particularly in the educational sphere'.[16] However, Marquard's understanding of educational books was broad, and his main interest was in political publishing. Marquard was intensely involved in Liberal politics in South Africa; his book *The Black Man's Burden* (published under the pseudonym John Burger by Victor Gollancz's Left Book Club in 1943) has been described as a 'landmark' text, an 'argument for militant industrial struggle' amongst the African proletariat in South Africa.[17] He was also a founder of the student union NUSAS and a member of the Institute of Race Relations. Dubow regards Marquard as an important critic of the United Party in the mid-1940s, recounting how he warned Smuts's government in 1946 that it was dangerously ignoring the threat of the Nationalists, and subsequently 'implored Jan Hofmeyr to break away from Smuts in order to form a new left-liberal political party committed to some form of universal franchise and an end to the colour bar'.[18] Marquard was unsuccessful in his attempt to become nominated as a Liberal Association MP in the 1948 elections, but went on to become Vice President of the Liberal Party, founded in Cape Town on 9 May 1953, alongside Margaret Ballinger as President and Alan Paton as Co-Vice President.[19]

After the establishment of the Nationalist government in 1948, the new OUP branch was subject to an array of restrictions. The Suppression of Communism Act of 1950 prohibited the 'printing, publication and circulation of documents emanating from or reflecting the aims of communist organisations'. The Customs Act of 1955 strictly controlled the importation of material that was deemed to be objectionable in any way: the particular target of the customs officials was anti-apartheid work in cheap editions.[20]

David Philip was appointed as educational publishing assistant in the Cape Town branch in 1954. He was initially based in Salisbury, responsible for the sales and publishing programme in Rhodesia. His history of OUP in South Africa draws attention to the list that Marquard developed as editorial manager of the branch from 1947 to 1962, emphasising the high-profile authors published by the branch at this time. The list contained prestigious, academic publications that were mainly concerned with the historical, sociological, anthropological and literary context in South Africa, which were published for the white, tertiary-level market. Philip's history portrays Marquard as a heroic individual, who established a tradition in the South African branch of anti-apartheid publishing:

> Leo Marquard, the liberalised Afrikaner, was the ideal person to set up the local publishing division of the Oxford University Press in Cape Town. This he did with distinction, publishing or initiating such books as Alan Paton's *Hofmeyr*, Edgar Brookes's *Civil Liberty in South Africa*, *Langa* by Monica Wilson, *The South African Economy* by Desmond Hobart Houghton, *The Afrikaner Bond* by T.R.H. Davenport, and *The Roots of Segregation* by David Welsh, and himself writing the often-reprinted *Peoples and Policies of South Africa*.[21]

Philip's history makes it clear that this liberal publishing programme had to be supported by educational publishing: 'Leo Marquard was required by the Oxford University Press also to develop primary textbooks for black schools, especially in English and Xhosa; these became the backbone of the Oxford University Press's list and helped to subsidise the historical, anthropological and political books'.[22] Thus, Philip does not censure the involvement of OUP in Bantu education *per se*, but regards it as a necessary adjunct to their cultural academic programme, and a means of cross-subsidising this list.

The Nationalist government set about reforming 'Native Education' in the early 1950s. Marquard was invited in 1950 to complete a 'Questionnaire on Native Education' for the Senate Select Committee on Native Education.[23] Marquard's seven-page response argues that the expansion of European education to Africans was essential, and that African and European children should receive the same education: 'all our experience seems to show that it is environmental circumstances and not biological inheritance that are responsible for the existing differences between some Europeans and some Natives', in particular 'the laws of the land [that] discriminate against the Native'.[24] He described the 'hopeless inadequacy' of current 'Native Education' to meet the demand, urged for increased funding from general revenue, and for education to be freely available to Africans, who 'should not ... be expected to pay for a social service which is free to other members of the community'.[25]

Marquard's recommendations were disregarded in the Eiselen Report of 1951, which set out the Nationalist government's strategy for African education. The resulting Bantu Education Act of 1953 established government-controlled, separate black schools. It centralised African education under the Department of Native Affairs and the Department of Bantu Education, outlawed the creation of schools for Africans without government permission, and provided for the state gradually to assume control over mission schools.[26] The architects of Bantu Education declared that 'native education should be based on the principles of trusteeship, non-equality, and segregation; its aim should be to inculcate the white man's view of life, especially that of the Boer nation, which is the senior trustee'.[27] Dr Verwoerd, then Minister of Native Affairs, introduced the Act as follows:

> When I am controller of Native Education I will reform it so that the natives will be taught from childhood to realize that equality with Europeans is not for them. ... The Bantu must be guided to serve his own community. There is no place for him in the European community above certain forms of labour. ... Education must train and teach people in accordance with their opportunities in life – according to the sphere in which they live.[28]

Kallaway has urged caution in taking this notorious statement as a reflection of the practice in schools in the 1950s.[29] He argues that Bantu Education 'made provision for mass African education and, in addition, it addressed issues of culture, tradition, and language, now considered to be of vital importance to good educational practice, even if it did so in ways that were frequently condemned for having dubious political motivation'.[30] Nonetheless, African schools received at the outset one tenth of the funding of white schools per capita, and the disparity in government spending increased decade by decade. The net effect of this underfunding was overcrowded schools with inadequately trained teachers, and chronic shortages of books and equipment. In practice, there were not enough places for African students; 50 per cent of students entering the lowest primary grade were forced out before reaching the fourth year. Bantu Education, unlike white education, was neither compulsory nor free.[31] African parents and school boards or school committees were required to provide supplemental financing for their children's education, and while schoolbooks were free in white schools, in black schools parents had to pay for them.[32] According to David Johnson, 'secondary education was deliberately neglected because white labour was still able to meet the need for clerical, skilled and administrative workers'.[33]

In February 1955, Alan Paton asked Marquard to join an appeal he was involved with against Bantu Education, organised by the Africa Bureau in the UK. Marquard was invited to act as an advisor to the African Schools and Families Fund, which sought to support private schools for black students. Marquard refused the invitation, writing to Paton, 'I find myself in the rather difficult position of having to differ rather radically from my friends'.[34] He enclosed a copy of the letter he had written to the Africa Bureau, which explained his ambivalence about Bantu Education:

> I cannot agree that the Bantu Education Act 'virtually denies to African children the right to education as it is known in this country', or that it is 'a travesty of education', or 'a subtler form of slavery'. Incidentally, the implication of the statement is that all those who have 'compromised with this travesty of education' are either deluded or a willing party to the imposition of a subtle form of slavery.
> I cannot accept these statements or their implications. There are a great many things wrong with Bantu Education; but I believe that, having fought the Bill and lost, the best thing to do now is to accept the situation and to bend all energies to counteract its main danger – the growth of an embittered anti-white nationalism – to mitigate as far as possible its short-term inequalities, and to strengthen those parts of the Act that are, educationally, valuable. … In saying this, I am not forgetting the published statements of the Minister for Native Affairs on the aims of Bantu Education, nor am I unaware of the grave dangers for South Africa of the views of which he is so eloquent an exponent. But I think that those dangers must be met on the political field and not in the school room. … I regret having to differ from my friends; but there it is.[35]

Paton replied to Marquard on 17 March 1955:

> I am naturally sorry you could not advise the School Fund, but each must decide for himself. I admit the language of the statement is strong, yet bearning in mind the statements of Dr. Verwoerd, of the P.M., and Mr. de Klerk, I cannot but view the Bantu Education Act as an instrument of domination, and therefore I cannot tell myself that these strong statements are untrue. So long therefore as it is permitted to run private schools, I think they should be supported.[36]

In 1957, the Delegates and managers of OUP decided that educational publishing in South Africa was 'ripe for expansion', and that 'the expansion should be almost entirely in the area of education, rather than general, publishing'.[37] After being brought under state control, the market for 'Bantu' schoolbooks presented more opportunities for OUP than the white school market, in which it had few opportunities for getting books prescribed because of the Nationalist government's preferential treatment of three Afrikaner publishers: Nasionale Pers (Naspers), whose board included D.F. Malan, formerly Editor-in-Chief of its newspaper *De Burger*; Perskor, which had on its board of directors B.J. Vorster, and H.F. Verwoerd (the first editor of its newspaper, *Die Transvaler*); and HAUM De-Jager.[38]

Bantu Education created a homogeneous market, with books prescribed centrally, and OUP actively sought to be a supplier of prescribed books. Following approval of the text from the education department, the publisher then set a cheap price on the texts, and aimed to sell the books directly to the students. It was the potential number of sales direct to students rather than the guarantee of sales to an educational department that provided profit for the publisher. The majority of the textbooks and educational magazines were prepared again by Perskor and Naspers, who were the lead publishers in this market, but OUP and Longman Green had a share.[39]

African languages were the prescribed medium of instruction in primary schools, which meant that there was instantly a need for literature in these languages. Marquard was quick to recognise this gap in the market and the branch became involved in the publication of literature in the vernacular in the hope of prescription by the Education Department for use in schools. As Gérard notes, 'Although the real purpose of this aspect of the Act was to achieve a definite lowering of overall educational standards by confining the black child to the limits of his tribal outlook, on the other hand, a fast-growing market was created, almost overnight, for vernacular literary productions'.[40] There is no reference to these OUP publications in the archive files, but eighteen literary texts in Zulu, Sotho and Xhosa published by OUP Cape Town from 1957 to 1963 are deposited in the British Library. These were mainly poetry, drama and fiction in Xhosa, with two Zulu texts and one of Sotho poetry.

In addition to publishing literature for schools in African languages, the branch managed to gain a foothold in publishing language textbooks for Bantu Education, although schoolbook publishing was dominated by Afrikaner publishing houses. Profitable publications for the branch were language courses in Xhosa and English. OUP published a large series of *Oxford Xhosa Readers* and *Oxford Xhosa Grammars* dating from 1956. In addition, *The Oxford English Course for Bantu Schools* was written by George A. Wright specifically for this market and published in 1959. Johnson notes that 'the new syllabuses showed a dilution of the "standards" established for white schools. English teaching made adjustments to suit the demands of the different racially consti-tuted education departments', in particular with respect to 'state notions of black urbanization'.[41] Depicting rural African life, the language textbooks produced by OUP in no way challenged the mythology of apartheid. The text and illustrations in Standard 1 of the *Oxford English Course for Bantu Schools* were concerned with 'Things that live out on the veld', 'Herding cattle on the veld', 'Fetching a load of wood', 'A ride to the town' and 'Hoeing the mealies'. The illustrations were of Africans in stores, on the farm, and in the fields. The Standard 2 Pupil's Book consisted of folktales based on animals: 'Raincow and the King of the Baboons', 'The Honey Bird and the Mamba', 'Kalula and the Baboons', 'Mole and His Friend Swallow', and 'Porcupine and Dassie'.

The process by which the branch obtained prescribed-book status for its texts is indi-cated in the correspondence between Marquard and Fred Hawksley, the administrator of the Bantu Education Board in Durban. Marquard sent him potential publications, and Hawksley in turn would make recommendations to the Central Book Committee. For example, in 1961 Hawksley notified Marquard that Frederick French's *English in Tables* might be prescribed if the editorial errors contained within it were corrected.[42] A month later, the book was approved by the Inspector for Bantu Education in their C List, which meant that it was to be bought by teachers and used in teacher training.[43]

There was a strong correlation between the aims of Bantu Education and the British Colonial Office's 'Native Education' strategy. Kallaway identifies the English roots of the Bantu Education Policy, in particular through the Phelps Stokes Commissions of 1922–24, which attempted to provide an education that was adapted for African rural life, rooted in social and cultural values of African society.[44] That OUP was involved in publishing for 'Native Education' throughout British colonial Africa might explain the seamless transition in the South Africa branch to publishing for Bantu Education, which occurred without any documented opposition or debate within OUP.

Philip's history of the Cape Town branch depicts black educational publishing as a necessary means of funding the oppositional publishing; it does not examine the contradictions that this policy entailed. The anti-apartheid publishing of Marquard was funded by direct involvement in Bantu Education, which the African National Congress identified as 'the most dangerous of any of the oppressive laws'.[45] There were public protests against the education system from the mid-1950s onwards. The ANC decided upon an indefinite boycott of primary schools, which began on the East Rand in April 1955, and then spread to townships nearer Johannesburg and to the Eastern Cape.[46] There were then riots and boycotts in 1961, in Eastern Cape and Transvaal boarding schools: St John's College in Umtata, at Emmarentia Bantu High School at Warmbaths, then at Healdtown, Lovedale and Kilnerton.[47] To illustrate the contradictions in branch policy, Bantu Education was directly attacked in a publication that Marquard and Philip themselves commissioned and edited, Mary Benson's 1963 biography of Albert Luthuli, which quoted the ANC leader's condemnation of the educational system as 'brain washing on a grand scale... an attempt to enslave the minds and spirit of ten million people'.[48]

Constraints on Liberal Publishing, 1962–1970

In 1962, Marquard retired from the Branch, and Philip was promoted to Editorial Manager, under the continued branch management of Cannon. Philip's own history describes himself as carrying on the political tradition established by Marquard during the remainder of the decade: 'When in 1962 I succeeded Leo as editorial manager of Oxford University Press, there was already a formidable list of oppositional books, which I needed only to nurture and encourage'.[49] However, during these nine years as Editorial Manager, Philip was constrained in an unprecedented way by censorship legislation. In reality, the branch was unable to publish many 'oppositional' books in this decade and was forced to resort to London publication for several of their more critical publications. In addition, Cannon was meanwhile developing the branch in a different direction, which led to conflicting strategies within the publishing programme.

Following Sharpeville in 1960, the government introduced a range of ever-more punitive measures. In 1963, The Publications and Entertainments Act created the framework for the censoring of publications, films and public entertainment on the grounds of moral, religious, sociological or political undesirability. This was later reinforced by the more stringent Publications Act of 1974. Under the terms of the act, publication, printing and importing of undesirable publications could be prohibited and a blanket ban could be placed on a specific publisher. The system was administered by the government-appointed Directorate of Publications, headed by Judge Lammie Snyman, based in Cape Town. Publications could be submitted to one of the Publication Control Boards in the country, and the committee would reach a decision about the desirability of the publication without necessarily hearing any evidence, and without any legal argument. The production of publications that had been declared undesirable was a criminal offence, and distribution of the publication was also prohibited, and in cases of 'radical undesirability' the publications committee could declare that the mere possession of a publication was an offence.[50]

Overt censorship of publications was only one aspect of the legal arsenal adopted by the government. An effective means of silencing opposition was to issue a banning injunction. The Prisons Act of 1959 had already made it an offence to publish information about prisoners, and then, in 1962, the definition of sabotage was extended to include all anti-apartheid activities, making it a serious offence to quote or publish the work of a prohibited person. Indeed, all the previous publications of a banned person were simultaneously excluded from publication.[51] After 1964, customs officials became more rigorous and began scrutinising all books, rather than just invoices.

The Liberal Party was to come under sustained attack from Verwoerd's government in the early 1960s. Two years after his retirement from OUP, while he was still acting as an editor and advisor to the branch, Marquard was subjected to two security raids at his home in Stellenbosch. In July 1964, while his wife and daughter were alone, there was a pre-dawn raid. He wrote a letter published in the *Cape Argus* denouncing the attempt 'to assassinate our characters by smearing us as Communists or saboteurs'.[52] In a second raid on 18 March 1966, the Special Branch removed Marquard's files on the Defence and Aid Fund, an organisation set up to help dependants of detainees, which had been suddenly banned. The police also scrutinised his other documents, including the manuscripts that he was reading on behalf of OUP.[53] By 1968, the Liberal Party had disbanded in the face of the Prohibition of Improper Interference Act, which made parties with multi-racial membership illegal. Thereafter, liberalism in South Africa became, according to Rich simply 'a set of intellectual attitudes that had little political embodiment'.[54]

Throughout the 1960s, despite government censorship, Philip attempted to continue the anti-apartheid publishing tradition of Marquard. He published new books by Marquard's authors, and continued publication projects that Marquard had initiated.[55] Increasingly, however, the Cape Town branch had to rely on London to publish books that were in danger of being banned in South Africa. In 1960 there were concerns that Alan Paton might be detained. He had been commissioned a decade earlier to write a biography of Jan Hofmeyr. Anxiety intensified after 1962, when there were fears that Paton might be classed as a 'prohibited person' under the Sabotage Act, but in that case London would have taken on publication. In the event, Paton escaped a banning injunction and his *Hofmeyr* was published in Cape Town in 1964. But the branch was barred from publishing Benson's aforementioned biography of Luthuli, who had been banned in 1958. Philip requested that Rex Collings, in OUP London, should take it on, and he agreed, although he predicted that sales of the book would be low, given that it was cut off from its major market.[56] *Chief Albert Lutuli of South Africa* was published in 1964 in the Three Crowns Series.

Monica Wilson and Leonard Thompson's *Oxford History of South Africa* was, according to Philip, the 'foster child' of Marquard, although it was published long after his retirement. Editorial work was carried out in Cape Town but the two-volume *History* was published from the Clarendon Press in Oxford in 1969 and 1971. Leo Kuper's chapter 'African Nationalism in South Africa, 1910–1964' in the second volume contained quotations from banned people and unlawful organisations. Marquard, Philip and Cannon presumed that the volume would be banned on account of this one chapter, and argued that 'the availability of the work should not be jeopardised; ... that the chapter concerned was expendable in the interests of the availability of the rest of the work'.[57] The decision was made to publish the South African edition of the second volume with 52 blank pages where Kuper's chapter would have appeared, although the international edition was published intact. As a result the book was not banned, although the censor apparently argued that the missing pages were so annoying that he wished he could ban it. OUP has been criticised for being willingly silenced in this fashion, and for not even testing the system. Merrett writes that 'the publishers had achieved the state's purpose through a blatant act of self-censorship'.[58]

Censorship and Collaboration, 1962–1970

According to Philip, the OUP branch in Cape Town avoided any collusion with the government censors: 'To my knowledge when I was at the Press we never submitted anything to the censorship board, and we wouldn't have done'.[59] Marquard made a public speech at Rhodes University in 1962 against the impending Publications and Entertainments Act, which he argued would have a devastating effect on the book trade, in particular by encouraging publishers to submit their manuscripts to the censorship board before publication, to avoid losing money investing in books that would subsequently be banned: 'In that case, I cease to be a reputable publisher, and on my gravestone should be the inscription, Here lies a publisher by kind permission of the Government'.[60]

Yet, there is overwhelming evidence that Cannon, as Trade Manager of the Cape Town branch, submitted books before publication to the censorship board with alacrity. James Currey, editor at the Cape Town Branch in the early 1960s, claimed that Cannon 'welcomed the establishment of a censorship board because he said it made life easier for a publisher than self-censorship'.[61] Cannon demonstrated a concern to keep the branch afloat under increasingly difficult political and economic constraints, and to avoid anything that might affect the educational sales of the branch. He attempted to intercept inappropriate books before publication, rather than risk importing books that might subsequently be banned, and face financial loss as a result. For example, in February 1964, he submitted a proof copy of Lewis Nkosi's *The Rhythm of Violence* to the Publications Control Board in advance of the play's publication in the London-based Three Crowns series later that year. Cannon was informed in March 1964 that the publication was deemed 'indecent, obscene or objectionable and that the importation and circulation thereof is prohibited'.[62]

By 1968, Cannon was anxious to obtain advance galley proofs for all OUP books relating to Southern Africa, 'not only for vetting from a banning point of view but also for editorial purposes'.[63] In March 1970, Cannon sent a letter to Jannie Kruger, the Chairman of the Publications Control Board, that clearly described the process by which Cannon selected books from the UK for import:

> [we] invariably inspect proof copies of books to appear under the imprint of our Principals to decide if they will prove acceptable for sale in South Africa; and ... in turn, submit such proofs to you if we think that they are likely to be judged undesirable. ... I shall continue to act in this manner as I feel it is better for a book to be deemed undesirable before stocks arrive in this country than for it to be

subsequently placed under embargo and, if then prohibited, for copies to be returned to England.[64]

As an agent for several other British publishers in South Africa, many of the books submitted to the Board by OUP were from other publishers. For example, a proof copy of Richard Neville's *Play Power* was submitted to the board on 14 January 1970, shortly before publication in the UK by Jonathan Cape, and was subsequently banned on 6 February 1970. Further books that were submitted by the branch and subsequently banned included Lewis Nkosi's *Home and Exile* (banned July 1967), Robert S. de Ropp's *Sex Energy* (banned February 1970), Leonard Cohen's *Beautiful Losers* (banned March 1970), Regis Debray's *Strategy for Revolution* (banned May 1970), Massima Teodori's *The New Left: A Documentary History* (banned July 1970), and J.J. Head's *How Human Life Begins* (banned October 1970).[65] McDonald notes that many British publishers, including Gollancz, Collins, Faber, Heinemann, Penguin and OUP, were aware that their local representatives submitted proof copies of their books prior to publication, and claims that they 'adopted a ... pragmatic stance' and 'worked with the system to try to secure the release of some of their titles'.[66]

Publishing for 'Bantu' schools continued apace in the 1960s. In 1963, the first African sales representative was appointed, Richard Mnyakama, who moved between his home in Cape Town and the Transkei and Ciskei. In 1968, Everett Moahloli was appointed as Transkei representative, with an assistant, Godfrey Ndugane.[67] Cannon reported the branch's success in publishing for the Bantu Education Department in his Annual Report of 1968/9. He described the close links he was establishing in the Transkei, the first Bantustan, including the Department of Education in Umtata, the capital, and reported his success in getting schoolbooks prescribed for 'Bantu' examinations:

> In South Africa several of our Xhosa publications were prescribed for examinations and sales of Oxford English Course for Bantu Schools and Oxford Xhosa Readers were good. Both these series should reflect much better returns at the end of the current year as we now have two African representatives in the Transkei, introducing these books to schools in that enormous territory and maintaining close contact with the Department of Education in Umtata. *Their Secret Ways*, prescribed for a Bantu examination, was extremely popular, some 26,000 copies being sold.[68]

In April 1970, Cannon retired after 40 years with OUP in Cape Town.[69] Finding a replacement for Cannon proved difficult. Philip was expected to take on the position, but he turned it down: 'The number two whom we had all confidently expected to succeed refused, no-one suitable on the existing UK staff was prepared to take the job on'.[70] A South African living in the UK was appointed to the post, but pulled out at the last minute, and the London editor and poet Jon Stallworthy was seconded at very short notice to be caretaker manager at Cape Town for eight months from April to November 1970 while the company found a replacement.[71] Eventually, Neville Gracie, a retired lawyer and ex-mayor of Durban Westville, was appointed as General Manager for Southern Africa in November 1970.[72]

During the 1960s, balancing the branch's interests in cultural and economic capital became increasingly difficult. In the context of punishing censorship legislation, the publication of oppositional texts for a restricted academic market involved constant confrontation with the state, or avoidance of confrontation through publication in London, which led to loss of sales for the branch. By the end of the decade, the branch was in a state of financial crisis: publishing for Bantu education was successful, but was insufficient. Branch profits had declined from £21,624 in 1961 to a loss of £13,553 in 1968.[73] The situation provoked a crisis in the Cape Town branch and major dilemmas in London and Oxford regarding OUP's future in South Africa.

Crisis and Conflict, 1970–1972

By 1970, OUP's involvement in Southern Africa was not only a financial liability but increasingly a public relations liability. The international anti-apartheid movement meant that trade with other branches became difficult. India refused to let its goods be exported to South Africa, and the only way to get books through was for payment to go through London.[74] The New York branch was cautious about importing books from South Africa; regarding a new series of paperbacks launched from Cape Town, the New York branch manager commented: 'I would have to say that the words "Southern Africa" at the present time would incline many people in the United States to have a negative feeling towards the books'.[75]

The OUP Secretary, Colin Roberts, and the London Publisher, John Brown, corresponded about the future of the branch, and met privately with the Delegates in Oxford to discuss the Press's position. Brown initially prepared a one-page statement defending OUP's involvement in South Africa, for fear of it being 'attacked within the University for having any connexion with South Africa'.[76] This statement reiterated OUP's cultural mission in Africa, its educational role in publishing local books, including in African languages, and its commitment to scholarship through the publication of academic books on South Africa by Paton, Brookes and Macaulay. On reading it, Roberts decided that it should not be released, as it simply raised a series of difficult questions:

> the more I read it and reflect on it, the more I hope we are not questioned – not that I think our policy is not defensible, but that it would be hard to persuade those who do not wish to be persuaded of the rightness of it. ... To illustrate the difficulties, you comment that Cannon is an Englishman, but say nothing about Gracie. Should we add that he is a South African of English descent and also a member of the Liberal Party? Similarly with Marquard. If we were to draw attention to his admirable political record, it may arouse questions about others. The books published by the Branch you list should certainly count to us for righteousness. On the other hand, the mere fact that our books are sold in Rhodesia will be apt to cause trouble.[77]

Brown was quick to concede that public scrutiny of OUP's policy would be best avoided.

> Like you, I hope very much that we are not questioned. This, of course, is an entirely emotional matter, not open to reason. ... Gracie is not a member of the

Liberal Party because that, surely, is now banned, but he says he votes Progressive. Certainly he is very anti the National government, though I suspect that this may be based more on his English-speaking background than any truly liberal principles. Obviously we do take a risk with the appointment of a South African as manager and we shall certainly have to watch his publishing policy.[78]

Thus, avoidance of public debate about South Africa became the official management strategy. However, there was to be a major – and very public – crisis in the South African branch the following year.

From 1970, the management in Oxford put pressure on the Cape Town branch to confine its work to profitable publishing for African primary schools. This was part of a series of directives from Oxford that reinforced the principle that the cultural and scholarly endeavours of the Clarendon Press should be funded by the profits from the overseas markets.[79] The internal enquiry into the running of the OUP, resulting in the *Waldock Report* of 1970, reasserted that branch publishing should be strictly on a 'profit-making basis' to generate the 'financial resources of the Press'.[80] According to this report, OUP was the largest publishing house in the United Kingdom, with a turnover of well over £10 million per annum and a heavy dependence on its overseas income.[81] It was evidently imperative that the Cape Town branch should be brought into line with OUP's general branch publishing strategy.

Anthony Toyne of Ely House in London was sent on an extended visit to South Africa in 1969 and drew up a five-year plan for the branch, proposing expansion into Bantu Education through the publication of language courses, dictionaries and mathematics courses, which involved translating and revising existing texts. Brown then wrote to Philip in April 1970, insisting on a change of policy:

> It is, as you know, the policy of the Press that Branch publishing should be profi table, that the main emphasis should be on educational books but that the smaller proportion should be in the general field. ... But the weakness of the Branch from a financial point of view has been its comparative lack of success in the specifically educational field, no doubt due to a lack of capital and staff, and this is what I hope will be corrected.[82]

Philip found the shift towards publishing for profit alone intolerable and resigned in protest, as he explained in his autobiographical history: 'One of the reasons for my decision to leave OUP was that it had been made clear to me by OUP, Oxford, that I would be expected to publish almost exclusively school textbooks and I preferred tertiary and general publishing'.[83] Philip's history is a lament for the slow decline of the OUP in South Africa from oppositional academic publishing to mass schoolbook publishing, from financially disinterested publishing to profit-centred publishing. He attributes this smothering of editorial independence to profit-seeking management in Oxford, but in an interview also alludes to problems with the manager: 'I didn't want to continue publishing primary schoolbooks, especially as there was such a need for other books in South Africa. And Neville Gracie and I didn't get on'.[84] On resigning from OUP, Philip was involved in anti-apartheid publishing through his own imprint, David Philip Publishers (DPP) from 1971 to 2002, and took with him many OUP authors, most crucially Alan Paton.[85]

Following his sabbatical in the branch in Cape Town, Stallworthy returned to the UK concerned about the appointment of Gracie, and with major reservations about OUP's continuation in South Africa. He agitated for a further series of management meetings about the issue. John Bell, Manager of the Overseas Education department, describes this in a letter to Philip in July 1971, following news of his resignation:

> All of us are distressed at your leaving the Press and at the general wave of departures that have followed on Neville's taking over. As you must know, there have been anxious debates over the problem ever since Jon came back: debates from which he was I think rightly excluded, the Management Committee having to take the *responsibility for decisions* without involving Jon in any of the consequences. But of course his views have been known and taken into consideration.
>
> Clearly things have got much worse than had been anticipated by the Management Committee (though not to you and Jon). It may be that something cataclysmic was needed before Neville could build. But you must not think that we are not *all* in considerable distress that you have felt obliged to go: and that at present things are so unhappy.
>
> Having appointed Neville, we must let him run things his way for a fair time. He won't find it very easy here at the end of the month: there will be a lot of hard questioning. I doubt if Jon will feel disposed to talk to him at all. But this won't restore *you*, and this is the most miserable break of all. I am extremely sorry about it, and wait anxiously to hear of your future. You have had a rotten year, may the next be a happier one.[86]

The change of official policy with respect to South Africa is clearly described in correspondence between Alan Paton and John Brown, the London Publisher, in November 1973. Paton asked for a cancellation of his contract with OUP Southern Africa for the biography of Roy Campbell in the light of Philip's resignation: 'I must also be honest with you and say that I have no confidence in the present management of the OUP in South Africa, and am of the opinion that it would be antipathetic or merely indifferent to any work of mine'.[87] Brown agreed to cancel the contract and defended the transition of the branch towards Bantu Education publishing:

> Perhaps I can say that I think that you are wrong in your assessment of our present management in Cape Town because I suspect you have had only partial evidence. We did, however, in order to exist in South Africa and to satisfy the Delegates of the Oxford University Press, have to make some changes in policy of a kind which in easier circumstances we would not have had to make. Our publishing policy has changed and we are concentrating at the moment very much more on educational books for the Bantu schools at the expense of general publications.[88]

Stallworthy was appointed to All Souls College, Oxford, but evidently continued to campaign in the university over the situation in South Africa. In June 1972, he wrote to Colin Roberts to warn him that Herbert Hart, the legal philosopher and former Professor of Jurisprudence at Oxford, was planning to question OUP's operations in South Africa.[89] Hart wrote to Roberts asking about the conditions for black staff in the

Cape Town office, urging that a policy of equal pay for black and white should be adopted, along with educational facilities for black employees: 'I think we could be exposed to very adverse comment if we do less than we could for our black employees. I am sure that the matter should be given attention quite seriously soon and I would hate it if comments appeared in the newspapers showing that we had less concern than other companies operating in South Africa (this is not a veiled threat!).'[90]

Roberts replied to Hart that he agreed that 'there is no time to be lost' in considering the question: 'It seems to me there are three separate but interlocked issues: the justification for our presence in South Africa … our policy as an employer, and thirdly (something on which Jon Stallworthy has views and on which I have no direct information), the management of the branch'.[91] A meeting took place to discuss this, attended by Roberts, Brown, J.H.C. Thompson, Hart and Stallworthy, whose presence Roberts felt was necessary although 'Bruno [Brown] suggested that we meet without Jon Stallworthy on the ground that he is too emotionally involved'.[92] The outcome of this meeting in Oxford in 1972 has not been recorded in the archive, but evidently the decision was made that OUP should remain in South Africa. At this time certain other multinational publishers disinvested in the country in protest against its racial policies: Heinemann moved out in the 1960s, and McGraw Hill in the early 1970s.[93]

Publishing for Bantu Education, 1970s and 1980s

The main informant about the history of the Cape Town branch after 1970 is Gracie. He was the author of the annual branch reports, and he was interviewed for, and quoted extensively in, Riette Hart's unpublished 'Cape Town Branch: The Story of Oxford University Press Southern Africa', which was written for internal branch circulation in 1992, based on archival evidence and oral testimonies of branch staff.[94] Gracie forthrightly described the task facing him when he took over branch management:

> OUP is a 'foreign' company, and exchange regulations eventually didn't allow us to run an overdraft at all as this would amount to sending money out of the country. At the same time, there was no way that the Press could or would subsidize us when there was more and more pressure from some other branches to totally close down operations here. If we continued losing money this might be just the excuse they were looking for. It was therefore imperative that we build a 'cash cushion' to see us through.[95]

Gracie's Annual Reports for the years 1970 to 1974 testify to the importance of the Bantu Education market for the branch, and in particular the market in the Transkei. In the financial year 1970–1, 33,699 copies of Wright's *Oxford English Course* sold in the Transkei alone, and total sales of this title reached 64,806. Of 81,622 copies of Pahl's *Oxford Xhosa Readers* sold countrywide, 55,973 were sold in the Transkei. By 1972, Gracie was reporting that 'the major source of profit' came from these titles and affirmed the necessity for the branch to retain sales in this area.[96] In 1974 again, the majority of the profit from local publishing was from the sale of primary schoolbooks in the Transkei and Ciskei.[97]

In addition to publishing books locally, imported titles from Oxford were also prescribed for the Bantu Education Department. A memo from Gracie to Paul Binding in the Oxford Children's Book Department demonstrates the size of the Bantu Education market by 1977. Gracie anticipated that the London-published *Jason and the Golden Fleece* would be prescribed for the Standard 3 English examination of 1980. He estimated that 87,000 pupils would need the book, expecting sales of 50,000–60,000 copies, sold at a price of 95 cents per copy.[98] This would far outstrip the sales for books prescribed for white schools in the Cape Education Department, which Gracie estimated at about 7,000 pupils taking Standard 8.[99]

In 1974, the Publications Act amended the censorship legislation to provide for banning of all the output of a publisher and removed the right of appeal to the Supreme Court. The branch's response was to be even more cautious. Hart's history recognises the close relationship between the censors and OUP at this time:

> The Branch for most of these difficult years fortunately had a better relationship …
> with those officials who'd been appointed to protect the nation's morals against
> possible corruption. Alison Neis, who in the 1970s was responsible for handling
> the List of Objectionable Literature, says the Branch had a 'gentleman's
> agreement' with the customs officials that it would submit anything they were
> unsure of, with a covering letter, in case there were any queries at a later date.
> If necessary, as in the case of Prof. Dugard's prescribed book *Principles and
> Policy of South Africa*, quotes on the back cover were blanked out or cut out by
> hand.[100]

There was a sharp decline in historical, political and sociological texts, and those that were published had reduced print runs. The branch list became more commercial and the texts more anodyne. The few new titles that were acquired for the branch are indicative of its new direction. Gracie acknowledged in his report of 1972/3 that '[t]he tempo of editorial production of the Branch is still extremely slow and only four new works were published during the year'.[101] The only new publications were three economics texts and one school poetry collection. In 1973/4, Gracie wrote that 'Publishing activity was concentrated mainly on the production of new editions and impressions of existing books',[102] including Clarke's *Map Reading*, Kidd's *Wild Flowers of the Cape Peninsula*, and Victor Pohl's *Farewell the Little People*, a collection of the author's versions of Bushman tales, in which the 'almost extinct little people of Southern Africa' were compared to 'Lilliputians, fairies, gnomes and elflike creatures'.[103]

Gracie systematically rejected all political or controversial titles, and sent proposals instead to London or the Clarendon Press. Between 1975 and 1978 Gracie rejected several texts: Robert Shoen's *The Demography of an Apartheid Society*, which he described as a 'monograph dealing with the processes of economic development and population change in South Africa' – 'we shall not publish it in South Africa';[104] Pierre Hugo's *Working Within the System: A Study of Contemporary Coloured Politics in South Africa*;[105] and a sociology title, *Prejudice under Pressure* (a 'rather detailed report and analysis of the racial attitudes and thinking of white South African artisans') by Randall Stokes and Edward Feit.[106] In each of these cases, the editors in London and Oxford similarly rejected the proposals on the basis of the limited market the titles would have, and there is no evidence that they were published by other British or South African publishers.

The branch's publishing strategy was symptomatic of the general approach of multinational publishers in this era, according to Philip, who maintained that educational publishers in the UK – including OUP – ceased to publish texts from the UK that were critical of apartheid in South Africa. They were, he claimed, concerned about their relationship with the government over school textbook prescriptions: 'there was no more critical material coming from London. There was a concern amongst transnationals about their education publishing prescriptions, and not wanting to do anything that might damage this'.[107] The OUP archival evidence supports this argument. OUP in London and Oxford turned down the oppositional titles that had been rejected by the Southern African branch, although as a multinational publisher they had freedom to publish them. They gave market-based reasons for their decisions, but it appears likely that OUP's local involvement in Bantu Education led to a lack of commercial independence.

Gracie's strategy was a great economic success, but did not make him a popular manager. In interview with Hart, Gracie admitted that he kept a tight rein on the branch finances and 'he was often very disliked for this and other reasons'.[108] In 1970, when Gracie took over, the branch lost £13,704, but in the Annual Report of 1971/2 he could announce: 'A record profit has replaced the losses of the two previous years. This has been achieved by a ten per cent reduction in overhead expenses and by firmly turning down uneconomic publishing projects'. In this financial year the branch achieved a net profit of £18,702.[109] The fortunes of the branch in Cape Town continued to improve. Gracie was congratulated by Colin Roberts, Secretary of OUP, in 1973 on his success: 'Dear Neville, I am delighted to learn in such a substantial form that the Branch has had another successful year. I have not yet seen the figure, but shall look forward to doing so; meanwhile I shall have much pleasure in drinking the Branch's health'.[110] In 1974, Gracie announced: 'Profits in the last three years have now largely eliminated the losses incurred in the late sixties'.[111] Hart's history describes this period of economic success in the late 1970s:

> The Branch finances continued to flourish 'despite rampant inflation, the catastrophic fall in the price of gold, and a government clamp on private spending to offset astronomical public expenditure', and when sales exceeded £$1\frac{1}{4}$ million for the first time in 1977 every member of staff was presented with a bottle of champagne! This milestone was reached in spite of an imposition of 15% duty on imported goods in the same year.[112]

By 1979, turnover in the South African branch had reached £1.2 million, and net profits in the branch, which were repatriated to London, rose to over £120,000. Branch profit was based on sales of branch publications alone, and excluded the more significant profit from OUP books published in Oxford and London and sold through the Cape Town branch.[113] According to the Deputy Publisher in London, Philip Chester, 'by far the greater part of the turnover' of the African branches was derived from sales of books published in London, but this accrued to the general UK accounts, and was not broken down by individual markets.[114]

The South African branch was particularly important to the Press in view of the sudden loss of the most profitable branch markets in East and West Africa, which had been vital to OUP throughout the 1960s and early 1970s. The Nairobi branch turnover amounted to over £500,000 annually from 1969–1972, but declined sharply in 1973 with the economic crisis in the region.[115] The Nigerian branch turnover rose to a peak of £9.1 million in 1977, constituting 22 per cent of the total OUP turnover of £46 million, but the market failed in 1978 when the Press was forced to indigenise the business; this was followed by a general economic collapse.[116] In this context, the South African branch assumed particular significance. By 1984, Gracie wrote in *The Record*, 'The growth of SA Branch since 1970 has outstripped that of any other branch by more than twice'.[117] Around this time, Gracie made an offer of a management buy-out to Roger Boning, Director of the Press's Branch Headquarters in Oxford, which was rejected:

> Roger Boning turned my offer down as he said that, frankly, we had become too lucrative. Many of the other branches weren't doing very well at the time, the Press itself wasn't in wonderful shape, and they couldn't afford to lose Southern Africa.[118]

In 1987, there was an investigation by a senior OUP management team sent to Cape Town to decide if OUP should remain in the country, reportedly due to pressure from Oxford University students to disinvest from South Africa.[119] The outcome was a decision to remain in South Africa, although Gracie's management of the branch was evidently criticised. Gracie was bitter about the investigation and its conclusions, and he reported in the same interview with Hart that he decided to resign as a result, as he did not want to continue working under 'unpleasant' circumstances: 'I had had enough. OUP was here to stay. I felt that there were no real challenges left, and I didn't need to work, so I resigned some 18 months before my contract was due to expire'.[120]

Gracie's retirement took place in September 1987. He was temporarily replaced by Adam Butcher as manager of the African Region on 3 October, and James Clarke was then appointed as General Manager of the branch, with Kate McCallum as Educational Publisher from 1988. Clarke remained in post until 1990, and was replaced by Smuts Beyers, who had formerly worked for Maskew Miller Longman. In 1990 there was a further visit by press managers Sir Roger Eliot, Secretary to the Delegates and Chief Executive of OUP, and the historian and Delegate, Sir Keith Thomas. In Hart's words: 'On the conclusion of this visit, the message was clear: Oxford University Press, which had been in this country for three quarters of a century, had no intention of withdrawing from South Africa'.[121]

In 1993, the Commissioner for Inland Revenue revoked the tax exemption status of OUP in South Africa, arguing that 'OUP was a commercial undertaking conducting the business of a dealer in books and as a publisher thereof ', and was therefore deemed liable for taxation.[122] OUP contested the decision twice. The first appeal was in the Cape Provincial Division of the Supreme Court on 31 March and 1 June 1994; OUP's argument was that it should be exempt from tax because it promoted 'high standards of learning and of scholarship by the universal distribution of educational, scholarly and academic works' and 'carrie[d] on other activities in southern Africa through the OUP, namely the training of black teachers, curriculum development work, lobbying the local education department for the provision by the OUP of dictionaries and atlases to black schoolchildren and the teaching of dictionary skills, and involvement in public interest committees concerned with education'.[123] This appeal was unsuccessful, but following the further appeal to the Appellate Division on 24 and

30 November 1995, Chief Justice Michael Corbett ruled in favour of Oxford University. His judgement emphasised OUP's historical commitment to 'promote scholarship, education and culture' and its support of black education.[124]

Conclusion

This history of OUP in South Africa demonstrates a transformation in the relation between cultural and economic capital in the branch. Initially the branch functioned as a microcosm of the Press as a whole, whereby scholarly publications for the 'restricted' academic market were subsidised by the 'large-scale' educational market-place.[125] Stratification was on racial lines: cultural capital was accumulated through OUP's publications for the white academic and tertiary market, and economic capital through the profitable black educational market. However, by 1970, the Cape Town branch was under pressure to conform to the international publishing policy of OUP, by which it became not only self-supporting but a source of income for the Press as a whole. The branch was required to concentrate exclusively on the acquisition of economic capital; there was evidently a realisation that serving the liberal academic market in South Africa jeopardised its position in the country. As demonstrated, the result was, in effect, closure of the general and scholarly list and a focus on Bantu Education publishing.

The cross-subsidisation of economic and symbolic capital in the publishing industry is contradictory according to Bourdieu's model, but for OUP this global strategy was highly successful. Economic capital generated at the periphery supported the cultural endeavours in the metropole whilst symbolic capital accrued by the academic, Oxford-based Clarendon Press helped sell educational textbooks throughout Africa and Asia. OUP's expansion into Bantu Education in South Africa paid dividends: from a reported loss of £13,000 in 1970, branch turnover in 1979 reached an unprecedented £1.2 million.[126] Undoubtedly, this model of cultural production did entail a number of 'contradictions' and 'incompatibilities': after 1970, OUP South Africa was increasingly at variance with the liberal public profile promoted by OUP globally.[127] However, OUP were successful in veiling their commercial interests in South Africa under apartheid – in 'abstaining from fully revealing their self-interested goals'.[128] This was achieved partly through OUP Oxford's geographical separation from this profit-centre, but also through careful attention to its self-representation in South Africa.

Correspondence between the London Publisher and the Secretary to the Delegates indicates their concern to prevent public scrutiny of OUP's programme in the country. However, Gracie was permitted to 'run things his way for a fair time', despite protests and resignations, and it was 16 years before there was a management investigation of OUP's operation in the country. Since the end of apartheid, OUP in South Africa has sought to rebrand itself as an investor in black education and culture, as demonstrated in its arguments in the Supreme Court. The narrative constructed by OUP that ultimately protected its tax status in South Africa emphasised its cultural and educational mission while being more reticent about the economic imperative – and significant profits – underwriting this project. OUP is evidently keen to draw a line under its past in South Africa; this article aims to shed light on this occluded publishing history.

Notes

1. G. Moss, 'Publishing in Post-Apartheid South Africa', *Logos*, 4, 3 (1993), p. 141.

2. Examples include M. Trump (ed.), *Rendering Things Visible: Essays on South African Literary Culture* (Johannesburg, Ravan Press, 1990); G.E. de Villiers (ed.), *Ravan: Twenty-Five Years, 1972–1997: A Commemorative Volume of New Writing* (Randburg, Ravan Press, 1997); G.V. Davis and H.G. Ehling, 'Levelling the Playing Fields: An Interview with David and Marie Philip', in G.V. Davis (ed.), *Southern African Writing: Voyages and Explorations* (Amsterdam, Rodopi, 1994), pp. 133–42; G. Moss, 'The Life and Changing Times of an Independent Publisher in South Africa', *Logos*, 4, 3 (1993), pp. 144–6; G. Friedman and R. Blumenthal (eds), *A Writer in Stone: South African Writers Celebrate the 70th Birthday of Lionel Abrahams* (Cape Town, David Philip, 1998); and AD Donker, 'English-Language Publishing in South Africa', *English in Africa*, 10, 1 (May 1983), pp. 29–35.

3. P. Sutcliffe, *The Oxford University Press: An Informal History* (Oxford, Oxford University Press, 1978), inside book jacket.

4. P. Bourdieu, *The Rules of Art: Genesis and Structure of the Literary Field* (Cambridge, Polity Press, 1996), p. 142.

5. *Ibid.*, p. 145.

6. Archives of the Oxford University Press (hereafter AOUP), Three Crowns Misc. 1967–72, LOGE 000223, J. Bell to C. Lewis, 31 July 1969. All archival references and quotations are reprinted by permission of the Secretary to the Delegates of Oxford University Press. A 30-year embargo is in place on the OUP Oxford archive: files up to 1980 were consulted for this research.

7. Sutcliffe, *The Oxford University Press*, p. 213.

8. National English Literary Museum (hereafter NELM), File 2006.30.2.12, OUP CTB After 1969, R. Hart, 'Cape Town Branch: The Story of Oxford University Press Southern Africa' (unpublished paper, Cape Town, 1992), p. 1.

9. AOUP, South Africa Branch, 165 (1), Parnwell to Sisam, 19 October 1928.

10. AOUP, South Africa Branch, 165 (1), Parnwell to Milford, 8 April 1943.

11. *Ibid.*, Sisam to Milford, 25 August 1943.

12. J. Peires, 'Lovedale Press: Literature for the Bantu', *English in Africa*, 7, 1 (1980), quoted in P. Mpe and M. Seeber, 'The Politics of Book Publishing in South Africa: A Critical Overview', in N. Evans and M. Seeber (eds), *The Politics of Publishing in South Africa* (London, Hohger Ehling Publishing, 2000), p. 20.

13. W.R. Johnson, 'Education: Keystone of Apartheid', *Anthropology & Education Quarterly*, 13, 3 (Autumn 1982), p. 217.

14. J. Hyslop, *The Classroom Struggle: Policy and Resistance in South Africa, 1940–1990* (Pietermaritzburg, University of Natal Press, 1999), p. 2.

15. *Ibid.*, p. 3.

16. NELM, File 2006.30.2.1, OUP, David Philip Collection, L. Marquard to H. Milford, 29 January 1945.

17. P.B. Rich, *White Power and the Liberal Conscience: Racial Segregation and South African Liberalism 1921–1960* (Manchester, Manchester University Press, 1984), pp. 89–90.

18. S. Dubow, 'Introduction: South Africa's 1940s', in S. Dubow and A. Jeeves (eds), *South Africa's 1940s: Worlds of Possibilities* (Cape Town, Double Storey Books, 2005), p. 12.

19. R. Vigne, *Liberals against Apartheid: A History of the Liberal Party of South Africa, 1953–1968* (London, Macmillan, 1997), p. 21.

20. C. Merrett, *A Culture of Censorship: Secrecy and Intellectual Repression in South Africa* (Cape Town, David Philip, 1995), pp. 21, 34.

21. D. Philip, 'Book Publishing Under and After Apartheid', in *Book Publishing in South Africa for the 1990s: Proceedings of a Symposium Held at the South African Library, Cape Town, 22–23 November 1990* (Cape Town, South African Library, 1991), p. 11.

22. Philip, 'Book Publishing Under and After Apartheid'.

23. University of Cape Town Libraries (hereafter UCT), BC587, Leo Marquard Papers, E22.19, c. March 1950.

24. UCT, BC587, E22.20, Leo Marquard, 'Evidence before National Education Committee', January 1950, p. 2.

25. UCT, BC587, E22.20, Leo Marquard, 'Evidence' p. 5.

26. W.R. Johnson, 'Education', p. 219; Z. Ngwane, 'Apartheid Under Education: Schooling, Initiation, and Domestic Reproduction in Post-Apartheid Rural South Africa', in P. Kallaway (ed.), *The History of Education Under Apartheid 1948–1994: The Doors of Learning and Culture Shall Be Opened* (Cape Town, Pearson, 2002), pp. 276–7.

27. W.R. Johnson, 'Education', p. 219.

28. Cited in W.R. Johnson, 'Education', p. 219.

29. P. Kallaway, 'An Introduction to the Study of Education for Blacks in South Africa', in P. Kallaway (ed.), *Apartheid and Education: The Education of Black South Africans* (Johannesburg, Ravan Press, 1984), p. 4.

30. P. Kallaway, 'Introduction', in Kallaway (ed.), *The History of Education Under Apartheid*, p. 11.

31. W.R. Johnson, 'Education', p. 220.

32. M. Horrell, *A Decade of Bantu Education* (Johannesburg, South African Institute of Race Relations, 1964), p. 149.

33. D. Johnson, *Shakespeare and South Africa* (Oxford, Oxford University Press, 1996), p. 164.

34. UCT. BC587, C129.6, L. Marquard to A. Paton, 8 March 1955.

35. UCT, BC 587, C129. 7, L. Marquard to M. Benson, 8 March 1955.

36. UCT, BC 587, C129.8, A. Paton to L. Marquard, 17 March 1955.

37 NELM, File 2006.3.2.11, Cape Town Branch to 1969, Folder 2: D. Philip, notes relating to meeting with the Delegates, the Publisher, E. Parnwell and D. Neale, 30 August 1957; and 'Report by Anthony Toyne of Ely House (OE) after Extended Visit 1969', p. 1.

38 Mpe and Seeber, 'The Politics of Book Publishing', pp. 20–21.

39 Ibid., p. 20.

40 A.S. Gérard, African Language Literatures: An Introduction to the Literary History of Sub-Saharan Africa (Washington, DC, Three Continents Press, 1981), p. 207, quoted in Mpe and Seeber, 'The Politics of Book Publishing', p. 19.

41 D. Johnson, Shakespeare and South Africa, p. 170.

42 NELM, File 2006.3.2.11, David Philip Collection, L. Marquard to D. Neale, 21 February 1962.

43 NELM, File 2006.3.2.11., Inspector of Bantu Education to Chairman of the Central Book Committee, 6 March 1961.

44 Kallaway, 'Introduction', pp. 14–15.

45 'Rebusoajoang', 'Education and Social Control in South Africa', African Affairs, 78, 311 (April 1979), p. 235.

46 Hyslop, The Classroom Struggle, pp. 65–81.

47 Ibid., p. 97.

48 M. Benson, Chief Albert Lutuli of South Africa (Oxford, Oxford University Press, 1963), p. 25.

49 Philip, 'Book Publishing Under and After Apartheid', p. 12.

50 J. van der Vyver, 'General Aspects of the South African Censorship Laws', in T. Coggin (ed.), Censorship: A Study of Censorship in South Africa (Johannesburg, South Africa Institute of Race Relations, 1983), pp. 21–22.

51 Merrett, A Culture of Censorship, p. 50.

52 UCT, BC 587, A6.33; 'Marquard Tells of the Raid on his House', Cape Argus, 12 May 1964.

53 UCT, BC 587, A6.42, 'Graaff Questions Police Raids', Cape Times, 2 July 1964.

54 P.B. Rich, Hope and Despair: English-Speaking Intellectuals and South African Politics 1896–1976 (London, British Academic Press, 1993), p. 206.

55 Titles included B.A. Pauw, The Second Generation. A Study of the Family Among Urbanized Bantu in East London (Cape Town, Oxford University Press, 1963); S.T. van der Horst, African Workers in Town: A Study of Labour in Cape Town (Cape Town, Oxford University Press, 1964); P. Carsten, The Social Structure of a Cape Coloured Reserve: A Study of Racial Integration and Segregation in South Africa (Cape Town, Oxford University Press, 1966); and D. Welsh, The Roots of Segregation: Native Policy in Natal, 1845–1910 (Cape Town, Oxford University Press, 1971).

56 AOUP, Chief Albert Lutuli, 12031, R. Collings to D. Philip, 11 September 1962.

57 Philip, 'Book Publishing Under and After Apartheid', p. 12.

58 Merrett, A Culture of Censorship, p. 63.

59 Interview with D. and M. Philip by C. Davis, Cape Town, 5 April 2007.

60 UCT, BC 587, H2.33, L. Marquard, 'Writing under Permit', Rhodes University, 30 August 1962.

61 I. Essery, 'Politics and Publishing in South Africa: Interviews with Two Pioneers', Logos, 17, 3 (2006), p. 154.

62 Cape Town Archives Repository (hereafter CTAR), Publications Control Board (hereafter BCS) 41, 201/64, A. Van Wyk to Secretary for Customs and Excise, 17 March 1964.

63 AOUP, South Africa Branch, 165(1), J. Brown to the Secretary, 13 February 1968. Brown quotes from a memo sent by Cannon, in a handwritten postscript.

64 CTAR, BCS 100, 41/70, F. Cannon to J. Kruger, 18 March 1970.

65 CTAR, BCS 100, 41/70, Objectionable Literature: Various Publications Published by Oxford University Press Southern Africa.

66 P.D. McDonald, The Literature Police: Apartheid Censorship and Its Cultural Consequences (Oxford, Oxford University Press, 2009), pp. 105–6.

67 Hart, 'Cape Town Branch', pp. 14, 17.

68 AOUP, South Africa Branch Accounts 1928–1981, 'South African Branch Annual Report 1968/9', F. Cannon to the Delegates, November 1969.

69 Ibid., 'Southern African Branch Annual Report 1970–71', N. Gracie to the Delegates, 9 September 1971.

70 Ibid., 'South Africa Branch Trading Account Year Ended 31 March 1969', J. Brown to the Delegates, December 1969.

71 AOUP, 'Daughters of the Sun and Other Stories', File 911068, PB/ED 008138, Box OP9, J. Stallworthy to O. Egbuna, 3 March 1970.

72 Hart, 'Cape Town Branch', p. 17.

73 AOUP, South Africa Branch Accounts 1928–1981: F. Cannon, 'South African Branch Trading Account Summary, Year Ended 31st March 1961'; F. Cannon 'South African Branch Trading Account Summary: Year Ended 31st March 1968'.

74 Hart, 'Cape Town Branch', p. 18.

75 AOUP, South Africa Branch, 165 (1), The Manager of the New York branch to D. Philip, 21 October 1970.

76 Ibid., J. Brown to C. Roberts, 13 April 1970.

77 Ibid., C. Roberts to J. Brown, 14 April 1970.

78 AOUP, South Africa Branch, 165 (1), J. Brown to C. Roberts, 16 April 1970.

79 AOUP, Three Crowns Misc. 1967–72, LOGE 000223, J. Bell to C. Lewis, 31 July 1969.

80 'Report of the Committee on the University Press', Oxford University Gazette, 103, 27 (May 1970), p. 24.

81 Ibid., p. 27. According to Sutcliffe, The Oxford University Press, p. 268, 75 per cent of the Press's income was derived from exports and overseas branch income in 1967.

82 Hart, 'Cape Town Branch', p. 17.

83 Philip, 'Book Publishing Under and After Apartheid', p. 13.

84 Interview with D. and M. Philip by C. Davis, Cape Town, 5 April 2007.

85 Philip died on 16 February 2009; see obituary by R. Vigne, 'David Philip: Publisher Who Resisted Apartheid', *Independent*, 10 March 2009, available at http://www.independent.co.uk/news/obituaries/david-philip-publisher-who-resisted-apartheid-1641047.html, retrieved on 5 October 2010.

86 NELM, File 2006.30.2.16, J. Bell to D. Philip, 4 July 1971 (emphasis as in original).

87 NELM, File 2002.33.6.1: Paton and Alexander; Campbell: Selected Poems (Donker) 1982, A. Paton to J. Brown, 6 November 1973.

88 NELM, File 2002.33.6.1. J. Brown to A. Paton, 23 November 1973.

89 AOUP, South Africa Branch, 165 (1), J. Stallworthy to C. Roberts, 8 June 1972.

90 AOUP, South Africa Branch, 165 (1), H. Hart to C. Roberts, 7 June 1972.

91 AOUP, South Africa Branch, 165 (1), C. Roberts to H. Hart, 9 June 1972.

92 AOUP, South Africa Branch, 165 (1), C. Roberts to J. Thompson, 9 June 1972.

93 Mpe and Seeber, 'The Politics of Book Publishing', p. 22.

94 David Philip's copy of this history is lodged in the National English Literary Museum (NELM) in Grahamstown and a further copy is available in the OUP Oxford archive. This is my main source of information about OUP's history from 1980 to 1990.

95 Hart, 'Cape Town Branch', p. 22.

96 AOUP, South Africa Branch Accounts 1928–1981, 'South African Branch Annual Report 1971/2', N. Gracie to the Finance Committee, 31 July 1972.

97 AOUP, South Africa Branch Accounts 1928–1981, 'Southern African Branch Annual Report 1973/4', N. Gracie, 16 September 1974.

98 AOUP, File, LOGE 000096, LG12, Pkt 88 (2), Cape Town (General), N. Gracie to P. Binding, 10 March 1977.

99 AOUP, File, LOGE 000096, LG12, Pkt 88 (2), Cape Town (General), N. Gracie to I. Bossy, 18 November 1975.

100 Hart, 'Cape Town Branch', p. 21.

101 AOUP, South Africa Branch Accounts 1928–1981, 'Annual Report 1972/3', N. Gracie to the Finance Committee.

102 AOUP, South African Branch Accounts 1928–1981, 'Southern African Branch Annual Report 1973/4', N. Gracie, 16 September 1974.

103 V. Pohl, *Farewell the Little People* (Cape Town, Oxford University Press, 1968), Preface.

104 AOUP, Southern African Branch, 165(2), from 1976, N. Gracie to P. Sutcliffe, 30 December 1975.

105 AOUP, Southern African Branch, 165(2), from 1976, N. Gracie to P. Sutcliffe, 9 August 1976.

106 AOUP, Southern African Branch, 165(2), from 1976, 25 November 1976.

107 Interview with D. and M. Philip by C. Davis, Cape Town, 5 April 2007.

108 Hart, 'Cape Town Branch', p. 23.

109 AOUP, South Africa Branch Accounts 1928–1981, 'South African Branch Annual Report 1971/72', N. Gracie to the Finance Committee, 31 July 1972, p. 1.

110 AOUP, South Africa Branch, 165 (1), C. Roberts to N. Gracie, 22 June 1973.

111 AOUP, South Africa Branch Accounts 1928–1981, 'Annual Report 1973/4', N. Gracie.

112 Hart, 'Cape Town Branch', p. 25.

113 AOUP, South Africa Branch Accounts 1928–1981, 'South African Branch Trading Account Year Ended 31 March 1969', J. Brown to the Delegates, December 1969. Brown writes 'profits on the sales in the area accrue in the UK accounts and not the Branch accounts, which reflect profits on local publishing only'.

114 AOUP, Three Crowns Miscellaneous, LOGE: 000 223, 221 (3), 'Editorial General Session, Editorial Assistance to the Branches', P. Chester, June 1971. This financial arrangement is also illustrated by the branch profit and loss sheet for the year ending 21 March 1981, in which the branch annual turnover amounted to £910,662, of which £690,493 (75.8 per cent) was derived from sales of OUP titles from the UK. On these sales, the branch achieved a commission of ten per cent. In this financial year, the branch reported annual net profits of £120,899 (13.27 per cent of the annual turnover), but there is no record of the profit accrued to OUP in the UK from the sales of their titles in South Africa. See AOUP, South Africa Branch Accounts 1928–1981, 'Departmental Trading Accounts for the Year to 31 March 1981'.

115 AOUP, East Africa Branch Accounts 1964–73.

116 'Annual Report 1 April 1976 – 31 March 1977: Report of the Committee on the University Press', *Oxford University Gazette* (1977), Supplement.

117 Hart, 'Cape Town Branch', p. 29.

118 *Ibid.*, p. 31.

119 *Ibid.*, p. 30. The investigation team consisted of Professor Sir Roger Eliot (then chairman of the Finance Committee, subsequently Secretary to the Delegates of the Press), Sir George Richardson (Secretary) and Roger Boning.

120 *Ibid.*, p. 30.

121 *Ibid.*, p. 32.

122 Chancellor, Masters and Scholars of the University of Oxford v. Commissioner for Inland Revenue, Republic of South Africa Cape Provincial Division, 31 March and 13 June 1994, before Berman J. Tax Cases Volume 57 SATC 231, also cited as 1995 (3) SA 258, available at http://www.btinternet.com/~akme/berman.html, retrieved on 20 August 2010.

123 Chancellor, Masters and Scholars of the University of Oxford v. Commissioner for Inland Revenue.

124 C.J. Corbett, 'Judgement in Case no. 385/94 In the Supreme Court of South Africa (Appellate Division), in the matter between The Chancellor, Masters and Scholars of the University of Oxford and the Commissioner for Inland Revenue', 30 November 1995, p. 9, available at http://www.saflii.org/za/cases/ZASCA/1995/157.pdf, retrieved on 20 August 2010.

125 Bourdieu, *The Rules of Art*, p. 142.

126 AOUP, South Africa Branch Accounts 1928–1981, 'Southern Africa Branch Annual Report 1969–1970', N. Gracie.

127 Bourdieu, *The Rules of Art*, p. 145.

128 *Ibid.*, p. 142.

Caroline Davis

17 Re-ethicizing the Classroom
Pedagogy, the Public Sphere, and the Postcolonial Condition

Ajay Heble

Despite our diminishing faith in a public sphere that can function independent of corporate and commercial frames of reference and serve as a site for engaged debate, informed opinion, and oppositional activity, we need, as Andrew Ross suggests, to remember that the world of the academy, populated as it is with millions of citizens, constitutes a public in its own right. In spite of the powerful … influence of the private sector within higher education, he argues, internal conflicts [within the academy] can easily be defined as issues of public concern (1994, 260). In this paper, I want to open up questions about how ethically responsible work of public concern can emerge from an institution whose frames of reference are so massively determined by the goals and logic of business and industry. The text for my paper will be the classroom itself: specifically, a class replete with its own internal conflicts, which I taught in the 1995–96 academic year and which forced me to confront this very question and to recognize the urgency with which a commitment to the ethical value of our teaching practices needs to be seen as a vital part of our struggle for what Henry Giroux calls "the democratization, pluralization, and reconstruction of public life" (1993, 52).

Recent scholarship in a range of adjacent—and often overlapping—areas of study (pedagogy, postcolonialism, cultural studies, rhetoric and composition studies) points compellingly to the need for a reinvigorated understanding of our sense of purpose as teachers and scholars in the humanities. Indeed, if, with Mary Louise Pratt, we agree (as I do) that "three historical processes … transforming the way literature and culture are conceived and studied in the academy" are "globalization, democratization, and decolonization" (1995, 59), then we need, in light of these processes and their institutional consequences, to think anew about what we do in the classroom, and, perhaps more suggestively, about how and why we do it. Pratt, in fact, points out that these three salient

Ajay Heble, "Re-ethicizing the Classroom: Pedagogy, the Public Sphere, and the Postcolonial Condition." *College Literature*, 29(1), 2002: 143–160. © 2002 by West Chester University. Reprinted with permission of Johns Hopkins University Press.

Postcolonial Studies: An Anthology, First Edition. Edited by Pramod K. Nayar.
Editorial material and organization © 2016 John Wiley & Sons, Ltd.
Published 2016 by John Wiley & Sons, Ltd.

historical processes have facilitated, in the academy, "a broadening of subject matter which calls for shifts, among other things, in priorities and modes of accountability" (61). At issue here, it seems to me, is what Bruce Robbins calls "a new framing of the whole which revalues both unfamiliar and long-accepted genres, produces new concepts and criteria of judgment, and affects even those critics [and, by implication, teachers] who never 'do' world literature or colonial discourse at all—affects all critics, that is, by shifting criticism's whole sense of intellectual enterprise" (1992, 170) R. Radhakrishnan, similarly, urges us to think of "postcoloniality as everyone's concern, its ethicopolitical authority a matter of general concern and awareness and not the mere resentment of a ghetto" (1996, 178). And Amitava Kumar, too, suggests that postcoloniality needs to move beyond its scholarly affiliations with other fields of study into more purposeful engagements with "groups, organizations, or peoples united in struggles outside the walls of the academy" (1995, 232). The project underlying postcolonial pedagogy, these critics are suggesting, needs to be understood in the context of the social processes and institutional practices which frame (and are shaping) the production of knowledge both inside and outside the academy, its emancipatory aspirations and "ethicopolitical authority" reconfigured as part of a broader critical model of public discourse.[1]

Now, lest I seem overwhelmingly (and unrealistically) optimistic about the potential for postcolonial pedagogy to facilitate "debate, reflection, action, and moral-political transformation" (Benhabib 1992, 113) in the public arena, let me say a few words here both about the institutional and hegemonic constraints that have been impeding our ability to ethicize the classroom, and, more generally, about some of the factors that, in my mind, have *necessitated* the re-emergence of ethically-valenced models of inquiry in the context of pedagogy and critical practice in literary studies. There is, as Bill Readings has put it in his important book, *The University in Ruins* (and as the comments I referred to from Pratt and Robbins would also seem to suggest), a very real need for "the University to respond to the demand for accountability, while at the same time refusing to conduct the debate over the nature of its responsibility in terms of the language of accounting" (1996, 18). In asking us to distinguish between accountability and the language of accounting, Readings wants us to ask, How do we measure accountability without allowing education itself to be framed in the context and interests of a corporate logic and language, without, in short, buying into a rhetoric which participates in the very transformation of public institutions into marketplace commodities? "To whom and to what the University remains accountable are," says Readings, "questions we must continue to pose and worry over." But "appeals to accounting—whether in the form of numerically scored teaching evaluations, efficiency ratings, or other bureaucratic statistics—will only," he argues, "serve to prop up the logic of consumerism that [currently] rules the University" (1996, 134).

Readings's analysis of the shifts in the University's function—from being an inculcator of the idea of national culture to becoming, more recently, a transnational bureaucratic corporation—highlights not only "the decline of the national cultural mission that has up to now provided its *raison d'être*" (1996, 3) but also its increasing naturalization of corporate frames of reference. As John McMurtry points out,

> even the language of educational purpose has undergone a sea-shift of transformation into business terminology and the going discourse of the corporate culture— "resource units" for what used to be subject disciplines and their professors;

educational "consumers" for what used to be students and learners; "uniform standards" for what used to be the search for quality, depth, and originality; "program packages" for what used to be curriculum; "products" for what used to be graduates; "buying" ideas for what used to be the search for truth. It is difficult to avoid the conclusion that the educational process has been so pervasively subordinated to the aims and practices of business that its agents can no longer comprehend their vocation in any other terms. (McMurtry 1991, 211)

McMurtry's argument about the ability of corporate assumptions and practices to saturate our consciousness and thinking, and his concern that the institutionalization of such assumptions and practices may lead us to believe that they *go without saying* should, I think, give us some sense of the urgency for recovering an ethics in our classrooms: that is, in the face of massive corporate interests which are increasingly becoming naturalized and taken for granted, how best, we need to ask, can pedagogy provide a basis for intervention?

Another related (yet dissimilar) context that has significant bearing on our understanding of the questions I'm trying to open up here is postmodernism. Undoubtedly the dominant model of intellectual inquiry in our era, postmodernism, as I have argued elsewhere, has been tremendously valuable for oppositional critics because of its ability to expose the constructedness of positions that have been presented and accepted as natural and self-evident (Heble 1997). As Satya Mohanty points out, "for most of us today progressive politics—feminist, antiracist, anticolonialist, and so forth—has increasingly become identified with a critical and demystificatory [postmodern] project that not only interrogates the smugness of traditional claims to truth but is also skeptical of any attempt to seek objectivity" (1997, 16). For all its interrogations of prevailing values and systems of thought, though, postmodernism, with its suspicion of truth-claims, its skepticism of collective human goals, and its attempts to render unstable our grounds for judgment, runs the risk of being immobilizing for oppressed peoples. Mohanty, in fact, argues that this kind of skepticism leads ultimately to "serious confusion in cultural—and particularly cross-cultural—studies" (1997, 16). Seyla Benhabib, similarly, tells us that "postmodernism in its infinitely skeptical and subversive attitude toward normative claims, institutional justice and political struggles, is certainly refreshing. Yet, it is also debilitating" (1992, 15). What interests me in this paper is "the problem," to borrow Patricia Bizzell's apt phrasing, "of how to avow one's ideological agenda, or, I may as well say, moral values, in a postmodern philosophical climate that will not allow such values to be grounded, or justified" (1992, 29). If, as I suggested earlier, the increasing naturalization of corporate practices and priorities has made the re-emergence of ethically-informed teaching such an urgent task for educators, then a recognition of the limits of postmodern skepticism and suspicion has likely been the other key factor involved in fostering renewed interest in ethics as a model for pedagogy and critical inquiry.

That ethics is now a legitimate concern in literary studies is, for example, signalled by the fact that it is one of the terms that has been added to the revised edition of Frank Lentricchia's and Thomas McLaughlin's *Critical Terms For Literary Study*, a text that's widely used to teach theory in undergraduate classrooms. Its currency, I would suggest, bespeaks, at least in part, a dissatisfaction with what some might see as the moral bankruptcy of postmodernism: specifically, as many critics have compellingly argued, postmodernism's attack on the possibility of truth and objectivity sits uneasily with the urgent need to make judgments, to take stands on issues (see, for example, Chomsky 2000, 20).

If ethics, as Geoffrey Galt Harpham suggests in his entry on "Ethics" in Lentricchia and McLaughlin, "is the arena in which claims of otherness—the moral law, the human other, cultural norms, the Good-in-itself, etc.—are articulated and negotiated" (1995, 394), then ethically-inflected work (which ought to inform our thinking no matter what our discipline or our area of specialization[2]) is clearly one of the things that give postcolonial theory its particular critical edge. Radhakrishnan writes, "postcoloniality as a field could well be the arena where inequalities, imbalances, and asymmetries could historicize themselves 'relationally,' an arena where dominant historiographies could be made accountable to the ethicopolitical authority of emerging histories" (1996, 173). Or, in Ashis Nandy's words, "the recovery of the other selves of cultures and communities, selves not defined by the dominant global consciousness, may turn out to be the first task of social criticism and political activism and the first responsibility of intellectual stock-taking in the first decades of the coming century" (1989, 265). Thus to understand the ethical edge of postcolonial theory, its ability to negotiate and articulate claims of otherness, is, I would suggest, already to recognize its participation in reinvigorating our understanding of a critical model of public discourse.

* * *

My focus for the remainder of this paper will be on how to translate post-colonial theory into pedagogical practice, how best to establish the "criteria of obligation for making judgments" (McLaren 1995, 256) *in the classroom*. Hard methodological questions, I think, need to be asked about the practice of ethicizing the classroom. Specifically, how do we reconcile our responsibility, as teachers, to ensure that teaching and learning are, in Readings's words, sites of obligation and loci of ethical practices (1996, 154), with a commitment to democratizing the classroom, to creating participatory spaces for the shaping and the production of knowledge (hooks 1994, 15)? How, that is, do we negotiate between, on the one hand, a genuine insistence on and valuing of student expression (itself an ethical move?), and, on the other, our ethical responsibility to promote forms of inquiry and models of knowledge-production which challenge oppression, suffering, and injustice? And, in this context, what happens to democracy in the classroom (to engaged pedagogy, to "freedom of speech," to the preservation of expressive rights) when pedagogies which take as their point of departure what Satya Mohanty calls "the process of unlearning historically determined habits of privilege and privation, of ruling and dependency" (1995, 110) are forced to confront resistant (read: racist, sexist, homophobic) voices? What strategies can we develop that would enable us to negotiate in the classroom between our desire to promote free speech and the ethical imperative to prevent hate speech?[3]

These are, of course, highly challenging questions, and I can't pretend to be able to resolve them in the context of a single paper. What I would like to do, though, is to use specific accounts of teaching a particular class as a test case for measuring the efficacy (and the pitfalls) of deploying postcolonial categories of analysis in a (largely) resistant classroom. On the subject of resistant voices in the classroom, there is, indeed, an evolving body of critical work that uses psychoanalytic and Marxist frameworks to explore the extent to which teaching must necessarily be predicated on the disruptions and blockages that prompt its very undoing. Robert Con Davis, for example, in his introduction to the first of two special issues of *College English* devoted to this topic, draws on the psychoanalytic concept of resistance—defined by Freud as "that which 'interrupts the progress of analytic work'" (1987, 622)—to assert that "the resistance to reading and teaching is also the force that makes them possible … reading and teaching must in an important sense 'fail' before they succeed" (621). Can the resistances I've experienced with this class, I want to ask, be understood in any away as being instructive? I'd also like to use the specifics of this particular class as a way of opening up broader questions about how postcolonial pedagogy can best facilitate the kinds of purposeful public interventions that critics such as Radhakrishnan, Nandy, Pratt, and Robbins all see as central to its sense of intellectual purpose. I might add here that while the gesture of including consideration of a specific teaching situation may appear to be something of an uncustomary move to make in a paper that's largely been trafficking in the realm of theory, it is precisely this kind of attention to the specific material conditions of teaching that is absent from so much writing on critical pedagogy. As Maureen McNeil puts it,

> Critical pedagogical writing is a mixed blessing in this respect: it rallies teachers around the possibility of social and political change and can also provide important insights about what we are doing and not doing…. Yet much critical theory is rather vague about specific pedagogic activities and may discourage interrogation of the social relations around teaching itself. The rhetoric of social and political change which is so pervasive may too easily reassure writers and readers of critical pedagogic theory that they are educating for change. (McNeil 1997, 80)

While work by Giroux, bell hooks, and other theorists of critical pedagogy is genuinely salutary for its visionary sense of intellectual purpose and its inspirational insistence, via Paulo Freire, on democratizing the classroom, their essays frequently lack sustained attention to the specificities of the teaching and learning situations they describe. So, for example, when hooks talks about the need to "create participatory spaces for the shaping of knowledge" (1994, 15), she never really tells us what such a move would involve, nor does she connect that suggestion (which has to do with giving students a voice) with an earlier comment in which she describes a largely resistant class. What's missing is a rigorous account of the specific teaching strategies hooks evolved for altering the dynamics of a class which clearly was not committed to the engaged pedagogy their teacher was trying to promote.

The class that I'd now like to turn my attention to was also largely resistant, was also, that is, unwilling to share my commitment to an ethical pedagogy. The course, a full-year 200 level seminar in English called Honors Critical Practice (37–211/212) is, as I teach it, essentially an introduction to critical literacy and theory. It is a highly demanding course which asks students to think rigorously about the assumptions governing their reading practices, and which encourages a critical and methodological self-consciousness in their responses to and interpretations of texts (primarily literary and theoretical texts, but also media texts, texts of advertising, etc). In the past, I've had tremendous success teaching Honors Critical Practice. In fact, I've taught the course every year that it has been offered, and I consider it to be the single most important course in our curriculum (and, by far and away, my favorite one to teach because it is a particularly suitable place to put into practice the pedagogical principles I've been addressing). I'm filling in some of these contextual details partly because they speak to the enormous success of and amazingly high level of discourse in this course in all the other years in which I've taught it, but also because they'll help to account for my incredible sense of frustration and disappointment with the 1995–96 version of this class—perhaps the most difficult class I've ever taught (and also the class to which I devoted the most time and energy).

On several occasions, and especially around issues of gender, race, media literacy, and corporatism, the class became polarized: a number of (usually male) students would make insensitive, reactionary, and offensive comments which made other (usually female) students in the class feel at best uncomfortable and at worst threatened—comments which would deny, belittle, or make a travesty of the very real struggles (both within and outside the academy) to overcome inequality, suffering, and injustice. Any attempt from me or from other members of the class to respond only served to provoke the offending students to become defensive, to insist that what they had to say was justified, and that any attempt from me to shut them down was a violation of their right to freedom of speech and (though they didn't have the language to express it in these terms) of the very democratized classroom I was trying to promote. There were, in fact, times when I did intervene in rather heavy-handed ways (either through directly confronting students and asking them to think more rigorously about the implications and the consequences of their remarks or by rescheduling seminars and dedicating an entire class to trying to work out some of the tensions in the room). But it is clear to me that these strategies weren't all that helpful.

The two main pedagogical strategies I deployed (at times attempting to shut down the offending voices and at other times showing a willingness to allow all voices to be heard[4]) were, roughly speaking, parallel to the "[t]wo strong ethical traditions" that, according to Wayne Booth, "advise us in seemingly contrasting ways about how to address the deceptive heroes and villains, saints and sinners who offer themselves to us from our first years onward. On the one hand," says Booth, "we become virtuous by recognizing and then excluding or extruding evil. On the other hand, we become virtuous by an open embrace of all the 'goods' we meet, leaving to some process natural or supernatural the task of winnowing bad from good" (1988, 485). I've learned from this class that, again to borrow Booth's formulation, "we must both open ourselves to 'others' that look initially dangerous or worthless, and yet prepare ourselves to cast them off whenever, after keeping company with them, we must conclude that they are potentially harmful. Which of these opposing practices will serve us best at a given moment will depend on who 'we' are and what the 'moment' is" (1988, 488). In retrospect, though, I am not happy with the ways in which I handled the tensions and divisions in that classroom, and if I were to be confronted with a similar class again in the future, I'm not sure I'd have any ready-made answers about how to respond. While Booth's context-dependent formulation, his insistence that ethical criticism should always be "embedded in the lives of particular persons at particular moments" (1988, x), is salutary, I'm still struggling to determine how his insights might help translate into strategies to prevent or to deal with similarly disruptive classroom situations in the future. Indeed, as Black legal scholar Patricia Williams notes,

> The dilemma I face at this moment in the academic world is this: if I respond
> to or open discussion about belligerent or offensive remarks from students in

my classes, I am called 'PC' and accused of forcing my opinions down the throats of my students—and of not teaching them the 'real' subject matter [in my case, literary texts in themselves].... If I follow the prevalent advice of 'just ignoring it,' then I am perceived as weak, humiliated, ineffectual, a doormat. (Williams 1996, 83)

What, then, is to be done? I must confess that I offer this essay, in part, as a record of failure: there's no conversion narrative here, no happy ending, no inspired account of students progressing towards some newly discovered form of critical consciousness. If hitherto I have been inclined to perceive my strengths as a teacher to reside primarily in my commitment to fostering genuinely interactive learning environments where students come to value their own ideas and insights, this class taught me just how ineffective I could be at intervening in polarized settings. Student comments on course evaluations voiced similar concerns. "The instructor," wrote one student, "seemed to let his own biases intrude upon discussions. Sometimes it seemed that he was clearly supporting one student's ideas over another's. I feel it important that an instructor express his views, but the class seemed polarized, at times, and needed a facilitator." Another student concurred: "at times [the instructor] got too involved in taking sides."

Is it possible, I want to ask, *not* to take sides when students are literally yelling at one another across the floor in the classroom (in this class, the men would tend to group themselves on one side of the room, the women on the other), or when they would talk to me in lengthy private interviews about how threatened and violated they were feeling because of what their classmates said in class? If, with Patricia Bizzell, I insist on seeing "all my classroom work as deeply imbued with my moral values" (1992, 284), if I too see everything I do in the classroom as being informed by my commitments to social justice, then pretending to remain neutral in the midst of fractious classroom debates just doesn't seem a viable option. Doesn't one, in such situations, have to take sides, doesn't one have to "teach one's values forthrightly" (Bizzell 1992, 288)?

An instructor's involvement in taking sides on heated issues, however, does not, as the remarks I've quoted from student evaluations will suggest, always make for wise pedagogy. Something else, or at least something more, is needed if pedagogy is to enable a radical reconceptualization of the role that ethics can play in public life. I'm not exactly sure what that "something" is (and if Booth is correct, then much, of course, will have to depend on the specifics of context), but what I'm now realizing is that, despite my failures, I've learned an important lesson from that class. Not only did the polarized settings force many of us (myself included) to make judgements and announce commitments, but, perhaps more importantly, they taught me that students and teachers alike need to work on sharpening and invigorating our understanding of the way in which our judgments and commitments are grounded in complex patterns of social and historical relevance.

Let me try to be more precise. For privilege to be unlearned in the classroom, part of what is at issue, I think, is that teachers need to find new ways to unsettle powerfully entrenched and institutionalized notions of individualism. In that class, for example, many of the students (particularly the male students) continued to cling to the belief that they were genuinely self-willed, freethinking individuals. At times, this belief would manifest itself in their insistence that they were free to say what they liked, without having to take any real responsibility for their comments. In a section of the course on gender and language, one student spoke of the way in which his friend, a high school history teacher, was forced, at the behest of his publisher, to change all uses of the word "fisherman" in his textbook on 19th century fishing in Newfoundland to something more gender-neutral. The student's point was that such instances of gender-neutral language result in a distortion of history, that there were, in fact, no women fishing in Newfoundland in the 19th century. Another student concurred, suggesting, by way of a rather trivial and equally extreme example from the television show *Benny Hill*, that we can often go too far in our attempts to "equalize" language. I should perhaps add that these comments were made in the context of an already deeply polarized room. Whereas with a more tightly knit class, such comments might well have passed by relatively unnoticed, these students were immediately called to task for their remarks, both by some of the women in the class and by me. How are we to understand such remarks, we asked, when we know that "[r]ecent pedagogic research has found account after account of resistance to feminists in the classroom and resistance to discussing male privilege and social inequality" (Bauer and Rhoades, 1996, 95)? When we tried to suggest that their comments, in the context of such a fraught classroom, were belittling, that their extreme examples ran the risk of denying the legitimacy of very real (and monumentally important) historical and contemporary struggles to overcome the intolerable facts of suffering and inequality, the two male students (with the other men now jumping to their defense) became even more insistent that they were justified in their comments. Later, still feeling justified, one of the offending students wrote me a long letter saying he was perfectly within his rights to say what had popped into his head in that classroom, and that he had not meant to offend anyone. In fact, he implied the *Benny Hill* reference was just an example, and a neutral example at that; it didn't necessarily express views that he shared.

My point in belaboring these specific classroom moments is to suggest that as teachers we need to impress upon our students the need for them to take serious responsibility for what they say in class (and, by implication, out of class). Students need to recognize that even seemingly offhand or "neutral" remarks can be profoundly oppressive and debilitating, and to see how the defense of their autonomy as individuals can have troubling consequences. "Language," after all, as Mikhail Bakhtin writes, "is not a neutral medium that passes freely and easily into the private property of the speaker's intentions; it is populated—overpopulated—with the intentions of others" (1981, 294).

I've used various classroom strategies to encourage students to think about the social implications of their use of language, and to challenge their received assumptions about individualism. One thing I have started doing, as a result of that class, is to require all students to go public with their journal entries. Instead of asking students to submit their journals only to me, I now have them post their weekly entries on-line as part of an ongoing computer conference for all students in the class to read and debate. In some ways, this is only a small shift, but it *does*, I think, make students aware of the fact that they are part of a larger community. In dialogue with that community, students often find purposeful ways to confront (and indeed to interrogate) the complex forces governing their assumptions and beliefs. Similarly, I insist that a large portion of their in-class seminar work involve collaborative activity. Again, collaborative work, I've found, forces students to move outside the individualism and isolationism fostered by more traditional kinds of academic assignments (term papers, tests, exams, etc.). In place of pedagogical efforts geared towards a narrative of autonomy—a narrative which, in Readings's terms, enables students to think that they are acquiring "a certain freedom, a position of self-sufficient identity" (1996, 157)—we need, moreover, to encourage our students to confront the networks of power and privilege that make self-sufficiency even thinkable. Educator and critic Sherene Razack is forthright on this point: "the free, autonomous individual who acts in his or her own self-interest can only do so while standing on the back of someone else" (1998, 30). Or, as Readings succinctly puts it, independence is "the end of dependence, the end of obligated relations to others" (1996, 157).

Along with rethinking the nature and function of the kind of research and assignments we ask our students to complete, we can, of course, seek to shatter myths of individualism through our very choice of course content. I'm thinking here not only of the need to teach texts from cultures other than our own (though this too is certainly important, as I'll suggest in a moment), but also, in light of the arguments I've cited from Robbins, Pratt, and Radhakrishnan, of how, more broadly, the goals and the tools of analysis of postcolonial pedagogy can ethicize and humanize all of us, whether or not we even "do" world literature. The kind of unlearning of privilege that Mohanty has in mind must, in short, take place on several fronts, including, significantly, those that are closest to (rather than furthest from) us. One text that I've found particularly resonant in this regard is Daniel Brooks and Guillermo Verdecchia's extraordinary play, *The Noam Chomsky Lectures*. This Canadian play, indeed, deals with issues and events immediately familiar to pretty well all of my students, yet it tends to have a profoundly defamiliarizing effect. Particularly when read alongside Chomsky's own compelling work on the media, the play forces students to recognize just what is at stake in the media's hegemonic control over the production and the distribution of knowledge. Far from being autonomous, self-willed, and freethinking individuals, students, as a result of these readings, are able to recognize just how massively their own frames of reference are determined by corporate interests and priorities. Moreover, they can begin to see the extent to which they too are complicit in the impoverishment and suffering of others.

The texts we teach can also go some distance to unlearning privilege in the classroom if, as Martha Nussbaum advises, we seek out "literary experiences in which we ... identify sympathetically with individual members of marginalized or oppressed groups." Nussbaum continues: "If one of the significant contributions of the novel to public rationality is its depiction of the interaction between shared human aspirations and concrete social circumstances, it seems reasonable that we should seek novels that depict the special circumstances of groups with whom we live and whom we want to understand, cultivating the habit of seeing the fulfillment or frustration of their aspirations and desires within a social world that may be characterized by institutional inequalities" (1995, 92–93). This kind of sympathetic engagement with the Other is, in fact, often seen as central to the purpose of post-colonial pedagogy. In an essay entitled "A Pedagogy of Post-colonial Literature," for example, Lindsay Pentolfe Aegerter puts it thus: "I am fully convinced that students can come to a clear understanding of poststructuralist and feminist notions of socially-constructed subjectivity, and of postcolonial perspectives that reveal the presence of 'the self' in 'the other' ... if they can find personal and cultural connections to those peoples they would otherwise perceive as antithetical to them" (1997, 144). I certainly teach texts that would permit (and, indeed, encourage) such identifications and connections, but I remain slightly uneasy with Nussbaum's and Aegerter's suggestions. To what extent, I find myself wondering, will sympathetic engagement with fictional characters who are epistemologically or ontologically remote from our own areas of experience, simply function as a kind of surrogate for actual encounters with real-life "others" in the daily world of our lived experience? Isn't there something to be said for Lennard Davis's provocative suggestion, in *Reading Novels*, that novel reading is a private activity that inhibits rather than facilitates social change, that novels, in effect, can provide "a false or surrogate example of change that might satisfy any external need or desire for change" (1987, 19). I wonder too about another broad set of questions about how best to handle academic (and often elitist) expressions of affiliation with marginalized and oppressed peoples. As Kathleen Weiler asks,

> What obligation do we as educators have to include the histories and cultures of those not only different from ourselves, but about whom we may ourselves be miseducated or ignorant? How can we as teachers acknowledge our own histories and privileges without taking a position of interpreter and expert about the words and lives of those whose experience are [sic] very different from our own? (Weiler 1993, 222)

These, again, are highly complex ethical questions; my point in rehearsing them here is to suggest that they are precisely the kinds of questions we need to open up and confront when we teach and discuss texts from traditions and cultures other than our own. After all, as Jim Merod writes, the "way critics of a radical inclination assert themselves professionally, as morally and politically adept people, will ... determine what kind of involvement literary scholarship and critical theory can have, directly or indirectly, with oppressed and unrepresented people" (1987, 156).

I've attempted to outline a number of different strategies for ethicizing the classroom. With the exception of requiring students to post on-line journal entries for their peers to read, these were all things that I tried with (or texts that I taught in) my 211–212 class in the 1995–96 academic year. Still, as I've suggested, the class remained polarized, and its conflicts (with all due respect to Gerald Graff's important book) remained unteachable. While the problems that emerged out of that particular, if unrepresentative, version of 37–211/212 were never resolved, they brought home to me some compelling reasons for insisting that students be made accountable to what Radhakrishnan calls "the ethicopolitical authority of emerging histories." Such accountability, I've been implying, goes hand-in-hand with the need for students to recognize the extent to which they may not be as truly self-willed, as autonomous, or as freethinking as they might believe. Students, in fact, need to see that such recognition can actually be enabling. In Kathleen McCormick's words, "conceiving of the self as an interdiscursive subject rather than a free individual can (paradoxically) enable students to develop greater agency than they might otherwise have had; such a radical reconception of the self may lead students not only to examine the various discursive practices which have helped to produce them, but to work more actively within and against them" (1994, 146). "Agency," she suggests, "follows only from a meta-awareness of why (to some extent) one has the beliefs, assumptions and habits one does" (148). Most of my students that year, unfortunately, did not get to such a point, never even approximated that stage of self-consciousness.

Why? Again, I can't be sure, but my suspicion is that my failure to ethicize that classroom had something to do with contexts (some of which I touched on at the outset of this paper) outside the academy. Just as, in Shirley Nelson Garner's words, "[t]ransforming antifeminist culture within the academy means, ultimately, transforming antifeminist culture outside the academy" (1996, 201), this class and its problems also brought home to me just how much postcolonial pedagogy—pedagogy which takes as its point of departure what Satya Mohanty, in that phrase I quoted earlier, calls "the process of unlearning historically determined habits of privilege and privation, of ruling and dependency"—is a matter of contemporary *public* urgency. In an era of widespread inequality, privation, and injustice, when subjugated knowledges struggle for legitimacy only to be met with various forms of institutional disparagement and intolerance, pedagogy can carry an impressive ethical (and if Andrew Ross is correct, public) force.

Dealing, even if unsuccessfully, with this resistant class, taught me, then, that there's something vital at stake in the kinds of pedagogical interventions that postcolonial etiquettes of reading are working to facilitate, something, perhaps, that has to do with my recognition of the ways in which education itself is connected with oppressive structures in the larger society, and with how education (as Readings, McMurtry and others have convincingly demonstrated) has functioned to reinforce and naturalize dominant spheres of knowledge production. But there's something else, I think, that gives urgency to our task. If, as Bruce Robbins argues, "the common assumption for all of us who begin, in the study of colonial and postcolonial culture, with the intolerable facts of global suffering and injustice ought surely to be … that progress is an absolute necessity" (1994b, 33), then progress, it seems to me, can only be won through tough coalitional struggles for public legitimacy. We've reached a historical moment where, in Michael Keefer's words, "the formerly unspeakable is not merely being spoken, but shouted from the rooftops: radio talk-show host Bob Grant, for example, has lifted his ratings on New York's WABC to new heights by calling blacks 'savages' and denouncing Martin Luther King as a 'scumbag'" (1996, 3). Mary Louise Pratt, in an essay on the Western Culture Debate at Stanford, mentions a similarly disturbing set of attempts to legitimize, first in the name of freedom of speech and then in the name of ignorance, oppressive (in this case homophobic and racist) models of conduct. After a student was expelled from his residence for "a year of disruptive activity directed especially toward a gay resident assistant," "ten fraternity brothers, in defense of the expelled student's freedom of speech, staged a silent vigil" which "seemed to deliberately invoke the customs of the Ku Klux Klan" (1994, 62). The students later, as Pratt points out, "claimed complete ignorance of the associations their vigil invoked" (1994, 62). Her conclusion about this series of incidents is, I think, worth quoting at length because, again, it gives us some sense of just how pressing our task, as educators, is:

> If it is possible for young adults to leave the American educational system ignorant of the history of race relations in the United States (not part of standard Western culture curricula), then something needs to change. And if a person who knows the history of race relations and their symbolizations feels free to reenact racist rituals of mockery or intimidation, something needs to change. At the same time, blame must be placed where it belongs. In pleading ignorance,

the students were following the example of many of the country's own leaders, for whom ignorance had become an acceptable standard of public life. Throughout their high school and college years these students had looked to a president who consistently showed himself to be both ignorant and utterly comfortable with his ignorance. (Pratt 1994, 62)

Pratt's comments and examples go some distance in accounting for the factors that produced the racism and sexism in my class. In Ontario, where I live and teach, the Conservative government, led by Mike Harris, has, through its actions and policies, sanctioned ignorance, intolerance, and irresponsibility: indeed, through rolling back employment equity legislation and labor laws, and cutting funding to women's shelters, it has, I would argue, made ignorance and intolerance acceptable standards of public life. The kind of dismantling of social democratic policies and programs we're seeing in Ontario (as indeed throughout Canada) should be sufficient measure of the urgency with which postcolonial strategies for re-ethicizing the classroom need to been seen as part of the struggle for access to public legitimacy. Chandra Mohanty argues that "as we develop more complex, nuanced modes of asking questions and as scholarship in a number of relevant fields begins to address histories of colonialism, capitalism, race, and gender as inextricably interrelated, our very conceptual maps are redrawn and transformed" (1991, 3). In its ongoing participation in the transformation of conceptual categories, and with its continuing efforts to put ethical pressure on dominant spheres of knowledge production, postcolonial pedagogy invests teachers with a responsibility to initiate forms of solidarity which will help bring about progress, and help facilitate change both in the current distribution of social relations and in the public understanding.

Notes

[1] Contemporary scholarship in rhetoric and composition studies often offers an analogous argument. Patricia Donahue and Ellen Quandahl, for instance, point to the way in which teachers of composition and rhetoric strive to "give students specific analytical methods for reading the world, for understanding the terms of linguistic power, for resisting oppressive authority" (1989, 15). Similarly, James Berlin reminds us that "in teaching writing we are providing students with guidance in seeing and structuring their experience with a set of tacit rules about distinguishing truth from falsity, reality from illusion" (1987, 7). See also Carolyn Ericksen Hill: "though cultures and minds do live within their own systems of ideas, only those minds and cultures that stay open to different ones can be fully rhetorical in an ethical way" (1990, 35).

[2] See Wayne Booth's important book, *The Company We Keep: An Ethics of Fiction* (1988). Booth argues that "we can no longer pretend that ethical criticism is passé. It is practiced everywhere, often surreptitiously, often guiltily, and often badly, partly because it is the most difficult of critical modes, and partly because we have so little serious talk about why it is important, what purpose it serves, and how it might be done well" (1988, 19).

[3] Henry Louis Gates's essay in a collection on academic freedom takes up this question of whether and how restrictions on hate speech are compatible with our desire to promote freedom of inquiry and expression. Gates tells us that "[t]he byword among many black activists and intellectuals is no longer the political imperative to protect free speech but the moral imperative to suppress hate speech. And therein hangs a tale" (119). See also Ronald Dworkin's discussion, in that same volume, of instances where we might need to compromise the right of free speech "in deference to other rights that are, in context, more urgently or centrally at stake" (1996, 196). "Though academic freedom is," Dworkin writes, "a profound value … it is nevertheless only one value among many. … How do we choose when academic freedom conflicts with something else that is also important, like equality and decency?" (191).

⁴ Hill grapples with a similar set of issues. "How was it possible," she asks, "to stand in the middle of a commitment, yet still stay open enough to negotiate with positions contrary to it…. Right timing of speaking up and staying silent would have to be involved" (1990, 36).

Works Cited

Aegerter, Lindsay Pentolfe. 1997. "A Pedagogy of Post-colonial Literature." *College Literature* 24.2 (June): 142–50.

Bakhtin, M. M. 1981. *The Dialogic Imagination: Four Essays.* Trans. Caryl Emerson and Michael Holquist. Austin: University of Texas Press.

Bauer, Dale, with Katherine Rhoades. 1996. "The Meanings and Metaphors of Student Resistance." In *Antifeminism in the Academy*, ed. VèVè Clark, Shirley Nelson Garner, Margaret Higonnet, and Ketu H. Katrak. New York: Routledge.

Benhabib, Seyla. 1992. *Situating the Self: Gender, Community and Postmodernism in Contemporary Ethics.* New York: Routledge.

Berlin, James. 1987. *Rhetoric and Reality: Writing Instruction in American Colleges, 1900–1985.* Carbondale: Southern Illinois University Press.

Bizzell, Patricia. 1992. *Academic Discourse and Critical Consciousness.* Pittsburgh: University of Pittsburgh Press.

Booth, Wayne. 1988. *The Company We Keep: An Ethics of Fiction.* Berkeley: University of California Press.

Brooks, Daniel, and Guillermo Verdecchia. 1991. *The Noam Chomsky Lectures: A Play.* Toronto: Coach House.

Chomsky, Noam. 2000. *Chomsky on MisEducation.* Ed. Donaldo Macedo. Lanham, MD: Rowman and Littlefield.

Davis, Lennard J. 1987. *Resisting Novels: Ideology and Fiction.* New York: Methuen.

Davis, Robert Con. 1987. "Freud's Resistance to Reading and Teaching." *College English* 49.6: 621–27.

Donahue, Patricia, and Ellen Quandahl. 1989. "Reading the Classroom." In *Reclaiming Pedagogy: The Rhetoric of the Classroom*, ed. Patricia Donahue and Ellen Quandahl. Carbondale: Southern Illinois University Press.

Dworkin, Ronald. 1996. "We Need a New Interpretation of Academic Freedom." In *The Future of Academic Freedom*, ed. Louis Menand. Chicago: University of Chicago Press.

Garner, Shirley Nelson. 1996. "Transforming Antifeminist Culture in the Academy." In *Antifeminism in the Academy*, ed. VèVè Clark, Shirley Nelson Garner, Margaret Higonnet, and Ketu H. Katrak. New York: Routledge.

Gates Jr. Henry Louis. 1996. "Critical Race Theory and Freedom of Speech." In *The Future of Academic Freedom*, ed. Louis Menand. Chicago: University of Chicago Press.

Giroux, Henry. 1993. *Living Dangerously: Multiculturalism and the Politics of Difference.* New York: Peter Lang.

Harpham, Geoffrey Galt. 1995. "Ethics." In *Critical Terms for Literary Study.* 2nd ed., ed. Frank Lentricchia and Thomas McLaughlin. Chicago: University of Chicago Press.

Heble, Ajay. 1997. "New Contexts of Canadian Criticism: Democracy, Counterpoint, Responsibility." In *New Contexts of Canadian Criticism*, ed. Ajay Heble, Donna Palmateer Pennee, and J.R. (Tim) Struthers. Peterborough, ON: Broadview Press.

Hill, Carolyn Ericksen. 1990. *Writing from the Margins: Power and Pedagogy for Teachers of Composition.* New York: Oxford University Press.

hooks, bell. 1994. "Engaged Pedagogy." In *Teaching to Transgress: Education as the Practice of Freedom.* New York: Routledge.

Keefer, Michael. 1996. *Lunar Perspectives: Field Notes from the Culture Wars.* Toronto: Anansi.

Kumar, Amitava. 1995. "Postcolonial Tour 93 (All Major U.S. Cities)." In *Order and Partialities: Theory, Pedagogy, and the "Postcolonial,"* ed. Kostas Myrsiades and Jerry McGuire. New York: SUNY Press.

McCormick, Kathleen. 1994. *The Culture of Reading and the Teaching of English.* Manchester: Manchester University Press.

McLaren, Peter. 1995. *Critical Pedagogy and Predatory Culture: Oppositional Politics in a Postmodern Era.* London: Routledge.

McMurtry, John. 1991. "Education and the Market Model." *Journal of the Philosophy of Education* 25: 209–17.

McNeil, Maureen. 1997. "'It Ain't Like Any Other Teaching': Some Versions of Teaching Cultural Studies." In *A Question of Discipline: Pedagogy, Power and Praxis in Cultural Studies*, ed. Joyce E. Canaan and Debbie Epstein. Boulder, CO: Westwood.

Merod, Jim. 1987. *The Political Responsibility of the Critic.* Ithaca: Cornell University Press.

Mohanty, Chandra Talpade. 1991. "Introduction: Cartographies of Struggle: Third World Women and the Politics of Feminism." In *Third World Women and the Politics of Feminism*, ed. Chandra Talpade Mohanty, Ann Russo, Lourdes Torres. Bloomington: Indiana University Press.

Mohanty, Satya P. 1997. *Literary Theory and the Claims of History: Postmodernism, Objectivity, Multicultural Politics.* Ithaca: Cornell University Press.

___. 1995. "Epilogue. Colonial Legacies, Multicultural Futures: Relativism, Objectivity, and the Challenge of Otherness." *PMLA* 110 (January): 108–18.

Ajay Heble

Nandy, Ashis. 1989. "Shamans, Savages and the Wilderness: On the Audibility of Dissent and the Future of Civilizations." *Alternatives* 14: 263–78.

Nussbaum, Martha. 1985. *Poetic Justice: The Literary Imagination and Public Life*. Boston: Beacon.

Pratt, Mary Louise. 1995. "Comparative Literature and Global Citizenship." In *Comparative Literature in the Age of Multiculturalism*, ed. Charles Bernheimer. Baltimore: Johns Hopkins University Press.

___. 1994. "Humanities for the Future: Reflections on the Western Culture Debate at Stanford." In *Falling into Theory: Conflicting Views on Reading Literature*, ed. David Richter. Boston: Bedford Books.

Radhakrishnan, R. 1996. *Diasporic Mediations: Between Home and Location*. Minneapolis: University of Minnesota Press.

Razack, Sherene H. 1998. *Looking White People in the Eye: Gender, Race, and Culture in Courtrooms and Classrooms*. Toronto: University of Toronto Press.

Readings, Bill. 1996a. *The University in Ruins*. Cambridge: Harvard University Press.

Robbins, Bruce. 1994. "Introduction: The Public as Phantom." In *The Phantom Public Sphere*, ed. Bruce Robbins. Minneapolis: University of Minnesota Press.

___. 1994b "Secularism, Elitism, Progress, and Other Transgressions: On Edward Said's 'Voyage In.'" *Social Text* 40 (Fall): 25–37.

___. 1992. "Comparative Cosmopolitanism." *Social Text* 31/32: 169–86.

Ross, Andrew. 1994. "The Fine Art of Regulation." In *The Phantom Public Sphere*, ed. Bruce Robbins. Minnesota: University of Minnesota Press.

Weiler, Kathleen. 1993. "Feminism and the Struggle for a Democratic Education: A View from the United States." In *Feminism and Social Justice in Education: International Perspectives*, ed. Madeleine Arnot and Kathleen Weiler. London: Falmer.

Williams, Patricia. 1996. "Talking about Race, Talking about Gender, Talking about How We Talk." In *Antifeminism in the Academy*, ed. VèVè Clark, Shirley Nelson Garner, Margaret Higonnet, and Ketu H. Katrak. New York: Routledge.

Part Four
Nation, Space, Identity

Postcolonialism's concern with history is perhaps matched in intensity of focus and depth of engagement only by its attentiveness to questions of nationalism, national identity (geopolitical as well as cultural), and belonging. The essays in this section examine geographical spaces that have come into the postcolonial sightline only recently — Ireland, Canada, Israel–Palestine, and India's Northeast. Threats to or neglect of spaces then mutate, mostly by discursive amplification, into threats to identity and belonging, even as regional, local, communitarian, and national identities evolve as threatened identities.

As postcolonial studies across Asia, Africa, and South America continue to grapple with colonial pasts of various nations, critiques have pointed to an awkward assumption at the heart of the field: the easy slippage from "white" to "colonizer." This slippage ignores the internal racisms that have always marked intra-European relations across countries and cultures. Aniko Imre points to the troubling-troubled Irish identity of being colonized *whites* before moving on to a discussion of what might be

Europe's internal others — white races who did not participate in colonization and were themselves colonized, such as the Gypsies. Whiteness is, in Imre's study, contested and plural, and increasingly the self-representations by the Romani (Gypsy) people invite us to reconsider "whether the postcolonial nation-state is the only relevant category in terms of which we should examine issues of whiteness." Similar questions of whiteness, hybrid identities, and national belonging need to be examined within the institutional frameworks where literary texts, such as Asian Canadian, are studied/taught, argues Lily Cho's essay. Focusing less on the cultural histories of the people than on the forms of pedagogy and analysis, Cho considers the relevance of the rubric of "diaspora" as a possible way to examine these texts. Diaspora studies' own engagements with postcolonialism might fruitfully enable one to study the tensions of the Canadian nation state and the migrants' concerns with "belonging," she argues. Eóin Flannery turns to Ireland and examines utopian postcolonial critiques and their construction of Ireland. Flannery argues that such critiques

Postcolonial Studies: An Anthology, First Edition. Edited by Pramod K. Nayar.
Editorial material and organization © 2016 John Wiley & Sons, Ltd.
Published 2016 by John Wiley & Sons, Ltd.

appropriate the "Utopian dynamism of historical Irish anti-colonial thought and action," where the utopian dimension has assimilated, even as it contributes to, an international postcolonial critique. This involves, Flannery proposes, seeing the past as a utopian resource and not a burden. Nandana Dutta's study of the writings from Northeast India – with its history of secessionist movements, identity politics, and often antagonistic relationship with "mainland" India – demonstrates how a "narrative of neglect" is endemic to the region's self-representations. Such a narrative, Dutta shows, serves political expediency and generates economic benefits, even as it constantly embodies "aspirations, dejections, despair, frustrations, and anger." Like Flannery,

Dutta too is mindful of particular appropriations of the past in the form of (disaffected, subnational, or, as in the case of Flannery, utopian) discourses that then are constitutive of the region's relations with the rest of the nation-state. In another "troubled" region, Palestine–Israel, Rebecca Stein sees the discourse of Jewish leisure under attack from Palestine militancy as enabling an invisibilizing of the daily losses and daily suffering caused by Israeli onslaughts on the Palestinians. The Israeli café serves, Stein notes, as a metonym for the larger political field, the nation itself. The targeting of the café was treated as a threat to Israeli citizenship even as the consumers and workers in the café evolved into new national subject positions.

18   Whiteness in Post-Socialist Eastern Europe

The Time of The Gypsies, The End of Race

Anikó Imre

Whiteness and Nationalism in Eastern Europe

"I BELIEVE AMERICA TAUGHT our son's killer to hate African-Americans." This is how Camille Cosby's controversial article starts in the July 8, 1998, issue of *USA Today* (Cosby, 15A). "Presumably," she continues, "Markhasev did not learn to hate black people in his native country, the Ukraine, where the black population was near zero. Nor was he likely to see America's intolerable, stereotypical movies and television programs about blacks, which were not shown in the Soviet Union before the killer and his family moved to America in the late 1980s" (15A). Cosby levels a passionate charge against the racist foundations of the American nation, a charge that "opened a real dialogue on race" (Cohen 1998, 26). However, her statement also echoes two highly debatable assumptions: that certain forms of racism are specific to particular groups and historical situations, and that film and media shape ethnic and racial identities in predictable ways.

Bell hooks also addresses these assumptions when she recalls discussing Wim Wenders's film *Wings of Desire* (1988) with white friends:

> *Wings of Desire* evoked images of that imperialist colonizing whiteness that has dominated much of the planet. This image was reinforced by the use of non-white people as colorful backdrop in the film, a gesture that was in no way subversive and undermining in that much of the film was an attempt to represent white culture in a new light. Encountering white friends raving about

Imre Anikó, "Whiteness in Post-Socialist Eastern Europe: The Time of the Gypsies, the End of Race," in Alfred J. Lopez, ed., *Postcolonial Whiteness: A Critical Reader on Race and Empire*. Albany: State University of New York Press, 2005, pp. 79–102. Reprinted by permission of State University of New York Press.

Postcolonial Studies: An Anthology, First Edition. Edited by Pramod K. Nayar.
Editorial material and organization © 2016 John Wiley & Sons, Ltd.
Published 2016 by John Wiley & Sons, Ltd.

Anikó Imre

the magic of this film, I would respond by saying it was just "too white." They would give me that frustrated "no racism again, please" look that is so popular these days and explain to me that, after all, Berlin is a white city. (hooks 1991, 167)

Hooks writes that this film made her think about "white culture" not simply in terms of skin color, but rather "as a concept underlying racism, colonization, and cultural imperialism" (166). This is a useful starting point, but it ignores the fact that whiteness is far from being a monolithic concept. Irish culture, for instance, contests the conflation of white and colonizer. And there are predominantly white cultures that have not directly participated in historical processes of colonization and imperialism. In countries of Eastern Europe, most people would probably still insist that issues of colonization and race are not relevant to the region, despite the fact that, similar to Berlin, these places are much less "white" than they used to be. Since the end of socialism, as a result of large-scale Eurasian migrations, a massive onslaught of global media, and the fervor of the neo-fascist, racist persecution of Gypsies and racialized foreigners, a new awareness of racial difference has emerged in the post-Soviet region. But, despite the variety of colors that are now present on the streets and screens of Poland, Slovakia, the Czech Republic, or Hungary, whiteness as a moral category has remained transparent. Its politics and aesthetics have remained beyond analysis.

In the following, I will first attempt to explain why this is so. I will argue that white supremacy's function in the constitution of East European national identities is rooted much deeper than either these nations' official self-representations or the Western media portrayal of recent ethnic confrontations would suggest. Since the end of socialism, much of the struggle over ethnic and racial representation has taken place in, and under the influence of, films and other media, indigenous as well as imported. However, this has happened without adequate analysis or even acknowledgment of the constitutive role that media representations have played in the shifting relationships of national, ethnic, and racial majorities and minorities. I will analyze East European representations in which whiteness appears contested and contestable, "as a process, not a "thing," as plural rather than singular in nature" (Frankenberg 1997, 1). The changing situation of Gypsy, or Romani, minorities within Eastern Europe provides a useful lens through which we can examine how whiteness has been called upon to provide legitimacy to the post-socialist nation-state. In the concluding part of this chapter, I will point to new, transnational Gypsy self-representations that address the racial foundations of East European nations and, at the same time, prompt us to ask whether the postcolonial nation-state is the only relevant category in terms of which we should examine issues of whiteness.

The Return of The Racist Repressed

Judging by the recent racist outbursts of ethnic nationalism in Eastern Europe and the former Soviet Union, the question appears to be less whether discourses of colonization, race, and, in particular, whiteness, are relevant to the functioning of East European societies, but rather how such discourses have managed to stay submerged for so long. With the collapse of socialism, East Europeans have suddenly awakened from their relative imprisonment within the Soviet Bloc to find their national boundaries vulnerable to influences from a world that had moved on to an increasingly transnational order. They have been confronted with the possibility that identities are far from taken-for-granted, not the least because of the power of global communication and information networks. It is not surprising that, emerging from the discredited communist rhetoric of egalitarianism and internationalism, East Europeans have fallen back on nationalism as a "source of self-confidence, an ideological substitute for the vanished certainties of the communist era" (Tismaneanu 1994,102). As Vladimir Tismaneanu writes,

> Postcommunist nationalism is ... a political and ideological phenomenon with a dual nature. As an expression of historical cleavage, it rejects the spurious internationalism of communist propaganda and emphasizes long-repressed national values. On the other hand, it is a mental construct rooted in and marked by Leninist authoritarian mentalities and habits. Its targets are primarily forces that champion pro-Western, pluralist orientations, but also individuals or groups perceived as alien, different, potentially destructive of a presumably homogeneous ethnic body (such as immigrant, Gypsy, or gay minorities). Nationalist discourse demonizes the West and insists on rejecting any attempts to turn postcommunist nations into "the external proletarian armies" of the capitalist metropolis. (106)

Dominant East European political groups have resorted to nationalist manipulation and mobilization in order to maintain their monopoly on power (105). The unquestionable goal of "preserving the nation" against alien influences has played out in terms of the preservation of national cultures, primarily in print and broadcast media. The call to save the national culture has often been issued in the name of a resistance to the demonic values conveyed by "cultural imperialism," associated with consumerism, global media homogenization, and multiculturalism. However, this does not mean the rejection of the West as a whole. Rather, the binary logic of nationalism has dictated that the West be split in two: authentic and false; old and new; sophisticated and mass-oriented. Influences deemed "harmful" for the nation are associated with the United States, in opposition to good old "authentic" European values.

This dichotomy has several advantages for the political and cultural elite. First of all, the "return to Europe," which has become an indispensable slogan for East European political campaigns (Iordanova, "Balkans," 2000), allows discourses of imperialism and racism to remain unexamined within nationalism. East European nations' unspoken insistence on their whiteness is one of the most effective and least recognized means of asserting their Europeanness. The fact that racism has surfaced at the end of the cold war is, precisely, an indication that the Eurocentric, black-and-white self-image of East European nations is under contestation, along with concepts such as national destiny and national character. The "new-old nationalisms" of Eastern Europe (Eisenstein, *Hatreds*, 45), and the accompanying "new racisms" (Žižek, "Ez van"; "A Leftist Plea") betray the very insecurity of modernist nationalisms in their confrontations with the postmodern, transnational media and economy.

The insistence on the invisibility of whiteness, and on an absolute "color line" between white and nonwhite, provides the foundation for a series of rigid, hierarchical binary divisions in East European national ideologies: truth/lie, human/inhuman, high culture/mass culture, individual/collective, and scientific/superstitious. Of course, these dichotomies have been the very devices with which the West naturalized its hierarchical relationship to its colonies (Shohat and Stam 1994, 201). Indeed, in a sense, Eastern Europe has adopted racism and nationalism from the West: On the one hand, as the Bulgarian theorist Alexander Kiossev puts it, East European nations, "on the periphery of civilization," came into existence and have survived through a process of "self-colonization." These nations voluntarily accepted the superiority of European Enlightenment ideas of rationality, progress, and racial hierarchy (18). On the other hand, similar to its relationship to third world nations, "Europe" has been far from innocent of imposing its imperial master narratives on the populations of Eastern Europe: the "Other Europe" has provided a favorable, admiring mirror even after the end of actual imperial ventures to Asia and Africa. It has remained a resort for living out forbidden or unrealizable fantasies without taking full responsibility for them.

This process continues under the cover of liberal democracy, occasionally surfacing in such contradictions as the effective media "racialization" and subsequent abandonment of the Balkans, and the simultaneous, some-what hypocritical Western diplomatic protests against the legal and political inequality of Gypsy minorities in Eastern Europe. In the first case, the Western media coverage of the war in Yugoslavia— one of the hotbeds of the "ethnic conflicts" that have burst into violence in postcommunist Eastern Europe since 1989—insisted on distancing the war from Western, rational frame-works of interpretation. The confrontations were represented as the results of ancient, internal and unresolvable tribal disagreements (Iordanova, "Balkans"; Ó Tuathail 1996, 191–95; Ravetto 1998, 47; Žižek, "Ez van"). In the second case, while the European Union has set future East European member states strict standards for improving the political and economic situation of ethnic minorities, the borders of "Europe" are increasingly protected from "alien invasion." There are "Gypsy ghettos" in Italy, and ethnic violence is on the rise in Austria and Germany.[1]

One of the primary difficulties of using Western theories of ethnicity, race, and colonialism to mark whiteness and contest ethnocentric nationalisms in Eastern Europe is that in East European languages, state politics, and in social scientific studies of Eastern Europe, the category of "race" has remained embedded within that of "ethnicity." Most studies of East European nationalisms continue to approach their subjects in terms such as "political" and "ethnic" (Kennedy 1994, 27). The failure—or refusal—to distinguish race from ethnicity deflates the state's violence and the social policies that accompany prejudices against a racialized group (Shohat and Stam, 183). Race and racism continue to be considered concepts that belong exclusively to discourses of coloniality and imperialism, from which Eastern Europe, the deceased "second world," continues to be excluded, and from which East European nationalisms are eager to exclude themselves. For instance, seeing my interest in the current racist backlash against the Roma, white Hungarians repeatedly anticipated my "American" reaction, and vehemently warned me not to set up an analogy between Gypsies in Eastern Europe and African Americans in the United States. I have been told not to confuse a racial minority, whose ancestors were forced into slavery, with an East European "historical," ethnic minority such as the Roma; not to force the "white guilt" that Americans "rightly" feel about the extinction of Native Americans on innocent East Europeans, for whom both colonization and whiteness are distant concepts; and not to hold up misguided American racial policies such as affirmative action as ideals for Eastern Europe, freshly liberated from the burden of censorship. At the same time, in Hungarian, it is perfectly acceptable to use the phrase "It's not for white people" to describe hard physical labor, and it is considered to be free of contradiction to say, "I hate Gypsies, but I am not a racist."

This point returns us to the questions of why Ennis Cosby's murderer did not need to see American media images to become a racist, and why Wim Wenders and other white European masters of high culture are held in so much critical regard throughout Eastern Europe. It is true that direct imperialism, and its necessary consequence, colonialism—understood in a narrower, historical sense as the forceful domination and economic exploitation of a distant land—bypassed East European cultures.[2] However, imperialism as the "theory, and the attitudes of a dominating metropolitan center ruling a distant territory" (Said 1993, 9) has thoroughly influenced the formation of East European nations. The latter came into existence by adopting the models of European national and imperial development. Models and symbols of imperial "Europeanness," which were imported by traveling intellectuals and disseminated primarily by schools and universities, have been in great demand in Eastern Europe for centuries (Kiossev 2000, 18). The concept of "cultural nationalism"[3] usefully describes this "eastern type of development," formulated as a desire to be European, demonstrating "an overwhelming concern for fictions and symbols" in the absence of the "proper," European political institutions of the nation state (Csepeli 1991, 328).

In a sense, of course, nationalism is always a product of colonization (Balibar 1991, 89), and racism has been both an ally and a product of the colonization process (Stam and Spence 1976, 35).[4] Edward Said explains that the cultural exchange between Europe and the "Orient"—India, Egypt, or the Ottoman world, for instance—was initially a mutual process. However, as imperial economic interests had gained in importance, it became necessary to justify Europe's natural superiority to colonized cultures along racial lines (Said and Burgmer, "Bevezetés," 2000). The subsequent institutionalization of racism became a crucial component of East European nationalisms, as well, the "Europeanness" of which was in question from the start.[5] Since Eastern Europe's participation in imperialism has been fantasmatic, rather than based on direct contact with others, it has operated by national consensus, unfettered by anticolonialist critique and white guilt.

Wimal Dissanayake sums up the relationship of nationalism to colonization: "Nationalism simultaneously extends the range and depth of colonialism, offers resistance to it, subverts its imperatives and determinants, and reproduces it in subtle and not so subtle ways" (Dissanayake 1994, ix). In Eastern Europe, these functions have been distributed along the geographical West-East division: the resistance to and the subversion of colonialism have been reserved for invasions from the East (the Tartars, the Ottoman Empire, the Soviets), while eager reproduction has characterized the self-colonizing relationship to Europe.[6] The United States has recently become a third player in this paradigm, standing for a simplified understanding of neocolonialism and media imperialism.

Whiteness has stayed unmarked, embedded in Hungarianness, Bulgarianness, and other nationalities. As Zillah Eisenstein writes in relation to recent events in Bosnia, nationalism in Eastern Europe functions as a form of racism (*Hatreds*, 48).[7] Unlike Frantz Fanon, Haile Gerima, or Edward Said, for whom watching *Tarzan* provoked a schizophrenic "crisis of identity" (Stam and Spence, 157), East Europeans have never had to doubt whom to cheer for, and never confused themselves with cannibals.

Racism has remained, perhaps, the most poorly articulated factor in the relationship between official ideologies and people's fantasies during and since communism. Instead of theorizing the postcommunist transition in the context of (post)coloniality, discourses of market and democracy currently appropriate the rhetoric of public debates in Eastern Europe—further confirming the racialized/gendered/sexualized silences that are prerequisites to building and maintaining nation-states (Eisenstein, *Hatreds*, 43). As Eisenstein writes, "Democracy, when used on behalf of nationalist rhetoric, allows racism to flourish. In many of the east european post-communist nations, freedom of speech has allowed hatred toward jews, roma, and other ethnic minorities to be spoken openly" (49).

This is not to say, of course, that one should simply substitute "ethnicity" for "race." "Ethnicity" is useful in that, in contrast to "race," it implies the constructedness of the subjectivites and identities it describes (Hall 1997, 378). Ethnicity is "fictive" (Balibar 1991, 96) in the sense that it is continually crossed and reinvented by racial, linguistic, class, gender, sexual, religious, and other identities. However, as Stuart Hall argues, this constructedness is a double-edged sword. It can usefully shift a politics of race from the assumption of essentialist racial homogeneity to a politics of solidarity based on the recognition of differences within ethnic groups—as Hall's study of the emergent British "new ethnicities" demonstrates (Hall 1997, 378–79). However, in order to employ ethnicity in the interests of racialized minorities, the notion of ethnicity needs to be "decoupled" from the way it functions in the dominant discourses of the state, from "its equivalence with nationalism, imperialism, racism": discourses that have taken advantage of the flexibility of "ethnicity" in order to disavow the realities of racism (379).

In postimperial and postcolonial cultures of the third world, where the realities of racial difference and racism have been impossible to disavow in the long run, the shift in cultural politics from "natural" racial identities to provisional ethnic positionalities has been engaged and discussed for decades. In Eastern Europe and studies of Eastern Europe, however, where racism has survived fossilized under the surface of "ethnic" and "national" relations, a similar shift has not taken place. Therefore, in order for racialized minorities, most prominently the Roma, to decolonize the "ethnic" label imposed on them, and transform themselves into Hall-style "new ethnicities" on the non-innocent ground of differences within similarities, it seems necessary for them to come into representation first. Their status of the stereotyped other needs to be acknowledged and analyzed in terms of political and economic injustice, which has been carried on for centuries with the help of racist representations. And conversely, the invisibility of the dominant national minorities, grounded in the assumption of the absolute superiority of "whiteness," needs to be foregrounded within a wide range of cultural representations.

The dichotomies that sustain primordial nationalisms and perpetuate the hegemony and moral transparency of whiteness have begun to be eroded in the process of the transition from state socialism to global capitalism, from resistant nationalism to transnational neocolonialism, from the terror of European, white, male high culture to the terror of American popular culture. The cohesion of the nation-state and the validity of nationalism are under attack by transnational flows of immigrants and images. As elsewhere in the world, in Eastern Europe the "national genie" is becoming "increasingly unrestrained by ideas of spatial boundary and territorial sovereignty," where "key identities and identifications now only partially revolve around the realities and images of place" (Appadurai 1993, 413–14). This situation is bound to expose contradictions in the nation-state's claim to authenticity, and unsettle the unspoken racialized hierarchy of nationalism.

Whiteness and The Romans

The most formidable challenge to the invisible support that whiteness has provided East European nationalisms has come from the changing situation of the Romani. The Romani, or Gypsies,[8] have come to play a complex role in the processes of the postcommunist transition. On the one hand, the insecurity of postauthoritarian societies has induced a search for scapegoats, often reviving dormant or unacknowledged racial prejudice (Pók 1998, 531–33). The Romani have made for perfect scapegoats: They have lived in East European states for centuries, maintaining their diverse diasporas and resisting nation-formation and assimilation to the majority nation[9] (Hancock 2001), while the majority of them lack economic and political power. Longing for pure, ethnocentrically based national identities (Salecl 1994, 20; Ravetto 1998, 43), post-socialist East European states have leveled unparalleled discrimination and violence against Gypsies.[10] In the general atmosphere of nationalist revival, the Roma communities' "transnational" character has continued to be stigmatized as nomadic and backward.[11] At the same time, the desired European Union membership and the relative accessibility of Roma-related state policies to foreign media make the East European state more vulnerable and accountable than it was before. It is clear that the serene, European, democratic national front that the state attempts to present is, precisely, a front, which covers up boiling racial tension within the nation.

The white, national majority's relationship with Romani minorities is fraught with contradictions that threaten to expose the unstable boundaries of East European nationalisms. The post-1989 backlash against East European Roma is a symptom of the inevitable realization that nationalism is becoming obsolete under the pressure of the transnational, and that its crucial component, racial purity, is an illusory construction. Violently distancing themselves from Gypsies is an effort by "true" East Europeans to deny their own impurity, the fact that they are often equated with Gypsies in the West.[12] Part of the reason why East Europeans treat the Roma as exoticized and pre-civilized creatures is that they are treated as "Gypsies" by the Western media.[13] At the same time, the Canadian authorities discovered in the early 1990s that "white" Hungarians were posing as Gypsies in order to be granted refugee status in Canada, which the Hungarian prime minister simply denied ("Hungarians" 2000). This is an utterly ironic proof of the fragility and even the reversibility of the rigid racial hierarchy that nationalism constructs, in the post–cold war era of global mobility.

Comparing Hungarian and Gypsy narratives of origin yields further, ironic proof that nations are not products of natural destinies rooted in language, race, soil, or religion (Appadurai, "Patriotism," 414). Both tribes derive from Asia, migrated westwards, mixed genes and languages with those of many other tribes along the way, and eventually settled in Eastern Europe. In addition, although some Gypsies have more distinctive ethnic features, many are physically indistinguishable from Hungarians. Some scholars maintain that, genetically, Gypsies today are predominantly European.[14] Hungarian nationalism, however, simply disavows these similarities and turns differences into evidences of two diametrically opposed kinds of national characters.

The precise details of the travels of the nomadic tribes who could be considered the ancestors of Hungarians—such as the site of the "ancient homeland" or the identity of linguistic relatives—are still a matter of myth and ongoing debate. Of course, the factual value of these arguments is not as important as the political profit that national elites can gain from the idea of such spectacular progress from Asia to Europe. As opposed to the *myth* of national origin, which is concerned with the long journey through Eurasia, the official *history* of the Hungarian nation as such begins "precisely" in AD 896, with the European settlement of the tribes. Hungarian historiography has focused on the European performance of Hungarians (see László 1981). The contrast between the pre-civilized Asian past and the progressive European past (and future) of the nation has been naturalized not only through the sexual division between active men and passive women, but also through a literal adoption of and insistence on what Anne McClintock calls the "Family Tree of Nations," an essential part of the ideological foundation of European imperialism:

> In the image of the Family Tree, evolutionary progress was represented as a series of anatomically distinct family types organized into a linear procession, from the "childhood" of "primitive" races to the enlightened "adulthood" of European imperial nationalism. ... The merging of the racial evolutionary Tree and the gendered family into the Family Tree of Man provided scientific racism with a simultaneously gendered and racial image through which it could popularize the idea of linear national Progress. (McClintock 1995, 359)

Since national consciousness, throughout Eastern Europe, has been closely tied to the fate of the national language, the debates about the origins of the Hungarian language have been saturated with the racial politics of nationalism. An early historian of the language claimed that Hungarian "united the bold figurative character of the East with the sobriety of the West" (Sherwood 1996, 27). The "Turkish-Finnish war" of the late nineteenth century divided intellectuals and the general public alike as to which linguistic kinship would be more desirable to establish. The Finno-Ugric family of languages is frequently represented by a tree model that bears a conspicuous similarity to the Family Tree of Man: It ranks related languages according to the extent of their westward progress. The group that made it the farthest from the Asian steppes are unquestionably the Hungarians, with the Finns as second best (see Benkö and Imre 1972; Engel 1990, 27–49; László 1981).[15] The "temporal anomaly" within nationalism— "veering between nostalgia for the past and the impatient, progressive sloughing off of the past" (McClintock, 358–59) thus implies a sense of natural superiority to cultures to the east of Hungary, which compensates for an equally strong sense of inferiority toward cultures in Western Europe.

The "tribal," "nomadic," "Asian" part of the Hungarian national story is represented, retroactively, as at once a mythical resource and a conscious preparation for the founding event of the nation: the "Settlement." It was territorial conquest that began the magical transformation of nomadic tribes into a unified nation. The claiming and defending of the territory are precisely the acts that supposedly make all Hungarians inherently superior to all Gypsies, since the latter have never had a serious interest in forming nation-states. Since the Gypsies' plight was never glorified by the sacred act of "settlement," which would have transformed them from "tribe" into "nation," they can only be represented in pejorative, deeply prejudiced ways in the Eurocentric language of modern nationalisms. Since Hungarians and Gypsies share vague, nomadic origins and the "trope of the tribe" (Appadurai, "Patriotism," 422–23), Hungarian nationalism has to insist on the act of territorial settlement as a distinctive event, and on locking Gypsies into stereotypes that characterize them as "still" nomadic,[16] backward, and genetically averse to "progress." Furthermore, while Hungarian national ideology regards the genetic heterogeneity of the nation as scientific proof of its "strength," Gypsies' genetic and cultural heterogeneity is considered proof of degeneration, inability to achieve collective stability.

The Romans as Gypsy

There is a special urgency to looking at the situation of Gypsies through the lens of critical theories of representation. Even more than in the case of other marginal or minority groups, the reality of Gypsy life is overshadowed by stereotypes of Gypsies throughout the world. Gypsies exist for most people as pickpockets, musicians, or fairy tale characters, invariably associated with dark powers or, at best, a simple, easy life unfettered by the responsibilities of the modern citizen. As Ian Hancock puts it,

> Just as no one would question the fear of trolls and goblins or argue for their rights, the fear of Gypsies likewise goes unchallenged. … [B]ecause of a history of exclusion of Roma from education and because of cultural restrictions on greater integration of Roma in the mainstream, the Gypsy image has taken on a life of its own and Romani populations have been administered and studied through the filter of that image. (Hancock)

According to György Kerényi, in Hungary, "the half million Roma exist only as a people with a Gypsy existence and identity. Being a Gypsy is an exclusive and indelible mark, which allows no other role" (Kerényi 1999, 147). Nationalist and racist stereotypes of Gypsies in Eastern Europe—and else-where—are wrapped in the images of the subhuman, and thus manage to evade ideological critique. It is impossible to reestablish the often severed connections between the socioeconomic and the cultural spheres without taking seriously representations of Gypsies.

Postcommunist film and media have shown a revived interest in the image of the Gypsy.[17] In Hungary alone, since 1989, nineteen feature and documentary films have been produced with Gypsy-related topics, whereas during the three decades between 1960 and 1989 only nine were made altogether ("Roma-filmek" 1999). These films fall into two broad categories: one consists of documentaries of Gypsy life, which intend to "bring silenced voices to the center of the debate" (Portuges, 197) and wish to "correct the record" (Iordanova 2001, 3). András Salamon's *Városlakók* (1997), which depicts the ordeals of urban Gypsies within a white majority, or Tamás Almási's *Meddö* (1995) about helpless, unemployed Gypsy communities in the north of Hungary, are outstanding examples. However, the majority of these films have not been made by Romani filmmakers (Iordanova 2001, 3). Most of them unavoidably approach their subject with the questions, and often the answers, of the white majority. In a similar vein, even though issues of Romani minorities have recently had more exposure in the dominant news media than before, "the representation of Gypsies is dominated by conflicts: unemployment, crime, and other social problems" (Gyurkovics 1999, 22).

Representations in the second category revive the romanticized image of the free-spirited, childish Gypsy (Iordanova 2001, 3). Hancock notes the recent increase in the representation of the Gypsy as an illiterate, inarticulate buffoon on Bulgarian, Romanian, or Slovakian television screens. Like turn-of-the century black and white minstrels in America, such characters are played by white people, and they help maintain a status quo that invariably renders the Roma figures of fun (Hancock). The Gypsy as the "dancing slave" has been recently reinvented in Hungary as well. While Gypsy characters are indispensable to popular jokes and cabarets—mostly representing the simple-minded petty criminal—they have no part to play in soap operas, talk shows, or commercials, where dominant cultural values of the nation are reflected, created, and confirmed (Kerényi 1999, 147).

Most of the recent "Gypsy" films are populated by what Erzsébet Bori appropriately calls "screen Gypsies" (Bori 1998):

> Screen Gypsies—in contrast with real ones, who are as heterogeneous in their language and history as in their lifestyles and values—are quite alike all over the world: their souls are made of songs, and their hearts are made of gold; they live in picturesque and photogenic poverty, and survive on the surface of ice; they fear God and the police, because their passionate temperament and indestructible vitality make them prone to violating the Ten Commandments and state laws. (Bori 53)

Films about screen Gypsies draw on the international romantic stereotypes of "Gypsy freedom, music, flower-patterned skirts, wild emotions, and horses" (Rádai 1999, 21)—images that have very little to do with the recent past of actual East European Roma, and nothing to do with their present. The recent renaissance of the romanticized, vagrant Gypsy in Hungary is a mimicry of Western stereotypes and a commercial attempt to market Hungarian cultural products.

However, instead of distinguishing Gypsy and non-Gypsy cultures, images of "screen Gypsies" further confuse the two in the eyes of the West. This is especially true in Hungary, where the Roma constitute more than 5 percent of the population (Barany 1998, 322). Gypsy music is a touristic emblem of Hungarian culture, and the Western media portray the "Wild East" as Hungarians portray Gypsies (Portuges, 198).[18]

The film *Romani kris* (*Gypsy Law*) (dir. Bence Gyöngyössy, 1997), made in German-Hungarian-Bulgarian co-production, received Hungary's feature film nomination for the Oscar, and was awarded a First Film Prize at the 1997 Montreal Film Festival. With a shrewdly calculated marketing strategy, it combines Gypsy romanticism with the captivating story and the high cultural credentials of *King Lear*. It takes place within a Roma community somewhere in Hungary, at an undefined time during the last fifty years. Most of the story unfolds in retrospect, as remembered by the aging Gypsy patriarch Lovér/Lear, played by Djoko Rosic. Lovér is an exile in the present, wondering around with his faithful companion Tamáska, the sensitive and musically-inclined village fool, looking for his youngest daughter to ask for her forgiveness before he dies.

The retrospective narrative begins in an idyllic extended family environment that does not resemble any actual Gypsy community during communism. Gypsies are one with nature; the music never stops, and grandfather is full of fantastic stories to tell the children. The trouble starts when a "white man from town" arrives with the order that, in the name of modernization, the Gypsies need to move into town. In a moment of collective passion, "typical" of hot-blooded Gypsies, Lovér murders the urban messenger. The crime is temporarily covered up, but the murderer is tortured by his own conscience, which is embodied in his youngest and most honest daughter, Sarolta, a stunning "Gypsy beauty" with long dark hair and a natural talent for dancing. Sarolta refuses to dance for her father at his birthday party—a drawn-out, fully exoticized Gypsy celebration—foreshad-owing the troubles that will inevitably strike as a result of breaking the law. And so the story continues until the father has been punished enough to be redeemed, and to be reunited with the "good" Sarolta. As a Hungarian review says, *Romani kris* is a not-too-original fairy tale at its best, and kitsch at its worst: "What does it have to do with Gypsies, what does it want from them, and what does it want to say about, or through them? (And to whom?) It is not a good enough reason that this is what the world is interested in right now" (Bori, 53).

Even more interesting are those films that romanticize Gypsy characters to continue a tradition in which Gypsies are used as allegorical expressions of the nation. In this case, although allegory is intended to set up a barrier between Gypsies and the "real" nation, the analogical connection still calls attention to the similarities between the two groups and leaves these films open to deconstructive critique. One of the seminal texts of this tradition is the epic allegorical poem *"A nagyidai cigányok"* ("The Gypsies of Nagyida"), written by cherished nineteenth-century poet János Arany. The poem satirically commemorates the failed revolution of 1848, venting a bitter disappoint-ment about the humiliated ideas of national independence, which many leading intel-lectuals of the times shared. While the poem blames Hungarians themselves for the failure of nationalism, the guilt is projected into Gypsy characters. They are full of high ideals, but action remains limited to talking about dreams and to satisfying bodily needs. The critical revival of *"A nagyidai cigányok"* in the 1990s cannot be a coincidence, considering the current and similarly frustrated transitional moment. Both moments call for Gypsy characters to carry the disavowed, undesirable features of the Hungarian nation, and, thereby symbolically purify "real," that is, white, Hungarians. In a recent Hungarian deconstructionist conference, devoted entirely to the interpretation of *"A nagyidai cigányok,"* several papers hinted at the historical parallel, but none of them reflected on the political implications of inventing and appropriating images of a racialized ethnic group in order to achieve an intellectual-national catharsis.[19]

A number of recent Hungarian films cast Gypsy or other racialized characters in order to reflect on the changing portrait of the nation or the changing role of the national intellectual. Livia Szederkényi's award-winning feature film, *Paramicha* (1993) is an avowedly "intellectual" film. Szederkényi explains how she searched for years to find the right protagonist, who could be the filmmaker's, or, in general, the intel-lectual's, mirror. Szederkényi says she had tried to find somebody through whom she could "understand herself":

> And, suddenly, it occurred to me that [this character] must be Chinese. Because I needed someone who is just there. Here. Simply. And you can see him. And

then I remembered Gauguin, and why he went where he did, and then it became clear where I needed to go. I don't know why it had taken me so long; it was so evident. ... (Csáky 1994, 16)

This logic led Szederkényi to an old Gypsy man in a small village, who appeared perfect for the role.

On a small scale, Szederkényi reproduces the process of the imperialist self-construction of whiteness "on the backs of equally constructed Others" (Stam and Spence, 636). The fact that she thought of a Chinese character first betrays Orientalist reflexes, which are "second nature" to Hungarian intellectuals. Szederkényi sees a certain analogy between the Chinese and Gypsies, but this realization does not compel her to examine her own position, which is analogical to that of a European imperialist.[20] The only factor that decides in favor of a Roma character is his geographical closeness, which supposedly increases his "knowability." It is significant that Gauguin's modernist self-exile from European civilization to Tahiti serves as the vehicle for the analogy: the reference to modernist high culture automatically ensures political immunity. One is reminded, again, of hooks's claim that whiteness is a cultural value intimately bonded to the aesthetics of European high culture.[21]

If Gypsies exist predominantly as "images" in the cultural fabric (Hancock), it is evident that improving the alarming situation of the Romani is contingent on confronting harmful stereotypes. It is not so clear how to go about this, however. Hancock suggests that "in order for things to change, the Gypsy image must be deconstructed and replaced by a more accurate one—in the bureaucratic structures as well as in the textbooks" (Hancock 2001). But this corrective impulse faces the same danger that Cosby's corrective impulse faces in the case of media representations of African Americans. How does one draw the line between "accurate" and "positive" images? And how does one aim for accuracy in the case of such a diverse and dispersed group?

These are crucial questions, since the media has become a mirror in which white majority and Gypsy minority see each other. In the emerging discussion about ethnic representation in the media, the example of American multicultural representation recurs. "White" (and almost by definition, male) politicians, sociologists, journalists, and filmmakers seem to agree that the American way of "positive discrimination"—allowing images of Gypsies on the screen, and encouraging Romani cultural productions—is irrelevant to Hungarian circumstances, if not harmful (Turcsányi 2000). The arguments warn of the dangers of "mixing the aesthetic with the political"[22] and privileging skin color over talent. Most transparent of all, some think it is impossible for Gypsies to represent themselves in the media, since very few of them have learned the profession, and those who have lost their Romani identity in the process of necessary assimilation (Rádai, 20). In other words, Gypsies are to blame if they do not assimilate in order to learn media trades, but it is also their fault if they do assimilate and cease to be "authentic" Gypsies.[23]

Even in the liberal press, which claims to be more sympathetic to Roma concerns, descriptions of the Romani's situation often implicitly blame the victim. "Positive" articles—headed by titles such as "Gypsies Get Down to Work"—often simply reinforce negative stereotypes by presenting the "good," "civilized" Roma as the exception to the rule (Kerényi, 146).

The problem with striving for representational accuracy is that it perpetuates racial essentialism. While my purpose has been to make race visible as a category that has silently underlined and supported racism, I am aware that stopping at the point of reinstalling "race" would fix ethnic minorities in their subordinate positions. How does one separate race and racism without reproducing the latter's essentialism in the former? Race is an essentially racist category: it is a product of racism and, as such, it inevitably carries racist assumptions and structures. For this reason, Paul Gilroy calls for a rethinking of the politics of antiracist theorizing and antiracist activism. Gilroy claims that the usefulness of race as an analytical category has come to an end because of the profound transformations that have taken place in the last few decades in the way the body is understood, largely as a result of the emergence of molecular biology, digital processing, and other technologies (Gilroy 1998, 840):

> These new ways of seeing, understanding and relating to our selves point to the possibility that the time of "race" may be coming to a close. This possibility brings new dangers, but it also brings new hope to a situation in which, as Zygmunt Bauman has argued persuasively, a task-oriented relation to the corporeal constitutes the primal scene of postmodernity as an emergent sociological formation in the overdeveloped world. (840)

Gilroy is aware of the polemical nature of his argument, especially of the charge that renouncing "race" might be interpreted as a betrayal of the antiracist solidarities achieved precisely in the name of racial connections. However, as he points out, the taken-for-granted bond between antiracist activism and intellectual work on race has significantly changed in the last twenty years, not the least due to the intervention of corporate multi-culturalism and its cultures of simulation, which have reevaluated racial difference on a commercial basis (842–43). Gilroy asks academics working in Ethnic and Racial Studies to reexamine their professional interests, the degree of their possible complicity in the reification of racial difference (842). The same questions can and should be asked of academics working in East European Studies, and of politicians involved in decisions concerning ethnicity and race in Eastern Europe. I consider the category of "race" to be of limited, temporary usefulness only. It is indispensable to foregrounding the racist violence of "innocent" ethnic and national representations, but it will always remain complicit in the processes that justify racist violence.

It seems that those forms of Romani self-representation that have had the most political impact are less concerned with racial essentialism and correct images, but, instead represent Gypsy "authenticity" in new, hybrid, transnational and multicultural forms. These forms foreground how "whiteness" and "the national" are naturalized in the aesthetics sanctioned by dominant culture. "Roma rap," for instance, initiated by the Gypsy group *Fekete Vonat* ("Black Train"), may be characterized as the Roma's own, ironic use of global media. Like the Irish working-class musicians of *The Commitments* (1991, d. Alan Parker), who play soul and call themselves "the blacks of Europe," *Fekete Vonat* draws on images and sounds associated with African Americans for self-representation. While members of the group do not disavow the stereotype that Romani have music in their veins, *Fekete Vonat*—and the Gypsy groups that have sprung up in their wake—defy canonized and commercialized "Gypsy music" by mixing various musical styles as well as languages, including Romani. Roma rap is at once part of global cultural expression and specific to the "local Harlem," the 8th district of Budapest (Fáy 1999, 24). Their lyrics, which embed racial politics in humor and irony, address white and Gypsy audiences alike. Members of *Fekete Vonat* say in an interview: "Our lyrics talk about our problems as Gypsies, and the problems of Gypsy people in general. This is one of the things that makes this music Roma rap. … We also try to attack everyday racism, and throw back in the gadjes'[24] face what they say about us, Roma" ("Roma rap," my translation).

Many Romani musicians have successfully entered the international music scene recently. Ironically, this has increased their popularity and respectability in Eastern Europe.[25] Roma rap is becoming part of the "world beat" which, Arjun Appadurai claims, is an excellent example of "fundamentally postnational and diasporic" cultural forms ("Patriotism," 426), and is a very different response to global media imperialism than the defensive refusal of globalization by the nationalistic Hungarian cultural elite. Roma rap resembles the cannibalistic, carnivalistic aesthetic of many third world groups, which "pick through capitalist leavings, and use them ironically as a strategy of resistance" (Shohat and Stam, 307–309).

Paris-based Romani filmmaker Tony Gatlif's film *Latcho Drom* (1993) is a similar attempt at subverting stereotypes without didacticism. *Latcho Drom*, which means "Safe Journey," is a film without dialogue. It traces the history of Romani migration from northern India through North Africa and Eastern Europe to Spain through musical vignettes, which feature many different Gypsy groups and musical styles against changing backdrops. It is an ironic history conveyed through music, which mocks narratives of origin designed to confer authenticity on people and places. The strength of Gypsy identity, according to Gatlif, is precisely the Gypsies' ability to survive across great diversity.

Many Gypsy intellectuals and scholars of Gypsy culture claim that the time of the Gypsies has arrived at the beginning of the millennium. One reason for this is exactly that Gypsies are not obsessed with national mythologies, with absolute collective roots. It is true that most Gypsies are not in a position to invent their own identities freely, either. Yet the transnational nature of Gypsy communities foreshadows a "new type of community," for which there is yet no vocabulary (Vajda and Kende, 2000). There is no proper terminology available, because

> [a]lthough many antistate movements revolve around images of homeland, of soil, of place, and of return from exile, these images reflect the poverty of their (and our) political languages rather than the hegemony of territorial nationalism. Put another way, no idiom has yet emerged to capture the collective interest of many groups in translocal solidarities, cross-border mobilizations, and postnational identities. Such interests are many and local, but they are still entrapped in the linguistic imaginary of the territorial state. (Appadurai, "Patriotism," 418)

Although, in the lack of new vocabulary, East European "territorial states" are currently trying to force the Romani into the vicious cycle of opposing ethnocentrism with ethnocentrism, such attempts have not been too successful. More and more Gypsy intellectuals emerge who are more likely to embrace antiessentialist and anti-nationalist paradigms (Vajda and Kende). Even if positing a common origin and emphasizing a common language will be necessary to come into representation and gain legitimacy within the current hegemony of the nation-state (Hancock), the Romani's outsider position and great linguistic and cultural diversity will constantly undermine the legitimacy of the nation-state as we know it. Most white Hungarians continue to despise, fear, and exclude from the nation real Roma, but romanticize them in movies that they hope to distribute on the global market. In this contradictory process, Hungarians undermine their own effort to protect the traditional boundaries of nation and ethnicity. Conversely, when some Roma reject identities imposed on them by dominant society—those of the victim, the criminal, and the romantic savage—and recreate their "authentic" culture in hybrid images and sounds, they affirm antiessentialist identities with the strategies of *mestizaje* and *creolité* in Caribbean and Latin American cinemas: strategies with which "marginalized groups try to find leaks in the systems of representation and turn them into floods" (Shohat and Stam, 316).

East European ethnocentrisms and nationalisms are permeated by such leaks. The geographical, political, and economic instability and inferiority of the region has nurtured a desperate insistence on primordialisms. The fact that the operation of racial and racist categories is invariably effaced at state and individual levels alike is a sign that the naturalness of these categories is highly unstable. In the current time of transformation, ethnic and racial representations are extremely vulnerable to contestations, to revelations that they perform, and not faithfully reflect, reality. My ultimate goal in this chapter has been to contest the often spontaneously unraveling biological essentialisms inherent in the discursive performances of white supremacy. They provide prime examples for Appadurai's claim that the invention of tradition and ethnicity becomes a slippery search for certainties, and is regularly frustrated by the fluidities of transnational communication ("Disjuncture," 325). The new global culture is not unequivocally beneficial, since it has also brought new refugee-flows and ethnocide. But for East European Roma, even if the state retains control over access to political rights and economic opportunities, global culture provides formerly unavailable cultural outlets for the expansion of suppressed hope, and nurtures fantasies that implicitly question the primacy of the national.[26] The introduction of new theoretical models will help reveal the extent to which the reigning old models are appropriated by intellectuals and the state in the service of a white, nationalistic majority. New models will hopefully begin to liberate such studies from the "shackles of highly localized, boundary-oriented, holistic, primordialist images of cultural form and substance" (335).

Notes

[1] See for instance Connelly, 1997; "From Bad"; Solimano and Mori 2000; Lawday 1991; Bade and Anderson 1997; and Bering-Jensen 1993.

[2] The Habsburg Monarchy was rather parochial, uninterested in the acquisition of distant territories (Anderson, 107).

[3] For a detailed discussion of cultural nationalism (as opposed to "political nationalism"), see Hutchinson 1987, especially 12–19 and 30–36.

[4] I rely on Edward Said's distinction between "imperialism" and "colonialism." Said considers the two related terms with different emphases: Colonialism, "the implanting of settlements on distant territory," is almost always the consequence of the imperialism. "In our time, direct colonialism has largely ended; imperialism ... lingers where it has always been, in a kind of general cultural sphere as well as in specific political, ideological, economic, and social practices" (*Culture*, 9).

5 Similar to its imperial model, East European white supremacy has sought proof of its power in unchanging mirrors of racial others. But the instability of Eastern Europe's geographical position has had to be counterbalanced by the idealization of Europe—the tower of civilization—on one side, and the projection of backward, exotic Asia on the other. The Hungarian language, similar to other East European languages, abundantly reflects this racialized geography: "European" is the synonym of "modern, civilized," while "Asian" connotes "primitive" and "uncivilized." See Iordanova's "Balkans," which reflects on a similar use of "Europe" in the Balkans.

6 Along a different division, women and femininity have represented the "love" of nation—or the nation in its most lovable, European form. Hate, however, has been transferred to racialized outsiders to the east and south, and within the nation (Eisenstein, *Hatreds*, 51–52).

7 The implication of East European nationalisms in the discourses of imperialism, colonialism, and racism is an almost entirely unexplored area for research. Such research would examine the "vast colonial intertext" and "widely disseminated set of discursive practices" in which colonialist representation is rooted (Stam and Spence, 636) in Eastern Europe. The communist era would be a treasure house of such research: not only had European civilization not ceased to be the object of desire and the only credible source of information about other cultures, but it had become particularly valued precisely because the connections with Europe were severely restricted and monitored by the state. At the same time, the state maintained a peaceful symbiosis between communist internationalism and Eurocentric nationalism.

8 "Convening in London in 1971, the first World Romany Congress condemned ethnic appellations traditionally applied to Gypsy groups, including cziany, Gypsy, gitano, and zigeuner, adopting instead "Roma" or "Rom" as a self-chosen ethnonym (Kurti, qtd. in Portuges n.d., 201). While this is an important step, it does not automatically erase the difficulty of naming without perpetuating prejudices. In Hungary, both "roma" and "cigány" are such prejudiced names. Romany groups use both as self-designation. See also Tanaka, and Hancock.

9 East European states offered the Romani only one option: to transform themselves into an obedient "national" or "ethnic" minority and copy the progressive model of their "Europeanized" mother-nations. The Romani's continuing refusal to assimilate to the white national majority amounts to a rejection of the claim that nation forming following the European model is the only enlightened progressive prospect for a group. For centuries, Gypsies have managed to maintain their smaller, non-national community affiliations within various nation-states and refused to adopt the monolithic racial and racist categories which dominant discourses had tried to impose on them.

10 Since 1989, news of atrocities committed against East European Roma proliferated: an innocent Romani woman was beaten to death in front of her children in Slovakia (Johnson 2000). A Czech city built a wall to separate Romani homes from Czech ones (Johnson). A Hungarian high school organized a segregated graduation ceremony for its Romani students (Kerényi 1999, 143). Daily examples of police brutality, prejudiced education, unlawful evictions, and various other forms of blatant discrimination abound.

11 In Hungary, as in most East European socialist states, the anti-Gypsy campaign started as early as the 1980s, when the socialist order was about to collapse and unemployment and inflation appeared to be increasingly menacing realities. The media, in service of the state, were instrumental in trying to rebuild a crumbling national unity by representing the Roma in terms of age-old negative stereotypes (Kerényi 142).

12 Recently, the Romanian Ministry of Foreign Affairs issued a memorandum, which advises all public officers to address all Romani as "Tigani," or Gypsies, despite the pejorative connotations of the word, and despite the fact that Gypsy organizations identify themselves by other nonpejorative names such as Rom, Romani, or Rromani. The government does not hide the fact that the motivation behind the memorandum is to prevent the confusion of Romanians with Rroma. "Romania's reputation" is at stake in the eyes of the world. See Tanaka.

13 As Catherine Portuges writes, hatred of Gypsies unites Eastern and Western Europe. See Portuges 212.

14 Werner Cohn, Wim Willems, and Judith Okely, for instance. See Hancock.

15 See some of the authorative books on the history of Hungarians and the Hungarian language. (Benkö and Imre 1972; Engel 1990; László 1981.)

16 The stereotype of the vagrant Gypsy still flourishes, even though only about 5 percent of the entire Gypsy population in Europe (estimated between 7 and 8.5 million) lead an itinerant life (Tanaka 2000).

17 Some of the films that have earned international recognition are *Time of the Gypsies* (1989, dir. Emir Kusturica); *Montenegro* (1981, dir. Dusan Makavejev); and *Latcho Drom* ("Safe Journey") (1993, dir. Tony Gatlif). Dina Iordanova provides a detailed account of postcommunist "Gypsy" films in her book, *Cinema of Flames* (2001, 213–34).

18 For instance, in the classic Hollywood film, *Golden Earrings* (Mitchell Leisen, 1947), Marlene Dietrich plays a seductive and wild, vagrant Hungarian-Gypsy woman, true to the exotic stereotype. Another well-known example is *The Wolf Man* (1941), which features (the Hungarian) Bela Lugosi, a Gypsy called "Bela," who turns into a werewolf. The ease with which the West collapses Hungarian and Gypsy cultures into one would shock most Hungarians.

19 For a representative analysis, see Müllner 1998.

20 Of course, this is not to say that modernist art is by definition imperialist. On this question see Said and Burgmer 2000, 7.

21 *Csajok* (*Bitches*, 1993), a film made in a German-Hungarian co-production by the Hungarian Ildikó Szabó, shows admirable sensitivity to its three female protagonists, but has no qualms about representing racialized characters in the most stereotypical light—predominantly for comic effect. The film portrays sometimes mercilessly naturalistic, at other times widely unrealistic, tragicomic moments from the lives of three women who try to escape from failed marriages. While most characters are on the verge of insanity, from the women's points of view, men appear especially driven by uncontrolled emotions. Most of the men are simultaneously violent and childish. Interestingly, this combination of features is frequently represented by racialized alter-egos that the men invent for themselves. Enikö's lover, for instance, imagines that he is an Indian chief, and he expects everyone to participate in his grossly exoticized, Hollywood-style fantasy. In a similarly oversimplified flash, we see a group of half-naked, "tribal" Africans drumming away in the small apartment of Juli's parents. We know so little about the inhabitants of the household that the Africans convey only a sense of irrationality. But the most revealing instance of representational violence is a long scene in which Barbara, a young actress, takes Enikö and Juli to a Gypsy celebration. It is hinted that Barbara herself is of Gypsy origin, because she knows her way around, and has romantic ties with the "Gypsy king," a tall and powerful man with a parodically long moustache and an excessively colorful shirt. While Enikö and Dorka drink and watch, Barbara, who is carried away by Gypsy romanticism and alcohol, begins a ritual, erotic dance with the man. The dancing ritual leads to a mating ritual, to which the film only alludes. In the next scene, Barbara awakens sober and in disbelief, runs home—to her drunken husband—and frantically cleanses herself in the bathtub, in disgust. It is unmistakable, and presented by the film with sympathy, that she has undergone a maturing process in which she, the actress living in her various roles, has been forced to separate dreams from reality. The "other Gypsy" that she saw through the cloud of alcohol was the material of dreams, while the reality is the racial contamination that she tries to get rid of.

22 This is a conspicuously hypocritical claim, since East European art of the last fifty years has been saturated with national politics. It is obvious that the minority politics of ethnicity is not considered of the same weight and value as the politics of the nation.

23 There are practically no Roma faces on television or among the producers of TV programs. "If a foreigner ignorant of East European matters were asked to watch Hungarian television—except for the news—for a while, he wouldn't have the slightest idea that there are Gypsies living in this country" (Gyurkovics, 23).

24 A Gypsy term for white people.

25 A review of an international musical festival, held in Budapest in August 2000, notes that most of the Hungarian participants were Roma. It also predicts that, similar to many of their predecessors, some of these Romani musicians will end up with contracts with well-known Western groups. Klezmatics. "Filmszakadásig." *Magyar Narancs*, 30 December 2000: 27.

26 "The critical point is that both sides of the coin of global culture today are products of the infinitely varied mutual contest of sameness and difference on a stage characterized by radical disjunctures between different sorts of global cultural flows and the uncertain landscapes created in and through these disjunctions" (Appadurai, "Disjuncture," 334).

References

Alexander, Jacqui, and Sandra Mohanty, eds. 1997. *Feminist genealogies*. New York: Routledge.

Anderson, Benedict. 1992. *Imagined communities: Reflections on the origin and spread of nationalism*. London: Verso.

Appadurai, Arjun. 1993. Patriotism and its futures. *Public Culture* 5:411–29.

___. 1994. Disjuncture and difference in the global cultural economy. In *Colonial discourse and postcolonial theory*, ed. Patrick Williams and Laura Chrisman, 324–39. New York: Columbia University Press.

Bade, Klaus J., and Lieselotte Anderson. 1994. Immigration and social peace in united Germany. *Daedalus* 123, no. 1: 85–97.

Balibar, Etienne. 1991. The nation form: History and ideology. In *Race, Nation, Class*, ed. Etienne Balibar and Immanuel Wallerstein, 86–105. London: Verso.

Barany, Zoltan. 1998. Ethnic mobilization and the state: The Roma in Eastern Europe. *Ethnic and Racial Studies* 21, no. 2: 308–27.

Benkö, Loránd, and Samu Imre, eds. 1972. *The Hungarian language*. Paris: Mouton.

Bering-Jensen, Henrik. 1993. A flood of strangers in estranged lands: Neo-Nazi attacks on refugees and foreigners in Germany. *Insight on the News* 9, no. 1: 6–14.

Bori, Erzsébet. 1998. *Vászoncigányok* (Screen gypsies). *Filmvilág* 41, no. 10: 53.

Brinker-Gabler, ed. N.d. *Writing new identities*. N.p.

Cohen, Richard. 20–27 July 1998. Camille Cosby's complaint. *The Washington Post Weekly*, 26.

The Commitments. 1991. Alan Parker, director. Paramount.

Connelly, Joel. 14 January 1997. In Eastern Europe, new gains vie with old ways. *Seattle Post-Intelligencer*, A5.

Cosby, Camille. 8 July 1998. America taught my son's killer to hate blacks. *USA Today*, 15A.

Anikó Imre

Csajok (Bitches). 1993a. Ildikó Szabó, director. Hungary/Germany.

Csáky, M. Caliban. 1994. *Van* (There is). *Filmvilág* 37, no. 9: 15–19.

Csepeli, György. 1991. Competing patterns of national identity in postcommunist Hungary. *Media, Culture, and Society* 13: 325–339.

Dissanayake, Wimal. 1994. Introduction: Nationhood, history, and cinema: Reflections on the Asian scene. In *Colonialism and nationalism in Asian cinema*, ed. Wimal Dissanayake, ix–xxix. Bloomington: Indiana University Press.

Eisenstein, Zillah. 1996. *Hatreds: Racialized and sexualized conflicts in the twenty-first century*. New York: Routledge.

Engel, Pál. 1990. *Beilleszkedés Európába a kezdetektöl 1440-ig* (Europeanization, from the beginnings to 1440). Budapest: Háttér Kiadó.

Fáy, Miklós. 1999. Mit ér a vér, miszter fehér? (What is your blood worth, Mr. White?). *Filmvilág* 42, no. 1: 24.

Frankenberg, Ruth, ed. and Intro. 1997. Introduction: local whitenesses, localizing whiteness. In *Displaying whiteness: Essays in cultural criticism*, 1–33. Durham: Duke University Press.

Gates. Nathaniel, ed. 1997. *Cultural and literary concepts of race*. New York: Garland.

Gilroy, Paul. 1998. Race ends here. *Ethnic and Racial Studies* 21, no. 5: 838–47.

Golden Earrings. 1947. Mitchell Leisen, director.

Gyurkovics, Tamás. 1999. *Cigányok ideje* (The Time of the Gypsies). *Filmvilág* 42, no. 1: 22–24.

Hall, Stuart. 1997. New ethnicities. In *Cultural and literary concepts of race*, ed. Nathaniel E. Gates, 373–382. New York: Garland.

Hancock, Ian. 18 July 2001. The struggle for the control of identity. http://www.geocities.com/Paris/5121/identity.htm.

hooks, bell. 1991. *Yearning: Race, gender, and cultural politics*. London: Turnaround.

Hungarians disguised as Roma. 4 July 2000a. *Budapest Sun*, 4–5.

Hutchinson, John. 1987. *The dynamics of cultural nationalism*. London: Allen and Unwin.

Intellectuals support Zamoly Roma. 1 September 2000b. http://www.romapage.hu/eng/hiren028.htm.

Iordanova, Dina. 2000. Are the Balkans admissible? The discourse on Europe. *Balkanistica* 13: 1–35.

____. 2001. *Cinema of flames: Balkan film, culture, and the media*. London: BFI.

James, Beverly. 1995. The reception of American popular culture by Hungarians. *Journal of Popular Culture* 29, no. 2: 97–107.

Johnson, Eric. 25 August 2000. *Beating death of Romany mars Slovakia's image*. United Press International.

Kapitány, Gábor and Ágnes. 1995. Changing world-views in Hungary, 1945–1980. *Journal of Popular Culture* 29, no. 2: 33–43.

Kennedy, Michael D. 1994. An introduction to East European ideology and identity in transformation. In *Envisioning Eastern Europe: Postcommunist cultural studies*, ed. Michael D. Kennedy, 1–45. Ann Arbor: University of Michigan Press.

Kerényi, György. 1999. Roma in the Hungarian media. *Media Studies Journal* 13, no. 3: 140–47.

Kiossev, Aleksandar. 2000. Megjegyzések az önkolonizáló kultúrákról (Notes about self-colonizing cultures). *Magyar Lettre Internationale* 37 (Summer): 7–10.

Klezmatics. 30 December 2000. *Filmszakadásig* (Until the film tears). *Magyar Narancs*, 27.

László, Gyula. 1981. *Ostörténetünk (Our ancient history)*. Budapest: Tankönyvkiadó.

Latcho Drom. 1993. Tony Gatlif, director. France. 1993.

Lawday, David. 9 December 1991. No immigrants need apply. *U.S. News and World Report* 111, no. 24, 46–49.

McClintock, Anne. 1995. *Imperial leather: Race, gender, and sexuality in the colonial context*. London: Routledge.

Meddö (Barren). 1995. Tamás Almási, director. Hungary.

Montenegro. 1981. Dusan Makavejev, director. Sweden/UK.

Nichols, Bill, ed. 1976. *Movies and methods*. Berkeley: University of California Press.

Ó Tuathail, Gearóid. 1996. *Critical geopolitics*. Minneapolis: University of Minnesota Press.

Paramicha (Tale). 1993. Livia Szederkényi, director. Hungary.

Pók, Attila. 1998. Atonement and sacrifice: Scapegoats in modern Eastern and Central Europe. *East European Quarterly* 32, no. 4: 531–47.

Portuges, Catherine. Hidden subjects, secret identities: Figuring Jews, Gypsies, and gender in 1990s cinema of Eastern Europe. In *Writing new identities*, ed. Gisela Brinker-Gabler, 196–215. N.p., n.d.

Pynsent, Robert B., ed. 1996. *The literature of nationalism: Essays on East European identity*. Basingstoke: Macmillan and Company.

Rádai, Eszter. 1999. *Ugyanolyanok vagyunk mint te* (We are just like you). *Filmvilág* 42, no. 1: 18–22.

Ravetto, Kriss. 1998. Mytho-poetic cinema: Cinemas of disappearance. *Third Text* 43: 43–57.

Romani kris/Cigánytörvény (Gypsy law). 1997a. Bence Gyöngyössy, director. Hungary.

Roma-filmek (Romani Films). 1999. *Filmvilág* 42, no. 1: 42.

Roma rap: avagy beindult a Fekete Vonat (Roma Rap, or the *Black Train* is on its Way). 3 July 2000. *Amarodrom*. http://www.amarodrom.hu/archivum/98/vonat.html.

Romany studies to be offered in Hungary. 25 August, 2000. *RFE/RL*. Budapest: N.p.

Said, Edward W. 1989. *Orientalism*. New York: Knopf.

____. 1993. *Culture and Imperialism*. New York: Knopf.

Said, Edward, and Christopher Burgmer. 2000. *Bevezetés a posztkoloniális diskurzusba* (Introduction to Postcolonial Discourse). Trans. Zsolt Farkas. *Magyar Lettre Internationale* 28.

Salecl, Renata. 1994. *The spoils of freedom: Psychoanalysis and feminism after the fall of socialism.* London: Routledge.

Sherwood, Peter. 1996. A nation may be said to live in its language: Some socio-historical perspectives on attitudes to Hungarian. In *The literature of nationalism: Essays on East European identity*, ed. Robert B. Pynsent, 27–39. Basingstoke: Macmillan and Company.

Shohat, Ella. 1997. Post-third-worldist culture: Gender, nation, and the cinema. In *Feminist genealogies*, ed. Jacqui Alexander and Sandra Mohanty, 183–209. New York: Routledge.

Shohat, Ella, and Robert Stam. 1994. *Unthinking Eurocentrism: Multiculturalism and the media.* New York: Routledge.

Solimano, Nicola, and Tiziana Mori. 2000. A Roma ghetto in Florence. *UNESCO Courier*, 40.

Stam, Robert, and Louise Spence. 1976. Colonialism, racism, and representation: An introduction. In *Movies and Methods*, ed. Bill Nichols, 632–49. Berkeley: University of California Press.

Stam, Robert. 1997. *Tropical multiculturalism: A comparative history of race in Brazilian cinema and culture.* Durham: Duke University Press.

Tanaka, Jennifer. 11 June 2000. Roma in Romania: Struggle for self-identification. *Patrin Web Journal.* http://www.geocities.com/Paris/5121/rroma.htm.

Time of the Gypsies. 1989. Emir Kusturica, director. UK/Italy/Yugoslavia.

Tismaneanu, Vladimir. 1994 Fantasies of salvation: Varieties of nationalism in postcommunist Eastern Europe. In *Postcommunist cultural studies*, ed. Michael D. Kennedy, 102–24. Ann Arbor: University of Michigan Press.

Turcsányi, Sándor. 17 July 2000. *Kell a romantika: Romani kris—Cigánytörvény* (We need romanticism: Romani kris—Gypsy law). *Amarodrom.* http://www.amarodrom.hu/archívum/98/romani.html.

Vajda, Róza, and Kende Ágnes. 17 July 2000. *A gázsók minding megtalálják a maguk rossz cigányát* (The Gadjo will always find their own bad gypsy). *Amarodrom.* http://www.amarodrom.hu/archívum/98/thomas.html.

Városlakók (Urbanites). 1997. András Salamon, director. Hungary.

Wolf Man, The. 1941. George Waggner, director. Paramount.

Žižek, Slavoj. 1998. A leftist plea for 'Eurocentrism.' *Critical Inquiry* 24, no. 4: 988–1009.

Žižek, Slavoj, and Dorothea Schuler. 18 August 2000. *Ez van, ezt kell szeretni?* (This is it, we'd better like it?). Trans. Éva Karádi. *Magyar Lettre Internationale* 28. http://c.3.hu/scripta/scripta0/lettre28/02zizek.htm.

19 Asian Canadian Futures
Diasporic Passages and the Routes of Indenture

Lily Cho

This paper traces possible future directions for Asian Canadian literature within the rubric of Asian diasporic studies and is written in the spirit of the tremendous sense of possibility that I see for Asian Canadian literature. Asian Canadian literature is, of course, not a new phenomenon. As Donald Goellnicht observes in his overview of the emergence of Asian Canadian literature as a field, despite the long history of Asian Canadian writing, "we in the academy seem to operate in an almost perpetual state of *announcing* Asian Canadian literature, a literature that has taken, from our snowblind perspective, twenty to twenty-five years to be 'born'" (2). Goellnicht makes clear that he is referring to the institutional space of Asian Canadian literature rather than the literary works themselves, and that his article is "an exploration of the ways in which institutional formations and practices in North America have attempted to discipline and contain various Asian ethnic groups and their cultural production as well as … the possibilities for resistance to such containment within those institutional formations" (3). Following Goellnicht's meditations on institutional formations, this paper explores the institutional futures of a field whose arrival needs less and less to be announced.

While personal histories are not necessarily reflective of institutional ones, they can sometimes be instructive for considerations of institutional shifts. Writing this paper has been an opportunity to reflect upon my own embarrassingly thin training. Having undertaken over a decade of postsecondary work in Canadian universities, primarily in Departments of English, I could not take any courses in Asian Canadian literature. Moreover, the idea of being an "Asian Canadianist" was, until recently, virtually unthinkable. When I wrote my doctoral candidacy exams, Asian Canadian literature was not something in which I could declare a specialization (I was guided toward established fields such as Canadian and postcolonial literatures). And it would never have occurred to me that, at the close of my graduate work, major Canadian

Lily Cho, "Asian Canadian Futures: Diasporic Passages and the Routes of Indenture." *Canadian Literature,* 199, 2008: 181–201. Reprinted by permission of Canadian Literature.

universities would be hiring—or have stated intentions of hiring—in fields such as Asian Canadian literature, Asian diasporic literature, and Asian North American literature. Partly because of these institutional shifts, and largely because of the hard work of many activists and scholars, Canadian scholars are now in the curious position of considering the pasts and the futures of a field that, until recently, did not have a defined institutional existence.

I do not recount this personal institutional history in order to celebrate the seeming rise of Asian Canadian literature in Canadian academic institutions. Rather, I wonder what the exercise of cautious optimism might look like. Unlike the institutional location of Asian American literature, our fledgling institutional location means that internal critique must always be balanced with the necessity of nurturing Asian Canadian and Asian North American literature as it establishes a toehold in the academy. Goellnicht's metaphor of Asian Canadian literature as having emerged from a "protracted birth" suggests precisely what I suspect is a collective sense of the fragile newness of the field. While the metaphoric references to the relative youthfulness of Asian Canadian literature as a field are useful and, in many ways, unavoidable for thinking through our current institutional moment, I cannot help feeling a little wary of depending too much on the developmental narrative that they imply. Asian Canadian scholarship needs a sense of its institutional histories in order to get a sense of where it might go next. And yet, even as I too rely on considerations of the field in terms of develop-mental narratives, I sense that it is also a field which is looking for ways of thinking through these histories that are attentive to the lessons of postcolonialism and the perils of Western historiography.

Perhaps one approach might involve imagining directions for the field that benefit from the work that has been done in fields such as Asian American studies, Asian Australian studies, postcolonial studies, and diasporic studies. Asian Canadianists can draw from related fields, partly because most of the critics who have pioneered so much of the work in this field come to it, by necessity, through side doors and back doors, bringing with them a commitment not only to this literature but also to a wide range of critical projects. We can draw from these multiple fields of inquiry to make serious interventions not only within the Canadian academy but also internationally. As Goellnicht points out, Asian Canadian literature as a field emerges from a different history than Asian American literature (3). This difference registers as an enabling one when we take up the possibilities of our own distinct intellectual and institutional histories. People who work in Asian Canadian literary criticism come not only from fields that might be considered to be related, such as postcolonial and Canadian literature, but also from Romanticism, eighteenth-century, and comparative literature. Rather than seeing these interests as distinct from the study of Asian Canadian literature, we can exploit these eccentricities of location by building a field that is broadly affiliative. We can use these intellectual interests to put pressure on Asian Canadian literature by pushing this literature toward more comparative contexts.

One of the possibilities that I want to explore in this paper is that of approaching Asian Canadian literature through the rubric of diaspora. I suggest that Asian Canadian literature must retain its affiliation with diasporic concerns and remain open to its ties to postcolonial studies because a rigorous exploration of the politics and culture of indenture and its aftermath needs to be at the centre of Asian Canadian literary studies specifically and of Asian diasporic studies in general. In this paper, I will be referring most specifically to Chinese Canadian communities, but I hope that some of my comments will have relevance for other Asian communities in Canada.

Because diasporic studies is, like Asian Canadian studies, a relatively new field, let me briefly outline how I understand its significance. The recent resurgence of the term "diaspora" in the Western academy has arisen out of a profound perplexity regarding the cultural spaces and products of peoples who have been displaced by oppression and violence. I suggest that, if the term is to retain its potential for powerful critique, it cannot float away from the constitutive sadnesses of dislocation. Furthermore, I propose that the term in contemporary discussion would be productively used as a way of thinking through subjectivities that emerge from the displacements of colonial and imperial oppression. In this sense, I understand diasporic studies as constitutively related to postcolonialism. As Rebecca Walsh notes, "the study of diaspora is frequently inseparable from the study of postcolonialism and imperialism in its various forms" (2). In "Rethinking Diaspora(s): Stateless Power in the Transnational Moment," Khachig Tölölyan admits some fears about the ways in which diaspora as a concept has become unhinged, in both enabling and disabling ways, from its classical usage. Warning of the dangers of allowing the term to become too expansive and inclusive, he suggests that, "Without some minimum stringency of definition, most of America—or Argentina, or New Zealand, or any modern immigrant-nation—would just as easily be a diaspora" (30). The need for stringency of definition lies in the perils of a collapsing of transnational and diasporic subjects where the use of the diasporic concept beyond its classical sense may result in "the inadvertent complicity between some diasporicists and transnationalists in the attack on the nation-state" (29).

In differentiating between transnationalism and diaspora, I want to highlight the ways in which the state of diasporic migrancy is framed by social and political precariousness. It is not that all migrants exist in a precarious state but that migrancy carries within it the potential for precariousness. This is a precariousness amplified by race, sexuality, gender, and class. What stands out for me in this marking, though, is the way in which the words *go home* carry specific valences for some communities more than others. For some, the injunction to go home carries with it a profoundly different capacity for pain, humiliation, and political disempowerment. Vijay Mishra notes in "The Diasporic Imaginary: Theorizing the Indian Diaspora" that, "As long as there is a fascist fringe always willing to find racial scapegoats for the nation's own shortcomings and to chant 'Go home', the autochthonous pressures towards diasporic racial exclusivism will remain" (426). Mishra describes the sense of "familiar temporariness" that marks what he has called the old Indian diaspora, the diasporic community that is the legacy of indentured labour in the West Indies (426). In this idea of a "familiar temporariness," we can begin to read for the kind of precariousness that lies within racially marked diasporic communities. For example, a fourth- or fifth-generation Chinese Canadian might still be asked to "go home" in a way that a fourth- or fifth-generation white Canadian will never be. In the context of the Chinese diaspora, I therefore focus on a diaspora marked most explicitly by race but inescapably defined by issues of class, sexuality, and gender. I focus on a racialized diaspora because the Chinese diaspora has been defined throughout the social and historical archive by race first. As the history of race riots and race-based legislation such as the head tax and the exclusion act illustrates, the Chinese Canadian community has been attacked primarily on the basis of its Chineseness, even though issues of class, sexuality, and gender—especially evident in the promulgation of the idea of a degenerate bachelor society that has taken jobs away from upstanding and hard-working white men—are crucially imbricated in the targeting of Chinese immigrants.[1]

In distinguishing the diasporic from the transnational, I am also arguing for a racialized differentiation that turns on class and is profoundly connected to colonial displacement. Jana Evans Braziel and Anita Mannur call for distinctions to be made by identifying "the political risks entailed in different forms of movement and migration as well as between transnationalism (which can describe NGOs, multinational corporations, and dissident political organizations, as well as individuals) and diaspora (which is a human phenomenon)" (15). While the distinction between the human and the non-human (are NGOs, multinational corporations, and dissident political organizations not human?) is slippery and thus potentially misleading, Braziel and Mannur do point to the importance of thinking through the nexus of the diasporic and the transnational. In their introduction to *The Powers of Diaspora: Two Essays on the Relevance of Jewish Culture*, Jonathan Boyarin and Daniel Boyarin warn against "an exclusive focus on the diasporic as *transnational*" because they suggest that we also consider the possibilities of diasporas existing within states (23). They refer specifically to the experiences of Natives in North America. Boyarin and Boyarin suggest that we need to keep the concept open to displacements that are compelled by colonialism but that are not necessarily transnational. As Aihwa Ong's *Flexible Citizenship: The Cultural Logics of Transnationality* makes clear, the issues that attend on thinking through the experiences of privileged, multiple-passport-carrying subjects can be most productively engaged through the rubric of transnationalism. As she notes in "Cyberpublics and Diaspora Politics among Transnational Chinese," "The term 'transnationality' better describes the variety of cultural interconnections and trans-border movements and networks which have intensified under conditions of late capitalism" (85).

Ong's *Buddha Is Hiding: Refugees, Citizenship, the New America* attempts to address the "other Asians"—those who are not among the "new affluent Asian immigrants" of her previous study of flexible citizenship.[2] However, as the delineation "other Asians" suggests, Ong's discussion in *Buddha Is Hiding* understands the migratory underclass as the other side, or the underside if you will, of transnationalism. For Ong, the underclass Asian migrant constitutes a problem for citizenship and thus illuminates the ways in which "citizenship rights have become partially disembedded from the nation" (286). While her discussion usefully highlights the need for a "transnational moral economy" that takes into account the failure of the discourse of citizenship to protect those most vulnerable to the abuses of power, what remains less clear are the conditions of dislocation and racialization that connect one generation of Asian immigrants and another as well as those connections across Asian communities differentiated by ethnicity and class. It is not just that pan-Asian politics might still provide a place for thinking about the construction of communities in dislocation but also that we need to think through the historical connections between Asian diasporic communities and the histories of European colonialism and imperialism. Rather than thinking of this underclass as the underside of transnationalism, we might understand these subjects within a rubric that sees them as more than the dark side of a transnational dream.

The history of Chinese diasporic trajectories is intimately linked to the history of colonialism. As Jenny Sharpe notes, "The designation of postcolonial as an umbrella term for diaspora and minority communities is derived in part from an understanding of decolonization as the beginning of an unprecedented migration from the former colonies to advanced industrialist centers" (105). However, as the trajectory of Chinese indentured labour shows, diaspora begins not only with the end of colonialism but also with its instigation. The nineteenth and twentieth centuries marked the mass exodus of dispossessed communities who were bound by indenture and slavery. I believe that we need to foreground this history of dispossession and dislocation not because it is "history" in the Western historiographic sense but because these are pasts that are constitutive of our present. It would be a mistake to think of the indentured Asian labourer as an unfortunate feature of a forgettable past. The march of history does not proceed so smoothly. We cannot risk losing sight of the ways in which the racisms of the past continue to shape the racisms of our present.

Approaching Asian Canadian literature within the rubric of diasporic studies, as I have briefly outlined it, encourages interventions such as comparative work between multiple sites of Asian migration, comparative work between minority communities, and explorations of the relationship between slavery and indenture as formative features of certain diasporic subjectivities. I should say that these are not interventions that diasporic studies necessarily enables but ones that I see as potentially enabled by a diasporic perspective.

First, attention to the routes of indenture of Asian Canadian immigration facilitates comparative work between the multiple sites of Asian migration. I think not only of communities in Australia or the US but also, for example, of those that emerged from the sugar plantations in Cuba and the Caribbean, the railway workers in South America, and the miners in South Africa. That is, we could understand early Asian Canadian migration within a complicated and overlapping set of trajectories. In emphasizing the routes of migration, I am not advocating a rejection of the need to engage with the nation-state. I am, however, suggesting that we need to think of Asian Canadian migration as deeply connected to a whole series of movements and migrations. The colonial archive abounds with instances of these connections. For example, part of the decision to import Chinese indentured labour to South Africa in the early-twentieth century was based on consultation with the *Report of the Royal Commission on Chinese Immigration in Canada* submitted to the Canadian Parliament in 1885 as well as the experience of Chinese labour in Australia and the US. Persia Crawford Campbell notes that

> on Feb. 14, 1903, the Witwatersand Labour Association, under the aegis of the Chamber of Mines, asked Mr. Ross Skinner to proceed to California and the Far East to investigate
>
> 1. the conditions under which indentured Chinese labourers might be employed on the Rand;
> 2. the possibility of obtaining such labour;
> 3. its suitability to supplement the present inadequate Kaffir supply. (171)

The representations of Chineseness that circulate in one country are not limited to those national contexts. Canada consults Australia and the US; South Africa consults all of the former. The representation of the experience of Chinese workers in nineteenth-century Canada in British colonial administrative documents such as the

Report of the Royal Commission on Chinese Immigration in Canada directly shaped the experiences of Chinese workers who would end up in South Africa working in the gold mines. Moreover, one of the aims of the Royal Commission report was that of situating Chinese immigration in Canada in the context of Chinese immigration in Australia and the US:

> It will also be part of the duties of the Commission to examine the evidence submitted in Australia, California and Washington and to condense and collate it and submit it with its report to Parliament so that the Parliament of Canada may have, in a convenient shape, together with the researches of the Commissioners, all the information which the legislative bodies of the United States and Australia had when they undertook the work of legislating on this question. (Canada viii)

It makes perfect sense that one arm of colonialism would consult with another and that they would work in tandem to produce politically coherent forms of legislating not only Chinese immigration but also Chineseness itself, as one would have to be able to differentiate those who are Chinese from other forms of Asianness in order to legislate around it.[3] But this is also precisely the reason why we need to think through the connections between Chineseness in Canada and elsewhere.

The shaping of Chineseness in Canada is not distinct from the mechanisms of colonialism and its dislocating forces. Throughout the history of the recent mass migrations of Chinese people, one form of exploitation has been used to justify another. The experience of one migrant population has implications for those of another. We need to think about Chineseness not as an identity formed solely in relation to the Canadian state; we also need to think about the formation of the Canadian state through imperialism and colonialism and the relationships between other colonized spaces. British imperialists did not see Chinese populations in Canada as distinct from those in Australia, South Africa, or Hong Kong; in order to understand this history of racialization, we need to think of it in terms of the construction of Chineseness in Canada and to think of this construction as deeply connected to Chineseness elsewhere. We might also consider the possibilities of resistance across these spaces. Might the routes of indenture have also been trajectories for the circulation of information, tactics for survival, strategies of resistance? As Peter Linebaugh and Marcus Rediker demonstrate with detailed clarity in *The Many-Headed Hydra*, the transatlantic routes of slavery were also a means for the passage of information among subaltern populations. These are possibilities we have yet to fully consider in terms of the trans-Pacific passages of indenture.

Second, a diasporic perspective displaces the primacy of the relationship between white and nonwhite groups, shifting the emphasis to the relationships among minority groups. "Asia" and "Canada" are not the only cultural, historical, or geographical entities that constitute Asian Canadian subjectivities. One of the tasks of Asian Canadian and diasporic criticism lies in a serious engagement with the kinds of relationships between minority communities that texts such as SKY Lee's *Disappearing Moon Cafe* and Fred Wah's *Diamond Grill* explore. In addition to the complicated whorls of a personal history that involves Chinese, Swedish, Scottish, and Irish crossings and mixings, *Diamond Grill* depicts interactions between Japanese, First Nations, Doukhobor, Jewish, and Chinese communities. Similarly, Lee's novel opens with a love story between a Chinese man and a First Nations woman. These are not necessarily relationships that we need to recuperate as celebratory examples of minority interactions. As Tseen-ling Khoo argues, "the particular colonial oppressions and legacies of Canada's indigenous groups are situations for which Asian-Canadians can express sympathy and some forms of solidarity but cannot claim to share" (177). Khoo goes on to note that she is "not advocating a hierarchy of victimage; rather [she] want[s] to iterate the strategic quality of coalitions and their potential for contingent but powerful effects" (177). Indeed, both Wah's use of the term "half-bred poetics" to describe "the activity and dynamics of the site of the hyphen" ("Half-Bred" 95) and Lee's depiction of First Nations communities suggest that these are deeply complicated and vexed relationships and interactions—a point that Rita Wong explores in detail in her contribution to this special issue. But it is precisely this messy, discomfiting space that we need to explore in our criticism. At this point in cultural criticism, the issue is not about whether a particular representation is good or bad, or accurate or inaccurate. However, I hope that a diasporic perspective on Asian Canadian literature might bring forward more discussion of the kinds of dynamics that unfold in texts that invite precisely these complex discussions on the uneven relationships between minoritized groups.

Recognizing and examining the uneven relationships between minority groups might curtail some of the inevitable binarism that seems to be already implied in the notion of "Asian Canadian" studies. The past two decades of diasporic and minority discourse criticism have already suggested the need to consider the multiplicity of the interactions from which concepts such as Asian Canadian emerge. This work points to thinking about racialization as a set of differential relations that cut across each other. In *Cartographies of Diaspora: Contesting Identities*, Avtar Brah asks, "How ... are African, Caribbean, South Asian and white Muslims differentially constructed within anti-Muslim racism in present-day Britain? Similarly, how are blacks, Chicanos, Chinese, Japanese or South Koreans in the USA differentiated within its racialised formations? What are the economic, political, cultural and psychic effects of these differential racialisations on the lives of these groups?" (185). In response to these questions, Brah argues, "Of central concern in addressing such questions are the power dynamics which usher in racialised social relations and inscribe racialised modes of subjectivity and identity. [Her] argument ... is that these racisms are not simply parallel racisms but intersecting modalities of *differential racialisations marking positionality across articulating fields of power*" (185–86). This attention to the positionality of differentially racialized communities recalls Abdul JanMohamed and David Lloyd's discussion of minority discourse as a theoretical project that "involves drawing out solidarities in the form of modes of repression and struggle that all minorities experience separately but experience precisely as minorities. ... 'Becoming minor' is ... a question of position: a subject-position that in the final analysis can be defined only in 'political' terms—that is, in terms of the effects of economic exploitation, political disenfranchisement, social manipulation, and ideological domination on cultural formation of minority subjects and discourses" (9). JanMohamed and Lloyd call attention to the structural situation of minority communities and the urgency of understanding these positionings as a dialogue between minorities. Brah has noted that minority discourse, unlike the Black Power movement and its reorienting of the connotations of blackness, has not been successful in shifting the meaning of minority; she "remain[s] skeptical that ... any moves that perpetuate the circulation of the minority/majority dichotomy will not serve to reinforce the hegemonic relations that inscribe this dichotomy" (189). While we must remain attentive to the possibilities of re-entrenching the very binaries that we seek to disrupt, the overall project of understanding minorities in relation to one another rather than simply in opposition to whiteness remains one that we must continue to work toward.

In highlighting the relationships among minority communities, we can problematize the presumption of a trajectory where the Asian is always already foreign. Instead of understanding the "home" of diasporic trajectories as primeval localities that expel people into new places that are becoming increasingly culturally mixed as a result, a diasporic perspective demands an understanding of the *construction* of home and arrival in diasporic trajectories. Not doing so naturalizes the idea that diasporic peoples come from a space of racial homogeneity and arrive at spaces that are becoming increasingly multicultural because of other people "like them" without ever questioning the autochthonous claims of those "who were there first." In the case of the Chinese diaspora, taking for granted the trajectory of "home" and "arrival" naturalizes the idea that China is a uniformly "Chinese" country, that Chinese diasporic communities ultimately come from China (even if there are multigenerational detours through Indonesia, Vietnam, South Africa, and so on), and that white people originate in Canada. In challenging the autochthonous claims of whiteness, this perspective also refuses to naturalize the relationship between the nation-state and ethnicity, between the People's Republic of China and Chineseness.

Third, a diasporic perspective on Asian Canadian literature illuminates the relationship between indenture and slavery, between Asian Canadian communities and black Canadian communities. I suggest that we need to think through the historical and cultural relationships between slavery and indenture. While slavery has commonly been understood as a foundational event of black diasporic culture, the relationship between Asian indentured labour to the Americas and Asian diasporic culture has yet to be fully explored. When slavery was "abolished" in European colonies in the mid-nineteenth century, there was a concerted effort to recruit indentured labour from India and China to take the place of slave labour. As documents as diverse as the Canadian *Report of the Royal Commission* and *The Cuba Commission Report: A Hidden History of the Chinese in Cuba* show, Asian labourers were specifically targeted for indenture because of their perceived docility or pacific nature. What was known as *la trata amarilla* ("the yellow trade") in Spanish colonies and the "coolie" trade in anglophone colonies supplanted the slave trade.[4]

Furthermore, an analysis of the journey of indentured labourers from Asia to the New World opens up the possibilities for thinking about the connections between black and Asian diasporas, Atlantic and Pacific subjectivities. I have been struck by the realization that many of the ships used to carry slaves across the Atlantic were used to transport indentured labourers across the Pacific. Moreover, all of the ships used to transport indentured labourers copied precisely the architecture of slave ships: "iron gratings over hatch-ways, walls between crew and coolie quarters, armed guards, [and] cannons trained on hatchways" (Applied History Research Group). The legacy of these architectural forms raises all kinds of questions about the relationship between the Middle Passage and the Pacific passages of indenture. It is not just that Asian indentured labourers were subjected to similar incarceratory forms as slaves from

Africa but also that the very differences between these forms are also profoundly suggestive for our considerations of the construction of black and Asian diasporic subjectivities.

Not only were the same ships often used, but, looking at logbooks and shipping routes, we can see that Asian indentured labourers also passed through the now infamous Middle Passage across the Atlantic.

When I first began this research, I assumed, wrongly, that an examination of nineteenth-century Asian migration would largely be one of looking at trans-Pacific routes. However, this assumption is based on the bias of twentieth-century air travel and the supposition of migration to North America alone. As Cutler's map of common nineteenth-century shipping routes shows, some ships—particularly those headed to ports such as Vancouver, San Francisco, or Callao from Asia—did indeed traverse the Pacific. Yet many other ships left Asia and sailed *west* across the Indian Ocean, round the Cape of Good Hope, and across the *Atlantic*.

If, following the pioneering work of Paul Gilroy in *The Black Atlantic*, we take seriously the importance of routes for thinking about diasporic cultures, then understanding the routes of Asian indenture means understanding the black Atlantic as *formative* of Asian diasporic cultures, not only in the sense that black slavery precedes the mass migration of Asian indentured labourers but also, more importantly, in the sense that black Atlantic formations can be understood as *constitutive* of Asian diasporic formations. That is, the black Atlantic was not solely black, and Asian diasporic movements were not solely transpacific.

Asian American critics such as Gary Okihiro and Lisa Yun have long argued for the importance of thinking about Asian diasporas in relation to black diasporas. In *Margins and Mainstreams: Asians in American History and Culture*, Okihiro argues that "the migration of Asians to America cannot be divorced from the African slave trade, or from the coolie trade that followed in its wake" (47). In his recognition of the connections between coolie and slave histories, Okihiro warns against emphasizing the differences rather than the similarities between these coercive forms of labour migration. Lisa Yun and Ricardo Laremont argue that "The terms 'coolie' or 'indentured labourer' … obfuscate the very political and experiential nature of coolies" (101). Comparing the cost of slave and coolie labour in nineteenth-century Cuba, Yun and Laremont demonstrate that coolie labour was significantly cheaper than slave labour and note that the conditions of work for coolies were no different and sometimes even worse than for those of slaves from Africa (107–09). "Because of malnourishment and abusive conditions, over fifty percent of coolies died *before* their eight-year contract ended. The average life span of an African slave on a sugar plantation was twenty years" (Yun and Laremont 113). These statistics are horrifying enough to suggest that it would not be mistaken to understand the indenture of Chinese labourers within the terms of slavery.

My point here is not that slavery and indenture shared similar features or that the horrors of slavery did not end with abolition. There has been a tendency to think of the black and Asian diasporas as distinct partly because of legal differences between these two forms of forced labour[5] but also because these legal differences are also reinforced by the supposition of distinctly separate geographical passages. Understanding Pacific passages as linked to Atlantic passages enables an understanding of the relationship between Asian and black diasporic subjectivities. If the Middle Passage has been a crucible for the emergence of contemporary black identity, Asian Canadian scholars would be amiss in not also looking at the ways in which these routes lie within the histories of some Asian migrant populations. Asian Canadian scholarship needs to untangle the spatial overlap that marks both the displacement of slavery by indenture and the congruence of these experiences.

Investigating the routes of indenture offers an opportunity to think about the passage itself as deeply transformative and to meditate on what these transformations might be for diasporic cultures. The average journey from Macao to Havana took more than half a year. What happened in that time? What kinds of bonds were formed, and which communities emerged from these experiences? How do they resonate in contemporary culture? In "(B) ordering Naipaul: Indenture History and Diaspora Poetics," Vijay Mishra argues "that any account of the production and reproduction of diaspora culture must begin with the ships of the passage: 'indenture lives in dates and distances,' writes Arnold Itwaru in his poem 'We have Survived' (293)" (196). Taking up Henri Lefebvre's provocative declaration that "No space ever vanishes utterly, leaving no trace" (164), Mishra suggests that "the ship was a space that outlived its original design" (198). It carries a resonance, the memory of confinement, passage, and trans-formation, beyond that of the journey itself. Displacements and migrations are not simply about people moving from one place to another. Rather, the processes of dis-placement carry within them a memory tied to the materiality of ships, of passages, of the months and days spent at sea in abysmal conditions and under constant threat. Diasporas are formed not only by the act of moving from place to another but also by what happens along the way. After all, no one is born a coolie. One *becomes* one through experiencing the spaces of imperial confinement—the ship's hold, the barracks of embarkation, and those of arrival. This becoming is a process of subjection from which slave and indentured subjectivities emerge in the "living memory" of incarcera-tion (Gilroy 198).[6] Within this process of becoming, of subject formation and the attendant resistances to these incarceratory forms of subjectivization, we can decipher the transformations from which diasporic subjectivities might emerge.

Contemplating the relation between what we might think of as "indenture passages" for Asian diasporas and contemporary experiences of displacement, we come to the problem of old and new diasporas. In 1996 issues of *Textual Practice*, Vijay Mishra and Gayatri Spivak, in separate essays, mark out the distinction between old and new diasporas. In "The Diasporic Imaginary," Mishra suggests that "the old Indian diasporas of the sugar plantations" who "make up a single group of dispersed and territorially disaggregated bodies" can be distinguished from the "new" Indian diasporas, which "are part of a global odyssey as they renegotiate new topographies through the travails of travel" (427, 435). Similarly, Spivak asks in "Diasporas Old and New: Women in the Transnational World," "What were the old diasporas, before the world was thoroughly consolidated as transnational? They were the results of religious oppression and war, of slavery and indenturing, trade and conquest, and intra-European economic migration which, since the nineteenth century, took the form of migration and immigration to the United States" (245). While this distinction between old and new diasporas has not been significantly taken up in subsequent discussions of diaspora and postcoloniality, I want to return to it because these categories open up a way of understanding the heterogeneity of diasporic communities while still attending to the continuities of specific historical experiences of displacement. Mishra notes that drawing out a distinction between old and new Indian diasporas in his essay is more than "a purely heuristic desire for a neat taxonomy" ("Diasporic Imaginary" 442). He draws "attention to the complex procedures by which diasporas negotiate their perceived moment of trauma and how, in the artistic domain, the trauma works itself out" (442). Mishra's identification of the old Indian diaspora with the traumas of indenture passage points to ways in which the experience of the passage shapes diasporic communities. Implicit within the distinction between old and new diasporas lies the problem of involuntary and voluntary displacement. Extending Spivak's and Mishra's project, I suggest that the "old" diasporas of indenture and slavery are not fully distinct from the "new" ones of jet-fuelled transnational mobility. Rather, these diasporas are contemporaneous and can draw attention to the ways in which the past is constitutive of the present.

While both Mishra and Spivak make the distinction between old and new diasporic subjects, my sense is that we cannot so easily separate them. That is, one is constitutive of and defined against the other. Contemporary Asian Canadian literature grapples with these connections and ruptures of old and new diasporic experiences. Lee's *Disappearing Moon Café* juxtaposes the narratives of characters such as Kae Ying Woo and Hermia Chow against old diasporic characters such as Wong Gwei Chang and Lee Mui Lan. Wah's *Diamond Grill* meditates on the connections between his father's experience of becoming Chinese and his own. Lydia Kwa's *This Place Called Absence* explores the connections between Wu Lan, a psychologist living in Vancouver, and Lee Ah Choi and Chow Chat Mui, two prostitutes in nineteenth-century Singapore. In *Salt Fish Girl*, Larissa Lai pushes the edges of the old and the new, staging the connection between Nu Wa in ancient China and Miranda, who lives in a future that is yet to come. These texts attempt to think through the relation between the old and new experiences of migration and displacement as a function of what it means to be in diaspora. They take up what it means to feel connected to one place and be in another while also attending to what it means to be in one moment in history and still feel the presence of another.

It is this question of history that marks for me the urgent relation between Asian Canadian literary criticism and postcolonial historiography. As Stephen Slemon notes in "Post-Colonial Critical Theories," postcolonial theory consistently questions the category of history. Taking up Eduardo Galeano's retelling of the Spanish conquest of South and Central America through the figure of the poet and the "remembering of colonial history, at its most brutal and abject, in a language of smell, touch and taste" (109), Slemon argues that

> The intellectual challenge for post-colonial critical theory is to attempt to come to know the story of colonial and neo-colonial engagements in all their complexity, and to find ways to represent those engagements in a language that can build cross-disciplinary, cross-community, cross-cultural alliances for the historical production of genuine social change. That is how [Slemon reads] Eduardo Galeano's message about the poet of conquest, who seeks out history in the stones of the river, who teaches history in the smell of the wind. (114)

Whether this postcolonial engagement takes place through the subaltern historiography or colonial discourse analysis, it never lets go of the question of the subject of history and the subjective experiences of the past, of history as it resides in the memory of the senses. While there is still much work to be done in examining the relationship between postcoloniality and Asian Canadian literature, we might begin with postcolonialism's commitment to this question of the subject of history. Asian Canadian literary studies cannot take for granted the subject of its engagement and must continue to wrestle with constructions of race and ethnicity as well as the historical contingencies of those constructions. Asian Canadian literature is not simply a multicultural subsection of something bigger called Canadian literature. It is more than just a piece of the Canadian literary puzzle. Rather, it situates Canadian literature within a complex and delicate global network of routes and passages that are at once cultural and historical. Asian Canadian literature reaches outward across the Pacific and beyond as much as it reaches inward toward the heart of the Prairies; it reaches backward through the histories of displacement and forward to futures that we have yet to imagine.

I am aware of the problem of flattening out the multiple histories of Asian indenture. Not only are there significant differences in the histories of Indian and Chinese labouring communities, but there are also important differences between the experiences of Chinese indentured labourers. That is, the experience of working on the Canadian Pacific Railway is not the same as that of hauling guano in Peru, which is not the same as that of working on the sugar plantations in Cuba, and so on. Some labourers travelled on the credit-ticket system, some as indentured labourers, some as contract labourers. However, my sense is that we need to explore the similarities, the ways in which these histories of displacement create common cultural formations. One of the challenges of diaspora theory is to think through what David Scott, in reference to Kamau Braithwaite, calls "an obscure miracle of connection" (*Refashioning Futures* 106)—how it is that one of the effects of the isolating experience of displacement is that of a powerful sense of connection to communities that are not even necessarily bound by nation, race, or class.

We might also keep in mind that the differentiations between the forms of the exploitation of Chinese labour (credit-ticket, contract, outright indenture, and so on) are distinctions that have been engendered by colonial and imperial bureaucracies. I suggest that, at least in the case of labourers imported from Asia for reasons of economy and ease of exploitation, the divisions between voluntary and involuntary, contract and indenture, are false ones. As postcolonial historians such as Madhavi Kale and Gyan Prakash have noted, the categories of free and unfree labour emerged out of colonialism and imperialism. Prakash's *Bonded Histories: Genealogies of Labour Servitude in Colonial India* argues that the discourse of freedom is tied to notions of the individual subject, while Kale notes that the very category of labour and its place in British history "were forged in the crucible of empire" (3–4). Reading the archive of Indian indenture through the lens of race and gender, Kale proposes that

> The articulation of gender, race and nation or colonial status is what made indentured labor so crucial to the crystallization of "free labour" ideology. Indentured labour was peculiarly suited to imperial post-emancipation conditions because it recognized and implicitly capitalized on racial differentiation—indeed racial hierarchy—within the empire by contributing to naturalizing, universalizing a bourgeois-imperial sexual division of labor that was not only predicated on but also reproduced women's banishment to the domestic: to domestic labor, space, identity. (174)

The differentiation of race and its hierarchization, as well as the gendering of labour, made possible a postemancipation system of labour exploitation that can ostensibly hold to the principles of abolition without relinquishing a reliance on unfree labour. It is not that indenture was necessarily slavery under a different name (although those who advocated the end of indenture, such as the commissioners of the *Cuba Commission Report*, certainly declared it to be such) but that indenture, as Kale notes above, "crystallized" notions of freedom that made possible the dichotomization of free and unfree labour.

I began with a sense of the multiple possible futures of Asian Canadian literature, and it seems as though I have ended up in the past. However, in Fred Wah's apt words, "this rusty nail has been here forever in fact the real last spike is yet to be driven" (*Diamond Grill* 165). The "rusty" traumas of displacement and discrimination remain unredressed. The question of the future is also that of the past. As David Scott observes in *Conscripts of Modernity: The Tragedy of Colonial Enlightenment*, our imaginings of the future shape our relations to the past. He notes that postcolonial studies has anchored much of its imaginings of a postcolonial future in a Romantic vision of anticolonial struggle (in which "Romantic" refers precisely to the heritage of European literary Romanticism). This unacknowledged reliance upon a Romantic narrative of anticolonial struggle and anticolonial revolutionary figures such as Toussaint L'Ouverture leaves postcolonial studies with an unresolved longing for a future already belied by the tragedies of postcolonial governance. Writing about the problem of the future, Scott suggests "that alleged histories of the present (postcolonial or otherwise) tend to elide the problem of 'futures' in historical temporality": "I do not mean by this that they are non- (or anti-) utopian in formulation (though they typically are this too). I mean, rather, that these histories tend *not* to inquire systematically into the ways in which the expectation of—or longing for—particular futures helps to shape the kind of problem the past is constructed as for the present" (31). Scott points to the crucial role of desire in the relation of the past to the future and how our longings for particular futures shape our understandings of the past.

While postcolonial studies, as Scott suggests, longs for anticolonial revolution and revolutionaries rooted in a disavowed Romanticism, Asian Canadian literary studies seems to be uncertain about its own desires. It exists not in longings unfulfilled and unrequitable but in the peculiar ache of longings that have yet to be articulated. As Goellnicht notes, almost wistfully, we do not have an explicit history of revolution or struggle upon which to base the emergence of the field: "Asian Canadians never attained the status of a mass, panethnic social movement but remained localized groups, primarily in Vancouver or Toronto, or focused on the issues of a single ethnic group" (9). Unlike Asian American studies, Asian Canadian literary criticism does not emerge directly from U.S. countercultural political movements such as the civil rights struggle, the anti–Vietnam War protests, or the Third World strikes. However, not knowing the shape of our longings does not necessarily result in an elision of the question of the future. Rather, existing within this ache of longing for a future that has yet to be articulated enables a different kind of temporal relation. It can be, as I have been suggesting in this essay, a relation that imagines a future out of the precariousness of displacement. If what we long for shapes our understanding of what we think we know, then we must attend to the longings shot through Asian Canadian literature for community, for redress, for the right to embrace the sadnesses of history as much as the pleasures of memory. The work of the present continues to be that of understanding the proleptic power of forgotten and suppressed pasts.

Notes

[1] There has been a series of race riots targeted against Chinese immigrants in Canadian history, including the 1907 Vancouver riot, which caused enough concern at both local and national levels that Wilfrid Laurier, the prime minister at the time, stepped in to police the situation. For detailed discussions of anti-Chinese riots and anti-Chinese legislation (the two often went hand in hand), see Li; Roy; Ward; and Wickberg et al.

[2] Ong observes in the prologue to *Buddha Is Hiding* that, "In *Flexible Citizenship*, I suggest that new affluent Asian immigrants—relocating their families and wealth to North America, while pursuing business interests in Asia—represent a new kind of disembodied citizenship. This is a parallel study of the 'other Asians'—Southeast Asian war refugees—who flowed in at roughly the same time, and it will focus on the practices that embed these newcomers in specific contexts of subject-making" (xiv).

[3] For a more extensive discussion of Chineseness and the significance of the head tax legislation in Canada, see Cho.

[4] See Hu-DeHart for a discussion of Asian diaspora populations and the history of indenture in Latin America. Also see Helly for *The Cuba Commission Report*.

[5] As Hu-DeHart argues, we cannot ignore the legal differences between slavery and indenture no matter what similarities there were in terms of material conditions: "it is important to separate actual physical treatment from legal status. A well-treated slave was still chattel for life by law" (83).

[6] In the final chapter of *The Black Atlantic: Modernity and Double Consciousness*, Gilroy writes of "the living memory of the changing same" (198). His notion of this "living memory"—which changes and yet remains tied to the continuities between the past and the present—offers an important way of understanding the presence of the history of slavery in memory of contemporary black diasporic subjects.

Works cited

Applied History Research Group, University of Calgary. 2001. U of Calgary. 29 Apr. 2003. <http://www.ucalgary.ca/applied_history/tutor/migrations/five4.html>.

Boyarin, Jonathan, and Daniel Boyarin. *Powers of Diaspora: Two Essays on the Relevance of Jewish Culture*. Minneapolis: U of Minnesota P, 2002.

Brah, Avtar. *Cartographies of Diaspora: Contesting Identities*. London: Routledge, 1996.

Braziel, Jana Evans, and Anita Mannur. "Nation, Migration, Globalization: Points of Contention in Diaspora Studies." *Theorizing Diaspora*. Ed. Braziel and Mannur. London: Blackwell, 2003. 1–20.

Campbell, Persia Crawford. *Chinese Coolie Emigration to Countries within the British Empire*. London: King and Son, 1923.

Canada. *Report of the Royal Commission on Chinese Immigration in Canada*. Ottawa, 1885.

Cho, Lily. "Rereading Head Tax Racism: Redress, Stereotype, and Antiracist Critical Practice." *Essays on Canadian Writing* 75 (2002): 62–84.

Cutler, Carl. *Greyhounds of the Sea*. New York: Halcyon, 1937.

Gilroy, Paul. *The Black Atlantic: Modernity and Double Consciousness*. Cambridge, MA: Harvard UP, 1993.

Goellnicht, Donald C. "A Long Labour: The Protracted Birth of Asian Canadian Literature." *Essays on Canadian Writing* 72 (2000): 1–41.

Helly, Denise, ed. *The Cuba Commission Report: A Hidden History of the Chinese in Cuba*. 1876. Baltimore: Johns Hopkins UP, 1993.

Hu-DeHart, Evelyn. "Latin America in Asia-Pacific Perspective." *What Is in a Rim? Critical Perspectives on the Pacific Region Idea*. Ed. Arif Dirlik. 2nd ed. New York: Rowman, 1997. 251–78.

JanMohamed, Abdul, and David Lloyd. "Introduction: Towards a Theory of Minority Discourse." *The Nature and Context of Minority Discourse*. New York: Oxford UP, 1990. 1–16.

Kale, Madhavi. *Fragments of Empire: Capital, Slavery, and Indian Indentured Labor Migration in the British Caribbean*. Philadelphia: U of Pennsylvania P, 1998.

Khoo, Tseen-ling. *Banana Bending: Asian-Australian and Asian-Canadian Literature*. Montreal: McGill-Queen's UP, 2003.

Kwa, Lydia. *This Place Called Absence*. Winnipeg: Turnstone, 2002.

Lai, Larissa. *Salt Fish Girl*. Toronto: Allen, 2002.

Lee, SKY. *Disappearing Moon Café*. Vancouver: Douglas, 1990.

Lefebvre, Henri. *The Production of Space*. Trans. Donald Nicholson-Smith. London: Blackwell, 1991.

Li, Peter. *The Chinese in Canada*. Toronto: Oxford UP, 1988.

Linebaugh, Peter, and Marcus Rediker. *The Many-Headed Hydra*. Boston: Beacon, 2001.

Mishra, Vijay. "(B)ordering Naipaul: Indenture History and Diaspora Poetics." *Diaspora* 5.2 (1996): 189–237.

___. "The Diasporic Imaginary: Theorizing the Indian Diaspora." *Textual Practice* 10.3 (1996): 421–47.

Okihiro, Gary. *Margins and Mainstreams: Asians in American History and Culture*. Seattle: U of Washington P, 1994.

330

Lily Cho

Ong, Aihwa. *Buddha Is Hiding: Refugees, Citizenship, the New America*. Berkeley: U of California P, 2003.

___. "Cyberpublics and Diaspora Politics among Transnational Chinese." *Interventions* 5.1 (2003): 82–100.

___. *Flexible Citizenship: The Cultural Logics of Transnationality*. Durham, NC: Duke UP, 1999.

Prakash, Gyan. *Bonded Histories: Genealogies of Labor Servitude in Colonial India*. Cambridge, UK: Cambridge UP, 1990.

Roy, Patricia. *A White Man's Province: British Columbia Politicians and Chinese and Japanese Immigrants 1858–1914*. Vancouver: U of British Columbia P, 1989.

Scott, David. *Conscripts of Modernity: The Tragedy of Colonial Enlightenment*. Durham, NC: Duke UP, 2004.

___. *Refashioning Futures: Criticism after Postcoloniality*. Princeton, NJ: Princeton UP, 1999.

Sharpe, Jenny. "Is the United States Postcolonial?" *Diaspora* 4.2 (1995): 181–199.

Slemon, Stephen. "Post-Colonial Critical Theories." *Postcolonial Discourses: An Anthology*. Ed. Gregory Castle. London: Blackwell, 2001. 99–118.

Spivak, Gayatri. "Diasporas Old and New: Women in the Transnational World." *Textual Practice* 10.2 (1996): 245–269.

Tölölyan, Khachig. "Rethinking Diaspora(s): Stateless Power in the Transnational Moment." *Diaspora* 5.1 (1996): 3–36.

Wah, Fred. *Diamond Grill*. Edmonton: NeWest, 1996.

___. "Half-Bred Poetics." *Faking It: Poetics and Hybridity*. Edmonton: NeWest, 2000. 71–96.

Walsh, Rebecca. "Global Diasporas: Introduction." *Interventions* 5.1 (2003): 1–11.

Ward, W. Peter. *White Canada Forever: Popular Attitudes and Public Policy toward Orientals in British Columbia*. Montreal: McGill-Queen's UP, 1978.

Wickberg, Edgar, et al. *From China to Canada: A History of the Chinese Communities in Canada*. Toronto: McClelland, 1983.

Yun, Lisa. "Under the Hatches: American Coolie Ships and Nineteenth-Century Narratives of Pacific Passage." *Amerasia Journal* 28.2 (2002): 38–61.

Yun, Lisa, and Ricardo Laremont. "Chinese Coolies and African Slaves in Cuba 1847–74." *Journal of Asian American Studies* 4.2 (2001): 99–122.

20 Ireland, Empire and Utopia
Irish Postcolonial Criticism and the Utopian Impulse

Eóin Flannery

A Response

The idioms and the methodologies of 'Utopia' have always been explicit and implicit in both projects of colonial acquisition and expansion, and in the differential projects of anti-colonial theory and practice. Yet there has never been an adequate commerce of ideas established between the respective contemporary fields of Utopian studies and postcolonial studies. However, in a recent essay in this journal, the postcolonial scholar, Bill Ashcroft, attempted to bridge the theoretical hiatus between the two fields.[1] In 'Critical Utopias' Ashcroft essentially provides a literary critical mapping of how 'the Utopian' has figured in the literary art of Anglophone colonial, anti-colonial and postcolonial crucibles. Ashcroft's summary Utopian/postcolonial survey takes its theoretical impetus, naturally enough, from a conversation between Ernst Bloch and Theodor Adorno in 1964, in which Adorno adumbrates the repressed knowledge that each individual harbours of a possible Utopia – we know that a better *possible* world exists, but we are ideologically persuaded that the possible is actually the impossible.[2] In addition to foundational thinkers such as Bloch and Adorno, Ashcroft also enlists other theorists of the Utopian, including Herbert Marcuse and Fredric Jameson. The survey is not confined to theoretical utopias, however, as Ashcroft subsequently traverses a variety of historical times and spaces in divining traces of literary Utopian dynamism in colonial contexts. Invoked in this generous inventory are: Thomas More's originary *Utopia*; Shakespeare's *The Tempest*; and Defoe's *Robinson Crusoe* – the latter two, of course, are representative of the Utopian colonial project, but are also read as texts that are capable of producing their own Utopian counter-narratives of anti-colonial resistance. In contemporary terms, Ashcroft straddles the Indian sub-continent; Africa

Eóin Flannery, "Ireland, Empire and Utopia: Irish Postcolonial Criticism and the Utopian Impulse." *Textual Practice*, 24(3), 2010: 453–481. Reprinted by permission of Taylor & Francis Ltd.

Postcolonial Studies: An Anthology, First Edition. Edited by Pramod K. Nayar.
Editorial material and organization © 2016 John Wiley & Sons, Ltd.
Published 2016 by John Wiley & Sons, Ltd.

and the Caribbean, specifically: Salman Rushdie; JM Coetzee; Edouard Glissant; Aime Cesaire; Derek Walcott; and Edward Kamau Brathwaite. Ashcroft's intervention is distinguished by its concentration on what are, putatively, canonical texts of postcolonial literary studies. And while the species of utopia canvassed by Ashcroft is one that seeks to undermine the naturalised centrality of 'History' as discourse, there is an implicit assumption in such a parade of writers of a 'postcolonial History', or 'post-colonial Tradition' within its literary branch. Regardless of this initial point of contention, the virtue of Ashcroft's essay is its dedication to the necessary relevance of Utopian literary critical; literary historical; and historiographical strategies to debates within postcolonial studies. Yet, as I have indicated, in this speculative initiative by Ashcroft these critical strategies seem to be predominantly confined to literary horizons and there is little engagement with neo-Marxist critiques within postcolonial studies itself. These features may be consequences of the fact that the range of Utopian theorists referred to may be foundational, but it is not extensive. While the employment of Bloch is naturally instructive and a contemporary Utopian critic such as Tom Moylan is summarily cited, there is no reference to seminal figures within the Utopian field such as: Lyman Tower Sargent; Ruth Levitas; Darko Suvin; Lucy Sargisson; Krishan Kumar; Barbara Goodwin; Gregory Claeys; Raffaella Baccolini and Vincent Geoghegan.

Finally, with respect to the postcolonial aspects of Ashcroft's piece; the essay commits a familiar error of omission, one that seems to have been redressed in many publications on postcolonial studies but that does persist. The case of Ireland as either a Utopian, postcolonial or Utopian-postcolonial case-study is neither addressed nor alluded to at any stage. Such an oversight is disappointing given Ireland's protracted colonial history and its exemplary role as an early twentieth century pioneer in anti-colonial theory and practice. Furthermore, Ireland has a distinguished history office Utopian writing, mythology and political philosophy, which would clearly enrich any discussion of the commonalities of the fields of Utopian studies and postcolonial studies.[3] The purpose of the present essay is to respond to Ashcroft's provocative critical alignment of the Utopian and the postcolonial, and to furnish necessary modifications and supplements to the argument developed therein. With this in mind, my argument will accent the inherently Utopian cast of much of the recent and ongoing literary historical; literary critical; historiographical; and theoretical writing within contemporary Irish postcolonial studies. In providing an effective metacritical survey of these Utopian-postcolonial vectors in Irish literary and cultural studies, this essay will address the implicated inter-disciplinary projects that constitute the field of Irish postcolonial studies. The ensuing metacritique argues that not only are some of the major strands of Utopian postcolonial critique focused on interrogating the philosophical limits and lacunae of the contested legacies of 'Enlightenment' thought; British imperial discourses; and bourgeois Irish nationalism, but they are also involved in tracking the Utopian energies of subaltern Irish nationalisms and in retrieving the work and reputations of Irish anti-colonial thinkers, writers and activists in light of contemporary international postcolonial theory and activism. At root, the discussion displays the urgency with which postcolonial critics have approached, and attempted to appropriate, the Utopian dynamism of historical Irish anti-colonial thought and action in their own Utopian engagements with the prevailing political and economic conjuncture in Irish society. These projects are by no means homogenous and it is not to be concluded that they are easily woven together as fractions of a sanctioned critical consensus within

Irish postcolonial studies. They are representative of a viable critical mass within Irish criticism that accepts the legitimacy of Utopian imagination, and that has gleaned valuable lessons from the historiographical, often subalternist, methodologies of international postcolonial studies. In sum, the present essay has a particular focus on matters that pertain to the utopic in terms of the literary historical and the historiographical within Irish postcolonial studies, and will, one hopes, catalyse future interventions that might engage with other facets of Irish colonial history and postcolonial criticism.

Ireland and Utopia

In his polemical book, *The End of Utopia*, the American historian Russell Jacoby suggests that the Utopian ideals that once nourished intellectual dissent and activated movements for radical social change have been largely abandoned in a world that is content to doze in a state of blissful compliance and comfortable political apathy.[4] In this book Jacoby provides a general assault on the moribund nature of intellectual engagement with the presiding politico-economic conjuncture, particularly that pursued by those resident in the Western academy. In his estimation, the parameters of contemporary critical commentary have been foreshortened and there is no desire to overhaul radically the mechanisms of exclusion and inequality that are the trademark of the current world economic system. All of which, according to Jacoby, is an abdication of the Utopian responsibilities and possibilities of intellectual labour. As a series of intellectual projects that trades on its antagonistic relations to the homogenising dynamics of the historical and contemporary global capitalist system, post-colonial studies is emphatically implicated in Jacoby's polemic. As Jacoby argues: 'The dearth of economic and sociological analyses, the inflation of cultural approaches, the assumption that cultures fundamentally diverge, the failure or inability to consider the forces of assimilation … and the lack of any political vision or alternative'[5] are a depressingly familiar feature of contemporary intellectual debate. Without rigorous conceptual clarity, an economy of linguistic opacity has stepped in to fill the gap – an economy motored by the decentring modes of poststructuralist theories. And while the instability and elusiveness championed and practiced by 'theoretical' interventions can be adjudged as legitimate strategies of subversion in culturalist challenges to representational domination or elision, for Jacoby intellectual vacuity is the net result. In his conclusion, such tactical ambiguity does not embody any sense of subversion, but is characteristic of 'the timid conclusions, chalky language and toothless concepts'[6] of culturalist criticism. In the end, there is merely a cosmetic attempt to broaden the constituencies of participation and the terms of access to hierarchical wealth; an insidious domestication of dissent. Such a prospect constitutes a dereliction of a Utopian intellectual responsibility and stands as an aborted imaginative impulse.

The content and tenor of Jacoby's argument seem apposite to recent historical and theoretical appraisals of Ireland's colonial and postcolonial histories, as well as to assessments of Irish social and economic histories since the 'immaculate conception' of the Celtic Tiger economy, and its attendant boons and burdens. As Peadar Kirby has argued in his essay 'Contested Pedigrees of the Celtic Tiger', the phenomenon of the Celtic Tiger has been readily seized as an object ripe for narration; for strategic emplotment within certain legitimate hermeneutic codes.[7] Kirby's meta-historical interrogation of the Celtic Tiger's pedigree highlights the extent to which this period in recent Irish social and economic history has been seized for narrative justification. The economic vigour that has been, and remains to a lesser degree, has unquestionably brought unprecedented fiscal wealth to many social constituencies to which it would have been here-to-fore unknown. But, as Kirby concludes, the same wave of economic buoyancy has served to exacerbate the gap between those with relative wealth and those in relative poverty. While the financial largesse of the Celtic Tiger period is often, crudely, popularly perceived as a Utopian arrival – an affirmation of the progressive tenets of liberal modernisation that were invested in by successive Irish administrations since the 1960s – as Kirby suggests, these affective pleasures of desire and satisfaction are confined to sections of Irish society, while a whole raft of the population remains confined to states of anxiety and frustration. In the sense, the Utopian impulse belongs to the latter and has merely mutated into a hollowed-out repetition of the eternal present in the former. The Celtic Tiger has nourished a false convergent genus of desire – which is, in its truly Utopian guise, a heteronymous and quite specific mode of wish fulfilment. The present has been eroticised as the apotheosis of historical progress; there is no appetite for alternatives and under such dispensations, as the necessary faculties of Utopian desire are easily jettisoned. Kirby's critique belongs to a Blochian tradition of Utopian thought, which asserts the existence of the Utopian within despair – a longing that stretches out of the present towards an unseen, imagined future. A future that, as my discussion of the work of several of the leading Irish postcolonial critics urges, is significantly moulded by the energies of the past, or, as Raffaella Baccolini suggests in a Benjaminian reading of the relationship between the past and the present, which itself is reminiscent of that detailed in much Irish postcolonial writing:

> The Utopian value of memory rests in nurturing a culture of memory and sustaining a theory of remembrance. These actions, therefore, become important elements of a political, Utopian praxis of change, action, and empowerment: indeed, our reconstructions of the past shape our present and future. Memory, then, to be of use to Utopia, needs to dissociate itself from its traditional link to the metaphor of storage and identify itself as a process.[8]

While Kirby's essay primarily focuses upon the narrative schematisation of the Celtic Tiger period in Irish history, it is equally a version of the literary-critical methodologies that have been brought to bear on the histories of Irish modernisation under the auspices of postcolonial studies. Kirby specifically objects to Rory O'Donnell's narration of the history of the Celtic Tiger; he rejects the manner in which such narrative manoeuvring becomes part of a self-fulfilling prophesy, namely the celebration of the continued success of Irish modernisation.[9] In many ways, Kirby's critique is informed by the theoretical scepticism that is characteristic of many interventions within postcolonial studies. The 'image' of Celtic Tiger Ireland and its representation approaches the condition of a 'naturalised' system of semiotics – it is a brand, a product, a series of events that must be marshalled (narrated) in order to project and to protect a commodity. In his concern with how the Celtic Tiger is portrayed as the legacy of, and the ultimate testimony to, Ireland's subscription to capitalist modernisation, Kirby's work is allied to some of the most cogent critiques of the limitations of such a socio-economic trajectory. Not only does Kirby reference Luke Gibbons and Declan Kiberd, but he skilfully exercises their differential postcolonial readings of Irish culture to perform a convincing counter-argument to that canvassed by those commentators on Irish society who adhere to the modalities and the accruals of modernisation.

Under the aegis of this internally differentiated constituency, often referenced as 'revisionist', the 'past' is treated with a level of suspicion – it is ruthlessly narrated as contributive to, or as inhibitive of, the momentum of Irish modernisation. Similarly, the social and cultural institutions that are adjudged to have embodied outmoded or discredited social, cultural or political beliefs are subjected to unforgiving opprobrium in dismissive historical representations. Irish history, in this world-view, has been diachronically moving towards such a potential economic miracle under the watchful eye of the politico-economic forces of liberal capitalist modernisation. Equally, the economic uniformity, cultural convergence and social fragmentation that these vectors of social progress entail are necessary agents of the general prosperity that prevails. Kirby's anxiety is that the economic success that Ireland feasted upon for a decade, and that in truth is still evident despite recent downturns, bleaches the nation of any impulse towards a coherent sense of identity. With the historiographical and critical assaults on erstwhile social institutions, such as religion and nationalism as two major examples, now almost complete, and their relative banishment to nostalgia or historical exile, economic success now becomes the index of personal belonging and national identity. As a consequence any resources, or will, towards egalitarian social transformation in Ireland become very difficult to sustain and in many ways are bribed out existence. The present conjuncture in Ireland evidences little or no will to equalise society; there is little motivation to re-imagine in any lateral political or cultural sense, as it is far easier to luxuriate in the transient benefits of economic wealth. Kirby's conclusion suggests that Ireland needs a transfusion of Utopian critique if it is to be lulled out of this consumerist concussion:

> The resituating of the state in this era of neo-liberalism so that it becomes subservient to market forces fatally undermines its ability to embody a project of social transformation. This shift is clearly evident in the Irish case as the state is increasingly seen to serve the needs of an economic elite while neglecting the growing inequality that is undermining the cohesion of society.[10]

From a postcolonial perspective, then, how do such Utopian ideas and ideals cohere with the variegated historical, literary and theoretical projects of its field? Initially the Marxist heritage of postcolonial studies; the field's concentration on historical and contemporary systematic oppression and disenfranchisement; and the discursive and historiographical re-representation and retrieval of what are often termed 'subaltern' constituencies and cultural practices chime with the ethical and material spirit of Utopian thought. The imagination of a better future is very much bound up with the re-appropriation of the past and the unearthing of alternative historical practices and experiences. In the Irish case, Joe Cleary argues that the accumulated projects of postcolonial studies represent a critique of theories of modernisation, which, he argues, are at root latter day incarnations of the rapacity of imperialism and its own battery of legitimating narrative codes.[11] Cleary's own work is deeply influenced by Jameson and offers pessimistic readings of the social and cultural implications of Ireland's uncritical embrace of a form of capitalist modernisation and itself intersects with both the political spirit, and many of the arguments, dealt with below in my extended discussion of the Utopian impulses of Irish postcolonial studies. It is beyond the scope of this essay to address all of the divergent opinions expressed and emotions exercised in evaluating the relative merits and demerits of Ireland's economic wind-fall, but I do want to address this one strand of cultural criticism that pre-dates, but that is also synchronous with the period of Ireland's recent prosperity, namely postcolonial studies.

In his introduction to the recently published special Irish number of *Utopian Studies*, Tom Moylan, the editor, alludes to the often underappreciated fact that 'individual scholars have written about Utopian aspects of Irish culture'.[12] Moylan's point here explicitly refers to critics who have divined historical and literary historical traces of a Utopian impulse within Irish culture. Enumerated on Moylan's Irish Utopian roll-call are critics such as Colin Graham; Luke Gibbons; Declan Kiberd; Carmen Kuhling; Ralph Pordzik; and Michael Griffin. While pressures of space do not permit Moylan to elaborate on the specifics of each of these scholars, it is sufficient that a well-established Utopianist, such as Moylan acknowledges the Utopian motives of some of the most progressive critical thinkers and practitioners in contemporary Irish studies. In addition, it is note-worthy that the majority of Moylan's named critics have been instrumental in both the formative stages and, the later, metacritical critique of Irish postcolonial studies. While many historians, literary critics, economists and sociologists in Ireland have, often legitimately, raised objections to the political temper, cultural methodologies or historiographical procedures of Irish postcolonial studies, the implicit Utopian roots and geist of this suite of theoretical and historiographical resources has never been fully explored. Moylan's 'Introduction' is both salutary, and overdue, in its diagnosis of the Utopian spirit of many of the interventions within Irish postcolonial studies. Indeed, to illustrate further the increasing timeliness of ideational exchange between the fields of Utopian studies and postcolonial studies within an Irish context, elsewhere Moylan consciously invokes a number of recent publications within the field of Irish studies, which bear the theoretical watermark of postcolonial critique. Detailing the agenda of The Ralahine Centre for Utopian Studies at the University of Limerick, of which he is director, in 2006 Moylan states:

> Our project aims to stimulate research in all areas of Irish culture. And, as we discover the Utopian nature of each of our research objects, we will also seek to understand the role that social dreaming has played throughout Irish history, so that we can see more clearly how the Utopian, as opposed to the instrumental, process of 'reimagining' or 'reinventing' Ireland (to borrow from two recent titles) has brought us to where we are today and how it might affect where we might be going.[13]

As we shall discuss below, Moylan's intentions are vital elements of much recent postcolonial writing about Ireland; the Utopian impulse is both divined in previous moments of Irish history and it is deemed necessary to confrontations with the contemporary.

Ireland, Empire and Enlightenment

In *The Wretched of the Earth*, Frantz Fanon outlines the underlying violence that marks the colonial encounter and that similarly structures the relationship between the settler-coloniser and the native-colonised. He writes:

Their first encounter was marked by violence and their existence together – that is to say the exploitation of the native by the settler – was carried on by dint of a great array of bayonets and cannons. The settler and the native are old acquaintances. In fact, the settler is right when he speaks of knowing 'them' well. For it is the settler who has brought the native into existence and who perpetuates his existence.[14]

The combined projects of Irish postcolonial studies are concerned with explicating that very process through which an Irish colonial 'native' was brought into existence; in other words, these heteronymous critical projects interrogate the political, cultural and economic discourses through which imperial modernity imposed itself on Ireland, and how it was forced to engage with, and in many cases obliterate, indigenous forms of 'counter-modernity'. Fanon's violence, enacted in this extract through military weaponry, is tracked within Irish postcolonial studies by scholars who strive to unearth, and to redeem, moments and patterns of Irish 'radical memory'; alternative modernity and counter-modern 'tradition'. The external imposition of imperial modernity in Ireland was a laterally traumatic experience, under which the cultural resources of the indigenous population were sundered or surrendered under the demands of a coercive colonial social programme. The cultural undergirding of Irish culture was consigned to history as a progressive and unrelenting teleological historical schema was grafted onto Irish society. The synchronicity of modernisation and imperialism is a primary concern of many Irish postcolonial critics and historians. The historical process of modernisation is not homogenous, but it does strive for homogeneity. Yet throughout the history of economic and political modernisation, there is always evidence of recalcitrance to its hegemony. Modernisation is not an inert state but an ongoing historical process that strives to achieve a sense of political and economic conformity. It is easy, then, to identify its shared interests with imperialism, which is underwritten by a similar accumulative desire. Indeed Saree Makdisi locates an explicit link between modernisation and imperialism at the end of the eighteenth-century and the beginning of the nineteenth-century, arguably the formative period of modern 'high' British imperialism. In Makdisi's view:

Modernization can in this sense be understood as the purest form of imperialism; this conviction is based on the fact that modernisation 'occurs at once in large-scale sweeps and bursts, but also in terms of the micrological, the quotidian…In effect, the project of modernization begins at the very moment a new territory is defined as pre-modern.[15]

One of the dominant strains of Irish postcolonial thought in contemporary Irish criticism is concerned with exposing the ways in which imperial modernity, itself only one route out of Enlightenment thought, was made manifest in Ireland in the nineteenth century, and in teasing out the many ways in which a distillation of modernisation theory realised, and retained, its dominance in both the political and cultural management of Irish society, particularly in the latter half of the twentieth century. It is significant that Irish postcolonial studies has striven not only to reject a universal type of Enlightenment, granted it does bear ferocious critical ire for its Scottish variant, but has eagerly sought out traces of alternative Enlightenment thinking that is an aggregation of indigenous circumstances and international Republican principles. The multicultural solidarity divined in the cultural politics of these late eighteenth century projects has also been mapped onto the political and cultural terrain of twentieth century Irish society, in which modernisation theory and its advocates are deemed to have hitched their wagon to a similarly universalising and exclusionary social programme as that promulgated in the most limited forms of Enlightenment thought.

The renewed Irish interest in critiquing dominant strands of Enlightenment thought, most vehemently its Scottish declension, and in co-opting alternative versions of Enlightenment to postcolonial projects has been noted by the eighteenth century scholar David Denby. Denby's essay 'Ireland, Modernization and the Enlightenment Debate' engages with these very matters, and focuses on an important volume of essays co-edited by Gibbons: *Reinventing Ireland: Culture, Society and the Global Economy.*[16] The editorial consensus of this latter publication rejects the passive acceptance of liberal universal principles in Irish society, and adheres to a breed of cosmopolitan egalitarianism.[17] Denby usefully sets out the terms of the so-called 'Enlightenment debate' that is no longer confined to the precincts of moral and political philosophy but has been transported to the sites of postcolonial debate. It is worth quoting Denby at length in order to grasp the basic concerns of this debate and then to translate its relevance to current conversations in Irish cultural criticism. He begins: 'The term 'Enlightenment' can be said to operate as a token, a coded signifier, and, simplifying only a little, as something which calls upon us to take sides'. Facing off against each other in this ideological confrontation are those who support the underlying tenets of Enlightenment thought: 'the liberals and probably the Marxists'; and those constituencies that are opposed: 'the neo-Aristotelians, some of the communitarians and the ecologists, the postmoderns'.[18] Underlying these juxtaposing ideological positions are contrary readings of the universalist rhetoric of the Enlightenment, and again this is usefully glossed by Denby:

> What in one idiom can be read as universal human rights, democratic sovereignty ... a rational, scientific and secularizing approach to the planning of modern societies, and a belief that human beings can effect progress through such planning, can be rewritten in another language as an exploitative human domination over nature, an atomistic definition of the human individual which cuts people off from tradition and community ... the 'Enlightenment project' has been so confident in the universality of its description of the human condition that it has had no compunction about exporting that model around the world, through colonization and now in the form of economic and cultural globalization.[19]

The validity of postcolonial critical approaches has been their consistent antagonistic stance against such cultural and political uniformity; postcolonial studies, including its literary, historical and theoretical facets, impress the agency of the local and the marginal both in spatial-geopolitical terms and in the temporal sense of historical, archival and non-archival recovery. As Luke Gibbons, Kevin Whelan, and David Lloyd demonstrate, there are indigenous forms of modernity or instances of radical tradition that offer affective, and effective, affronts to the self-validating logic of narrow versions of Enlightenment thought. Nevertheless, as Denby argues subsequently it is self-defeating to merely reject the philosophical heritage of the late eighteenth century Enlightenment. Recourse to a purely relativist, postmodern system of ethics, aesthetics or historiography is equally narrow in its prodigious playfulness. And in this criticism Denby largely echoes with the postcolonial retrieval of valuable elements of Enlightenment thought in Irish studies. As will become clear there are discernible affinities between Denby's conclusions and the most progressive contributions to Ireland's postcolonial Enlightenment debate. Specifically Denby suggests that 'in a context where historical and contemporary issues have become so explicitly entwined, historical writing must enable a dialogue between past and present, in which, among other things, the coherence and potentialities of the past, unclear to those who lived at the time, become clear to us with the benefit of hindsight'.[20] It is this school of postcolonial thought within Irish studies that I intend to address, an affiliated grouping that has disinterred 'elements of Enlightenment history which have been obscured or insufficiently emphasised' and has cast them 'back into full view as part of the contemporary dialogue'.[21]

The impacts of Enlightenment thought and those of imperially driven processes of modernisation on Ireland have been key concerns for many Irish postcolonial critics; this has primarily centred around figures such as Seamus Deane, Gibbons and Whelan, each of whom has looked to illustrate the ways in which Irish culture and society was adjudicated to be deviant from the dominant strains of 'rationality' and, latterly, 'sociability' characteristic of enlightened social collectives. These critics are by no means uniform in their historical and philosophical convictions and/or sources, but each does look to exemplary figures in late eighteenth-century Irish society for corrective guidance in their respective postcolonial projects. Deane, in particular and characteristically, was at the vanguard of the philosophical resuscitation of the work of Edmund Burke, having completed his doctoral work on Burke at Cambridge in the late 1960s and subsequently employed Burke as a critical compass in much of his subsequent literary historical output. Equally, and as Conor McCarthy has cursorily demonstrated, Deane, and Irish postcolonial studies at large, owe a debt to the philosophical work of the Frankfurt School of Critical Theory, especially that of Theodor Adorno and Walter Benjamin.[22] The critical pessimism of Adorno can be traced in Deane's dismissive view of imperial modernity as it impacted on Irish colonial society; the rational functionalism and the universalising dogma of individual sociability based on cultural similarity are primary among these critical targets.[23]

The watermarks of Burke's work are also evident in Gibbons' most recent work on postcolonial ethics and it is to Gibbons' work that I want initially to draw attention. Gibbons has taken Deane's lead and recuperated a version of Burke that is critical of the excesses of British imperialism, a Burke that offers philosophical guidance in the formulation of an egalitarian postcolonial moral economy based on differential solidarity. While Gibbons' major publication on Burke is a relatively recent venture, the spirit of postcolonial solidarity has been a consistent feature of his work for many years.[24] But Gibbons does not confine his philosophical mining of the late eighteenth century to the work of Burke; he also locates a resistant egalitarian cultural politics in the political, non-confessional agenda of the Republican United Irish movement. The United Irishmen represent a strand of what Gibbons has termed 'a postcolonial Enlightenment'; an Enlightenment that is supportive of indigenous cultures, one that respects the cultural currency of the so-called 'traditional' or 'obsolescent' societies.[25] Gibbons views the movement as a viable historical instance and source of cross-cultural solidarity based on civic, non-confessional Republican principles. The political and cultural accommodation offered by the United Irishmen is one that embraces the idealistic notion of an accessible civic public sphere. Combining an effective critique of Scottish Enlightenment thought with a Utopian and postcolonial investment in the cultural politics and ethics of the United Irishmen's project, he states:

> New concepts of history, and related stages theories of development were among the most important contributions of the Scottish Enlightenment to Western intellectual culture. What is not often realised, however, is that in opposing progress to primitivism, and civility to barbarism, the Scottish intelligentsia were concerned to dispel the threat not only of a distant, exotic 'other', but also the savage on their native shore, in the form of Gaelic, Catholic culture.[26]

By way of contrast to such a prescriptive, stadial calibration of histories, cultures, and creeds, Gibbons posits the egalitarian impulses of the United Irishmen who 'sought to embrace this despised social order, including it within their democratic vision of a new Ireland rather than relegating it to the fate of "doomed peoples"'.[27] There are overt Utopian dynamics behind the failed but enduring principles of United Irish egalitarian democratic principles, in Gibbons' estimation, and it is plausible that such historical precedence can transfuse the convergent politics of contemporary Ireland. For Gibbons, the United Irish programme participates in the contemporary postcolonial interrogation of 'the limits of the Enlightenment'.[28] As he concludes: 'Part of the postcolonial (or postmodern) critique of the Enlightenment has been precisely its condescension, if not racist hostility, towards 'native' cultures: by gesturing towards new versions of cultural interaction and religious tolerance, the United Irishmen may be seen as pre-empting this critique but without rejecting the powerful emancipatory vision of the Enlightenment in the process'.[29]

In his major study of Edmund Burke, *Edmund Burke and Ireland: Aesthetics, Politics and the Colonial Sublime*, Gibbons attempts to establish a philosophical framework through which postcolonial solidarity or cross-colonial sympathy can blossom outside of the strict moral parameters of mainstream enlightened 'modern' philosophy. Traversing a range of political philosophy, visual aesthetics and Scottish Enlightenment political economy, Gibbons concludes that Burke's writings on the sublime in his *Enquiry* coupled with the dual effect of his personal linkage to the native Catholic population in Ireland and Warren Hastings' campaign of bloody imperial rule in India contribute to Burke's modification of standard Enlightenment beliefs and is a tangible endorsement of an anti-imperial position. Burke's work, for Gibbons, is not simply a crude rejection of the founding structures of this discourse, but constitutes a 'radical extension of Enlightenment thinking'.[30] Gibbons' advancement of Burke as an exemplar of this brand of alternative Enlightenment has international resonances in the work of Sankar Muthu, whose book *Enlightenment Against Empire* charts equivalent undervalued trajectories in late eighteenth century political philosophy and who concludes his book with resolutely postcolonial and Utopian sentiments by arguing that:

> if a central reason to study the history of political thought is to gain the perspective of another set of assumptions and arguments that are shaped by different historical sensibilities and directed toward distinct political phenomena, and thus to

defamiliarize our otherwise complacent political and ethical beliefs and priorities, then the study of Enlightenment anti-imperialism offers productive opportunities for such a task.[31]

Such directions have traditionally given way in accounts (both positive and negative) of the Enlightenment to more limited versions. Muthu's reclamation of Diderot, Kant and Herder is based on his conviction that their legacies as figureheads of the Enlightenment have been ill-served by its widespread condemnation as a philosophical resource for a universal morality, which legitimated vile colonial expropriation, genocide and disenfranchisement. In some ways, Gibbons strikes an equal blow for Burke in his work, voicing a more nuanced version of Burke's work, one that is amenable to radical historiographical and ethical projects under the rubric of liberatory postcolonial studies. The radical nature of Gibbons' Burke is evident in Gibbons' assertion that Burke's recalibration of the mainstream Enlightenment 'sought to arouse our sympathies not just for (corporal) violations of our human nature ... but also for fundamental breaches of cultural integrity which addresses questions of cultural difference, and which thus challenge the parochial emphasis on 'sameness' which often passes for cosmopolitanism'.[32] The homogenising impulses of modernity, as diagnosed within postcolonial studies, therefore can take instruction from Burke's broadly inclusive sympathetic sublime 'which crosses cultural boundaries', and through which 'members of other cultures can be induced to feel a sense of moral outrage with an intensity not unlike members of the aggrieved society themselves'.[33]

Under the civilisational imaginary of the Scottish Enlightenment, there was little 'sympathy' for cultural 'others'; similarity and a communion of social standards was the accepted universal norm. Such a philosophical school demanded a renunciation of 'local' tradition and an amelioration or sundering of anachronistic social systems. The arrow of history was firmly pointed towards a preordained future and those communities that failed to keep step, or were incapable of keeping step, with its progress were either to be consigned to the oblivion of the past, or abstracted into the consolatory topographies of romantic nostalgia. Cultural difference, then, was not to be countenanced and sympathetic feeling, or moral outrage, were not transferable across these social borders. Yet as Gibbons amply outlines, Burke's newly hewn programme of anti-imperial social justice and moral solidarity provides a corrective to such exclusionary cultural politics. The sufferings of oppressed others, who reside in cognate contexts of colonial occupation is central to this Burkean idea; the severity of suffering can be felt across oceans and continents and is a potential germ of anti-colonial resistance. As Gibbons concludes, alluding to the cross-continental reach of Burke's anti-imperial vision:

the logic of Burke's position is in fact to extend the ethical basis of the Enlightenment, bringing the imaginative reach of sympathy to regions excluded from mainstream Enlightenment thought. For Burke, this involved a profound, troubled engagement with the plight of colonized peoples whether in Ireland, India, or America, an extension of cross-cultural solidarity to those cultures that were doomed, according to Enlightenment theories of progress, to the dustbin of history.[34]

Gibbons' refraction of Burke's writings and political speeches in terms of early anti-colonial discourse were anticipated, to a degree, in Saree Makdisi's pioneering study of British Romanticism and empire in his 1998 book *Romantic Imperialism: Universal Empire and the Culture of Modernity*. Makdisi presents a powerfully argued critique of British imperialism, proposing that the counter-rational aesthetic impulses of Romanticism embodied signal affronts to the relentless spate of imperial modernity. Indeed for our present purposes, it is apposite that Makdisi focuses on Burke's contradictory relationship to the machinations, and logic, of Britain's imperial mission. Makdisi's reading of Burke's most famous intervention in the administration of British India, the trial of Warren Hastings, is figured in terms of a conjunction between Burke's political philosophy, his aesthetic writings and his ethics. For Makdisi, Burke's vigorous declamations of Hastings' administration of British holdings in India are wedded to his conceptualisation of the sublime, a point also raised in his study by Gibbons. Makdisi argues that Burke's emphatic 'differentiation' of India as a physical, cultural and moral 'Other' is best understood in terms of the sub-continent's sublimity; in other words, 'Burke's respect for the cultural difference of India is inextricably caught up with his fear of India'.[35] According to this argument, in Burke's view Hastings' great crime was not to be part of an exploitative imperial mission, but simply that his methods of administering that mission in India were excessive in their violences. There is no doubt, in Makdisi's reading of Burke, that the necessity for the imperial link was ever questioned by Burke; the Indian population is incapable of self-governance and consequently requires political and moral tutelage under the benevolent imperial order. The core of Makdisi's argument is that Burke's critiques of British imperialism were founded on his disapproval of *how* the empire was governed and never on the issue of whether imperial expansion was a morally objectionable matter in and of itself. While Burke was sensitive to the existence of pronounced differences in the moral and cultural patterns of British and Indian societies and insisted upon the fact that these specificities should be respected, there is a sense in Makdisi's case that the superiority of British civility is always assumed. Nested within Burke's writings on British imperialism there is a discernible trace of generosity towards the colonial 'other'. While the colonial mission is taken for granted, Burke does betray a radical sympathetic urge towards under the shadow of this mission. It is at this point that we can divine some convergence between Makdisi and Gibbons, and their respective versions of the 'colonial Burke'. Yet Gibbons is insistent in his espousal of Burke as a precursor of contemporary postcolonial ethics, while Makdisi concludes that Burke's attitude to Britain's oppressed colonial subjects was one that was marked by an abiding contradiction. He concludes:

> Burke's impassioned … speeches on India are characterized by an underlying tension between, on the one hand, his universalistic claims about the trans-cultural and univocal 'nature' (and hence 'rights') of humankind; and, on the other, his repeated invocation of a version of polygenesis as well as the contemporaneous scientific … concepts of preformationism and anti-mutationism, according to which 'improvement' in level and status, whether for species, for individuals, for societies, or for classes, is impossible.[36]

Through this comparative positioning of Gibbons' and Makdisi's respective versions of Burke's ethics, politics and aesthetics, we can conclude that Gibbons' Utopian configuration of a 'postcolonial' Burke does not go uncontested. But equally, it demonstrates the necessity of bringing *Irish* postcolonial and *Irish* Utopian readings into established, and often dominant, interpretations of histories of colonialism and Utopianism; processes which can allow for productive, and enabling mutual trade and/or tension.

Revival, Rising and Utopia

In his critique of Celtic Tiger Ireland, which is alluded to above, Kirby juxtaposes the contemporary economic success with the lateral dynamism of the Irish Revival at the end of the nineteenth century and the beginning of the twentieth century. Kirby exposes what he believes is an essential shallowness inherent to many of the contemporary celebrations of the recent time of economic prosperity. And in his analysis, he is dismissive of the alleged achievements and legacies of the contemporary 'revival' in comparison with the earlier period of social transformation:

> What characterised Ireland's invention in the period 1890 to 1920 was a strong civil society, mobilised in a rich variety of social, political, cultural and economic organisations promoting through vigorous political means the building of an economy based on native capabilities and resources to serve the good of society at local, regional and national level and creating a rich and inclusive 'imagined community' to which the majority could, with pride, owe allegiance.[37]

For Kirby, the earlier period is distinguished by its adherence to a suite of egalitarian Utopian principles, which underlay the anti-colonial nationalist trajectories of many of these social and cultural movements. Informed by a sense of crisis, these enterprises invested heavily in creativity in all spheres of social, cultural and political imagination. Yet by way of undistinguished comparison, 'the resituating of the state in this era of neo-liberalism so that it becomes subservient to market forces fatally undermines its ability to embody a project of social transformation'.[38] In contemporary Ireland desire, that necessary ingredient of Utopian thought and action, has been usurped, blunted or crassly satiated. The absence of radical Utopian impulses in contemporary Irish society is a failure of both form and content – we are satisfied to subscribe to the mechanisms of and to the daily material rewards accrued within this system. And for Kirby that heralds nothing more than a complacent acquiescence with inequality and social disfunction.

It is instructive that he should invoke the economic and cultural creativities of the Irish Revival period as exemplary of what he terms 'native capabilities and resources' as a counterpoint to his lament for the dereliction of Utopian social imagination in contemporary Ireland. And it is to this period that we turn now – a period retrieved and celebrated in much greater detail by Declan Kiberd and PJ Mathews as one of neglected social possibilities by the post-Independence Irish Free State, but one that was infused with radical Utopian energies in its prime, and that retains such exemplary Utopian dynamism. My focus in this section is on another strain of Utopian retrieval within Irish postcolonial studies. While, as we have noted, the discussion thus far has spotlighted an array of unrealised potentials, this section deals with Utopian impulses that did yield concrete and enduring results – moments of Utopian purchase – within the social reality of Irish political, economic and cultural life, some of the legacies of which are still evident in Irish society and others that have, lamentably, been neglected. Specifically, we will address the work of Kiberd and Mathews, both of whom configure their critiques of late nineteenth and early twentieth century Irish society in resolutely postcolonial, and, it seems, Utopian, terms. Most explicitly, both critics treat the period of the Irish Revival of the 1890s and early decades of the 1900s as a time of intense and profitable Utopian imagining and activism in Ireland.

While Kiberd's work has alluded more generally, if over a longer time-frame, to the richly Utopian cast of the skein of social movements that were active during the Irish Revival, Mathews' work has provided a singular, focused assessment of these projects. Mathews' *Revival: The Abbey Theatre, Sinn Fein, The Gaelic League and the Co-operative Movement* is, as the title evidences, a materialist argument that each of these movements were never mutually exclusive, but were part of a broad Utopian energy that informed Irish political, cultural and economic life at the end of the nineteenth and beginning of the twentieth centuries. Mathews' assessment asserts its materialism overtly and it is unmistakeably postcolonial in its exposure of the anti-colonial and nationalist enterprises of the Revival. But equally he lauds the tenacious Utopianism of each of the projects as singular undertakings and as collective, or at least imbricated, exercises. Indeed Mathews' postcolonial methodology intersects considerably with John McLeod's recently coined agenda for postcolonial studies. In his editorial to *The Routledge Companion to Postcolonial Studies*, McLeod argues:

> To enter into postcolonial studies is to engage in a self-conscious process of contestation; it is to contend often with both the *form* and *content* of prevailing knowledge … It is a concept which helps us to frame and ask questions from a particular, interested vantage, and which secures a Utopian ethics at its heart.[39]

Such a manifesto for postcolonial studies is reflected in both Mathews' and Kiberd's engagements with the Irish Revivalist movements. Both are keen to redress the neglect and distortion of the Revival's achievements in post-Independence historical accounts, and both stress the Utopian imagination of the earlier period in its 'revival' and creation of viable economic and cultural forms. Their contiguous critiques underscore the disingenuous ways in which the combined enterprises of the Irish Revival were processed in later historical and literary historical renditions of the period – renditions that tarnished or obscured the fertile Utopian heritage of Irish anti-colonial nationalism and, it seems, impoverished the reservoirs of social imagination in Ireland up to the present day. In fact, the Utopian and combative nature of McLeod's version of postcolonial studies seems fitting to the entire range of Utopian postcolonial projects undertaken in recent Irish postcolonial critiques.

Mathews opens his account of the Irish Revival with an unalloyed declaration of his intentions – which largely centre on the contention that there has been a large degree of misrepresentation and miscomprehension in previous accounts of the period:

> The broad aim is to open up the early productions of the Irish theatre movement to the discursive and material complexities of their historical moment and to explore the degree to which they were influenced by, and in turn influenced, the

dynamics of the Irish Revival. Central to this manoeuvre is the belief that the early Irish theatre initiative can be usefully understood as an important 'self-help' movement that has much in common with comparable projects such as the Gaelic League, the Irish Agricultural Organisation Society (IAOS) and Sinn Fein … The purpose of this book is to recover these connections and reveal the degree to which a progressive self-help ethos was subscribed to across a range of cultural and social initiatives during the Irish Revival.[40]

In an effort to rescue the Irish theatre movement, and its pioneers, Yeats, Synge, Gregory, Martyn *et al.*, from the consolations of the abstract, the mystical, the esoteric, Mathews views this theatrical movement as clearly in tune with and contributive to the more 'material' self-help activism of the period. At a general level, Mathews positions the aggregation of social and cultural projects as testimony to an Irish declension of what Paul Gilroy has theorised as 'alternative modernity'.[41] These variegated, yet interlaced, projects 'were not achieved by adopting colonial models of modernization', but were fashioned by an understanding that the so-called traditional does not translate as 'anachronistic' or 'dormant', or 'obsolete' – contrarily, tradition is comprehended 'as a stimulus towards innovation and change rather than a barrier to it'.[42] Mathews' introductory comments invoke a range of theoretical and historiographical intersections: from the internationally postcolonial in Gilroy to the 'nationally' postcolonial, Lloyd and Whelan, with respect to the notion of the alternatively modern; and to recent Utopian writing on memory and social change in the work of Baccolini and Elspeth Probyn. But equally the exchange between the past and the present that was such a dynamic feature of these social movements partakes of a radical Utopianism. These initiatives, as Mathews outlines, seek nothing less than the wholesale structural re-imagination of Irish society in its cultural, social and political forms and strove to negotiate such change in natively produced Utopian idioms.

What was witnessed in the evolving 'self-help' culture in Ireland during the 1890s was an imaginative alternative to such formal political stasis. Again Mathews highlights the dynamism of these projects as they turned to local, traditional resources as assertions of renewed political agency and cultural empowerment. In his view:

Central the endeavour was the realization that the Irish had accepted London as the centre of culture and civilization for too long and that the time had come for the Irish people to regenerate their own intellectual terms of reference and nar-ratives of cultural meaning … [and] it is hardly surprising that the revival would eventually produce a movement which would take the self-help ethos to its most radical conclusion by advocating an alternative politics.[43]

While the precise species of 'alternative politics' that would emerge as a legacy of this series of social endeavours has, itself, been fiercely contested, '[with] the development of the national institutions and the emergence of a new wave of nationalist newspapers, an infrastructure was put in place which allowed the "imagining" of the Irish nation'.[44] Here Mathews consciously alludes to Benedict Anderson's conceptualisation of the imaginative fabrics of national identities, but, in fact, Mathews extends his narrative and, in distinction to Anderson, Mathews believes that it was a conjunction of nationalist newspaper publications together with the birth of the national theatre movement that furnished the public and the performative spaces of the imagination of Irish national identities. Crucially, these combined phenomena house discernible Utopian energies, and in many respects cohere with Valerie Fournier's assessment that 'Utopianism is not a blueprint for a 'perfect society' but may be better conceptualised as a movement of hope. It undermines dominant understandings of what is possible and opens up new conceptual spaces for imagining and practicing possible futures … it is about opening up visions of alternatives rather than closing down on 'a' vision'.[45] The mobile, generative forces of Utopianism clearly manifest in the series of cultural, social and political movements addressed by Mathews. They were imaginative, interrogative and pioneering – each pulses with desire and hope for change, much perhaps nascent and prospective. In Mathews' case the Utopian projects of the Revival are intimately bound up with pursuit of a national identity – yet such was the multifaceted nature of that series of projects that no single strain of Irish identity gained unilateral consensus. The variously consonant and dissonant voices and projects of this Utopian nexus compete, inform and challenge the formulation of Irish identity; projects which are, of course, at root Utopian in their energies, if 'not explicitly utopias themselves'.[46] And, as we have established, this was not an Irish identity that simply leeched its conceptual and practical framework from British precedents. As Mathews outlines, both modern social and cultural practices – farming; theatre, journalism; and education – were fastened to 'traditional' native Irish practices in such a way that a historically informed present might mould an alternative route(s) to a modern Irish society. Re-iterating his presiding contention, Mathews draws our attention to the urgency of grasping the *material* impacts of the cultural quarters of the Irish Revival and the extent to which the entire Revival movement proffered a viable alternative politics during this period. The intimacy of British colonialism, the proximity of the colonial mainland and the penetration of its exercises created the conditions for such Utopian thought. Frontiers and borderlands that are coloured by conflict, occupation, usurpation and oppression demand a Utopian politics to imagine beyond such proximate threat. And Mathews' postcolonial reading of the Revival period is a signal intervention in the reclamation of such Utopian energies that were characteristic of the combined Irish nationalist movements. As he concludes:

> One of the most remarkable features of this period is the extent to which the dynamic energies of a loosely aligned self-help revivalism emerged as an alternative sphere of influence to the realm of crisis-ridden parliamentary politics … [these] activities were inherently political and played an important role in Irish decolonization.[47]

The very title of Kiberd's seminal postcolonial intervention, *Inventing Ireland*, invokes the idea of the Utopian; it bespeaks a *process* of imagination, of industry and of movement, just as Fournier gestures to above. And in his diverse, and copious, readings of the literary and cultural twentieth century in Ireland, Kiberd charts the multifarious Utopian 'inventions' in literary form and content across the entire landscape of the literary canon. In particular, Kiberd asserts the remarkable cultural Utopianism of the Revival period, as well as that of Wilde the proto-modernist and of Joyce the postcolonial modernist. Kiberd, in a sense, performs an act of recovery and redress in his readings, which are significantly pitched against the political and cultural orthodoxies of, first, the Counter-Revival, and second, the more contemporary literary historical and historiographical work of revisionist literary critics, historians and journalists. Characteristically, asserting the aborted legacies of the Utopian dynamisms of the Revivalists, Kiberd contends that:

> In 1922 the urges of national possibility froze, with the country's teachers cast as curators of a post-imperial museum, whose English departments were patrolled by zealous custodians anxious to ensure that nothing changed very much. Down the corridor, many curators of the postcolonial Gaelic museum, known as the Irish Department, made equally certain that no radical revisions occurred, no compromising contacts with other cultures.[48]

There is a degree of facetiousness to Kiberd's remarks in this extract, but, regardless, the spirit of his conclusion contributes to, and draws upon, widely held criticisms of the conservative mind-sets and social programmes of the newly independent Irish Free State. In telling contrast to the richly assimilative practices of the Revival period, this era of new found national independence sanctioned little beyond insularity. Defence became central rather than imagination; consolidation superseded creativity. In Kiberd's assessment the provocative Utopian energies of the nationalist movement were squandered in a surge of conservative stability. The cultural and political creativity of a raft of Irish writers and activists, it seems, was disowned and there was a lateral failure to exploit and build upon the momentum of this branch of Irish Utopianism. Emblematic of this field of Irish Utopianism, in Kiberd's survey, are many of the canonical figures of twentieth century Irish writing, including Yeats and Joyce. Their cultural documents and practices symbolise the unyielded possibilities referred to above by Kiberd.

All of the foregoing material is, as we have outlined, qualitatively Utopian in its differential relation to Ireland's experiences and legacies of British imperial modernity. And as if to confirm such a trend, Cleary recently concluded that within Irish Studies:

> Postcolonial studies…while broadly internationalist in its outlook, has been dis-positionally more sympathetic to the radical republican, republican socialist, and other dissenting minoritarian elements in Irish history … for postcolonialists, the recovery of the memory of radical struggles in the past is an important element of any commitment to building contemporary modes of social consciousness and social analysis that extend beyond the limits of nationalism.[49]

As we have seen, each of the interventions strives to underscore the Utopian trajectories of past moments in Irish history and, implicitly, attempts to resurrect such Utopian energies in the present. As Cleary notes, and as Whelan terms it, Irish postcolonial studies is infused with a commitment to the Utopian possibilities of 'radical memory' – a concept that has been given lateral applications in recent Irish postcolonial scholarship. Rather than broaching the past as a calcified showcase of continuous failure and defeat, such 'radical' memorial Utopianism visits the past as a vivifying repertoire of political, cultural and ethical options in the present and towards the future. In Whelan's terms 'radical memory deployed the past to challenge the present, to restore into possibility historical moments that had been blocked or unfulfilled earlier'.[50] And in keeping with

Kirby's dim view of the prevailing conjuncture in which Irish society finds itself, to which it has firmly subscribed to, interventions that compel Irish studies to travel in these imaginative critical directions seem all the more pressing. Crystallising the Utopian animus of these rememorative strategies at a general level, and drawing on Bloch, Vincent Geoghegan's conclusion resonates with the Utopian assertions present in Irish postcolonial studies:

> Much political contestation is already driven by group and individual memories, and these memories fuel the various alternatives proposed ... These memories provide much of the raw material for the vital Utopian dimension of their politics. To the extent that these memories reveal shared values and experiences, the basis is established for the assertion of historical universals. It thus opens the door for a Utopianism which is grounded in the historically evolving memories of groups of individuals. The future, in this conception, is not a return to the past but draws sustenance from this past. Memory is the means in the present to ground the future in the past.[51]

In this spirit and to conclude this essay, I want to consider the historical figure whose writings and thought have been harnessed most recently, and most suggestively, within Irish postcolonial studies, and who can be stabled with many of the revivalist figures detailed in Mathews' study: the 1916 martyr, James Connolly. Indeed the centrality of Connolly to Irish socialist anti-colonial consciousness, as well as to mid-twentieth century international neo-colonial Marxist theory is boldly signalled by the biographer of Connolly's son Roddy, Charlie McGuire:

> Connolly believed that it had been the British bourgeoisie that had introduced capitalism into Ireland, breaking up finally the last remnants of the old Gaelic communal system, and that it continued to profit in the present day from exploitation of Irish resources and from the labor power of Irish workers. He believed that the capitalist economic system was the real basis of British power and control in Ireland.[52]

For Connolly, Irish national freedom without socialism is a still-born idea; Ireland did not possess a dynamic, transformative bourgeoisie capable of radical social change. Rather the indigenous Irish version was dependent on British economic control, so, therefore, in Connolly's view 'nationalism without socialism ... is only national recreancy'.[53] Such was the depth of Ireland's coerced integration into the economics of British capitalist imperialism that a profound structural social revolution was required in order that Ireland realises genuine national liberty, both political and economic. In these sentiments, we can see that Connolly's work is proleptic of later national liberationist theorists and also of subsequent Marxist thought on the insidious nature of neo-colonialism. Without conflating historical contexts, or geographical specificities, ties might be made between Connolly's pioneering conjunction of national liberation and socialist democracy in his critique of colonialism and his anticipation of the inequities of neo-colonialism in an Irish context with figures such as Fanon; Mao; Nkrumah; and Trotsky. As 'the first theorist of neo-colonialism', the link he (Connolly) proposed 'between British capitalist penetration of Ireland, the nature of the social, economic, and political structures this created, and the consequences of all this for the Irish independence struggle anticipated by several decades the efforts of those who develop fully the theory of neo-colonialism'.[54]

Connolly's reclamation as an intellectual precursor of, and resource for, contemporary postcolonial theory, though, is not confined to its Irish variant. In his seminal survey of the field, *Postcolonialism: An Historical Introduction*, Robert Young invokes Connolly's work, and positions his thinking on the correlation between the national struggle and the socialist struggle against the materially exploitative mechanisms of imperial modernity in the same philosophical continuum as that of the most radical Marxist figures of the twentieth century, such as Lenin; Mao, Cabral and Guevara.[55] While Young's discussion of Connolly may be revealing, it is, nonetheless, cursory. Yet subsequent to Young's inclusion of Connolly in his extended genealogy of the radical historical informants of contemporary postcolonial studies, a number of significant pieces have appeared on Connolly in Young's journal, *Interventions*. Beginning with a special number on 'Ireland's Modernities', which included two essays that dealt with Connolly, and resulting with a special number dedicated to Connolly, the journal has provided a forum through which Young's initial summary remarks have been elaborated upon by critics and literary historians from within the field of Irish studies.[56]

Primary among the recent efforts in the archival reclamation of this radical Utopian thinker is the work of the American scholar, Gregory Dobbins.[57] In a series of historically and theoretically rigorous publications, Dobbins has essayed the pioneering contributions of Connolly to early twentieth-century Irish nationalist and international Marxist thought; his proleptic anticipation of the work of mid-century anti-colonialists and national Marxists such as Fanon, Cabral and Guevara; his mining and problematisation of complacent and State-affirming notions of the Irish 'national' archive and the 'national tradition'; and canvassed the methodological relevance of Connolly's political historiography to critiques of contemporary Irish society and its own legitimating historical and cultural narratives. Dobbins' work is qualitatively different from many of the other acts of historical re-representation discussed heretofore, but the methodology endorsed by Dobbins significantly intersects with that practiced in the broader field of Irish postcolonial studies. Indeed Dobbins' positioning of Connolly's legacy embraces both form and content in its explication of Connolly's radical anti-colonial critique of historiographical practice and in Dobbins' conviction that Connolly himself represents a mis-construed figure within histories of Irish anti-colonial nationalism and the Irish labour movement. In effect, 'Connolly's work has been forced to fit into pre-existing categories which elide or obfuscate the complexity'[58] of his work. Typically, Connolly's legacy has been tethered to a narrowly conceived, and discredited, strand of romantic Irish nationalism, a fact which has obscured his deft theoretical negotiation of the politics of the local and specific (Irish nationalism) and the politics of the international and the structural (Marxism).

So if Connolly's revolutionary thought has been eclipsed and/or disfigured in twentieth-century historical accounts of Irish nationalist history, what is there to recommend a corrective re-appraisal of this thought? How can Connolly's early twentieth-century national Marxism inform contemporary readings of Irish colonial histories, and in what ways can such thinking pressurise the dominant modes of social policy and programming in Ireland today? In opening up such prospects, we might turn, initially, to David Lloyd, who, it seems, has seized upon Connolly's, and, of course, Dobbins', works as evidence of, even corroboration of, his previous, and ongoing, work on the narration of Irish history.[59] For Lloyd, Connolly is the exemplary historian of Irish subalternity, the diviner of the fragmented pulses of Irish counter-modernity, which Lloyd has theorised so effectively, but has been reproached as lacking empirical or historical substance. In Connolly, Lloyd's theoretical Utopianism seems to have located a historical precursor:

> Connolly…discerns in the attachment of the Irish working classes to a past form of social organization a mode of resistance to colonial capitalism that can form the basis of a radical social movement rather than an obstacle to be removed by the passage through prescribed stages of modernization. In this he anticipates many of the ways in which subaltern historiographers and postcolonial theorists have critiqued the developmental progressivism that informs not only imperial ideology but also nationalist movements.[60]

In this extract, Connolly is further co-opted into the field of postcolonial studies; Lloyd advances Young's summoning of Connolly into the field with the added affiliation of the Indian subaltern studies collective. Just as Lloyd, Young, Dobbins and others attempt to wrest Connolly from a tapered historiographical valence within revisionism, Connolly was acutely aware of the value and the need to research and to voice the unheeded political and cultural formations of pre-colonial Irish history. Not as bland forms of regressive nationalist propaganda or consolatory nostalgia, but as expressions of enduring cultural difference, which could provide 'a ground for further radicalisation and the possibility of imagining alternatives without … having to pass through the homogenizing stage of modernization and rationalization'.[61] It is a Utopian historio-graphical practice that depends on the excavation of the past, of memories in the service of new political and ethical constellations. As Moylan maintains this rememorative axis within Utopian thought is crucial; for him 'another important element in the Utopian method is *memory*, in particular that form of memory that is productive rather than consoling and disempowering'.[62] The past can yield enabling lessons, which are corrective of the diachronicity of imperial historical narratives. The past, as we have consistently seen, retains catalytic Utopian energies and 'the recognition of, and reflection on, past struggles can inform the contemporary process so that it becomes imbued with an educated grasp of previous campaigns even as it proceeds with the work of negation, revision, transformation'.[63]

Both Dobbins and Lloyd present Connolly as a pioneer in what have become the methodologies of postcolonial historiography within Irish postcolonial studies. Connolly's proto-subalternist historiography partook of the Utopian 'radical memory' outlined above by Whelan. For Dobbins and Lloyd such work of reclamation is both historiographically inclusive and politically subversive, and represents a valuable trace of resistant Irish Utopian memory. Of equal value is Dobbins' belief that while Connolly's work is both exemplary and instructive in its relation to Irish postcolonial studies, it is also seen as a potential informant of critical discussions on the economic and cultural imprints of the 'Celtic Tiger' years. Though in this respect Dobbins is keen to assert that Connolly's work is very much of its time and should not be seamlessly transplanted onto the contours of contemporary Irish political debate. Nevertheless, the combative historiographical methodologies pioneered by Connolly can be considered Utopian in their own time, but also as available Utopian resources in our time too. Contemporary retrievals of Connolly's legacies and examples are patently Utopian in their own right. As Dobbins speculates:

> The critical rediscovery of Connolly began not only after the advent of postcolonial theory in Ireland but also after the emergence of a full-blown globalized economy in Ireland during the period of the so-called Celtic Tiger. It is reasonable to wonder whether the recent re-articulation of Connolly's theoretical interventions is in part motivated by opposition to the newly dominant neoliberal values of the Celtic Tiger.[64]

Conclusion

In this 'Response' to Bill Ashcroft, we have discussed the historiographical and literary historical retrieval office Utopian potentials within Irish cultural and political history by contemporary postcolonial critics. Largely, such critics take a pessimistic view of the Irish experience of British imperial modernity and conclude that Ireland's interface with the processes of social and economic modernisation in the nineteenth century were characterised by the experience of trauma, dislocation and disenfranchisement. In other words, modernisation under British imperial rule was grafted onto Irish society by an externally based occupying force. In this strand of postcolonial critique, a range of resources are reclaimed as unrealised potentials and as potential informants of contemporary postcolonial interrogations of the current politico-economic conjuncture. Spanning the philosophical and political subtleties of Edmund Burke; the civic republicanism of the United Irish movement; the imbricated political, cultural and social movements of the Irish Revival; the Socialist nationalism of James Connolly, as well as the recalcitrant local practices of counter-modern social formations mined by Connolly's proto-subalternist historiography, it is evident that the Utopian agents unearthed by postcolonial critics are both copious and highly differentiated. This suite of postcolonial critiques constitutes a range of unrealised potentials, as evidence of the persistence and viability of 'radical memory'. A situation where the past is no longer a burden in the present, nor is it quarantined from the present, but is a spur to innovation and imagination in political, social, cultural and ethical fields. It is the past as Utopian resource. In fact, as Kirby's argument above details, there is an acute need for such historical and philosophical Utopian thought in contemporary Ireland, wherein political apathy and assent have become the norms. The value of the Utopian strain within Irish postcolonial studies is precisely its impatience with the prevailing conjuncture of political and economic interests. In this sense, all of these critical endeavours are energised by the 'fundamental dynamic of ... Utopian politics (or of any political Utopianism) ... [which] aims at imagining, and sometimes even at realizing, a system radically different from this one'.[65] As is clear, Ireland's histories of Utopian, colonial, anti-colonial and postcolonial theory and practice are vital informants of and participants in any future debate on the possible historical and/or contemporary transactions between Utopian studies and postcolonial studies. My 'Response', therefore, has been intended as a supplement to Ashcroft's initial intervention, but also as a reminder that Ireland should not be easily elided from postcolonial debates, as it so often has been.

Notes

1 Bill Ashcroft, 'Critical Utopias', *Textual Practice*, 21.3(2007), pp. 411–431.

2 Ernst Bloch, *The Utopian Function of Art and Literature: Selected Essays*, trans. Jack Zipes and Frank Mecklenberg (Minneapolis, MN: University of Minnesota Press, 1989), p. 4.

3 For a summary introduction to Ireland's Utopian histories see, Tom Moylan, 'To Stand with Dreamers: On the Use Value of Utopia', *The Irish Review*, 34(2006), pp. 1–19; and ed. Tom Moylan, *Utopian Studies – Special Issue: Irish Utopias* 18.3(2007), *passim*.

4 Russell Jacoby, *The End of Utopia: Politics and Culture in an Age of Apathy* (New York: Basic Books, 1999).

5 Jacoby, *The End of Utopia*, pp. 55–56.

6 Ibid., p. 60.

7 Peadar Kirby, 'Contested Pedigrees of the Celtic Tiger' in Peadar Kirby, Luke Gibbons and Michael Cronin (eds), *Reinventing Ireland: Culture, Society and the Global Economy* (London: Pluto Press. 2002), pp. 21–37.

8 Raffaella Baccolini, 'Finding Utopia in Dystopia: Feminism, Memory, Nostalgia, and Hope' in Tom Moylan and Raffaella Baccolini (eds), *Utopia Method Vision: The Use Value of Social Dreaming* (Bern: Peter Lang, 2007), p. 172.

9 See Rory O'Donnell, 'Public Policy and Social Partnership' in Joseph Dunne, Attracta Ingram and Frank Litton (eds), *Questioning Ireland: Debates in Political Philosophy and Public Policy* (Dublin: IPA, 2000), pp. 187–213.

10 Kirby, op. cit., p. 35.

11 Joe Cleary, *Outrageous Fortune: Capital and Culture in Modern Ireland* (Dublin: Field Day, 2006).

12 Tom Moylan, 'Introduction: Tracking Utopia in Irish Culture(s)', *Utopian Studies – Special Issue – Irish Utopias*, 18.3(2007), p. 295.

13 Tom Moylan, 'To Stand with Dreamers: On the Use Value of Utopia', p. 16.

14 Frantz Fanon, *The Wretched of the Earth* (London: Penguin, 1967), p. 28.

15 Saree Makdisi, *Romantic Imperialism: Universal Empire and the Culture of Modernity* (Cambridge: Cambridge University Press, 1998), p. 182.

16 David Denby, 'Ireland, Modernization and the Enlightenment Debate', *The Irish Review*, 31(2004), pp. 28–39.

17 Peadar Kirby, Luke Gibbons and Michael Cronin, eds., *Reinventing Ireland: Culture, Society and the Global Economy* (London: Pluto Press, 2002).

18 Denby op. cit., p. 29.

19 Ibid., pp. 29–30.

20 Ibid., p. 31.

21 Ibid.

22 See Conor McCarthy, 'Seamus Deane: Between Burke and Adorno', *The Year-book of English Studies*, 35.1(2005), pp. 232–248.

23 Seamus Deane, *Strange Country: Modernity and Nationhood in Irish Writing since 1790* (Oxford: Oxford University Press, 1997).

24 For example see his 'Unapproved Roads: Ireland and Post-colonial Identity' *Transformations in Irish Culture* (Cork: Cork University Press, 1996), pp. 171–180 and 'Guests of the Nation: Ireland, Immigration and Postcolonial Solidarity' in Meaghan Morris and Brett de Bary (eds), *'Race' Panic and the Memory of Migration* (Hong Kong: Hong Kong University Press, 2001), pp. 79–102.

25 Luke Gibbons, 'Towards a Postcolonial Enlightenment: The United Irishmen, Cultural Diversity and the Public Sphere' in Clare Carroll and Patricia King (eds), *Ireland and Postcolonial Theory* (Cork: Cork University Press, 2003), *passim*.

26 Ibid., p. 83.

27 Ibid.

28 Ibid.

29 Ibid.

30 Luke Gibbons, *Edmund Burke and Ireland: Aesthetics, Politics and the Colonial Sublime* (Cambridge: Cambridge University Press, 2003), p. 116.

31 Sankar Muthu, *Enlightenment Against Empire* (Princeton: Princeton University Press, 2003), p. 283.

32 Gibbons, op. cit., p. 116.

33 Ibid.

34 Ibid., p. 113.

35 Makdisi, op. cit., p. 106.

36 Ibid., p. 103.

37 Kirby, op. cit., p. 28.

38 Kirby, op. cit., p. 35.

39 John McLeod, 'Introduction' in John McLeod (ed.), *The Routledge Companion to Postcolonial Studies* (London: Routledge, 2007), p. 8.

40 PJ Mathews, *Revival: The Abbey Theatre, Sinn Fein, The Gaelic League and the Co-operative Movement* (Cork: Cork University Press, 2003), p. 2.

41 See Paul Gilroy, *The Black Atlantic: Modernity and Double Consciousness* (London and New York: Verso, 1993), pp. 187–223.

42 Mathews, op. cit., p. 2.

43 Mathews, op. cit., p. 9.

44 Ibid, p. 10.

45 Valerie Fournier, 'Utopianism and the Cultivation of Possibilities: Grassroots Movements of Hope' in Martin Parker (ed.), *Utopia and Organization* (Oxford: Blackwell, 2002), p. 192.

46 Lyman Tower Sargent, 'Utopianism and National Identity' in Barbara Goodwin (ed.), *The Philosophy of Utopia* (London: Frank Cass, 2001), p. 88.

47 Mathews, op. cit., p. 34.

48 Declan Kiberd, *Inventing Ireland: The Literature of the Modern Nation* (London: Vintage, 1995), p. 561.

49 Joe Cleary, 'Amongst Empires: A Short History of Ireland and Empire Studies in International Context', *Eire-Ireland*, 42.1 and 42.2(2007), p. 43.

50 Kevin Whelan, 'The Memories of "The Dead"', *The Yale Journal of Criticism*, 15.1(2002), p. 60.

51 Vincent Geoghegan, 'Remembering the Future' in Jamie Owen Daniel and Tom Moylan (eds), *Not Yet: Reconsidering Ernost Bloch* (London: Verso, 1997), p. 31.

52 Charlie McGuire, 'Irish Marxism and the Development of the Theory of Neo-Colonialism', *Eire-Ireland*, 41.3 and 4(2006), p. 114.

53 Ibid., p. 115.

54 Ibid., p. 119.

55 Robert J.C. Young, *Postcolonialism: An Historical Introduction* (Oxford: Black-well, 2001).

56 'Ireland's Modernities', David Lloyd (ed.), *Interventions* 5.3 (2003) and 'Postcolonial Connolly', Catherine Morris and Spurgeon Thompson (eds), *Interventions* 10.1(2008).

57 Among Dobbins' published work on James Connolly are: 'Connolly, the Archive and Method', *Interventions*, 10.1(2008), pp. 48–66; 'Whenever Green is Red: James Connolly and Postcolonial Theory', *Nepantla: Views from the South*, 1.3(2000), pp. 605–648; and '"Scenes of Tawdry Tribute": Modernism, Tradition and Connolly' in P.J. Mathews (ed.), *New Voices in Irish Criticism* (Dublin: Four Courts Press, 2000), pp. 3–12.

58 Dobbins, '"Scenes of Tawdry Tribute": Modernism, Tradition and Connolly', p. 6.

59 See David Lloyd, *Anomalous States: Irish Writing and the Post-colonial Moment* (Dublin: Lilliput Press, 1993); and *Ireland after History* (Cork: Cork University Press, 1999), especially pp. 19–36; 37–52; and 77–88.

60 David Lloyd, 'Why Read Connolly?', *Interventions*, 10.1(2008), p. 121.

61 Ibid.

62 Tom Moylan, 'Realizing Better Futures, Strong Thought for Hard Times' in Tom Moylan and Raffaella Baccolini (eds), *Utopia Method Vision: The Use Value of Social Dreaming* (Bern: Peter Lang, 2007), p. 217.

63 Ibid., pp. 217–218.

64 Dobbins, 'Connolly, the Archive and Method', p. 51.

65 Fredric Jameson, *Archaeologies of the Future: The Desire called Utopia and Other Science Fictions* (London and New York: Verso, 2005), p. xii.

21 Narrative Agency and Thinking about Conflicts

Nandana Dutta

...ethnicity should be viewed as the social and political creation of elites who draw upon, distort and sometimes fabricate materials from the cultures of the groups they wish to represent in order to protect their well being or existence or to gain economic and political advantage for their groups as well as for themselves.[1]

Assam's turmoil in the last three decades has been the result of narratives, about it generated by the centre and narratives about itself generated in response. How does one explain such a claim? One could examine public utterances from the nineteenth century onwards about Assam's relationship with the rest of India—a Jyoti Prasad Agarwalla or an Ambikagiri Roychowdhuri, both acknowledging the value of alignment, albeit in different ways, and imagining a great nation of which Assam is a part. Or one might look at the political relationship in the post-Independence era, when the rhetoric about indifference and neglect is fuelled by Nehru's infamous reply to very real fears about invasion by China and immigrant influx from East Pakistan communicated to him by the then chief minister, Gopinath Bordoloi. Or one might study this narrative in its maturity in the last three decades which saw the situation in Assam coming to a boil as a result of the neglect of political, economic, and social issues over the entire post-Independence period. This third option is the one I choose to look at in this essay, noting how the narrative of neglect works, what are the political/ideological investments made in it, and how it is manipulated in different situations. Along with scholarship on the sources and dimensions of the situations in the Northeast, it is also necessary to look at the continuation of the situations of conflict, the repetition of the same kinds of problems all over the region—in other words, the 'sustenance' of conflict. One of the possible sources of such sustenance is the way we have represented

Nandana Dutta, "Narrative Agency and Thinking about Conflicts," in Sanjib Baruah, ed., *Beyond Counter-Insurgency: Breaking the Impasse in Northeast India*. New Delhi: Oxford University Press, 2009, pp. 124–144. Reproduced by permission of the author.

ourselves, our history and our identity, that is, the role played by narrative, by the story of self, a way of self-projection manifested in the discursive climate of the region—the perpetuation of the problem through attachment to a particular story.

Awareness of how narratives are constructed, refurbished, elaborated, and disseminated, and the significant contributions of mediators—both intellectual and political—in adding or subtracting aspects, is a necessary adjunct to understanding the atmosphere of turmoil and an important step that waits to be taken. In fact, the examination of this 'matured' narrative and the acknowledgment of its constructedness also points to ways in which such manipulation may actually involve the injection of selected elements into the grand narrative, and not only the injection of the politically expedient ones. It is quite possible that the politically expedient element is also the socially, culturally, and economically beneficent one. The following incident is an example of the way in which a silent shift occurs in a narrative in which a whole society has invested in, the actual acknowledgment of the shift sliding under the assertions of the new narrative as if the other older one never was.

On 21 January 2006, the *Assam Tribune* reported a statement made by Samujjal Bhattacharyya, advisor and chairperson, North East Students' Organisation (NESO), and Tapan Gogoi, general secretary, All Assam Students' Union (AASU) on the treatment meted out to a particular singer on ZEE TV's music reality show *Sa Re Ga Ma Pa*.

> Last night's episode of *Sa Re Ga Ma Pa* has exposed the plot against Debojit which is only because of the fact that he happens to come from Assam and the North East.
>
> Debojit's case betrays the fact that for a section of mainstream India, particularly for those who matter, there is no India beyond Kolkata. Debojit has established that nothing can suppress talent. Now it is for the people to give a fitting reply to the conspiracy against Debojit and thereby ensure that he scales new heights in the world of music. (pp. 1,3)

The statement is worth noting for several reasons. First, of course, it emphatically repeats the conspiracy leitmotif that is implicit in the narrative of neglect and alienation that has characterized centre/state, mainstream India/northeastern periphery relations. Second, as subsequent events and further statements revealed, Debojit's victory was ensured; a 'fitting reply' was given. But the third point that emerges from this statement is the most interesting. In taking up the case of this particular young man as a representative of 'Assam and the Northeast' the speakers inducted a new element into their political discourse. Subtly and naturally, without drawing special attention to the fact, they elided over the traditional Barak Valley/Brahmaputra Valley binary. (Debojit hails from the predominantly Bengali-speaking town of Silchar in the Barak Valley.) The manner in which this shift was achieved lends support to the argument that this article seeks to present about the way a discourse may be constructed, changed, and manipulated, and the role that influential figures through their public pronouncements play in such makings.

A dramatic example of the use/deployment of discourse is provided by the Field Day project in Ireland which, among other engagements, publishes pamphlets interpreting the Irish nationalist aspiration against the 'contemporary colonialism' by Britain (Deane 1990: 8). In his Introduction to *Nationalism, Colonialism, and Literature*—

the three essays on nationalism and the role of cultural production as a means to understanding colonization—Seamus Deane writes of the need for a 'new discourse' to enable a 'new relationship between our idea of the human subject and our idea of human communities' (ibid.: 3). The Field Day Theatre Company which steers the production of this 'new discourse' is specially engaged in the study of Irish culture as politically produced, and it therefore pays particular attention to 'interpretations' and discursive interventions. As Deane tells us, 'The general trend has been to analyze the various rhetorics of coercion and liberation that are so evident in modern Irish litera-ture (particularly in Yeats and Joyce), in modern Irish political and legal discourse and practice, as well as in the systems of interpretation that have mediated these' (ibid.: 14). The Field Day example points to the existence of such a field of discursivity where various kinds of narratives are afloat. The similarity with the Northeast lies in the per-ception of the situation of centre–periphery (and not necessarily in the actual political dynamics involved) which is also the perception of a 'contemporary colonialism'.

Conflicts in the Northeast have been the result of a dissatisfaction with the ruling mindset at the centre—with the centre's inadequate understanding of centre—periphery relationships; with limp and shortsighted policies most commonly perceived as 'exploitation' of northeastern states for their rich natural resources of tea, oil, and timber; and the 'indifference' to its problems with intra-state and international borders. Jairam Ramesh analyses government policies towards the Northeast as struc-tured by four different paradigms succeeding one another from the 1950s onwards:

1. The *culture paradigm*: 'that the Northeast is a phenomenally diverse mosaic of cul-tures which have to be preserved and enriched'.
2. The *security paradigm*: 'the Northeast … as a strategically significant region … in a geopolitical sense of India's role in East Asia and Southeast Asia'.
3. The *politics paradigm*: 'the diverse tribal cultures and diverse sub-nationalities required participation in "mainstream" democratic process … new states began to be formed'.
4. The *development paradigm*: 'that if we build schools, bridges, internet centres, IITs and refineries, the people will be happy' (Ramesh 2005: 17, 18).

These approaches over the years have merely fed the complex of problems around the issue of border: border transgressions, territorial integrity, and intra-state dissensions.

The historical development of a northeastern narrative about itself, constituted from these elements, is manifested in what is most immediately discernible as the 'nar-rative of neglect', encapsulating aspirations, dejections, despair, frustrations, and anger. Its circulation and regular attrition from the realm of general and individual articulations has given this narrative a status that puts it virtually beyond the reach of critical scrutiny-a new narreme (or little narrative element) sparked off by a fresh event or political decision unquestioningly added to it and not necessarily calling the narra-tive into question. Apparent in the functioning of this narrative is the manner in which—like all narrative or discursive representation—it has come to stand in for the 'real', the situation of 'conflict' or the 'problem of the Northeast' subsumed under this influential narrativization (as Hayden White [1981] would nuance it, the telling of the story by an identifiable agent transformed into the story *telling itself*). As one surveys the ground of conflict the question that repeatedly asks itself is: How do we simultaneously achieve integration and difference? This is a question that addresses the peculiar reality of being an integral part of a national formation while being diverse and fractured in ways that demand repeated reorientations of policy.

This narrativization has been both *enabling*—in the articulation of the 'problems of the Northeast' (addressing the perception is as important as addressing the reality of individual problems)—and *obstructive*, because it has frozen into the form and shape of 'knowledge', making it extremely difficult to look beyond its cognitive framework. Therefore, the second aspect of this narrative recognition of the area and its problems is of how it is made or arrived at. This may be a primordialist mode, borrowed from a group's conception of itself; alternatively, it may be the constructivist mode of the scholar, the commentator, or the politician which consciously or deliberately intervenes in the formation of discourses. The latter is probably the only possible mode especially because the constructed nature of the discourse has so often been ignored, sunk as it is into a kind of understructure, somewhat out of the range of scrutiny.

C.A. Bayly, in a study of indigenous nationalisms in South Asia, refers to the way distance or proximity to the imperial centre in India determined the kind of nationalism that emerged; the normative power of the imperial culture felt differently depending on where a people and a region were based (Bayly 2001: 38). This is an insight that one might bring to bear on the relationship of India's border states, in this case the Northeast, to the centre. Harekrishna Deka, writing about the Assamese mindset, notes how Assam became a non-player on the national field because of such 'distance from the centre' and instead became the victim of a political psychology that failed to 'address micro-level inequalities and needs of a people living in a geopolitical unit away from the centre' (Deka 2005: 191).

People in states furthest away from the centre, because of poor communication links, geographical distance, difficult terrain, and therefore emotionally alienated from the discourse of nationalism and identity legitimized by the centre, seek their own ways of expressing sentiments of attachment to a land and to the formation of their identity. This is an explanation that accounts partly for the sense of difference felt and sought to be sustained as empowering and imperative.

Recent narratives about the Northeast are, however, worth a fresh look because the shift I describe in the Debojit incident is in fact making itself felt in other areas as well. What one might call a trans-border exercise is apparent in the organization mentioned earlier called NESO, an organization of student bodies of all the northeastern states which most dramatically made its unity visible to the public eye in the joint felicitation offered to the young man Debojit who virtually transcended his Silchar/Bengali identity to become the iconic representative of all young talented northeasterners who needed to stand tall and make themselves heard on the national scene. The other little noticed and little commented upon aspect of this episode is one which, in the background of the separatist sentiment floated by the ULFA, has its own delicious ironies. By supporting Debojit in a 'national' and nationally televised music show, instead of logically ditching or ignoring him, the NESO and its constituents publicly jettisoned the earlier narrative of Assamese–Bengali confrontation, announced their wish to be counted as part of the Indian nation, and demanded recognition of the talent of these northeasterners who were also Indians (Debojit actually becoming the 'voice of India' that the TV channel had announced was the object of the entire exercise)—an act that not only offered a tacit political alternative but also set up a dialogue with the 'rest of India' represented on the show itself by all those voices in the audience who expressed doubt about the north-eastern voice being the truly Indian voice that the programme purported to be seeking. Prior to this episode, the significant inclusion of the Sattriya dance of Assam as a classical Indian dance form like Oddisi, Kathak, and Bharatnatyam by the Sangeet Natak Akademi (a process worth studying for the kind of ideological pressures that led up to its culmination) had similar potential for 'use' as a link by scholarship on the region but perhaps because it did not have the reach of the popular cultural exercise that generally shatters hierarchization, it was largely left alone.[2]

The shift is also apparent in two other large policy changes in the approach to the Northeast, one of which, the so-called Look East policy, is already in the process of a somewhat shaky implementation and is also the subject of serious debate. The second source of a possible shift in the self-construction of the Northeast is the new emphasis on tourism, 'an economic engine in the development of postcolonial societies' (Bruner 2005: 4). Both of these I take up later within the discursive context of this argument as sources of new narrative components that might be usefully and productively added to the narrative. And yet the idea of linkages across borders is as old as the migrations of the human race.

In giving myself the onus of rethinking and scrutinizing the way we generally respond to conflicts and the way we respond to conflicts here and now, I take recourse to a narrative consciousness, activating narrative at two levels of understanding—one at the level of critique and the other at the level of experience, that is, the discourse of *conflict assessment* as distinguished from the discourse of *conflict*. My 'object of study' is something pervasive but nebulous and difficult to actually pin down to any single or specific source (obviously it does not appear fully formed in any single utterance or cultural form)—the narrative by which a people and a society live or negotiate their relations with others. I am compelled to find a method of study that will legitimize the object itself but that will inevitably circle round the question: why is such a narrative important; does it really 'exist' or is it in process always, though silent until it is deployed? In addressing these questions of the Northeast narrative one discovers that it is impossible to access it in its overarching form except through its manifestations in small individual narratives that play with some aspects of it. As the Debojit episode—or the narrative representation of it by Samujjal Bhattacharyya and Tapan Gogoi, and the narrative interpretation under which it appears in this essay—shows, we have here an example of a 'narrative of what happened' but the episode itself is inseparable from its narration. From this methodological tangle it is evident that the 'event' is inaccessible except through its narrative existence in the consciousness of a people or an individual who may mediate it in this particular way to a people. And the repetition/reiteration of the narrative is also the process of its change and its taking on fresh components as it adapts and comes closer to the imagination of those who begin to depend on it as an articulation of identity. At the same time, however, I admit that this narrative as 'object of study' is, in a most intriguing way, inaccessible, enjoining the critic/observer to constitute it in the process of studying it and adding to the problem of 'assumption' of the slant already borne by the object or 'transcending' it.

Implicit in this recognition of narrative are three key areas of narrative theory:

1. *The story–discourse debate* that hinges on the difficulty of pinning down that first version or ur-narrative, because the only access we have to it is through its little manifestations, not in neat chronological development.

2. *The relations between narrative and psychoanalysis*, the most useful element of which is the model offered by the talking cure—the retelling of a story with components being added or erased, until the best story coincides with the patient being cured.
3. *The distinction between narrating and narrativizing* is the last key area in the logical sequence to the above two aspects where the story 'telling itself' commonly has a greater weight because it points to the way things 'really are' rather than to an identifiable manipulator of a narrative but where its critique shows how all narratives including the ones that pretend to be telling themselves, all have narratorial agents.

The 'neglect narrative' as I read it shows all three positions in action as it were. There is no single overarching narrative which carries all its components; rather it is an amalgamation of little narratives that feed into it. It has grown in strength and become discernible through reiteration and when I assert that such narrative reiteration is a reason for conflict, I also have in mind the insertion into it of selected elements and the emergence of a new story whose reiteration could also be the beginnings of a solution—another story, a story that is therapeutic, a better story of ourselves to live by.[3] And thirdly, the 'neglect narrative', as we live it, has erased its agents in becoming more convincing for a people and an alternative probably also has to be able to narrative itself and not merely be narrated in order to be convincing as a story to live by. At the same time, it is as well to point out that recognizing agency in a narrative's fashioning is the necessary first step to deliberately and selectively participating in the fashioning of that 'good' narrative. And Samujjal Bhattacharyya's 'insertions' in the Debojit incident is as much an example of such agency as is Mamoni Raisom Goswami's 'peace curriculum' for the universities of the Northeast.[4]

Narratives of Resistance

Acknowledging the sensitive nature of national–regional relationships—basic to the situation of conflict and providing the occasion for the emergence of the kind of identity noted in the Northeast is an entry point into the modes of talking and thinking about conflicts. In the larger picture, a historical view of South Asia shows how ethnic plurality contests nation-building processes. A 'unified national identity' or national integration, 'a national identity that coincides with state divisions' but does not reflect ethnic divisions—these general themes find place in several studies of the region and are comprehensively represented by a work like *Ethnicity and Nation-Building in South Asia*.

> For a long time, given the ethnic plurality of South Asia, post-colonial nation-building approaches focused almost exclusively on creating a unified 'national identity' based around either common political values and citizenship or a putative majoritarian 'ethnic' identity. The overall aim of both approaches has been to produce a pulverized and uniform sense of national identity to coincide with state boundaries that seldom reflect ethnic divisions on the ground (Phadnis and Ganguly 2001: 13).

And against 'the development of an all-country identity', ethnic diversities though recognized as social givens, were perceived as evoking primordial, sectional loyalties and consequently hampering the developmental processes of the country in general and 'national integration' in particular (Phadnis and Ganguly 2001: 146).

The coming into being of the modern state as also the demands of the globalized economy are antagonistic to the continuation of older, less modernized modes of living represented by ethnic groups and this is evident in the case presented by Adeel Khan (2005) who notes 'the role of the interventionist modern state in creating, hardening and radicalizing national sentiment' among the Baluch, Pakhtun, Sindhi, and the Mohajir. Such polarization and discomfort over homogenization, foundational to the narrative of neglect, are reflected in readings of the Northeast. A collection of essays edited by B.C. Bhuyan (1992) contains essays titled 'Nationalist and Subnationalist', 'Integration in the North East', 'Problems and Prospects of National Integration in the North East', and 'Economic Integration' all registering the dominant obsession in these rather obvious linguistic preferences. Udayon Misra's book on the Naga and Assamese sub-nationalist movements is revealingly titled *The Periphery Strikes Back* (2000)—a title that is virtually repeated in a later essay, 'The Margins Strike Back: Echoes of Sovereignty and the Indian State', that also recalls some of those favourite signposts of the neglect narrative: the exchange of letters between Gopinath Bardoloi and Jawaharlal Nehru over refugee influx, Nehru's 'defence reasons' for not setting up a refinery in Assam, and his virtual abandonment of the entire region to Chinese forces during the 1962 Chinese aggression (Misra 2005: 271).

A similar rhetoric sounds through Sanjib Baruah's book *India Against Itself* (1999) even as it analyses sub-nationalist aspirations that express themselves in conflicts and makes a nuanced and detailed examination of centre–state, national–sub-national configurations, a version of which appeared as Assamese micro-nationalism in a 1994 paper titled '"Ethnic" Conflict as State-Society Struggle' (Baruah 1994).

Patricia Mukhim, Khasi journalist and social activist, writing in the special Northeast issue of *IIC Quarterly*, approaches the problem of the location of the Northeast in a predictable resistance to the much-flogged 'unity in diversity' thesis and makes the following observation:

> When India became free, the various tribes of the North-eastern region were made to sign the Instrument of Accession into the Indian Union by coercion. ... It is but natural that freedom from British rule was seen as a mere exchange of masters. The perception remains that India with its sheer might, has co-opted all smaller independent principalities into itself (Mukhim 2005).

This is revealing because it suggests that in identifying the locus of resistance, the target of resistant discourse is as important as the process of resistance itself or what is sought to be put in its place. By once again harking back to the terminology of unity and diversity the door is shut on fresh approaches, on the possibility of asking other questions, and perhaps in accessing other concepts of nationhood. In contrast, by jettisoning these familiar terms the new narrative of transnationalism, in this case represented by the Look East Policy and the Tourism Policy document, does seem to have the potential to chart a new direction.

Mukhim's essay, especially its introductory section, provides another example of the reiteration of the 'neglect narrative':

How can a region within a country be considered a 'difficult region'?... This coterie of bureaucrats/technocrats and politicians from the *Hindi heartland* who have no understanding of the special sensitivities of the North-eastern region actually write the plan documents for the country. Plans that are most unsuitable for the region and therefore not implementable (Mukhim 2005: 178–9).

The problem of inadequate examination of the popularity of the neglect narrative is evident in the subsequent claim that,

in the last two decades ... people living in central India ... have suddenly developed a keen interest ... A ministry (DONER) with the North East suffix was created to ostensibly give the people of this region a feeling that they were being looked after. But this condescension and patronage is resented because the benefits flowing out of that ministry do not reach the people (Mukhim 2005: 179).

The echoes of 'us and them', 'Northeast and rest of India', and accusations of exploitation, ignorance, indifference about faulty implementation of policies, and perhaps most importantly, condescension—all components of the neglect narrative—are heard here.

The perception of neglect is the dominant impression sought to be created by Hiranya Kumar Bhattacharyya (former police officer and sympathetic observer of the 'Assam movement against foreigners') when he quotes Rajmohan Gandhi and Myron Weiner. Rajmohan Gandhi says: 'The rest of India does not see us. If seen we are not recognized. If recognized we are not remembered. And are not heard. This has been the charge of the citizens of the North-east against the Indian majority' (Bhattacharyya 2001: 1). Weiner also articulates a similar observation: 'The Assamese often think of themselves as a "forgotten" and "neglected" state within the Indian Union and as a neglected people in danger of being overwhelmed by migrant peoples and absorbed by neighboring states' (ibid.).

How does one *not* continue to reiterate them, *not* continue to make the same accusations that make the entire approach predictable—a kind of 'boy who cried wolf' syndrome that drowns the voice from its auditors or renders the situation invisible? While the intellectual, as Edward Said suggests, must function as a kind of 'public memory' to recall what is forgotten or ignored (Said 2001: 503) (the circumstances of accession might qualify as such an event), such recollections for the instrumental purpose of ventilating a grievance, is hardly productive for a better centre–state relationship, or for the transcendence of discontent.

In his study of Manipur, P.T. Hitson Jusho (2004: 103) identifies the following as sources of unrest: tribal consciousness, a central administration replacing customary laws, the jostling of several ethnic groups within the same territory and the consequent generation of majority–minority questions, and finally, in an emotive gesture that takes his analysis out of the realm of the critical, 'the indifferent attitude of the state towards the hill people' (p. 103). In marked contrast, the Mizo problem analysed by Phadnis and Ganguly (2001) is traced to the more impersonal and objective 'political and economic policies'. One might, in a similar vein, trace ethnic problems to colonial legacies, the federal structure of the Indian state, etc., none of which carries the same emotion. This hybrid text represents the sentiment that has been predominant in the region. It also ties in with my argument about the native intellectual who is responsible for the discourse and who can therefore be a powerful nodal factor in its 'adulteration' or manipulation.

A collection of essays (written during the decade 1953–63) by Bolairam Senapati (2000), an intellectual of the Tiwa or Lalung tribe of Assam, offers support not only to the persistent fascination for the binary argument, but allows glimpses of the many facets of the relationship that a minority community may have with a majority, showcasing a situation where the narrative spreads internally into the 'dominant community–minority community' site. In an era that precedes the violent turn in present-day conflicts, Senapati contributes to the predominant discourse on the tribal–non-tribal relationship. He too speaks of the 'indifferent attitude' (*abahelito manobhab*) of non-tribals towards tribals. Drawing on the imperialist policy of divide and rule he speaks of political attempts to divide tribals pushing the entire tribal fraternity towards destruction—a point that, he urges, must be appreciated by tribal leaders and immediate interventionist steps taken.[5] The grievance against the majority community is addressed very differently from how it would be today: for example, an essay in the volume, titled 'Asomiya Jati Gathanat, Tiwa Sakaler Abadan' (The Contribution of the Tiwas to the Formation of the Assamese Race), is an invitation to the community to feel good and comfortable about its relationship—a feeling the majority should be able to accommodate as a way out of potential conflict situations. On the other hand, a comment from 'the other side' could very well add fuel to the paranoiac in the discourse. Prafulladatta Goswami adopts the position that 'the Indian way of life has touched communities all over the country'. He speaks of cultural synthesis and admits that 'there are differences but there is a large common ground where the Brahman and the so-called tribal meet' (Goswami 1983: 1). This echoes the integrative nationalist sentiment and is inimical to the desire of the ethnic community for a distinctive identity.

That conflicts can be fuelled and sustained by articulations is evident in the early strains of the narrative of marginalization heard in the pieces by Jnananath Bora—'*Kamrup aru Bharatvarsha*' (Kamrup and India) and '*Asom Desh Bharatborshar Bhitarat thakiba Kiyo*' (Why Should Assam Remain within India): 'The Assamese have always lived in a distinct country with its own distinct administration and never seen Assam as a part of India … India's history is not our history. … our people consider themselves to be outside India. Like Burma, Afghanistan or Thailand, Assam has always been a neighboring country of India' (quoted in Misra 2001: 33). This is echoed in a statement from *Sadin* (an Assamese daily): 'The government of India policy in this region is to destroy the struggles of the indigenous peoples of the area' and (with regard to military mobilization against militant groups like the ULFA) 'destroy the Assamese nation' (quoted in Baruah 1999: 164).

The elements that characterize conflicts are apparent in these narratives. For example, the fears that precede conflicts are at the following levels: social (demographic change and therefore profile change of communities); political (a minority group's demands going unrepresented); economic (the cornering of limited job opportunities, the exploitation of resources); or cultural (fears of traditional distinctiveness or identity being lost, music, dance, the arts getting adulterated, cuisine tempered, weaving cultures transformed). The threat perception therefore involves one community besieged by another community that by its proximity or its intrusion may engulf the other—a fear manifested most recently in the attacks on people of Bihari origin, but also evident in the hostility expressed towards outsiders or intruders in several northeastern states, or in strict border control achieved by inner line permits. All of this at the psycho-social level has meant a suspicion of the other, the assumption of the rhetoric of neglect, marginality and distance, dissemination and use of narratives of discontent, and the desire for exclusive homelands expressed through calls for autonomy or secession. Each of the above is an issue of border and requires a creative understanding of the concept.

The examples of critique and emotive expression are founded on the assumption of exclusivity—the 'homeland thesis' most recently brought to our attention by the Dimasa–Karbi conflict in Karbi Anglong. The conception of homeland that is generally assumed is the traditional one of a well-marked territory that coincides with social and cultural boundaries. Surprisingly, even when faced with crises of huge proportions—the taking of life and the torching of homes and property—the crisis situation does not seem to have radicalized thinking which is still trapped in binarism: homeland/loss of homeland without the ability to imagine the in-between.

The questions that arise out of the texts referred to earlier, I believe, demand serious and engaged reflection, not immediate pat answers: What is it that one selects as the target of resistance in a narrative of the self? Which element of the past does one select and how does one therefore read that past? The urgent need is to go back and look at how we came to be the way we are instead of once again offering the same narrative about marginalization as weakness. How does one connect to the theories of marginalization as a position of strength? The necessity of a theoretical or conceptual infusion into thinking about the region really legitimizes itself in these circumstances.

Countering the above discourse which is essentially circumscribed or bounded is one that is open and transgressive, borrowing its terms from an international rhetoric of transnationalism and travel. This is beginning to be evident in government policy for the Northeast (especially in the Look East Policy and the new thrust in tourism) and is matched by a recognition from 'below' that the material conditions of our times have always been liminal; we have always lived without strict and definite borders.

Towards Narrative Shifts

In the process of rethinking both the sources of conflicts and their derivatives it would appear that an obsession with issues relating to borders is the defining framework of the neglect narrative—whether it is the relationship with the centre, borders shared with other states or international borders, and communities territorially and culturally bordering on each other—spawning fears of homogenization and its derivative, invisibility, or its opposite, otherization. Ethnic movements for statehood or autonomy have 'a territory orientation with the vision of a "homeland"' (Phadnis and Ganguly 2001: 217); and such orientation is generally exclusivist and therefore dependent on a border. However, this material dimension of the term is only the first step into what I see as a border-consciousness necessary to the understanding and rethinking of conflicts—border as a trope that could be a 'creative space of resistance' (Rosaldo 1989) or the liminal, in-between space (Bhabha 1994) that is the postcolonial's most empowering site, the space where new identities can be forged or disciplines radically challenged.

Against such preoccupations it would appear that the alternative narrative has to speak of a new conception of borders, evince a degree of comfort with multiple identities, and recognize that the agency for transforming the narrative is there to be taken. Recent racial riots in France offer a searing example of the price of keeping a section of the population invisible—France's Muslim minorities, ghettoized in the seedy suburbs of Paris, are also rendered invisible by the state policy of denying Muslim girls the right to wear the hijab or the burqa in schools or in public places, thereby homogenizing them into mainstream French society. In this section my attempt is to find a way of keeping such invisibility or homogenization (the end point feared by most communities in strife) at bay by examining what might constitute an alternative narrative.

Already audible in the narrative shift is a border consciousness that is fertile ground for the introduction of concrete elements that would shape the new narrative and take self-conception in a different and more positive direction. If the Debojit episode is a kind of test case, it is obvious that selected elements can be inserted into the narrative to address the basic grievances. Since the narrative shift addresses (and has to address) the questions of intra-regional relationships, the internal dynamics of the majority and the minority communities (in the case of Assam, the Assamese in their interactions with the Bodo, Karbi, Rabha, Mising, Lalung, and the Dimasa), historical dissensions about the exclusivity of borders, and the influx of outside elements or transgression of these borders, the deployment or access to a conceptual framework is necessary both for the understanding and the 'use' of the narrative. Travel theory developments suggest that tourism, which is a welcome transgression of borders, may well be that area. With the tourism option the exclusivist idea is subtly transgressed and common elements that affect communities, cutting across borders, introduced. Travel theory indeed positions tourism as a 'crucial component in the construction of transnational culture' (Kaplan 1996: 47). And Kaplan cites Donald Horne: 'Tourism as a manifestation of a crisis in reality insists upon proof of the authentic' (ibid.: 60). The compulsion to cater to this desire for the authentic must radicalize the visited culture, compel a re-examination of its status/identity, culture, and enable strong new constructs as well as encourage freedom from old and fixed ones.

James Clifford invites a rethinking of tribal cultures in conjunction with a diaspora discourse of simultaneous 'rootedness and displacement' (Clifford 1997: 254), bypassing the polarity of these concepts. He claims, with examples taken from living museums and tribal cultures that, 'If tribal groups survive it is now frequently in artificially reduced and displaced conditions, with segments of their populations living in cities away from the land' (ibid.). Such a condition is true of tribal groups in the Northeast as well, with substantial numbers existing outside their traditional territories or even outside the region, therefore stressing the importance of understanding how it is possible to live without borders and yet sustain one's sense of rootedness to a culture. The discourses of transnationalism and multiple identity may provide an understructure that a new discourse of the Northeast might build on.

Transnationalism is a version of migration theory that has induced a radical rethinking within the discipline of anthropology. It not only invites unfreezing of borders between states, disciplines, and peoples, but also thereby unsettles the fixity of subject–object positions, of observer and observed, of migrant and host.

Transnationalism is defined as 'a social process whereby migrants operate in social fields that transgress geographic, political and cultural borders', a process facilitated by modern modes of transportation and telecommunications. 'From a transnational perspective, migrants are no longer "uprooted" but rather move freely back and forth across international borders and between different cultures and social systems'

(Brettell 2000: 104), something that the Look East policy also purports to do. In the disciplinary site, transnationalism is 'part of an effort to reconfigure anthropological thinking so that it will reflect current transformations in the way in which time and space [are] experienced and represented' (Glick Schiller et al. in Brettell 2000: 104). And it involves a 'general move in anthropology away from bounded units of analysis and localized community studies' and instead looks at social action in a 'multidimensional global space with unbounded, often discontinuous and interpenetrating subspaces' (ibid.). Anthropology's taking on board of a contemporary political reality and its resulting transformation is worth attending to because it points to a way of intellectual engagement that is necessary. But equally significant for this argument is the genera- tion of a new and adventurous rhetoric, the entry of which into our thought horizons must be transformative for the way in which we view our society in crisis and free ourselves from the traps of outmoded thinking.

The second area of radical change comes out of multiculturalist theories of identity, particularly the concept of multiple identity. Multiple identity is a function of border crossing, of transgression and of the breaching of the borders of single identities by difference and *différance*. The 'subjective experience of any social group membership depends fundamentally on relations to memberships in other social groups' (Hames- Garcia 2001: 103). Hames-Garcia takes his examples from race, gender, and sexual identifications which are never singly held but run into one another; but the same enmeshing can also be seen among nation–state–ethnic group identities—a fact that could prove useful in the process we are engaged in. 'What does it mean to be understood exclusively in terms of one's race, gender or sexuality? It means that one is understood in terms of the most dominant construction of that identity' (ibid.: 104). We could very well be back at the same point of misconceptions about the Northeast. Hames-Garcia quotes Maria Lugones ('Purity, Impurity and Separatism') who demonstrates how separating something into pure parts is an act of domination. 'By contrast, she views "impurity" as a way of resisting the social forces of reification. Lugones' paradigmatic example of impurity (curdling) is mestizaje or racial mixing which asserts its impure (undivided) multiplicity and rejects separation into pure, discrete parts' (ibid.: 120).

Behind the process of discovering multiple identities is the acknowledgment of the 'reality of experience and its construction' (ibid.: 109) that has come to be known in literary–theoretical circles as post-positivist realism and that 'self-consciously uses linguistic (and theoretical) mediation to come to a truer, revisable understanding of non-reified multiplicity and its wider social context' (ibid.: 118). The crucial area in this position is that of the acceptance of theoretical and linguistic construction with the help of which one might understand and find oneself as an individual ('consciousness- raising' is an important example)—crucial because with this preliminary recognition which is at the same time a discursive recognition, it is possible to imagine the usability of a discourse or narrative and its deployment for suitable action. The holding of these two theoretical positions, transnationalism and multiculturalism, on one's intellectual horizon is a step towards the insertion of their relevant aspects into thinking about the Northeast since it must be admitted that the isolation or alienation of scholarship about the Northeast from an international discourse that relies so productively on theoretical awareness about these issues has been one of the major reasons for the continuance of the neglect narrative.[6]

Narrative Agency and Thinking about Conflicts

New Narratives and Their Possibilities

In the Look East policy and the Tourism Policy document, we have samples of narratives that are empowering because they perform a multidimensional role, echoing but also reshaping and supplementing the existing narrative of self through a tacit dialogue with ideas of transnationalism and travel, involving radical rethinking of the issue of borders and fruitfully engaging with the reality of the multiculturalist situation of the Northeast, lip service to which has been one of the causes for both invisibility and discontent. The underlying caveat about pervasiveness and elusiveness that discomfits this essay still holds because in none of these textual complexes is it actually possible to see the new narrative at work; rather, components of it play about in interpretative positions. However, the narrative of neglect that is predicated on the assumption of the fundamental divide between cultural and political homogeneity and the infinitely heterogeneous is discernibly shifting, taking on elements that are new interpretations of many older ideas relating to borders and closure of boundaries. Jairam Ramesh's dramatic pronouncement that 'we need to really start becoming schizophrenic'—which he explains as 'political integration with the rest of India and economic integration with the rest of Asia' (Ramesh 2005: 19)—is a sharpening of the new narrative that is already heard in the several dimensions of the Debojit incident.

One of the articulations of the Look East policy appears in the special issue of the journal *Seminar*. The rhetoric that is being generated in the new scenario is of particular interest. The establishment line on the policy is announced by Rajiv Sikri, secretary (East) of the Ministry of External Affairs (MEA). He says that it 'envisages the Northeast region not as the periphery of India, but as the centre of a thriving and integrated economic space linking two dynamic regions with a network of highways, railways, pipelines, transmission lines crisscrossing the region' (quoted in Baruah 2005b: 12). Whether it is a question of the Northeast supplying hydroelectric power to its cross-border neighbours, of reviewing water transportation, or of projecting the Northeast as a tourist destination for the Asia-Pacific region, in all of these programmes for the future are heard echoes of that alternative discourse that is slowly taking shape. What may also be of interest is that this policy retrieves and refurbishes one of those attractive components of the old identity narrative—the historical links with East and Southeast Asia.

The Tourism Policy document announces plans to involve stakeholders at the infrastructural levels of hospitality, transport, and maintenance of tourism sites— positive economic interventions that would ensure continuance of the transborder narrative. The two thrust areas are eco-tourism and integrated tourism circuits which might involve a tourist itinerary like the following through several states of the Northeast: Shillong (Meghalaya); Guwahati, Kaziranga, Tezpur, Bhalukpong (all in Assam); Tawang (Arunachal Pradesh); Majuli, Sivasagar (Assam); and Kohima (Nagaland), openly rejecting a state-centred approach and highlighting the positive and quite natural breaching of borders and boundaries, indeed inviting transgression of borders and active economic collaboration across states.

A final element in the document that connects with the question of narrative shifts and agency is the intention to 'plan, and implement a professionally managed integrated communications strategy to be called the "National Tourism Awareness Campaign"' (National Tourism Policy 2002: 13), indicating a mode that would be used to inject a new impetus into the Northeast narrative about itself, through which a more enabling narrative may take shape.[7]

The tourism option offers an emphatic transformation in the area of borders, closure and exclusivity, especially evident in thinking on the ethnographic dimension of travel. The anthropologist/ethnographer Ed Bruner who led a group of tourists to view his own professional site, Bali, speaks of a 'touristic borderzone' which is 'a site for the invention of culture on a massive scale' (Bruner 2005: 193). Such cultural production may also be the route to the preservation of many of the institutions and rituals of a culture that are at risk in the conditions of modern living but that are still perceived as necessary ways for a culture to distinguish itself or keep its separate identity. One of Bruner's examples of such invention is the Balinese frog dance devised for tourists in Batuan in the 1970s which, in the 1980s, was performed at a Balinese wedding: 'What began in tourism entered Balinese ritual' (ibid.: 199). While Bruner speaks only of forms that are invented purely for the sake of tourists, we might borrow his implication of constructedness in under- standing how local cultural forms may gain visibility through such a process. Such outright or overt invention is not immediately apparent here, but the demands of tourism and the necessity of providing an 'authentic' experience of the culture of a group among whom the tourist may travel, could very well aid the preservation and consolidation of cultural or social forms. On a visit to the Lalung dominated Morigaon district of Assam, to study its folk literature, a group of us from the English department of Gauhati University had a discussion with local leaders on the institution of the 'boys' dormitory'[8] (common in many tribal societies). We were told that with the new and growing assertion of ethnic identity, the institution which had virtually stopped functioning was being revived and we were actually shown one such dormitory that was in the process of construction—certainly not for regular use but as a mark of cultural distinctiveness that could be displayed. The pressure of presenting such an 'authentic' experience, a corollary of successful tourism, is likely to urge a revival of many dormant forms of cultural practice— dance, music, cuisine, weaving—that in turn should offer economic opportunities and cultural visibility.

Both these new narratives carry the potential to energize the existing narrative out of its apathy. But what they provide is the hope of insidious change in surface and material conditions, addressing and keeping alive difference, embedding into the narrative of the Northeast questions of ethnic visibility, recognition, and admiration, that should be corollaries of difference or distinctiveness. Of special interest therefore is the idea of circuits in the Tourism Policy document which rather than being state- or region-centred highlights borders and boundaries and yet sees them as positively breachable.

The desire, the reality, the investment in one kind of discourse against another, all of these are functions in the evolution of any narrative that seeks to express the Northeast. It would be naïve to suggest that such narrative manipulation can be an exclusive solution to the turmoil of the Northeast. Policy changes, political vision, and timely action are the fundamentals but narrative may be employed as an aide.

Nandana Dutta

Notes

¹ Paul Brass in Phadnis and Ganguly (2001: 26).

² Harekrishna Deka notes that there is simultaneously a centripetal and a centrifugal force working in Assam's relations with India—protonationalism balanced by cultural bonding (2005: 191–2)—a view that echoes the writings of cultural icons like Ambikagiri Roychowdhuri and Jyoti Prasad Agarwalla, both of whom acknowledge cultural links of the state with the rest of India, and may also be traced in the belief expressed by Prafulladatta Goswami about 'Indian' influence on all communities (quoted later in this essay).

³ Harekrishna Deka (2005) revealingly uses the term 'mind management' (p. 199) as he also identifies a 'neglect syndrome' that is 'not imaginary' in his analysis of the Assamese mind.

⁴ Goswami, well-known Assamese writer and now negotiator between the ULFA and the Government of India, made this suggestion in a paper titled 'North–East India: The Education, Militancy and Peace Linkage' presented at a seminar on 'Road to Peace and Progress in South Asia: Learning from the Neighborhood'.

⁵ See 'Obstacles in the Relationship of Tribals and Non-Tribals', in Senapati (2000: 39). Translation and paraphrase is mine.

⁶ The rationale for such use of a theory is in fact provided by the multiple identities of the Northeast and is available in the earlier narrative of Assameseness in the dual concepts of 'jati' and 'mahajati' used productively by a generation of early twentieth-century Assamese thinkers while referring to Assam and India, with no contradiction perceived in one also being the other. I particularly have in mind the writings of Ambikagiri Roychowdhuri (1986) on these two concepts.

⁷ All of these programmes are fluid in that they invite each state to formulate the details of their own particular policies (eschewing the top-down traits of most central policies)—moves that seem to be already under way in several states as evidenced, for example, in the Tourism Policy Document of the Government of Meghalaya which echoes the National Tourism Policy vision of welfare, participation, employment generation, etc., and also mentions schemes for loans to youths to provide several different kinds of tourism support.

⁸ The boys' dormitory is an institution in many tribal communities that is now mostly defunct. Young boys would be taken from their families and brought up together. Here, they would study, eat and sleep, learn the crafts of the tribe, and often when necessary help out a family by bringing in the crops or lend their collective strength in some other sphere of activity. It was an exercise in developing community feeling, leadership qualities, and responsibility. In some tribes there has also been a tradition of girls' dormitories.

References

Baruah, Sanjib, 'The Problem', *Seminar* (Special issue on 'Gateway to the East: A Symposium on Northeast India and the Look East Policy'), 550, June, pp. 12–16, 2005b.

Baruah, Sanjib, *India Against Itself: Assam and Politics of Nationality*, Philadelphia University of Pennsylvania Press and New Delhi: Oxford University Press, 1999.

Baruah, Sanjib, 'Ethnic' Conflict as State-Society Struggle: The Poetics and Politics of Assamese Micro-Nationalism', *Modern Asian Studies*, 28 (3), pp. 649–71, 1994.

Bayly, C.A., *Origins of Nationality in South Asia: Patriotism and Ethical Government in the Making of Modern India*, New Delhi: Oxford University Press, 2001 [1998].

Bhabha, Homi, *The Location of Culture*, London and New York: Routledge, 1994.

Bhattacharyya, Hiranya Kumar, *The Silent Invasion: Assam versus Infiltration*, Guwahati & Delhi: Spectrum Publications, 2001.

Bhuyan, B.C., *Political Development of the North East*, Vol. II, New Delhi: Omsons Publications, 1992.

Brettell, Caroline B, 'Theorizing Migration in Anthropology', in Caroline B. Brettell and James F. Hollifield (eds), *Migration Theory: Talking Across Disciplines*, New York and London: Routledge, 2000.

Bruner, Edward H., *Culture on Tour: Ethnographies of Travel*, Chicago & London: University of Chicago Press, 2005.

Clifford, James, *Routes: Travel and Translation in the Late Twentieth Century*, Cambridge, Mass. & London: Harvard University Press, 1997.

Deane, Seamus, 'Introduction', *Nationalism, Colonialism, and Literature*, Minneapolis: University of Minnesota Press, 1990.

Deka, Harekrishna, 'The Assamese Mind: Contours of a Landscape', *IIC Quarterly* (New Delhi: India International Centre Quarterly), 32 (2&3), pp. 189–202, 2005.

Goswami, Praphulladatta, *Essays on the Folklore and Culture of North-Eastern India*, Guwahati: Spectrum, 1983.

Hames-Garcia, Michael R., 'Who are Our Own People: Challenges for a Theory of Social Identity', in Paula Moya and Michael R. Hames-Garcia (eds), *Reclaiming Identity*, Hyderabad: Orient Longman, 2001.

Hitson Jusho, P.T., *Politics of Ethnicity in North East India (With special reference to Manipur)*, New Delhi: Regency Publications, 2004.

Kaplan, Caren, *Questions of Travel: Postmodern Discourses of Displacement*, Durham and London: Duke University Press, 1996.

Khan, Adeel, *Politics of Identity: Ethnic Nationalism and the State of Pakistan*, New Delhi and London: Sage Publications, 2005.

Misra, Udayon, *The Periphery Strikes Back*, Shimla: Indian Institute of Advanced Study, 2000.

Mukhim, Patricia, 'Where is this North-east?' *IIC Quarterly* [New Delhi: India International Centre Quarterly], 32 (2&3), pp. 177–88, 2005.

National Tourism Policy, Department of Tourism, Government of India, 2002.

Phadnis, Urmila, and Rajat Ganguly, *Ethnicity and Nation-Building in South Asia*, New Delhi: Sage, 2001 [1989].

Ramesh, Jairam, 'Northeast India in a New Asia', *Seminar*, 550, pp. 17–21, June 2005.

Rosaldo, Renato, *Culture and Truth: The Remaking of Social Analysis*, Boston: Beacon, 1989.

Said, Edward W., *Reflections on Exile*, New Delhi: Penguin Books India, 2001.

Senapati, Bolairam, *Atitar Sandhanat* (In Search of the Past), Jagiroad: Tiwa Mathonlai Takhre, 2000.

White, Hayden, 'The Value of Narrativity', in W.J.T. Mitchell (ed.), *On Narrative*, Chicago: University of Chicago Press, 1981.

22   The Ballad of the Sad Café
Israeli Leisure, Palestinian Terror, and the Post/colonial Question

Rebecca L. Stein

Long after the arguments in Edward Said's *Orientalism* (1978) have acquired both academic and popular currency, the degree to which Said's *The Question of Palestine* (1979) remains a bold intervention into dominant US discourse on the Middle East seems remarkable. At the most rudimentary level, Said's text aimed to establish the very existence of Palestine and the Palestinian people, and to trace the genealogy of their displacement—both materially from their land and figuratively from the landscape of both Israeli and US history and collective memory. No less pressing, at the time of the text's publication, was the relatively uncharted work of systematically inserting Zionism into the history of European imperialism. In 1979, at a time when the signifier *Palestine* still resounded with insurgence for many US audiences, *The Question of Palestine* was both a courageous project and, as Said noted in the text's introduction, a rather lonely one—the loneliness of one who articulates the heretofore unsaid.[1] While the existence of the Palestinian people is no longer in question in the present, an aura of insurgence still haunts Said's colonial claim. Indeed, it is only very recently that academics, journalists, and activists in the United States have been authorized to speak openly about the coloniality of the Zionist project without the threat of sanction, without the need to defend against the charge of anti-Semitism—and, for Jewish critics, that highly problematic label of "self-hater," which has long done the work of disciplining Jewish dissent and delimiting the terms of intelligible Jewish identity.

    Yet the parameters of permissible discourse about Zionism and the Jewish state have indeed shifted in the last few decades—and quite markedly at the turn of the millennium alone. The genesis of this shift has been multiple. Certainly, it has been

Rebecca L. Stein, "The Ballad of Sad Café: Israeli Leisure, Palestinian Terror, and the Post/colonial Question," in Ania Loomba, Suvir Kaul, Matti Bunzl, Antoinette Burton, and Jed Esty, eds., *Postcolonial Studies and Beyond*. Durham, NC: Duke University Press, 2005, pp. 317–336. Reproduced by permission of Duke University Press.

Postcolonial Studies: An Anthology, First Edition. Edited by Pramod K. Nayar.
Editorial material and organization © 2016 John Wiley & Sons, Ltd.
Published 2016 by John Wiley & Sons, Ltd.

enabled by the success with which the Palestinian national movement and resistance struggle of the 1980s and early 1990s managed to export its historical claims, demands, and images of defiance into the US arena. The Oslo Accords of 1993, for all their flaws, bestowed international legitimacy on the Palestinian struggle for self-determination in relatively unprecedented ways. So, too, must one credit the World Conference against Racism of 2001, with its popularization of an anticolonial critique of the Zionist project. But it is certainly the magnitude of Israeli violence and repression in the years following the dissolution of the (so-called) peace process that enabled–indeed, required–this vocabulary to emerge in new ways and with new force. The spring of 2002 constitutes a dramatic case in point: amid the largest and most brutal Israeli incursion into the Occupied Palestinian Territories since the 1967 war, US audiences bore witness to a significant change in the texture of popular discourse. What exploded onto the screens of televisions, and in the pages of newspapers, was not merely the language of "military occupation" and (to a lesser degree) "colonialism" but also word of "war crimes," "ethnic cleansing," and even "genocide"—language deployed, particularly in the aftermath of the Israeli incursion into Jenin, as a way to name and make sense of Israel's military presence in the West Bank and the Gaza Strip. Certainly, some of these terms proved much more accurate than others. Nonetheless, what merits attention is the fact of their collective emergence within a discursive landscape that had long been fiercely policed for anything that smacked of anti-Israeli sentiment.

All of this does not mean to suggest the wholesale radicalization of US discourse and politics on Palestine during the period under discussion. In the spring of 2002, as Israeli fatalities mounted from a campaign of Palestinian militarism inside the state's 1967 borders, US audiences also witnessed a frightening return to classic Zionist rhetorics, and racist defenses of the Jewish state, particularly from within the mainstream Jewish American community. Of course, Israel's official discourse on the need for self-defence in the face of Arab terror proved a newly persuasive one for a US public still stinging from the pain and affront of September 11, 2001. What one witnessed was a polyphonic discursive sphere in which the language of Zionist coloniality and Palestinian terror competed for space and audibility within the mainstream media in relatively unprecedented ways. These complications—and, at times, contradictions— were exemplified in the language of President Bush, who lent his support to the Israeli administration in their battle against "terror" even as he experimentally deployed the term *Palestine*—a term bearing the marks of the Palestinian struggle for self-determination.

Taking my cue from this moment of discursive ambivalence and possibility in the US media, and building on the tradition of (post)colonial criticism that we have inherited from Said and others, this essay investigates the ways in which mainstream Israeli print media responded to this same moment—that is, the moment of heightened Palestinian militarism and escalating Israeli violence in the Occupied Territories in the spring of 2002. I am interested in a rather unlikely narrative that circulated in Hebrew- and English-language newspapers of this period.[2] As Israel's occupation grew in intensity, violence, and scope, and as Israelis were faced with a virtually unprecedented wave of Palestinian "suicide bombings" against civilian targets inside the state,[3] Israeli newspapers began to talk a lot about *leisure*. In order to dramatize and render intelligible the Israeli experience of Palestinian militarism, and the radical ways in which it had transformed daily life, the mainstream media told a story of Jewish leisure practices, and consumer patterns more generally, under attack.[4] At the center of this discourse stood the café or the coffeehouse, a central institution of Israeli bourgeois public life (and arguably of colonial metropolitan culture in broader terms),[5] now targeted by Palestinian militants in relatively unprecedented ways.

Yet the Israeli investment in the café as an index of Palestinian violence far exceeded its material status as terror's target. In the Israeli media, cafés as signs became heavily burdened with symbolic meaning—configured as superlative instances and indices of Israel in a time of crisis. Cafés were asked to carry a metonymic charge: to stand in for the Jewish nation-state and its fragility. The story of cafés under attack thus did the work of representing and managing popular anxiety about the mounting threat of Palestinian terror. Cafés also performed the labor of deflection; by telling the story of the current moment through an account of Israeli leisure institutions under attack, the café discourse elided not merely the concurrent Israeli violence against Palestinians in the West Bank and Gaza, where the toll on daily life was much more severe, but the histories of Israeli aggression and dispossession of which the current crisis was constitutive. The grossly myopic focus on Israeli loss in the face of enormous violence and devastation in the West Bank certainly constituted the narrative's greatest offense.

When one reads the café as metonym, a multiple set of story lines emerges in the Israeli media. Some are unsurprising—such as the stories of good citizenship and patriotism that respond to this moment of national threat by enunciating through a discourse on leisure-based consumption. One also sees a set of restorative narratives that take the café as their occasion to reembed the dominant (and fictional) terms of Israeli nationness. This essay pays particular attention to the moment at which Israeli violence returns to the narrative from which it had been expunged. I will argue that the press's account of leisure under attack was haunted by precisely that which it sought to refuse—namely, the historic and enduring injustices of the Israeli settle national project. To read the leisure narrative thus is by no means to refuse the very real and lasting trauma with which cafés have been associated in the lives of many Israelis. Rather, it is to consider how cafés—both as institutions and as signs—have been asked to carry the burden of this trauma and in tandem, of the Israeli aggression and vitriol of this political moment, well as the histories with which they resonate.

This essay draws heavily on postcolonial theory, particularly the (in) famous textual strategies and analytics of Homi Bhabha and his project of reading the texts of Western imperialism against their grain with an eye to their ambivalences, indeterminacies, and double-sessions. For Bhabha "ambivalence" was a way to name the "conflictual economy of colonial discourse," the perpetual slippages of its authority (epistemological and other wise), the impossibility of a seamless disavowal of its violence.[6] In adapting Bhabha's reading strategy for my study of Israeli political culture, I want to tell a rather different story of ambivalence—its locations, histories, and subjects. Rather than resting on the conflictual economy of the psyche on the sign, the forms of ambivalence that I am tracing within the mainstream texts of Israeli settler-nationalism are highly situated and historical. My aim is not to position the café narrative—or the print media, by extension–as a superlative site of ambivalence/resistance. Rather, it is to suggest that it functions as a quotidian instance of a broader political field, that what haunted the pages of Israeli newspapers in the spring of 2002 were precisely those instabilities/ aporias at issue in other, more explicitly political narratives, spaces, and institutions (e.g., on the floor of the Israeli parliament; in the official policies and rationales of

Israeli politicians, demographers, and military strategists; in the texts of state-sponsored history books). In the broadest terms, then, I deploy postcolonial analytics to document the ways in which dominant Israeli discourse at the turn of the twenty-first century has made sense of the enduring coloniality of the Israeli national project–that is, the forms of coloniality that remain at play within the Occupied Territories and within the state itself, and the histories of coloniality on which these forms build and with which they resonate.

Reading the Café

To understand the leisure narrative, one must first grasp the political landscape out of which it emerged. The narrative took shape in the Israeli media during the spring of 2002, at a time when violence was erupting in new forms, and with new intensity, in Palestine and Israel. The second Palestinian uprising, a response to the failures of the Oslo process and the growing poverty and unemployment in the Occupied Territories, was in its second year. Unlike the first uprising (1988–93), this second one was growing increasingly militarized. Beginning in the winter of 2001, in a response to the Palestinian uprising, the Israeli Defense Forces (IDF) had gone on the offensive in the West Bank, shelling and demolishing houses, razing orchards and crops. In tandem, the Israeli government (now under the leadership of prime minister Ariel Sharon, elected in February 2001) was continuing to expand the settlement infrastructure and to fortify the military closure of the West Bank, effectively restricting Palestinian movement both in and out of Israel, and between towns and villages in the West Bank. Extrajudicial killings by the state of (so-called) wanted Palestinians were also on the rise. By the end of February 2002, Israeli forces had killed more than one thousand Palestinians by these and other means. In response to the Israeli offensive, armed Palestinian groups and individuals escalated their attacks against Israeli installations in the Occupied Territories and began to move their struggle increasingly inside the Green Line. By February of 2002, some 250 Israelis, the vast majority of them civilians, had been killed.[7] Inside the state, the rising death toll and growing fear of random violence profoundly altered daily life and popular politics, fueling the political shift to the right. Many Israeli Jews spoke of the need for self-defense at all costs.

The café discourse emerged most powerfully in the wake of March 9, 2002, after a young Palestinian bomber detonated his charge in a crowded café (Café Moment) in an affluent West Jerusalem neighborhood. The blast proved strong and deadly, killing eleven men and women and injuring some fifty others. In the days that followed the bombing, the café became a shrine of sorts, a place of secular homage.[8] Neighborhood mourners decked the sidewalk and the demolished storefront with flowers and memorial candles, and young girls gathered to recite psalms for the dead, their bodies draped in the Israeli flag—scenes which harkened back to the popular acts of public memorialization (therein, performative acts of citizenship) that followed the 1995 assassination of prime minister Yitzhak Rabin. Israel had experienced attacks like these before, most recently during the wave of bus bombings of the mid-1990s—a response to the Hebron massacre of 1994, the assassination of a prominent Hamas leader by Mossad agents in 1996, and to the (so-called) peace process more generally.[9] Yet in the winter and spring of 2002, the scope and form of Palestinian militarism began to change. Now, bombings became far more frequent, and they struck new kinds of targets. Bombers began to set their sights on places of middle-class consumption and leisure in the very heart of the Israeli metropole—including a pizzeria, a hotel lobby, a supermarket, a disco, and a number of cafés. While cafés were not unprecedented targets, they were becoming more frequent ones in the spring of 2002—a change that many Israelis understood as a concerted shift in Palestinian strategy. In addition to the bombing of Café Moment, the month of March 2002 alone witnessed a bombing at a Tel Aviv coffeehouse (claiming far fewer lives) and word of a thwarted attack at another Jerusalem venue, prevented by a vigilant waiter. Nonetheless, the greatest number of attacks, and subsequent lives lost, from Palestinian bombings occurred at the more traditional sites of dense working-class assembly, such as army and settler installations in the Occupied Territories and inside Israel, open-air markets, and public buses—the latter remaining the favored site of militarism, as it had been for nearly a decade.

Yet in the mainstream Israeli media, the perception of Palestinian militarism and its preferred targets was otherwise. As the death toll from bombings mounted in March and early April, the Israeli press turned its attention to the café as the locus of Palestinian terror. The image of the Jewish state under fire was illustrated through a story of leisure and its loss—the loss of the café as a space of daily, ritualized consumption. The popularity of this narrative reached its peak in the weeks prior to the most brutal phase of the Israeli incursion, which began on March 29, 2002. Nonetheless, the narrative circulated at a time of disproportionate violence, when Israeli aggression in the West Bank was exacting a much greater toll on the daily lives of Palestinians.

Consider an article from *Ha'aretz* newspaper—the Hebrew daily of the Israeli intelligentsia. On March 10, the day following the Café Moment bombing, the newspaper broke from its standard idiom of reportage to decry in highly personalized form both the cost in human life and the violence afflicted on the Israeli way of life, with the café at its center: "This is our café," began the article, which was featured prominently on the first page of the newspaper, just below its masthead: "We came here in the morning for an espresso and a croissant. We came here in the evening for a [beer]. To grasp what is left of normalcy, of our secular sanity. To grasp at what is left of our way of life."[10] From the vantage of an intimate eyewitness, the paragraphs that followed surveyed the scene of death and destruction in the immediate aftermath of the blast. In blunt staccato prose, the article narrated the landscape of carnage: "the smell of burning," the "charred human flesh," fragments of human bodies amid the shattered glass, the screams of the evacuated survivors, the stillness of the dead. In turn, it offered a forceful political critique, lambasting the Left for naming settlement building and military occupation as the cause of the current political crisis. The author disagreed, telling his alternative political narrative through the figure of the café: "When the police sappers walk among the dead youth, searching for another explosive device, it does not seem to be so [a War for the Peace of the Settlements].[11] It seems very, very different. Maybe the War for Moment [Café]? Maybe the War for a chance of a Western society to survive in the Middle East? … [W]e can no longer keep fooling ourselves. This is a war about the morning's coffee and croissant. About the beer in the evening. About our very lives."

That a piece like this—in its highly editorial prose, in its lyrical eulogy—should appear on the front page was indeed unusual for a newspaper committed to the serious reporting of the *New York Times* variety.[12] Yet this was only the most dramatic instance of a discourse becoming ubiquitous in Israeli media of this moment, one that recurred with an almost absurd repetitiveness, returning to the same tropes and story lines. Print media and talk shows alike decried the sacrifice of cafés to Palestinian terror. In melancholic tones, they chronicled the "chilling quiet" that had befallen café districts in Tel Aviv and Jerusalem. In defiance, they spoke of the ad hoc efforts of residents to "take back the cafés" in their neighborhoods,[13] and hailed victims of café bombings as exemplary Israeli citizens, as the "Everyman, [as] mainstream Israel." In turn, the figure of the coffeehouse was used to narrate the decline of the peace process and thus to tell the story of the current political moment: "[The] Oslo peace agreement meant that we should be able to have a cup of coffee in Baghdad. Instead it has turned out that we cannot even have a cup of coffee in Tel Aviv."[14] So ubiquitous was the café discourse that it became the subject of Israeli bumper stickers, made its way into the political rhetoric of the Israeli housing minister,[15] appeared in Ariel Sharon's national address from the Knesset floor,[16] and was exported into the US media, where it circulated in similar—although less pervasive—ways. The café narrative acquired a complicated performative status; its very citation seemed to produce the effects of a pledge of allegiance—marking the speaker as in and of the Israeli nation-state.

Many of these accounts, particularly those appearing in the English-language media, borrowed from the post-September 11 narrative of defiance through consumerism, whereby the abnegation of normal consumptive patterns was deemed a victory for terrorists (as in, "If we don't go out for drinks, then 'they' win").[17] Die-hard customers were portrayed as heroes who persevered in the face of Palestinian terror—evidence of the lasting power of the Israeli people in the face of this assault on their existence. "If you want to understand [the state of Israel], come to Caffit [café] for breakfast," read an Israeli editorial from early April. "This is a people that aren't going away. They are not even going to stop drinking coffee."[18] Several daily papers interviewed the dedicated patrons that returned to their favorite coffee bars in the face of the current crisis: "Just about the most patriotic thing you can do now is go out and have a drink."[19] Burdened with new symbolic import, those cafés that remained open for table service became privilege sites for the performance of national allegiance. One's very presence in a café was rendered a superlative act of loyalty to the state in its battle against terror. Consumption itself became an act of defiance, and the consumer, the defiant citizen.

More than leisure practices were at issue. Also under fire was the posibility of public assemblage in café spaces. It was thus with considerable shock that West Jerusalemites learned of local plans to convert coffeehouse into take-out only facilities. Consider the following testimony of a Jewish Jerusalem resident, published as a personal essay on the crisis in a weekly Israeli magazine: "While [picking up] my son [after school] … I [ran] into [a] neighbor, who told me that the Aroma Café … had moved all its table and chairs so customers could no longer sit there. At first I didn't really understand what she was saying, and she had to repeat herself before I let the reality of that statement sink in: Aroma had become a take-out place."[20] As the ones mentioned before, this story was a rather pervasive one. The emergence of café take-out became a matter of national importance that was covered by all major Israeli daily newspapers, as it reflected a radical shift in the landscape of civil society.[21] True to Habermas's telling, take-out threatened the space and possibility of social intercourse itself. The Israeli public feared an erosion of the public sphere—the loss of those spaces in which, through consumption, disparate patrons were rendered social equals and consumer-subjects became citizens.

While the loss of cafés threatened with a loss of citizenship and its practices, the threat of violence in café spaces (and the discourse that attended it) also inaugurated a new set of national subject positions. Not only consumers but also workers in the café sector were being called to duty for the nation-state in new ways. The Israeli press was particularly attentive, in this regard, to the case of a young West Jerusalem waiter who detected a Palestinian man armed with explosives at the entrance of a crowded coffeehouse ("Hero of the day," he was hailed by one popular Hebrew daily).[22] As the labor of racial profiling—of discerning terrorist from tourist—increasingly became the domain of café employees, labor in this leisure sector was increasingly marked with the semiotics of patriotic citizenship. Indeed, as the café acquired the status of a battleground,[23] the difference between waiters and armed guards began to blur; all were being conscripted into this war, all were being hailed not merely as citizens but as citizen-*soldiers* in new ways.

Thus it was that cafés became a kind of staging ground for many of the larger political questions and issues of the moment. One such issue was the problem of the border. At this moment, much of the Jewish Israeli public appeared united on the need to enclose the nation-state, to fortify and render it insular, not merely with armed checkpoints and border police, or with military closures and visa restrictions to keep Palestinians out, but with heavily fortified walls that would demarcate and protect (or so the story went) the edges of the nation-state.[24] Campaigns of Palestinian militancy inside the 1967 borders generated the desire for such enclosures even as they betrayed them as impossible fantasies. It was both in partial recognition of this fantasy and of the desire to preserve it that borders began to proliferate and move inward, to the heart of the public sphere—becoming "borders" of restaurants, shopping malls, and cafés. Now, waiters performed not merely as soldiers but as border guards of sorts. The café and its thresholds began to function as a kind of national enclosure writ small.

Cafés and Zionist Fantasy

As I have noted, cafés were not the only institutions targeted by Palestinian militants over the course of the last decade. In strictly numeric terms, both regarding attacks and lives lost, the public bus had long constituted the favored locus of Palestinian vio-lence. The choice of buses as targets began in earnest in the mid-1990s as Palestinian militants worked to disrupt the initial workings of the Oslo peace process.[25] Yet as an institution, the bus failed to capture the Israeli imagination, to acquire symbolic value, to become mobilized as national instance. This is not to suggest an Israeli failure to take buses seriously as loci of terror. After each attack, conversation about the need to avoid bus travel would invariably proliferate in the Israeli media, and the number of users would precipitously decline (at least among populations with the means to travel otherwise). And at times of political extremity or during an election period, buses have been called into service as mobile billboards (in 1994, after the assassination of Rabin, calling on the Jewish Israeli public to preserve "tolerance" and say no to violence; in 2002, calling on the public to reelect Ariel Sharon). Yet buses have not been burdened with a set of national meanings exceeding their functional status. They could serve as *messengers* of meaning, but they did not themselves become inscribed, as signs, with meaning—they were not hailed as placeholders of the nation-state.

Why, then, the café? As an institution, it has long enjoyed a privileged place in the history and mythology of the Israeli nation-state.[26] Cafés, which proliferated in Tel Aviv from the very inception of the city in the early 1900s, were both a staple of the urban landscape (installed in large numbers along the city's main boulevards) and proved crucial in producing the space and geographical imagination of Tel Aviv as an explicitly *Western* city, that is, a city made in the likeness of Western European cosmopolitan centers and defined against the supposed premodernity of its urban neighbor, the Palestinian city of Jaffa.[27] In collective Ashkenazi memory, the story of Zionist cultural and intellectual life of the 1940s and 1950s remains intimately tied to café society (where, "sitting cheek by jowl, would be authors, architects, artists, public figures, actors and all the rest of the intelligentsia").[28] The labors of some of Israel's most important cultural figures (famously, poet Natan Alterman) is popularly traced back to particular Tel Aviv coffeehouses (e.g., Café Cassit). In turn, select Jerusalem cafés (e.g., Café Atara) are celebrated for their service to the early Zionist militias.[29] At issue is the importance of the café in the history of the Jewish state and the fabric of secular, Zionist modernity.[30]

Cafés continue to do important symbolic national work in the present. The European-style café remains a defining feature of Tel Aviv's urban, Ashkenazi centers, continuing the process of demarcating and safeguarding the Western character of Israeli cosmopolitanism—a character growing increasingly phantasmatic in the face of the ever expanding nonwhite, and non-Israeli, working-class peripheries. Moreover, the mainstream Israeli and Jewish-diasporic imaginations of the city and its subjects remain linked to this leisure institution ("This is a city in which you are what your Friday café is," wrote the *Jerusalem Post* in 1989).[31] In West Jerusalem, where coffeehouses have historically been less plentiful, cafés have been asked to do a different kind of work in the late twentieth and early twenty-first century: not merely to demarcate an explicitly Western form of cosmopolitanism but to preserve a *secular* Israeli geography within a city increasingly dominated by religious interests and communities. In recent decades, those cafés that have remained open on Saturday, in violation of religious dictates to the contrary, have become privileged fronts in the battle between the city's secular and religious populations—occasional targets of religious violence and, in turn, icons of secular defiance.

What these histories and discourses share with the leisure narrative of 2002 is the story of the café as an explicitly Western form of cosmopolitan modernity. The coffeehouse memorialized by the press in 2002 was always a European space and institution, a purveyor not merely of coffee per se but of espresso and croissant, a locus not merely of popular Israeli congress but of bourgeois Western society and taste.[32] In highly literal terms, such representations proved accurate: the cafés that received foremost media attention—and, indeed, those that bore the brunt of Palestinian violence during this period—were located in affluent Ashkenazi neighborhoods heretofore outside the daily circuits of the conflict and its violences. But at issue, again, is the way in which the story of European cafés was asked to function metonymically. The fiction of the metonym was twofold. First, it worked to obscure the historic and iconic status of the coffeehouse in the Arab world and the multiple kinds of Arab coffeehouses (both Palestinian and Mizrahi) that marked the Israeli landscape in the present.[33] But more pointedly, the fiction cohered in the ways in which the café as Euro-Jewish institution was installed to tell the story of the character and composition of a nation-state that, given both its Palestinian and Mizrahi histories, had never been. In the year 2002—as Israeli demographers continued to warn of rising Arab birthrates, the growing community of foreign workers, and the magnitude of the Russian Christian immigration inside the state—this proved a particularly fragile fiction that required vigilant making and remaking in the face of its dissolution.

Empty Landscapes

Perhaps the most ubiquitous trope in this discursive regime was that of *emptiness*—a trope that appeared with remarkable frequency in the Israeli press of this period. In this moment of random and frequent public violence and pervasive fear, the trope certainly told the truth of Israeli public space: in the aftermath of the March 9 bombing, cafés remained empty, as, indeed, did most places of leisure. Numerous articles began their accounts of the current political crisis with a visual sweep of the depopulated urban landscape.[34] They spoke of half-empty cinemas and dwindling numbers of consumers in shopping malls; of restaurants, pubs, and clubs, all suffering from lack of customers. They chronicled the new ease of barhopping on a Saturday night, as a popular route that once took several hours could now be covered in fifteen minutes— due to deserted venues and plentiful parking.[35] Articles noted the "chilling quiet [that had] taken control of [Israeli cities]," and the large number of armed guards outside cafés and restaurants, "watching empty places."[36] They spoke of popular bohemian neighborhoods, where parking was usually at premium, in which now "only a few hardy souls are out wandering the streets."[37]

I do not question the "truth" of these accounts. At issue, again, is their very ubiquity—the fact that the Israeli media invested so heavily in these desolate scapes as a way to enunciate the national crisis.[38] To begin with, the story of emptiness did the work of substitution; it functioned to obscure other landscapes of desolation and other kinds of empty scapes, particularly urban ones, coming into being at this political moment. Perhaps most striking in this regard, and largely ignored by the press, was the sudden absence from Israeli urban centers of Palestinian Arabs, who stayed away in fear of racial profiling by police and armed security guards and of the mounting anti-Arab rage of the Jewish population. Equally apparent, particularly in West Jerusalem, were the declining numbers of Arab residents using public transportation and entering Jewish neighborhoods or shopping districts, deterred by the racist slogans posted outside downtown businesses: "We do not employ Arabs." Or, "Enemies should not be offered livelihood."[39] These other modalities of emptiness, and these fantasies of a city stripped clean of Arabs, went largely unrecorded in the mainstream media, trumped by images of Jewish suffering and absence.

Yet the trope of emptiness also drew on a long discursive history, borrowing from, and resonating with, that most freighted of narratives about the history of the Jewish state, and that most classic of colonial tropes: the myth of "empty land." Empty land represents one of the founding narratives of the early Zionist movement as propagated in the work of Theodore Herzl, Hayyim Nahman Bialik, Max Mandelstamm, and others.[40] As in the larger colonial archive on which this narrative relied, "emptiness" marked the premodern: the sign of a place outside time and history, waiting, indeed beckoning, for Western intervention and development.[41] The founding of Tel Aviv was narrated through this story—that of a European city born out of sand—"an outpost of civilization against barbarism," in Herzl's famous words.[42] Of course, Jaffa was a thriving seaport at the time of Zionist settlement, as Jewish settlers were quick to discover. And much of the rural landscape of Palestine—imagined as uncultivated and sparsely populated—was densely settled by Palestinian Arabs, distributed throughout most of the fertile and cultivable regions.[43] As Zachery Lockman reminds us, early Zionist accounts of emptiness in the Palestine context should also be read metaphorically: not merely as testimonies of a place without people (for this fiction was easily discounted by a tour of the environs) but of a place without "a people," without the recognizable makings of a modern nation(-state).[44] Nonetheless, much of the violence that both preceded and followed Israeli state formation has turned on efforts to repair the gap between this fantasy and its countervailing reality—the effort to produce emptiness where there was none, both through the material dispossession of Palestinians and the more symbolic efforts to remove their traces from the landscape.

In much the same way did the trope resonate with the fantasies of emptiness articulated and enacted in contemporaneous Israeli policy—through new tactics and strategies of dispossession and the reinvigoration of old ones. More pointedly, it gestured toward the reemergence, in Israeli political culture of 2002, of the concept of mass population transfer of the Palestinian population as a means of political solution.[45] As some Israeli analysts argued, the violence and inhumanity of the Israeli incursion into the Palestinian territories seemed motivated by a proximate goal. On this issue, far-right members of the Israeli parliament were clear; should Palestinian violence escalate into a regional war, they warned, Palestinians should anticipate another 1948, another massive expulsion from their homes and lands.[46] Nor were Palestinians from the Occupied Territories the only population identified in such fantasies of ethnic cleansing; rather, in a radical revision of the transfer ideology as it had circulated in the Jewish Israeli political imagination heretofore, Israeli Jews were beginning to imagine the same for the Palestinian citizens of the state.[47]

I want to take seriously the ways in which the story of the empty leisure landscape, as told and retold in the Israeli media, resonated with these histories and contemporary fantasies of Palestinian dispossession. There is an uncanniness here, a way in which the ubiquitous narrative of the empty city both recalled and rehearsed, almost feverishly, the aftermath of such a dispossession—the strange scene of a once inhabited landscape rendered desolate. And yet, there is a crucial reversal at work: Jews, not Palestinian Arabs, were the ones missing from cafés, the once crowded pubs, and restaurants. Such a reversal functioned, perhaps, in recognition of the ways in which another war of dispossession would necessarily rebound into the Jewish state with untold violence.

This narrative transposition deserves careful consideration.[48] Borrowing rather loosely from Gayatri Spivak and her work in reading the British imperial archive against its grain, one can construct the *manifest* terms of the café narrative in terms of a single sentence: "They [the Palestinians] have emptied our cafés."[49] As did Spivak's formulation,[50] I aim to illustrate the kinds of displacements at work here—the "ideological dissimulation of imperialist political economy" at play in Israeli political culture of this period, and the shapes that such dissimulations take through the story of leisure.[51]

When one reads the café narrative against its grain, in articulation with the political landscape from which it emerged, it appears that the sentence requires a transposition that returns to the referent for which *café* functions as metonym: "We [the Israelis] have emptied their nation." Read thusly, the story of leisure seems to function not only as a site of deflection and nation making, but also as confession for the past and fantasy about the future.

Postcolonialities and Palestine/Israel

My aim in this essay is, in part, to foster the relatively incipient conversation between theory and the case(s) of Palestine and Israel. To point to the incipient nature of this conversation is not to deny the generations of activists and scholars (including those in Israel) who have boldly insisted on the coloniality of the Zionist project—both on the historic links between the modern project and other European colonial endeavors and the colonial nature of the Israeli state and its occupation in the present.[52] Rather, it is to note the enduring reluctance of most Palestine/Israel scholars, a handful of important exceptions notwithstanding,[53] to take up the postcolonial theoretical rubric. At issue, in part, is the general theoretical conservatism of Middle East studies—a by-product, in part, of its cold war legacy. Yet the logics of postcoloniality as theoretical/historical rubric are also to blame notably, the well-remarked vagaries of the key term and the ways in which much early postcolonial scholarship failed to adequately heterogenize "the postcolonial" as temporal, historical, and/or geographical index. As many scholars have noted, one product of this failure was a blurring of the differences between nation-states that had undergone decolonization, and those that had transformed into territorialized settler nation-states—states that now enjoyed independence, even as they remained on settled territory and maintained many forms of colonial privilege over conquered populations.[54]

It is for these and other reasons that the notion of a "postcolonial Israel" fails to tell a clear historical narrative—failing to account, for example, for the tensions between Israel's declaration of independent statehood in 1948 and the ways in which Palestinians who remained in the area of the emergent state continued to, as Joseph Massad has noted, "inhabit these spaces as colonial spaces." Of course, since 1967, the problem has become more difficult still.[55] At issue are both settler-nation and military occupation—two different and yet concurrent forms of coloniality, distinct and yet intimately imbricated. In addition, Israeli modalities of coloniality do not only take shape at the fault lines of "Arab versus Jew." As the work of Ella Shohat and Smadar Lavie teaches us,[56] a historically nuanced postcoloniality would also need to consider the ways that Arab Jews (or Mizrahim) were made to live as second-class citizens within a state founded on the notion of Euro-Jewish normativity. What this suggests, as Massad notes, are the ways in which the singularity of the term *postcolonial* radically fails to illustrate the complexities and multiple forms of coloniality (or its postness) in Palestine/Israel in any given time and space.

Interestingly, the historical problems of bringing postcoloniality to the Palestine/Israel context were reinforced by the ways in which Palestine and Palestinians became referenced within postcolonial literature of the early 1990s—the moment of the ascendance of this rubric within the humanities. What one sees at this time, particularly in the work of Homi Bhabha, are highly parenthetical detours through the Palestine/ Israel case as a way to tell the story of postcoloniality writ large. In such detours, "the Palestinian" is offered up as a seemingly self-evident instance of displacement, home-lessness, or abjection. While "the Israeli" is denied a similarly metonymic status in such literature, it is the absent present that makes such examples possible—implicitly marked as the selfsame locus of power/dominance against which the abject of "the Palestinian" (in its supposed singularity) takes shape. Consider, for example, the conclusion of *Location of Culture*, where Bhabha reflects on Frantz Fanon's story of "the Dirty Nigger": "Whenever these words are said in anger or in hate, whether of the Jew in the estaminet in Antwerp, or of *the Palestinian on the West Bank*, or the Zairian student eking out a wretched existence selling fake fetishes on the Left Bank … whenever and wherever I am when I hear a racist, or catch his look, I am reminded of Fanon's evocative essay 'The Fact of Blackness' and its unforgettable opening lines."[57] What is being offered here, as Amit Rai has argued, is a chain of subalternity that threatens to flatten the play of difference: "[Bhabha's] equation of all liminal and dom-inated groups and subjectivities also risks collapsing their social identities into an ontological correspondence which reduces their distinct struggles into analogous experiences of marginalization."[58] Of course, it is the availability of "the Palestinian on the West Bank" to appear in this list that interests me. This figure—simultaneously situated ("on the West Bank") and legible as a generality (an instance of "the Palestinian people")—takes its place amid the "whenever and wherever" of racism, illustrating a case with generalizable effects. The very legibility of "Palestinian" as parenthetical instance depends on the presumption of a singular referent, bearing radically circum-scribed meaning.[59] Invisible in this and other similar asides are the forms of Palestinian history that do not conform to such a story of abjection, the histories and daily ways of being Palestinian that are cosmopolitan, located, enfranchised. Invisible, in turn, are the subaltern subjects and histories that cannot be mapped as easily onto the binary terms of occupier/occupied (e.g., Palestinians with Israeli citizenship, Arab Jews, Palestinian refugees). My point here is not to protect the cosmopolitan Palestinian subject, but to open up a more varied and internally conflictual landscape of power and identity in the Palestine/Israel case, to make conceptual space for those communities, histories, and subjects who have been rendered invisible by the work of "the exemplar" and its presumed singularity.

In the light of such critiques, why take recourse to postcolonial theory as a way to study Palestine/Israel? In methodological terms, the poststructural theories of power/ knowledge on which postcolonial theory builds force a productive rethinking of the normative paradigm of so-called conflict studies with its static story of power/resistance and politics. They offer, instead, an account of the political that radically multiplies both the sites of power and the places and technologies of its refusal. Perhaps most crucially, the mapping of Israel/Palestine onto the global and diachronic geography of the post-colonial refuses to abide by the terms of Israeli exceptionalism. The kind of colonial comparativism in which postcolonial theory engages mounts an important challenge to this most recalcitrant of Israeli state and popular discourses—an argument with at least a half century of violent effects. To insist on situating Israel/Palestine within this broader colonial geography is not only to enable a tracing of legacies of similitude (in terms of colonial violence, institutions, and cultural logics) but also to imagine the possibility of a decolonized future.

Notes

Thanks to editors of this volume for their sharp engagements with successive formulations. A shorter version of this essay was presented at Amherst College in 2002 and appeared in Theory and Event 6, no. 3 (2003), available at http://muse.jhu.edu/journals/tae/v006/6.3stein.html. Thanks also to Joel Beinin, Tom Dumm, Judith Frank, Andrew Janiak, Andrew Parker, and Shira Robinson for their critical readings.

1   Said writes: "To the West, which is where I live, to be a Palestinian is in political terms to be an outlaw of sorts, or at any rate very much an outsider. But that is a reality, and I mention it today only as a way of indicating the peculiar loneliness of my undertaking in this book." Said, The Question of Palestine, xviii.

2   This essay focuses on a variety of different Israeli newspapers, both Hebrew- and English-language, including Ha'aretz (the newspaper of the Israeli intelligentsia, often likened to the New York Times), Yedi'ot Aharonot, Ma'ariv (Israel's largest circulating Hebrew dailies), and the Jerusalem Post (an English-language daily with a considerably smaller circulation). All of these newspapers have a national rather than regional or city-specific identity, meaning both that they are consumed across Israel and speak in the idiom of the national, rather than that of the regional.

3   My quotes are meant to signal the ideological nature of this phrase, replete with a story of Islamic and/or Arab fanaticism and its disavowal of the value of human life.

4   Innumerable thanks to Shira Robinson, with whom I discussed the political economy of leisure. See Robinson, "My Hairdresser Is a Sniper."

5   I am particularly thinking of the place of the café in the battles for decolonization in the Algerian and Irish contexts. Gillo Pontecorvo's Battle of Algiers (1965) stages this battle most graphically.

6   Homi K. Bhabha, The Location of Culture, 85. Note that many scholars, among them Robert Young, argue that the problem with Bhabha's "ambivalence" rests in the story of "agency" it tells, whereby the postcolonial reader is inscribed as the primary agent of struggle in a seeming refusal of material acts of resistance (or, in Young's telling, "resistance by colonized peoples"). I take issue with such objections, whereby "real" politics is thought to rest beyond textual politics. See Young, White Mythologies, 149.

7   Amnesty International, Israel and the Occupied Territories.

8   Etgar Lefkowitz, "Hundreds Turn Bombed Café into Shrine," Jerusalem Post, March 11, 2002.

9   I am referring to the Baruch Goldstein massacre at the Ibrahimi Mosque in February of 1994 and the assassination of Yahya Ayyash in Khan Yunis in January of 1996.

10 In the following, all unmarked translations from the Hebrew are mine.

11 This was a central slogan of the Israeli Left during 2002, one which blamed settlement building and the military occupation for the wave of violence. The slogan punned on the state name for the Lebanon war ("War for the Peace of Galilee").

12 Despite the ubiquity of this narrative, it had its critics, some of whom were published in the Israeli press. For a critical response to this article, see Roman Bronfman, "The Terrorist Ruined His Morning Coffee," Ha'aretz, March 13, 2002.

13 Kelly Hartog, "Taking Back the Cafés," Jerusalem Post, March 29, 2002.

14 This quote from an Israeli soldier patrolling the streets of Bethlehem appeared in the foreign press: Peter Beaumont, "'I Don't Want to Be Here … But What Would You Do?'" Observer, April 7, 2002.

15 Natan (Anatoly) Sharansky, "An Open Letter," Israel Resource Review, April 9, 2002.

16 In a speech on April 8, 2002, before a special session of the Israeli parliament, Sharon said: "The murderous gangs have a leader, a purpose, and a directing hand. They have one mission: to chase us out of here, from everywhere, from our home in Elon Moreh, and from the supermarket in Jerusalem, from the café in Tel Aviv and the restaurant in Haifa." New York Times, April 9, 2002; emphasis mine.

17 This imported September 11 logic became particularly apparent in the Israeli English-language media of this moment. For example, a Jerusalem Post article quoted a Jewish Israeli mother and son on the merits of eating out: "We can't stop living our normal lives. That's what they [the Palestinian bombers] [sic] want us to do. If we change what we do, then they win." Ruth Mason, "Personal Lessons in Coping," Jerusalem Post, March 20, 2002; emphasis mine.

18 Hirsh Goodman, "Blood, Sweat, and Cappuccino," Jerusalem Post, April 8, 2002.

19 Lefkovitz, "Hundreds Turn Café into Shrine."

20 Ruth Mason, "Personal Lessons in Coping."

21 See Shirli Golan-Meiri, "Aroma Branches in Jerusalem Forbid Sitting in Their Spaces" [in Hebrew], Yedi'ot Aharonot, March 11, 2002; Lili Galili, "Jerusalem Becomes a City of Take-Out" [in Hebrew], Ha'aretz, March 11, 2002; and Efrat Weiss, "It's Impossible to Stop This Moment" [in Hebrew], Yedi'ot Aharonot, March 10, 2002.

22 See Efrat Weiss and Sharon Ropa, "Suicide Bomber Detained on Emek Rafayim Street in Jerusalem" [in Hebrew], Yedi'ot Aharonot, March 7, 2002; and Etgar Lefkovitz, "Waiter Foils Jerusalem Café Bombing," Jerusalem Post, March 8, 2002.

23 Ha'aretz put it this way: "People's fear is totally rational; if there are about 30 recreation venues in Jerusalem, and each week one explodes, then going out to recreate is really going out to the front lines." Yoash Foldesh,

"Certain Half-Deserted Streets," *Ha'aretz English Edition*, March 17, 2002.

24 For a discussion of the fence in the Israeli press of 2002, see Haim Ramon, "Should a Security Fence Be Built between Israel and the West Bank?" *Jerusalem Report*, February 25, 2002; and Miriam Shaviv, "The Siege of Jerusalem," *Jerusalem Post*, February 1, 2002.

25 It should be noted that buses became targets as early as the 1950s and then reemerged in the 1970s. But it was only in the 1990s that they turned into popular and repeat targets.

26 The iconic status of the café has spawned two recent plays about Israeli history that take the café as their organizing principle: *And Off We Went to Cassit Café* [in Hebrew], by Hanna Marron (performed at the Herzilya Theater Ensemble in the winter of 2002), and *Let's Dance*, by Eldad Lidor, with choreography by Gaby Aldor, (performed at the Hebrew-Arabic Theater of Jaffa).

27 LeVine, *Overthrowing Geography*.

28 Helen Kaye, "Ghosts of the Past," *Jerusalem Post*, February 5, 2002.

29 Herb Keinon, "Culture in a Cup," *Jerusalem Post*, July 28, 2000; Greer Fay Cashman, "Jerusalem's Downtown Café Atara Closing for Good," *Jerusalem Post*, December 22, 2000.

30 For an instance of the iconic status of the café, see, Matan Shiram et al., "Over a Cup of Coffee" [in Hebrew] (Jerusalem: Shiram CMA Ltd., 2000).

31 David Louison, "A Café Society," *Jerusalem Post*, January 6, 1989.

32 For discussion of the cultural politics of Ashkenazi dominance, see Shohat, "Sephardim in Israel."

33 Hattox, *Coffee and Coffeehouses*.

34 Avirama Golan, "The City Turns Its Back" [in Hebrew], *Ha'aretz*, March 10, 2001; and Galili, "Jerusalem Becomes a City of Take-Out."

35 Shira Ben-Simon, "Nightlife Is Dying" [in Hebrew], *Ma'ariv*, April 4, 2002; Noam Vind, "Nowhere to Run" [in Hebrew], *Ma'ariv*, April 4, 2002; Hartog, "Taking Back the Cafés"; Mouin Khalbi, "Here, the Best in the World" [in Hebrew]. *Ma'ariv*, April 10, 2002; and Yoash Foldesh, "Certain Half-Deserted Streets."

36 Galili, "Jerusalem Becomes a City of Take-Out."

37 Hartog, "Taking Back the Cafés."

38 Additional references to emptiness include the following: Yair Etinger and Anshel Pepper, "From Day to Day, the Residents Say, the City Is Being Erased" [in Hebrew], *Ha'aretz*, March 22, 2002; Hagit Almakis and Shirli Menzley, "Spot-check Finds: Large Number of Restaurants and Cafés in Holon and Bat Yam Are Empty and Unprotected" [in Hebrew], *Ma'ariv*, April 4, 2002; Etgar Lefkovitz, "Attacks Leave Capital's Restaurants, Cafés Empty," *Jerusalem Post*, March 12, 2002; and Ilan Shahar, "Whoever Doesn't Have to, Doesn't Go Downtown" [in Hebrew], *Ha'aretz*, March 22, 2002.

39 Neve Gordon, "Where Are the Peaceniks?" *Nation*, April 29, 2002, 4–5.

40 For a recent discussion of the contours of this classic Zionist trope, see Piterberg, "Erasures." Also see Raz-Krakotzkin, "Exile within Sovereignty"; and Raz-Krakotzkin, "Exile within Sovereignty (Continued)."

41 Pratt, "Scratches on the Face of the Country."

42 Herzl, *The Jewish State*, 96.

43 Khaldi, *Palestinian Identity*, 101.

44 Lockman, *Comrades and Enemies*, 26–31.

45 See Blecher, "Living on the Edge." A poll taken by the Jaffee Center for Strategic Studies in the fall of 2001 reported that some 46 percent of Israel's Jewish citizens favored transferring Palestinians out of the territories. See Amnon Barzilai, "More Israeli Jews Favor Transfer of Palestinians, Israeli Arab Poll Finds" [in Hebrew], *Ha'artez*, September 17, 2001.

46 Such were promises made by far-right Knesset member Effi Eytan who, in 2002, openly supported Palestinian mass population transfer. See Ari Shavit, "Dear God, This is Effi," *Ha'aretz Internet Edition*, March 23, 2002, available at http://middleeastinfo.org/article290.html.

47 The Jaffee Center Poll also reported that some 31 percent of Jewish Israelis favored transferring Arabs with Israeli citizenship out of the country. Ibid. Barzilai, "More Israeli Jews Favor Transfer of Palestinians."

48 Thanks to Matti Bunzl and Jed Esty for pushing me in this direction.

49 I am building on Gayatri Spivak's "Can the Subaltern Speak?"

50 For example, "White men are saving brown women from brown men." Spivak, "Can the Subaltern Speak?," 296.

51 Ibid., 297.

52 An early Jewish Israeli critic of the colonial nature of the Zionist movement was Mazpen, an Israeli socialist organization, which emerged in the 1960s. A 1972 treatise argued that "the Israeli Jews constitute a society of settler-colonialists, and the Zionist state is the instrument that procures benefits for them based on the denial of these benefits to Palestinians." Bober, *The Other Israel*, 192. Quoted in Silberstein, *The Postzionism Debates*, 85.

53 The foundational work of Edward Said has been crucial in enabling such scholarship, as has the work of Ella Shohat, Smadar Lavie, and Joseph Massad.

54 See, for example, McClintock, "The Angel of Progress"; and Shohat, "Notes on the Postcolonial."

55 Massad, "The 'Post-colonial' Colony."

56 For example, Lavie, "Blow-Ups in the Borderzone"; Shohat, "The Invention of the Mizrahim"; and Shohat, "Sephardim in Israel."

57 Bhabha, *Location of Culture*, 236; emphasis mine.

58 Rai, "'Thus Spoke the Subaltern …'," 167.

59 A similar logic informs McClintock's parenthetical list of "abject zones (*the Israeli Occupied Territories*, prisons, battered women's shelters)." McClintock, *Imperial Leather*,

Rebecca L. Stein

72; emphasis mine. Marianna Torgovnick refers to the "art-world equivalent of the Palestinians" (an artistic form perpetually "wandering the globe"). Torgovnick, *Primitive Passions*. And John Gillis makes a gesture toward "those,

like the Palestinians … [who] are forced to contend with multiple identities and multiple memories, as they are moved from place to place, time after time." Gillis, *Commemorations*, 16; emphasis mine.

References

Amnesty International, *Israel and the Occupied Territories: The Heavy Price of Israeli Incursions*. April 11, 2002. Archived at www.amnestyusa.org/countries/Israel_and_occupied_territories/reports.do.

Bhabha, Homi K. *The Location of Culture*. London: Routledge, 1994.

Blecher, Robert. "Living on the Edge: The Threat of Transfer in Israel and Palestine *Middle East Report* 225 (2002). Available at www.merip.org/mer225/225_blec.html.

Gillis, John, ed. *Commemorations: The Politics of National Identity*, Princeton, NJ: Princeton University Press, 1994.

Herzl, Theodore. *The Jewish State*. New York: Dover, 1988.

Khaldi, Rashid. *Palestinian Identity: The Construction of Modern National Consciousness*. New York: Columbia University Press, 1997.

Lavie, Smadar. "Blow-Ups in the Borderzone: Third World Israeli Authors' Gropings for Home." *New Formations*, no. 18 (1992): 84–105.

LeVine, Mark. *Overthrowing Geography, Reimagining Identities: A History of Jaffa and Tel Aviv, 1880 to the Present*. Berkeley: University of California Press, 2005.

Lockman, Zachery. *Comrades and Enemies: Arab and Jewish Workers in Palestine, 1906–1948*. Berkeley: University of California Press, 1996.

Massad, Joseph. "The 'Post-colonial' Colony: Time, Space, and Bodies in Israel/Palestine." In *The Pre-occupation of Postcolonial Studies*, ed. Fawzia Afzal-Khan and Kalpana Seshadri-Crooks, 311–46. Durham, NC: Duke University Press, 2000.

McClintock, Anne. "The Angel of Progress: Pitfalls of the Term Postcolonial." *Social Text*, nos. 31–32 (1992): 84–98.

McClintock, Anne. *Imperial Leather: Race, Gender, and Sexuality in the Colonial Contest*. New York: Routledge, 1995.

Piterberg, Gabriel. "Erasures." *New Left Review*, no. 10 (2001): 31–46.

Pratt, Mary, Louise. "Scratches on the Face of the Country; Or, What Mr. Barrows Saw in the Land of the Bushman." In *"Race," Writing, and Difference*, ed. Henry Louis Gates Jr., 138–62. Chicago: University of Chicago Press, 1985.

Rai, Amit. "'Thus Spoke the Subaltern…': Postcolonial Criticism and the Scene of Desire." *Discourse* 19, no. 2 (1997): 163–93.

Raz-Krakotzkin, Amnon. "Exile within Sovereignty" [in Hebrew]. *Theory and Criticism*, no. 4 (1993): 23–56.

Raz-Krakotzkin, Amnon. "Exile within Sovereignty (Continued)" [in Hebrew]. *Theory and Criticism*, no. 5 (1994): 113–32.

Robinson, Shira. "My Hairdresser Is a Sniper." *Middle East Report* 223 (2002). Available at www.merip.org/mer/mer223/223_robinson.html.

Said, Edward W. *Orientalism*. New York: Vintage, 1978.

Said, Edward W. *The Question of Palestine*. New York: Vintage, 1979.

Shohat, Ella. "The Invention of the Mizrahim." *Journal of Palestine Studies* 29, no. 1 (1999): 5–20.

Shohat, Ella. "Notes on the Postcolonial." *Social Text*, nos. 31–32 (1992): 99–113.

Shohat, Ella. "Sephardim in Israel: Zionism from the Standpoint of Its Jewish Victims." *Social Text*, nos. 19–20 (1988): 1–35.

Silberstein, Lawrence J. *The Postzionism Debates: Knowledge and Power in Israeli Culture*. New York: Routledge, 1999.

Spivak, Gayatri Chakravorty. "Can the Subaltern Speak?" In *Marxism and the Interpretation of Culture*, ed. Cary Nelson and Lawrence Grossberg, 271–313. Urbana: University of Illinois Press, 1988.

Torgovnick, Marianna. *Primitive Passions: Men, Women, and the Quest for Ecstasy*. New York: Knopf, 1997.

Young, Robert. *White Mythologies: Writing History and the West*. London: Routledge, 1990.

Part Five
Transnationalism and Cosmopolitanism

Moving beyond the territorial organization of the nation-state while at the same time locating the nation within the spaces of globalization, this section carries essays that foreground transnational and cosmopolitan identities in literature and culture. Walter Mignolo seeks to clarify the many interlinked terms – cosmopolitanism, globalization, and the transnational – in his essay, focusing in particular on what he terms "decolonial cosmopolitanism." Mignolo argues that, in sharp contrast to earlier forms of both globalization and cosmopolitanism, we need to also account for the "cosmopolitanism from below" so as to distance it from the European imperialist project (which was coterminous with older cosmopolitanisms). This would involve the forging of "links between the commonality of colonial experiences between people with uncommon local histories." Arif Dirlik is interested in Asian American (and other ethnic transnational) literature for embodying the link between fiction and history, but also as offering "a challenge not only to historical ways of thinking, but also to the ways in which we have

organized the study of the world in terms of nations, areas and regions." Examining the ethnography of culture as embedded in literary texts, Dirlik ponders the problems associated with conceptualizations of ethnic identities, especially in the context of transnationalism. Vivienne Jabri's essay works through a similar set of concerns, especially around the problematic of the nation-state, but from the perspective of international relations. Jabri postulates a political cosmopolitanism whose idea(l)s are premised upon internationalism and solidarity. Solidarity for Jabri is a way of escaping the nation-state. This political cosmopolitanism is also, in Jabri's formulation, postcolonial for it "problematises taken-for-granted frameworks of knowledge relating to the international order, conceptions of human solidarity, and the sources of violence and oppressive practices." Pnina Werbner, entering the debate from anthropology, studies the concept of cultural hybridity – a key topic in postcolonial studies, especially after Homi Bhabha. Werbner focuses on "organic" and "intentional" hybridity and is concerned with the

Postcolonial Studies: An Anthology, First Edition. Edited by Pramod K. Nayar.
Editorial material and organization © 2016 John Wiley & Sons, Ltd.
Published 2016 by John Wiley & Sons, Ltd.

limits of such hybrid aesthetics and practices in the globalizing world. While intentional hybridity can be the instrument of social renewal and reform, Werbner draws attention to its capacity/ tendency to offend communities by producing "monsters," whereas organic hybridity, wherein a culture hybridizes itself unconsciously, emerges from the lifeworld of that community.

23   Cosmopolitanism and the De-colonial Option

Walter D. Mignolo

I

I.1

In 2000, I published an article in *Public Culture* titled "The Many Faces of Cosmo-polis: Border Thinking and Critical Cosmopolitanism" (Mignolo 2000). The starting point was to brazen out "cosmopolitanism" with "globalization." For, indeed, is not globalization cosmopolitan? And, in reverse, is not cosmopolitanism global by definition? It appears then, and in retrospect, that "globalization" was a term introduced in the vocabulary of political theory and political economy when markets were de-regulated and profit was equated with growth. "Globalization" became, in the 1980s, the replacement for "development" that invaded the field of political theory and political economies approximately from 1950 to 1975. But once the theories of Milton Friedman began to take hold in the late 1970s, and were institutionalized by Ronald Reagan and Margaret Thatcher in the 1980s, "globalization" was the rhetorical term to describe imperial designs in the remaking of global coloniality. Global coloniality, the darker side of globalization, explains the frequent concern with the fact that, during the past quarter of a century, globalization also meant the expansion of the poverty line and the growing divide between the have and have-nots. Cosmopolitanism, instead, was a term re-invigorated by progressive humanists of liberal, postmodern, and Marxist bent. Furthermore, cosmopolitanism was mainly a concern of Western intellectuals and scholars. I did not encounter any interest in Bolivia and Ecuador for example, and I wonder what cosmopolitanism may mean in the Middle East or in Central Asia. Cosmopolitanism, like globalism, was also unidirectional.

Thus, I was asking myself, what is the place of "cosmopolitanism" in the dreary scenario at the end of the twentieth century? My response, at the time of writing (late

Walter D. Mignolo, "Cosmopolitanism and the De-colonial Option." *Study in the Philosophy of Education,* 29, 2010: 111–127. Used by permission of Springer Science+Business Media.

1990s) and its publication (mid 2000), started from Immanuel Kant's cosmopolitan ideals (and, by extension, with enlightenment, clear cosmopolitan ambitions) co-existing with his notorious racist underpinnings. So, the question was, how could cosmopolitanism be possible when the designer of the project had a hierarchical view of humanity around the planet? It became clear to me then, that "cosmopolitanism" was willingly or not a project of Western expansion (that is today what we describe as "globalization," see above), whose implementation was through the "civilizing mission" rather than by free market in economy and democracy in politics. In that regard, Kant's cosmopolitan ideals were as imperial as the late twentieth century's march through free-trade, military bases, and "spreading democracy," one of the preferred expressions of the politically defunct ex-President George W. Bush. I believed, however, that Kant was an honest and true believer.

Once I reached this conclusion, I set myself to explore the issue in two directions: one historical and the other co-eval with particular "faces" of cosmopolitan projects. Historically, I realized that Kant's cosmopolitanism was co-eval with the declaration of The Rights of Man and of the Citizen. While cosmopolitanism was a world (or global) project, The Rights of Man and of the Citizen was concerned with what would be the modern (and European) nation-states. It doesn't take too much effort to conclude that The Rights of Man and of the Citizen in France and, by extension, in England and Germany, formation of the modern nation-state would become—directly or indirectly—linked to cosmopolitan projects. How come? If The Rights of Man and of the Citizen in Europe were to warrant the civil security of Man (let's say, of human beings) and that the civil security of Man was tied up to citizenship, then The Rights worked in two complementary directions. One was chronological, as The Rights of Man and of the Citizen are necessary to secure the life of the citizens under secular rule of governmentality within the history of Europe itself. The other was geographical, as The Rights will become the measuring stick to judge social behavior that, according to Western standards, are un-civilized and, therefore, violates the rights of Man outside Europe. The silent assumption was that there was no violation of the rights of citizens, because there was no such social role outside Europe. Thus, the civilizing mission and cosmopolitanism appeared to be the underlying project of secular Western expansion.

9/11, 2001 was the first wake-up call and not only for globalization, but for cosmopolitanism as well. It was, perhaps, the first global event that put a halt to the dreams of Kantian cosmopolitanism, but also revealed the imperial underpinnings of the Kantian vision and legacy.

I.2

"Cosmopolitanism" was a buzzword in the late 1990s and continues to be in the first decade of the twenty-first century. Why the such widespread interest in "cosmopolitanism?"

I see four main motivations:

1. One was the previous widespread concerns and limits of "national thinking." Nationalism was what cosmopolitanism was trying to overcome. Cross-cultural and planetary dialogs were argued as ways toward the future, instead of leaping to

defend and enclose the borders of the nations. Immigration contributed to the surge of cosmopolitanism. Nationalists saw immigration as a problem; cosmopolitans as an opening toward global futures.

2. The second motivation was the need to build arguments that, moving away from nationalism, did not fall into the hands of neo-liberal and economic globalization. That kind of global world was not what cosmopolitans liked to support at the end of the twentieth century. Thus, one of the strands of cosmopolitan thinking, confronting globalization, was caught in between honest liberalism opposed to neo-liberal globalization and a renovated Marxism that saw new global players invited to think cosmopolitanism beyond the international proletarian revolution.

3. A third motivation, related to the first two, was to move away from closed and monocultural conceptions of identity supporting State designs to control the population by celebrating multiculturalism. At this level, cosmopolitanism focused on the individual: the person was invited to see herself as an open citizen of the world, embodying several "identities." In a word, it was a liberal conception of cosmopolitanism born out of dissent simultaneous with the formation in Europe of the modern nation-states. That legacy has been translated into an ideal of flexible and open cultural citizenship simultaneous with the process of neo-liberal globalization.

4. The fourth motivation, compatible but also distinct from the second, was the legal proposal putting on the agenda "cosmopolitanism from below" that was eventually connected with the agenda of the World Social Forum.

II

In his lectures on *Anthropology from a Pragmatic Point of View* (published toward the end of his life, [Kant 1996], Kant brought cosmopolitanism in the section devoted to the "characters of the species." The characters of the species, in relation to his cosmopolitan ideas and ideals, shall be understood in relation to two preceding sections: "the character of the nations" and the "character of races." The characters of the nations are limited to six European nations: France, England, and Germany in the first round; Italy, Spain, and Portugal in the second round. Kant arrives at the frontier of "nations" encloses this section stressing its limits:

> Since *Russia* has not yet developed definite characteristics from its natural potential; since *Poland* has no longer any characteristics; and since the nationals of European Turkey never have had a character, nor will ever attain what is necessary for a definite national character, the description of these nations' characters may properly be passed over here.[1]

Kant then moves to the "character of races," which is a short section in which "nature" takes the place of "nations" in the previous section. Kant delimits the question of races by focusing instead on "the character of species." And in this section, the character of the species "human" (of the race animals), deserves close scrutiny. Cosmopolitanism then comes into the picture in the section "basic features concerning the description of the Human Species' Characters." And here is how Kant envisioned cosmopolitanism, quoted at length:

> The human race taken collectively (as the entire human species) is a great number of people living successively and simultaneously. **They** cannot be without peaceful co-existence, and yet they cannot avoid continuous disagreement with one another. Consequently, **they** feel destined by nature to develop, through mutual compulsion and laws written by **them,** into *a* **cosmopolitan society** (*cosmopolitanisms*) which is constantly threatened by dissension but generally progressing toward a coalition.
>
> The cosmopolitan society is in itself an unreachable idea, but it is not a constitutive principle (which is expectant of peace amidst the most vigorous actions and reactions of men). It is only a **regulative principle** demanding that **we yield generously** to the **cosmopolitan society as the destiny of the human race;** and this not without reasonable ground for supposition that there is a natural inclination in this direction.[2]

The idea and the horizon of a cosmopolitan society is predicated, by Kant, on the bases of a previous consideration that he has established between freedom and law, the two pivots or pillars of any civil legislation: "If authority is combined with freedom and law, the principles of freedom and law are ensured with success".[3] And he considers four conceivable combinations of authority with freedom and law:

1. Law and freedom without authority (anarchy);
2. Law and authority without freedom (despotism);
3. Authority without freedom and law (barbarism);
4. Authority, with freedom and law (republic).[4]

Needless to say, Kant privileges the last one. And, therefore, cosmopolitan ideals presuppose the republican organization of society in which authority goes hand in hand with freedom and law. As Kant himself recognizes it, cosmopolitanism is an idea which may become despotic and anarchic if authority with freedom and law in place A is considered to be the ideal of social organization for B, C, D, E, F, G. And this was precisely the presuppositions underlying Kant's ideals envisaging a global order that he conceived as cosmopolitan.

III

There is still another aspect which we need to bring to the foreground in order to understand the implications of a cosmopolitan social order that were put forward in the eighteenth century.

In his landmark book *Cosmopolis. The Hidden Agenda of Modernity*, Toulmin (1990) brought the idea of a cosmo-polis into new light—cosmo-polis as a significant aspect of the hidden agenda of modernity. Why the hidden agenda? What motivated Toulmin to write this book was the moment when he understood that the image of *modernity* which he had learned in England in the 1930s and 1940s were faulty, partial, and overtly celebratory. Toulmin uncovers two dimensions of the idealistic and triumphal image of modernity ingrained mainly in protestant Europe. One is that the seventeenth century, far from being a golden age of Europe that prompted the advent of science and philosophy, was a moment of economic crisis marked by the decay of the Spanish empire and the not-yet flourishing of a new imperial era. Holland was enjoying a moment of commercial glory, but Western Christians were killing each other in the Thirty Years' War. The second aspect underlined by Toulmin, prompted by his early reading of Michel de Montaigne's *Essais*, was to the humanistic tradition (that is, not just the advent of modern science and secular philosophy with Galileo, Bacon, and Descartes), but the humanistic tradition initiated during the European Renaissance breaking away from the theological and epistemological control of the Church and the Papacy. That, in a nutshell, is the hidden agenda in which modernity and cosmo-polis appears in Toulmin's argument in that humanistic vein, although, of course, mixed with scientific models of the world. Precisely, cosmo-polis or the polis (society) was organized following the model of the *cosmos* that physics and astronomy were making available at the time.

Thus, Toulmin adumbrates the issue in the following manner:

> We are here concerned, not with "science" as the modern positivists understand it, but with a *cosmopolis* that gives a comprehensive account of the world, so as to bind things together in "politico-theological," as much as in scientific or explanatory, terms (Toulmin 1990, p. 128).

Toulmin explains that the reconstruction of European society after the Thirty Years' War was based on two pillars or principles: *stability* and *hierarchy*. *Stability* applied to inter-relations among sovereign nations. Sovereign nations were a conception in the mind of European thinkers (like Kant, for example), and it applied to the very society in which they were dwelling and thinking. Thus, beyond the realm of sovereign nations (which were basically the six modern and imperial European nations [Germany, England, France, Spain, Italy, and Portugal, with Holland interregnum]).[5] The imperial question was not in the picture of stable relations among sovereign nations in the process of becoming states. *Hierarchy* applied to the internal organization of society or within the internal organization of each individual state. But, again, the presupposed totality was that of the six or seven Western European countries.

Toulmin further explains—and reminds us—that by 1700, social relations (hierarchy) within nation-states were defined *horizontally* based on super-ordination and subordination of class relations: "Social stability depended on all the parties in society 'knowing their place' relative to the others, and knowing what reciprocal modes of behavior were appropriate and rational".[6] The planetary model of society was based on the hierarchical relations within nation-states and it was, Toulmin observes, "explicitly *cosmopolitical.*" How come?

> Without such a justification—Toulmin observes—the imposition of hierarchy on 'the lower orders' by 'the better sort' of people would be arbitrary and self-serving. *To the extent that this hierarchy mirrored the structure of nature, its authority* was self-explanatory, self-justifying and seemingly rational.[7]

Here, we encounter *authority* and *law* (posited by Kant), but not yet *freedom*. Let's take one step further and see how the *polis* can be organized following the model of the *cosmos*. In this light, we understand that the undisclosed assumption was that:

a. The *hierarchical organization* of each nation (*polis*) state shall follow the model provided by the law of the *cosmos*;
b. The *stability relations* among nation-states shall also be modeled on the law of nature (cosmos) that serves the model for the organization of each state within itself (polis).

Thus, Toulmin puts it this way:

> The philosophical belief that nature obeys mathematical "laws" which will ensure its stability for so long as it pleases God to maintain it, was a socially revolutionary idea: both *cosmos* and *polis* (it appeared) were self-contained, and their joint 'rationality' guaranteed their stability. As recently as 1650, people worried that the World was grinding to its End: by 1720, their grand children were confident that a rational and omniscient Creator had made a world that ran perfectly.[8]

The idea was shortly after that (by 1776) applied to the economy and the belief took hold that economic transactions were guided by an "invisible hand" which, like God or Nature, regulated and balanced the field of forces. This idea lasted until the Fall of 2008, when Wall Street exploded, blowing off the fingers of the invisible hands and depriving them from playing the strings and guiding the marionettes.

IV

If *cosmopolitan* ideals shall be maintained *in* and *for* the twenty-first century, *cosmopolitanism* shall be accountable for its crimes: the very foundation of *cosmopolitanism*, as envisioned by Kant and explained by Toulmin, was in complicity with the formation of European imperial powers and of European expansion in America, Africa, and Asia, as well as with the continuation of Europe in the United States, as Hegel was anticipating.[9] To maintain *cosmopolitan ideals*. we (i.e., all those who engage in this project) have to decolonize cosmopolitanism, which means moving toward a de-colonial cosmopolitan order no longer modeled on the law of nature discovered by science. *De-colonial cosmopolitanism* shall be *the becoming of a pluri-versal* world order built upon and dwelling on the global borders of modernity/coloniality. In what follows, I explain this idea. I will proceed by taking a step back from the seventeenth century, where Toulmin learned that "modernity" planted its seed toward the Renaissance, where Toulmin discovered humanism as modernity's hidden agenda beyond the celebration of science and secular philosophy. And I will take a step forward toward the formation of the United States and the transformation of European cosmopolitan ideals in the early twentieth century, when massive immigration from Europe agitated the quiet waters of two centuries of Pilgrim's pro-creation, Native American repression, and enslaved African exploitation.

About 130 years before Immanuel Kant pronounced his lecture on anthropology from a pragmatic point of view (1772–1773), the need of international law emerged in the consciousness of Western Christians. While in Europe the Trent's Council was setting the stage for a bloody scenario that will consume Western Christian Europe until the Peace of Westphalia (1648), ending both the Thirty Years' War that piggy-backed on the 80 years war between Spain and the Netherlands, legal theologians at the University of Salamanca were starting their long journey to solve two interre-lated problems: to what extent Indians in the New World were Human and to what extent, as a consequence, they have property rights. Far from the mind of Castilian was to just think for a minute that property rights was not universal, and that in the Inca and Aztec civilizations, as well as in other existing communities in the Caribbean, natives do not relate to land as property by as Mother Earth (Pachamama was the name in Aymara and Quechua). Francisco de Vitoria and his followers were con-fronting, during the second half of the sixteenth century, issues of a history parallel to and intertwined with the internal history of Europe that Kant framed in terms of nation-state and national characters. This double history, its imperial and colonial side, were certainly at work in the seventeenth century, but as Toulmin has elegantly narrated in the first chapter of his book, only the bright side of imperial European history was transmitted to his generation, in England, in the 1930s and 1940s.

Dwelling in a secular era, Kant revamped the Greek word *cosmopolis* and gave it a different meaning. Greek philosophers were not thinking next to modern science, Christian religious war, and modern imperial colonialism. Greek *cosmopolis* has more in common with Quechua-Aymara *Tawantinsuyu* (the world [cosmos and the city] organized in four *suyus* or sections) than with Kant's *cosmo-polis*. However, one could surmise that *Tawantinsuyu* could have served equally well to imagine a global and social organization of the Human species. And, as a matter of fact, Guaman Poma de Ayala did exactly that 250 years before Kant when he laid out his *Nueva Corónica y Buen Gobierno* and proposed to Philip III an organization of "The Indies of the New World" (as Guaman Poma de Ayala referred to the mixed co-existence of Inca and Spanish rule in the Viceroyalty of Perú and the Inca Tawantinsuyu).[10] The organization of the first imperial/colonial society since the sixteenth century was meant to solve a cosmo-political problem of a particular kind: the formation of modern/colonial inter-state relations and inner-state social organization (stability and hierarchy).

Toward the end of the sixteenth century, that is, merely 50 years from the moment Spaniards were able to gain control of Tawantinsuyu and began to build the Viceroyalty of Peru, was not very much time to figure out what to do in a new situation in the history of human kind. Guaman Poma knew his own history and the history of the world he read in Spanish authors, mainly those writing on the New World. The internal organization of Tawantinsuyu he solved by giving one *suyu* to each of the existing ethnicities at his time: Spaniards, Indians, Moors, and Blacks. On the other hand, the world was remapped according to Tawantinsuyu: he drew a map and then divided it into two parts. On the upper part, he located Tawantinsuyu and in the lower part, Spain. However, Spaniards did not see themselves below Tawantinsuyu and they prevailed. Prevailing, however, did not mean that the forces of history were killed forever. The current process of re-writing the Constitution in

Bolivia and Ecuador, and the entire discussion on the pluri-national state is nothing else than the continuation of the problem Guaman Poma saw emerging 500 years ago when the territory of Incas and Aymaras became a mix of ethnicities. His de-colonial political treatise was, and remains, exemplar: he did not propose to co-exist with the *enemy*. On the contrary, the very idea of the *enemy* was not in his mind. Thus, one of the first steps of de-colonial cosmopolitanism is to get rid of the idea of *friends and enemies*, in which *the political* finds its raison-d'etre. Carl Schmitt's proposal only makes sense with European "political theology," that is, in the secular-ization of Christian theology, in which the world was already divided between Christianity and "those barbarians who hate it and want to destroy it."

The problem is not minor, and the whole idea of de-colonial cosmopolitanism is at stake.

IV.2

"Cosmopolitanism" was not a term in use in the sixteenth and seventeenth centuries. The "idea," however, was there in theological, rather than secular terms. Kant's concep-tion of cosmo-polis presupposed the already existing "typus orbis terrarum" mapped by Abraham Ortelius in 1570.[11] In other words, "cosmopolitanism" in the eighteenth century (in the sense of a human polis modeled on the law of the cosmos) is the secular version of a word that did not exist but that we can invent: "Christianism." Christianism did not image society regulated by the law of the universe (quite the contrary, Christianity was against scientific discoveries—as we know through Galileo's trial—but none the less, imagined a society modeled according to Christian views of divine and natural laws). In the last analysis, it was the same: secular thinkers who dethroned God and replaced it with Science and Reason and placed themselves in the driver's seat of civilization. So, let's go back in search of the Christian version (sixteenth and seven-teenth centuries) and the foundation of secular cosmopolitanism (eighteenth and nineteenth centuries).

The concept of "good governance" recently entered the vocabulary of interna-tional relations and international law. Paradoxically, the term is not used in the sense proposed by Guaman Poma, and even less in the sense that the Zapatistas in Southern Mexico use the term ("Juntas de Buen Gobierno," "Council of Good Governance"), but in the implied version elaborated by legal theologians of Salamanca. Thus, there is a direct line connecting the emergence of international law in the sixteenth century (there is no such a thing before then) with cosmopol-itan ideals in the eighteenth century and with good governance and development in the twentieth century promoted by the United Nations and the World Bank. Not by chance, the Universal Declaration of Human Rights, in 1948, came at the time in which such institutions were being created and, therefore, Human Rights, good governance, and development began to work in tandem towards the new version of "Christianism" and "cosmopolitanism," now baptized as "globalism." "Globalism," like "cosmopolitanism," names a vision rather than a process (e.g., globalization). Interestingly enough, what words highlight and hide is different in the three succes-sive and now coexisting imperial projects. Christianization and globalization are accepted words. However, "cosmopolitanization" is not accepted by the Thesaurus, which doesn't accept "Christianism" either.

The continuity from the sixteenth to the twenty-first century, that is, the formation, consolidation, and expansion of Western ideals and civilizations, is one of the central theses of the project modernity/coloniality (Grosfóguel 2008). The theses is the following: the process of governing the Indies, managing the riches and controlling the population, forcing Spaniard and Portuguese first, then British, French, and German intellectuals, merchants, and officers of the State to invent both discourses and managerial technologies that introduced transformations of scale in relation to previous technologies of control, in Europe, and introduced others unknown until then. The end result was the formation, during the sixteenth century, of the *colonial matrix of power*.

The colonial matrix of power has been described in four interrelated domains of practices and arguments (as well as laws, edicts, institutions, and implicit and explicit assumptions):

1. The management of the control of subjectivities emerged first in the Spanish encounter with natives. The church and the monastic orders took over the management and control of subjectivities by converting Indians to Christianity and teaching them Spanish and also by controlling the Spanish and Portuguese population, and their descendants, in the formation of colonial societies.

2. The control of authority, shared between the papacy and the monarchy, was established by a series of law and edits, such as El Tratado de Tordesillas (1394), by which the Pope donated the Americas to Spanish and Portuguese monarchs; by the infamous Requerimiento, by which Spaniards gave themselves the right to expropriate lands and by the establishments of Viceroyalties from Mexico to Peru and the River Plate. International law came about as a need to regulate the inter-actions between European foreigners and native Indians.

3. The control of the economy was organized first around the exploitations of mines and the creation of *encomiendas*, by means of which Spaniards obtained lands and Indians to work on it. Later on, plantations in the Caribbean accelerated the slave trade and the exploitation of labor. By the end of the seventeenth century, the economy engendered a set of discourse that will engender, in the eighteenth century, the emergence of political economy.

4. The control of knowledge was managed by several means. First of all, the already existing printing press that allowed Europeans to publish and circulate reports, narratives, treatises, and debates about the New World. Indians did not have the same possibility and, therefore, whatever they said and thought was either unheard or, if it was heard, it was through Iberian first and then French and British travelers, historians, or philosophers in later centuries. And the same hap-pened with millions of enslaved Africans transported to the New World, and with Africans in Africa who did not have any say in the debate, until late in the eighteenth century, when the ex-enslaved had the opportunity to write and be published. And, secondly, the control of knowledge was managed through the installation of colleges, monasteries, and universities.

These four domains are all and constantly interrelated and held together by the two pillars of enunciation: *the racial and patriarchal foundation of knowledge without which the colonial matrix of power would not have been possible to be established.* Racism and patriarchy took the form of Christian theology (regardless of whether Catholic or Protestant principles are defended or critiqued) and manifested itself in the theo-politic of knowledge. Since the eighteenth century, the secular science of philosophy (regardless of whether different schools of thought confronted each other) displaced (but did not replace) theology and grounded itself in secular reason and egology. When France and England, for example, displaced Spain and Portugal in the leadership (or when the United States displaced England after WWII), the colonial matrix of power was transformed and was adapted to the new circumstances, but the basic principles in the control of knowledge remained. Another story appears when, for example, the confrontation is not between England and Spain, but between all of the Western Christian countries of the Atlantic and the Islamic countries of the Middle East. In the former case, the dispute was, and still is, for the control of the colonial matrix of power. In the second case, the confrontation is between countries, agents, and institutions that built and controlled the colonial matrix and countries, agents, and institutions that were destined to be controlled by it. Thus, "good governance" meant the imperial management of authority and the control of knowledge directly related to good governance. International law sprang out of the necessity to justify the control of Indians and justify the expropriation of their lands.

IV.3

Francisco de Vitoria was celebrated mainly among Spanish and other European scholars for being one of the founders of international law. His treatise, *Relectio de Indis*, is considered foundational (de Vitoria 1532). The idea of the *Orbis Christianus* (or the Christian cosmos) was not new. It was the legacy of the Roman Empire; particularly from the moment Constantine brought together Christianity with *Imperium* (e.g., dominium), to which later on England will claim their own inheritance and more recently, the United States. The novelty of the sixteenth century was the emergence of a part of humanity (named Indians by Christians) and lands (named Indias Occidentales, New World, and, later on, America). The historical and colonial foundation of international law was, at the same time, the foundation of *rights and racism* as we know it today. Let's see how.

Central in Vitoria's argument is the question of *ius gentium* (rights of the people or rights of nations). At Vitoria's time, a distinction was made between divine, human, and natural law. By divine law, the Pope was the ultimate sovereign, above the monarch—more precisely, between God and the monarch. Vitoria was a humanist and he rejected divine law. Nations, that is, communities of people, were bound by natural law and, therefore, they all have the *rights* of the *people*. Thus, there was no difference for Vitoria between Spaniards and Indians in regard to *ius gentium*. The problem appeared when he had to find a reason to legally authorize Spaniards to take possession of Indian lands. Vitoria found his way out by recognizing that the Indians are human but they "lack" something. Lack and excesses were two constant features of Indians, as well as non-Christians, to locate their correspondence with the standard model of humanity. Thus, although bound and equal to Spaniards in the domain of *ius gentium*, Indians were sort of childish and needed the guidance and protection of Spaniards.

At that moment, Vitoria inserted the colonial difference into international law. *Orbis Christianus* encountered its limits, limits that will remain when secular cosmopolitanism recast the imperial project and set the stage for the civilizing mission. Anthony Anghie has provided an insightful analysis of the historical foundational moment of the colonial difference.[12] In a nutshell, the argument is the following; Indians and Spaniards are equal in the face of natural law, as both, by natural law, are endowed with *ius gentium*. In making this move, Vitoria prevented the Pope and divine law from legislating on human issues. That is, it deprived the Pope of its sovereignty. Natural law endows the monarch and the state as sovereign. The question now is whether Indians who, like Spaniards, are endowed with *ius gentium* by natural (and not divine) law are sovereigns. If they are sovereigns, then wars with Indians will be ruled by international law legislating between two sovereign states. Vitoria's foundational move consisted in this:

By bracketing divine law and putting the Pope out of legislation of human affairs, he established natural law as the ultimate sovereign. Society shall be governed according to natural law and, at the time where science (astronomy and physics) were in its inception and not on good terms with theology, the interpretation of natural law was in the hands of legal theologians, like Vitoria himself. Now, by natural law, all human beings were born equal—a principle to which no one will object—and because of it, are all endow with *ius gentium*, with the rights of people or nations. Vitoria devoted the first two of the three sections of *Relectio de Indis* to defend the rights of Indians (to whom he consistently refers to as "los bárbaros," "the barbarians") not to be dispossessed or invaded, and put a halt to Spaniards' anxiety to invade and dispossess.

However, once Vitoria established the distinction between "principes Christianos" (and Castilian in general) and "los bárbaros" (the barbarians), and he made his best effort to balance his arguments based on the equality he attributed to both people by natural law and *ius gentium*, the entire discussion is based on Spaniards' *rights and limits* toward "the barbarians" to expropriate or not, to declare war or not, to govern or not. Vitoria frequently offers counter or parallel examples imagining what would happen if, instead of Christians and barbarians, the situation would be between French and Castilians without calling attention to the difference. The difference is that communication and interactions between the French and Castilians are established on the assumption of two sovereign nations or people, in which case in any litigation, both parties will have a saying. On the contrary, communication and interactions between Christians and barbarians are one-sided: *the barbarians have no saying in whatever Vitoria said because barbarians are deprived from sovereignty even when they are recognized as equal per natural law and ius gentium.*

The move is foundational in the legal and philosophical constitution of the modern/colonial world and will be maintained through the centuries, modified in the vocabulary from barbarians to primitives, from primitives to communists, from communists to terrorists. Thus, *Orbis Christianus*, secular cosmopolitanism, and economic globalism are names corresponding to different moments of the colonial matrix of power and distinct imperial leadership (from Spain to England to the United States). These are the many faces of cosmo-polis that I outlined in my previous article tackling the question of rights (of people, of man, and of the citizen and of humans) to flag the limits of imperial cosmopolitan projects.

Anthony Anghie made two decisive points about Vitoria and the historical origins of international law:

> My argument, then, is that Vitoria is concerned, not so much with the *problem of order among sovereign states but the problem of order among societies belonging to two different cultural systems*. Vitoria resolves this problem by focusing on the cultural practices of each society and assessing them in terms of universal law of *jusgentium*. *Once this framework is established*, he demonstrates that the *Indians (e.g., barbarians in Vitoria's vocabulary) are in violation of universal natural law*. **Indians are included within a system only to be disciplined.**[13]

Three limits to cosmopolitan ideals (from *Orbis Christianus* to globalism) deserve attention. The first is that the distinction between two cultural systems has not been proposed by Indians (or barbarians), but by Vitoria unilaterally. Unilateralism in this particular case means that *the colonial difference* was inscribed in the apparent equality between two cultures or nations endowed by natural law with *ius gentium*. The colonial difference was mainly and foremost *epistemological*. That is, by recognizing equality by birth and by natural law, Spaniards and barbarians are ontologically equals. However, epistemically, barbarians are not yet ready to govern themselves according to the standards established by *human law*. And here is where Vitoria's distinction between divine, natural, and human law pays its dividends.

The second is that the framework is there to regulate its violation. And when violation occurs, then the creator and enforcers of the framework had a justification to invade and use force to punish and expropriate the violator. This logic was wonderfully rehearsed by John Locke in his *Second Treatise on Government* (1681). One can say that "coloniality," in Vitoria, set the stage not only for international law but also for "modern and European" conceptions of governmentality. It seems obvious that Locke did not get as much from Machiavelli as from the emergence of international law in the sixteenth century, and in the way that Vitoria, and his followers, settled to discuss both the question of "property" and "governance" in the interaction between Christians and the barbarians. Machiavelli was thinking politically in the conflicted Italy of the first half of the sixteenth century. His concern was to advise the Prince as how to obtain or maintain power and how to regulate conflict in Italy, not between Spaniards and the barbarians! So, for Machiavelli, there was no "thief," like in Locke, or violators of natural law, like in Vitoria.

The third is that the "framework" is not dictated by divine or natural law but by human interests, and, in this case, the interests of Christian Castilian males. Thus, the "framework" presupposes a very well located and singular locus of enunciation that, guarded by divine and natural law, it is presumed to be universal. And third, the universal and unilateral frame "includes" the barbarians or Indians (a principle that is valid for all politics of inclusion that we hear today) in their difference, thus, justifying any action that Christians will take to tame them. The construction of *the colonial difference* goes hand in hand with the establishment of *exteriority*: the invented place outside the frame (barbarians) that is brought into the frame in order to secure the control of the frame (civilized) and to legislate. *Exteriority* in other words, is the outside, invented in the process of building the inside. In order to do so, you have to control the enunciation both institutionally and conceptually.

Anghie made a second single observation that coincides with one of the basic principles upon which de-colonial thinking and the analytic of modernity/coloniality has been built:

Clearly, then, Vitoria's work suggests that the conventional view in which sovereignty doctrine was developed in the West and then transferred to the non-European world is, in important respects, misleading. *Sovereignty doctrine acquired its character through the colonial encounter.* This is the darker history of sovereignty, which cannot be understood by any account of the doctrine that assumes the existence of sovereign states.[14]

Anghie points toward a radical epistemic shift necessary to de-colonize the inherited view of Eurocentered modernity. That is, that international relations based on the concept of sovereignty emerged in Europe, after the Peace of Westphalia, to regulate an emerging inter-state system, within Europe where states were considered to be sovereign. This is the local and regional situation in which Kant was thinking cosmopolitanism. But beyond the heart of Europe, as we saw above, when Kant faces Russia, Turkey, and Poland, what he faces is indeed the *colonial difference*. And the *colonial difference*, at the time of Kant, was refashioned in two complementary directions:

1. Orientalism, as analyzed by Edward Said, was nothing else other than updating the colonial difference of secular Europe with the Orient, that Vitoria had already established Christian Europe and the barbarians.
2. The invention of the South of Europe (clear in Kant and Hegel) recast the colonial difference into *internal imperial difference*: the emerging imperial countries (England, Germany, France, now leading the European Union), separated themselves from Christian and Latin countries (France occupying an intermediary position, but also taking the leadership of the Southern Latin countries—Italy, Spain, and Portugal).

Kant's cosmopolitanism was cast under the implicit assumptions that, beyond the heart of Europe was the land of those who had to be brought into civilization and, in the South of Europe, the Latin and Catholic countries, some of them—like Spain and Portugal—too close to the Moors and with mixed blood.

Now, if we jump from the era of European "cosmopolitan" modernity and the civilizing mission (with England and France leading the way) to a post-modern world guided by "globalism," we have the sketch of the continuity and diachronic accumulation of the rhetoric of modernity (salvation, conviviality, prosperity, and freedom) and its darker side, the logic of coloniality (discrimination, racism, domination, unilateralism, exploitation). What is "globalism?" Manfred Steger introduced suggestions that globalism—is "an Anglo-American market ideology that reached its zenith in the 1990s—was inextricably linked to the rising fortunes of neoliberal political forces in the world's sole remaining superpower (Steger 2006, 12). It is anchored in neo-liberalism, a doctrine associated with the ideas developed after WWII by Hayek and Milton Friedman—in radical confrontation with the state-regulated economy of the Soviet Union—implemented by Ronald Reagan and Margaret Thatcher and brought to their disastrous consequences by the spectacular collapse of Wall Street in September–October 2008. The extreme interest of globalism, in relation to the previous periods of theological international law and secular state and interstate regulations after Westphalia (Locke, Kant), is that, while the first (*Orbis Christianus*) has Christian theology (divine, natural, and human law) as the overarching frame and the second (secular cosmopolitanism) had secular philosophy and science (the physical law of the cosmos unveiled by from Copernicus and Galileo to Newton) to regulate society and imagine a cosmopolitan world, the third (globalism) had an "invisible hand" regulating economy. The "invisible hand" introduced by Adam Smith—during the same years that Kant was imagining cosmopolitanism and conviviality—as the regulator of economic transactions, always had, for me, a hidden complicity with Vitoria (and Christian) divine and natural laws.

Thus, when we move from "good governance" in the sense that Vitoria and Locke imagined it (the first through international law, the second regulation national-state) to globalism, we put *homo economicus* in the front row (instead of Christian and civilized confronting the barbarians) and the underdeveloped at the other end. At this point, "bar-barians" of all kinds lose their appeal and their forces: globalism is not so much concerned with taming the barbarians and in the legality of international relations, but in reducing costs and increasing gains. Thus, barbarians were replaced by "communists" first and by "terrorists" later: the forces that prevent *homo ecnomicus* from becoming global.

Questions related to the nature of humanity, of who is human or less human and who is more, lose their relevance. What counts are people who can work and consume disregarding their religious belief, their skin color, or their sexuality. "Globalism" is the global sharing of a particular type of economy disregarding, once again, whether the leaders of that economy are Saudi Arabians, Indonesian Muslim, Hindu Indians, Orthodox and Slavic Russians, or White and Christian French, British, and Anglo-Americans. *Orbis Christianus*, cosmopolitanism, and globalism are, then, different versions in the long history of Western imperial expansion, to the point, today, of having loosened the grip it had on the colonial matrix of power under dispute.

V

De-colonial cosmopolitanism proposes a double departure, a radical shift in the geopolitics of knowing and being. The scenarios in which de-colonial cosmopolitanism could be thought out and acted are the following:

1. The transformation of the mono-centric (and unilateral) Western world from the sixteenth century establishment of the colonial matrix of power to 2000. In that period, the colonial matrix of power that we created was consolidated, augmented, and controlled by Western imperialism (Spain, England, and the United States basically). Since 2000, approximately, the colonial matrix of power is under dispute. We are witnessing the transformation of a mono-centric to a poly-centric world sharing the same type of economy, capitalist of [sic] economy. However, poly-centricity appears at the level of control of political authority, control of knowledge, and control of subjectivity (e.g., gender, sexuality, religiosity, etc.). At the time of writing this article, the meeting of the G20 is taking place in Washington to rectify the Wall Street disaster. However, while the G20 would

agree on many points regarding the economy, there is no question that China and the United States, India and Brazil, Saudi Arabia and Germany, etc., would have contentions in other arenas, from political to epistemic and religious issues. Furthermore, countries like Iran and Venezuela, economically powerful and capitalist, are not part of the G20 precisely because contentions are played out in the domain of controlling authority, subjectivity, and knowledge.

2. A poly-centric capitalist world is not, of course, a de-colonial world: a world that has dispensed with the colonial matrix of power and the colonial and imperial differences regulating the field of forces in the modern/colonial world. De-colonial cosmopolitanism is not so much (yet) thought out and activated in the sphere of the state (perhaps with exceptions like Evo Morales in Bolivia), but in the domain of what Partha Chatterjee describes as "political society" (Chatterjee 2004, 27–52). That is, the sphere of the "civil society" described by Hegel in the framework of liberal cosmopolitanism and the secular order of society has been expanded, mainly in the twentieth century, by the eruption and disruption of the "political society," part of which is described as "social movements." De-colonial cosmopolitanism shall be placed in the sphere of the political society, although not necessarily the entire sphere of political society would be de-colonial. De-colonial projects and de-colonial cosmopolitanism are defined in relation to the definition of coloniality, that is, of the formation and transformation of the colonial matrix of power as described above.

De-colonial cosmopolitanism dwells in the borders, in *exteriority*, in the colonial difference. While cosmopolitanism, in its different versions (*Orbis Christianus*, globalism), were concocted and enacted in and from the "center" (that is, in the heart of Western imperial countries and histories), de-colonial cosmopolitanism is a proposal from the "margins." The margins are places, histories, and people whom non-being Christian and secular Europeans, without dwelling in that particular history, were forced to deal with it, from the "barbarian Indians" and enslaved Africans in the sixteenth and seventeenth centuries, to China and India in the nineteenth century, Iran and Iraq in the twentieth, since oil was discovered. I am not saying that all Indians and Afro-descendants in America, Chinese and Indians, Iranians and Iraqis will get up and rise in arms, harmoniously and unified against the evil forces of Western modernity. I am just saying that de-colonial projects are emerging from colonial modernities, that is, non-European subjects who had to deal with European modernity in spite of themselves. Inhabitants of colonial modernities have an array of options. In one extreme, there is the assimilating option and the contribution to Westernization of their backward countries. The other is enrolling and adapting Marxism to detach from European modernity and capitalism. Another would be to enroll in theologies of liberations, in places where theology entered mainly as an imperial force. And still another will be the de-colonial option. The de-colonial option starts from narrating a silenced history, the history of the formation and transformation of the colonial matrix of power.

The de-colonial option is the connector, the spine of de-colonial cosmopolitanism, the links between the commonality of colonial experiences between people with uncommon local histories—Indians in India and the indigenous in America, New Zealand, and Australia; Chinese struck by the Opium War and by neo-liberalism and the legacies of Maoism in struggles of liberations. In summation, de-colonial cosmopolitanism is the cosmopolitanism that emerges from the de-colonial option and cut across—at the same time that respects—identities *in* life and politics: all human beings confronting—at different scales—the consequences of modern/colonial racism and patriarchy have something in common, beyond their religious, ethnic, gender, sexuality, nationalities, and languages. Frantz Fanon had a name for them/us: les damnés de la terre. The de-colonial option materializes in multiple trajectories where identities emerge. But, beyond identities, the commonality that identifies people and communities for being "not quite human" runs like a thread across identities, connecting (rather than uniting) many projects and trajectories in a global process of de-colonial cosmopolitanism, toward the horizon of pluri-versality as a universal project.

Mehrzad Boroujerdi (Boroujerdi 1996) distinguished between "Orientalism in reverse" from "Nativism." In the first case, subjects that became oriental objects in Western knowledge responded by making the West the other. By so doing, "Orientalism in reverse" accepts the rule of the game and attempts to change the content—not the terms—of the conversation. "Nativism" in Boroujerdi's conceptualization is something different. The term "Nativism" here may surprise members of the cosmopolitan club. Let's first listen and then comment upon:

> Nativism stands in the same relation to Orientalism in reverse as Eurocentrism does to Orientalism proper. Both Nativism and Eurocentrism provide an ontological and epistemological umbrella under which it becomes possible to develop a theory of history and a political platform. Whereas Eurocentrism does advocate such ideas as the uniqueness and superiority of the West and its unequivocal manifest destiny, Nativism champions the cause of abandoning, subverting, and reversing these same meta-narratives and master codes. *Nativism was born of the lamentable circumstance of colonialism and the agonizing milieu of the post-World War II period of decolonization.* It represents a cultural reflex on the part of many Third World intellectuals from Southeast Asia to the Caribbean eager to assert their newly found identities (1996, 14; italics mine).

The reader may suspect that we are here confronting another essentialist proposal. The interesting aspect of the proposal is that Frantz Fanon comes up, for an Iranian intellectual, as the paradigmatic example of "Nativism." Boroujerdi doesn't offer any specific reference or quotation as to why Fanon would be a paradigmatic example of "Nativism." I suspect that he has in mind statements like this one:

> I am ready to concede that on the plane of factual being the past existence of an Aztec civilization does not change anything very much in the diet of the Mexican peasant of today … But it has been remarked several times that this passionate search for a national culture which existed before the colonial era finds its legitimate reason in the anxiety shared by native intellectuals to shrink away from that Western culture in which they all risk being swamped. Because they realize they are in danger of losing their lives and thus becoming lost to their people, these men, hotheaded and with anger in their hearts, relentlessly determine to renew contact once more with the oldest and most pre-colonial springs of life of their people (Fanon, 1963, 209–210).

Let's then translate "Nativism" into "Localism" and be clear that locals have been conformed by the formation and transformation of the colonial matrix of power.

The point is, then, that Localism emerges because of the advent of a powerful intellectual and political elite, some of them still linked to Europe through Marxism but in the colonies, and some plainly already decolonial. Localism, crossed and conformed by historical forces (in this case, Persia, Islam, the Western creation of the Middle East as a region, and the Middle East becoming part of the Third World) then emerges as a pluri-versal response and confrontation with universal Eurocentrism.

Eurocentrism, in the last analysis, is Western localism (or perhaps "Nativism" is a good name for Eurocentrism), with a global design that became synonymous with universalism. Thus, Kant cosmopolitanism and its legacy propose the universalization of Western Nativism/Localism. And the Marxist left, for better or worst, belongs to that world. And this is a challenge for cosmopolitanism. On the contrary, non-Western localism is plural, since there are many multiple memories and colonial wounds infringed by racism, ways of life, languages, beliefs, experiences connected to the West, but at the same time, not subsumable to it. Localism (which shall not be confused with "national fundamentalisms" or "Nativism from the right") should be pluri-versal and, therefore, decolonial. Since Localism originated "from the lamentable circumstance of colonialism," or better yet, of the logic of coloniality common to different Western imperial/colonial expansion (Spain, France, England) and its surrogates after the sixteenth century (imperial Russia, Soviet Union, Japan), a trademark of localism is the decolonial thread that connects and makes pluri-versality a global project. De-colonial localism is global or, if you wish, cosmopolitical. Thus, we arrive at the paradoxical conclusion that, if cosmopolitanism shall be preserved in the humanities goal toward the future, it should be "cosmopolitan localism," an oxymoron no doubt, but the Kantian project of one localism being the universal is untenable today. "Cosmopolitan localism" is another expression for pluri-versality as a global project. Kantian's legacies shall be reduced to its proper localism and stripped of its imperial/global pretensions. Recognizing the "idea" doesn't mean accepting its implementation. Cosmopolitanism can only work if there is no master global design, but a global agreement in which no one will rule without being ruled. It is a tough call for those who believe that his/her party, religion, or ideology is the best for everybody and has to be imposed for the well-being of all and for universal peace. A tough but realistic call now that the global political society is growing and is on its feet; it is aware that the era of being ruled and obeying, or being repressed for disobeying, is reaching its limit.

Notes

1 Kant 1996, op.cit., p. 235.
2 Kant, op.cit., p. 249, bold added.
3 Kant, op.cit., p. 248.
4 Kant, op.cit., p. 248.
5 Holland had a flourishing commercial interregnum in the seventeenth century, but Dutch is not one of the top 10 languages with the larger number of speakers. Portuguese is in seventh place, above Italian and French, and below Arabic and Bengali.
6 Toulmin, op.cit., p. 133.
7 Toulmin, op.cit., p. 133.
8 Toulmin, op.cit., p. 133.
9 Crimes that have been covered in velvet and shoveled out of the main stream, by the beautifully written and well advertised essay Cosmopolitanism. Ethics in a World of Strangers, by Kwame Anthony Appiah (Appiah 2006).
10 Guaman Poma de Ayala Nueva Corónica y buen Gobierno was finished in 1516, presumably composed during a period of two decades. See de Ayala (1985).
11 See Abraham Ortelius's world map (Ortelius 1570).
12 On the topic, see Anghie (1999), Mignolo (2000), and Weik (2007).
13 Anghie, op.cit., p. 102, emphasis added.
14 Anghie, op.cit., p. 103. emphasis added.

Walter D. Mignolo

References

Anghie, A. (1999). Francisco de Vitoria and the colonial origins of international law. In E. Darian-Smith & P. Fitzpatrick (Eds.), *Laws of the postcolonial* (pp. 89–108). Ann Arbor: University of Michigan Press.

Appiah, K. A. (2006). *Cosmopolitanism. Ethics in a world of strangers*. New York: W.W. Norton.

Boroujerdi, M. (1996). *Iranian intellectuals and the West—The tormented triumph of nativism*. Syracuse: Syracuse University Press.

Chatterjee, P. (2004). *The politics of the governed. Reflections on popular politics in most of the world.* New York: Columbia University Press.

de Ayala, F. G. P. (1985). Nueva Corónica y Buen Gobierno ([1617], 1985). In J. V. Murra & R. Adorno (Eds.). México: Fondo de Cultura Económica.

de Vitoria, F. (1532/1989). *Relectio de Indis*. Madrid: Consejo Superior de Investigaciones Científicas y Técnicas.

Fanon, F. (1963). *The wretched of the earth* (Constance Farrington, Trans.). New York: Grove Press.

Grosfóguel, R. (2008). Transmodernity, border thinking, and global coloniality. Decolonizing political economy and postcolonial studies. In *Eurozine;* http://www.eurozine.com/articles/2008-07-04-grosfoguel-en.html.

Kant, I. (1996). *Anthropology from a pragmatic point of view* (Victor Lyle Dowdell, Trans.). Carbondale: Southern Illinois University Press.

Mignolo, W. D. (2000). The many faces of cosmo-polis: Border thinking and critical cosmopolitanism. *Public Culture,* 12(3), 721–748.

Ortelius, A. (1570). *Typus Orbis Terrarum.* http://nla.gov.au/nla.map-rm2044.

Steger, M. (2006). *Globalism. Market ideology meets terrorism.* New York: Rowman and Littlefield.

Toulmin, S. (1990). *Cosmopolis. The hidden agenda of modernity.* New York: Free Press.

Weik, A. (2007). "The uses, hazards of expatriation": Richard Wright's cosmopolitanism in process. *African American Review,* 41, 459–475.

24 Solidarity and Spheres of Culture

The Cosmopolitan and the Postcolonial

Vivienne Jabri

The concept of solidarity comes into the frame in International Relations in the context of the English School and in the wider normative discourse around liberal internationalism, cosmopolitanism, and communitarianism.[1] It is hence a widely used (and assumed) concept, focusing attention on the conditions that generate cross-national ties, variously defined in articulations of support and responsibility towards members of other societies. Where realism, with its emphasis on the state as an abstract entity functioning within a system of states, assumes the potential for solidarity between states that is born of necessity, these other discourses assume a moral content built respectively on rules of mutuality, universality, and historical cultural learning. Debates and contests around the sources of moral agency apart, at the heart of discourses around solidarity is the assumption that the realm of the international, a location defined in terms of sovereign statehood, is somehow reined in, challenged, by another realm, that of the human. Expressions of solidarity are of interest to the scholar of International Relations exactly in their location at the nexus between the international and the human, a problematic, transnational, and indefinable location where the political takes place beyond the confines of the sovereign state.

The aim of this article is to explore the concept of solidarity in relation to the sphere of the international.[2] It specifically focuses on the implications of different forms and conceptions of solidarity for the structure of the international and its late-modern transformations. The article confines its investigation to modes and articulations of solidarity that transcend the bounds of community and state, concentrating instead on distinctly liberal and cosmopolitan interpretations. Its treatment of cosmopolitanism is by no means exhaustive, for the purpose here is to explore the politics of solidarity, its modes of expression, and its implications for global politics. The article suggests that

Vivienne Jabri, "Solidarity and Spheres of Culture: The Cosmopolitan and the Postcolonial." *Review of International Studies*, 33, 2007: 715–728. Reproduced by permission of Cambridge University Press.

within these discourses, solidarity may be conceived in two analytically distinct forms: (1) the liberal cosmopolitan, and (2) the political cosmopolitan. The aim is to argue that these different forms of solidarity have wholly different implications for the landscape of international relations, so that where the former is located in a transcendent sphere of humanity, a sphere generative of late-modern transformations away from sovereign statehood and towards some notion of a universal realm of community, the latter stresses instead a distinctly political conception of solidarity, one that places emphasis on critique and local expressions of resistance against exclusionary practices. Where the former is distinctly hierarchical in its conception of the international order and its agents, the latter acknowledges relations of power and structures of domination generative of discourses and practices that assume the realm of the human as a sphere of governmental operations, including specifically military interventions. The article seeks ultimately to locate a distinctly political conception of solidarity within a postcolonial interpretation of the international, an interpretation that problematises taken-for-granted frameworks of knowledge relating to the international order, conceptions of human solidarity, and the sources of violence and oppressive practices.

The primacy of interventionist warfare and varieties of military/policing actions in the post-Cold War context has brought into sharp focus issues relating to the 'government' of the international sphere, issues that acquired particularly urgent salience in the aftermath of the events of September 11th 2001 and subsequent transnational acts of violence directed at major European and non-European cities. The interventions of the late twentieth and early twenty-first centuries were/are variously defined in terms of humanitarian wars, liberal wars, and preventive wars, these often being conflated into the terminology of the so-called 'war against terrorism', irrespective of the origins of this last formulation. From the first Gulf War, to the interventions in the Balkans, Africa, and latterly Afghanistan and Iraq, all somehow articulated in the language of human rights, the rescue of populations, and the protection of humanity at large.[3] Within particular moral framings of the wars of the recent past and present, high technology warfare is deemed to be in the service variously of human rights, humanity, women, progress, peace, and civilisation itself. Given the nature of such interventions, including as they do not simply military and policing operations, but ambitions for state-building, war is no longer confined to the battlefield, but moves and shifts into the minutiae of the social, economic, and political life of recipient societies. It is in this sense that, as we will see below, the government of the international order comes into sharp relief, as does the place of war therein. This is then the context within which discussions of solidarity acquire resonance, for this is a context that calls attention to our understandings of distinctly modern conceptions of the international sphere, of political community, and articulations of political subjectivity, each of which in turn is affected differently through different modes of solidarity.

The 'international' as a political sphere is a distinctly modern construct, historically defined in terms of relations between sovereign states and the regulatory practices constitutive of an international order of states.[4] Both realism and international liberalism relied on this conception of the modern international, so that state sovereignty, irrespective of its contested claims, came to form the underpinning principal of international law, of conceptions of political community, and aspirations within Europe and beyond towards self-determination based on the political nation. As foremost political sociologists have shown, the modern European state, as a primary institution of modernity, came to encompass the consolidation of power over a specified territory and population, providing the institutions that regulated relations with other states while at the same time servicing the expansion of capital globally.[5] War played a major part in the pacification of societies, in relations between states, and in enabling colonial dispossession. The modern period at the same time witnesses the emergence of universal conceptions of humanity and its institutionalisation in the discourse of human rights and its positive articulation in laws of war and humanitarian law. The sphere of the international, from the Hague Conventions to the Geneva Conventions, to the Universal Declaration of Human Rights, to subsequent conventions against torture, against race and gender discrimination, all form the armoury of a formidable discourse of rights that is now globally acknowledged and recognised, if not fully ratified by all states. Practices and expressions of solidarity have in the past just as they are now formed and enabled by some conception of this realm of the human, irrespective of constructed boundaries around states or cultures. Just as these international treaties and conventions are drawn upon in practices and expressions of solidarity, so too they in turn were a product of situated struggles, campaigns, and acts of resistance the culmination of some of which came to constitute the norms and values which inform the basis of judgment and responsibility today.

It is this realm of the human and its historically transcendent force that brings into sharp focus the question of solidarity, its conditions of possibility, and its implications for the sphere of the international. I want to argue that the ways in which solidarity is understood, formulated and practised will have a profound impact on how solidarity is related to structures of domination globally. As I state above, the article argues that we might usefully understand solidarity in two distinct ways, the liberal cosmopolitan and the political cosmopolitan.[6] Each of these, as will be seen below, presents different implications for our understanding of the international and each of them sits differently in relation to postcolonial societies. What is presented below is then a postcolonial reading of solidarity and its different modes of articulations in international relations.

Solidarity and Liberal Cosmopolitanism

There is much written on understandings of cosmopolitanism in International Relations, from its philosophical foundations to its meaning in situated practices. What is of interest in the present context is how cosmopolitanism relates to social and political solidarity conceived in global terms and one of the most powerful articulations of cosmopolitanism is distinctly liberal in its conception of politics and political agency.[7] The ontological underpinning of liberal thought, namely the rational autonomous individual and a post-Enlightenment society premised on the institutionalisation of procedural resolutions of social conflict, has over time informed renditions on liberalism that have global aspirations. Such aspirations related to the construction of a liberal international economic order, or the wider political institutions the purpose of which was the regulation and maintenance of the international order through established rules and procedures, including those that sought to define the place of the individual in relation to the state and these wider global institutions.

Liberalism assumes some notion of what Guess refers to as an 'overriding con-sensus' suggestive of a certain 'minimal and tacit agreement in values and normative conceptions' that bind liberal society together.[8] This minimal and tacit agreement draws upon a background of intellectual thought and a self-understanding that assumes individual autonomy as being constitutive of a rationally defined social arrangement. The idea of autonomy is seen as the basis of liberal toleration of different forms of life, individual choices of lifestyle, expression and association. It is in this sense that liberalism comes to constitute the apotheosis of modernity, the liberation of the individual self from religious edicts, tradition, and situated culture. In estab-lishing individual autonomy as the centrepiece of liberal thought, the modern self could emerge into a rationally constituted public arena distinct from a private realm of concrete affiliations, of family, church, tradition, and so on. The assumption of an overriding consensus informs recent discourses around social cohesion in the liberal multicultural state and what constitutes a distinct European identity in a post-September 11th context where social cohesion and the integration of migrant communities has come into question. It also informs intellectual interventions that have sought to estab-lish a clear blue line between the continuing European project of modernity and the re-emergence of religious doctrine across the Atlantic and elsewhere (including certain multicultural spaces in Europe) as a basis for public policy.[9]

The liberal conception of solidarity is hence geared towards certain core elements now so deeply rooted as constitutive of the liberal democratic state that deviations from this consensus, both within the liberal polity and beyond, must be subject to explanation or justification. As John Gray notes, while some liberal philosophies assume the baseline of the above core elements to be metaphysically derived, those more historically oriented, such as Quentin Skinner, recognise the historical genesis of contemporary articulations of ideas relating to individual liberty and pluralist tolera-tion.[10] When liberalism sheds its metaphysical orientation it comes to be recognised as a distinct historical project, itself born of contest, so that any conception of solidarity rendered in liberal terms is one that accepts the historical underpinnings of consensus around particular preferences in opposition to others. While there is much in liberal thought that relies on a Kantian metaphysics, from Rawls's *Theory of Justice* to its cos-mopolitan articulation in Beitz and others, it is hence entirely wrong to suggest that all liberal thought is devoid of a conception of the struggles and contestations that have come to define a distinctly liberal understanding of modern political subjectivity and the social formations emergent from a distinct historical era. This then provides a base-line from which we might understand solidarity in liberalism as a distinctly culturalist understanding so that we can articulate a culture of liberalism expressive of particular preferences and possessing particular cultural boundaries and affiliations. It is this culturalist understanding of liberalism that then enables us to understand the tensions that emerge when (1) liberalism assumes humanity at large within its purview of operations, and (2) when liberalism comes face to face with practices and orientations that a liberal self-understanding opposes.

When liberalism assumes humanity within its remit of operations it comes to be framed in terms of cosmopolitanism, transcending the domestic/international divide, seeking instead to articulate a political and a moral project of solidarity that has global aspirations. While certain authors stress the moral imperative that binds humanity as a location of free and equal individuals, others articulate a desire for a transformed juridico-political order that is distinctly cosmopolitan in its orientation, so that the remit of law and of political institutions is no longer limited to the sovereign state, but extends beyond, into a wider polity of humankind. To suggest a cosmopolitan polity is hence to imply an institutional articulation of a global social consensus that is not simply of a tacit and minimal kind, but one that sees its ultimate expression in what Habermas refers to as cosmopolitan law and Linklater refers to as a post-Westphalian political community.[11] The statute of the International Criminal Court, the European Convention on Human Rights, both now ratified in a number of domestic jurisdictions, the Universal Declaration of Human Rights, the UN Convention Against Torture and the wider body of humanitarian law, all are constitutive of a modern conception of humanity as a location of not simply moral conduct, charitable affiliation and empathy, but of a positive legal and political public sphere where the self is no longer subject to the state and its actions, but has this wider legal and political connection, both in terms of answerability and in terms of protection. These forms of institutionalisation may hence be seen as the solidification of what Dallmayr refers to as a 'general consensus on moral norms' the centrality of which is human rights.[12]

When this consensus is seen in distinctly political terms, cosmopolitanism acquires a historical orientation that recognises the genesis of the construct of humanity in conflict and contestation. The 'transformation of political community' as phrased in Linklater's work, comes to be understood in terms not simply of a dialogue between difference, but in terms of the mechanics of how such transformation takes place in the actuality of the historical process where what is involved is, as Bonnie Honig highlights, no less than a political and a moral project of 'ordering subjects, institutions, and values'.[13] This ordering may indeed be dialogical, but when scrutinised historically, the experience of the postcolonial world, both in history and in the contemporary twenty-first century, is predominantly violent and structured in inequality and domination.

The Postcolonial Critique of Liberal Cosmopolitanism

Liberal cosmopolitanism assumes a community of humankind solidified in institutional frameworks of law that pitch cosmopolitan right against sovereign right. Its driving force is a historical project of modernity that sees the individual self as autonomous and hence as a holder of rights protected in a transformed global order where sovereign impunity comes face to face with a legally enshrined cosmopolitan law that can hold sovereigns to account. This post-Westphalian ordering of the world is both emergent from and is constitutive of global articulations of solidarity born of the actions of progressive social movements as well as states. How then would such a framework of thinking and practice be vulnerable to a powerful postcolonial critique?

What at first hand appears to constitute an emancipatory political project, one that expresses solidarity with the mass of humankind subjected to violence, poverty, and unjust practices, can be read as a project that is itself complicit in these very practices. For postcolonial authors writing in International Relations, the liberalism that is assumed to be at the heart of the project of modernity was only possible through practices of dispossession that defined colonial expansion. Furthermore, and as Siba

Grovogui has argued, the experience of modernity in colonial and postcolonial times is one that is deeply influenced by historical subjugation and practices, discursive and institutional, put in place in colonial times and the immediate postcolonial period.[14] Just as Europe was moving towards a consensus built upon liberal norms, so too it was at the same time involved in the direct violation of other societies and their autonomy. When scrutinised from the postcolonial angle, therefore, the experience of modernity acquires a wholly different narrative.

The historical record of liberalism apart, a postcolonial critique may also look closely at the elements that constitute the liberal cosmopolitan project and reveal through doing so the inherent hierarchies that are assumed in this conception of solidarity. As we saw above, the liberal cosmopolitan project seeks to redefine the international sphere so that sovereign right gives way to cosmopolitan right where, as Linklater puts it, 'significant national powers are transferred to international legal authorities'.[15] When we look into the drivers behind such transformations, we see a significant role for progressive social movements in Linklater and Habermas among others. However, and crucially, we also see significant transformative agency attributed to specific societies that are deemed to possess the 'moral resources', according to Linklater, that drive progress towards a cosmopolitan order, namely societies that exhibit constitutional modes of governance, democratic accountability, and 'sophisticated' understandings of dialogical communicative practices. However, given the focus on intervention, the liberal cosmopolitan project is not merely confined to dialogical practices but seeks the juridical transformation of the international order, so that those in possession of the above resources are also accrued the political authority to intervene in the name of cosmopolitan right. As witnessed in cases such as Bosnia and East Timor, such authority may derive from a number of locations, from international institutions, to coalitions of states, to a complex network of non-governmental organisations, all engaged in what is in effect an international (indeed cosmopolitan) civil service that took charge of governance functions engaged in shaping, or disciplining, previously conflict-ridden societies. However, as these and other cases of intervention indicate, the overwhelming capacity that defines transformative agency is military and each intervention accrued legitimacy by liberal cosmopolitan authors is one that has involved the use of armed forces, including in the cases of Kosovo, Iraq, Afghanistan, full-scale warfare.[16] The assumption that underpins liberal cosmopolitan thought is that the agents capable of achieving the constitution of a post-Westphalian political community and its juridical underpinning are liberal democratic states which are in turn placed in a hierarchical relationship with other states. When this distinction is assumed to be the dynamic force behind the transformation of the international away from the sovereignty principle and towards a cosmopolitan order, the liberal democratic state, indeed states that dominate the contemporary global order, are conferred greater legitimacy to act in the name of human rights, and hence humanity at large.

It becomes apparent from the above that liberal cosmopolitan conceptions of solidarity assume the primacy of human rights as the underpinning basis for the constitution of humanity as a legitimate sphere of operations, and hence of the right to intervene in the name of cosmopolitan right. Capacity and legitimacy are formative of what is conceived as the agency implicated in the transformation of the international sphere towards a cosmopolitan order built on human solidarity while being

constitutive itself of such solidarity. As we see from discourses of humanitarian intervention, war comes to be a formative, constitutive moment in the transformation
of the international into a liberal global polity, one that is rule-governed and domesticated, and built upon an assumed consensus on what constitutes the human. What
becomes apparent is that far from defining a shift away from sovereign right, this
liberal cosmopolitan articulation of solidarity simply reasserts the sovereignty of
the most powerful, those possessing the capacity to act, states that, in other words,
have global reach. Within this liberal cosmopolitan framework of knowledge, war
is expressive of solidarity even when it may also be interpreted as a regulatory
practice, a technology of government,[17] that aims at the wholesale transformation of
societies deemed 'failed' as well as the international system as a whole.

The liberal cosmopolitan standpoint sees itself, even in warfare, as acting on behalf
of humanity, in solidarity with those whose very humanity is violated. In thus
perceiving its remit, it assumes a certainty of purpose and is anxious in portraying
such certainty in representation. Acting on behalf of humanity, its remit is immediately universal, conferring to itself a legitimacy that is itself assumed to derive from
this universal space. The subject of liberal cosmopolitanism is hence by definition
always just, always human, an enlightened, modern being whose engagement in violence is justifiable exactly through the elements that constitute the self-understanding
of the liberal cosmopolitan subject, namely the just, the human, the enlightened, and
the modern. The liberal cosmopolitan understanding of solidarity bases its project on
a moral imperative that is global and being so relies on capacities that are global in
reach. Every action undertaken in the name of humanity, in the name of a cosmopolitan
order, is constitutive of that order, defined in juridical and political terms. Such action,
therefore, is not born of law, but is constitutive of law, a violent moment that confers
to its agents the capacity to judge and the capacity to act. As Richard Falk and others
have highlighted, humanitarian intervention, war conducted in the name of humanity,
is located at the limits of law, indeed has no place in law, and yet is interpreted by the
liberal cosmopolitan as potentially constitutive of law.[18] Humanitarian intervention
inscribes populations targeted as recipients of care and protection even as those very
populations are at the receiving end of high technology capacities of warfare that
define and indeed constitute liberal cosmopolitan agency.

From the postcolonial viewpoint therefore, the solidarities expressive of such
agency are always hierarchically constituted, not simply in terms of technological and
material resource capacity, but in a self-understanding that sees itself in moral terms,
constructed in terms of saving others, just warriors engaged in the rescue of other,
distant populations. As the postcolonial critique highlights, the condition of possibility
for such constructions is a certain dislocation from history, enabling a distanciation
from the complicities generative of the conditions that are rendered in terms of
humanitarian necessity. As Sara Ahmed has highlighted, the carers' moral positioning
removes them as the agents 'behind the injuries'.[19] The discursive grammar behind
such a politics of forgetting is one that is framed in terms of progress and civilisation,
a distinctly liberal articulation that is self-legislating and self-legitimising, while being
at the same time universalising in its remit. The self in this sense comes to assume the
universal, indeed represents the universal realm of the human, so that any oppositional discourse appears to somehow locate itself outside this universal domain.
However, it is exactly in the historical specificity of the liberal project that such claims

to universality come to be vulnerable to this postcolonial critique, for to understand liberal cosmopolitanism as a distinctly historical and political project, is to suggest, indeed acknowledge, that this is a project that now sees itself in confrontation with other political projects, especially those that proclaim a different cultural under-standing of lived experience and normative expectations.

The hierarchies I point to above, namely those of capacity and morality, are hence at the same time also culturally articulated, even as such articulation is more often than not implicit in the discourse and the inscriptions conferred to liberal self and other. While it is all-too-easy to draw upon a 'clash of civilisations'[20] formula in interpreting contemporary global confrontations, what is significant to highlight is that cultural difference has somehow replaced race as a primary marker of difference and enmity in global politics. As Paul Gilroy highlights, the racialisation of culture, in its multiform locations, from the Balkans conflicts, to the Middle East, to US foreign policy, to the formulations of Huntington and Condoleezza Rice, comes to constitute the 'organising principle that underpins contemporary schemes of racial classification and division'.[21] Missions to modernise, civilise, and liberalise come to be associated with modes of ordering the hierarchies of which are culturally defined in terms of a liberal West that is fully modern and cosmopolitan and the rest steeped in the constraining particularities of tradition. Just as liberal cosmopolitanism sees itself as the driver of the project of modernity, what it appears to deny, as postcolonial critics argue, is that this very project is experienced differently across the globe, a project that is at once both enabling and constraining. This differentiation in the experience of modernity has both institutional and discursive manifestations and nowhere is this differentiation more apparent than in the experience of the modern state. While the Western conception of modern political community has been constructed around the limits of the modern sovereign state, the postcolonial experience is exactly conceived in terms of the vulnerability of these limits. Conceptions of political community, of justice and legitimacy, as the basic tenets of politics, acquired a modern expression in anti-colonial struggles, but such struggles were not only aimed at the colonial power, but looked inwards as well in relation to modes of expression that perceived politics in relation to locality and a transnational sphere of affiliation. It is in this sense that post-colonial societies always emerge as anomalies or failures with respect to modernity and its organising principles.[22] Liberal cosmopolitan solidarity may hence express a recognition of cultural diversity, it is nevertheless steeped in a hierarchically culturalist discourse whereby, as Inayatullah and Blaney point out, 'the cultural conceptions of Western liberals are constructed as normal or natural in relation to today's "barbarians", the marginalised and anarchical peoples and regions, perpetually on the road to mature liberal selfhood.'[23]

Confronted with a powerful postcolonial critique, the universalising remit of liberal cosmopolitanism emerges as a project complicit in the perpetuation of structures of domination generative of the very conditions which are then framed in a discursive politics of human solidarity. The charge goes further, however, and highlights the systems of knowledge that confer legitimacy to modes of representation that elevate the liberal self in relation to the 'rescued' other. In relation to the question of solidarity and its conditions of possibility in this unequal terrain, the challenge is to articulate a mode of international politics, indeed a cosmopolitan politics, that is at once both internationalist in orientation as well as being cognisant of the inequalities that constitute the terrain of the human. A distinctly political cosmopolitanism is therefore self-consciously historical in its self-understanding, is responsive to and indeed acknowledges its location not just in the struggles of modernity and its paradoxes, but in the engagement of particularities that define the postcolonial condition in global terms, and not simply in terms that locate postcoloniality somehow elsewhere. Any consensus that is assumed therefore is one that emerges as a result of a hegemonic battle of sorts, where the universal is not assumed, but is rather always in negotiation.

Solidarity and Political Cosmopolitanism

The question of social solidarity comes to acquire salience when the universal is no longer thought of simply in normative terms, but comes to be the arena wherein political contestation takes place. Solidarity of the cosmopolitan form must hence assume not simply a terrain of an undefined, depoliticised humanity at large, but rather an articulation of political agency that is self-consciously particular in its choices of affiliation. Where liberal cosmopolitanism acknowledged cultural diversity while at once both relegating cultural affiliation to the private sphere and defining difference in culturally hierarchical terms, political cosmopolitanism acknowledges itself in distinctly cultural terms and hence recognises other modes of cultural articulation as being equally located in the public sphere and hence of equal political worth, potentially engaged in a sphere of contestation. Understood in political cosmopolitan terms, solidarity assumes a political agency that has the politics of mobilisation at its core, where the case has to be made in a complex global arena wherein the universal is a contested space.

This final section of the article seeks an alternative reading of cosmopolitanism, therefore, one that moves the terms of discourse away from interventionist hierarchies and their associated violent and exclusionary practices. I want to argue that this alternative expression of solidarity seeks a socialisation of the international without the dangers of undermining societies and their desires and aspirations for self-determination. As highlighted elsewhere,[24] this mode of cosmopolitanism recognises that while identities are important, so too is equality as significant a political project, both locally and internationally. Crucially, this form of political cosmopolitanism locates its discourse and its genesis firmly in an *imminent critique* of modernity. It is imminent in that it is constitutively modern, formed and constituted by the discourses and institutions of modernity, centred as these are on modern subjectivity, the state, and a global capitalist order. It is, furthermore, imminently *critical* in that it recognises that the modern state, the global capitalist order, and the realm of the human are differently experienced in relation to enablement and constraint both internally in relation to differences of class and gender as well as externally in relation to the colonial legacy as formative of the modern project itself. A solidarity that is emancipatory in its politics hence recognises its political subjectivity in distinctly modern terms, while articulating a critique of the very discourses and institutions that give it form. This critique is at the same time postcolonial in its definition, for it recognises at one and the same time both what Spivak refers to as the 'epistemic violence'[25] that constitutes systems of knowledge that deny their location in structures of domination and the continuities of colonisation and dispossession that define late modern international politics.

Any understanding of the dynamics of solidarity in the political cosmopolitan sense recognises its location in relation to the discourses and institutions of modernity and their differential implications across the global arena. As the article argues above, liberal renditions of solidarity express a hierarchical conception of the international defined in terms of capacities, moral worth, and cultural subjectivity. Even as liberal cosmopolitanism proclaims recognition of difference, it is, as argued above, premised on a historical supremacy of liberal modes of being and social organisation.

The challenge for a mode of solidarity emergent from political cosmopolitanism is exactly the rejection of a hierarchical conception of agency, organisation and being, while retaining some view of the possibility of connection and affiliation beyond the boundaries of culture and state. This conception of solidarity does not rely on any total-ising discourse that assumes humanity at large, nor does it have a self-understanding that is grand in scale or reliant on armed intervention as the manifestation of care. Recognising the continuities, epistemic, discursive, and institutional, that generate daily struggles, daily manifestations of inequality, this form of solidarity occurs through local campaigns that may accrue wide solidarities through political mobilisa-tion. Any solidarities emergent from the wider global arena draw their inspiration from local agents and their preferences. As Walker highlights in a much forgotten, but nevertheless invaluable early text, this form of solidarity does not assume an 'easy universalism' nor an emergent 'global community'.[26] Rather, political agency emerges in the situated context of local struggles and the contingent political mobilisations that may draw external support. There is no claim here of a universal consensus consti-tuting a humanity at large, nor is there any assumption made in relation to the constitution of an emergent juridically under-written political community defined in terms of a domesticated international arena. Solidarity in this sense is not reliant on a dialogue the rules of which are always already in place. This is rather an understanding of solidarity that acknowledges political agency in terms of the specificities of political choice, and the dynamics that enter into and constitute political mobilisation.

Nevertheless, political cosmopolitanism by definition also assumes the global as a location of politics, and the question emerges as to how to conceptualise a distinctly global political agency that is not vulnerable to the postcolonial critique articulated earlier in this article. One way in which such agency may be conceived is in the recog-nition, or indeed acknowledgement, that the universal as a terrain of social and economic interaction is already in place, already subject to political action and mobili-sation. The space of the universal in this sense is as much a source of differential vul-nerabilities as it is a space wherein potential modes of solidarity in the struggle against vulnerabilities might take place. There is no necessary assumption here of a universal political community writ large that, as highlighted by Balibar, comes to constitute a new mode of exclusion.[27] However, there persists what Balibar refers to as a 'fictive' form of universality, one that has historically enabled the gradual shift away from primary identifications (ethnic, religious, tribal) and towards a higher political formation (the secular state) instrumental in both the 'individuation' as well as the 'normalisation' of the self. In place of conceiving the project of modernity as being located in the emergence of the autonomous self, this conception recognises the dialectic of moder-nity, namely the liberation of the self and the emergence of practices and institutions that seek the regulation of the self. This recognition of individuation as the product of increasingly abstract and universal modes of organisation, namely the modern state, suggests, for Balibar, the historical possibility of a solidarity of strangers unencumbered by ties of tradition. Nevertheless, while the modern state suggests the possibility of exactly such a solidarity of strangers, it at the same time is historically a product of the normalising practices that include the conforming, but exclude forms of subjectivity deemed beyond such normality, namely the foreigner, the un-integrated, the homosexual, and others who are then subjected to discriminatory practices. Crucially for the political cosmopolitan conception of solidarity, however, the state comes to represent a fictive universality that 'leads dominated groups to struggle against discrimination or inequality in the very name of the superior values of the community: the legal and ethical values of the state itself.'[28] This liberating aspect of the modern state and the particularistic tensions it generates is especially apparent in the protections accrued to women as against traditional practices that seek to target their lives and bodies. Any universalising move is hence always and at the same time a moment of struggle and contention. The articulation of the universal is hence always a space of contention, whether its articulation comes in the form of the real, the fictive or indeed the aspirational. This last is expressive of what Balibar refers to as a 'right to politics', an insurrectionary mode of articulation that imagines emancipation through collective effort and not through external imposition. Solidarity is hence always a solidarity of claims and a solidarity of effort, driven aspirationally through some conception of an otherwise to the present while drawing on and constituting the fictive universality that is the modern state and the modern global arena. This is, however, distinctly a 'solidarity without creating a community'.[29]

Conclusion

This article has focused attention on the question of cosmopolitan solidarity and its expression in two distinct forms, what I have referred to as the liberal and the political. Where liberal cosmopolitanism assumes its operational remit in humanity at large, drawing its inspiration from normative constructs relating to humanity, human rights, and humanitarianism, political cosmopolitanism resists any such grand designs on the universal, preferring instead an engagement with situated struggles and expressions of resistance. The article suggests that while the former expression of cosmopolitanism is vulnerable to a powerful postcolonial critique, primarily due to its hierarchical conception of political, moral, and cultural agency that differentiates the 'carer' or protector from the protected, it generates in its wake not just systems of knowledge that constitute epistemic violence, but practices, including warfare, that perpetuate systems of dominations articulated in the contemporary era in resurgent colonial practices wherein dispossession, of agency, of local assertions of difference, and of material resources is represented in discourse in terms of a modernising imperative conducted in the name of humanity at large.

The aim has been then to articulate a conception of solidarity that can meet the postcolonial challenge while retaining the idea of a cosmopolitan mode of political expression, one that recognised the possibility of a universal location of politics, but one that did not assume a juridical remit nor indeed the emergence of a global political community underwritten by law. The article has suggested that this form of cosmopolitan solidarity defines itself in terms of an imminent critique of modernity, recognising its discourse as at one and the same time both modern in its generation, and hence related to modernity's institutions, and critical of the totalising and exclusionary force of modernity's legacy, specifically its colonial legacy. What has emerged therefore is a conception of cosmopolitan solidarity that, far from aiming to reshape societies into an image of liberalism and the liberal self, recognised the terrain of the universal as a location of contestation and struggle. The universalism assumed in this latter conception is conceived in relation to lived experience rather than being conceived in totalising terms. Thinking of political cosmopolitanism in terms of an imminent critique of modernity enabled both a recognition of modernity's liberating potential – in the constitution of firstly a modern subjectivity that could extract itself from the constraints of tradition, and secondly of modern institutions, specifically the modern state as the expression of a solidarity of strangers wherein the citizen could claim rights beyond traditional forms of affiliation – and the tensions, conflicts and inequalities historically associated with the modern legacy.

The article has argued that political cosmopolitanism is a distinctly modern project and as such seeks to retain some notion of the universal, while recognising the implications of its universalising moves. Borrowing variously from Walker, Balibar, as well as the postcolonial critique that I present of liberal cosmopolitanism, the article conceives of solidarity as a positive concept, one that is constitutively built upon the idea of a collective effort, the capacity to act, the capacity to define the limits of affiliation, while retaining some element of 'negativity', not just that associated with resistance and non-conformity, but the idea that there is always an excess that remains uncaptured by the concept.[30] What is provided above is in many ways also a negative conception of solidarity; to use Balibar, solidarity without community, a mode of thinking where politics is assumed to happen with others, but one which does not lapse into reifying its own particularity as universality.

Notes

1. See, for example, Nicholas Wheeler's *Saving Strangers: Humanitarian Intervention in International Society* (Oxford: Oxford University Press, 2002), for the English School, while Charles Beitz and Simon Caney provide accounts of moral conduct framed by cosmopolitan ethics. See respectively, Charles Beitz, *Political Theory and International Relations* (Princeton, NJ: Princeton University Press, 1999) and Simon Caney, *Justice Beyond Borders: A Global Political Theory* (Oxford: Oxford University Press, 2005).

2. The arguments presented in this article derive from a detailed investigation into late-modern war and its implications for global politics. See Vivienne Jabri, *War and the Transformation of Global Politics* (London and New York: Palgrave Macmillan, 2007).

3. There is here a wide and varied literature on war, humanitarianism, and prevention deemed to be in the service of humanity. Authors who see liberal wars in terms of the transformation of the international order include Anne-Marie Slaughter, 'International Law in a World of Liberal States', *European Journal of International Law*, 6 (1995),

Lawrence Freedman, 'The Age of Liberal Wars', *Review of International Studies*, 31 (2005), and Jean Bethke Elshtain, 'International Justice as Equal Regard and the Use of Force', *Ethics and International Affairs*, 17 (2003).

4. For a conception of the international as a modern construct, see R. B. J. Walker, *Inside/Outside: International Relations as Political Theory* (Cambridge: Cambridge University Press, 1993).

5. Anthony Giddens, *The Nation-State and Violence* (Cambridge: Polity Press, 1985), Michael Mann, *The Sources of Social Power*, vol. II (Cambridge: Cambridge University Press, 1993); and Charles Tilly, *Coercion, Capital and European States AD 990–1990* (Oxford: Blackwell, 1990).

6. There is, of course, a wide literature on cosmopolitanism and debates/classifications therein. See especially Fred Dallmayr, 'Cosmopolitanism: Moral and Political', *Political Theory*, 31 (2003), pp. 421–42.

7. Beitz, *Political Theory and International Relations*

8. Raymond Guess, 'Liberalism and its Discontents', *Political Theory*, 30 (2002), p. 327.

9 Of particular significance here is the public agreement between Jacques Derrida and Jurgen Habermas on the distinctiveness of the European project of modernity and its indebtedness to the Enlightenment. See interviews conducted by Giovanna Borradori in her *Philosophy in a Time of Terror: Dialogues with Jurgen Habermas and Jacques Derrida* (Chicago, IL and London: University of Chicago Press, 2003).

10 John Gray, 'Pluralism and Toleration in Contemporary Political Philosophy', *Political Studies*, 48 (2000), pp. 323–33. For a distinctly historical understanding of liberalism, see Quentin Skinner, *Liberty before Liberalism* (Cambridge: Cambridge University Press, 1988).

11 See especially, Jurgen Hagerman, 'Kant's Idea of Perpetual Peace, with the Benefit of Two Hundred Years' Hindsight', in James Bohman and Matthias Lutz-Bachmann (eds.), *Perpetual Peace: Essays on Kant's Cosmopolitan Ideal* (Cambridge, MA and London: The MIT Press, 1997). On post-Westphalian political community, see Andrew Linklater, *The Transformation of Political Community* (Cambridge: Polity Press, 1998).

12 Fred Dallmayr, 'Cosmopolitanism: Moral and Political', *Political Theory*, 31 (2003), p. 427.

13 Bonnie Honig, 'Difference, Dilemmas and the Politics of Home', in Seyla Benhabib (ed.), *Democracy and Difference: Contesting Boundaries of the Political* (Princeton, NJ: Princeton University Press, 1996), p. 258.

14 Siba N. Grovogui, 'Regimes of Sovereignty: International Morality and the African Condition', *European Journal of International Relations*, 8 (2002), pp. 315–38.

15 Linklater, *The Transformation of Political Community*, p. 171. For a critique of Linklater along the lines outlined, see Beate Jahn, *One Step Forward, Two Steps Back: Critical Theory as the Latest Edition of Liberal Idealism*, Millenium, 27:3 (1998), pp. 613–42.

16 Jabri, *War and the Transformation of Global Politics*, pp. 94–135. For a conceptualisation of liberal interventions in relation to peacebuilding, see Oliver Richmond, *The Transformation of Peace* (London and New York: Palgrave Macmillan, 2005).

17 For this Foucaultian inspired conception of war as a technology of government, see Vivienne Jabri, 'War, Security and the Liberal State', *Security Dialogue*, 37 (2006). See also Michael Dillon, 'Cared to Death: The Biopoliticised Time of Your Life', *Foucault Studies*, 2 (2005).

18 Richard Falk, 'Legality and Legitimacy: the Quest for Principled Flexibility and Restraint', *Review of International Studies*, 31 (2005).

19 Sara Ahmed, 'Collective Feelings Or, The Impressions Left By Others', *Theory, Culture & Society*, 21 (2004), pp. 25–42.

20 As formulated in Samuel P. Huntington's Clash of Civilisations and the Remaking of World Order (New York: Simon and Schuster, 1996).

21 Paul Gilroy, *After Empire: Melancholia or Convivial Culture* (London and New York: Routledge, 2004), p. 39.

22 See especially Edward Said's powerful critique of Western and especially American representations of the Arabs and the Middle East as a region. Edward Said, 'The Arab-American War: The Politics of Information', in his *The Politics of Dispossession* (London: Chatto and Windus, 1994).

23 Naeem Inayatullah and David Blaney, *International Relations and the Problem of Difference* (London and New York: Routledge, 2004), p. 117.

24 Jabri, *War and the Transformation of Global Politics*, pp. 163–89.

25 Gayatry Chakravorty Spivak, *A Critique of Postcolonial Reason: Toward a History of the Vanishing Present* (Cambridge, MA and London: Harvard University Press, 1999), p. 277.

26 R. B. J. Walker, *One World Many Worlds: Struggles for a Just World Peace* (Boulder, CO and London: Lynne Rienner and Zed Books, 1988), p. 102.

27 I draw this triptych of the universal, as 'real', 'fictive', and 'ideal', from Etienne Balibar's *Politics and the Other Scene* (London: Verso, 2002), pp. 148–70.

28 Balibar, *Politics*, p. 161.

29 Balibar, *Politics*, pp. 167–8.

30 For an excellent rendition on philosophies of negativity, see Diana Coole, *Negativity and Politics* (Routledge, London 2000).

25   Literature/Identity

Transnationalism, Narrative and Representation

Arif Dirlik

When I suggested the above title for this article, my intention was to pursue further a question I had raised in earlier writings: that of the relationship between narrative form and the construction/reception of cultural identity as it appears in Asian-American writing. I will still address this question, but from a perspective that foregrounds the relationship between literature and history. The discussion is restricted to issues thrown up by the appropriations, denials and subversions of history in literary work; most importantly in the blurring of distinctions between fiction and history. The question of the relationship between history and literature, I argue below, is not an academic question of disciplinary boundaries, a question of scholarly versus creative work, or an abstract question of culture; it is most importantly a political question, as it compels attention to the fundamental issue of the implication of writing in configuring the boundaries between the public and the private.

Ethnic or transnational literatures present a challenge not only to historical ways of thinking, but also to the ways in which we have organized the study of the world in terms of nations, areas and regions. While the challenge is to be welcomed for forcing a rethinking of history and its complicity in power, those who would dismiss history, celebrate the blurring of the boundaries between fiction and history, or simply privilege literary over historical constructions of identity, often overlook the indispensable critical insights compelled by a consciousness of historicity. The blurring of boundaries between fiction and history, moreover, calls into question not only the identity of history but also the identity of literature. As literature has been placed at the service of exploring ethnic and transnational (or diasporic) identities, the construction of identities in literary work has been confounded with the ethnography of culture, subjecting the writer to pressures that subvert the autonomy of creative work. Compounding this confusion is the question of the cultural

Arif Dirlik, "Literature/Identity: Transnationalism, Narrative and Representation." *Review of Education, Pedagogy and Cultural Studies*, 24, 2002: 209–234. Reprinted by permission of Taylor & Francis Ltd.

belonging of literature as it is divorced from earlier associations with nations and national languages.

This is especially important when it comes to questions of cultural identity and representation, which are of primary concern here. There has been a renewed tendency over the last decade or so to reify cultures through the equation of cultural with national, regional or civilizational boundaries. While the goal of most ethnic or transnational writing has been to break down such boundaries, is it possible that dehistoricization of the explorations of identity in such writing, and the language in which such exploration is articulated, contribute to the reification of cultural identity, however contrary that may be to the intentions of its authors? The question is evident in the controversies among writers and critics over the status of the history in fiction. It is necessary, I think, to place these discussions in a broader social and ideological context, and to relate the issues they raise to a broader field of discourse of which they are both constituents and beneficiaries. The necessity of attentiveness to historicity in cultural discussion and criticism, always an important issue, has acquired a new urgency with the tragic events of September 11.

The Chinese-American writer and poet, Russell Leong, remarks in an interview that

> there's the view of history as grandiose, the "sweep of history," but most history is made up of the lives and actions of ordinary people and really not the "heroic" in the sense that it's even recorded … The grand sweep of history is for traditional historians, and that presupposes that history is linear, and that it's going someplace, and that there's a beginning and an end, a goal located within a master narrative. But many times, when you're just living life, you're not sure of its end point, or its beginning, or the middle.[1]

Leong is a historically minded writer, and what he has to say about history is not so much a rejection of it as an insistence on incorporating history in literary work to bring to the understanding of the past and the present elements that are left out of history or that may be impossible to contain within historical categories. Likewise, for Karen Tei-Yamashita, a Japanese-American writer, the preference for literature grows out of a sense of the insufficiencies of history: "With straight history, you … couldn't express the emotion. You couldn't express those extra things that illustrate history … I also wanted to bring in a feeling for the sense of place, that scene, the smell."[2] In the case of these two authors, history and literature complement one another, each making up for the lack in the other. If in the process the boundary between history and literature becomes blurred, it is to the enrichment of both. Such is not always the intention underlying the questioning of history. The Burmese-American writer, Wendy Law-Yone asserts that "history, after all, is the version of the victors … Literature, on the other hand, documents the version of the conquered. I'm on the side of literature."[3]

While none of these statements may be taken as representative or typical of Asian-American writers, together they represent a range of attitudes toward history that extends from a desire to bring history and literature together to the benefit of both, to the repudiation of history for its complicity in hegemony, oppression and erasure of ethnic pasts and sensibilities, in which case literature has to take over in the construction of the past. This privileging of literature in the case of ethnic and diasporic populations in general is evident in the following lines from Azade Seyhan in her *Writing Outside the Nation*:

> As cultures collide, unite, and are reconfigured in real and virtual spaces in unprecedented ways, postcolonial, migrant, and border-crossing theorists and artists fine-tune received critical traditions in order to safeguard historical and cultural specificities. Ultimately, every theory of postcolonial, transnational, or diasporic literature and art is most convincingly articulated and performed by works of literature and art themselves. Literature as an institution and literary fiction as an expression of human experience predate their theoretical articulation, a truism perhaps best exemplified by Aristotle's *Poetics*. Literature as social document resists the erasure of geographical, historical, and cultural differences.[4]

What happens to literature when it is converted into a "social document" is a problem that the author conveniently overlooks. It is a point to which I will return below, as it is crucial to the plight of the ethnic writer. Here I would like to note that there is something puzzling about this privileging of literature (if we overlook the vulgar objection of institutional self-interest, which is not to be dismissed for its vulgarity, but distracts from more important questions), and charges, as in the case of Law-Yone that history speaks for power while literature provides a voice for the oppressed and marginalized. I do not share some professional historians' reluctance to recognize the important ways in which literature contributes to voicing experiences erased or simply ignored in historical ways of knowing and representation or find objectionable the blurring of the boundaries between literature and history. It seems necessary to note, nevertheless, that there is a profound confusion in such statements of the conditions that attended the emergence of modern historiography as we know it (historicism, so-called) and the actual practice of history—which is a confusion that is common to certain tendencies in postcolonial criticism to the point of having turned into a cliché. Such charges seem to speak to a past historiography that set the standards for contemporary historiography where issues of fact and fiction are concerned, but they otherwise overlook the very significant ways in which contemporary historical practice has broken with its origins, in many ways paving the way for postcolonial criticism. Gender, ethnic, and social histories as they have unfolded since the 1960s could hardly be charged of complicity with power, as they led the way in challenging inherited assumptions concerning history and have been charged by conservative historians of undermining "Western civilization." It is arguable that any work of history that has claims to significance needs to attend to questions of politics, power and public consciousness. But that is not the same thing as a categorical assertion of history's complicity in power and oppression. If historians do anything these days, it is to call into question the relationship of their disciplinary legacy to power, and to bring into history those who were excluded from it by virtue of race, culture, and gender. The more important problem, it seems to me, lies else-where.

To elucidate this concern, I would like to turn here to the discussion of the problem of narrative by Hayden White, whose work lies at the origins of much of the contemporary discussion of the relationship between history and literature. In a discussion of narrative in nineteenth-century European historiography, White observes that

"Hegel ... insisted that a specifically historical mode of being was linked to a specifically narrative mode of representation by a shared 'internal vital principle.' This principle was, for him, nothing other than politics." He then goes on to quote Hegel to the effect that

> We must suppose historical narrations to have appeared contemporaneously with historical deeds and events. Family memorials, patriarchal traditions, have an interest confined to the family and the clan. The uniform course of events that such a condition implies is no subject of serious remembrance ... It is the state that first presents a subject matter that not only is *adapted* to the prose of history, but involves the production of such history in the progress of its own being.

What is of interest here is White's brilliant invocation of Hegel to deconstruct the problem of narrative in nineteenth-century historical thought. As he puts it,

> Hegel's views on the nature of historical discourse had the merit of making explicit what was acknowledged in the dominant practice of historical scholarship in the nineteenth century; namely, an interest in the study of political history, which was, however, often hidden behind vague professions of an interest in narration as an end in itself. The *doxa* of the profession, in other words, took the form of the historical discourse—what it called the true story, for the content of the discourse—while the real content; politics, was represented as being primarily only a vehicle for an occasion of storyteliing ... It is in this respect, rather than in any overt espousal of a specific political program or cause, that nineteenth-century professional historiography can be regarded as ideological. For if ideology is the treatment of the form of a thing as a content or essence, nineteenth-century historiography is ideological insofar as it takes the characteristic form of its discourse, the narrative, as a content—namely, narrativity—and treats "narrativity" as an essence shared by both discourses and sets of events alike.[5]

What White has to say accords closely with current criticisms of the European historical tradition to which contemporary historiography is heir; which is not very surprising, as he was one of the first to point out the relationship between ideology and historical narrative. We may add also that the reference to politics in Hegel's statement is not just to any kind of politics, but the politics of the state, which informs critiques of history for its complicity with power. We need also to remember that this was the basis for Karl Marx's critique of Hegel, and his insistence that it was civil society and not the state that was the ultimate location of politics.

What is more to the point, however, is the relationship to which White points between narrative form and ideology, which, read reflexively, has much to tell us about contemporary forms of narrative that, concerned with narrative as an end itself, also disguise the relationship between narrative form and politics. There is more than meets the eye in the contemporary rejection and suspicion of history, and the valorization of fictional forms of representation, which may have less to do with history and literature as alternative forms of narrative than with alternative forms of politics. The appropriation of history for literature implies also the privatization of history—and of the political function history has served—replacing politics conceived as public activity by politics conceived as identity politics, privatized and yet fraught with implications for our understanding of what is public and what is private. Where Hegel and nineteenth-century historians pointed to the state and the public realm (identified with the state) as the location for history, the privatized literary version of history locates it in what Hegel regarded as the private realm, "the family and the clan." The argument that it is literature rather than history that fulfills the needs of the oppressed and marginalized perpetuates the Hegelian prejudice that history belongs to the state, while it also privatizes the political needs of those who are left out of state-centered histories. In the process, it yields the public realm to the state. This is often accompanied, in the case of ethnic groups, by a displacement of political questions to the realm of culture. Cultural politics, moreover, easily lends itself to the reification of cultural identity as culture is evacuated of history.

The confounding of politics and cultural narrative is apparent in Azade Seyhan's identification of the distinctive feature of what she describes as "diasporic narratives":

> In the broadest sense, then, "diasporic narratives" discussed in this study represent a conscious effort to transmit a linguistic and cultural heritage that is articulated through acts of personal and collective memory. In this way, writers become chroniclers of the displaced whose stories will otherwise go unrecorded. Literature tends to record what history and public memory often forget. Furthermore, it can narrate both obliquely and allegorically, thereby preserving what can be censored and encouraging interpretation in the public sphere. Through the lens of personal recollection and interpretation, the specificity of class, ethnic, and gender experiences gains a stature that is often erased.[6]

It is not at all apparent to this reader why history cannot undertake the task of recovering what has been forgotten or "censored" in public memory, or force a reinterpretation of "the public sphere." It seems to me that this is what gender and ethnic historiography has been all about. The question, moreover, is not merely a question of forgetting, suppression or censorship in memory, but the very real historical denial of citizenship and, therefore, political participation to certain groups on the basis of gender, ethnicity, race and culture; with the result that they could be excluded without much ado from any history written as a celebration of the state's progress in time, which conveniently overlooked the suppression of difference that was an inextricable part of this progress. In the case of so-called "diasporic" populations, they could find a place in history only to the extent that they were assimilated, and could be seen to have contributed, to such progress; which, again, was impossible so long as they were denied political participation. The recovery of the historical presence of these groups is a challenge not only to state-centered conceptions of politics, but also to history written around the state. It adds the challenge of transnationality to a provocation first mounted in the name of citizenship. The challenge does not indicate the impossibility of history, but calls for a different kind of history.

All this, however, may be irrelevant to the agenda implied by Seyhan, which does not only privilege literature over history, but also the private over the public, while easily glossing over the question of "personal and collective memory" by throwing them together, erasing in the process the contradictory relationship between the two. Seyhan is quite right to stress the importance of personal memory in "diasporic" writing. But her celebration of personal memory, and reification of the "ethnic" or "diasporic," obviates the need to explore further the contradiction between the personal and the collective, as well as between history and memory. The appropriation for literature of the social and the historical may be celebrated as a blurring of the boundaries of conventional categories, but it also burdens literature with tasks that may undermine the autonomy of the individual writer; just as the conflation of the personal and the collective raises the question of the public (and, therefore, political) responsibility of the literary work in the representation of collective consciousness.

It may be argued that literature has been endowed all along with such responsibility in its association with the nation. Timothy Brennan writes that,

> It was the *novel* that historically accompanied the rise of nations by objectifying the "one, yet many" of national life, and by mimicking the structure of the nation, a clearly bordered jumble of languages and styles. Socially, the novel joined the newspaper as the major vehicle of the national print media, helping to standardize language, encourage literacy, and remove mutual incomprehensibility. But it did much more than that. Its manner of presentation allowed people to imagine the special community that was the nation.[7]

Brennan's reference in the last line is to Benedict Anderson, who pointed in his *Imagined Communities* to the correspondence between "the 'interior' time of the novel" and the "'exterior' time of the reader's everyday life," which "gives a hypnotic confirmation of the solidity of a single community, embracing characters, author and readers, moving onward through calendrical time."[8]

Where there is some assumption of cultural and linguistic homogeneity, as in the case of national culture, the individual work of literature may still claim a unique voice through or in opposition to the national culture. The situation is somewhat different in the case of minority and transnational literatures in a heterogeneous cultural and linguistic context—heterogeneous not only in the composition of the transnationalized national society, but in the constitution of the minority group itself. In such a context, the very affirmation of diversity burdens the unique creative voice with the additional task of social and cultural interpretation, of mediating not only between different spaces but different times. Within such a context "the characters, the author and readers" do not belong in the same spatiality or temporality, and "the interior time of the novel" does not confirm but challenges "the 'exterior' time of the reader's everyday life"—where the very language in which the novel is written, while it is seemingly the very same national language, nevertheless calls for translation because its idiom now includes the legacies of many other languages. More is at issue in this situation than the identity of literature. The issue, ultimately, is that of the status of the nation itself as political and cultural form. Whether this situation calls for the denial of the nation, as is fashionable these days, or its reconceptualization, is a question I will take up below by way of conclusion.

The burden of translation that transnationalization imposes upon the writer has been recognized by Asian-American writers and critics alike. One such critic, King-kok Cheung, writes that,

Like most artists of color, authors of Asian ancestry in the United States face a host of assumptions and expectations. Because their number is still relatively small, those who draw inspiration from their experiences as members of a minority are often seen as speaking for their ethnic groups. Because their work is frequently treated as ethnography by mainstream reviewers, many in the Asian American communities hold them accountable for an authentic "representation."[9]

The most dramatic illustration of Cheung's observation is the celebrated controversy occasioned by Maxine Hong Kingston's *Woman Warrior*, published in 1976, that remains alive after two decades. Submitted by the author as a work of fiction, the book was marketed by the publisher as autobiography—bringing the author no end of grief, and distracting from what is a powerful meditation on growing up as a Chinese-American woman in Stockton, California. The mere naming of the genre converted an imaginative piece of work into a "social document," raising fundamental questions about personal and collective memory, fiction and history, the relationship of Chinese Americans to their society of origin and even the nature of Chinese society itself. Kingston herself has queried, in total frustration, "Why must I 'represent' anyone besides myself? Why should I be denied an individual artistic vision?"[10] But as another critic, David Li, points out:

> Once *The Woman* Warrior is labeled as nonfiction, it is understood by convention to be a real narrative of real events. The consequence is actually twofold. On the one hand, it invites the audience to identify it as an account of real life. On the other hand, it dissuades the possibility of interpreting it as a symbolic act. Therefore, the generic definition can have the effect of depriving Asian American expression of its credibility as imaginative art and reducing it into some subliterary status, serving the role of social scientific data, an encompassing reflection of Asian American totality.[11]

Li's point is well taken, and many participants in the discussion of this work have pointed to the publisher's labeling of the book as a major factor in its "misreading," which to more uncompromising critics also appears as evidence of Kingston's complicity in the misrepresentation of her work. This is a serious problem that has not stopped with Kingston's work. Publishers in recent years have repeatedly classified fictional or semi-fictional works by Asians under "Asian Studies," thrown together in catalogues Asian and Asian-American writers, and placed writings on Asian America among "Asian peoples." How such labeling affects the reading of these works is not self-evident, but we must suppose that it plays some part in the reading, where the works are placed in bookstores and libraries, and how it may influence decisions in course adoption.

And yet it is worth pondering if the reading of *The Woman Warrior* by critics or readers would have been affected substantially, had it been labeled fiction. Amy Tan's works are marketed under fiction/literature, and yet that has not stopped readers from treating them as accounts of "Chinese" life and etiquette. She says in a 1999 essay that,"I am alarmed when reviewers and educators assume that my very personal, specific, and fictional stories are meant to be representative down to the nth detail not just of Chinese-Americans but, sometimes, of all Asian culture."[12]

Autobiography is a problematic genre. Li is correct to point out that, by convention, autobiography suggests real events and historicalness. After all, autobiography is personalized history, and is expected for that reason not only to tell us something about history but also to comply with historiographical rules of evidence. This is what we expect, at any rate, of autobiographies by public personages, as when a Henry Kissinger writes his memoirs.

But it would be misleading to place a work such as *The Woman Warrior* in the same category as public autobiography, because that is not what it strives to be; it does not take for granted a historical subjectivity that then acts to make history, but rather relates the construction of identity out of social and cultural fragments. That may be the reason why, as autobiography, it has lent itself to readings that find in it a narrative of Asian-American history and an ethnography of Chinese culture, but has been vulnerable also to accusations by Chinese-American critics of hijacking Chinese-American history and grossly distorting "the facts" of Chinese society.

It seems to me that autobiography, writing the self, can also include self-exploration the point of departure for which is not necessarily the outside, public worlds but the construction of the self's interiority; which may include stories, fantasies, perversions, and assorted deployments of the imagination which may not stand the empirical test of history or ethnography, but are no less the real, therefore, in the construction of the self. *The Woman Warrior* is evidently this kind of autobiography, one that explores the inner world and self-construction of a young Chinese-American woman as she sorts through fantasies, stories, and a variety of social and cultural encounters.

Viewed from this perspective, we may include among Kingston's questions cited above another, perhaps more fundamental, question: is the ethnic writer permitted to have an autonomous interiority, or is s/he condemned to represent the ethnic collectivity in the senses, in David Li's terms, both of "standing for" and "acting" or "speaking for."[13] Phrased differently, and less abstractly, what mode of expression best offers the greatest hope of escaping the ethnic prison-house? While the phrasing here foregrounds the personal and the subjective, I would like to underline its political implications, because the question presupposes the separation once again of the personal and the collective, the private and the public; in other words, a move away from identity politics toward a politics informed by public consciousness.[14]

It would be pretentious for me to try to answer this question, and somewhat contrary to my premises here, as so-called ethnic writers differ immensely from one another and must face the problem from different situational perspectives. On the other hand, it is somewhat easier to identify the circumstances and narrative strategies that reinforce identity politics, and facilitate appropriations of individual for collective consciousness, while obstructing the formulation of a publicly informed politics. Crucial in either case is the way culture comes into play in the articulation of identity.

Some of these circumstances are products of the racialization and culturalization of the ethnic writer in the dominant ideology of the larger society. In her study of the concept of representation, Pitkin tells us that in its earliest usages, representation conveyed the sense of embodiment, "as when a virtue seems embodied in the image of a certain face," or as "church leaders [were] seen as the embodiment and image of Christ and the Apostles."[15] This sense of representation has not quite disappeared. The racialized body, or any other marker of race or foreignness, such as names, is taken to authorize the writer (or anyone else for that matter) to stand or speak for the group of which s/he is allegedly a member by virtue of physical appearance or some other trait, regardless of how remote the connection of the author to the society of origin, or how complicated the composition of the group. In the case of a Chinese American such as Kingston or Tan, the writer is taken as the "embodiment" of an abstract "Chineseness" that defies historicity, in which Orientalist notions of a dehistoricized and desocialized Chinese culture are blended imperceptibly with supposedly racial traits, producing a notion of culture that is "almost biologized by its proximity to 'race.'"[16] The identification justifies the qualification of the author to speak for something called Chinese, but also the containment of what s/he has to say in an originary "Chineseness," where it is no longer clear whether ethnic identification is a cultural privilege or a cultural prison-house. This is also where an oppressive and hegemonic culturalism becomes barely distinguishable from a liberal and benign multiculturalism, which may valorize "Chineseness" differently, but is otherwise subject to the same conceptual protocols; most importantly in the abstraction of the idea of culture, and in the failure to define its boundaries.[17]

The racialization and culturalization of Chinese Americans is not new, but is in fact a legacy of Orientalism with a long history. On the other hand, it derives additional force from recent developments, which have created an ideological environment that favors ethnicization. The emergence of multiculturalism in response to ethnic self-assertion is itself one of these new developments. Equally important is the part multiculturalism plays in the commodification of culture and ethnicity. I have referred already to the marketing of books, and how that affects the labeling of literature. In recent decades, ethnicity and culture have become major concerns of marketers and corporate management. As one sociologist observes wryly, "in an age that celebrates diversity and multiculturalism, it has become almost a civic duty to have an ethnicity, as well as to appreciate that of others."[18]

Unlike in an earlier period of hegemonic Orientalism, in other words, ethnicity appears in contemporary United States society as a desirable trait, and ethnics themselves participate freely in the promotion and marketing of the cultures of their societies of origin. Contemporary migrations, moreover, nourish the re-ethnicization (or reaffirmation of cultural roots) of populations that only a few decades ago were concerned mostly to assert their places in United States society and history, which is especially pertinent in the case of Asian Americans whose increasing prominence was fueled by Pacific Rim discourse. At the broadest level, the ideology of globalization extends multiculturalism globally, reviving the reification of cultures as civilizations in an earlier modernization discourse, though with some ambiguity now over its consequences: clash of civilizations versus peaceful coexistence in mutual recognition of difference.[19]

My immediate concern here is with ethnic complicity in cultural reification. The reception of ethnic writing in the dominant culture, and the contribution to it of the ideological environment, are crucial questions, but they do not exhaust the problem. One of the most astute critics of Asian-American literature, Sau-ling Wong, has observed that there is a history in Asian-American literature of autobiography as guided tour of China and Chinatown, in which "the individual's life serves the function of conveying anthropological information."[20] The most prominent beneficiary of the contemporary valorization of ethnicity may be Amy Tan, whose writings have enjoyed phenomenal success, been placed among American classics, and invoked exuberant comparisons with the likes of Leo Tolstoy. Whatever merit Tan's writing may have, there is good evidence also that she has benefited immensely from the ethnic touch. In a brilliant analysis of Tan's novels, the same critic, Sau-ling Wong, writes with reference to Tan's deployment of "Chinese" details:

> Are the reviewers simply misguided when they laud Tan's "Convincing details"? Not at all. The details are there, but their nature and function are probably not what a "Common sense" view would make them out to be: evidence of referential accuracy, of the author's familiarity with the "real" China. Rather, they act as gestures to the "mainstream" readers that the author is familiar with the kind of culturally mediated discourse they have enjoyed, as well as qualified to give them what they expect. I call these details "markers of authenticity," whose function is to create an "Oriental effect" by signalling a reassuring affinity between the given work and American preconceptions of what the Orient is/should be.[21]

Wong observes shrewdly that anti-Orientalist gestures in Tan's writing do not undermine, but further contribute to the impression of her authenticity as cultural mediator. I referred above to Tan's own complaint about being placed in this role; which is less than convincing in light of what we must assume to be her compliance in the marketing of her works. Her name and the very "Chinese" cover of her latest book, *The Bonesetter's Daughter*, now grace the tins of "Mandarin Orange Spice Green Tea," complete with a recipe, marketed by The Republic of Tea in book-stores such as Borders, an honor never accorded the likes of Leo Tolstoy.

Chinese-American critics of the manipulation of literary work by publishers, reviewers, readers and tea-peddlers themselves are not immune to complicity in the reification of Chineseness. The criticism of *The Woman Warrior* for its representation of things Chinese, and *its* representation to the reading public as autobiography and, therefore, history, quickly spilled over into a discussion of "Chineseness"; what was or was not authentically Chinese, whether or not Chinese myths were immune to historical and social interpretation, and questions of masculinity and femininity in Chinese culture. The very invocation of "China" in a discussion of a work of Chinese-American literature was indicative of the erasure of the spatial and historical distance that separated Chinese Americans from the society of origin, rendering competing Chinese-American visions of China into alternative visions of a China without history—in the process reifying Chineseness at the risk not only of denying Chinese differences but also bracketing their own histories.[22]

The question of ethnic complicity in cultural reification may be a product ultimately of the language of writing and representation within its social and political situation. In a critical evaluation of *The Woman Warrior*, Amy Ling refers to "the dialogic dilemma" of Asian-American writers. As she puts it, "In applying Bakhtin to *The Woman Warrior*, one may read the entire text as an extended exploration of the internal dialogism of three words: *Chinese, American*, and *female*. Each term carries a multitude of meanings in dialogue, if not open warfare, with each other ... The entire book is devoted to an exploration of these words in an attempt at a self-definition that, finally, is never definitive in the sense of complete, conclusive, static."[23] Ling's analysis is perceptive and to the point, but in spite of its recognition of the overdetermined nature of the very terms of the dialogue, remains trapped in the limits set by those terms, possibly because of an unwillingness to look beyond a social situation in which a "Self-Other" confrontation sets the stage for cultural and political imagination. A question worth raising here is whether it is the culturally fragmented self that finds expression in the dialogue she analyzes, or whether it is the insistence on such a dialogue that fragments the self, making for the "dialogic dilemma" to which she refers. Ling's point of departure in the discussion is similar to the problem indicated in the statement by King-kok Cheung that I cited above: the predicament of Asian-American writers "writing of the cultural specificities of their own cultural back-grounds [who] are forced into the language of anthropological ethnography and thereby partake of the hierarchical binaries of Same and Other, Normal and Exotic, Advanced and Backward, Superior and Inferior"; in other words, the creative writer as "native informant." While the analysis that follows denies the "conclusive, complete and static," the role she assigns to the Asian-American writer and critic seems to be premised upon the static—as when she writes that the role "of all minority writers in this society, if we wish to be understood by a majority audience, cannot help but be that of cultural explainers until such time as everyone is informed of the myriad cultures that make up the United States. ... We have no choice, except of course, if we choose to speak only to others exactly like ourselves."[24] The "myriad cultures" apparently do not refer to myriad divisions within each sphere of cultural ethnicity, as her analysis of Kingston's work would suggest, but different ethnic cultures defined by a space of "others exactly like us." Hence, once again, the writer and critic appear as cultural interpreter or bridge, foregrounding in the very act of interpretation the intelligibility and, therefore, the internal coherence, if not homogeneity, of the culture to be interpreted. Ling underlines the importance of unequal power in creating this situation, which may hardly be doubted, but she ignores the equal importance of a social situation in which hybridity has become a valuable social asset as "it has become almost a civic duty to have an ethnicity." It is interesting that it is the language of the cultural rather than the social that stands out in her analysis, as it does in much critical analysis these days. Unlike "social," which stresses the here and now, "cultural" facilitates the connecting of the experience of the here and now with some originary point of departure somewhere, drawing attention away from the historically concrete unfolding of identity (its dialectics) to its entrapment in confrontations of abstract cultural belongings (its dialogics). The two versions speak to different historical circumstances with different social and political expectations. But they are not mutually exclusive, at least I do not think so. But closing the gap between them requires a different kind of language than has dominated cultural discussion in recent decades, a language that is more cognizant of the historicity of the cultural, which in turn is premised on a politics driven not by questions of cultural identity but questions of social and public responsibility.

A transnational perspective on the identity of Chinese-American literature may help elucidate the problem I have in mind here. In a fascinating examination of the reception of Kingston's work in China, the Hong Kong literary critic K.C. Lo has analyzed efforts in Taiwan and the People's Republic of China to appropriate Kingston for a Chinese national cultural sphere.[25] Lo writes that

> the claim of cultural particularity is not only confined to the writing of national
> literature but also closely associated with the translation of other literatures into

its cultural code. The recent scholarship and translation of Chinese American and Chinese diaspora literatures in Mainland China and Taiwan always highlight the appeal to the cultural origin or cultural commonality of these "Chinese" literary works written in English. The affirmation of cultural nationalism in the translation constitutes a means of reinventing the Chinese nation and the unified Chinese self in the changing environment of the twentieth century. If [a] Western reader of Chinese literature in English is more interested in politics than in literary work itself, the Chinese translations of Chinese American novels are also prone to stressing more their cultural and ethnic identification than their artistic achievement or creativity. ... While asserting the continuity of Chinese cultural tradition in a transnational setting and prolonging the myth of national unity, the Chinese translations of the Chinese American fictions could contain and diffuse the cultural hybridity and heterogeneity of the "homeless" Chinese immigrants and their descendants. Cultural distinctiveness and difference found in Chinese American literature could be neutralized, or even erased in translation.[26]

In light of charges brought against her by Chinese-American critics of distorting Chinese culture and history, it must have been heartening for Kingston to read in the introduction to the Mainland translation of *China Men* that "this work of Kingston has dealt with the suffering of Chinese immigrants in America relatively well. If it can be called a fiction, I would prefer to call it a history of Chinese written in blood and tears."[27] While these same critics alleged, moreover, that the autobiographical form of *The Woman Warrior* placed her in the tradition of Euro American missionary writing on China, she was more than pleasantly surprised by being placed by Mainland writers in a Chinese canon. As she put it in her interview after her first visit to China in 1984,

> A poet told me that I was the only Chinese that was writing in the tradition of the *Dream of Red Chamber* because here is Wittman [the protagonist of her then new work, *Tripmaster Monkey*] as the effete, young man battling to keep his manhood among the matriarchy, the twelve women of that book. And, in part of the conference, they were telling us that there was a "roots" literature movement in China—because during the Cultural Revolution they cut off the roots. So they had cut off their ties to the West, and cut off the bindings of feudalism, the imperial arts and all that. But then they weren't left with anything. ... And I spent this lifetime working on roots. So what they were saying was that I was their continuity. ... But, God, I felt so terrific. Because they were telling me that I was part of a Chinese canon. And here I was writing in English."[28]

It is a statement of redemption, as with those Chinese Over-seas who go to China to awaken all of a sudden to their slumbering Chineseness. It appears from what Kingston was told by Chinese writers that the Chinese literary canon, having lost its connection to its past at home, took a detour through California to discover its continuity through a Chinese-American writer. Here is literature deterritorialized in order to establish cultural continuity of sorts, but at the price of the abstraction of culture from place and time. What is also interesting is that Kingston ignores the antifeminist implications of the reference to the *Dream of the Red Chamber* and finds invigorating her identification as quintessentially "Chinese," which within a United States context constitutes a "mis-reading of her book."

What is equally interesting, where the identity of literature is concerned, is the reinterpretation of the form and content of literature in order to sustain a sense of national cultural belonging. A pioneer translator of Chinese American works into Chinese (and a long time professor of Chinese in the United States who has relocated to Hong Kong) writes that

> Although Chinese American literature is written in English, its content is—no matter it is positive or negative—a resonance of Chinese memory since its writers are Chinese descendants. Therefore I see it as part of my research field … What determines the "nationality" of literature is not its language, but its content … So I consider Chinese American literature a branch of Chinese literature.[29]

Lau's statement is reminiscent of Salman Rushdie's argument that Indian literature is as Indian as Indian literature in any other Indian languages.[30] But the two cases are different. Whether it is a legacy of colonialism or not, English in India has a long history, and within the boundaries of the nation. In the case of China, English is the language of Chinese with their own histories outside of China and requires translation back into Chinese. Here the claiming of English language literature for Chineseness requires a different kind of rupture in the national narrative—where not a continuing legacy, but "descent" provides the recuperation as Chinese of memories written elsewhere—foregrounding once again a cultural unity that can be sustained by racializing Chineseness in the language of nation and culture.

Language and history, in other words, no longer serve as markers of the identity of literature, as they did in the case of national literatures. Migrants writing in the language of the place of arrival need to be translated so that their works may be comprehended both in the place of departure and the place of arrival. In the former case the translation is literal, from one language into another. But translation is necessary even within the same language. An interesting illustration of this is to be found in the case of Emine Sevgi Ozdamar, a German writer of Anatolian origin. Ozdamar writes in German, and the "Germanness" of her writing has been recognized in the literary prizes that she has been awarded. On the other hand, her German is so loaded with Turkish idiom and references to the Turkish past that it requires translation to make it comprehensible to the German reader.[31] In a case such as this one, language does not serve as a marker of belonging either in the place of departure or the place of arrival, but becomes an object of investigation itself.

This may be a problem for all ethnic or diasporic literature. Transnationalization has created a new kind of literature that is not easily identifiable in earlier terms of national literature. On the other hand, transnationality is itself haunted by its origins in nations, and transnational literature faces the predicament of serving as the site for a new politics of literature. National claims on literature have not disappeared, but now take the form of the racialization and culturalization of the writer in both the society of departure and the society of arrival. Ironically, the very diversity and contradictoriness of such claims (what constitutes an authentic national or cultural identity) may be taken as evidence of the vacuity of such claims. As David Li has observed, the literary works of writers such as Frank Chin and Maxine Hong Kingston, taken as articulations of Chineseness, represent instead different ways of constructing Chineseness and, therefore, point to differences among the populations so-named.[32] As Lo puts it

> The dialectic of control and resistance occurs in the translation of Kingston's stories. If dialectic is understood as the grasping of the opposites in a whole-ness, then the Chineseness asserted in the translation of Chinese American literature can only actualize itself by alienating itself, and restore its self-unity by recognizing this differentiation as nothing other than its own manifestation. The only possible way to weave or re-weave the Chinese cultural tapestry in the transnational era, I believe, is to recognize the multiple differences in its culture's worldwide peregrination.[33]

And the only way to such a recognition, I would like to add, is to remind ourselves constantly of the constructedness of ethnicity and culture, which also makes them available for articulation to new circumstances. A basic premise of critical cultural studies is that the recognition of difference is crucial to the transformation of politics (and the public sphere). This transformation also requires a recognition of the historicity of cultural legacies so as to allow creative responses to new historical circumstances.[34] This seems to be forgotten easily in language that reifies both culture and ethnicity, possibly because of their entanglement in political struggles, where the recognition of the historicity of ethnicity or culture runs up against the requirements of some kind of ethnic and cultural unity in the struggle against hegemony.

There are good reasons for cultural self-assertion in this struggle, but a distinction needs to be drawn nevertheless between culture as a prison-house of origins, and culture as a living expression of populations engaged in the transformation of the public sphere. If they are not to issue in renewed essentialisms, political demands on culture need to be accompanied by a recognition that terms such as Asian American, Chinese American or whatever, however important politically, are ultimately devoid of substantial cultural meaning and do not stand the test of empirical historical reality—except the transformative politics they enable. They also confound social, political and cultural differences, as well as differences of temporality, displacing it all to a realm of culture in which national or civilizational boundaries are supreme. The recognition of Chinese differences necessitates a recognition not just of differ-ences between Chinese in China and Chinese Overseas, but place-based differences within China and the United States. Why, for example, do we speak of Chinese Americans instead of Cantonese Stocktonites or Beijing New Yorkers? Or, to take it to an even more basic level, why not Taishanese-Tucsonese (referring to a friend of mine)? Why is the Taishan Guangzhou, Macao or Hong Kong passage any less significant, in cultural terms, than the passage to the United States, since it entails bridging the gap between the countryside and the city, which also includes over-coming language differences? And what happened to a Chinese who moved upon arrival from San Francisco to Salt Lake City? The point here is that cultural crossings entail many boundary crossings; and yet our language of analysis revolves mostly around national (Chinese-American) or civilizational (Chinese-Western) boundaries.

The term "Chinese" is itself very complicated, as the last statement implies, as it encompasses references to territory, nation, culture, and race, which are often thrown together without further analysis.

The differences are temporal as well. In what sense is a Chinese who migrated to the United States in the nineteenth century (when both societies were still in the process of national formation) the same as a Chinese who migrates to the United States in our day? The Chinese who arrived in the United States in the nineteenth century were subjects of the Manchu Qing Dynasty, which was subsequently repudiated by the rise of nationalism around the turn of the twentieth century, which was to change and complicate the political/cultural identity of the population. The Chinese who arrived in the United States from the 1920s to the 1950s (admittedly few, because of exclusion laws) were products of a revolutionary situation. Contemporary Chinese immigrants are from a variety of Chinese societies around the world, which are products of a century of war, colonialism, migration, and revolution—not to speak of newfound success in the capitalist world economy. They also land in a society that has come a long way from a century ago, culturally and ideologically, which in its self-conception encompasses the entire globe in its sovereignty. The immediate reference for "assimilation" (which is no longer expected, at least officially) in this new society may be not American culture in general, which has become increasingly problematic, but Chinese America. These migrants also follow diverse trajectories; with some hapless Chinese immigrants, "the illegals," having to take worldwide detours to make it to the United States, only to find the gates shut, while others find themselves welcomed enthusiastically because of the talents and capital they bring with them.

The list could go on. The point here is to underline the importance of historicity in the sense both of time and place in the deployment of such terms as ethnicity, diaspora and culture, and descriptive vocabulary such as Chinese or Asian American. An individual creative writer is free to choose the terms of his or her own exploration of being Chinese American, but the terms chosen have important historical and political implications nevertheless.

Two implications of these observations need to be drawn out. The first concerns the question of the nation. It has become fashionable in recent years to declare the end of the nation as a political or cultural entity, which is informed more often than not by economic transnationalization and its social consequences, which seem to be most readily apparent in motions of peoples across national boundaries. These motions have confounded not only national boundaries, the argument goes, but have also facilitated flows between intranational ethnicities and "global ethnoscapes."[35] A more nuanced version of this argument has been proposed by Basch, Glick-Schiller and Szanton-Blanc, who, while recognizing the continued power of the nation, have observed the emergence of new transnational social formations which they name "transnations," which have an existence of their own but also serve as sites of struggle between nations which seek to appropriate their "transnationality" to further national ends.[36]

What is problematic about all such arguments is not the phenomenon of transnationalism, but the assumption that crucial to transnationalism is "deterritorialization," which renders transnationalism into an off-ground concept, undermining any concrete explanatory power it may have to offer. The term "transnationalism" itself derives its meaning from the continued existence of nations, which is built into its semic struc-ture. The notion of "deterritorialization" ignores that even transnationals live in places (though they may move from one place to another); and that what they understand by transnationality (if they, in contrast to scholars, indeed understand their situation as such) or their cultural self-identification may be impossible to grasp without reference to the particular places they inhabit and the particular trajectories of "transnationality." What is in question here is the reification of "transnationalism" (or kindred concepts such as "diaspora") which glosses over the many place-based cultural formations that accompany transnationalization. Transnations, nations, places may all have their histories of which we need to be aware, but these are not histories that exist separately from one another; they are intertwined and intersect in concrete locations. The point is to understand what is at work in these locations and their implications not just culturally, but more significant, politically.

One common way to overcome political challenges presented by conjunctures of the transnational, the national, and the place-based is to displace the challenge to the realm of culture. Ironically, even as transnationality serves to question the viability of the national, a seemingly ingrained habit of cultural and political thinking easily leads back to the national (or, in some cases, civilizational) culture of origin as the ultimate identifying feature of the transnational or diasporic formation; which perpetuates an ahistorical culturalism, rendering the transnational or diasporic population into extensions of nations of departure, and aliens in nations of arrival. Their stories are then told as private stories of diaspora-family narratives—rather than as stories of public struggles that seek not so much to challenge the existence of the nation as to redefine its culture and politics. A transformative cultural politics is in the process rendered into privatized accounts of cultural nostalgia and lack, or a cultural "insider-ism," which qualifies the population in question for service as "bridges" between cultures, in which the issue more often than not is not culture *per se* but deployments of culture for political and economic ends. No wonder that efforts at ethnic recognition and identity with public goals have become indistin-guishable from, or even swallowed by, neoliberal versions of globalization and trans-nationalism. It may not be very surprising that the marketing of ethnicity and culture, and the valorizations of diasporas, have coincided with the intensification of practices and ideologies of globalization from the 1980s—not just in the United States but elsewhere, as in the People's Republic of China, where re-opening or incorporation into the global economy also endowed Chinese Overseas with a new significance as "cultural capital." Public struggles over the meaning of ethnicity and culture, or to create a new political culture, are by no means dead, but they have to contend with a new context which offers alluring ideological temptations to deter-ritorialization in the valorization of cultural roots that defy history, and rewards for cultural hybridity that enable the "bridging" of distances between cultures conceived once again in ahistorical (and reductionist) differences. The latter, need-less to say, makes difficult a conception of culture as ongoing activity, the goal of which is to reaffirm public sociability in concrete contexts. What it offers instead is culture as an object of consumption, where the rewarding of private memory serves to conceal the alienation of the cultural from the political.

The second implication concerns the issue of translation, where the difficulties of translation in literature to which I referred above are metonymic of a broader cultural problem. Translation most immediately invokes the foreignness of the languages it mediates, and this is the meaning attached to it in much of the discussion I have outlined. This says less about the literary works in question than about the political and cultural context of their production; once again a legacy of habits of thinking about literature as an expression or producer of national culture conceived in fantasies of homogeneity.[37] It is this habit that informs the alienation and exoticization of "ethnic" literature such as the Chinese American, which is echoed in the "ethnic" writer's readiness to assume the role of bridge or interpreter between cultures; to assume the role, as in some of the instances cited above, as a "representative" of Chinese culture for non-Chinese readers. This is also what makes possible the reading of this literature as "ethnography" of the alien other.

This is, of course, not the only possible understanding of translation. A conception of the nation that allows for diversity of histories (*not* cultures) in the making of the nation allows for other possibilities as well. It is only to recognize an empirical truism to state that a work by a Kingston or a Chin is a work about growing up in Stockton or the San Francisco Bay Area, produced by a writer writing in those locations in various inflections of the languages of those same locations. If China enters the picture, it is a China invented in the process of imagining the trajectories that brought those writers to the very act of writing. If translation is necessary to make their experiences intelligible to non-Chinese-American readers, that translation is not a translation of one foreign language or culture into another, but a translation between languages and cultural experiences that are products of the same locality and their broader national environment. And if there is ethnography at work, it is an ethnography not of China or Chineseness, but of locations in California with its diverse populations; an ethnography, in other words, of American society as it appears in those locations. How this literature gets to be exoticized as a consequence of hegemonic cultural relations within United States society does not need much comment. A German writer of Anatolian origin queries poignantly, "Germany long ago became part of us German Turks. Now a question is being posed that we cannot answer alone. Are we also a part of Germany?"[38] It is a question that has greater poignancy in a society that prides itself on its diversity, and prides itself on its cultural openness, that sees in such works an ethnography not of itself but of some society across the ocean, and, in the process, consigns the "ethnic" writer to the realm of private memory while retaining firmly in its grasp claims to public culture.

What may require a more urgent explanation at the present juncture is the apparent willingness of "ethnic" writers to embrace this role assigned to them. There are complicated reasons, some of which I have referred to above. Here I would like to underline one of those reasons that has been a basic concern in the discussion: the reification of ethnic cultures in neoliberal multiculturalism, which is part of a global reification of cultures (that makes it possible to view Kingston as a quintessentially Chinese writer). One of the challenges to cultural understanding presently, not just in the United States but globally, is the difficulty of distinguishing benign efforts to reaffirm cultural autonomy and preserve cultural difference from the economic and political manipulations of culture both from within and without the cultures so named. Recognition of difference in intention, unfortunately, does not make it any easier to distinguish the various uses of culture in practice; especially as these various efforts seem to share a basic tendency to identify culture with social, political and even fictive entities such as ethnicities, nations and civilizations, which facilitate the identification of boundaries to cultures, but at the very high cost of erasing their historicity in both a spatial and a temporal sense. Equally important in either case is the displacement of political questions to the realm of culture, that is entangled in a widespread uncertainty over the meaning of the public sphere.

Within the United States, these terms that define boundaries of difference are the legacies of the struggles of the 1960s that brought Chinese Americans, as well as other groups, into cultural and political recognition in the United States. A term such as "Asian American" first appeared not as a term of cultural but of political identity. As far as we know, the term was coined by the distinguished Japanese-American historian Yuji Ichioka in the heat of political struggles in Berkeley/Oakland sometime in 1968. It is not that cultural identity was not important for those such as Ichioka, but that cultural identity was not conceived to be detachable from politics. And the goal of politics was transformative; transformative both of the constitution of the public in the United States, and of public consciousness, including the consciousness of those who were encompassed by the term "Asian American."[39] History was deemed essential to this goal, as is evident from the titles of a bibliography of Japanese-American history by Ichioka ("A Buried Past") and a comparable one by Him Mark Lai ("A History Reclaimed").[40]

The privatization of history in literature enriches our understanding of the diversity of historical experiences of Asian Americans, or any other group for that matter. The substitution of the private for the public is another matter, because it runs the risk of substituting for a socially and historically informed idea of culture one that is deterritorialized and abstract, which may make it more manipulable in the expression and exploration of identity, but it is then also more amenable for the same reason to appropriation for culturalist practices of one kind or another beyond the intentions of the author. This is quite evident in the painful recognition by ethnic writers of the treatment of their work as ethnography that erases individual and social complexity.

In a situation of transnationalism, we might note, conceptualization of ethnic groups in terms not of their social standing and social differences, but in terms of some imaginary cultural unity, is also the first step to their reappropriation into reified cultural claims of nations and civilizations. The term "transnational" itself is not without problems. If it captures the contradictions created by the coexistence of globalizing tendencies with continued claims to national and civilizational cultural homogeneity, it also conceals the importance of viewing contemporary social, political, cultural and even economic processes translocally—which is crucial to deconstructing the claims of abstract cultural entities with the concrete practices of everyday life. This may be the key not only to "rescuing history from the nation," as the title of a recent study goes, but perhaps more importantly to rescuing the nation from history.[41] History has served to bolster the claims of the nation-state, as literary critics argue, but the converse is also true. Nations, having created imaginary histories in their legitimation, also find themselves trapped by their own creation, unable to conceive of themselves in ways other than what that history will permit. If literature may be of help in rescuing the nation from history, history in turn may be indispensable in guarding against the entrapment of literature in culture.

Notes

1   "Russell Leong," Interview by Robert B. Ito, in King-kok Cheung (ed), *Words Matter: Conversations with Asian American Writers* (Honolulu: University of Hawai'i Press, 2000), pp. 233–250, p. 237.

2   "Karen Tei Yamashita," Interview by Michael S. Murashige, in Cheung, pp. 320–342, p. 336.

3   "Wendy Law-Yone," Interview by Nancy Yoo and Tamara Ho, in Cheung, pp. 283–302, pp. 301–302.

4   Azade Seyhan, *Writing Outside the Nation* (Princeton and Oxford: Princeton University Press, 2001), p. 7.

5   Hayden White, "Narrative in Contemporary Historical Theory," in Hayden White, *The Content of the Form: Narrative Discourse and Historical Representation* (Baltimore and London: The Johns Hopkins University Press, 1987), pp. 26–57, pp. 29–30.

6   Seyhan, *Writing Outside the Nation*, p. 12.

7   Timothy Brennan, "The National Longing for Form," in Homi Bhabha, *Nation and Narration* (London and New York: Routledge, 1990), pp. 44–70, p. 49.

8   Benedict Anderson, *Imagined Communities: Reflections on the Origins and Spread of Nationalism* (London and New York: Verso, 1995), p. 27.

9   Cheung, "Introduction," *Words Matter*, pp. 1–17, pp. 1–2.

10 Maxine Hong Kingston, "Cultural Mis-readings by American Reviewers," in Laura E. Skandera-Trombley (ed), *Critical Essays on Maxine Hong Kingston* (New York: G.K. Hall & Co., 1998), pp. 95–103, p. 101.

11 David Leiwei Li, "Re-presenting *The Woman Warrior*: An Essay of Interpretive History," in Skandera-Trombley, *Critical Essays on Maxine Hong Kingston*, pp. 182–203, pp. 189–190.

12 Amy Tan, "Why I write," *Literary Cavalcade* 51.6 (March 1999) :10–13, p. 11.

13 Li, p. 190.

14 An important, if highly personalized, account of the implication of ethnic cultural belonging in the confrontation between the public and the private is offered in an autobiography by Richard Rodriguez, *Hunger of Memory: The Education of Richard Rodriguez* (New York: Bantam Books, 1982), especially in chapter 1. Rodriguez's identification of ethnic cultural belonging with the private and assimilation with the public is too clear-cut and mechanical and overlooks the part played by ethnic cultural self-assertion in the dialectics of the public sphere. On the other hand, his stress from the late seventies on the ways in which ethnicity/race were coming to overshadow all other modes of identity, and ethnic/racial inequality all other inequalities, pointed to a fundamental question which, if anything, has retreated even further in cultural discussion since then with the diffusion of neoliberal assumptions and ethnicization of politics even among many self-styled radicals. Not surprisingly, Rodriguez also questions the category of an "ethnic literature" (p. 7).

15 Hannah F. Pitkin, *The Concept of Representation* (Berkeley: University of California Press, 1967), "appendix on etymology," pp. 242–252, pp. 242–243.

16 Paul Gilroy, "'The Whisper Wakes, the Shudder Plays' : Race, Nation and Ethnic Absolutism," in Padmini Mongia (ed), *Contemporary Postcolonial Theory: A Reader*, (London: Arnold, 1996), pp. 248–274, p. 263.

17 For three important, and personalized, discussions of "Chineseness," see Ien Ang, "On Not Speaking Chinese: Postmodern Ethnicity and the Politics of Diaspora," *New Formations*, No. 24 (Winter 1994: 1–18; Ien "Can One Say No to Chineseness? Pushing the Limits of the Diasporic Paradigm," *boundary 2*, 25.3 (Fall 1998): 223–242; Rey Chow, "Introduction: On Chineseness as a Theoretical Problem," *boundary 2*, 25.1 (Fall 1998 :1–24. For a more light-hearted discussion, see, Selina Li Duke, "Representing China," *Quadrant*, 42.6 (June 1998): 62–66.

18 Robert Wood, cited in Marilyn Halter, *Shopping for Identity: The Marketing of Ethnicity* (New York: Schocken Books, 2000), p. 9.

19 For further discussion of these problems, see Arif Dirlik, "Modernity as History," *Social History* (in press), and Arif Dirlik, "Markets, Culture, Power: The Making of a 'Second Cultural Revolution' in China," *Asian Studies Review*, 25.1 (March 2001): 1–33.

20 Sau-ling Cynthia Wong, "Autobiography as Guided Chinatown Tour? Maxine Hong Kingston's *Woman Warrior* and the Chinese-American Autobiographical Controversy," in Skandera-Trombley, *Critical Essays on Maxine Hong Kingston*, pp. 146–167, pp. 156–157.

21 Sau-ling Cynthia Wong, "'Sugar Sisterhood': Situating the Amy Tan Phenomenon," in David Palumbo-Liu (ed), The *Ethnic Canon: Histories, Institutions, and Interventions* (Minneapolis, MN: University of Minnesota Press, 1995), pp. 174–210, p.187.

22 Kingston's critics are many (and they are not all male) but among them, Frank China has been the most persistent. For his comprehensive criticism of Chinese-American writers, including Kingston and Tan, see, "Come all Ye Asian American Writers of the Real and the Fake," in Jeffrey Paul Chan, Frank China, Lawson Fusao Inada, and Shawn Wong, *The Big AIIIEEEEE!* (New York: Meridian Books, 1991), pp. 1–91.

23 Amy Ling, "Maxine Hong Kingston and the Dialogic Dilemma of Asian American Writers," in Skandera-Trombley, *Critical Essays on Maxine Hong Kingston*, pp. 168–181, p. 172.

24 Ibid, pp. 168–169.

25 Kwai-Cheung Lo, "Reaffirming 'Chineseness' in the Translation of Asian American Literature: Maxine Hong Kingston's Fictions in Taiwan and Mainland China," *Translation Quarterly*, Nos. 18 & 19(2000): 74–98.

26 Ibid., p. 78–79.

27 Ibid., p. 87.

28 Marilyn Chin, "Writing the Other: An Interview with Maxine Hong Kingston," in Paul Skenazy and Tera Martin Jackson (eds), *Conversations with Maxine Hong Kingston* (Jackson, MI: University Press of Mississippi, 1998). Quoted in Lo, p. 82.

29 Joseph Lau, quoted in Lo, p. 81.

30 Salman Rushdie, "Damme, This is the Oriental Scene for You!" *The New Yorker*, June 23 & 30 (1997): 53–61.

31 See her *Life Is a Caravanserai—Has Two Doors—I Came in One—I Went Out the Other*, tr. by Louise Von Flotow (London, England: Middlesex University Press, 2000). Ozdamar's Turkish idiom has been captured successfully by the translator in the English translation as well. For a perceptive analysis of Ozdamar's work, see Seyhan, *Writing Outside the Nation*, chapters 4 and 5.

32 David Leiwei Li, "The Production of Chinese American Tradition: Displacing American Orientalist Discourse," in Shirley Geok-lin and Amy Ling (eds), *Reading the Literatures of Asian America* (Philadelphia: Temple University Press, 1992), pp. 319–331.

33 Lo, pp. 92–93.

34 Cultural studies, in other words, are significant not for allowing celebrations of cultural difference but for recognizing an autonomous part to cultural activity in political transformation. SeeLawrence Grossberg, "Identity and Cultural Studies: Is That All There Is?" in Stuart Hall and Paul Du Gay (eds), *Questions of Cultural Identity* (Thousand Oaks, CA: Sage Publications, 1997), pp. 87–107. See, also, the collection of essays in Henry Giroux, *Impure Acts: The Practical Politics of Cultural Studies* (New York: Routledge, 2000).

35 Arjun Appadurai has been the most articulate proponent of this notion of transnationalization. See the essays in his *Modernity at Large: Cultural Dimensions of Globalization* (Minneapolis, MN: University of Minnesota Press, 1996), especially, "Global Ethnoscapes: Notes and Queries for Transnational Anthropology," pp. 48–65.

36 Linda Basch, Nina Glick Schiller and Christina Szanton Blanc, *Nations Unbound: Transnational Projects, Postcolonial Predicaments, and Deterritorialised Nation-States* (New York: Gordon and Breach, 1994).

37 For a discussion challenging the identification of literature with national culture, see, Simon During, "Literature— Nationalism's Other? The Case for Revision," in Homi Bhabha, *Nation and Narration*, pp. 138–154.

38 Zafer Senocak, "War and Peace in Modernity: Reflections on the German-Turkish Future" (tr. by Martin Chalmers and Leslie A. Adelson), in Senocak, *Atlas of a Tropical Germany: Essays on Politics and Culture, 1990–1998*, tr. and ed. By Leslie A. Adelson (Lincoln, NE: University of Nebraska Press), pp. 83–98, p. 98.

39 Yuji Ichioka's recollections are available in his "A Historian by Happenstance," *Amerasia* 26.1 (2000): 33–53. For comparable recollections of Chinese American struggles, see Him Mark Lai, "Musings of a Chinese American Historian," in the same issue, pp. 2–30.

40 Yuji Ichioka, et al., *A Buried Past: An Annotated Bibliography of the Japanese American Research Project* (Berkeley and Los Angeles: University of California Press, 1974), and the sequel, Yuji Ichioka and Eiichiro Azuma, *A Buried Past II: A Sequel to the Annotated Bibliography of the Japanese American Research Project Collection* (Los Angeles: UCLA Asian American Studies Center, 1999); Him Mark Lai, *A History Reclaimed: An Annotated Bibliography of Chinese Language Materials on the Chinese of America* (Los Angeles: Asian American Studies Center, 1986).

41 Prasenjit Duara, *Rescuing History from the Nation: Questioning Narratives of Modern China* (Chicago: The University of Chicago Press, 1995).

26   The Limits of Cultural Hybridity
On Ritual Monsters, Poetic Licence and Contested Postcolonial Purifications

Pnina Werbner

We are by now all too familiar with critiques of 'colonial anthropology', from Asad's (1973) early deconstructivist exposure of British anthropology's apparent collusion with the colonial project, to the denunciation by the authors of *Writing culture* of modernist anthropology's false claims to ethnographic authority (Clifford 1988; Clifford & Marcus 1986; Marcus & Fischer 1988).[1] The most recent assault has come from postcolonial studies; as in the quotation above, colonial anthropologists, among others (Bhabha lists Montesquieu, Barthes, Kristeva, Derrida, and Lyotard), are accused of denying oppositional agency to the 'other', the power to signify, negate, and initiate historic desire. Yet while these critiques urge us to recognize the historicity of culture, they appear to construct their own historical narrative through an act of amnesia, an erasure from memory and history of a particular strand of British social anthropology that moved away from descriptions of enclosed cultures to an open and explicit focus, from 1940 onwards, on colonial administration, race relations, urbanization, labour migration, 'tribalism', political ethnicity, and social movements. Dominant in this trend were anthropologists associated with the Rhodes-Livingstone Institute in Central Africa (on 'the Manchester School', as it came to be known, see Hannerz 1980; R. Werbner 1990).

The erasure is significant. However, here I want to go beyond that act of forgetfulness in order to argue that the infinitesimal details of a local culture with its seemingly arcane rituals and mythologies, as studied by key modernist anthropologists, were also ways of reflecting upon oppositional agency, transgression, and cultural reflexivity. Far from denying the very possibility of critical consciousness, modernist anthropology afforded insight into how, in apparently closed societies, ritual performances and myths enacted ambivalences of power and paradoxes of sociality.

Pnina Werbner, "The Limits of Cultural Hybridity: On Ritual Monsters, Poetic Licence and Contested Postcolonial Purifications." *Journal of the Royal Anthropological Institute*, 7(1), 2001: 133–152. Reprinted by permission of John Wiley & Sons Ltd.

Cultural hybridity, liminality, and transgression, key tropes animating my argument, have dominated recent writings in cultural and postcolonial studies. In many senses this has revitalized the focus on topics of enduring interest to anthropology and illuminated them in news ways. As in some of my earlier work (e.g. P. Werbner 1997a), I attempt here to recover these metaphors for anthropology. One key criticism often levelled against the notion of cultural hybridity is that it assumes the prior existence of whole cultures, a vision of culture much discredited in contemporary anthropology. Against that I pose the possibility that cultures may be grasped as porous, constantly changing and borrowing, while nevertheless being able to retain at any particular historical moment the capacity to shock through deliberate conflations and subversions of sanctified orderings. My argument rests on a key distinction made by Bakhtin between 'organic' and 'intentional' hybridity. To illustrate this distinction, let me turn first to a ceremony in 1938, the opening of a bridge in modern Zululand, as it was described by Gluckman (1958 [1940]).

In his fine-grained description, Gluckman (1958: 11) reveals that the ceremony was a cultural mishmash. It was organized by the Chief Native Commissioner (CNC), who added exotic touches to a basically technocrat-modernist European ceremony. The key moment of the ceremony was the cutting, by the CNC's car, of a tape stretched across the bridge. The car was preceded by Zulu warriors singing the *ihubo*. Most of the important Zulu were dressed in European riding clothes, while the Zulu king wore a lounge suit (1958: 5). The guard at the bridge was dressed in full Zulu war regalia, while most of the other Zulu men who were pagans were dressed in 'motley combinations of European and Zulu dress' (1958: 5). There were royal Zulu salutes and blessings and European hand-clapping and hymns, speeches in a mixture of languages, English and Zulu, and, after the ceremony was over, the whites retired to drink tea, the Zulus to drink traditional beer and eat the sacrificial meat, one beast being donated by the CNC to the people, the other three by the people to their king. The CNC was sent traditional beer across the bridge, the king a cup of tea in the opposite direction. A group of Christians from a Zionist separatist sect, dressed in European clothes, sang Christian hymns from the river bank. Some of these acts were clearly spontaneous and unplanned. Gluckman describes in detail the intricate spatial mixings and separations of whites and blacks before going on to discuss their broader sociological significance for an understanding of power and race relations in South Africa in 1938.

Several key issues concern us here, emanating from Gluckman's (1958: 25) point that the event was a harmonious one, with structural conflicts between black and white kept in abeyance. There was a shared interest in the bridge that cut across the dominant cleavage of black and white. The project was successfully initiated by the CNC and built by Zulu men with voluntary labour to provide access to a local maternity hospital during the rainy season. The bridge was generally felt to be a good thing. The common celebration was a moment of 'co-operation and communication' and, even though interdependency was founded in the final analysis on the 'superior force of the White group', participants formed 'a single community of two co-operating' groups (1958: 25). Invoking Fortes, Gluckman proposes, against 'culture-contact' theorists, that in studying social change the anthropologist 'must work with communities rather than customs ... [with] a unit of life ... of common participation in the everyday political, economic and social life' (1958: 51). Such conflictual communities form a single, organized culture, he argues, rather than a social aggregation of heterogeneous cultural groups, as Malinowski would have it. Importantly, then, for Gluckman, as indeed for Fortes and Schapera, social relations, even those marked by hierarchy and domination, nevertheless are constitutive of culture: not as a unified, homogeneous set of beliefs, but as a fragmentary, contradictory, and conflict-ridden social formation.

Analysing the opening of the bridge from this perspective allows us to grasp the *naturalness* of the events making up the ceremony for participants, despite its apparently incongruous juxtaposition of disparate cultural elements and customs. The whites took it for granted that they should be drinking tea on the banks of the Black Umfolosi River, just as the blacks took for granted the vehicular cutting of the tape and the sacrificial beast offered them by the CNC. This naturalness of what Hobsbawm and Ranger (1963) have aptly called an 'invented tradition' is one that Bakhtin (1981: 358) refers to as 'organic hybridity': 'unintentional, unconscious hybridization is one of the most important modes in the historical life and evolution of languages. We may even say that language and languages change historically primarily by means of hybridization, by means of mixing of various "languages".' In such situations of mixing, Bakhtin (1981: 360) goes on to say, 'the mixture remains mute and opaque, never making use of conscious contrasts and oppositions ... [Yet] such unconscious hybrids have been at the same time profoundly productive historically: they are pregnant with potential for new world views, with new "internal forms" for perceiving the world.'

In his analysis, Gluckman (1958: 61) recognizes that as conflicts between black and white sharpened, new configurations of existing cultures tended to surface as means of social and political mobilization which stressed cultural difference, an argument that later came to be known through the work of Cohen (1969) as 'political ethnicity'. Yet, as I argue below, such social movements, even when they announce their cultural purity and sharp distinction, are necessarily hybrid culturally, since they arise from within the new social and cultural configurations of the historically transformed, organically hybridized community.

The harmony of the ceremony was necessarily an ambivalent one, given the pervasive inequalities and separations between white and black. This ambivalence, the unstable meanings, the *hybridity* of the bridge ceremony, did not simply derive from the fusing of disparate cultural elements, each bearing its own fixed cultural meaning. As Bhabha (1994: 119) insightfully recognizes, hybridity may be produced by a 'doubling up of the sign', a 'splitting' which is 'less than one and double'. The same object or custom placed in a different context acquires quite new meanings, while echoing old ones. The Zulu warrior standing guard as policeman at the bridge is not a Zulu warrior. Drinking tea in the middle of the veld is quite unlike tea in Surrey on a Sunday afternoon. In this sense, hybridity is unconscious, yet disturbing and interruptive. It renders colonial authority, Bhabha proposes, ambivalent, uncertain.

This reminds us that the bridge ceremony is not just a 'unit of life' but a ceremony, a staged and framed aesthetic production. According to Bakhtin (1981: 359), 'an intentional hybrid is first of all a *conscious* hybrid', that is, 'an encounter, within the area of an utterance, between two different linguistic consciousnesses, separated from one another by an epoch, by social differentiation or by some other factor' (1981: 358).

Hence, the intentional, novelistic hybrid is not only an individualized mixing of two socio-linguistic consciousnesses, but 'the collision between differing points of view on the world that are embedded in these forms' (1981: 360). Intentional hybrids are thus 'inevitably dialogical' (1981: 360). Bakhtin (1981: 361) argues, moreover, that such intentional hybrids are 'double voiced', encapsulated within the framework of a single utterance. Similarly Bhabha (1994: 36), drawing on Derrida, also stresses the performative dimensions of cultural enunciation: 'the *place of utterance* – is crossed by the *différance* of writing … [which ensures] that meaning is never simply mimetic and transparent'.

The ceremonial opening of the bridge defines a liminal space in which both intentional and organic hybridities, conscious and unconscious, are played out. The policeman in warrior clothes, like the warrior dance before the car, are intentional hybrids. But much else in the ceremony is unreflexive and spontaneous. Seen from Bhabha's perspective, both types of hybridity (he does not distinguish them) frame a 'third space' in which the ambivalences of the colonial encounter are enacted. Bhabha (pers. comm.) uses liminality, like hybridity, to refer to the moment or place of untranslatability, the limit where a thing becomes its alterity. He draws on Benjamin's argument that accurate translation is impossible, since the intentionality of words is lost in translation; no translation can exhaust the meanings of the original, especially because those meanings themselves are subject to future historical revision. Yet translations can, according to Benjamin (1992: 70–82), *extend* the translating language and create new meanings in it. In the colonial encounter, then, it is not just the colonized who are subjected to Western ways; the colonizers too are transformed, while the colonized deploy borrowed forms to tell their own, distinct narratives which 'unsettle' and 'subvert' the cultural authority of the colonizers (Bhabha 1994: 102–22; see also Nandy 1983).

In anthropology, too, the liminal has been described as transformative and transgressive through the conjoining incommensurables: human and god, boy and man, male and female, and so forth. In Turner's (1967: 97) words,

> the neophytes are neither living nor dead from one aspect, and both living and dead from another. Their condition is one of ambiguity and paradox, a confusion of all customary categories … Liminality may perhaps be regarded as the Nay to all positive structural assertions, but as in some sense the source of them all, and, more than that, as a realm of pure possibility whence novel configurations of ideas and relations may arise.

Turner's theory of liminality, while drawing on van Gennep, has to be read in the broader theoretical context of the Manchester School, which stressed that social relations in tribal societies were characterized by endemic structural conflicts: between groups, between different principles of social organization, between rules and norms, and between classificatory categories. 'Every social system is a field of tension, full of ambivalence, of co-operation and contrasting struggle' (Gluckman 1963: 127). Normally, such contradictions are left unmarked in everyday life through a process of 'situational selection', a term derived from the work of Evans-Pritchard. But such conflicts and struggles surface symbolically and are 'dramatized' in ritual. They are often marked by obscenities and the breaking of taboos. Paradoxically, however, the outcome and explicit aim of such transgressive performances is to achieve the blessing, fertility, and social unity of the community (Gluckman 1963: 126). Bakhtin (1984) uses a similar argument in his analysis of grotesque realism in European medieval carnivals.

Gluckman called these symbolic ritualizations of underlying conflicts 'rituals of rebellion'. In relation to such rituals, he raises a question relevant to my argument. Why are such transgressive performances *vis-à-vis* figures of authority licensed in tribal societies for the sake of communal blessing, whereas in urban civilizations, as in Europe today, national ceremonies are 'marked by adulation only'? (Gluckman 1965: 258; for his full analysis, see 250-64) His answer is that in small-scale, face-to-face societies, the nature of authority is very often not in doubt, even if the incumbency of specific rulers is; whereas in our societies, with their large complex structures, the very constitution of authority is a matter of intense struggle. In this article I raise a similar question in relation to Islamic societies. Why were rituals of transgressive hybridity licensed in intimate, face-to-face Muslim societies, whereas once exposed to processes of globalization, such hybridities came to be regarded as sinful and dangerous?

As we have seen, intentional hybridity as an aesthetic is inherently political, a clash of languages which questions an existing social order. In anthropological theory, intentional hybridity, I propose, refers to the conflation or transgression of culturally constructed categories in ritual and myth, as much as to the aesthetic encounter between cultures. Culture itself is, of course, a constructed category, subject to continuous processes of organic hybridization. Nevertheless, at any given moment social and cultural categories are naturalized as givens of the social order, and it is these naturalized categories that form the basis for aesthetic, intentional hybrids, often transgressive and oppositional.

I begin my discussion of Muslim societies with an example of intentional hybridity in the ritual masquerade following the Eid sacrifice among Berbers in Morocco. The ritual, I suggest, reveals that cultures produce their own indigenous forms of critical reflexivity and satire. Yet in a globalizing society, I argue, hybridity and transgression, while being potential tools of resistance which upturn taken-for-granted hierarchies, play dangerously on the boundary and can thus become a source of offence. In post-colonial diasporas, minorities often draw on culture strategically to fight for recognition and against discrimination and oppression. But this raises the question, what are the creative limits of cultural hybridity? When, in what situations, does the use of intentional hybrid aesthetic forms overstep the boundaries of acceptability, to be experienced by vulnerable minorities as painful mockery? In relation to this, the final part of the paper considers the critique by anthropologists of postcolonial hybridity theory that arose especially after the publication of *The Satanic Verses*, and which raised also the more general question of the limits and possibilities of communication across cultures.

Order and Hybridity

Although a fully fledged field of comparative postcolonial literary studies has only emerged recently, there are important parallels to be drawn between its themes and some of the central ideas about ritual of modernist anthropology. Modernist anthropology was concerned above all with social ordering and social reproduction. But in thinking about order it discovered disorder: betwixt-and-between moments and liminal spaces, mythical hybrid monsters and ritual clowns, matter out of place, joking relations that attacked hierarchies.[2] As early scholars, from Durkheim and Mauss to

Lévi-Strauss, recognized, even the most rudimentary hunter-gatherer and neolithic societies were *classifiers*: they ordered the world in terms of broad categories – of above and below, male and female, carnivores and herbivores, domestic and wild, young and old, hot and cold, us and them. Whatever did not fit neatly into these arbitrary but compelling classificatory schemes was experienced as problematic. It was matter out of place (Douglas 1966) and, as such, extremely dangerous, hedged with taboos, *haram*, both sacred and yet often defiling. Ambivalent, cross-over figures and moments were perceived to be extremely powerful, both for good and evil (Douglas 1975). Gods and sorcerers were equally hybrid, their classificatory categories mixed: but whereas the gods brought life and fertility, the sorcerers brought death and barrenness.

There were several strands to the way the argument developed about order and disorder, liminality and hybridity. Turner, as we have seen, analysed the liminal period of rites of passage as transformative moments in which incongruous elements were juxtaposed, often 'doubled up', plucked – with all their physiological and emotional connotations – out of the everyday world. The liminal phase was also, according to Turner, a time of reflexivity. The neophytes were confronted with sacred, often esoteric, figurines and masks that mixed elements from disparate domains, often magnified and exaggerated. These monstrous images enabled them, Turner speculated, to reflect critically on the very constitution of their societies.

Douglas's work drew on Lévi-Strauss's (1966; 1969) theory of totemic classifications. In his study of myth, Lévi-Strauss (1963) argued that myths were cultural attempts to resolve the fundamental contradictions or dilemmas that classificatory schemes threw up, since each society had a multiplicity of such schema for ordering the world. These were ordered in homologous systems of contrast and similarity, for example male: female as above: below. But given the complexity of the homologies across the different classificatory schemes, and given the constant need to override the reality of our cultural grounding in nature, cultural schema generated their own classificatory aporias. Myths were ways of transcending these aporias, and hence often focused on monstrous creatures or clowns that embodied the contradictions and dilemmas that culture itself had invented.

In addition to her work on anomaly, Douglas also extended earlier theories on customary joking relations in tribal societies. Joking partners were licensed to behave outrageously, throw excrement, make overt sexual gestures and advances, swear and abuse, steal food and create havoc, all without causing offence. Yet the very same joking partners also helped with funeral arrangements. As first formulated by Radcliffe-Brown (1940; 1949), joking managed ambivalences and ambiguities in relations between affines or joking clans. Douglas (1968; 1975) went further. Joking, she proposed, attacks hierarchy and exposes the taken-for-granted authority structures of a society for what they are: cultural constructions. Hence joking releases human spontaneity from the shackles of customary norms and constraints and heightens consciousness of the relativity of all culture and morality.

More recent work has built on these early modernist insights to develop further a theoretical understanding of the place of ritual monsters and clowns in the ritual process. Highlighting the betwixt-and-between qualities of ritual clowns, Handelman stresses their continuous oscillation between opposites (1990: 242), so that they embody flux, process, uncertainty, a 'deep instability', the very boundary itself (1990: 243 *passim*).

The reification of these opposed qualities in a single figure means, Handelman (1990: 245) suggests, that ritual clowns have the capacity to 'mould context to the logic of [their] own composition'.

But ritual monsters are not only objects of intellectual reflection and consciousness. As later theories recognize, they actively mediate sacred exchange and symbolic transactions across boundaries. Hybrid figures effect a movement of ritual qualities between spaces, subjects, and communities. In doing so, they bring the tangible boons of fertility, life, *baraka*, power, into a community, and remove dirt, pollution, decay away from it. As R. Werbner (1989: 61) has argued:

> In ritual for purification and healing, the movement from disorder to order requires boundary crossing. This is often achieved by figures beyond the community's moral universe who are tricksters or clown like. They may be wild, obscene, and sexually licentious; they are often transvestite, and often the epitome of an authority alternative to that paramount within the community. Nevertheless, the figures do not merely dramatise disorder. In ritual performance, as go-betweens come from afar, they are agents of change, of purification and healing. They serve as means for directing sacred exchange across the community's moral universe.

Such ritual hybrid figures are found very widely. I turn first to an example from rural Morocco.

Ritual Licence in Morocco

Every year after the Great Eid sacrifice, young Berber men in remote communities of the High Atlas mountains celebrate the ritual of Bilmawn (this is the name given by Hammoudi 1993). In this ritual masquerade, one (or sometimes two) men dress up in sacrificial goat- and sheepskins, their head inserted in a goat's head, horns and all. Bilmawn is an androgynous figure. On his back hang a phallus and testicles, on his chest a large, single breast. Westermarck reported that he is also called 'the lion with sheepskins' (from R. Werbner 1989: 62). He is accompanied by several ritual masqueraders representing Jews, with their leader being the rabbi. The Jews' masks are smeared with flour and egg, and decorated with hairs from the sacrificial hides. A third figure is that of a slave. Known as Ismakh, he wears a black goat burnous, while all the other ritual masqueraders wear grey goatskins (Hammoudi 1993: 58).

The masqueraders are allowed almost unlimited licence. They swear and attack onlookers, enact sexual copulation in public in front of women, enter the women's homes while the men of the house are absent, demand or steal food. According to Hammoudi, who studied the ritual in 1981, these sacrificial goat clowns even satirize Qur'anic verses. As part of their routine they enact ploughing, harvesting, and a mock wedding. During the whole time in which they take over the village, senior men are banished and it becomes the domain of young men, women, and children. The masqueraders scatter great sacks of ash over the people and their houses. They themselves roll in the soot of the great cooking-pots which heat the ablution waters at the mosque. The ash from the fires of the ablution is an accumulation of a whole year of burnt firewood. One may speculate that these remains of the burning in the mosque are powerfully imbued with *baraka*. Hence, despite their licentious and transgressive behaviour, as they scatter the ash and flail the people with their hooves and skins, the sacrificial clowns bring desired blessing to each and every household.

The sacrificial clowns are clearly hybrid figures; they combine the attributes of human and animal, male and female, Muslim and Jew, free man and slave, young and old. They turn the world topsy-turvy and back to front. The ritual itself has been reported by a long line of ethnologists and travellers who visited Morocco. Early scholars mostly attempted to interpret it as a pre-Muslim fertility rite. Hammoudi, the most recent to study the ritual, rightly objects to this view, arguing that the sacrifice and the masquerade are linked together and cannot be understood apart from each other. Yet he too fails, in my view, to grasp fully the symbolic and structural transformations effected by the clowns as metonymic carriers of powerful purity and impurity while being, at the same time, inversions of the official Islamic sacrificial rite.

Let us recall that when the clowns appear, the sacrifice has already taken place in all its sober formality. The Eid sacrifice is an occasion of purification and expiation in which the sacrificer and the community reaffirm their bond with Allah. Why, then, the need to incorporate this otherness beyond the boundary?

Reflecting on Westermarck's (1968 [1926]) account of the ritual at the turn of the century, R. Werbner (1989: 61–2) argues that boundary-crossing, while powerful,

> is dangerous, and [hence] these trickster figures are sometimes violent or out of control, and physically attack people around them … they demand symbolic gifts which are lavished upon them with generosity … Through their performance, ordeals are created, the passing of which gives members of the community around the wild or alien figures a sense of having moved towards a higher plane of existence. Here, the unclean is the purifier; the transgressor of moral norms, the agent of moral renewal; the victim, the victimiser; the predator, the agent of sacrifice.

Moreover, we cannot understand the hybrid sacrificial goat and lion clowns of the ritual without noting that they are the bearers of a powerful sexuality, dangerous but fertilizing. Wrapped in the sacred skin of the sacrificial animal and smeared with the sacred soot and ashes of the ablution waters, they embody the gross sexuality necessary for human and natural reproduction, as sanctified and divinely sanctioned. They inseminate and impregnate through mock battles, mock copulations, and sacred exchanges of nurture and substance. They then depart, *carrying the dirt and pollution of the old year with them*. In this sense they are both ordeals to be transcended and purifiers. As Bakhtin (1984) too has argued in his study of carnival, sexuality and the lower body, excluded from the realm of formal religion, are reincorporated through the enactment of lower-status figures, animals or strangers. But importantly in this case, these transgressive figures are first imbued (via the soot) with the power of the sacrificial act itself, and the connection to God it has effected.

Hammoudi (1993: 65) tells us that people were reluctant to speak of the masquerade at other times, because 'that is when people do and say obscene things'. This is, of course, the way such liminal, taboo-breaking moments are usually treated. In the 1980s, however, the ritual was under a very different sort of threat, this time from

Muslim reformists who wanted to eliminate it entirely. They argued, much like the old ethnologists, that the ritual was un-Islamic, *bida*, unlawful innovation. One man told Hammoudi (1993: 66): 'these are customs from before … these are the *jahiliya* … The people are Muslim, and all of a sudden they call themselves Jews and rabbis! It is not possible. And then, someone who imitates a people afterwards belongs to that people!' The battle is pitched between the purist reformers and the traditionalists, those who want to continue the ritual, each with their own vision of what constitutes authentic cultural and religious authority (1993: 167).[3]

Impure and Pure: Intentional and Organic Hybridities

Ritual clowns and monsters are very much like avant-garde works of art or novels: they are meant to shock, to inseminate, to impregnate, to bring otherness from beyond the boundaries into established routines of daily life. They are *intentional* hybridities; they work to transform, to revitalize, to create new ordeals to be transcended. They generate, as Bhabha has rightly proposed, liminal spaces, betwixt-and-between tropes that render authority structures ambivalent. But what are the limits of such hybridities? When are they part of the revitalizing process of social renewal, as they appear to be in rural Morocco, and when are they experienced as an unacceptable attack on all that is sacred, as they seemed to be by the Islamist reformists? Secondly, is there something about the postcolonial condition that makes such intentional hybrids especially threatening to some, whereas before they were accepted as a bit of fun, a good laugh, a moment of hedonistic liberation that did not really threaten to undermine the social order?

New religious fundamentalist movements of purification, whether Jewish, Christian, Hindu, Buddhist, or Muslim are, somewhat paradoxically, themselves hybrids of modernity. They are regimented and bureaucratized, scripturalist and procedural. They take to a new *modernist* extreme the inherent tendency of all religions to classify right and wrong, good and evil, the acceptable and the unacceptable, the normal and the transgressive. They allow for no exceptions, no anomalies, no betwixt-and-betweens. They seek to own the instruments of governance and the state in order to exploit its technologies of power.

Some have argued that nationalism too, the archetypal institution of modernity, seeks purity and homogeneity. The boundaries of the nation-state, unlike those of the old dynastic or religious empires, are clearly demarcated. An inherent tendency of nationalism is thus to turn racist, to expunge, marginalize, or subordinate internal strangers as malignant and impure matter out of place (see Bauman 1989). But this simplifies the complex and highly dynamic relation between national belonging and citizenship. Citizenship often allows room for cultural heterogeneity, for religious pluralism, cultural hybridity, or multiculturalism. Moreover, the nation is itself a negotiated and highly contested social order, marked by intense conflicts between classes, lifestyles, political ideologies, religious affiliations, regional loyalties, town and country, men and women. There is a good deal of critical debate within democratic nation-states even before migrants, ethnics, or religious minorities enter the picture. The past itself is a contested terrain for different national fractions. This is true even of European nationalisms, the only ones which posit a 'natural' cultural or linguistic homogeneity as the *raison d'être* for the very existence of the nation. Postcolonial nationalisms are almost always, by contrast, linguistically and ethnically plural. Or, as in the postcolonial Middle East, neither language, religion, nor culture divide the Arab nations, yet they remain, and perceive themselves to be, discrete political entities.

Leaving aside for the moment, then, the important question of nationalism, let us consider the two contrasting hybrids presented here so far: the sacrificial goat clowns of the Eid masquerade and the Muslim reformists who want to abolish them as polluting the purity of Islam. These represent the two contrasting types of hybridization posited by Bakhtin: the one intentional, the other organic.[4]

As we have seen, we may say that despite the illusion of boundedness, cultures evolve historically through unreflective borrowings, mimetic appropriations, exchanges, and inventions. There is no culture in and of itself. As Ahmad (1995: 18) puts it, the 'cross-fertilisation of cultures has been endemic to all movements of people … and all such movements in history have involved the travel, contact, transmutation, hybridisation of ideas, values and behavioural norms' (see also Sahlins 1999). At the same time, and this amplifies Bakhtin's point, organic hybridization does not disrupt the sense of order and continuity: new images, words, objects, are integrated into language or culture unconsciously. But organic hybrids do begin to render prior structures of authority ambivalent; in this sense, they are 'pregnant with potential for new world views' (Bakhtin 1981: 360).

Islamist and reform movements, I propose, are *unconscious* hybrids of modernity. Self-consciously they reject any kind of syncretic amalgamation as *bida*, and they particularly reject the ethical norms of a perceived Western modernity. Instead, they turn back to the past, to the glorious period of Islam at its foundation. But their very bureaucratic structure and modes of operation and dissemination are modernist.

As organic hybrids of modernity which seek purity, the Islamists are particularly hostile to any intentional aesthetic or religious hybrids that are meant to shock, change, challenge, revitalize, or disrupt order through deliberate, intended fusions of unlike social languages and images. They reject the ironic double consciousness created by intentional hybrids.

Bakhtin's distinction is useful for theorizing the simultaneous coexistence of both cultural change and resistance to change in religious, ethnic, or migrant groups and in postcolonial nation-states. What is felt to be most threatening is the deliberate, provoc-ative aesthetic challenge to an implicit social order and identity. Yet the same aesthetic may also be experienced, from a different social position, as revitalizing and 'fun'. Such aesthetic interventions are thus critically different from the routine cultural borrowings and appropriations by national or diasporic groups that unconsciously create the grounds for future social change. Demotic discourses deny boundaries, while the dominant discourses of the very same actors demand that they be respected, as Baumann (1997) has argued.

The danger that the aesthetic poses for any closed social universe with a single monological, authoritative, unitary language is that of a heteroglossia 'that rages beyond the boundaries' (Bakhtin 1981: 368). Intentional heteroglossias relativize singular ideologies, cultures, and languages. By contrast, the notion of organic hybrid-ization casts doubts on the viability of simplistic *scholarly* models of cultural holism, the idea that we should study a 'unit of custom' rather than a 'unit of life'.

The Limits of Cultural Hybridity

The objection of Islamists to fun and hybridity is comprehensible in terms of the very narrow yardsticks of religious authenticity that they have set themselves. But what are the limits of cultural hybridity for ordinary people? When do ritual masquerades cease to be revitalizing and enjoyable and become unacceptable? When and why do hybrid postcolonial novels cease to be funny and entertaining and become deeply offensive? After all, poetry, including satirical and agonistic poetry, has long been an integral institution in many Muslim societies.

Writing about Moroccan poetry, Geertz (1983: 117) describes it as 'morally ambiguous because it is not sacred enough to justify the power it actually has and not secular enough for that power to be equated to ordinary eloquence'. The Moroccan oral poet, speaking in Arabic, a sacred language, 'inhabits a region between speech types which is at the same time a region between worlds, between the discourse of God and the wrangle of men'.

In other words, Moroccan oral poetry is a hybrid of social discourses in the Bakhtinian sense, and as such disturbing and interruptive.[5] Hence poets must tread a fine line between delightful transgression and real offence. To judge the response of their audience, they must share a whole number of implicit understandings, experiences, and emotional sensitivities to art, poetry, religion, and life. Geertz (1983: 99 *passim*) calls this aesthetic complex a local 'sensibility'. Extending his insight, we may argue that only someone who fully has such a local sensibility can play upon and transgress a local aesthetic without causing offence. However outrageous the Eid ritual sacrificial goat clowns are, they still observe limits; beyond those limits their actions may arouse hostility or even violence.

But postcolonial societies are no longer intimate societies with 'local' aesthetic sensibilities and, as Gluckman would have it, relatively stable notions of legitimate authority. Aesthetic communities are formed in them through and around mass-produced class and sub-cultural consumer goods and 'neo-tribal' lifestyles (Maffesoli 1995). Moreover, as Bourdieu (1984; especially 1993) in particular has argued, the field of high art has been reconstituted as a discrete field of taste and distinction for a discerning and knowledgeable elite of expert critics. It is a field in which competitive innovation and creativity are accorded high value, and in which novelty and avant-garde transgression are highly rewarded. There is thus, he proposes, a constant attempt to create *disjunctions* between elite tastes and those of the *petit bourgeois* masses. At the same time, even avant-garde novelists would like to reach a mass readership.

Postcolonial diasporic literature in English is produced partly within this rarefied postmodern atmosphere, in which novelists such as Salman Rushdie or Hanif Qureshi are part of a wider cosmopolitan literary cohort of writers, novelists, and poets (see Fowler 2000). Like novelists, postcolonial critics too are included within this enchanted circle of refined tasters. The special contribution that South Asian diasporic writers and critics have made to hybridity theory has been, in their own words, to elaborate the hybrid figure of the postcolonial migrant and, alongside that, to create and invent a hybrid literary style that draws on Indian subcontinental words, images, and tropes and weaves them into the English language in delightfully funny, provocative, or disturbing ways.[6] The originality, in particular, of Rushdie's contribution to the world of English literature, measured by elite canons of high taste, has been breathtaking.

Postcolonial novels, Bhabha has argued, serve to 'interrupt' pure narratives of nation. For Bhabha (1994: 142, 158), nationalism is never homogeneous and unitary, it is the liminal space created by the permanent *performative* transgression of national grand narratives, eternal and 'pedagogic', by the 'shreds and patches' of the quotidian 'daily plebiscite' of many national voices, by cultural discourses from the margins. Drawing on Derrida, Bhabha locates agency in the act of interruptive enunciation, as we have seen. As Gilroy (1993: 126, 161-2) also argues, what this does is to create a 'double consciousness', a split subject, a fractured reality–doubly framed (Bhabha 1994: 214). To an anthropologist this echoes familiar tropes. Liminal masks, possessed 'lions' or sacrificial goats, ritual clowns as anomalous creatures from beyond the boundaries, all create such double consciousnesses, except that here the discursive setting is the nation and the marginal, hybrid, anomalous, betwixt-and-between, highly potent creatures are postcolonial migrants; or their creative works of high culture.

One might even suggest that the transgressive and reflexive nature of the modern novel is equivalent to the kinds of 'rituals of rebellion' I have described here, an insti-tutionalized, symbolic form of opposition to the established order. In the case of the novel, this sanctified symbolic interruption is one enshrined by 'enlightened' modern bourgeois society. As such, the novel creates dialogical hybridity and reflexiveness without necessarily being seen to pose a serious threat to a liberal social order. One has only to think of the elaborate ceremonials of publicity accompanying the launch of a new novel, its aesthetic design and set-aside spaces (it must not, of course, either be destroyed or taken too seriously) to unmask its hidden ontology: a ritualized object, hedged with taboos, a modern-day equivalent of liminal sacra, of boundary-crossing pangolins or humanized sacrificial goats.

Artistic creativity is not, however, only the prerogative of cosmopolitan post-colonial elites. In Britain there is also a local diasporic poetry in the vernacular, Urdu. *Mushairas*, poetry readings, are extremely popular among Pakistani settlers. Although not written in Arabic and hence not quite as sanctified linguistically as their Arabic counterparts, Urdu poetry combines high art and satire in an unstable, critical, and potentially transgressive mixture. The bigger *mushairas* include Urdu poets renowned both locally and internationally. Much of the poetry is love poems, *ghazals*, which often deploy stock, formulaic phrases, but now and then poets pro-duce commentaries on the diasporic condition itself. Especially good poems are greeted with loud shouts of appreciation. I use two poems recorded at one such event in Manchester, both by local poets, as an example. The first is clearly written from the perspective of a politically conscious proletarian (words in inverted commas were spoken in English):

Migrant Seasons
Friends, in a 'hotel'[a] I have worked and toiled
For my belly, I carried a bucketful of soil[b]
Consumed by summer heat in the deep cold of winter[c]
I wasted my hard-earned labour on 'pubs', 'clubs', and girls.

[a] restaurant
[b] worked extremely hard
[c] suffering the heat of the cooking in cold winters

A second poem reveals the sense of loss and nostalgia which first generation Pakistani migrant settlers experience:

'*Why is it that only I cannot sleep?*'
The bed is warm and the room is cosy
No fear of tomorrow, no work worry
'Ruby' is sleeping, so is 'Rosy'
'Cheeky' is asleep, so is 'Nosy'[a]
It is only I who cannot sleep
Why is it that only I cannot sleep?

[a] nicknames of his children, born and brought up in Britain

The fifth and sixth lines are famous, written by the poet Mirza Ghalib, the nineteenth-century Urdu poet who witnessed the decline of Muslim power and the rise of British colonialism. In the original version the previous line was 'I know death will come one day'. Stunned by the scale of the loss, Ahmed (1997: 45) tells us, 'in an often quoted verse, perhaps one of the first political poems in Urdu, Ghalib vividly reveals the darkness of the Muslim mind confronting the disintegration: "There is no hope in the future / Once I could laugh at the human condition / Now there is no laughter"', and elsewhere (1997: 172), '"There is no solution in sight / Once there was mirth in the heart / Now nothing makes me smile"'.

The poet implicitly evokes the despair of the colonial experience in lamenting his exile:

They all are happy, speaking English
With sweet 'Lancashire' 'accents'.
They do not understand us, nor we them
Even 'communication' is broken
'Ti, tu, ta, tatar'[b] – I do not understand
Why is it that only I cannot sleep?

We cry not just about speaking –
Eating, drinking, washing, sleeping,[c]
How easy to be without God,
How can one be *with* God?[d]
We cannot see our way through this
Why is it that only I cannot sleep?

I went to the 'GP' to tell my woes
They all sleep, but I cannot
So what have you been thinking of?
Only of what has been gained and lost[e]
But even thinking helps me not
Why is it, Oh healer, that only I cannot sleep?

I took a 'valium' last night
I even put 'baan'[f] on my eyes
I've done all I can to find a remedy
Talking about Rumi, Sanai, and Razi[g]
Now no talk helps
Why is it that only I cannot sleep?

I even watched 'television'
And all the 'season' 'Christmas' 'films'
What is the cause of my dead heart?
Having performed the 'recitation'
Still, the heart's voice fails
Why is it that only I cannot sleep?

We like to display our piety
While doing deeds that should not be done
Having done them, we repent
And we repent our repentances
Nor do we feel ashamed
Why is it that only I cannot sleep?

[b] terms of address in Urdu
[c] All these are different in England.
[d] The poet implies that his children have lost their faith, and living with them he himself
  has difficulty retaining his Islamic faith in Britain.
[e] by coming to England
[f] an ointment
[g] names of famous Muslim poets

Both of these hybrid poems mix English and Urdu words and phrases satirically, while commenting ironically on the predicaments of a poet's exile, in which dreams of success have been displaced by a reality of sweating in restaurant kitchens or failing to communicate with one's children. At the same time, the second poem also expresses a sense of pain and nostalgic yearning for a less hybrid culture and faith. The question is: is this yearning in some sense wrong? Theories that celebrate hybridity as an attack on cultural essentialism and criminalize culture as a source of evil fail to recognize that the matrices of culture are also, for subjects themselves, the matrices of ethical value, responsibility, and shared sociality (see also Lévi-Strauss 1994: 422–3).[7] In the present deconstructive moment, any unitary conception of a bounded culture is pejoratively labelled naturalistic and essentialist. But the alternatives seem equally unconvincing: if 'culture' is merely a false intellectual construction, an inauthentic nostalgic imaginary, or a bricolage of artificially designed capitalist consumer objects, this leaves most postmodern subjects stripped of an ethical life world. One might even argue that cultural hybridity is powerful *because* it originates from that life world and the orders and separations it prescribes. Moreover, ethnic and religious minorities use culture strategically as a rallying banner to demand equal rights and symbolic citizenship in the public domain. Culture thus becomes a tool in an emancipatory battle.

The Satanic Verses

The question of culture versus hybridity came to the fore in debates about the Muslim response to the publication of *The Satanic Verses* and the offence it evidently caused Muslim feelings. *The Satanic Verses* was a book about hybridity written in a hybrid mode that challenged both pure theories of religion (Islamic fundamentalism) and pure theories of the nation (racism or cultural racism). But it seemed to spill over beyond the ritualized, sacred domain of high art and to become a political intervention which generated intolerance rather than tolerance. Partly as a result, a critical anthropological literature has evolved that reflects on the limitations of the postcolonial celebration of cultural hybridity and religious syncretism, as though these were panaceas for religious communalism, ethnic racism, and cultural intolerance.

Criticizing a tendency of elite Indian intellectuals such as Nandy (1983; 1990) to see a prior religious syncretism (Hindu, Muslim, or Buddhist) as more tolerant than current fundamentalist Hindu religious revivalist movements, van der Veer (1994) has argued that syncretism disguises inequalities under a veneer of openness and universal eclecticism. There is always, he maintains, a dominant or hegemonic element in syncretic cults, for example, Sufi saints' cults in South Asia or Gandhian universalism, and in practice also unequal participation and inclusion of different groups in such discourses. In relation to *The Satanic Verses*, van der Veer (1997: 102) criticizes Bhabha's (1994: chap. 11) celebration of the book as a great text of migration and self-renewal, and argues that its provocative insulting of the Prophet and the Qur'an simply intensified the marginalization of a Muslim underclass in Britain and Europe, already suffering racism and economic subordination. The image of fanatical Muslims, which their collective response to the novel provoked, set back the course of race relations in Britain and Europe, he says, by many years.

Echoes of van der Veer's position are found in other work by anthropologists, all of whom stress the vulnerability, backwardness, and deprivation of a Muslim diasporic underclass in Britain. It was the sense of alienation and marginalization of this underclass, the argument goes, that pushed them to defend their culture and sacred icons against what was perceived to be a deliberate insult (Asad 1993; Fischer & Abedi 1990; Friedman 1997). Fischer and Abedi (1990) see this response as part of an ongoing class war in Muslim society itself, in which satirical poetry has always been used as a dissenting tool by intellectual elites, while being rejected by *petit bourgeois* conservatives. Friedman (1997) focuses on postcolonial intellectuals in the West whom, he argues, are a small, self-congratulatory elite having little notion of the problems faced by proletarian migrants living in urban poverty. The same point is echoed by Ahmed (1992: 164–6) in his critique of the snobbery and cronyism of this relatively secularized, South Asian Muslim elite. The disjunction and lack of communication between elites and masses is also one stressed by Fowler (2000), who suggests that Rushdie as a novelist was primarily responsive to the demands of the art field for avant-garde innovation. In his ivory tower, he failed entirely to anticipate the wholly negative response to the novel by fellow Pakistanis in Britain, even though the novel was supposedly about them and even though it narrates almost prophetically the reaction to it.

My own response to the book has been somewhat different. First, I have seen no grounds for describing local Pakistanis as merely an underprivileged, deeply religious underclass. In my observation, Pakistanis in the diaspora form an aesthetic community which celebrates 'fun' in the forms of music, dance, satire, and masquerade, much to the disapproval of a relatively small group of religious reformists. Pre-wedding *mehndi* (henna) celebrations by women include ritual masquerading and clowning, in which the women often dress up as disgusting old men and in which arranged marriage, sexuality, and men in general are spoofed and satirized, while romantic love is celebrated in singing and sensual dancing (P. Werbner 1986; 1990: chap. 9; see also Raheja & Gold 1994). The satirical spoofing of Pakistani inter-generational relations in British Pakistani movies such as 'East is East' exemplifies Asian celebration of self-critical, transgressive laughter. Cricket and, as we have seen, poetry readings, are extremely popular pursuits (on cricket and hybridity, see P. Werbner 1996b; 1997b). In addition, Pakistanis in the diaspora consume an unadulterated diet of Bombay films and of audio-cassettes of film music, *bhangra*, or jazzed-up *qawwali* Sufi devotional singing, which are all extremely popular.

My reading of *The Satanic Verses* also differs from the usual run of interpretations. I have argued (P. Werbner 1996a) that the figure of the Prophet depicted in the novel is one of tolerance and almost-perfection, set against a host of counter-selves who are all deeply flawed. The confrontation with, and ultimate execution of, the poet Baal, a figure who is, for most of the novel, entirely devoid of moral fibre despite his artistic talents, highlights the ambiguous authority of amoral poetry *vis-à-vis* religious morality, without resolving this dilemma fully. It also raises the question of the limits of tolerance.

The Satanic Verses is not, then, simply a novel that celebrates hybridity, epitomized by that familiar trope of diasporic writing, the figure of the postcolonial migrant. If this were all the novel was, it would not be worth defending. For Rushdie, migration, *hijra*, is a more profound experience of conversion and ethical search for a new reality. But even if we take the novel as a serious critique of religious intolerance and not just a postmodern spoof, this does not do away with the question of whether it should have been written, and written in such an obscure way that its serious meanings are completely lost to all but a tiny minority of readers. The fact that it appears to be a sacrilegious attack on Islam and the Prophet makes this the truth of the novel for the majority. Given the clash of emotional aesthetics that the novel has created, and the deep offence it generated even among elite and relatively liberal, fun-loving Muslims (at least in Britain), the question that needs to be asked is not whether it challenges a puritanical religious fundamentalism. The real question is this: in a global context, when does transgressive hybridity facilitate, and when does it destroy, communication across cultures for the sake of social renewal?

Conclusion

How does one tread the line of acceptable interruptive hybridity in the post-colonial world? This is a world in which all identities are 'palimpsest', overlaid and reinscribed (Bauman 1997). Given these historical inscriptions and reinscriptions of different subjective identities, differentially positioned, the analysis of postcolonial struggles for authority in public life presents a daunting challenge (see R. Werbner 1996: 4). Debates about cultural hybridity necessarily rest on notions of right and wrong. But in reality, hybridity is not essentially good, just as cultural essentialism is not intrinsically evil. When women or minorities struggle to gain recognition for 'their' culture in the public domain, they are making legitimate claims to symbolic citizenship in the nation-state.

More than just celebrating hybridity, we need to ask whether cultural movements are critical and emancipatory or conservative and exclusive, whether they recognize difference and allow cultural creativity, or deny the right to be different. But poetic licence is not unlimited; to be effective, it must walk the fine line between social languages so that humour is not read as painful mockery. It must retain a local sensibility in a globalizing world. Otherwise, rather than leading to a double consciousness, a global cultural ecumene (Hannerz 1996) which some scholars optimistically evoke, such hybrid transgressions can lead only to a polarization of discourses.

One of the important points arising from the anthropological study of ritual hybrids is that critical consciousness does not necessarily emerge solely from the encounter between discrete cultures or from a position of strangerhood on the margins of the nation. A key issue is that of reflexivity within, as well as in the encounter between, cultures. Ewing (1997: 20) has argued against the assumption by some anthropologists and sociologists of 'a prior [pre-colonial] existence of an unreflective plenitude in which tradition is hegemonic and simply reproduced'. So, too, there have been many instances in the history of the English novel, for example, in which transgressive critiques of the social order have come from within, from English novelists, just as indigenous Moroccan poetry and ritual serve to heighten consciousness of a local moral order beyond the West.

This is where an anthropological theory of hybridity is crucial. It makes clear that the encounter of order with disorder, however culturally constructed, is always contextual and sited, no matter if this be in the micro-political gendered and generational divisions of village life or in the meeting of a local culture and Western colonialism, as in the ceremony by the bridge in modern Zululand. Whether cultural hybridity is generative and fertilizing depends on how its varied audiences interpret it. For some, multiculturalism, cultural borrowings and mixings, constitute an attack on their felt subjectivity. In a world in which local people feel their culture to be under threat from globalizing Western cultural forces or from incoming stranger migrants, interruptive hybridity may be experienced not as revitalizing and fun, but as threatening a prior social order and morality. The line between respect and transgression, as anthropologists studying joking relations have long recognized, is an easy one to cross. This is ever more so in postcolonial nations and the ambivalent encounters they generate.

Notes

1 By 'modernist anthropology' I refer to anthropological theories based on systematic empirical research, encompassing a variety of approaches, including the interpretivist.

2 Hence Stallybrass and White (1986: 193), drawing explicit connections between Bakhtin's theory of carnivals and modernist anthropological theorists like Lévi-Strauss, Gluckman, Leach, Turner, and Douglas, comment: 'It was not by accident … that an anthropology which began by exploring the ordering mechanisms of social classification was led onto the question of pollution rites and filth'.

3 Post-Renaissance bourgeois attempts to suppress the grotesque realism of popular culture are discussed by Stallybrass and White (1986: 9 passim, 193–4).

4 For a discussion of this distinction as critical to hybridity theory, see also Young (1995: 21–5).

5 Interestingly, Bakhtin (1981) denies that poetry can be hybrid, a characteristic he attributes to the novel.

6 Ironically, it was Rudyard Kipling, an English colonial writer, who initiated this exuberant linguistic hybridization, for instance in Kim.

7 Thus Lévi-Strauss (1994: 422) says: 'one has to agree to pay the price: to know that cultures, each of which is attached to a lifestyle and value system of its own, foster their own peculiarities, and that this tendency is healthy and not – as people would like to have us think – pathological'.

References

Ahmad, A. 1995. The politics of literary postcoloniality. *Race and Class* 36: 3, 1–20.

Ahmed, A.S. 1992. *Postmodernism and Islam: predicament and promise*. London: Routledge.

___ 1997. *Jinnah, Pakistan and Islamic identity: the search for Saladin*. London: Routledge.

Asad, T. (ed.) 1973. *Anthropology and the colonial encounter*. London: Ithaca Press.

___ (ed.) 1993. *Genealogies of religion*. Baltimore: Johns Hopkins University Press.

Bakhtin, M. 1981. *The dialogic imagination* (trans. C. Emerson & M. Holquist). Austin: University of Texas Press.

___ 1984. *Rabelais and his world* (trans. H. Iswolsky). Bloomington: Indiana University Press.

Bauman, Z. 1989. *Modernity and the Holocaust*. Cambridge: Polity Press.

___ 1997. The making and unmaking of strangers. In *Debating cultural hybridity: multicultural identities and the politics of anti-racism* (eds) P. Werbner & T. Modood, 46–57. London: Zed Books.

Baumann, G. 1997. Dominant and demotic discourses of culture: their relevance to multi-ethnic alliances. In *Debating cultural hybridity: multi-cultural identities and the politics of anti-racism* (eds) P. Werbner & T. Modood, 209–25. London: Zed Books.

Benjamin, W. 1992 (1973). *Illuminations* (ed. H. Arendt, trans. H. Zohn). London: Fontana.

Bhabha, H.K. 1994. *The location of culture*. London: Routledge.

Bourdieu, P. 1984. *Distinction*. London: Routledge & Kegan Paul.

___ 1993. *The field of art production*. Cambridge: Polity Press.

Clifford, J. 1988. *The predicament of culture*. Cambridge, Mass: Harvard University Press.

___ & G. Marcus (eds) 1986. *Writing culture*. Berkeley: University of California Press.

Cohen, A. 1969. *Custom and politics in urban Africa*. London: Routledge & Kegan Paul.

Douglas, M. 1966. *Purity and danger*. London: Routledge & Kegan Paul.

___ 1968. The social control of cognition: some factors in joke perception. *Man (N.S.)* 3, 361–76.

___ 1975. *Implicit meanings*. London: Routledge & Kegan Paul.

Ewing, K. 1997. *Arguing sainthood: modernity, psychoanalysis and Islam*. Durham, N.C.: Duke University Press.

Fischer, M. & M. Abedi 1990. *Debating Muslims*. Madison: University of Wisconsin Press.

Fowler, B. 2000. A sociological analysis of *The Satanic Verses* affair. *Theory, Culture and Society* 17: 1, 39–62.

Friedman, J. 1997. Global crises, the struggle for cultural identity and intellectual porkbarrelling: cosmopolitans versus locals, ethnics and nationals in an era of de-hegemonisation. In *Debating cultural hybridity: multi-cultural identities and the politics of anti-racism* (eds) P. Werbner & T. Modood, 70–89. London: Zed Books.

Geertz, C. 1983. *Local knowledge*. London: Fontana.

Gilroy, P. 1993. *The Black Atlantic: modernity and double consciousness*. London: Verso.

Gluckman, M. 1958 (1940). *Analysis of a social situation in modern Zululand (Rhodes-Livingstone Papers 28)*. Manchester: University Press for the Rhodes-Livingstone Institute.

___ 1963. *Order and rebellion in tribal Africa*. London: Cohen & West.

___ 1965. *Politics, law and ritual in tribal society*. Oxford: Basil Blackwell.

Hammoudi, A. 1993. *The victim and its masks* (trans. P. Wissig). Chicago: University Press.

Handelman, D. 1990. *Models and mirrors: towards an anthropology of public events*. Cambridge: University Press.

Hannerz, U. 1980. *Exploring the city*. New York: Columbia University Press.

___ 1996. *Transnational connections*. London: Routledge.

Hobsbawm, E. & T. Ranger (eds) 1963. *The invention of tradition*. Cambridge: University Press.

Lévi-Strauss, C. 1963. *Structural anthropology* (trans. C. Jacobson & B. Grundfest Schoepf). London: Penguin.

___ 1966. *The savage mind*. London: Weidenfeld & Nicholson.

___ 1969. *Totemism* (trans. R. Needham). London: Pelican.

___ 1994. Anthropology, race and politics: a conversation with Didier Eribon. In *Assessing cultural anthropology* (ed.) R. Borowski, 420–9. New York: McGraw-Hill Inc.

Maffesoli, M. 1995. *The time of the tribes*. London: Sage.

Marcus, G. & M. Fischer 1986. *Anthropology as cultural critique*. Chicago: University Press.

Nandy, A. 1983. *The intimate enemy: loss and recovery of self under colonialism*. Delhi: Oxford University Press.

___ 1990. The politics of secularism and the recovery of religious tolerance. In *Communities, riots and survivors in South Asia* (ed.) V. Das, 69–93. New Delhi: Oxford University Press.

Radcliffe-Brown, A.R. 1940. On joking relationships. *Africa* 13, 195–210.

___ 1949. A further note on joking relationships. *Africa* 19, 133–40.

Raheja, G.G. & A.G. Gold 1994. *Listen to the heron's words: reimagining gender and kinship in North India*. Berkeley: University of California Press.

Sahlins, M. 1999. Two or three things that I know about culture. *Journal of the Royal Anthropological Institute (N.S.)* 5, 399–422.

Stallybrass, P. & A. White 1986. *The politics and poetics of transgression*. Ithaca, N.Y.: Cornell University Press.

Turner, V. 1967. *The forest of symbols*. Ithaca, N.Y.: Cornell University Press.

Van der Veer, P. 1994. Syncretism, multiculturalism and the discourse of tolerance. In *Syncretism/anti-syncretism: the politics of religious synthesis* (eds) C. Stewart & R. Shaw, 196–211. London: Routledge.

___ 1997. 'The enigma of arrival': hybridity and authenticity in the global space. In *Debating cultural hybridity: multi-cultural identities and the politics of anti-racism* (eds) P. Werbner & T. Modood, 90–105. London: Zed Books.

Werbner, P. 1986. The virgin and the clown: ritual elaboration in Pakistani weddings. *Man (N.S.)* 21, 227–250.

___ 1990. *The migration process: capital, gifts and offerings among British Pakistanis*. Oxford: Berg.

___ 1996a. Allegories of sacred imperfection: passion, hermeneutics and magic in *The Satanic Verses*. *Current Anthropology* 37 (Anthropology in Public, supplement), 55–86.

___ 1996b. Fun spaces: on identity and social empowerment among British Pakistanis. *Theory, Culture and Society* 13: 4, 53–80.

___ 1997a. Introduction: the dialectics of cultural hybridity. In *Debating cultural hybridity: multi-cultural identities and the politics of anti-racism* (eds) P. Werbner & Modood, 1–25. London: Zed Books.

___ 1997b. 'The Lion of Lahore': anthropology, cultural performance and Imran Khan. In *Anthropology and cultural studies* (eds) S. Nugent & C. Shore, 34–67. London: Pluto Press.

Werbner, R. 1989. *Ritual passage, sacred journey*. Washington, D.C.: Smithsonian Institution Press.

___ 1990. South-Central Africa: the Manchester School and after. In *Localizing strategies: regional traditions of ethnographic writing* (ed.) R. Fardon, 152–81. Edinburgh: Scottish Academic Press.

___ 1996. Introduction: multiple identities, plural arenas. In *Postcolonial identities in Africa* (eds) R. Werbner & T. Ranger, 1–26. London: Zed Books.

Westermarck, E. 1968 (1926). *Ritual and belief in Morocco*, vol. 2. New York: University Books.

Young, R. 1995. *Colonial desire: hybridity in theory, culture and race*. London: Routledge.

Part Six
Gender and Sexuality

Focusing on the intersection of race and gender, the essays in this section range across four domains: fashion and lifestyle, torture, spirituality, and masculinity. Reina Lewis' essay, an exercise in postcolonial cultural studies but also in globalization and fashion studies, documents how veiled shop assistants in Britain might be treated as linking Muslim consumer societies to Middle Eastern modernities. Deterritorialized concepts of multi-ethnic religious communities in England's cities, in Lewis' reading, enable the remaking of spaces where a "woman's adoption of particular veiling habits will have an effect on the perceived and experienced identities of other women both in her immediate vicinity and in all the spaces discursively touched by her actions." Mark Leopold's essay on Idi Amin harnesses psychoanalysis to anthropology in order to suggest that Amin's notoriety might be studied within a model of "charismatic hyper-heterosexuality." Leopold also notes that this construction of the "evil" Amin could be traced not simply to European representations of the racial Other (in the stereotype of the "Oriental despot") as the "not inconsiderable dark side of the British colonial fantasy," but to African dis-

courses too, as well as to what Leopold deems to be Amin's "feminized position of the subaltern ... as a longtime non-commissioned officer in the British army." Within the broadly left postcolonial frame the spiritualist position offers an interesting shift. Addressing the double bind of race and gender in the Native American woman's context, Jaimes Guerrero's essay proposes a native feminist spirituality – spirituality not being a traditional inclusion in postcolonial studies makes this an important intervention – that revives native kinship patterns. The essay also sees such a "Native Womanism" as possessing an ecocritical edge that therefore is at once an instrument to be deployed against patriarchy and also a Eurocentric history of "tribalism" that, as Guerrero argues, operates as a myth that "distorts the genuine meaning of communalism in traditionally-oriented Native American societies" where this communalism is "the basis of Native nationhood." Moving away from questions of spirituality and community toward a wholly different order of things, Melanie Richter-Montpetit, examining the Abu Ghraib visuals, argues that the systemic torture in the "war on terror" was made possible by the United

Postcolonial Studies: An Anthology, First Edition. Edited by Pramod K. Nayar.
Editorial material and organization © 2016 John Wiley & Sons, Ltd.
Published 2016 by John Wiley & Sons, Ltd.

States' gendered and raced cultural script. The system that incorporated white *women* into these horrific practices – in an odd aberration of ideologies of "gender equality" – in Richter-Montpetit's argument, rehearses the Western world's colonial "save civilization itself" fantasy and reproduces its "racist discourse and its concomitant practices of domination, expropriation and exploitation."

27   Veils and Sales

Muslims and the Spaces of Postcolonial Fashion Retail

Reina Lewis

Saturday August 6 2005

One month after the bombs in London, and Oxford Street is buzzing with shoppers. Retail figures are down and travel on the tube has diminished by a third, but the sales are in full swing and bargain hunters are not to be deterred. Walking from Oxford Circus to Marble Arch reveals a significant number of visibly "Muslim" women: girls in tight jeans with patterned scarves over their hair cluster around the makeup counter in Top Shop; older women in embroidered shalwar kameez with filmy dupatta thrown loosely over their heads mooch around Debenhams; hip twentysomethings in black boot-cut trousers and skimpy T-shirts wear their black head wraps tight with a fashionable ghetto-fabulous tail cascading down their backs from their high topknots as they check out bargains in Mango; clusters of young women in black jilbabs move around the accessories department of Selfridges looking at handbags, perhaps to augment the selection worn over wrists and shoulder; in Marks and Spencer Marble Arch, mothers in black abayas with niqabs over their faces select children's clothes. On the street, in the cafes that now increasingly line the pavements of this and other British high streets, women in various forms of veiling are highly visible, bearing these (generally presumed to be) most easily recognizable and decodable signs of religious and cultural identity. And in their activities as consumers the women in hijab, and not in hijab, are likely to be served by shop assistants who also veil. A trawl down the street reveals women in British Home Stores in cream jilbab working alongside female colleagues in uniform blouses; in Marks and Spencer, young women wear the uniform issue long-sleeved shirt with a store-issued (non-branded) black scarf pinned close about their heads; in New Look, young women keep the changing rooms under control in colored headscarves worn over the items from this season's selection that constitute the store's "feelgood fashion" uniform choices. All this in a month when assaults on Muslims, or those perceived as Muslim,

Reina Lewis, "Veils and Sales: Muslims and the Spaces of Postcolonial Fashion Retail." *Fashion Theory*, 11(4), 2007: 423–441. © 2007 Reina Lewis. Used by permission of Berg, an imprint of Bloomsbury Publishing plc.

Postcolonial Studies: An Anthology, First Edition. Edited by Pramod K. Nayar.
Editorial material and organization © 2016 John Wiley & Sons, Ltd.
Published 2016 by John Wiley & Sons, Ltd.

have increased dramatically from the police figures of this time last year, and in a week when some Muslim "leaders" have been quoted in the press advising women that they should relinquish their veils if their public prominence makes them likely targets for abuse or attacks.

And in this context writing about shopping, fashion, and veils seems ever more appropriate as a way of decoding some of the bewildering issues experienced in contemporary postcolonial spaces. Simply to pitch those three terms together generates immediate interest because veils are seen by those outside veiling communities, and sometimes by those inside, as inimical to fashion and largely as outside of the commercial circuits of the fashion industry. With shops, or fashion shopping, operating as an indicator of modernity, and with Islam often presented as resistant to modernity, the presence of veiled shop girls becomes a potent mix of two contrasting spatial and social codes, often still interpreted as a temporal clash. The perceived opposition between Islam and modernity that surfaces periodically in British political discourse was reactivated after the July 2005 bombs as politicians and commentators worried about the non-integration of Muslim populations. Though anxious discussions about alienated "Muslim youth" (understood primarily in the masculine) shifted the focus to the perceived threat posed by Muslim young men, the image of the veiled Muslim woman continued ubiquitous. In a discourse that tried to address the presence of Muslims as part of Britain, differences of religious or ethnic identity were frequently depicted as both spatial and temporal (with, for example, concern that foreign imams were not equipped to prepare young Muslims for life in "modern" Britain).

But the temporal nature of perceived religious differences also structures many varieties of Islamic revivalist discourse, reversing the values ascribed to the opposition between Islam and commerce, "tradition" and modernity, modesty and fashion. Yet, whilst revivalist identities are often positioned as self-consciously oppositional to Western consumption, the commercial development and distribution of new forms of Islamic dress (such as the Turkish *tesettür*) demonstrates that religious identities are increasingly experienced and expressed through the self-conscious consumption of goods marked (and marketed) as the opposite of secular/Westernized commodities and lifestyles (Navaro-Yashin 2002; Secor 2002; on lifestyle, Miller *et al.* 1998).

To understand the complexities of the Oxford Street scene requires a historicized awareness of these apparently conflicting sartorial and consumer frameworks and the variety of specific/local and generic/supranational spatial practices that they involve. Specific spatial relations include most obviously the geographies of the shop and the other consumption practices facilitated by the West End location, all encountered as part of the area's multicultural (and international tourist) demographic. At the same time, these territorialized experiences are positioned by the presence of the veil, a spatializing practice underpinned by the deterritorialized Islamic concept of the supranational multi-ethnic religious community of believers, the umma.

Participants in Oxford Street consumption move through these different spatial regimes with varying degrees of self-consciousness and acquiescence and are seen by diverse audiences there and in the spaces they encounter in their journeys to and from this largely non-residential quarter of the city. To unpick the conditions that permit and constrain the legibility of their dressed bodies we must turn to histories of gendered consumption in the formation of Western and non-Western modernities.

The creation of women as consumers has long been seen as a central element of Western modernity (Benson 1986; Lancaster 2000; Wilson 2003). With the development in the second half of the nineteenth century of the department store as a space for respectable female luxury expenditure, and the blossoming of consumption as a facet of female subjectivity, the notion of shopping for pleasure has become a widespread component of female experience. Shopping for the nonessential, and for clothing especially, has significance for the constitution and performance of modern femininities that is recognized around the world. The spatial relations in the shop, between staff and between staff and customers, are inevitably related to the spatial relations outside the shop, as bodies move from one space to another, performing different elements of their identities as they go (from daughter at home, to worker in the shop, to consumer in the lunch-hour perusal of other retail outlets, to passenger on public transport) only some elements of which are legible to the external observer and all of which require different cultural competencies to be decoded.

But through all this the veil, in all its forms, suffers from an almost generic illegibility in that the dress acts of most veiling women in the UK are observed by a majority non-veiling and non-Islamic audience who cannot adequately deduce the significance of their veiling choices. Women who veil are almost inevitably read as Muslim by a majority audience—even though there are in Britain substantial established communities of Hindus and Sikhs whose female members will also often veil. In a situation where the expression through dress of ethnicity and religion are often united in the minds of their practitioners (Dwyer 1999), the likelihood of veiled women being presumed Muslim by those outside their communities is high.[1] As such, Islamophobic prejudice or well-intentioned protectionism will rain on any woman who veils, regardless of her actual ethnic or religious identity. Although "the" veil is often fetishized as a thing in itself, this garment (in all its varieties) can, like all dress, best be understood as what Joanne Entwistle calls a "situated bodily practice" (2000: 3). Clothes and fashions acquire social meaning through being worn on dressed bodies whose ability to present in socially appropriate ways relies on the internalization of learned "techniques of the body"—literally how to hold oneself, to walk, to dress (Mauss 1973 in Entwistle 2000: 14). Nobody is born knowing how to walk in high heels, but many women in Western cultures learn the body management necessary to enact this particular gender-specific and socially sanctioned embodied practice. Wearing any form of veil similarly requires the development of particular techniques of body management, such as the processes by which Hindu girls in an Indian village "learn" to wear the veil, progressing from the lighter half-sari adopted in late childhood to the complex techniques demanded by stricter forms of face and head covering as they grow towards marriageable age (Tarlo 1996).

Not only is dress an embodied practice, it is also spatialized and temporal—dressed bodies are given meaning though their location in specific times and places which have their own rules of dress and comportment. Space is not an inert entity in which things just happen, it is dynamic, and the different places that dressed bodies inhabit are relational, acquiring distinction and meaning from their relationship to what lies "beyond" (Massey 1994). Individuals, therefore, never belong to only one spatial community: they engage with overlapping sets of spatial relations whose socializing effects produce differences of gender, sexuality, class, race, and ethnicity.

But for veiled bodies, the diverse audiences that witness their spatialized dress practices provide additional complications. The veiled body in the contemporary postcolonial city travels across what Anna Secor usefully names as different "veiling regimes:" "spatially realized sets of hegemonic rules and norms regarding women's veiling, which are themselves produced by specific constellations of power" and which vary in terms of "formality, enforcement, stability, and contestation" (Secor 2002: 8). These regimes of veiling, which also include the normatization of non-veiling, inhere in different spaces and are enforced and challenged to varying extents (officially by state police in Saudi Arabia, or unofficially by the regulatory role of gossip and elders in close-knit minority ethnic communities in London). Combine the socializing dynamism of space with the concept of spatialized veiling regimes, and the veiled woman—sometimes presented as the passive victim of patriarchal cultures—emerges as an agent actively negotiating the spaces she encounters.

Women, with varying degrees of "choice" in different contexts, can be understood to exercise a series of cultural and subcultural competencies in their adherences to and destabilizations of veiling regimes, often moving between different regimes in the space of a single day and over the course of their lives. But the performative elements that make up these veiled manifestations are not universally comprehensible. This is where the traveling of bodies in the postcolonial city becomes so significant: the veiling and non-veiling inhabitants of a district like Southall in West London (that has a long-established and substantial South Asian community) may well be sufficiently familiar with their South Asian neighbors to distinguish between the dress (and regional affiliations) of Hindu, Sikh, or Muslim women, but when the veiled woman moves beyond the district she is likely to be incorporated within a discourse that— operating without the spatialized cultural competencies that might render her "legible" in Southall—frames her as Muslim.

Veiling as a Spatial System

The veil is not just a garment that is worn in particular locations: it is itself a spatializing device that facilitates the gender segregation of society for those communities that adhere to codes of gender seclusion. There are several misconceptions about the veil that need to be addressed: first, although the veil is today predominantly associated with Islam, it is a garment that is pre-Islamic in origin and one that has been adopted by diverse religious and ethnic communities, especially in the Middle East. Secondly, in the Middle East, the veil often signified status rather than piety or ethnic allegiance. Thirdly, there is no single garment that equates to the veil: different versions of clothing that are held suitably to preserve modesty in gender-mixed environments have been adopted by different communities (often with different names for the same garment). Furthermore, the form of these garments or combinations of garments changes over time, quite often within the lifespan of a single woman. Thus, attempts to legislate which type of body covering is properly Islamic can only be seen as partial and located. Fourthly, the veil is intended primarily as outerwear, as a garment that preserves modesty between the sexes when outside the gender secluded space of the Islamically structured home (or when non-familial men are present in the domestic space, as may be case more often these days). It is this last element that brings us most closely to questions of spatiality.

As Fatima Mernissi (1985) has argued, the veil can be understood as a sartorial mechanism by which the gender seclusion of the harem system—the Islamic organization of domestic space that keeps a distance between women and those men to whom they are not closely related—is extended beyond the harem walls. Based on the presumption of an active female sexuality, harem seclusion and the veil serve to keep men and women separated to protect the community from the chaos of *fitna*, or uncontrolled sexual energy that would be released by inappropriate sexual contact.

For the Islamic world, harem and veiling, properly understood, require codes of modesty from both genders: men as well as women should dress modestly, and should deport their bodies in ways that will not prompt inappropriate cross-sex contact. Thus for women in territories largely governed by Muslim habits of body management, the wearing of a veil constitutes a legible display that prompts similarly respectful performances from male bodies in her vicinity, such as not staring at her face. In a Western postcolonial environment of mixed religious, genders, and ethnicities, there is no such social contract. (Ironically, one of the behaviors that was held retrospectively to mark out the "extremist" tendencies of one of the London bombers was his habit in his recent ultra-orthodox incarnation of refusing to meet the eyes of any woman in public. This practice, when repositioned to postcolonial, post-industrial northern England, read as misplaced zealotry to others in his community, rather than as good modest manners).

The harem space from which the veiled woman emanates has often been misunderstood in the West as a sexualized domain, seen within Orientalist fantasy as more akin to a brothel or sexual prison than to the domestic home (Lewis 1996). Since Western observers, unless they were female, could not visit these segregated domains, it was common until recently to regard the harem as a "private" space, cut off from the public world of politics and commerce. But to project the Western ideology of the separate spheres onto the Islamic household was inaccurate on a number of counts. For those elite sections of the population who lived in vast, architecturally divided households, the harem was not an isolated sphere but the space of family life, punctuated by female visitors and traders (Graham-Brown 1988). In less elite households, the harem quarters were where income generating as well as domestic household labor took place. Segregation did not and does not necessarily mean isolation: within a set of seclusionary spatial relations organized around different notions of public and private women constitute their own public, with attendant networks of patronage and power appropriate to the social status of the household (Peirce 1993). In the late nineteenth and early twentieth century elite women in the modernizing centers of Istanbul and Cairo were a vibrant public for each other's political and cultural activities crucial to the negotiation and development of regional modernities (Lewis and Micklewright 2006)—and consumption was one of the key arenas through which different modernities were worked out.

Dress as a Temporal Practice: Veiling, Shopping, and Non-Western Modernities

In the development and representation of modernities in what might broadly be called the Muslim world, the veil in particular and female dress in general were a source of continual tension in debates about modernity and its compatibility with Islam from the early nineteenth century. As in subsequent and contemporary discussions, the

Reina Lewis

figure of woman stood for both defense of tradition and the march of modernity. For modernizing rulers like Mohamad Ali in Egypt (reigned 1805–49) and successive Ottoman sultans who sought to harness the advantages of modern Western technologies (from railways to cameras), the social behaviors that accompanied Western commodities were not necessarily to be emulated. The indigenization of Western technologies and goods was therefore a process of selective adaptation rather than straightforward adoption (Frierson 2000), as Ottoman-style leaders adapted Western imports to suit local social mores. For example, the baroque facade that appeared to promise a Western-style interior would often surround a conventional Islamic organization of interior space (Göçek 1996). The arena where most people encountered Western goods was in the home and most of this selective cross-cultural consumption was directed by women.

It was through clothing that Western designs were most pressingly brought to bear on non-Western bodies. Women of the Egyptian and Ottoman royal families and the progressive elites that surrounded them had access to Paris fashions from the mid-nineteenth century, ordering direct from Paris and commissioning copies from local seamstresses who visited the harems. Fashion designs were seen in the imported European press and the Ottoman and Egyptian women's press (Baron 1994; Frierson 1999). Apart from complete toilettes of the latest French styles, women increasingly altered conventional Ottoman garments to include elements of Western styling, such as the addition of a definite waistline to the previously loose-fitting *entari* (a shift-like garment) that had by the 1890s been almost universally remodeled to accommodate the now ubiquitous corset. But as these modifications were to indoor rather than outerwear, the curious Western observer did not see them, and if they did, were rarely equipped to understand their significance (Micklewright 2000). Western clothing and goods that were seen were most often bewailed by Westerners as a sad absence of picturesque local "costume" (Lewis and Micklewright 2006) in a version of "imperialist nostalgia" (Rosaldo 1993) that allowed Westerners to position themselves as the experts on and guardians of "real" oriental dress and to sneer at the "vulgarity" of Ottoman cultural hybridity.

Whether individual's use of Western commodities signaled a conscious or only a vague sense of modernity or progressiveness (Duben and Behar 1991), by the turn of the twentieth century most sectors of the urban population were regularly engaging with Western goods. The ways in which Muslim women encountered Western fashion items reveals the extent to which local modernization processes contributed to and relied on the development of new (gendered) spatialities.

Women from segregated households in Istanbul and Cairo and other major cities started to go out to shop, in the bazaars of the old city quarters and, in Istanbul, to the shops of Pera, the international quarter. These excursions were made possible by a combination of two potentially conflicting spatial relations: the modernizations of the Tanzimat reforms that aimed in part to open up mixed gender spaces outside the home, and the Islamic conventions of the veil. Though this meant that veiled women were increasingly more visible on public streets, the nuanced social stratification of who was seen where and engaged in which consumer activities was often only perceptible to inside observers. Lelya Sazhammeffendi, writing about her youth in the household of Sultan Abdulmecit in the 1850s and 1860s, recalls that when the imperial princesses visited the Grand Bazaar their shopping was managed through a partial seclusion in the Bazaar's mosque, a space understood as socially restricted by the other elite (but not royal) ladies, who took care "never to stop in any of the dependencies of the Mosque in order not to give the impression of imitating the Imperial Harem" (Lelya Sazhammeffendi 1920 in Lewis and Micklewright 2006: 181). In Alexandria by the 1890s, the young Hoda Shaarawi, later a prominent nationalist and feminist leader, was thrilled to visit the new department store—a spatial incursion achieved only after substantial negotiations with her parents' household. "[A]shamed" of the scene caused by her overzealous eunuch and the retinue that accompanied her, Shaarawi eventually persuaded her mother to visit the store at which point permission to shop alone was granted (Shaarawi 1987 in Lewis and Micklewright 2006: 192).

Recognized by themselves and their male peers as both potentially liberating and potentially dangerous, engaging in fashion innovation and visiting department stores or dressmakers outside the home were key elements of Middle Eastern modernities for many women. Sumptuary legislation concerning women's dress in the last decades of the Ottoman Empire focused on outerwear as the visible symbol of women's propriety, subjecting it to a variety of often-contradictory imperial decrees. These were implemented with mixed degrees of success across the empire and, even within the capital, depended for their effect on the class and generational characteristics of particular districts (Davis 1986). Women's outerwear was more likely to change in response to the garments underneath, developing to accommodate trends in the adaptation of Western styles, so that the silhouette seen in public in one year would be the loose cape-like *çarşaf* (preferred for its ability to house wide puffy belle époque sleeves), whist the closer-fitting *feraçe* returned to favor in the early years of the twentieth century. Head coverings also varied in response to fashions in hairstyles, with *yaşmaks* hovering fetchingly over bouffant Edwardian coiffures, only to be discarded for closer-fitting versions of the *çarşaf* that skimmed close to the face to reveal a lick of flapper curl in the 1910s and 1920s (Lewis 2004). Local custom and practice was often more effectively regulatory than imperial edicts. The prominent Turkish nationalist and feminist Halide Edib ran up against an unofficial but stringently enforced regime of veiling when visiting a poor area in the fashionable "modern" *çarşaf* of her class through which the threatening street children could discern her modishly bouffant hair. Narrowly avoiding being stoned, Edib on subsequent trips remembered to wear a "loose old-fashioned" *çarşaf* that was "never pinned … so tight as to make the form of my head and hair apparent" (Edib 2005[1926]: 362).

Local wardrobe decisions were understood to have international ramifications. Ottomans and Egyptians were well aware that the image of the veiled harem lady was seen by the West as an indicator of the state of civilization of their entire society and took pains to counter Orientalist stereotypes, often through attention to the dressed visibility of Muslim women. By the 1920s, in a version of modernity that was to become increasingly and aggressively secular, the new Turkish republic under Mustapha Kemal (Atatürk) used the public presence of unveiled female bodies to advertise its modernity to itself and to the West, specifically aiming to disassociate itself from the old-style image of the secluded *hanim* (lady). Still regulating religion, but displacing it to the domestic sphere, the Kemalist modernization project relied on the public performance of educated unveiled femininity as a route to national social emancipation through Westernizing secularization (Göle 1996). When Demetra Vaka Brown, a Greek Ottoman-American, returned to a war-torn and occupied Istanbul in 1922 to interview the first generation of unveiled shop girls, it is clear that they were motivated by a sense of participating in a project of nation building—and that this imbued with honor their public unveiled retail labor (Vaka 2005[1923]). But to what extent are contemporary British shop girls in veils heirs to these insurrectionary activities?

Regulating Bodies in Space: Shop Dress Codes

All the fashion retail outlets listed at the start of this article can be found in most British high streets and shopping malls. Unlike the independent boutique, these companies require their staff to dress according to a uniform code, be it branded in-house uniforms, selections from the current range, or the mix of store uniform and franchise merchandise worn in the department store.

Associated with the rise of women as shop workers in the last quarter of the nineteenth century, shop dress codes (and later uniforms) were designed to establish the respectability of their largely female staff. Often accompanied by strict rules about behavior, dress codes created an identity for the establishment through the regulation of employees' bodies inside and outside the store. Within an often paternalistic management style (especially in the large department stores), the respectability of shop work as a form of employment was one of the attractions for working-class women who saw it as a step up, and for middle-class women who were reassured that the propriety of social relations in the store would help make shop work a respectable career (Lancaster 2000). Women's dress at work was a key factor in the manufacture of these decorous social relations, whilst association with the glamour and modernity of fashion retail was itself a lure (that continued into the twentieth century; Winship 2000).

Today, in relation to the veil, UK employers are bound by the new British regulations concerning discrimination at work. The previous legislation outlawing racial discrimination could not cover Muslims as such, extending only to those faith communities established in law as an ethnic group, such as Jews or Sikhs. For the multi-ethnic Muslim population, it needed the 2003 Employment Equality (Religion or Belief) Regulations to extend protection against discrimination at work, or in vocational training. Significantly, the law covers discrimination "on the grounds of perceived as well as actual religion or belief (i.e. assuming—correctly or incorrectly—that someone has a particular religion or belief)" (http://www.dti.gov.uk/er/equality). The emphasis on perceived religion attests to a state recognition of the instability and potential illegibility of performances of religious identity.

For shop workers this means that the employer now has an obligation to permit and to facilitate the expression of religious identity as defined by employees and therefore must not discriminate against or in any way treat differently an employee who wishes to wear a veil. An employee's right to expression is limited by the provision for unspecified exceptions, and, when I started on this project in 2004, my discussion with the British arbitration service ACAS revealed that were as yet no cases concerning the veil at work in the public domain. At that time it was generally anticipated that exceptions to the new regulation would be in terms of health and safety: for example, a Sikh man might not be permitted on safety grounds to wear a *kirpan* (ritual sword) when working in an airport. In the early stages of this work, but after the London bombs, my straw poll of human resources departments at high-street employers found a widespread acknowledgment that women could wear a veil "if their religion demanded it." This is a situation specific to Britain: for employees of international retailers who work in branches elsewhere in the world, clothing rights at work (beyond those permitted by individual companies, some of whom have an equal opportunities code of practice) are subject to local state law. Whilst recent changes to British law have been designed to bring British regulation in line with the European Employment Equality Directive (2000), for employees in other EU states who find themselves denied the right to wear a veil the European Court of Human Rights will provide the point of last appeal. However, since my initial inquiries, the situation in the UK has changed and veiling has featured so prominently in debates about social inclusion and belonging that I cannot imagine employers being willing or able casually to answer questions about veiling at work. Recent court cases have made Muslim veiling a prominent employment issue, and have shifted the focus from covering the head to covering the face.

Since the 1980s, policies of multiculturalism in Britain have permitted the "tolerance" of visible signs of ethnic and religious diversity—in stark contrast to the aggressive secularism of the (Muslim) republic of Turkey and the (Catholic) republic of France. But in the early years of the twenty-first century, challenges to accepted UK veiling regimes by young women revivalists have tested the sartorial limits of multiculturalism. In 2002, teenager Shabina Begum took her Luton school to court after being refused permission to wear a *jilbab* rather than the uniform option of shalwar kameez and headscarf (that had been negotiated with the area's large South Asian community). Contested up to the House of Lords, where she eventually lost (http://www.publications.parliament.uk/pa/ld/ldjudgmt.htm), Begum's actions in seeking to distinguish herself through the assertive performance of a revivalist identity had obvious implications for other Muslim girls in the UK. Where some have "up-veiled" in solidarity, others have been compelled to wear an unwanted *jilbab*, once the alibi of school uniform was eroded (Hari 2005).

In 2006, the issue of the niqab hit the British press when Jack Straw, a Labour MP and former Foreign Secretary, revealed that he asked women wearing a face veil to remove it during consultations in his constituency office. Briefing the national press about an article he had written for the local paper of his Midlands constituency, Straw characterized the niqab as "a visible statement of separation and difference," arguing that it was an obstacle to communication in that "the value of a meeting, as opposed to a letter or phone call, is that you can—almost literally—see what the other person means, not just hear what they say" http://www.telegraph.co.uk/news/main.jhtml?xml=/news/10/06/nveils106.xml).

At the same time two court cases that questioned the ability of women in niqabs to carry out professional duties hit the news within weeks of each other, feeding the ferment of commentary and demonstration. In one, the young teaching assistant Aisha Azmi lost her case at industrial tribunal (appeal pending) against the school that sacked her for wearing a niqab in the classroom. The school, that had hired her to help non-native speakers improve their English language, claimed that the children needed to see as well as hear her forming the words. In the other, legal advocate Shabnam Mughal won a partial victory over the judge in an immigration tribunal, who suspended proceedings when she refused to remove her niqab. In an interim decision Mr Justice Hodge, president of the Asylum and Immigration Tribunal, advised that the niqab be permitted in court unless a judge's inability to hear meant that "the interests of justice are not served" (*The Independent* November 10 2006: 23).

Couched not in terms of health and safety, but on the assertion that the niqab impedes verbal and visual communication these challenges to veiling habits normatize Western modes of body management and, in the case of Straw especially, naturalize the culturally specific presumption that visual expression is an accurate guide to inner feeling. At the time of going to press, these challenges to expressions of faith-based identities are provoking widespread cultural crises for minority and majority communities. Whilst face covering of any form is a minority practice among the UK veiling population, this intense focus on the niqab has effectively shifted the common-sense definition of the "veil" from head covering to face covering—with an attendant ratcheting up of political activity. Revivalist young women take up the niqab as a badge of anti-establishment honor, whilst the government issues consultation documents specifically offering schools the opportunity to ban niqabs from their premises.

Spaces of Fashion

Non-Western clothing has until recently often been relegated to the domain of dress, or worse, costume—a form of clothing presented as the unchanging expression of essential-ized collective cultural identities antithetical to the fast-paced turnover of individuating style typical of Western fashion. Without entering into counter-arguments about the dynamism of non-Western dress (see Barnes and Eicher 1992), it is helpful here to locate the Western fashion system as a historically and geographically specific set of dress prac-tices tied to particular conditions of production, distribution, and consumption (Entwistle 2000). Rooted in the development of modernity and characterized by rapid changes in style, fashion arises in situations of potential social mobility offering the subject a tech-nique of dressing with which "self consciously to construct an identity suitable for the modern stage" (Entwistle 2000: 75).

In the Middle East, local fashion circuits evolved as part of indigenized consumer cultures (Durakbaşa and Cindoğlu 2002), often with the overt politicization of consumer practices typical of non-Western modernities. In the new Turkish republic, the Kemalists promoted the unveiled "daughters of the republic" (Durakbaşa 1993) as a sign of the nation state's successful modernity. The nascent consumption habits of the late Ottoman era were appropriated to extend to the rest of the population a lifestyle that signified Westernized "civilization" and modernity—specifically positioning the veiled body as the opposite of modernity and, by inference, of civilization (Göle 1996).

However, in Turkey and elsewhere since the late 1970s, the presumed exile of the veiled woman from the spaces of modernity has been challenged by what has now become a range of politicized Islamist dress practices. Whilst earlier forms of revivalist dress pioneered in Egypt in the mid-1970s were made at home by activists (El Guindi 1999), by the 1990s in Turkey the emergence of an Islamic bourgeoisie had led to the development and manufacture of Islamic products and services distributed and consumed as part of an Islamic lifestyle. For the Turkish state, the assertive spatial practices of veiled educated Islamist women who demand a place in state education and institutions is a contradiction in terms. Intervening in the public domain, Islamist women cover themselves in distinc-tive ways (*tesettür*), using their plain "raincoats" and closely pinned, often patterned, headscarves to distinguish themselves from the looser headscarf (*başörtüsü*) associated with rural immigrant women (Secor 2002). That for many young Islamist women this sartorial choice marks them out as different from their mothers is precisely the point: like other forms of revivalist dress, their new form of veiling seeks to present itself as a doctrinal choice based on personal knowledge of the holy texts.

The poster girl of the internationalist Islamist movement, the *tesettür*-clad woman's style, and practices of spatial incursion travel the globe via the new magazines and websites that support the emergent Islamist consumer. Replacing mainstream/secular style intermediaries, Islamist journalists emphatically represent veils as fashion, with reports of new veiling trends (following the seasonal colors of international fashion) that secure veiling as a form of individuating self-expression explicitly tied to modern lifestyle consumer culture (Kılıçbay and Binark 2002). As an embodied dressed subject in the urban spaces of contemporary cities, the Islamist woman stands simultaneously as an emblem of a supra-national Islamist collectivity and as evidence of the "latent individualism" emerging among the increasingly autonomous female elite cadres of the revivalist movements (Göle 1996: 22). In Britain, too, Islamic consumers can be guided by the recent development of Muslim lifestyle media (such as the magazine *Emel*, established 2003) and pro-*hijab* websites. Training in the management of veiled bodies, that might otherwise have been localized through female relatives and community observers, is provided increasingly by the Internet (and Islamic societies at college and university) as the often young Islamist adherents take up veiling practices at odds with the habits of home norms and their mothers' generation. In postcolonial Britain women who veil (for any reason) operate within overlapping spatialities and competing but mutually constituting dress systems, including international *tesettür*, UK diaspora dress conventions, and the "mainstream" fashion system.

The spatialized relations of the contemporary globalized fashion industry are integral to and influenced by the dress choices of veiling women. Whilst expanding numbers of retail outlets whether actual (in the UK or abroad) or virtual, offer the chance to consume primarily through ethically Muslim businesses, in the UK as elsewhere, most Muslim women wear the veil in conjunction with non-Islamic fashion. But veiling women are not positioned simply in a dichotomous relationship between ethnic and mainstream fashion; the "cross-fertilization" between the two (Jones and Leshkowich 2003) creates interwoven production–consumption circuits and veiling regimes (on "designer" headscarves, see Balasescu 2003). As the Islamic lifestyle market diversifies, women may simultaneously find themselves excluded by the new subcultural taste communities of Islamist "cool" (Boubekeur 2005), and included by the periodic "trickle-up" of ethnic dress into the mainstream. Signaling both the influence of diaspora street style and of the vitality of diaspora fashion entrepreneurship (see Puwar and Raghuran 2003), the repositioning of "traditional" dress as temporarily fashionable can enable new formulations of diasporic cultural authenticity (Mani 2003) at the same time as it can reinforce social divisions between those who wear "Asian chic" as fashion or as habit (Leshkowich and Jones 2003).

Conclusion: Selling Spaces

Although the mainstream may well presume to relegate Asian dress back to the temporally alien zone of the unfashionable, Dwyer and Crang suggest that interacting with commodity culture can offer minority fashion designers and consumers a "matrix for the fashioning of ethnicities" (2002: 411). Their argument that ethnic identities are not essential and preexistent but are achieved socially and relationally, gives renewed significance to the bodily performances of veiled women. Demarcating differences between groups as well as within groups, one woman's adoption of particular veiling habits will have an effect on the perceived and experienced identities of other women both in her immediate vicinity and in all the spaces discursively touched by her actions.

Just as school students know that they are judged in relation to the veiling practices of other students and teachers (Dwyer 1999), the appearance behind the shop counter of a veiled body immediately repositions the other bodies around it. Staff can find themselves having to explain to non-Muslim colleagues why they do not veil, or veil in a different way, and potentially having to justify their choices to other co-religionists on the workforce. Similarly, the self-presentation of shop staff may facilitate comfortable retail geographies for Muslim consumers, as shoppers and workers circulate cultural knowledges about which stores are likely to have veiled staff and or be Muslim friendly employers. If, as David Gilbert (2000) argues, garments are rendered meaningful by the manner of their acquisition (shopping with friends, good advice from an assistant) as much as by their design or even their wearing, then the presence of the veiled shop assistant becomes an important element of the shopping process. As Deborah Leslie notes, fashion is "a commodity whose production is highly globalized, but whose display, marketing and ultimate consumption is localized on the body" (2002: 62). The embodied geographies of interactive service sector work require staff (waiters, shop assistants, or merchant bankers) to perform gendered social identities suitable to the product being sold (McDowell and Court 1994). Whilst the self-conscious performance of the required identities can be pleasurable for employees (sharing in the cultural capital of the work location), it is also potentially alienating (Crang 1994). When the body of the assistant is veiled fashion retail's overinvestment in the bodies of its staff (far more than other areas of retail) raises new questions about staff selection, training, and retention.

Inside and outside the store the occurrence of dress acts within relational spatial frameworks—"encompassing more than one individual body" (Secor 2002: 7)—connects shopper and retailer to each other and to bodies in places beyond their particular location. The trajectories of individual shopping processes undo the apparently bounded space of a single store (carefully demarcated by the uniformed bodies of its staff) so that it loses its spatial integrity, becoming, as Louise Crewe puts it, "a tapestry of different spaces, woven together to comprise personal accumulated shopping geographies" (2003: 355). But in context where the polysemic potential of dress acts supersedes the control of wearers (with *tesettür* sometimes adopted out of social aspiration rather than piety; White 2002), it is not only majoritarian observers who may "fail" to decipher individual women's veiling intentions. With the political and discursive creation post-7/7 of new categories for British Muslims of "moderate" and "extremist," recent attempts by the courts to arbitrate between acceptable and unreasonable forms of veiling play out across the bodies of Muslim women the wider debate about nationality and belonging—often premised on essentialized categories of gender and identity. Given the alarming hypervisibility accorded to the veiled woman, the reminder that women who veil (in any way and for any reason) operate within overlapping spatialities and competing but mutually constituting dress systems may be a way to think through some of the bewildering challenges of dress politics in postcolonial Britain.

Note

[1] This article concerns itself specifically with Muslim forms of veiling, and generically with the ways in which veiled bodies are incorporated as Muslim within a dominant discourse. For reasons of space, I have restricted my comparative geographical and temporal focus to the modernizing centers of the late Ottoman Empire and the modern Turkish Republic.

References

Barnes, R. and J. B. Eicher (eds). 1992. *Dress and Gender: Making and Meaning.* Oxford: Berg.

Balasescu, Alexandru. 2003. "Tehran Chic: Islamic Headscarves, Fashion Designers, and New Geographies of Modernity." *Fashion Theory* 7(1): 39–56.

Benson, Susan Porter. 1986. *Counter Cultures: Saleswomen, Managers, and Customers in American Department Stores 1890–1940.* Urbana and Chicago, IL: University of Illinois Press.

Boubekeur, Amel. 2005. "Cool and Competitive: Muslim Culture in the West." *ISIM Review (International Institute for the Study of Islam in the Modern World)* 16: 12–13.

Crang, Philip. 1994. "It's Showtime: On the Workplace Geographies of Display in a Restaurant in Southeast England." *Environment and Planning D: Society and Space* 12: 675–704.

Crewe, Louise. 2003. "Geographies of Retailing and Consumption: Markets in Motion." *Progress in Human Geography* 27(3): 352–62.

Davis, Fanny. 1986. *The Ottoman Lady: A Social History from 1718–1918.* New York: Greenwood Press.

Duben, Alan and Cem Behar. 1991. *Istanbul Households: Marriage, Family and Fertility, 1880–1940.* Cambridge: Cambridge University Press.

Durakbaşa, Ayşe. 1993. "*Reappraisal of Halide Edib for a Critique of Turkish Modernization.*" Unpublished PhD thesis, Department of Sociology, University of Essex.

Durakbaşa, Ayşe and Dilek Cindoğlu. 2002. "Encounters at the Counter: Gender and the Shopping Experience." In Deniz Kandiyoti and Ayşe Saktanber (eds) *Fragments of Culture: The Everyday of Modern Turkey*, pp. 73–89. London: I. B. Tauris.

Dwyer, Claire. 1999. "Veiled Meanings: Young British Muslim Women and the Negotiation of Differences." *Gender, Place and Culture* 6(1): 5–26.

Dwyer, Claire and Philip Crang. 2002. "Fashioning Ethnicities: The Commercial Spaces of Multiculture." *Ethnicities* 2(3): 410–30.

Edib, Halide Adivar. 2005[1926]. *Memoirs of Halidé Edib.* Piscataway, NJ: Gorgias Press.

Entwistle, Joanne. 2000. *The Fashioned Body: Fashion, Dress and Modern Social Theory.* Cambridge: Polity.

Frierson, Elizabeth B. 1999. "Cheap and Easy: The Creation of Consumer Culture in Late Ottoman Society." In Donald Quataert (ed.) *Consumption Studies and the History of the Ottoman Empire 1550–1922*, pp. 243–60. New York: State University of New York Press.

Frierson, Elizabeth B. 2000. "Mirrors Out, Mirrors In: Domestication and Rejection the Foreign in Late-Ottoman Women's Magazines." In Dede Fairchild Ruggles (ed.) *Women, Patronage, and Self-Representation in Islamic Societies*, pp. 177–204. New York: State University of New York Press.

Gilbert, David. 2000. "Urban Outfitting: The City and the Spaces of Fashion Culture." In Stella Bruzzi and Pamela Church Gibson (eds) *Fashion Cultures: Theories, Explorations and Analysis*, pp. 7–24. London: Routledge.

Göçek, Fatma Müge. 1996. *Rise of the Bourgeoisie, Demise of Empire: Ottoman Westernization and Social Change.* New York: Oxford University Press.

Göle, Nilüfer. 1996. *The Forbidden Modern: Civilization and Veiling.* Ann Arbor, MI: University of Michigan Press.

Graham-Brown, Sarah. 1988. *Images of Women: The Portrayal of Women in Photography of the Middle East 1860–1950.* London, Quartet.

El Guindi, F. 1999. "Veiling Resistance." *Fashion Theory* 3(1): 51–80.

Hari, Johann. 2005. "Multiculturalism is Not the Best Way to Welcome People to Our Country." The Independent August 5 2005: 35.

Jones, Carla, and Ann Marie Leshkowich. 2003. "Introduction: The Globalization of Asian Dress: Re-Orienting Fashion or Re-Orientalizing Asia." In, Sandra Neissen, Ann Marie Leshkowich and Carla Jones (eds) *Re-Orienting Fashion: The Globalization of Asian Dress*, pp. 1–48. Oxford: Berg.

Kılıçbay, Barış and Mutlu Binark. 2002. "Consumer Culture, Islam and the Politics of Lifestyle." *European Journal of Communication* 17(4): 495–511.

Lancaster, Bill. 2000. *The Department Store: A Social History*. Leicester: Leicester University Press.

Leshkowich, Ann Marie and Carla Jones. 2003. "What Happens with Asian Chic Becomes Chic in Asia?" *Fashion Theory* 7(3–4): 281–300.

Lewis, Reina. 1996. *Gendering Orientalism: Race, Femininity and Representation*. London: Routledge.

Lewis, Reina. 2004. *Rethinking Orientalism: Women, Travel and the Ottoman Harem*. London: I. B. Tauris.

Lewis, Reina and Nancy Micklewright (eds). 2006. *Gender, Modernity, Liberty: Middle Eastern and Western Women's Writings, a Critical Sourcebook*. London: I. B. Tauris.

Leslie, Deborah. 2002. "Gender, Retail Employment and the Clothing Commodity Chain." *Gender, Place and Culture* 9(1): 61–76.

McDowell, Linda and Gill Court. 1994. "Performing Work: Bodily Representations in Merchant Banks." *Environment and Planning D: Society and Space* 12: 727–750.

Mani, Bakirathi. 2003. "Undressing the Diaspora." in Nirmal Puwar and Parvati Raghuram (eds) *South Asian Women in the Diaspora*, pp. 117–36. Oxford: Berg.

Massey, Doreen. 1994. *Space, Place and Gender*. Cambridge: Polity Press.

Mernissi, Fatima. 1985. *Beyond the Veil: Male–Female Dynamics in Muslim Society*, 2nd edn. London: al Saqi Books.

Micklewright, Nancy. 2000. "Public and Private for Ottoman Women of the Nineteenth Century." In Dede Fairchild Ruggles (ed.) *Women, Patronage, and Self-Representation in Islamic Societies*, pp. 155–76. New York: State University of New York Press.

Miller, Daniel, Peter Jackson, Nigel Thrift, Beverley Holbrook and Michael Rowlands. 1998. *Shopping, Place and Identity*. London: Routledge.

Navaro-Yashin, Yael. 2002. "The Market for Identities: Secularism, Islamism, Communities." In Deniz Kandiyoti and Ayşe Saktanber (eds) *Fragments of Culture: The Everyday of Modern Turkey*, pp. 221–253. London: I. B. Tauris.

Puwar, Nirmal and Parvati Raghuram (eds). 2003. *South Asian Dress in the Diaspora*. Oxford: Berg.

Rosaldo, Renato. 1993. *Culture and Truth: The Remaking of Social Analysis*. London: Routledge.

Secor, Anna J. 2002. "The Veil and Urban Space in Istanbul: Women's Dress, Mobility and Islamic Knowledge." *Gender, Place and Culture* 9(1): 5–22.

Tarlo, Emma. 1996. *Clothing Matters: Dress and Identity in India*. London: C. Hurst and Co.

Vaka, Demetra (Mrs. Kenneth Brown). 2005[1923]. *The Unveiled Ladies of Stamboul*. Piscataway, NJ: Gorgias Press.

White, Jenny. 2002. "The Islamist Paradox." In Deniz Kandiyoti and Ayşe Saktanber (eds) *Fragments of Culture: The Everyday of Modern Turkey*, pp. 191–220. London: I. B. Tauris.

Wilson, Elizabeth. 2003. *Adorned in Dreams: Fashion and Modernity, revised and updated version*. London: I. B. Tauris.

Winship, Janice. 2000. "Culture of Restraint: The British Chain Store 1920–39." In Peter Jackson, Michelle Lowe, Daniel Miller and Frank Mort (eds) *Commercial Cultures: Economies, Practices, Spaces*, pp. 15–34. Oxford: Berg.

28 "Patriarchal Colonialism" and Indigenism

Implications for Native Feminist Spirituality and Native Womanism

M. A. Jaimes Guerrero

One perspective on "feminism" among Native American women is that the emphasis has been on individuality as conceived by early Western feminists who wanted more equality with men in the prevailing patriarchal sociopolitical structures in U. S. American society and who premised their struggle on democratic ideals for gender equity (Jaimes 1998, 413–39 or Jaimes 1999a, 1–25; see also Jaimes and Halsey 1992). Starting with the suffragettes, women among the upper and middle classes demanded the vote for "white" women within this historical legacy of the women's movement (Kerber and De Hart 1999, Introduction), but they were not concerned with other "women of color" in this democratic pursuit. Therefore, Native American women perceived this early feminism as a reaction to an existing patriarchal sociopolitical system not concerned with the racialized oppression—as a result of Euroamerican racism—of other marginalized women and subcultural groups of "ethnic minorities," such as Native Americans as tribal peoples, or with the impact of U. S. colonialism on their traditional ways of life. Feminists of these earlier and more exclusive times were focused on challenging sexism and the chauvinistic behavior of men, in general, toward women in mainstream populations. These feminists were generally more educated in Euroamerican hegemony, married, and of the middle class, in contrast to their "women of color" counterparts.

The Myth of "Tribalism" and U. S. Colonialism

The meaning of "tribalism" is often connoted with conformity and the subservience of the individual to the group, because each individual group member must follow group culture and rules, with little or no independent thinking—an almost "infantile"

M. A. Jaimes Guerrero, "'Patriarchal Colonialism' and Indigenism: Implications for Native Feminist Spirituality and Native Womanism." *Hypatia*, 18(2), 2003: 58–69. Reprinted by permission of John Wiley & Sons Ltd.

behavior posture. On the more positive side, tribalism connotes kinship and protection, meeting group members' needs for community and acceptance. This is the case among Native tribes, other ethnic groups, and other extended family traditions—including even gangs and athletic teams. Other terms attributed to the "tribal order" include magic, rituals, mysticism, animism, protection of ancestral or cultural traditions, myths, rights of kinship, and sacred places (Moyer 2000). Generally speaking, tribalism is not considered to reflect a high level of maturity or civilization within the Euroamerican hegemony; indeed, it is often considered to be primitive or savage, and therefore backward and uncivilized.

In this Eurocentric way of thinking, Native peoples and their cultures were often described as a "tribe" or as a "tribal people" in the same way in which groups of animals are named (such as a "gaggle of geese" or a "pack of wolves")—as a subspecies lesser than "white" or Anglicized humankind (Churchill 1992, 22–33). A more current definition of the term "tribe," from the *OED*, is "A group of persons forming a community and claiming common ancestry. A particular race of recognized ancestry; a family ... the families or communities of persons having the same surname. ... A race of people; now esp. to a primary aggregate of people in a primitive or barbarous condition, under a headman or chief" (*OED* 1985, s.v. "tribe"). In this hegemonic context, Native American peoples are seen, therefore, as dependent "tribes" with inferior cultures as compared to the Euroamerican dominant culture—as subordinate constructs, referred to in the U. S. Supreme Court's 1831 Marshall Decision as "domestic dependent nations" (Churchill and Morris 1992, 18). As a result of U. S. colonialism and patriarchal structure, the traditional authority of Native American women has been systematically disempowered up to the present time.

Native Americans, on the other hand, see themselves as "a People" and refer to themselves as such in their respective indigenous languages through the group names for themselves. For example, "Dine" (Navajo) and "Lakota" (Sioux) mean "the peoples." According to *Webster's Dictionary* (1969), a "people" is defined as: "*1. A body of persons united by a common character, culture, or sentiment; the individuals collectively of any characteristic group, conceived apart from the unity of the group as subject to common government (that is, as a state) or as issued from common stock (that is, as a race or tribe). 2. A race, tribe, or nation; as, the peoples of Europe* (Webster's 1969, s.v. "people"). The *OED* (1985) states the meaning of a "people" thus: "*A body of persons composing a community, tribe, race, or nation. ... Sometimes viewed as a unity, sometimes as a collective of number. ... The persons belonging to a place or occupying a particular concourse, congregation, company, or class. ... Those to whom any one belongs; the members of one's tribe, clan, family, community, association, church, etc., collectively. ... The common people, the commonality. ... The whole body of enfranchised or qualified citizens, considered as the source of power; esp. in a democratic state, the electorate. ... Men or women indefinitely; men and women, persons, folk*" (*OED* 1985, s.v. "people").

In these definitional configurations of the British/American English language, with its Germanic roots, it is evident how the Eurocentric lexicon is used in the dominant/subordinate construction of the colonizer and the colonized, with imperialist aims, monopolistic agendas, and even duplicitous confusion as to which "people," as a population entity, calls itself a nation or state, thus subjugating "the other" to marginal status as an "ethnicity" or "tribe," with corresponding subcultural or minority sociopolitical status.

Through the acceptance of the United Nations charter and other human rights instruments, the self-determination of all peoples is a nearly universally accepted aspiration in modern times. This inherent right of self-determination of peoples, however, has only been recognized with the realization that colonialism is an abhorrent obstacle to the desired liberty of all humanity. Colonialism is a theoretical construct in Euroamerican international law, and its meaning can only be defined in the context of the Eurocentric paradigm as an imperialist doctrine: colonialism is the "control by one power over a dependent area of people. It is also construed as a policy advocating or based on such control" (*Webster's* 1969, s.v. "colonialism"). In this definitional context, the colonizer is "an animal or plant which has [not] quite established itself in a place where it is not indigenous" (*Webster's* 1969, s.v. "colonizer"). Hence, the colonist or colonialist is a usurper, "one who takes part in founding a colony" (*OED* 1985, s.v. "colonialist") where other peoples and their respective territorial nation-hoods have already been established. Therefore, the colony is established as a predatory process of colonialism in order to gain dominion over the earlier inhabitants, their land, and its natural resources. Half of the Native population was women, and among them were those who held formidable spheres of authority and leadership as Clan Mothers. Moreover, there has been an inevitable cost to the colonizers due to their actions as invading transgressors—a loss of humanity for themselves as well as others.

On the historical precedence that premises European and U. S. colonialism, Native scholars in international law and politics have noted the colonialist distinction made between Christians and others. Stigmatized as infidels (or worse, as heretics), indigenous peoples have been labeled as non-Christians and denigrated as pagans, savages, or heathens. Native legal scholar Glenn T. Morris writes, "As an extension of the Roman legal principle, *territorium (res) nullius*, "… a 'discoverer' could legally occupy a territory that was already inhabited (by 'infidels') and extend Christian sovereignty over it" (1992, 58). In response to Spanish colonial law, Morris also notes that the first known European documents addressing the question of dominion over the "New World" were the *Papal Bulls* of Pope Alexander VI. Such documents acknowledged the right of the sovereigns of Castille and Aragon to acquire and Christianize the islands and *terra firma* of the new regions. The issuance of these religio-political laws created immediate tensions and international legal debates that would remain unresolved in Europe from their inception to the present (Churchill and Morris 1992, 59). The situation of the European Irish constituted an anomaly in the usual imperialist situation of Christian-over-"pagan," because historical events in Western Europe led to the colonization and consequent subjugation of the predominantly Catholic Irish after the authority of the Catholic Church was overthrown in Britain by the Anglican Protestant Church. In ancient times, however, Celtic peoples were also subjugated as "pagans" by British imperialists.

Morris continues:

> The historical antecedents of the legal rights of indigenous peoples may be found centuries prior to the European arrival in the Western hemisphere. After the establishment of the Holy Roman Empire, but prior to the colonial travels of various peoples to the "New World" … distinctions drawn by Europeans between the known world were generally in terms of Christians and infidels. …

Although the [U. S.] claims that its national legislature possesses such rights under the "plenary power doctrine," its assertion is not unlike similar claims by other colonizing states that have maintained their relations with colonized peoples are purely domestic issues. ... The roots of the assertion that the [U. S.] possesses exclusive domestic jurisdiction over its relations with indigenous nations can be found in [its] case law and the self-serving legislation that often accompanied it. Asserting such claims, however, does not accord them acceptance under law. ... While it is true that the [U. S.] Congress has passed thousands of laws in the area of U. S.- indigenous affairs, to suggest that the unilateral acts of a legislature can diminish the national sovereignty of [these historical] nations ... seems an unjustifiable conclusion. ... By 1820 ... the power of the [U. S.] had been consolidated ... to the extent that many indigenous nations were vulnerable to military invasion by U. S. forces. The expansion of the U. S. was fueled by a racist philosophy ... [therefore] the [U. S.] Americans [as colonialists] believed that through divine ordination and the natural superiority of the white race, they had a right (and indeed an obligation) to seize and occupy all of North America. (1992, 58–67)

The imposition of colonialism on Native peoples and their land-based cultures has conferred a unique status as designated tribal nations with "quasi-sovereignty" within the United States. These Federal-Indian relations were based on treaties and other agreements, negotiated as land transactions between approximately 400 "federally-recognized" Native groups and the United States. (Churchill and Morris 1992, 13–21). What the historical texts conveniently leave out, in terms of the impact of aggressive colonization on a disrupted people, is the question of the impact and cost of this disruption on these Native peoples and their land-based cultures. This inquiry also needs to be contextualized in postcolonialist terms regarding concerns over biocolonialism and biopiracy (see Jaimes Guerrero forthcoming).

Will Durant, a prolific Marxian scholar, authored (with his wife, Ariel, whose contributions he would only later acknowledge) a ten-volume Eurocentric "history of civilization" in which he observes, with regard to what he terms "village communities," that the individual was hardly recognized as a separate entity in natural (that is, indigenous) society. Within such a context, he notes, kin-ship was valued over virtually all other possible forms of social organization, and power was derived from consent rather than from more abstract sources of a "right" to domination: "primitive" societies functioned essentially on the basis of cooperation, collective enterprise, and communal custom, according to this view. The social form in question, Durant implies, had much more to commend it by way of its humanity than any of its more "modern" counterparts, and might accordingly be considered something of a model for emulation in a world beset by ruthless competition, the extreme brutality of a hierarchy and class inequality, and global warfare. Remarking that this comparatively idyllic social existence had once been virtually universal, he muses that it should certainly be possible for "modern man"—with all "his" material and intellectual attainment—to do as well (1954, 21–35).

Of course, despite his benignly good intentions and obvious accuracy of much of his analysis—more than likely influenced by Karl Marx's notion that early indigenous peoples practiced a form of "primitive communism" (Marx, in Durant 1954, 21, 35)—

Durant is still engaging in the fundamentally Eurocentric error of treating indigenous peoples and cultures as artifacts of the past, as if they no longer exist. In actuality, this model of the collective, communal, natural, or indigenous society was and is still very much in evidence; it is a cultural tradition that is available for present as well as historical consideration (see Jaimes 1992).

On Indigenous Kinship and Traditional Communalism

In an historical context, the Eurocentric definition of "tribalism" operates as a myth that distorts the genuine meaning of communalism in traditionally-oriented Native American societies, and such communalism is the basis of Native nation-hood, premised as it was on matrilineal lines of kinship and descent for most if not all Native peoples prior to the impact of U. S. colonialism and patriarchy on their indigenous lifeways. These communal models of indigenous governance granted women respect and authority; exemplary of the gender egalitarianism practiced by many Native societies is their use of both matrifocal and patrifocal (to use anthropological terms) councils to negotiate consensus and make decisions in times of peace and war. Native women also more often lived longer than the men, so they enjoyed longevity in their elder status and thus provided matrilineal conti-nuity in their roles as "Clan Mothers" who determined role responsibilities among all members through collective cultural practices and reciprocal kinship traditions (for example, among the Iroquois Confederacy in the Eastern Woodlands; among the Southwest Pueblos and Navajo/Dine; and among the Great Plains Tribal Nations in the Dakotas). These Native practices constituted Native nationhoods that were, and are, distinct from modern nationalism and present-day corporate nationalism (Jaimes˙Guerrero 1999a).

Theresa Halsey, a Dakota woman among the Great Plains Peoples, points out that their concept of kinship is different from the traditional Western one. She states, "When we live in our community, it is called a *tiyospaye*, [meaning] a group of tipis. This community was very important to us because that is where we found our strength and knowledge of knowing who we are and where we come from. We no longer live in tipis but still believe in this concept" (personal correspondence, 2002). Halsey quotes Ella Deloria's ethnographic *Waterlily* on traditional Dakota living: "'Any family could maintain itself adequately as long as the father was a good hunter and the mother an industrious woman. But socially, that was not enough; ideally it must be part of a larger [extended] family, constituted of related households ... [as in kinship]. In the camp circle such groups placed their tipis side by side where they would be [within] easy reach for cooperative living. In their closeness lay such strength and social importance as no single family, however able, could or wished to achieve entirely by its own efforts'" (Deloria 1988, 20). Halsey continues, "I agree with Ella Deloria ... when she says: 'the ultimate aim of Sioux life, stripped of accessories, was quite simple; one must obey the kinship rules; one must be a good relative. No Dakota who has participated in that life will dispute that. In the last analysis every other consideration was secondary—property, personal ambition, glory, good times, life itself. Without that aim and the constant struggle to attain it, the people would no longer be Dakota in truth. They would no longer even be human. To be a good Dakota was to be humanized, civilized. And to be civilized was to keep the rules imposed by kinship for achieving civility, good manners, and a good sense of responsibility toward every individual dealt with. Thus only was it possible to live communally with success; that is to say, with a minimum of friction and a maximum of good will'" (Deloria 1988, 20).

Halsey quotes Deloria: "'We also had social kinship which were relationships based on the Sioux cultural concept that relationships can be based on patterns of thought and behavior and be equally as binding as relationship of blood, unlike the western concept of blood relatives. A good example of this is when Blue Bird and her grandmother lost their family to an enemy war party and the people of their kind who spoke their dialect, took them in and adopted the newcomers like relatives'" (Deloria 1988, 20).

On the great relevance of the traditional role of Aboriginal women, Warren Goulding, via e-mail in 2002, quoted Winona Wheeler, an Aboriginal woman and Acting Dean of Saskatchewan Indian Federated College in Saskatchewan, Canada: "'It's a contemporary translation of a traditional role. ... Women were not dependent on men, their role was very much in balance with men.'" Goulding observes:

> History has much to teach us about the role of women in First Nations communities and family, how they share the responsibilities and duties with men and elders, and how it evolved that the status of women was diminished and, in the eyes of some Church leaders and European men, demonized. Wheeler says the primary focus of women prior to the arrival of the European fur traders was to protect the family and to act as breadwinners, as she describes kinship relations: "Imagine four circles. There is a little circle in the center with the babies and children. Around the circle is another one, with Elders, grandfathers, grandmothers. Around that circle are the women and then around them are the men. The men formed the first line of protection, they protected all from danger and their primary focus was the entire community, the sustenance of the entire community. ... The next line of protection was the women and their focus was on family, then the Elders who were raising the children. ... There was a balance and no one job, no one role was more important than the other. Especially among Plains societies, which were egalitarian, [as] everyone's role was equally valued."

Goulding notes, "The arrival of the Europeans brought out massive societal changes, the negative impacts of which are being felt today."

Even though these are only two illustrations of the concept of kinship in traditional Native/Aboriginal societies, and both are particular to the Great Plains cultures, there are main themes that reverberate among all indigenous peoples in North America, in the United States and Canada, and which include the Pueblo Peoples of the Southwest states (such as Arizona, Colorado, New Mexico, Utah, and Texas) and elsewhere. Among these recurring themes that denote indigenous kinship are communalism; egalitarianism; reciprocity with others and with nature; and a complementary relationship between women and men, with special respect granted to children and elders.

On "Patriarchal Colonialism"

The impact of both U. S. colonialism and patriarchy on Native American peoples, especially on women, has been to accomplish a further erosion of their indigenous rights as the earliest groups in the Americas. For Native American women, this has meant a double burden because they must deal with both racist and sexist attitudes, and with the discrimination that results from such prejudices. This can be described as "patriarchal colonialism," and deconstructing it demands an understanding of U. S. American colonial history as a legacy that brought over Eurocentric notions of the inferiority of other non-white or non Western "races," and of all women in general, versus the presumed superiority of the Anglicized, Euroamerican male. A synonym for patriarchy is paternalism; yet patriarchal structures and attitudes are indicative of a more systemic hegemony in the prevailing chauvinism of postcolonial times, as juxtaposed with the racism characteristic of U. S. colonialism.

In this context also arises a need to address the impact of what can be termed "transnational colonialism" as practiced among third world peoples, as the result of NAFTA and other modern transnational arrangements. In response, a global indigenous resistance emerging to resist a new wave of genocide linked with ethnocide and ecocide; within the Native Feminist and Native Womanist movements that are a part of this resistance, Native and indigenous women are in activist and leadership roles, campaigning for indigenous liberation in life and land struggles.

Native American Women and Indigenism:
For Native Feminist Spirituality

This emerging global indigenous movement, in which Native American women and their (inter)national organizations are actively engaged, also involves the preservation of Native spirituality. Among these Native or indigenous women's organizations are Women of All Red Nations (WARN) and the Indigenous Women's Network (IWN), both of which send delegates to (inter)national conferences and United Nations forums to advocate for the human rights of all indigenous peoples. The IWN was prominently represented at the 1985 Women's International Conference in Beijing, China, as well as working on inter-American alliances and coalitions with a delegation of Indigenous Peoples of the Western Hemisphere. This hemispheric inter-American organization is calling for more bioethics—and specifically within the cultural context of Native spirituality, in what is criticized as "biocolonialism" and "biopiracy" of targeted indigenous peoples throughout the Americas (as well as elsewhere). Such terms are used by indigenous delegates and activists as protestors against this genome research that lacks bioethics, and with Native women leading this charge. The geneticists, themselves, use the term "bioprospecting," as agents in the Human Genome Diversity Project(s), while referring to their objectified subjects as "isolates of historic interest" (see Jaimes*Guerrero forthcoming 2003).

In a literal sense, *indigenism* means "to be born of a place," but for Native peoples, it also means "to live in relationship with the place where one is born," as in the sense of an "indigenous homeland." In this cultural context, an indigenous member has the responsibility to practice kinship roles in reciprocal relationship with his or her

M. A. Jaimes Guerrero

bioregional habitat, and this is manifested through cultural beliefs, rituals, and ceremonies that cherish biodiversity (that is, human culture in relationship to bioregion): this is the context of a Native Land Ethic and Native Spirituality. If one moves or migrates, as an individual or as part of a group, one is expected to practice this bioethic in a new environment respectful of the bioregion in its biodiversity. This is also manifested in the sacred images of what I refer to as the "feminine organic archetypes" found in *all* Native creation stories and geomythology. Examples of such figures include the Corn Mother and Daughter, Spider Woman, and Changing Woman of Southwest Pueblo cultural lore (see Jaimes Guerrero 1999a).

This is a main principle of what can be called a "Native Feminist Spirituality" that is in the context of Indigenism and Ecofeminism, and which advocates for Native women's cultural rights in contemporary times, in terms of one's subjective agency within the existing patriarchal and postcolonialist globalizing U. S. society. This patriarchal colonialist situation is a result of a "trickle-down patriarchy" in male-dominated tribal politics under the guise of "tribal sovereignty" that is at the expense of Native women (see Jaimes 1998). My conceptualization of "Native Womanism" advocates for more "historical agency" in reenvisioning a pre-patriarchal, pre-colonialist, and pre-capitalist U. S. society, as well as for Native women's self-determination in reclaiming their indigenous (that is, matrilineal/matrifocal) roles that empower them with respect and authority in indigenous governance (see Jaimes Guerrero 1999a).

A Call for "Native Womanism": From Sacred Kinship Traditions

The term "womanist" was inspired by novelist Alice Walker's *In Search of Our Mothers' Gardens: Womanist Prose* (1983), in which she calls for "women to love women" (Walker 1999, Introduction). I interpret this in both literal and figurative ways, in terms of restoring the *female principle* to challenge the prevailing colonialist and patriarchal denigration of women and nature. I have added to Walker's equation the denigration of Natives by considering them to be "tribal peoples" according to Western conceptions—what I term above as "patriarchal colonialism." In this vein, it has been historically documented that Native men were perceived as emasculated by Spanish colonialists and other chroniclers; Native men were considered less masculine according to androcentric European standards which placed women beneath men and held them to be the property of men, along with children, servants/slaves, animals, and all of nature. Similarly, Native or indigenous women were viewed as exotic and erotic females who had the power to seduce any man into promiscuity and even to turn their own men into "eunuchs" (see Jaimes Guerrero 1999b). But what the sexist Western Europeans mistook as the subjugation of Native men to their women was actually the gender role dynamics of an egalitarian society that valued both women and men. It was Aristotle, according to Lewis Hanke (1959), who first wrote that all women—as well as all children, slaves/servants, and animals—were to be the property of male heads of patriarchal households.

"Native Womanism" also has an ecological perspective, because there is also a connection between the denigration and subordination of women and the corresponding degradation and subjugation of nature through acts of ecocide (the erosion of the natural environment or ecosystem). Each aspect of this *feminized* subordination of nature, Natives, and women is a manifestation of the denigration of the *female principle*, and this engendered-female principle of subordination can be contextualized as "strands in the web of imperialism."[1] This denigration of the *female principle* is the result of the patriarchal colonialism that has been imposed on Native peoples and others in the process of conquest as part of an imperialist agenda. This intersection among nature, Natives, and women, therefore, also serves as a means of illustrating advancing genocidal agendas, because genocide (the destruction or erosion of a people) is often inextricably linked with ethnocide (the destruction or erosion of their cultures) and with ecocide (the destruction or erosion of their environment) (see Jaimes˙Guerrero forthcoming).

In challenging this feminized subjugation, which is anti-female and anti-woman, I call for the historical agency of "Native Womanism," for a broader scope of the issues concerning Native women, and as a result of the impact of U.S. colonialism as well as patriarchy in their life and land struggles. This call is also in order to preserve and restore the sacred kinship traditions among these bioregionally-based indigenous peoples and their respective cultures, to envision precolonialist and prepatriarchal times, which promotes a prospective vision for a more humane and gender-egalitarian future exemplary of "being Indigenous."

Note

[1] This phrase is the tentative title of one of my papers currently in progress.

References

Churchill, Ward. 1992. Naming our destiny: Towards a language of Indian liberation. *Global Justice* 3: 22–33.

Churchill, Ward, and Glenn T. Morris. 1992. Table: Key Indian laws and cases. In *The state of Native America: Genocide, colonization, and resistance*, ed. M. Annette Jaimes. Boston: South End Press.

Deloria, Ella. 1988. *Waterlily*. Lincoln: University of Nebraska Press.

Durant, Will. 1954. Our oriental heritage. In *The story of European civilization.* Vol. 1. New York: Simon and Schuster.

Hanke, Lewis. 1959. *Aristotle and the American Indians.* Bloomington: Indiana University Press.

Jaimes, M. Annette, with Theresa Halsey. 1992. American Indian women: At the center of indigenous resistance in North America. In *The state of Native America: Genocide, colonization, and resistance*, ed. M. Annette Jaimes. Boston, Mass.: South End Press.

Jaimes, M. Annette. 1992. La raza and indigenism: Alternatives to autogenocide in North America. In *Global Justice* 3 (2–3): 4–19.

Jaimes*Guerrero, M. A. 1998. Savage hegemony: Feminist and indigenous women's alliances. In *Talking visions: Multicultural feminism in transnational age*, ed. Ella Shohat. Cambridge: M. I. T. Press.

___. M. A. 1999a. Red warrior women: Exemplars of indigenism in 'Native womanism.' *Asian Women* 9: 1–25.

___. M. A. 1999b. Savage exotica, erotica: Media imagery of Native women in 'Hollywood' cinema. In *Native North America: Critical cultural perspectives*, ed. Renee Hulan. Nova Scotia, Canada: ECW Press, St. Mary's University.

___. M. A. forthcoming 2003. Biocolonialism and "isolates of historic interest:" An overview of the human genome diversity project on targeted indigineous peoples/ ecocultures. In *The protection of indigenous intellectual property rights*, ed. Mary Riley. Walnut Creek, Calif.: AltaMira Press.

Kerber, Linda K., and Jane Sherron De Hart, eds. 1999. *Women's America: Refocusing the past.* 5th ed. New York: Oxford University Press.

Morris, Glenn T. 1992. International law and politics: Toward a right to self-determination for indigenous peoples. In *The state of Native America: Genocide, colonization, and resistance*, ed. M. Annette Jaimes. Cambridge: South End Press.

Moyer, Bill, on D. Beck and C. Cowan. 2000. Spiral dynamics: Mastering values, leadership, and change, exploring the new science of memetics. n.p.

Walker, Alice. 1999. *In search of our mothers' gardens: Womanist prose*. San Diego: Harvest.

29 Sex, Violence and History in the Lives of Idi Amin

Postcolonial Masculinity as Masquerade[1]

Mark Leopold

Idi Amin Dada, President of Uganda from 1971 to 1979, has become an icon of evil in contemporary Euro-American society. In 2001, he was the only living person to be included in Channel 5's TV series *The 50 Most Evil Men and Women in History* (Twiss 177–89), and he is a staple character in books with titles like *The World's Most Evil People* (Castleden), *The World's Most Evil Dictators* (Law), *The World's Most Evil Men* (Blandford and Jones) and *Monsters* (Montefiore). Amin's name has become a universal point of reference whenever African political dictatorship is mentioned, even those as different from Amin himself as Robert Mugabe. Since his death (in exile in Saudi Arabia) in 2003, his reputation has, if anything, grown more sinister, with the Oscar-winning movie *The Last King of Scotland*, based on the novel by Giles Foden, only one recent example of his notoriety.

Most Ugandans and historians of Uganda agree that Amin's rule was a crucial period in the collapse of Ugandan society. The three main reasons for this were the economic destruction caused by his expulsion of almost all the Asian population of the country, the internal disorder created as a result of undisciplined military rule, and his habit of making powerful external enemies, both in East Africa and internationally. However, most analysts, Ugandan and Euro-American, also agree that Amin's predecessor and successor, Milton Obote, was responsible for at least as many, if not more, deaths than Amin (see, for example, Hansen and Twaddle, *Uganda Now* 3). Moreover, unlike Obote during his second regime, Amin did not specifically set out to wipe out entire civilian populations defined on tribal grounds. Nor is Obote's earlier expulsion of the Kenyan Luo remembered alongside Amin's of the Asians, although the former were considerably larger in number.[2]

Mark Leopold, "Sex, Violence and History in the Lives of Idi Amin: Postcolonial Masculinity as Masquerade." *Journal of Postcolonial Writing*, 45(3), 2009: 321–330. Reprinted by permission of Taylor & Francis Ltd.

Genocide is not the word for Amin's rule; it was far more chaotic than that. He simply killed or caused to be killed those who got in his way, while allowing his troops considerable licence to carry out personal grudges and further their economic aims. Although Amin specifically targeted soldiers from the Acholi and Langi tribes in the army, because he suspected their loyalty was to Obote, he never undertook mass pogroms against Acholi or Langi civilians in their home areas. Obote, on the other hand *did* attempt to exterminate large, racially defined groups of civilians, both in West Nile itself and among the Baganda of the Luwero Triangle in the south of the country.[3] The description of Amin by the British writer Denis Hills, who was jailed and nearly executed for writing it, as a "village tyrant" (333) is not the whole truth. Amin was certainly more than that. But it is a whole lot closer to the truth than depicting him as a Hitlerite monster. And meanwhile Obote has never been portrayed as an icon of African evil for our time.

Why should have Amin acquired such notoriety? It is easy to see him as a figure who all too conveniently fits colonial stereotypes of "the African": violent, unedu-cated, "primitive", a colonial fantasy figure exemplifying the image of the continent as a "heart of darkness". In this article, I argue that the popular image of Amin unites many of our society's ideas about the nature of evil, fitting what anthropolo-gists term a western folk model. However, as I will show, African intellectuals and writers have been key participants in developing this image. Crucial, in both the European and the African material, is the depiction of Amin in terms of a charis-matic hyper-heterosexuality.

One reason for the image is that Obote was always a modernist, with scant respect for African tradition. He could talk the language of world diplomacy, and that of socialism. Amin, an uneducated soldier with an accent which, in any of his several languages, was painful to the southern Ugandan ear,[4] not only seemed to be a primitive reversion but to glory in such a role. He immediately became famous, as well as notorious, in Britain for his grandiose anti-colonial statements (often, it seems likely, deliberately rather than accidentally funny), delivered in an English quickly parodied, notably by Alan Coren in his long-running column in *Punch* magazine, which was written in a kind of grotesque parody of West African or African American English (see Coren, *Bulletins*; *Further Bulletins*). It would be a mistake, however, to see Amin's image as simply a kneejerk response of British racism, although some African commentators did portray it as such in the 1970s.[5] In fact, as we shall see, some of the most caricatured pictures of Amin as a primi-tive reversion came from African writers, some of whom indeed celebrated such an image as much as he did himself. This image of tribal atavism runs through virtually all the extensive literature on Amin.[6] Throughout his rule and subse-quently, both his supporters and his detractors have emphasized the point that he was a creature of his ethnicity: that the source and inspiration of his regime lay in his heredity. This worked in two ways: in the more popular texts, a racist anthropology related Amin's atrocities to the traditional ways of his tribe; in the more academic work, his origins are seen to link his actions through deep, perhaps submerged, historical roots, to aspects of the Nile Valley or wider African past. Either way, the literature stresses the links between Amin's ethnicity, his gender, and his sexuality, creating an image that is probably unique among the world's dictators.

In the first place, suitably for a fantasy figure, there is some dispute over Amin's precise origins, although he is always seen as associated with the West Nile district of Northwest Uganda. Most accounts suggest that he was born in the small town of Koboko, very close to both the Congo and Sudanese borders, of a Muslim father from the Kakwa tribe and a Lugbara mother. However, he seems sometimes to have claimed to have been born near Kampala (see Kiwanuka; Mutibwa), while hostile commentators frequently suggest he may not have been born in Uganda at all (Smith; Harrell-Bond). In the cruder work, the Kakwa are depicted as particularly ferocious. Amin's former commanding officer in the British army calls them a "warrior tribe" (Grahame 9) and tells us that they and other West Nile tribes engaged in "sacrifices of animals and humans" (12). Henry Kyemba, a Baganda who worked for Amin as a senior civil servant and cabinet minister, goes further still:

> Amin's bizarre behaviour [...] derives partly from his tribal background. Like many other warrior societies, the Kakwa, Amin's tribe, are known to have practised blood rituals on slain enemies. These involve cutting a piece of flesh from the body to subdue the dead man's spirit or tasting the victim's blood to render the spirit harmless [...]. Such rituals still exist among the Kakwa. [...]
> Amin's practices do not stop at tasting blood: on several occasions he has boasted to me and others that he has eaten human flesh. [...] H]e went on to say that eating human flesh is not uncommon in his home area. (Kyemba 109–10)

George Ivan Smith wrote that "there is strong evidence that Amin and his henchmen did engage in this sort of thing, but as an instrument of terror, not as a tribal custom" (34), but he went on to explain that "people in thin, arid⁷ places such as the Kakwa area of Uganda would engage [...] in the shedding of the blood of animals or even human beings. The witchcraft in which blood is shed is stronger than the witchcraft of berries and roots" (40), and that "Amin's mother was a Lugbara. She was known to be steeped in witchcraft, consulted by soldiers from the barracks for that, and for other services" (42).

Another approach is to explain the supposed violence of the West Nilers in terms of the relatively stateless, acephalous nature of their traditional societies. Amin's first biographer, the Anglo-Irish aristocrat Judith, Lady Listowel, perhaps unsurprisingly, traces the problem to Amin's lack of social advantages:

> The Kakwa have a great respect for personalities, but not for rank or position. They never had chiefs or recognized clan leaders. [...] A chiefless African society can have disadvantages. Among the Baganda [...] a chief's headquarters was in every sense the centre of tribal life [...] Parents sent their children to the chief's enclosure to be his men- and maid-servants as only in that way could they obtain advancement. [...] Amin could have had no such training because the Kakwa had no chiefs. Some of his recent measures illustrate all too well that he had to leap from a peasant background into the complicated politics of the modern world without any intermediate feudal preparation. (Listowel 12)

If the "Kakwa"-based explanations, in Mahmoud Mamdani's damning phrase, were "parading Amin as some sort of anthropological oddity" (*Imperialism and Fascism* 32), another set of explanations based on his West Nile background portrayed Amin as an *historical* oddity, a resurgence of primeval African tradition. This approach reaches its most intellectually interesting form in the work of Ali Mazrui, which will be discussed in more detail below. First, though, it is necessary to discuss an aspect of Amin's ethnicity which indeed has historical reverberations. The first contact the people of West Nile had with outsiders possessing radically different technologies came with slave raids in the first half of the 19th century, carried out by groups of soldiers, most of whom were themselves slaves, who would seize children and adults to refresh their ranks, or for onward sale in the slave markets of North Africa and the Middle East. Western powers, particularly Britain which had its own aims in the region, sought to stamp out the practice, and by the 1870s, the Anglo-Egyptian regime which theoretically ruled the area which was to become the Sudan sent armed forces, many of whom were themselves former slave soldiers (see Leopold, "Legacies"). One such group was commanded by a German doctor turned Muslim convert, known as Emin Pasha.[8] In the late 1880s, an Islamic insurrection, known to colonial history as the Mahdi's rebellion, caused Emin Pasha and his troops to be driven up the Nile to the area which later became known as West Nile.

In 1889, Emin was "rescued" by the explorer Henry Stanley, in a major international media event which became the inspiration for Joseph Conrad's novella "Heart of Darkness", described by Chinua Achebe as the "dominant image of Africa in the Western imagination" (261). Most of Emin's soldiers remained behind, to be picked up a few years later by Captain Frederick Lugard of the Imperial British East Africa Company. Lugard regarded these people as the best material for soldiery in Africa, and he used them in his successful attempt to carve out what was to become modern Uganda. These people became known as "Nubi" or "Nubians". Many of them were later integrated into the Fourth Battalion of the King's African Rifles (4 KAR) and fought for the British in East Africa and elsewhere. From the days of the slave armies, they had been Muslims and, in fact if not in theory, the Muslim identity became one which many West Nile Ugandans and others adopted when they moved to towns, became traders or joined the army, providing that they converted to Islam, and spoke KiNubi (a form of vernacular Arabic) and/or KiSwahili.

Others inherited Nubi status. Like his father, Idi Amin was a Nubi, born and brought up in British military service, and many commentators have seen his Nubi roots as determining, in part, his violent behaviour, just as others have explained it in terms of his Kakwa nature.[9] The journalist David Martin, for example, says in his 1974 biography of Amin that:

> among their fellow countrymen they enjoyed an unenviable reputation of having one of the world's highest homicide rates. The Nubians were renowned for their sadistic brutality, lack of formal education, for poisoning enemies and for their refusal to integrate, even in the urban centres. (14)

While Grahame, who, as Amin's commanding officer in 4 KAR, commanded many Nubian troops, gives this gloss on Nubi history:

> For close on twenty years [after Lugard took them into his forces] the Nubians became the most feared and influential ethnic group in Uganda, mercilessly suppressing uprisings and tribal disputes at the behest of their British masters. (9)

To be a Nubi was to lay claim to a martial tradition:

> [Amin's mother] was a Christian from the Lugbara tribe, while his father was a Moslem and a Kakwa. Like many West Nilotes, Idi Amin therefore had complex ethnic and religious affiliations for, as a Kinubi-speaking Moslem whose ancestors had come from the Sudan, he was also allowed to consider himself a Nubian. To these people Lord Lugard had given the epithet of "the best soldiery in Africa". (23)

This extraordinary ethnicity is invariably described in exclusively masculine terms: the idea of a female "Nubian" is almost a contradiction in terms. With the Nubi, ethnicity becomes a way of talking about gender; they are seen as inherently male just as they are inherently soldiers. It is clear, then, that one can explain Amin's violence by either the Kakwa's traditional lack of a state or the Nubi's historical involvement in the colonial state. Some writers are unsure whether murder and cannibalism are characteristically Kakwa or Nubi phenomena. Smith tells us that:

> The southern Ugandans are particularly contemptuous of the southern Sudanese and Nubis (not of other northern tribes) as wild and uncivilized. It is from them that we have reports of Amin and his Nubis tasting the blood of their victims and eating their livers and the explanation that such a custom is either a Nubi or a Kakwa one. (34)

Another, key set of associations deployed in both popular and academic work on Amin concerns gender and sexuality. Amin is portrayed as the epitome of masculinity, defined in terms of both violence (the warrior ethos) and a charismatic heterosexuality. Lady Listowel describes meeting him for the first time:

> I looked into the smiling face of a tall, muscular officer with shrewd eyes, who invited me to a cup of coffee. He was a hulking figure of a man and I was fascinated by his hands – beautiful, slim hands with long, tapering fingers. (7)

Amin was a famous sportsman in his army days (he was heavyweight boxing champion of Uganda in 1951–52). According to his commanding officer, Iain Grahame, his "physique was like that of a Grecian sculpture, and no matter to what form of athleticism he turned his hand, he excelled and he conquered" (34). After a particularly exhausting route march:

> As we finally passed the finishing post, Idi Amin was marching beside me at the head of the column, head held high and still singing. […] Across one shoulder

were two bren guns and over the other was a crippled askari. It reminded me of a translation of another KAR marching song:

> It's the Sudi,[10] my boy, it's the Sudi
> With his grim-set, ugly face:
> But he looks like a man and he fights like a man
> for he comes of a fighting race (39)

Amin's former Minister for Health, Henry Kyemba, in his book *A State of Blood* (which appears to have been a major source for *The Last King of Scotland*) characterized his rule as follows:

> Besides his five wives, Amin has had countless other women, many of whom have borne him children. His sex life is truly extraordinary. He regards his sexual energy as a sign of his power and authority. He never tries to hide his lust. His eyes lock onto any beautiful woman. His reputation for sexual performance is so startling that women often deliberately make themselves available. […]
>   Besides his official wives there are at least ten unofficial ones. […] Amin's casual affairs are too numerous to count. His sex life has extended into all corners of the administration. No ministry or department has been left untouched. In my own ministry [Health] I had to cope with his frequent approaches to nurses. […]
>   Amin's sex life and his working life are two sides of the same coin. […] His treatment of women has its counterpart in his treatment of the country. His urge to dominate by force, his vindictiveness, his peacock flamboyance – all suggest that he has seized and ravaged the country as he has possessed his scores of women. (163–65)

The popular books on Amin, then, consistently represent him in terms of masculinity, violence and sexuality, linked to an atavistic racial primitivism and a frontier historical tradition, which are both exemplified by his West Nile origins. Perhaps surprisingly, though, these themes are pursued most obsessively not in the popular literature on Amin but in the academic work of the renowned Tanzanian-born political scientist Ali Mazrui.[11] Mazrui's writings about Amin as they developed over the 1970s and 1980s are complex and sometimes contradictory – matching, in this respect, their subject. He invokes the British historian Terence Ranger's early arguments about the relationship between "primary" and "secondary" resistance movements in Africa, suggesting that:

> It is General Idi Amin rather than Dr Milton Obote who is the true successor to those early warriors in Bunyoro, Acholi, as well as West Nile, who reached for their spears to strike a blow, however weak, against European imperialism. (Mazrui, "Resurrection" 67)

Mazrui developed a pan-African theory of "the warrior", exemplified by Amin, whom he described as "in an important sense, a reactivation of the ancestral assertiveness of warrior culture" ("Warrior Tradition" 77). As such, Amin simultaneously exemplified heterosexual masculinity:

What should not be overlooked is the sexual dimension of the warrior culture. [...] The statement "he is a real man" could mean either he is sexually virile, or he is tough and valiant. [...]

In some African societies, special sexual rites [*sic*] were accorded to warriors. [...] Given the link between manliness and warfare there could also be an easy link between violence and sexuality. (Mazrui, "Resurrection" 71, 73)

Historically, this link was exemplified by the Zulu king, Shaka, but:

Whereas Shaka had defined manliness in terms of sexual abstinence, Amin has seen it in terms of virile promiscuity. [...] A new Shaka has indeed cast his shadow across the African continent – but committed to virile masculinity, rather than to celibate manliness. (81–83)

The sexual, the military and the political are merged in this masculine paradigm:

When we relate charisma to the warrior tradition in Africa, there is one quality which demands particular attention. We call this quality political masculinity. [...]

The political masculinity of the General does not lie merely in his size, though he is impressively tall and broad. Nor does it lie merely in his insistence that he fears no-one but God. Yet these factors are part of the story, combined with the additional factor that an affirmation of fearlessness and an athletic build have indeed been part of the total picture of martial values within African political cultures. (Mazrui, *Soldiers* 149)

While Mazrui's papers on this theme usually include a token reminder that the warrior tradition is a cruel one, the overall tendency of his work in the 1970s was to celebrate both that tradition and its then exemplar, Idi Amin.[12]

How does this ultra-masculine, violent, hyper-(hetero)sexuality help in explaining the image of Amin as an icon of evil? The anthropologist Jean La Fontaine has written that:

In most of the societies anthropologists have traditionally studied, inhuman evil is personified in the form of the witch. Whatever the local term that is translated "witch" by anthropologists, it refers to those who commit acts perceived as transgressing the fundamental moral axioms on which human nature, and hence social life, is based. The sins attributed to witches may vary somewhat in their detail and emphasis according to the culture in question, but they commonly concern sex, food and killing. (La Fontaine 14)

La Fontaine, originally an anthropologist of Uganda, wrote this in the context of a study of "satanic ritual child abuse" in the UK, but the general point applies well to Amin's image as hyper-sexualized murderous cannibal.

This kind of evil involves an *excess* well beyond normal "badness" or anti-social behaviour, even of normal killing and murder. In the European philosophical tradition, this is akin to Emmanuel Kant's notion of "radical evil". Kant's essay "Religion within the Limits of Reason Alone" (1793) sought to re-create in secular form a version of the theological concept of original sin, an "'insurmountable wickedness', the 'radical evil' that inhabits the heart of man and which he can 'by no means wipe out'" (qtd in Copjec viii). Kant no sooner proposed this than he dropped the idea but, in the mid-1990s, the concept was adopted by a group of neo-Lacanian psychoanalytic theorists, in an attempt to develop the ideas in Lacan's 1959–60 seminar series on the ethics of psychoanalysis and his essay "Kant with Sade". In these, reading Kant in the light of de Sade's perversions of human reason, Lacan developed Freud's concept of the death instinct into an analysis of a kind of pleasure in evil (Lacan, "Kant"; *Ethics*; see the critique in Staten). The concept of radical evil implies an excess beyond normal human badness, however bad that may be, to something which seems inhuman. It is a move beyond the simple dualism of good/bad, and one which animates the various inhuman, externalized incarnations of evil so familiar to anthropologists of a wide range of societies: monsters, witches and so on. The Freudian approach implies the awful suspicion that the source even of radical evil may ultimately lie inside us, "inhabit[ing] our hearts" – or our Ids – rather than being attributable to an externalized "Them".

The best known of this group of neo-Lacanians is the eclectic Slovenian philosopher Slavoj Žižek, who has returned to the subject of radical evil a number of times (e.g. *Tarrying*; "Selfhood"; *Plague*), the first of which is the most germane to this article. For Žižek, Kant is right to stress that human evil (qua radical evil) is an a priori rather than an empirical phenomenon. However, in shying away from what he termed "diabolical evil", that is, evil as a deliberate ethical choice, Kant, according to Žižek, is resisting the implications of the concept of radical evil, on which, by a complex dialectical process, depends any possibility of the good:

> Evil is another name for the "death-drive" for the fixation on some Thing which derails our customary life-circuit. By way of Evil, man wrests himself from animal instinctual rhythm, i.e. Evil introduces the radical reversal of the "natural" relationship. […] When Hegel, in his *Lectures on the Philosophy of Religion* conceives of the very act of becoming human, the passage of animal into man, as the Fall into sin, he is more penetrating [than Kant]: the possible space for Good is opened up by the original choice of radical Evil which disrupts the pattern of the organic substantial Whole. (*Tarrying* 96)

What is most relevant, for present purposes, in Žižek's analysis, is his application of the concept of radical evil to political issues:

> From the standpoint of the precapitalist corporate society, capitalism is Evil, disruptive, it unsettles the delicate balance of the closed, precapitalist economy. […]

However, once capitalism achieves a new balance of its self-reproductive circuit and becomes its own mediating totality, i.e. once it establishes itself as a system which "posits its own presuppositions", the site of evil is radically displaced: what now counts as "evil" are precisely the left-overs of the previous "Good"; islands of resistance, of precapitalism which disturb the untroubled circulation of Capital, the new form of Good. (99)

Žižek goes on to apply the notion in the course of a discussion of how western liberalism creates its opponents as "barbaric" (written, of course, before "9/11" and the subsequent demonization of Islam):

The traditional liberal opposition between "open" pluralist societies and "closed" nationalist-corporatist societies founded on the exclusion of the Other has thus to be brought to its point of self-reference; the liberal gaze itself functions according to the same logic, in so far as it is founded upon the exclusion of the Other to whom one attributes the fundamentalist nationalism. [...]

This antagonistic splitting opens up the field for the Khmer Rouge, Sendero Luminoso and other similar movements which seem to personify "radical Evil" in today's politics; if "fundamentalism" functions as a kind of "negative judgement" on liberal capitalism, as an inherent negation of the universalist claim of liberal capitalism, then movements such as Sendero Luminoso enact an "infinite judgement" on it. [...] In other words, far from presenting a case of exotic barbarism, the "Radical Evil" of the Khmer Rouge and the Senderistas is conceivable only against the constitutive antagonism of today's capitalism. (223–24)

Taking off from this analysis, it is possible to reconceptualize Amin's relationship to his history and that of his fellow West Nilers, "the best material for soldiery in Africa". Amin, in such a view, represents the not inconsiderable dark side of the British colonial fantasy. Rather than exemplifying *Africa* as a heart of darkness, he represents western society's own dirty little secret. As Achebe noted about Conrad's book, the real source of the European fear of Africa is not the latter's imaginary otherness but its real similarity: "What thrilled you was the thought of their humanity – like yours [...] Ugly" (254). In a similar vein, Jacqueline Rose has written: "On what is the belief in the infantile nature of the Primitive founded if not on a moment of projection?" (Sachs *Black Hamlet*).

This also suggests that Amin's hyper-masculinity was itself a colonial masquerade, not just in the sense of a spectacular performance but in precisely the same sense that Lacan describes femininity as a masquerade. As Ellie Ragland-Sullivan puts it, Lacan is "proposing the masquerade as the very definition of 'femininity' precisely because it is constructed with reference to a male sign" (49). Both positions, the ultra-feminine and the hyper-masculine, presuppose their opposite. In Amin's case, this "opposite" of his hyper-masculinity is the feminized position of the subaltern. For him, the latter term applies very literally; as a long-time non-commissioned officer in the British army he was very much the historical child of that army and the state it represented. His Oedipal struggles with this severe father were well represented (whatever its other flaws) in *The Last King of Scotland*. Every account of Amin is infected with fantasy (including those of his fellow West Nilers I spoke with in the mid-1990s).[13] His role as an icon of evil is thus not reducible to historical "fact" but to an historical Imaginary, behind which lie the crude realities of political power in colonial and postcolonial society.

Notes

1 This article is dedicated to the memory of Rena Grant (1959–92).

2 See, for example, Mazrui, "Casualties"; Mamdani, "Asian Expulsion". Larger still was the expulsion of the Banyarwanda (originally from Ruanda) under the Obote II regime in the 1980s (ibid. 87).

3 The basic texts on the recent history of Uganda remain the collections edited by Holger Bernt Hansen and Michael Twaddle (*Uganda Now*; *Changing Uganda*; *Developing Uganda*).

4 On southern Ugandan attitudes to the people of the North and Northwest, see Leopold, "War in the North".

5 See, for example, Godwin Matatu in *Africa* 37 (September 1974).

6 Jamison's bibliography lists 406 "scholarly, research-level works [on Amin and on Uganda during his rule] in English and housed in libraries in North America" (xiii). Even before his overthrow, one academic commentator remarked on Amin's position as "Africa's most publicised ruler" and remarked on the number of academic discussions of his rule (Woodward 153).

7 In fact, although considerably drier than southern Uganda, rainfall levels in West Nile are higher than those of, for example, England.

8 "Emin" is the Turkish version, and "Amin" the Arabic form, of a fairly widespread Muslim name meaning "Faithful".

9 On the Nubi, and on Amin's Nubi identity, see especially Southall, "General Amin and the Coup"; Mazrui, "Resurrection", *Soldiers and Kinsmen*, "Religious Strangers"; Soghayroun; Rowe; Woodward; Johnson "Sudanese Military Slavery", "Structure of a Legacy"; Hansen; Kokole. See also Leopold, *Inside West Nile*, "Legacies of Slavery".

10 Sudi = Sudanese = Nubi. Wendy James (pers. comm.) points out that this verse builds on the original Arabic connotation of "Sudanese" as synonymous with "black" or even "slave". It is one of the ironies of Ugandan history that it has there come to have connotations of "Arab" and "Muslim". Of course, on both counts it implies "other".

11 Much of this work, as Mazrui explains in the introduction to *Soldiers and Kinsmen*, was first written while at close quarters to Amin, teaching at Makerere at a time when the latter was an active Chancellor, who frequently sought to test academic and student opinion concerning his policies. The book was published, however, after Mazrui had left Uganda; by 1975 he was at the University of Michigan.

12 This might in part be explained by the occasional explicit references he makes to contemporary American Black Power movements. It should be said that Mazrui's account of Amin was fiercely contested at the time by a Makerere colleague, the anthropologist Aidan Southall, in a number of articles (particularly "General Amin and the Coup", "Bankruptcy").

13 See Leopold, *Inside West Nile*.

Works cited

Achebe, Chinua. "An Image of Africa: Racism in Conrad's 'Heart of Darkness'." *Joseph Conrad: Heart of Darkness*. 1977. Ed. Robert Kimbrough. New York: Norton, 1988. 251–62.

Blandford, Neil, and Bruce Jones. *The World's Most Evil Men*. London: Octopus, 1985.

Castleton, Rodney. *The World's Most Evil People: The Epitome of Evil*. London: Time Warner, 2005.

Copjec, Joan. "Introduction." *Radical Evil*. Ed. Joan Copjec. London and New York: Verso, 1996.

Coren, Alan. *The Collected Bulletins of President Idi Amin*. London: Robson, 1975.

Coren, Alan. *The Further Bulletins of President Idi Amin*. London: Robson, 1975.

Grahame, Iain. *Amin and Uganda: A Personal Memoir*. London: Granada, 1980.

Hansen, Holger Bernt. "Pre-colonial Immigrants and Colonial Servants. The Nubians in Uganda Revisited." *African Affairs* 90.2 (1991): 559–80.

Hansen, Holger Bernt, and Michael Twaddle, eds. *Changing Uganda*. London: Currey, 1991.

Hansen, Holger Bernt, and Michael Twaddle, eds. *Developing Uganda*. Oxford: Currey, 1998.

Hansen, Holger Bernt, and Michael Twaddle, eds. *Uganda Now*. London: Currey, 1988.

Harrell-Bond, Barbara E. *Imposing Aid: Emergency Assistance to Refugees*. Oxford: Oxford UP, 1986.

Hills, Dennis. *The White Pumpkin*. London: Allen, 1975.

Jamison, Martin. *Amin and Uganda: An Annotated Bibliography*. Westport, CT and London: Greenwood, 1992.

Johnson, Douglas H. "The Structure of a Legacy: Military Slavery in Northeast Africa." *Ethnohistory* 36.1 (1989): 72–88.

Johnson, Douglas H. "Sudanese Military Slavery from the Eighteenth to the Twentieth Century." *Slavery and Other Forms of Unfree Labour*. Ed. Louise Archer. London: Routledge, 1988. 142–55.

Kiwanuka, Semakula. *Amin and the Tragedy of Uganda*. Munich and London: Weltforum, 1979.

Kokole, O.H. "Idi Amin, 'the Nubi' and Islam in Ugandan Politics, 1971–1979." *Religion and Politics in East Africa*. Ed. Holger Bernt Hansen and Michael Twaddle. London: Currey, 1995. 45–55.

Kyemba, H. *A State of Blood: The Inside Story of Idi Amin*. London: Corgi, 1977.

La Fontaine, Jean S. *Speak of the Devil: Tales of Satanic Abuse in Contemporary England*. Cambridge: Cambridge UP, 1998.

Lacan, Jacques. *The Ethics of Psychoanalysis 1959–60: The Seminar of Jacques Lacan Book VII*. London: Tavistock/Routledge, 1992.

Lacan, Jacques. "Kant with Sade." *October* 51 (1989): 63–114.

Law, Diane. *The World's Most Evil Dictators: The Lives and Times of History's Worst Tyrants*. London: Paragon, 2006.

Leopold, Mark. *Inside West Nile: Violence, History and Representation on an African Frontier*. Oxford: Currey; Santa Fe: School of American Research Press; Kampala: Fountain, 2005.

Leopold, Mark. "Legacies of Slavery in North West Uganda: The Story of the 'One-Elevens'." *Africa: Journal of the International African Institute* 76.2 (2006): 180–99.

Leopold, Mark. "'The War in the North': Ethnicity in Ugandan Press Explanations of Conflict, 1996–97." *The Media of Conflict: War Reporting and Representations of Ethnic Violence*. Ed. Tim Allen and Jean Seaton. London and New York: Zed, 1999. 219–43.

Listowel, Judith. *Amin*. Dublin and London: IUP, 1973.

Mamdani, Mahmoud. *Imperialism and Fascism in Uganda*. London: Heinemann, 1983.

Mamdani, Mahmoud. "The Ugandan Asian Expulsion Twenty Years On." *And Fire Does Not Always Beget Ash: Critical Reflections on the NRM*. Ed. Mahmoud Mamdani. Kampala: Monitor, 1995. 79–90.

Martin, David. *General Amin*. London: Faber, 1974.

Mazrui, Ali A. "Casualties of an Underdeveloped Class Structure: The Expulsions of Luo Workers and Asian Bourgeoisie from Uganda." *Strangers in African Societies*. Ed. W.A. Shack and E.P. Skinner. Berkeley and London: U of California P, 1979. 261–278.

Mazrui, Ali A. "Religious Strangers in Uganda: From Emin Pasha to Amin Dada." *African Affairs* 76.302 (1977): 21–38.

Mazrui, Ali A. "The Resurrection of the Warrior Tradition in African Political Culture." *Journal of Modern African Studies* 13.1 (1975): 67–84.

Mazrui, Ali A. *Soldiers and Kinsmen in Uganda: The Making of a Military Ethnocracy*. Beverly Hills and London: Sage, 1975.

Mazrui, Ali A. "The Warrior Tradition and the Masculinity of War." *The Warrior Tradition in Modern Africa*. Ed. Ali A. Mazrui. Leiden: Brill, 1977. 69–81.

Montefiore, Simon Sebag. *Monsters: History's Most Evil Men and Women*. London: Quercus, 2008.

Mutibwa, P. *Uganda since Independence: A Story of Unfulfilled Hopes*. London: Hurst, 1992.

Ragland-Sullivan, Ellie. "The Sexual Masquerade: a Lacanian Theory of Sexual Difference". *Lacan and the Subject of Language*. Ed. E. Ragland-Sullivan and M. Bracher. New York and London: Routledge.

Rowe, J.A. "Islam under Idi Amin: A Case of Déjà Vu?" *Uganda Now*. Ed. Holger Bernt Hansen and Michael Twaddle. London: Currey, 1988. 267–79.

Sachs, W. "Introduction." By J. Rose. and S. Dubow. *Black Hamlet*. 1937. Baltimore and London: Johns Hopkins UP, 1996. 38–67.

Smith, George Ivan. *Ghosts of Kampala*. London: Weidenfeld, 1980.

Soghayroun, Ibrahim. *The Sudanese Muslim Factor in Uganda*. Khartoum: Khartoum UP, 1981.

Southall, Aidan. "The Bankruptcy of the Warrior Tradition." *The Warrior Tradition in Modern Africa*. Ed. Ali A. Mazrui. Leiden: Brill, 1977. 166–76.

Southall, Aidan. "General Amin and the Coup: Great Man or Historical Inevitability?" *Journal of Modern African Studies* 13.1 (1975): 85–105.

Staten, H. "'Radical Evil' Revived: Hitler, Kant, Luther, Neo-Lacanianism." *Radical Philosophy* 98 (1999): 6–15.

Twiss, Miranda. *The Most Evil Men and Women in History (The Book of the Channel Five TV Series)*. London: O'Mara, 2002.

Mark Leopold

Woodward, Peter. "Uganda and Southern Sudan." *Uganda Now*. Ed. Holger Bernt Hansen and Michael Twaddle. London: Currey, 1988. 224–38.

Žižek, Slavoj. *The Plague of Fantasies*. London and New York: Verso, 1997.

Žižek, Slavoj. "Selfhood as Such is Spirit: F.W.J. Schelling on the Origins of Evil." *Radical Evil*. Ed. Joan Copjec. London and New York: Verso, 1996. 1–29.

Žižek, Slavoj. *Tarrying with the Negative: Kant, Hegel and the Critique of Ideology*. Durham, NC: Duke UP, 1993.

30 Empire, Desire and Violence

A Queer Transnational Feminist Reading of The Prisoner 'Abuse' in Abu Ghraib and the Question of 'Gender Equality'

Melanie Richter-Montpetit

[I]n the outskirts of the world … the system reveals its true face.

(Eduardo Galeano cited in Slater 2004: 20)

This article looks at some of the discourses and practices surrounding the detainee 'abuses'[1] in Abu Ghraib prison in Iraq, 2003, at the hands of US soldiers. With the help of a queer transnational feminist lens I examine the ways in which the acts of torture were conducted as well as the ways in which they were represented in official and more critical discourses. I address three questions: first, how can we account for the highly sexualized character of many of the 'abuses'? Second, given the conclusions of a large body of feminist literature on the link between violence and 'militarized *masculinity*', how is it possible that officers and low-ranking male-identified soldiers deliberately engaged *female*-identified soldiers in the torture of the detainees? Third, is the participation of female-identified soldiers a sign of gender equality as feminist theorist and social justice activist Barbara Ehrenreich (2004a, 2004b) has suggested?

Dominant discourses paint the acts of violence in Abu Ghraib as either the obscene but exceptional example of some low-ranking soldiers gone mad or as the direct result of the 'state of exception', the suspension of the rule of law in the global 'war on terror'. In contrast, Ehrenreich, an advocate of women's full inclusion into the US armed forces, suggests that the pictures depicting Lynndie England and other female soldiers enacting acts of torture on the bodies of detainees in Abu Ghraib prison are horrifying and constitute a sign of 'gender equality' (Ehrenreich 2004a, 2004b).

Melanie Richter-Montpetit, "Empire, Desire, Violence: A Queer Transnational Feminist Reading of the Prisoner 'Abuse' in Abu Ghraib and the Question of 'Gender Equality.'" *International Feminist Journal of Politics*, 9(1), 2007: 38–59. Reprinted by permission of Taylor & Francis Ltd.

Melanie Richter-Montpetit

This article departs from all three of these positions. I argue that the ways that the violences were enacted on the bodies of detainees follow a pre-constructed hetero-sexed, racialized and gendered script. The pleasure that the seven convicted military prison guards took in torturing detainees is grounded in colonial desires, similar to the nineteenth-century colonial fantasy of the 'White Man's burden'. The effect of these violences and violations is to (re)produce the current misogynist, racialized, heterosexed and classed neo-liberal World DisOrder, and therefore the torturing female-identified soldiers are *not* a sign of 'gender equality'.

Reading these discourses through a queer transnational feminist lens, I try to connect different sites of Empire, among them states and markets with bodies, the household, anti-queer politics and military and civilian prisons. My framework and argument draw on a growing body of literature self-identifying as transnational feminism(s) (e.g. Grewal and Kaplan 1994; Kaplan *et al.* 1999; Shohat 1999), which poses a direct challenge to Euro-American liberal feminist theory and praxis and its assumption that 'Sisterhood is Global' (see Mohanty 1984; Mendoza 2002). Rooted in postcolonial and women of colour feminisms, these works bring together feminist approaches to political economy and discourse analysis in order to trace and contest the 'uneven and dissimilar circuits of culture and capital' across 'boundaries of nation, race, and gender' and the ways in which they constitute and are constituted by old and new forms of colonialism/imperialism (Grewal and Kaplan 2000).

While the issue of sexuality[2] has been largely undertheorized in much transnational feminist writing,[3] my approach foregrounds explicitly queer interventions into the hegemonic sex/gender system, or 'heterosexual matrix' (Butler 1990), which challenge the notion of a stable male/female and heterosexual/homosexual dichotomy. Central to this article is a notion of sexuality that conceptualizes heteronormativity not as a discrete relation of domination, but as intersecting with, and indivisible from, other power relations.

While many of the current debates on bodies treat bodies and desire(s) merely as discursive or cultural phenomena, my inquiry into the gaps, silences and suppressions surrounding the 'detainee abuses' in Abu Ghraib seeks to un-cover the linkages 'between Western [practices of] representation and knowledge on the one hand, and Western material and political power on the other' (Moore-Gilbert 1997: 34). It is only by uncovering some of the social contradictions underlying these seemingly autono-mous social practices that we can produce knowledge that allows us to transform existing social relations of exploitation and oppression (Ebert 1996: 7).

The subject-matter of this article lies at the intersection of multiple areas of study, such as International Relations, Sociology, Political Science and Political Economy. My framework differs significantly from the hegemonic discourses in these literatures. Historically, their liberal versions in particular have been heavily shaped by moderniza-tion theory and its obsession with achieving 'political stability' based on western liberal polities. I favour a transformative approach that conceives of the social world as dynamic and of (non-violent) conflict and contradiction as potentially progressive.

Moreover, the hegemonic discourses in the above-mentioned (themselves compart-mentalized) fields of study tend to compartmentalize the social world and to treat its fragments in isolation from one another. Instead, I envision social phenomena as an overdetermined amalgam of mutually constitutive social processes. Hence, the violences enacted on the bodies of detainees are not 'reducible to discrete elements, but rather [are] a complex [and often contradictory] phenomenon whose constituent parts have an organic unity', to borrow from Ake's observation on the nature of underdevelopment (1981: 6, my addition). The social crises leading to the outbreak of these micro-level violations and violences are deeply embedded in the larger social order. As long as this 'order', with its underlying relations of inequality, is not transformed, the kinds of violences performed on the bodies of Abu Ghraib prisoners cannot be overcome.

Drawing on the insight of Edward Said (1993) and other postcolonial scholars, that Empire is not only about the accumulation of wealth, but also about 'a deeply held belief in the need to and the right to dominate others *for their own good*, others who are expected to be grateful' (Razack 2004: 10, emphasis in original), I argue that the torture and murder of prisoners were acts of colonial violence, firmly rooted in a continuum of racialized, (hetero)sexualized, classed violence. This continuum of violence reaches back in time to the modern 'civilizing mission' and outward in space to link the imperial violence enacted on the bodies of people of colour, Muslims, queers and women in the 'mother' country/'homeland', with the perceived moral righteousness or even duty of the US Empire to bring (liberal) democracy to the 'dark corners of the earth' (Bush 2002a) in the 'war on terror', the war 'to save civilization itself' (Bush 2001e). Making legible some of the larger social relations at work in the events at Abu Ghraib is not intended to exonerate the military prison guards, but rather to show how our desires are not just a question of individual preference.[4]

I will start off with an exploration of the Bush administration's foreign policy discourse, which I term the 'save civilization itself'-fantasy. I will show how, through this national fantasy and its interpellated subject-positions ('Whiteness'), the discursive representation of the US nation-state and its citizens as benign defenders of 'civilization itself' made sense. With the help of a queer transnational feminist lens, I will then seek to forge a meaningful narrative to conceive of the ways the different acts of torture were conducted.

'Operation Iraqi Hope', 'Whiteness' and the National 'Save Civilization Itself'-Fantasy

It is my claim that the violences enacted on the bodies of prisoners in Abu Ghraib are embedded in the linguistic and non-linguistic practices of the 'save civilization itself'-fantasy.[5] Grounded in a long history of colonial practices and desires, this hegemonic fantasy should not be read as merely offering legitimacy to the US Empire's 'war on terror', but as a site where imperial power is (re)produced.

Discourses are not closed systems, but overlap and are open-ended. They draw on elements of other discourses; hence a newly emerging discourse always contains traces of past discursive formations (Hall 1996: 202). The successful deployment of ruling class ideas, such as the 'save civilization itself'-fantasy, depends on these ideas being embraced by the subaltern classes as the unquestioned, taken for granted, 'common sense' (Gramsci 1971). This 'common sense' provides frames of intelligibility that make certain practices, identities and desires appear 'natural', possible and desirable, to the exclusion of other practices and identities, thereby helping secure the societal *status quo* (Doty 1996; Weldes 1999). Yet what exactly constitutes 'common sense' at a specific historical juncture is not simply imposed by dominant groups, but involves unceasing processes of contestation and (re)negotiation between various social forces, which, however, do not operate on a level playing field (Gramsci 1971: 421).

The struggle over the production of meaning does not only involve the consent of subaltern groups, but also the *(re)production* of subject-positions from whose location within the discursive formation the fantasy actually makes sense. In fact, I theorize the relationship between a discursive formation, its subject-positions and their desires as mutually constitutive and continuously (re)enacted. Following Althusser (1971), the process of constructing and locating identities or subject-positions can be understood as 'interpellation'. Borrowing from Jutta Weldes' inquiry into the 'Cuban missile crisis', I argue that the 'save civilization itself'-fantasy successfully interpellated the 'abusive' prison guards, as well as the majority of the US electorate in the last presidential elections, 'because it represents events as occurring in a world of familiar objects and familiar threats forged of conventional, already familiar articulations. Its common-sense character was and is secured by interpellating most Americans into familiar and acceptable subject positions' (Weldes 1999: 121). In this section, I will explore some crucial linguistic and non-linguistic aspects of the 'world of familiar objects and familiar threats' on which the currently hegemonic national fantasy draws.

Following the killings of 9/11, the official reasoning of the current Bush-administration for its pursuit of the 'Global War on Terror' and its attack on Iraq in particular, has oscillated between self-defense (in terms of a response to 9/11 or a search for 'Weapons of Mass Destruction') and humanitarian intervention (in the form of 'Operation Iraqi Freedom'). In this 'war', the Bush-administration announced a permanent state of emergency, which has suspended the UN Charter's prohibition of force and the Geneva Convention on the treatment of Prisoners of War. The justification for the breach of international law is self-defence: President Bush claims that 'the civilized world faces unprecedented dangers' (Bush 2002b). 'We act to defend ourselves and deliver our children from a future of fear' (Bush 2001e). Bush argues that this war is a total war, as the 'threat [from terrorism] cannot be appeased. Civilization itself, the civilization we share, is threatened' (Bush 2001e). Therefore, '[w]e wage a war to save civilization, itself. We did not seek it, but we must fight it – and we will prevail' (Bush 2001d).

This discourse essentializes and then pitches the 'civilized' nations in diametrical opposition to the 'terrorist'/'foreign fighter' 'who dwells in the dark corners of the earth' (Bush 2002a) or 'rogue states' such as Iraq. In this permanent state of war, '[y]ou are either with us or you are against us' (Bush 2001c). The epistemological and ontological distinction between the two enemy camps 'puts the Westerner in a whole series of possible relationships with the Orient without ever losing him the relative upper hand' (Said 1994: 7). The trope of 'rogue states' draws on the orientalist idea of the duplicitous character of 'orientals' who cannot be trusted, and henceforth diplomacy and other 'civilized' ways of interaction are not appropriate – the only language 'they' understand is violence. This representation of 'orientals' and the 'Orient' has been circulating in western discourses since classical times and continues to shape western responses to the Middle East (Said 1994, 1997; Moore-Gilbert 1997: 39–40).[6]

The 'save civilization itself'-fantasy builds on the idea of 'American exceptionalism', whose theological and secular components date back (at least) to the rise of European colonialism and the 'discovery' of the New World. From the story of Europe's destined conquest of America at the hands of Christopher Columbus, followed by the American Puritans' divinely ordained 'errand in the wilderness', to the secular ideology of a 'Manifest Destiny' to expand westward to the Pacific coast (Spanos 2000: 22) and the Cold War 'defender of the Free World'-discourse, the American national identity has been constructed around,

> a long story – a story we continue, but whose end we will not see. It is the story of a new world that became a friend and liberator of the old, a story of a slave-holding society that became a servant of freedom, the story of a power that went into the world to protect but not possess, to defend but not to conquer.
>
> (Bush 2001a)

The religious dimension of the fantasy feeds on the faith that the USA is the land of the chosen people, the 'redeemer nation' (Tuveson 1968), handpicked by God to defend freedom and 'save civilization itself'. As Bush put it: 'This is our calling. This is the calling of the United States of America, the most free nation in the world. A nation built on fundamental values that rejects hate, rejects violence, rejects murderers, rejects evil' (Bush 2001b). 'We have a special responsibility to defend freedom' (Bush 2002a); 'we've been called to a unique role in human events' (Bush 2002b).

This narrative constructing US national identity as peaceful and 'the most free nation in the world' obscures the fact that, historically, the internal and external civilizing missions of 'the New World' (and the 'Old Europe') were based on systematic violence against Other(s)[7] and the extraction of their labour – from the genocide of the indigenous Americans to the transatlantic slave-trade, and from the mass lynchings in post-bellum South to the ongoing 'war on drugs' and the post-9/11 'war on terror'.

In the context of the latest invasion and occupation of Iraq, this rhetoric obscures the violence unleashed by the Allies' own 'Weapons of Mass Destruction' (such as depleted uranium and 'daisy cutters') and the outright robbery of Iraqi riches, among them the large-scale privatization of Iraq's state-owned industries. The extreme neo-liberal makeover of the Iraqi economy imposed by the US-led Coalition Provisional Authority, which includes the adoption of a 15 per cent flat corporate tax rate and the right for foreign investors to repatriate 100 per cent of the profit (Klein 2004), altered every economic policy of the Hussein-government except for the ones 'restricting trade unions and collective bargaining' (Klein 2004). A World Bank (2004: 2) report on Iraq recommends the launch of a public relations campaign to 'educate' the 97 per cent of the Iraqi population who, according to its survey, have not yet understood the supreme superiority of a free-market development model. Like his nineteenth-century colonial predecessor, today's 'White man', 'Davos-man', is getting generous compensation for shouldering his 'burden' of bringing 'civilization' to others.

To conclude this part of my argument, the 'save civilization itself'-fantasy articulated by the Bush-administration represents 'Operation Iraqi Hope' as an altruistic civilizing mission, creating the discursive space for the subject-position 'Whiteness'. I argue that the prison guards/soldiers were not just passively 'hailed' into this subject-position, but that their willingness to identify with the 'save civilization itself'-fantasy was embedded in their desire to enact 'Whiteness'. As 'freedom-loving' First World citizens from 'the most free nation in the world', they saw themselves as civilizing the Third World oriental or 'hajji'[8]/'raghead'[9]/'sand nigger'. In the next section, I will focus on the actual torture practices of the soldiers, and the ways in which the violence involved was portrayed and (re)produced in US military investigations and public discourses.

A Queer Transnational Feminist Reading of the Torture Practices

The 'save civilization itself'-fantasy operates not only to interpellate individual soldiers but also to structure the four official US military reports into the 'detainee abuses' (two published together as Fay and Jones 2004; see also Schlesinger *et al.* 2004; Taguba 2004). One such report declares that, after the events of 9/11, 'the President, the Congress and the American people recognized we were at war with a different kind of enemy' (Schlesinger *et al.* 2004: 6). It cites approvingly US General Abizaid's orientalist testimony before a Senate Committee on 19 May 2004: 'Our enemies kill without remorse ... Their targets are not Kabul and Baghdad, but places like Madrid and London and New York' (Schlesinger *et al.* 2004: 28). This narrative obscures the resistance the 'coalition troops' face in both Afghanistan and Iraq as well as the fact that the population in these two countries is most affected by the ongoing strife between the US-led 'coalition troops' and the 'terrorists'.

Moreover, by pitching western cities in diametrical opposition to eastern cities seen as Other, Abizaid's testimony and its recounting in the report serve to (re)construct the line of conflict in international relations in a way that separates and homogenizes the civilized West on the one side and Bush's 'dark corners of the earth' on the other. Concretely, in these 'dark corners of the earth', which represent 'a complex and dangerous operational environment' (Fay and Jones 2004: 6), 'there are no safe areas behind "friendly lines" – there *are* no friendly lines' (Schlesinger *et al.* 2004: 57, emphasis in original). This narrative clearly recalls Manifest Destiny's trope of 'Indian country'.[10] In this national fantasy of the global 'war on terror', 'tens of thousands of men and women in uniform strive every day under austere and dangerous conditions to secure our freedom and the freedom of others' (Schlesinger *et al.* 2004: 18). In their quest to 'preserve the freedoms and liberties that America and our Army represents throughout the world' (Fay and Jones 2004: 6), and in 'supporting the Iraqi people' (Fay and Jones 2004: 33), they 'confronted a faceless enemy whose hatred of the United States knew no limits' (Fay and Jones 2004: 12).

In stark contrast to the seemingly benign intentions articulated in this hegemonic national fantasy, the four reports came to a similar conclusion whereby between October and December 2003, 'numerous incidents of sadistic, blatant, and wanton criminal abuses were inflicted on several detainees' in Abu Ghraib prison (Taguba 2004: 16).

At this point, we should note a large body of feminist literature challenging the supposed exceptionalism of 'sadistic, blatant, and wanton criminal abuses' among soldiers in war zones and at home (see Seifert 1996; Barrett 1999; Whitworth 2004). This feminist scholarship on militarism suggests that being a soldier is, 'in short, about violence and about preparing people to destroy other human beings by force' (Whitworth 2004: 151). Yet the problem goes beyond military training, it is about what constitutes becoming and being a soldier – it is about *militarized masculinity*. Drawing on Cynthia Enloe, Whitworth (2004: 16) argues that militaries rely on a certain kind of 'ideology of manliness' in order to function well, an ideology premised on violence and aggression, individual conformity to military discipline, aggressive heterosexism, misogyny and racism. The military compensates the soldier for subordination and physical stress with the promise of community, and physical and emotional toughness (Whitworth 2004: 16).

Militarized masculinity is inherently fragile, due to the discrepancies between the 'myths and promises' associated with militarized masculinity as experienced and enacted in military training as well as in simulations of warfare, and the lack of control in the actual lives of soldiers (Whitworth 2004: 166). Whitworth further argues that, through violence and the denigration of Others who undermine their promised entitlements, soldiers seek to (re)constitute their militarized masculine self. Following Whitworth, I suggest that the various forms of torture enacted by the soldiers on the bodies of Abu Ghraib detainees were a way of reasserting control and reconstituting the soldierly Self, particularly after the 'emasculating' events on 9/11 and the daily resistance against the occupation of Iraq.

The heavy involvement of female-identified soldiers in the torture of prisoners seems to stand in clear contradiction to feminist theories of militarized masculinity. How can we make sense of this tension? I argue that we can do so if we understand 'Operation Iraqi Hope' as a colonial endeavour, the racialized encounter between prison guards and detainees as a colonial one and the torturing of detainees as acts of colonial violence rooted in the desire to enact 'Whiteness'.[11] I will now turn to the ways the acts of torture were staged.

According to the military reports male detainees were 'sodomized' by prison guards, forced to 'masturbate themselves' and/or 'perform indecent acts on each other' (Fay and Jones 2004: 72), such as simulating and/or performing oral or anal 'sex' on fellow male detainees. The prison guards also arranged naked male detainees in a human pyramid, in such a way 'that the bottom guys [sic] penis would touch the guy on tops [sic] butt' (Taguba 2004), and called them names such as 'gay'. Many of these 'homosexual acts' = 'indecent acts' were photographed and/or videotaped. Moreover, the soldiers stripped male detainees and forced them to wear female underpants, often on their heads.

I suggest that these torture practices are embedded in colonial narratives and practices that, first, paint the colonies or 'dark corners of the earth' as feminized and 'spatially spread for male exploration' (McClintock 1995: 23) or 'penetration'; and, second, equate the lack of potency and domination of the male body (and the nation) with femininity and male 'homosexuality'.

From the 'discoveries' of the Middle Ages on, the racialized sexualization of colonial conquests played a central role in western imperialisms in terms of constructing boundaries along the intersecting lines of class, gender, race, nation and civilization in ways that helped regulate the larger social 'order', and in particular helped organize the exploitation of labour. 'For centuries, the uncertain continents – Africa, the Americas, Asia – were figured in European lore as libidinously eroticized' (McClintock 1995: 22). Sex was considered the Other of civilization – 'a threat to social order, modernity and the nation, a threat to progress' (Binnie 2004: 17). Within these 'porno-tropics for the European imagination', as McClintock (1995: 22) puts it, 'women figured as the epitome of aberration and excess' and female sexuality was often depicted as cannibalistic (McClintock 1995: 27). Moreover, the first European conquerors of the New World often depicted indigenous men as sodomites – perverts that deserved to be penetrated and killed (Trexler 1995). In these colonial fantasies, the 'Arabic Orient' constituted the site of particular sexual excess (see Said 1994; Boone 2003).

In the late nineteenth century, the western colonial projects coincided and intersected with the rise of 'scientific' racism and its systematic racialization of Others in the colonies *and* in the mother country. In the colonies, '[t]he personage of the savage was developed as the Other of civilization and one of the first "proofs" of this otherness was the nakedness of the savage, the visibility of its sex' (Mercer and Julien cited in Somerville 2000: 5). 'Back home', the twin processes of sexualization and racialization constructed internal Other(s) – the degenerate European races such as the Jews and the Irish, prostitutes, the unemployed, the insane (McClintock 1995: 50) and homosexuals. These intersecting processes helped erect and police the boundaries between the imperial elites and the European and non-European subaltern, and served to rationalize, to render 'natural', the concomitant acts of exclusion and violence.

The hetero-patriarchal association of the penetrated body as passive and feminine, and of the penetrator as virile and masculine has played, and continues to play, a significant role in military conquests of the US Empire. It intersects clearly with racialized notions of inferiority and superiority. For example, during the 1991 Gulf War, US airforce soldiers scribbled messages on their bombs, such as 'Mrs Saddam's sex toy', 'a suppository for Saddam' and 'bend over Saddam' (Progler 1999).

In this hetero-patriarchal narrative, to be feminized and sexualized by a female-identified soldier is deemed particularly humiliating for the colonized male body (and his nation). In the court martial of army reservist Charles Graner, witnesses reported that female soldiers were instructed by officers to 'shout abuse' (Reid 2005). As I will elaborate below, I do not suggest that the 'female' soldiers were puppets in the service of racialized hetero-patriarchy, but rather that their motivations were located in colonial desires. The deliberate involvement of 'females' in Abu Ghraib (and Guantanamo Bay), which also included 'a female Soldier … press[ing] a broom against his [a male-identified detainee's] anus' (Fay and Jones 2004: 77), intersects with racist orientalist discourses that depict acts of sexualized violence against 'men' at the hands of 'women', as well as 'homosexual sex' and its simulation, as particularly humiliating for 'oriental' men.

An example of this can be seen in an article by high-profile investigative journalist and commentator, Seymour Hersh, in the *New Yorker* newspaper. Hersh's article was the first to offer a detailed analysis countering the Bush-administration's 'few bad apples' thesis on the prisoner 'abuse' in Abu Ghraib. Hersh (2004) argues that '[s]uch dehumanization is unacceptable in any culture', but then continues to say that 'it is especially so in the Arab world. Homosexual acts are against Islamic law'. This reasoning conflates 'homosexuality' with dehumanization, as well as all inmates with 'Arabs' = 'the Arab world' = 'Islamic' = 'Fundamentalist'; it also obscures how terror against queers in the alleged 'most free nation in the world' is systemic and state-sponsored.[12]

Among the current anti-queer sexual politics of the Bush administration is the attempt to pass a constitutional amendment limiting marriage to unions between 'men' and 'women'. Bush (2004a) declared that a ban on same-sex marriage was a matter of 'national importance' because the union of a man and woman in marriage is 'the most fundamental institution of civilization'. Same-sex marriage threatens 'the basis of an orderly society' (Bush 2004b) and 'the welfare of children' (Bush 2004a) – ultimately it threatens civilization itself. In fact, the only times Bush conjures up threats to civilization are in the 'war on terror' and the 'war on same-sex marriage'.[13] Moreover, the anti-queer sexual politics of the Bush administration are not limited to defending marriage, but are aimed at fighting non-normative sexualities *tout court*.[14] For example, queer organizations in New York City have reported a dramatic increase in anti-queer violence since the Bush administration's aggressively anti-queer agenda (Goldstein 2004).

Today, federal law prohibits openly gay men and lesbians in the US military. Between 1994 and 2003, nearly 9,500 members of the US armed forces were discharged under the 'don't ask, don't tell, don't pursue' policy (Associated Press 2005). Moreover, it was not until 2003 that the US Supreme Court struck out the 'anti-sodomy' laws of fourteen US states and the military, which had criminalized consensual anal sex in the 'private' sphere.[15]

Against the backdrop of the institutionalized aggressive heteronormativity of the US nation-state, particularly within its military, it should not be surprising that the prison guards set the stage for their acts of violence and humiliation according to an aggressively homophobic script. In the following, I zoom in a little closer on the discursive practice of referring to 'homosexual sex' and 'sodomy', which, I suggest, helps erase certain aspects of the violences.

The four official investigations, as well as the US mass media, over-whelmingly reported that male detainees in Abu Ghraib were forced to have or simulate 'homosexual sex' or 'sodomy'. The way this discourse frames these acts of violence as 'sex' and not rape recalls the orthodox interpretation that male rape of female bodies is about too much testosterone and/or the irresistible 'sexiness' of the victim/survivor (see Brownmiller 1975; Seifert 1993). However, there is also a large contemporary body of literature, including work by non-feminists and military psychologists, which argues that rape is about violence and domination, making the Other lose control over her or his body, particularly her or his sexuality (see Marlowe 1983; Goldstein 2001).

But there is something else to it. The following poem by Miriam Axel-Lute (2001: 15) captures well the violent erasures of the sodomy discourse. The poem is about the 'sodomizing' of Abner Louima, a Black man from Haiti by White supremacists of the New York Police Department in 1997:

> They Never Call It Rape
>
> Even the sympathetic media
> say Abner Louima
> was 'sodomized'
> by the police
> in a bathroom
> after being beaten.
>
> Sodomized
> as if the terrible part
> was his ass
> and not the splintering
> toilet plunger handle
> they used.

Axel-Lute's poem shows how the use of the language of 'sodomy' obscures the brutality and the concomitant pain inflicted by ramming a toilet plunger handle up a rectum with so much force that it actually splinters. The poem conveys how the

Melanie Richter-Montpetit

anxiety of the sodomy discourse, with its focus on the 'ass', silences the concrete violation as an act of racist violence against a racialized body.

Turning to the ways in which the acts of torture seem to be grounded in colonial desires, I would begin by highlighting the numerous reports and pictures of detainees being forced to crawl and to bark. Some of the most (in)famous pictures show army reservist Lynndie England holding a crawling prisoner on a leash like a dog. This logic of equating the Barbarian Other with animals also operated in the speeches of President Bush. On several occasions he announced that he would 'smoke them out of their caves' (2001f) in the 'dark corners of the earth' (2002a).

I want to make two points about the articulation of racialized difference through animal imagery. First, animals are wild and dangerous and need to be tamed/civilized – the most domesticated animal in the Euro-American context is the dog. Yet even when domesticated, a dog is still a dog.[16] Second, historically, colonial Europe ascribed lust to animals – raw, untamed/uncivilized sexuality (Hoch 1979: 51). In one of the courts martial, a witness testified that when he saw 'two naked detainees, one masturbating to another kneeling with its [sic] mouth open', one of the perpetrators, former civilian prison guard Staff Sergeant Ivan L. Frederick II, told him: 'Look what these *animals* do when you leave them alone for two seconds' (cited in Hersh 2004, my emphasis). The Fay-Jones Report describes a picture depicting naked detainees who were forced to masturbate and then were 'ridden like animals' (2004: 78).

Another instance revealing how much the soldiers imagined themselves to be in a civilizing mission is the inscription and picture on the door of one of the prison cells. One of the detainees was incarcerated in a 'totally darkened cell measuring about 2 m long and less than a metre across, devoid of any window, latrine or water tap, or bedding' (Fay and Jones 2004: 66). On the door to this 'room' was the inscription 'the Gollum' and a picture of said character from the Hollywood trilogy 'Lord of the Rings'. In the movie, Gollum is portrayed as dangerous, irrational, ugly and naked; it hates sunlight and its warmth and, because of that, seeks refuge in a dark cave. Gollum is a murderer, constantly lying, and finally betrays the heroes. As he is irredeemably irrational, the only language he understands is violence. In fact, the only time in the film that Gollum speaks anything close to the truth is when he gets tortured.

I suggest that the 'coalition' soldiers in their quest for 'saving civilization itself' saw themselves in a struggle between Good and Evil, like the heroes in 'Lord of the Rings'. Their 'save civilization itself'-fantasy was enacted in a 'dangerous enemy land' (Schlesinger *et al.* 2004), where regular mortar attacks on Abu Ghraib prison were part of the guerilla-style resistance to the occupation 'of a different kind of enemy' (Schlesinger *et al.* 2004: 6), including suicide-bombings. 'Gollum' is duplicitous, a common trope in orientalist discourses. He needs to be tortured in order to become truthful, thus rendering the torture of his body a *civilizing* act.

Forced nudity, at times for several days, was a 'seemingly common practice' (Fay and Jones 2004: 68). The soldiers videotaped and photographed the naked bodies. The practice of forced nudity draws on the colonial imaginary discussed earlier, according to which the first 'proof' of the Barbarian Other's primitivism is the open display of its genitals. Like colonial travellers and late modern tourists, the soldiers sought to enact 'Whiteness' by capturing the 'exoticism' of the Other with the help of video and photo camera.

Over the period of three months, the soldiers took around 1,800 pictures of their acts of violence. These pictures also depict grinning soldiers giving thumbs up to the camera next to the wounded, naked flesh of the detainees, strongly evoking the trophy pictures of colonial hunters standing proudly next to their prey.[17] Immortalizing the moment of triumph over the beast with the help of pictures allows them to relive the triumphant moment of 'Whiteness' and to share it with friends and family.[18] One of the pictures depicting naked detainees stacked in a 'pyramid' was used as a screensaver on the computer in the office of the prison guards (Fay and Jones 2004: 78).

Both the Taguba and Fay-Jones reports mention pictures depicting two female detainees lifting their shirts and thereby exposing their breasts. Yet these pictures have not been published in the European or American media, nor did I find any journalist demanding that they be published. Against the backdrop of the publication of photos portraying in graphic detail the sexualized violence against male detainees, the silence concerning these pictures of women and the acts they depict should arouse our 'feminist curiosity' (Enloe 2004).

The Fay-Jones Report (2004: 91) mentions that the two women were 'arrested for suspected prostitution' and states that '[t]here is no evidence to confirm if these acts were consensual or coerced'. Interestingly, none of the four reports, including Fay-Jones, ever raised the question of whether or not nudity was possibly forced on *male*-identified detainees. Also, this incident is the only one out of the four reports mentioning the 'crime' that a 'criminal detainee' was charged with. Clearly, the uncertainty of the Fay-Jones Report about whether or not these acts of nudity were consensual or coerced has to do with the alleged deviant sexual behaviour of the two racialized women. In a similar vein, the Taguba Report (2004: 17) mentions an MP (Military Policeman) 'having sex' with a female detainee. Due to the limited scope of this article I cannot further explore this rampant silence on sexualized violences enacted on female-identified detainees. However I suggest the need for further research to examine this issue in the light of the historical 'unrapeability' of black female-identified bodies (see Davis 1981; hooks 1997, 1998; Bakare-Yusuf 1999) and western representations of 'oriental' women as mysterious (e.g. veiled) and lascivious (e.g. in the harem).

As my reading through a queer transnational feminist lens has shown, the sexed racialization of acts of violence against detainees in Abu Ghraib was not an aberration. The same kind of violent practices are reported from military installations in Afghanistan, Guantanamo Bay, other US-led Iraqi prisons and US civilian prisons. The US prison-industrial complex is characterized by a grossly disproportionate incarceration of racialized bodies, and particularly of Black males. Rape, trafficking in inmates for sex, forced nudity, crawling naked, being hooded and made to wear women's underwear are part and parcel of the civilian prison experience in the 'most free nation of the world' (see Butterfield 2004). Charles Graner, deemed one of the main perpetrators in Abu Ghraib, had previously worked as a guard in a civilian prison in the USA, where he is alleged to have put razor blades into the food of an inmate. Before his departure to Iraq, he was quoted as saying, 'I can't wait to go kill some sand niggers' (Black Commentator 2004). The new racist slur 'hajjis', which collapses Arab/Iraqi/Muslim/Taliban, is now so commonsensical among US soldiers in Iraq that it is even used in official military documents (Rockwell 2005).

My analysis of the acts of torture comes to the conclusion that they were staged according to a misogynist, heterosexed, racialized script. Enacting violences on the bodies of Abu Ghraib prisoners reasserted not only the perceived control of the individual, militarized Selves of the seven soldiers in the photographs, but also allowed them to enact 'Whiteness' – and thereby re/produce the identity and hegemony of the US Empire and its heterosexed, racialized and classed World (Dis)Order.

This brings me back to Ehrenreich's argument that 'the photos of abuse' in Abu Ghraib prison are 'a sign of gender equality'. Ehrenreich (2004b) bases her analysis on the 'fact' that three out of the seven prison guards involved, as well as the prison director, the top US intelligence officer in Iraq and the National Security Advisor, were 'women'. An advocate of women's full inclusion in the military, Ehrenreich (2004b) admits that she 'did have some illusions about women'. While she 'never believed that women were innately gentler and less aggressive than men', she had hoped that once women achieved a critical mass in the military, they would change the institution over time (Ehrenreich 2004b: 1).

I do not think that the participation of the three female-identified military prison guards in the acts of torture constitutes a sign of gender equality. Ehrenreich's reading is based on a problematic liberal framework of equality and freedom, embedded in a hetero-normative ontology that maps a bipolar notion of 'gender' onto a bipolar notion of sexed bodies, and flirts with a certain essentialism about femininity (and masculinity) which seems based less on nature than nurture.

Ehrenreich's notion of subjectivity obscures how 'gender' is always already racial-ized, classed and sexualized, to mention just a few 'markers'. The gendered subjectivity to which she refers is reminiscent of the (supposedly) universal feminist subject 'woman' conjured by dominant strands of the first- and second-wave feminist movement(s) in Europe and North America. This monolithic notion of 'woman' and its accompanying single-issue politics raise the question 'gender equality *for whom* and *at the cost of whom?*' and have been contested for being implicitly marked as White heterosexual able-bodied and middle-class (see Moraga and Anzaldúa 1981). In a similar vein, Ehrenreich's notion of 'gender' erases not only the racialization of the female-gendered subject (namely White), but also the possibility of this subject being racist and/or homophobic.

As my analysis of the sexed, racialized torture practices has shown, the 'save civili-zation itself'-fantasy, that is, the hegemonic national fantasy envisaging the First World civilized Self bringing (liberal) democracy to the Third World Other incapable of self-determination, and the subject-position 'Whiteness', depend on the association of femininity with subordination, weakness and passivity, in short, inferiority. While the (hetero)sexualized humiliation of racialized men at the hands of White western women disrupts the fictitious clear-cut male/female dichotomy underpinning this fantasy, the violent practices constitute merely a reversal of that logocentrism, they do not displace it. To remain within Ehrenreich's problematic framework, the female-identified soldiers ironically contributed actively to gender *in*equality.

Moreover, I think Ehrenreich's hope of taming/'civilizing' the military is an illusion. The military cannot be transformed, as its mission is to prepare and organize its workers to kill people; the reproduction of the 'New World Order' continues to depend heavily on the deployment of military force. As discussed earlier, physical violence and aggres-sive Othering play a constitutive role in the construction of the soldier Self.

In sum, the acts of violence perpetrated by the female-identified soldiers on the bodies of prisoners should be located within colonial desires. Given the systematic, simulta-neously racialized and heterosexed character of the acts of torture, and given that their effect is to re/produce the identity and hegemony of the US Empire and its heterosexed, racialized and classed World (Dis)Order, the participation of the three female-identified soldiers is not a sign of 'gender equality'. Further, as Whiteness and the concomitant World (Dis)Order are also a classed project,[19] both female- and male-identified prison guards occupy the subject-position 'White but not quite' (Agathangelou 2004).

Though none of the torture pictures published depict soldiers of colour, the Fay-Jones Report (2004: 77, 80) twice mentions 'Black soldiers' engaging in torture of prisoners, and one of the seven soldiers convicted of prisoner 'abuse' self-identifies as a Black male. These reports do not contradict my argument that the soldiers desired and enacted a fantasy of 'racial' supremacy. I argue that the essentially *colonial* character of 'Operation Iraqi Hope', the commonsensical fantasy of the First World civilized Self that brings (liberal) democracy to the Third World Other incapable of self-determination, creates discursive space for the interpellation and participation of the sexed, classed and racialized bodies of some of the US Empire's internal Others.[20]

Conclusions

'Operation Iraqi Hope' is part of the Bush-administration's 'save civilization itself'-fantasy, 'the story of a power that went into the world to protect but not possess, to defend but not to conquer' (Bush 2001a). This national fantasy constructed discursive space for the subject-position 'Whiteness', the 'freedom-loving' and 'civilized' westerner, citizen of 'the most free nation in the world', who intervenes in Iraq to defend civilization itself and benevolently to sort out the problems of the Third World Other or 'sand niggers' who are unable to take care of themselves. The desire of the soldiers to have themselves interpellated by the 'save civilization itself'-fantasy was rooted in their desire to enact 'Whiteness', the racist fantasy and practice of 'racial' supremacy over 'hajjis' and 'sand niggers', a pleasure clearly conveyed by the smiling faces giving thumbs up on hundreds and hundreds of pictures.

That these pictures were emailed to friends and family back home shows the *common-sense* character of the perception of 'Operation Iraqi Hope' as a colonial and civilizing mission, and hence the moral righteousness of the associated acts of violence, from the 'ordinary' violence of warfare, to the unexpiated daily killings of civilians at road checks, to state-sanctioned prison torture.

The participation of female-identified soldiers in the acts of misogynist, racialized and heterosexed violence against colonized bodies and territories is not a sign of 'gender equality', as Barbara Ehrenreich suggests. Rather these practices make visible how White western women's participation in empire-building – in this case by occupying typical male-identified positions – may disclose certain social contradictions underpinning imperial discourse; however, they do not challenge the hegemony of the 'save civilization itself'-fantasy but (re)produce this racist discourse and its concomitant practices of domination, expropriation and exploitation.

Notes

1. All four official US investigations belittle the acts of torture as 'prisoner abuses'.

2. 'Sexuality' in this article refers to both a field of knowledge and an erotic practice.

3. Among the transnational feminists incorporating sexuality studies are Alexander (1991, 1994) and Puar (1998).

4. Due to the limited scope of this essay, my reading of the events surrounding the torture of prisoners

Melanie Richter-Montpetit

in Abu Ghraib focuses largely on the US Empire's hege-monic foreign policy discourse, the 'save civilization itself'-fantasy. As I will elaborate below, I do not concep-tualize discourse or imperial power as monolithic and pro-duced merely in a top – down fashion. In fact, this essay is part of a larger project in which I seek to explore how alternative narratives and identification-practices compli-cated or interrupted the workings of the 'save civilization itself'-fantasy in Abu Ghraib, e.g. the multiple and poten-tially contradictory positionings of soldiers themselves due to their gendered, classed and/or racialized subjec-tivities in other social, historical and spatial contexts as well as the prisoners' contributions towards, and contesta-tions of, this discursive formation.

5 I use fantasy instead of discourse or ideology because it captures better the contribution of our dreams and unconsciousness to the inter-subjective creation of our life worlds and the ways we get to know ourselves. See Yegenoglu (1998: 2) for a discussion on 'the risk of psy-chologizing structural processes by reducing them to individual psychological motivations'; see Grewal (2001) on the Eurocentrism of (Lacanian) psychoanalysis.

6 Said has been rightly critiqued for not accounting sufficiently for variances between and within different national ori-entalisms, for example due to the gendered (Lowe 1991) and heterosexed (Boone 2003) nature of colonial discourses.

7 On the racialization of the non-western Other in US foreign policy, see Hunt (1988) and Doty (1996).

8 This racist slang directed at the homogenized Arab/Muslim/Iraqi/Taliban Other draws on the Arabic word for Muslims who have undertaken the pilgrimage to Mekka ('haj') (Rockwell 2005).

9 There are reports that US drill sergeants use chants of 'burning turbans' and 'killing ragheads' to prepare their recruits in the 'war on terror' (Rockwell 2005).

10 I owe this thought to Razack's (2004) exploration of the discursive effects of constructing Somalia as 'Indian country' in her insightful book on Canada's 'Somalia Affair'.

11 Razack (2004) makes a similar argument in the context of the quasi-peacekeeping operations of the Canadian military in Somalia.

12 In fact, while it was only in 2003 that the US Supreme Court struck down 'anti-sodomy' legislation, the Iraqi Criminal Code did not explicitly criminalize 'homosexu-ality' until 2001 (Brown 2005). Rather than engaging in a discussion about which country is more aggressively homophobic, I want to problematize Hersh's construction of the homophobic Other that ultimately secures the Self as more 'civilized' and benign.

13 I am grateful to Mark B. Salter for pointing this out to me.

14 Among these practices are Bush's attempt in February 2005 to re-nominate prominent anti-queer activist Bill Pryor for the federal court of appeal and the 2001 Global Gag Rule restricting funding for family planning.

15 For a good discussion on how the recent decriminali-zation of 'sodomy' sanctions only a particular form of 'homosexuality', see Ruskola (2005).

16 I am grateful to Carmen Sanchez for pointing this out to me.

17 Taking trophy pictures of the violences enacted on the bodies of 'Third World people' seems to be a common practice in peacekeeping missions involving western soldiers (Razack 2004: 53).

18 In fact, the seven prison guards accused of 'abusing' detainees emailed pictures of their acts of violence to friends and family back home (Hersh 2004).

19 Several gross orthographic mistakes made by the seven MPs offer a hint of the appalling class divide in US society reflected in military recruitment. For example, none of the 'civilizing' prison guards noticed that they had misspelled the word 'Rapest' [sic] when spraying it on one of the naked prisoners. In another instance, an MP log indicated that a detainee was 'neked' [sic] (Fay 2004: 89).

20 For other studies exploring the interpellation of internal Others into colonial fantasies, see Lewis (1996) and Yegenoglu (1998) on White women and Razack (2004) on racialized soldiers.

References

Agathangelou, A. M. 2004. *The Global Political Economy of Sex: Desire, Violence, and Insecurity in Mediterranean Nation States*. New York: Palgrave MacMillan Press.

Ake, C. 1981. *A Political Economy of Africa*. Harlow, Essex: Longman.

Alexander, M. J. 1991. 'Erotic Autonomy and a Politics of Decolonization: An Anatomy of Feminist and State Practice in the Bahamas Tourist Economy', in Alexander, M. J. and Mohanty, C. T. (eds) *Feminist Genealogies, Colonial Legacies, Democratic Futures*, pp. 63–100. New York: Routledge.

Alexander, M. J. 1994. 'Not Just Anybody Can Be a Citizen: The Politics of Law, Sexuality and Postcoloniality in Trinidad and Tobago and the Bahamas', *Feminist Review* 48: 5–23.

Althusser, L. 1971. *Lenin and Philosophy, and other Essays*. London: New Left Books.

Associated Press. 2005. '"Don't Ask, Don't Tell" Hurts Military, Study Says.' Available at http://www.msnbc.msn.com/id/7025815/ (accessed 25 March 2005).

Axel-Lute, M. 2001. *Souls like Mockingbirds*, self-published. Available to purchase from http://www.mjoy.org/poetry/order.html

Bakare-Yusuf, B. 1999. 'The Economy of Violence: Black Bodies and the Unspeakable Terror', in Shildrick, M.

(ed.) *Feminist Theory and the Body*, pp. 311–23. New York: Routledge Press.

Barrett, F. J. 1999. 'Die Konstruktion Hegemonialer Männlichkeit in Organisationen: Das Beispiel der US-Marine', in Eifler, C. and Seifert, R. (eds) *Soziale Konstruktion*, pp. 71–91. Münster: Verlag Westfälisches Dampfboot.

Binnie, J. 2004. *The Globalization of Sexuality*. London: Sage.

Black Commentator. 2004. 'Mass Incarceration and Rape: The Savaging of Black America.' Available at http://www.doublestandards.org/bc1.html (accessed 24 March 2005).

Boone, J. A. 2003. 'Vacation Cruises; Or, the Homoerotics of Orientalism', in Lewis, R. and Mills, S. (eds) *Feminist Post-Colonial Theory: A Reader*, pp. 460–86. New York: Routledge.

Brown, E. T. J. 2005. 'Iraq: Sexual Orientation, Human Rights and the Law.' Available at http://www.sodomylaws.org/world/iraq/iqnews003.htm (accessed 12 November 2005).

Brownmiller, S. 1975. *Against Our Will: Men, Women and Rape*. New York: Simon & Schuster.

Bush, G. W. 2001a. 'President George W. Bush's Inaugural Address.' Available at http://www.whitehouse.gov/news/inaugural-address.html (accessed 24 March 2005).

Bush, G. W. 2001b. 'President Unveils "Most Wanted" Terrorists.' Available at http://www.vote-smart.org/speech_detail.php?speech_id=3571 (accessed 26 March 2005).

Bush, G. W. 2001c. 'President Welcomes President Chirac to White House.' Available at http://www.whitehouse.gov/news/releases/2001/11/20011106-4.html (accessed 24 March 2005).

Bush, G. W. 2001d. 'President Discusses War on Terrorism: Address to the Nation.' Available at http://www.whitehouse.gov/news/releases/2001/11/20011108-13.html (accessed 26 March 2005).

Bush, G. W. 2001e. 'President Bush Addresses the UN.' Available at http://www.internationalwallofprayer.org/A-032-President-Bush-Addresses-UN-Nov-10-2001.html (accessed 26 March 2005).

Bush, G. W. 2001f. 'President Freezes Terrorists' Assets: Remarks by the President, Secretary of the Treasury O'Neill and Secretary of State Powell on Executive Order.' Available at http://www.whitehouse.gov/news/releases/2001/09/20010924-4.html (accessed 11 September 2006).

Bush, G. W. 2002a. 'First Priority Is the Military.' Available at http://www.whitehouse.gov/news/releases/2002/01/20020123-13.html (accessed 24 March 2005).

Bush, G. W. 2002b. 'President Delivers State of the Union Address.' Available at http://www.whitehouse.gov/news/releases/2002/01/20020129-11.html (accessed 26 March 2005).

Bush, G.W. 2004a. 'President Calls for Constitutional Amendment Protecting Marriage.' Available at http://www.whitehouse.gov/news/releases/2004/02/20040224-2.html (accessed 24 February 2006).

Bush, G. W. 2004b. 'President's Radio Address.' Available at http://www.whitehouse.gov/news/releases/2004/07/20040710.html (accessed 26 February 2006).

Butler, J. 1990. *Gender Trouble: Feminism and the Subversion of Identity*. New York: Routledge.

Butterfield, F. 2004. 'Mistreatment of Prisoners Is Called Routine in US', *The New York Times*. Available at http://www.nytimes.com/2004/05/08/national/08PRIS.html (accessed 23 March 2005).

Davis, A. 1981. *Women, Race and Class*. New York: Random House.

Doty, R. L. 1996. *Imperial Encounters*. Minneapolis, MN: University of Minnesota Press.

Ebert, T. L. 1996. *Ludic Feminism and After: Postmodernism, Desire, and Labour in Late Capitalism*. Ann Arbor, MI: The University of Michigan Press.

Ehrenreich, B. 2004a. 'Barbara Ehrenreich's Commencement Address at Barnard College.' Available at http://www.longviewinstitute.org/research/ehrenreich/becommencement (accessed 30 August 2006).

Ehrenreich, B. 2004b. 'Prison Abuse. Feminism's Assumptions Upended. A Uterus is Not a Substitute for a Conscience. Giving Women Positions of Power Won't Change Society by Itself.' *LA Times* , 16 May, section M: 1.

Enloe, C. 2004. *The Curious Feminist: Searching for Women in a New Age of Empire*. Berkeley, CA: University of California Press.

Fay, G. R. and Jones, A. R. 2005. 'The Investigation of Intelligence Activities at Abu Ghraib.' Available at http://www4.army.mil/ocpa/reports/ar15-6/AR15-6.pdf (accessed 11 September 2006).

Goldstein, J. S. 2001. *War and Gender: How Gender Shapes the War System and Vice Versa*. Cambridge, MA: Cambridge University Press.

Goldstein, R. 2004. 'The Hate That Makes Men Straight: Psychoanalysts Probe the Roots of Homophobia.' Available at http://www.villagevoice.com/news/9851,goldstein,2411,1.html (accessed 30 August 2006).

Gramsci, A. 1971. *Selections of the Prison Notebooks of Antonio Gramsci*. Trans. Q. Hoare and G. N. Smith. New York: International Publishers/London: Lawrence & Wishart.

Grewal, I. 2001. 'Global Identities: Theorizing Transnational Studies of Sexuality', *GLQ: A Journal of Lesbian and Gay Studies* 7 (4): 663–79.

Grewal, I. and Kaplan, C. (eds). 1994. *Scattered Hegemonies: Postmodernity and Transnational Feminist Practices*. Minneapolis, MN: University of Minnesota Press.

Melanie Richter-Montpetit

Grewal, I. and Kaplan, C. 2000. 'Postcolonial Studies and Transnational Feminist Practices', *Jouvert* 5 (1). Available at http://social.chass.ncsu.edu/jouvert/v5i1/grewal.htm (accessed 30 August 2006).

Hall, S. 1996. 'The West and the Rest: Discourse and Power', in Hall, S., Held, D., Hubert, D. and Thompson, K. (eds) *Modernity: An Introduction to Modern Societies*, pp. 184–227. Cambridge: Blackwell Publishers.

Hersh, S. M. 2004. 'Annals of National Security: Torture at Abu Ghraib', *The New Yorker*. Available at http://www.newyorker.com/printables/fact/040510fa_fact (accessed 26 March 2005).

Hoch, P. 1979. *White Hero Black Beast: Racism, Sexism and the Mask of Masculinity*. London: Pluto Press.

hooks, b. 1997. 'Selling Hot Pussy: Representations of Black Female Sexuality in the Cultural Marketplace', in Conboy, K., Medina, N. and Stanbury, S. (eds) *Writing on the Body: Female Embodiment and Feminist Theory*, pp. 113–28. New York: Columbia University Press.

hooks, b. 1998. 'Naked Without a Shame: A Counter-Hegemonic Body Politic', in Shohat, E. (ed.) *Talking Visions: Multicultural Feminism in a Transnational Age*, pp. 65–74. New York: MIT Press.

Hunt, M. H. 1988. *Ideology and US Foreign Policy*. New Haven, CT: Yale University Press.

Kaplan, C., Alarcón, N. and Moallem, M. (eds). 1999. *Between Woman and Nation: Nationalism, Transnational Feminism, and the State*. Durham, NC: Duke University Press.

Klein, N. 2004. 'Baghdad Year Zero: Pillaging Iraq in Pursuit of a Neocon Utopia', *Harper's Magazine*. Available at http://www.harpers.org/BaghdadYearZero.html (accessed 24 March 2005).

Lewis, R. 1996. *Gendering Orientalism: Race, Femininity and Representation*. New York: Routledge.

Lowe, L. 1991. *Critical Terrains*. Ithaca, NY: Cornell University Press.

McClintock, A. 1995. *Imperial Leather: Race, Gender, and Sexuality in the Colonial Project*. New York: Routledge.

Marlowe, D. H. 1983. 'The Manning of the Force and the Structure of Battle: Part 2 – Men and Women', in Fullinwider, R. K. (ed.) *Conscription and Volunteers: Military Requirements, Social Justice, and the All-Volunteer Force*, pp. 189–99. Totowa, NJ: Rowman & Allanheld.

Mendoza, B. 2002. 'Transnational Feminisms in Question', *Feminist Theory* 3 (3): 295–314.

Mohanty, C. T. 1984. 'Under Western Eyes: Feminist Scholarship and Colonial Discourses', *Boundary* 2 (12 & 13): 333–57.

Moore-Gilbert, B. 1997. *Postcolonial Theory: Contexts, Practices, Politics*. London: Verso.

Moraga, C. and Anzaldúa, G. 1981. *This Bridge Called My Back: Writings by Radical Women of Colour*. Watertown: Persephone Press.

Progler, Y. 1999. 'Racist and Degrading Graffiti Rooted in America's Military Culture.' Available at http://www.muslimedia.com/archives/special99/graffiti.htm (accessed 25 March 2005).

Puar, J. K. 1998. 'Transnational Sexualities: South Asian (Trans)nation(alisms) and Queer Diasporas' in Eng, D. L. and Hom, A. Y. (eds) *Queer in Asian America*, pp. 405–22. Philadelphia, PA: Temple University Press.

Razack, S. 2004. *Dark Threats and White Knights: The Somalia Affair, Peacekeeping and the New Imperialism*. Toronto: University of Toronto Press.

Reid, T. R. 2005. 'Guard Convicted in the First Case from Abu Ghraib: Graner Faces 15 Years for Abusing Iraqis.' *Washington Post*, 15 January, Section A: 1. Available at http://www.washingtonpost.com/wp-dyn/articles/A9343-2005Jan14.html (accessed 24 March 2005).

Rockwell, P. 2005. 'Army Reservist Witnesses War Crimes: New Revelations about Racism in the Military.' Available at http://www.inmotionmagazine.com/global/pr_adelgado.html (accessed 30 August 2006).

Ruskola, T. 2005. 'Gay Rights vs. Queer Theory: What Is Left of Sodomy After Lawrence vs. Texas?', *Social Text* 23 (3–4, 84–5): 235–49.

Said, E. 1993. *Culture and Imperialism*. New York: Alfred Knopf.

Said, E. 1994. *Orientalism*. New York: Vintage Books.

Said, E. 1997. *Covering Islam: How the Media and the Experts Determine How We See the Rest of the World*. New York: Vintage Books.

Schlesinger, J., Brown, H., Fowler, T. K. and Homer, C. A. 2004. 'Final Report of the Independent Panel to Review Department of Defense Detention Operations', Arlington, VA. Available at http://www.defenselink.mil/news/Aug2004/d20040824finalreport.pdf (accessed 26 March 2005).

Seifert, R. 1993. 'Krieg und Vergewaltigung: Ansätze zu einer Analyse', in Stiglmayer, A. (ed.) *Massenvergewaltigungen – Krieg Gegen die Frauen*. Frankfurt/Main: Fischer Taschenbuch Verlag: 85–108.

Seifert, R. 1996. *Militär, Kultur, Identität: Individualisierung, Geschlechterverhältnisse und die Soziale Konstruktion des Soldaten*. Bremen: Edition Temmen.

Shohat, E. (ed.). 1999. *Talking Visions: Multicultural Feminism in a Transnational Age*. Cambridge, MA: MIT Press.

Slater, D. 2004. *Geopolitics and the Post-Colonial: Rethinking North–South Relations*. Oxford: Blackwell Publishing.

Somerville, S. B. 2000. *Queering the Color Line: Race and the Invention of Homosexuality in American Culture*. Durham, NC & London: Duke University Press.

Spanos, W. V. 2000. *America's Shadow: An Anatomy of Empire*. Minneapolis, MN: University of Minnesota Press.

Taguba, A. 2004. 'Article 15–6 Investigation of the 800th Military Police Brigade.' Available at http://www.npr.org/iraq/2004/prison_abuse_report.pdf (accessed 21 September 2006).

Trexler, R. C. 1995. *Sex and Conquest: Gendered Violence, Political Order, and the European Conquest of the Americas*. Ithaca, NY: Cornell University Press.

Tuveson, E. L. 1968. *Redeemer Nation: The Idea of America's Millennial Role*. Chicago, IL: University of Chicago Press.

Weldes, J. 1999. *Constructing National Interests: The United States and the Cuban Missile Crisis*. Minneapolis, MN: University of Minnesota Press.

Whitworth, S. 2004. *Men, Militarism, and UN Peacekeeping: A Gendered Analysis*. Boulder, CO: Lynne Rienner.

World Bank. 2004. *Reconstructing Iraq*. Working Paper Series, Executive Summaries.

Yegenoglu, M. 1998. *Colonial Fantasies: Towards a Feminist Reading of Orientalism*. Cambridge: Cambridge University Press.

Part Seven
Science, Environment, Development

Speaking of the "formless threats whose fatal repercussions are dispersed across space and time," such as environmental pollution, the destruction of nature, and the overexploitation of resources, Rob Nixon brings together postcolonialism's concerns with national identity, sovereignty, and territory with environmentalism's concerns about nature, soil, water, and resources. Tracing colonialism's and now transnational bodies' destruction of the environment in Africa and other parts of the world as well as local environmental campaigns, Nixon argues that "cinematic catastrophe" overshadows more calamitous violence (which he calls "unphotogenic"), but that to ignore the latter is even more severely detrimental to society's disenfranchised. In the same category of examining systematic resource exploitation, John Merson's essay analyzes the rise of the International Genetic Order. Bioprospecting is a form of biocolonialism that extends and expands older forms of natural exploitation, this time under the guise of research and as a part of intellectual property regimes. Indigenous genes and knowledges might be appropriated, but the search for a more equitable order is also being simultaneously proposed under UN-led biodiversity initiatives, says Merson. Elizabeth DeLoughrey's study of ecosystem ecologies traces the field's origins to US atomic testing, and demonstrates how myths of biological "isolates" transformed tropical islanders into the sites of radiation experiments. The "island as isolate" functioned, she writes, as "a conceptual rubric ... vital to a historical moment that brought together newly acquired island territories, the development of ecosystem concepts of closed space, and nuclear militarism that relegated these islands to laboratories." Thus racialized colonialism and racialized science merge in the essay's analysis of nuclear testing and biomedicine. Extending the arguments about science and technology to include gender, Sandra Harding begins with the assumption that "gender and racial/colonial categories still co-constitute each other" today. Yoking together feminism and postcolonial studies, Harding examines the role of women native informants

Postcolonial Studies: An Anthology, First Edition. Edited by Pramod K. Nayar.
Editorial material and organization © 2016 John Wiley & Sons, Ltd.
Published 2016 by John Wiley & Sons, Ltd.

for pharmacologists, botanists, and other such (male) inventors/discoverers. Harding reiterates the need to use standpoint methodologies – which are gendered, looking at women's lives in the midst of "development" or "modernization" – as well as the need to recognize multiple sciences that societies produce at very local levels with traditional knowledge.

31   Slow Violence, Gender, and the Environmentalism of the Poor

Rob Nixon

To address the challenges of slow violence is to confront the dilemma Rachel Carson faced over forty years ago in seeking to dramatize what she called "death by indirection" (32). Carson's subjects were biomagnification and toxic drift, forms of oblique, slow-acting violence that, like climate change and desertification, pose formidable imaginative difficulties for writers and activists alike. How, in an age that venerates the instant and the spectacular, can one turn attritional calamities starring nobody into stories dramatic enough to rouse public sentiment? In struggling to give shape to an amorphous menace, both Carson and reviewers of *Silent Spring* resorted to a narratological vocabulary: one reviewer portrayed the book as exposing "the new, unplotted and mysterious dangers we insist upon creating all around us," (Sevareid 3) while Carson herself wrote of "a shadow that is no less ominous because it is formless and obscure" (238).[1]

To confront what I am calling slow violence requires that we attempt to give symbolic shape and plot to formless threats whose fatal repercussions are dispersed across space and time. Politically and emotionally, different kinds of disaster possess unequal heft. Falling bodies, burning towers, exploding heads have a visceral, page-turning potency that tales of slow violence cannot match. Stories of toxic buildup, massing greenhouse gases, or desertification may be cataclysmic, but they're scientifically convoluted cataclysms in which casualties are deferred, often for generations. In the gap between acts of slow violence and their delayed effects both memory and causation readily fade from view and the casualties thus incurred pass untallied.

The long dyings that ensue from slow violence are out of sync not only with our dramatic expectations, but with the swift seasons of electoral change. How can leaders be goaded to avert catastrophe when the political rewards of their actions will be reaped on someone else's watch, decades, even centuries from now? How can environmental storytellers and activists help counter the potent forces of political self-interest,

Rob Nixon, "Slow Violence, Gender, and the Environmentalism of the Poor." *Journal of Commonwealth and Postcolonial Studies*, 13(2)–14(1), 2006–2007: 14–37. Reprinted by permission of Georgia Southern University.

procrastination, and dissembling? We see such dissembling at work, for instance, in the afterword to Michael Crichton's 2004 environmental conspiracy novel, *State of Fear*, where he argues that we need twenty more years of data gathering on climate change before any policy decisions can be made (626). For his pains, Crichton, though he lacked even an undergraduate science degree, was appointed to President Bush's special committee on climate change.

The oxymoronic notion of slow violence poses representational, statistical, and legislative challenges. The under-representation of slow violence in the media results in the discounting of casualties—from, for example, the toxic aftermaths of wars— which in turn exacerbates the difficulty of securing effective legal measures for preemption, restitution, and redress.

The representational challenges are acute, requiring creative ways of drawing public attention to catastrophic acts that are low in instant spectacle but high in long-term effects. To intervene representationally requires that we find both the iconic symbols to embody amorphous calamities and the narrative forms to infuse them with dramatic urgency. In an age of degraded attention spans it becomes doubly difficult to focus on the toll exacted, over time, by ecological degradation. We live, as Microsoft executive Linda Stone puts it, in an age of "continuous partial attention" (qtd. in Friedman A27). Fast is faster than it used to be and story units have become concomitantly shorter. In this cultural milieu, the intergenerational aftermath becomes a harder sell. So to render slow violence visible entails, among other things, redefining speed: we see such efforts in talk of accelerated species loss, rapid climate change, and in attempts to recast "glacial"— once a dead metaphor for slow—as a rousing, iconic image of unacceptably fast loss.

Efforts to infuse slow violence with an urgent visibility suffered a setback in America with the events of 9/11, which reinforced a narrow image of what it means to be at risk—as a nation, a species, and a planet. The fiery spectacle of the collapsing towers was burned into the national psyche as *the* definitive image of violence, exacerbating for years the difficulty of rallying public sentiment against attritional violence like global warming, a threat that is both incremental and exponential. Condoleezza Rice's strategic fantasy of a mushroom cloud suspended over America if the United States failed to invade Iraq and topple Saddam Hussein gave further visual definition to the idea of cataclysmic violence as something explosive and instantaneous, a recognizably cinematic, pyrotechnic event.[2]

The representational bias against slow violence has statistical ramifications; under-represented casualties—human and environmental— are the casualties most likely to be discounted. We see this, for instance, in the way wars whose lethal repercussions sprawl across space and time are tidily book-ended in the historical record. A 2003 *New York Times* editorial on Vietnam reported, "during our dozen years there, the U.S. killed and helped kill at least 1.5 million people" ("Vietnam" A25). That simple word "during," however, shrinks the toll: hundreds of thousands survived the war years, only to lose their lives prematurely to Agent Orange. In a 2002 study, the environmental scientist Arnold Schecter recorded dioxin levels in the bloodstreams of Bien Hoa residents at 135 times the levels of Hanoi's inhabitants, who lived far north of the spraying (Schecter 516). The afflicted include thousands of children born decades after the war's end. More than thirty years after the last spraying run, Agent Orange continues to wreak havoc as, through biomagnification, dioxins build up in the fatty tissues of pivotal foods like duck and fish and pass from the natural world into the cooking pot and from there to ensuing human generations. "During": a small word, yet a powerful reminder of how easily the belated casualties of slow violence are habitually screened from view.

The Green Belt Movement and Sustainable Security

Kenya's Green Belt Movement, founded by Wangari Maathai, serves as an animating instance of collective mobilization against slow violence, in this case the incremental violence of desertification and deforestation. At the heart of the movement's activism stand these urgent questions: What does it mean to be at risk? What does it mean, long term, to be secure? How can we most effectively represent, acknowledge, and counter the violence of delayed effects?

The recent appearance of Maathai's memoir, *Unbowed*, provides an opportunity to assess the strategies that the Green Belt Movement devised to challenge foreshortened definitions of environmental and human security. What has emerged from the Green Belt Movement's ascent is an alternative narrative of national security that challenged the militaristic, male version embodied and imposed by Kenya's President Daniel arap Moi, during his twenty-four years of authoritarian rule from 1978 to 2002. The Green Belt Movement's rival narrative of national security has sought to foreground the longer timeline of slow violence, both in exposing environmental degradation and in advancing environmental recovery.

The Green Belt Movement had modest beginnings. On Earth Day in 1977, Maathai and a small cohort of the likeminded planted seven trees to commemorate Kenyan women who had been environmental activists (Lappe and Lappe 1). By the time Maathai was awarded the Nobel Peace Prize in 2004, the movement had created 6,000 local tree nurseries and employed 100,000 women to plant thirty million trees, mostly in Kenya, but in a dozen other African countries as well (*Unbowed* 175). The movement's achievements have been both material—providing employment while helping anchor soil, generate shade and firewood, and replenish watersheds—and symbolic, by inspiring other reforestation movements as far afield as India. As such, the Green Belt Movement has symbolized and enacted the conviction that, as Lester Brown has declared in another context, "a strategy for eradicating poverty will not succeed if an economy's environmental support systems are collapsing" (1).

Early on, Maathai alighted on the idea of tree planting as the movement's core activity, one that over time would achieve a brilliant symbolic economy, becoming an iconic act of civil disobedience as the women's struggle against desertification segued into a struggle against illicit deforestation perpetrated by Kenya's draconian regime. Neither desertification nor deforestation posed a sudden threat, but both were persistently and pervasively injurious to Kenya's long-term human and environmental prospects. The symbolic focus of mass tree plantings helped foster a broad alliance around what one might call issues of sustainable security, a set of issues crucial not just to an era of Kenyan authoritarianism, but to the very different context of post-9/11 America as well, where militaristic ideologies of security have disproportionately and destructively dominated public policy and debate.

The risk of ignoring the intertwined issues of slow violence and sustainable security was evident in many American responses to the March 2003 invasion of Iraq, which was widely represented as a clean strategic and moral departure from the ugly spill-ages of total warfare. Even many liberal commentators adhered to this view. Hendrik Hertzberg, writing in *The New Yorker*, declared that

> Whatever else can be said about the war against the Iraqi dictatorship that began on March 19th, it cannot be said that the Anglo-American invaders have pursued anything remotely resembling a policy of killing civilians deliberately. And, so far, they have gone to great tactical and technological lengths to avoid doing it inadvertently... What we do not yet know is whether a different intention, backed by technologies of precision, will produce a different political result. (15)

This war, Hertzberg continued, was not the kind that "expanded the battlefield to encompass whole societies" (15). Like most American media commentators at the con-flict's outset, Hertzberg bought into the idea that so-called smart bombs exhibit a mor-ally superior intelligence.[3] What he failed to observe, trailing behind those luminous technologies of precision streaking across the sky, was the shadow of imprecision that for years, decades, generations will claim the lives of random civilians through the lethal legacy of depleted uranium munitions and unexploded cluster bombs. Wars that have receded into memory often continue, through their active residues, to maim and slaughter for generations. Depending on the ordnance and strategies deployed, a quick "smart" war may morph into a long-term killer, leaving behind landscapes of dragging death.

The battlefield that unobtrusively threatens to encompass whole societies is of direct pertinence to the conditions that gave rise to Kenya's Green Belt Movement. The movement emerged in response to what one might call the violence of staggered effects in relation to ecologies of scale. From the perspective of rural Kenyan women whose local livelihood has been threatened by desertification's slow march what does it mean to be secure in space and time? As Maathai notes,

> ... during the rainy season, thousands of tons of topsoil are eroded from Kenya's countryside by rivers and washed into the ocean and lakes. Additionally, soil is lost through wind erosion in areas where the land is devoid of vegetative cover. Losing topsoil should be considered analogous to losing territory to an invading enemy. And indeed, if any country were so threatened, it would mobilize all available resources, including a heavily armed military, to protect the priceless land. Unfortunately, the loss of soil through these elements has yet to be perceived with such urgency. (*The Green Belt Movement* 38)

What is productive about Maathai's reformulation of security here is her insistence that threats to national territorial integrity—that most deepseated rationale for war—be expanded to include threats to the nation's integrity from environmental assaults. To reframe violence in this way is to intervene in the discourse of national defense and, hence, in the psychology of war. Under Kenya's authoritarian regime, the prevail-ing response to desertification was a mix of denial and resignation; the damage, the loss of land, went unsourced and hence required no concerted mobilization of national resources. The violence occurred in the passive voice, despite the regime's monu-mental resource mismanagement.

Desertification results in part, of course, from global forms of violence— especially human-induced climate change, to which rural Kenyan women contribute little and can do very little to avert. But the desert's steady seizure of once viable, fertile land also stems from local forms of slow violence— deforestation and the denuding of vegetation—and it was at those junctures that the women found a way to exert their collective agency. As the drivers of the nation's subsistence agriculture, women inhabited most directly the fallout from an environmental violence that is low in immediate drama but high in long-term consequences.

Resource bottlenecks are difficult to dramatize and, deficient in explosive spectacle, typically garner little media attention. Yet the bottlenecks that result from desertification can fuel conflicts for decades, costing (directly and indirectly) untold lives. Certainly, if we take our cues from the media, it is easy to forget that, in the words of the American agronomist, Wes Jackson, "soil is as much a nonrenewable resource as oil" (141). International and intranational contests over this finite resource can destabilize whole regions. Soil security ought to be inextricable from national security policy, not least in a society like Kenya, which, since the arrival of British colonialists in the late nineteenth century, has lost 98 percent of its anchoring, cleansing, and cooling forest cover (Maathai, *Unbowed* 281).

The Theatre of the Tree

The Green Belt Movement's achievements in engaging the violence of deforestation and desertification flow from three critical strategies. First, tree planting served not only as a practical response to an attritional environmental calamity, but to create, in addition, a symbolic hub for the political resistance and for media coverage of an otherwise amorphous issue. Second, the movement was able to articulate the discourse of violent land loss to a deeper narrative of territorial theft, as perpetrated first by the British colonialists and later by their neo-colonial legatees. Third, the Green Belt Movement made strategic use of what I call intersectional environmentalism to broaden their base and credibility in Kenya and abroad.[4]

The choice of tree planting as the Green Belt Movement's defining act proved politically astute. Here was a simple, pragmatic, yet powerfully figurative act that connected with many women's quotidian lives as tillers of the soil. Desertification and deforestation are corrosive, compound threats that damage vital watersheds, exacerbate the silting and dessication of rivers, erode topsoil, engender firewood and food shortages, and ultimately contribute to malnutrition. Maathai and her allies succeeded in using these compound threats to forge a compound alliance among authoritarianism's discounted casualties, especially marginalized women, citizens whose environmental concerns were indissociable from their concerns over food security and political accountability.

At political flashpoints during the 1980s and 1990s, these convergent concerns made the Green Belt Movement a powerful player in a broad-based civil rights coalition that gave thousands of Kenyans a revived sense of civic agency and national possibility. The movement probed and widened the fissures within the state's authoritarian structures, clamoring for answerability within what Ato Quayson, in another context, calls "the culture of impunity" (73).

The theatre of the tree afforded the social movement a rich symbolic vocabulary that helped extend its civic reach. Maathai recast the simple gesture of digging a hole and putting a sapling in it as a way of "planting the seeds of peace" (Selva 9). To plant trees was metaphorically to cultivate democratic change; with a slight vegetative tweak, the gesture could breathe new life into the dead metaphor of grass roots democracy. Within the campaign against one-party rule, activists could establish a ready symbolic connection between environmental erosion and the erosion of civil rights. At the heart of this symbolic nexus was a contest over definitions of growth: each tree planted by the Green Belt Movement stood as a tangible, biological image of steady, sustainable growth, a dramatic counter-image to the ruling elite's kleptocratic image of "growth," a euphemism for their high-speed piratical plunder of the nation's coffers and finite natural resources. As William Finnegan has observed in a broader international context,

> … even economic growth, which is regarded nearly universally as an overall social good, is not necessarily so. There is growth so unequal that it heightens social conflict and increases repression. There is growth so environmentally destructive that it detracts, in sum, from a community's quality of life. (48)

There is something perverse about an economic order in which the unsustainable, ill-managed plunder of resources is calculated not as a loss of GNP but as productive growth.

To plant trees is, in the fullest sense of the phrase, to work toward cultivating change. In an era of widening social inequity and unshared growth, the replenished forest offered an egalitarian and participatory image of growth—growth as sustainable over the long haul.[5] The Moi regime vilified Maathai as an enemy of growth, development, and progress, all discourses the ruling cabal had used to mask its high speed plunder. Saplings in hand, the Green Belt Movement returned the blighted trope of growth to its vital, biological roots.

To plant a tree is an act of intergenerational optimism, a selfless act at once practical and utopian, an investment in a communal future the planter will not see; to plant a tree is to offer shade to unborn strangers. To act in this manner was to secede ethically from Kenya's top down culture of ruthless self-interest. A social movement devoted to tree planting, in addition to regenerating embattled forests, thus also helped regenerate an endangered vision of civic time. Against the backdrop of Kenya's winner-takes-all-and-takes-it-now kleptocracy, the movement affirmed a radically subversive ethic—an ethic of selflessness—allied to an equally subversive time frame, the long duree of patient growth for sustainable collective gain.

By 1998, the Moi regime had come to treat tree planting as an incendiary, seditious act of civil disobedience. That year, the showdown between the Green Belt Movement and state power came to a head over the 2,500-acre Karura Forest. Word spread that the regime was felling swathes of the public forest, a green lung for Nairobi and a critical catchment area for four rivers (Maathai, *Unbowed* 262). The cleared, appropriated land was being sold on the cheap to cabinet ministers and other presidential cronies who planned to build luxury developments—golf courses, hotels, and gated communities—on it. Maathai and her followers, armed with nothing but oak saplings, with which they sought to begin replanting the plundered forest, were set upon by guards and goons wielding pangas, clubs, and whips. Maathai had her head bloodied by a panga; protestors were arrested and imprisoned.

The theatre of the tree has accrued a host of potent valencies at different points in human history, as both the planting and the felling of forests have become highly charged political acts. In the England that the Puritans fled, for example, trees were markers of aristocratic privilege; hence on numerous occasions, insurrectionists chopped or burned down those exclusionary groves. As Michael Pollan notes, "after the Restoration, replanting trees was regarded as a fitting way for a gentleman to demonstrate his loyalty to the monarchy, and several million hardwoods were planted between 1660 and 1800" (194). To early American colonists, tree felling was typically viewed as an act of progress that often doubled as a way of improving the land and claiming it for one's own.

Since the early 1970s, a strong but varied transnational tradition of civil disobedience has gathered force around the fate of the forest. In March 1973, a band of hill peasants in the isolated Himalayan village of Mandal devised the strategy of tree hugging to thwart loggers who had come to fell hornbeam trees in a state forest on which the peasants depended for their livelihood. This was the beginning of a succession of such protests that launched India's Chipko movement. Three years later, in the Brazilian Amazon, Francisco Chico Mendes led a series of standoffs by rubber tappers and their allies who sought to arrest uncontrolled felling and burning by rancher colonists (Guha 115–24). In Thailand, a Buddhist monk was jailed when he sought to safeguard trees by ordaining them, while Julia Butterfly Hill achieved celebrity visibility during her two-year tree sit to protest the clear cutting of endangered California redwoods.

What distinguished the Green Belt Movement's approach was the way that, in protesting deforestation, they went beyond the standard strategies of civil disobedience (sit ins, tree hugging, or chaining themselves to trees), turning instead to active reforestation as the symbolic vehicle for their civil disobedience. Under an undemocratic dispensation, the threatened forest can be converted into a particularly dramatic theatre for reviving civic agency because it throws into relief incompatible visions of public land. To Kenya's authoritarian president, the forest was state-owned, and because he and his cronies treated the nation as identical to the state, he felt at license to fell national forests and sell off the nation's public land. To the activists, by contrast, the forest was not a private presidential fiefdom, but commonage, the indivisible property of the people. The regime's contemptuous looting of Karura Forest was thus read as symptomatic of a wider contempt for the rights of the poor.

The Green Belt Movement's campaign to replant Karura assumed a potency that reverberated beyond the fate of one particular forest; their efforts served as a dramatic initiative to repossess, for the polity, not just plundered public land and resources, but plundered political agency. Outrage over the Karura assaults soon swelled to students and other disaffected groups in Nairobi until the regime was forced to suspend its attacks on both the women and the trees. In this way, the theatre of the tree fortified the bond between a beleaguered environment and a beleaguered polity.[6]

For those who perpetrate slow violence, their greatest ally is the protracted, convoluted vapor trail of blame. If slow violence typically occurs in the passive voice—without clearly articulated agency—the attritional deforestation of Karura and other public lands offered a clearer case than say, desertification, of decisive accountability. The Green Belt Movement's theatre of the tree inverted the syntax of violence by naming the agents of destruction. Through the drama of the axed tree and the planted sapling, Maathai and her allies staged a showdown between the forces of incremental violence and the forces of incremental peace; in so doing they gave a symbolic and dramatic shape to public discontent over the official culture of plunder. Ultimately, Maathai saw in the culture of tree planting a way of interrupting the cycle of poverty, a cycle whereby, as she put it, "poverty is both a cause and a symptom of environmental degradation" (Pal 5).

Colonialism, Mau Mau, and the Forest in National Memory

In using the theatre of the forest to reanimate political debate around ideas of sustainable growth, grassroots democracy, erosion of rights, and the seeds of change, Maathai and her resource rebels also tapped into a robust national memory of popular resistance to colonialism, above all, resistance to the unjust seizure of land.[7] Maathai's memoir doesn't engage this question of anti-colonial memory directly, but it is surely pertinent to the political traction that her movement attained, given the particular place of the forest in Kenya's national symbolic archive of resistance. The confrontation, during Moi's neo-colonial rule, between the forces of deforestation and the forces of reforestation was played out against the historic backdrop of the forest as a redoubt of anti-colonialism, an heroic place which, during the Mau Mau uprising from 1952–1958, achieved a mythic potency among both the British colonialists and those Kenyans—primarily Kikuyu—who fought for freedom and the restitution of their land.[8]

In the dominant colonial literature about Mau Mau (political tracts, memoirs, and fiction), the forest appears as a place beyond reach of civilization, a place of atavistic savagery where "terrorists" banded together to perform degenerate rites of barbarism.[9] For those Kenyans who sought an end to their colonial subjugation, the forest represented something else entirely: it was a place of cultural regeneration and political refusal, a proving ground where resistance fighters pledged oaths of unity, above all, an oath to reclaim, by force if necessary, their people's stolen land.

The forest thus became the geographical and symbolic nexus of a peasant insurrection, as a host of Kenyan writers, Meja Mwangi, Wachira, Mangua, and Ngũgĩ wa Thiong'o among them, have all testified.[10] From an environmental perspective, *A Grain of Wheat*, Ngũgĩ's novel of the Mau Mau uprising, is particularly suggestive. As Byron Caminero-Santangelo observes, most of the novel's British characters work at the Githima Forestry and Agricultural Research Station, an institution whose official aims are to advance agriculture and conservation, but which was founded "as part of a new colonial development plan" (702). The novel unfolds in part, then, as a clash between rival cultures of nature: between nature as instrument of colonial control (under the guise of development) and nature as a sustaining animist force, an anti-colonial ally of Mau Mau forest fighters pledging oaths of liberation.[11]

The gender politics of all this are complex and compelling. In the 1950s, the forest served as a bastion not just of anti-colonialism, but also of warrior masculinity. Thirty years later, it was nonviolent women, armed only with oak saplings and a commitment to civil disobedience, who embodied the political resistance to neo-colonialism. So the showdown at Karura reprised the anti-colonial history of forest resistance in a different key: now the core fighters—Maathai's "foresters without diplomas"—were female and unarmed.[12] Does this double rescripting of resistance help explain the particularly vicious backlash from Kenya's male political establishment?

Intersectional Environmentalism, Gender, and Colonial Conservation

The colonial backdrop to the achievements of the Green Belt Movement surfaces not just through the memory of Mau Mau forest fighters but also through the contrast between colonial conservation and what I'm calling intersectional environmentalism. Maathai was never a single-issue environmentalist: she sought from the outset to integrate and advance the causes of environmental, women's, and human rights. The Green Belt Movement emerged in the late 1970s under the auspices of the women's movement: it was through Maathai's involvement in the Kenya Association of University of Women that she was first invited to join a local Environment Liaison Centre and from there was approached by representatives from the United National Environmental Programme, which led in turn to ever widening circles of international access (Maathai, *Unbowed* 120).

Maathai's intersectional approach to environmental justice contrasted starkly with the dominant colonial traditions of conservation, which had focused on spectacular megafauna.[13] That sharply masculinist tradition—in Kenya and, more broadly, in East and Southern Africa—was associated with forced removal, with the colonial appropriation of land, and with an anti-human ecology. That tradition remains part of Kenya's economic legacy, a legacy associated not just with human displacement, but in contemporary Kenya with local exclusion from elite cultures of leisure.

In ecological as in human terms, Maathai's angle of approach was not top down: instead of focusing on the dramatic end of the biotic chain—the elephants, rhino, lion, and leopards that have preoccupied colonial hunters, conservationists, and foreign tourists—she drew attention to a more mundane and pervasive issue: the impact of accumulative resource mismanagement on biodiversity, soil quality, food security, and the life prospects of rural women and their families.

As Fiona Mackenzie demonstrates, the grounds for such resource mismanagement were laid during the colonial era when conservationist and agricultural discourses of "betterment" were often deployed in the service of appropriating African lands. Focusing on colonial narratives about the environment and agriculture in the Kikuyu reserves between 1920 and 1945, Mackenzie traces the effects of the colonial bureaucracy's authoritarian paternalism, of what James C. Scott calls "the imperial pretensions of agronomic science" (264). Not least among these deleterious effects was "the recasting of the gender of the Kikuyu farmer ... through a colonial discourse of betterment that was integrally linked to the reconstruction of agricultural knowledge" (Mackenzie 700).[14] Thus—and this has profound consequences for the priorities of the Green Belt Movement—colonial authorities failed to acknowledge women as primary cultivators. This refusal had the effect of diminishing the deeply grounded, adaptable knowledge, both ecological and agricultural, that women had amassed.

Maathai's refusal to subordinate the interwoven questions of environmental and social justice to the priorities of either spectacular conservation or industrial agriculture has proven crucial to the long term adaptability of the Green Belt Movement, allowing it to regenerate itself by improvising alliances with other initiatives for sustainable security and democratic transformation. Although it was the theatre of tree-planting that initially garnered Maathai and her allies media attention and international support, they continued to expand the circles of their activism, mobilizing for campaigns that ranged from the release of Kenya's political prisoners to debt forgiveness for impoverished nations. The Green Belt Movement's intersectional strategy helped integrate issues of attritional environmental violence into a broad movement for political answerability that in turn helped lead to democratic elections in Kenya in 2002.

The positioning of the Green Belt Movement at the crossroads between environmental rights and women's rights made historic sense. Women in Kenya have born the brunt of successive waves of dispossession, dating back to the late nineteenth century, when the British colonialists shifted the structures of land ownership to women's detriment. Previously, land had belonged inalienably to the extended family or clan; with the introduction of colonial taxation that same land became deeded to a male deemed to be head of the household. As taxation forced more and more Kenyans into a wage economy, and as (first under colonialism and later under neo-colonial structural adjustment) cash crops like tea, coffee, and sugar cane shrank the arable land available for food production, women became disproportionately marginalized from economic power. In the resultant cash economy, men typically owned the bank accounts (Jeffries 7).

Rural women suffered the perfect storm of dispossession: colonial land theft, the individualizing and masculinizing of property, and the experience of continuing to be the primary tillers of the land under increasingly inclement circumstances, including desertification and the stripping of the forests. As forests and watersheds became degraded, it was the women who had to walk the extra miles to fetch water and firewood, it was the women who had to plough and plant in once rich but now denuded land where, without the anchorage of trees, topsoil was washed and blown away. In this context, the political convergence of the campaigns for environmental and women's rights in Kenya made experiential sense: women inhabited the betrayals of successive narratives of development that had brutally excluded them. The links between attritional environmental violence, poverty, and malnutrition was a logic that they lived. So when the Moi regime laid claim to Karura Forest and Uhuru Park for private "development" schemes, Maathai was able to mobilize women who historically had been at the raw end of plunder that benefited minute male elites, whether colonial or neocolonial in character.

It is a measure of the threat that this intersectional environmentalism posed that in 1985 the regime demanded—ultimately without success—that the women's movement and the green movement disengage from one another (Maathai, *Unbowed* 179). What the regime foresaw was that these women tending saplings in their rural nurseries were seeding a civil rights movement that could help propel a broader campaign for an end to direct and indirect violence in the name of greater political answerability.

Environmental Agency and Ungovernable Women: Maathai and Carson

Maathai and Carson each sought, in their different cultural milieus, to shift the parameters of what is commonly perceived as violence. They devoted themselves to questioning shibboleths about development and progress, to making visible the overlooked casualties of accumulative environmental injury, and to mobilizing public sentiment—especially among women—against the self-satisfaction and profitable complicities of a male power elite. Both writer-activists questioned the orthodox, militarized vision of security as sufficient to cope with the domino effects of exponential environmental risk, not least the intergenerational risk to food security.[15] Indeed, both saw the militarization of their societies—Cold War America of the late 1950s and early 1960s and Moi's tyrannized Kenya of the 1980s and 1990s—as exacerbating the environmental degradation that threatened long-term stability locally, nationally, and transnationally.

Retrospectively, it is easy to focus on the achievements of these two towering figures: the social movements they helped build, the changes in perception and legislation their work wrought, Maathai's Nobel Peace Prize, the selection of *Silent Spring* as the most influential work of nonfiction of the twentieth century. Yet it is important to acknowledge the embattled marginalization and vilification both women had to endure at great personal cost in order to ensure that their unorthodox visions of environmental violence and its repercussions gained political traction. Their marginality was wounding, but emboldening, the engine of their originality.

Carson and Maathai were multiply extra-institutional: as female scientists, anomalies for their time and place; as scientists working outside the structures and strictures of the university; and as unmarried women. On all fronts, they had to weather *ad feminam* assaults from male establishments whose orthodoxies were threatened by their autonomy.

Although Carson had a master's degree in biology, financial pressures and the pressures of caring for dependent relatives prevented her from pursuing a PhD. Her background was in public science writing; she had no university affiliation at a time when only one percent of tenured scientists in America were women (Lear 254). But by the time she came to embark on *Silent Spring*, her best-selling books on the sea had given her some financial autonomy. Carson's institutional and economic independence freed her to set her own research agenda, to engage in unearthing, synthesizing and promoting environmental research that had been suppressed or sidelined by the funding priorities of the major research institutions, whose agendas she recognized as compromised by the entangled special interests of agribusiness, the chemical and arms industries, and by the headlong rush to profitable product development.

Carson's detractors questioned her professional authority, her patriotism, her ability to be unemotional, and the integrity of her scientific commitment to intergenerational genetic issues, given that she was a "spinster." "Why is a spinster with no children so concerned about genetics? She is probably a Communist," a former U.S. Secretary of Agriculture intoned (qtd. in Lear 429).

Hostile reviewers dismissed Carson's arguments as "hysterically overemphatic" ("Pesticides") and as "more emotional than accurate" (qtd. in Lear 461).[16] The general counsel for Velsicol, a Chicago chemical company, accused Carson of being under the sway of "sinister influences" whose purpose was "to reduce the use of agricultural chemicals in this country and the countries of western Europe, so that our supply of food will be reduced to east-curtain parity" (Lear 417). Other commentators deduced that "Miss Rachel Carson's reference to the selfishness of insecticide manufacturers probably reflects her Communist sympathies" (Lear 409). Carson's nemesis, the chemical industry spokesman, Dr. Robert White-Stevens—who gave twenty-eight speeches against *Silent Spring* in a single year—opined that "if man were to faithfully follow the teachings of Miss Carson, we would return to the Dark Ages" (qtd. in "The Silent Spring of Rachel Carson"). In the ultimate vilification of Carson as embodying a model of irrational female treachery, a critic in *Aerosol Age* concluded, "Miss Carson missed her calling. She might have used her talents in telling war propaganda of the type made famous by Tokyo Rose and Axis Sally" (DAD).[17]

Twenty-five years on and Maathai's opponents were brandishing even more outrageous *ad feminam* threats and insinuations against an autonomous female scientist who threatened the political and environmental status quo. Maathai was not a "spinster," but she was a divorcee, a label her opponents wielded against her relentlessly. Like Carson, she was represented as overly emotional and unhinged, an unnatural woman, uncontrollable, unattached, without a husband to rein her in and keep her (and her ideas) respectable. If the chemical-agricultural establishment sought to dismiss Carson, who lacked a PhD, as unqualified to speak, Kenya's power elite tried to discredit Maathai—the first woman in East or Central Africa to receive a doctorate in any field—as suspiciously overqualified, as a woman who had to be brought down because she was overreaching.[18] When she led the protests against government plans for the private "development" of Uhuru Park, one parliamentarian declared, "I don't see why we should listen to a bunch of divorced women." Another politician portrayed her as a "madwoman"; a third threatened to "circumcise" her if she ever set foot in his district (Selva 8).

As a highly educated woman scientist, an advocate of women's rights, and a proponent of environmentalism for the poor, Maathai was vulnerable on multiple fronts to charges of inauthenticity and, like Carson, of unpatriotic behavior. A cabinet minister railed against Maathai as "an ignorant and ill-tempered puppet of foreign masters" (qtd. in Motavelli 11). Another criticized her for "not being enough of an African woman," of being "a white woman in black skin" (Maathai, *Unbowed* 110). Such critics typically adhered to a gender-specific nativism: as Maathai notes, Kenyan men freely adopted Western languages, Western dress, and the technological trappings of modernity, while expecting women to be the markers and bearers of "tradition" (111).[19] President Moi (who imprisoned Maathai several times) chastised her for being "disobedient" (115); if she were "a proper woman in the African tradition—[she] should respect men and be quiet" (196).[20]

As Kwame Anthony Appiah has observed, the charge of inauthenticity is an inherently unstable one:

> … nativists may appeal to identities that are both wider and narrower than the nation: to 'tribes' and towns, below the nation-state; to Africa, above. And, I believe, we shall have the best chance of re-directing nativism's power if we challenge not the rhetoric of the tribe, the nation, or the continent, but the topology that it presupposes, the opposition it asserts. (55)

This is certainly borne out in Maathai's case: she fell foul of proliferating "uns"— unAfrican, unKenyan, unKikuyu, unpatriotic, ungovernable, unmarried, unbecoming of a woman. But through her intersectional environmentalism she sought to circumvent the binaries of authentication. One strategy she used to sidestep such oppositional topologies was to seek out local currents of environmental practice that were consistent with notions like biodiversity, the commons, and ecological stewardship, but not necessarily reducible to them. In this way she could also try to defuse accusations that she was a Western agent of "green imperialism."

The vehemence of the attacks on Maathai and Carson are a measure both of institutionalized misogyny and of how much is at stake politically, economically, and professionally in keeping the insidious dynamics and repercussions of slow violence concealed from view. While personally vulnerable, Maathai and Carson were threatening because they stood outside powerful systems of scientific patronage, academic intimidation, and silencing kickbacks. Their cultural contexts differed widely, but their extra-institutional positions allowed them the scientific autonomy and political integrity to speak out against attritional environmental violence and help mobilize against it.

Conclusion

If Maathai's nativist detractors sought to discredit her as an enemy of national development, she also faced, when awarded the 2004 Nobel Peace Prize, a different style of criticism from abroad. Carl I. Hagen, leader of Norway's Progress Party, typifies this line of aggressive disbelief: "It's odd," Hagen observes, "that the [Nobel] committee has completely overlooked the unrest that the world is living with daily, and given the prize to an environmental activist" (qtd. in Tyler, "In Wartime" A5).[21] The implications of Hagen's position are clear: nineteen months into the Iraq War, and amidst the war in Afghanistan, the wider "war on terror," the tumult in the Middle East, Congo, Sudan and elsewhere, to honor an environmentalist for planting trees was to trivialize conflict resolution and to turn one's back on the most urgent issues of the hour.

Maathai, however, sought to recast the question of urgency in a different time frame, one that challenged the dominant associations of two of the early twenty-first century's most explosive words: "preemptive" and "terror." The Green Belt Movement focused not on conventional *ex post facto* conflict resolution but on conflict preemption through nonmilitary means. As Maathai insisted, "many wars are fought over natural resources. In managing our resources and in sustainable development we plant the seeds of peace" (qtd. in Tyler, "Peace Prize" A5).[22] This approach has discursive, strategic, and legislative ramifications for the "global war on terror." Most of our planet's people face more immediate terrors than a terrorist attack: creeping deserts that reduce farms to sand; the incremental assaults of climate change compounded by deforestation; not knowing where tonight's meal will come from; unsafe drinking water; having to walk five or ten miles to collect firewood to keep one's children warm and fed. Such quotidian terrors haunt the lives of millions immiserated, abandoned, and humiliated by authoritarian rule and by a purportedly postcolonial new world order. Under such circumstances, slow violence, often coupled with direct repression, can ignite tensions, creating flashpoints of desperation and explosive rage.[23] Perhaps to Hagen and others like him, tree planting is conflict resolution lite; it lacks a dramatic, decisive, newsworthy military target. But Maathai, by insisting that resource bottlenecks impact sustainable security at local, national, and global levels, and by insisting that the environmentalism of the poor is inseparable from distributive justice, has done more than forge a broad political alliance against Kenyan authoritarian rule. Through her testimony and through her movement's collective example, she has sought to reframe conflict resolution for an age when instant cinematic catastrophe has tended to overshadow violence that is calamitous in more insidious ways. This, then, is Wangari Maathai's contribution to the "war on terror": building a movement committed, in her words, to "reintroducing a sense of security among ordinary people so they do not feel so marginalized and so terrorized by the state" (qtd. in Quist-Arcton 1).

Coda

The aftermath of Kenya's December 2007 elections has witnessed inter-ethnic killings and counter-killings and the displacement of hundreds of thousands of citizens. The surface trigger of this cataclysm was electoral fraud. However, it is crucial to recognize the broader, over-determined forces—including environmental; class; gender; and generational and economic forces, internal and global—that contributed to this apparent outburst of ethnic fundamentalism. Kenya's post-electoral violence, as David Anderson points out, "has an ethnic element, but tribalism is a description of these events not an explanation" ("Kenya's Agony" 5).

Because slow violence is unphotogenic, makes for undramatic copy, and requires a long attention span, when rapid, direct violence erupts it is far easier for the media to briskly ascribe it to "atavistic ethnic hatreds" than to track the deeper, systemic roots. The post-electoral killings and mass displacements far from being atavistic are more accurately to be read as expressing profound contradictions within Kenya's modern state.

Unequal access to resources—land, jobs, power, and hope—do exist among Kenya's forty-two ethnicities. However, by far the most glaring chasm separates the elite and the poor of all ethnic backgrounds. Despite a much-lauded average five percent growth during President Mwai Kibaki's five-year term, almost half of Kenya's thirty-six million people survive on $1,200 per annum or less, while cabinet ministers annually take home on average around $155,000 (Nyambura-Mwaura).

Together the discourses of "economic growth" and "atavistic tribal hatreds" camouflage a gross failure of distributive justice that has a profound environmental component. Kenya is both a "success story" and one of the world's most unequal societies: it ranks 152nd in terms of equitable distribution of wealth. Whatever his relative advances over the tyranny of the Moi years, Kibaki failed to address the long duree of dispossession that has left land and wealth concentrated in the hands of a few. If Kenya is a democracy, it remains a plutocratic democracy with an almost imperial presidency whose excessive powers exacerbate a winner-takes-all mentality.

Wangari Maathai, reflecting in her memoir on the Rift Valley violence that engulfed the 1992 elections, noted how readily environmental stresses could heighten the kind of desperation that was easily manipulated by a power-hungry political elite (*Unbowed* 236–37). Officially, the cycles of post-electoral violence have been inter-ethnic, yet they have been inflamed in large part by the convergence of increasing numbers of mobile pastoralists and sedentary agriculturalists on increasingly degraded land. This competition for stressed space, one should note, has both a rural and an urban manifestation. Together, the expansion of tea plantations and other vast estates of industrial scale, export-oriented agriculture, the unaddressed colonial legacy of over-concentrated land (exacerbated by neo-colonial cronyism), and deforestation and desertification have put the squeeze on subsistence, driving hundreds of thousands of the rural poor toward the cities, often less out of hope than out of the sheer impossibility of surviving in the countryside. As a result—especially in Nairobi—extreme wealth and extreme poverty live in combustible proximity, where the acute stratification of the city readily takes on ethnic dimensions. In the city's Kibera slum, some areas have 80,000 inhabitants per square kilometer, while in the glossy suburb of Karen only 360 inhabitants live in a comparable area (Vasagar 6). It is no coincidence, then, that the Rift Valley and the Nairobi slums have become epicenters of intolerance and brutality.

In an incisive essay called "Hitting without Violence," the exiled Ugandan writer, Kalundi Serumaga argues, "Kenya was and is an atrocity a long time made and a catastrophe a long time coming." The result is poor-on-poor violence. "If you kill a cop," Serumaga observes, "ten will come back; if you kill a child of the rich, your fellow poor will be offered reward money to find you. If you kill a fellow poor 'non-you' you have found the perfect victim." Thus cynical political elites in both major parties have fomented proxy wars, waged by the poor in a desperate bid for power at all costs.[24]

These proxy wars have a deep-seated gender dimension, as warrior masculinity becomes the dominant mode of conflict and the primary media image of inter-ethnic relations. Whether it is Kikuyu Mungiki criminal gangs dismembering Luos in the Nairobi slums or bow-and-arrowed Kalenjin warriors stalking "alien" Kikuyus in the Rift Valley, images of immediate, spectacular inter-ethnic male violence dominate the media's explanatory script. Yet questions need to be asked about the extreme marginalization of women from Kenya's political elite and about the near-invisibility in the media of the leading role women have played in initiating reconciliation and engaging the underlying slow violence that keeps fueling fresh cycles of overt brutality.

"Local disasters," writes Wai Chee Dimock, "are the almost predictable side effects of global geopolitics. They are part of a larger distributive pattern—a pattern of unequal protection that Ulrich Beck calls the global "risk society"—with the risk falling on the least privileged, and being maximized at just those points where the resources have been most depleted" (18). Dimock is reflecting here on the aftermath of Hurricane Katrina, yet her words apply with equal force to contemporary Kenya, where local and transnational structures of slow violence sustain tinderbox conditions that a cynical political elite can readily ignite at great cost to the society's systemically disenfranchised.

Notes

[1] Although Carson had almost nothing to say on the subjects of colonialism and race, her work speaks powerfully to the environmentalism of the poor precisely because of her concern with the complicity of the military-industrial complex in concealing toxicity, with discounted casualties, and with the transnational fallout of lethal actions that are often remote in space and time.

I'm adapting the term "the environmentalism of the poor" from Guha and Martinez-Alier's groundbreaking work on that subject (3–16).

[2] In this context, one recalls that the public furor stirred up by *Silent Spring* overlapped with another high water mark of American paranoia, the Cuban Missile Crisis. Carson exhorted an America awash with paranoia to take charge of its fears by changing the way it lived, by acting differently in the short term to reduce long-term catastrophic risk. Carson redirected some of the national anxiety away from the Red Peril to the aerosol Doom perched on the kitchen shelf. By revealing how small, domestic choices could help secure a more inhabitable world, *Silent Spring*

altered the landscape of fear—and ultimately, the laws as well.

3 The insistence that Shock and Awe was the beginning of a war unprecedented in its humanitarian precision was heard across the political spectrum. Donald Rumsfeld, most memorably, insisted that the futuristic weaponry that the United States deployed in the war exhibited "a degree of precision that no one dreamt of in a prior conflict," resulting in bombings that were morally exemplary:

> The care that goes into it, the humanity that goes into it, to see that military targets are destroyed, to be sure, but that it's done in a way, and in a manner, and in a direction and with a weapon that is appropriate to that very particularized target. ... I think that will be the case when ground truth is achieved. (U.S. Department of Defense)

4 For a related and insightful discussion of what she calls "articulated categories," see Anne McClintock (4ff).

5 The time frame here is crucial. With the help of international donors, Maathai put in place a system whereby each woman was paid a modest amount not for planting a tree, but for keeping it alive for six months. If it were still growing at that point, she would be remunerated. Thus the focus of the group's activities was not the single act of planting but maintaining growth over time.

6 A major precursor to the conflict over Karura had occurred in 1989. The regime had been steadily appropriated and privatizing parts of Nairobi's Uhuru Park, which Maathai has likened to New York's Central Park and London's Hyde Park as a vital green space, a space for leisure and for political gatherings. When Maathai learned that the ruling party was to erect a sixty-story skyscraper for new party headquarters and a media center in Uhuru Park, battle was joined. Green Belt activists spearheaded a successful movement to turn back the regime's efforts to privatize public land under the deceptively spectacular iconography of national development. The regime would not forgive Maathai for humiliating them in this manner.

7 I've adapted the phrase from Al Gedicks' book, *Resource Rebels: Native Challenges to Mining and Oil Corporations*.

8 For the history of the forest fighters, see Elkins, Maloba, and especially Anderson (*Histories of the Hanged* 230–88).

9 For the most comprehensive discussion of this literature, see Maughan-Brown.

10 The Mau-Mau uprising was far from being an undivided revolt: numerous fault lines opened up at times, not least between educated nationalist leaders and the predominantly peasant forest fighters.

11 In many Kenyan novels about the Mau Mau period, the forest fighters are depicted with a cloying if understandable romanticism. On the complex and varied legacies of colonial cultures of nature, one notes Maathai's admiration for the Men of the Trees, an organization founded in Kenya in the 1920s that brought together British and Kikuyu leaders to promote tree planting (Maathai, *Unbowed* 131).

12 Although the initial resistance came from the Green Belt Movement, the resistance spread to the streets of Nairobi, where it was taken up by a broad swath of the population, particularly students, both female and male.

13 See Beinart and Coates, Carruthers, and Mackenzie.

14 Mackenzie, like Beinart, stresses that among the colonial officialdom were some dissident voices who recognized the value and applicability of local agricultural and environmental knowledge (Mackenzie 710–14).

15 An important distinction should be made between the routes that Carson and Maathai took to their writing and their activism. Carson was a lifelong writer who remade herself as an activist late in life, after she traded her lyrical voice (which she'd honed as a celebrant of marine life) for the voice of elegy and apocalypse in *Silent Spring*. Maathai's trajectory was in the opposite direction: an activist all of her adult life, she became a writer of testimony only in her later years.

16 Additionally, a review by Carl Hodge was entitled "*Silent Spring* Makes Protest Too Hysterical."

17 I am grateful to Lindsay Woodbridge for first drawing my attention to this review in her fine unpublished senior thesis, "The Fallout of Silent Spring."

18 This misogyny, together with the regime's authoritarian intolerance of dissent, had profound professional and financial repercussions for Maathai. In 1982, after teaching at the University of Nairobi for sixteen years, she decided to run for parliament. To do so, she was told she had to resign from her job at the university. She was then promptly informed by the electoral committee that she was disqualified (on a trumped up technicality) from running for parliament. So, twelve hours after resigning as chair of the university's Department of Veterinary Anatomy, Maathai asked for her job back. Under pressure from the regime, the university refused to reemploy her, denying her, moreover, all pension and health benefits. Maathai, a forty-one year old single mother with no safety net, was thrown out onto the streets. One notes that, in 2005, shortly after Maathai was awarded the Nobel Prize, the very university that had treated her so appallingly tried to cash in on her international fame by awarding her an honorary doctorate in science.

19 For a more elaborate account of the burden of traditionalism placed on women in the context of a Janus-faced modernity, see McClintock, pages 294–300.

20 There are echoes between the nativist arguments mounted against her by President Moi and the arguments of her ex-husband, Mwangi, who testified in court that he was divorcing her because she was ungovernable: "too educated, too strong, too successful, too stubborn, and too hard to control" (Maathai, *Unbowed* 146).

21 Morten Hoeglund, a member of Norway's Progress Party, concurred with Hagen, arguing "the committee should have focused on more important matters, such as weapons of mass destruction" (Selva 9).

[22] See, for example, Maathai's insistence that, through a focus on reforestation and environmental resource management, "we might preempt many conflicts over the access and control of resources" (*Unbowed* xvi).

[23] In Kenya, which boasts some forty ethnicities, the sources of ethnic tension are complex, but have often been especially explosive along the fault lines between pastoralists and farmers where resources are over-stressed. Divisive politicians have manipulated these tensions to their advantage during, for instance, the violence that beset the Rift Valley, Nyanza, and Western prov-inces in the early 1990s and, more broadly, during the aftermath of the disputed national elections of 2007. The slow violence of resource depletion, a mistrust of government, and political leaders who play the ethnic card can easily kindle an atmosphere of terror that fuels social unrest.

[24] Compare this with Daniel Branch's observation that "Kibaki and his clique stole an election in the knowledge that the people who would pay the penalty for their actions would almost certainly be from their own power base, the Kikuyu in the Rift Valley" (Branch 27).

Works Cited

Anderson, David. *Histories of the Hanged: The Dirty War in Kenya and the End of Empire*. New York: Norton, 2005.

___. "Kenya's Agony." *Royal Africa Society On-line*. 10 January 2008: 1–9. 15 January 2008. <http://www.royalafricansocietyorg/index.php?option=com_content&task=view&id=443>.

Appiah, Kwame Anthony. *In My Father's House*. New York: Oxford University Press, 1992.

Beinart, William, and Peter Coates. *Environmental History: The Taming of Nature in the U.S.A. and South Africa*. London: Routledge, 1995.

Branch, Daniel. "At the Polling Station." *London Review of Books* 24 January 2008: 26–27.

Brown, Lester R. "The Price of Salvation." *Guardian* 25 April 2007: 1–4.

Caminero-Santangelo, Byron. "Different Shades of Green: Ecocriticism and African Literature." *African Literature: An Anthology of Criticism and Theory*. Eds. Tejumola Olaniyan and Ato Quayson. Oxford: Blackwell, 2007. 698–706.

Carruthers, Jane. *The Kruger National Park: A Social and Political History*. Pietermaritzburg, South Africa: Allen, 1995.

Carson, Rachel. *Silent Spring*. 1962. Boston: Houghton Mifflin, 1992.

Crichton, Michael. *State of Fear*. New York: Avon, 2004.

DAD. "Controversial Book by Rachel Carson Lives Up to Advance Warnings." *Aerosol Age*. October (1962): 81–82, 168.

Dimock, Wai Chee. "World History According to Katrina." *States of Emergency*. Eds. Russ Castronovo and Susan Gillman. Forthcoming, 2009.

Elkins, Caroline. *Imperial Reckoning: The Untold Story of Britain's Gulag in Kenya*. New York: Holt, 2005.

Finnegan, William. "The Economics of Empire: the Washington Concensus." *Harper's* May (2003): 41–54.

Friedman, Thomas. "The Age of Interruption." *New York Times* 5 July 2006: A 27.

Gedicks, Al. *Resource Rebels: Native Challenges to Mining and Oil Corporations*. Cambridge, Mass: South End Press, 2001.

Guha, Ramachandra. *Environmentalism: A Global History*. New York: Longman, 2000.

Guha, Ramachandra, and Juan Martinez-Alier. *Varieties of Environmentalism: Essays North and South*. London: Earthscan, 1997.

Hertzberg, Hendrik. "The War in Iraq." *The New Yorker*. 27 March 2003: 15.

Hodge, Carl. "Silent Spring Makes Protest Too Hysterical." *Arizona Star* 14 October 1962: 14.

Jackson, Wes. "The Agrarian Mind. Mere Nostalgia or a Practical Necessity?" *The Essential Agrarian Reader*. Ed. Norman Wirzba. Washington, DC: Shoemaker and Hoard, 2003. 140–53.

Jeffries, Stuart. "Kenya's Tree Woman." *Mail and Guardian* 28 February 2007: 7–8.

Lappe, Anna, and Frances Moore Lappe. "The Genius of Wangari Maathai." *International Herald Tribune* 15 October 2004: 1–2.

Lear, Linda. *Rachel Carson: Witness for Nature*. New York: Holt, 1997.

Maathai, Wangari. *The Green Belt Movement: Sharing the Approach and the Experience*. New York: Lantern Books, 2003.

___. *Unbowed: A Memoir*. New York: Knopf, 2006.

Mackenzie, A. Fiona D. "Contested Ground: Colonial Narratives and the Kenyan Environment, 1920–1945." *Journal of Southern African Studies* 26 (2000): 697–718.

Maloba, Wunyabari O. *Mau Mau and Kenya: An Analysis of a Peasant Revolt*. Bloomington: Indiana UP, 1998.

Maughan-Brown, David. *Land, Freedom and Fiction: History and Ideology in Kenya*. London: Zed Press, 1985.

McClintock, Anne. *Imperial Leather: Race, Gender and Sexuality in the Colonial Contest*. New York: Routledge, 1995.

Motavelli, Jim. "Movement Built on Power of Trees." *E: The Environmental Magazine*. July–Aug. (2002): 11–13.

Ngũgĩ, wa Thiong'o. *A Grain of Wheat*. London: Heinemann, 1967.

Nyambura-Mwaura, Helen. "Seeds of Class War Sprout in Kenya's Crisis." *Mail and Guardian* 13 February 2008: 15–16.

Pal, Amitabh. "Maathai Interview." *The Progressive* May (2005): 3–5.

"Pesticides: The Price of Progress." *Time* 28 September 1962: 45.

Pollan, Michael. *Second Nature: A Gardener's Education*. New York: Dell, 1991.

Quayson, Ato. *Calibrations*. Minneapolis: University of Minnesota Press, 2003.

Quist-Arcton, Ofeibea. "Maathai: Change Kenya to Benefit People." *All Africa.com*. 1 January 2003. 10 November 2007. <http://www.greenbeltmovement.org/a.php?id=130>.

Schecter, Arnold, et al. "Agent Orange and the Vietnamese: the Persistence of Elevated Dioxin Levels in Human Tissues." *American Journal of Public Health* 85 (1995): 516–22.

Scott, James C. *Seeing Like a State: How Certain Schemes to Improve the Human Condition Have Failed*. New Haven: Yale University Press, 1998.

Selva, Meear. "Wangari Maathai: Queen of the Greens." *The Guardian* 9 October 2004: 7–9.

Serumaga, Kalundi. "Unsettled—Hitting Without Touching." *Liberation Lit*. 18 February 2008. <liblit.wordpress.com/2008/02/18/unsettled-by-kalundi-serumaga>.

Sevareid, Eric. "An Explosive Book." *Washington D.C. Star*. 9 October 1962: 3.

"The Silent Spring of Rachel Carson." *CBS Reports*. 3 April 1963. Transcript.

Tyler, Patrick E. "Peace Prize Goes to Environmentalism in Kenya." *New York Times* 9 October 2004: A1, A5.

___. "In Wartime, Critics Question Peace Prize for Environmentalism." *New York Times* 10 October 2004: A5.

United States Department of Defense. "DoD News Briefing—Secretary Rumsfeld and Gen. Myers." Friday, 21 March 2003.

Vasagar, Jeevan. "Bulldozers Go in To Clear Kenya's Slum City." *Guardian* 20 April 2004: 6.

"Vietnam in Retrospect." *New York Times* 23 March 2003: A25.

Woodbridge, Lindsay. "The Fallout of Silent Spring." Senior Thesis. U of Wisconsin-Madison, 2007.

32 Postcolonial and Feminist Philosophies of Science and Technology

Convergences and Dissonances

Sandra Harding

Feminist and postcolonial science and technology studies (STS) both emerged in the third quarter of the last century, though each had important forerunners. The agendas of these two intellectual currents and their related social movements are similar in important respects and thus would seem to be complementary. Both argue that the perspectives and interests of their particular constituencies are not well served by modern Western science and technology philosophies, policies, or practices. The global social progress promised by modern Western philosophies of science has resulted in economic, political, social, and cultural regress for them. Both offer alternatives that they claim are better grounded in realistic understandings of knowledge production processes, more comprehensive, and better able to serve the peoples on behalf of whom each speaks. Thus each is politically as well as intellectually engaged.

Yet this kind of complementarity is too weak. Additional reasons for each to be interested in the projects of the other can come from recognition that their constituencies are overlapping and their discourses are interlocked. At least half of the ex-colonized and those still under the control of neo-colonialism and neo-imperialism are women and their dependants. And a majority of the world's women and their dependants are among ex-colonized peoples and those still controlled by neo-colonialism and neo-imperialism. Furthermore, the dominant discourses that these social movements criticize (as well as the ones that they use) are deeply imbricated or locked into each other: colonialism, imperialism, and male supremacy have persistently represented gender in racial or colonial terms and racial and colonial relations in gender terms. Gender and racial/colonial categories still co-constitute each other today. Because of their overlapping constituencies and interlocking discourses, it would seem that each of these science and technology movements will have to depend upon the successes of the other if it is to achieve its own professed goals. In this sense they are *strongly complementary*.

Sandra Harding, "Postcolonial and Feminist Philosophies of Science and Technology: Convergences and Dissonances." *Postcolonial Studies*, 12(4), 2009: 401–421. Reprinted by permission of Taylor & Francis Ltd.

Some scholars in each field have made significant explorations into at least some part of the concerns of the other. Certainly such explorations have increased in recent years. Yet the results of these forays still feel scattered and undertheorized. They appear more as 'add ons' to the prevailing conceptual framework of each rather than as the transformations of these frameworks necessary to fully engage with the full range of issues and the innovative insights of both postcolonial and feminist science and technology studies. To be sure, even such 'add-ons' are often difficult to do and produce illuminating results. To be able to see that one European woman, Maria Sibylla Merian, was among the great scientist-voyagers to the Americas (so far, the only one so identified) enlarges our understandings of women's opportunities and risks in sciences of the era while providing additional evidence of the importance to European sciences of research done in the colonies.[1] But it does not fundamentally challenge the assumption that women played marginal roles in the development of European sciences of the era, in particular through the colonial and imperial 'voyages of discovery.' It does not challenge the opinion that the ones who did were entirely of European origin, and that European sciences owe no significant debts to knowledge of the natural world accumulated by indigenous peoples. Most scholars reporting on Merian's entomology have not focused on how deeply her work depended on the accumulated knowledge of indigenous peoples, and especially indigenous women.[2]

Of course, each of these social movements, with its distinctive intellectual currents, is internally heterogeneous. The terms 'feminist' and 'postcolonial' are themselves highly contested *within* groups committed respectively to ending male-supremacy and Western-supremacy. Political, disciplinary, institutional, and regional cultural histories and commitments create strikingly different analyses and agendas for different groups within each social movement. Thus it can seem a futile project to try to get into productive coalitions such diverse and internally conflicted social movements and to integrate their conceptual frameworks in ways satisfactory to all. Nevertheless, I think it valuable to focus on several commonalities and dissonances in the ways these groups have conceptualized their projects. This can be a useful step toward creating intellectual and political spaces for the coalitions necessary for progressive social transformations.

Here I suggest that these two social and intellectual movements seem committed to conflicting understandings of the relevant social relations, the relevant sciences, and questions about who can and should be agents of the kinds of radical historical change for which each calls. (There are important exceptions to this charge, as we will see.) Under such circumstances, neither social movement can deliver the benefits it envisions to the majority of those to whom it has professed accountability. The intellectual and political projects of each must more deeply engage the insights and innovations of the other if each is to leave behind its still prevalent and self-damaging discriminatory assumptions and practices, intended or not. Section 2 delineates the conflicting conceptions of relevant social relations, sciences, and agents of progressive social transformation. Section 3 examines two literatures where such challenges have been met. Sections 4 and 5 identify unfamiliar logics of research and a couple of unresolved issues for these STS projects which nevertheless need not block coalitions between them. Philosophical issues are at stake here insofar as the three conflicting understandings and the two "logics of research" imply metaphysical, epistemological, and philosophy of science differences.

But first, what are feminist STS and postcolonial STS? I will presume readers are familiar with general outlines, at least, of the larger Western feminist social movements of the late twentieth century and the intellectual currents in which their STS are rooted. And that readers are familiar with one or another (at least) of the many different histories and geographies of postcolonialisms, their political struggles and intellectual currents. I leave until section 5 a brief discussion of this issue of the divergences in genealogies of postcolonialism since, in my view, while this diversity affects how various streams of postcolonial STS have developed, it does not seem to shape the issues that are the focus here, namely the disconnects between postcolonial and feminist conceptual frameworks.

Here I briefly identify for readers unfamiliar with one or the other of these two kinds of STS projects some of their central themes.

What are Feminist and Postcolonial STS?

From their beginnings one can find in both the gender-focused and the postcolonial STS the understanding that scientific and technological projects are co-constituted with their social orders, as Northern science and technology studies came to put the point sometime later.[3] That is, no sciences and technologies are or could be autonomous and value-free, as the rhetoric of 1950s modernization theory and its science policy held.[4] Interests in particular kinds of scientific and technological projects are created as part of social transformations, while such social transformations are shaped and directed in part by the kinds of scientific and technological projects that can be put in service to their goals, explicit or implicit. To put this point another way, feminism and postcolonialism both argue in effect that how we live together both enables and limits what we can know, and vice versa. Thus when new kinds of persons 'step on the stage of history' to rearticulate how they see themselves and the world, new kinds of sciences, philosophies of science, and epistemologies are both generated and also relied on by their listeners. Of course this insight about the relation between what we do and what we can know is not far from an important conventional feature of scientific method: how one interacts with the world around us both enables and limits what one can know about it.[5]

It should be noted that both of these intellectual and social movements positioned themselves against the policies and practices of modern Western sciences as well as the dominant Western epistemologies and philosophies of science and technology that justified them. So neither began in any articulated relation to the other. Their strong complementarity could not be recognized within the androcentric world of early postcolonial STS and the Eurocentric world of early feminist STS. Furthermore, neither movement is contained by geographical location, citizenship, or the ethnic or gender identities of its participants: Western scholars have made important contributions to postcolonial STS, and men have made important contributions to feminist work in this field.

Gender and science themes

From its beginnings, gender and science projects in the West pursued five main research trajectories. These were often initiated by groups with different kinds of disciplinary, political, or institutional interests in scientific and technological research. (1) Where are (and have been) women in the social structures of modern Western sciences, and why have there been so few of them in the arenas of the design and management of scientific and technological research? (2) How and why have 'sexist sciences' taken on projects of providing empirical support for the claimed inferiority of women? (3) How have technologies and the applications of the results of scientific research been used against women's equality? Women's health, reproductive, and environmental concerns were among the earliest such focuses. (4) How do scientific and technological education—pedagogy and curricula—restrict women's development as scientists and engineers? (5) What is problematic about the epistemologies, methodologies, and philosophies of science that produce and support such sexist and androcentric practices?[6]

These issues all remain important almost four decades later—unfortunately. In some areas significant progress has been made—for example, in increasing access for women to scientific educations, publications, organizations, lab and classroom jobs, and at least token presences in policy contexts. Moreover, significant changes in health and reproductive policies have occurred for women in already advantaged groups. Yet the changes have been mostly for the worse for women in Africa, South Asia, and other places around the globe. Today it is widely recognized that Western and especially US economic and political policies have greatly contributed to the increased threats to environments, health, and life itself experienced by the vast majority of the world's citizens who are women, and their dependants (as well as adult men), around the globe. An important achievement of feminisms has been their development of epistemological and methodological approaches that deeply transform 'the logic of scientific inquiry' and its familiar regulative ideals. These approaches have been widely adopted in the social sciences and some fields of biology and medical research.[7] Nevertheless, such feminist work has been largely marginalized in the mainstream science studies movements in the North.[8] If they are not 'studying women,' these researchers seem to think that gender issues are irrelevant to both the worlds they examine and the assumptions guiding their own work.

These five areas of feminist work in the North were slower to gather steam among researchers and activists from other parts of the world. When they did address such issues, it was in contexts of scientific and technological practice that were often ignored in Western gender and science projects. For example, achieving science literacy for girls in many 'Third World' countries requires enlarged agendas when school fees restrict poor families' educational investments to sons, or when girls are needed to help out full-time in domestic work (for example, caring for smaller children, fetching water, tending livestock). Moreover the effects of the applications and technologies of Western sciences are different in the political economies of the developing world than in Europe and the US. Finally, in the upper classes in some aristocratic societies, women will tend to get the same education as their brothers. Class, not gender, is the more salient enabler of education. This greater educational equity can also be the case in societies that enforce extreme gender segregation. In such cases girls will need to be trained as doctors, lawyers, and teachers for women and girls since interactions between the genders are severely restricted.[9]

Colonialism, imperialism, science and technology

In spite of its diversity, much of this work has focused on one or another of four themes.[10] One project has developed counter-histories of the achievements of modern Western sciences and technologies. For example, it asked if there were causal relations between the development of modern sciences in Europe and the 'voyages of discovery.' Here researchers have shown how the success of each in fact depended upon the success of the other. The voyagers needed an astronomy of the Southern hemisphere and better oceanography, climatology, and cartography to make their way to and from the Americas and Asia. They needed better knowledge of the flora, fauna, geography, geology and indigenes of the lands they encountered, as well as of the nature of and remedies for unfamiliar diseases. They needed what would come to be known as economic botany—the 'big science' of the seventeenth and eighteenth centuries—to make their voyages profitable. And the sciences, in turn, needed the economic and political support supplied by their assistance in the projects of the voyages. They also needed access to the world that became possible as European navies commanded the seas, enabling novel observations and comparisons of nature's order in different locations, as well as appropriation of indigenous knowledge for the advancement of modern Western sciences.[11] Indeed it has been suggested that increased focus on these kinds of European scientific projects would change what has traditionally been conceptualized as 'the Scientific Revolution'.[12]

A second topic has been a critical reevaluation of the legacies of traditional knowledge, many of which were eradicated and/or appropriated by the Western societies. Others have survived and continue to provide valuable resources to both societies too poor to access modern Western knowledge systems, and also societies that prefer to maintain elements of their traditional knowledge systems alongside, or integrated with, Western knowledge systems.[13] A third focus has been on the residues and resurrections of colonial and imperial science and technology relations since independence. This has occurred primarily through the carrots and sticks provided by First World financial and development policies and practices, but it is also due to the immense difficulty of escaping the ingrained habits, practices, and residual material conditions of those colonial and imperial relations, even when the perpetrators try to do so. One important focus here has been in critical modernity studies (see below). Finally, the postcolonial STS have persistently explored possible ways to move forward in their own science and technology projects yet within the difficult conditions set by global political and economic policies and circumstances, a point to which I return.

Sites of Dissonance

Three questions reveal conflicting understandings of the worlds in which these two STS projects are engaged.

What are the relevant social relations?

As historians pointed out some four decades ago, recognizing women to be fully human—as fully human as their brothers—undermines traditional historical methodological assumptions in three ways. First, chronologies grounded only in men's lives ignore the most significant changes in women's lives, and they ignore the effects that the conditions of women's lives have had on men's lives. Indeed, women's conditions have tended to regress at precisely the moments marked in conventional histories as highpoints of 'human progress.' Even worse, it was precisely because of the features identified as progressive that women's lives regressed. For example, women lost rights and opportunities in the Renaissance that they had earlier possessed; and in state formation in 1776 and evidently at every other time women have lost legal and political rights they possessed in earlier periods, including in the democratic revolutions of eighteenth-century Europe and recent independence movements of newly postcolonial states.[14] Second, sex/gender is one of the most significant determinants of a person's rights and responsibilities within any and every culture, though in different ways in different cultures. And, third, conventional theories of social change have failed to account for the transformations they intend to chart insofar as they ignore women's role and fate in such processes.[15]

Postcolonial STS tend to rely on traditional historical methodology in this respect with just such inadequate consequences for their accounts. With important exceptions, the relevant social relations for postcolonial STS are those of presumedly gender-free imperialism, colonialism, nation-building, and the local apparently gender-free resistances to such processes under colonial and imperial rule, or under the neo-colonialism and neo-imperialism that have characterized global social relations since the independence of these new states. When gender issues do appear, it is as the need for attention to 'women's concerns,' but virtually never are the kinds of epistemological, methodological or philosophy of science issues identified above engaged. As long as only men are in view, these accounts assume that consideration of gender relations is irrelevant to understanding what is happening. Consequently, postcolonial theory cannot understand colonial, imperial, postcolonial, or today's neo-colonial and neo-imperial processes as long as its practitioners obscure the presence of women and the gendered characteristics of knowledge practices that align primarily with men's interests and desires.

Yet Western feminist STS only rarely see the social relations of colonialism and imperialism as having anything to do with women's experiences of Western scientific and technological work. These scholars seem to think that as long as they are focused only on Western women, social relations of colonialism and imperialism are irrelevant to the sciences and technologies they observe. With important exceptions, they rarely attend to non-Western women's experiences of Western sciences and technologies, or such women's activities in their own knowledge production legacies. Such assumptions leave Western feminisms ignorant of both the history and practices of sciences and technologies around the globe, and of women's participation in and experiences of such histories and practices. To put the point another way, Western feminisms do not treat non-Westerners as fully human insofar as they ignore colonial and imperial social relations. Of course, neither do mainstream histories and philosophies of science.

What are the relevant sciences?

For Western feminists, the relevant sciences have been almost entirely modern Western ones. (See exceptions below.) Courageous and brilliant work has been accomplished here in addressing the gender dimensions even of the sciences thought least susceptible to social fingerprints, such as physics and chemistry.[16] Yet, with significant exceptions, the history of modern Western sciences and their practices today is only rarely set in the context of colonialism and imperialism or their contemporary residues and resurrections. And indigenous knowledge traditions, whether in the West or elsewhere, seem for the most part to be beyond the horizons of this work. Western feminist work largely is unaware of the counter-histories, the successes of indigenous knowledge, the arguments for a world of sciences, or the residues and resurrections of colonial and imperial science relations today. Consequently, the critical view of modern Western sciences and technologies that is specifically from the standpoint of non-Western societies is also missing.

For the postcolonial scholars, indigenous traditions, critical perspectives on modern Western sciences, and the design of science and technology policies and practices that integrate the best of both worlds are central projects. They have produced diverse accounts of possible future relations between indigenous and modern Western scientific knowledge systems.[17] Yet there has been almost no focus on women's domains of producing scientific and technological knowledge, or on the distortions in Western and non-Western projects originating in the absences of women from their design and management.

Who can and should be the subjects of progressive historical transformation?

Neither movement seems to think it necessary to center members of the other group in the design and management of its projects. Only a few women, such as Donna Haraway[18] and Vandana Shiva[19], appear in the citations of contemporary postcolonial science studies scholars. On the other hand, postcolonial literature is virtually completely absent from Western feminist work. Each seems to consign the other's work to the horizons of its own spheres of interest. The other's voices are hardly ever heard except as 'special interests.' The others are never represented as at the forefront in conceptualizing goals and strategies that will benefit all, including but not limited to those purportedly 'special interest' groups themselves. Yet neither can deliver social progress to its professed constituencies without attention to the full range of issues addressed by postcolonial and feminist science and technology studies. The two powerful conceptual frameworks must be conjoined.

Conjoining Conceptual Frameworks

Two clusters of studies, at least, have conjoined feminist and postcolonial STS frameworks in different ways.[20] These studies escape the challenges of discriminatory conceptions of the relevant social relations, sciences, and desirable agents of historical change. One cluster charts effects of gender relations on the scientific and technological projects of colonialism and imperialism before the formal end of European colonial rule, and the other studies the effects of gender relations within the Third World 'development' policies and practices that began after World War II. Both kinds of work have raised new questions that go beyond the separate agendas of feminist and postcolonial STS.

Effects of colonial and imperial gender relations on scientific and technological inquiry

The absence of women in positions of funding, sponsoring, designing, and managing scientific and technological projects within Western colonial and imperial contexts has influenced the direction and content of scientific inquiry both 'at home' in Europe and

North America and abroad. Since societies and their sciences co-constitute each other, it should not come as a surprise to discover that the gender relations of the societies sponsoring and conducting scientific and technological research in colonial and imperial contexts would shape the nature of the knowledge such inquiries produced. The absence of women in these kinds of directorial positions affected the selection of scientific problems, hypotheses to be tested, what constituted relevant data to be collected, how it was collected and interpreted, the dissemination and consequences of the results of research, and who was credited with the scientific and technological work. Three kinds of projects have been initiated.

First, indigenous women may have been the majority of 'native informants' about indigenous pharmacologies and economic uses of local botanies. As Harris points out, 'For most societies relying upon a mixture of hunting, gathering, and small-scale agriculture, women tended to be the chief custodians of botanical knowledge. In fact, we know that Joseph-Francois Lafitau's "discovery" of Canadian ginseng in 1716 was merely a matter of asking a Mohawk medicine woman to find the plant for him'.[21] Maria Sybylla Merian, whose meticulous depictions of caterpillars and other insects of Suriname (as well as of Europe) were cited appreciatively by Linneaus, said that she learned much about these insects and the plants on which they fed from the indigenous women who were her servants in Suriname, one of whom she brought back to Europe to assist her in accurately representing the insects, plants, and their uses. Londa Schiebinger maps this procedure more generally in the Caribbean.[22]

Second, nature itself was perceived, categorized, and represented through gender stereotypes characteristic of particular eras. For example, notions of courtship and gendered sexual behaviors were attributed to flowering plants and to animals in the nineteenth century.[23] Third, racial distinctions were often gendered: '... certain physical and climatic features were associated with manly and martial races, others— particularly the tropics—with femininity. Such ideas served to legitimate and explain the imperial order'.[24]

Finally, once one recognizes that all male groups also have gender relations (that is, that it is not just when women appear that gender issues are relevant), a range of existing and possible masculinity studies come into focus. One question here is: how was the search for knowledge itself gendered as manly, and how did that gendering function to legitimate scientific work as it also delegitimated women's participation in it? Canizares-Esguerra[25] points to the chivalric gendered values of imperial sciences in Spain, but also England and France, visible in the many depictions of the scientist/explorer as a knight (pp 67–69). Mary Terrall[26] has analyzed the seventeenth- and eighteenth-century similar British production of 'Heroic Narratives of Quest and Discovery'; and Rhodes describes the rhetoric of masculinity within the missionary work of the Jesuits—their reports of trials of strength and endurance that made their work a masculine science.[27] Sharon Traweek has described the persistence of this hyper-masculinization of scientific work in late twentieth-century high-energy physics laboratories.[28] Donna Haraway has looked at the exercises in manly colonial game-hunting which provided animals for scientific study and museum display And she has looked at how meanings of manly competition and control of women and 'lesser males' shaped the primate experiments designed by the founder of modern primatology.[29] She also describes the very different kinds of national interests in primates, and different methodologies, characteristic of primatology enterprises in India and Japan.

Harris points to another question here.[30] Within the structure of all-male colonial and imperial projects, how was a gendered division of labor created—that is, between different groups of men—and what were its effects on the production of scientific knowledge and the careers of these men? The powerful public spaces of Jesuit activity 'were occupied almost exclusively by university-educated, ordained, professed fathers,' who accounted for 'more than 95% of the entire Jesuit scientific corpus' (p 78, n31). 'The duties and spaces of lay brothers, by contrast, were almost exclusively domestic. They were accepted into the Society to tend to the "temporalities" of cooking, cleaning, caring for the sick, and generally minding the day-to-day business of Jesuit houses' (p 78). One of the Jesuits' most successful enterprises was the production of 'catalogs of medicinal recipes and handbooks for the healing arts' (p 78), and the consequent business that the ordained priests did in medical consultations with powerful figures in China, among other places. While it was the lay brothers, employed as apothecaries, who produced these catalogs and handbooks, they published little of interest in the scientific circles of the day. They did 'what could be defined as the "women's work" of the Society' (p 78). Indigenes were among the lay brothers.

These studies situate their accounts at the point where gender and colonial/imperial relations are co-constituting each other. The sciences of interest are modern Western ones and the array of (other) regional ones, and the influences and exchanges between them. And the agents of scientific and technical change are not restricted to European men.

Meanwhile, studies of the masculinization of modernization theory, policy, and practices, and their articulation in post-World War II Third World development, reveal the co-constitution of masculine and both neo-liberal and some forms of left 'progressive' identities.

The masculinization of modernization and development

Because men's criteria for social progress have so systematically ignored the contributions to such processes by women as well as the effects of such processes on them, it should come as no surprise that Western policies and practices of modernization and development have had socially regressive effects on women. Two literatures here are especially relevant to STS: gender and modernization theory and the women and development debates.

Modernization theory was articulated first by the founders of social science in the late nineteenth century and then updated in the 1950s to justify the Third World development projects of Northern states and the various international agencies they designed and directed. Four themes consistently linked social progress to the dissemination of the North's scientific rationality and technical expertise, to the constitution of new kinds of masculinities, and to the necessity of a public/private division of social domains. First, men must leave behind them loyalties to women, families, kin, households, and the nature that sustains them, as they leave for the metropolitan sites of modernity and urbanization. Their primary responsibilities cannot be to their birth-worlds, but must shift to the newly forming modern worlds. Second, economic and political activities, located in households and kin relations in pre-modernity, must be extracted from households to a 'public sphere,' leaving the 'private sphere' of the household severely politically and economically weakened. Third, scientific rationality and technological expertise function as one-way 'time machines' that transport men and all of the institutions of society except the family into the modern, public sphere. Finally, this kind of social transformation is presented in naturalizing, evolutionary terms; this is how the human species evolves from its childhood in tradition to its maturity in modern civilizations, according to modernization theory.[31]

The consequences of modernization theory often are not good for women anywhere or for non-Western men in traditional societies. Such peoples are positioned in the childhood of the species. Their activities and loyalties are located on the horizons of modernity, where they are barely intelligible to modern thought. The welfare of women and households is abandoned by public institutions as a condition of modernization. Women and households are identified as drags on economic growth and political progress, and as 'externals' to economies and their political systems, their welfare undeserving of serious consideration, sometimes deserving gracious handouts, but never positioned as active agents of social progress. Furthermore, male-supremacy and European/white-supremacy are used to metaphorize each other. Women are 'outside civilization,' non-European men are not really manly. Thus the oppression of each lives on as a natural fact inside representations of the oppression of other. Finally, this literature enables us to see that what has been called the epistemological crisis of the West is actually also the epistemological crisis of masculinity.[32]

To turn to a second literature, the mostly sad story of First World so-called development policies for the Third World provides a good illustration of what feminists object to in modernization theory and policy. Development was conceptualized from its origins as bringing social progress through the transfer to the Third World of First World scientific rationality and technical expertise. How have development projects affected women? Answers to this question were articulated first within the lively feminist theoretical debates of the 1970s and 1980s. The 'Women in Development' projects began with Ester Boserup's path-breaking account of *Women's Role in Economic Development*.[33] Boserup documented the bad consequences of development on women's lives. Her work stimulated liberal feminists' efforts to integrate women into development projects as workers. These feminist projects adhered to the tenets of modernization theory. But by the early 1980s, marxist feminists were arguing that this liberal framework was problematic in that it isolated gender inequality from the economic structural relations that made such inequality profitable. One of their influential 'Women and Development' focuses was on the exploitation of women by multinational corporations.

However, the socialist feminist 'gender and development' accounts, also emerging in the 1980s, stressed the importance of addressing the limitations of both approaches. It emphasized issues of women's inequality in both domestic and wage-labor spheres, and the interplay between them. And it also insisted on 'masculinity studies.' Gender studies must not be a matter only of 'studying women.' Gender is a relation, like class or race. Men's lives are deeply implicated in the conditions of women's lives, as whites' lives are in the lives of people of color, and the lives of the rich are in the lives of the poor. Moreover, by the end of the 1980s, a fully-articulated integration of feminist environmental issues into these analyses had produced the 'Women, Environment, and Sustainable Development' movement.[34] Yet to this day, the Boserup-inspired liberal approaches are still favored in those national and international development agencies that deign to pay any attention at all to 'women's issues.' This should come as no surprise since such approaches fit into the neo-liberal assumptions that have been directing these institutions in ways that more radical approaches do not.

One of the most striking analyses in the latest stage of this work appeared in a series of studies by Maria Mies and her colleagues.[35] Mies argued that it was the appropriation of women's and peasants' land rights and labor for export production that made a major contribution to the increased gross national productivity in newly developed societies (and a huge contribution to increased wealth of Western-based multinational corporations and the First World-controlled global financial system). It was in the First World that 'reproduction' should be controlled, since the vast majority of Third World peoples were not permitted even to reproduce themselves. Rather, they and their children had to go hungry and die young in order to provide ever more goods for the already greedy and bloated over-advantaged groups in the First World. Mies here not only contested the liberal feminist accounts, but also turned the tables on the marxist analyses. She justified a critical attack on marxist-inspired accounts in a logic that originated in nineteenth-century marxism, as she placed women and peasants at the center of competent analyses of late twentieth-century global political economies in the way that Marx had placed industrial workers at the center of analyses of capitalism's political and economic relations.

These accounts of modernization and development theory and practice, while only rarely explicitly focused on science and technology issues as they appear in either the postcolonial or the Northern feminist accounts, nevertheless do address them. First, Western scientific rationality and technical expertise, from the conceptualization, direction, and management of which women have been excluded, are always positioned as the 'motor' that drives both modernization and development. So the failures of both projects raise questions about the adequacy of such sciences and technologies to advance social progress. These accounts challenge the 'triumphalism' of standard historical and philosophic accounts of Western sciences and technologies that justify the public support and huge expenditures that the latter require. Second, the conjoining of feminist environmentalism to socialist feminist analyses of the political economy raised the issue of the faulty concept of limitless natural resources assumed by Western philosophies of science.[36] Third, the feminist modernization and development criticisms started off thinking about the global political economy from the standpoint of the daily lives of women and peasants, who were the least visible actors in this political economy in the modernization theory that directed development policies. These inquiries undertook the standpoint methodological/epistemological strategy, to which I shortly turn.

In these criticisms of modernization and Third World development theories, policies, and practices, gender and colonial/imperial social relations co-constitute each other. The fates of 'traditional' knowledge and of Western scientific rationality and technical expertise are mapped together in relation to each other. And those who have borne most of the costs and received fewest of the benefits of these First World agendas are represented as actual and potential agents of valuable knowledge for everyone, and of progressive social transformations. Thus the conceptions here of relevant social relations, relevant sciences, and desirable agents of progressive social transformations integrate feminist and postcolonial standpoints.

Looking forward: engaging with 'strange logics' of research

Especially challenging for each movement is to engage with what appears to be a strange 'logic of scientific inquiry' in the other movement. Strange to postcolonial researchers and activists is to start out thinking about any and every issue—not just 'women's issues'—from the standpoint of the women affected by it. Strange for Northern feminist work is to think within a framework in which modern Western sciences are just one among many valuable scientific legacies.

Standpoint methodology

The concept of an epistemological/methodological 'standpoint' arose first in Marxian writings about the importance of the 'standpoint of the proletariat' for revealing how the political economy of industrial capitalism actually worked to accumulate wealth in the lives of the already advantaged and misery in the lives of the workers, contrary to conventional accounts of economics of the day (and still of our day, alas). In feminist hands, the standpoint strategy directed researchers to start off thinking about their any and every project 'from women's lives' instead of from the conceptual frameworks of their disciplines.[37] Those frameworks had been designed to answer questions for the dominant social institutions (including research disciplines), from the design and management of which women had been excluded. It was those institutions that sponsored, funded, and monitored natural and social science research. Thus it should not have been surprising to note that these dominant conceptual frameworks engaged in the 'conceptual practices of power,' in Dorothy Smith's words.[38]

Standpoint projects 'studied up'; that is, they started off thinking about a situation from the women's lives involved, but attempted to explain the high-level institutional decisions and practices responsible for initiating and maintaining such situations. In this respect they differed from the ethnographies that were frequently parts of such projects, and with which they were often mistakenly conflated.[39] Standpoints are not to be conceptualized only as 'perspectives'; they are intellectual and political achievements, not ascriptions. They require critical, scientific study to see beneath the everyday social relations in which all were forced to live, and political struggles to gain access to the sites (the board rooms, the command centers, the policy circles) where one could see how decisions were made that directed and maintained sexist and andro-centric social relations. This was a project that strengthened the standards for 'good method' in the natural as well as the social sciences. Similarly it produced revisions of other regulative ideals of the sciences: 'strong objectivity,' 'robust reflexivity,' and expanded standards for rationality.

This epistemology and methodology has remained controversial throughout its more than three decades of development.[40] It is positioned at the convergence of central global intellectual and political quandaries for the West. Critics tend to try to assimilate it to some other positivist or anti-positivist position that they disparage, though its logic resists such assimilation. Its increasingly wide dissemination keeps its controversiality well-fueled, enabling, as one observer put the point, new polemics about relations between experience and knowledge.[41]

Largely influenced by this feminist work, standpoint methodologies have by now been adopted across the social sciences, such mixed social/natural sciences as environmental and health studies, many areas of biology, and technology studies. However, their strategy—their 'logic of inquiry'—has an organic quality in that it seems to appear whenever a new group tries to rearticulate its own knowledge-needs against the practices of inquiry projects that serve powerful groups. Indeed, one could say that the field(s) of postcolonial studies is grounded in just such a methodology. In all of its diverse varieties, it starts off thinking about colonialism and imperialism from the situations of those who have borne most of the costs and received fewest of the benefits of such exploitative and violent institutional practices.

For postcolonial movements and their intellectual projects, however, the feminist version of standpoint theory violates their assumption that while the exploitation of women by colonialism and imperialism must be ended, it is men who do, will, and must lead the way to postcolonial futures. Indeed, rejections of feminism as just one more Western cultural imperialism—obscuring anti-male-supremacist organizing by women around the globe—often constitute an obstacle to this feminist methodological and epistemological project. Yet standpoint methodology/epistemology may be too Western to be fully useful elsewhere quite apart from this particular gender issue. After all, it is positioned against what are perceived as 'positivist' regulatory ideals and practices in Western-origin natural and social sciences. It was formulated initially within the Marxian and Enlightenment philosophic and methodological legacies, even as it protests significant aspects of them. Positivism is not one of the most problematic aspects of many Third World societies, as philosopher Uma Narayan pointed out about India several decades ago. Moreover, she noted that standpoint theory's appeal to the value of women's experience can lose its critical edge in societies that conceptualize sex/gender differences as fundamentally complementary rather than hierarchical (and regardless of whether such differences are in fact treated as hierarchical).[42] My point is that there are other ways to articulate research projects that can distribute their benefits more effectively to least advantaged groups. Yet postcolonial resistance to thinking from the standpoint of women's lives, whatever the anti-male-supremacist conceptual framework within which such a project is located, remains an obstacle to the integration of postcolonial and feminist projects, and in my view this is a loss for both social movements.

Multiple sciences, multiple modernities

The postcolonial perspectives enable us to see the nature and value of recognizing 'a world of sciences'—that is, multiple scientific and technological traditions, each exquisitely adapted to regional needs and interests.

Here the central argument is that modernization is not identical to Westernization, contrary to Western exceptionalist and triumphalist assumptions. Rather, most— admittedly not all—peoples around the world now live in societies that have left feudalism or earlier economic/political forms. Moreover, the global reach of Western modernity's environmental destruction, toxic dumps, and arms industries, not to mention its production of pandemics and refugees, permeates even societies that have received no benefits from Western modernity. It would be reasonable to say that every society today lives in global modernity, even if only in the darkest corners of its effects.[43]

Thus modernity is not only disseminated from West to 'rest.' It is also independently produced within each and every society. Whether arriving from outside or inside a society—or, more likely, through negotiations between inside and outside—it must be 'sutured' into existing economic, political, cultural, psychic, and material worlds. Thus modernity will always take on distinctive local features in its multiple regional appearances. And it always tends to appropriate and reshape to its own ends the social hierarchies that exist. Feminist and postcolonial projects will always be multiple and distinctively local if they are to serve those escaping local male-supremacist and Western-supremacist histories. And such escapes require direct attention; they do not arrive either from modernization itself or from struggles against just one of the multiple social hierarchies within which most peoples around the globe live.[44] With important exceptions, feminist STS has tended to adopt either the universalist or relativist understandings of scientific and technological work that were the only alternatives offered in the older 'exceptionalist' positivist legacies. It, like the rest of Western STS, has not yet fully engaged with the reality that modern Western scientific traditions are just one of many viable and desirable ones around the globe, albeit the most powerful ones, at least to a significant extent because of the economic/political systems in which they live and travel.

Unresolved issues

There are at least a couple of unresolved internal tensions which present problems for contemplated alliances between the two movements. I point to just three of them here: criticizing the Enlightenment conceptual framework while using it; the conflicts and tensions between divergent accounts of the genealogy of postcoloniality and post-colonial theory; and the difficulty of completely demarcating gender differences from sex differences.

At least some postcolonial theorists seem far more willing to commit themselves to abandoning the conventional regulative ideals of modern Western sciences than Western feminist scientists and scholars have been. While feminism has of course criticized androcentric alignments and agendas in these ideals and their uses, its concerns have been to revise and transform the existing regulative ideals for more intellectually and politically defensible scientific inquiries. Much Western feminist science work has focused on improving women's access to the kinds of knowledge that they need and want as they live within the modern West. Indeed, for many science studies scholars Western feminist accounts, especially standpoint approaches, are too firmly lodged within the offensive Enlightenment and its modern commitments to objectivity, rationality and 'good method,' or else they are criticized as committed to an epistemological relativism which fails to engage with global power relations. In either case, critics fail to grasp the third position, neither objectivist nor relativist in conventional terms, that many feminist science scholars prefer.

Postcolonial critics appear much more ambivalent about the relation of their work to Enlightenment regulative ideals. There are three important positions here. One advocates that non-Western cultures in effect 'delink' from Western sciences and develop regional sciences out of the fertile ground of their own traditions.[45] At the opposite extreme, nationalist projects, including those inspired by dependencia theories, often enthusiastically adopt as their own goals the kind of scientific rationality and technical expertise hailed in the West.[46] So too do other kinds of scholars and policy makers convinced of the necessity of a kind of 'realpolitik' that perceives Western sciences as too widely and deeply entrenched in global political economies to be disenfranchised or even transformed except by 'add-ons' from other knowledge systems.[47] A third position clearly recognizes that, on the one hand, one cannot simply abandon modern Western sciences and their philosophies. On the other hand, these can be radically transformed through integration with regional legacies so as to enable the flourishing of a multiplicity of knowledge-traditions and the societies that depend upon them.[48] Indeed, perhaps we should conclude that a main focus of postcolonial STS in perpetuity will remain the delicate task of undermining the Enlightenment notions of science and technology that have been so useful to colonial and imperial projects while advocating radically transformed versions of them on behalf of better sciences and technologies. This third position is much like the prevailing feminist one mentioned above. Perhaps this should come as no surprise since both in effect use standpoint strategies, whether or not they name them as such. They each start off from the concerns and lives of oppressed groups to explain those groups' and others' knowledge production processes in ways that reveal what the oppressed groups need to know about them. Neither the delinking nor the overt relativist positions are easy to find in feminist science and technology work.

A second internal problem in postcolonial theory is discerning just what should count as the legitimate genealogies of postcoloniality and postcolonialism.[49] This is related to disputes over what should count as relevant colonialities, and what are the relations between colonialism and imperialism. Four major kinds of sites of oppression seem to attract leading clusters of these disputes. Which geographic locations provide the models of colonialism being criticized? (Settler colonies, the Indian subcontinent, Africa, Latin America? What about Eastern Europe and China?) How far back in history can the roots of postcoloniality be found? (Only since the end of official Western rule since World War II? Or since successful Latin American independence struggles, or in struggles during colonial eras?) What are the disciplinary priorities of the account? (Cultural, economic, political, or epistemic?) What kinds of institutions, their cultures and practices, are the primary focus? (Universities, national, regional and international governmental agencies and projects, corporations, including the European trading corporations, the Jesuits?) And then there are the focuses on resistance to distinctive kinds of oppression at these various sites (class, gender and race most notably). The accounts of political and intellectual resistance in each of these sites are so illuminating that I suggest that we should all feel obligated to assume that there is not and cannot be only one kind of right story here.

Several observations are relevant. The fact that groups invest in particular histories, geographies, disciplinary, and institutional accounts of anti-racism, anti-colonialism, anti-imperialism, and their more recent forms suggests that the term 'postcolonialism' will and always must be contested; such contestations are a productive process. Second, science and technology issues are rarely centered in such histories; they usually fail to make any appearance in them at all, though the broader Enlightenment epistemologies are usually contested. Moreover, the priorities of some of these histories are less welcoming than others to science and technology issues. For example, many cultural studies scholars including historians tend to conceptualize the Enlightenment and consequently also resistances to Western colonialism and imperialism as first and foremost political events about democratic governance; their exceptionalist and triumphalist attitudes toward Western sciences remain untouched by such concerns. Third, with the exception of the feminist postcolonial science and technology studies discussed in the section above on conjoining conceptual frameworks, these diverse accounts of the genealogy of postcolonialism are pretty much equally resistant to prioritizing women's issues. I take the three disconnects between assumptions about the relevant social relations, the relevant sciences, and the relevant historical actors to be applicable to most of these otherwise conflicting discussions of postcolonialism.

There is one challenge for feminisms that deserves mention. How come everywhere we look in history and culture we always find gender relations? Are they inside history or outside it, in nature? Let me distinguish this issue from a related one. It is a problem that Western feminists tend erroneously to generalize from their own situations to those of Third World women, and that Western feminists also tend to essentialize an 'average Third World Woman' who is poor, ignorant, completely a victim of local and global patriarchies, and whose purportedly miserable conditions consequently reveal the progressiveness of Western women.[50] These are serious problems which many feminists have addressed for some two decades, and yet which persist in blatant and less obvious forms in contemporary feminist accounts.

However, there is a kind of extreme form of this issue only occasionally glimpsed in such critiques: are the social relations of gender inside human history, or not? Do they come down to a matter of embroideries on biological difference? Of course this would be anathema to feminists, who have struggled for some four decades to document and analyze how women and men 'are made, not born' (in contrast to females and males, which are born in many species). Yet wherever one looks back in history and across cultures, one seems to find always already there women and men, femininity and masculinity, and their accompanying gender hierarchies. Is gender only a colonial imposition outside the West? Certainly Western ways of thinking about it and Western insistence on enforcing everywhere Western norms are such an imposition.[51] Yet another possibility is that gender differences are not as separable from sex differences as feminists have assumed—for reasons different from those given in traditional biological reductionism.

The way out of this discouraging fate for hard-working and already beleaguered social determinists will probably be to put the issue another way: the insistence on the sex-difference vs. gender-difference distinction seems to reinstate the nature vs. culture, genes vs. environment binary that has been so vigorously criticized by scientists recently with respect to race as well as sex/gender,[52] and which has become indefensible in Western science studies. The solution cannot be to go back to the old biological determinist accounts of gender differences. However, a more complex and nuanced biology/history/sociology, in which nature and culture are always fundamentally inseparable, is not yet available. Of course wheresoever culture exists, it will on occasion be valuable to focus on one rather than the other.

Conclusion

Both postcolonialisms and feminisms are theoretical and political projects on-the-move. They both do and must have transitional features in that they must still function as oppositional projects within the worlds that produced them while at the same time envisioning and acting to produce very different kinds of social, material, and intellectual worlds. Such attention to their powerful 'others' that generated them leaves limiting marks on their future-oriented theories and practices. Yet several literatures have begun to meet such challenges; they have conjoined feminist and postcolonial conceptual frameworks to produce analyses that illuminate issues of interest in both intellectual currents. Moreover, these schools of thought are and must remain permanently internally plural, and thus full of internal tensions and conflicts, since the still colonial, imperial and male-supremacist worlds they oppose take different forms in different times and places. The latter continually try to recuperate their losses to these emancipatory intellectual and political movements through new forms of resistance to and cooptation of their demands, as the former continually try to recuperate their original radical energies and visions in social worlds always already poised to contain them yet again. One could say that feminist and postcolonial movements expand the Copernican revolution as they decenter and parochialize dominant ways of thinking about the production of scientific and technological knowledge and their familiar philosophic assumptions.[53]

Recognition of these challenges points toward better futures. This is a particularly auspicious political moment in which to advance the radically progressive agendas developed in these two science and technology movements. Such projects contain the resources to develop more robust and productive dialogues and alliances.

Notes

1 Ella Reitsma, *Maria Sibylla Merian & Daughters: Women of Art and Science*, Zwolle: Waanders Publishers, n.d. [2008].

2 See Londa Schiebinger, 'Prospecting for Drugs: European Naturalists in the West Indies,' in Londa Schiebinger and Caludia Swan (eds), *Colonial Botany*, Philadelphia: University of Pennsylvania Press, 2005.

3 Steven Shapin and Simon Schaffer, *Leviathan and the Air Pump*, Princeton: Princeton University Press, 1985; Sheila Jasanoff (ed), *States of Knowledge: The Co-Production of Science and Social Order*, New York: Routledge, 2004.

4 David Hollinger, *Science, Jews, and Secular Culture*, Princeton: Princeton University Press, 1996.

5 See, for example, Ian Hacking, *Representing and Intervening*, Cambridge: Cambridge University Press, 1983.

6 Examples of this relatively early work include: Boston Women's Health Collective, *Our Bodies, Ourselves*, Boston: New England Free Press, 1970 (later editions published by Random House); Anne Fausto-Sterling, *Myths of Gender: Biological Theories about Women and Men*, New York: Basic Books, 1994; Donna Haraway, *Primate Visions: Gender, Race, and Nature in the World of Modern Science*, New York: Routledge, 1989; Sandra Harding, *The Science Question in Feminism*, Ithaca, NY: Cornell University Press, 1986; Sandra Harding, *Whose Science? Whose Knowledge?* Ithaca, NY: Cornell University Press, 1991; Sandra Harding and Merrill

Hintikka (eds), *Discovering Reality*, Dordrecht: Kluwer Academic Publishers, 2003; Ruth Hubbard, M S Henifin and Barbara Fried (eds), *Biological Woman: The Convenient Myth*, Cambridge, MA: Schenkman, 1982; Evelyn Fox Keller, *Reflections on Gender and Science*, New Haven, CT: Yale University Press, 1984; Helen Longino, Science as Social Knowledge, Princeton: Princeton University Press, 1990; Carolyn Merchant, *The Death of Nature: Women, Ecology, and the Scientific Revolution*, New York: Harper and Row, 1980; Margaret Rossiter, *Women Scientists in America*, vols 1 and 2, Baltimore: Johns Hopkins University Press, 1982/1995; Londa Schiebinger, *The Mind Has No Sex: Women in the Origins of Modern Science*, Cambridge, MA: Harvard University Press, 1989; Londa Schiebinger, *Nature's Body: Gender in the Making of Modern Science*, Boston: Beacon Press, 1993; Ethel Tobach and Betty Rosoff (eds), *Genes and Gender*, vols 1–4. New York: Gordian Press, 1978, 1979, 1981, 1984; Judy Wajcman, *Feminism Confronts Technology*, University Park: Penn State University Press, 1991. Of course the medical establishment's disparaging and often erroneous opinions about women's bodies were the object of much early gender and science work.

7 Sandra Harding 'Rethinking Standpoint Epistemology: What is 'Strong Objectivity'?', in L Alcoff and E Potter (eds), *Feminist Epistemologies*, New York: Routledge, 1992.

8   Mario Biagioli (ed), *The Science Studies Reader*, New York: Routledge, 1999.; Sheila Jasanoff, Gerald E Markle, James C Petersen and Trevor Pinch (eds), *Handbook of Science and Technology Studies*, Thousand Oaks, CA: Sage, 1995; Edward J Hackett, Olga Amsterdamska, Michael Lynch and Judy Wajcman, *The Handbook of Science and Technology Studies*, 3rd edn, Cambridge, MA: MIT Press, 2007. But see the greater attention to such issues in Sal Restivo (ed), *Science, Technology and Society: An Encyclopedia*, New York: Oxford, 2005.

9   Sandra Harding and Elizabeth McGregor, 'The Gender Dimension of Science and Technology,' in Howard J Moore (ed) *UNESCO World Science Report*, Paris: UNESCO, 1996.

10 Examples of relatively early work include: Michael Adas, *Machines as the Measure of Man*, Ithaca, NY: Cornell University Press, 1989; Lucille H Brockway, *Science and Colonial Expansion: The Role of the British Royal Botanical Gardens*, New York: Academic Press, 1979; Susantha Goonatilake, *Aborted Discovery: Science and Creativity in the Third World*, London: Zed Books, 1984; Sandra Harding (ed), *The 'Racial' Economy of Science: Toward a Democratic Future*, Bloomington: Indiana University Press, 1993; Daniel R Headrick (ed), *The Tools of Empire: Technology and European Imperialism in the Nineteenth Century*, New York: Oxford University Press, 1981; David Hess, *Science and Technology in a Multicultural World: The Cultural Politics of Facts and Artifacts*, New York: Columbia University Press, 1995; James E McClellan, *Colonialism and Science: Saint Domingue in the Old Regime*, Baltimore: Johns Hopkins University Press, 1992; Ashis Nandy, *The Intimate Enemy: Loss and Recovery of Self under Colonialism*, Delhi: Oxford University Press, 1983; Joseph Needham, *Science and Civilization in China*, 7 vols, Cambridge: Cambridge University Press, 1956–2004; Ziauddin Sardar (ed), *The Revenge of Athena: Science, Exploitation, and the Third World*, London: Mansell, 1988; Helaine Selin (ed), *Encyclopaedia of the History of Science, Technology, and Medicine in Non-Western Cultures*, 2 vols, Dordrecht: Springer, 2008; Vandana Shiva, *Staying Alive: Women, Ecology and Development*, London: Zed Books, 1989; Vandana Shiva, *Monocultures of the Mind: Perspectives on Biodiversity and Biotechnology*, New York and Penang: Zed Books and Third World Network, 1993; Third World Network, 'Modern Science in Crisis: A Third World Response,' in S Harding (ed), *The Racial Economy of Science*, Bloomington: Indiana University Press, 1993 (Penang, Malaysia: Third World Network and Consumers' Association of Penang, 1988). See also Warwick Anderson and Vincanne Adams, 'Praemoedya's Chickens: Postcolonial Studies of Technoscience', in Edward J. Hackett, Olga Amsterdamska, Michael Lynch and Judy Wajcman (eds), *The Handbook of Science and Technology Studies, Third Ed*, Cambridge, MA: Massachusetts Institute of Technology, 2007; Sandra Harding, *Is Science Multicultural? Postcolonialisms, Feminisms, and Epistemologies*, Bloomington: Indiana University Press, 1998; and Sandra Harding (ed), *Science and Technology Beyond Postcolonial Theory*, forthcoming.

11 David Hess, *Alternative Pathways in Science and Industry: Activism, Innovation, and the Environment in an Era of Globalization*, Cambridge, MA: MIT Press, 2007. Hess refers to this process as the 'primitive epistemic accumulation' of early modern Europe.

12 Steven J Harris, 'Long-Distance Corporations and the Geography of Natural Knowledge,' Configurations, 6(2), 1998, pp 269–304; J M Blaut, *The Colonizer's Model of the World: Geographical Diffusionism and Eurocentric History*, New York: Guilford Press, 1993.

13 Catherine A Odora Hoppers (ed), *Indigenous Knowledge and the Integration of Knowledge Systems*, Claremont, South Africa: New Africa Books, 2002; Selin, *Encyclopedia*.

14 Joan Kelly-Gadol, 'The Social Relations of the Sexes: Methodological Implications of a Women's History', *Signs: Journal of Women in Culture and Society*, 1(4), 1976, pp 810–823; Carole Pateman, *The Sexual Contract*, Palo Alto, CA: Stanford University Press, 1988.

15 Kelly-Gadol, 'The Social Relations'.

16 Keller, *Reflections on Gender*; Elizabeth Potter, *Gender and Boyle's Law of Gases*, Bloomington: Indiana University Press, 2001; Sharon Traweek, *Beamtimes and Life Times*, Cambridge, MA: MIT Press, 1988.

17 Susantha Goonatilake, *Toward a Global Science: Mining Civilizational Knowledge*, Bloomington: Indiana University Press, 1998; Hess, *Science and Technology*; Hess, *Alternative Pathways*; Hoppers, *Indigenous Knowledge*; Laura Nader (ed), *Naked Science: Anthropological Inquiry into Boundaries, Power, and Knowledge*, New York: Routledge, 1996; Third World Network, *Modern Science*.

18 Donna Haraway, *Primate Visions*; Donna Haraway, 'Situated Knowledges: The Science Question in Feminism and the Privilege of Partial Perspectives,' in *Simians, Cyborgs, and Women*, New York: Routledge, 1991.

19 Vandana Shiva, *Staying Alive*; Vandana Shiva, *Monocultures of the Mind*.

20 I am focused here on existing literatures that engage feminist postcolonial science and technology issues. Another route into identifying such issues is to look at the literatures that do address feminist postcolonialism and tease out where the science and technology issues are hinted at or should appear. This kind of process is what led me to insist on the importance to feminist STS of the women in development literatures and their successors mentioned below. For three differently valuable attempts to construct either feminist genealogies of postcolonialism or genealogies of feminist postcolonialism, none of which directly address science and technology issues (though epistemological concerns are often visible), see Reina Lewis and Sara Mills (eds), *Feminist Postcolonial Theory: A Reader*,

New York: Routledge, 2003; Rajeswari Sunder Rajan and You-me Park, 'Postcolonial Feminism/Postcolonialism and Feminism,' in Henry Schwarz and Sangeeta Ray (eds), *A Companion to Postcolonial Studies*, Oxford: Blackwell, 2000; Robert J C Young, *Postcolonialism: An Historical Introduction*, Oxford: Blackwell, 2001, Chapter 25.

21 Steven J Harris, 'Jesuit Scientific Activity in the Overseas Missions, 1540–1773', *Isis*, 96, 2005, pp 71–79, 77–78.

22 Schiebinger, 'Prospecting for Drugs'.

23 Schiebinger, *Nature's Body*.

24 Mark Harrison, 'Science and the British Empire', *Isis*, 96, 2005, pp 56–63, 59; Nancy Stepan, 'Race and Gender', *Isis*, 77, 1986, pp 261–277.

25 Jorge Canizares-Esguerra, 'Iberian Colonial Science', *Isis*, 96, 2005, pp 64–70.

26 Mary Terrall, 'Heroic Narratives of Quest and Discovery', *Configurations*, 6(2), 1998, pp 223–242.

27 Elizabeth Rhodes, 'Join the Jesuits, See the World: Early Modern Women in Spain and the Society of Jesus', in John W O'Malley, Gauvin Alexander Bailey, Steven J Harris and T Frank Kennedy (eds), *The Jesuits, II: Cultures, Sciences, and the Arts, 1540–1773*, Toronto: University of Toronto Press, 2005; reported in Harris, 'Jesuit Scientific Activity'.

28 Traweek, *Beamtimes and Life Times*.

29 Haraway, *Primate Visions*.

30 Harris, 'Jesuit Scientific Activity'.

31 Rita Felski, *The Gender of Modernity*, Cambridge, MA: Harvard University Press, 1995; Sandra Harding, *Sciences from Below: Feminisms, Postcolonialities, and Modernities*, Durham, NC: Duke University Press, 2008; Alice Jardine, *Gynesis: Configurations of Woman and Modernity*, Ithaca, NY: Cornell University Press, 1985; Catherine V Scott, *Gender and Development: Rethinking Modernization and Dependency Theory*, Boulder, CO: Lynne Rienner Publishers, 1995.

32 Felski, *The Gender of Modernity*; Harding, *Sciences from Below*; Jardine, *Gynesis*; Scott, *Gender and Development*.

33 Ester Boserup, *Women's Role in Economic Development*, New York: St Martin's Press, 1970.

34 Rosi Braidotti, Ewa Charkiewicz, Sabine Hausler and Saskia Wieringa, *Women, the Environment, and Sustainable Development*, Atlantic Highlands, NJ: Zed Books, 1994; Irene Tinker, 'The Making of a Field: Advocates, Practitioners and Scholars,' in Irene Tinker (ed), *Persistent Inequalities: Women and Development*, Oxford: Oxford University Press, 1990; Nalini Visvanathan, Lynn Duggan, Laurie Nisonoff and Nan Wiegersma (eds), *The Women, Gender and Development Reader*, London: Zed Books, 1997; see also Joni Seager, *Earth Follies: Coming to Feminist Terms with the Global Environmental Crisis*, New York: Routledge, 1993; Joni Seager, 'Rachel Carson Died of Breast Cancer: The Coming of Age of Feminist Environmentalism', *Signs: Journal of Women in Culture and Society*, 28(3), 2003, pp 945–972.

35 Maria Mies, *Patriarchy and Accumulation on a World Scale: Women in the International Division of Labor*, Atlantic Highlands, NJ: Zed Books, 1986.

36 Braidotti, Charkiewicz, Hausler and Wieringa, *Women, the Environment, and Sustainable Development*; Seager, *Earth Follies*.

37 Sandra Harding (ed), *The Feminist Standpoint Theory Reader*, New York: Routledge, 2004.

38 Dorothy E Smith, *The Conceptual Practices of Power: A Feminist Sociology of Knowledge*, Boston: Northeastern University Press, 1990; Dorothy E Smith, *Institutional Ethnography: A Sociology for People*, Lanham, MD: Rowman and Littlefield, 2005.

39 But see Smith, *Institutional Ethnography* for a critical ethnography.

40 Sandra Harding, 'Introduction: Standpoint Theory as a Site of Political, Philosophic, and Scientific Debate', in Sandra Harding (ed), *The Feminist Standpoint Theory Reader*, New York: Routledge, 2004.

41 Fredric Jameson, '*History and Class Consciousness* as an "Unfinished Project"', *Rethinking Marxism*, 1(1), 1988, pp 49–72; Harding, *The Feminist Standpoint*.

42 Uma Narayan, 'The Project of a Feminist Epistemology: Perspectives from a Non-western Feminist', in Susan Bordo and Alison Jaggar (eds), *Gender/Body/Knowledge*, New Brunswick, NJ: Rutgers University Press, 1989; Walter D Mignolo, *The Darker Side of the Renaissance: Literacy, Territoriality and Colonization*, Ann Arbor: University of Michigan Press, 1995; Walter D Mignolo, *Local Histories/Global Designs*, Princeton: Princeton University Press, 2000.

43 S N Eisenstadt and Wolfgang Schluchter (eds), 'Early Modernities', Special Issue, *Daedalus*, 127(3), 1998; S N Eisenstadt (ed), 'Multiple Modernities,' Special Issue, Daedalus 129(1), 2000, see especially 'Multiple Modernities,' pp 1–30; Third World Network, 'Modern Science in Crisis'.

44 Sandra Harding, *Sciences From Below*, Durham: Duke University Press, 2008.

45 Samir Amin, *Delinking: Towards a Polycentric World*, New York: Zed Books, 1990. Third World Network, 'Modern Science in Crisis'.

46 Catherine V Scott, *Gender and Development*.

47 Goonatilake, *Toward a Global Science*.

48 Dipesh Chakrabarty, *Provincializing Europe: Postcolonial Thought and Historical Difference*, Princeton: Princeton University Press, 2000; Mignolo, *Local Histories*.

49 There are dozens of collections of essays seeking to establish the legitimacy of some particular kind of genealogy of postcolonialism. For a comprehensive collection containing excerpts from many of the 'classic' analyses, see the five volumes of Diana Brydon (ed), *Postcolonialism: Critical Concepts in Literary and Cultural Studies*, vols I–V, New York: Routledge, 2000. There are also many anthologies and review essays

Sandra Harding

debating the origins, nature, and future of such debates and tensions. For three sources of the many illuminating discussions about the usefulness and desirable domains of the concept of postcolonialism, see David Theo Goldberg and Ato Quayson (eds), *Relocating Postcolonialism*, New York: Blackwell, 2002; Ania Loomba, Suvir Kaul, Antoinette Burton and Jed Esty (eds), *Postcolonial Studies and Beyond*, Durham, NC: Duke University Press, 2005; and early issues of *Postcolonial Studies* (1998ff).

50 Chandra Talpade Mohanty, 'Under Western Eyes: Feminist Scholarship and Colonial Discourses,' in Chandra Talpade Mohanty, Ann Russo and Lourdes Torres (eds), *Third World Women and the Politics of Feminism*, Bloomington: Indiana University Press, 1991; Gayatri Spivak, 'French Feminism in an International Frame', in her *In Other Worlds*, New York: Routledge, 1987.

51 Oyeronke Oyewumi, *The Invention of Women: Making an African Sense of Western Gender Discourses*, Minneapolis: University of Minnesota Press, 1997.

52 See, for example, Anne Fausto-Sterling, 'The Bare Bones of Sex: Sex and Gender', *Signs: Journal of Women in Culture and Society*, 30(2), 2005, pp 1491–1528; Evelyn Fox Keller, *The Mirage of a Space between Nature and Nurture*, Durham: Duke University Press, 2009.

53 Chakrabarty, *Provincializing Europe*.

33 The Myth of Isolates

Ecosystem Ecologies in the Nuclear Pacific

Elizabeth M. DeLoughrey

The Age of Ecology began on the desert outside Alamogordo, New Mexico on July 16, 1945, with a dazzling fireball of light and a swelling mushroom cloud of radioactive gases.

– Donald Worster, *Nature's Economy*[1]

Laboratories generate so many new objects because they are able to create extreme conditions and because each of these actions is obsessively inscribed.

– Bruno Latour, *Science in Action*[2]

While many scholars have explored the rise of ecological thought, few have traced the close relationship between the rise of the Age of Ecology and the Atomic Age, the multi-constitutive relationship between radioactive militarism and the study of the environment.[3] Donald Worster's foundational book *Nature's Economy* suggests that nuclear weapon fallout catalyzed public consciousness about the pollution of the environment, while others suggest that the planetary extent of this militarized radiation inspired the modern concept of globalism itself.[4] Worster's history of environmentalism gives us a vital starting point for assessing the paradox of how Cold War science was utilized to both destroy and conserve nature. Here I build upon his work to examine how American ecosystem ecology, one of the most influential models of environmental thought, was created by scientists funded by the Atomic Energy Commission (AEC), particularly in its surveys of the radioactive aftermath of its Pacific Island nuclear tests. American environmentalism and militarism are paradoxically and mutually imbricated, particularly in their construction of the isolate. Thus the ecosystem paradigm relies on the idea of a

Elizabeth M. DeLoughrey, "The Myth of Isolates: Ecosystem Ecologies in the Nuclear Pacific." *Cultural Geographies*, 20(12), 2012: 167–184. Reprinted by permission of SAGE.

closed system, a concept that was constituted by the island laboratory and the irradiated atoll and perpetuated by the aerial view utilized by AEC films to introduce US viewers to the newly acquired island territories in the Pacific Islands. As I will explain, the production of the myth of the biological and geographical isolate has ethical implications, contributing as it did to the AEC's justifications for human radiation experiments on Marshall Islanders for 40 decades.[5]

In 1947, David Lilienthal, head of the AEC, declared that '[t]he atom is center of reality at council tables ... all over the world. No nation in the world can make decisions these days without thinking of the atom.'[6] While a mere five atomic weapons had been detonated on earth by then, new uses of the atom were creating dramatic political, scientific, and environmental changes. Since the end of the First World War, nuclear physics grew exponentially; by the 1940s the field was being cultivated by the enormous budgets of the Manhattan Project (1942–46) and the Atomic Energy Commission (1946–74). Although it is not often recognized, these political shifts made a remarkable impact on studies of the environment, a field that was initially considered a 'soft' science consisting of 'butterfly chasers'[7] until it began to engage with a 'big science' like physics. While nuclear physicists focus on the subatomic and inanimate world, and ecologists privilege observable and living matter, the 20th-century crisis of nuclear fallout brought these disparate fields together. This is remarkable because the new field of quantum physics determined that the subatomic world was not legible if one used the models and laws of classical matter. So while an emergent quantum physics was breaking away from its roots in natural history (*physis* means nature), ecologists sought to bring the fields together by using two key concepts: the island isolate and the flow of energy. Both research concepts grew out of an unprecedented era of US militarization, sustained and often funded by the AEC.

The concept of the island or isolate was vital to ecosystem ecology from the very beginning. In popularizing the new term 'ecosystem' in 1935, the botanist Alfred George Tansley drew from the field of physics to describe the relationship between organisms and their habitat, arguing that one might conceptually isolate ecosystems as a model to study 'the universe as a whole down to the atom.'[8] He explained: 'The point is to isolate ecosystems mentally for the purposes of study so that the series of *isolates* we make become the actual objects of our study, whether the isolate be a solar system, a planet ... or an atom. The isolation is partially artificial, but it is the only possible way we can proceed.'[9] Key to this new conceptual rubric was the theme of isolation, a model that had been deployed in the 19th century to propose the theory of evolution, and which re-energized the longstanding colonial understanding of the island as a laboratory.[10] Tansley's invocation of the atom as a synecdoche for ecosystem ecology was prescient: in less than 20 years, the American militarization of science would usher in a new era of ecological thought drawn from the notion of isolated landscapes permeated with nuclear radiation.

Ecosystem Ecology

The theoretical connections made between physics and ecology were largely attributed to AEC-funded research during the Cold War. Joel Hagen has traced out what he calls the 'symbiosis ... between atomic energy and ecosystem ecology,' particularly as it was organized by brothers Eugene and Howard (Tom) Odum, the field's 'founding father(s)'[11] It is important to note, as do Chunglin Kwa and Stephen Bocking, that it was not the AEC that pioneered this shift in ecological thought. Instead, the development of radiation ecology was due to public pressure on the agency to clean up its nuclear waste and to efforts by some AEC-funded scientists.[12] Global atmospheric levels of militarized radiation (fallout) were alarming the public to such an extent that the field of 'Health Physics' was created to determine the impact on human bodies,[13] and secret AEC projects such as Operation Sunshine were established to collect cadavers, fetuses, and human limbs from mortuaries around the world to measure radioactive traces in bone and tissue.[14] Like the Manhattan Project before it, the AEC was notoriously resistant to publically admitting any danger from nuclear tests. In fact, the military head of the Manhattan Project, Lieutenant General Leslie Groves, lied to a Special Senate Committee on Atomic Energy in 1945, testifying in the wake of the radiation deaths of Nagasaki and Hiroshima that 'they say it is a very pleasant way to die.'[15] This was counter to the ample evidence of gruesome radiation deaths from the radium dial painters of the 1920s, nuclear accidents in AEC laboratories, and the military's study of postatomic casualties in Japan.[16] Although the AEC's stance was to publically deny any human or environmental impact from the nuclear tests, as early as 1952, two years before the first thermonuclear weapon, the head of Brookhaven Laboratory's Health Physics Division admitted that 'the days of undisturbed natural background (radiation) are gone perhaps forever, as a result of the continuing detonations of atomic bombs.'[17]

With the rapid expansion of nuclear testing in the Cold War and the subsequent radiological contamination of the planet, the AEC contracted a number of biologists to study the radioactive fallout from the newly acquired American territories in the Marshall Islands (Micronesia).[18] Appropriated under the unprecedented concept of a US-Navy controlled 'Trust Territory' (Article 82 under the UN Charter), Micronesia became a nuclear colony under President Truman's doctrine of oceanic colonialism. Thus at the start of the Cold War the US enacted a state of exception to appropriate an enormous portion of the Pacific to detonate hundreds of deadly weapons, rationalized by the misconception of island isolation. Of course, the radioactive by-products of these weapons were never contained to a presumably isolated atoll and were distributed globally.[19] In claiming Micronesia and expanding the American exclusive economic zone, Truman tripled the territorial size of the United States.[20] Although the land-base of Micronesia is 846 square miles, the oceanic territory, vital to US naval and airforce transit, represents three million square miles.[21] By 1946, the AEC began relocating islanders in order to detonate atomic and hydrogen weapons in the atolls, turning the Marshall Islands into a 'Proving Ground.' With the advent of the far more powerful hydrogen weapons, the AEC in 1954 cordoned off an enormous area of the Pacific, banning the passage of ships or planes for 400,000 square miles.[22] This was in direct contradiction to the international law principle of freedom of the seas, which stipulated unrestricted international access for navigation, fisheries, submarine cables, and flight above the high seas.[23]

Eugene and Howard Odum were sent to Enewetak Atoll in 1955, and thus the field of what they termed 'radiation ecology' began in the Pacific with their study of a chain of islands that functioned as an AEC laboratory for nearly 50 nuclear weapons tests between 1948–58. So irradiated was the marine life in Bikini Atoll that the fish produced auto-radiographs; impressing their own images onto photographic plates and film.[24] By the time the Odums arrived for their six-week study, 18 nuclear weapons had been detonated at Enewetak and Bikini Atolls. This began with Operation Crossroads, tests *Able* and *Baker* at Bikini Atoll in 1946, weapons that so irradiated the islands that the Bikinians, originally asked to vacate for a few weeks, were permanently displaced from their homeland. The extensive radioactive fallout from the *Baker* shot became a scandal and caused President Truman to cancel the third test of the operation. According to Paul Boyer, 'it was Bikini, rather than Hiroshima and Nagasaki, which first brought the issue of radioactivity compellingly to the nation's consciousness.'[25] Operation Sandstone was staged in 1948 and Operation Greenhouse, a series of four nuclear explosions, was executed in 1951. Richard Grove has argued that Europeans utilized their tropical island colonies as botanical laboratories or greenhouses for experiments in transplantation and hybridization.[26] The name of this 1951 operation overtly labeled the islands as a contained ecological space, a 'greenhouse' for experiments in nature/physics. Ironically, AEC films of these test areas demonstrate that the islands are denuded of botanical life; they are paved over for military transport and anything but green.

The Odums arrived shortly after Operation Ivy, another naturalizing and 'green' title for deadly experiments in nature/physics. This important test was known for the world's first thermonuclear (hydrogen weapon) explosion called *Mike*, a 12-megaton device that produced a mushroom cloud 25 miles high and 100 miles wide. *Mike* blew the island of Elugelab out of existence, leaving a 6200 foot wide crater, giving new meaning to the term 'zero-island'. In the words of the AEC film *Operation Ivy*, 'in the early months, Elugelab was just another small naked island of the atoll but by midsummer, it began to look like the thing it was selected for: a shot island.'[27] As such, the repeated production of island craters suggests the AEC's nuclear testing program was dependent on an island laboratory that then became its opposite. In the words of E.B. White in *The New Yorker*, the 'laboratory was a paradise' and they conducted 'an experiment in befouling the laboratory itself.'[28]

The most controversial test of all, the reason why the AEC started to increase its funding to the field of radioecology, was Operation CASTLE, a series of six nuclear explosions at Enewetak and Bikini Atolls in 1954 that featured the notorious 15-megaton thermonuclear weapon *Bravo*, which left a crater (or 'anti-island') 6500 feet wide and 250 feet deep. Hydrogen weapons are some of the radioactively 'dirtiest' of nuclear devices due to their outercasing of uranium^{238}, which has a half-life of over 200,000 years.[29] As is well documented, *Bravo* covered the surrounding islands with radioactive strontium, cesium, and iodine, and became an ecological and political relations disaster. In addition to exposing a Japanese fishing vessel to lethal levels of radiation that killed its crew and created a transpacific ban on consuming fish, *Bravo's* fallout exposed hundreds of Marshall Islanders to nuclear radiation, contributing to countless miscarriages, leukemia deaths, thyroid cancers, and the kind of chromosome damage that knows no temporal or genealogical limit. It covered the neighboring island of Rongelap with radioactive 'snow' and permanently displaced its residents due to continuing lethal levels of cesium^{137}, even 40 years later.[30] The 1954 Petition from the Marshallese People Concerning the Pacific Islands: Complaint Regarding Explosions of Lethal Weapons within Our Home Islands, an 'urgent plea' to the UN to cease the tests due to extreme radiogenic illness and land displacement, went unheeded.[31]

In the clinical words of the AEC film *Operation Castle*: 'These islands, functioning as *accidental total fallout collectors*, gave us our first real clues to the vast area affected by contamination from a high yield surface burst.'[32]

Estimated at one thousand times the force of the bombs dropped on Hiroshima and Nagasaki, *Bravo* has been called the worst radiological disaster in history. In addition to spreading lethal levels of radiation over 5000 miles of the Pacific,[33] *Bravo*'s fallout was detected in the rain over Japan, in lubricating oil of Indian aircraft, in winds over Australia, and in the sky over the United States and Europe.[34] It caused the radiogenic illness of the crew of a Japanese freighter 1200 miles away.[35] Designed as a weapon of radiological warfare, *Bravo* catalyzed a worldwide out-cry against the H-bomb and forced the AEC to more thoroughly assess the radiation impact of its weapons testing program.[36] In the antinuclear activism that followed, the militarized island became configured as a synecdoche for the world. The irradiated atoll, as an 'anti-island' or 'zero-island,' became a catalyst and signifier for a global consciousness about an increasingly militarized planet.[37]

Western colonizers had long configured tropical islands into the contained spaces of a laboratory, which is to say a suppression of island history and indigenous presence. This generation of AEC ecologists embraced nuclear testing as creating a novel opportunity to study a complete eco-system through the trace of radiation. As the Odums remarked, '[s]ince nuclear explosion tests are being conducted in the vicinity of these inherently stable reef communities, *a unique opportunity* is provided for critical assays of the effects of radiations due to fission products *on whole populations and entire ecological systems* in the field.'[38] Although Enewetak and Bikini were already heavily irradiated, the Odums injected additional radioactive isotopes in order to study ecological metabolism. While it seems paradoxical for ecologists to celebrate the 'opportunities' provided by irradiated landscapes and displaced peoples, Frank Benjamin Golley, one of Odum's colleagues, remarks that they all 'seemed oblivious to the connection between ecosystem research and the military activity of the U.S.'[39]

Of course, AEC-funded ecologists were also studying the radioactive impact of non-island sites, such as nuclear power plants, nuclear dumps, and the impact of weapons tests in the continental US.[40] Yet I want to underline the importance of the island as isolate as a conceptual rubric as vital to a historical moment that brought together newly acquired island territories, the development of ecosystem concepts of closed space, and nuclear militarism that relegated these islands to laboratories. Understood as a 'landmark in ecological research,'[41] the Odums' work on the irradia-tion of Enewetak's coral reefs provided ecologists with a model of a structured, self-regulating ecosystem and the first theorization of shared resource relationships in nature, which they termed 'mutualism.'[42] As such, systems ecology emerged from the field of 'radiation ecology' in the Pacific Islands.[43] The concept of the closed system or isolate was tied closely to the colonization of islands and rendering them into nuclear laboratories. After researching in Enewetak and publishing about what he termed the 'strontium ecosystem,' Howard Odum coordinated a research grant from the AEC to irradiate El Verde, a tropical rainforest in Puerto Rico, which killed various plants, trees, animals and birds. Describing a project that irradiated the forest with cesium[137] and strontium[85], Odum, senior researcher at the University of Puerto Rico's AEC-run Nuclear Center, concluded that the El Verde forest was an ideal 'teaching laboratory.'[44] Ironically, one of the major catalysts for the study was the discovery in 1962 of high fallout levels in the El Verde mountains from the atmospheric testing of nuclear weapons in the Pacific Islands.[45] As such, their model of the ecological or biological isolate was already rendered a fabrication by the global distribution of militarized radioactive fallout.

An American empire of tropical islands, circling the globe from the Pacific to the Caribbean, became a strategic space for military experimentation and the production of new scientific epistemologies like ecosystem theory. The militarization of the atom created the new availability of radioactive isotopes, allowing the Odums and their contemporaries to study nuclear fallout and waste sites as well as to introduce radioactive tracers into the environment to determine how energy was transformed in a presumably contained system. By comparing Enewetak and Puerto Rico, Howard Odum hoped to use the concept of *energy* as a 'universal principle' of any ecosystem.[46] Thus, ecosystem theory encodes a tension between the ways in which the island is thought to contain and concentrate space, and the concept of energy, which is understood in relation to mobility and transmission. The AEC's support of ecosystem ecology must be considered influential to 20th-century theories of energy and space, particularly when we consider the islands that were subjected to Cold War irradiation. This is how Howard Odum came to conclude that 'ecological and bio-chemical cycles' are 'driven by radiant energy.'[47] It seems no coincidence that the enormous energy released by the splitting of the nucleus of an atom suddenly became a universal framework for understanding any isolated system. As Chunglin Kwa argues, the Odums hoped that this model of how energy moves between elements of nature would 'revolutionize' ecology.[48] Since to revolutionize is to break from institutional models rather than to assimilate them into the nuclear politics of the military state, one could not really say the Odums' work 'revolutionized' ecology, but it certainly catalyzed remarkable institutional expansion. AEC-funded research laboratories and over 50 programs in radiation ecology (radioecology) were organized in universities and at nuclear power sites all over the United States, creating what Golley terms an 'invisible college'[49] and catapulting ecosystem ecology into a veritable institution.[50]

From our contemporary viewpoint, the ecologists' obliviousness to the militarization of their research may seem incredulous. Yet this militarization of space also permeated the language of ecosystem ecology. For instance, Eugene Odum's 1957 article, 'Ecology and the Atomic Age,' argued that:

> science advances on a *broad front* … It is analogous to the advance *of an army*; a breakthrough may occur anywhere, and when one does it will not *penetrate* far until the *whole front* moves up. Thus, ecologists need not feel bashful about *attacking ecosystems* so long as they observe the rules of good science.[51]

Although Eugene Odum is considered an inspiration to the environmental movement because his theories integrated humans into natural systems,[52] his Cold War writing demonstrates the mutual permeability of the militarization of the island laboratory, science, and the language of ecosystems. In bracketing off ethics in this war for knowledge, Odum's model of the ecosystem positions laboratory space outside of history (i.e. human presence) and accountability, encouraging scientists to 'attack' environments already devastated by nuclearization. This grammar of assault is possible because of an American empire sustained by the concept of an isolated and ultimately disposable laboratory, at once conceptually isolated from indigenous presence and yet, as recent research demonstrates, also demanding human subjects for experimentation.

Visualizing the Laboratory

I would like to turn to how islands were conceived by their continental visitors in order to tease out this relationship between the concept of the laboratory and the ecosystem. Since ecosystem ecology is modeled on the concept of a closed system, it is no coincidence that island colonies were chosen for nuclear tests and their radioactive surveys. While often deemed peripheral to modernity, we know that islands have in fact been at the center of the development of modern ecological thought. As I mentioned, historian Richard Grove has demonstrated how tropical island colonies all over the globe served as vital laboratories and spaces of social, botanical, and industrial experiment in ways that informed 17th- and 18th-century modernity and the conservation movement that followed. I would like to propose a similar relationship between the militarized American island colonies of Micronesia and their constitution of atomic modernity and the field of ecosystem ecology.

Just as the AEC manipulated landscapes in an era of what Ward Churchill calls 'radioactive colonialism,' the new field of ecosystem ecology emphasized the management of the environment in a way that could be extended to social relations.[53] Thus, the ecosystem is based on the concepts of the closed system, stabilization, and control. In the words of historian Gregg Mitman:

> Ecology not only appropriated military funds, it also appropriated the cybernetics narrative that emerged from military research on aircraft-missile guidance systems. The ecosystem blurred the distinction between inorganic and organic by reducing everything to energy as the common denominator. Nature had become a system of components that could be managed, manipulated, and controlled.[54]

Part of this process of communicating the significance of the newly acquired Pacific territories to the average continental American was through film, particularly the use of an aerial view that demonstrated how the island could be 'managed, manipulated, and controlled.' The conversion of populated islands into ahistorical laboratories of radiological experiment is particularly visible in AEC films of the 1950s, newsreels that were released to American audiences that utilized aerial surveillance as vital to the scientific and military control of the Marshall Island atolls. While some have argued that the development of the 20th-century aerial view could lead to a new transnational consciousness and to the blurring of the boundaries between nations, Gillian Beer points out that the aerial view of an island reinscribes the concept of boundedness, since 'centrality is emphasized and the enclosure of land within surrounding shores is the controlling meaning.'[55]

Elsewhere I have argued that the production of the isolated island requires the erasure of the technologies that enable mobility. In other words, this concept of isolation suppresses the ships and airplanes that make travel to islands possible.[56] Thus, the tropical island is configured as distant and isolated even as it becomes accessible – through print, photography, or film – to the reader/viewer. With the democratization of air travel in the mid-20th century, the vision of islands shifted from a 'deck-eye' view of an arrivant ship to an aerial view. The US military films of Micronesia excessively employ an aerial view that renders the atolls into a panopticon, thus domesticating (and destroying) new territories for the consumption of the American public. For instance, in the film *Operation Greenhouse* (1951), the AEC employs an aerial view to juxtapose the modernity of American science – the master lab at Los Alamos – against the purportedly ahistorical and depopulated Marshall Islands, which are viewed with detachment from a military plane. As such, modernity is seen to be exported from the US to 'distant and primitive' yet vitally important 'test islands … a giant lab in the middle of an ocean.' To quote from this Hollywood-produced film:

> One of the proving grounds is an outdoor laboratory: Enewetak Atoll in the Pacific. This Trust Territory of the United States has been used before as a testing ground for Operation Sandstone (1948). But three years have passed, three years to bring new and improved atomic weapons to this secluded equatorial land … Since Enewetak is a distant and primitive area, men have to leave their stateside laboratories and homes for a period of months. [*Image of an American man with suitcase entering his car and waving goodbye to son and dog*]. Now the proving grounds come alive like a university campus when students return from a summer holiday … [*aerial view of islands from military plane*] these are the dormitories of 'Enewetak university' … individual test islands, seemingly like so many science buildings on college grounds.[57]

In its persistent references to flight and aerial images of the islands, this film harnesses what Denis Cosgrove has termed the 'Apollonian eye', a gaze that is 'synoptic and omniscient, intellectually detached'[58] as it surveys a colonial island laboratory and presents it as an extension of the long reach of the arm of the US Air Force. As Cosgrove and Fox point out, 'widespread familiarity with the aerial view in the postwar years came not only from actual flights, but also – for most people – from photographs … newsreels and movies.'[59]

It is no coincidence that the first inter-continental ballistic missile (ICBM) developed in subsequent years was called Atlas; as Cosgrove has demonstrated, aerial vision has long been tied to conceptualizations of the globe and often to territorial claims over it.[60] The airplane radically changed the perception of space and time, producing an 'aerial subjectivity',[61] a cosmic view or aerial gaze born out of colonial mapping practices and tied to the often violent geopolitics of knowledge accumulation.[62] 'The airman's vision evolved into a powerful trope not only for military strategy … but also for political shaping of the postwar global order.'[63] This was particularly important for the large oceanic spaces of the Pacific, which were visualized aerially in US military films. Released in 1951, *Operation Greenhouse* predates the *Apollo* space mission photographs of the earth (1969–71) so a photographic global vision was not yet possible. However it is prefigured in these US military surveillance films in which the island is a world, a microcosm of the potential global destruction that would be unleashed should this nuclear warfare be expanded to other targets outside the Pacific Island colonies.[64]

While 'vision has been the privileged sense in Western science' for centuries[65] it was through airplane technologies since WWI that new ideas of space, vision, photography, and patriotic nationalism came together.[66] Flight and cinematic photography emerged nearly simultaneously and are constitutive of modern war.[67] Ernst Junger has argued that 'war making and picture taking are congruent.'[68] That was certainly the case in the Pacific Proving Grounds, where the 1946 Operation Crossroads test at Bikini Atoll was recorded by 1,500,000 feet of film and over 1 million still pictures.[69] Paul Virilio has argued that 'if you can see a target you can destroy it'[70] and this seems to be confirmed by the US nuclear tests in the Marshall Islands, where islands become, in Godfrey Baldacchino's words, 'tabulae rasae, potential labs for any conceivable human project.'[71] As Baldacchino and others have argued, the Pacific Islands have long been fashioned as laboratories for western colonial interests, from the botanical collecting of James Cook's voyages to Darwin's theories of evolution to structural anthropology.[72] In the words of one historian, 'the Pacific and its peoples were both a *laboratory* for the study of human prehistory and a major *testing ground* for Enlightenment and subsequent science.'[73]

Ecosystems ecology drew from the grammar of the AEC and its nuclear tests and therefore it is not surprising that it focused on energy as a universal means of exchange and that it upheld the concept of isolated spaces. While the film *Operation Greenhouse* juxtaposes the complex laboratories and lives of Los Alamos with the depopulated and defoliated Enewetak Atoll in ways that emphasize that they are bringing 'new and improved atomic weapons to this equatorial land' – that is to say civilization to the savages, an old colonial trope – we see the ways in which space is not, as Johannes Fabian might say, coeval.[74] In this narrative, modernity emanates from the US colonial center, visible in the way in which the camera lingers on the uniformed officers, airplanes, and laboratory space, and is being imported to the tropical island, bereft of history and indigenous inhabitants. Thus it produces a paradox, a 'distant and primitive area' yet at the same time a place of 'individual test islands' much like the 'science buildings on college grounds.' In positioning Los Alamos as a 'modern pueblo' as much as an 'atomic city' and 'isolated mesa,' the film *Operation Greenhouse* unwittingly suggests the ways in which indigenous appropriation and erasure in both the American west and its new frontier, the Marshall Islands, are constitutive in visualizing and creating the concept of the isolated laboratory.

Rethinking the ways in which science used the isolated island concept to produce some of the most apocalyptic technologies on earth challenges both the assumption of the primitive ahistorical island and what constitutes the laboratory itself. For instance, David Livingstone's *Putting Science in its Place* argues that there are four distinct spaces of science: The space of manipulation (the lab); the space of expedition (the field); the space of presentation (museum); and the space of circulation (the archive).[75] *Operation Greenhouse* suggests that these spaces were condensed in the Pacific Proving Grounds. The space of masculine expedition, signaled in the film by the Los Alamos scientist leaving his boy and dog to travel to the Pacific, is not a field so much as 'a giant lab in the middle of an ocean.' The excessive photographic documentation of the Pacific nuclear tests, where the high speed camera and color film were developed, suggests that the 'field' is also the space of presentation and of circulation, in which one tropical island stands in for the next, a virtual archive of nuclear irradiation, and a virtual island laboratory. Yet the visual production of nuclearization has amnesic effects. This is precisely the structure of erasure theorized by Teresia Teaiwa about how extreme visibility, evidenced in the ways in which the bikini bathing suit emerged from nuclear colonialism and suppressed the histories of 's/pacific' islands.[76]

Metaphoric Displacement

Teaiwa's groundbreaking work on the historical and semantic production of the radiation-prone bikini helps us understand the function of 'objectification through excessive visibility,'[77] a process of erasure that is fundamentally tropological. As a form of trope, metaphor moves from one object to another – in this case, island to laboratory – in a way that foregrounds resemblance and renders what might be invisible visible.[78] But metaphor is equally about displacement, subsuming other possible modes of relation between objects and suppressing the ways in which the island is not a laboratory and vice versa.[79] Metaphor is how nonhuman nature is rendered knowable and, following Girard Genette, the way that 'language spatializes itself' so that space becomes language and thus articulates itself to us.[80] Thus remote islands of the Pacific, for American viewers, become legible by likening them to island laboratories. This displaces the inhabitants of these islands who must be suppressed in order to naturalize the islands as nuclear testing zones and laboratories, bereft of human history. Thus in the AEC's aerial surveillance films, images of the Marshall Islanders have been removed, their housing and cemeteries plowed down. Even the foliage has been bulldozed 'for elbow room' as one AEC film declares, fashioning a laboratory and also a tropical playground for soldiers to play volleyball and sunbathe.[81] Marshall Islanders rarely appear in these films, except a brief appearance of displaced Bikinians where the narrator declares, 'the islanders are a nomadic group, and are well pleased that the Yanks are going to add a little variety to their lives.'[82] Generally speaking, the human subjects who appear in these films are American scientists at work with instruments, generals explaining military exercises to the audience, and servicemen – future Atomic Veterans – at leisure on the beach. Such images anticipate Teaiwa's theorization of what she terms 'militourism,' the mutual constitution of the tourist and military industry in the Pacific Islands.[83] In erasing the presence of the islanders, AEC newsreels instead celebrate the collection of scientific data, the nuclear yield, and the size of craters or 'zero islands' left behind. Employing an Apollonian eye, the films encourage the US audience to become vicarious masters of all they surveyed, inscribing a new era of empire.

Native Pacific Studies has long emphasized a horizontal view produced from the centrally located voyaging canoe, in which the islands, ocean and stars are seen to move towards the voyager.[84] Vicente Diaz's theorization of the 'moving island' foregrounds the dynamism of animate space, a place from which we might glean the 'currents' of militarization 'across spatial and temporal boundaries,' to borrow from Setsu Shigematsu and Keith Camacho.[85] In contrast, the aerial gaze of these AEC films displaces horizontal island stories – the complex social and historical relations between the islands, the creation of nuclear nomads and the political legacies of the displacement, as well as the history of the AEC's collection of the islanders' biomaterial without consent for decades after the tests. The island as laboratory metaphor – and the aerial gaze – displace the most criminally and ethically negligent results of these 67 nuclear tests in the Marshall Islands, such as the occupation and contamination of the environments and people of the western Pacific and the denial of their well-being by a Cold War superpower that held them 'in trust,' as assured under UN Article 73. Moreover, the AEC medical experiments conducted on the Marshallese are in violation of the 1949 Geneva Convention and the 1998 Rome Statute of the International Criminal Court.[86]

The recent work of Barbara Rose Johnston and Holly Barker has brought to light disturbing evidence that suggests intentionality of radiation exposure. For instance, the Rongelap islanders had been relocated for previous nuclear tests but not for *Bravo*, even though this test was designed to spread radiation. The Rongelapese were covered in radioactive fallout and not evacuated for three days even though neighboring servicemen were removed within 24 hours. While the US had blamed the fallout on a last-minute weather change, recently declassified documents demonstrate that the Navy knew about the wind shift towards Rongelap hours before the nuclear test.[87] In the language of the AEC, the boundedness of this chain of islands was thought to allow the division of 'test' and 'control' groups to indicate radiation exposure, but as recent work demonstrates, all 28 Marshall Islands were seriously contaminated with fallout, not merely the four islands indicated by the AEC.[88] (In fact, one of the northern Marshall Islands has been declared by the AEC as uninhabitable for 25,000 years.)

The declassification of a 1957 memo from Brookhaven National Laboratory's medical researcher Dr Robert Conard, the doctor in charge of testing and caring for the hundreds of Marshallese exposed to radiation, has confirmed suspicions that it was the islanders as much as the environment that were subject to an AEC experiment. To his colleagues he wrote, 'The habitation of these people on the island will afford most valuable ecological radiation data on human beings.'[89] Arguments like this appear elsewhere in AEC records. For instance, the director of the AEC Health and Safely Laboratory described neighboring Utirik Atoll in 1956 as 'by far the most contaminated place in the world' but that it will be 'very interesting' to get data from the environment and islanders when they are returned there. Referring to genetic tests about the impact of radiation on fruit flies and mice, he observed of the Marshall Islanders: 'While it is true that these people do not live, I would say, the way Westerners do, civilized people, it is nevertheless also true that these people are more like us than mice.'[90] As Mbembe observes about the state of exception that characterizes the racism of colonial rule, 'in the eyes of the conqueror, *savage life* is just another form of *animal life*, a horrifying experience, something alien beyond imagination or comprehension.'[91]

Johnston and Barker's work not only brings to light how the Marshall Islands were used as living ecological laboratories but also documents that the Rongelapese were used for human subject research for four decades without their knowledge or consent.[92] From 1954 until their removal by Greenpeace from contaminated Rongelap in 1985, the islanders were studied by AEC scientists but not always treated and rarely informed about the nature of their illnesses. For instance, when the Rongelapese were first exposed to *Bravo* fallout, some with radioactive burns over 90 percent of their bodies and causing skin to peel down to the bone, they were not given pain medication.[93] With the declassification of the AEC's Project 4.1, 'Study of Response of Human Beings Exposed to Significant Beta and Gamma Radiation Due to Fallout from High Yield Weapons,' evidence has come forward that scientists collected blood, tissue, bone marrow and teeth samples for decades – extracting even perfectly healthy teeth – to measure bioaccumulation without consent.[94] When Rongelapese women began giving birth to babies without skulls and without skeletons ('jellyfish babies' and 'grape babies'), infants with severe brain damage and missing limbs, scientists informed them that these miscarriages and defects were 'to be expected in a small island population.'[95] Although scientists from the AEC Division of Biology and Medicine had ample evidence of the extensive radiological contamination of Rongelap, they allowed the islanders to return in order to deflect criticism of the AEC's atmospheric testing program, and thus exposed the islanders to another 22 nuclear tests on Enewetak and possibly to biological weapons tests.[96] Moreover, they did not warn against the consumption of certain plants, animals, and fish that bio-accumulate and concentrate deadly levels of cesium[137], strontium[90], and iodine[131], the most lethal isotopes to humans.[97]

Over the course of 67 nuclear tests, many of which were designed to spread deadly radioactive isotopes, the Marshall Islanders were exposed to over 8 *billion* curies of iodine-[131]. Comparatively, the Chernobyl accident, widely known as one of the world's worst radiological accidents, released 50 million curies.[98] Their return home exposed the Rongelapese to another three decades' worth of additional radiological contamination without ample medical treatment, except for annual visits from AEC director Robert Conard, which Barker and Johnston have shown were visits focused on sampling bones and tissues. Even more disturbingly, this population, perhaps the most radiogenically exposed and studied people on earth, was subjected to the injection of radioactive isotopes without their knowledge or consent.[99] Despite the excessive surveillance and documentation of their radiogenic illnesses, to this day the majority of affected islanders have been refused access to their medical records and have inadequate medical treatment. The Department of Energy Advisory Committee on Human Radiation Experiments concluded in reviewing this history 'that the AEC had an ethical imperative to take advantage of the unique opportunity posed by the fallout from *Bravo* to learn as much as possible about radiation effects in humans.' In light of this response we can understand why, as Linda Tuhiwai Smith observes, '"research" is probably one of the dirtiest words in the indigenous world's vocabulary.'[100]

After decades of suffering, the Rongelapese magistrate Nelson Anjain had this to say in an April 1975 letter to Conard:

> Your entire career is based on our illness. We are far more valuable to you than you are to us. You have never really cared about us as people – only as a group of guinea pigs for your government's bomb research effort. For me and for other people on Rongelap, it is life which matters most. For you it is facts and figures. There is no question about your technical competence, but we often wonder about your humanity ... We want medical care from doctors who care about us, not about collecting information for the US government's war makers ... America has been trying to Americanize us by flying flags and using cast-off textbooks. It's about time America gave us the kind of medical care it gives its own citizens ... We no longer want you to come to Rongelap.[101]

While ecosystem ecology did not catalyze the AEC's decision to detonate 67 nuclear weapons in the Marshall Islands and to study radiological data on humans, we must raise the vital question as to how, as a methodology and system of thought, it sustained the concept of isolation, despite all evidence to the contrary. Elsewhere AEC studies of the same era were experimenting with radioactive isotopes on indigenous peoples in the Amazon and Alaska based on a similar concept of the 'biologically discrete.'[102] This model of isolation perpetuates the neat division of 'test' and 'control' groups, and the presumed isolation of the Marshall Islands colonies from the continental US and its responsibility to the rule of law. As I have argued elsewhere, the colonial concept of island isolation has worked – to effectively – to suppress the ongoing history of military expansion and new forms of colonialism.[103]

Ecosystem ecology, with its emphasis on closed systems, management, control, and equilibrium, drew tremendous support in part because it was appealing to the military, which sought to expand its weapons testing program, and to industry, which began working with the AEC to capitalize on the opportunity to build more nuclear plants.[104] Although it was discarded as a scientific model in the 1960s for more dynamic approaches to the environment, as late as 1968 Glenn Seaborg, the Chairman of the AEC, had this to say in a press release:

> While Bikini is best known as a weapons testing site, it has also contributed significantly to man's knowledge of the long term effects of radiation on an environment. During the years when radiation levels were too high for people to live there permanently, the AEC sponsored several scientific studies on the atoll. In fact, Bikini truly served as a living ecological laboratory.[105]

Metaphor not only connects two disparate entities but validates and naturalizes this new relationship and thus is crucial to constructing new paradigms of knowledge.[106] This has not been lost on theorists of the lab such as Bruno Latour, who has long argued against the concept of the bounded laboratory, and Isabelle Stengers, who argues 'isolation is a dangerous game, and those who can purify their objects in fact intervene actively in the significance of the object they observe.'[107] Clifford Geertz has observed that the 'the natural laboratory notion has been ... pernicious, not only because the analogy is false' since parameters are always porous, but because the data is no more pure or fundamental.[108] In *Nuclear Playground*, Stewart Firth deconstructs the island laboratory metaphor, arguing

> [t]he nuclear bomb men have always assumed that atolls and deserts are a long way from anywhere. But they are wrong. Nuclear explosions in the atmosphere, which occurred frequently in the Pacific Islands between 1946 and 1975, were global in effect ... In preparing for war we were poisoning our planet and going into battle against nature itself.[109]

The lie of isolation has indeed been a dangerous game, to the Marshall Islanders especially, and beyond. Due to these thermonuclear weapons, the entire planet is permeated with militarized radiation. *Bravo* and the subsequent 2000 or so nuclear tests on this planet, Eileen Welsome observes, 'split the world into "preatomic" and "postatomic" species.'[110] Radioactive elements produced by these weapons were spread through the atmosphere, deposited into water supplies and soils, absorbed by plants and thus into the bone tissue of humans all over the globe. The body of every human on the planet now contains strontium[90], a man-made by product of nuclear detonations[111] and forensic scientists use the traces of militarized radioactive carbon in our teeth to date human remains (as before or after the 1954 *Bravo* shot).[112] At very conservative estimates, these nuclear weapons tests have produced 400,000 cancer deaths worldwide.[113]

There is a long history of using the myth of island isolation to mystify the extent of the military irradiation of the planet and to deflect from what many would suggest are human rights violations in the Marshall Islands. As a transoceanic culture, Pacific Islanders have not historically harbored a binary division between land and sea nor have they conceived of their islands, before colonialism, as peripheral to an American metropolitan center. With this horizontal view, we might say that many in the region might wish for *more* isolation from the United States and its expanding military (especially given the post 9/11 build-up in Hawai'i and Guam). The late anthropologist Epeli Hau'ofa has importantly argued against the colonial concept of isolated islands and brought our attention to a dynamic 'sea of islands' long connected by histories of migration, nuclear colonialism and globalization. A world of islands.[114] Thanks to their irradiation, we all carry a small piece of that island world in our bones.

Notes

1   D. Worster, *Nature's Economy: A History of Ecological Ideas*, 2nd ed. (Cambridge: Cambridge University Press, 1994), p. 339.

2   B. Latour, *Science in Action: How to Follow Scientists and Engineers through Society* (Cambridge, MA: Harvard University Press, 1987), p. 90.

3   In addition to Worster, vital contributions connecting the US rise of ecology with federal nuclear weapons programs include S. Bocking, M. Klingle, C. Kwa, F. Golley, J. Hagen, S. Kingsland, and S. Kirsch.

4   Worster, *Nature's Economy*, p. 339; E. DeLoughrey, 'Radiation Ecologies and the Wars of Light.' *Modern Fiction Studies* 55(3), 2009, pp. 468–495; J. Masco, 'Bad Weather: On Planetary Crisis.' *Social Studies of Science* 40(1), 2010, pp. 7–40.

5   This essay traces military developments under the jurisdiction of first the Manhattan Project (1942–46), then the Atomic Energy Commission (1946–74), and finally the US Department of Energy (1974–present).

6   Quoted in Daniel Lang, *From Hiroshima to the Moon* (New York: Simon and Schuster, 1959), p. 89.

7   S. Bocking, *Nature's Experts: Science, Politics, and the Environment* (New Brunswick, NJ: Rutgers University Press, 2004), p. 18.

8   A. Tansley, 'The Use and Abuse of Vegetational Concepts and Terms', in D. Keller and F. Golley (eds), *The Philosophy of Ecology* (Athens, GA: University of Georgia Press, 2000), p. 64.

9   Tansley, 'Vegetational Concepts', p. 64.

10 The concept of isolation has been vital to theories of ecology, evolution, and the laboratory. The works of Charles Darwin and Charles Lyell are famous for utilizing the concept of the biological isolate and this was developed by Robert MacArthur and Edward Wilson in their influential *The Theory of Island Biogeography* (Princeton, NJ: Princeton University Press, 1967). Recent work in island studies has called attention to and problematized the notion of the island isolate: see Richard Grove's *Green Imperialism: Colonial Expansion, Tropical Island Edens and the Origins of Environmentalism 1600–1860* (Cambridge: Cambridge University Press, 1995); Hau'ofa's 'Our Sea of Islands', in A. Dirlik and R. Wilson (eds), *Asia/Pacific as Space of Cultural Production* (Durham, NC: Duke University Press, 1995); and G. Baldacchino's 'Coming of Age of Island Studies', *Tijdschrift voor Economische en Sociale Geografie*, 95(3), 2004. This is further discussed in the introduction to E.M. DeLoughrey's *Routes and Roots: Navigating Caribbean and Pacific Island Literatures* (Honolulu, HI: University of Hawai'i Press, 2007).

11 J. Hagen, *An Entangled Bank: The Origins of Ecosystem Ecology* (Piscataway, NJ: Rutgers University Press, 1992), p. 101.

12 C. Kwa, 'Representations of Nature Mediating between Ecology and Science Policy: The Case of the International Biological Programme', *Social Studies of Science*, 17(3), 1987, pp. 413–42, pp. 418–21; S. Bocking, 'Ecosystems, Ecologists and the Atom: Environmental Research at Oak Ridge National Laboratory', *Journal of History of Biology*, 28(1), 1995, pp. 1–47.

13 Bocking, 'Ecosystems', p. 4.

14 E. Welsome, *The Plutonium Files: America's Secret Medical Experiments in the Cold War* (New York: Dial Press, 1999), p. 30.

15 Quoted in Welsome, *Plutonium Files*, p. 118.

16 Welsome, *Plutonium Files* and C. Caufield, *Multiple Exposures: Chronicles of the Radiation Age* (Toronto: Stoddard Publishing Co., 1988).

17 F. Cowan, 'Everyday Radiation', *Physics Today*, 5(10), 1952, pp. 10–16, p. 14.

18 See M. Klingle, 'Plying Atomic Waters: Lauren Donaldson and the "Fern Lake Concept" of Fisheries Management', *Journal of the History of Biology*, 31(1), 1998, pp. 1–32.

19 On Micronesian history, see D. Hanlon, *Remaking Micronesia: Discourses over Development in a Pacific Territory, 1944–1982* (Honolulu, HI: University of Hawai'i Press, 1998) and R. Rogers, *Destiny's Landfall: A History of Guam* (Honolulu, HI: University of Hawai'i Press, 1995). On the state of exception see Giorgio Agamben's *State of Exception* (Chicago, IL: University of Chicago Press, 2005) which addresses how sovereign power declares a state of emergency to transcend the rule of law. This radioactive contamination of the entire planet ushers in an unprecedented era of what Achille Mbembe in another context terms 'necropower,' 'where sovereignty consists fundamentally in the exercise of a power outside the law (*ab legibus solutus*) and where "peace" is more likely to take on the face of a "war without end."' A. Mbembe, 'Necropolitcs', *Public Culture*, 15(1), 2003, pp. 11–40, p. 23.

20 Micronesia is the size of continental US, so combined with the EEZ and 3.9 billion acres of submarine land and resources this triples the territorial US (National Academy of Sciences, 1989), p. 1. UNCLOS and its importance to reconfiguring the Pacific as an Americanized space is explored in DeLoughrey, *Routes and Roots*.

21 E. Margolis, 'The Hydrogen Bomb Experiments and International Law', *The Yale Law Journal*, 64(5), 1955, pp. 629–47, p. 630.

22 Margolis, 'The Hydrogen Bomb', p. 631.

23 Margolis, 'The Hydrogen Bomb', p. 634.

24 P. Boyer, *By the Bomb's Early Light: American Thought and Culture at the Dawn of the Atomic Age* (Chapel Hill, NC: University of North Carolina Press, 1994), p. 92.

25 Boyer, *Bomb's Early Light*, p. 90. For more on the impact on Bikini, see Boyer, *Bomb's Early Light*; S. Firth, *Nuclear Playground* (Honolulu, HI: University of Hawai'i Press, 1987); J. Niedenthal, *For the Good of Mankind: a History of the People of Bikini and Their Islands* (Majuro, Marshall Islands: Bravo Publishers, 2001); R. Stone, *Radio Bikini* (Robert Stone Productions, 1988); J. Dibblin, *Day of Two Suns: Nuclear Testing and the Pacific Islanders* (London: Virago, 1988); T. Teaiwa, 'Bikinis and Other s/pacific n/oceans', *The Contemporary Pacific*, 6, 1994; and J. Weisgall, *Operation Crossroads: The Atomic Tests at Bikini Atoll* (Annapolis, MD: Naval Institute Press, 1994).

26 See Grove, *Green Imperialism*.

27 *Operation Ivy* (United States Air Force Lookout Mountain Laboratory, Air Photographic Charting Service, Hollywood, California, 1952).

28 Quoted in Boyer, *Bomb's Early Light*, p. 91.

29 M. Stephenson and J. Weal, *Nuclear Dictionary* (London: Longman, 1985), p. 79; R. Jungk, *Brighter than a Thousand Suns: A Personal History of the Atomic Scientists* (New York: Harcourt Brace, 1958), p. 310.

30 On *Bravo* see Dibblin's *Day of Two Suns*, Firth's *Nuclear Playground*, D. O'Rourke's *Half-Life* (O'Rourke and Associates Filmakers Pty, 1986), H. Barker, *Bravo for the Marshallese: Regaining Control in a Post-Nuclear; Post-Colonial World* (Belmont, CA: Wadsworth, 2004), and B. Johnston and H. Barker, *Consequential Damages of Nuclear War: The Rongelap Report* (Walnut Creek, CA: Left Coast Press, 2008).

31 Johnston and Barker, *Consequential Damages*, pp. 18–19.

32 My emphasis. *Military Effects Studies on Operation Castle* (United States Air Force Lookout Mountain Laboratory, Air Photographic Charting Service, Hollywood, California, 1954).

33 *Operation Castle Commander's Report* (Lookout Mountain Laboratory, US Air Force, Hollywood, California, 1954), <http://www.archive.org/details/CastleCommandersReport1954>.

34 Jungk, *Thousand Suns*, p. 310.

35 Margolis, 'The Hydrogen Bomb', p. 637.

36 C. Kwa, 'Radiation Ecology, Systems Ecology and the Management of the Environment', in Michael Shortland (ed.), *Science and Nature* (Oxford: British Society for the History of Science, 1993), pp. 213–49, p. 215.

37 On antinuclear activism in the Pacific, see Firth, *Nuclear Playground*, Teaiwa, 'Microwomen: US Colonialism and Micronesian Women Activists', in D. Rubenstein (ed.), *Pacific History: Papers from the 8th Pacific History Association Conference* (Mangilao, Guam: University of Guam and Micronesian Area Research Center, 1992).

38 My emphasis. H. Odum and E. Odum, 'Trophic Structure and Productivity of a Windward Coral Reef Community on Eniwetok Atoll', *Ecological Monographs*, 25(3), 1955, pp. 291–320. See also V. Kuletz's discussion of the Odums, *The Tainted Desert: Environmental Ruin in the American West* (New York: Routledge, 1998), p. 249. Biologist Lauren Donaldson found in the irradiated Pacific atolls 'an unparalleled opportunity to study the role of trace elements' in the environment (quoted in Klingle, 'Atomic Waters', p. 11).

39 F. Golley, *A History of the Ecosystem Concept in Ecology* (New Haven, CT: Yale University Press, 1993), p. 105.

40 See for instance S. Bocking, 'Ecosystems', S. Kirsch, 'Ecologists and the Experimental Landscape: The Nature of Science at the US Department of Energy's Savannah River Site', *cultural geographies*, 14(4), 2007, pp. 485–510.

41 Hagen, *An Entangled Bank*, p. 105.

42 Hagen, *An Entangled Bank*, pp. 104, 105.

43 Kwa, 'Radiation Ecology', p. 213.

44 H. Odum, 'Preface', in H. Odum and R. Pigeon (eds), *A Tropical Rain Forest: A Study of Irradiation and Ecology at El Verde, Puerto Rico* (Oak Ridge, TN: United States Atomic Energy Commission, National Technical Information Service, 1970), p. x.

45 H. Odum, 'Introduction to Section F', in H. Odum and R. Pigeon (eds), *A Tropical Rain Forest: A Study of Irradiation and Ecology at El Verde, Puerto Rico* (Oak Ridge, TN: United States Atomic Energy Commission, Division of Technical Information, 1970), pp. F1–F7, C–17. See also A. Lugo, 'H.T. Odum and the Luquillo Experimental Forest', *Ecological Modelling*, 178, 2004, pp. 65–74.

46 P. Taylor, 'Technocratic Optimism, H.T. Odum, and the Partial Transformation of Ecological Metaphor after World War II', *The Journal of the History of Biology*, 21(2), 1998, p. 229. See also Kuletz, *The Tainted Desert*, pp. 248–58.

47 H. Odum, 'The Stability of the World Strontium Cycle', *Science*, 114(2964), 1951, pp. 407–11, p. 407.

48 Kwa, 'Radiation Ecology', p. 213.

49 Golley, *The Ecosystem Concept*, p. 74.

50 Hagen, *An Entangled Bank*, p. 112.

51 My emphasis, E. Odum, 'Ecology and the Atomic Age', *ASB Bulletin*, 4(2), 1957, pp. 27–9, p. 28.

52 S. Kingsland, *The Evolution of American Ecology 1890–2000* (Baltimore, MD: Johns Hopkins University Press, 2005), p. 185.

53 W. Churchill, 'Geographic of Sacrifice: The Radioactive Colonization of Native North America', in W. Churchill (ed.), *Struggle for the Land: Native North American Resistance to Genocide, Ecocide and Colonization* (San Francisco, CA: City Lights Books, 2002), pp. 239–91, p. 239.

54 G. Mitman, *The State of Nature: Ecology, Community, and American Social Thought, 1900–1950* (Chicago, IL: University of Chicago Press, 1992), p. 209.

55 G. Beer, 'The Island and the Aeroplane: The Case of Virginia Woolf', in Homi Bhabha (ed.), *Nation and Narration* (London: Routledge, 1990), pp. 265–90, p. 265.

56 See DeLoughrey, *Routes and Roots*.

57 *Operation Greenhouse* (Lookout Mountain Laboratory, US Air Force, Hollywood, California, 1951), <http://www.archive.org/details/OperationGreenhouse1951>.

58 D. Cosgrove, *Apollo's Eye: A Cartographic Genealogy of the Earth in the Western Imagination* (Baltimore, MD: Johns Hopkins University Press, 2001), p. 2.

59 D. Cosgrove and W. Fox, *Photography and Flight* (London: Reaktion Books Ltd, 2010), p. 59.

60 Cosgrove, *Apollo's Eye*.

61 Waldheim quoted in P. Adey, *Aerial Life: Spaces, Mobilities, Affects* (Oxford: Wiley-Blackwell Publications, 2010), p. 10.

62 C. Kaplan, 'Mobility and War: The Cosmic View of US "Air Power"', *Environment and Planning A*, 38, 2006, pp. 395–407; P. Adey, *Aerial Life*. My thanks to Mimi Sheller for her references on aerial vision.

63 Cosgrove, *Apollo's Eye*, pp. 242–3.

64 Matthew Farish has an interesting argument about the decentralization of the American city in response to fears of nuclear attack that might be suggestively placed in a dialogue with the highly focalized space of the atomic test island. M. Farish, 'Disaster and Decentralization: American Cities and the Cold War', *cultural geographies*, 10(2), 2003, pp. 125–48.

65 Cosgrove, *Apollo's Eye*, p. 26.

66 Cosgrove, *Apollo's Eye*, p. 236.

67 Cosgrove, *Apollo's Eye*, p. 242.

68 Quoted in S. Sontag, *Regarding the Pain of Others* (New York: Farrar, 2003), p. 66.

69 *Hollywood's Top Secret Film Studio, Radio Bikini*. As one AEC film observed, 'one of the most important and dramatic elements in the dropping of the bomb is the photographic element' (quoted in Stone, *Radio Bikini*).

70 P. Virilio, *War and Cinema: The Logistics of Perception* (London: Verso, 1989), p. 4.

71 G. Baldacchino, 'Islands, Island Studies', *Island Studies Journal*, 1(1), 2006, pp. 3–18, p. 5.

72 As I discuss in *Routes and Roots*, functionalism, which is based on studying how individual parts fit the body of the whole community, is tied very closely to the bounded island concept and ecosystem ecology.

73 My emphasis, K.R. Howe, *The Quest for Origins: Who First Discovered and Settled New Zealand and the Pacific Islands* (Harmondsworth: Penguin Books, 2003), p. 23.

74 J. Fabian, *Time and the Other: How Anthropology Makes its Object* (New York: Columbia University Press, 2002).

75 D. Livingstone, *Putting Science in its Place: Geographies of Scientific Knowledge* (Chicago, IL: University of Chicago Press, 2003), p. 180.

76 Teaiwa, 'Bikinis', p. 90.

77 Teaiwa, 'Bikinis', p. 89.

78 P. Ricoeur, *The Rule of Metaphor: The Creation of Meaning in Language* (London: Routledge, 2003), p. 34.

79 Ricoeur, *The Rule of Metaphor*, p. 110.

80 Ricoeur, *The Rule of Metaphor*, p. 147.

81 *Nuclear Test Film – Operation Sandstone – Navy* (Department of Energy, 1948), <http://www.archive.org/details/gov.doe.0800003>.

82 *Nuclear Exiles* (National Geographic Society, 1987). See the work of Nathan Atkinson, 'Newsreels as Domestic Propaganda: Visual Rhetoric at the Dawn of the Cold War', *Rhetoric and Public Affairs*, 14(1), 2011, pp. 70–101, who demonstrates the control and sanitization of images of the Bikinians.

83 T. Teaiwa, 'Reading Paul Gauguin's *Noa Noa* with Epeli Hau'ofa's *Kisses in the Nederends*: Militourism, Feminism, and "Polynesian" Body', in Vilsoni Hereniko and Rob Wilson (eds), *Inside Out: Literature, Cultural Politics and Identity in the New Pacific* (Lanham, MD: Rowman and Littlefield, 2001), pp. 249–69.

84 Turning to geology, oceanography, and histories of voyaging, Diaz and Kauanui have argued against colonial

models of island isolation to demonstrate that the 'Pacific is on the move,' understood in terms of tectonics, human migration, and a growing field of scholarship in V. Diaz and J. Kauanui, 'Native Pacific Cultural Studies on the Edge', *The Contemporary Pacific*, 13(2), 2001, pp. 315–42, p. 317.

85 S. Shigematsu and K. Camacho, *Militarized Currents: Toward a Decolonized Future in Asia and the Pacific* (Minneapolis, MN: University of Minnesota Press, 2010), p. xv.

86 Johnston and Barker, *Consequential Damages*, p. 196. Mbembe's description of the necropolitics of the colony are relevant here: 'the colonies are zones in which war and disorder, internal and external, figures of the political, stand side by side or alternate with each other.' They are 'the location par excellence where the controls and guarantees of judicial order can be suspended – the zone where the violence of the state of exception is deemed to operate in the service of "civilization."' Mbembe, 'Necropolitics', p. 24.

87 Johnston and Barker, *Consequential Damages*, p. 96. Merril Eisenbud, an AEC scientist later observed: 'There are many unanswered questions about the circumstances of the 1954 fallout. It is strange that no formal investigation was ever conducted. There have been reports that the device was exploded despite an adverse meteorological forecast. It has not been explained why an evacuation capability was not standing by, as had been recommended, or why there was not immediate action to evaluate the matter when the task force learned (seven hours after the explosion) that the AEC Health & Safety Laboratory recording instrument on Rongerik was off scale. There was also an unexplained interval of many days before the fallout was announced to the public.' Oral history interview, <http://www.hss.energy.gov/healthsafety/ohre/roadmap/achre/chap12_3.htm>.

88 See Barker, *Bravo for the Marshallese*, and Johnston and Barker, *Consequential Damages*, p. 28.

89 R. Conard, *Medical Survey of Rongelap and Utirik People Three Years after Exposure to Radioactive Fallout* (Upton, NY: Brookhaven National Laboratory, 1958), quoted in G. Johnson, *Collision Course at Kwajalein: Marshall Islanders in the Shadow of the Bomb* (Honolulu, HI: Pacific Concerns Resource Center, 1984), p. 13.

90 Quoted in B. Johnston, '"More Like Us than Mice": Radiation Experiments with Indigenous Peoples', in B. Johnston (ed.), *Half-Lives & Half-Truths: Confronting the Radioactive Legacy of the* Cold War (Santa Fe, NM: School for Advanced Research Press, 2007), p. 25.

91 Mbembe, 'Necropolis', p. 24.

92 The Department of Energy (formerly the AEC) Advisory Commission on Radiation Experiments determined in 1995 that the AEC did conduct a few non-therapeutic tests on the Marshallese but as they had no access to materials

that were later declassified, they stated that there was no evidence of deliberate exposure or experimentation. See Johnston and Barker, *Consequential Damages*, pp. 30–1 and the ruling here: <http://www.hss.energy.gov/healthsafety/ohre/roadmap/achre/chap12_3.html>.

93 Johnston and Barker, *Consequential Damages*, p. 231.

94 Johnston and Barker, *Consequential Damages*, p. 156.

95 Johnston and Barker summarizing comments made by the AEC in response to complaint letters from the Rongelapese, *Consequential Damages*, p. 24.

96 See Johnston, 'More Like Us Than Mice', p. 40.

97 Johnston and Barker, *Consequential Damages*, pp. 119–21.

98 Johnston and Barker, *Consequential Damages*, p. 19.

99 See Johnston and Barker, *Consequential Damages*, pp. 153–6, and ACHRE <http://www.hss.energy.gov/healthsafety/ohre/roadmap/achre/chap12_3.html>.

100 ACHRE <http://www.hss.energy.gov/healthsafety/ohre/roadmap/achre/chap12_3.html>. L. Smith, *Decolonizing Methodologies: Research and Indigenous Peoples* (London: Zed Books, 2006), p. 1.

101 Johnston and Barker, *Consequential Damages*, p. 139.

102 See B. Johnston, 'Half-Lives, Half-Truths, and Other Radioactive Legacies of the Cold War'.

103 See DeLoughrey, *Routes and Roots*.

104 Golley, *The Ecosystem Concept*, p. 3.

105 US Atomic Energy Commission Official Memorandum, 1 August 1968, <http://www.hss.doe.gov/Healthsafety/IHS/marshall/collection/ihp/ …/B34.PDF>.

106 See R. Boyd, 'Metaphor and Theory Change: What is "Metaphor" a Metaphor for?', in A. Ortony (ed.), *Metaphor and Thought* (Cambridge: Cambridge University Press, 1979), pp. 356–408, and T. Kuhn, 'Metaphor in Science', in A. Ortony (ed.), *Metaphor and Thought* (Cambridge: Cambridge University Press, 1979), pp. 409–19.

107 B. Latour, 'Give Me a Laboratory and I will Raise the World', in M. Mulkay and K. Knorr-Cetina (eds), *Science Observed: Perspectives on the Study of Science* (London: SAGE, 1983), p. 17.

108 C. Geertz, Interpretation of Cultures (New York: Basic, 1973), p. 22.

109 Firth, *Nuclear Playground*, p. 3.

110 Welsome, *Plutonium Files*, p. 299.

111 Caufield, *Multiple Exposures*, p. 132.

112 See K. Spalding et al., 'Forensics: Age Written in Teeth by Nuclear Tests', *Nature*, 437(7057), 2005, pp. 333–4.

113 J. Masco, *The Nuclear Borderlands: The Manhattan Project in Post-Cold War New Mexico* (Princeton, NJ: Princeton University Press, 2006), p. 27.

114 See Godfrey Balacchino's important collection of the same title *A World of Islands* (Malta: Agenda Publishers, 2007).

34 Bio-Prospecting or Bio-Piracy

Intellectual Property Rights and Biodiversity in a Colonial and Postcolonial Context

John Merson

> *Lands long given up to imperial enterprise suffer by imperial withdrawal for two related reasons. Unless their economies remain neo-colonial, they are ill equipped to bear the loss of habitual modes of employment. Nor can they rapidly overcome habits of dependence ingrained by long subservience to the will, as to the interests, of others.*
>
> —David Lowenthal, "Empires and Ecologies:
> Reflections on Imperial History"

IN DISCUSSING THE SHIFT FROM COLONIAL TO POSTCOLONIAL science, it has been customary to make a distinction between settler countries, such as Canada, North America, Australia, Argentina, and New Zealand, and those where the indigenous populations were colonized, including India, Malaysia, Indonesia, Korea, and Africa. Countries such as China, Japan, and Thailand, although independent, were nonetheless economically shaped by the policies of imperial powers throughout the nineteenth and early twentieth centuries.[1]

The economic development of settler cultures, particularly the United States, provided new market structures and mechanisms for funding innovative research. However, this was rarely the case in nonsettler colonies, where the indigenous population and environment were primarily exploited for cheap labor and natural resources. Even following independence, the ability to link local scientific research with the economy remained limited, owing to cultural ambivalence, a low level of industrialization, and lack of private-sector support.[2]

Jon Merson, "Bio-Prospecting or Bio-Piracy: Intellectual Property Rights and Biodiversity in a Colonial and Postcolonial Context." *Osiris*, 2nd series, 15, 2000: 282–296. Reprinted by permission of The University of Chicago Press.

In the heady days of decolonization following the end of the Second World War, India, Indonesia, Korea, Malaysia, and many African states placed under national control the fledgling scientific and technological research facilities that had once served their colonial masters. However, with the exception of South Korea and Taiwan, the shift from colonial to postcolonial science has meant very little in terms of the capacity to use the tools of research to shape economic development. Most newly decolonized states invested heavily in education, and especially in the training of scientists and technicians. However, their reliance on import substitution schemes for the transfer of industrial technology provided few opportunities for local technicians to innovate in the application of science. Exceptions to this general rule can be found, notably in agriculture. Yet even where local plant breeding and agricultural extension services were maintained, by the 1960s they were subsumed by the imperatives of industrialized agriculture that came with the green revolution. Although it increased yields, the green revolution also reinforced dependency on foreign technical advisers and industrial inputs such as high-yielding plant varieties, chemical fertilizers, insecticides, and herbicides, along with farm machinery and irrigation systems.

As countries gradually opened their economies to the global trading system in the second half of the twentieth century, an international division of labor emerged. The poorer ex-colonial countries of Africa, Asia, and Latin America continued to play the traditional role of suppliers of cheap primary resources in exchange for advanced industrial goods and military technology. Despite the postwar establishment of the United Nations, the World Bank, and the International Monetary Fund (IMF), whose charters were ostensibly to help emerging nation-states find an equal place in the new international economic order, the global division of labor has reduced many of these states to a neo-colonial economic status.

This situation was reinforced in the 1970s due to declining commodity prices, population growth, and increased costs of imported industrial goods.[3] As Third World governments confronted a rising level of public debt, they were forced by the World Bank and the IMF to emphasize the production of cash crops for the export market, and to adopt structural adjustment programs that led to cutbacks in public-sector expenditure. This was disastrous for local scientific research and indigenous technological development. It also meant that with ever-burgeoning populations and often corrupt ruling elites, natural resources were exploited with ruthless disregard for the environmental consequences. Tropical forest ecosystems were destroyed at an unprecedented rate to make way for plantation agriculture: beef in the Brazilian Amazon, wood pulp in Thailand, and palm oil in Indonesia.

In this sense, globalization has created a situation in which, despite the rhetoric of national sovereignty, most developing countries remain in a condition of dependency. This paper will review some of the difficulties faced by developing nations as they attempt to move beyond a neo-colonial relationship within the global trading system towards a legitimate place in the corporate research networks that dominate production in the emerging biotechnology industries. This is particularly critical in the case of the economically poor but biologically rich nations of the tropical and subtropical regions.

John Merson

Biotechnology and The Convention on Biodiversity

The tropical regions of the world, which occupy only six percent of the earth's surface and are economically the poorest and least developed, contain the greatest diversity of the world's fauna and flora. The biologist Edward O. Wilson has estimated that at the beginning of the 1990s, human activity had already eliminated 55 percent of original forest cover in the wet tropical regions. Since then we have been reducing the remaining 45 percent at a rate of around 1 percent per annum, or an acre per second.[4]

In 1992, amid growing international concern that the economic pressures on developing countries in the tropical regions were leading to destruction of a large part of the earth's biological heritage, the United Nations mounted its historic Rio Earth Summit on Environment and Development. The passage at Rio of an International Convention on Biological Diversity, and its ratification by most countries within the UN system, was a remarkable achievement. In the colonial context, biological resources had been regarded as being part of the global commons and were not subject to property rights, except where specific plant breeding occurred. The drafters of the convention believed that the best strategy to protect biological and genetic resources was to give states explicit property rights.

The Convention on Biodiversity was therefore an attempt to encourage Third World governments to conserve their existing forests or to harvest them sustainably. The argument conservationists put forward was that the long-term commercial value of these biological resources to the world's chemical, pharmaceutical, and biotechnology industries was much greater than their value for extracted timber and agriculture, especially as tropical soils can have short-term use for agricultural production. In support, botanists pointed out that at least seven thousand of the most commonly used drugs in Western medicine are derived from plants. Much of this comes from the biologically rich environments of the tropics, and is worth U.S. $32 billion a year in sales worldwide. However, while Third World countries supply and maintain the bulk of these resources, they receive only U.S. $551 million in return.[5]

To appreciate the significance of this landmark agreement, it is necessary first to review the use and development of biological resources during the colonial and postcolonial periods. For even though the convention is a well-meaning attempt to address some of the global inequalities that are a legacy of colonialism, defining genetic and biological resources as state property has opened a Pandora's box of controversy and complexity.

Science and The Colonization of the Natural World

The collection and trade of plants for use as foods, drugs, or insecticides dates back to the earliest hunter-gatherer communities. The knowledge and use of local plants was important in the development of medical practices. One of the earliest documented compendiums of medicinal plants was the *Pen Ts'ao* by the Chinese herbalist Shen Nung. Written in 2500 B.C., it listed some 366 plant drugs, some of which, like ephedra, were also used in the West. A thousand years later, the *Ebers Papyrus* listed opium, aloes, and henbane among the drugs in use in Egypt in 1500 B.C. By A.D. 78, Dioscorides, in his *De Materia Medica*, described 600 plants including specific extracts such as aloe, ergot, and opium. While many of these materials were traded throughout the ancient world, it was not until the development of European colonial empires that moving plants from one side of the globe to another took on real economic significance.[6]

Within fifty years of such American crops as the potato, maize, and tobacco arriving in Europe, they were also being cultivated in China. Cotton and cane sugar transferred from India to the Caribbean and the Americas formed the basis of the plantation system in the New World. By the late seventeenth century, the Dutch East India Company plantations in Java had given the Netherlands an international monopoly on spices such as pepper, cloves, and cinnamon, and also political control of Java itself. However, the growth of the administrative and trading port of Batavia brought new diseases to the Dutch, such as malaria, dengue fever, and a range of bacterial infections unknown in Europe. As Leonard Blusse has documented, the old city of Batavia was abandoned in 1730 because of the inability to control the disease being spread by severe pollution of the city's canal system.[7] Pollution from sugar manufacture and the system's failure to flush out sewage turned the canals into breeding grounds for tropical diseases against which the Europeans had neither immunity nor drugs.

New medicines were thus sought not only to find cures for diseases that racked the growing cities of Europe, but also to sustain colonial communities in remote parts of the world. By the time of James Cook's voyages to the South Pacific, the British Admiralty saw the inclusion of botanical research under Joseph Banks and his Swedish colleague Carl Solander as a legitimate part of a voyage of exploration.

In the late eighteenth and early nineteenth centuries, the establishment of botanical gardens in Europe and in the colonies was of growing scientific, medical, and agricultural importance. Botanical gardens at Kew and Leiden became major centers for adapting economic and medicinal plants from around the world for cultivation. Botanical gardens established in the colonies were to become part of a sophisticated international network. In Java, for instance, the famous botanical gardens at Bogor and the scientific institutes in Bandung became major centers of research, at times eclipsing metropolitan centers in Holland. In Australia, botanical gardens were primarily concerned with the adaptation of European food crops to alien environments, and only later became centers for the collection and scientific exploration of native plants. As Linden Gillbank has observed, "imperial powers sought to control the cultivation of useful plants, with colonial botanical gardens providing crucial testing grounds for the suitability of plants to new climates. The Australian botanical gardens were part of a well controlled network of British colonial gardens which manipulated global botanical resources for the economic interests of Britain."[8]

The transfer of plant and animal species from one colonial region to another led to both enormous profit and environmental disaster. Establishing plantations for tea in Ceylon and India, and for South American rubber trees in Malaysia, provided a lasting economic foundation for Britain's imperial aspirations, especially after the valuable tropical timber resources had been exploited. Despite Brazil's efforts to stop the export of rubber-tree seeds and seedlings in the late nineteenth century, within twenty years of the first rubber trees being planted in Malaysia, Brazil's share of the rubber trade had dropped from 98 percent to virtually nothing.[9] The growing imperial and international market for rubber, tea, coffee, sugar, cotton, and wool meant that colonial administrations were actively encouraging the clearing of forested regions to make way for these lucrative export crops. It also meant that biological research was largely focused on crossbreeding to develop plants suited to specific environmental conditions.

By the late nineteenth century, the destruction of forest ecosystems in Australia had become so extensive that Frederick von Mueller, director of the Melbourne Botanical Gardens, argued for the need to preserve biodiversity. "Floral Commons ... should be reserved in every great country for some maintenance of the original vegetation, and therewith for the preservation of animal life concomitant to peculiar plants."[10] It is perhaps ironic that colonists and scientists could talk of the principle of a "floral commons" when, in reality, the expansion of European property laws to the colonies meant the appropriation of lands and resources commonly held and used by aboriginal communities.

The Growth of Biochemical Knowledge

The nineteenth-century application of the experimental methods of science to the extraction of active agents from biological material played a crucial role in establishing the chemical industry, particularly in Germany. Extracting and identifying the active pharmacological agents from many of the better-known plants yielded major advances in medical treatment. In 1803, the German pharmacist Freidrich Serturner experimented with the newly discovered techniques of isolating organic acids. He tried the technique on opium and ended up not with an acid but the first alkaloid. This led not only to the development and use of morphine in the control of pain, but also to the discovery of the active pharmaceutical agents in a number of other important medicinal plants, many derived directly from colonial sources. Quinine was first extracted in 1819, atropine in 1831, cocaine in 1860, ergotamine in 1918, and tubocurarine in 1935.[11] The medical importance of these new alkaloids, especially the use of quinine in combating the debilitating effects of malaria in the colonies, cannot be underestimated. As with rubber seedlings from Brazil, many South American states attempted to prevent the export of cinchona bark or seedlings (from which quinine is derived), but with little success. The dominance of European powers, and the disregard for intellectual property rights other than those possessed by European industry, made such efforts fruitless.[12]

Institutes for the study of tropical diseases and medicine began to emerge towards the end of the century. The impact of European diseases on native populations was also a major concern for colonial administrations. The documentation of local medical practices, and the use of native plant material, soon became part of the process of fighting disease.[13] The value of new drugs and the internationalization of the chemical and pharmaceutical industries led to a far more systematic exploration of the plants used by native peoples under colonial rule.

Medicine in the colonies was not concerned only with the plight of colonists and natives. The introduction of sheep, cattle, horses, pigs, and poultry was a risky business given their transfer to very different environments and ecosystems. Again, diseases unknown in Europe meant that crossbreeding for resistance was critical. Overcoming new animal diseases gave veterinary medicine a unique and critical role in the economic survival of colonial agriculture.[14]

Intellectual Property Rights and Biological Resources

The colonial assumption that all plant and genetic resources were part of a "common biological heritage" was at least tacitly accepted until 1930, when the United States passed the Plant Patent Act. This legislation, which allowed for the patenting of asexually reproduced plants, was passed mainly under pressure from plant breeders in the ornamental garden market. However, it opened a Pandora's box on plant breeder's rights. In the 1940s, Europeans passed laws allowing for the protection of sexually reproduced plants. By 1961, international trade in hybrid species had grown to the point where an international convention on plant breeder's rights, known as the UPOV Convention, was established by the Union for New Varieties of Plants.[15] With the development of recombinant DNA techniques, the genetic engineering of new varieties of agricultural plants became a reality, leading to the patenting of genetically engineered strains of common agricultural crops such as cotton, soybeans, and corn. These new varieties, with built-in resistance to common pests, offered economic advantages in terms of reduced reliance on chemical inputs. As a result, they tended to undermine the value of traditional varieties held within farming communities as common property. This clash between property law and customary rights also arose as pharmaceutical and agrichemical corporations began to explore the medicinal plants used by traditional communities around the world.

The environmental problems caused by the overuse of synthetic fertilizers, insecticides, and herbicides meant that there was a constant search for new and less-damaging chemical compounds. By the 1970s the search for new biodegradable insecticides was a major goal, especially given adverse publicity and consumer concerns about residues of the organochlorine and phosphate insecticides in common use. The development of one of the best known of these new bio-insecticides, Bio-Neem, illustrates the problems of equity that arise when communally held intellectual property is used to create products for the international market.

In 1971 an American timber importer, Robert Larsen, became interested in the wide-spread use of the berries of the neem tree (*Azadirachta indica*) by villagers throughout India. For over two thousand years, the oil from the neem has been used in India as an insecticide, a fungicide, a contraceptive, and an antibacterial agent. Over a number of years at his company headquarters in Wisconsin, Larsen carried out experiments on the extraction of azadirachtin from neem oil, which he found to be a powerful insect growth inhibitor. In 1985 he took out a patent on his process of extracting azadirachtin, which he then sold to W. R. Grace & Co. in 1988. In 1993, after considerable R & D, Grace released a new bio-insecticide called Bio-Neem or Margosan-O. Its active ingredient, azadirachtin, has unique characteristics as a bio-insecticide in that it is lethal to at least two hundred types of insects, as well as to species of mites and nematodes, yet it is completely harmless to birds, mammals, and beneficial insects such as bees. Given the huge demand for the product, especially for the control of greenhouse pests throughout America, Grace entered into a deal with a private Indian firm, P. J. Margo, to start a neem processing plant in Karnataka, in South India. The plant was soon processing twenty tons of neem seeds a day and the new insecticide was taken up in greenhouses across the United States, from California to Florida.

Dr. Martin Sherwin, president of Grace's commercial development division in Florida, argued that Indian industry was set to benefit from further development of this product. The W. R. Grace patent, he argued, created a more valuable resource from neem. Before 1988, neem berries were processed primarily for oil, which was used as a surfactant in medicinal soaps and other domestic products, and the berries' waste material was then sold as a fertilizer. The Grace patent involved a three-stage extraction process that produced azadirachtin along with both the oil and the fertilizer.[16] This, by any account, was a considerable improvement. As a consequence, six Indian companies followed suit and set up operations based on separate patents taken out in India for azadirachtin extraction.

With the bio-insecticide industry estimated to be worth around $1 billion, the demand rose for neem berries collected from over fourteen million trees throughout India. But the small-scale, local neem-oil industry was in no position to compete with the technological resources and industrial power available to W. R. Grace. Following 1993's General Agreement on Tariffs and Trade–Trade-Based Intellectual Property (GATT–TRIPS) agreement, India and other developing countries were given until 1998 to develop an intellectual property system compatible with other trading nations, in order to protect their interests in international patents such as Grace's. While patenting options and intellectual property rights had been available to Indian manufacturers, no legal mechanism recognized the collective intellectual property interests of traditional users. On these grounds, critics such as Vandana Shiva argued that the Grace patent fell little short of "bio-piracy."[17] W. R. Grace has not, as yet, even tried to extend its United States patent to India because of the commercial risks and political sensitivity involved. The company's industrial and global market dominance provides it with sufficient security.

European intellectual property law was not designed to represent knowledge held collectively, as is the case with neem. "Indigenous heritage," to use Dr. Erica-Irene Daes's term, tends to fall outside the normal patenting and other commercial/legal mechanisms.[18] However, international concern about protecting intellectual property held collectively within traditional indigenous cultures has led a number of Third World countries, such as the Philippines, to develop sui generis legislation. There is no doubt that the innovations involved in the W. R. Grace patent are a legitimate improvement on the methods of extracting azadiractin from neem oil. But in the view of Tony Simpson and Vanessa Jackson, lawyers specializing in intellectual property rights, the World Trade Organization TRIPS agreement, which aims to provide international protection for such patents, provides no recognition of the intellectual property interests of the community in India that first discovered and used neem-based products. In their view, such disregard for cultural knowledge

> will deepen the North/South rift, with ensuing unfair and unequal exchange; the agreement will facilitate increased occurrence of bio-piracy of biological and genetic resources from indigenous peoples; and communities and cultures may be irreversibly damaged by the forced introduction of foreign concepts of intellectual property law (such as the concepts of exclusive ownership and alienability), and the further erosion of their means of self determination.[19]

The Merck/Inbio Deal

The case of neem illustrates the conflict that commonly arises when traditional industries confront the commercial and technological power of a global corporation like W. R. Grace. However, there have been cases in which global corporations entered into more equitable relationships with Third World countries in the development of new chemical and pharmaceutical products.

In 1991, the Central American nation of Costa Rica had a GNP of about $5.2 billion, only slightly more than half the $8.6 billion in annual sales of pharmaceutical giant Merck Corporation. Yet in the same year, Costa Rica's National Biodiversity Institute, INBio, signed a bio-prospecting agreement with Merck worth $1.135 million over two years. This strategy was designed to help maintain the rich biodiversity locked in Costa Rica's national parks and forestry reserves, which represent 27 percent of the country. Despite its tiny size, Costa Rica holds around 4 percent of the world's diverse range of plants and animals.

The Merck/INBio joint venture was the first in what has now become a growing trend of agreements involving biologically rich but economically poor countries. From INBio's point of view, this deal gave them not only much-needed finance but also access to advanced screening technology and training for their researchers. It has also allowed local villagers in forest areas to be trained as "parataxonomists" and to participate in the scientific identification and collection of species, building on extensive traditional knowledge of the fauna and flora. Dr. Anna Siddenfeld, who was in charge of research at INBio in 1991, argued that the great value of the deal was Merck's transfer of assaying technology to INBio, and the training of staff in its use. "Data from the work of the first group indicates that 15 parataxonomists generate well in excess of 50,000 prepared specimens a month, and the inventory collection at INBio at present contains more than two and a half million specimens."[20] It has not only helped Costa Rica to justify the preservation of its forest ecosystems, but also to begin the enormous task of accurately documenting its diverse range of plants and animals. The value-added element in this sort of *in situ* screening is that the royalty returns to INBio and Costa Rica are trebled in the case of a successful project. "It is common to receive royalties of 1–6% of net sales for unscreened chemical samples, 5–10% for material backed by preclinical information on its medical activity, and 10–15% for factional and identified material with effective data."[21]

Through this experience, INBio has been put in a position to explore and develop products with other international groups, but from a position of relative strength. For example, INBio has fostered the development of Costa Rica's first bio-insecticide industry in conjunction with the British Technology Group (BTG). It is a nematocide produced from the seeds of a leguminous tree found in Costa Rica's dry tropical forests. This was developed in conjunction with Dr. Dan Jonstone after the discovery that the seeds of this tree were not eaten by either birds or animals. After eight years of testing at the Royal Botanical Gardens at Kew, chemists isolated a pyrolidine alkaloid called DMDP. This alkaloid is both nontoxic to humans and biodegradable, so it can be sprayed on plants at very low doses to protect the roots from attack by nematodes. (The only other chemical protection suitable for tropical conditions requires extensive application and is highly toxic.) BTG has taken out a patent on the product in conjunction with

INBio, and Costa Rica will be producing the new bio-insecticide locally. If successful, this product could give Costa Rica a new industry in the cultivation and harvesting of raw materials, and in the processing and production of the final product. Trials are being carried out in Costa Rica on tropical plants, and in Britain on temperate crops such as tomatoes and potatoes.

Costa Rica's experience demonstrates the logical connection between the maintenance of biodiversity in forest ecosystems and the development of profitable new industries. This example is often used to vindicate the arguments put forward by those drafting the Convention on Biodiversity. It also demonstrates what can be achieved where there is genuine North/South collaboration.

Since Costa Rica's success, a number of bilateral deals have been struck between large pharmaceutical/chemical companies and state bio-prospecting agencies. Mexico's National Biodiversity Commission was set up in 1992, and similar institutions have been established in Peru and Brazil. The Indonesian government and the Asian Development Bank have agreed to establish a Biodiversity Marketing and Commercialisation Board. In Australia, the AMRAD Corporation established similar bio-prospecting agreements with the Tiwi people of the Northern Territory in 1994, and formed the Northern Lands Council in 1995 for collecting and assaying specimens on aboriginal land. More recently, these agreements have extended to the Malaysian state of Sarawak (in 1996 and 1998).[22] Pharmaceutical companies around the world are developing similar agreements. Some, like the Sharman Corporation of San Francisco, have targeted remote tribal communities and are using their traditional plant medicines as the basis for developing new drugs. Others, like the U.S. National Cancer Institute and the British company Biotics Ltd., are acting as brokers between research groups in developing countries that are independently exploring their indigenous pharmacopoeia, such as in China, and the international drug companies looking for new chemical compounds or genetic materials.

The Biodiversity Convention and Indigenous Rights

The Biodiversity Convention agreed to at Rio, and subsequently ratified by most of the 160 countries present, represents an important step in trying to overcome the colonial heritage that is inherent in the economic and technological power relations around the globe. It could be argued that the enthusiasm with which so many Third World countries embraced the convention reflects their very real concern over their loss of control. Critics of the GATT–TRIPS agreement, such as Shiva and Narji, argue that the economic forces driving globalization are leading to a form of neo-colonialism.[23] They cite the fact that global corporations, such as W. R. Grace and Merck, have the capital to dominate and shape international markets. However, Dr. Lyn Capporal, the Merck representative involved in setting up the deal with Costa Rica, points out that while Merck might be the largest pharmaceutical company in the world, it controls only 5 percent of the world market, and has far less power then its critics imagine.

It is still unclear whether the countries that were signatories to the convention, will find the principle of property rights over the biological and genetic resources within their territories meaningful enough to encourage the conservation of biodiversity. For many economic, legal, and scientific factors may weaken and undermine the anticipated benefits. Some of these factors are reflected in the pronounced inequality, in both scientific and industrial resources, that exists between the countries holding the bulk of the world's biodiversity and the global agrichemical and pharmaceutical corporations most capable of making use of it. Also, while the convention focuses on giving property rights to states, it also recognizes that in many cases the maintenance of biodiversity rests in the hands of indigenous communities that have been part of the ecological balance for many thousands of years. The convention refers to the need to protect the interests of these indigenous communities as part of any conservation strategy.[24] However, the state ownership of biological and genetic resources may simply reinforce past patterns of appropriation and dispossession. Consider, for example, the situation of the Australian aborigines.

The Mabo High Court decision of June 1992, which recognized aboriginal land ownership prior to European settlement, destroyed the illusion that Australia had been *terra nullius*, or an empty land, as colonists had conveniently believed. Their contention that aborigines had had no land use or traditions of ownership meant that the country was available for settlement without the colonial government having to enter into treaties or purchase agreements. In reality, archaeological research by Rhys Jones has shown that aboriginal systems of land management ("fire stick farming") had transformed the Australian environment from the time of their arrival around sixty thousand years ago.[25] Evidence of this practice was first reported by James Cook as early as the 1770s, and by the explorer Ernest Giles over a century later (in 1889):

> The natives were about, burning, burning, everywhere burning; one would think they were the fabled salamander race, and lived on fire instead of water.[26]

The regime of burning the land in a mosaic pattern in cycles of up to thirteen years was responsible for preventing raging fires from destroying valuable fruit-bearing trees, as well as useful plants and animals.[27] In other words, the traditional biodiversity of Australia, particularly its unique fire-dependent or -tolerant species, could well be considered a byproduct of aboriginal culture. This fact was observed as early as 1838 when Sir Thomas Mitchell, surveyor general of New South Wales, noted the change in vegetation that had occurred as a result of the aboriginals being forced off the land areas around Sydney.

> Kangaroos are no longer to be seen there; the grass is choked by underwood; neither are there natives to burn the grass … the omission of the annual periodical burning by natives, of the grass and young saplings, has already produced in the open forests nearest Sydney, thick forests of young trees, where, formerly, a man might gallop without impediment, and see whole miles before him.[28]

The significance of the Mabo decision is that, in recognizing aboriginal traditions of land ownership, and that their land management practices shaped the biodiversity across large areas of the country, it can therefore be argued that this biodiversity is, in part, an artifact of aboriginal culture. Clear evidence of this is to be found in the continued use of a system of mosaic burning to maintain biodiversity in the famous World Heritage Kakadu National Park in Arnhem Land. For aborigines still living close to their land, this burning practice is often referred to as "looking after the country."

As a consequence of the Convention on Biodiversity, a number of Australian states have passed legislation claiming ownership of all native botanical and genetic resources within their jurisdiction. However, while articles of the convention specifically state that indigenous interests and rights are to be taken into account, these have yet to be recognized in state legislation. Similar conflicts of interest will be found in many countries as stakeholders identified by the convention begin to assert their rights. There are other factors associated with the past international movement of plant species that could make the convention's notion of property rights difficult to implement. For example, many ornamental and economic plant species are held either in gene banks as germ plasm, or in botanical gardens and arboretums around the world. Often these have been in such collections for hundreds of years and the location of the original specimen is no longer known. Biotechnology companies, concerned about the increased complexities of obtaining bio-prospecting agreements in many Third World countries, are turning to these vast collections. For example, in 1996 the United States biotechnology company Phytera signed agreements with seven European botanical gardens to obtain seeds and tissues from tropical plants in their collections. While this contravenes the spirit of the 1993 Convention on Biodiversity, it has not been legally challenged. The deal involves Phytera paying the gardens $15 per plant specimen delivered and 0.25 percent of the profit from products derived from the specimens. The gardens involved will get 2.5 percent if products are developed under license from Phytera.[29]

In the case of food plants, the free international flow of germ plasm is essential for scientists and plant breeders in both rich and poor countries alike, as they develop new species to keep ahead of resistance to disease and climate change. But as Balick and Kloppenburg argue, "Third world plant breeders can have access to the USDA's gene bank—[but] in practice, 'free exchange' is not the even-handed opportunity its proponents have made it out to be, and the benefits of collecting biochemical and genetic information have accrued to the North in extremely disproportionate fashion."[30]

Of equal importance has been the operation of gene banks under an agreement between the Consultative Group on International Agricultural Research and the UN Food and Agriculture Organisation. This global network of international agricultural research centers represents the world's largest collection of germ plasm for crops and forestry. Six hundred thousand accessions are made available to researchers free of charge each year, with many of these going to developing countries.[31] This system is now governed by trustees from sixty countries, with funding flowing from forty countries. With the transformation of agriculture and the increasing loss of global biodiversity, this international network of gene banks is an essential asset, but the value of free access is clearly a matter of an individual country's knowledge and resources.

The efforts of overzealous governments to use claims of ownership to stem the free flow of germ plasm and genetic materials may backfire on their own scientists and plant breeding programs, creating what has been called a "seed war." However, some Third World groups argue that these gene banks should operate on a fee system. Like the copyright laws that govern the international use of music or art, the banks could provide some return to the country whence the germ plasm originated. While this would be in the spirit of the Convention on Biodiversity, it could prove to be a commercial nightmare for both plant breeders and the emerging biotechnology industry.

This complex environment of competing interest groups has led Balick and Kloppenburg to observe that a "New International Genetic Order is clearly in the offing. The degree to which this altered order is truly 'new,' or whether it is simply a kinder or gentler version of the old exploitative relationship, remains to be seen."[32]

Conclusion

In considering the legacy of colonialism, there is an obvious tendency to blame the colonial powers for the scientific, technological, and economic underdevelopment plaguing many Third World countries. Despite the rhetoric, decolonization has not resulted in any fundamental changes in the locality of scientific and technological innovation. The countries' dependence on the research and development of the advanced economies of Europe, the United States, and Japan is, if anything, greater now than during the colonial era. This is largely due to the integration of most of the world's economies following the Second World War and, more recently, to the ending of the cold war. This dependency is particularly true of agriculture and biotechnology following the genetic engineering revolution of the 1970s and 1980s. This transformation led to large-scale capital investment in the biosciences, which have followed high-energy physics into becoming "Big Science."[33] The financial returns from the global marketing of new agrichemicals and pharmaceuticals are so great that corporations such as Novartis are prepared to invest $250 million in an Institute for Functional Genomics in La Jolla, California, and the Wellcome Trust and other pharmaceutical companies in Britain are putting $45 million into a major research project addressing diagnostic nucleotide polymorphism. The scale of these investments means that highly centralized international research teams will dominate the applied market in many fields of biotechnology, leaving behind small groups of scientific researchers in ex-colonial countries. Even in Australia, New Zealand, Canada, and India, where there have been strong traditions of biological research, these changes could reduce applied research to niche or peripheral fields.

The era of globalization has seen the emergence of corporations having international dominance in key markets, such as W. R. Grace, Monsanto, Merck, and Microsoft. Their global networks of production and distribution have led to increasing standardization and the accentuation of inequalities.[34] In the case of the cotton industry, countries that once had independent agricultural and research traditions now face a situation in which all inputs—from seeds and fertilizers to insecticides, herbicides, and machinery—are imported from international agribusiness firms. These same corporations also buy back the crop for processing in the industrialized centers of the North. The only stake that "peripheral" nation-states have in the final product is in providing labor, land, and water to the "core" industry group, all of which represent low value-added returns.[35] While critics have described this situation as neo-colonial in that it perpetuates the traditional colonial condition of technological and economic dependency, there is one obvious difference. We are no longer discussing colonial empires, but rather a global market system that the world community accepts as being in everyone's long-term interest, even though it has engendered transnational corporations of unprecedented economic power. This being the case, multilateral agreements through the United Nations system, such as the Convention on Biodiversity and the WTO/TRIPS protocols, may be the only realistic strategy to redress the economic inequalities that are the root cause of the high levels of environmental destruction in Third World countries.[36] Reshaping or redefining rights and interests within the global trading system may eventually lead to more constructive and beneficial relationships, along the lines of the Merck/INBio deal.

For the scientific community, the shift towards viewing the world's biological and genetic resources as the property of nation-states, rather than as part of the global commons, is only just beginning to sink in. Some have argued that the Convention on Biodiversity is unworkable and unenforceable, given the geographical distribution of species across political boundaries and the vast dispersion of plants and animals around the world. Others contend that the loss of biodiversity in the tropical and subtropical regions of the world is so great that the convention must be made to work, or at least serve as the starting point for alternative strategies that can halt the destruction.

Allying mechanisms to protect our biodiversity with the legitimate interests of the world community in using its genetic riches is something that will be battled out in courts and legislative assemblies well into the next millennium. What many call bio-prospecting, others in the Third World call bio-piracy, in that they see the real benefits of any discovery ultimately flowing into the coffers of global chemical and pharma-ceutical companies, and not to the knowledge and resource providers.

Ethnobotanists and biotechnology enthusiasts argue that the future returns from forest and wetland ecosystems could be enormous. The successful development of a new drug that could halt the scourge of AIDS, or of a valuable new agrichemical compound, could be worth hundreds of millions in royalties each year. At the same time, the WTO/TRIPS system of intellectual property rights is coming up against very real problems. These flow from trying to make antiquated patent and copyright systems apply to everything from genetic information in living organisms to the collective knowledge and property rights of indigenous peoples. While the 1993 Convention on Biological Diversity is flawed by internal contradiction and legal loopholes, it is nonetheless an important start in trying to halt the annihilation of the world's ever-diminishing range of plant and animal life. One thing is clear: unless the convention becomes part of a much broader process of overcoming the colonial and neo-colonial legacy of entrenched global inequality, there is little likelihood of its objectives ever being realized.

Notes

1 Alfred W. Cosby, *Ecological Imperialism: The Biological Expansion of Europe, 900–1900* (Cambridge: Cambridge Univ. Press, 1986); and Ian Inkster, *Science and Technology in History* (London: Macmillan, 1991).

2 For an account of the problem in Indonesia, see Steven Hill, Anthony March, John Merson, and Falatehan Siregar, "Science and Technology: Partnership in Development,"

in *Expanding Horizons: Australia and Indonesia into the 21ˢᵗ Century* (Australia: East Asia Analytical Unit, Department of Foreign Affairs and Trade, 1994).

3 Susan George, *A Fate Worse than Debt* (Harmondsworth, U.K.: Penguin, 1990).

4 Edward O. Wilson, "Biodiversity, Prosperity and Value," in *Ecology, Economy, Ethics: The Broken Circle*, eds. F. Herbert

Bormann and Stephen R. Kellert (New Haven/London: Yale Univ. Press, 1991), pp. 3–10.

5 The Crucible Group, *People, Plants and Patents: The Impact of Intellectual Property on Trade, Plant Biodiversity, and Rural Society* (Ottawa: International Development Research Centre,1994).

6 Varro E. Tyler, "Natural Products and Medicine: An Overview," in *Medicinal Resources of the Tropical Forest: Biodiversity and its Importance to Human Health*, eds. Michael J. Balick, Elaine Elisabetsky, and Sarah A. Laird (New York: Columbia Univ. Press, 1996), pp. 3–10.

7 Leonard Blusse, *Strange Company: Chinese Settlers, Mestizo Women and the Dutch in VOC Batavia* (Amsterdam: Foris Publications, 1986), pp. 15–34.

8 Linden Gillbank, "The Life Sciences: Collections to Conservation," in *The Commonwealth of Science: ANZAAS and the Scientific Enterprise in Australasia 1888–1988*, ed. Roy MacLeod (Melbourne: Oxford Univ. Press, 1988), p. 100.

9 L. H. Brockway, "Plant Science and Colonial Expansion: The Botanical Chess Game," in *Seeds and Sovereignty*, ed. Jack R. Kloppenburg (Durham, N.C.: Duke Univ. Press, 1988), pp. 49–66.

10 Frederick von Mueller, "Inaugural Address," *Report of the American Association for the Advancement of Science* (Melbourne, 1890), vol. 2. As quoted in Gillbank, "The Life Sciences" (cit. n. 8), p. 117.

11 Tyler, "Natural Products and Medicine" (cit. n. 6), p. 4.

12 Calestous Juma, *The Gene Hunters: Biotechnology and the Scramble for Seeds* (Princeton, N.J.: Princeton Univ. Press, 1989).

13 The 1898 Cambridge Anthropological Expedition to the Torres Strait is an example of one of the first systematic anthropological explorations. See A. Herle and J. Philp, *Torres Strait Islanders* (Cambridge: Univ. of Cambridge Museum of Archaeology and Anthropology, 1998).

14 For an interesting account of colonial veterinary policy and practices, see William Beinart, "Vets, Viruses and Environmentalism at the Cape," in *Ecology and Empire: Environmental History of Settler Societies*, eds. Tom Griffiths and Libby Robin (Melbourne: Melbourne Univ. Press, 1997), pp. 87–101.

15 The Crucible Group, *People, Plants and Patents* (cit. n. 5), pp. 55–65.

16 As stated in a 1994 interview with the author and broadcast on an Australian Broadcasting Corporation Radio's National Science Show program, "Gene Prospecting," 18 Feb. 1995.

17 Vandana Shiva, "Biodiversity, Biotechnology and Profit: The Need for a People's Plan to Protect Biological Diversity," *The Ecologist*, 1990, 20, 2:44–7.

18 Dr. Erica-Irene Daes is the United Nations' special rapporteur for the Subcommittee on Prevention of Discrimination and Protection of Minorities, and is chairperson of the Working Group on Indigenous Populations. As quoted in Tony Simpson and Vanessa Jackson, "Effective Protection of Indigenous Cultural Knowledge: A Challenge for the Next Millennium," *Indigenous Affairs*, 1998, 3:45.

19 *Ibid.*

20 Ana Sittenfeld, "Tropical Medicinal Plant Conservation and Development Projects: The Case of the Costa Rican National Institute of Biodiversity (INBio)," in Balick, Elisabetsky, and Laird, *Medicinal Resources of the Tropical Forest* (cit. n. 6), p. 336.

21 Walter Reid *et al.*, "Biodiversity Prospecting," in *ibid.*, p. 161.

22 From AMRAD Prospectus, 1998.

23 Vandana Shiva and G. S. Nijar, a lawyer with the Third World Network, view enforced compliance with the GATT–TRIPS agreement, as well as the Organization for Economic Cooperation and Development's proposed Multilateral Agreement on Investment, as reinforcing neo-colonial economic relations between the North and South.

24 Articles 8j and 10c.

25 Rhys Jones, "Fire Stick Farming," *Australian Natural History*, Sept. 1968, 16, 3:224–8.

26 Tim Flannery, *The Future Eaters* (Sydney: Reed, 1994), p. 217.

27 This was clearly demonstrated after aboriginal tribes were forced off the pasture lands west of the Great Dividing Range. Forest scrub returned, creating conditions in the early part of the nineteenth century allowing for some of the most destructive bush fires in the colonies' history.

28 Sir Thomas Mitchell, cited in Flannery, *The Future Eaters* (cit. n. 26), p. 220.

29 *New Scientist*, 29 June 1996.

30 Jack R. Kloppenburg and Michael J. Balick, "Property Rights and Genetic Resources: A Frame-work for Analysis," in Balick, Elisabetsky, and Laird, *Medicinal Resources of the Tropical Forest* (cit. n. 6.), p. 181.

31 The Crucible Group, *People, Plants and Patents* (cit. n. 5), p. 92.

32 Kloppenburg and Balick, "Property Rights and Genetic Resources" (cit. n. 30), p. 183.

33 The emergence of biological "Big Science" is similar to the transformation of physics in the 1960s as outlined in John Ziman, *The Force of Knowledge* (Cambridge: Cambridge Univ. Press, 1976).

34 Robert Reich, *Work of Nations: Preparing Ourselves for the 21st Century* (New York: Knopf, 1991).

35 This use of the concept of "core and peripheral states" is drawn from the work of C. Hamelink, "Information Imbalance: Core and Periphery," in *Questioning the Media*, eds. John Downing *et al.* (London: Sage Publications, 1990).

36 For a useful discussion of this issue, see Larry Hempel, *Environmental Governance: The Global Challenge* (Washington, D.C.: Island Press, 1996).

Part Eight
Globalization, Digital Cultures, Identity

Globalization's reliance on information and communications networks also produces new forms of identity-making, contests, hegemonic practices, and resistances. The essays in this section deal with the many appropriations of digital culture, for hegemonic "informational capitalism," identity-building, and social identity, but also in some cases by formerly colonized cultures for resistance or for memory projects of individual communities. Rita Raley's essay on "eEmpires" draws links between technology and capitalism where there is, in the rhetoric of techno-corporates, enough allusion to historical empires. Raley goes on to examine how the "British colonial epistemology of science and an American postindustrial, neocolonial epistemology of IT" merge to produce the system's performativity. Winifred Poster's study of call centers and BPO workers notes how global credit industries work to extract emotional labor from the "Global South." The new credit economy of the late twentieth century, argues Poster, ensures that the consumer is "comfortable" in her/his online transactions by "decoupl[ing] emotional zones from their locational moorings and then root[ing] them in new sites." Rohit Chopra's essay focuses on the Hindutva appropriation of digital technologies in order to present a "primordial" image of Hindu identity. While this appropriation is in keeping with the Hindu majority's long existent control of fields of cultural and knowledge production, we can also discern a subaltern (Dalits, the historically oppressed "lower castes" of Hindu society) appropriation of this same "primordiality discourse" online. Positioning new media and mixed-reality media technologies as something that might help indigenous people to organize the archive itself, Elizabeth Povinelli argues that particular web protocols built into the digital design in the two sample archives she studies determine the logic of what gets to be archived, and how. These protocols prevent the outsider from masquerading as a cultural avatar, even as all files on the archive are geotagged, thereby linking the data to the land or territory of the indigenous people.

Postcolonial Studies: An Anthology, First Edition. Edited by Pramod K. Nayar.
Editorial material and organization © 2016 John Wiley & Sons, Ltd.
Published 2016 by John Wiley & Sons, Ltd.

Part Eight
Globalization, Digital Cultures, Identity

35 Global Primordialities

Virtual Identity Politics in Online Hindutva
and Online Dalit Discourse

Rohit Chopra

This article broadly addresses the online representations of the identity politics discourse of two Indian communities: an elite community of Hindu nationalists and the subaltern community of Dalits. The respective claims about Hindu and Dalit identity, as expressed on select Hindu nationalist and Dalit websites, are remarkably similar in several respects, despite their deep ideological differences. Both online discourses voice their arguments in the vocabulary of the global human rights movement. Dalit sites speak of the ongoing holocaust perpetrated against Dalit communities by upper-caste Hindus, while Hindu nationalist sites assert that Hindus have been the victims of genocide at the hands of Islamic invaders. Each online discourse articulates political claims not on grounds of citizenship, but rather of original territorial inhabitation of the Indian nation and the globe. Both types of online discourse seek to locate the histories of the respective communities as chapters of subordination in a world-historical narrative of domination and resistance. These shared characteristics between the two online discourses may not necessarily be representative of online Indian discourse at large. However, why the similarities should exist at all between the online expressions of two identity politics movements that are radically opposed in their political aspirations is a question worth examining. As this article hopes to show, the consonance between the two discourses is far from accidental but can be grasped with reference to key changes in India during the 1990s, in particular the value accorded to information technology (IT) by the Indian state and society following the liberalization of the Indian economy in 1991, and the ascendancy of Hindu nationalism as a powerful political and cultural movement.

This article's thesis is that developments in the Indian technological and cultural fields in the 1990s have enabled the emergence of a new mode of representing collective

Rohit Chopra, "Global Primordialities: Virtual Identity Politics in Online Hindutva and Online Dalit Discourse." *New Media & Society*, 8(2), 2006: 187–206. Reprinted by permission of SAGE.

identity – which this article terms 'global primordiality' – that explains the curious commonalities between Dalit and Hindu nationalist websites. In the technological field, the quality of globality is now validated as a desirable attribute of Indian identity. In the cultural field, the quality of primordiality is proposed as the basis on which Indian communities can stake a claim to cultural ownership of the nation. Typically, the proposition of global primordiality finds expression in cyberspace, where the realms of technology and culture intersect. However, the model of global primordiality is not shaped in equal measure by Dalits and Hindu nationalists. The primary authors of the practice are Hindu nationalists who also occupy a privileged position as elites in the Indian technological field. In its participation in cyberspace, Dalit discourse may tend to mirror this dominant mode of cyber-representation, even as it remains opposed to the ideology of Hindu nationalism.

Following Castells, the internet and, by extension, cyberspace are conceptualized here as continuous with society, 'an extension of life as it is, in all its dimensions and all its modalities', shaping as much as reflecting social existence (2001: 118). Castells states that while the 'internet has been appropriated by social practice, in all its diversity', at the same time 'this appropriation does have specific effects on social practice itself' (2001: 118). The article employs a cultural studies framework; the websites selected for analysis are understood as discursive objects or 'texts' located in economies of technology and culture that are at once economies of power. The methodology is that of close reading of selected virtual texts with reference to the cultural sociology of the technological practice of the Hindu nationalist and Dalit communities.

The article is structured as follows. Drawing on Bourdieu's theorizations of the field and capital, first it describes changes in the Indian technological and cultural fields since the 1990s. Second, it offers a close reading of selected Hindu nationalist and Dalit websites, with the objective of demonstrating how both types of online discourse express the logic of global primordiality through a rewriting of Indian history. Finally, it concludes with some speculations on the precise role of the internet in contributing to expressions of identity.

The Logic of Globality and Primordiality: Technological and Cultural Fields in India Since the 1990s

According to Bourdieu, social space can be theorized as made up of autonomous (although often overlapping) fields that correspond to different spheres of activity and practice, such as the cultural, economic, social and political (Thompson, 2001). Participants in each field compete over resources – capital – specific to that field. Given the relative autonomy of fields from one another, value or capital in one field does not invariably translate into value in another field, although different types of capital can be traded or cashed in according to specific rates of exchange between fields. Each field has a semi-objective structure, an operational logic that orients how capital may be accumulated and exchanged. The logic of each field is constituted historically and reflects the interests of the dominant groups in the field, those that possess the maximum amount of capital. While autonomous and relatively stable, fields are not immune to being reshaped dramatically by external events. The definition of capital and the logic of the field may be altered by, say, a radical shift in state policy, a path-breaking technological innovation or the situation of war, when some kinds of technology suddenly gain in value. Depending on changes in the field, dominant groups may retain their privilege, lose it or have to share it with new elites.

Reflecting the aspirations of Nehru, the technological field in independent India was constituted through a socialist model of economic planning that emphasized industrial development and heavy state investment in technological education and research. The structure of the field was shaped also by the policy imperatives of self-sufficiency and egalitarian distribution of the material benefits of technology. The dominant groups of participants in the technological field in post-independence India were primarily middle and upper-class, upper-caste, English-speaking urban elites (Chopra, 2003). In post-independence India, there was a disjunction between the ideal-ized conception and actual functioning of the technological field. In practice, the accumulation of technological capital was dependent upon a structure of privileged access to the field, consonant with social hierarchies of class, caste, educational ability and fluency in the English language (Chopra, 2003).

With the liberalization of the Indian economy in 1991, neoliberalism replaced socialism as the policy framework for technological development. National self-sufficiency, through technology or other avenues, is now sought to be achieved within a paradigm of global economic interdependence. IT products and services aimed at global and domestic markets now occupy the pride of place once granted to industri-alization as the motor of the Indian economy. As Greenspan observes, 'Inside India, there is no doubt that the IT industry has created jobs, strengthened exports and made substantial contributions to economic growth' (2004: 109). India's value for the global economy is perceived as significantly dependent on its IT capabilities. As Sachs et al. state, 'India is becoming one of the most important players of the world in the IT sec-tor and it is the fastest growing foreign exchange earner for the country' (2000: xi). The internet, in particular, is viewed as both agency and symbol of the benefits of liberal-ization and technological development. Wolcott and Goodman note that 'the Internet is central to the new vision of India as an IT power in many respects' (2003: 565). The importance of the internet stems from its 'core' role in IT development, its potential to profoundly change the nature of business and private communication, its wide-spread reach and the fact that it is an agent of change in related 'technologies, government policies, laws and services' (2003: 566). The internet is one of the main attractions for American and European companies to set up back office operations in Indian metropolitan areas, in addition to other factors such as the ample availability of labor, low wages and low satellite communication costs (Sachs et al., 2000: xi–xii). The Indian central government and numerous Indian state governments seem to agree on the potential of IT and the internet for socio-economic development. Several Indian states have implemented ambitious e-literacy and e-governance initiatives. National and state government projects are in the process of bringing the benefits of IT and the internet to rural Indian communities. For example, the Warana Village experiment, jointly undertaken by the national government, the Maharashtra state government and the Warana Vibhag Shikshan Mandal, aims to effectively use information and communication technologies (ICTs) including the internet, for the socio-economic development of 70 villages near Warana Nagar in the Kolhapur and Sangli districts of Maharashtra. The Indian government has ambitious plans to provide 1 million internet kiosks all over the country by 2008 (Singh, 2000: i).

However, access to IT and the internet is the privilege of an elite in liberalized India. Keniston points out that, for 'Indians who speak no (or little) English, the barriers to the Information Age are almost insuperable' (2004: 15), given that English is the language in which the bulk of operating systems, software and websites are accessible. The reach of the internet is far more modest than its instrumental value in driving economic reforms. As of 2000, India could boast only 27 million telephone lines for a population of more than 1 billion (Bagchi, 2000). India had an estimated 3.8 million internet subscribers as of September 2002 and an estimated 9.8 million users as of March 2002 (Wolcott and Goodman, 2003: 607–8). By February 2005, the total number of telephone subscribers had increased to 97.03 million (IndiaStat, 2005a). But as of March 2004, the number of internet subscribers had increased to no more than 4.55 million, still a tiny fraction of India's vast population (IndiaStat, 2005b). As Wolcott and Goodman note, while the internet usage base has grown at a fast pace since 1995, 'in the context of the entire country, usage of the internet remains low' (2003: 608). All major Indian cities are wired through internet service providers (ISPs), but rural areas suffer from 'extremely limited' access (2003: 609). Internet usage is limited to an 'urban core' and the predominant users of the Indian internet are the educated middle classes. It is worth noting here that the Indian 'middle classes' are actually socio-economic elites and can be defined broadly as the top 25 percent income-earning segments of Indian society (Vanaik, 2002: 228). According to different parameters, the elite Indian 'middle classes' number anywhere between 100 and 250 million (Vanaik, 2002: 228). Almost 90 percent of all websites visited by Indians are in the English language (Wolcott and Goodman, 2003: 612). Internet reach in the academic and health sectors remains low overall at less than 10 percent, while it has reached moderate levels recently for the commercial and government administrative sectors (Wolcott and Goodman, 2003: 613).

The chief beneficiaries of the technological field in liberalized India are still largely English-speaking, middle- and upper-class and urban groups. But there have been important changes in the internal configuration of the agenda-setters in the field. Keniston has described the emergence of a new elite group in India comprised of workers in high-tech professions. The 'digerati', as Keniston calls them, are 'the beneficiaries of the enormously successful information technology (IT) industry and the other knowledge-based sectors of the economy, such as biotechnology and pharmacology' (2004: 17). Interestingly, the digerati are privileged over equally well-educated workers in other fields of science and technology, such as chemical engineers. Affluent, cosmopolitan and globally mobile, the status of the digerati derives from their technological education and expertise, not from caste, wealth, or social privileges (Keniston, 2004). Through its policies of economic and technological development since the 1980s, but especially the 1990s, the Indian state has endorsed non-resident Indians (NRIs) working in technology as an immensely valuable resource of human capital for the Indian nation (Chakravartty, 2001). Muppidi (2004), in fact argues that with liberalization the NRI has been inscribed in state discourse as the most authentic incarnation of post-colonial citizenship. Indian expatriates, such as students and professionals, are also a key segment for promoting the growth of internet usage (Wolcott and Goodman, 2003).

In the reconfigured Indian technological field, the accumulation of expertise in IT, access to and use of IT have been defined as global practices. The technological capital gained by the use of information technologies is deemed valuable by the Indian state and society because it is globally valid currency, placing its possessors in a position of privilege, even dominance, in the technological field. The principle of globality is therefore enshrined as the logic of the technological field; it determines the allocation of value to different activities within the field and the circuits along which technological capital may be accumulated or traded. The centrality granted to globally encashable technological capital in the developmental vision of the neoliberal Indian state means that the principle of globality (taken as value for the global marketplace, global location and global mobility) confers social status on those who represent or embody it. Consequently, a principle of technological reason – the ascription of value based on expertise in the specific domain of technological practice – is redefined as a broader and more fundamental principle of social reason. The policy outlook of the Indian state and the power of new communities of technological elites have thus resulted in the affirmation of globality as a desirable attribute of Indian social identity since the 1990s.

During the same decade the rise of Hindu nationalism, more than any other event, has been responsible for the increased importance granted to claims of primordiality in cultural and political discourse in Indian society. Contemporary Hindu nationalism is associated with a group of related organizations, including the Rashtriya Swayamsevak Sangh (RSS), Bharatiya Janata Party (BJP), Vishwa Hindu Parishad (VHP) and Bajrang Dal (BD). The BJP is a political party while the other groups call themselves cultural or social organizations. All the organizations share a commitment to the ideology of Hindutva. Formulated in the early 1920s by Veer Savarkar, a militant nationalist leader of the Indian anti-colonial freedom struggle, Hindutva is premised on a primordialist argument that equates authentic Indianness with Hindu cultural origins. For Savarkar, Hindutva, rooted in the Aryan civilization of ancient India, stood for a cultural ethos that exceeded Hinduism as a religion. Hindus were members of a nation who shared a race, culture and territorial origin. However, this imagined community – at once, nation, 'race' and cultural community – did not encompass all the inhabitants of India. For Savarkar, Indian Muslims, Christians, Parsis and Jews were outsiders; they could never be truly Indian since their faiths had originated outside the subcontinent.

Marginalized in Indian politics after independence, Hindu nationalism has resurfaced as a popular and powerful movement in the last two decades. Since the 1980s, Hindu images have begun to appear with higher frequency in advertising, television series and films; Hindu 'values' have gained greater prominence as an element of the rhetoric of many political parties, including the supposedly secular Congress; and the public functions of the secular Indian state have been marked increasingly by the presence of Hindu rituals. Following victory in the 1999 elections, the BJP led the coalition National Democratic Alliance government through its full term until the following election in 2004.[1] Sympathetic to Savarkar's claims, the resurgent Hindu nationalist movement has continued to target Indian religious minorities, especially Muslims and Christians. Hindu nationalists argue that such minorities should publicly accept that Hinduism is the historical/cultural ground of their identity. The movement has also been responsible for anti-Muslim and anti-Christian violence throughout the 1990s. In the academic and educational fields, it has sought to 'correct' what it calls Leftist bias in the writing of Indian history. The Hindutva historical-cum-historiographical endeavor typically describes the period of Mughal rule in India as an age of Islamic

Rohit Chopra

despotism; it reconstructs the history of India as a mythic narrative of Hindu resistance to Islam and Christianity and glorifies the role of Hindu nationalists in the Indian freedom struggle. As Sarkar argues, the 'systematic, consistent and generalized' (2002: 244) project of the Hindu nationalists to control the production of Indian history is motivated by its 'insistence on a homogenised, unitary and aggressive Hindu bloc' (2002: 258) – that is, a cultural essentialist notion of Hindu identity.

The reach of the Hindu nationalist movement is not restricted to the cultural field. However, the attempt to secure legitimacy for the logic of primordiality, central to the grand narrative of Hindu nationalism, is primarily a contestation that is cultural in nature. Hinduness is presented as a form of cultural capital that is sought to be made convertible into other kinds of capital. The Hindu nationalist movement intervenes in social space at the point where the cultural field overlaps with various other fields, such as the political, educational, economic and technological. It seeks to inscribe the primordialist argument – as a principle of cultural reasoning – as part of the logic of accumulation of capital in every field, that is, as a more widely applicable principle of social interaction and exchange. Hinduness, or the quality of primordiality, is thus authorized as a desirable attribute of Indian identity.

There appears to be a significant overlap between the respective profiles of the 'primordialists', the community of Hindu nationalists in the cultural field and the 'globalists', the community of participants in the technological field. Scholars agree that the core support for the Hindu nationalist movement is drawn from India's middle classes or Indian elites (Corbridge and Harriss, 2000; Hansen, 1999; Vanaik, 2002). Corbridge and Harriss view Hindu nationalism as an 'elite' revolt, reflecting 'the interests and aspirations especially of the middle classes and upper castes' (2000: xix). They also note that India's urban socio-economic elites have provided strong support for the BJP in the 1996 and 1999 general elections in India. Such elites, as specified earlier, are among the prime beneficiaries of the reconfigured technological field in liberalized India. A strong bastion of support for Hindu nationalism is an overseas, largely US-based, Hindu population (Das, 2002; Lal, 2001; Rajagopal, 2000). The IT professionals feted by the Indian state are well represented among the diasporic Hindu nationalists. The internet, in particular, seems to be the chosen medium for the Hindu nationalists working in technology to promote Hindutva. 'The much touted thousands of computer and software experts', who count among the recent Indian migrants to the US, 'help maintain over five hundred VHP Web sites (www.vhp.org) with their messages of Hindutva, Hindu history and Muslim-bashing' (Mazumdar, 2003: 240). Rajagopal notes that 'with the proliferation of software engineers from India, the internet has become a site for expansion' of Hindu nationalist discourse (2000: 484). According to Lal (2001), many Hindu nationalist websites are produced by politically and culturally conservative Indian software programmers in the US, who present themselves as historical authorities online.

The overlap between the groups of technology workers and Hindu nationalists indicates the existence of an elite community located in India and the US that views both globality *and* (Hindu) primordiality as desirable attributes of Indian identity. Viewed through the prism of the technocultural imaginary that combines both these qualities, technological expertise is recast in terms of a primordialist cultural ability. As Chakravartty notes, 'corporate networks between India and the United States promote a cyber-capitalist rereading of Hindu values, locating the success of high tech

Indian entrepreneurs in essential characteristics associated with ethno-religious identity' (2001: 343). 'For example, Indian competence in the internet economy', the author observes, 'is associated with the "web of interrelations" that tie together Indian families across national borders' (2001: 343). Conversely, as we will see shortly, the framework of global primordiality also rephrases characteristics of cultural identity in the idiom of a model of global significance.

Along with the rise of elite groups of Hindu nationalists and technological communities, the 1990s in India saw the ascendancy of the subaltern Dalit community as a political force. The term Dalit refers to the historically oppressed and disempowered caste groups of 'Untouchables'. Placed outside the four-fold caste system of traditional Hinduism, the Untouchables were treated as lacking caste itself and, hence, any place in society. These disempowered and disenfranchised caste groups are constitutionally termed 'Scheduled Castes' (SCs). The practice of untouchability has been banned in India since independence in 1947, but casteism is an enduring fact of Indian social existence, widely prevalent among all religious communities. As per the 1991 census, the SCs numbered 138 million or 15.8 percent of the Indian population. Dalit groups are predominantly rural and poor. As Shah notes, 84 percent of SCs inhabit rural areas and most of them work the land. Almost 13 percent are landless, while the bulk of land-owning Dalits are 'small and marginal farmers' (Shah, 2001: 18). Among the more than 2 million Indian bonded laborers who practically work as slaves, 'SCs labourers constitute a sizeable number, if not a majority' (2001: 18–19). The Indian constitution does not recognize as SCs or Dalits those former Untouchables who have converted to Islam or Christianity. Hindu, Sikh and Buddhist Dalits can avail of the affirmative action policies of the Indian state, but Muslim or Christian 'Dalits' cannot.

As Sikand (2003) notes: 'Recent decades have witnessed a remarkable upsurge in radical Dalit assertiveness'. As a rights struggle, the Dalit movement has influenced other non-elite groups too, notably 'the Other Backward Classes (OBCs), who form over half the Indian population, as well as the Christians and Muslims, most of whom share, in terms of social and economic background, much in common with the Dalits' (Sikand, 2003). In the complex game of Indian electoral politics, Dalits have gained in importance as a political constituency, with the rise of Dalit regional parties such as the Bahujan Samaj Party (BSP). However, the Dalit movement has not managed to establish itself as a coherent alternative to the BJP or congress at the national level. The Dalit vote, as indeed the non-elite Indian vote at large, continues to be fractured along regional, religious, linguistic and ideological grounds.

Whether the Dalit movement is understood as a subaltern Hindu revolt or as a wider cause bringing together various non-elite groups, the argument about primordiality does not appear to be central to Dalit discourse. The Dalit movement is primarily an intervention to reshape the Indian political field, seeking to translate numerical strength into political capital through the structure of democracy as a means of challenging and breaking the hegemony of upper-caste Hindus in the institutions of government. To the extent that the movement has succeeded in altering the Indian political field, this success reflects both a fight for constitutional and human rights and an opportunism endemic to the field. For example, in the 1990s the BSP twice entered into a governing alliance with the Hindu nationalist BJP in the Indian state of Uttar Pradesh. As its profile might suggest, the largely poor and rural Dalit community is marginalized in the technological and cultural fields. Omvedt (2001) speaks of 'the upper-caste dominance in the professions, business, culture and the world of Information Technology'. Dalits are near invisible at the Indian Institutes of Technology, India's premier technological institutions (People's Union for Civil Liberties, 2001). Pointing out that private sector IT firms in India have been reluctant in adopting affirmative action policies to increase Dalit presence, Omvedt wryly notes that Indian cyberspace seems particularly populated by the Indian elite. 'If upper caste Brahmins have always seemed to live in a world of philosophy and abstraction', she argues, 'the electronic "virtual" realm of IT seems somehow especially appropriate for them' (Omvedt, 2001). In contrast, millions of Dalits 'have very little access' to the medium of the internet (Vundru, 2001). With reference to the characteristics of the Indian cultural and technological fields described above, we now turn to a reading of Hindu nationalist and Dalit websites.

Online Hindu Nationalist and Dalit Discourse as Cyberhistoriography

The analysis of global primordiality as a mode of representing collective identity is based on a reading of six sites, three representing Hindu nationalist discourse and three representing Dalit discourse.[2] One site from each discourse purporting to archive historical materials on the Hindu and Dalit communities has been included, specifically the Library of Hindu History (www.hindunet.org/hindu_history/hist_index.html) and the Ambedkar Library on Dalitstan (www.dalitstan.org/books/index.html). In addition, there are two sites from each discourse which categorically address the Hindu/Dalit holocaust and genocide: the Online Hindu Holocaust Memorial Museum (http://sarvadharma.org/Museum/HinduHolocaustWelcomePage.htm) and the Hindu Holocaust Museum (www.mantra.com/holocaust/); and the Sudra Holocaust Museum (www.dalitstan.org/holocaust/index.html) and the Brahminist Genocides Index (www.dalitstan.org/journal/genocide/genocide.html). Hereafter, the first Hindu nationalist holocaust site is referred to as the Sarvadharma Museum and the second as the Mantra Museum. The principle of selection followed is simply that the sites should reflect the 'lay' discourse of Hindu nationalists and Dalit communities at large, i.e. the websites should be produced outside the ambit of academic or professional specialization. The cross-section of online discourse chosen here does not qualify as a statistically representative sample. However, this article hopes to show that these websites embody the social logic of global primordiality, which manifests itself as a virtual rewriting of Indian history or cyberhistoriography.

The very choice of the terms 'holocaust' and 'genocide' on both online discourses indicates a two-fold strategy aimed at two distinct audiences. One type of assumed reader of the sites is the enlightened global citizen, possessed of a cosmopolitan universalism and well-educated about the world, whose political sympathies are likely to be stirred by the terms 'holocaust' and 'genocide'. This intended reader may be Indian or non-Indian, Hindu or non-Hindu, Dalit or non-Dalit. Once persuaded of the evidence, this reader, impelled by their conscience, may well further the political cause of the victim community. The second type of assumed reader is community-specific, Hindu nationalist or Dalit, but nevertheless is one who is (presumably) globally mobile or located in transnational circuits. This reader must be socialized into describing the history and condition of the Hindus or Dalits in a terminology that would be immediately resonant and comprehensible in any socio-cultural context in the world. The global relevance of the Hindu holocaust is additionally invoked through locating the victimization of Hindus in a comparative frame with other similar events in world history, for example, the holocaust of the Jews, Armenians, Native American populations and pagan peoples of Europe. A similar contention is found in a text in the Ambedkar Library, *The Bible of Aryan Invasions*, which references the ethnic cleansing of the indigenous populations of South America and the Jews while describing the extermination of the indigenous peoples of India (including Dalits) at the hands of the invaders who introduced Brahminism to the subcontinent (Naidu, 1999).

If the logic of globality is expressed through a frame of comparison, the logic of primordiality manifests itself through two exceptionalist claims about the history of Dalits and Hindus respectively. The first claim concerns the long duration and magnitude of the holocaust or genocide with its origins in antiquity. As the Sarvadharma Museum declares, the '1000-year long holocaust' has resulted in the extermination of 'many millions' of Hindus. The agents of the ongoing holocaust are a succession of invaders beginning with the Greek Alexander, but most notably Muslims and Christians. On both the Sarvadharma Museum and the Mantra Museum, the Islamic invasions of India and duration of Muslim rule of the Indian subcontinent are singled out as the longest, most sustained and unrelentingly brutal phase of the genocide of Hindus. This contention is repeated in articles accessible through the Hindu Library of History (Vyas, 1994–2003a, 1994–2003b). The Dalitstan website (from which the Sudra Holocaust Museum is linked), speaks of the '2000-year long Sudra' holocaust, while the museum itself is dedicated itself to 'the memory of millions of slain Sudroids', a category that includes Dalits among other Indian communities. A section of the museum that focuses on the 'modern' phase of the Dalit genocide states that Hinduism, '[t]he religion based on caste system has annihilated millions of Dalits over the centuries' and that Dalit killings continue unabated (Sudra Holocaust Museum, 2001). On the document, the number of Dalits killed in just the last 50-odd years since Indian independence in 1947 is listed as 1 million and those enslaved as 40 million. On the home page of the Brahminist Genocides Index site, Brahmanism or upper-caste Hinduism is described as responsible for the annihilation of not only Indian Dalits but also Indian Muslims and Christians. Both types of sites present the argument that the Hindu/Dalit holocaust has been unparalleled in human history, exceeding in its severity and toll various other genocides and holocausts.[3]

The second, related, line of reasoning reflecting the logic of primordiality is that the holocaust of the Hindus and Dalits is not merely the extermination of a particular Indian community, but the decimation of one of the oldest cultures known to humanity. In both sets of websites, it is asserted or implied that Dalits/Hindus are ur-communities of the subcontinent and the original inhabitants of the Indus Valley settlement, a civilization dating back to around 2300 BC. On the Sarvadharma Museum website, Hinduism – which is used interchangeably and synonymously with 'Indian civilization' – is described as the only one of the 'great ancient civilizations' that has survived the 'onslaught of the western Abrahamic monotheist religions' (Hindu Holocaust Memorial Museum, nd). A text in the Ambedkar Library describes Dalits as one group within a larger 'Indo-Negroid' or 'Sudroid' race, which is defined as an aboriginal, indigenous, black population of India that is genetically, culturally and linguistically closely related to 'Africoid' and 'Australoid' communities (Rao, nd). The suggestion is that of a pan-national community, resembling the core proposition of the Afro-Dalit project, the 'premise that Dalits are part of the African diaspora and that they are the first settlers in the Indian subcontinent' (Prashad, 2000). The implication of the arguments on the websites about the destruction of an ancient, original people of the earth is that the Dalit/Hindu holocaust and genocide is tantamount to a veritable destruction of humanity itself.

Contestation about the original peoples of the subcontinent also manifests itself in the form of diametrically opposed positions, seen on the websites as indeed, 'offline', with regard to the propositions of the Aryan Invasion Theory. This theory, long primarily the preserve of the academic discipline of Indology, proposes that Vedic Hinduism was brought to the Indian subcontinent by fair-skinned European tribes who conquered the indigenous dark-skinned Dravidians of the region. The Aryans destroyed the Indus Valley civilization, pushing the majority of the native population to the southern part of India. The subordination of indigenous populations was institutionalized through the caste system, which allowed the Aryans to preserve their dominance even as they assimilated with segments of the native community. The theory implies that Brahmins and upper-caste Hindus are descendants of Aryan ruling groups while lower caste and Untouchable communities are descendants of the original vanquished communities. The theory has not been unchallenged; an alternate reading of the evidence, considered credible by archaeologists, historians and Indologists, proposes that Aryans entered India through successive waves of migration, not invasion.

Hindu nationalist sites are invested in disputing the idea that Aryans were invaders, since the notion strongly undermines the grounds of their objection to Indian Muslims and Christians. Similarly, they challenge the claim that Aryans were outsiders of any kind, since that argument gives the lie to the core proposition of Hindutva that Vedic Hinduism is the indigenous historical-cultural basis of Indian society. Instead, the movement is committed to the propagation of the Indo-Saraswati theory, according to which Vedic Hinduism originated within a civilization that chronologically predates the Indus Valley civilization but is culturally contiguous with it. Thus, on the Library of Hindu History, a section is dedicated to articles that problematize the Aryan Invasion Theory (Hindu Library of History, 2003). Dalit sites, conversely, defend the Aryan Invasion Theory with vigor, rejecting not just the Indo-Saraswati theory but also the alternative reading of Aryan migration to India. Several texts in the Ambedkar Library employ the framework of the Aryan Invasion Theory in their arguments, explicating in detail the actions of Aryan invaders and their consequences for Dalit and other indigenous Indian communities (Nadar, 1999; Naidu, 1999; Tudu, nd).

The modality of global primordiality on both Dalit and Hindu nationalist websites takes shape as a cyberhistoriographic endeavor where the necessary rewriting of Indian history becomes a form of political activism. Dalit sites point to the misrepresentations of a politically motivated 'Brahminist' history that denies the fact of the Sudra holocaust and the Aryan Invasion Theory, while the well-worn Hindutva grouse against Marxist hegemony in Indian history-writing is found on articles and sites linked to the chosen Hindu nationalist sites (Gandasa, 2000; Walia, nd). The mode of global primordiality rests on an erasure of two specificities: first, elision of the particular problematics of evidence to make the case for the respective holocaust and genocide of the Hindus and Dalits; second, effacement of the specificity of the Indian *state*. The complexities of the subcontinent's early history are ignored as Dalit/ Hindu history is presented, on the basis of weak evidence, in terms of a universal history of suffering and, at the same time, as a founding moment in this history. The Dalit and Hindu holocausts are both global and primordial in this sense. While the Indian *nation* is manifest in the discourse as the cultural property of the Dalit/Hindu communities and as a cultural essence that is synonymous with humanity itself – part, as it were, of the very soul of humankind – what is conspicuously absent in both discourses is any serious attempt to engage with the institutions of the independent Indian state. There is no argument, for example, that addresses Hindu nationalist or Dalit claims in terms of the constitutional rights or concept of citizenship offered by the Indian state. The state as an institution is subordinate to the original 'nations' of the Hindus or Dalits, even as the globe is imagined as consisting of such 'nations' or 'peoples' instead of nation-states.

The expression of global primordiality described above corresponds well with the mode of social identity authorized by the dominant elites in the cultural and technological fields – those Hindu nationalists who produce, use and participate in online technologically-powered identity discourse. The cyberhistoriographic imperative that locates history and identity in simultaneously global and primordial terms seems apposite for the Hindu nationalist project of 'correcting' history, its assertion of original inhabitation of the Indian nation and its rhetoric of victimization at the hands of invaders. Certainly, these issues are pertinent to the Dalit movement, yet the energies of the movement are focused also on other matters more urgent to its cause. The question remains, then, why Dalit discourse should resemble Hindu nationalist discourse so closely in its respective expressions in cyberspace.

A theoretical clarification about a structural property of fields may explain the resemblance and near-identity between the discourses. According to Bourdieu, the struggle for accumulation of capital within a field can be understood as a game played by participants according to the rules of that field. Bourdieu states that to participate in the game is to accept tacitly the rules of the game. It is to be 'interested' and 'absolutely invested' in the game (1997: 11). Participation, in turn, is an affirmation of the logic of the field. Even if a player wishes to challenge the stakes by which capital is defined in a field, they can do so only by playing according to those very stakes. Every player in the game validates the existing principle of accumulation as legitimate through the simple act of participation. This means that as subaltern groups seek to accumulate capital in a field, they must utilize those very strategies, techniques and choices that are beneficial to dominant groups, at least until the point where the former can accumulate a critical mass of capital to redefine the rules of the game. Thus online Dalit discourse cannot be understood as merely imitating online Hindu nationalist discourse. Rather, since Hindu nationalists in the arena of cyberspace have authorized a form of reasoning – the mode of global primordiality – as a form of virtual technological/cultural capital, Dalit intervention in cyberspace may be compelled to restructure its arguments in the same form to accumulate more capital. This article concludes by addressing briefly the question of the role that the internet may have played in promoting this particular form of reasoning and, more generally, in enabling expressions of identity.

Conclusion: Locating the 'Virtual' in Virtual Identity Politics

In this article, following Castells (2001), the construct of 'Indian' cyberspace has been located within the context of wider social processes and forces such as globalization, national technology policy and changes in the sphere of culture and politics. Castells (2000) has described the internet as a central feature of the 'network society' that has crystallized over the second half of the 20th century due to innovations in computing and telecommunications, transformations in the workforce and nature of work and the social impact of the mass media. He argues that in the network society, practically every dimension of contemporary society operates in terms of flows – of capital, information and technology, as well as images, sights and sounds. The internet facilitates and contributes to such flows, even as it might transform them. He also contends that privileged groups in a network society are comprised of a spatial grid of transnational elites whose decisions dictate the flows of different resources (Castells, 2000). Castells' argument about transnational elites squares with the assessment, offered earlier in this article, about the role of Indian socio-economic elites as agents of a new form of articulating social identity in cyberspace. This article's suggestion is that, in addition to the particularities of the cultural and technological fields in India, the dynamics and mechanics of flows of information on the internet also contribute to the shaping of the mode of global primordiality as a paradigm of representing identity.

The globality of the internet suggests that the medium may promote an increasingly standardized logic of social practice, including a vocabulary or mode of expression of communal or group identity. The point here is that if that a particular practice translates into any kind of capital, it can be repeated quickly and legitimated as an axiom of virtual behavior. This may not necessarily happen; indeed, such a practice may be ignored or die out. But the interactive nature and wide reach of the medium suggest that consensus about the value or utility of an act or opinion can emerge within a relatively short duration and on a relatively large scale. At the same time, thanks to this very feature of the rapid circulation of knowledge via the medium, information exchange on the internet is characterized by the borrowing of ideas, concepts and stratagems *across* movements which, ironically, may be polar opposites in their political objectives, commitments and values. In this manner, internet discourse may be characterized by the somewhat paradoxical quality of standardized hybridity, a bricolage across borders. The modality of global primordiality in online Dalit discourse and Hindu nationalist discourse reveals this quality; it reflects a standardized vocabulary of 'genocide' and 'holocaust', a borrowing of the terms from the history of other communities and the cross-fertilization between Dalit and Hindu nationalist discourse in terms of strategies of representation and argument. The flow of information on the internet may help to accelerate the entrenchment of dominant logics in the technocultural domain of cyberspace.

Relatedly, while the quality of standardized hybridity creates the space for a vastly expanded realm of strategic and tactical possibilities, it may promote also a relativization of truths where it becomes difficult to assess the credibility of truth claims, especially to distinguish between apparently similar kinds of claims. The Hindu nationalist and Dalit sites are a case in point, embodying the problem of apparent equivalence in the logic of their respective political assertions and objectives. The ongoing historical oppression of Dalits, if not the genocide or holocaust, at the hands of upper-caste Hindus is a legitimate fact, unlike the Hindu nationalist claim of ongoing historical oppression at the hands of Muslims. One would be hard-pressed, however, to make that case just on the basis of the arguments on the two types of websites, given the similarities in the form of reasoning employed in both types of online discourse. At the same time, however, the relativization of truth claims – enabled by the tools and resources of the internet – is also a provincialization of truth claims. One might argue that on the Dalit sites, the absolutist arguments of the Hindu nationalist movement are deconstructed through a confrontation with their inverted doubles, logically identical but substantively antithetical. Indeed, here may lie the political value of the internet; inasmuch as the glut of information in cyberspace muddies the line between knowledge and 'noise', it may help also to unmask the atrocity of noise masquerading as knowledge.

The cyberhistoriographic rewriting of Dalit and Hindu history in the mode of global primordiality encapsulates the ambivalent effects of the internet in promoting flows of discourse. The sites reveal the pros and cons of the tenor of standardized hybridity and typify the problematic relativization/provincialization of truth claims. In addition, the websites represent another paradox: they stand for a democratization of the production of historical knowledge and the tools of representation, even though the product of this wider democratization may result in the endorsement of patently undemocratic values, as seen on Hindu nationalist websites. The internet may seem far removed from the realm of concrete political action and practice but, as suggested by the contestations on Dalit and Hindu nationalist sites, it is by no means a rarified ether that voids all causes of political urgency. If representation on the internet or cyberspace is subject to a politics of disembodiment, it is also subject to a politics of reconstitution in which the medium is implicated. The new modes of imagining identity thrown up by cyberspace may create new problems of thinking politics and conceptualizing praxis, but equally they may offer fresh solutions to problems, old and new.

Notes

1. Following the 1996 national elections, the BJP spearheaded a short-lived coalition government that lasted 13 days. A BJP-led government, formed after national elections in 1998, lasted for about a year. In the 2004 national elections, the Congress emerged as a surprising winner with the maximum number of seats. The congress leads the current coalition United Progressive Alliance government. The BJP received 21.48 percent of the vote in 2004 as compared to the congress share of 26.21 percent (for details of the 2004 election, see Indian Election, 2005).

2. The three Dalit sites chosen here are part of the Dalistan Organisation portal (www.dalitstan.org). They may be viewed also as three sections of the same umbrella website or information gateway.

3. 'The massacres perpetuated by the Aryans in India during the 1000 years of the Vedic Dark Ages are unparalleled in history, exceeding the Holocaust of the Jews by the Nazis (which was inspired by the Vedic Aryans) and the slaughter of the South American native populations by the invading Spaniards and Portuguese. Almost all of the 5 million inhabitants of the Indus Valley perished, besides unnumbered others' (Naidu, 1999).

A near identical quote by Francois Gautier is found on the Hindu Holocaust Museum website homepage: 'The massacres perpetrated by Muslims in India are unparalleled in history, bigger than the holocaust of the Jews by the Nazis; or the massacre of the Armenians by the Turks; more extensive even than the slaughter of the South American native populations by the invading Spanish and Portuguese.' (Hindu Holocaust Museum, 2003)

References

Bagchi, P. (2000) 'Telecommunications Reform and the State in India: the Contradiction of Private Control and Government Competition', *CASI Occasional Paper 13*, URL (consulted September 2004): http://www.sas. upenn.edu/casi/reports/Bagchipaper120000.htm

Bourdieu, P. (1997) *Pascalian Meditations* (trans. R. Nice). Stanford, CA: Stanford University Press.

Castells, M. (2000) *The Rise of the Network Society* (2nd edn). Oxford: Blackwell.

Castells, M. (2001) *The Internet Galaxy: Reflections on the Internet, Business and Society*. Oxford: Oxford University Press.

Chakravartty, P. (2001) 'The Emigration of High-Skilled Indian Workers to the United States: Flexible Citizenship and India's Information Economy', in W.A. Cornelius, T.J. Espenshade and I. Salehyan (eds) *The International Migration of the Highly Skilled: Demand and Supply and Development Consequences in Sending and Receiving Countries*, pp. 325–49. La Jolla, CA: Center for Comparative Immigration Studies.

Chopra, R. (2003) 'Neoliberalism as *Doxa*: Bourdieu's Theory of the State and the Contemporary Indian Discourse on Globalization and Liberalization', *Cultural Studies* 17(3–4): 419–44.

Corbridge, S. and J. Harriss (2000) *Reinventing India: Liberalization, Hindu Nationalism and Popular Democracy*. Malden, MA: Blackwell.

Das, A.N. (2002) 'The End of Geography: Nationalism in the Era of Globalization', in R. Starr (ed.) *Nations Under Siege: Globalization and Nationalism in Asia*, pp. 31–62. New York: Palgrave.

Gandasa, K. (2000) 'Brahminist Historical Propaganda', in *Collapse of the Brahminist Empire* (ch. 4), Ambedkar Library, URL (consulted September 2004): http://www. dalitstan.org/books/gandasa/gandasa4.html

Greenspan, A. (2004) *India and the IT Revolution: Networks of Global Culture*. New York: Palgrave.

Hansen, T.B. (1999) *The Saffron Wave: Democracy and Hindu Nationalism in Modern India*. Princeton, NJ: Princeton University Press.

Hindu Holocaust Memorial Museum (nd) 'Historical Overview', URL (consulted September 2004): http://sarvadharma.org/Museum/history/histories.htm

Indian Election (2005) 'Results Update', URL (consulted March 2005): http://www.indian-elections. com/resultsupdate/

IndiaStat (2005) 'Table: Number of Subscribers in Cellular (including WLL) and Fixed Line in India (2000 to 2005)', URL (consulted November 2005): http://www.indiastat.com/india/ShowData.asp?secid = 368487&ptid = 19279&level = 4

IndiaStat (2005) 'Table: Number of Internet Subscribers in India (March 2000–2004)', URL (consulted November 2005): http://www.indiastat.com/india/ ShowData.asp?secid = 291283&ptid = 143&level = 3

Keniston, K. (2004) 'Introduction: the Four Digital Divides', in K. Keniston and D. Kumar (eds) *IT Experience in India: Bridging the Digital Divide*, pp. 11–36. New Delhi: Sage.

Lal, V. (2001) 'The Politics of History on the Internet: Cyber-Diasporic Hinduism and the North American Hindu Diaspora', in M.R. Paranjape (ed.) *In Diaspora: Theories, Histories, Texts*, pp. 179–221. New Delhi: Indialog Publications.

Library of Hindu History (2003) Aryan Invasion Theory links, URL (consulted September 2004): http://www. hindunet.org/hindu_history/ancient/aryan/aryan_link. html

Mazumdar, S. (2003) 'The Politics of Religion and National Origin: Rediscovering Hindu Indian Identity in the United States', in V. Kaiwar and S. Mazumdar (eds) *Antinomies of Modernity: Essays on Race, Orient, Nation*, pp. 223–60. Durham, NC: Duke University Press.

Muppidi, H. (2004) *The Politics of the Global*. Minneapolis, MN: University of Minnesota Press.

Nadar, S. (1999) 'Brahmin Gold', *Dalitstan Journal* 1(2), URL (consulted November 2004): http://www.dalitstan. org/books/b_gold/index.html

Naidu, U. (1999) 'Early Vedic Aryan Invasions: Aryan Invasions & Genocide of Negroes, Semites & Mongols, The Bible of Aryan Invasions, Vol. II', *Dalitstan Journal* 1(2), URL (consulted November 2004): http://www. dalitstan.org/books/bibai/bibai2.html

Omvedt, G. (2001) 'Untouchables in the World of IT', *Panos London Online*, URL (consulted May 2004): http://www.panos.org.uk/newsfeatures/featureprintable. asp?id = 1177

People's Union for Civil Liberties (2001) 'Dalits at the Indian Institutes of Technology', *PUCL Bulletin*, URL (consulted July 2004): http://www.pucl.org/reports/ National/2001/dalits.htm Prashad, V. (2000) 'Badges of Color: an Afro-Dalit Story', *Znet*, URL (consulted September 2004): http://www.zmag.org/zmag/articles/ march2000prashad.htm

Rajagopal, A. (2000) 'Hindu Nationalism in the US: Changing Configurations of Political Practice', *Ethnic and Racial Studies* 23(3): 467–96.

Rao, H. (nd) 'The Sudroid (Indo-Negroid) Race', *Ambedkar Library*, URL (consulted September 2004): http://www.dalitstan.org/books/sudroid/

Sachs, J.D., A. Varshney and N. Bajpai (eds) (2000) 'Preface to the Paperback Edition', in *India in the Era of Economic Reforms*, pp. vii–xvii. New Delhi: Oxford University Press.

Sarkar, S. (2002) *Beyond Nationalist Frames: Postmodernism, Hindu Fundamentalism, History*. Bloomington, IN: Indiana University Press.

Shah, G. (2001) 'Introduction: Dalit Politics' in G. Shah (ed.) *Dalit Identity and Politics: Cultural Subordination and the Dalit Challenge, Volume 2*, pp. 17–43. New Delhi: Sage.

Sikand, Y. (2003) 'The "Dalit Muslims" and the All-India Backward Muslim Morcha', *Qalandar: Islam and Interfaith Relations in South Asia*, URL (consulted September 2004): http://www.islaminterfaith.org/sep2003/article.html

Singh, H.S. (2000) 'Ways and Means of Bridging the Gap Between Developed and Developing Countries', paper presented at the Panel on Information Technology and Public Administration, United Nations, New York, 26 September, URL (consulted July 2003): http://unpan1.un.org/intradoc/gros/public/documents/APCITY/UNPAN014648.pdf

Sudra Holocaust Museum (2001) 'Genocide of Dalits in the Indian Union (1947ff.)', URL (consulted September 2004): http://www.dalitstan.org/holocaust/bharat/idxbhar.html

Thompson, J.B. (ed) (2001) 'Editor's Introduction', in P. Bourdieu, *Language and Symbolic Power* (trans. G. Raymond and M. Adamson), pp. 1–31. Cambridge, MA: Harvard University Press.

Tudu, S. (nd) 'The Destruction of Indian Civilizations', URL (consulted June 2004): http://www.dalitstan.org/books/destruction/destruction.html

Vanaik, A. (2002) 'Consumerism and New Classes in India', in S. Patel, J. Bagchi and K. Raj (eds) *Thinking Social Science in India: Essays in Honour of Alice Thorner*, pp. 227–34. New Delhi: Sage.

Vundru, R.S. (2001) 'On Their Way to the Information Highway', URL (consulted June 2004): http://www.ambedkar.org/chandrabhan/Ontheir.htm

Vyas, S. (1994a) 'Hindu Genocide in East Pakistan', Hindu Library of History, URL (consulted September 2004): http://www.hindunet.org/hindu_history/modern/hindu_bangla.html

Vyas, S. (1994b) 'Hindu Kush Means Hindu Slaughter', *Hindu Library of History*, URL (consulted September 2004): http://www.hindunet.org/hindu_history/modern/hindu_kush.html

Walia, C.J.S. (nd) '*Rewriting Indian History* by Francois Gautier', *IndiaStar Review of Books*, URL (consulted September 2004): http://www.indiastar.com/wallia10.htm

Wolcott, P. and S. Goodman (2003) 'Global Diffusion of the Internet I: Is the Elephant Learning to Dance?', *Communications of the Association for Information Systems* 11: 560–646 (available at: http://mosaic.unomaha.edu/India_2003.pdf).New Media & Society 8(2)

36   Hidden Sides of the Credit Economy

Emotions, Outsourcing, and Indian Call Centers

Winifred R. Poster

Scholars remark that it is not necessarily 'rational' for consumers to get into debt and/or pay it back (Elster, 1989). The purpose of this analysis is to explore the sociological sources of the credit accumulation process. In particular, I examine how the process of acquiring and sustaining consumer credit requires emotion work – a navigation of thoughts, identities, and most importantly, feelings, to persuade citizens to plunge into debt. These non-material items are the crucial link between the firms who seek the debtor, and the action of the consumer signing onto it.

This is the story of the people who do that work – the 'emotional hitmen' of credit. Just like Perkins's (2004) 'economic hitmen' (clandestine officials for intergovernmental agencies in the Global North who secure large, often unpayable, loans by state governments in the Global South[1]), the process of securing debt from the public requires its emissaries and staff. Emotional hitmen are central to credit industries, as unseen actors who spend their days convincing consumers to acquire debt from private firms, and then urging or threatening them into making the payments. They manage the 'softer' side of credit – peoples' personal stories, biographies, family and work situations, etc. – which condition their ability to pay back loans.

Increasingly, these workers operate in transnational fields. Outsourcing has sent the customer service work of credit from the US to India. Particularly since the 2000s as white-collar work became digitally mobile, firms have been transferring key aspects of the credit industry – debt consolidation, collections, telemarketing sales – to the Global South. Just like the economic hitmen then, these emotional hitmen operate in a global platform. The path is different, however. Instead of moving linearly from Global North to South, they switch back as a cross-border boomerang: these credit firms hire Indian employees to target *their own* customers in the US.

Winifred Poster, "Hidden Sides of the Credit Economy: Emotions, Outsourcing, and Indian Call Centres." *International Journal of Comparative Sociology*, 54(3), 2013: 205–227. Reprinted by permission of SAGE.

This analysis is based on case studies of three Indian call centers, where employees in India handle credit service on the phone for US customers. Research involved ethnographic observations and intensive interviews with 85 workers, managers, and officials in the Northern region of India.

I will argue that Indian call centers signify a nexus for three dynamics in the contemporary economy: globalization, emotions, and credit. While the literature has yet to connect these forces conceptually, I show how they intersect. To start with, *emotions are integral to credit*. Managers train employees to utilize particular types of emotion work to secure credit: appeals to customers' intimacies (deep sensitivities and anxieties about money, family, self, etc.) and their moralities (ethics about finance and sense of honor about paying debts). Second, *credit is a driver of outsourcing*. This industry has served historically as the founder, and continues to be the primary client base of offshore customer services in India. Third, *outsourcing facilitates the emotional components of credit work*. Moving these functions from the Global North to South enables credit firms to access highly skilled and inexpensive workers, and monitor their emotions rigorously in the ongoing labor process.

I will argue that Indian call centers reveal the globalization of an affect economy. In what Hochschild (2003) refers to as 'emotional imperialism', Northern credit firms use outsourcing to extract emotional labor from the Global South. Expanding on this thesis, I argue that outsourcing shifts not only where firms get their emotional labor, but in some ways, how they construct it.

Following my discussion of the literature and research sites below, I delve into each of these three segments of the credit-emotion-outsourcing cycle. Next I recount the tension it creates for credit firms, as outsourcing presents a *transnational cognitive dissonance* in the meanings of credit and consumption. In turn, the call centers respond by re-nationalizing Indian moralities and intimacies of credit to those of the US. Finally, I discuss implications for our understandings of these intersecting forces, especially for Indian workers and US consumers.

Literature

Previous studies have examined separately (or in pairings) the three dynamics of credit, emotions, and outsourcing. Rarely have they considered them as an interactive set, however. Here I discuss how this leaves gaps in the literature, and what we can learn by viewing them more integrally.

First, *credit has been absent from the outsourcing literature*. This is especially true for the research on Indian call centers. The last decade has seen a wealth of studies in this area, yet few focus on the specific industries that are involved, or the substantive context of the work. When I began my own fieldwork, in fact, credit was not a focal point. It became quickly apparent to me, however, that credit is what employees are often doing on the phone with customers. Thus, I will show how credit and outsourcing are not coincidental, unrelated events. They are emerging and growing together, and have implications for the emotional dynamics of customer service in Indian call centers.

Second, *the emotions literature has yet to explore the full range and impact of credit*. As a foundation, the sociological literature gave us the concept of 'emotion work', revealing how employers often ask workers to invoke, perform, and deliver particular emotions as part of the job. Hochschild (1983) featured bill collectors, significantly, in her seminal study of emotion work. She shows how bill collectors are the heel versus the toe of the service industry, performing the opposite role of emotion work from that of the flight attendants, who work for the same larger company. They deflate rather than enhance the status of the customer; they insult and coerce rather than smile and comfort. Later, Sutton (1991) found that credit firms encourage bill collectors to present a general tone of urgency, with contingencies for irritation, anger, calmness, and warmth depending on customer mood. A primary focal point of this literature, then, is the emotions that workers should display when interacting with consumers.

With outsourcing, we see a broader view of the credit industry, and in turn, an expansion in the emotion work of credit. I will show how it occurs in locations beyond the home country of the firm (in this case, the US), and how it involves more than just collections and debt repayment. As a characteristic of globalization, outsourcing 'compresses' (Castells, 2000) diverse credit activities in call centers. Global call centers integrate functions of sales, financing, and collections, exposing credit for the wide-ranging process that it is – intimately tied to the rise of consumption, service, and financialization (Sassen, 2008). As these call centers do more than collections, their employees have to learn skills beyond being stern and deflating the status of the customer. They require emotional strategies that get at the heart of cross-credit functions. In my study, they appear as *intimacies and moralities*, involving less emphasis on emotional display by the worker, and more emphasis on the complex navigation of feelings of the consumer.

Outsourcing impacts the emotions of credit through a second globalizing imperative – 'dispersion'. Simultaneous to the compression dynamic above, outsourcing spreads and distances the relations of credit (in this case, between employee and customer) across national boundaries. This process exposes a geography of emotions (Ahmed, 2004) within credit. As call center managers find, the exchanges between employee and customer have groundings in localized meanings and interpretations. Transnational settings reveal, quite critically, how the emotions themselves (those on display and under target) are not about credit alone, but are reflective of 'American' feelings of credit (i.e. believing that credit is a social imperative, feeling that it is a morally good thing to do, etc.). Moreover, this global dispersion invokes additional types of emotions within the credit exchange by the consumer – feelings about outsourcing as a process. This study will illustrate how nationalized emotions of credit surface in Indian call centers.

My third critique is that *emotions are missing from the outsourcing literature*. Researchers often study outsourcing for its material foundations. Economists, for instance, note the importance of global labor arbitrage for outsourcing, as firms move their jobs to countries where hiring workers is less expensive, where they can save on rent and physical infrastructures, and where they receive exemptions from legal regulations.

Many studies are revealing the *nonmaterial* sides of outsourcing, however. Arvidsson (forth-coming) notes how traditional 'tangible' assets are becoming more unstable and problematic. To bolster market capabilities and power therefore, firms are turning to 'intangible assets'. These include 'affective investments such as reputation, goodwill, or employee motivation' (pp. 3 and 7). Particularly with the rise of the service industry, firms are trading and exchanging emotions for corporate value in the global economy.

This changes the scope of what global firms seek from their workers. It involves what Hochschild (2003) calls the 'new emotional imperialism'. In contrast to colonial era imperialism, which involved extracting material resources from the Global South, emotional imperialism involves extracting immaterial resources: love, care, and feelings. Transnational industries in domestic service, teaching, and nursing illustrate this process, as they import workers physically from the Global South to provide care and other positive emotions to children, families, patients, students, etc., in the North (Ehrenreich and Hochschild, 2003).

In a similar way, US credit industries turn to Indian workers to provide intimacy and morality talk for US consumers. As they send customer service to India, US credit firms move emotion work from Global North to South. *Indian call centers, therefore, show how credit firms are shifting the geographic source of where they get their emotional labor.*

It's important to note how this stage of imperialism rests on that of previous eras. The contemporary global credit industry, in particular, benefits from British colonialism in India in many ways, not the least of which are the English language policies that have diffused through a large portion of middle-class society. The ability of the white-collar labor force to speak English is a key factor that draws firms to India, and enables them to articulate the emotions of credit to their consumers, despite indigenous language differences.

I will elaborate on Hochschild's concept to argue that, for credit, emotional imperialism refigures not only the location of the labor force but transforms aspects of the emotion work itself. Some kinds of emotions are more easily transportable within emotional imperialism (care, love, etc.). Others, like those of credit, are less so. Firms and their workers have to modify them while extracting them. *Through the outsourcing of call centers to India, there is a re-nationalization of meanings and feelings of credit, as workers mobilize the intimacies and moralities across borders.*

In sum, to provide a more integrated view of these three factors – credit, emotions, and outsourcing – this study explores their inter-connections and cyclical relations in Indian call centers.

Research Methods, Sites, and Sources

I use the approach of global ethnography (Burawoy et al., 2000) to illuminate the dynamic. This methodology helps the researcher to see the macro within the micro, and to explore how global forces act through and from local sites. Thus, while this study is not comparative across the US and India, it captures the agency of actors from both places in the single settings of Indian call centers.

I conducted my study at a time when this industry was taking off, from late 2002 to early 2004. Fieldwork involved ethnographic case studies of Indian call centers in the northern region of India near New Delhi: in particular, the neighboring cities of Noida (state of Uttar Pradesh) and Gurgaon (state of Haryana). This triadic region is where the call center industry began, and still has one of the largest concentrations of organizations. Three call centers were the focus of the fieldwork (Table 1). I selected them through several informants – one through personal connections, another recommended by an industry association, and the third recommended by a government official. The firms represent variations within this industry in terms of size, ownership,

Table 1 Characteristics of call center firms, workers, and jobs

	SmallCo	MiddleCo	BigCo
Firm characteristics			
Ownership	Subcontractor (Indian-owned)	Joint venture(co-ownership)	Transnational (US-owned)
Number of employees (rounded)	40	200	3,000
Founding year of firm	2003	2001	2000
Employee characteristics			
Highest educational level[a]	High school	College	Post-college
Age (years)[a]	22	22	26
Time in job (months)[a]	1.4	6.8	11.1
Training and rewards			
Length of training (weeks)	No training	3.5 to 4	6 to 14
Percent of training on style (e.g. emotion) versus process (e.g., details of product or service)	–	75 to 86	50
Annual salary[a] (converted from rupees)	$4,536	$5,076	$7,044
Rewards and incentives	Party at work; dinner outing to a restaurant	Certificate; name on notice board; pizza and ice cream; cash	CD players; cash; trips to the US for training

[a] Listings and figures are averages for each firm.

and global positioning (altered names to indicate this): BigCo, a multinational firm with about 3000 employees; MediumCo, a joint venture firm with a US company having about 200 employees; and SmallCo, an Indian-owned firm with 40 employees.

My methods involved interviews and observations. At these three firms, I conducted 50 formal (semi-structured) interviews with calling agents. This includes about 15 from each firm (with a handful of interviews from a few additional firms for more breadth of comparison). Interviews were conducted in English and lasted about an hour. Sample selection was based on employee lists provided by the human resource department. I chose respondents chosen randomly, although balancing samples according to gender and occupational level. My sample is mostly male, at about 60–70 percent, which is illustrative of the national distribution. Most of the population is also young, highly educated, and urban. (I changed the names of informants to protect their anonymity. At the request of call center managers, I also changed names of some of the US firms contracting the services.)

I talked to other types of informants as well, through more informal, unstructured interviews. This includes 20 interviews with HR managers, quality control personnel, recruiters, trainers, nurses, etc. I conducted another 15 interviews outside these firms with experts and professionals from the community, such as representatives of industry associations, government officials, and employee associations. To get a feel for the experience of call center work, I observed the 'production floor', attended training seminars, joined agents for dinner in the cafeteria, etc.

The routines of call center work are highly structured and standardized. A typical day in call center involves sitting for eight hours on the phone in front of a computer. Shifts are very rigid, with precise meal and rest breaks. On average, workers make hundreds of calls a day. This depends, however, on the particular 'campaign': a tech support employee could spend an entire shift on a single call; a telemarketer may make 20,000 calls a day (van Jaarsveld and Poster, 2012). Some campaigns can involve scripts for employees to recite and follow, which can dictate explicitly the type of emotions to convey. Given that the main activity of the work is talking, the components of that talk – including emotions – become critical measures for how supervisors evaluate the jobs and determine the quality of the service that employees are providing.

To explore the US actors in the story, the credit corporations, consumers, etc., I did additional research between 2009 and 2012. This involved analyzing websites of credit, debt, and call center companies, and 'webinars' (or online videos) about their products and programs. Below I describe the three interrelated dynamics of globalized credit, starting with the impact of the credit industry on outsourcing as a process.

Credit as a Driver of Outsourcing

Credit, sales, and debt are massive industries. In 2011, revenues in US credit cards firms were $154.9 billion, and revenues in collections were $12.2 billion. Credit card companies are the 'engine' of the banking industry, making more money on the fees than on the goods they are selling (Schechter, 2007). Most debt with collections agencies is for credit cards, but it may be shifting to cell phones, medical care, utilities, etc. In collections, there are 140,000+ workers, each of whom collects on average $245,000. The impact on consumers is profound. Total consumer debt was $11.44 trillion in 2012. Broken down, that is more than $30,000 per household. Seventy-seven percent of households are in debt. One in seven US citizens is being pursued by a debt collector (*Huffington Post*, 2012).

Corporate mobility and the history of credit

Organizational mobility has been a consistent theme in the history of credit. When the industry was taking off in the late 1970s, firms like Citibank moved operations and workers regionally – from high-interest East Coast states to low-interest Midwestern ones (Bergman and Rummel, 2004). The next phase at the turn of the millennium has been cross-border. The strategy now involves maximizing profit through transnational outsourcing.

Credit and banking firms play significant roles in the story of outsourcing. This is especially evident when focusing on the case of India, which is one of their key destinations. The very first outsourcers were credit card firms like American Express, which set up in the 1980s. GE Capital International Services, the financial and services wing of General Electric (later spun-off as Genpact), would become the major force for outsourcing in India. This firm had the largest work-force of all the Indian call centers by 2003, with 12,000 employees (see Table 2).

GE Capital launched this industry in two ways. For one, it 'pioneered business process outsourcing' (according to the company website). In what would become

Table 2 Top five outsourcing employers in India, 2003 and 2011

2003			2011		
Company	Number of employees	Country ownership	Company	Number of employees	Country ownership
GE Capital (now Genpact)	12,000	US	Tata Consultancy Services	226,751	India
Standard Chartered Bank	4,500	UK	Infosys	145,088	India
JP Morgan Chase	3,000	US	Wipro	136,734	India
American Express	2,000	US	Cognizant Technology Solutions	130,000	US
HSBC Banking and Financial Services	2,000	UK	HCL Technologies	21,985	India

Note: Some figures for 2003 are estimates. Sources include: NASSCOM (2003, 2012), Simhan (2012).

a standard term, BPO involves transfer of back office tasks (human resources, finance, accounting, etc.) and/or front office tasks (customer service) from firms to offshore locations. Second, GE Capital would introduce voice functions to Indian BPO operations, by adding phone capabilities to the existing data transmission work. Enabling direct person-to-person communication, this firm opened the path of *transnational* customer service for the credit industry. It is significant then, that the groundings for outsourcing would emerge from US finance firms.

Soon other banking companies from the US and Europe followed, in conjunction with the opening of markets to foreign firms by the Indian government in the early 1990s. The largest of these firms were JP Morgan Chase, Standard Chartered Bank, and HSBC Bank (Table 2). The attraction for US companies in particular has been India's large English-speaking, highly skilled, and inexpensive workforce. These firms became a model for other industries, showing how to save costs (in rent, infrastructure, labor, etc.) by moving to India. Indian industry association NASSCOM boasts that firms can save 40–50 percent of their operating costs through outsourcing.

Advances in information and communication technology around the year 2000 boosted the outsourcing process substantially. With data and network capabilities, firms could offshore white-collar work on a mass scale for the first time, as they had been doing with manufacturing for decades. This included both upper-tier software research and development work, and lower-tier clerical and customer service work. Many Indian-owned firms sprung up to handle the ensuing offshore contracts, and ignited a rapid growth of local players in the industry. Now, Indian firms dominate the field: Tata Consultancy Services, Infosys, Wipro, and HCL Technologies (Table 2). The US is main market for the Indian export industry: 61 percent of the spending comes from contracts in the US, followed by Europe (30%, mostly the UK), Asia and Pacific (6%), and others (2%) (NASSCOM, 2008).

Credit not only launched this industry, it continues to be its main driver. At present, two-thirds of the business of Indian back office outsourcing is in sales, credit, or debt. The largest segment of Indian export revenues – by far, at 40 percent – is in banking, financial services, and insurance. This sector is so dominant it has its own acronym: BFSI. An additional 27 percent comes from telecommunications, high-tech, and retail sectors (NASSCOM, 2008). Indian firms, furthermore, are more likely to do banking and telemarketing than those in other outsourcing destinations: 70 percent of firms in India are reported to be working in this field, while those in other countries of the Global South average closer to 50 percent, and those in the Global North average about 30 percent (Holman et al., 2007).

The movement of credit overseas has had profound effects on economies of the sending and receiving countries. From the US side, 80 percent of Fortune 500 companies now outsource some of their functions abroad, and 50 percent outsource to India in particular. For the Indian side, revenues in BPO exports are significant and rising steadily, from $4.6 billion in 2005 to $16 billion in 2012 (NASSCOM, 2012). There are roughly 800+ outsourcing firms in India, employing 2.8 million workers. It's important to note, however, that the vast majority of US customer service work is performed onshore. Although US call centers are now stable in their growth or else on the decline, they are still outnumber those in India substantially.

Offshore subcontracting and the consolidation of credit work

The process of subcontracting compresses and integrates the strands of emotion work in credit together. Domestically, call centers tend to be more homogenous in their credit work. In-house call centers focus on a single corporation and its defined set of products, services, etc. Likewise, out-of-house (third party) call centers typically specialize around a particular credit service (i.e. collections, telemarketing, etc.), even if they take contracts from many firms.

Indian call centers, in contrast, are a grab-bag of customer service. As they are under pressure to attract as many 'campaigns' (or corporate contracts) as possible, they become a receptacle for many functions in the global economy. They accept many types of credit processes, from many types of firms, and from many different countries (although for simplicity's sake here, I focus on just the US). In my study, employees perform a range of campaigns – mortgage insurance, cell phone and television sales, debt consolidation, computer sales, etc.

Accordingly, call center workers do several key activities that mediate credit and debt processes. To start with, they directly sell credit lines, large and small, to consumers. They handle mortgages, insurance, and credit cards. They work for banks, enforcing fees on savings and checking accounts. Second, they sell everyday products to consumers. This may be an item with a one-time payment or multiple payments. It may also be a service that has an indefinite life and therefore continuous payments. Some of these transactions, quite critically, involve buying a tangible product *and* buying credit for it. An example is a cell phone, which often involves purchasing a phone and then activating the payments for the ongoing service. Some retail companies have their own credit divisions to handle these accounts, others are affiliated with an external bank. Finally, the third major activity of call centers is collections, wherein consumers pay on those debts. Employees take payments from debtors and their answer questions. They sell debt consolidations plans. They seek out debtors who refuse to pay.

Organizationally then, there is a fluidity between the various parts of credit. Workers within an Indian call center usually shift from one campaign to another. A particular campaign will occupy a group of workers for a set amount of time, days, weeks, months, etc. Then they will change. Even if workers do not encounter these different types of credit work within the same firm, they inevitably do so as they 'job-hop' across firms.

In this way, Indian call centers reveal how the dynamics of credit operate as stages or components of the same larger process of consumption – first, individuals buy products and services; second, obtain credit to do so (sometimes within the very process of the sale); and then pay on those debts. I consider all three as a unit, and for the sake of simplicity, refer to them under the label of 'credit'.

Emotional Routines of Transnational Credit

Given this compression of credit functions in Indian call centers, managers in my study searched for emotional strategies that would work across all of them. Rather than targeting a particular phase of credit and its corresponding emotion from the employee (e.g. politeness in sales, or meanness in collections), trainers and supervisors often chose core tactics that they could standardize for many campaigns. The emotional hitmen in my study performed two main tasks: creating intimacies for trust in credit exchanges, and activating moralities of credit. So, while emotional displays by the employee still matter to these managers (as Sutton and others have shown), the emotional routines of credit here are more about delving deeply into the psyche of the customer. This process tends to be more indirect, circuitous, and instrumental, and requires employees to go through the intermediary of the mind and bio-history of the customer.[2]

Intimacies of credit

The emotion work of credit first involves becoming personal with the customers. Arjun Raina, a celebrated call center trainer who had conducted sessions at BigCo, speaks of this in terms of moving through spaces of intimacy. In his book *Speaking Right for a Call Center Job*, he recommends that employees 'enter the customer's emotional zone' (2004: 177). Workers should bond with the customer in order to move him/her toward the sale or payment. Significantly, this does not involve adopting a blanket emotional style, but rather tailoring emotional control to the individual habits, tastes, and quirks of customers. Three stages (and sub-stages) of emotion work facilitate this intimacy.

Scoping and counter-positioning. First, employees investigate the customer's emotional, mental, and physical state. As Srijesh at BigCo describes, it is a form of amateur psychoanalysis:

> You probe and then you find out. If you think the person needs this kind of treatment, is not well, is really down, we go by that line. But if we see that he's fine, he is sitting in his office just inquiring, [then] be very professional and very

normal. We gauge what other person's physical condition is, and what the psychological condition at that point in time would be when he is making that call … What I do usually is when I talk to them, make a couple of basic questions. And a couple of minutes into the talk, rough images form: Ok, this sort of person. According to that image, you try and be with him or her.

The employee scopes out the conditions, hopes, and fears of the consumer – sometimes just by his/her voice.

Srijesh also points out an important follow-up strategy in this quote: emotional counter-positioning. Employees coordinate their own demeanor and tone with that of the customer. Mohan recounts the process used at SmallCo. He uses sounds in the customer's voice and language to analyze emotion, beginning with the very first word uttered from his/her mouth:

> We can only judge a person by his voice – what kind of mood he is in. Like if I pick up the phone and [he] says, 'hello' sounding in a good mood, [then] I say 'hello' in a rough mood. If someone says 'hello' very, very harshly, [then] I say, 'Hi sir this is Jamie Lawson' being very soft. Why? Because that guy's in anger. See if one is hot and the second one is cold, then they can do something. If he is hot, I am hot: clash. He is cold, I am cold: clash. One has to be high, one has to be low. So when the costumer is high, you be low: you can make a deal. But if he is high, and you're high, there is just going to be argument, which the costumer never has to go for.

Mohan fashions his own mood in a very particular and somewhat unexpected way: not parallel to that of the customer, but opposite. His experience tells him that congruent emotional states are counterproductive for credit work, lead to 'arguments'. Instead, he crafts his emotional state to mirror the customer. This is not a simplistic or straightforward process of emotional matching (e.g. a pleasant-sounding worker for a pleasant customer). It is a more finessed strategy of counterbalance in order to gain control and 'make a deal'.

Emotional steering. Once workers have pinpointed the psyche of the customer and adjusted their own emotional counter-stance, they move into the second step: steering the customers' emotions. This is how employees subtly push consumers toward the credit transaction. Pradeep at MiddleCo explains:

> You come across thousands of people every month. You have never seen that person in front of you; you have just heard his voice. But you can very well understand the psyche of that person, as well as his natures, his preferences, how sort of a person he is, what sort of his likings and dislikings. … Basically, telemarketing [is] just to understand the psyche of the customer. *If you can understand the psyche of the customer, you can get a sell out of him*. It's not a problem. It's completely not a problem. (Emphasis added)

When employees understand the customer deeply, they can sell.

Emotional steering for credit can move in many directions. If employees want to invoke pleasant feelings in the consumer, they search for ways to bond and then close the deal. To insiders like Srijesh at BigCo, this is called rapport-building: 'To build rapport, I see if that person's date of birth is something very close by, or just passed, or maybe his car is a nice one, maybe the registration number is fascinating ... I remember one day, one of the policy holders, the last three digits of his mobile phone number were 007, so I just shared a couple of [James] Bond things with him.' Workers are trained to scan consumer information on their computers, and use any tidbit – even a registration number – to make an intimate, emotional connection.

Then the employees present 'positive' emotions to create an impulse to buy. The trainer at MiddleCo said during a session: 'We are not manipulating. That's a negative word. Create the value of the need. *Present* the benefits rather than *telling* the benefit of the product. Build the value. Phrase it positively.' This is the nuanced way the emotional steering works: creating and building the value emotionally.

The other side of steering is redirecting negative emotions from the customer, especially those expressing anger or opposition to the firm. Sonali from MiddleCo summarizes this strategy concisely: 'Keep quiet. Let them speak. Then do rapport-building.' It involves allowing the customer to express their feelings without responding or intervening. Controlled venting is how employees like Aditya at BigCo talk about this: 'Over a period of time, you learn how to manage such customers... So all you have to do is give them like 2 minutes to vent it out, so they can say what they're saying. You have to be active listener to that ... After that, you just need to take the control of the call ... And it becomes easy to handle.' This tactic may seem passive, but it is carefully planned. Venting allows the emotional outburst to diminish on its own, while enabling the employee to bypass the content of the communication and accountability for it. Aditya points to this when stating that venting helps employees 'take control of the call' and hence the customer.

In a more subtle (but still manipulative) manner, trainer Raina refers to this process as skilled indulgence: 'Sometimes, a customer will take the conversation into an emotional zone away from business needs. You need to indulge the customer a little before you bring the person back on track. That skilled indulgence is rapport and establishes the human bond' (2004: 176–177). His emphasis on keeping the customer on track is indicative of how workers direct consumers towards credit.

Trickery and deception. At this point, the worker may engage in a third step: using 'tricks' on the customers to alter their emotional state, change their outlook, and increase their propensity for purchasing and signing onto debt. This is done through careful word play, as Vinod at SmallCo describes:

> *Telemarketing is playing with words most of all* ... Suppose you have a campaign to sell a camera. A camera is the type of [product] you don't need every day. If you bought a camera, you use it once in a month, or once in a blue moon. You won't be ready to buy at that time. So we need to make those rebuttals, to create the necessity again. So that is the creativity, to make the person think: It has got that zoom, it has got focus, it has got night vision, etc. (Emphasis added)

Employees use language to 'create a necessity' for consumption. With clever talk, they make the customers believe that they have a desire or need for buying the item.

Workers use tricks for another reason: to confuse. This is especially common with bigger purchases and credit accounts, which involve more anxiety and therefore require more sophisticated tricking. At MiddleCo, an employee named Shuba describes her practices when selling mortgages:

> Mortgage is a very personal issue [when] you take a loan … to buy a new home or something. Some people don't feel comfortable in discussing the mortgage. They are very finicky, so you have to be in a very professional tone. People will ask, 'how [did] you come to know we are on a mortgage?' *So you have to play the tricks, you have to play with words.* 'We just prepared an analysis area that people staying in your area, most of them have property under mortgage, so probably your property is under mortgage too.' It is very interesting, we have to play with the words. But you have to be very cautious about what you are saying. (Emphasis added)

Call centers have vast amounts of data on their consumers, even private information like whether they have a mortgage and what the details are. Concealing this pre-phone call analysis is part of the employee's job. Yet, workers are skilled in developing narratives and linguistic strategies – on the spot – to hide the practices of their US clients and Indian managers. As we will see, there are additional kinds of deception common in Indian call centers as well.

These tactics, which employees direct at the intimate vulnerabilities of consumers, become the centerpiece of the emotional hitman's job. They may vary their emotional tone within and across the stages of credit (e.g. more politeness in the initial calls of debt collection, more aggressiveness down the line, etc.). And in fact, employees like Gaurav at SmallCo told me that their tone should be multi-layered: 'the collection agent should convince the person softly and harshly – both – to make that person convinced they should pay off the company'. However, the basic strategies of gaining intimacy to secure credit from the consumer remain constant. Employees use skills of scoping, steering, and trickery throughout the credit process, and as such, call centers teach them together as part of the same general training for all employees.

Moralities of credit

Emotional hitmen use a second fundamental tactic to sway customers into credit – morality. Employees appeal to consumers' sense of loyalty, honor, and ethics about money. This strategy differs from the previous one in that workers are not *creating* particular emotions (happiness, calmness, etc.). Rather they are *activating* a pre-existing set of social norms concerning or affecting credit. As Bob Johnson explains: 'There's a lot of things that motivate people: you know, you can attack pride, fear, integrity, what's the person's honor.'

Call center employees use a range of moralities to 'motivate' customers to pay or purchase. Some of the moralities are favorable or socially approved. An example is personal and financial responsibility, especially among the poor. Banks target the poor because they are the most profitable consumers, according to Senator Elizabeth Warren who was founding director of the US Consumer Financial Protection Bureau (Scurlock, 2006). Indeed, even though interest rates for credit rise with greater impoverishment, the poor are still likely to make payments (however small) on their loans (Schechter, 2007). Some industry experts believe this reflects an ethic concerning debt.

Credit firms depend on other kinds of positive moralities, like 'brand loyalties'. These are affinities that consumers develop for specific companies and services. With long-term patronage of a bank, credit card company, retailer, etc., consumers may feel motivated to pay, buy, or borrow from them.

On the flip side, the credit industry also relies on immoralities. For example, financial institutions count on the stigma of bankruptcy. Bankruptcy is one of the only options for consumers to get out of severe debt, but it also carries a mark of dishonor or failure. Many debtors wait to file three to five years after they have become broke, just for this reason (Schechter, 2007). Another immorality is humiliation. Employees draw on the mere act of being pursued by a debt collector to shame consumers. At People's First Recoveries, the second owner Chris Winkler and one of his employees recount the procedure (Scurlock, 2006):

STAFF MEMBER: Basically what you can do with this [software] is you type in their social security number. It's gonna give me every previous address that he's been at back up to 20 years [and] possible neighbors.
OWNER: It's not illegal for us to call your neighbors and try to get a message to you, have a neighbor trying to get you to call back. You know, how embarrassing is that to somebody, if they have to get a message through a neighbor.
STAFF MEMBER: I find it more effective if you actually reach a relative of theirs, because obviously that's a little more embarrassing.

Employees are given sophisticated technology to track down a customer's neighbors and relatives. By calling them and simply asking to pass on a message from a debt collector, they disgrace and exert more pressure on the customer.

Gaining popularity within this industry is a certain type of morality: obligations to family who have passed away. Death, bereavement, and grief (and for that matter, dead consumers themselves) are increasing targets of credit firms. I became curious about this when observing training sessions at both BigCo and SmallCo. They teach that bereavement is a highly sensitive emotion, and conquering feelings about death is the ultimate call center achievement. If employees can sell something to, or get collections payments from, someone who is in mourning, they've mastered the emotional hitman job. Gaurav at SmallCo describes:

They train us that the person [customer] is getting direct care, and you get personal … If they say someone in their family died, you say: 'Must be so painful for you.' Because if you say 'So sorry', it doesn't help them. Why is [he] 'so sorry'? They understand he is pretending, since you don't know the person that just died. But if you say: 'It is so painful', they understand that *you know* it was painful to them. So [you say]: 'It might be painful for you', and after that, 'I am sorry I called you, but will you be able to give me that information you are trying to give?'

Emotional authenticity in the display of empathy is paramount in this process. The worker has to sound emotionally sincere in understanding the customer's grief. At the same time, the employee must craft words to navigate *around* the emotions of death, and move the conversation toward the economic transaction (in this case, divulging credit information).

Moreover, grief is key for unlocking other kinds of credit from consumers – like the finances of family left behind. 'Deceased collections' has become a niche market within this industry in the US: 'Dead people are the newest frontier in debt collecting, and one of the healthiest parts of the industry' (Streitfeld, 2009). Collections agents draw upon feelings of familial responsibility to the dead in asking living relatives to pay off those debts. Phone workers at firms like DCM Services in the US tap into consumer moralities: by paying the debt, 'they are honoring the wishes of their loved ones' (Streitfeld, 2009). Some are trained in psychological counseling techniques including 'the five stage of grief'. Workers look specifically for the bargaining stage. They are told by training managers: 'You get to be the person who cares.' This is not just faked caring. Workers transform themselves from the hired hand who is exploiting human tragedy to its opposite – the savior and the only one who provides genuine concern and solutions. Emotions are the linchpin that enables this flipped role.

These tactics are so successful that they distract consumers from the obvious question: whether they are legally required to pay debts for their deceased relatives. The answer is often no. Yet, workers in the death collections industry – even those from law firms – admit that they rarely disclose this information 'upfront', and only do so 'if family members ask' (Streitfeld, 2009). This is another example of the deceptive tactics of phone workers to sway customers into paying.

Outsourcing as Conduit for the Emotion Work of Credit

The process of outsourcing facilitates – and enhances – this emotion work of credit for US firms.[3] It is no accident that they have been flocking to India, and other Global South nations like South Africa, the Philippines, and Argentina. Call center labor in India costs as little as a tenth of that of countries like the US, with median annual salaries of $2,444 versus $29,000, respectively. The range of Indian salaries is somewhat higher in my study, averaging from $4,536 at SmallCo, $5,076 at MiddleCo, to $7,044 at BigCo (Table 1). Still, because of the comparative reduction in wages, US firms benefit financially from outsourcing. Paying call center workers takes up merely 35–45 percent of total organizational expenses in countries like India and Brazil, but as much as 65–70 percent in North America and Europe. The implications are vivid when seen through the eyes of the employees. In a single month, an Indian call center worker collects close to a million dollars in fees for GE Capital, while earning $7 a day (Gulati, 2005).

My argument, however, is that credit firms gain more than just a cheaper labor force through outsourcing. *Global business strategies provide credit firms with specialized resources to inculcate, enforce, and regulate emotions within their employees (and in turn, consumers).* Outsourcing to India in particular contributes to the emotion work of credit for US firms in three ways.

Hiring emotionally intelligent workers

First, credit firms gain access to a desired labor force for performing emotional labor. This happens through the competencies they receive from a higher-skilled and often higher-class workforce. Most call center employees in India have completed some college (Table 1), while those in the US (on average) have barely received high school diplomas. In comparative studies, India ranks the highest on educational levels of new recruits. Firms in India are 50 percent more likely to hire a workforce primarily comprising college graduates, relative to call centers in North America, Europe, etc. My sample includes employees with even higher educational and professional credentials, like former architects, engineers, and hotel managers. Formal education, then, is one of the filtering mechanisms that the Indian call center industry uses to deliver not just a cheaper product, but a superior one.[4] It conveys their concerted, self-conscious attention to the phenomenon of emotional labor. Particularly, it reflects their attempt to secure more sophisticated mental and affective capacities among the workers – an 'emotionally intelligence' (Bachman et al., 2000) – for handling the nuanced strategies of credit.

Furthermore, outsourcing provides credit firms with organizational resources for sustaining this workforce. Indian call centers tend to nurture their workforces with a greater range of incentives to motivate and encourage stability than in the US. In India, call center employment is almost completely full-time (at 97%), as in other global south countries like South Africa (at 88%). US firms, in contrast, are far less likely to do so. Full-time employment is found in only 59 percent of out-of-house call center firms, and at best, in 81 percent of in-house units (figures approximate). Instead, US firms rely more on part-time and temporary workers. On top of this, Indian firms are likely to attract and retain workers with extensive benefits and perks. All the firms in my study provide employees with hot meals and transportation to and from work. They also give many bonuses and incentives (Table 1), ranging from parties and dinner outings, to gifts and cash, to international trips.

In turn, call center firms in India are more likely to keep around their high-skilled workforce relative to similar third-party firms in the US. Indian firms are almost 12 percent less likely to lose their workers annually to quits and dismissals, and 4 percent less likely to face employee absenteeism, than US out-of-house call centers (and with only marginal difference to in-house call centers). Even though Indian attrition is high compared to many countries, these workers are more motivated to show up and perform than in comparable US contexts. Such factors point to a call center workforce in India that is more easily hirable, trainable and better equipped to handle the intimacies and moralities of credit.

Regulating emotion work

Outsourcing aids the credit industry in a second critical way: in regulating the emotional labor of their customer service. Indian call centers invest heavily in developing the emotional intelligence of their workers, more so than comparable US firms in many ways. It happens through targeted organizational procedures for emotional vetting and training.

Indian call centers, to start with, rigorously screen workers for emotionality before they get to the job. Workers are tested during the selection process for their psychological states, emotional qualifications, and their ability to carry out interactions with consumers. Call center firms in the Global South are generally much more likely to administer these tests than those in the Global North, with India as the outlier among them: while the average is 50 percent in most countries of the global sample, it is 75 percent among Indian call centers.

At BigCo, the screening is done through psychometric tests. These typically assess skills like: cognitive and mental ability, verbal aptitude, and 'the "big five" personality traits: extroversion, agreeableness, conscientiousness, openness to experience, and emotional stability' (Jenkins, 2001). BigCo managers not only administer these tests in-house, they send out crews to do so in the smaller cities of India (like Lucknow and Chandighar) from where they recruit. At MiddleCo, hiring assessments are made on the basis of several emotional criteria, including listening skills, telephone etiquette, politeness, and tone. For some firms, like SmallCo, the stakes for these initial emotional screenings are even higher. Vetting during recruitment is their *only* means of ensuring emotional skill on the job (as opposed to the many follow-up procedures discussed next). Managers fire workers who do not perform according to the emotional standards within a month of their hiring.

Next, Indian firms devote extensive resources towards emotional and communicative types of training. Indian workers spend more than twice the amount of time on initial training as those in the US – 4.7 weeks versus 2.3 weeks (in out-of-house call centers). Indian employees also experience more ongoing training: 10 days or more a year on average (similar to other Global South countries like South Africa, Korea, and Brazil), versus six days a year on average in the Global North countries (like Canada, Germany, Spain, etc.). In my study, this varies by size of firm (Table 1). SmallCo has no training at all, as the CEO reported it was too expensive for his budget. MiddleCo spends 3.5 to 4 weeks. Large firms commit the most: BigCo devoted an average between six and 14 weeks. Some of their credit campaigns take up to six months of training, as the firm's Vice President for Human Resources informed me.

Much of this 'extra time' in training goes towards accent and language skills (i.e. learning American English as opposed to Indian English), and increasingly so. However, very often, managers focus this training on emotional labor. What especially surprised me when observing these sessions is how little time trainers spend on the details of the credit product or service that is being sold. Rather, they devote most of the class time to the *style* of the communication, including its emotional qualities (Table 1): BigCo allocates 50 percent of the training on style, while MiddleCo allocates up to 86 percent. At MiddleCo, this 'soft skills' training module includes sales, customer handling, and tele-etiquette, and emotional presentation of tone, enthusiasm, and mood.

Monitoring emotion work

Outsourcing aids the emotional labor of credit firms in a third way: in the observing and evaluating the emotions of customer service work. Managers listen to live or recorded calls in part to track emotional performances of employees. While they are looking for things like employee fraud, etc., they are also checking on the effectiveness of emotional labor through measures of talk time, adherence to scripts, and friendliness in providing service. Indian call centers do this monitoring (in some cases) twice as much as those in the US. Indian employees experience electronic monitoring in 92 percent of their work time, whereas US call centers average only 50 percent (in-house) or 68 percent (out-of-house). Plus, in the global sample of 17 countries, Indian firms stood alone in monitoring workers daily, whereas the others did so on average weekly or monthly.

Finally, employers use highly sophisticated technologies to monitor and analyze the emotional performances of employees. As I've shown elsewhere (Poster, 2011), some rely on automatic 'emotion detectors' in the computer software. These programs use sound wave frequencies and key word searches determine the types of emotions that workers are projecting to consumers, and how well they are integrating those feelings into conversations.

Transnational Dissonance in the Emotions of Credit

Moving the customer service of credit overseas can create problems, however. US firms face a dilemma of how to transfer the emotions of credit to India, what I call a transnational dissonance. Here is where we see a geography to the emotions of credit, and how employers attempt to manage this disparity by re-nationalizing the intimacies and moralities.

Emotional labor scholars borrow the term 'cognitive dissonance' from the field of psychology to describe an internal discord between one's inner self and the outward display of feelings for a job (Hochschild, 1983). In the case of outsourced credit industries, we see another kind of cognitive dissonance – in the meanings and feelings about debt and finance. Within a global context, this discord is not internal (within individuals), but external (between actors in the US and India).

Conflicting moralities

We see this transnational dissonance, to begin with, in the moralities of credit. In the US, the general population has acquiesced to the idea of credit. This is evident in the large rates of those indebted (even if they disagree with it, or have trouble paying it back). US firms push the moralities further, positing credit as a social good.

Yet in India, credit has not penetrated the wider society in the same way, especially as an accepted principle for household routines.[5] The idea of consumer credit is still relatively unfamiliar to many Indians, despite the rapid growth of the middle class over the last few decades and the rise in disposable incomes. Indians, until very recently, have been characterized as 'conservative savers' (Kazmin, 2010) and 'used to living within their means' (Varma, 2007: xix). This outlook is partly grounded in the practical realities of Indian banking: under the era of state-run institutions, personal credit and home loans were generally unavailable to the public. However, this changed in the mid-1990s with the shift towards neoliberal policy by the government, and the subsequent entrance of foreign financial industries into the market. As a case in point, the number of credit cards quadrupled over the 2000s (Varma, 2007), yielding Citigroup 3.3 million customers (Timmons, 2007). Still, the statistics on credit in India remain strikingly low. Out of 100 adults, approximately two have a credit card, 13 have a debit card, and 40 have a bank account (Roy, 2010). This leaves India with one of the lowest rates of credit card ownership in the world (Timmons, 2007).

Indian lifestyles, in turn, are less embedded with notions of consumption and buying things (Ganguly-Scrase and Scrase, 2009). Many scholars are skeptical that expanding job opportunities and incomes have led to meaningful changes in consumerism, even though Indians have been buying more than they used to (Fernandes, 2006). Not only are Indians more hesitant to sign on to credit than consumers in the US, they are more hesitant to repay: 1 in 10 cards are charged off due to stoppage in payment, versus 1 in 25 in the US (Timmons, 2007). Thus, the whole process of credit – from getting credit, to buying things, to paying it back – are less central to daily life in India.[6] Credit is not a moral imperative in India, or at least an assumed practice, the way it is in the US.

This makes hiring Indian employees as representatives of credit a tricky task. Employers have to teach and instill US moralities of credit in Indian workers. As part of the 'extra training' in Indian call centers, employees undergo extensive sessions on 'cultural training'. The name suggests a broad-based curriculum but in practice, it is really about credit, finance, and consumption.

Managers and trainers teach US credit morality in several ways. First come the foundations: the *normative value* of credit and consumption and the *instinct of promoting* credit to others. To help implant these notions within Indian employees, call center trainers try to make consumption and credit personal. They use carefully selected metaphors to draw upon workers' routines and experiences: for instance, how to see *all* relationships (not just their encounters on the phone) through the lens of customer service. The SmallCo President explains his philosophy:

> We try to incorporate a kind of a culture where each one is customer to someone or the other. For example, the *agent* is performing not only for their client, they are also … a customer to quality [department]. Another example, a *new candidate* who has just walked in and has already joined, they are customers for our HR department. The *person in the kitchen* who is trying to prepare some tea or coffee, he should put in so much of love and affection in his preparation, because to people who he is going to serve [i.e. the employees], they are customers for him. Get my point? Each one is a customer to someone or another.

By seeing everyone in their lives as a customer, employees are more likely to internalize consumption and prioritize service above all else.

Teaching the morality of credit to Indian workers next includes a crash course on the *substance* of American consumerism (i.e. what Americans are buying and what it means to them). Indian workers get some of this in their daily lives outside the firm, through the pervasive marketing of US products, music, films, media, etc. However, employers dig much deeper into the intricacies of credit.

Training sessions at MiddleCo, for instance, methodically go through the key points of US consumerism. Employees learn what brands and corporate logos Americans feel loyal to and why. When discussing 'stores', they learn the names of major retailers like Walgreens and Albertsons. In 'eateries', they learn about McDonalds. Trainers lecture on what money means in the US, and the routines of spending. A 'dollar table' on the overhead projector shows currency conversion rates and what you can buy with a dollar bill. In 'customs and attitudes', workers learn that American consumers don't like to divulge personal information, and that they are individualistic. In 'lifestyle', they learn about traffic and how almost everybody owns their own car. And then, there are the formal institutions of American consumer society. Umesh, the MiddleCo Training Manager, teaches the centrality of 'finance' to the 'life of the common man', including his/her relation to 'banking, financial institutes'. Filling in the knowledge base of

Indians on consumption in the US helps workers to overcome the transnational disso-nance in credit. It enables these workers to internalize and then articulate the logic, practice, and morality of credit in US society.

Conflicting intimacies

However, there is a second complication of outsourcing: a transnational dissonance in the intimacies of credit. In the words of call center trainer Raina, outsourcing disturbs the 'comfort zones' of consumers. Indeed, as found in other research, foreignness compromises a sense of security and invokes anxiety for some consumers (Mirchandani, 2012). This is particularly true when they are discussing issues of finance, purchasing, and service.

As research shows, US customers prefer to talk on the phone with someone of their own nationality. Thelen and colleagues (2010) have been studying US attitudes towards outsourcing and service, and have found a trend of 'service ethnocentrism'. Sometimes US consumers have political objections to outsourcing itself, in terms of beliefs about keeping jobs in the country and retaining employment opportunities. However, they also express two clearly nationalized themes: foreign enmity beliefs (that offshore workers are not familiar enough with American culture to provide effective services), and nativist beliefs (that workers in one's own country are generally superior, e.g. smarter, more helpful, etc.). Moreover, Thelen and colleagues find that these feelings, when charted against types of service, are more associated with financial-related activ-ities (like taxes) and less so with problem-solving activities (like computer help-desks). Customer service encounters involving money, in other words, heighten the ethnic/national unease among US consumers.

This means that the work of credit in global contexts involves unique types of consumer emotions than those mentioned in the earlier sections – this time, morality about outsourcing and anxiety about foreigners.

Manufacturing cognitive consonance in credit. In response, outsourcing firms attempt to recreate this comfort zone for consumers by altering the identities of their workers. The managerial solution for transnational dissonance is making the narratives of credit parallel. Firms try to refashion Indian personas into those of the US in attempt to achieve cultural consonance.

Indian call centers in my study require workers (in greater and lesser extents) to disguise their nationality and adopt another nationality, during the course of the conversation. In what I call 'national identity management' (Poster, 2007), employers ask workers to use American names, adopt American accents, and convey through idle conversation and prepared scripts that they are in fact in the US. Managers often assert, and workers re-articulate, that acting American helps in sales. Lokesh at SmallCo explains that he needs to *become* an American in order to sell to them:

> I can sell you something only when you want it. Like I am selling you a pen, I need to create a need in you, that you become … wanting enough to get a pen. Whether you need it or not, I need to *make* you a need … If I am selling you a pen, *I need to come to be in your position, putting [my]self in the customer's shoes. Then you really need to be an American*. (Emphasis added)

Employees not only need to 'get personal' with the customer (as noted earlier), they need to be in the 'position' of the customer, and in particular, 'in the customer's shoes' as 'an American'. Outsourcing nationalizes the intimacies of credit work.

Posing as an American, therefore, enables employees to foster an intimacy with consumers and re-establish the comfort zone. A female training manager at SmallCo, Anjali, describes:

> We have to know everything [about the US], because we don't want the client to think we are not knowledgeable. Because there is a relationship between everything. We don't want the clients [i.e. customers] to feel bad – that she is speaking rubbish and we are not understanding it. *I want my client [customer] to understand that I am as much caring as his people back home. Though it's an official talk, we need to make a level of comfort zone, so the person thinks yes, they are talking to someone on the outside, but they are not a stranger.* (Emphasis added)

The markers of American accent and name serve as an emotional guarantee that the level of care will be equal to that in the US. They enable Anjali to be an outsider 'but not a stranger' (read: an unsympathetic and unscrupulous foreigner) to the consumer. National identity management eases the anxiety of foreignness (or in other words, the service ethnocentrism) for consumers. It helps build the trust so that customers are more confident in the credit transaction.

In this way, outsourcing may re-nationalize the emotions of credit – not directly in the transfer of campaigns from the US to India – but subsequently and indirectly in managerial responses to this transnational dissonance.

Implications

The emotions of credit are apparent in far more than the discourses of managers and employees of these firms. As shown above, they are integral to organizational structures and practices, including hiring, training, and the applications of resources. In addition, emotions are crucial mechanisms of job hierarchies and career ladders.

For instance, some credit activities require more advanced emotional and linguistic skills than others, and in turn, accrue higher wages. Employers track workers into jobs according to eight verbal-emotional-communicative 'competencies' (based on scores from psychometric tests and evaluations of emotional skill in training sessions). Emotional categories include things like stress tolerance, interpersonal relation, and customer focus. Linguistic categories include things like speed, pacing, and articulation of speech. Umesh, as one of these managers, showed me a diagram of how MiddleCo carries out this matching process:

> This is my competency chart which we have right now … These are the competencies in different campaigns and what kind of rating is required there. … For example here, if you see … in Campaign X, we need 'articulation' in the person to be 'average'. That means if his articulation is between 40% and 60%, then it's ok… In Campaign Y, you need to be 'excellent', 80% or above. You need to be *very* articulate to speak. In Campaign Z, probably, you again need to be average.

Through this formalized process, managers link emotional skill to organizational rewards. It complements the bonuses, games, parties, etc. (Table 1) that managers use to recognize employees who achieve targets on sales, new accounts, debt repayment, etc.

When workers *don't perform* their emotional tasks, furthermore, managers react with organizational disciplines. Some workers abstain deliberately, as they object to the emotional deception and manipulation of customers (Poster, 2007). Other workers are just not skilled at it. In turn, there are punishments for doing emotion work poorly (i.e. for the *non*-emotional hitmen) that go along with the many rewards for doing it well (Sutton, 1991). Managers at MiddleCo bump workers off higher-paying campaigns onto lower-paying campaigns requiring lower emotional-verbal competencies. At firms like SmallCo, they weed these workers out within the first few days on the job. At MiddleCo and BigCo, which have more technological resources, managers regularly fire workers who have low scores on quality control and electronic monitoring systems.

Theoretically, these cases studies show the distinctiveness of credit as a form of emotion work within the wider context of outsourcing. Employees recount how working for credit campaigns is different from that of other types of customer service in Indian call centers. From her previous experience, Meena at BigCo recounts how tech support generally requires much more 'politeness' on the part of the employee. She says that when customers call for help with their computers, 'You need to be sounding sweet, sounding good with the customers, everything like that. Even if you are right and the customer is wrong, you have to be sounding genuinely good to that person.' Pradeep at MiddleCo explains why. In tech support, 'a customer always calls the company or the customer care executive when he's in trouble. And he always shouts on you, and you have to calm them down, "No sir, actually this is that, this is that," you know. It becomes really very, very difficult.'

Indeed, presentation of self and displaying pleasant emotions are highly integral to the job of *providing services* like fixing a computer. The customer is paying for that service, and along with it, the emotional offerings of the worker (which can be a measure of the quality of that service). For credit, however, the goal of the job is typically *not* to provide a service, nor even to help the consumer (despite their title of 'customer care representative'). The aim is the reverse – to *get something from the consumer*. Even though credit is a similarly outsourced task, the emotion work can be very different.

These case studies reveal dynamics in the other direction as well – like the impact of outsourcing on the emotion work of credit. Outsourcing may not affect all parts of this labor – like the core emotions involved with the work. As Sutton (1991) documents, for instance, displaying a sense of urgency in collections may be a standard practice that cuts across organizations and locations. I expect, in a similar, way that the targeting of intimacies and moralities may surface in other call centers, not just those in India.

Still, outsourcing adds new layers to the emotions of credit, by compressing credit functions within organizations, and dispersing the participants globally. It inserts a *transnational* dimension to the relations (which in this case link customers in the US to workers in India). This means that workers not only manage consumer feelings about *credit*, but also their feelings about *globalization* (including foreigners, Indians, and outsourcing itself). Workers explain how interacting with consumers in the US compared to India changes the emotional demands of the job. Hemant at MiddleCo had this experience in selling Citibank credit cards both locally and internationally:

> Citibank customers [in India] are ... very good customers. ... They never abuse on the calls. Whatever the problems, they tell us in a very gentle manner or a very polite manner. But when I switched over to this industry [for the US], ... the customer abuses you. And you don't have the ok [to respond]. That's the way it is. I know it's a part of my job, but [at the end] of the day, it hurts you. It hurts me. I don't know about other person, but it hurts me.

More importantly, outsourcing exposes managers (especially) to the idea that the emotions of credit have geographies. As call centers become the meeting point for credit actors in various parts of the world, managers and staff encounter these different affects and discourses of credit. This is where we see a transnational dissonance of credit – something that other call center studies may overlook by virtue of the local empirical base. Even though US firms choose India as an outsourcing destination partly for its large English-speaking population, a common language is not enough to overcome this transnational dissonance. It is not sufficient to ensure smooth communications between Indian employees and US customers, in a practical sense of understanding accents, but also in a conceptual sense of understanding the meanings of credit.

The transformation in emotions of credit, therefore, may not be a direct result of outsourcing, per se, but rather a by-product of managerial responses to it, and in particular, to the transnational dissonance in credit. Facing pressure from US clients, Indian call center managers attempt to create the congruence artificially, by re-nationalizing the intimacies and moralities of credit. Their employees need to know what kind of moral commitments Americans are sensitive to, in order to tap into consumers' anxieties about and leanings towards credit. They need to learn the language of consumption in the US, and become aware of the cultural embeddedness of those principles. Moreover, in some cases, they also have to pose (explicitly or implicitly) as Americans themselves.

Conclusion

Indian call centers illustrate an under-recognized side of credit – the utilization of emotions by firms and employees to get consumers to enter into, stay on, and pay back debt. Unlike the previous research on emotion work in credit, I find that employees direct these tactics externally as well as internally. Employees use intricate emotional strategies to target consumer intimacies and moralities. They do emotional investigative work to figure out what consumers' personal sensitivities are, and exploit their emotional motivations for paying. They tap into consumer ethics concerning debt, and lean upon their sense of honor, status, and respectability.

This builds on sociological insight regarding the long tradition in American society of probing into the psychological fears of everyday people for economic purposes. Weber (1930) showed how early American religious leaders encouraged people to save compulsively, by fueling anxieties about the afterlife. The US economy benefitted from this practice of wealth accumulation and savings, as it became a springboard for growth at the time. In the 21st century, we see the targeting of public anxieties for an opposite purpose. Credit firms urge US citizens to spend and become indebted rather than to save. Here's where the emotional hitmen become useful. As mediators between firms and the public, customer service workers have an important role in achieving the ends of credit. They assist credit firms in dissipating consumer hesitancy to spend and become indebted. They ascend many emotional hurdles among the consuming public – counter-moralities of *avoiding* debt, or inabilities to pay due to declining real wages, job fragmentation, recession, etc., as much of the middle class is experiencing.

In this study, several dynamics intersect to achieve these ends for US credit firms – globalization, outsourcing, and emotions. They affect each other in succession or as a cycle: emotions are a key tool of credit work, the credit industry is a driver of outsourcing, and outsourcing helps to achieve the emotional strategies of credit. Their relations may not be *exclusive* (i.e. emotion work is not limited to credit; outsourcing involves more than credit work alone, etc.). Rather, this study aims to show how such factors are increasingly operating together. The methodology of global ethnography enables us to reveal and explore these connections, by viewing the macro and the micro in a single site (or set of sites).

Further, when interconnected this way, these three forces work to the advantage of the credit industry and to the disadvantage of consumers and workers. Profits of the credit industry have been increasing steadily since the first decade of offshoring of customer service. Yet, I have tried to show that their gains are more than material. Firms receive emotional payoffs from outsourcing, revealing an emerging affect economy in credit. Outsourcing to India provides credit firms with specialized resources to inculcate, enforce, and regulate emotions within their employees (and in turn, consumers).

On the other hand, US consumers are the recipients of emotional targeting, as employees probe, prod, and sway their sensitivities and anxieties in the interests of credit. They are victims of many kinds of deception, as workers 'trick' them with their words, or omit crucial information (such as legal exemptions from paying debts of deceased family members). Finally, the costs for Indian employees may not be material, as their wages tend to be higher than those of other service professions. However, their losses may be bodily and affective. This includes an emotional toll from taking on the emotional hitman role, especially when they are morally against it. In addition, employees handle the burden of resolving the transnational dissonance of credit. They contend with both abuse from customers due to their hostilities towards outsourcing, and requirements from managers to submerge and reconfigure their national identity.

Theoretically, this study reveals how the 'new emotional imperialism' applies in the information age. Unlike the global nannies of Hochschild's study who express emotions through direct touch, these workers do so through digital phone lines. They also *remain* in the Global South rather than physically moving to the Global

North, traveling instead through what Aneesh (2006) calls a 'virtual migration'. Still, the constant is that *Global North firms mine workers in the Global South for their feelings and emotional capacities*.

Moreover, while some kinds of affect may be universal (like love, in the case of transnational nannies), the affect of global credit and call centers is more specific. Thus, elaborating on the concept of emotional imperialism, I show how credit firms modify these emotions while extracting them. *Through the process of outsourcing customer service work to India, firms re-nationalize of meanings and feelings of credit.* In order to make the consumer comfortable for the transaction, employees decouple emotional zones from their locational moorings and then root them in new sites. Likewise, they mobilize intimacies and moralities of debt across borders. This dynamic is evident in the political realm too, as creditor nations like Germany draw on morality to urge debtor countries like Greece to pay back loans in the recent recession.

While this study has provided a glimpse into the nascence of the outsourcing industry in the early 2000s, many things have changed since then. For instance, scholars like Mirchandani (2012) and Nadeem (2011) have documented an organizational retrenchment away from stricter forms of national identity management in India. When it comes to the debt industry, we might see that some key practices may remain, like the nationalized training *in credit*. Still, it would be valuable to explore more recent emotional dynamics in Indian call centers. Another development is that outsourcing has gained momentum in other countries, with the Philippines equalizing if not overtaking the number of call centers as India. Does the character of the emotion work change as offshoring pathways move to other regions of the Global South? Documenting the contours of credit intimacies and moralities in call centers around the world (and from credit firms emerging from other counties in the Global North) would be fruitful for answering such questions.

Notes

1. I use the terms 'Global North' and 'Global South' to draw attention to inequalities among countries that tend to be mapped out (at least partially) on geographic lines (i.e. US, Canada, Europe, and Japan versus Central/South America, Africa, South/Southeast Asia, etc.). I recognize that these concepts also have many flaws, however.

2. To emphasize the pervasiveness of these core emotional strategies for credit customer service in many parts of the world, I draw upon illustrations in the US as well. Later, I describe what is more distinct and contextual about this work in India.

3. To highlight why US firms choose call centers abroad versus those at home, I situate my ethnographic findings below in two quantitative studies conducted in the early 2000s: a comparative study of call centers, *The Global Call Center Report* (Holman et al., 2007), analyzing 17 countries across North America, Europe, Asia, and Africa; and

a section of that project which focuses on the India and US cases in particular (Batt et al., 2006). This comparison shows the representativeness of my case within India, as well as how Indian call centers differ from those in the Global North.

4. I thank one of the reviewers for elucidating this point for me.

5. In making this transnational comparison, my aim is not to essentialize differences in meanings of credit in India and US, or to privilege the national above the local or global in this process. Rather, the purpose is to situate these dynamics in their contexts, and explore how transnationalism is altering the degrees of both social distance and crossover between these two countries.

6. Interest rates and fees in India are as high as 50 percent – higher than the upper bound in the US, at 30 percent. This is yet another deterrent to the social acceptance of credit in India.

References

Ahmed S (2004) Affective economies. *Social Text* 22(2): 117–139.

Aneesh A (2006) *Virtual Migration*. Durham, NC: Duke University Press.

Arvidsson A (forthcoming) General sentiment: How value and affect converge in the information economy. *Sociological Review*.

Bachman J, Stein S, Campbell K and Sitarenios G (2000) Emotional intelligence in the collection of debt. *International Journal of Selection and Assessment* 8(3): 176–182.

Batt R, Doellgast V and Kwon H (2006) Service management and employment systems in U.S. and Indian call centers. In: Collins SM and Brainard L (eds) *Brookings Trade Forum 2005*. Washington, DC: Brookings Institution Press, pp. 335–372.

Bergman L and Rummel D (2004) *Secret History of the Credit Card*. PBS Frontline TV documentary.

Burawoy M, Blum JA, George S, Gille Z, Gowan T, Haney L, Klawiter M, Lopez SH, O Riain S and Thayer M (2000) *Global Ethnography: Forces, Connections, and Imaginations in a Postmodern World*. Berkeley: University of California Press.

Castells M (2000) *The Rise of the Network Society*, 2nd edn. Malden, MA: Blackwell Publishing.

Ehrenreich B and Hochschild AR (eds) (2003) *Global Woman: Nannies, Maids, and Sex Workers in the New Economy*. New York: Metropolitan Books.

Elster J (1989) *Solomonic Judgements: Studies in the Limination of Rationality*. Cambridge: Cambridge University Press.

Fernandes L (2006) *India's New Middle Class*. Minneapolis: University of Minnesota Press.

Ganguly-Scrase R and Scrase TJ (2009) *Globalisation and the Middle Classes in India*. Abington: Routledge.

Gulati S (2005) *Nalini by Day, Nancy by Night*. Women Make Movies, documentary film.

Hochschild AR (1983) *The Managed Heart: Commercialization of Human Feeling*. Berkeley: University of California Press.

Hochschild AR (2003) Love and gold. In: Ehrenreich B and Hochschild AR (eds) *Global Woman*. New York: Metropolitan Books, pp. 15–30.

Holman D, Batt R and Holtgrewe U (2007) *The Global Call Center Report*. Ithaca, NY: ILR School, Cornell University.

Huffington Post (2012) Debt collectors pursue one in seven Americans, 2 February. Available at www.huffingtonpost.com.

Jenkins A (2001) *Companies' Use of Psychometric Testing and the Changing Demand for Skills: A Review of the Literature*. London: London School of Economics and Political Science.

Kazmin A (2010) Indians struggle to repay credit card debt. *Financial Times*, 21 January.

Mirchandani K (2012) *Phone Clones*. Ithaca, NY: Cornell University Press.

Nadeem S (2011) *Dead Ringers*. Princeton, NJ: Princeton University Press.

NASSCOM (2003) *Strategic Review 2003*. New Delhi, India: NASSCOM.

NASSCOM (2008) An overview of the IT-BPO sector in India. Powerpoint presentation, NASSCOM.

NASSCOM (2012) *Strategic Review 2012*. New Delhi, India: NASSCOM.

Perkins J (2004) *Confessions of an Economic Hitman*. San Francisco, CA: Berrett-Koehler Publishers.

Poster WR (2007) Who's on the line? Indian call center agents pose as Americans for U.S.-outsourced firms. *Industrial Relations* 46(2): 271–304.

Poster WR (2011) Emotion detectors, answering machines and e-unions: Multisurveillances in the global interactive services industry. *American Behavioral Scientist* 55(7): 868–901.

Raina A (2004) *Speaking Right for a Call Center Job*. New Delhi: Penguin Books.

Roy M (2010) *Report on Trend and Progress of Banking in India 2009–10*. Mumbai: Reserve Bank of India.

Sassen S (2008) Two stops in today's international division of labor: Shaping novel labor supplies and employment regimes. *American Behavioral Scientist* 25(3): 457–496.

Schechter D (2007) *In Debt We Trust*. Globalvision, documentary film.

Scurlock J (2006) *Maxed Out*. Trueworks, documentary film.

Simhan TER (2012) Staff count in top four firms set to touch 6 Lakh this year. *The Hindu Business Line*, 1 September.

Streitfeld D (2009) So you're dead? Don't expect that to stop the debt collector. *New York Times*, 4 March, pp. A1, A15.

Sutton RI (1991) Maintaining norms about expressed emotions: The case of bill collectors. *Administrative Science Quarterly* 36(2): 245–268.

Thelen ST, Boonghoo Y and Magnini VP (2010) An examination of customer sentiment toward offshore services. *Journal of the Academy of Marketing Science* 39(2): 270–289.

Timmons H (2007) Credit cards get a hostile reception in India. *New York Times*, 5 July.

van Jaarsveld D and Poster WR (2012) Call centers: Emotional labor over the phone. In: Grandey A, Diefendorff J and Rupp DE (eds) *Emotional Labor in the 21st Century*. Mahwah, NJ: LEA Press, pp. 153–174.

Varma PK (2007) *The Great Indian Middle Class*. New Delhi: Penguin Books India.

Weber M (1930) *The Protestant Ethic and the Spirit of Capitalism*. New York: Charles Scriber's Sons.

37 eEmpires

Rita Raley

I really want it to be called "UntoCaesar.com."
 —Kaleil Isaza Tuzman, *Startup.com*

It is the flow of money, moving quickly and silently to those who are sufficiently wise and creative to establish themselves as players in this new arena.
 —Steffano Korper and Juanita Ellis, *The E-Commerce Book: Building the E-Empire*

e=M-C-M

The eEmpire has definitively entered our lexicon, both as concept and as semantic construction, with "e" continuing to operate as the value-added, universal signifier of the brave new wired world. The signifier "e," as this essay will demonstrate, cannot be located under one set of stable descriptors. Rather, it must be understood as a fluid and intersecting set of forces, practices, technologies, and events. It is not a singular entity, but comprises communicative networks, electronic commerce, modes of production, and global financial markets. With numerous precursors, most notably associated with Microsoft, the Electronic Empire suggests a triumphant narrative of technology and capitalism.[1] However, it goes beyond that to suggest a speculative departure from the material conditions of production and circulation and toward informationalism. Such a speculative departure constitutes the now-dominant mode and stage of capital—a philosophical appraisal anticipated by Marx[2] and reanimated by Giovanni Arrighi and Fredric Jameson. The Electronic Empire has different rhetorical registers, ranging from cultural studies to ordinary advertisements. A visual analysis of a recent commercial will outline my critical treatment of the electronic empire and the thematic terrain of this essay.

Rita Raley, "eEmpires." *Cultural Critique*, 57 (Spring), 2004: 111–150. Reproduced by permission of University of Minnesota Press.

Beginning in April 2001, the eBusiness software company Computer Associates repeatedly ran a thirty-second advertisement entitled "Empire" on the Rupert Murdoch–owned Fox network, self-consciously combining a cyberpunk aesthetic with the elements of a sword-and-sandal picture and formally resembling both an inspirational corporate video and a promotional QuickTime movie.[3] The commercial is made all the more remarkable by the visual absence of the computer as fetish object, yet the mechanism is message via its operation as interface and substrate. The verbal script illustrates what initially appears to be a morphological shift from classical Rome to the global electronic empire, which is communicated with even greater complexity by the visual iconography. Both in its audio and visual tracks, it establishes a direct, continuous, and naturalized link connecting the Roman empire, the British empire, and the contemporary eBusiness at the center of Wall Street: the shared governing idea, after all, is the controlling of new domains through new technologies. Concluding with a voice-over whose celebratory and pedagogic intonations are replicated throughout the commercial tech sector, the script runs as follows:

> Roar of the crowd: "Caesar, Caesar, Caesar."
> Caesar: "Hail, Romans! Today our nation is great, far greater than it has
>   ever been." [punctuated by camera shutters and flashes]
> Voice-over: "If you manage it correctly, even the largest empire will
>   adapt and continue to thrive. Our software has helped more companies
>   evolve their infrastructure than anyone else on earth. Hello, tomorrow.
>   We are Computer Associates, the software that manages eBusiness."

The sense of continuity, inheritance, and an evolution from the historical empire to the contemporary American electronic empire is further facilitated by the visual trajectory of the commercial. Marked by all of the signifiers of imperial Rome, it begins with Caesar's march through a palatial stateroom and out through majestic curtains onto a balcony to address the multitudes below.

That address and the unfolding narrative are equally marked by all of the signifiers of digital culture: the address is simultaneously projected onto a giant high-resolution screen, while the production cameras pan quickly to show that those in the audience not cheering are equipped with their own high-tech camera equipment. A helicopter descends as if from the outtakes of *The Matrix,* and the urban landscape picked up by the rapid cuts and sweeping cameras includes London city buses, taxis, bobbies, and citizens of both the Roman and the British empires. In order to evoke the fiction that the re-enacted empire is global, then, the phantasmagorical urban landscape is also powerfully resonant of the imaginative Far East of William Gibson, an exoticized colonial-era Bombay, and the futurist Los Angeles of Ridley Scott. Such a historical and technological compression is augmented by a comparable pastiche of architectural styles: in a panorama shot, Caesar speaks from and alongside neo-classical buildings; the London Houses of Parliament and Big Ben are visible at the end of the extensive mall; and, further emphasizing the teleology from Rome to contemporary finance capital, he concludes his triumphant appearance with an equally triumphant exit over a bridge leading to Manhattan, Wall Street, and the afterlife of empire, the passage into New York overseen by an iconic statue of Caesar in the place of the Statue of Liberty.

And, with the destruction of the twin towers now in mind, the narrative and semiotic arc that begins with Ionic columns and culminates with the now-memorialized New York skyline clearly communicates the symbolic and material value of these towers and their embodiment of empire and finance capital. In that it materializes and fuses the territorial city with the apparatuses of media, "Empire" both advertises and enacts the electronic empire in its collapse of the historical and the contemporary within the frame of the commercial itself.

Notwithstanding its formal density, there are no negative connotations of empire here; neither are the links between business and empire hidden. In its partially ironic celebration of gladiatorial capitalism and well-managed empires, the commercial, like the CEO of the fallen Internet company documented in the film *Startup.com*, embraces an ideology of empire presented as inherent to the ruth-lessness of business: in order to survive, rule, and "manage correctly," material strength, power, and compliance are required by nation and corporation alike. (The emperor's march, after all, is itself presided over by Praetorian guards and a variety of armed soldiers and all of the visible manifestations of crowd and riot control.) That survival should be a Darwinian survival is evinced by the verbal rhetoric of evolution and adaptation, which in part indicates a retreat to the biological and material and a flinching back from a wholesale embrace of the electronic.

My essay examines this kind of organic paradigm and its relation to various speculative visions of the futures, logic, and possible destruction of capitalist history; of late finance; and of informational capitalism. It reviews the current field of study of technology, information, and global capitalism, and it reviews the idea of the American century—beginning with Henry Luce's manifesto on the rights and responsibilities of America as a new world power—yet it is embedded in both the literal and the metaphoric idea of the network and so looks to the question of new, uncertain, and future reincarnations. In this respect, my essay addresses both the material transformations that the electronic age has brought about and our means of analyzing these transformations.

While this essay is not directly about communications and computer companies and microchips, it is about the operation of networks such as CHIPS: a private-sector clearing house and money-movement system that handles over 242,000 bank-to-bank transactions and business payments per day, which correlates to an average daily circulation of $1.2 trillion.[4] An electronic system that purports to handle over 95 percent of all global dollar payments must necessarily turn for its administration to software specialists, programmers, and systems analysts, but in some respects the system authenticates, regulates, and generates itself. It does this partly by assigning every participant a net position of debit or credit at the end of the day so as to stabilize the instantaneous movement of stateless money. (The CHIPS system assigns each participant a universal identification number [UID] that tracks account and bank information.) The system also operates as an information database that helps to set monetary value and coordinates the very financial transactions that it needs to operate. The worldwide financial telecommunications system called SWIFT functions alongside CHIPS by standardizing and facilitating the automation of payment messages between networked banks. Both systems regulate transactions, financial data, and themselves; both are purely instrumental and commodifiable.[5] As is the case for Claude Shannon's mathematical theory of communication, neither can account for either the creation or the significance of financial information. Both are in a sense meaningless; rather, their function and performance are their meaning.

We might move from this specific instance of economic self-regulation and self-governance to more general conceptions of the operational principles of the global financial markets. Michael Pryke and John Allen draw on Georg Simmel's philosophy of money in their analysis of derivatives, the merger of technology and money, speed, and the new forms of money post–Bretton Woods, and they suggest that money "has made itself adaptable to a new set of circumstances and, in so doing, seeks to 'impose its rhythm and pace' on the contents and co-ordinates of life" (2000, 270). Strongly echoing Lyotard's commentary on the status of truth and knowledge in a postmodern moment, Jean-Marie Guéhenno further argues that functionality constitutes the significance and structure of the principal financial markets, which lack a "clear architecture," generally lack a "territorial logic," and are, as he notes, "increasingly defined by the rules by which they run themselves."[6] Such operationalism is precisely the mode of the network, which is simultaneously organizational model and killer app of the global informational society.[7]

The transition into the informational, network society has in general terms been articulated, and the critical work linking technological change and capitalist and social development is appropriately expansive, as is the critical work delineating the period in which information is the prime commodity and source of value, productivity, and power.[8] From the representative opening lines of Daniel Bell's treatise on the postindustrial society (1973), to Simon Nora and Alain Minc's report to the president of France (1978), to the first volume of Manuel Castells's trilogy devoted to the Information Age (1996), a revolutionary transition has been announced. This technological revolution paradoxically "centered around information technologies, [and] began to reshape, at accelerated pace, the material basis of society" (Castells 1996, 1). Operating within a language of revolution symptomatic of their retroactive situation within a general Enlightenment, progressivist paradigm—and echoing Henry Luce's declaration that "ours is a revolutionary century," but revolutionary in science and industry—numerous works have set out both to predict and document as precisely as possible the scope, scale, and general consequences of the "computerization of society."[9] One general question asked in the discourse concerns revolution and historical change itself. Is our current moment, in other words, structurally and paradigmatically different from the moment of the telegraph, the printing press, or the railway, or do we remain within the same technology of empire and the same capitalist system?[10] As Nick Dyer-Witheford proposes, the idea of revolution is central to the discourse on the information society because it has rewritten the Marxist "notion of historical progress toward a classes society … but reinscribe[d] technological advance rather than class conflict as the driving force in this transformation" (1999,37). The ideological and conceptual rifts within the historical assessments of the informational and electronics revolution are well documented, and lines are generally drawn between promoters and skeptics, and between harbingers of the new and historians of precursors. (The latter would argue that the electronic revolution is on par with earlier technological revolutions, and its transformative effects, therefore, not qualitatively different.) Accounts of these continuities and of transformations, shifts, and epistemological ruptures alike can be traced through academic and mass-market texts, managerial manifestoes, and cyberlibertarian treatises.[11]

The grand narrative of this informational society holds that global capitalism is at once facilitator and structural logic, especially as both capital and society have progressed, ascended, or mutated from earlier stages of mercantile capitalism and finance capital.[12] Castells, for example, uses the phrase "informational capitalism" to describe the new "techno-economic system," the structure of which was ultimately determined by the neoliberalism of the 1980s.[13] In contrast to the evolutionary and transformational narrative of the new information economy, Arrighi has articulated a theory of finance capital that holds it to be fundamentally cyclical, and as such, "a recurrent phenomenon which has marked the capitalist era from its earliest beginnings in late medieval and early modern Europe" (1994, ix). The moment when capital takes flight from production and becomes speculative constitutes its third and final stage. This last and highest stage is recurrent, and the long twentieth century—the title of Arrighi's study—is just one of four systemic cycles of accumulation that he identifies within capital's lifespan.[14] So it is that we have the basic operational logic of capital for Arrighi: regeneration, a thesis that comes from his exegesis of Marx.

According to Marx's formula for capital, value had an "occult" power of self- and automatic expansion, that of being able to augment or "add value to itself" (Marx 1995, 98). Such a quality of self-reproduction would, in the mid-nineteenth century, almost necessarily be described in quasi-biological terms: so, value "brings forth living offspring, or, at the least, lays golden eggs" and operates in the guise, mode, and form of money so as to bring about "its own spontaneous generation" (98). Marx suggests that value, while always linked to material labor, nonetheless postures as capital and commodity and implicitly emerges as auto-generative and "self-multiplying," as that which lays its own golden eggs (1973, 537). Jameson's amplification of the third stage of Marx's formula, C-M, picks up on this abstraction. In his commentary on the passage from commodity-form to money-form—"it must spend some time as a cocoon before it can take off as a butterfly" (Marx 1973, 548–49)—and Arrighi's own exegesis of this stage, Jameson notes: "Capital itself becomes free-floating. It separates from the concrete context of its productive geography.... Now, like the butterfly stirring within the chrysalis, it separates itself from that concrete breeding ground and prepares to take flight" (1997, 251).

These biological metaphors for the evolutionary movements of capital are appropriately creative in their vision of birth via meta-morphosis and the shedding of a decayed structure, echoing as they do Joseph Schumpeter's famous theory of the birth, regeneration, and essential truth of capital, that of "creative destruction."[15] In concrete terms, creative destruction suggests the dislodging of one product or process by another, such as the replacement of mimeograph machines by photocopiers. For Schumpeter, capital operates according to a biological process of "industrial mutation," whereby the economic structure "incessantly revolutionizes … *from within,* incessantly destroying the old one, incessantly creating a new one" (1950, 83). But what exactly is the relation between revolution and a biological paradigm? Schumpeter's formulation suggests that a certain degree of destruction is inherent to any systemic change and that there can be no change without energy, but situating capital within a biological paradigm allows him also to speculate both on genesis and its corollary, termination or degeneration. It places him within a dialectical model of growth and decline.[16] Linking capital to organic matter lends it continuity and coherence on a path from genesis to decay and eventual death. It further suggests a process of self-reproduction, with capital giving birth to its own offspring, laying its own golden eggs, or decomposing and reorganizing its own larval tissues.

Such a vision of auto-generation reaches an apotheosis in Marx's figural reading of commodities and money's power, both of accrual and origination, which is part of the same general formula for capital. "However scurvy they may look, or however badly they may smell," he writes, commodities "are in faith and in truth money, inwardly circumcised Jews, and what is more, a wonderful means whereby out of money to make new money."[17] This is of course value's "occult" power: literally hidden, concealed, and secret. Circumcision here may serve as an identificatory marker, but an inward circumcision is also suggestive of Schumpeter's mutation "from within." By implying that the potential for procreation lies almost exclusively within the system, Marx suggests that capital has the capacity, perhaps the genetic material, both to reproduce and to destroy itself.[18] Arrighi performs a similar analysis with his explicative suggestion that capital already has an inherent "'flexibility' and 'eclecticism'" rather than consisting of "concrete forms" (1994, 4). Such a critical move assimilates the unpredictability, uncertainty, and indistinctness of the "after-life" of the current cycle of capitalist accumulation—the long twentieth century marked by the ascendance of information as a commodity—to the flexibility and mobility of the network.

The impetus of this essay, then, is to situate the Electronic Empire within the network, both as object and facilitator. My starting point is Arrighi's argument that capital is bound to perpetual and cyclical mutation and to regeneration, with capital read as a viral epidemic that is nearly impossible to vaccinate against. But biological and genetic metaphors do not provide a fully adequate lens through which to view the operational logic of the current financial markets or with which to project along a diachronic axis so as to imagine the ends and the futures of capital, U.S. capitalism, and historical epoch. Because it cannot account for the complexity of global, neoliberal capitalism, the organic is a limited and insufficient figure with which to trace a strategic and conceptual break from the rhetoric and paradigms of the American century. The limitations of organic metaphors within economic discourse have also been identified by J. K. Gibson-Graham, who focuses specifically on the representation of the economy as an organic body. In a collaborative study of capitalism "as we know it," Gibson-Graham (Katherine Gibson and Julie Graham writing in one voice) critiques the dominant articulation of capitalism within the Marxian tradition as unified, singular, and totalizing (1996, 253–65). This tendency to read capitalism as a unified, self-reproducing organism is manifest, Gibson-Graham suggests, in the physiological metaphors used to characterize the economy.[19] Such a reading, in her view, fails to account for capitalism as a "disaggregated and diverse set of practices unevenly distributed across a varied economic landscape" (117). Reconceptualizing capitalism in terms of heterogeneity, fragmentation, and permeability, rather than organic unity, requires that we recognize noncapitalist economic practices, and it also allows for a more widely integrative notion of revolutionary praxis.

Tariq Ali has suggested that the "old empires developed organically." The Electronic Empire, on the other hand, develops non-organically. Thus, in contrast to the organic figures and evolutionary paradigms so prevalent in current critical theory of capital, information, and Empire, I would like to suggest that the automatism of the network is instead paradigmatic for our period, the speculative stage of finance capital, and thus befits our move into the twenty-first century. Mid-World War II, nearly post-Depression and coterminous with Luce, Schumpeter suggested in *Capitalism, Socialism, and Democracy* (1942) that, when we are dealing with capitalism, "we are dealing with an organic process" (83). However, sixty intervening years have brought us to a point whereby we must now consider the process as not inorganic, but nonorganic. The nonorganic is a complex system that has energy, movement, and dynamism. It is not biologically alive, but neither is it an inert, inanimate, material structure: it functions like an organic entity, yet it is not. In order to speak to the Electronic Empire, the apparatus of our time, we need the figure of the network, that which subtends the organic and the nonorganic. The inchoate, indeterminate abyss beyond the long twentieth century may, in my view, best be articulated in terms of the electronic network, that which writes, coordinates, and implements its own rules of operation.

The Electronic Empire

However tenuous or temporary their claims to unprecedented wealth and hegemony, the IT (information technology) and mass-media markets continue to be delineated as electronic empires, part of them evil, with colonial and anticolonial tactics of territorial warfare replaced both by vicious and constant competition and by industrial espionage.[20] So, too, are these markets delineated as the province of the new class, the wealth not of nations but of innovative, "wise and creative" and often renegade individuals, whether they be "Silicon Samurai," tycoons, teenage hackers, or ordinary players.[21] The IT market in particular—the domain of eCommerce—has been particularly dominated by emergent corporations and emergent technologies, and it consists of both Net-based transactions and the goods themselves.[22] It is the main site of U.S. managerial and corporate capitalism, and, as has been extensively articulated, it functions with information as its chief commodity.

Popular opinion may have it that the speculative bubble has burst and the market destabilized, but in fact most recent qualitative research shows that eCommerce is not just surviving but growing, particularly in the area of b2b, the direct linking of buyers and sellers.[23] As almost any industry article will argue, the power of the IT or "e-conomic" market is not registered on the NASDAQ, nor does it lie with its current dominant interface, the Web. And, as prone as market and economic commentary is to forecasts, judicious commentators will acknowledge that the exact form and contour of the impact of IT is as yet unknown and uncertain, and that it is even unpredictable without analogies to past technological developments, usually electricity, the printing press, and the assembly line. What we do know is that the IT network is pervasive and invasive; that it promises to go anywhere and allow everyone access; that its strength is its mobility, flexibility, and reprogrammability; and, most important, that its value increases as it grows, as knowledge is accumulated, more computers are linked to the system, and information processing becomes more complex. IT network and market alike, in other words, are themselves self-generating—a feature epitomized by the composition and programming of the Windows NT operating system with its own code.[24]

The linking of IT and the new technologies with imperialism and the concept of Empire has given us new historical descriptors, among them the virtual empire, the virtual universal, and my concept of choice, the Electronic Empire, chosen because of its resonance with the electronic network and with computer processes. The electronic, as well, signifies the commodity itself and the means of circulation. It is, in other words, a communicative network. Although organically or biologically based computing developments may eventually make electronics obsolete, in the present moment we can say that electronics, especially microprocessing, has made other technological developments possible (e.g. digital telecommunications, bioengineering, biotech, materials science) and has historically been not just bound to but also constitutive of the concept of Empire. However, thus far within cultural criticism, information technology has been linked to empire primarily by way of both parallelism and pretext. Debbie Lee and Tim Fulford, for example, analyze the Microsoft-sponsored Web site and adventure magazine, *Mungo Park*, which shares its name with the eighteenth-century Scottish explorer who mapped parts of the interior of Africa during two famous and chronicled expeditions.[25] They argue that such an instance of naming is not simply fortuitous but rather suggests that the logic of empire and neocolonialism is intrinsic to monopolistic software companies. But this radical extension of the meaning of "virtual empire," such that it encompasses a British colonial epistemology of science and an American postindustrial, neocolonial epistemology of IT, attenuates the force of the insight, and there are other links one might establish between the electronic and the empire.

The industry understanding of "eEmpire" suggests a convergence of electronics and commerce, marked by the elimination of geographical boundaries for the client base and global sales and marketing, and by the extension of communication and information networks into what are imagined as highly improbable spaces. Put simply, according to a well-circulated business guide, the Electronic Empire is "the newest pairing of global business and top-notch technology."[26] Yet for industry, Electronic Empire is not just the convergence of global business and technology, but also the integration of technologies, whereby various modes of consumption may be synchronized and syncretized into one platform (as in the convergence of e-mail, shopping, entertainment, and information). From the perspective of the mainstream media and much academic writing in the area of communication, cultural, and media studies, the Electronic Empire signifies the control of distribution and of content by a few familiar transnational corporations: Viacom, AOL Time Warner, Sony, Disney, GE, and Seagram, with companies such as Microsoft and Intel controlling the standards, performance, and distribution of digital technologies.[27] Oliver Boyd-Barrett has formulated a thesis of media imperialism that calls for the extensive study of the "colonization of communications space" based on a political concern with U.S. hegemony and ideology, with detailed empirical analyses of generic media imperialism. Such colonization, for Boyd-Barrett and others, differs over temporary and geographic horizons, differs in the intensity of imposition, dependence, and resistance that it generates, and differs according to media forms and governmental regulation. The difference is in degree and kind.

Herbert I. Schiller's assessment of *Mass Communications and American Empire* in 1969 remains remarkably relevant and worth repeating here because he hints at a mode of empire that is not strictly territorial but networked: "If free trade is the mechanism by which a powerful economy penetrates and dominates a weaker one, the 'free flow of information,' the designated objective incidentally of UNESCO, is the channel through which life styles and value systems can be imposed on poor and vulnerable societies."[28] For Schiller, the issue is information imperialism, specifically with reference to U.S.

hegemony and the "invasions," exportations, and impositions of information. He thus uses the notion of electronic empire to signify an "informal" empire based on the ideology of free trade, such that controlling the flows of information and communication amounts to controlling the world economy and hence the world. For him the concept is metaphoric, albeit with profound material effects, and it lies behind the American ideology of concern, freedom, cultural exchange, and benevolence, an ideology present from Luce to the Coca Cola refrain, "I'd like to teach the world to sing." (We know well that the Project for the New American Century is not articulated in terms of benevolence, but in terms of dominance and military strength.) For such a problem as the American century, one must necessarily return to Schiller's observation that "to 'own' a century is to own an empire," but qualitatively new economics and electronics alike need revisiting if we are now to articulate the connections between them. Thirty years on, academic and popular critics still abide by the persistence of U.S. media hegemony, and such a position is almost unavoidable (H. Schiller 1969, 2; Boyd-Barrett 1984, 162). In fact, the popular electronic empire—that of IT and mass-media market domination—is symptomatic of the synecdoche of the economic realities of globalism, whereby part of the world substitutes for the whole, a claim made with respect to the putative ascendancy of the United States and/or the West. This synecdoche is generally corroborated and its threat of cultural homogenization viewed as a nightmarish possibility that must be countered if pedagogy and the idea of critique are to be resuscitated.

The threat of corporate imperial takeover also motivates Daya Thussu's intervention, which is similarly bound to the age of basic cable and TV satellites. In the eponymous *Electronic Empires*, he uses "empire" to refer to the command of content and the sheer massification and extension of transnational media corporations, comparable to the imperial institutions and administrators of the nineteenth century only in their geographic and cultural ambition. Their aim, he says, "is not to subject alien populations to imperial dictates but to persuade consumers, through their global electronic networks, to use their media or buy the products advertised and to accept as inevitable the global progress of the market."[29] McChesney makes a similar diagnosis of commercial media as a constitutive and reflective component of global capitalism: "The rise of a global commercial media system is closely linked to the rise of a significantly more integrated 'neo-liberal' global capitalist economic system" (1998, 27). Thussu as well argues that the emergence of a new and "corporate colonialism" of mass broadcast media no longer means the accrual power and capital for the state, but that capital accrues power for itself. With a similar focus, A. Sivanandan follows Harold Innis in claiming a coextensiveness of empire and media monopolies and argues: "It is no longer the ownership of the means of production that is important, but the ownership of the means of communication. Not Britannia, but Murdoch, rules the waves. What I am talking about here is the centralization of power behind a democratic facade" (Sivanandan 1997, 288; Innis 1950, 9).

The rhetorical power of the analogy notwithstanding, in our current critical and technological moment, and in light of the significant scholarly work on the historical meaning of imperialism, we might say instead that the old imperial paradigm is no longer applicable precisely because that stage of capitalist and territorial accumulation and that episteme (with an attendant understanding of race and nation) has given way and mutated into a "global networked and information society." In the new mode of

Empire, power may be consolidated by transnational corporations, but the logic of power is capitalist and not territorial.[30] Finance capital, to return to Jameson, is "free-floating," mobile, and "footloose" (Jameson 1997, 251; Cerny 1994, 337). The ascendance of finance over "real" material goods and the separation of capital from the "concrete context of its productive geography" facilitates this shift from imperial territory to "modulating networks of command."[31] This understanding of the capitalist logic of power works in concert with many articulations of the emergent mode of empire. For example, Guéhenno envisages a future in which "Rome will no longer be in Rome, and no territorial given, no dominant group, will be able to impose itself. This empire will be neither a supernation nor a universal republic. It will not be governed by an emperor" (1995, 47). Similarly, Thussu notes that the "virtual empires of the electronic age do not depend on territorial conquest" (1998, 1). However, in his implicit reference to Murdoch as the new emperor, he has recourse to an Enlightenment-era notion of a single controlling human entity: "the digital globe under construction by Murdoch will lead to empires which have no territories but span the world, with the potential of being more powerful than the territorial-based ones of the past" (6). (Even the "colonization of communications space" involves a figurative space, territory that is mediatized, dematerialized, commodified, and the province of speculation.) We might go further to observe that the current incarnation of Empire presents us with an interface between the territorial and the nonterritorial. Territories are certainly less materially situated than they are subject to recurrent proclamations of definitive, yet arbitrary, boundaries; thus, on the one hand, there are continual battles for territory (Kashmir, Israel-Palestine). But, Empire depends on entrepreneurial zones and high-tech corridors, which suggests a gridded networking of territory, as with the electronic and physical movement of military bases across national borders.

Within a capitalist logic of power, the nation-state acquires a kind of temporary obsolescence. In spite of one of the more prevalent dramas within the Western imagination, which stages a national contest between American capital and that of the Far East, usually Japan, the new mode of Empire does not maintain the nation-state as either categorical foundation or operational center.[32] Michael Hardt, Antonio Negri, and numerous others suggest that it is not simply that the nation-state has lost power and that the United States no longer occupies the center of an imperial order, which is itself defunct, but also that a supranational economic, political, and communicative network has ascended in its place. Hardt and Negri put the point succinctly: *"The United States does not, and indeed no nation-state can today, form the center of an imperialist project. Imperialism is over"* (2000, xiii–xiv). The discourse on financial globalization tends to corroborate this challenge to the power of nation-states and testify to their undermining by financial markets. Philip G. Cerny provides a representative claim: "financial markets, not states, represent the closest thing to a new hegemony in the contemporary international system" (1994, 339).[33]

To go further than the displacement of the nation-state from the position of center requires noting that the very notion of a center has become meaningless. Instead we have nodes within interconnected financial and informational networks—"centers" for the coordination, standardization, and transmission of payment messages. These centers often battle for control within the network, as with the efforts of Al-Jazeera and CNN to develop competing archives to store and produce the "truth" of a dominant cultural memory. The network, then, is by nature a counternetwork and thereby embodies contradiction, internal contest, and multiplicity.[34] For instance, even transnational corporations maintain nodal centers that often grow in size, importance, and complexity relative to the corporations's own rhizomatic development and expansion. In this respect, I find productive the syncretic concept of Empire delineated by Hardt and Negri, which not only "establishes no territorial center of power and does not rely on fixed boundaries or barriers," but is also "a *decentered* and *deterritorializing* apparatus of rule that progressively incorporates the entire global realm within its open, expanding frontiers" (xii).[35] We have seen other instances of the claim for Empire's decentered and a-territorial quality. What Deleuze and Guattari's paradigm contributes to this analytic is the sense that the new mode and system of Empire has its own forces of operation. Imperial power no longer maintains a positive, "actual and localizable terrain or center"; rather, it is "distributed in networks, through mobile and articulated mechanisms of control" (Hardt and Negri 2000, 384). Displacing Caesar and Murdoch from the helm, Empire now operates itself. In terms of practice, then, the Electronic Empire signifies the convergence of global capitalism and the new technologies and thus the complete imbrication of media and market and control over the content and distributive flows of the communication networks. But the concept of the Electronic Empire is more complexly paradigmatic, encompassing as it does the ascendance of information, the mode and operational logic of the network, and neoliberal global capitalism. It is in fact the paradigmatic concept for the moment beyond or after the American century.

The Age of Electronic Networks

In his wide-ranging study of world-economies, Fernand Braudel meditates upon the periodic movements and conjunctural rhythms of history, contemplates our existence in both the short and the long term, within periods that precede and outlive us, and then asks whether it is "possible to identify a finite plane or body which, being the site of a movement, fixes its time-span" (83–85). The question is apposite: can we identify a point of closure, an end, an afterlife—temporal, geographic, psychic, or otherwise— perhaps a post-American century, or a fourth wave? But, what exactly is at an end: is it history; finance capital; "culture," now ceded to the commercial; the nation; a particular conception of imperialism; the organic body (supplanted or overcoded by biotech); the human; politics (replaced by a categorically different reign of the image and of spectacle); the century of "total war"; the 'real'; the (old) mass media; or industrial and material productivity (supplanted by information, symbols, and the immaterial)? What indeed will be the replacement mythologies, or will a non-mythology function in that capacity?[36]

Is, in other words, the American century, or U.S. hegemony or U.S. capitalism, an infinitely expanding idiom, or has the idiom, and its time, expired, its spectacular and apocalyptic conclusion elegiacally captured on tape on September 11? A different version of this question comes from Arrighi in *The Long Twentieth Century*, in which he addresses the most recent systemic cycle of accumulation, the temporal unit named in the title of the book, and asks whether capitalist history has reached its ends with U.S. capitalism, whether "the structures of US capitalism constitute the ultimate limit of the six centuries-long process through which capitalist power has attained its present, seemingly all-encompassing scale and scope?"[37] The answer he gives is no: the ends are more imaginable than realizable, and capitalism will undoubtedly survive in new forms, in new guises.[38] Both its own "spontaneous generation" and its own destruction are, as Arrighi says elsewhere, coded into capital's "genes" (1990, 55–56).

Schumpeter's main argument holds that it is the successful and regenerative runs of capitalism, and not its crises and failures, that damage and potentially short-circuit it, much like the successful run of the butterfly, which after all dies shortly after its metamorphosis. The power of this insight notwithstanding, Schumpeter's basic premise about capitalism still holds, even through the doubts of Arrighi and other theorists of late capitalism and economic globalization on the question of its ultimate survival: capitalism "not only never is but never can be stationary."[39] Such is the fundamental logic of finance capital, echoed as well in Gertrude Stein's oft-quoted axiom on the durability and perpetuity of money—"The money is always there but the pockets change"—a sentiment accepted as axiomatic precisely like the fundamental physical law echoed in my first section title ($e=mc^2$). It is not just the pockets that change, however, but also the form, matter, and function of capital, as well as its mode of circulation. This is the crux of the regeneration thesis, both for Marx and for Arrighi, and in a different sense for contemporary CEO-turned-financial-guru Walter Wriston, who suggests that the virtual and immediate changing of pockets in the late twentieth century constitutes a theoretical, essential, and ontological difference, such that money is in fact still here, but now has a qualitatively different power of mutability: "The increased volition of money gives you a difference in kind—not just degree. It's like a piece of lead: you put it on your desk, it's a paperweight; put it in a gun, it's a bullet" (Marx 1973, 536, 667–68; Wriston quoted in Bass). Although it is not my primary concern here, more substantive academic commentary on the range and targets of these guns is required—on the damage inflicted on "human material" by the mechanisms of production—and this is largely the province of a recent article by Jerry Harris, who, in the context of an exposé of the operations of informational capitalism, as well as of its comparatively under-documented material consequences and abuses, hits upon a particularly apt metaphor for the regenerative operation of capital: "Like a man in a sinking ship looking for a way out, capitalism found in information technology a life boat to a new world of profits" (1998/1999, 34). It would indeed be a ship seeking passage to a "new world of profits," suggestive as it is of other inaugural moments of Empire and world economy.

If it is the case, as it is also for Arrighi and Jameson, that capital is bound to inevitable regeneration, doomed to repeat and exhaust the three stages of accumulation, production, and speculation (M-C-M), the question before us is what lies beyond the limit of U.S. capitalism and the American century; it is even whether they have in fact reached their limit. One could argue that the recent display of U.S. military power was compensatory and suggests that U.S. economic and cultural hegemony is coming to an end.[40] An analysis of this problem, however, must necessarily veer into the imaginative rather than the descriptive, and appropriately enough, into speculation.[41] It makes perfect conceptual sense, then, that Arrighi and Beverly Silver together figure the after-life of U.S. hegemony as "a yet unknown destination" (1999, 35). Terence Hopkins and Immanuel Wallerstein also comment upon the dynamic and diachronic quality of a historical system, which "is evolving second by second such that it is never the same at two successive points in time" (1996, 8). Further, they suggest that the "trends" that disturb the equilibrium of the system eventually destabilize it in a permanent fashion, in effect creating a "real 'crisis,' meaning a turning point so decisive that the system comes to an end and is replaced by one or more alternative successor systems" (8). The form and content of this crisis—the disequilibrium and bifurcations of the system—is unpredictable and approximately Borgesian: as Hopkins and Wallerstein note, "there is always more than one possibility at this point, and there is no way of determining in advance what the outcome(s) will be. All one can do is assess the likelihood that we are approaching a bifurcation (or are already in the midst of one)" (8–9). It is also the case for Arrighi that the futures of world systems should resemble forking paths, that the regeneration of capital comes with an escape clause, a set of parenthetically noted alternative futures (which I will come to) for the histories and futures of capital. Capitalism's futures, in other words, are marked by a significant degree of indeterminacy. Because the outcomes of capitalist history are essentially unknowable, the moment of its end, its futures, the afterlife, and the subsequent cycle of accumulation have all been thought in terms of crisis, turbulence, unpredictability, chaos.[42]

For Hobsbawn and Wallerstein, this crisis is prefigured in the upheavals of 1989.[43] And, though the outcomes of capitalist history are not determinable in advance, for Arrighi, the ends of capitalism are imaginable in bifurcating apocalyptic visions: "finally, to paraphrase Schumpeter, before humanity chokes (or basks) in the dungeon (or paradise) of a post-capitalist world empire or of a post-capitalist world market society, it may well burn up in the horrors (or glories) of the escalating violence that has accompanied the liquidation of the Cold War world order. In this case, capitalist history would also come to an end but by reverting permanently to the systemic chaos from which it began six hundred years ago and which has been reproduced on an ever-increasing scale with each transition" (1994, 356). For Arrighi, like for Braudel in his meditation on the beginnings of world economies, the ends of capitalism haunt it from its inception in the fourteenth century. Schumpeter's rhetoric of internal mutation is apropos here: capitalism bears within itself the elements of its own destruction and the capacity to bring itself to crisis. Capitalism's dynamic quality and tendency toward destructive biological shifts was, for Schumpeter, understandable in terms of extreme weather phenomenon: creative destruction manifests as a "perennial gale" (1942, 84, 87). In that he theorized the evolutionary movements of capitalism in terms of cataclysmic discontinuity, then, Schumpeter's organic paradigm was fundamentally unstable.[44]

The rhetoric of "systemic chaos" and of complexity was not available to Schumpeter, but it permeates the discourse on global or neoliberal capitalism. Given the sheer range of disciplinary schema brought to bear on the problem of the "global," it is not surprising that it lacks a certain semantic and analytic clarity, but the more germane and also ubiquitous models for our historical period, the current cycle of accumulation, the world system, and even global culture comment directly upon this lack of clarity and suggest that the "global" and the global economy are best understandable in terms of abstraction, elasticity, unknowability, and complexity.[45] For example, Bill Maurer draws on the discourse linking economics to computer science and evolutionary biology in order to understand the architectures of offshore finance as "complex, networked, evolving, and adaptive systems" (1995, 114–15). As another example, Fernando Coronil similarly critiques the new forms of wealth by citing Bankers Trust CEO Charles Sanford's disquisition on "particle finance," which analogizes the speculative futures of capital to quantum physics and modern biology, with the attendant implication of unpredictability.[46]

The discourse of complexity theory has also been incorporated into the discourse on Empire, which, for Hardt and Negri, "cannot be represented by a juridical order, but it nonetheless is an order, an order defined by its virtuality, its dynamism, and its functional inconclusiveness" (41). And, for Guéhenno, the age of networks is in fact "the age of complexity … an age of incompletion and disequilibrium" (49). Richard Lee also works with the dialectic of order and disequilibrium to outline the conceptual and critical links between computer systems and world systems: "Since the late 1960s, dynamical-systems research has led to a reconceptualization of the world as one of complexity, determinate but unpredictable: order within chaos (strange attractors); order out of chaos (dissipative structures); visual representation of pathological functions and natural forms exhibiting non-integer dimensions (fractal geometry)" (1996, 197). While a delineation of the analytic conjunctions between scientific paradigms, specifically those related to computer systems, and those of world systems would require a more detailed study, we may say by way of an overview that it seems particularly appropriate that the dynamism and flexibility of world system and network society alike should find its descriptive embodiment in complexity theory: both turn to excess and the remainder, that which cannot be captured by, or forecast within, the system. The global system, in other words, cannot ultimately be contained in, or explained by, discursive structures. Linking system, category, and historical period alike to complexity theory marks a productive and powerful anxiety about both knowing everything and about the unknown. As Castells notes in *The Power of Identity*, "the turbulence of information flows will keep codes in a constant swirl"—an energy and movement that is nonorganic by interpretation and not by essence (1997, 360).

The Electronic Empire is not particularly locatable or containable, but it nevertheless has effects that can be discerned. It does not easily align with the watchwords, or adjectival buzzwords, of what is called the world economy and cannot as such be integrated, total, systematized, synchronized, compatible, balanced, or complete. Jameson speaks of the contemporary world system in terms of an "impossible totality" and the only "dimly perceivable" (1991, 38). The Electronic Empire epitomizes his account of the contemporary world system in this respect, rather than that of Hopkins and Wallerstein, who describe it as "a single, imperfect, organic whole, each vector quite dependent on the others" (2). To go further than the "dimly perceivable," we have only to posit that the Electronic Empire is not only neither organic nor whole, but arguably not even a system at all. Rather, it is a loose assemblage of relations characterized by another set of terms: flexibility, functionality, mobility, programmability, and automation.

The paradigm for such an assemblage is the network, which involves new geopolitical orderings, a reconfigured sense of center and periphery and an attendant complication of the world-system idea. Networks are by nature connective, suggestive of traceable and identifiable affiliations, alliances, and group politics, and their connective tissues provide a fantasy of community, of sociality, of collectives, of utopias.[47] Annelise Riles notes that "the Network offers a poignant case study of institutionalized utopianism, an ambition for political change through communication and information exchange, of universalism *after* cultural relativism" (2000, 3). The need to reimagine a nontechnicist and nonmercantile internationalism or a philosophical and ethical universalism is not unique to our moment, but the substitutive figure of the network as a complex interconnective system has a particular currency, resonance, and ubiquity within the context of coalition building and the events of September 11 (including the need to fix Al Qaeda as a mappable network), as well as the expansion of mass media and communication, information, and electronic technologies over the course of the last two centuries.[48] It follows, then, that Armand Mattelart's *Networking the World* would trace the network back to Henri Saint-Simon and the dawn of the age of modern corporate administration as a way to historicize not just a contemporary figure, but also a contemporary understanding of globalization and global social organization: "In this project of planetary restructuring, the network, as a model of rationality, became the emblematic figure of the new organization of society."[49] In a related analysis of the city of London, Andrew Leyshon and Nigel Thrift employ the figure of the "actor-network" to describe the constitutive function of communities of everyday social practices associated with finance.

Jameson has followed Ernest Mandel and suggested that the global network is the emblematic figure of late capitalism, that "the whole new de-centered global network of the third stage of capital itself" constitutes "a network of power and control even more difficult for our minds and imaginations to grasp."[50] Such a "great global multinational and decentered communicational network" must for Jameson necessarily involve new spatial and geopolitical arrangements that the individual mind can neither wholly perceive nor wholly chart (44). The complexity of the networked world system, while allowing for new and reconfigured local connective links, as well as circuits of transmission and exchange, quite simply escapes our totalizing representation and our cognitive reach.[51] For Jameson, then, the "network" is implicitly, as it is explicitly for me, the means to give a provisional, flexible, and paradoxically concrete form to the complexity and abstraction of neoliberal global capitalism. So, too, does it evince the general quality of communications space, which, as Boyd-Barrett notes, is its "astonishing elasticity" (1998, 163). The network, then, is not static but mobile and highly changeable, of which technical and cultural re-encoding, the disappearance of servers, and the constant change of DNS entries and Web addresses are fitting symptoms.

Thus, in its conceptual and figural manifestation as a network, the Electronic Empire maintains a mutable configuration of command and control; it has "lost its pivot"; and it is without point of origin and end, even given the frequent and fantastic imagining of its apocalyptic destruction. Situated in its unsituatedness, it is rather "always in the middle, between things, interbeing, intermezzo" (Deleuze and Guattari 1980, 6, 25). Rather than dichotomies and binary distinctions, then, the network of Empire presents interstices, interconnecting lines, and autonomous flows. The paradigm of "acentered systems" within *A Thousand Plateaus* is itself paradigmatic: "finite networks of automata in which communication runs from any neighbor to any other, the stems or channels do not preexist, and all individuals are interchangeable, defined only by their state at a given moment—such that the local operations are coordinated and the final, global result synchronized without a central agency" (17).

Even though the electronic imperial network does not yield to a single, central agency, there are still various forces at work trying to co-opt its movement. Former chair and CEO of Citicorp/Citibank Walter Wriston speaks to the paradox: "Money goes where it is wanted and stays where it is well treated. ... This huge pool of money is destabilizing. It can move instantly, and it does. ... But money really has no volition of its own. It all depends on the people who own it and use it" (Bass). But the notion that there is a single, central agent, whether nation, subject, or corporation, operating the network of Electronic Empire is contestable. It is, as an asset manager and former International

Monetary Fund official notes, "extremely powerful. Nobody can stand in front of it."[52] Although the instantiation of knowledge and administrative monopolies, the "expert system," and various control apparatuses indicate the desire and attempt to manage, restrain, and centralize the operations of the network of global capital, it nevertheless remains the case that it is marked by aleatory movement and general unpredictability. Further, the network has the capacity to evade its own annihilation in a worldwide systems crash, so that ultimately "no breakdown, no sabotage is decisive."[53]

The events of September 11 have been strongly illustrative of this idea. While one might have expected that the leveling of the towers and the bombing of the Pentagon would result in a disruption of the network circuits, precisely the opposite has been the effect. Indeed, the electronic network is not disrupted by but constituted around such events, which it has the capacity to absorb, rework, and replay. This knitting function indicates that the electronic network corresponds to the new mode of Empire, which is, as Hardt and Negri articulate, a "machine for universal integration" (191). Again, however, Empire is less a machine or "apparatus of rule," which would suggest some kind of human agency or supervisor at the controls, than it is a system.[54] This systemic integration is manifest in the set of communication networks that comprise the Electronic Empire, networks that, as I have previously stated, are responsible for the circulation of finance and information in the period of late capitalism.

In either its old or its current manifestation, then, the concept of Empire is an "indication of the efficiency of communication" (Innis 9). This insight has a place within Mattelart's rich and essentially axiomatic understanding of communication and information technologies as instrumental facilitator of Empire, economic, and cultural power alike. However, the new system of Empire need not necessarily operate through domination, subjection, and imposition, albeit under the guise of "free flow," because it now operates through insinuation, which is a modal switch of power and consists of hosts accepting rather than rejecting or being forced to accept. As a counterpoint and strong reminder of the continued material force of the "old" empire, Arrighi and Silver ask whether globalization and "the phoenix of high finance … can rule the roost without the support of strong states more effectively than it has in the past."[55] Mixed metaphor notwithstanding, the use of the phoenix as figure is significant because finance capital is continually imagined as emerging in a new form from the ashes, shell, structure, or chrysalis of the old.

It is these properties of malleability, mutation, and adaptation that will lead Jameson to link capital to a virus in his reading of Arrighi, wherein he describes the movements of late capitalism in similar terms, with metaphors drawn from biology and genetics: "the system is better seen as a kind of virus (not Arrighi's figure), and its development is something like an epidemic (better still, a rash of epidemics, an epidemic of epidemics)" (1997, 249). In the displacement of capital onto a battle of viruses, or their exponential magnification as epidemic, or better still, a plague, there is an attendant promise that capitalism might indeed carry a fatal disease and bear within itself the elements of its own destruction. Pryke and Allen articulate the potential for disruption in similar terms: monetized time-space is that "through which 'infections' may pass simultaneously" (2000, 270). Indeed, the promise of a future vaccination against this infectious disease and the very idea of biological mechanisms of self-protection and self-preservation serve as a screen for the whole repertoire of tactics Mattelart and others have in mind when they speak of resistance to the forces of global media and capital. But, as Hardt and Negri suggest via their commentary on the viral spread and regeneration of the imperial order, not only is vaccinating against the global network of capital impossible, but transmittal and contamination are inevitable: *"The age of globalization is the age of universal contagion,"* they note, and the Empire is formed partly "on the basis of its capacity to develop itself more deeply, to be reborn, and to extend itself throughout the biopolitical latticework of world society" (41).

This, however, is the mode of the network: an autotelic, auto-generative, and autodidactical "smart" system that drives the global economy and provides its most appropriate figure. Informational capitalism mutates not as an unavoidably communicable virus, but as a nonorganic, electronic network whose operative criterion is performativity. Lyotard notes that the computer "could become the 'dream' instrument for controlling and regulating the market system, extended to include knowledge itself and governed exclusively by the performativity principle. In that case, it would inevitably involve the use of terror" (1984, 67). The electronic network operates according to the Lyotardian technological performative in that its very nature and truth is constituted by its performance and efficiency.[56] The networked structure of information and technologies exists in the moment of "the great unknown" (Arrighi and Silver), and it is differentiated and defined by its rules of operation. It has its own operating force and thus Lyotard's conception of terror is also a necessary component: the function is that which rules the waves. The general belief at the end of the long twentieth century is that capital itself is given to mutation and flexibility, not to self-destruction, but to autotelic reproduction and regeneration. This is the mode of the network, which is forced to function or else it risks being destroyed. It must perform, not optimally or creatively, but basically. The difference is the nonorganic, networked status of Empire and (late) capital, no longer linked to the organicism of the body—Marx's commodities as "inwardly circumcised Jews" or Marshall McLuhan's "nervous system" in a "global embrace"—but coded in the form of the electronic network. Organicism merely disguises a progressivist narrative, and we can perhaps imagine a conceptual break with Enlightenment paradigms of growth and progress and with nineteenth-century paradigms of degeneration (equally organicist and biological) only in terms of a complex network with unknown effects. But, as this essay has tried to demonstrate, one thing we can say about the nature of the network is that it retains an inherent plasticity and carries along with it the power to reconstitute itself.

Notes

An earlier version of this essay was written for the "After the American Century" conference at the Center for the Humanities, Oregon State University (April 18–20, 2001). I am grateful to Paula Rabinowitz for the invitation to participate. Russell Samolsky was of incalculable assistance throughout the many stages of composition. Also, Alan Liu, Lois Cucullu, Jennifer Jones, and Jani Scandura commented on different versions of the essay and gave me invaluable ideas and suggestions for its improvement.I am also grateful to the anonymous reviewer for *Cultural Critique* who referred me to a wealth of useful material on global finance and economic discourse. Karen Steigman, my research assistant at the University of Minnesota, found some key material particularly related to eCommerce.

1. See Wallace and Erickson 1992; Drummond 1999; Andrews 2000; Tsang 2000.
2. Marx's famous delineation of a general formula for capital and of the difference between money and capital, or what Jameson calls the "expanding dialectic of accumulation," comes partly in volume 1, part 2, chapter 4 of *Capital:*

"The simplest form of the circulation of commodities is C-M-C, the transformation of commodities into money, and the change of the money back again into commodities; or selling in order to buy. But alongside of this form we find another specifically different form: M-C-M, the transformation of money into commodities, and the change of commodities back into money; or buying in order to sell. Money that circulates in the latter manner is thereby transformed into, becomes capital, and is already potentially capital" (1995, 93–94). Also see the chapter on capital in *Grundrisse*. See Jameson 1997,250.

3   Stills and a RealVideo version of the Young and Rubicam "Empire" spot were stored on the Computer Associates Web site, http://www.cai.com/ hellotomorrow, through August 2001. A sixty-second version of the spot was also completed and aired with a more detailed "classical" opening and extended street scenes. I am grateful to Russell Samolsky for alerting me to this commercial. The cyberpunk aesthetic is all the more suggestive in that a proposal calling for the testing of *interplanetary* Internet protocols was put before the standard-bearing Internet Engineering Task Force at the time the commercial was airing. See Robert Lemos, "Internet Gurus Aim for the Stars" (May 24, 2001), http://news.cnet.com/news/0-1003-200-6029873.html?tag=dd.ne.dhm.nl-sty.o.

4   Clearing House Interbank Payments Company, CHIPCo, http://www. chips.org. In *The Twilight of Sovereignty* (1992), Walter Wriston makes a representative comment on the extent to which the telecom network began radically transforming the global financial markets with the introduction of Reuters's video terminal, "Monitor," in 1973; see especially 40–42, 59–61. On the topic of "e-money," or "virtual money," and its informationalism, see Ingham 2002; Leyshon and Thrift 1997, especially 20–22; Solomon 1997; Hart 2001; and, in a futurist context, Kelly 1995, 203–29.

5   With regard to regulation, Masao Miyoshi briefly considers the role of CHIPS in relation to the weakened power of national banks. On the theme of self-facilitation, Ingham notes that "circuits of economic exchange obviously have been able to create their own *media of exchange*" (1993, 139). Payment systems, in other words, require a network, hardware, and software.

6   Guéhenno 1995, 54. Also see Richard J. Barnet and John Cavanagh's discussion of "money without a home" (1994, 385–402). Employing a somewhat literal definition of the deterritorial in their discussion of financial markets and monetized time-space, Pryke and Allen conclude that money "has become increasingly deterritorialized … as previously separate financial markets have lost their regulatory and geographical distinction" (2000, 282). In response, much contemporary work on global capital markets and the hazards of derivatives calls for the international and national regulation of speculative trading, e.g. Tickell 2000.

7   In *The Rise of the Network Society*, Castells notes that "one of the key features of informational society is the networking logic of its basic structure" (1997, 21). Barnet and Cavanagh cite *New York Times* writer Peter Passell on the reliance of global banking and financial systems on electronic communications networks. Passell also uses the language of the body to characterize the operation of the network: it is "the computer system that is the heart of global capitalism" (387). Leyshon and Thrift use the same metaphor, but figure the city of London as the electronic "heart" of the "international imperium of commercial capital" (1997, 336).

8   For one example of work linking technological change and capitalist development, see Castells 2000, 52–74. Also see Jessop 2001. Similar themes are evident in Jessop 2002. Representative of the many varied commentators on the order of information, economist and scholar Jean-Pierre Dupuy names the postindustrial society as the "informational society" in "Myths of Informational Society," (Woodward 1980,3–17). Management theorist Peter Drucker names the substance of the world economy as "information capitalism," a globalized world that is in actual fact Westernized (1993, 166). Walter Wriston delineates the shift from material commodities to information as the "new source of wealth" (1992, 19, 55–73). Hardt and Negri summarize earlier work on the qualitative shift from the assembly line to the network and outline three modes of production, which now predominantly tends toward becoming "informationalized" (2000, 286). Finally, Castells outlines the crucial differences between information and informational in *Network Society* (1996, 21).

9   Henry Luce 1941, 28. Alvin Toffler names roughly the same epistemological and chronological period, which is "post-smokestack" and originates in the mid-1950s, as the "third wave." See *The Third Wave* (1980) and *Powershift: Knowledge, Wealth, and Violence at the Edge of the 21st Century* (1990). In *The Gutenberg Galaxy: The Making of Typographic Man* (1962), Marshall McLuhan argues that new technologies will result in the end of print culture and ultimately forge a new and more democratic society. An exemplary and frequently cited claim that the digital revolution is precisely that—a revolution—and also uniform and homogenous in character is made by Nicholas Negroponte in *Being Digital* (1996).

10 An early study of the possible connections here, with particular reference to Canada, is George Grant, *Technology and Empire* (1965). I would come down on the side of rupture, difference, variation (as would many theorists of information and the informational society such as Daniel Bell, Castells, and Hardt and Negri), rather than on the side of strict continuity and extension (as would other neo-Marxists such as David Harvey, Herbert Schiller, and Immanuel Wallerstein), although I would abide by the idea that the network and the global both have a more extensive and prolonged history than popular commentary might

suggest. On the long-term discourse of the network, see Armand Mattelart, *Networking the World, 1794–2000* (2000). In order to trace the network society back to the eighteenth century, he performs an analysis of the internationalization of communication by surveying the literal networks of telegraph transmissions, railway lines and rail gauges, the metrical system, undersea cables, radio communication, telephone lines, cinema and images, and electricity. Leyshon and Thrift similarly trace the origins of the contemporary networked, telematic city back to the telegraph (1997, 323–54).

11 The popularization of these discussions in Europe and the United States was initiated, in some sense, by Nora and Minc's report to the President of France; Marc Porat's nine-volume report, *The Information Economy: Sources and Methods for Measuring the Primary Information Sector (Detailed Industry Reports)* (1977); Daniel Bell, *The Coming of Post-Industrial Society: A Venture in Social Forecasting* (1973); Michael L. Dertouzos and Joel Moses, eds., *The Computer Age: A Twenty-Year View* (1979); Christopher Evans, *The Mighty Micro: The Impact of the Computer Revolution* (1979); Joseph Weizenbaum, *Computer Power and Human Reason* (1976); and the continual recovery, "translation," and reference to the work of Norbert Weiner, particularly *The Human Use of Human Beings: Cybernetics and Society* (1950).

12 On the ascendance of finance capital over mercantile capitalism and the export of commodities, see Lenin's essay on imperialism.

13 *Network Society* 18–21, 143–4. In a related analysis, Dan Schiller focuses on the role of neoliberal policies in facilitating "an epochal political-economic transition" into "digital capitalism" (1999, xvii). Dyer-Witheford also points out that the expansion of the global financial markets is "inseparable from the expansion of information technology" (1999, 139).

14 Eric Hobsbawm speaks of a short twentieth century (1914–1991) abbreviated by two decades of crisis and culminating in the collapse of communist regimes and subsequent political instability and uncertainty. See Hobsbawm 1994, 10–11. Similarly, Wallerstein designates 1989 as the end of the modern world system begun in the "long" sixteenth century.

15 Schumpeter 1950, 83. For a comparison of Schumpeter and Marx's views of capitalism's future, see Elliott 1980.

16 See Chamberlin and Gilman 1985.

17 *Capital: An Abridged Edition*, part 2, chapter 4 (99). Another link can be made to Ricardo's concept of the "organic structure of capital," which, according to Schumpeter, concerns the relation between "constant and variable capital" (1950, 26). Though it is not concerned with Marx or this passage, extended commentary on the representation of the Jewish body and circumcision as a "marker" of incompleteness, identity, and difference "within the parameters of 'healthy' or 'diseased'" can be found in Gilman 1991, 155.

18 Among the many subsequent exegeses of *Capital* on this point, see Benjamin Lee and Edward LiPuma on capital's "self-propelling treadmill structure" and the economy as "an autonomous, self-regulating system" (2002, 208) and Robert Heilbroner: "capitalism's most striking historical characteristic is its extra-ordinary propensity for self-generated change" (1993, 41).

19 Kathleen Woodward also notes the prevalence of the biological metaphor in 1970s analyses of the self-replicating quality of information, partly beginning with Daniel Bell's commentary on information as that which reproduces itself: "Underlying the process of the reproduction of information are metaphors drawn from biology and fission, both of which proceed at an exponential rate. ... We speak of an information explosion that triggers an ever-accelerating growth in information" (Woodward 1973, xv).

20 However, the rhetoric of the old imperialism remains: Dan Schiller argues that the Internet and "cyberspace itself is being rapidly colonized by the familiar workings of the market system" (1999, xiv).

21 See Forester 1993, 2–5 and 201–7. Forester's concerns are Japanese business and economic strategies and the corresponding displacement of the United States and Europe, facilitated by the corporate weakness and haplessness of the Americans, which is epitomized by the famous episode of regurgitation: "Unless the West learns the lessons of Japan's high-tech business strategy and changes course, there is a grave danger that America and Europe could become little more than industrial museums—and Japan's economic triumph will be complete" (x).

22 For recent industry information on eCommerce and e-conomics, see Pam Woodall, "Untangling e-conomics," *The Economist*, September 21, 2000, http://www.economist.com/surveys/showsurvey.cfm?issue=20000923. Also see the U.S. Department of Commerce Report, *Digital Economy 2000*, http://www.esa.doc.gov/dezk.htm. Finally, the NRF Forrester Online Retail Index lists the most recent business and technology consumer data (http://www.forrester.com/NRF/1,2873,0,00.html). It is worth noting that the claims for the power of the "new" postindustrial society, the information age, and the computerized society, were made at a time of more severe economic recession and while the United States was losing the war in Vietnam (all calling into question the putative power of the "American century").

23 See the latest data from the independent emerging-technology research firm, Forrester (http://www.forrester.com/ER/Press/Release/0,1769,533,00.html). In February 2001, 13.5 million U.S. households made online purchases totaling $3.4 billion. By 2004, Forrester predicts that global Net commerce—including b2b (business-to-business) and b2c (business-to-consumers)—will reach $6.8 trillion on the strength of the Asian Pacific and European markets. See http://www.forrester.com/ER/Press/Forrfind/0,1768,0,00.html.

24 For an account of the work of software engineer David Cutler and the Microsoft programming team, see Zachary 1994.

25 http://www.mungopark.com. See also Mungo Park, *Travels in the Interior Districts of Africa* (1799). For Lee and Fulford, the matter at hand is representation, which is why their concern is with virtuality (2000, 3–28).

26 Korper and Ellis 2000, xiii. Also see Barnet and Cavanagh 1994. For extensive, academic, and rigorous studies of the convergence of telecommunications, computers, and global business in the 1990s, see Bradley, Hausman, and Nolan 1993.

27 In late 2000 and early 2001, Monash University and the Australian Broadcasting Corporation sponsored a thirteen-part radio series on the digital revolution and included one segment on "electronic empires," with scholars such as Dan Schiller and Robert McChesney participating. Transcripts are available from http://www.abc.net.au/pipeline/radio/programs/prog4.htm. Also see Daya Thussu 1998, as well as Herman and McChesney 1997.

28 Herbert Schiller 1969, 8–9. Schiller's text is an inaugural and still-influential study of the economic and political functions of mass communications in the United States up to 1968. His primary concern is the integration of commercial communications and U.S. business interests and with the cultural consequences of the global broadcast of American images.

29 Thussu 1998, 1. Miyoshi takes a similar general position in "A Borderless World?" (1993): "Cable TV and MTV dominate the world absolutely" (747). However, a critical space must open here to address the space outside of these communication networks and those, often in the south, who do not have access to the equipment required to receive MTV, CNN, or Murdoch's Star TV network. On the development of Murdoch's electronic empire, see Rohm 2002. For Murdoch's News Corporation's vast holdings and the equally vast and diversified Disney and Time Warner, see McChesney 1998, 27–46. Extensive and detailed analysis of the problem of imperialism, communication, and "global ideological control" may also be found in Mattelart and Siegelaub 1979.

30 For an expansive articulation of the two logics of power, see Harvey 2003.

31 Jameson 1997, 251; Hardt and Negri 2001, xii. Žižek pursues the point further to note that capital and commodities may be mobile, but the circulation of people is rigidly controlled (2002, 149). Trebor Scholz and Carol Flax make the same argument in their hypermedia work, *Tuesday Afternoon* (2001), http://rhizome.org/object.rhiz?4069.

32 Guéhenno also suggests that the new idea of empire "describes a world that is at once unified and without a center" (1995, xii). In contrast, Luce envisions "America as the dynamic center of ever-widening spheres of enterprise, America as the training center of the skillful servants of mankind" (1941, 39). In the new imperial contest, the empire as such is not industrial but postindus-trial and linked to IT and to knowledge work. See Arrighi 1994 and Arrighi and Silver 1999, 5–15; see the latter also on the contest between capital and the nation-state.

33 This hegemony, Cerny argues, was "legislate[d] away" as states gradually relinquished nonliberal capital controls (1994, 321). In his comprehensive study of the function of states within the process of financial globalization, Eric Helleiner (1994) also shows that the post–World War II international economic order did not directly produce global financial markets; rather, industrial states played a significant role in the liberalizing of capital controls and the deregulating of domestic markets. Wood similarly argues that capitalism depends on the "extra-economic coercion" of territorial states (2003, 9–25).

34 Dyer-Witheford's reading of the information age as the new battle-ground in the contest between capital and its laboring subjects is apposite here. In his articulation of the relevance of Marxism in the current moment, Dyer-Witheford suggests that the networks of communication that facilitate the instantaneous circulation of capital also facilitate resistance and "oppositional networking" (1999, 155). These "circuits of struggle" both promote increased control and provide the means by which social organizations and antiglobalization movements can develop and strengthen (124–28, 147–64, 232–38).

35 On the decentered quality of Empire and the new world order, Hardt and Negri are also preceded by Frederick Buell's *National Culture and the New Global System* (10–11). At this point the secondary criticism on *Empire* is too extensive to review here, although Balakrishnan is exemplary. The concept of the multitude is frequently regarded to be the great contribution of Hardt and Negri's text, and it has reintroduced many productive questions about social multiplicity and agency. Laclau notes that *Empire* fails to provide "any coherent theory of political subjectivity," but I read this as a sign of their investment in the relations between an autotelic network system and the collective power of the multitude to trigger massive changes in that network (2001, 8).

36 Catherine Bargh, Peter Scott, and David Smith catalog the many distinguishing features, complexity among them, attributed to the "new society" in their *Governing Universities: Changing the Culture?* (1996, 13).

37 Arrighi 1994, 19. In the study, he periodizes the long twentieth century with respect to finance capital: "As this approximate and preliminary periodization implies, consecutive systemic cycles of accumulation overlap, and although they become progressively shorter in duration, they all last longer than a century; hence the notion of the 'long century,' which will be taken as the basic temporal unit in the analysis of world-scale processes of capital accumulation" (6–7). Arrighi's periodization of the long twentieth century is based on three periods of crisis: the Great Depression of 1873–1896, the thirty-year crisis of 1914–1945, and the economic crisis of the 1970s.

[38] In contrast, Samir Amin argues that the current crisis of the world system "reveals that the polarization of the world really constitutes a historic limit for capitalism" (1992, 13).

[39] Schumpeter, 82. Schumpeter summarizes his position vis-à-vis Marx in a 1949 address: "Marx was wrong in his diagnosis of the manner in which capitalist society would break down; he was not wrong in the prediction that it would break down eventually" (424–25). Though they focus primarily on the efforts to prolong hegemony, and not on the successful hegemonic runs, Hopkins and Wallerstein suggest a systemic logic similar to that articulated by Arrighi for what they call the capitalist world-economy, whereby "the very efforts made to prolong the power themselves tend to undermine the base of the power, and thus start the long process of relative decline" (1996, 9).

[40] On the new Empire and the contemporary relations between American military and economic power, see Wallerstein 2003; Joxe 2002; Wood 2003; Mann 2003.

[41] Moreover, an analysis of the interface between global capitalism and new technologies could only really be in the mode of the speculation, partly because there are no strict answers for these questions, partly because of the uncertain futures of the market, but also because the market and capital itself exist now in the mode of global financial speculation, as do the new technologies, which cannot eliminate (or shake off) either vaporware or the system of initial public offerings (IPOs).

[42] Arrighi and Silver review the criticism linking chaos theory to changes in the global political economy, especially 21–26. Also see Amin 1992. In contrast, Joxe draws on the rhetoric of equilibrium in his commentary on the question of the "end of capitalism" (2002, 189).

[43] Hopkins and Wallerstein begin *The Age of Transition* with the extended question, "The World-System: Is There a Crisis?" Also see Hobsbawm, *The Age of Extremes*, and Arrighi and Silver, 2.

[44] I am grateful to Alan Liu for pointing me to this passage in Schumpeter as a means to bridge organicism and the language of complexity. The importance of rhetoric and speech performance in Schumpter's analysis is underscored by Robinson.

[45] For (often indirect) allusions to a complexity model, with implications of the inconclusive, unpredictable, and nontotalizable, for the "global," global culture, and global orderings, see Ó Tuathail 1996, 15; Hardt and Negri 2000, 41; Richard Lee 1996, 197; and Arrighi and Silver 1999. Alvin and Heidi Toffler make very general use of the chaos and complexity paradigms in *War and Anti-War: Making Sense of Today's Global Chaos* (1993). Ulf Hannerz also loosely links global culture to complexity theory by arguing that "people like the cosmopolitans have a special part in bringing about a degree of coherence; if there

were only locals, world culture would be no more than the sum of its separate parts" (1996, 111).

[46] Coronil 2001, 79. Also Sanford 1994.

[47] For one reverential tribute to the values and virtues of interdependence, reimagined as "connexity," see Geoff Mulgan, *Connexity: How to Live in a Connected World* (1997). An academic precursor for his work is that of French anthropologist André Leroi-Gourhan, who has argued that in precapitalist social systems, space has the property of "connexity"—wherein any two points can be connected by a psychic and experiential continuous path—which suggests that space is not experienced as discrete or isolated. See *Le Geste et la parole* (1964). For the place of networks in utopian thinking, particularly on "the ideology of redemption through networks" dating at least from Michel Chevalier, a follower of Claude-Henri de Saint-Simon and prophet of the "circulating civilization," see Mattelart, *Networking the World*, especially 16–21, 117–20. Lee and Fulford remark on the possibilities of networks as well (2000, 4).

[48] For efforts to think and imagine an ethical universalism, at times in conjunction with a contemporary cosmopolitanism, see Robbins 1999 and Cheah and Robbins 1998, for whom, according to Robbins, "*cosmopolitics* represents one effort to describe, from within multiculturalism, a name for the genuine striving toward common norms and mutual translatability that is also part of multiculturalism" (12–13). For a call to read the mechanisms and practices of communications through the lens of community rather than through market economics, see Carey 1997.

[49] Mattelart 2000, 15. See also Ionescu 1976 and Taylor 1975.

[50] See Ernest Mandel's tripartite structure of capitalism in his *Late Capitalism* (1978), on which Jameson builds in *Postmodernism*. For the quoted text, see Jameson 1991, 38. On Mandel, see Nick Heffernan, *Capital, Class, and Technology in Contemporary American Culture* (2000). For a similar claim for the coextensiveness of networks and the global market, see Dan Schiller, especially xiv.

[51] For a discussion of critical, and fictional, geopolitics, see Arrighi, Hui, Ray, and Reifer 1999; Ó Tuathail 1996; Parker 1998; and O'Loughlin 1994.

[52] Quoted in Collier 1996. Reiterating this basic point, Hardt and Negri name three sources of global control: the bomb, ether, and money (345).

[53] Guéhenno, 120. On the expert-system and knowledge monopolies, see Harold Innis on the hoarding of IT information (1950, 210); Sean Cubitt on Net culture's "fully administrable knowledge world" (1998, 12); and Armand Mattelart on technicians and experts (1994, 229).

[54] Hardt and Negri, xii. Mark Poster's critique of Hardt and Negri is that the multitude-as-new-proletariat thesis presumes a liberal humanist subject. Because they are not attuned to the technological specificity of digital information, Poster suggests, their text remains mired in a problematic of another episteme—the subject—and does

not fully engage with the radical rearticulation, if not evacuation, of the subject prompted by the rise of intelligent machines. "The Information Empire," *Comparative Literature Studies* (forthcoming).

55 Arrighi and Silver 10. Their discussion of "a dominant state [that] becomes the 'model' for other states to emulate and thereby draws them into its own path of development" (27) follows the critical path of Gramsci on hegemony and George Modelski and William R. Thompson (1995). With respect to the reconfiguration of the function of the state vis-à-vis contemporary

capitalism, Harris also notes, "[Transnationals use] government to help penetrate new markets, keep labour and environmental costs low and subsidise their global activities. This is not the disappearance of states, but the redefinition of their role" (33).

56 By extending speech-act theory to economic practices, Lee and LiPuma (2002) investigate the performativity of capital. I am grateful to the anonymous reviewer for *Cultural Critique* for directing me to this discussion of another performative.

Works Cited

Ali, Tariq. "Globalization: For Whom? By Whom?" Plenary Presentation. Towards a Critical Globalization Studies Conference. University of California, Santa Barbara. May 2, 2003.

Amin, Samir. *Empire of Chaos*. New York: Monthly Review Press, 1992.

Andrews, Paul. *How the Web Was Won: How Bill Gates and His Internet Idealists Transformed the Microsoft Empire*. New York: Broadway Books, 2000.

Arrighi, Giovanni. "Marxist Century—American Century: The Making and Remaking of the World Labor Movement." In *Transforming the Revolution*, ed. Samir Amin, 54–95. New York: Monthly Review Press, 1990.

___. *The Long Twentieth Century: Money, Power, and the Origins of Our Times*. New York: Verso, 1994.

Arrighi, Giovanni and Beverly J. Silver. *Chaos and Governance in the Modern World System*. Minneapolis: University of Minnesota Press, 1999.

Arrighi, Giovanni, Po-keung Hui, Krishnendu Ray, and Thomas Ehrlich Reifer. "Geopolitics and High Finance." In *Chaos and Governance in the Modern World System*, ed. Giovanni Arrighi and Beverly Silver, 37–96. Minneapolis: University of Minnesota Press, 1999.

Balakrishnan, Gopal. *Debating Empire*. New York: Verso, 2003.

Bargh, Catherine, Peter Scott, and David Smith. *Governing Universities: Changing the Culture?* Buckingham: Open University Press, 1996.

Barnet, Richard J., and John Cavanagh. *Global Dreams: Imperial Corporations and the New World Order*. New York: Simon & Schuster, 1994.

Bass, Thomas A. "The Future of Money." *Wired* 4, no. 10 (October 1996). http://www.wired.com/wired/archive /4.10/wriston.html.

Bell, Daniel. *The Coming of Post-Industrial Society: A Venture in Social Forecasting*. New York: Penguin Books, 1973.

Boyd-Barrett, Oliver. "Media Imperialism Reformulated." In *Electronic Empires: Global Media and Local Resistance*, ed. Daya Thussu, 157–76. London: Arnold, 1998.

Bradley, Stephen P., Jerry A. Hausman, and Richard L. Nolan, eds. *Globalization, Technology, and Competition*. Boston: Harvard Business School, 1993.

Braudel, Fernand. *The Perspective of the World*. Trans. Siân Reynolds. London: Collins, 1984.

Buell, Frederick. *National Culture and the New Global System*. Baltimore: Johns Hopkins University Press, 1993.

Carey, James. "Communications and Economics." In *James Carey: A Critical Reader*, ed. Eve Stryker Munson and Catherine A. Warren, 60–75. Minneapolis: University of Minnesota Press, 1997.

Castells, Manuel. *The Rise of the Network Society*. Oxford: Blackwell, 1996.

___. *The Power of Identity*. Oxford: Blackwell, 1997.

___. "Information Technology and *Global Capitalism*." In *Global Capitalism*, ed. Will Hutton and Anthony Giddens, 52–74. New York: The New Press, 2000.

Cerny, Philip G. "The Dynamics of Financial Globalization: Technology, Market Structure, and Policy Response." *Policy Sciences* 27 (1994): 319–42.

Chamberlin, J. Edward, and Sander L. Gilman. *Degeneration: The Dark Side of Progress*. New York: Columbia University Press, 1985.

Cheah, Pheng, and Bruce Robbins, ed. *Cosmopolitics: Thinking and Feeling beyond the Nation*. Minneapolis: University of Minnesota Press, 1998.

Collier, Robert. "Bullish Investors Pouring Billions Back into Mexico." *San Francisco Chronicle, July 5, 1996.

Coronil, Fernando. "Toward a Critique of Globalcentrism: Speculations on Capitalism's Nature." In *Millennial Capitalism and the Culture of Neoliberalism*, ed. Jean Comaroff and John L. Comaroff, 63–87. Durham, NC: Duke University Press, 2001.

Cubitt, Sean. *Digital Aesthetics*. London: Sage, 1998.

Deleuze, Gilles, and Félix Guattari. *A Thousand Plateaus*. Trans. Brian Massumi. Minneapolis: University of Minnesota Press, 1980.

Dertouzos, Michael L., and Joel Moses, ed. *The Computer Age: A Twenty-Year View*. Cambridge: MIT Press, 1979.

Drummond, Michael. *Renegades of the Empire: How Three Software Warriors Started a Revolution behind the Walls of Fortress Microsoft*. New York: Crown Publications, 1999.

Drucker, Peter. *Post-Capitalist Society*. Oxford: Butterworth-Heinemann, 1993.

Dyer-Witheford, Nick. *Cyber-Marx: Cycles and Circuits of Struggle in High-Technology Capitalism*. Urbana: University of Illinois Press, 1999.

Elliott, John E. "Marx and Schumpeter on Capitalism's Creative Destruction: A Comparative Restatement." *Quarterly Journal of Economics* 95, no. 1 (August 1980): 45–68.

"Empire." Television Advertisement for Computer Associates. Young & Rubicam Advertising. Aired in April 2001.

Evans, Christopher. *The Mighty Micro: The Impact of the Computer Revolution*. London: Victor Gollancz, 1979.

Forester, Tom. *Silicon Samurai: How Japan Conquered the World's IT Industry*. Cambridge: Blackwell, 1993.

Gibson-Graham, J. K. *The End of Capitalism (As We Knew It)*. Cambridge: Blackwell, 1996.

Gilman, Sander L. *The Jew's Body*. New York: Routledge, 1991.

Grant, George. *Technology and Empire*. Toronto: House of Anansi, 1965.

Guéhenno, Jean-Marie. *The End of the Nation-State*. Trans. Victoria Elliott. Minneapolis: University of Minnesota Press, 1995.

Hannerz, Ulf. *Transnational Connections*. New York: Routledge, 1996.

Hardt, Michael, and Antonio Negri. *Empire*. Cambridge, MA: Harvard University Press, 2000.

Harris, Jerry. "Globalisation and the Technological Transformation of Capitalism." *Race and Class* 40, no. 2/3 (1998/1999): 21–35.

Hart, Keith. *Money in an Unequal World*. New York: Texere, 2001.

Harvey, David. *The New Imperialism*. New York: Oxford University Press, 2003.

Heffernan, Nick. *Capital, Class, and Technology in Contemporary American Culture*. London: Pluto Press, 2000.

Heilbroner, Robert. *21st Century Capitalism*. New York: W. W. Norton, 1993.

Helleiner, Eric. *States and the Reemergence of Global Finance: From Bretton Woods to the 1990s*. New York: Cornell University Press, 1994.

Herman, Edward S., and Robert W. McChesney. *The Global Media*. London: Cassell, 1997.

Hobsbawm, Eric. *The Age of Extremes: A History of the World, 1914–1991*. New York: Vintage, 1994.

Hopkins, Terence K., and Immanuel Wallerstein. *The Age of Transition: Trajectory of the World-System, 1945–2025*. London: Zed Books, 1996.

Ingham, Geoffrey. "New Monetary Spaces?" In *The Future of Money*, 123–45. Paris: Organisation for Economic Co-operation and Development, 2002.

Innis, Harold A. *Empire and Communications*. Oxford: Clarendon Press, 1950.

Ionescu, Ghita, ed. *The Political Thought of Saint-Simon*. New York: Oxford University Press, 1976.

Jameson, Fredric. *Postmodernism, or, the Cultural Logic of Late Capitalism*. Durham, NC: Duke University Press, 1991.

___. "Culture and Finance Capital." *Critical Inquiry* 24 (autumn 1997): 246–65.

Jessop, Bob. "The State and the Contradictions of the Knowledge-Driven Economy." In *Knowledge, Space, Economy*, ed. J. R. Bryson, P. W. Daniels, N. D. Henry, and J. Pollard, 63–78. New York: Routledge, 2001.

___. "The Globalization of Capital." *Rethinking Marxism* 14, no. 1 (spring 2002): 97–117.

Joxe, Alain. *Empire of Disorder*. Trans. Ames Hodges. Los Angeles: Semiotext(e), 2002.

Kelly, Kevin. *Out of Control: The New Biology of Machines, Social Systems, and the Economic World*. Cambridge, MA: Perseus Publishing, 1995.

Korper, Steffano, and Juanita Ellis. *The E-Commerce Book: Building the E-Empire*. San Diego: Academic Press, 2000.

Laclau, Ernesto. "Can Imperialism Explain Social Struggles?" *diacritics* 31, no. 4 (winter 2001): 3–10.

Lee, Benjamin, and Edward LiPuma. "Cultures of Circulation: The Imaginations of Modernity." *Public Culture* 14, no. 1 (2002): 191–213.

Lee, Debbie, and Tim Fulford. "Virtual Empires." *Cultural Critique* 44 (winter 2000): 3–28.

Lee, Richard. "Structures of Knowledge." In *The Age of Transition: Trajectory of the World-System, 1945–2025*, ed. Terence Hopkins, Immanuel Wallerstein. 178–206. London: Zed Books, 1996.

Lenin, Vladimir I. *Imperialism, the Highest Stage of Capitalism*. London: Pluto Press, 1996.

Leroi-Gourhan, André. *Le Geste et la parole*. Paris: Albin-Michel, 1964.

Leyshon, Andrew, and Nigel Thrift. *Money/Space: Geographies of Monetary Transformation*. New York: Routledge, 1997.

Luce, Henry. *The American Century*. New York: Farrar & Rinehart, Inc., 1941.

Lyotard, Jean-François. *The Postmodern Condition: A Report on Knowledge*. Trans. Geoff Bennington and Brian Massumi. Minneapolis: University of Minnesota Press, 1984.

Mandel, Ernest. *Late Capitalism*. London: Verso, 1978.

Mann, Michael. *Incoherent Empire*. New York: Verso, 2003.

Marx, Karl. *Grundrisse*. Trans. Martin Nicolaus. New York: Penguin Books, 1973.

___. *Capital: An Abridged Edition*. Ed. David McLellan. New York: Oxford University Press, 1995.

Mattelart, Armand. *Mapping World Communication: War, Progress, Culture*. Minneapolis: University of Minnesota Press, 1994.

Rita Raley

___. *Networking the World, 1794–2000.* Trans. Liz Carey-Libbrecht and James A. Cohen. Minneapolis: University of Minnesota Press, 2000.

Mattelart, Armand, and Seth Siegelaub, ed. *Communication and Class Struggle. Vol. 1, Capitalism, Imperialism.* New York: International General, 1979.

Maurer, Bill. "Complex Subjects: Offshore Finance, Complexity Theory, and the Dispersion of the Modern." *Socialist Review* 25, no. 3–4 (1995): 113–45.

McChesney, Robert W. "Media Convergence and Globalisation." In *Electronic Empires: Global Media and Local Resistance,* ed. Daya Thussu, 27–46. London: Arnold, 1998.

McLuhan, Marshall. *The Gutenberg Galaxy: The Making of Typographic Man.* Toronto: University of Toronto Press, 1962.

___. *Understanding Media: The Extensions of Man.* New York: McGraw-Hill, 1964.

Miyoshi, Masao. "A Borderless World? From Colonialism to Transnationalism and the Decline of the Nation-State." *Critical Inquiry* 19 (summer 1993): 726–51.

Modelski, George, and William R. Thompson. *Leading Sectors and World Powers: The Coevolution of Global Economics and Politics.* Columbia: University of South Carolina Press, 1995.

Mulgan, Geoff. *Connexity: How to Live in a Connected World.* London: Chatto & Windus, 1997.

Negroponte, Nicholas. *Being Digital.* New York: Vintage, 1996.

Nora, Simon, and Alain Minc. *The Computerization of Society: A Report to the President of France.* Cambridge: MIT Press, 1980.

O'Loughlin, John. *Dictionary of Geopolitics.* Westport, CT: Greenwood Press, 1994.

Ó Tuathail, Gearóid. *Critical Geopolitics: The Politics of Writing Global Space.* Minneapolis: University of Minnesota Press, 1996.

Park, Mungo. *Travels in the Interior Districts of Africa.* London: James Humphreys, 1799.

Parker, Geoffrey. *Geopolitics: Past, Present, and Future.* London: Pinter, 1998.

Porat, Marc. *The Information Economy: Sources and Methods for Measuring the Primary Information Sector (Detailed Industry Reports).* OT Special Publication 77–12 (2). 9 vols. Washington DC: U.S. Department of Commerce, Office of Telecommunications, May 1977.

Poster, Mark. "The Information Empire." *Comparative Literature Studies* (forthcoming).

Pryke, Michael, and John Allen. "Monetized Time-Space: Derivatives—Money's 'New Imaginary'?" *Economy and Society* 29, no. 2 (May 2000): 264–84.

Riles, Annelise. *The Network Inside Out.* Ann Arbor: University of Michigan Press, 2000.

Robbins, Bruce. *Feeling Global.* New York: NYU Press, 1999.

Robinson, Joan. Review of *Capitalism, Socialism, and Democracy. Economic Journal* 53 (December 1943): 381–83.

Rohm, Wendy Goldman. *The Murdoch Mission: The Digital Transformation of a Media Empire.* New York: John Wiley, 2002.

Sanford, Charles. "Financial Markets in 2020." Federal Reserve Bank of Kansas City (1994): 1–10. http://www.kc.frb.org/publicat/econrev/pdf/1q94sanf.pdf.

Schiller, Dan. *Digital Capitalism: Networking and the Global Market System.* Cambridge, MA: MIT Press, 1999.

Schiller, Herbert I. *Mass Communications and American Empire.* New York: Augustus M. Kelley, 1969.

Schumpeter, Joseph A. *Capitalism, Socialism, and Democracy. 1942.* New York: Harper & Row, 1950.

Shannon, Claude E., and Warren Weaver. *The Mathematical Theory of Communication.* Urbana: University of Illinois Press, 1949.

Sivanandan, A. "Heresies and Prophecies: The Social and Political Fallout of the Technological Revolution." In *Cutting Edge: Technology, Information Capitalism, and Social Revolution,* ed. Jim Davis, Thomas A. Hirschl, and Michael Stack, 287–96. New York: Verso, 1997.

Solomon, Elinor. *Virtual Money: Understanding the Power and Risks of Money's High-Speed Journey into Electronic Space.* New York: Oxford University Press, 1997.

Startup.com. Dir. Jehane Noujaim and Chris Hegedus. Noujaim Films, 2001.

Taylor, Keith, ed. *Henri Saint-Simon (1760–1825): Selected Writings on Science, Industry and Social Organisation.* New York: Holmes and Meier, 1975.

Thussu, Daya Dishan, ed. *Electronic Empires: Global Media and Local Resistance.* London: Arnold, 1998.

Tickell, Adam. "Dangerous Derivatives: Controlling and Creating Risks in International Money." *Geoforum* 31 (2000): 87–99.

Toffler, Alvin. *The Third Wave.* London: Collins, 1980.

___. *Powershift: Knowledge, Wealth, and Violence at the Edge of the 21st Century.* New York: Bantam Books, 1990.

Toffler, Alvin, and Heidi Toffler. *War and Anti-War: Making Sense of Today's Global Chaos.* New York: Little, Brown and Company, 1993.

Tsang, Cheryl D. *Microsoft First Generation: The Success Secrets of the Visionaries Who Launched a Technology Empire.* New York: Wiley, 2000.

Wallace, James, and Jim Erickson. *Hard Drive: Bill Gates and the Making of the Microsoft Empire.* New York: Wiley, 1992.

Wallerstein, Immanuel. *The End of the World as We Know It.* Minneapolis: University of Minneosta Press, 1999.

___. *The Decline of American Power.* New York: The New Press, 2003.

Weizenbaum, Joseph. *Computer Power and Human Reason*. New York: W. H. Freeman, 1976.

Weiner, Norbert. *The Human Use of Human Beings: Cybernetics and Society*. New York: Avon, 1971.

Wood, Ellen Meiksins. *Empire of Capital*. New York: Verso, 2003.

Woodward, Kathleen, ed. *The Myths of Information: Technology and Postindustrial Culture*. London: Routledge and Kegan Paul, 1980.

Wriston, Walter. *The Twilight of Sovereignty: How the Information Revolution Is Transforming Our World*. New York: Charles Scribner's Sons, 1992.

Zachary, G. Pascal. *Show-Stopper! The Breakneck Race to Create Windows NT and the Next Generation at Microsoft*. New York: Free Press, 1994.

Žižek, Slavoj. *Welcome to the Desert of the Real*. New York: Verso, 2002.

38   The Woman on the Other Side of the Wall

Archiving the Otherwise in Postcolonial Digital Archives

Elizabeth A. Povinelli

I

It is a justifiably famous, if enigmatic story. In "The Library of Babel," Jorge Luis Borges portrays the universe as a vast honeycombed library in which every book that ever was or ever will be written, every thought that has been or could be thought, is contained in its randomly organized, often senseless manuscripts. Because there is nothing outside the library, its inhabitants suffer dangerous illusions of what is knowable. If everything that can be known is contained within the library and yet the library's contents are unknown, the illusion emerges that it might be possible to know the library as a whole—a totality with a single law organizing its disparate parts. Perhaps a book will be found that provides the catalog of the entire library, and this will be the key to its universal knowledge. Or perhaps an encyclopedic knowledge of one region of the library, or just one of its hexagon-shaped rooms, would be sufficient to unlock the logic of the whole. Quite famously, a radical sect of librarians seeks to burn all books that seem to them to contain nothing but gibberish in hopes of making the task of comprehension more manageable. But what if one day, much to their surprise, a stranger walked in from the other side of one of the hexagon-walled rooms carrying a new book or embodying a different memory and practice? Where would she have come from if an outside to the library has been categorically excluded? And how could her book be incorporated into the theories of knowledge that had assumed the closed world of the library, and more: had assumed that all knowledge and all thought were contained in the traditions of the book? Would she or it have to be

Elizabeth Povinelli, "The Woman on the Other Side of the Wall: Archiving the Otherwise in Postcolonial Digital Archives." *differences*, 22(1), 2011: 146–171. © 2011, Brown University and *differences: A Journal of Feminist Cultural Studies*. Republished by permission of the copyright holder, and the present publisher, Duke University Press.

Postcolonial Studies: An Anthology, First Edition. Edited by Pramod K. Nayar.
Editorial material and organization © 2016 John Wiley & Sons, Ltd.
Published 2016 by John Wiley & Sons, Ltd.

burned? Or could a new library, or a new bookcase or a new alcove in the old library, be built that could shelve this book or her embodied memory? Is the problem the book, the woman, her memory, or the idea of a singular and total universe?

This essay probes a set of problems that have emerged as Indigenous and non-Indigenous colleagues and I have struggled to create a postcolonial digital archive in rural northwest Australia. This archive does not as yet exist. If it existed as it is currently conceived, it would organize mixed (augmented) reality media on the basis of social media and operate it on smart phones. The smart phones would contain a small segment of the archive. And this segment would be geotagged so that it could not run unless the phone was proximate to the site to which the information referred. The pitch we present for the project to potential donors and supporters goes something like this:

> Our project implements and investigates "mixed reality technology" for re-storying the traditional country of families living on the quasi-remote southern side of the Anson Bay area at the mouth of the Daly River in the Northern Territory. More specifically, it would create a land-based "living library" by geotagging media files in such a way that media files are playable only within a certain proximity to a site. The idea is to develop software that creates three unique interfaces—for tourists, land management, and Indigenous families, the latter having management authority over the entire project and content— and provide a dynamic feedback loop for the input of new information and media. We believe that mixed reality technology would provide the Indigenous partners with an opportunity to use new information technologies to their social and economic benefit without undermining their commitment to having the land speak its history and present in situ. Imagine someone preparing for a trip to far north Australia. While researching the area online, she discovers our Website that highlights various points of interest. She then downloads either a free or premium application to her smartphone. Now imagine this same person in a boat, floating off the shore of a pristine beach in the remote Anson Bay. She activates her smartphone and opens the application and holds up her smart-phone to see the video coming through her phone's camera. As she moves the phone around she sees various icons representing stories or videos available to her. She touches one of these icons with her finger and the story of the indigenous Dreaming Site where she finds herself appears; she can also look at archival photos or short animated clips based on archived media files. The archive is a living library insofar as one of its software functions allows new media files to be added, such as a video of people watching the videos of the place.

When we pitch this project to libraries, granting agencies, and private donors, some questions we are asked include: "How does this way of archiving Indigenous knowledge affect Indigenous traditional culture?" "Can Indigenous people actually shape and run such a project?" "In what sense is it of interest to libraries and their mission to house significant, publicly accessible knowledge?" "In what sense is this an archival project?" "What will be included and what excluded?"

When we evoke the archive, what are we conjuring by way of inclusion and exclusion? What, for instance, is the difference between an archive and a collection or between an archive and a hoard or between an archivist and a collector and a hoarder? What is altered when the archive is housed in a library, in a classified state vault, in a dour professor's office, or provided a GPS coordinate so that it can be accessed only in a certain place with a specific piece of technology? I have a collection of earrings that I have found on the streets of New York City. It is one of the things I do—I collect discarded earrings, often to the chagrin of my friends, digging them out of the rot that accumulates in the seams of pavements. Why I do this—or, less agentially, why my eye catches these accidentally discarded objects and why my hands reach down and scoop or dig them up—is one question. But another question, more relevant to the task at hand, is: under what conditions would this collection of lost jewelry become an archive or a part of an archive? Am I an archivist, a collector, a hoarder? Does it matter whether I've indexed my earrings or simply thrown them onto a shelf in my study? Similar questions arise about any number of collections ranging from mint condition Barbie dolls to tongue suppressants.

Every collection, if taken too far—by necessity a vaguely defined borderland— threatens to mark the collector as having a "condition," in the case of hoarding, the mental disorder *disposaphobia:* the compulsion to keep and hide; to cherish and conceal; to be surrounded by increasing abundance yet to be increasingly deprived as the treasured objects slowly seal the subject into an ever more restricted zone of movement. Earrings are hopefully far too small to present a real threat to me. But hoarding other objects—stacks of newspapers, old underwear, or empty plastic Diet Coke bottles— compromises life even if, under the right media conditions, it can create new cycles of wealth and restriction, if not necessarily for the hoarder. Take, for instance, the popular American television show *Hoarders* or Song Dong's critically renowned MOMA exhibit *Waste Not*. *Hoarders* tries to distinguish between a collector and a hoarder on the basis of a disorder of the will. Hoarders are unable to part with their belongings even when these belongings seriously disrupt everyday functions and relations. Indeed, strictly speaking, the belongings no longer belong to the person. The person has become the exhausted archivist who cannot shut the book return. She belongs to the books. *Waste Not* takes a less psychological point of view on hoarding. Beijing-based Song Dong disgorges the complete contents of her mother's home, amassed over fifty years in conformity to the concept *wu jin qi yong*, "waste not," which allowed people to survive the hardships of the transition from the Mao to the post-Mao economy.

But while taking different stances on the sources and meanings of collections and hoards, these two shows may well become part of another circuit of collection, archiving, and restriction. *Hoarders* will enter and be registered in the archive of twenty-first-century American pop television, perhaps at the Film and Television Archive at UCLA; *Waste Not*, in the Museum of Modern Art's archive of art exhibits. An archivist will have to manage their selection, catalog, preservation, and accessibility. And, having been entered into these archives, these shows will become the material for new writings, collections, hoards, and archives, which, if significant, will be recycled back into these or other archives, slowly sealing the library into an ever more cramped space. Compact bookcases will be installed. Remote storage spaces will be built, new jobs created for shuttling objects back and forth. And the accounting of all of these activities will create their own archives. And so it goes in "the social life of things" (Appadurai). Collections threaten to become hoards, which might become archives, which are stuffed into libraries or state vaults, which threaten to produce the surreal spectacle of Borges's exhausted archivists of the Library without end. Who might be in better need of an intervention than these archivists who toil in an "indefinite and perhaps infinite of hexagonal galleries," neither hoarders nor collectors, but rather mere managers of the universe of things that cannot be disposed of and that keep spawning new things? And why wouldn't they dream of an endless expanse of digital space where there seems no limit to what can be stored and what can be found—if someone can pay the storage fees? Isn't our project part of this dream, a social media–based method of allowing an endless series of new cartographies to be formed and circulated?

II

Acknowledging the impossibility of stilling these incessant definitional quandaries and categorical peregrinations, some scholars, such as Jacques Derrida and Michel Foucault, have tried to understand the archive as a kind of power rather than a kind of thing. For Derrida, "archontic power" is the name we give to the power to make and command what took place here or there, in this or that place, and thus what has a place in the contemporary organization of a law that appears to rule without commanding (*Archive*). Archival power authorizes specific forms of the future by domiciling space and time, the here and now relative to the there and then; us as opposed to them. And it does so by continually concealing the history of the manipulation and management of the documents within existing archives. Cribbing from Foucault, power archives itself in the sense that the sedimentation of texts provides a hieroglyph and cartography of dominant and subjugated knowledges (*Archaeology*). But for Derrida, archival power is not merely a form of authorization and domiciliation of space and time, and not merely a sedimentation of texts that can be read as an archaeology of power. It is also a kind of iteration, or drive. It is what compels Borges's librarians to look ceaselessly for the document that will give an account of the total and thus final truth of *this place* and yet not disturb the organization of power that makes this place as such. Thus archival power depends not only on an ability to shelter the memory of its own construction so as to appear as a form of rule without a command but also on a certain inexhaustible suspicion that somewhere another, fuller account of this rule exists. Maybe a door will open and a woman will appear.

In the shadow of these discussions, scholars such as Anjali Arondekar, Michel Rolph Trouillot, Ann Laura Stoler, and the Subaltern Studies Collective have noted that archives are not sites of knowledge retrieval but of knowledge production. Archives are not recorded moments of history but monuments of states, colonies, and empires. In this view the archive is, as Foucault argued, an index of historical struggle. Whether of Barbie dolls and tongue suppressants or of piles of trash and formations of life, all archives seek to ensure the endurance of something, its temporality and territorial expression. The task of the postcolonial archivist would seem to be clear. The post-colonial archivist is charged with finding lost objects, subjugated knowledges, and excluded socialities within existing archives or to repatriate exiled objects, knowledges, and socialities. For instance, in "Digitization, History, and the Making of a Postcolonial Archive of Southern African Liberation Struggles," Allen Isaacman, Premesh Lalu, and Thomas Nygren argue that when modifying "archive," the term *postcolonial* signals "the need for scholars to overcome the traces of colonialism and apartheid that persist through forms of knowledge production" (59).

If the archive is meant to preserve or challenge the present organization of power by authorizing and domiciling contested histories, then one of the major problems the archive faces, whether national, colonial, or postcolonial, is the preservation of the documents that will be or are domiciled. How does one support the endurance of what must be preserved? The U.S. Congress addressed the problem of the endurance of the paper archive when in 1988 it initiated the "brittle books" program. It requested that the National Endowment for the Humanities begin microfilming millions of volumes subject to a "slow fire" as the acidic levels in older paper slowly turned books to ash. And more recently, increasingly large portions of library budgets are dedicated to migrating digitized information across ever-changing hardware and software platforms. But landfills of "critical evidentiary material" in the form of "thousands of personal papers, pamphlets, photographs, newspapers, and other critical documents not in secure repositories are inadvertently destroyed" well before they reach an archive because the archons have decided that they are not relevant to this or that domiciliation (Isaacman, Lalu, and Nygren 56). They have no perceived public significance. And a far vaster—indeed an infinite—library of knowledge never migrates from its organic form (memory, bodily praxis) to a standard text form (book, audio, or video recording). No more than the thousands of pamphlets, these organic forms are not perceived to be relevant, or relevant enough, to the domiciliation of authority. Isaacman, Lalu, and Nygren single out this vast array of memory as of particular relevance to the postcolonial archive in South Africa. "With the passing of time, more and more elders who played critical roles in the armed struggle have died, as have the women and men who served as ordinary foot-soldiers. Gone with them are their personal narratives, which could have provided a valuable interior view of the combatants' experiences" (56).

But if "archive" is the name we give to the power to make and command what took place here or there, in this or that place, and thus what has an authoritative place in the contemporary organization of social life, the *postcolonial archive* cannot be merely a collection of new artifacts reflecting a different, subjugated history. Instead, the post-colonial archive must directly address the problem of the endurance of the otherwise within—or distinct from—this form of power. In other words, the task of the postcolonial archivist is not merely to collect subaltern histories. It is also to investigate the compositional logics of the archive as such: the material conditions that allow something to be archived and archivable; the compulsions and desires that conjure the appearance and disappearance of objects, knowledges, and socialities within an archive; the cultures of circulation, manipulation, and management that allow an object to enter the archive and thus contribute to the endurance of specific social formations. The shaping of objects entering the archive presents a number of new questions. What kinds of managements—trainings and exercises of objects and subjects—are necessary for something to be archived? Does an object need to become "an object" within a certain theory of grammar before it can be locatable? What kinds of manipulations simply make the objects within the archive more usable but never touch their status as an archived collection, say, the way an archive is rearranged when moved from an office or home into a library, or, say, when the creation of a digital index mandates the Web-based document be marked with metadata? Rearranging the stacking and boxing; providing an index; providing metadata that allows search functions: why don't, or how do, these acts of reassemblage touch the status of the archive? And at what moment or to what degree does the "manipulation" of an archive transform it from an archive into something else, such as a scholarly work that draws on an archive but is not itself an archive—or is not until that scholar's entire work and conditions of work are themselves deemed archivable, turning something that used an archive into a second-order archive? The building of the postcolonial archive is not, in other words, engaged in the same kind of reading practice that defined the hermeneutic tradition of the book, but is a different kind of interpretative framework that focuses on the generative matrix in which archival forms, practices, and artifacts carry out their routine ideological labor of constituting subjects who can be summoned in the name of a public or a people (see Gaonkar and Povinelli).

The dream is that, if done properly and with a rigorous and firm commitment, the postcolonial archive will create new forms of storage and preservation and new archival spaces and time, in which a social otherwise can endure and thus change existing social formations of power. The woman who suddenly walks through the wall into the honeycombed library will not merely find a place on the shelf but will build a new kind of shelf, maybe a digital shelf, not really a shelf at all, especially if the shelf appears and disappears according to where one is standing. Maybe this shelf will house a digital archive or itself be in the digital archive as a metadata standard. But then, won't her appearance initiate a new problem? And does this "new problem" signal an actual new problem or rather the old power of the archive? After all, what makes archival power such a difficult force to grapple with is that archival power is not *in the archive*, nor can it be contained to the archive, whether old or new media, brick and mortar or virtual library. As Derrida argues in *Archive Fever*, archival power works against every given archive. It produces—or is—a compulsion to dig deeper into and beyond every given archive, to dream of the person who will open a wall to an alcove that cannot be opened, so that some final document can be found hidden among the infinite Library, a document that would decide fate or be the final arbiter of a power that claims to be outside given power and, at the same time, the final and most effective mask of given power. In this place, the archive is a kind of Lacanian desire, always dissatisfied with its object, always incessantly moving away from every textual artifact, the thrill of discovery quickly giving over to the anomie of lack, propelling the archivist into more and more collections.

III

If the purpose of a postcolonial archive is to support subjugated knowledge, help alternative socialities endure, and challenge the formation of power that national and colonial archives promote and conceal, then some of the best attempts at achieving these goals can be found in recent Australian Indigenous digital archival projects. There are numerous projects underway. They experiment in archival form, computer hardware interfaces, and software applications. Some projects run on local networked computers; others on password-protected Web sites. All seek to support an Indigenous way of life, whatever that might mean in the present and the anticipated future, even as all of them challenge dominant archival logics. Given the centrality that territory and history play in settler colonies like Australia, it is hardly surprising that these archival projects seek to support alternative cultural beliefs about and social protocols concerning the domiciliation, territorialization, and authorization of historical knowledge. While other old and new media archives might meet archival power obliquely, Indigenous archives directly confront the ontological and geontological presuppositions on which they are based. Before discussing our project, let me mention two others.

We can begin with Kim Christen and Chris Cooney's Web project, "Digital Dynamic across Cultures," in *Ephemera*, an issue of *Vectors: Journal of Culture and Technology in a Dynamic Vernacular*. In their authors' statement, Christen and Cooney note their desire to encode "the unique systems of belief and of shared ownership that underpin Warumungu knowledge production and reproduction, including a system of 'protocols' that limit access to information or to images in accordance with Aboriginal systems of accountability." Christen is an anthropologist who has worked with the Central Australian Warumungu in and around Tennant Creek for over a decade. Cooney is a digital media designer. *Vectors* is an experiment in electronic scholarly publishing. Many if not most scholarly electronic journals merely reproduce the print version in a Web-accessible form that allows content to be downloaded onto and printed off a computer. (Or the journal skips the original print version altogether, simply allowing Web-accessible downloading.) Few journals make use of even the most limited new media capabilities, such as supplementing the online print version of an essay with sound or video files (say, if *differences* asked me— or made it mandatory for me—to provide an audio file of the dog stories I discuss toward the end of this essay for its online version). The journal *Vectors* attempts to move beyond even this supplementary logic. It seeks to create a new kind of authorial voice and argumentative form in the interactive region between new and old media, programmer/designer and scholar, and the exposition and performance of theory. What is produced is not so much an essay as an interactive site. If designed effectively, the *Vectors* collective believes the argument of an essay will emerge as the "reader" explores the site. This form of media allows Christen and Cooney to stage the coauthorization of Indigeneity as it emerges across the complex actors in the digital archive.

The argument that "Digital Dynamic" seeks to make through its dynamic interface is twofold. On the one hand, the project challenges liberal assumptions about the role of systemized, intentional human agency in knowledge production, retrieval, and circulation. As in all of the projects in *Vectors*, the argument of "Digital Dynamic" is "run" by a database and algorithm. In this sense, the database, vis-à-vis the anthropologist and designer, is the immediate author of the argument. The database is populated with photographic, video, and audio files from Christen's extensive Warumungu archive. But the archivist—the actor, or actant—was not Christen, or not fully and finally Christen, but an algorithm and database, built by Cooney and other staff at *Vectors*. This algorithm pulled from Christen's entire archive "a representational assortment of content" that then populated the database. Every time a visitor logs into the site, another randomized algorithm shifts the material available to her and, in the process, according to Cooney and Christen, precludes the possibility of the user being able to "systematically [...] know 'the Other.'" This dual algorithmic function allows "enough content for Kim [Christen] to make her point but not too much so as to overwhelm the user" and allows "each visit to the site" to be unique even though the "different assortment of content" makes the same argument ("Digital Dynamic"). It is as if Christen and Cooney were intentionally confounding the librarians of Borges's imagination.

On the other hand, "Digital Dynamics" puts pressure on the presumed sociality of the archive. The project implicitly contrasts two forms of sociability: stranger sociability and kinship sociability. Stranger sociability is a way of knowing how to go about navigating and interacting in the world and circulating things through the world—from buying an ice cream cone to sitting in a movie theater—with people to whom one has no known relationship beyond being, as we put it in creole, *stranger-gidja*, strangers to each other. As Michael Warner has noted, whereas in an earlier European context, a stranger might have been a "mysterious" or "disturbing presence requiring resolution," in the context of contemporary publics, strangers can be, and indeed must be, "treated as already belonging to our world" (56). Stranger sociality forms the basis of the modern public as a dominant social imaginary and mode of identification. Thus in their everyday practices of being—their political imaginary, market interactions, and intimate aspirations—everyone acts as a stranger to other strangers. (In various Web environments, such as Second Life, the avatar stylizes stranger sociability.) In contrast, kinship sociability, such as among the Warumungu, imposes a very different condition on the circulation of things, humans, nonhumans, objects, narratives, ideas, and so on. The circulation of knowledge and its biproducts are based on thickly embedded social relations that are constantly negotiated within and across the social categories that compose them and their territorial substrate and expression. No one is fixed in any singular identity, and humans are and can become nonhuman agents (when they die they become *nyuidj* who inhabit the landscape, and when alive are already the descendants of specific kinds of posthuman creatures). But these movements of being are not achieved by abstracting the person from her social skin. They are achieved by thickening this skin and its imaginings. Images and other textualized forms are never detachable from these thick social worlds; there is not an image and an image-handling and interpreting subject, but only the co-constitution of the materiality and meaning of each.

Christen and Cooney attempt to make these points in an interactive rather than an expository way. The point is not simply to tell readers that the divide between stranger and kinship sociabilities exists, but to have them experience their place in this division as they attempt to navigate the Warumungu archive. When a user enters the site, a pop-up screen tells her that "access to certain elements of Warumungu culture is restricted." And as she explores the site she "may come across images, videos or other content that have been partially or completely blocked from view." The viewer is then urged to learn more about the protocols for Warumungu sociality and to "Enjoy!" (This enjoyment button is especially interesting insofar as it simultaneously incites the jouissance of the other and counters the notion that the social restriction of the subject is against enjoyment.) When the user clicks on "protocols" at the bottom of the screen, she is told, although there is no Warumungu word that translates as protocol, that the use and circulation of cultural knowledge (tangible and intangible) is based on restrictions (what one cannot do) and acting guidelines (what one must do to act responsibly) and that these protocols are especially important when outsiders engage with Warumungu people and their knowledge. After reading this pop-up screen (or simply hitting "close" without reading it), the user sees Warumungu territory represented as a set of interactive dots (think here of the ubiquitous "dot paintings" of central Australia). Each dot represents a place and is surrounded by other dots that represent events and activities. Which dots appear depends on what the algorithm selects. If a user selects the "Patta" dot ("Patta" is the Warumungu name for Tennant Creek) and if the algorithm has generated the constellation "women's ceremony," and if the user clicks on "women's ceremony," another pop-up screen tells the user that Warumungu women sang and danced at the opening of a new rail line in Tennant Creek and that while the performance was "open" to outsiders, photographs and video shouldn't be taken without the permission of the traditional owners and performers. Once again, the viewer is urged to "learn more about this protocol" by clicking on "learn more about this protocol." And so it goes as a user moves around the archive.

Thus, from the moment the user opens the archive, a metadiscourse about the circulation of cultural knowledge and its social forms and formations confronts her. At once and at the same time, the archive addresses a mass "you" who are assumed not to be a part of the Warumungu knowledge public; makes it impossible for this mass second person to continue further without interacting with the screen of exclusion (even if users don't read the pop-up screens, they have to do something to get rid of them); and positions this stranger as a voyeur in another social world. The site insists that "you-the-stranger" are now within a differently organized social world in which all people, except "you," have a place based on territorially embedded kinship and ritual relations. It insists that the social rules that organize the access and circulation of information in "your" world do not work in this world. You cannot purchase this information, nor can you gain this information in any way that sidesteps the social and cultural protocols of the Warumungu. Your ancestry and ritual status is what matters here. And insofar as it does, the user cannot feel unencumbered by social identity. Rather than the new media freeing the viewer from her social skin and allowing her to become a cultural avatar it fixes her social identity as stranger, outsider, voyeur, and suspect. One can here see why librarians would ask us how this kind of archive relates to the mandate to support publicly available information. Warumungu knowledge and its power to territorialize people are not organized on the basis of the *demos*. Knowledge does depend on accidents of birth—even as, from a Warumungu point of view, no birth is simply an accident. As a result, the postcolonial archive will never be compatible with the colonial archive because it opposes the sense of limitless public access to knowledge on which the colonial archive is based—and it exposes how all archives restrict access to all sorts of material based on the assumption that free access is free of social figuration.

But it would be wrong to imagine these modes of sociality as civilizational contrasts rather than spaces of ongoing negotiation and experimentation. Strangers are a constant presence among the Warumungu in places like Tennant Creek. Some but not all of these strangers are absorbed into local kinship cosmologies. They are given specific kinship or ritual relations and encouraged to act on the basis of these ascribed relations. But both socialized strangers and strangers who remain unsocialized bring new modes of knowledge production, storage, and manipulation with them: mobile phones, Bluetooth connectivity, laptop computers, MP3 players, and so on. Moreover, Indigenous teenagers are often in advance of their non-Indigenous teachers in terms of their use and understanding of new media sites. Helen Verran and Michael Christie have examined a set of new social forms and socio-ethical issues that emerge when Indigenous communities use new media to learn about and represent their countries. More specifically, they have proposed a software program called TAMI (texts, audio, movies, images) that would allow Indigenous communities to create their own new media narratives of place. TAMI would use novel base-code to flatten the ontological presuppositions of the metadata organizing most digital archives. In a standard digital database, metadata is used to structure, define, and administer electronically organized data. For instance, metadata might refer to the time and date a piece of data was created; to the file-type (.mov,.doc,.mp3); to the author, title, or location of the original document; to the type of object (plant, animal, person, place, event); or the relationships that exist among various metadata categories. In the semantic web, ontological space is composed of syntactically organized metadata. (The semantic web expands the properties and classes, the relations between classes, properties of scale and equality, as well as a richer array of properties to the metadata.) The only a priori ontological distinction Verran and Christie hope would be in play in their database would be the distinction between texts, audios, movies, and images. The idea is to allow for "parents, children, teachers, grandpas and grandmas generating and collecting digital objects of various types. It sees users as presenting and representing their places and collective life by designing and presenting/performing collections for many sorts of purposes" without predetermining the purpose or end of this assemblage and reassemblage.

Although Verran and Christie were never able to garner the money needed to finance the building of TAMI, it was nevertheless a controversial project. The debate pivoted over the effect that computer-based learning through "databases and other digital technologies" would have on local Indigenous commitments to collective "embodied in-place experience" (Verran 102). Would TAMI displace the ontological assumptions of metadata only to undermine the geontological properties of Indigenous knowledge? Verran acknowledges this as a pressing concern given that, on the one hand, for many Indigenous persons, "the notion of being in the world has human existence as an outcome or expression of place" and, on the other hand, when lodged on computers, learning about country can happen far away from the country one is learning about. The fear that a local Indigenous geontology is incompatible with modern technology is itself part of a more general fear each advance in technology triggers both for the civilizational trajectory of "Western culture" and for the authenticity of the Other (see Darnton and Roche). This sense of incompatibility and contagion is especially heightened when dealing with so-called oral cultures. For example, the fear of epistemological and ontological contagion was rampant in Australia in the 1980s during a set of highly contested Indigenous land claim hearings that included rural and urban claimants, the highly literate, and the partially literate. Opponents of specific Indigenous claimant groups would pose the question of how claimants came to know what they knew about the land under claim. Had they learned what they knew through "traditional" methods such as collective practices in-country supervised and initiated by elders? Or had they learned through the solitary practice of book reading? As Verran notes, this suspicion of textually mediated Indigenous learning is exacerbated in computer archiving even though "Aboriginal people are already, in their own places and their own ways, beginning to explore the knowledge management possibilities for themselves" (104). And this is the vital difference of Verran and Christie's project: given the right software conditions, can the new media allow Indigenous Australians to repurpose their ways of being in the land and becoming for the land according to their own desires, including their desire to become fluent in the new media and perhaps alter what in-place learning is?

In critical ways, our augmented reality project lies precisely in the geontological space that Verran calls "embodied in-place experience." But locating ourselves here does not solve the problems associated with Verran and Christie's project, and it opens a new set of concerns. Members of the project understand human existence to be an outcome of being in place and in other humans. But they also understand place-existence to be an outcome of being in humans and other places. What is at stake here is not merely a set of protocols for circulating knowledge but also how knowledge is a way to create and maintain the cosubstantiality of forms of being. In other words, the point is not knowledge per se but the purpose of knowledge. Knowledge about country should be learned, but abstract truth is not the actual end of learning. Learning—knowing the truth about place—is a way to refashion bodies and land-scapes into mutually obligated bodies. The French philosopher Pierre Hadot's work on the post-Socratic concept of ascesis, self-transformation, might come to mind at this point. The refashioning of self cannot be separated from an entire host of relations with place, including material transfers: eating, pissing, shitting, sweating in a place and sending matter back into soil; and semiotic transfers: speaking to place and reading the semiotic interplay of place. And it includes forms of embodiment over time, which non-Indigenous strangers may think of as a culturally inflected way to refer to memory, with memory understood as a psychological state of storing, retaining, and recalling information. But these in-place beings are not memories. They are not psychological states. Places absorb the spirit of specific people, *nyuidj*, who then appear to living people. Over time, the specificity of the person is slowly lost and absorbed into a more general kinship or linguistic category (Povinelli, "Poetics").

The design of our project intends to secure the digital archive to this alternative sociology and geontology and their subsequent modes of domiciliation, authoriza-tion, and territorialization. Our archive relies on social media so that its content can be concealed and exposed, expanded and contracted according to the dialogical conditions of a social network. And each one of these social networks would create its own cartographic imagining of geographic space and being. Would this network, however, be composed according to kinship rather than friendship assumptions? Moreover, in standard GPS cartographic projects, space is coded according to a number of features, say, coding a GPS-generated map in terms of climate change, water cover, or tree coverage. Maps are then laminated on top of each other to understand the dynamic relationship among these environmental forms. But our "maps" would not necessarily rely on the notion of a geographically correct substrate. As a result, the various maps cannot be coordinated. Place may appear distended. In-place-beings might move or be moved as they sense and respond to the presence of any number of human and nonhuman beings. Indeed, space may appear as the result of the networks' agreements and disagreements about the social meanings, locations, and purposes of various kinds of human and nonhuman agents.

While this might seem interesting, a significant problem emerges when we place the technical nature of this new archive in the actual social conditions of using the archive. If all files within the augmented reality archive must be geotagged to be played (i.e., media is given a set of GPS coordinates that mandate that all knowledge is in-place knowledge), doesn't this mean that some substrate of the geographically correct continues to inform the archive? Moreover, given the cost of traveling to the places in which the archive would be located, one ironic result could be that non-Indigenous people would be able to visit these sites more than the makers of the archive. They might end up being the woman who emerges from the other side of our wall, overwhelming the site with their experiences.

All of these projects are part of a virtual *explosion* (or, a *virtual* explosion) in the construction of postcolonial digital archives in Australia. Each of them, though in very different ways, attempts to utilize a specific matrix of circulation not merely to move a new set of "objects" through the matrix of circulation but to model a novel form of sociability in it. Many of these archives are responding to other initiatives directly funded and managed by federal, state, and territory government agencies. For instance, the Department of Local Government, Housing, and Sport, through the auspices of its Library Information Services and specifically its new Library Knowledge Centres, has established ten Indigenous digital archives in remote communities throughout the Northern Territory and hopes to establish more with a grant from the Gates Foundation. These knowledge centers are themselves based on a piece of software called Ara Irititja ("stories from a long time ago") developed for the Anangu Pitjantjatjara communities in Central Australia. The Ara Irititja Web site notes that an "important feature of the database is its ability to restrict access to individual items" to protect "cultural sensitivities."[1] Of central concern to the Anangu is their ability to "[restrict] access to some knowledge on the basis of seniority and gender." And so the Ara Irititja software integrates "these cultural priorities into the design of its digital archive." In an earlier version of the public Web site, a user could click on the link provided, read the introduction or click "skip introduction," and enter the archive. To edit the archive, a user needed a password, but even without one a visitor could still enter and move around it. Inside the archive, an algorithm based on kinship, ritual, gender, and territorial identities controlled what could be selected and seen.

All of these projects attempt to counter a dominant logic governing online archives. To understand how these postcolonial archival projects present a counterdiscourse to the dominant logic governing online archives, one need simply enter the online archive "pictureaustralia.org" and type "Aboriginal ritual" or "Aboriginal ceremony." Photos that should never be seen by the uninitiated or by one gender or another are immediately available to anyone with a computer, an Internet connection, and the ability to type these three simple words. In short, the postcolonial digital archive opposes not merely those who would argue for all intellectual knowledge to circulate freely in an open information commons, including scholars such as Lawrence Lessig, who would nuance the concept of an open information commons by distinguishing between intellectual property and intellectual nonproperty, but also those who believe that a public is ever abstracted or abstractable from its social features.[2] The Warumungu and Ara Irititja sites force readers to have a social skin, to make stranger sociality an impediment to information access/acquisition and thus knowledge production and circulation.

But as closely as these various postcolonial digital archives strive to match local protocols about knowledge acquisition, retrieval, and circulation with new media forms of the same, the media matrix in which Indigenous protocols, knowledges, and objects circulate demands they conform to certain conditions that seem to appear and disappear as one moves across three interactive regions: code, interface (information arrays), and screen. In other words, all of these subjugated knowledges enter the demanding environment of digital information (Gaonkar and Povinelli). To be sure, the Internet is a dynamic space and thus what is being demanded is under constant construction. We are currently witnessing the movement from the "read-write" Web (Web 2.0) to the semantic web (or Web 3.0). But this dynamism is not formless. It continues to demand that "things" conform to whatever conditions of entry, movement, location, and export prevail. For instance, to tabulate and access information within a digital database, the information must be configured to be readable by an underlying code and the software that serves as the intermediary between the code and the user interface. Take, for example, JavaScript, which the journal *Vectors* uses. JavaScript relies on a Boolean logic of "NOT," "AND," and "OR" operations (or gates), standard if()/then() functions, and various object-detection protocols. (There are also "NOR," "NAND," "XOR," and "XNOR" gates.) Software allows a computer to find "objects," decide on events, and apply functions. The location of objects, the advent of an event, and the application of function are constantly occurring in the digital background as a person navigates online. When, for instance, you go to the *Vectors* site, a piece of code examines your computer to see if it is compatible with JavaScript or another piece of software. If the "object" exists, in this case JavaScript, then the condition becomes true and a block of code is executed, allowing the computer to run a JavaScript-based site.

It is out of these basic logical building blocks that software designers create applications. Cross-cultural archives present an intriguing problem for many designers—and the enjoyment of trying to solve novel environments needs to be noted. Indeed, the user is not the only human agency addressed by the command: "Enjoy!" This point was brought home to me during a conversation I had when on a fellowship at *Vectors*. As part of the weeklong seminar, the director of the Sustainable Archives and Library Technologies at UCSD led a workshop. During the long conversation, the topic drifted to the problem of cultural sensitivity and knowledge access and circulation in digital archives. The director was quite happy to discuss this problem and had been working with some Australian archivists on Indigenous knowledge and digital preservation. It was exciting, if at times quite challenging, he said, to write software that reflected local rules for knowledge access, circulation, and storage. From his perspective, the first thing a designer had to do was sit down with the right people, have them explain local rules for storage, access, and circulation, and then program these rules into a set of protocols in the languages of "if()/then()" gates. If a person is a woman, then she has access to this part of the archive. If a person is a relative of the person referred to or represented in a text, that person would have a coded set of rights to that text. (In Ontological Web Language, OWL, the woman would be a class within the subClassOf and would hasGender and hasRelative that would open or close the flow of information.) I asked, "How do you know who the right people are? What if there are disagreements about the rules and protocols?" The director was curious, engaged, thoughtful, and hardly surprised by this query. He certainly didn't need a lecture from me that "cultures" are not homogenous. He responded that if there were disagreements, a designer could use a set of "if ... then" functions to model this disagreement among subgroups. But, I persisted, what if the disagreement is of the following: "yes you can make a digital archive; no you can't."

I use this anecdote to suggest how seductive this game of gates is. Notice that my "challenge" was within the logic of the machine itself: "yes ... no." In other words, across our parley, knowledge is reduced to rules for locking and unlocking information into streams of circulation. The challenge is to configure social life into a set of discrete objects that can be found or not-found (true/false). The challenge is to find out what the minimal abstract qualities of the objects are and then what their rules for access and combination are. Once one solves these challenges and configures life so that it fits this form, then a designer can write code to reflect "social context." The code can even "learn" ("If the same serial number hits this site in this place x number of times, give her more information") and have a "social conscience" ("If this credit card contributes x amount of money to progressive Indigenous causes, give it more information"). In our project, information could be weighted according to the number of visits to a site with extra information released each time a visitor returns to a site. But learning, conscience, and context are construed within a specific metasocial framework: a social writing of the social as a problem of informational access and circulation; of the correct combinations to lock and unlock informational flows, as if knowledge production produced objects. The social context is written in a language that can be accessed by any computer anywhere—exactly the critique Verran and Christie tried to counter. We return to what at first appeared to be a strong division within digital space between those for and against an open commons to find that all digital commons, colonial or postcolonial, must be written in a code that assumes the social is a set of rules that can be written to operate independent of social context.

IV

Thus we see that the specific circulatory matrix of the new media places a number of conditions on how an object must allow itself to be configured as a condition of its circulation. What this configuration entails, and how the configuration might change—or how the matrix itself might change as it absorbs and shapes new materials—is only one part of what is at stake in building a postcolonial archive that will challenge archival power. It is certainly true that deep within the recesses of the new media are presuppositions about information and its sociability, on top of which the postcolonial software seeks to write a new history. And it is equally true that this specific matrix of circulation fashions the edges and expressions of information as the price of entering and circulating through this specific cultural form. But there are other conditions shaping and thus helping direct the futurity of things entering, exiting, and remaining in the postcolonial digital archive. Here, we might return to Isaacman, Lalu, and Nygren's lament that the organic ground of the postcolonial archive—the people whose personal narratives are the loci of memory as archive—is not being sustained long enough every day to transfer the archive as embodied knowledge and memory into textual knowledge and memory.

Take, for instance, the social environment in which my colleagues and I must build our augmented reality project. I first began talking with Indigenous colleagues and friends in 2005 about what to do with my extensive archive. At that time, the politics of recognition were still a dominant discourse of Indigenous-Settler relations. To be sure, the conservative Liberal-National alliance had controlled federal government for nine years, gaining the Senate and thus holding unchecked power in parliament in 2004. During this time, the prime minister, John Howard, had made serious discursive inroads into the self-evident worth of the recognition of Indigenous culture and of the bureaucratic structure that had accumulated around this self-evident good.

In 1996 his government had cut $470 million from support of Indigenous programs, claiming all Australians were equal and should be treated equally. In 1999 he refused to apologize for past wrongs done to Indigenous people, including the Stolen Generation. (The Stolen Generation refers to the extended period during which Aboriginal and Torres Strait Islander children were removed from their parents.) Howard claimed that present Australians should not be held responsible for the actions of past Australians. Further, he and others in his government argued that government policies such as the Stolen Generation had been intended to help, not harm, Indigenous people and should not be judged according to present values and views. In 2002 his government initiated a review of the parallel governing body, the Aboriginal and Torres Strait Islander Commission, and in 2004 abolished it, claiming corruption, nepotism, and incompetence.

But the decisive turn in the public politics of recognition occurred in 2007. The federal government pushed for the release of the *Little Children Are Sacred* report of the Northern Territory Board of Inquiry into the Protection of Aboriginal Children from Sexual Abuse.[3] The report was careful to disambiguate Indigenous social and cultural traditions from contemporary sexual abuse. The federal government was not. The Howard government seized the opportunity to make a frontal assault on the underlying notion of cultural recognition as such. Aboriginal culture had been exposed. Indigenous gender relations and ritual practices were based on premodern attitudes and trajectories. The paternalistic attitude of the 1950s was revealed to have been prescient. The shocking stagnation of Indigenous life from the perspective of health, education, morbidity, and employment was not a failure of government and state care but of Indigenous culture (Povinelli, "Culture"). Conservative papers staged Indigenous gender oppression and articulated it to other highly stereotyped gender oppressive cultures.

It would be hard to underestimate how this sex panic roiled public opinion about the truth and destiny of Indigenous culture. It seems safe to claim that this sex panic contributed to a sudden questioning of the previously unquestioned support of Indigenous culture. The veneer of spirituality referred to and nurtured by intersecting discourses of popular culture (one thinks of a long list of films and books, *The Last Wave, Picnic at Hanging Rock, Where the Green Ants Dream*), high art (see Myers), tele-visual pedagogy (shows on the ABC and SBS as well as on the National Indigenous Network), and law (legislation and rulings referring to Aboriginal land-based spirituality as the basis of culture) was suddenly overlain with the specter of sexual abuse. Once traditional culture with associated sexual abuse, a subsequent hegemonic link could be made between entrepreneurial (neoliberal) modernity and sexual remedy. This link was made, and supported, by the conservative government until it was ousted in 2007. And it continues to be made by conservative advocates in the national press and liberal or previously liberal-leaning multiculturalists (Sutton). According to these pundits, what Aboriginal people want is to be liberated from the oppressive weight of an outdated culture.

The articulation of Indigenous tradition to social deviance legitimized a material reorganization of government and private spending in relation to Indigenous people and communities. The Howard government loudly proclaimed the withdrawal of state support of remote Indigenous life to deprive Indigenous people of the supposed conditions of a sexualized culture and to force them into market-based goods and values. If Indigenous people wanted continued financial support for life outside the mainstream of the market economy, they would have to turn to that economy for financing. Communities were forced to sign ninety-nine-year leases over their lands if they wanted to continue to receive infrastructural improvements and educational support. They were no longer allowed to control who entered their communities. And the police presence in communities radically increased.

It was in these new conditions that members of our project had to make decisions about how, why, and to what end things should enter the digital archive and be allowed to circulate across various kinds of kin networks and stranger publics. Take, for instance, two narratives we considered inserting into the digital archive. The first tells the story of some dogs who moved across country trying to cook cheeky yams. (This kind of yam must be cooked or soaked to leach out the arsenic in it.) As they move across the landscapes trying again and again to consume the yams, the dogs slowly transform from an original, more human figure to their current dog form. At one site the dogs try to make a fire by rubbing fire sticks together. Because it is the rainy season, all the dogs do is dig deep holes that fill with water (becoming water wells) and, in the process, lose their fingers. At another place, famished, they decide to eat the yams without cooking them, subsequently burning their tongues and losing their ability to speak human language.

Some of these stories have already been published and circulate in the reading public. But as far as I know, the location of these sites is not indicated. Nor is it made clear how the various stories contribute to the larger cartography of the region. It would be wrong to assume that this cartography is "one." Anyone who is Indigenous, or works with Indigenous people, knows that every landscape is a complex dynamic between local contested cartographies and geontologies. Indeed, the point of composing this postcolonial digital archive is to allow for variation, contestation, change over time in narrative form and purpose and in changing environments (say, if the features have been dramatically changed by erosion of land development). That is to say, there is nothing particularly unusual about the issues raised by this story of dogs and their prehistory.

If there is nothing unusual about the issues raised by this story of dogs and their prehistory, another story presents the problem of the figuration of such stories before they enter the archive. This second narrative also performatively entails the geontology of the region's land and seascape. But this narrative is about a young woman who, having dressed as a man to go hunting, encounters an older man who, discovering the truth of her sex, fights her, rapes her, and then departs. This narrative presents some similar issues as the narrative of the famished dogs: the same internal disputes, metapragmatic functions, geontological background assumptions. But this time these issues are located at the intersection of national narratives about the scandalous revelation that rather than spirituality, it is sexuality, and a violent, predatory sexuality, that lies at the heart of Indigenous culture. What is "the truth" of this narrative? What parts that might have been backgrounded during the heyday of cultural recognition are now foregrounded? This reorganization of foreground and background is not countered by pointing out that countless stories of sexual and physical violence can be found in the spiritual texts of the religions of the book, often said to be the civilizational ground of Western culture.

How will our project configure these narratives to address the different viewing publics? Perhaps we could have a password-protected space within the social media where various versions of the narratives would be located. While editing these narratives might solve the present problem of a suspicious public, does it touch archival power? Here we remember that archival power is not merely what is in the archive, how this *what* is subtly or not so subtly shared and qualified, and how to preserve various organic grounds of memory. Archival power is also, and perhaps most profoundly, about the orientation of truth to some lost trace of the real. We return not only to Derrida but also to Borges and his librarian/archivists who construct various theologies of the book to isolate the singular truth of the library. As Derrida suggested, archival power is best understood in relation to the archival drive that every actual archive initiates. Archival power is a kind of Lacanian dissatisfaction with every actual source material, an incessant movement beyond every actual archival presentation. Having levels within our digital archive would heighten the intensity of this drive rather than lessen it. It does, however, increase the seduction of the project for capital and public interests. And this is not without own value. But it is not a value that works against the archival grain.

Years ago, when I first began discussing what to do with my archive, some older Indigenous men and women, as well as some younger ones, told me to burn it and bury it. Their reasoning was straightforward from one perspective. If no one acted in a way that kept what was in my archive alive, then it was simply dead matter that should be treated like other dead matter and returned to the ground from which it came. Of course, other reasons were also present: rage at a life, desire to be done with struggle, rejection of certain aspects of local being in the world. Burn the archive. But this was not a universal opinion. Others said that the purpose of having sat and poured this knowledge onto paper and tape and into me was to store it for their children and grandchildren. They were reflecting not merely some rote belief that Indigenous culture should "pass down through the generations" but a deeper understanding of the difficulties of navigating the various demands they faced as young people and that their children face today.

This is not a romantic notion of parenting. Present in this knowledge was also rage and resentment, including rage and resentment at me for having the complex means and wherewithal to sit and be a storage container as others died, were killed, or crippled themselves with substances. And in this was also my rage and resentment for having found myself in a position of obligation I do not seem able to let go of—with all the consequences on personal relations there and elsewhere. I have on many occasions thought of burning the archive myself and justifying it with the permission I was given. "Burn it," they said. I am tempted to join the sect of Borges's library that burns every book that would appear as gibberish.

But even then I would be preserving an archival trace—"they said." Neither editing nor burning the archive will touch archival power. I would have to burn my own history, never have existed; and theirs as well. Unless I do, someone somewhere, some text, here or there will remember that there were people who knew something and perhaps left some part of this something behind, maybe in a book or an attic or on the ground. And this something somewhere will finally tell us what our universe means without us having to stop and look around and ask, what is here now?

Notes ——

Postcolonial Digital Archives

¹ See http://www.irititja.com.
² See also the *Creative Commons* at http://creative commons.org.

³ The Northern Territory Government Web site provides the full report, which was released on June 15, 2007, at http://www.inquirysaac.nt.gov.au/.

Works Cited

Appadurai, Arjun. *The Social Life of Things: Commodities in a Cultural Perspective*. Cambridge: Cambridge UP, 1988.

Arondekar, Anjali. *For the Record: On Sexuality and the Colonial Archive in India*. Durham: Duke UP, 2009.

Borges, Jorge Luis. "The Library of Babel." *Collected Fictions*. Trans. Andrew Hurley. New York: Penguin, 1998. 112–18.

Born, Georgina. "The Social and the Aesthetic: For a Post-Bourdieuian Theory of Cultural Production." *Cultural Sociology* 4.2 (2010): 171–208.

Christen, Kim, and Chris Cooney. "Digital Dynamic across Cultures." *Ephemera*. Spec. issue of *Vectors: Journal of Culture and Technology in a Dynamic Vernacular* 2.1 (2006). http://vectorsjournal.org.

Darnton, Richard, and Daniel Roche. *Revolution in Print: The Press in France, 1775–1800*. Berkeley: U of California P, 1989.

Derrida, Jacques. *Archive Fever: A Freudian Impression*. Chicago: U of Chicago P, 1998.

Dong, Song. *Waste Not*. Museum of Modern Art. *Projects 90*. New York. 24 June-7 Sept. 2009.

Foucault, Michel. *The Archaeology of Knowledge and the Discourse on Language*. New York: Pantheon, 1982.

Gaonkar, Dilip Parameshwar, and Elizabeth A. Povinelli. "Technologies of Public Forms: Circulation, Transfiguration, Recognition." *Public Culture* 15.3 (2003): 385–97.

Hadot, Pierre. *What Is Ancient Philosophy?* Cambridge: Belknap, 2004.

Hoarders. Arts and Entertainment Network. 2008–present.

Isaacman, Allen F., Premesh Lalu, and Thomas I. Nygren. "Digitization, History, and the Making of a Postcolonial Archive of Southern African Liberation Struggles: The Aluka Project." *Africa Today* 52.2 (2005): 55–77.

Lessig, Lawrence. "Reclaiming a Commons." Keynote Address. Building a Digital Commons. Berkman Center, Cambridge, MA. 20 May 1999.

Myers, Fred. *Painting Culture: The Making of Aboriginal High Art*. Durham: Duke UP, 2003.

Povinelli, Elizabeth A. "The Crisis of Culture and the Arts of Care: Indigenous Politics in Late Liberalism." *Culture Crisis: Anthropology and Politics in Remote Aboriginal Australia*. Ed. Jon Altman and Melinda Hinkson. Sydney: U of New South Wales P, 2010. 17–31.

———. "The Poetics of Ghosts: Social Reproduction and the Archive of the Nation." *The Cunning of Recognition: Indigenous Alterities and the Making of Australian Multiculturalism*. Durham: Duke UP, 2002. 187–234.

Stoler, Ann Laura. *Along the Archival Grain: Epistemic Anxieties and Colonial Common Sense*. Princeton: Princeton UP, 2010.

Sutton, Peter. *The Politics of Suffering: Indigenous Australia and the End of the Liberal Consensus*. Melbourne: Melbourne UP, 2010.

Trouillot, Michel Rolph. *Silencing the Past: Power and Production of History*. Boston: Beacon, 1995.

Verran, Helen. "The Educational Value of Explicit Noncoherence: Software for Helping Aboriginal Children Learn about Place in Education and Technology." *Critical Perspectives, Possible Futures*. Ed. David W. Kritt and Lucien T. Winegar. Lanham: Lexington, 2007. 101–24.

Verran, Helen, and Michael Christie. "Using/Designing Digital Technologies of Representation in Aboriginal Australian Knowledge Practices." *Human Technology: Interdisciplinary Journal of Humans in ict Environments* 3.2 (2007): 214–27.

Warner, Michael. "Publics and Counterpublics." *Public Culture* 14.1 (2002): 49–90.

Index